REAL WORLD EXAMPLES: REALITY CHECKPOINTS

Industrial Organization

Contemporary Theory and Empirical Applications

Fourth Edition

Lynne Pepall

Dan Richards

George Norman

Blackwell Publishing

BLACKWELL PUBLISHING
350 Main Street, Malden, MA 02148-5020, USA
9600 Garsington Road, Oxford OX4 2DQ, UK
550 Swanston Street, Carlton, Victoria 3053, Australia

The right of Lynne Pepall, Dan Richards, and George Norman to be identified as the authors of
this work has been asserted in accordance with the UK Copyright, Designs, and Patents Act 1988.

This fourth edition first published 2008 by Blackwell Publishing Ltd

1 2008

Library of Congress Cataloging-in-Publication Data

Pepall, Lynne, 1952–
    Industrial organization : contemporary theory and empirical applications / Lynne Pepall,
Dan Richards, George Norman. – 4th ed.
        p. cm.
    Includes bibliographical references and index.
    ISBN 978-1-4051-7632-3 (hardcover : alk. paper)   1. Industrial organization.
I. Richards, Daniel Jay.   II. Norman, George, 1946–   III. Title.

    HD31.P377 2008
    658.1–dc22

                                                                2007039115

A catalogue record for this title is available from the British Library.

Set in 10/12pt Times
by Graphicraft Limited, Hong Kong
Printed and bound in the United States of America
by Sheridan Books, Inc.

The publisher's policy is to use permanent paper from mills that operate a sustainable forestry policy, and
which has been manufactured from pulp processed using acid-free and elementary chlorine-free practices.
Furthermore, the publisher ensures that the text paper and cover board used have met acceptable
environmental accreditation standards.

For further information on
Blackwell Publishing, visit our website at
www.blackwellpublishing.com

Short Contents

Contents

Figures

Tables

About the Authors

Lynne Pepall is Professor of Economics and Dean of the Graduate School of Arts and Sciences at Tufts University. Professor Pepall received her undergraduate degree in mathematics and economics from Trinity College, University of Toronto, and her Ph.D. in economics from Cambridge University in England. She has written numerous papers in industrial organization, appearing in the *Journal of Industrial Economics, International Journal of Industrial Organization, Journal of Economics and Management Strategy, Economic Journal, Canadian Journal of Economics, Economica*, and the *American Journal of Agricultural Economics*. She has taught industrial organization and microeconomics at both the graduate and undergraduate levels, at Tufts University since 1987. Professor Pepall lives in Newton, Massachusetts, with her two sons, a dog, three rabbits, and her husband, a co-author of this book.

Dan Richards is Professor of Economics at Tufts University. Professor Richards received his A.B. in economics and history from Oberlin College and his Ph.D. in economics from Yale University. Professor Richards has written numerous articles in both macroeconomics and industrial organization, appearing in the *American Economic Review, Quarterly Journal of Economics, Journal of Industrial Economics, Economica*, the *B. E. Journals in Economic Analysis and Policy, Canadian Journal of Economics*, the *Journal of Money, Credit, and Banking*, and the *American Journal of Agricultural Economics*. He came to Tufts in 1985 and has taught at both the graduate and undergraduate levels. He served as Director of the Graduate Program in Economics from 1989 through 1998, and has also served as a consultant to the Federal Trade Commission. From 1996 to 2005 he taught in the Sloan Fellows Program at MIT's Sloan School of Management. Professor Richards lives in Newton, Massachusetts, with his two sons, a dog, three rabbits, and his wife, a co-author of this book.

George Norman holds the William and Joyce Cummings Family Chair of Entrepreneurship and Business Economics at Tufts University. He came to Tufts in 1995 from Edinburgh University, where he had served as head of the department of economics. Prior to that, Professor Norman was the Tyler Professor of Economics at the University of Leicester (England). Professor Norman attended the University of Dundee (Scotland) where he was awarded the M.A. in economics with first class honors. He received his Ph.D. in economics from Cambridge University. His more than 70 published articles have appeared in such professional journals as the *American Economic Review, Review of Economic Studies, Quarterly Journal of Economics, Journal of Industrial Economics,* and *International Journal of Industrial Organization.* He is currently an Associate Editor for two journals, the *Bulletin of Economic Research* and *Regional Science and Urban Economics.* He is also on the editorial board of the *B.E. Journals in Economic Analysis and Policy.* In addition to this book, Professor Norman has written and edited, either alone or in collaboration with others, 17 other books. Professor Norman has taught courses in industrial organization and microeconomic theory at both the graduate and undergraduate levels. He has also taught introductory economics, corporate strategy, international economics, and entrepreneurship. Professor Norman lives in Newbury, Massachusetts, with his wife Margaret who, while *not* a co-author, has provided invaluable support and assistance in his work on this book.

Preface to the Fourth Edition

We are greatly pleased by the publication of the fourth edition of *Industrial Organization: Contemporary Theory and Empirical Applications*. It confirms our view that students want to learn the essentials of modern industrial organization and, more generally, the process of economic modeling and empirical application. There are immediate insights that come from thinking rigorously through the implications of strategic interaction. However, one of the most important lessons from studying industrial organization is understanding how to construct a rational economic argument whose implications are, in principle, able to be empirically tested. We believe that this edition of our textbook teaches this lesson successfully with its new emphasis on empirical applications.

Overall, the organization of the book remains the same as the previous edition. We have updated the checkpoints so that they remain contemporary illustrations of the underlying analysis. We have also done some pruning to make room for important new contributions and insights. Chapter 3 now includes a more formal presentation of Sutton's (1991) analysis of the relationship between sunk cost and market structure. Similarly, Chapter 8 now includes a discussion of the recent work by Evans and Salinger (2005) and Evans (2006) on competitive bundling and tying. In Chapter 14 we have eliminated the lengthy discussion of possible collusion in a market with two non-cooperative Nash equilibria. Instead, that chapter now includes a formal model of optimal antitrust policy in regard to cartels. This theme is continued in Chapter 15 where we have an extended discussion of the role of leniency or amnesty programs in inducing cartel members to confess their activities. Chapter 16 begins with the "merger paradox," but now includes the recent work by Fauli-Oller (2000) and others on sequential mergers as ways to resolve this paradox. In Chapter 20, we have added a section on the Anderson and Renault (2006) model of suppressed advertising content. In Chapter 23 we now give a more formal derivation of the Gilbert and Shapiro (1990) and Klemperer (1990) results on optimal patent length and breadth. We also note briefly the recent work by Lerner and Tirole (2004) on efficient patent pools.

The major innovation in this edition is, however, the new emphasis on empirical industrial organization. Fourteen of our 25 chapters now conclude with an in-depth treatment of a relevant empirical investigation. These sections are called Empirical Applications. For the most part, they are expositions of regression-based studies. However, there are also some non-regression-based analyses. Chapter 3 offers the first Empirical Application with a review of Harberger's (1954) study and the many studies that followed on the welfare losses from market power. While this is an old controversy, it serves to introduce students to the idea that important hypotheses can be tested using data in combination with calculations rooted in formal economic analysis. Chapter 4 also has an empirical case study. Here, we focus on the classic work of Christensen and Greene (1976) that helped initiate the estimation of cost functions and, specifically, the translog cost relation. This is a very accessible piece and it allows the instructor to take the student through the basic steps of deriving a cost function from a production relationship, input price data, and the assumption of cost minimization. It also helps students gain some familiarity with regression analysis.

The next Empirical Application comes in Chapter 7. Here we use the short study by Stavins (2001) to demonstrate the role of price discrimination in airline markets. The application helps to document the nature of airline price discrimination and to explore its strategic use in product differentiated competition. In Chapter 10 we provide another empirical analysis of a product differentiated market in a presentation of Hastings' (2004) study of competition in the southern California retail gasoline market. This application serves nicely to make clear that the nature of consumer preferences and, specifically, whether the relevant differentiation is horizontal or vertical, is an important empirical question. It also serves to illustrate the role that regression analysis can play in isolating the effect of a specific treatment or policy intervention.

Chapters 12 and 13 address predatory conduct, and in Chapter 13 we present the recent Ellison and Ellison (2006) study of possible predation by pharmaceutical firms who are about to face generic competition due to expiration of their patents. Among other features, the two-stage procedure in this study—first, testing markets for the likelihood of entry and, then, testing for entry-deterring conduct in those markets where entry is most probable—helps to make clear how careful we must be in identifying any sort of predatory conduct. In addition, this Empirical Application alerts students to the problems that accompany the use of limited dependent variables.

Both Chapters 14 and 15 are on collusion and price-fixing and each has an extended Empirical Application. Chapter 14 presents Kwoka's (1997) clever analysis of the price effects of collusive bidding in real estate auctions in Washington, D.C. In Chapter 15, we review the recent Hinloopen and Soetevent (2006) study of the impact of antitrust policies that grant leniency or amnesty to the first cartel member to confess. This application makes clear that such policies potentially wield a double-edged sword. While they make confession more likely once a cartel is under suspicion, the fact that they offer an escape from punishment for at least one firm may also encourage the formation of cartels in the first place. A further advantage of the Hinloopen and Soetevent (2006) study is that it is based on experimental analysis, and hence, introduces students to the use of this alternative empirical technique.

The next extended discussion of empirical work comes in Chapter 16. Here we present the technique of merger simulation. This application has two major benefits. First, it demonstrates how economic modeling indicates which parameters are needed for evaluating the likely post-merger market outcome. Second, because the effects of merger simulation are relatively sensitive to key elasticity estimates, the application also makes clear how and why economists can differ in their evaluation of a merger. We drive this point home more forcefully by also including a brief review of the Staples and Office Depot merger and the very different conclusions reached by different economists in that case.

Chapter 17 focuses primarily on vertical mergers, and in the Empirical Application we go over the recent study of vertical integration in the ready-mixed concrete industry by

Hortaçsu and Syverson (2006). Chapter 19 includes an Empirical Application on vertical contracts. In this case, it is the study by Sass (2005) of exclusive dealing in the U.S. domestic beer market. Both applications offer clear and accessible results that serve to emphasize that contemporary industrial organization practice involves data analysis. The Sass (2005) study has the added benefit of introducing students to the Seemingly Unrelated Regressions technique.

Chapter 21 on advertising includes an application on Ackerberg's (2001) empirical analysis of the introduction of a new yogurt product by Yoplait in the late 1980s. This application demonstrates perhaps more clearly than any other that when we have access to very detailed data, we can, if great care is taken, distinguish the validity of two competing hypotheses. Here the question is whether advertising works by raising prestige or by providing information. Moreover, because this study uses logit analysis, it gives us a second chance to present to students the underlying logic of empirical models that use limited dependent variables.

We also have included Empirical Applications in Chapters 22 and 23, which are on research and development (R&D). The focus of Chapter 22 is R&D competition under various degrees of spillover from one firm's innovative efforts to the productivity of its rivals, and we conclude this chapter with Keller's (2002) empirical study of such spillovers at an international level. Among other benefits, this application helps students understand how research in one area of economics may have implications for policy in other areas. It also introduces students to the idea of non-linear regression. In Chapter 23, which is on patents, we now include an Empirical Application on the Hall and Ziedonis (2001) study of patenting behavior in the U.S. semiconductor industry during the 1980s and 1990s. This application provides a neat illustration of how to identify the sources of dramatic changes in industrial conduct. It also briefly introduces students to the Poisson distribution.

Our final Empirical Application comes in Chapter 24. Here we describe Gandal's (1994) early test for network externalities in the market for spreadsheet software. Although a little older than most of our other empirical studies, this piece is very accessible. Moreover, it has the additional advantage of introducing students to the notion of hedonic regressions and, subsequently, the construction of a hedonic price index.

Our goal in revising the textbook for this edition was to expand and update the material covered. Generally speaking, we have included new material by becoming more efficient and without making extensive cuts to the content covered in previous editions. The updating of theory combined with the inclusion of the fourteen Empirical Applications makes the text more reflective of contemporary theory and practice in industrial organization.

ACKNOWLEDGMENTS

Our students at Tufts have been extremely helpful and we owe each of them a great deal of thanks. In addition, the comments of formal reviewers, instructors, and simply those who wished to be helpful have been very insightful. Among this group, we wish to give particular thanks to:

Sheri Aggarwal, University of Virginia

Simon Anderson, University of Virginia

David Audretsch, Indiana University

Gary Biglaiser, University of North Carolina, Chapel Hill

Giacomo Bonanno, University of California at Davis

Stacey Brook, University of Sioux Falls

Erik Brynjolfsson, MIT

Henry W. Chappell, Jr., University of South Carolina

Yongmin Chen, University of Colorado, Boulder

Darlene Chisholm, Suffolk University

Coldwell Daniel III, University of Memphis

Larry DeBrock, University of Illinois

Greg Ellis, University of Washington

Glenn Ellison, MIT

Stephen Erfle, Dickinson College

Robert M. Feinberg, American University

Anne Harper Fender, Gettysburg College

Sara Fisher Ellison, MIT

Mark R. Frascatore, Clarkson University

Luke Froeb, Vanderbilt University

S. N. Gajanan, University of Pittsburgh

Ian Gale, Georgetown University

Paolo Garella, University of Bologna

Gerald Granderson, Miami University of Ohio

Arne Hallam, Iowa State University

Mehdi Haririan, Bloomsburg University

Justine Hastings, Yale University

Barry Haworth, University of Louisville

Hugo A. Hopenhayn, University of Rochester

Peter Huang, University of Pennsylvania

Stanley Kardasz, University of Waterloo

Phillip King, San Francisco State University

Robert Lawrence, Harvard University

John Logan, Rutgers University

Nancy Lutz, Virginia Polytechnic Institute

Howard Marvel, Ohio State University

Catherine Matraves, Albion College

Deborah Menegotto, Tufts University

Eugenio J. Miravete, University of Pennsylvania

Jon Nelson, Pennsylvania State University

Craig Newmark, North Carolina State University

Debashis Pal, University of Cincinnati

Nicola Persico, University of Pennsylvania

Raymond Raab, University of Minnesota

Steve Rubb, Bentley College

Tim Sass, Florida State University

Nicholas Schmitt, University of Geneva

Sarah Stafford, William and Mary

Greg Werden, Department of Justice

William C. Wood, James Madison University

James Zinser, Oberlin College

Zenon Zyginont, Reed College

The authors would also like to thank the following reviewers:

Phoebe Chan, Wheaton College, Massachusetts

Yongmin Chen, University of Colorado, Boulder

Jeremy Fox, University of Chicago

Christos Genakos, Selwyn College, University of Cambridge

John Kwoka, Northeastern University

Qihong Liu, University of Oklahoma

Nancy Lutz, Virginia Technical College

Jill McCluskey, Washington State University

Michael Noel, University of California, San Diego

Jennfer Offenberg, Loyola Marymount University

Yochanan Sachmurove, University of Pennsylvania

Philip Schmidt-Dengler, London School of Economics

Dan Showalter, Southwest Texas State University

Andrew Sweeting, Northwestern University

Frederick Tiffany, Wittenberg University

Gianlugi Vernasca, University of Essex

Madeline Zavodny, Agnes Scott College, Georgia

Here at Tufts, Debra Kendrick has given us outstanding secretarial assistance and support. The editorial staff at Blackwell Publishing, especially George Lobell, have provided excellent and much-needed editorial guidance. Graeme Leonard's production editing is outstanding.

Of course, we owe the greatest debts to our family members. Lynne and Dan are thankful for the help, support and inspiration from their increasingly independent sons, Ben and William. George would like to thank his wife Margaret for her patience, help, and humor, which are indispensable to his work. For these and countless other reasons, we affectionately dedicate this book to our loved ones.

Part I
Foundations

We begin our study of industrial organization by reviewing the basic building blocks of market analysis. The first chapter provides a road map for the entire enterprise. Here, we describe the central aim of industrial organization, namely, the investigation of firm behavior and market outcomes in settings of less than perfect competition. We emphasize that an understanding of strategic interaction is a critical component of this analysis.

In Chapter 2, we review the basic microeconomics of the two polar textbook cases of perfect competition and pure monopoly. These two cases help introduce basic supply and especially demand considerations. They also permit us to present the notions of consumer surplus, producer surplus, and total surplus that are necessary for any complete valuation of market outcomes.

Having introduced the concept of market power and its exploitation in Chapter 2, Chapter 3 focuses on how we might identify those markets in which such abuse is likely to be a problem. Structural measures of concentration are a common way to make this identification and so this is an obvious place to introduce such measures as the n-firm concentration ratio and the Herfindahl–Hirschman Index. However, we also take the additional step of introducing the most explicit measure of monopoly price distortions, namely, the Lerner Index. This includes an extended empirical application explaining the many attempts at measuring the economy-wide welfare loss from such distortions beginning with Harberger (1954).

Finally, in Chapter 4 we turn to a discussion of some of the reasons that cause markets to exhibit the structural conditions that make perfect competition unlikely. Chief among these are cost considerations and it is in this chapter that we explore cost concepts most formally. We review the notion of marginal cost that has already been introduced and then turn our attention to those remaining cost concepts that most directly relate to market structure such as sunk costs, average cost, and both scale and scope economies. We also explore the implications of endogenous sunk cost as emphasized by Sutton (1991). As in Chapter 3, Chapter 4 also includes an empirical piece, based here on the early work of Christensen and Greene (1976). Our aim here is twofold. First, we wish to show formally how to derive a cost function from the application of profit-maximizing principles to a specified production function. Second, we wish to introduce the basic notion of regression analysis and how one can (and should) use theory to guide and inform empirical investigations.

1

Industrial Organization: What, How, and Why

A sample of business news stories from the late 1990s and early twenty-first century includes the following: Coke and Pepsi found themselves in the middle of a severe price war. Visa and MasterCard were found guilty of trying to monopolize the bank credit card business. Complaints from computer manufacturers, Dell and Gateway, led to the discovery of an international cartel in dynamic random access memory (DRAM) and subsequent guilty pleas. Companies from all industries, but especially those in the finance and telecommunications sector, e.g., AOL and Time-Warner, had embarked on a huge merger spree in which two or more firms consolidated into one.

Students often feel that there is a considerable gap between stories like those just described and the economics they study in the classroom. This is so despite the fact that most modern texts include real world applications. Indeed, it is difficult to think of a contemporary economics textbook that does not include examples drawn from practical business experience. Nevertheless, it is still far from unusual to hear remarks such as "economics is too abstract" or "this wasn't covered in the microeconomics that I studied."

This book is very much in keeping with the modern practice of illustrating the applications of economic theory. Our aim is, however, more ambitious than just showing that economics can illuminate the everyday events of the business world. Our goal is to develop a way of thinking about such experiences—a mental framework that permits students to form hypotheses about the mechanisms underlying such events and to consider how to test those hypotheses against empirical evidence. Of course, we cannot offer a framework for analyzing all economic phenomena, but we can develop one that applies to a large class of events including the ones described above. That framework rests solidly on modern game theory and the class of events to which it most readily applies falls under the heading of industrial organization.

1.1 WHAT IS INDUSTRIAL ORGANIZATION?

What is industrial organization? For a large number of people, the answer to that question is far from clear. Indeed, on a recent and long, cross-Pacific flight the question elicited a wide set of responses when put to several of our fellow passengers. Most supposed that the field had something to do with business. A few thought it was rooted in psychology and possibly applied to human resource management. One thought it dealt with the pattern of international trade. Actually, each of these answers has a grain of truth. Yet each is also wide of the mark. While the field of industrial organization does touch on many aspects of business life, it has come to have a fairly precise meaning in economics. Simply put, industrial organization is that branch of economics that is concerned with the study of imperfect competition.

Since you are reading this book, the chances are very good that you have had some economics classes, especially microeconomics classes, already. As a result, you have probably been exposed to the concept of perfect competition—that somewhat utopian vision of markets populated by numerous small firms and characterized by economic efficiency. You are also likely to have read about the most obvious counter-example, a pure monopoly. The case of a market dominated by one firm alone offers a clear contrast to the ideal of perfect competition. But what happens when the truth lies, as it almost always does, between these two polar extremes? What happens when there are two, or three, or several firms? How do competitive forces play out when each firm faces only a limited number of rivals? Will prices be driven to (marginal) costs, or will advertising and other promotional tactics avert this outcome? Will research and development of new products and processes be the major source of competitive pressure? If so, how do monopolies come about? If firms can obtain monopoly power, can they also devise strategies to maintain such power? Is it possible to keep new competitors from coming into the market?

Industrial organization forms the analytical core that economists use to answer these and many other related questions. Economists long ago worked out the analytics of perfect competition. What happens under the more common setting of imperfect competition—how close to or how far from working like the perfectly competitive market—is much less settled. This less settled domain is the field of industrial organization.

There is a good reason why industrial organization does not yield clear and simple answers regarding what happens in imperfectly competitive markets. When we describe a market as less than perfectly competitive that still leaves open a wide range of possibilities. It could be a duopoly market with only two firms, or perhaps a market dominated by one large firm competing with many very small ones. The products of the different firms may be identical, as in the case of cement manufacturers, or perhaps highly differentiated, as in the case of cosmetics. Entry by new firms may be easy, as in the restaurant business, or difficult, as in the automobile industry. This variety of possible market characterizations means that it is very difficult to make broad, unambiguous statements about imperfectly competitive markets.

Matters become even more complicated when we consider the decisions that the management of an imperfectly competitive firm must make. Start with perhaps a simple case such as a florist setting the price for a dozen roses. Should the price rise on Valentine's Day? Should the price for a dozen be exactly 12 times the price of a single rose? Or should the prospective buyer of flowers get a break if he or she buys in quantity?

Consider Jody Adams, the chef at one of the Boston area's top restaurants, Rialto. Jody must choose the complete menu of entrees and appetizers that the restaurant will serve at the start of each season as well as set the price of each menu entry. In making this choice, she must evaluate the cost and availability of different ingredients. For example, what seafood and vegetables are in season and can be served fresh? What price should she set for a la carte items and for the fixed price meal? Should she make available special dishes for those with food allergies? How extensive a wine list should she maintain? These decisions make clear that product design decisions are certainly as important as pricing decisions. A critical design choice by Microsoft to package its Web browser, Internet Explorer with its Windows operating system and to sell the two as one product was perhaps the primary reason for Internet Explorer's success against Netscape. It also played a major role in the government's later decision to pursue antitrust charges against Microsoft.

Price and product design choices are not the only decisions that firms make, however. Another choice concerns promotional effort. For example, in 2002 the soft-drink giant, Pepsi, paid over $200 million to replace Coca Cola for the rights to be the official soft drink of the National Football League.[1] By winning this contract, Pepsi gained the right to use the logos of the Super Bowl and other league properties in ads, signs, and banners. However, for this right it paid more than double the amount Coca-Cola had been paying. Was this a wise decision? A similar decision concerns what markets to enter. Southwest Airlines decided in the late 1990s that the time was right to begin service to points in the Northeast. What made this the right time and what tactics should Southwestern have employed to guarantee the success of this venture?

Firms make tough decisions like the ones just discussed on a daily basis. Industrial organization economists analyze those decisions and try to derive some predictions from that analysis to help us understand market outcomes. We also try to test those predictions using modern econometric analysis.

1.2   HOW WE STUDY INDUSTRIAL ORGANIZATION

One reason that analyzing imperfect competition is difficult is because of the interdependence that characterizes the firms' decisions in their markets. When Southwest Airlines considers offering services to Boston, it has to recognize that this will have a non-trivial effect on the other airlines that serve the Boston market. They may react by cutting fares, or by changing their flight times, or perhaps by cutting back on the Boston service so as to avoid a glut on the market. Similarly, when Pepsi thinks about putting in a high bid to become the National Football League's official soft drink, it has to wonder how Coke will respond. Will it bid even higher? If it does, should Pepsi raise its bid still further? Or what if Coke decides to respond to the advertising advantage that Pepsi gains by launching a price war in the soft drink market?

Imperfect competition is played out against a background of interdependence or, what economists call, a setting of strategic interaction. This means that determining a firm's optimal behavior is also difficult. Because the firms are likely to be aware of the interdependency of their actions, each firm will wish to take into account its rivals' response to its action. Yet that response will also depend on how the rivals think the first firm will react to their reaction and so on. A firm in this situation needs to "put itself in its rival's shoes" to see how the rival will respond to different actions that the firm could take. The firm must do this in order to figure out what its best course of action is. To understand the logic of strategic interaction we use game theory. Game theory provides us with the necessary framework for an analysis of settings in which the participants or players recognize that what they do affects other players and, in turn, what other players do affects them. It is for this reason that much of the recent work in industrial organization uses game theory to understand market outcomes under imperfect competition. While not all of the analysis in this book relies

---

[1]   See B. McKay and S. Fatsis, "Pepsi Scores One on Coke, Gaining Sponsorship Rights to the NFL," *Wall Street Journal*, March 29, 2002, p. B5.

on game theory, a good bit of our discussion is aimed at developing and applying the logic of game theory to market settings.

Game theory permits us to analyze strategic interaction in both a clear and logically consistent manner. For this reason, it has become an indispensable tool in industrial organization. It is equally important, however, to recognize that game theory and, more generally, the understanding of strategic interaction serves a broader goal of understanding what industrial organization is about. This perhaps is best expressed by reference to a quote from John Maynard Keynes who wrote insightfully, "the theory of economics does not furnish a body of settled conclusions immediately applicable to policy. It is a method rather than a doctrine, an apparatus of the mind, a technique of thinking which helps its possessor to draw

Reality Checkpoint

Show Time!

Perhaps no example of strategic interaction is more common than the annual or even seasonal game television networks play in scheduling their programming. The objective is to get the highest "average audience" rating as calculated by the A. C. Nielsen Company and defined as the percentage of homes with a television that is tuned to a program during an average minute of prime time viewing. This value determines the advertising fees that a network can charge and, hence, is crucial to the network's profit. Indeed, scheduling strategy is understood throughout the broadcast market as a crucial element in network success and a variety of well-known tactics have emerged over the years. These include: (1) *quick openers*—starting the evening with one's strongest shows to set up the rest of the viewing night; (2) *infant protection*—the avoidance of scheduling promising new shows to compete with strong rival programming and/or using an existing strong network show to serve as a lead-in for the new one; (3) *counterprogramming*—scheduling say a police show in a slot where the major competition is a comedy; and (4) *bridging*—scheduling shows an hour long or longer so that competing shows of an hour's length begin in the middle of the scheduled program.

For example, the current ratings champ on network television is Fox's *American Idol* now in its sixth year and which runs on both Tuesday and Wednesday evenings from January to May. Indeed, *Idol* is so popular that it could lose half of its audience and still be rated in the top ten. It also serves as a strong lead-in for an already popular Fox show, *House*.

Part of the response of other networks has been to reschedule their best shows to avoid being crushed. ABC moved its hit *Lost* from a 9:00 p.m. start on Wednesdays to a 10:00 p.m. start after *Idol* finishes. ABC also decided to reschedule its popular reality show *Dancing with the Stars* so that it runs on Monday and Tuesday evenings and does not start until May when *Idol* goes off the air. NBC similarly moved its shows *Earl* and *The Office* from Tuesday nights to Thursday nights to escape the *Idol* juggernaut.

Industry executives openly admit that the anticipation of the arrival of *Idol* in January makes it particularly difficult for new shows that premier in September. The slots the networks have most available for a new show are precisely those vacated by the existing shows, namely, the ones that compete directly with *Idol*. This means that any new show that starts on Tuesday or Wednesday nights in September has to fear that it is living on borrowed time and ratings unless it can quickly establish a loyal following. Even then, its best hope is that it will be moved in January away from the *Idol* dominated times. Otherwise, the new show is likely to suffer the same fate of all but a few *Idol* contestants: "I don't mean to be rude, but . . ."

Sources: B. Carter, "For Fox Rivals, 'American Idol' Remains a Schoolyard Bully," *New York Times*, February 20, 2007, p. C1.

correct conclusions."[2] The same can be said of modern industrial organization. It is a technique of thinking. To be precise, it is a means of thinking strategically and applying the insights of such analysis to model imperfect competition.

Of course, no model is a complete description of reality. A complete detailing of each aspect of the actual marketplace would be far too lengthy and unwieldy to be of much use. Instead, any market model is like a road map. It is a deliberate simplification of a very complicated terrain, omitting some features and thereby emphasizing others. The aim of the model is to capture and make transparent the essential features of the interaction among firms. In this light, to say that the real world is more complicated than the model is no criticism. Indeed, if the modeling achieves its aim of making clear the underlying structure and the principles governing the market outcome, then its abbreviated portrait of the real world is its strength.

Whether or not a particular theoretical model is a good proxy for real world outcomes can be determined by testing the predictions of the model against actual data and observational evidence. Armed with ever-increasingly sophisticated statistical techniques, such testing has also become an essential part of the field of modern industrial organization. Throughout this book, you will find numerous Reality Checkpoints designed to illustrate the applicability of the concepts in question. In addition, you will find a number of recent empirical studies offering evidence on the validity of the various models.

The combination of theory and evidence provides a useful guide to the likely outcome of strategic interaction in a variety of settings. In each such case studied, the basic interpretation of the model and associated data is that "this is how to think about what happens in an imperfectly competitive market when." This is how we do industrial organization.

1.3   WHY? ANTITRUST AND INDUSTRIAL ORGANIZATION THEORY

The text of the principal U.S. antitrust statutes is given in the Appendix to this chapter. Suffice it to say at this point that such legislation came early to the United States with the passage of the first major antitrust law—the Sherman Act—in 1890. This predates much of the formal modeling of imperfect competition and, certainly its dissemination. However, economists had had an intuitive grasp of the potential problems of monopoly power as far back as Adam Smith. In his classic, *The Wealth of Nations* (1776), Smith had written on both collusion among ostensibly rival firms and on the raw exercise of monopoly power:

> People of the same trade seldom meet together, even for merriment or diversion, but the conversation ends in a conspiracy against the public, or in some contrivance to raise prices.
> The monopolists, by keeping the market constantly understocked, by never fully supplying the effectual demand, sell their commodities much above the natural price.

By the late nineteenth century, many Americans had become convinced that a few large firms and trusts, such as Standard Oil and American Tobacco, had exploited their market power in just the ways Smith had forecast. A consensus emerged—one that has endured throughout the history of antitrust legislation—that some form of legal framework was needed to maintain competition in the market place. Moreover, while few people had any understanding of formal economics, there was a reasonably wide familiarity with the sentiments of Adam Smith.

---

[2]   Keynes (1935).

Thus it was that popular sentiment, reinforced by shrewd Smithian insight, led to the enactment of the first U.S. antitrust law, the 1890 Sherman Act. Indeed, it is somewhat remarkable just how directly the concerns of Adam Smith are reflected in the two primary sections of the Sherman Act. Section 1 prohibits contracts, combinations, and conspiracies "in restraint of trade." Section 2 makes illegal any attempt to monopolize a market. The view that government institutions were necessary to achieve these aims was also later reflected in the Clayton and Federal Trade Commission Acts.

Antitrust policy, in the beginning, focused primarily on prosecuting and preventing collusive agreements to raise prices under the authority of Section 1. Early cases such as the *Trans-Missouri Freight Association* and the *Addyston Pipe* case of 1897 and 1898 respectively, established this tradition and it remains a centerpiece of antitrust policy to this day[3] as evidenced by the successful prosecution of agricultural products giant, Archer Daniels Midland, the world's two largest auction houses, Sotheby's and Christie's, the international pharmaceutical giant, Hoffman-LaRoche, and the DRAM manufacturers mentioned at the start of this chapter.

However, unlike the Section 1 statute, the enforcement of Section 2 on monopolization has been more limited. Despite wide public perception that many of the giant firms emerging from the Industrial Revolution had abused and exploited their monopoly power, it was 12 years before one of these, the Standard Oil Company of New Jersey, was prosecuted under Section 2.[4] That case eventually led to the famous Supreme Court ruling in 1911 that Standard Oil had illegally monopolized the petroleum refining industry. Similar findings against other trusts, including most notably the Tobacco Trust,[5] followed quickly. Yet unlike the price-fixing cases, these monopolization decisions were less clear about what actions were illegal. In particular, the court established a "rule of reason" framework for monopolization cases that permitted the courts to examine not only whether monopolization of an industry had occurred but, if so, what the market context was surrounding the formation of that monopoly and the business practices used to achieve it. Only if this additional inquiry found an explicit intent to monopolize or an obvious exploitation of monopoly power was there a true violation.

Practically speaking, the rule of reason approach meant that there was a lot of ambiguity in exactly what actions were illegal. This had two important results. First, those who feared that such a legal framework might weaken antitrust enforcement were motivated to pursue additional reforms so that Section 2 of the Sherman Act would not become a "paper-toothed tiger."[6] This led in 1914 to the passage of the Clayton Act meant to stop monopolization in its incipiency by limiting the use of a number of business practices such as rebates, tying, and exclusive contracts that were employed by Standard Oil in establishing its dominance. Section 7, which was later amended in the 1950s, was passed to prevent anticompetitive mergers.

It also led to passage of the Federal Trade Commission Act in 1914 that established an administrative agency, the Federal Trade Commission (FTC), endowed with powers of investigation and adjudication to handle Clayton Act violations. As later amended this Act also outlawed "unfair methods of competition" and "unfair and deceptive acts or practices." Creation of the FTC gave antitrust policy a second arm of law enforcement in addition to that provided by the Justice Department (DOJ).

---

[3]   *United States v. Trans-Missouri Freight Association*, 166 U.S. 290 (1897) and *United States v. Addyston Pipe & Steel Co.*, 85 F. 271 (6 Cir. 1898).

[4]   *Standard Oil Co. of New Jersey v. United States*, 221 U.S. 1 (1911). See also, Posner (1971).

[5]   *United States v. American Tobacco Co.*, U.S. 221 U.S. 106 (1911).

[6]   Berki (1966), p. ix.

The second major result stemming from adoption of a rule of reason approach emerged later with the *U.S. Steel* case of 1920. In that case, the Court made clear that in its view "the law does not make mere size an offense or the existence of unexerted power an offense—it does not compel competition nor require all that is possible."[7] As a result, the Court found U.S. Steel—a firm that through a series of mergers had grown to control over 70 percent of U.S. steel-making capacity—innocent of any antitrust violations.

The U.S. Steel decision had a major impact on both the steel industry and the U.S. legal framework. For our purposes, however, the reason that this case was so important is that it served as a major intellectual stimulus to the field of industrial organization. For the conclusion to which many analysts were led by the 1920 decision was that without a good economic road map by which to understand imperfect competition, the making of antitrust policy was a difficult proposition at best. It was the subsequent effort to provide that road map that initiated the field that we now call industrial organization.

Economists such as Edward Chamberlin (1933) and Edward Mason (1939), both at Harvard, led the way. In their view the microeconomics of the time offered little guidance either to policy makers or the legal system as to what evidence might be useful in determining the likely outcome that a market would produce. The Supreme Court's dismissal of the government charges of monopolization in the *U.S. Steel* case was based on an argument that no exploitation of monopoly power or intent to monopolize had been shown. Only U.S. Steel's large market share had been documented and, "*the law does not make mere size an offense*" [emphasis added]. Unless there was good reason to believe that a large market share offered strong evidence of monopolization, or until there was a coherent argument that identified other observable characteristics that in turn implied illegal behavior, the court's decision had a fair bit of justification.

More generally, economists at that time realized that any informed legal judgment would require some practical way to determine from observable evidence whether the industry in question was closer to perfect competition or closer to monopoly. Accordingly, they viewed the highest priority of industrial economics to be the determination of whether and how one could infer illegal behavior from either firm size or other structural features. It was to provide this policy guide that the field of industrial organization began to emerge. The very name of the field—industrial organization—dates from this time.

Early work therefore focused on a set of key questions: how is the production of the industry organized? How is the market structured? How many firms are there and how large are they relative to each other? Are there clear barriers to entry? It was recognized from the outset, however, that answering these questions would not be enough to provide the legal framework needed by legislators and courts to determine whether or not the antitrust laws had been violated. Achieving this goal required not only that an industry's structural features be revealed but that clear links between structure and market outcomes also be identified. That is, industrial economists needed to obtain data on prices, profits, and market structure, and then use these data to identify statistical relationships between various market structures, on the one hand, and industrial performance, on the other.

This was the agenda explicitly announced by Edward Mason who, in 1939 wrote, "The problem, as I see it, is to reduce the voluminous data concerning industrial organization to some sort of order through a classification of market structures. Differences in market structure are ultimately explicable in terms of technological factors. The economic problem,

---

[7]   *United States v. United States Steel Corporation*, 251 U.S. 417 (1920).

however, is to explain, through an examination of the structure of markets and the organization of firms, differences in competitive practices including price, production and investment policies."[8] In sum, the early industrial organization economists viewed their goal as one of establishing links between market structure, on the one hand, and the conduct of firms in the market, on the other. In turn, that conduct would determine the likely outcome or performance of the market in terms of economic efficiency or general social welfare. For this reason, this early approach is typically referred to as the Structure–Conduct–Performance or SCP approach. Presumably, if the outcome for a particular industry given its structure was sufficiently bad, legal action was justified either to alter the conduct that structure would otherwise generate or, if necessary, to change the structure itself.

The basic principle behind the SCP paradigm was that perfect competition and monopoly are usefully viewed as opposite ends of a spectrum of market structures along which all markets lie. One natural measure of market structure is the degree of concentration, or the percentage of market output produced by the largest firms in an industry. Accordingly, the practice of industrial economics at that time became one of, first, accurately describing the structure of different markets and, second, deriving empirical relations between structures and outcomes in terms of price–cost margins, innovative efforts, and other performance measures. Research focused on examining statistically the broad hypotheses on market structure and performance implied by the SCP paradigm. Here, structure was often identified with the degree of concentration or the percentage of total market output accounted for by the few largest firms. Finding a road map for policy was interpreted to mean providing numerical answers to questions such as how much would a bit more concentration or a bit higher entry barriers raise price above cost.

In pursuit of the SCP quest, the 1930s and 1940s witnessed numerous studies attempting to document and to measure the link between industrial performance, say profitability, and an industry's structural features, such as concentration. In some respects, this goal was met. For example, looking at a cross-section of industries each with a different structure and a different overall profitability, scholars found some positive correlation between the industry's profit rate and extent to which production was concentrated in the hands of just a few firms. Further studies found a similar positive link between advertising and profitability. The first finding gave support to the view that an industry in which there was more than one but still just a few, large firms was indeed somewhat close to the monopoly pole. The second finding was interpreted as evidence that firms used advertising to build customer loyalty and, thus, to deter other firms from entering the market. In turn, this permitted the incumbent firms to enjoy monopoly power and profit.

1.3.1   The "New" Sherman Act and the Dominance of Structure-based Analysis

The early findings of SCP scholars increasingly seemed to suggest that perhaps a firm's "mere size" could imply a legal offense if it is sufficiently large. The real question then became whether or not these developments would influence antitrust law. This question was answered in the affirmative with the 1945 *Alcoa* decision.

Alcoa was by far the largest aluminum manufacturer in North America. It had been prosecuted for antitrust violations a number of times prior to the 1945 case. In fact, so large a

---

[8]   Mason (1939), pp. 61–74.

number of Supreme Court justices in 1945 had had previous litigation experience with Alcoa that they could not participate in this proceeding with the result that the Supreme Court lacked a quorum to hear the case. Hence, the 1945 decision was issued by a special panel of three circuit court judges. In a key decision, this panel overturned the finding of innocence by the lower district court and found Alcoa guilty of monopolization under Section 2 of the Sherman Act. An explicit consideration for the Court was the issue of size.[9] Alcoa's market share depended critically on how one measured the market, and much attention was given to this issue. Ultimately, the Court defined Alcoa's relevant market to be primary aluminum ingot production. Using this definition, the Court found that Alcoa supplied 90 percent of the market. In effect, this decision was a major policy validation of the SCP approach.

Other cases also reflecting a newly found concern over market domination by large firms soon followed. In 1946, the Supreme Court found the big three tobacco companies, American Tobacco, Ligget & Myers, and R. J. Reynolds, that controlled 75 percent of domestic cigarette production, guilty of monopolization.[10] A number of similar cases continued over the next 20 years, culminating with such well-known ones as the 1962 *Brown Shoe* case and the 1964 case against the Grinnell Corporation. All of these cases gave increasing weight to market structure as an indictment of proposed or past actions.[11] The (in)famous price discrimination case of *Utah Pie* (1967) may also be read as an indictment of any outcome in which a few large firms come to dominate the market.[12] In that case, the Court viewed the pricing strategies of the bigger nationwide companies to be evidence of predatory intent against a smaller firm primarily because the shares of the larger firms grew over a four-year period. In short, the period from 1945 into the late 1960s reflects the growing dominance of the SCP framework as the major intellectual influence on antitrust policy.[13]

As noted, this "New" Sherman Act policy found its intellectual support in the cross-industry analyses of the SCP approach. Because our understanding of the potential pitfalls of empirical research has grown tremendously, as has our ability to do much more sophisticated empirical analysis that avoids those pitfalls, it is probably fair to say that these early studies are no longer highly regarded by economists. There are, in fact, many problems with these early findings some of which we will discuss more fully below. It should be equally clear, however, that historically the early SCP studies were quite influential. Indeed, their influence ranged beyond the U.S. Particularly after the Second World War, the influential role of the U.S. served to spread the U.S. antitrust approach. This was particularly true for Japan and West Germany. In both countries, the sustained presence of U.S. forces was accompanied by strong decartelization measures. However, explicit legislation aimed at preserving competition found support in other countries as well. (See, e.g., Please 1954.) Britain passed its Monopolies Act in 1948. In 1957, the initial Common Market agreement, the Treaty of Rome, that established the European Community for Steel and Coal included Articles 65 and 66 that explicitly forbade agreements aimed at restricting the "normal operation of competition" and even outlawed "unauthorized concentrations" of market power (Resch 2005). These policy initiatives reflected a similar, and probably earlier spread of the SCP approach to industrial economists around the world. (See for example, Stern 1955.)

---

[9] *United States v. Aluminum Co. of America (ALCOA)*, 148 F.2d 416 (2 Cir. 1945).

[10] *American Tobacco Company v. United States*, 328 U.S. 781 (1946).

[11] *Brown Shoe Co. v. United States*, 370 U.S. 294 (1962) and *United States v. Grinnell Corp.*, 236 F.Supp. 244 (D.R.I. 1964).

[12] *Utah Pie Co. v. Continental Baking Co., et al.*, 386 U.S. 685 (1967).

[13] For an excellent survey of antitrust history see Mueller (1996).

However, there was at least one key difference between American antitrust policy and that of its international associates. Outside the U.S. there was a general suspicion that unfettered competition was not necessarily the ideal to which antitrust policy ought to aspire. Instead, there was some presumption that state regulation and even state ownership were useful tools for curbing the abuse of market power. In this context, it is worthwhile noting that the U.S. is a much larger country than say, Canada, or even Japan and the U.K. Hence, its markets tend to be bigger as well. As a result, if the minimum size necessary for efficient operation is the same in all countries, firms that achieve that size will have much larger market share in nations outside the U.S. In turn, this gives more potential for market abuse and Europeans may have been particularly sensitive to this concern. Faced with a choice between large efficient firms that may abuse their power or small, inefficient ones that cannot, the third option of large firms directed by the state on behalf of the public may have seemed a good alternative.

1.3.2   The Tide Changes: The Chicago School and Beyond

Matters began to change in the 1970s. In part, this reflected a growing awareness among academic scholars that the SCP paradigm had important failings. One of these was that the vast array of empirical findings that the SCP researchers had amassed was actually subject to different interpretations. For example, consider the frequent finding that firms with large market shares tend to earn greater profit. This could be taken as a verification of the basic SCP view that the larger a firm's market share, the greater its monopoly power and the higher its profit. However, a more benign interpretation of this evidence is also possible. It could be that the most efficient or the lowest-cost firm gains the largest share of the market, so that both large size and healthy profit are simply reflections of a firm's superior technology or talent.[14]

Other problems also became important. While accounting profit is easily obtained measuring the truly relevant economic profit is far more difficult. Other measurement issues such as defining the relevant market and distinguishing between short run and long run can also be difficult to resolve.

What was really unsatisfactory about the SCP approach, however, was that in considering its middle link—firm conduct—little or no attention was paid to strategic interaction. Something of an exception in this regard was the work of Joseph Bain (1956), a former student of Edward Mason, who made many important contributions to the field. A skilled scholar with a keen eye for actual business practice, Bain was among the first to realize that an industry could not be completely defined by its concentration. In particular, Bain understood that beyond the market configuration of the industry's existing firms we also needed to understand the ability of new firms to enter the market. Even a highly concentrated industry might be forced to price competitively if there were new firms ready and able to enter and compete away the profit of any firm pricing above the competitive level. This was an important insight. Indeed, this idea played a central role in the "contestability" theory developed much later by Baumol, Panzar, and Willig (1982). Bain's point though is really a two-edged sword. The ease with which new firms can enter is at least partially the result of actions taken by

---

[14]   As shown later, this is a standard result in a Cournot model in which costs differ across firms. Specifically, if P is market price, η is the market demand elasticity at that price, and c_i and s_i are the ith firm's unit cost and market share, respectively, then it must be the case that: $\dfrac{P - c_i}{P} = \dfrac{s_i}{\eta}$. Lower cost firms will have larger market shares, larger profit margins, and larger total profit.

the firms already in the market. That is, incumbent firms can pursue strategic actions meant to influence the entry decisions of other, potential rivals. In this case, structure is an outcome of conduct but one can not easily address this issue within the SCP framework. For all these problems, the cross-industry scholarship that provided the foundation for the aggressive antitrust policy of the 1950s and 1960s began to fall sharply in disfavor.

Moreover, the weaknesses in the SCP paradigm were accompanied by a discomfort that many felt concerning the more aggressive antitrust enforcements mentioned above. In the *Brown Shoe* case, for example, the Court disallowed the merger of two firms (Brown and Kinney) even though they only controlled about 5 percent of the national market (though a greater percent of individual local markets). Similarly, the *Utah Pie* case seemed to be a decision that did more to protect a specific competitor (Utah Pie) than to protect competitive forces.

The rising concern over flaws in both the SCP approach and the public policy it had fostered made possible a counter-movement led by lawyers and economists from the Chicago School such as Richard Posner, Robert Bork, and Sam Peltzman. These and other scholars began to point out that many of the practices that the courts had been viewing as harmful to competition and economic welfare could, when viewed through the lens of corporate strategy and tactics, be seen as actually improving economic efficiency and bringing benefits to consumers. This work initially focused on the vertical relationships either between a firm and its suppliers or between a firm and its distributors. Many such vertical contracts include restrictions such as those that grant franchisees exclusive territories, or that require distributors to sell at some minimum price. Chicago School economists argued that there were good economic reasons for these practices and that these restrictions actually brought benefits to consumers. Gradually, these arguments were successful and many practices that had been previously found to be *per se* or outright illegal the court now began to review for their "reasonability" on a case-by-case method.[15]

The Chicago School influence on vertical relationships soon spread to more of antitrust policy. In 1974, the U.S. Supreme Court rejected the government's efforts to block a large merger in a case involving the General Dynamics Corporation.[16] Many mergers that would previously have been prevented soon followed, justified on both grounds of cost savings and the potential for new entrants to constrain any attempt by the newly merged firm to exercise monopoly power. The government also lost several key cases accusing large firms such as Kodak and IBM of monopolization in violation of the Sherman Act. In addition, the precedent of the *Utah Pie* case was firmly rejected during these subsequent years. It became increasingly clear—most notably in the case involving a complaint by Zenith Corporation charging that seven Japanese television manufacturers had attempted to drive out competitors—that in the courts' view, efforts to eliminate rivals by pricing below cost rarely made sense.[17]

The Chicago School's contributions are difficult to underestimate and its legal influence is felt to this day. These scholars were right to point out the need to examine the logic and reasonability of a firm's conduct. However, they were hampered by the fact that, as of that time, no language or framework in which to view such strategic behavior on a consistent basis had yet been developed. Yet such a framework was emerging. Building on the work of Von Neumann and Morgenstern (1944) and Nash (1951), Nobel Prize laureates Reinhard

---

15 *See Continental T.V. Inc. v. GTE Sylvania, Inc.*, 433 U.S. 36 (1977), *State Oil v. Khan, et al.*, 522 U.S. 3 (1997) and, recently, *Leegin Creative Leather Products, Inc. v. PSKS, Inc.*, 551 U.S. _____(2007).
16 *United States v. General Dynamics Corp.*, 415 U.S. (1974).
17 *Matsuhita Electric Industrial Co. v. Zenith Radio Corp.*, 475 U.S. 574 (1986).

Selten, John Harsanyi, Michael Spence, and Thomas Schelling all made a number of crucial contributions that permitted game theory to become the language for modeling strategic interaction. As we noted earlier, the period since the 1980s has witnessed the rapid spread of game theory to analyze virtually every aspect of imperfect competition. As a result, the field of industrial organization has again been transformed and now reflects, at least in part, what some call a Post-Chicago view and what others simply refer to as the "new IO." [18]

We have already noted that there is much to be said for pursuing a game-theoretic understanding of the strategic interaction of firms. What is important to note at this point is that it was game theory that allowed us a way to model and analyze firm behavior in imperfectly competitive markets. Moreover, as game theoretic analysis spread through modern industrial organization its insights have, to some extent, led to a diminution of the Chicago School's impact. However, it would be wrong to identify the advent of game theory models and the new Post-Chicago approach as a total rejection of the Chicago School's work. For example, the Merger Guidelines adopted jointly by the Federal Trade Commission and the Justice Department have deep roots in the Cournot–Nash game-theoretic model that we describe more fully in Chapter 15. While these guidelines are far from permissive, they still allow for many more mergers than would ever have legally occurred in the "New Sherman Act" years of the 1950s and 1960s.

These developments have been accompanied by similar ones elsewhere. In 1997, the European Union adopted the Treaty of Amsterdam that amended the earlier Common Market treaties in keeping with its goal of full economic integration. Articles 81 and 82 of the treaty replaced articles 65 and 66 of the earlier Treaty of Rome and implemented language that was perhaps even more similar to that of the U.S. to be implemented by the European Commission Director-General for Competition. This reflected the widespread recognition that adoption of a common antitrust policy for all union members became a real necessity as European firms increasingly operated across European borders. Like its U.S. counterpart, European antitrust policy has incorporated much of the post-SCP learning. This has been perhaps particularly true for the courts that have questioned a number of early Commission decisions.

However, important distinctions do remain between the U.S. and European approaches with respect to specific cases, with Europe typically pursuing stricter and more aggressive enforcement. Thus, in 2001 the European Commission blocked GE's acquisition of Honeywell International even though the U.S. had already approved that merger somewhat earlier. Somewhat similarly, Microsoft was ordered by the European Commission in 2003 to offer a version of its Windows operating system that did not automatically include Microsoft's Media Player software as well as to provide the technical information to others that would allow them to develop programs fully compatible with the Windows platform. When Microsoft did not comply satisfactorily with these orders, the Commission levied substantial fines totaling hundreds of millions of dollars. While the U.S. had earlier found Microsoft guilty of antitrust violations, nothing in the final settlement of that case seemed nearly as harsh. These decisions and others perhaps reflect the historically greater mistrust Europeans have of large corporations that we mentioned earlier. They also show that debate about both the appropriate underlying economic analysis and the appropriate public policy remains lively and important.

---

[18]   Schmalensee (1988) provides a survey of the then "new IO" that is still relevant. Kovacic and Shapiro (2000) survey the influence of game theory on modern antitrust policy. Kwoka and White (2004) offer a discussion of recent antitrust cases.

In short, concerns over antitrust policy have been a major motivation for industrial economists since the modern inception of that policy in the late nineteenth century, through the emergence of the SCP approach in the mid-twentieth century and continuing to the present, Post-Chicago paradigm that is so prominent at the start of the twenty-first century. Throughout this time, competition has been regarded as a cornerstone of a free-market economy both in the U.S. and elsewhere. Hence, we want to know how firms compete when they have market power, what implication that competition has, and what the role of public policy might be in helping imperfectly competitive markets achieve outcomes closer to the competitive ideal. To put it as succinctly as possible, the reason why we study industrial organization is to understand market competition in all its dimensions.

Summary

Industrial organization is the study of imperfect competition. Industrial economists are interested in markets that we actually encounter in the real world. However, these real world markets come in many shapes and flavors. For example, some are comprised of a few large firms, some have one large firm and many smaller ones. In some, the products are greatly differentiated while in others they are nearly identical. Some firms compete largely by trying to keep prices as low as possible. In other markets, advertising and other forms of non-price competition are the dominant tactics. This range of possibilities has meant that over time, industrial economics has become a field rich with practical insights regarding real business behavior and public policy. This book is all about these developments.

Firms in imperfectly competitive industries need to make strategic decisions—that is, decisions that will have identifiable impacts on other participants in the market, be they rival firms, suppliers, or distributors. As a result, making any such choice must inevitably involve some consideration of how these other players in the game will react. Examples of such strategic choice variables include price, product design, decisions to expand capacity, and whether or not to invest heavily in research and development of a new product. This book presents the modern analysis of market situations involving such strategic interaction—an analysis that is rooted in non-cooperative game theory. We use this analysis to examine such issues as why there are so many varieties of cereals, or how firms maintain a price-fixing agreement, or how advertising and product innovation affect the nature of competition. We also describe how the predictions of these models have been tested.

Our interest is in more than just determining the profit-maximizing strategies that firms in a particular market context should adopt. As economists we are interested in the market outcomes that result when firms adopt such strategies, and whether those outcomes are close to those of the competitive ideal. If not, we then need to ask whether and how public policy can improve market allocations. Our hope is to convey the value of economic research and the gains from learning "to think like an economist." More generally, we hope to demonstrate the vitality and relevance of industrial organization, both in theory and in practice.

Problems

1. List three markets that you think are imperfectly competitive. Explain your reasoning.

2. Explain why a perfectly competitive market does not reflect a setting of strategic interaction.

3. The Appendix to this chapter lists the current, major antitrust laws of the U.S. Review Sections 2 and 7 of the Clayton Act. What potential threats to competition do these sections address?

4. Suppose that sophisticated statistical research provides clear evidence that, all else equal, worker productivity increases as industrial concentration increases. How would you interpret this finding?

5. Why do you think that the U.S. courts have consistently disallowed any form of price-fixing agreement among different firms but have been more tolerant of market dominance by one firm?

References

Bain, Joseph. 1956. *Barriers to New Competition.* Cambridge, MA: Harvard University Press.

Baumol, W. J., J. C. Panzar, and R. D. Willig. 1982. *Contestable Markets and the Theory of Market Structure.* New York: Harcourt Brace Jovanovich.

Berki, S., ed. 1996. *Antitrust Policy: Economics and Law.* Boston: D.C. Heath and Company.

Chamberlin, E. H. 1933. *The Theory of Monopolistic Competition.* Cambridge, MA: Harvard University Press.

Kaysen, Carl and Donald Turner. 1959. *Antitrust Policy.* Cambridge, MA: Harvard University Press.

Keynes, J. M. 1935. *The General Theory of Employment, Interest and Money.* New York: Harcourt Brace and Company.

Kovacic, W. E. and C. Shapiro. 2000. "Antitrust Policy: A Century of Legal and Economic Thinking." *Journal of Economic Perspectives* 14: 43–60.

Kwoka, J. E. and L. J. White. 2004. *The Antitrust Revolution: Economics, Competition, and Policy.* 4th edition. Oxford: Oxford University Press.

Mason, E. S. 1939. "Price and Production Policies of Large Scale Enterprise." *American Economic Review* 29: 61–74.

Mueller, Dennis C. 1996. "Lessons from the United State's Antitrust History." *International Journal of Industrial Organization* 14: 415–45.

Nash, J. 1951. "Noncooperative Games." *Annals of Mathematics* 54: 286–95.

Please, A. 1954. "Some Aspects of European Monopoly Legislation." *Journal of Industrial Economics* 3 (December): 34–46.

Posner, R. 1971. "A Statistical Study of Antitrust Enforcement." *Journal of Law and Economics* 13 (October).

Resch, A. 2005. "Phases of Competition Policy in Europe." University of California at Berkeley, Institute of European Studies, Working Paper 050401.

Schelling, T. 1959. *The Strategy of Conflict.* New York: Oxford University Press.

Schmalensee, R. 1988. "Industrial Economics: An Overview." *Economic Journal* 98: 643–81.

Stern, E. H. "Industrial Production and Profits in the United Kingdom and the United States." *Economic Journal* 3 (August): 1955.

Von Neumann, J. and O. Morgenstern. 1944. *Theory of Games and Economic Behavior.* Princeton: Princeton University Press.

Appendix

Excerpts from Key Antitrust Statutes

THE SHERMAN ACT

Sec. 1 Every contract, combination in the form of trust or otherwise, or conspiracy, in restraint of trade or commerce among the several States, or with foreign nations, is declared to be illegal. Every person who shall make any contract or engage in any combination or conspiracy hereby declared to be illegal shall be deemed guilty of a felony, and, on conviction thereof, shall be punished by fine not exceeding $10,000,000,000 if a corporation, or, if any other person, $350,000, or by imprisonment not exceeding three years, or by both said punishments, in the discretion of the court.

Sec. 2 Every person who shall monopolize, or attempt to monopolize, or combine or conspire with any other person or persons, to monopolize any part of the trade or commerce among the several States, or with foreign nations, shall be deemed guilty of a felony, and, on conviction thereof, shall be punished by fine not exceeding $10,000,000,000 if a corporation, or, if any other person, $350,000, or by imprisonment not exceeding three years, or by both said punishments, in the discretion of the court.

THE CLAYTON ACT, INCLUDING KEY AMENDMENTS OF THE ROBINSON–PATMAN ACT AND CELLER–KEFAUVER ACT

Sec. 2

(a) Price; selection of customers

It shall be unlawful for any person engaged in commerce, in the course of such commerce, either directly or indirectly, to discriminate in price between different purchasers of commodities of like grade and quality, where either or any of the purchases involved in such discrimination are in commerce, where such commodities are sold for use, consumption, or resale within the United States or any Territory thereof or the District of Columbia or any insular possession or other place under the jurisdiction of the United States, and where the effect of such discrimination may be substantially to lessen competition or tend to create a monopoly in any line of commerce, or to injure, destroy, or prevent competition with any person who either grants or knowingly receives the benefit of such discrimination, or with customers of either of them: Provided, That nothing herein contained shall prevent differentials which make only due allowance for differences in the cost of manufacture, sale, or delivery resulting from the differing methods or quantities in which such commodities are to such purchasers sold or delivered: Provided, however, That the Federal Trade Commission may, after due investigation and hearing to all interested parties, fix and establish quantity limits, and revise the same as it finds necessary, as to particular commodities or classes of commodities, where it finds that available purchasers in greater quantities are so few as to render differentials on account thereof unjustly discriminatory or promotive of monopoly in any line of commerce; and the foregoing shall then not be construed to permit differentials based on differences in quantities greater than those so fixed and established: And provided further, That nothing herein contained shall prevent persons engaged in selling goods, wares, or merchandise in commerce from selecting their own customers in bona fide transactions and not in restraint of trade: And provided further, That nothing herein contained shall prevent price changes from time to time where in response to changing conditions affecting the market for or the marketability of the goods concerned, such as but not limited to actual or imminent deterioration of perishable goods, obsolescence of seasonal goods, distress sales under court process, or sales in good faith in discontinuance of business in the goods concerned.

(b) Burden of rebutting prima-facie case of discrimination

Upon proof being made, at any hearing on a complaint under this section, that there has been discrimination in price or services or facilities furnished, the burden of rebutting the prima-facie case thus made by showing justification shall be upon the person charged with a violation of this section, and unless justification shall be affirmatively shown, the Commission is authorized to issue an order terminating the discrimination: Provided, however, That nothing herein contained shall prevent a seller rebutting the prima-facie case thus made by showing that his lower price or the furnishing of services or facilities to any purchaser or purchasers was made in good faith to meet an equally low price of a competitor, or the services or facilities furnished by a competitor.

(c) Payment or acceptance of commission, brokerage, or other compensation

It shall be unlawful for any person engaged in commerce, in the course of such commerce, to pay or grant, or to receive or accept, anything of value as a commission, brokerage, or other compensation, or any allowance or discount in lieu thereof, except for services rendered in connection with the sale or purchase of goods, wares, or merchandise, either to the other party, to an agent, representative, or other intermediary therein where such intermediary is acting in fact for or in behalf, or is subject to the direct or indirect control, of any party to such transaction other than the person by whom such compensation is so granted or paid.

(d) Payment for services or facilities for processing or sale

It shall be unlawful for any person engaged in commerce to pay or contract for the payment of anything of value to or for the benefit of a customer of such person in the course of such commerce as compensation or in consideration for any services or facilities furnished by or through such customer in connection with the processing, handling, sale, or offering for sale of any products or commodities manufactured, sold, or offered for sale by such person, unless such payment or consideration is available on proportionally equal terms to all other customers competing in the distribution of such products or commodities.

(e) Furnishing services or facilities for processing, handling, etc.

It shall be unlawful for any person to discriminate in favor of one purchaser against another purchaser or purchasers of a commodity bought for resale, with or without processing, by contracting to furnish or furnishing, or by contributing to the furnishing of, any services or facilities connected with the processing, handling, sale, or offering for sale of such commodity so purchased upon terms not accorded to all purchasers on proportionally equal terms.

(f) Knowingly inducing or receiving discriminatory price

It shall be unlawful for any person engaged in commerce, in the course of such commerce, to be a party to, or assist in, any transaction of sale, or contract to sell, which discriminates to his knowledge against competitors of the purchaser, in that, any discount, rebate, allowance, or advertising service charge is granted to the purchaser over and above any discount, rebate, allowance, or advertising service charge available at the time of such transaction to said competitors in respect of a sale of goods of like grade, quality, and quantity; to sell, or contract to sell, goods in any part of the United States at prices lower than those exacted by said person elsewhere in the United States for the purpose of destroying competition, or eliminating a competitor in such part of the United States; or, to sell, or contract to sell, goods at unreasonably low prices for the purpose of destroying competition or eliminating a competitor.

Sec. 3.

Sale, etc., on agreement not to use goods of competitor

It shall be unlawful for any person engaged in commerce, in the course of such commerce, to lease or make a sale or contract for sale of goods, wares, merchandise, machinery, supplies, or other commodities, whether patented or unpatented, for use, consumption, or resale within the United States or any Territory thereof or the District of Columbia or any insular possession or other place under the jurisdiction of the United States, or fix a price charged therefore, or discount from, or rebate upon, such price, on the condition, agreement, or understanding that the lessee or purchaser thereof shall not use or deal in the goods, wares, merchandise, machinery, supplies, or other commodity of a competitor or competitors of the lessor seller, where the effect of such lease, sale, or contract for sale or such condition, agreement, or understanding may be to substantially lessen competition or tend to create a monopoly in any line of commerce.

Sec. 7.

No person engaged in commerce or in any activity affecting commerce shall acquire, directly or indirectly, the whole or any part of the stock or other share capital and no person subject to the jurisdiction of the Federal Trade Commission shall acquire the whole or any part of the assets of another person engaged also in commerce or in any activity affecting commerce, where in any line of commerce or in any activity affecting commerce in any section of the country, the effect of such acquisition may be substantially to lessen competition, or to tend to create a monopoly.

2

Basic Microeconomics

The principal antitrust statutes in America were put into place over a hundred years ago. At that time economic theory offered little understanding of market outcomes beyond Adam Smith's original and intuitive insights. The formal modeling of those insights and of the benefits of competition versus monopoly were just beginning to appear in professional academic works, most notably, Alfred Marshall's *Principles of Economics*, vol. 1 (1890). A similarly rigorous understanding of what happens in that gray area between competition and monopoly would take some time to be developed and then some more time to be worked into the economics curriculum. Yet a sound understanding of the perfectly competitive and pure monopolized markets is, even by itself, quite insightful. Indeed, these models continue to provide useful starting points for interpreting much of what one reads about in the daily business press. They also reveal the primary intellectual force behind public policies designed to limit monopoly power. For all these reasons, we undertake in this chapter a review of the basic models of perfect competition and monopoly.

2.1 COMPETITION VERSUS MONOPOLY: THE POLES OF MARKET PERFORMANCE

Our review of the perfect competition and monopoly models is necessarily brief. We focus on firm profit-maximizing behavior and the resultant market outcome that such behavior implies. We take as given the derivation of an aggregate consumer demand for the product that defines the market of interest. This market demand curve describes the relationship between how much money consumers are willing to pay per unit of the good and the aggregate quantity of the good consumed. Figure 2.1 shows an example of a market demand curve—more specifically, a linear market demand curve, which can be described by the equation $P = A - BQ$. When we write the demand curve in this fashion with price on the left-hand side it is often called an inverse demand curve.[1] The vertical intercept A is the maximum willingness to

---

[1] The reason for this terminology is that traditionally in microeconomics, we think of quantity demanded as being the dependent variable (left-hand side of the equation), and price, the independent variable (right-hand side of the equation). However, when firms choose quantities and price adjusts to clear the market, it is preferable to put market price on the left-hand side, hence, the inverse demand function. Our discussion should make clear that the market demand curve can be thought of as the horizontal summation of the individual demand curve of each consumer. It is not, however, the horizontal summation of the demand curve facing each firm.

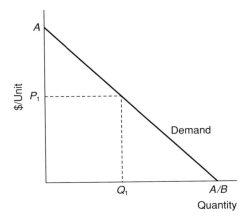

Figure 2.1   Market demand curve
The price P_1 is the marginal consumer valuation of an additional unit of output when current output is Q_1.

pay, or maximum reservation demand price that any consumer is willing to pay to have this good. At market prices greater than A, no one in this market wants to buy the product. As market price falls below A, demand for the product increases. For example, if the market price of the good is P_1 then consumers will desire to purchase a quantity Q_1 of the good. The price P_1 is the most any consumer would pay to consume the last or the Q_1th unit of the good. The price P_1 describes consumer willingness to pay at the margin.

When we draw a demand curve we are implicitly thinking of some period of time over which the good is consumed. For example, we may want to look at consumer demand for the product per week, or per quarter, or per year. Similarly when we talk about firms producing the good, we want to consider their corresponding weekly, quarterly, or annual production of the good. The temporal period over which we define consumer demand and firm production typically affects what production technologies are available to the firm for producing the good. The shorter the time period, the fewer options any firm has for acquiring or hiring more inputs for use in production. Following the tradition in microeconomics, we distinguish between two time periods: the short-run and the long-run production periods. The short run is a sufficiently short time period for the industry so that no new production facilities—no new plant and equipment—can be brought on line. In the short run, neither the number of firms nor the fixed capital at each firm can be changed. By contrast, the long run is a production period sufficiently long so that firms can build new production facilities to meet market demand.

For either the short-run or the long-run scenario we are interested in determining when a market is in equilibrium. By this we mean finding an outcome at which the market is "at rest." A useful interpretation of a market equilibrium is a situation in which no consumer and no firm in the market has an incentive to change its decision on how much to buy or how much to sell. The precise meaning of this definition may vary depending on whether we consider the short run or the long run. In either case, the essential feature is the same. Equilibrium requires that no one has an incentive to change his or her trading decision.

2.1.1   Perfect Competition

A perfectly competitive firm is a "price taker." The price of its product is not something that the perfectly competitive firm chooses. Instead, that price is determined by the interaction of all the firms and consumers in the market for this good, and it is beyond the influence of any one of the perfectly competitive firms. This characterization only makes sense if each firm's potential supply of the product is "small" relative to market demand for the product. If a firm's supply of a good were large relative to the market, we would expect that that firm could influence the price at which the good was sold. An example of a "small" firm would be a wheat farmer in Kansas or, alternatively, a broker on the New York Stock Exchange trading IBM stock. Each is so small that any feasible change in behavior leaves the prices of wheat and IBM stock, respectively, unchanged.

Because a perfectly competitive firm cannot influence the market price at which the good trades, the firm perceives that it can sell as much, or as little, as it wants to at that price. If the firm cannot sell as much as it wants to at the market price, then the implication is that selling more would require a fall in the price. But this would imply that the firm has some power over the market price—and so such a firm would not be a perfect competitor. If the firm can affect the price received by other producers, its actions have consequences that will affect other participants, leading the firm to engage in strategic behavior. Hence, to be a true perfectly competitive firm, the firm's output decision must not affect the going price. This feature may be illustrated in a graph by drawing the demand curve for a perfectly competitive firm as a horizontal line at the current market price. Note that a perfectly competitive firm faces a horizontal demand curve even though the market or industry demand curve describing demand faced by the entire industry is downward sloping.[2]

Like all firms, the perfectly competitive ones will each choose that output level which maximizes their individual profit. Profit is defined as the difference between the firm's revenue and its total costs. Revenue is just market price, P, times the firm's output, q. The firm's total cost is assumed to rise with the level of the firm's production according to some function, $C(q)$. It is important to understand that the firm's costs include the amount necessary to pay the owners of the firm's capital (that is, its stockholders) a normal or competitive return. This is a way of saying that input costs are properly measured as opportunity costs. That is, each input must be paid at least what that input could earn in its next best alternative employment. This is true for the capital employed by the firm as much as it is true for the labor and raw materials that the firm also uses. Generally speaking, the opportunity cost for the firm's capital is measured as the rate of return that the capital could earn if invested in other industries. This cost is then included in our measure of total cost, $C(q)$. In other words, the concept of profit we are using is that of economic profit and reflects net revenue above what is necessary to pay all of the firm's inputs at least what they could earn in alternative employment. The reason why this point is important is because it makes clear that when a firm earns no economic profit it does not mean that its stockholders go away empty-handed. It simply means that those stockholders do not earn more than a normal return on their investment.

A necessary condition for such profit maximization is that the firm chooses an output level such that the revenue received for the last unit produced, or the marginal revenue, just equals the cost incurred to produce that last unit, or the marginal cost. This condition for profit maximization holds for the output choice of any firm, be it a perfectly competitive one, or a monopoly. Since total revenue depends on the amount produced, marginal revenue is also

---

[2]   This follows from the definition of a perfect competitor. One may wonder how each firm can face a horizontal demand curve while industry demand is downward sloped. The answer is that the demand curve facing the industry reflects the summation of the individual demand presented by each consumer—not the individual demand facing each firm.

dependent on q as described by the marginal revenue function, $MR(q)$. Because the perfectly competitive firm can sell as much as it likes at the going market price, each additional unit of output produced and sold generates additional revenue exactly equal to the current market price. That is, the marginal revenue function for a competitive firm is just $MR(q) = P$. Similarly, because total cost is a function of total output, q, so the marginal cost function also depends on q, according to the function $MC(q)$. This function describes the cost incurred by the firm for each successive unit of output produced.

Diagrams like those shown in Figures 2.2(a) and 2.2(b), respectively, are often used to illustrate the standard textbook model of the perfectly competitive firm and the perfectly competitive market in which the firm sells. For any market to be in equilibrium, the first order condition mentioned earlier must hold for each firm. For a competitive market, this means that for each firm the price received for a unit of output exactly equals the cost of producing that output at the margin. This condition is illustrated in Figures 2.2(a) and 2.2(b). The initial industry demand curve is D_1 and the market price is P_C. A firm producing output q_C incurs a marginal cost of production $MC(q_C)$ just equal to that price. Producing one more unit would incur an extra cost, as indicated by the marginal cost curve MC that exceeds the price at which that unit would sell. Conversely, producing less than q_C would save less in cost than it would sacrifice in revenue. When the firm produces q_C and sells it at market price, P_C, it is maximizing profit. It therefore has no incentive to change its choice of output. Hence, in a competitive equilibrium each firm must produce at a point where its marginal cost is just equal to the price.

Total market supply, Q_C, is the sum of each firm's output, q_C. Since each firm is maximizing profit, the condition $P = MC(q_C)$, will hold for each firm. If demand for the product increases and the market price rises to say P_1, each firm will revise its production decision and increase output to q_1, where $P_1 = MC(q_1)$. This will increase total production to Q_1. Indeed, because the firms' production decisions are governed by costs at the margin, the marginal cost curve of each firm provides the basis for determining the total supply at any given market price. As the price rises, we work out how each firm adjusts its profit-maximizing output by moving up its marginal cost function to a point where $P = MC(q)$ at this new price. Then we add up all the firms' revised decisions and compute the total output now supplied. Repeating this exercise for various prices reveals the industry supply function indicating the total output supplied at any given market price. It is illustrated by the curve S_1 in Figure 2.2(b). Since for each firm price is equal to its marginal cost, it must be the case that at each point on the supply function for every firm the incremental cost of the last unit produced is just equal to that price.

Consider a simple linear example where each firm's marginal cost curve is linear instead of curved as shown in Figure 2.2(a). Specifically, let the marginal cost of each firm be: $MC(q) = 4q + 8$. Given a market price P, the optimal output for any one competitive firm is then q such that $4q + 8 = P$, implying that the optimal output for each such firm satisfies

$$q = \frac{P}{4} - 2.$$

If there are 80 such firms, total industry production Q at price P is 80 times q or $Q^S = 20P - 160$. Solving for P writes the resultant supply curve in the form implied by Figures 2.2(a) and 2.2(b) in which price appears on the vertical axis. This yields $P = 0.05Q^S + 8$. At a price of 8, each firm will produce zero output. Industry output will also be zero. A rise in P to 12 will induce each firm to raise its output to 1 unit, increasing industry output to 80. A further rise to $P = 16$ will lead every firm to raise its output to 2 units, implying a total supply of 160. We could repeat this exercise many times over, each time choosing a

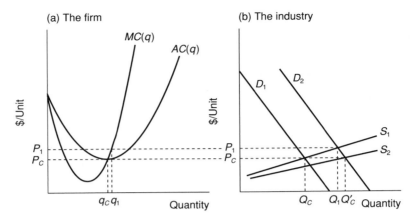

Figure 2.2   The long-run competitive equilibrium

Price P_1 is consistent with a short-run equilibrium in which each firm produces at a point where its marginal cost is equal to P_1. However, at P_1 price exceeds average cost and each firm earns a positive economic profit. This will encourage entry by new firms, shifting out the supply curve as shown in (b). The long-run competitive equilibrium occurs at price P_C in which each firm produces output level q_C and price equals both average and marginal cost.

different price. Plotting the industry output against each such price yields the industry supply curve. The important point to understand is that the derivation of that supply curve reflects the underlying first order condition for profit maximization—that is, each competitive firm choose a profit-maximizing level of output such that $P = MC(q)$.

In the example shown in Figures 2.2(a) and 2.2(b), the market initially clears at the price, P_C. Given the demand curve D_1, this equilibrium is consistent with the first order condition that each firm produce an output such that $P = MC(q)$. The requirement that each firm produces where marginal cost equals the market price is almost all that is required for a competitive equilibrium in the short run.[3] However, there is an additional condition that must be met in order for this to be a long-run competitive equilibrium. The condition is that in a long-run equilibrium each firm earns zero economic profit. This condition is also met in the initial equilibrium illustrated in Figure 2.2(a). At output q_C, each firm is just covering its cost of production, including the cost of hiring capital as well as labor and other inputs. In other words, a long-run competitive equilibrium requires that firms just "break even" and not earn any economic profit—revenue that exceeds the amount required to attract the productive inputs into the industry. This requirement can be stated differently. In the long run, the price of the good must just equal the average or per unit cost of producing the good. Again, both this zero profit condition and the further requirement that price equal marginal cost are satisfied in the initial equilibrium in which the industry demand curve is D_1 and the price is P_C.

If demand suddenly shifts to the level described by the demand curve, D_2, the existing industry firms will respond by increasing output. In so doing, these firms maximize profit by again satisfying the first requirement that they each produce where $P = MC(q)$. This leads

---

[3]   We say almost because there may be a distinction between average variable cost and marginal cost. No production will occur at all in the short run if the firm cannot produce at a level that will cover its average variable cost.

each firm to expand its production from q_C to q_1, thereby raising the market output to Q_1. However, this short-run response does not satisfy the zero profit condition required for a long-run competitive equilibrium. At price P_1, the market price equals each firm's marginal cost but exceeds each firm's average cost. Hence, each firm earns a positive economic profit of $P_1 - AC(q_1)$ on each of the q_1 units it sells.

Such profit either induces new firms to enter the industry or existing firms to expand production. This expansion shifts the industry supply curve outward until the equilibrium price again just covers average cost. Figure 2.2(b) illustrates this by the shift in the industry supply curve to S_2. As drawn, this shift reestablishes the initial price, P_C. Each firm again produces output q_C at which the industry price equals both the firm's marginal cost and its average cost. Of course, total industry output is now higher at Q'_C. While each firm is producing the output q_C, there are now more firms. The point is that in a long-run market equilibrium no firm has the incentive to change its production plan and in the long run, this means no firm wishes either to leave or to enter the market.

2.1

Assume that the manufacturing of cellular phones is a perfectly competitive industry. The market demand for cellular phones is described by a linear demand function:

$Q^D = \dfrac{6000 - 50P}{9}$. There are 50 manufacturers of cellular phones. Each manufacturer has

the same production costs. These are described by long-run total and marginal cost functions of $TC(q) = 100 + q^2 + 10q$, and $MC(q) = 2q + 10$.

a.   Show that a firm in this industry maximizes profit by producing $q = \dfrac{P - 10}{2}$

b.   Derive the industry supply curve and show that it is $Q^S = 25P - 250$.
c.   Find the market price and aggregate quantity traded in equilibrium.
d.   How much output does each firm produce? Show that each firm earns zero profit in equilibrium.

Practice Problem

Under perfect competition each firm's production of the good is small relative to the market. Now suppose that all these sellers become consolidated into one firm that is, by definition, a monopoly. Since the monopolist is the only supplier of the good, the monopoly is likely to be large relative to market demand. Specifically, the monopolist's demand curve is identical with the market demand curve. In complete contrast to the competitive firm, the monopoly firm is able to influence the price it receives for selling in this market. The monopolist's output decision will play a decisive role in determining the market-clearing price.

2.1.2   Monopoly

As shown in Figure 2.3, the downward slope of the monopolist's demand curve means that more production leads to a fall in price. For instance, a monopolist who was selling Q_1 units at price P_1 will find that increasing production to Q_2 units will cause the market price to fall from P_1 to P_2. The good news is that, by selling the additional output, the monopolist earns additional revenue. However, the bad news is that the original Q_1 units no longer sell at a price of P_1. Now, these units sell for only P_2 each. Often it is the case and we will assume

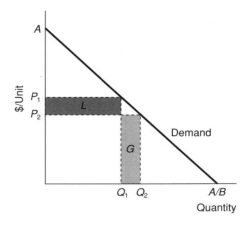

Figure 2.3   The marginal revenue from increased production for a monopolist
An increase in production from Q_1 to Q_2 causes a gain in revenues approximated by area G and a loss in revenues approximated by area L. The net change or marginal revenue is therefore $G - L$. Note, because the firm is a monopolist, this is also the net revenue gain generated by cutting price from P_1 to P_2.

it here that the monopolist cannot charge the first Q_1 customers a high price and the next $Q_2 - Q_1$ customers a lower price for the same commodity. The fact that such price discrimination is ruled out means that the monopolist must sell at the market-clearing price to all consumers and, therefore, that increases in the monopolist's total output will reduce the equilibrium market price.

Accordingly, the monopolist is very different from the competitive firm that reckons that every additional unit sold will bring in revenue equal to the current market price. Instead, the monopolist knows that every unit sold will bring in marginal revenue less than the existing price. Because the additional output can be sold only if the price declines, the marginal revenue from an additional unit sold is not market price but something less.

Marginal revenue for a monopolist is illustrated by the shaded areas G and L in Figure 2.3. These areas reflect the two forces affecting the monopolist's revenue when the monopolist increases output from Q_1 to Q_2, and thereby causes the price to fall from P_1 to P_2. Area G is equal to the new price P_2 times the rise in output, $Q_2 - Q_1$. It is the revenue gain that comes from selling more units. Area L equals the amount by which the price falls, $P_1 - P_2$, times the original output level, Q_1. This reflects the revenue lost on the initial Q_1 units as a result of cutting the price to P_2. The net change in the monopolist's revenue is the difference between the gain and the loss or $G - L$.

We can be more precise about this. Let $\Delta Q = Q_2 - Q_1$, and $\Delta P = P_1 - P_2$. The slope of the monopolist's (inverse) demand curve may then be expressed $\dfrac{\Delta P}{\Delta Q}$. If we describe this demand curve (which of course is also the market demand curve) as a linear relation, $P = A - BQ$, that slope is also equal to the term, $-B$, i.e., $\dfrac{\Delta P}{\Delta Q} = -B$. In other words, an increase in output ΔQ[4] leads to a decline in price ΔP equal to $-B\Delta Q$. Since total revenue is defined

---

[4]   Under perfect competition, firm output is different from industry output. So we use a lower case q to refer to firm output and an upper case Q for industry output. Under monopoly, firm output is the market output and so we use Q to describe both.

as price per unit times the number of units sold, we can write total revenue as a function of the firm's output decision, or $R(Q) = P(Q)Q = (A - BQ)Q$. As just shown in Figure 2.3, the change in revenue, $\Delta R(Q)$, due to the increase in output ΔQ, is the sum of two effects. The first is the revenue gain, $P_2 \Delta Q$. The second is the revenue loss, $Q_1 \Delta P$. Hence,

$$\Delta R(Q) = P_2 \Delta Q - Q_1 \Delta P = (A - BQ_2)\Delta Q - Q_1(B \Delta Q) \tag{2.1}$$

where we have used the demand curve to substitute $A - BQ_2$ for P_2 in the first term on the right-hand side. $MR(Q)$, is measured on a per unit basis. Hence, we must divide the change in revenue shown in equation (2.1) by the change in output, ΔQ, to obtain marginal revenue. This yields

$$MR(Q) = \frac{\Delta R(Q)}{\Delta Q} = A - BQ_2 - BQ_1 \approx A - 2BQ \tag{2.2}$$

Here we have used the approximation, $B(Q_1 + Q_2) \approx 2BQ$. This will be legitimate so long as we are talking about small changes in output, i.e., so long as Q_2 is fairly close to Q_1.

Equation (2.2)—sometimes referred to as the "twice as steep rule"—is quite important, and we will make frequent reference to it throughout the text. It not only illustrates that the monopolist's marginal revenue is less than the current price but, for the case of linear demand, also demonstrates the precise relationship between price and marginal revenue. The equation for the monopolist's marginal revenue function, $MR(Q) = A - 2BQ$, has the same price intercept A as the monopolist's demand curve but twice the slope, $-2B$ versus just $-B$. In other words, when the market demand curve is linear, the monopolist's marginal revenue curve starts from the same vertical intercept as that demand curve, but is everywhere twice as steeply sloped. The monopolist's marginal revenue curve must then lie everywhere below the inverse demand curve.

In Figure 2.4, we show both the market demand curve and the corresponding marginal revenue curve facing the monopolist. Again profit maximization requires that a firm produce

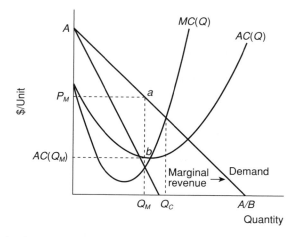

Figure 2.4 The textbook monopoly case
The monopolist maximizes profit by choosing the output Q_M at which marginal revenue equals marginal cost. The price at which this output can be sold is identified by the demand curve as P_M, which exceeds marginal cost. Profit is $abcd$. The competitive industry would have instead produced Q_C, at which point price equals marginal cost.

Derivation Checkpoint

The Calculus of Competition

For those familiar with calculus, the competitive firm's problem may be solved by first writing the firm's profit π as a function of its output q, or as $\pi(q)$ which, in turn, is defined as the difference between revenue $R(q)$ and cost $C(q)$. If we then recognize that revenue is just price times quantity or $R(q) = Pq$, we obtain:

$$\pi(q) = R(q) - C(q) = Pq - C(q)$$

Maximization of the firm's profit requires taking the derivative of the profit function with respect to q and setting it equal to zero. Recall however that the competitive firm takes P as given. Hence, the standard maximization procedure yields:

$$\frac{d\pi}{dq} = P - C'(q) = 0$$

Since $C'(q)$ is the change in cost as one more unit is produced it is precisely what we call marginal cost. Hence the profit-maximizing condition for the competitive firm is to choose the output q for which marginal cost $C'(q)$ equals price P.

For the monopoly firm, its output is the same as industry output Q and so its price is not given but instead declines with output as the firm moves down its demand curve. That is, the monopolist does not face a single price but instead a price function $P(Q)$, which is really the inverse demand curve. Hence, the monopolist's profit maximization problem is to choose output Q so as to maximize:

$$\pi(Q) = R(Q) - C(Q) = P(Q)Q - C(Q)$$

Again, standard maximization techniques yield:

$$\frac{d\pi}{dQ} = P(Q) + QP'(Q) - C'(Q) = 0$$

The sum, $P(Q) + QP'(Q)$, is the firm's marginal revenue. The monopolist will maximize profit by producing where marginal cost equals marginal revenue. For a linear demand curve of the form of $P(Q) = A - BQ$ we have $P'(Q) = -B$. Hence, in this case, the firm's marginal revenue is $A - BQ - BQ$, or $A - 2BQ$. The monopolist's marginal revenue curve has the same intercept as its demand curve but is twice as steeply sloped.

Note that the profit-maximizing condition above can also be written as

$$P(Q) - C'(Q) = -QP'(Q)$$

Dividing both sides by $P(Q)$ we then have

$$\frac{P(Q) - C'(Q)}{P(Q)} = -\frac{QP'(Q)}{P(Q)} = \frac{1}{\eta}$$

Where η is what economists call the elasticity of demand—a measure of how responsive the quantity demanded is to price movements. It is formally defined as:

$$\eta = \frac{P(Q)}{Q} \frac{1}{P'(Q)}$$

up to the point where the marginal revenue associated with the last unit of output just covers the marginal cost of producing that unit. This is true for the monopoly firm as well as for the perfectly competitive firm. The key and important difference here is that for the monopoly firm, marginal revenue is less than price. For the monopoly firm, the profit-maximizing rule of marginal revenue equal to marginal cost, or $MR(Q) = MC(Q)$, holds at the output Q_M. The profit-maximizing monopolist produces at this level and sells each unit at the price P_M. Observe that, at this output level, the revenue received from selling the last unit of output MR is less than the price at which that output is sold, $MR(Q_M) < P_M$. It is this fact that leads the monopolist to produce an output below the (short-run) equilibrium output of a competitive industry, Q_C.

We have also drawn the average cost function for the monopoly firm in Figure 2.4. The per unit or average cost of producing the output level Q_M, described on the average cost curve by $AC(Q_M)$, is less than the price P_M at which the monopolist sells the good. This means, of course, that total revenue exceeds total cost, and so the monopolist earns a positive economic profit. The monopoly profit is shown as the rectangle $P_M ab AC(Q_M)$. Furthermore, because the monopolist is the only firm in this market, and because we assume that no other firm can enter and supply this good, this market outcome is a long-run equilibrium. Each consumer buys as much as he wants to at price P_M and, given these cost conditions, the monopolist has no incentive to sell more or to sell less. Even in the long run, there is no tendency under monopoly for the market price to equal the unit cost of production.

Reality Checkpoint

Hung Up on Monopoly

It is not always easy to find examples of the classic monopoly behavior described in economics textbooks. However, Tyco International's control of the plastic hanger market in the late 1990s may have come pretty close. Retail firms such as J. C. Penney and K-Mart use only plastic hangers to display their clothing goods. Starting in about 1994, Tyco used mergers and acquisitions of rival firms to gain control of 70 to 80 percent of the market for plastic hangers. In a number of geographic regions, Tyco became the only plastic hanger firm available. In 1996, Tyco acquired a Michigan-based hanger firm, Batts, that was one of the largest suppliers to the Midwest region. Immediately thereafter, Tyco raised prices by 10 percent to all its customers. Some clients grumbled but most accepted the higher prices. Others though, such as K-Mart and VF (makers of Lee and Wrangler jeans) informed Tyco

that they had an alternative hanger supplier, namely, a company called WAF. For a brief moment, Tyco appears to have backed off raising the price. Yet the firm's underlying strategy soon became clear. In the fall of 1999, Tyco bought the WAF Corporation. Within a few months, it not only raised prices to all its customers again but, this time, it also added in a new delivery charge. Tyco also pursued an aggressive repurchase program so as to corner the market on used hangers. If it did not control the supply of this alternative to new hangers, Tyco would have faced increasing difficulty in charging a high price.

Source: M. Maremont, "Lion's Share: For Plastic Hangers You Almost Need to Go to Tyco International," *Wall Street Journal*, February 15, 2000, p. A1.

Practice Problem

2.2

Now suppose that the manufacturing of cellular phones, as described in Practice Problem 2.1, is monopolized. The monopolist has 50 identical plants to run. Each plant has the same cost function as described in Practice Problem 2.1. The overall marginal cost function for the multiplant monopolist[5] is described by $MC(Q) = 10 + Q/25$. The market demand is also assumed to be the same as in Practice Problem 2.1.

Recall $Q^D = \dfrac{6000 - 50P}{9}$

a. Show that the monopolist's marginal revenue function is $MR(Q) = 120 - 18Q/50$.
b. Show that the monopolist's profit-maximizing output level is $Q_M = 275$. What price does the monopolist set to sell this level of output?
c. What is the profit earned at each one of the monopolist's plants?

2.2   PROFIT TODAY VERSUS PROFIT TOMORROW: FIRM DECISION-MAKING OVER TIME

Both the competition and the monopoly models described in the previous section are somewhat vague with respect to time. While some distinction is made between the short run and the long run, neither concept explicitly confronts the notion of a unit of time such as a day, a week, a month, or a year, or of how many such units constitute say, the long run. To maximize profit in the long run requires, for example, only that the firm make all necessary adjustments to its inputs in order to produce at the optimum level, and then repeatedly choose this input–output combination in every individual period. From the standpoint of decision-making then, the long run is envisioned as a single market period and the assumption that the firm will seek to maximize profit is unambiguous in its meaning.

However, the recognition that the long run is a series of individual, finite time periods extending far into the future also raises the possibility that each such period will not be the same. Here, the choice may well be between taking an action that yields profit immediately versus taking an action that yields perhaps greater profit but not until many periods later. In such a setting, the meaning of maximizing profit is less clear. Is it better or worse to have more profit later and less profit now? How does one compare profit in one period with profit in another? Such questions must be answered if we are to provide a useful analysis of the strategic interaction among firms over time.

Sacrificing profit today means incurring a cost. Hence, the problem just described arises anytime that a cost is incurred in the present in return for benefits to be realized much later. Firms often face such a trade-off. A classic example is the decision to build a new manufacturing plant. If the plant is constructed now, the firm will immediately incur the expense

---

[5]   Strictly speaking, the monopolist is a multiplant one because he now has 50 plants to run. The profit-maximizing monopolist will want to allocate total production across the 50 plants in such a way that marginal cost of producing the last unit of output is the same in each plant. Therefore, the monopolist derives his overall marginal cost function in a manner similar to how we constructed the supply function for the competitive industry. This point is further explained in Chapter 3 in the section on multiplant monopolies.

of hiring architects and construction workers and the buying of building materials, machinery, and equipment. It will only be sometime later—after the plant is built and running smoothly—that the firm will actually begin to earn some profit or return on this investment.

In order to understand how firms make decisions in which the costs and benefits are experienced not just in one period but instead over time, we borrow some insights from financial markets. After all, the comparison of income received (or foregone) at different points in time is really what financial markets are all about. Think for a moment. If one buys some stock in say, Microsoft, one has to give up some funds today—namely, the price of a share in Microsoft times the number of shares bought. Of course, investors do this every day. Thousands of Microsoft shares are bought each day of the week. These investors are thus sacrificing some of their current income—which could alternatively be used to purchase a Caribbean vacation, or wardrobe, or other consumer goods—to buy these shares. Why do investors do this? The answer is that they do so in the expectation that those shares will pay dividends and will also appreciate in value over time. That is, stockholders buy shares of stock and incur the associated investment expense now, in the hope that the ownership of those shares will generate income as dividends and capital gains later.

In short, the financial markets are explicitly involved in trading current for future income. Accordingly, we can use the techniques of those markets to evaluate similar trades of current versus future profit that a firm might make. The key insight that we borrow from financial markets is the notion of present value or discounting. To understand the concept of discounting, imagine that a friend (a trustworthy friend) has asked to borrow $1,000 for 12 months. Suppose further that for you to lend her money requires that you withdraw $1,000 from your checking account, an account that pays 3 percent interest per year. In other words, you will have to lose about $30 of interest income by making this withdrawal. Although you like your friend very much, you may not see just precisely why you should make her a gift of $30. Therefore, you agree to lend her the $1,000 today if, a year from now, she pays you not only the $1,000 of principal but also an additional $30 in interest. Your friend will likely agree. After all, if she borrowed from the bank directly she would have to pay at least as much. The bank cannot afford to pay you 3 percent per year if it does not charge an interest rate at least as high when it loans those funds out. In fact, the bank will probably charge an interest rate a bit higher to cover its expenses. So, it makes sense for your friend to sign a contract (or perhaps just shake hands on the deal) requiring that you give her $1,000 today and that she give you $1,030 in 12 months.

Quite explicitly, you and your friend have just negotiated a trade of present funds for future funds. In fact, you have established the exact terms at which such a trade can take place. One thousand dollars today may be exchanged for $1,030 one year from now. Of course, matters would have been a bit different if the interest rate that your bank paid on deposits had been 5 percent. In that case, you would have asked your friend for $50 (5 percent of $1,000) in repayment beyond the $1,000 originally borrowed. That would have been the only repayment that would truly compensate you for your loss of the interest on your bank deposit. In general, if we denote the interest rate as r, then we have that $1,000 today exchanges for $(1 + r)$ times $1,000 in one year. If we now become even more general and consider an initial loan amount different from $1,000, say of Y, we will quickly see that the same logic implies that Y today trades for $(1 + r)Y$ paid in 12 months.

There is, however, an alternative way to view the transactions just described. Instead of asking how much money one will receive in a year for giving up $1,000 or Y now, we can reverse the question. That is, we can ask instead how much we have to pay today in order to get a particular payment one year from the present. For example, we could ask how much does it cost right now to buy a contract requiring that the other party to the deal pay us $1,030 in a year. If the interest rate is 3 percent, the answer is easy. It is simply $1,000. In fact, this is the contract with your friend that we just considered. You essentially paid $1,000 to purchase a promise from your friend to pay you $1,030 in one year. The intuition is that at an interest rate of 3 percent, the banks and the financial markets are saying that in return for a deposit of $1,000 they promise to pay $1,030 in one year. In other words, we can buy the contract we are thinking about for exactly $1,000 from the banks. There's no sense in paying more for it from anyone else, and no one else is going to accept less. Therefore, when the interest rate is 3 percent, the market is saying that the current price of a contract promising to pay $1,030 in one year is exactly $1,030/(1.03) or $1,000. Since price is just the economist's term for value, we call this the present value or, more completely, the present discounted value of $1,030 due in 12 months.

More generally, the present value of a piece of paper (e.g., a loan contract or share of stock) promising its owner a payment of Z in one period is just $Z/(1 + r)$. The term $1/(1 + r)$ is typically referred to as the discount factor and is often presented just as R. In other words, $R = 1/(1 + r)$. Hence, the present value of Z dollars one year from now is often written as RZ. The source of the adjective discount should be clear. Income that does not arrive until a year from now is not as valuable as income received today. Instead, the value of such future income is discounted. This has nothing to do with inflation and any possible cheapening of the currency over time. It simply reflects the fact that individuals prefer to have their consumption now and have to be paid a premium—an interest rate return—in order to be persuaded to wait.

What if the term of the loan had been for two years? Let us return again to our original example of a $1,000 loan at 3 percent interest. If your friend had initially asked to borrow the funds for two years, your reasoning might have gone as follows. Making a two-year loan to my friend requires that I take $1,000 out of my checking account today. Not making the loan means that the $1,000 stays in the bank. In this case, I will earn 3 percent over the next 12 months and, accordingly, start the next year with $1,030 in the bank. I will then earn 3 percent on this amount over the next or second year. Accordingly, by refusing my friend and keeping the funds in the bank, I will have on deposit $1,030(1.03) = $1,060.90 in two years. Therefore, I will only lend my friend the funds for two years if she in turn promises to pay me $1,060.90—the same as I could have earned at the bank—when the loan expires 24 months from now. Note that the amount $1,060.90 can be alternatively expressed as $1,000(1.03)(1.03) = $1,000(1.03)^2$. In general, a loan today of amount Y will yield $Y(1 + r)^2$ or YR^{-2} in two years. By extension, a loan of Y dollars for t years will yield an amount of $Y(1 + r)^t$ or YR^{-t} when it matures t years from now.

As before, we can turn the question around and ask how much we need to pay currently in order to receive an amount of Z dollars at some date t periods into the future. The answer follows immediately from our work above. It is $R^t Z$. How do we know this? If we put the amount $R^t Z$ dollars in an interest-bearing account today, then the amount that can be withdrawn in t periods is, by our previous logic, $(R^t Z)R^{-t} = Z$. So, clearly, the present discounted value of an amount Z to be received t periods in the future is just $R^t Z$.

The only remaining question is how to value a claim that provides different amounts at different dates in the future. For example, consider the construction of a plant that will, after completion in one year, generate Z_1 in net revenue; and then a net revenue of Z_2 two years from now; Z_3 three years from now, and so on. What is the present value of this stream of future net revenues? Well, the present value of Z_1 in one period is, as we know, RZ_1. Similarly, the present value of the Z_2 to be received in two periods is $R^2 Z_2$. If we continue in this manner we will work out the present value of the income received at each particular date. The present value of this entire stream will then simply be the sum of all these individual present values. In general, the present value PV of a stream of income receipts to be received at different dates extending T periods into the future is:

$$PV = RZ_1 + R^2 Z_2 + R^3 Z_3 + \ldots + R^T Z^T = \sum_{t=1}^{T} R^t Z_t \tag{2.3}$$

A special case of equation (2.3) occurs when the income received in each period Z_t is the same, that is, when $Z_1 = Z_2 = \ldots = Z_T = \bar{Z}$. In that case, the present value of the total stream is:

$$PV = \frac{\bar{Z}}{(1 - R)} (R - R^{T+1}) \tag{2.4}$$

An even more special case occurs when not only is the income receipt constant at $Z = \bar{Z}$, but the stream persists into the indefinite future so that the terminal period T approaches infinity. In that case, since the discount factor R is less than one, the term R^{T+1} in equation (2.4) goes to zero. Hence, when the stream is both constant and perpetual, the present value formula becomes:

$$PV = \bar{Z} \left(\frac{R}{1 - R} \right) = \frac{\bar{Z}}{r} \tag{2.5}$$

Thus, if the interest rate r were 3 percent, a promise to pay a constant $30 forever would have a present value of $PV = \$30/0.03 = \$1,000$. Note that for all our present value formulas, an increase in the real interest rate r implies a decrease in the discount factor R. In turn, this means that a rise in the interest rate implies a decrease in the present value of any given future income stream.

Again, it is important to remember the context in which these equations have been developed. Often firm decision-making has a temporal dimension. Indeed, our focus on long-run equilibria implies that we are considering just such decisions. Hence, we need to consider trade-offs that are made over time. An expense may need to be incurred now in order to reap additional profit at some future date or dates. The simple dictum maximize profit does not have a clear meaning in such cases. The only way of evaluating the desirability of such a trade-off over time is to discount, that is, translate the future dollar inflows into a current or present value that may then be compared with the current expense necessary to secure those future receipts. If the present value of the future income is not at least as great as the value of the necessary expense, then the trade-off is not favorable. If, for instance, a plant costs $3 million to build, and will generate future profit with a discounted present value of only $2 million, it is not a desirable investment, and we would not expect a rational firm to undertake it.[6] In short, our assumption that firms maximize profit must now be qualified to mean that firms maximize the present value of all current and future profit. Of course, for one-period problems, this is identical with the assumption that firms simply maximize profit.

---

[6] We have treated the problem as one of current expenses versus future receipts. Of course, future costs should be discounted as well.

Reality Checkpoint

Piracy on the High (Air)waves: Discounting, Monopoly Power, and Public Policy

In the United States, direct satellite television is largely provided by two services, Direct TV and the Dish Network. Subscribers to these services pay between $30 and $80 per month, depending on the package of TV programs they wish to view. In return, they get a satellite dish, receiver and decoder that permits them to view the programming in as many as four rooms in their house. In recent years, the number of satellite TV subscribers has grown rapidly to something on the order of 20 million. Yet even with this growth, satellite TV still has only about a third of the subscribers that its competitor, cable TV, has.

However, there is one category of subscriber in which satellite TV does outperform cable. This is the category of illegal, non-paying subscribers. The satellite TV firms have some idea as to how many dishes have been sold and installed over the years. Their estimate leaves them with about one to three million more dishes in place than actually subscribe to satellite services. The firms reckon that at least half of these represent users who obtain the service illegally by tapping into the satellite transmission.

To engage in such theft, the would-be airwaves pirate needs the basic hardware equipment—the dish and receiver—and also a smart card that tells the receiver what programs to decode. Anyone can buy such a smart card—new or used—on eBay.com and other sites. This is where the pirates enter the picture. A number of firms buy the smart card, then use hackers to break the code and write a script that tells the receiver to unscramble everything. Some illicit firms then simply sell the cards. Others sell the script that reprograms the card.

Of course, the satellite firms are aware of all this. They therefore periodically send out an Electronic Counter Measure (ECM) signal that puts out a new code and/or corrupts unauthorized cards. However, the best satellite pirates have become quite good at detecting when an ECM is coming and quickly write new scripts that restore the cards' operating ability.

How much are these illegal services worth? Consumers who subscribe to Direct TV or the Dish Network would expect to pay something like $75 per month for the complete package that includes all the channels of these networks. This typically includes the hardware, which is "rented" for free. Assume that the typical consumer has a current residence and therefore satellite TV horizon of five years. Then with an annual interest rate of 4 percent (compounded monthly) this implies a present value of about $4,114 for complete and legitimate satellite service over this time span. Illegal users pay about $225 to acquire their own hardware. They also pay about $25 to subscribe to the hacker services that provide them with updated scripts to keep their cards working. This works to a present value of just under $1,600, implying a saving of $2,500. However, illegal users do take some risks. Recently, the satellite firms have cracked down on the pirate companies and, in the process, obtained the lists of their customers. Those customers face very large potential fines. Typically, the satellite firms offer those caught the option of paying $5,000 to avoid further legal charges. Yet even with all their best efforts, the satellite firms reckon that the typical illicit consumer has at most a one-in-three chance of being caught and paying that fine. Thus, the expected value of the fine is $5,000/3 = $1,667. If it takes two years on average to catch the thief, then the present value of the fine—again assuming a 4 percent annual interest rate—is $1,540. Hence, an educated guess of the total expected cost to the illicit satellite user in present value terms is $1,600 + $1,667 = $3,267. Including the risk of getting caught has reduced the savings to $847. Even in a black market, consumers earn some surplus.

Source: D. Lieberman "Millions of Pirates Are Plundering Satellite TV," *USA Today*, December 2, 2004, p. C1.

However, we will need to be familiar with the idea of discounting and the present value of future profits in the second half of the book when we take up such issues as collusion and research and development, which often have a multiperiod dimension.

Suite Enterprises is a large restaurant supply firm that dominates the local market. It does, however, have one rival, Loew Supplies. Because of this competition, Suite earns a profit of $100,000 per year. It could, however, cut its prices to cost and drive out Loew. To do this, Suite would have to forgo all profit for one year and earn zero. After that year, Loew would be gone forever and Suite could earn $110,000 per year. The interest rate Suite confronts is 12 percent per annum, and so the discount factor is $R = 0.8929$.

a.   Is driving Loew out of the market a good "investment" for Suite?
b.   Consider the alternative strategy in which Suite buys Loew for $80,000 today and then operates the new combined firm, Suite & Loew, as a monopoly earning $110,000 in all subsequent periods. Is this a good investment?

2.3   EFFICIENCY, SURPLUS, AND SIZE RELATIVE TO THE MARKET

Now that we have described the perfectly competitive and pure monopoly market outcomes, it is time to try to understand why perfect competition is extolled and pure monopoly is guarded against by law. In both cases firms are driven by profit maximization. Also, in both cases the firms sell to consumers who decide how much they want to buy at any given price. What makes one market good and the other market bad? The answer to this question does not reflect any concern about too much profit or firms "ripping off" consumers. The answer instead lies in the economic concept of efficiency. In economics, efficiency has a very precise meaning. Briefly speaking, a market outcome is said to be efficient when it is impossible to find some small change in the allocation of capital, labor, goods, or services that would improve the well-being of one individual in the market without hurting any others.[7] If the only way we can make somebody better off is by making someone else worse off, then there is really no slack or inefficiency in how the market is working. If, on the other hand, we can imagine changes that would somehow allow one person to have more goods and services while nobody else has less, then the current market outcome is not efficient. As it turns out, that is precisely the case for a monopolized market. One can think of changes to the monopoly outcome that would yield more for at least one individual and no less for any other. However, as we'll see, market forces alone will not get us there in the case of the textbook monopolist.

It is readily apparent that, to implement our efficiency criterion, we need some measure of how well off consumers and firms are in any market outcome. For this purpose, we use the notions of consumer surplus and producer surplus. The consumer surplus obtained from consuming one unit of the good is defined as the difference between the maximum amount a consumer is willing to pay for that unit and the amount the consumer actually does pay.

---

[7]   This notion of efficiency is often referred to as Pareto optimality after the great Italian social thinker of the late nineteenth and early twentieth centuries, Vilfredo Pareto.

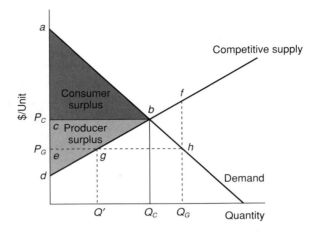

Figure 2.5   Competition maximizes the total surplus

At the competitive price P_C and output Q_C, consumers enjoy a surplus equal to triangle *abc*. Producers enjoy a surplus equal to triangle *cbd*. This is the maximum. Producing less would lose some of the total surplus given by triangle *abd*. Subsidizing production to output Q_G reduces the price to P_G. The required subsidy is *gfh*. Consumers gain additional surplus *cbge*. However, this amount represents a transfer of surplus from producers to consumers and, hence no net gain in total surplus. Consumers also gain the triangle *gbh*, but this is more than offset by the funds required for the needed subsidy. The remaining part of the subsidy equal to triangle *bfh* is a deadweight loss as resources valued more highly in alternative uses are transferred to the industry in question where the marginal value of output is only P_G.

Total consumer surplus in a market is then measured by summing this difference over each unit of the good bought in the market. Analogously, the producer surplus obtained from producing a single unit of the good is the difference between the amount the seller receives for that unit of the good and the cost of producing it. Total producer surplus in a market is then measured by summing up this difference over each unit of the good sold.

We illustrate these concepts in Figure 2.5. In the competitive outcome, Q_C units of the good are bought and sold. The maximum amount a consumer is willing to pay for the last unit, the Q_Cth unit, is just the equilibrium price P_C. However, the maximum amount a consumer is willing to pay for the first, the second, the third, and so on, up to the Q_Cth unit is greater than P_C. We know this because, at a given sales volume, the demand curve is a precise measure of the maximum amount any consumer is willing to pay for one more unit. Hence, the area under the demand curve but above the market equilibrium price P_C is surplus to consumers. It is a measure of how much they were willing to pay less what they actually did pay in the competitive outcome. This is shown in Figure 2.5 as area *abc*.

For competitive producers, the supply curve tells us the marginal cost of producing each unit.[8] Similar to consumer surplus, we can construct a measure of producer surplus. For each unit of the good sold, producer surplus is measured by the difference between market price P_C and the corresponding reservation supply price on the supply curve. By adding up this difference for each value of output up to the competitive output, we obtain total producer

---

[8]   Again, remember that the market supply curve is the horizontal summation of each competitive firm's marginal cost curve, and so the supply curve tells us exactly what is the opportunity cost to the firm of producing and selling each unit of the good.

surplus. This is illustrated by the area *cbd* in Figure 2.5. Note that when the equilibrium quantity, Q_C, of the good is produced and sold at price P_C, the total surplus or welfare to consumers and producers is given by the area *abd*.[9]

Suppose that an output greater than Q_C, say Q_G was produced in this market. For consumers to buy this quantity of the good, the price must fall to P_G. This rise in production and sales results in an increase in consumer surplus. Specifically, consumer surplus increases to *aeh*. Producer surplus, however, falls. Moreover, it falls by more than the increase in consumer surplus. Much of the rise in consumer surplus that results from moving to output Q_G—in particular, the shaded area *cbge*—is not an increase in total surplus. It simply reflects a transfer of surplus from producers to consumers. As for the additional increase in consumer surplus—the triangle *gbh*—this is clearly less than the additional decrease in producer surplus—the triangle *gfh*. Producers now receive a positive surplus only on the first Q' units produced. Because the gain in consumer surplus is less than the loss in producer surplus, the overall surplus at output Q_G is less than that at output Q_C. It is easy to repeat this analysis for any output greater than Q_C. In short, we cannot increase total surplus by raising output beyond the competitive level; we can only decrease it.

A similar thought experiment can be performed to show that output levels below Q_C also reduce the total surplus (see Practice Problem 2.4). This is because restricting output to be less than Q_C reduces consumer surplus by more than it raises producer surplus. Accordingly, the overall surplus at an output below Q_C must be smaller than the surplus under perfect competition. Note that saying that neither an increase nor a decrease in output from Q_C can increase the total surplus but only decrease it is equivalent to saying that the surplus is maximized at Q_C. Yet if we cannot increase the total surplus then we cannot make anyone better off without making someone worse off. That is, if we cannot make the size of the pie bigger, we can only give more to some individuals by giving less to others. Since this is the case under perfect competition, the perfectly competitive output level is efficient.[10]

Let's return to the cellular phone industry when it was organized as a perfectly competitive industry. Use the information in Practice Problem 2.1 to work out consumer surplus and producer surplus in a competitive equilibrium.

2.4

a. Show that when $Q_C = 500$ units and $P_C = \$30$ per unit then consumer surplus is equal to \$22,500 and producer surplus is equal to \$5,000. This results in a total surplus equal to \$27,500.

b. Show that when an output of 275 units is produced in this industry the sum of consumer and producer surplus falls to \$21,931.25.

Practice Problem

---

[9] Observe that the unit of measurement of the areas of consumer and producer surplus is the dollar. To work out the areas, you must take \$/unit as measured on the vertical axis times units on the horizontal axis. This gives you a measure in dollars, which is a money measure of the welfare created by having this good produced at output level Q_C and sold at price P_C.

[10] We focus here on the concept of allocational or static efficiency in which we examine the best way to allocate resources for the production of a given set of goods and services with a given technology. Dynamic efficiency, which considers the allocation of resources so as to promote the development of new goods and new production techniques, is addressed explicitly in Chapter 22.

2.3.1   The Monopolist and Producer Surplus

Now consider the monopoly outcome. We have suggested that this is inefficient. If this is the case, then it must be possible to show that by producing an output level different from the monopoly output Q_M, one individual can be made better off and no one else worse off. The way to show this is similar to the solution to Practice Problem 2.4 and is shown in Figure 2.6. This figure shows the competitive output and price, Q_C and P_C respectively, much as in Figure 2.5. However, in Figure 2.6 we also show what happens when the industry is monopolized. The monopolist produces output Q_M and sets price P_M. Consumer surplus is then the triangle *jax*. The monopolist's profit at Q_M is measured by area *jxzk*. The sum of these two surpluses is *axzk*. This is clearly smaller than the area *ayk*, which measures the total surplus obtained in the perfectly competitive outcome.

It is worth noting that while the total surplus is greater under perfect competition than it is under monopoly, the opposite holds true for producer surplus. True, a move from monopoly to competition gains the producer surplus *wyz*. But to achieve this gain requires setting the competitive price P_C and the consequent loss of the firm's surplus, *hjxw*. The loss is obviously greater than the gain.

Note that the reduction in consumer surplus that monopoly causes is not purely the result of an increase in the monopolist's surplus. Quite the contrary, the decline in total surplus alerts us to the fact that the monopolist's gain is less than the consumer's loss. In other words, as a result of moving from a competitive industry to one of monopoly, consumers lose more than the profit that the monopolist earns. They also lose an additional amount—the area *xwy* in Figure 2.6—beyond that part of their surplus that is transferred to the monopolist.

The area of the shaded triangle *xyz* is an exact measure of inefficiency under monopoly. The upper boundary of this triangle is comprised of points that lie on the consumers' demand curve. Every point on this boundary indicates the marginal value that consumers place on successive increases in output beyond Q_M. The lower boundary of this triangle traces out the

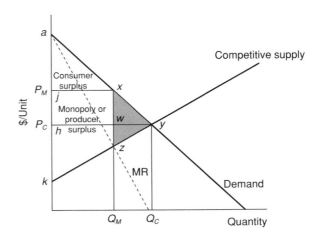

Figure 2.6   The deadweight loss of monopoly
The monopolist produces Q_M units and sells each at price P_M. A competitive industry produces Q_C units and each sells at a price of P_C. The deadweight loss caused by a move from competition to monopoly is triangle *xyz*.

marginal cost of producing this additional output. The triangle *xyz* thus reflects all the trades that generate a surplus which do not take place under monopoly. Within this triangle, the price consumers would willingly pay exceeds the cost of producing extra units and this difference is the surplus lost—that is, earned by no one—due to monopolization of the industry. If this additional output were produced, there would be a way to distribute it and make one person better off without lowering the profit of the monopolist or the welfare of any other individual. The triangle *xyz* is often referred to as the deadweight loss of monopoly. It is also a good approximation of the gains to be had by restructuring the industry to make it a competitive one.

The deadweight loss in Figure 2.6 is not due to the excess profit of the monopolist. From the viewpoint of economic efficiency, we do not care whether the surplus generated in a market goes to consumers—as it does under perfect competition—or to producers. The welfare triangle in Figure 2.6 is a loss because it reflects the potential surplus that would have gone to someone—consumers or producers—had the efficient output been produced. It is not the division of the surplus but its total amount that is addressed by economic efficiency.

Efficiency is a powerful concept both because of its underlying logic and because it is open to explicit computation. With appropriate statistical techniques, economists can try to calculate the deadweight loss of Figure 2.6 for a given industry. Hence, they can estimate the potential gains from moving to a more competitively structured market.

Practice Problem 2.5

Water is produced and sold by the government. Demand for water is represented by the linear function $Q = 50 - 2P$. The total cost function for water production is also a linear function: $TC(Q) = 100 + 10Q$. You will also need to work out both the average cost of production, denoted by $AC(Q)$, equal to the total cost of producing a quantity of output divided by that quantity of output, $TC(Q)/Q$, and the marginal cost of production, denoted by $MC(Q)$, which is the additional cost incurred to produce one more unit.

a.   How much should the government charge per unit of water in order to reach the efficient allocation?

b.   How much should it charge if it wishes to maximize profit from the sale of water?

c.   What is the value of the efficiency loss that results from charging the price in part b rather than the price determined in part a?

2.3.2   The Nonsurplus Approach to Economic Efficiency[11]

In considering the deadweight loss of monopoly, it is useful to pursue the question as to why the monopolist fails to earn that lost triangle of surplus. If it is there for the taking, why doesn't she go out and get it? After all, the monopolist is the only seller in the market. Shouldn't she be able to use her power to extract this additional profit?

Our concept of surplus provides a useful tool with which to consider this question. Suppose that the monopolist expands output from Q_M to the competitive level of Q_C. By doing so,

---

[11]   This section and the previous one make extensive use of the nonsurplus approach developed in Makowski and Ostroy (1995). It has had an important influence on our understanding of market participation. It also plays a central role in the business strategies advocated by Brandenburger and Nalebuff (1996).

the monopolist will indeed generate an increase in the total surplus exactly equal to the deadweight loss. That's the good news. The bad news is that the monopolist cannot appropriate all of this gain for herself. To begin with, some of the surplus generated by selling an additional $Q_C - Q_M$ units at price P_C will flow to those consumers lucky enough to buy these goods at this lower price. Yet many of these consumers were willing to pay more than P_C for this additional consumption. The surplus that these individuals enjoy as a result of acquiring the good while paying only P_C is surplus that the monopolist cannot claim. Moreover, the monopolist must confront a second problem as well. The monopolist cannot sell the same good at two different prices. If she tried to do so, she would find it very difficult to get anyone to buy at the higher price, P_M. Those who buy the product at the lower price P_C can make an easy economic profit by reselling the good to anyone to whom the monopolist tries to charge P_M. What this means is that selling the additional $Q_C - Q_M$ units requires that the price fall to P_C on every unit sold and not just on the extra $Q_C - Q_M$ units. Yet this price cut lowers the monopolist's profit on the initial Q_M units. It thereby further reduces the surplus that flows to the monopolist as a result of selling the extra $Q_M - Q_C$ units.

Indeed, even in our original equilibrium with output at Q_M, the monopoly firm was generating more total surplus than it was actually reaping as profit. To see this, just observe what would happen if the monopoly closed shop and left the market entirely. Not only would the monopoly profit be lost, but—and this is the crucial point—consumer surplus would vanish as well. Viewed in this light, we see that the monopolist always creates surplus that she does not get. If the monopolist could appropriate the entire surplus created in the market, then she would have an incentive to produce the output that maximizes that surplus—the efficient production level. It is a monopoly firm's inability to appropriate the surplus its production creates that leads it to choose an inefficient output level.

It may seem strange to say that a monopoly firm, which earns some surplus, underproduces just because it does not get the entire surplus when, by comparison, a competitive industry, in which each firm gets no surplus, achieves the efficient higher level of output. Remember, though, that we are making our comparisons at the firm level, not the industry level. The monopoly firm is a large producer relative to the market. Its choice of output materially alters the market supply and hence the market price. It thereby alters the surplus of consumers as well. This is not the case for the competitive firm. A perfectly competitive firm's supply is tiny relative to the market. Indeed, it is so small that its output decision has no effect on market price. Drop any one competitive firm from the market and nothing happens to either the market price or the industry's total output. That is what we mean in calling a competitive firm a "price-taker." But if the competitive firm cannot change the market price it also cannot change anyone's surplus. Again, this is not the case for the competitive industry overall. Taken together, all the firms in that industry do affect the total surplus. If we drop them all from the market, that total surplus will decline.

However, decisions are made at the level of the individual firm. So, we must look at the incentives facing a single competitive producer. Here we see that such a firm does capture the entire surplus its actions generate. It earns zero profit from its market participation and, as we have just seen, this is an exact measure of the contribution the firm makes to the total surplus. So, the perfectly competitive firm gets out of the market exactly what that firm puts in.

In contrast, the monopoly firm does not get the entire surplus that its participation in the market generates, even though it does earn a positive profit. As shown earlier, that profit is less than the surplus the monopolist generates. Since the monopoly firm gets less than what it puts in, it should not be surprising that its output choice is inefficiently small. We hasten to add that this approach to monopoly is not presented to garner sympathy for the monopoly

firm. Our aim is rather to clarify the source of inefficiency under monopoly. If the monopolist could collect as profit the entire surplus its production generates, it would have every
incentive to produce the efficient level of output.

Indeed, the real source of the monopoly problem is not the fact that only one firm is active
in the market. The true cause of the inefficiency is that the firm is large relative to the market size. To see this, consider a simple example in which the monopolist is a reproducer of
classic cars. Suppose that in particular, the monopolist in question is the only maker of reproductions of the classic 1939 Rolls-Royce Wraith. Suppose further that because of limited
supplies of parts and materials, the reproduction artist can only produce two such cars—
each at a cost of $80,000. Demand, however, is not so limited. There are 50,000 classic car
collectors in the world. Of these, the 200 who value the cars the most are each willing to
pay a price of $150,000—but not a penny more—to own precisely one of these autos.
The next 40,000 are each willing to pay $130,000 to own one car. The remaining 9,800 will
willingly pay $100,000 to own a reproduction Rolls-Royce Wraith. In short, the market is
characterized by some variety in consumer tastes.

The key point to note is that monopoly does not result in inefficiency. This is because
whether he produces and sells none or one or the maximum of two cars, the market price
of the reproductions will remain at $150,000 apiece. If the monopolist sells both cars, he
will sell them to two different buyers, each of whom is among the 200 collectors willing to
pay $150,000. If he decides to sell just one car, he again sells it for $150,000, this time dealing with only one buyer. Finally, if he sells no reproduced autos, no price will be recorded,
but there will be an implicit opportunity cost of $150,000 incurred for each car not produced
and sold. In short, the antique car producer cannot move the market price for one car away
from $150,000 even though he is a monopolist.

Note that any buyer who pays $150,000 for one of the cars enjoys a zero surplus from
the deal. The fact that $150,000 is exactly the maximum price that such a buyer is willing
to pay indicates that the buyer is essentially indifferent between purchasing the car at that
price and not buying it at all. In other words, such a buyer gets no surplus, implying that
the car builder appropriates the entire surplus that building and selling a reproduced Rolls
generates. Alternatively, if the monopolist were to leave—or, equivalently, not sell any cars—
the surplus enjoyed by all other market participants would be unchanged. So, whether the
monopolist sells both cars at the market-clearing price of $150,000, or whether he does not
participate in the market at all, his actions leave unchanged the surplus of each and every
other antique car market participant.

Obviously, the above story is a little contrived. Still, it serves to make the point that monopoly,
per se, is not the source of market inefficiency. The car firm owner has a monopoly, but its
supply of cars is small relative to the potential market. His situation is, therefore, similar to
the one that describes a perfectly competitive firm and not the standard monopolist. Just
like the perfect competitor, the car seller's decision on how many cars to sell has no effect
on the price. Matters would have been quite different had we assumed that there was only
one collector willing to pay $150,000 to own a classic Rolls-Royce, while all other collectors
were willing to pay only $20,000 apiece for such an automobile. In this second case, the
example is more like the standard monopoly case. The car owner's choice of how many cars
to sell affects the equilibrium price and the surplus of others as well.

The foregoing analysis that focuses on market actions and the surplus that they generate
is called the nonsurplus approach to understanding economic efficiency. It makes the important connection between the incentive to trade in a market and the efficiency of market trading. Firms are motivated by profit to trade. Under perfect competition, a single firm's (zero)

profit is equal to that firm's contribution to the surplus or welfare created by market trading. So, profit-maximizing behavior leads to an efficient market outcome. By contrast, the (large) monopoly firm's profit is less than the surplus created by market trading. Consequently, profit maximization under monopoly does not lead to an efficient market outcome.

Summary

We have formally presented the basic microeconomic analysis of markets characterized by either perfect competition or perfect monopoly. In both cases, the goal of any firm is assumed to be to maximize profit. The necessary condition for profit maximization is that the firm produce where marginal revenue equals marginal cost. Because firms in competitive markets take market price as given, price equals marginal revenue for the competitive firm. As a result, the competitive market equilibrium is one in which price is set equal to marginal cost. In turn, this implies that the competitive market equilibrium is efficient in that it maximizes the sum of producer and consumer surplus.

The pure monopoly case does not yield an efficient outcome. The monopoly firm understands that it can affect the market price and this implies that marginal revenue will be less than the price for a monopoly firm. If the market demand curve is linear, this difference is reflected in the

fact that the monopolist's marginal revenue curve has the same price intercept but is twice as steeply sloped as that demand curve. For the monopoly firm equating marginal revenue with marginal cost as required for profit maximization yields an output inefficiently below that of the competitive equilibrium. Resources are misallocated because too few resources are employed in the production of the monopolized commodity. The inefficiency that results is often called the deadweight or welfare loss of monopoly.

Pure competition and pure monopoly are useful market concepts. Whether they are also useful as a description of actual industries is another question. To answer that question we need some way to determine if a market is monopolized; or if it is quite competitive. That is, we need to develop some way to identify or to measure monopoly power. It is that issue that we address in the next chapter.

Problems

1. Suppose that the annual demand for prescription antidepressants such as Prozac, Paxil, and Zoloft is, in inverse form, given by: $P = 1,000 - 0.025Q$. Suppose that the competitive supply curve is given by: $P = 150 + 0.033Q$.
   a. Calculate the equilibrium price and annual quantity of antidepressants.
   b. Calculate (i) producer surplus; and (ii) consumer surplus in this competitive equilibrium.

2. Assume that the dairy industry is initially in a perfectly competitive equilibrium. Assume that, in the long run, the technology is such that average cost is constant at all levels of output. Suppose that producers agree to form an association and behave as a profit-maximizing monopolist. Explain clearly in a diagram the effects on (a) market price, (b) equilibrium output, (c) economic profit, (d) consumer surplus, and (e) welfare loss.

3. Suppose that the total cost of producing pizzas for the typical firm in a local town is given by: $C(q) = 2q + 2q^2$. In turn, marginal cost is given by: $MC = 2 + 4q$. (If you know calculus, you should be able to derive this expression for marginal cost.)
   a. Show that the competitive supply behavior of the typical pizza firm is described by: $q = \dfrac{P}{4} - \dfrac{1}{2}$.
   b. If there are 100 firms in the industry each acting as a perfect competitor, show that the market supply curve is, in inverse form, given by: $P = 2 + Q/25$.

4. Let the market demand for widgets be described by $Q = 1,000 - 50P$. Suppose further that widgets can be produced at a constant average and marginal cost of $10 per unit.
   a. Calculate the market output and price under perfect competition and under monopoly.

b. Define the point elasticity of demand η_D at a particular price and quantity combination as the ratio of price to quantity times the slope of the demand curve, $\Delta Q/\Delta P$, all multiplied by -1. That is, $\eta_D = -\dfrac{P}{Q}\dfrac{\Delta Q}{\Delta P}$. What is the elasticity of demand in the competitive equilibrium? What is the elasticity of demand in the monopoly equilibrium?

c. Denote marginal cost as MC. Show that in the monopoly equilibrium, the following condition is satisfied: $\dfrac{P - MC}{P} = -\dfrac{1}{\eta_D}$.

5. We mentioned Tyco International and its control of the plastic hangar market in the chapter. Suppose that the inverse demand for hangars is given by: $P = 3 - Q/16{,}000$. Suppose further that the marginal cost of producing hangars is constant at \$1.

   a. What is the equilibrium price and quantity of hangars if the market is competitive?
   b. What is the equilibrium price and quantity of hangars if the market is monopolized?
   c. What is the deadweight or welfare loss of monopoly in this market?

6. A single firm monopolizes the entire market for single-lever, ball-type faucets which it can produce at a constant average and marginal cost of $AC = MC = 10$. Originally, the firm faces a market demand curve given by $Q = 60 - P$.

   a. Calculate the profit-maximizing price and quantity combination for the firm. What is the firm's profit?
   b. Suppose that the market demand curve shifts outward and becomes steeper. Market demand is now described as $Q = 45 - 0.5P$. What is the firm's profit-maximizing price and quantity combination now? What is the firm's profit?
   c. Instead of the demand function assumed in part b, assume instead that market demand shifts outward and becomes flatter. It is described by $Q = 100 - 2P$. Now what is the firm's profit-maximizing price and quantity combination? What is the firm's profit?
   d. Graph the three different situations in parts (a), (b), and (c). Based on what you observe, explain why there is no supply curve for a firm with monopoly power.

References

Baumol, W. J., J. C. Panzar, and R. D. Willig. 1982. *Contestable Markets and the Theory of Market Structure*. New York: Harcourt, Brace, Jovanovich.

Brandenburger, A. and B. Nalebuff. 1996. *Co-opetition*. Cambridge: Harvard University Press.

Makowski, L., and J. Ostroy. 1995. "Appropriation and Efficiency: A Revision of the First Theorem of Welfare Economics." *American Economic Review* 85 (September): 808–27.

3

Market Structure and Market Power

The structure–conduct–performance paradigm, the old IO, starts with a given market structure and then investigates how firms behave in that kind of market. By contrast, the new IO has in some ways reversed the logic and begins by investigating how the firms' strategic behavior can affect the structure of the market. Yet despite these differences, the two approaches do agree that market structure or, the way the industry's producers are organized, affects what happens in the market place. A natural question that arises is how we can characterize a market's structure in a meaningful way.

In our review of basic microeconomics we saw that markets work well when firms are small relative to the size of the market. The idealized competitive market is one with numerous firms, each with a minimal market share. Yet such markets are relatively rare in the real world. Some markets have just 2 or 3 firms. Some have 10 or 12 of unequal size. In what ways is this difference important? If there are 20 firms, does it matter if one firm has 60 percent of the market and the other 19 have just a bit more than 2 percent each? Alternatively, can we measure market structure in such a way that enables us to make some inference of market power? Can we create an index that allows us to say how close or how far a market structure is from the competitive ideal? Because such a road map could be of great use to policy makers it is worthwhile to explore the question at length.

3.1 MEASURING MARKET STRUCTURE

One way to think about an industry's structure is to undertake the following, simple procedure. First, take all the firms in the industry and rank them by some measure of size from largest to smallest—one, denoting largest; two, the next largest; etc. Suppose, for example, that we use market share as a measure of size. We could then calculate the fraction of the industry's total production that is accounted for by the largest firm, then the two largest firms combined, then the three largest firms combined, and so on. This gives us the cumulative fraction of the industry's total output as we include progressively smaller firms. Plotting this relationship yields what we call a concentration curve. It is called a concentration curve because it describes the extent to which output is concentrated in the hands of just a few firms.

Figure 3.1 displays concentration curves for each of three representative industries, A, B, and C. The firms' ranked sizes are measured along the horizontal axis, again with the first

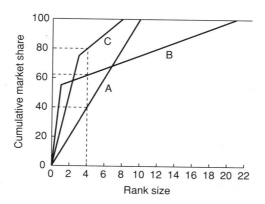

Figure 3.1   Some possible concentration curves

firm being the largest. The cumulative market share is measured on the vertical axis. For example, Industry A has 10 firms, each with a 10 percent market share. Industry B has 21 firms, the largest of which has a 55 percent market share. The remaining 20 firms all have a 2.25 percent share each. Finally, in industry C, there are three firms each with a market share of 25 percent and five firms each with a market share of 5 percent. For Industry B the vertical coordinates corresponding to the horizontal values 1 and 2 on this industry's concentration curve are 55 and 57.25, respectively. This reflects the fact that the largest firm has 55 percent of the market and the largest two firms have 57.25 percent between them.

Concentration curves are a useful illustrative device.[1] They permit one to get a quick sense of how industry production is allocated across firms from a quick visual inspection. However, often we need to summarize industrial structure with just a single parameter or index. One such popular index that focuses on the size of firms (relative to the industry) is the concentration ratio, CR_n, defined as the market share of the top n firms. In the United States, the most frequent choice is the four-firm concentration ratio, CR_4 or the percent of industry sales accounted for by the top four firms. For the three hypothetical industries described above, we can identify the CR_4 concentration very easily. All we need to do is draw a vertical line from the value 4 on the horizontal axis to the relevant concentration curve and from that point read horizontally to the vertical axis coordinate. As can be seen, CR_4 is 40, 61.75, and 80, for A, B, and C, respectively. A similar exercise yields the eight-firm ratio CR_8 that also is often reported. Its value for markets A, B, and C is 80, 70.75, and 100, respectively.

An n-firm concentration ratio then corresponds to a particular point on the industry's concentration curve. It follows that the principal drawback to such a measure is that it omits the other information in the curve. Compare, for example, the four-firm and eight-firm concentration ratios just given for the A, B, and C industries. Industry A appears more concentrated than does industry B using the CR_8 measure but less concentrated when evaluated with the CR_4 index.

---

[1]   Those familiar with the GINI coefficient typically used to measure income inequality will recognize the concentration curve as the industrial structure analog of the Lorenz curve from which the GINI coefficient is derived. For further details, see C. Damguard, "The Lorenz Curve," www.mathworld.wolfram.com/LorenzCurve.html.

Reality Checkpoint
Concentrating on Concentration

Just as we can measure the fraction of an industry's output accounted for by its largest firms, so we can measure the fraction of the economy's entire output, GDP, accounted for by its largest corporations. However, while it may make some sense to speak of a concentration index based on just the top four firms or top eight firms when speaking of a single industry, such a small number of firms would account for much too little of GDP to think seriously about. So, in the case of aggregate economic activity, we consider concentration ratios such as CR_{50} or CR_{200}. Such measures can be constructed using data from the Census Bureau's Census of Manufactures. Economist Lawrence White (2002) made such calculations for the U.S. for various years up to the end of the twentieth century. Some of his results are shown below.

These data suggest that, at least since the 1950s, aggregate concentration in manufacturing has shown no increasing or decreasing trend. It is approximately the same in 1997 as it was in 1958 whether one looks at the top 50, 100, or 200 largest firms. White shows that somewhat similar results obtain if one looks

Aggregate concentration for manufacturing (value added basis), selected years, 1947–97 (%)

Year	CR_{50}	CR_{100}	CR_{200}
1947	17	23	30
1958	23	30	38
1967	25	33	42
1977	24	33	44
1987	25	33	43
1992	24	32	42
1997	24	32	40

at all nonfinancial corporations, or focuses on shares of employment or profit. This of course does not mean that firms are not getting bigger. If each firm grows at the same rate as the economy, each of us will find ourselves employed in larger and larger organizations over time even though concentration is stable. White shows that this too has been happening and that the size of the average firm has, correspondingly, grown.

Source: L. White: "Trends in Aggregate Concentration in the United States," *Journal of Economic Perspectives* (Fall, 2002), 137–60.

An alternative to CR_n that attempts to reflect more fully the information in the concentration curve is the Herfindahl–Hirschman Index or more simply the HHI. For an industry with N firms, this is defined as follows:

$$\text{HHI} = \sum_{i=1}^{N} s_i^2 \tag{3.1}$$

where s_i is the market share of the ith firm. In other words, the HHI is the sum of the squares of the market shares of all of the firms in the industry. Table 3.1 illustrates the calculation of the HHI for industry C in our example. If we measure market share in decimal terms so that a firm with 25 percent of the market has a share $s_i = 0.25$, the HHI for industry C is 0.20. Compare this to a maximum value of HHI = 1.0, which would be the HHI if the industry were a pure monopoly with one firm accounting for all the output. However, the practice is often to measure the shares in percentage terms in which case the HHI for industry C is 2,000, which compares with a maximum, pure monopoly value of HHI = 10,000 when shares are measured in this way. For industries A and B, similar calculations yield HHI = 1,000 and HHI = 3,126.25, respectively.

Table 3.1   Calculation of the HHI for industry C

Firm rank	Market share (%) s_i	Squared market share s_i^2
1	25	625
2	25	625
3	25	625
4	5	25
5	5	25
6	5	25
7	5	25
8	5	25
Sum:	100	2,000 (HHI)

Like a concentration ratio, the HHI measure has its drawbacks. However, it does have one very strong advantage over a measure such as CR_4 or CR_8. This is that the HHI reflects the combined influence of both unequal firm sizes and the concentration of activity in a few large firms. That is, rather than just reflect a single point on the concentration curve, the HHI provides, in a single number, a more complete sense of the shape of that curve. It is this ability to reflect both average firm size and inequality of size between firms that leads economists to prefer the HHI to simple concentration ratios such as CR_4. In our example, industry B gets the highest HHI value because it is the one with the greatest disparity in firm sizes.

3.1

Practice Problem

Consider two industries, each comprising 10 firms. In industry A, the largest firm has a market share of 49 percent. The next three firms have market shares of 7 percent each, and the remaining six firms have equal shares of 5 percent each. In industry B, the top four firms share the bulk of the market with 19 percent apiece. The next largest firm accounts for 14 percent, and the smallest five firms equally split the remaining 10 percent of the industry.

a. Compute the four-firm concentration ratio and HHI for each industry. Compare these measures across the two industries. Which industry do you think truly exhibits a more competitive structure? Which measure do you think gives a better indication of this? Explain.

b. Now let the three second-largest firms in industry A merge their operations while holding on to their combined 21 percent market share. Recalculate the HHI for industry A.

3.1.1   Measurement Problems: What Is a Market?

Whether one uses a CR_4 or HHI as an overall measure of a market's structure, it should be clear that the ability to make such measurements at all is predicated upon our ability to identify a well-defined market in the first place. In truth, this is not often easy to do. Consider, for example, the automobile industry. Is the relevant market one for passenger cars? Or are specialized vehicles, such as motorcycles, vans, and pickup trucks also part of the picture? Or think of the beverage industry. Does Pepsi compete only against other carbonated

Table 3.2   Concentration measures for selected industries

Industry	CR$_4$	HHI
Breakfast cereals	82.9	2445.9
Soft drink mfg	47.2	800.4
Automobiles	79.5	2862.8
Textile mills	13.8	94.4
Paper mfg	18.5	173.3
Petroleum refineries	28.5	422.1
Petrochemical mfg	59.8	1187.0
Pharmaceuticals	32.3	446.3
Cement mfg	33.5	466.6
Aluminum sheet/plate/foil	65.0	1447.0
Computers and peripherals	37.0	464.9
Electric light bulbs	88.9	2849.0
Dolls, toys, and games	40.0	495.9
Aircraft	80.9	2562.2
Semiconductors	41.7	688.7
Telephone equipment	55.3	1061.1
Plastic pipes/fittings	24.8	241.3
Toiletries	38.6	564.2
Women's footwear	49.5	794.8
Household refrigerators	82.8	2161.6

Source: "Concentration Ratios in Manufacturing," Bureau of the Census, 1997; U.S. Census Bureau, Census of Manufactures, 2001, 2002

beverages, or should beverages such as fruit juices, iced teas, and flavored milk also be viewed as substitute products? Unless we have a clear procedure for answering such questions, any summary measure of market structure such as HHI will become an arbitrary statistic capable of being manipulated either upward or downward at the whim of the researcher. An analyst can then make CR$_4$ or HHI arbitrarily small or large by defining the market either broadly or narrowly.

In the United States, the Census Bureau is the custodian of the market definitions most frequently used. These definitions have recently changed somewhat in connection with the North American Free Trade Agreement. However, the logic underlying the earlier Standard Industrial Classification (SIC) definitions and the current North American Industry Classification System (NAICS) is essentially the same. The Census Bureau first categorizes the output of business units in the United States into broad sectors of the economy, such as manufacturing, primary metals, agriculture, and forestry products, each of which receives a numeric code. These sectors are then subdivided further, and each is given a two-digit code. The manufacturing sector, for example, is covered by codes 31–33. These are each disaggregated further into the three-digit, four-digit, five-digit and six-digit levels. Each additional digit represents a further subdivision of the initial classification. Primarily because of the method by which the data are collected—through surveys of companies—the basis of all subdivisions is the similarity of production processes, rather than, for example, the substitutability in consumption. The classification system permits the construction of concentration data. Before compiling these data, however, the Bureau must determine how to

Reality Checkpoint

Industries Aren't What They Used to Be!

In a press release issued on April 8, 1997, the Executive Office of the President of the United States announced the introduction of a new industry classification system. They stated that the new system will enable the North American Free Trade Agreement (NAFTA) partners—the United States, Canada, and Mexico—to better compare economic and financial statistics and ensure that such statistics keep pace with the changing economy.

The new system—the North American Industry Classification System (NAICS)—will replace the countries' separate classification systems with one uniform system for classifying industries. In the United States, NAICS will replace the current Standard Industrial Classification.

NAICS, a flexible system that will take into account changes in the global economy, will help to support more informed economic and trade policies, more profitable business decisions, and more cogent public discussion and debate.

The NAICS was fully in effect as of the 1997 Economic Census. One can review this data as well as the translation of the data from the older SIC classification system at the Census Bureau's website, http://www.census.gov.

Source: Executive Office of the President, Office of Management and Budget, Washington, D.C., April 8, 1997. Available on the Internet at: http://www.census.gov/epcd/naics/pressrel.html

categorize production plants that produce more than one product. Its basic procedure is to assign a plant on the basis of that plant's primary product, as measured by sales. Once all the establishments are so assigned, total sales are computed for each market. Market shares and concentration indices are then calculated. These data are published regularly by the Census Bureau. Table 3.2 shows both CR_4 and HHI for a sample of well-known industries.[2]

The two measures of industrial concentration, CR_4 and HHI, are highly correlated, implying that each gives roughly the same description of an industry's structure. Yet while the CR_4 and HHI measures often tell the same story, the crucial question is whether or not it is the right story.[3] That is, to what extent do the four-digit industry classification codes and the associated measures of market concentration conform to an economist's idea of a market?

Generally speaking, we would like to include production establishments in the same market if the products that they produce are closely substitutable in consumption. Typically economists measure substitutability in consumption by the cross-price elasticity of demand η_{ij}. This is defined as the percentage change in demand for good i that occurs when there is a 1 percent change in the price of another good j. The mathematical definition of this elasticity is

$$\eta_{ij} = \frac{\partial q_i}{\partial p_j} \frac{p_j}{q_i} \tag{3.2}$$

---

[2] Further details are available on the Internet at http://www.census.gov/epcd/www/naics.html.
[3] A quite readable discussion of the advantages and disadvantages of each ratio is available in Sleuwaegen and Dehandschutter (1986) and Sleuwaegen et al. (1989).

If this measure is large and positive then goods i and j would be considered to be reasonably close substitutes.[4] Because the Census approach groups establishments more on the basis of similarity in production techniques than on the basis of substitutability in consumption its market definitions do not always satisfy this criterion. For example, wood, ceramic tile, and linoleum are all used as flooring materials and therefore may be viewed as substitutes in consumption. Yet each is actually listed under a different three-digit NAICS code.

Other problems with the NAICS and similar classifications arise in connection with geographic considerations. The geographic boundaries of a market are just as vital to market definition as are the product boundaries. For example, virtually all newspapers operate in local markets where typically we find one or two other competitors at most. The fact that, taken as a nationwide industry, newspapers exhibit very low concentration measures may not be terribly relevant in terms of indicating the extent of choice available to consumers who purchase newspapers in a particular town or city.[5]

Another issue related to geography is foreign trade. When the volume of such trade is large, the relevant market may well be a global one instead of a domestic one. In addition, even if one looks at only the domestic market, the presence of foreign imports can mean that the measurement of market share will depend critically on whether one uses a production total or a sales total. Thus, General Motors, Ford, and Daimler-Chrysler account for roughly 80 percent of all domestic production, but closer to 60 percent of domestic sales as a result of automobile imports.

Finally, structural measures such as HHI and CR_4 have trouble reflecting the relationships between firms operating at different stages of the production process. The delivery of a final good or service to the customer often represents the last of many steps. These include the acquisition of the raw materials; their transformation into a semifinished good; the refinement of the semifinished good into a final consumer product and, thereafter, the retailing. In economics jargon, the initial raw materials phase is typically described as the upstream phase after which the product flows "downstream" through the various stages toward its final sale to the consumer. The relationship between upstream and downstream phases is therefore a vertical one, and there are several forms that this relationship can take. An upstream producer may own all the subsequent phases in which case we say the firm is vertically integrated. Alternatively, an upstream producer may offer franchising agreements or long-term contracts to downstream sellers. The existence and variability of such relationships can cause difficulty in measuring the structure of the market at any one stage of production. For instance, there are many bottling companies so that conventional measures of market concentration in the bottled, tin, and soft drink industry are rather low. In turn, this suggests a fairly competitive market. However, the reality is that most bottling companies do not compete with each other but, instead, are tied through strict franchise agreements to use one of the national upstream suppliers, such as Coca-Cola or Pepsi.[6] There is much less competition among bottlers than the concentration measure would suggest.

[4] However, the presence of a high monopoly price may inflate the cross-elasticity measure, a point originally emphasized by Stocking and Mueller (1955). That is, at the high price set by a monopolist, the cross-price elasticity may be large and indicate that other goods are substitutes when this would not be the finding had the monopolized industry been pricing competitively.

[5] This issue becomes even more complicated for an industry where large, national firms operate in many local markets. For example, the *New York Times* owns a controlling interest in the *Boston Globe* as well as in other newspapers. The Gannet group controls the newspapers in more than two dozen markets. The banking industry outside the United States reveals a similar pattern of national ownership of local branches.

[6] Some authors, for example, Gort (1962) and, more recently, Davies and Morris (1995), have tried to obtain a precise, quantitative measure of the extent of vertical integration.

In sum, interpreting the structural measures such as CR$_4$ and HHI is greatly complicated by a variety of factors such as regional markets, international trade, and vertical relationships. In addition, the standard approach of establishing categories on the basis of similarity in production techniques, rather than the degree to which they serve as substitutes in the eyes of consumers, means that most structural measures are far from ideal in terms of indicating the extent of market competition. Yet while it is well to recognize such limitations, it is equally important to recognize that some measures of industrial structure are probably better than none at all. Moreover, categorizing industries on the basis of closeness of shared production techniques does have its advantages. The most explicit theories of industrial structure link the configuration of an industry to the behavior of its production costs. Such a relationship only makes sense if the production technologies are sufficiently similar that we can make general, industry-wide statements about a typical firm's cost structure.

3.2 MEASURING MARKET POWER

Throughout this chapter, we have been thinking about market structure in the quite literal sense of how the industry's production of output is allocated across different firms. We have seen how summary statistics such as the CR$_4$ or HHI attempt to describe this configuration of firms in an industry much as a census taker might use similar statistics to describe the number and size of families in a geographic region. A large part of the motivation for these measures is the desire to summarize succinctly just where an industry might lie relative to the ideal of perfect competition. There is nothing wrong with this structural approach so long as one clear caveat is kept in mind. This is that a particular structure does not necessarily imply a particular outcome.

When we say that an industry is highly concentrated we are saying that the industry does not have many small firms, in contrast to the configuration that we associate with the competitive model. Does that necessarily mean then that prices charged in this industry are above what would prevail in a perfectly competitive market? The answer is not so straightforward. As we shall see in subsequent chapters, markets with even just two or three firms may come quite close to duplicating the competitive or efficient outcome.

The Lerner Index is one way to measure how well a market performs from an efficiency point of view. The Lerner Index LI measures how far the outcome is from the competitive ideal in the following way:

$$LI = \frac{P - MC}{P} \tag{3.3}$$

Because the Lerner Index directly reflects the discrepancy between price and marginal cost it captures much of what we are interested in when it comes to the *exercise* of market power. For a competitive firm, the Lerner Index is zero since such a firm prices at marginal cost. For a pure monopolist, on the other hand, the Lerner Index can be shown to be the inverse of the elasticity of demand—the less elastic the demand the greater is the price-marginal cost distortion. (See the Derivation Checkpoint, "The Calculus of Competition," in Chapter 2 for a formal derivation.) To see this recall that for a monopolist the marginal revenue of selling an additional unit of output can be written as $MR = P + \frac{\Delta P}{\Delta Q} Q$. For profit maximization we set marginal revenue equal to marginal cost, or $P + \frac{\Delta P}{\Delta Q} Q = MC$. Rearranging and dividing by price P we obtain

$$\frac{P - MC}{P} = -\frac{\Delta P}{\Delta Q}\frac{Q}{P} = \frac{1}{\eta} \tag{3.4}$$

where $1/\eta$ is the inverse of the elasticity of demand. The less elastic is demand, or the smaller is η, the greater is the difference between market price and marginal cost of production in the monopoly outcome. To drive the point home just a bit more deeply, recall that the perfectly competitive firm faces an infinitely elastic or horizontal demand curve. When such a large value is substituted for the elasticity term in equation (3.4) it implies a Lerner Index of 0. Again, the perfectly competitive firm sells at a price equal to marginal cost. Note too that the Lerner Index can never exceed 1 and that it can only hit this maximum value if marginal cost is 0.

For an industry of more than one but not a large number of firms, measuring the Lerner Index is more complicated and requires obtaining some average index. A particularly straightforward case in this regard is that in which the commodity in question is homogenous so that all firms must sell at exactly the same price. If this is so, then we can measure a market-wide Lerner Index as:

$$LI = \frac{P - \sum_{i=1}^{N} s_i MC_i}{P} \tag{3.5}$$

LI: a direct gauge of market power

Here, as before, s_i is the market share of the ith firm and N is the total number of firms.

The Lerner Index is a very useful conceptual tool and we will make reference to it throughout the remainder of this book. Like the CR_4 or the HHI, the Lerner Index is a summary measure. The difference is that the Lerner Index is not so much a measure of how an industry's production is structured as it is a measure of the market outcome. The greater is the Lerner Index, the farther the market outcome lies from the competitive case—and the more market power is being exploited. In this sense, the Lerner Index is a direct gauge of the extent of market competition.

Robert Hall (1988) uses a production theory approach to derive estimates of the Lerner Index for 20 broad manufacturing sectors in the U.S. These are shown in Table 3.3. Domowitz, Hubbard, and Petersen (1988) obtained similar but generally lower estimates of the Index using Hall's (1988) approach corrected for changes in raw material usage. Whereas Hall (1988) found an average price-cost margin of 0.577, Domowitz, Hubbard, and Petersen (1988) estimate the average to be only 0.37. Even this lower value, however, indicates a substantial degree of non-price-taking behavior.

Both the Hall (1988) and the Domowitz, Hubbard, and Petersen (1988) studies aim to get a sense of monopoly power in general, i.e., across a spectrum of industries. Hence, each is based on a cross-section of industries. Other studies, aimed at a narrower set of questions can also be useful. For example, Ellison (1994) tries to get evidence on game-theoretic models of cartel behavior. For this purpose, he studies railroad prices over time in the late nineteenth century. He estimates that, apart from price war periods, the Lerner Index was about 85 percent of what it would be under pure monopoly pricing. In other words, the collusive behavior of railroads at this time was capable of coming within 15 percent of the pure monopoly price distortion. Again, this is a considerable amount.

However, much like the structural indices, the Lerner Index also has its problems. To begin with, calculating the Lerner Index for an industry runs into the problem of market definition.

non-price-taking behavior

Table 3.3 Estimated Lerner Index for selected industries

Industry	Lerner Index
Food and kindred products	0.811
Tobacco	0.638
Textile mill products	0.214
Apparel	0.444
Lumber and wood	0.494
Furniture and fixtures	0.731
Paper and allied products	0.930
Printing	0.950
Rubber and plastic	0.337
Leather products	0.524
Stone, clay, and glass	0.606
Primary metals	0.540
Fabricated metals	0.394
Machinery	0.300
Electric equipment	0.676
Instruments	0.284
Miscellaneous mfg	0.777
Communication	0.972
Electric, gas, and sanitary services	0.921
Motor vehicles	0.433
Average	0.57

Sources: Hall (1988) U.S. Census Bureau, Census of Manufactures, 2002, and various studies

In this respect, the relevant industry-wide estimate of the Lerner Index can be just as difficult
to obtain as are good estimates of CR_4 and HHI.

Even when the market definition is reasonably clear, however, the Lerner Index is still
difficult to measure. It is one thing to count the number and estimate the sizes of the various firms in an industry. Measuring the elasticity of demand is trickier. Measuring marginal
cost is even more difficult. Unfortunately, even small changes in the assumptions one makes
about the data can lead to sizable differences in estimated price-cost margins as illustrated
by the differences between the Hall (1988) and Domowitz, Hubbard, and Petersen (1988)
estimates above. Indeed, Ellison's (1994) study relied on data studied earlier by Porter (1983).
Porter's (1983) estimate of the price distortion during collusive periods is only half as large
as Ellison's (1994) estimate.

Moreover, even when the Lerner Index is accurately measured its interpretation can
remain ambiguous. Suppose for example that each firm in an industry has to incur a one-
time sunk cost F associated with setting up its establishment. Assume further that each
firm's marginal cost is constant. Because each firm needs to earn enough operating profit
to cover its sunk cost, the equilibrium price level will need to rise above marginal cost.
That is, the Lerner Index will need to be positive. However, the more positive that difference is—the greater is the price-cost margin—the greater the number of firms that can cover
the one-time sunk cost. As a result, we might observe a high Lerner Index in a setting in
which there are numerous firms, none of which is very large. In such a case, the high Lerner

Index might erroneously indicate little competition even though no firm has any significant market power.[7]

Conversely, the Lerner Index might underestimate market power in settings in which cost-reducing innovations are important. Suppose for example that an industry has an old and not very efficient incumbent firm with high marginal cost. As long as demand is somewhat elastic, such a firm may have no choice but to price relatively close to marginal cost. At the same time, the incumbent has a great incentive to take whatever actions it can that will keep a low cost rival from entering the market. In this case, the Lerner Index deceptively indicates a fair bit of competition because price is low relative to the incumbent's marginal cost when the relevant but unavailable comparison is the price with the potential rival's lower marginal cost.[8]

3.3 EMPIRICAL APPLICATION
Monopoly Power—How Bad Is It?

A recurrent question in antitrust policy is just how costly imperfect competition is for the economy overall. If the losses from monopoly power are not large, then devoting any significant resources to antitrust enforcement to prevent such losses is probably not worthwhile. Such scarce resources would be better used in, say, increasing homeland security or providing relief to hurricane victims. If the economic costs of market power are large, however, then allocating resources to combat the abuse of that power is likely to be warranted. Hence, it would be useful if economists had some sense of just how serious the losses from monopoly power actually are.

In principle, economists have a clear measure of the economic loss caused by monopoly power. It is the deadweight loss or triangle that results from prices above marginal cost. In practice, however, measuring this loss is not so easy. This is because it requires getting estimates of cost and/or demand but, as with any estimate, these values are subject to some error. Unfortunately, rather small changes in the estimates can lead to rather large changes in the estimated welfare cost.

To understand the issues involved, let us start with the basic measurement of the welfare or deadweight loss that results from pricing above marginal cost. As shown in Chapter 2, this is the area whose height is given by the difference between price P and marginal cost MC, and whose base is given by the difference between the competitive output Q^C that would sell if $P = MC$ and the actual market output Q that sells at the actual price P. Hence, the welfare loss WL is:

$$WL = \frac{1}{2}(P - MC)(Q^C - Q) \tag{3.6}$$

It is convenient to express this welfare loss as a proportion of total sales revenue PQ to yield

$$WL' = \frac{WL}{PQ} = \frac{1}{2}\frac{(P - MC)}{P}\frac{(Q^C - Q)}{Q} \tag{3.7}$$

---

[7] See, for example, Elzinga (1989).
[8] Hovenkamp (1994), among others, has made this argument.

Remember that the elasticity of demand η is the proportionate increase in output in response to a given proportionate decrease in price. If the price were to fall from its current P level to the competitive level of $P = MC$, then output would rise to the competitive level of Q^C. That is:

$$\eta = \frac{(Q^C - Q)/Q}{(P - MC)/P} \quad \Rightarrow \quad \frac{(Q^C - Q)}{Q} = \eta \frac{(P - MC)}{P} \tag{3.8}$$

Since we also know that the industry Lerner Index is $(P - MC)/P$, we can rewrite equation (3.7) as:

$$WL' = \frac{WL}{PQ} = \frac{1}{2}\eta(LI)^2 \tag{3.9}$$

Now recall from equation (3.4) earlier in the chapter that, for a pure monopolist, the Lerner Index is given by: $LI = (P - MC)/P = 1/\eta$. Then, in this case, the deadweight loss relative to industry sales will be:

$$WL' = \frac{WL}{PQ} = \frac{1}{2}\frac{1}{\eta} \tag{3.10}$$

That is, for the perfect monopoly case, the deadweight loss as a fraction of current industry sales is simply one-half the Lerner Index or one over twice the elasticity of demand. The intuition is that as the demand elasticity increases, the welfare loss shrinks because other goods are increasingly viewed as substitutes to the monopolized commodity. Note further the sensitivity of the welfare loss to the elasticity estimate. An estimate that $\eta = 1.5$ produces a welfare loss equal to 33 percent of revenue. An estimate of $\eta = 2$ reduces this amount to 25 percent of revenue. That is, a 0.5 change in the elasticity estimate yields an 8 percent change in the welfare loss.

The first person to make calculations along the foregoing lines on a large scale was Arnold Harberger (1954). Using a sample of 73 manufacturing industries, Harberger (1954) took the departure of the five-year average industry rate of return from the five-year average for manufacturing overall as an approximation of LI. Because he worked with industry data, and because none of the industries was a pure monopoly, Harberger (1954) could not assume that his LI estimate is the inverse of elasticity of demand, as we did in equation (3.10). Instead, he combined his LI estimates with an assumed demand elasticity of $\eta = 1$ in equation (3.9). The dollar value of these estimated distortions is then given by multiplying WL' by industry sales PQ. When Harberger (1954) added these dollar values up and extrapolated the results across the entire economy he found a surprisingly small welfare cost of monopoly—on the order of one-tenth of 1 percent of Gross Domestic Product. Currently, the budget of the Justice Department and the FTC is between one and two-tenths of 1 percent of GDP. While much of this is for activities other than antitrust enforcement, the low value of Harberger's (1954) estimate still raised a serious question about the cost-effectiveness of antitrust policy.

Harberger's (1954) approach however did not go uncriticized. Bergson (1973) noted that Harberger's (1954) procedure essentially used a partial equilibrium framework to obtain a general equilibrium measure. He demonstrated that, in principle, this could mean that Harberger's (1954) estimate considerably understated the actual loss. Cowling and Mueller

(1978) used firm-level data for 734 companies in the United States and 103 companies in the United Kingdom. The use of firm-level data means that Cowling and Mueller (1978) could apply equation (3.10) directly. Their estimated monopoly welfare costs range from 4 to 13 percent of GDP in the U.S. and from 4 to 7 percent in the U.K. These are considerably larger than Harberger's (1954) estimates.

An important source of variation in Cowling and Mueller's (1978) analysis is how advertising costs are treated in measuring LI. This calls attention to the importance of the marginal cost measure in general in determining welfare losses. This issue has been addressed more recently by Aiginger and Pfaffermayr (1997). They start by recognizing that without the pressure of perfect competition, firms can operate in an industry with different cost efficiencies. Hence, the average industry marginal cost $\overline{MC}$ is very likely not the minimum average cost that would be enforced if perfect competition were the rule. Aiginger and Pfaffermayr (1997) then make use of a result (one that we shall derive in Chapter 9) from a standard oligopoly model. The result is that the industry price-cost margin measure using $\overline{MC}$ is equal to the industry Herfindahl–Hirschman Index, HHI (scaled from 0 to 1), divided by the elasticity of industry demand. That is:

$$\frac{P - \overline{MC}}{P} = \frac{HHI}{\eta} \quad \Rightarrow \quad \eta = HHI\left(\frac{P}{P - \overline{MC}}\right) \tag{3.11}$$

Substituting this result into equation (3.9), we obtain:

$$WL' = \frac{WL}{PQ} = \frac{1}{2}\left(\frac{P - MC}{P}\right)\left(\frac{P - MC}{P - \overline{MC}}\right)HHI \tag{3.12}$$

Note that the term $\left(\dfrac{P - MC}{P - \overline{MC}}\right)$ is greater than 1 because MC is the marginal cost that would prevail under competition. Aiginger and Pfaffermayr (1997) measure this competitive MC as the marginal cost of the most efficient firm in the industry under the assumption that this is the cost efficiency that would be required for competitive firms to survive. Effectively, their approach permits them to decompose the welfare cost of market power into two parts. One is the traditional welfare loss measure due to prices not equal to *industry* average marginal cost, $P - \overline{MC}$. The other is due to the fact that market power allows the survival of firms with higher than minimum costs, $\overline{MC} - MC$. Using data from 10,000 cement and paper firms in the European Union, Aiginger and Pfaffermayr (1997) find that the total welfare loss of market power in these industries is on the order of 9 to 11 percent of industry sales. Perhaps not surprisingly, they find that these welfare losses are largely due to the cost inefficiencies that imperfect competition permits. Thus, their estimate of the traditional welfare loss measure is on the order of 2 to 3 percent, while the cost inefficiency loss is on the order of 7 to 7.5 percent. Extrapolating these estimates to the entire economy would yield results that are considerably closer to the Cowling and Mueller estimates (1978) than those obtained by Harberger (1954).

In evaluating all of these estimates it is useful to bear in mind two caveats (at least). First, an implicit assumption in all these calculations is that it is feasible to have perfect competition in all industries. As we shall see in the next chapter, however, costs and technology make this an unlikely outcome. In this sense, the estimates of welfare losses due to monopoly price distortions are too high as there is no way in which all industries could be freed of such market power. Second, the measures are taken from data in which active antitrust enforcement has been the norm. In this sense, the measures are an understatement of the potential for monopoly-induced welfare losses. Had there been no antitrust enforcement, there would have presumably been more market power abuses and the associated welfare losses would have been greater.

Summary

This chapter has focused on the measurement of market structure and market power. We are very often interested in summarizing the extent to which an industry departs from the competitive ideal in a single number or index. The issue then becomes whether and how we can construct such a summary measure.

Concentration indices, such as the CR₄ or HHI, are explicit measures of a market's structure. Both look at firm shares as a fraction of the industry's total output. Both encounter important problems, such as the difficulty of accurately defining the relevant market. The HHI, however, is generally preferred by economists since it not only reflects the number of firms but also the differences in their relative sizes.

An explicit measure of market power is the Lerner Index. Since it is based on a comparison of price and marginal cost, this index directly addresses the extent to which the market outcome deviates from the competitive ideal. However, the need to measure marginal cost accurately, along with other measurement issues, makes the Lerner Index as difficult to employ as the structural indices. Estimates of the Lerner Index also serve as a useful starting point to estimate the actual efficiency costs of monopoly power. Many efforts have been made to do this for the entire economy in an attempt to get a general view as to how serious the problem of market power really is. These empirical studies have yielded a wide range of estimates of the aggregate deadweight loss as a percentage of GDP. The lower bound estimate is that monopoly power imposes only a small inefficiency cost of a few tenths of 1 percent of GDP. However, upper bound estimates range as high as 14 percent. A crucial parameter in such studies is the elasticity of demand assumed to be typical and whether costs are minimized.

As long as the foregoing problems are recognized, the CR₄, HHI, and Lerner Index measures are useful starting points to characterize an industry's competitive position. However, an industry's degree of concentration and price-cost margin do not materialize out of thin air. Instead, these indices all derive from the interaction of a number of factors. One of those factors is the nature of production costs. The role that technology and cost play in shaping the industrial outcome is examined in the next chapter.

Problems

1. The following table gives U.S. market share data in percentages for three paper product markets in 1994.

Facial tissue		Toilet paper		Paper towels	
Company	% share	Company	% share	Company	% share
Kimberly-Clark	48	Procter & Gamble	30	Procter & Gamble	37
Procter & Gamble	30	Scott	20	Scott	18
Scott	7	James River	16	James River	12
Georgia Pacific	6	Georgia Pacific	12	Georgia Pacific	11
Other	9	Kimberly-Clark	5	Scott	4
		Other	16	Other	18

  a. Calculate the four-firm concentration ratio for each industry.
  b. Calculate each industry's HHI Index.
  c. Which industry do you think exhibits the most concentration?

2. Consider again equation (3.11) that gives the Lerner Index as: $LI = HHI/\eta$ where η is the elasticity of demand. Now generalize this to the expression: $LI = \theta\,(HHI/\eta)$, where θ is a parameter to be estimated and that presumably varies across industries. Consider an industry with just four firms.
    a. What would be the value for θ if the firms in the industry collude to form a price-fixing cartel?
    b. What would be the value for θ if the firms in the industry act like perfect competitors?
    c. In general, what does the value of θ tell us about the degree of competition in an industry?

3. Monopoly Air is the sole provider of passenger air service between Eldorado and Erewhon. It flies two flights per day in either direction with the typical flight being about 85 percent booked. A new entrant, Upstart Airways, has announced plans to offer additional service in the Eldorado–Erewhon market. However, Monopoly Air has filed a complaint with the local transportation authority arguing that it is a natural monopoly and that additional air service will only cause losses for both parties. As evidence, Monopoly Air cites the fact that, even now, its planes are not fully booked. Hence, it argues that the market is not large enough to sustain two, efficient-sized air carriers.
    Evaluate the argument put forth by Monopoly Air. What problems do you see in its logic? What information would you ideally like to have in order to determine whether or not this market is a natural monopoly?

4. We defined the Lerner Index $LI = 1/\eta$ where η is the absolute value of the elasticity of demand. We also showed that LI can be alternatively expressed as $(P - MC)/P$. Use these relationships to show that LI can never exceed 1. What does this imply is the minimum demand elasticity we should ever observe for a monopolist?

References

Aiginer and Pfaffermayr. 1997. "Looking at the Cost Side of Monopoly." *Journal of Industrial Economics* 44 (September): 245–67.

Bergson, A. 1973. "On Monopoly Welfare Losses." *American Economic Review* 63 (December): 853–70.

Cowling, K. and D. C. Mueller. 1978. "The Social Cost of Monopoly Power." *Economic Journal* 88 (December): 727–48.

Davies, S. W. and C. Morris. 1995. "A New Index of Vertical Integration: Some Estimates for U.K. Manufacturing." *International Journal of Industrial Organization* 13 (June): 151–78.

Domowitz, I., R. G. Hubbard, and B. Petersen. 1988. "Market Structure and Cyclical Fluctuations in Manufacturing." *Review of Economics and Statistics* 70 (February): 55–66.

Ellison, G. 1994. "Theories of Cartel Stability and the Joint Executive Committee." *Rand Journal of Economics* 25 (Spring): 37–57.

Elzinga, K. 1989. "Unmasking Monopoly Power: Four Types of Economic Evidence." In R. Larner and J. Meehan, Jr., eds, *Economics and Antitrust Policy*. Westport, CT: Greenwood Press.

Gort, M. 1962. *Diversification and Integration in American Industry*. Princeton: Princeton University Press.

Hall, R. 1988. "The Relation between Price and Marginal Cost in U.S. Industry." *Journal of Political Economy* 96 (October): 921–47.

Harberger, A. 1954. "Monopoly and Resource Allocation." *American Economic Review* 45 (May): 77–87.

Hovenkamp, H. J. 1994. *Federal Antitrust Law Policy: The Law of Competition and Its Practice*. St. Paul: West Publishing.

Porter, R. 1983. "A Study of Cartel Stability: The Joint Executive Committee, 1880–1886." *Bell Journal of Economics* 14 (Autumn): 301–14.

Sleuwaegen, L. and W. V. Dehandschutter. 1986. "The Critical Choice between the Concentration Ratio and the H-Index in Assessing Industry Performance." *Journal of Industrial Economics* 35 (December): 193–208.

Sleuwaegen, L., W. V. Dehandschutter, and R. DeBondt. 1989. "The Herfindahl Index and Concentration Ratios Revisited." *Antitrust Bulletin* 34 (Fall): 625–40.

Stocking, G. and W. Mueller. 1955. "The Cellophane Case and the New Competition." *American Economic Review* 45 (March): 29–63.

4

Technology and Cost

Anyone who has observed the extensive growth of electronic commerce in recent years cannot fail to have noticed the low prices charged by many Internet firms. Egreetings Network, Inc., an Internet firm selling e-mail greeting cards, offers a case in point. In just one year, 1998, the firm lowered its price per card from $2.50 to just $0.50. A year later the company reduced its fees still further. Currently the firm charges less than 10 cents for some cards and gives others away for free. Such minimal pricing strategies are not uncommon in digital commerce. Many e-sellers permit customers to download their products either freely or for a very modest charge. The question that naturally arises is how such behavior can be profitable? Surely, these firms incur costs in producing their goods and services. How can they cover such costs while selling at such low prices?

Production costs are an important factor explaining firm behavior, as well as an important determinant of the industry's structure. The four firms—*General Mills*, *Kelloggs*, *General Foods* (*Post*), and *Quaker Oats* currently account for about 80 percent of sales in the U.S. ready-to-eat breakfast cereal industry. By contrast, the largest four manufacturers of games and toys account for 35 percent to 45 percent of these products—less if video games are included. In this chapter we introduce key cost concepts that are relevant to understanding industry structure.[1]

4.1 PRODUCTION TECHNOLOGY AND COST FUNCTIONS FOR SINGLE PRODUCT FIRM

What is a firm's technology? For our purposes, the firm's technology is a production relationship that describes how a given quantity of inputs is transformed into the firm's output. In this sense we adopt the traditional neoclassical approach to the firm in which a firm is solely envisioned as a production unit. The goal of this production unit is profit maximization, which, in turn, implies minimizing the cost of making any given level of output.

The neoclassical approach is not without its weaknesses. While it does indicate how the firm's production plan changes in response to changes in input and output prices, it says little about how that plan is actually implemented or managed. In other words, it says little about what happens inside the firm and, more specifically, about how the various competing

---

[1] Panzar (1989) presents a more extended review of this topic.

interests of management, workers, and shareholders are reconciled in the design and implementation of a production plan.[2]

Moreover, whatever happens within a firm it is clear that these internal relationships are different from the external ones that exist between the firm and those outside the firm such as customers and suppliers. A market typically mediates these external relationships. Customers and suppliers buy from and sell to the firm at market prices. Inside the firm, however, relationships are organized by non-market methods, such as hierarchical control. Thus, as eloquently argued by Nobel laureate Ronald Coase (1937), the boundary of the firm is really the boundary between the use of non-market business transactions and market ones. The question Coase then raised is what determines this boundary. Why is it that production of a good is distributed across many different firms instead of a few large ones? Indeed, what limits are there to having all production organized by one or a few giant, multidivisional and multiplant firms?

These are questions that the neoclassical view of the firm cannot fully answer because its focus on production costs narrowly defined leads it to ignore another important cost—the cost of transacting business. Coase (1937) was the first to raise the issue in his classic paper, "The Nature of the Firm," Hart and Moore (1990), Williamson (1975), and Hart (1990) are subsequent important contributions to these issues, as is Bolton and Scharfstein (1998). Yet while the neoclassical approach to firm size and market structure is not without its limitations, the approach does remain insightful. For our purposes, it is useful to be aware of the issues raised by the agency and transactions cost literature but to explore those concerns at all satisfactorily would take us beyond the boundary of this book. As long as its limitations are recognized, the neoclassical view of the firm will permit us to accomplish many of our objectives. So keep in mind throughout the following discussion that a firm is interpreted as simply a profit-maximizing production unit and not a complex organization.

4.1.1   Key Cost Concepts

Standard microeconomic theory describes a firm in terms of its production technology. A firm producing the quantity q of a single product is characterized by its production function $q = f(x_1, x_2, \ldots, x_k)$. This function specifies the quantity q that the firm produces from using k different inputs at levels x_1 for the first input, x_2 for the second input, and so on through the kth input of which x_k is used. The technology is reflected in the precise form of the function, $f(\ )$. In turn, the nature of this technology will be a central determinant of the firm's costs.

The firm is treated as a single decision-making unit that chooses output q and the associated inputs $x_1, x_2, \ldots, x_k$ to maximize profits. It is convenient to approach this choice by first identifying the relationship between a firm's output and its resulting production costs—which is simply the firm's cost function. That is, for any specific output $\bar{q}$ and given the prices $w_1, w_2, \ldots, w_k$ of the k inputs, there is a unique way to choose the level of each input $x_1, x_2, \ldots, x_k$ so as to minimize the total cost of producing $\bar{q}$. The firm obtains this solution by choosing that input combination that solves the problem:

$$\underset{x_i}{Minimize} \sum\nolimits_{i=1}^{k} w_i x_i \tag{4.1}$$

subject to the constraint $f(x_1, x_2, \ldots, x_k) = \bar{q}$.

---

[2]   See Milgrom and Roberts (1992) for a classic discussion of these issues.

If we solve this problem for different levels of output $\bar{q}$, we will obtain the minimum cost of each possible production level per unit of time. This relationship between costs and output is what is described by the cost function for the firm. We typically describe the firm's cost function by the expression $C(q) + F$, from which we can then derive three key cost concepts: fixed cost; average or unit cost; and marginal cost.

1. *Fixed cost*: The fixed cost concept is reflected in the term F. This term describes a given amount of expenditure that the firm must incur each period and that is unrelated to how much output the firm produces. That is, the firm must incur F whether it produces 0 or 1,000 units, hence the term, fixed. This is distinct from the variable cost portion described by $C(q)$ that does vary as output changes. Costs that may be fixed include interest costs associated with financing a particular size of plant and advertising costs. Note, however, that often these costs may be fixed only in the short run. Over a longer period of time, the firm can adjust what plant size it wants to operate and its promotional efforts. If this is true, then these costs are not fixed over a longer period of time.

2. *Average cost*: The firm's average cost is simply a measure of the expenditure per unit of production and is given by total cost divided by total output. This cost measure does depend on output; hence its algebraic representation is $AC(q)$. Formally, $AC(q) = [C(q) + F]/q$. We may also decompose average cost into its fixed and variable components. Average fixed cost is simply total fixed cost per unit of output or F/q. Average variable cost $AVC(q)$ is similarly just the total variable cost per unit of output, $C(q)/q$. Alternatively, average variable cost is just average cost less average fixed cost, $AVC(q) = AC(q) - F/q$.

3. *Marginal cost*: The firm's marginal cost $MC(q)$ is calculated as the addition to total cost that is incurred in increasing output by one unit. Alternatively, marginal cost can be defined as the savings in total cost that is realized as the firm decreases output by one unit. More precisely, marginal cost is the slope of the total cost function and so is defined by the derivative term, $MC(q) = dC(q)/dq$.

We now add a fourth key cost concept—*sunk cost*. Like fixed cost, sunk cost is a cost that is unrelated to output. However, unlike fixed costs, which are incurred every period, sunk cost is a cost that is incurred just once—typically as a prerequisite for entry. For example, a doctor will need to acquire a license to operate. Similarly, a firm may need to do market and product research or install highly specialized equipment before it enters a market. The cost of the license, the research expenditures and the expenditures on specialized assets are likely to be unrelated to subsequent output, so in this sense they are fixed. More importantly, should the doctor or firm subsequently decide to close down, only part of these specialized expenditures will be recoverable. It might be possible to sell the license to another doctor but probably not at the price that the first doctor paid. Similarly, the research expenditures are unrecoverable on exit and it will not be possible to sell the specialized assets for anything like their initial acquisition costs. For example, the kilns that are needed to manufacture cement have almost no alternative use other than as scrap metal. Much of the capital cost that Toyota incurred in building its U.S. car manufacturing plants—production lines, robots, and other specialized machinery—also had no other uses. By contrast, the airplanes used by JetBlue to open up a new route, say between Boston and Miami, can be redeployed if passenger traffic on that route turns out to be insufficient to continue its operation. Sunk costs, in other words, are initial entry costs that are unrecoverable if the doctor or firm chooses to exit the market.

4.1.2   Cost Variables and Output Decisions

Figure 4.1 depicts a standard textbook average cost function, $AC(q)$, and its corresponding marginal cost function, $MC(q)$. As discussed in Chapter 2, profit maximization over any period of time requires that the firm produce where marginal revenue is equal to marginal cost. Thus, with one important caveat, marginal cost is the relevant cost concept to determine how much the firm should produce. That caveat is that marginal cost is important for determining how much to produce *given* that the firm is going to produce any output at all.

Suppose for example that demand is very weak. In such a case, equating marginal cost to marginal revenue may result in price falling below average cost. If price is below average cost, the firm loses money on every unit that it sells. It cannot continue to do this in the long run. Hence, the firm will eventually shut down if price stays below average cost. Whether this shutdown happens sooner or later will depend on the relation between price and average variable cost, $AVC(q)$. If price exceeds average variable cost, the firm will continue to operate in the short run. If price is above average variable cost, the firm can make some operating profit on each unit that it sells and this provides funds to cover at least some of its fixed cost. However, if price is below average variable cost, then the firm will simply shut down immediately.

Consideration of price and average cost also allows us to identify the role played by sunk cost in the firm's decision-making. Again, profit per unit in any period is simply price less average cost, $P - AC(q)$. Total profit in any period is just the profit per unit times the number of units, $[P - AC(q)]q$. Before entering an industry, a firm must expect at least to break even. If entry incurs a sunk cost such as a licensing fee or research expense, then the firm will have to believe that it will earn enough profit in subsequent periods to cover that initial sunk cost. Otherwise, it will not enter the market. Formally, the discounted present value of the expected future profits must be at least as great as the sunk cost of entry. Note though, that once it has entered, the sunk cost is no longer relevant. Once the entry decision has been made and the sunk cost incurred, the best that the firm can do is to follow the prescription above: produce where marginal revenue equals marginal cost so long as in the short run price is greater than average variable cost, otherwise shut down. In the long run: produce where marginal revenue equals marginal cost so long as price is greater than average cost, otherwise exit. Sunk cost affects the entry decision—not the decision on how much to produce after entry has occurred nor the decision to exit.

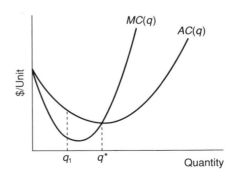

Figure 4.1   Typical average and marginal cost curves

In sum, the concept of average cost is relevant to whether the firm will produce positive output in the long run, and the concept of average variable cost is relevant to whether the firm will produce positive output in the short run. The concept of marginal cost is relevant to how much output the firm will produce given that it chooses to produce a positive amount. Sunk cost is relevant to the decision to enter the market in the first place.

4.1.3   Costs and Market Structure

Let's take a second, closer look at Figure 4.1. This figure illustrates an important relationship between average and marginal costs. Note that when marginal cost is less than average cost, as at output q_1, an expansion of output will lead to a reduction in average cost. Conversely, when marginal cost is greater than average cost, an expansion of output will lead to an increase in average cost. In the figure, marginal cost is less than average cost for all outputs less than q^*, and average cost falls throughout this range of output. Marginal cost is greater than average cost for outputs greater than q^* and average cost rises over this range of output. This feature is true for all cost functions. Average cost falls whenever marginal cost is less than average cost and rises whenever marginal cost exceeds average cost. A corollary of the just-described relationship between marginal cost and average cost is that the two are equal at the minimum point on the average cost function.

The basic cost relationships are illustrated with a hypothetical example in Table 4.1 (the parameter S in this table is explained below). This table provides measures of total, average, and marginal cost data for an imaginary firm.[3] As that table documents, average cost falls when it lies above marginal cost; rises when it is below marginal cost and (because the numbers are an approximation) is essentially equal to marginal cost at the minimum average cost value. Intuitively, if marginal cost is below average cost when average cost is falling but crosses above average cost when average cost is rising, then the crossing point at which the two are equal must be at the minimum average cost.

As noted above, firms have to expect to break even in order for production to be profitable. This means that both average cost and sunk cost play a role in determining market structure. We consider average cost first.

Table 4.1   Average and marginal cost

Output	Total cost ($)	Average cost ($/output)	Marginal cost (Δ$/Δ output)	Scale economy index (S)
5	725	145	—	—
6	816	136	96	1.42
7	917	131	104	1.26
8	1,024	128	113	1.13
9	1,143	127	123	1.03
10	1,270	127	132	0.96
11	1,408	128	151	0.85
12	1,572	131	—	—

[3]   Note: in Table 4.1, marginal cost is calculated as the average of the increase in cost associated with producing one unit more and the decrease in cost associated with producing one unit less.

Derivation Checkpoint
Average Cost, Marginal Cost, and Cost Minimization

Average cost is defined to be $AC(q) = C(q)/q$. Differentiate this with respect to output to yield:

$$\frac{dAC(q)}{dq} = \frac{q\dfrac{dC(q)}{dq} - C(q)}{q^2}$$

This can be simplified to:

$$\frac{dAC(q)}{dq} = \frac{q\left(MC(q) - \dfrac{C(q)}{q}\right)}{q^2} = \frac{[MC(q) - AC(q)]}{q}$$

The denominator of this term is positive. So, the slope of the average cost curve depends on the relation between marginal cost and average cost. If marginal cost exceeds average cost, the slope is positive. Raising output raises average cost. If average cost exceeds marginal cost, the slope is negative. Raising output lowers average cost. Minimum average cost is found where the slope of the average cost curve is zero. It is easy to see from the equation above that this occurs when average cost and marginal cost are equal.

Derivation of total and average cost functions assumes that firms produce each output level at minimum cost. A necessary condition for such minimization is that the following equation be satisfied for any pair of inputs i and j:

$$\frac{MP_i}{MP_j} = \frac{w_i}{w_j}; \text{ which is equivalent to } \frac{MP_i}{w_i} = \frac{MP_j}{w_j}$$

In other words, inputs should be used up to the point where the marginal product of the last dollar spent on input i equals the marginal product of the last dollar spent on input j.

The fact that average cost falls as output increases amounts to saying that the cost per unit of output declines as the scale of operations rises. It is natural to describe this state of affairs as one in which there are economies of scale. If, however, unit costs rise as production increases we say that there are diseconomies of scale. Fundamentally, the presence of scale economies or scale diseconomies reflects the underlying technology. Some factors of production simply cannot be scaled down to small levels of production. For example, provision of passenger rail service between Omaha and Lincoln, Nebraska, will require approximately 60 miles of track whether the number of trains per day is one or 20. As a result, a passenger train firm renting the track from the freight company that currently owns it will have to pay the same rent whether it has many passengers or just a few.

Yet it is not just the presence of large fixed costs that give rise to scale economies. For many productive processes there are efficiencies that come about just as a result of being larger. To begin with, size permits a greater division of labor, as Adam Smith noted over two hundred years ago.[4] This in turn permits specialization and more efficient production. Sometimes, the simple mathematics of the activity gives rise to important scale effects. It is well known, for example, that the cost of a container will rise roughly in proportion to its surface area (essentially, the radius squared), whereas its capacity rises roughly in proportion to its volume (essentially, the radius cubed). Thus, while a $10 \times 10 \times 10$ cube will hold 1,000 cubic feet, a $20 \times 20 \times 20$ cube holds 8,000 cubic feet. Since the cost in terms of materials and labor depends on surface area but output depends on volume, it follows that as container size increases there is a less-than-proportional rise in the cost. In turn, this implies that unit cost declines as output increases. Specifically, unit cost will fall by about 3 percent for every 10 percent increase in output.[5] For a variety of processes, such as distributing natural gas via a pipeline or manufacturing glass products in which molten glass is kept in large ovens, this relationship suggests that it will be less expensive per unit to operate at a large volume.[6]

Whatever the source of the scale economies, the fact that scale economies are measured by a falling average cost gives us a precise way to measure their presence. For we know that a declining average cost can only be observed if marginal cost is below average cost. Likewise, the presence of scale diseconomies or rising average cost requires that marginal cost be above average cost. Hence, we can construct a precise index of the extent of scale economies by defining the measure S to be the ratio $AC(q)/MC(q)$. That is, S is the ratio of average to marginal cost. S can also be shown (see the inset) to be the inverse of the elasticity of cost with respect to output. In other words, S measures the proportionate increase in output one obtains for a given proportionate increase in costs.

The more that S exceeds 1, the greater is the extent of scale economies. In such a setting, a 1 percent increase in output is associated with a less than 1 percent increase in costs. Conversely, when $S < 1$, diseconomies of scale are present. Increasing output by 1 percent now leads to more than a 1 percent increase in costs. Finally, when $S = 1$, neither economies nor diseconomies of scale are present. In this case, we say that the production technology exhibits constant returns to scale.

We define *minimum efficient scale* as the lowest level of output at which economies of scale are exhausted or, in other words, at which $S = 1$. In Figure 4.1 minimum efficient scale is q^*.

In Table 4.1, we can approximate the value of S at $q = 6$ as follows. The addition to total cost of increasing output from 6 to 7 is $101. The reduction in total cost of *decreasing* q by one unit is $91. So, an approximate measure of marginal cost at exactly $q = 6$ is the mean of these two numbers or $96. Average cost at $q = 6$ is $136. Accordingly, $S = 136/96 = 1.42$. S can also be estimated by dividing the percentage increase in total output by the percentage increase in total cost. For example, when output is increased from 6 to 7 the percentage increase is given by:

$$\frac{1}{6} \times 100\% = 16.67\%$$

[4]   Adam Smith's classic, *The Wealth of Nations*, includes a famous chapter on the division of labor and the productivity enhancement that this yielded at a pin factory.

[5]   The classic study by Chenery (1947) on natural-gas pipelines is an example of this technical relationship.

[6]   The technical explanations given here reflect the shortcomings of the neoclassical approach in that they do not make clear why the scale economies associated with a specific production technology must be exploited within a single firm. For example, two or more firms can own pipelines jointly. Indeed, there is growing support for the use of co-ownership or cotenancy, as an alternative to direct regulation in the case of natural monopoly. See Gale (1994).

Derivation Checkpoint

The Scale Economy Index and the Elasticity of Total Cost

The standard definition of the elasticity η_C of costs with respect to output is the proportionate increase in total cost that results from a given proportionate increase in output. This can be written as:

$$\eta_C = \frac{dC(q)}{C(q)} \bigg/ \frac{dq}{q} = \frac{dC(q)}{dq} \bigg/ \frac{q}{C(q)} = \frac{MC(q)}{AC(q)}.$$

As the scale economy index S is defined as the ratio of average cost to marginal cost, it follows that: $S = 1/\eta_C$.

Meanwhile, this output rise induces a percentage increase in total cost of:

$$\frac{917 - 816}{816} \times 100\% = 12.37\%$$

The ratio of these two percentages is then 16.67 percent/12.37 percent = 1.35. This is not far from the measure of S (= 1.42) that we obtained using the ratio of average to marginal cost. Indeed, if we could vary production more continuously and so consider the cost of producing 6.5 units, or 6.25 units and so on, the two measures would be virtually equal.

The ratio of the percentage change in total cost with respect to the percentage change in output is called the elasticity of cost with respect to output. What we have just shown is that the inverse of this ratio—the percentage change in output divided by the percentage change in cost—is a good indicator of scale economies. In other words, the inverse of the elasticity of cost with respect to output is a very good measure of S.

4.1

Confirm that at an output of $q = 11$, the scale economy index in Table 4.1 is indeed 0.85.

Practice Problem

How is the behavior of average cost or the extent of scale economies related to industry structure? Going back to Figure 4.1, we see that $S > 1$ for any level of output less than q^*. Scale economies are present at every output level in this range. By contrast, $S < 1$ for all outputs greater than q^*. Now suppose that we have other information indicating that demand conditions are such that the maximum extent of the market is less than q^* even if price falls to zero. We can then state that scale economies are present throughout the relevant range of production. Put another way, economies of scale are global in such a market.

If scale economies are global then the market is a natural monopoly. The term "natural" is meant to reflect the implication that monopoly is an (almost) inevitable outcome for this market because it is cheaper in such cases for a single firm to supply the entire market than for two or more firms to do so. For example, the least expensive way to produce the quantity $q*$ in Figure 4.1 is to have one firm produce the entire amount. If instead, two firms divided this production equally, so that each produced an output $q_1 = q*/2$, each of these two firms would have higher average costs than would the single firm producing $q*$.

The role of scale economies in determining market structure should now be clear. If scale economies are global, there will be no more than one firm in the market. Even if they are not global but simply quite large, efficiency may still require that all the production be done in one firm. More generally, the greater is the extent of scale economies—the larger the output at which average cost is minimized—the fewer firms that can operate efficiently in the market. Thus, large-scale economies will tend to result in concentrated markets.

Reality Checkpoint
Hotel Phone Costs May Be Fixed

Business travelers stopping at the Hampton Inn in Salt Lake City often find themselves powering down their cell phones and just relying on their room phone even though this is far more expensive. At some hotels, the cost of using the in-room phone can run as high $2 per minute or even more for domestic calls and ten or more times that amount for international calls. This compares with a near zero charge for cell phone calls. So, why does anyone use a hotel room phone?

The main answer is that cell phones do not always work. Reception can be poor and getting cell phone service simply may not be possible. For many travelers, the need to be in phone contact with others is such that they are willing to pay the high prices of hotel room phones. In turn, those high prices are necessary in part because of the fixed costs the hotels incur whether the phone is used a lot, a little, or not at all. These costs include a fixed rental fee for each line, the expense of employing operators, and the cost of maintaining equipment all of which is incurred regardless of the intensity with which room phones are used. The hotels charge a hefty fee, well above marginal cost, to earn those fixed costs back.

Unfortunately for the hotels, the advent of cell phones has sharply cut into their room phone revenue. In fact, operating profits per room phone per year in the U.S. fell from $644 in 2000 to $152 in 2004. This loss in revenue and profit may have led some hotels to go to rather unusual lengths to beat the cell phone competition. In 2003, the Scottish newspaper, the *Daily Record*, reported evidence that a local firm, Electron Electrical Engineering Services, was selling cell phone jamming devices to hotels and bed-and-breakfast establishments for between $135 and $200 apiece. These devices have the ability to block cell phone reception without the cell phone customer realizing it. All the customer will see is a message that "service is unavailable" in the location from which they are calling. Loreen Haim-Cayzer, the director of marketing and sales for Netline Communications Technologies in Tel Aviv, also acknowledged that her company had sold hundreds of cell phone jammers to hotels around the world, though none in the U.S. as far as she knew.

Of course, savvy phone users have another option. They can carry a phone card for use whenever their cell phone cannot get a signal. Those who do not, however, will have to rely on the in-room phone . . . and pay the associated fees. These customers may perhaps be forgiven then if they suspect that it is more than the costs of such phones that's fixed.

Source: C. Elliot, "Mystery of the Cell Phone that Doesn't Work at the Hotel," *New York Times*, September 7, 2004, p. C8; and C. Page "Mobile Phones Jam Scam," *The Daily Record*, August 26, 2003, p. 1.

4.2

Practice Problem

Consider the following cost relationship: $C = 50 + 2q + 0.5q^2$.

a. Derive an expression for average cost. Plot the value of average cost for $q = 4$, $q = 8$, $q = 10$, $q = 12$, and $q = 15$.

b. Marginal cost can be approximated by the rise in cost, ΔC, that occurs when output increases by one unit, $\Delta q = 1$. However, it can also be approximated by the fall in cost that occurs when output is decreased by one unit, $\Delta q = -1$. Since these two measures will not be quite the same we often use their average. Show that for the above cost relation, this procedure produces an estimate of marginal cost equal to $MC = 2 + q$.

c. Compute the index of scale economies, S. For what values of q is it the case that $S > 1$, $S = 1$, and $S < 1$?

4.2 SUNK COST AND MARKET STRUCTURE

Sunk costs also play a role in influencing market structure and one that is conceptually similar to the role of scale economies. Again, firms only enter a market if they believe that they can at least break even. This means that if there are positive sunk costs associated with entry, then firms must earn positive profits in each subsequent period of actual operation to cover those entry costs. If this is the case, entry will occur. Indeed, this view leads naturally to a definition of long-run equilibrium. Firms will stop entering the industry—and therefore the number of firms will be at its equilibrium level—when the profit from operating each period just covers the initial sunk cost that entry requires. Of course, the more firms that do enter an industry, the more competitive its pricing will be and the less profit a firm will make in any period of actual operation.

The foregoing logic permits us to see clearly the role of sunk cost in determining market structure. The higher the sunk cost, the fewer firms there will be in equilibrium. A high sunk entry cost requires that each firm that enters subsequently earns a fair bit of profit from its operations to repay the initial entry expense. This can only happen if the number of firms that enter is small so that competition is weak and price can rise above marginal (and average) cost.

To take a fairly simple example, imagine a market in which each firm produces an identical good and in which the elasticity of demand is exactly 1, or $\eta = 1$, throughout the demand curve. This means that the total consumer expenditure for the product is constant. A 1 percent decrease in price is balanced by a 1 percent increase in quantity sold. Denote this constant total expenditure as E. If P is the market price and Q is total market output, we then have: $E = PQ$. However, total output Q is also equal to the output of each firm q_i times the number of firms, N, i.e., $Q = Nq_i$. Putting these two relationships together we then obtain:

$$q_i = E/NP \tag{4.2}$$

Now recall the Lerner Index that we discussed in Chapter 3. If we assume that all firms are identical and that each has a constant marginal (and average) production cost c, then this index LI is given by: $(P - c)/P$. Since this index is a measure of the extent of monopoly power in the industry, it is natural to assume that it declines as the number of firms N gets larger. We formalize this idea by assuming that the industry Lerner Index is negatively related to the number of firms N as follows:

$$(P - c)/P = A/N^\alpha \qquad (4.3)$$

where A and α are both arbitrary positive constants. Finally, let's assume that firms only operate one period so that to break even requires that: $(P - c)q_i = F$, where F is the sunk entry cost.[7] Substituting this break-even requirement into equation (4.2) and combining that equation with equation (4.3) then yields that the equilibrium number of firms N^e at which each entrant just covers its sunk entry cost F, is given by:

$$N^e = \left[\frac{AE}{F} \right]^{\frac{1}{1+\alpha}} \qquad (4.4)$$

The intuition underlying equation (4.4) is straightforward. Industry structure is likely to be more concentrated in markets where sunk entry costs are a high proportion of expected consumer expenditures

4.3   COSTS AND MULTIPRODUCT FIRMS

Since scale economies are a description of the behavior of costs as output increases, investigating their existence in any industry requires that we measure the output of the firms in that industry. This is not always so easy. Consider, for instance, the case of a railroad. One possible measure of output is the rail ton-mile, defined as the number of tons transported times the average number of miles each ton travels. However, not all railroads carry the same type of freight. Some carry mainly mining and forestry products, some carry manufactured goods, and some carry agricultural products. In addition, through the first half of this century, many private U.S. railroads carried passengers as well as freight. Elsewhere in the world, this is still the case. Since all of these different kinds of services have different carrying costs, aggregating each railroad's output into a simple measure such as total ton-miles will confuse any cost analysis. Such aggregation does not allow us to identify whether cost differences between railroads are due to differences in scale or to differences in the kinds of service being offered.

The railroad example points to a gap in our analysis of the firm. In particular, it implies the need to extend the analysis to cover firms producing more than one type of good, that is, to investigate costs for multiproduct firms. This need is perhaps more important today than ever before. Evidence provided by Dunne, Roberts, and Samuelson (1988) and others indicates that the great majority of business establishments produce more than one product—often many more. The major automobile firms also produce trucks and buses. *Microsoft* produces both the Windows operating systems and several applications written for that system. Consumer electronics firms produce TVs, stereos, CD players, and so on. Measuring the output of these firms is clearly less than straightforward.

---

[7]   Alternatively, we could assume that F is the annualized value of the sunk entry costs.

Even when firms produce what might be considered a single basic product, they typically offer several varieties of that good. In the ready-to-eat breakfast cereal industry, the top four firms market over 80 brands of cereal. If we are to use the technological approach to the firm to gain some understanding of industry structure, we clearly need to extend that approach to handle multiproduct companies. In other words, we need to develop an analysis of costs for the multiproduct firm. The question then becomes whether we can derive average cost and scale economy measures for multiproduct firms that are as precise and clear as the analogous concepts developed for the single product case.

Derivation Checkpoint

Ray Average Cost and Multiproduct Scale Economies

Scale economies are always indicated by declining average cost. The relevant concept of average cost for a multiproduct firm is Ray Average Cost (RAC). If a firm has two products so that its cost function is $C(q_1, q_2)$ we may implicitly define total output q by the equations $q_1 = \lambda_1 q$, and $q_2 = \lambda_2 q$, where λ_1 and λ_2 sum to unity. Then Ray Average Cost is:

$$RAC(q) = \frac{C(\lambda_1 q, \lambda_2 q)}{q}$$

In the single-product case, the scale economy measure reflects the behavior of average cost as output expands. Similarly, for the two-product case, the issue is the behavior of RAC as output expands. Formally, this is given by derivative of RAC with respect to q. This is:

$$\frac{dRAC(q)}{dq} = \frac{(\lambda_1 MC_1 + \lambda_2 MC_2)q - C(\lambda_1 q, \lambda_2 q)}{q^2} = \frac{q_1 MC_1 + q_2 MC_2 - C(q_1, q_2)}{q^2}$$

where MC_i is the marginal cost of producing good i. It follows immediately that the sign of $dRAC(q)/dq$ is determined by the sign of the numerator of this expression. In other words, if $q_1 MC_1 + q_2 MC_2 > C(q_1, q_2)$ then $dRAC(q)/dq > 0$, while if $q_1 MC_1 + q_2 MC_2 < C(q_1, q_2)$ then $dRAC(q)/dq < 0$. Now define the ratio

$$S = \frac{C(q_1, q_2)}{q_1 MC_1 + q_2 MC_2}$$

The sign of the derivative above is then fully described by the value of S. If $S > 1$, this is equivalent to saying that Ray Average Cost decreases with output and so exhibits multiproduct increasing returns to scale. If $S < 1$, ray average cost is increasing, and so exhibits multiproduct decreasing returns to scale. If $S = 1$, neither scale economies nor diseconomies exist for the multiproduct firm. Note the similarity of this measure with our single-product scale economy index. In the single-product case, we measured scale economies by the ratio of average to marginal cost. This is more or less what we are doing here except that average cost is now measured by total cost divided by a weighted average of marginal cost. This is why we continue to use S to indicate scale economies. Moreover, while we have worked out this case for just the two-product firm, it easily generalizes to the case in which there are more than two products.

The answer to the foregoing question is that, subject to some restrictions, yes, we can. This is one of the major contributions of Baumol, Panzar, and Willig (1982). These authors show that the main restriction is that we measure average cost for a given mix of products, say two units of freight service for every one unit of passenger service in the railroad case. We can then measure average cost at any production level so long as we keep these proportions constant. This is what the Baumol, Panzar, and Willig (1982) call Ray Average Cost (RAC). They further show that we can derive a measure of scale economies based on the RAC measure that is conceptually quite similar to the scale economies measure for the single-product case. (See the Derivation Checkpoint: Ray Average Cost and Multiproduct Scale Economies.)

Perhaps the most important insight of Baumol, Panzar, and Willig (1982), however, is their introduction of the concept of economies of *scope*. Economies of scope are said to be present whenever it is less costly to produce a set of goods in one firm than it is to produce that set in two or more firms. Let the total cost of producing two goods, q_1 and q_2, be given by $C(q_1, q_2)$. For the two-product case, scope economies exist if $C(q_1, 0) + C(0, q_2) - C(q_1, q_2) > 0$. The first two terms in this equation are the total costs of producing product 1, passenger services for example, in one firm and product 2, say freight services, in another. The third term is the total cost of having these products produced by the same firm. If this difference is positive, then scope economies exist. If it is negative, there are diseconomies of scope. If it is 0, then there are neither economies nor diseconomies of scope. The degree of such economies, S_C, is defined by the ratio:

$$S_C = \frac{C(q_1, 0) + C(0, q_2) - C(q_1, q_2)}{C(q_1, q_2)} \tag{4.5}$$

The concept of scope economies is a crucial one that provides the central technological reason for the existence of multiproduct firms. Perhaps what is most important about scope economies, however, is that they give rise to multiproduct scale economies where we might not have expected any to exist. Looking at the production of only one product may not indicate any scale economy effects. However, if producing more of one product lowers the cost of producing another, then the firm may be able to lower its Ray Average Cost as it increases the production of both products.

Economies of scope can arise for two main reasons. The first of these is that particular outputs share common inputs. This is the source of economies of scope in the railroad example. There, the common factor is the track necessary to offer either passenger or freight rail service. Many other examples can be identified. For instance, a firm's advertising expenditures benefit all of its products to the extent that such advertising is intended to establish the firm's brand name. Similarly, if different products are manufactured with identical components —computer chips, for example—the manufacture of a whole range of such products allows the firm to take advantage of economies of scale in the manufacture of the components.

An alternative source of scope economies is the presence of cost complementarities. Cost complementarities occur when producing more of one good lowers the cost of producing a second good. There are numerous ways in which such interactions can take place. For example, the exploration and drilling of an oil well often yields not just oil but also natural gas. Hence, engaging in crude oil production will likely lower the cost of gas exploration. Similarly, a firm that manufactures computer software may also find it easy to provide computer consulting services.

Reality Checkpoint
Talk About Scope Economies, Holy Cow!

Economies of scope arise in many situations —including agricultural production. There is ample evidence that firms producing multiple crops are more cost efficient than firms specializing in just one or two crops. For firms that specialize in particular livestock, the gains from adding other livestock or crops seem to be less clear. However, this may be because livestock production itself already embodies many scope economies even when totally specialized.

Consider a cattle ranch. Raising cattle not only produces beef, but also leather. So, it is clearly cheaper for one farm to produce both products rather than for two farms to do each separately. Yet the scope economies of cattle

production do not stop there. Cattle carcasses are actually used in hundreds of processes. Glycerin and collagen are both cattle by-products. Other cattle body parts find their way into vaccines, animal feed, lubricants, asphalt, paper coatings, and fabric softeners. Imagine how much additional cost would be incurred if separate cattle stocks were maintained for the production of each of these goods.

Sources: V. Klinkenborg, "The Whole Cow and Nothing but the Whole Cow." *The New York Times*, January 20, 2004, p. 18; and C. Morrison Paul and R. Nehring, "Product Diversification, Production Systems, and Economic Performance in U.S. Agricultural Production," *Journal of Econometrics*, 126 (June, 2005), 525–48.

In our discussion of a multiproduct cost function such as $C(q_1, q_2)$, we did not distinguish between situations in which the two outputs are somewhat related, as is the case with passenger and freight rail service, and those where the two goods are substantially different products, say cologne and shirts. In the latter case, the two products use quite different production processes and the presence of scope economies seems less compelling. It seems more likely that scope economies will be found when the goods being produced use similar production techniques since then we are more likely to find shared inputs and cost complementarities.

We expect scope economies to be most prevalent in the joint production of different varieties of the same good, because in that case production similarities are strongest. For instance, the possibilities for cost savings due to sharing a common factor or due to cost complementarities seem clear in the case of a ready-to-eat cereal manufacturer producing many varieties of essentially the same wheat-based cereal product. It is probably also true for a firm such as Campbell's that produces a wide variety of prepared foods, most notably, soups. To consider these issues, we need to conceptualize more clearly the meaning of different varieties of the same good. For this purpose, we now introduce a model of product differentiation that will be used extensively in later chapters.

To speak about differentiated products in a rigorous way requires that we have some way to measure just how differentiated they are. One way to do this is to imagine that some particular characteristic is the critical distinguishing feature between different versions of the good. In the case of cars, this characteristic could be speed or acceleration. In the case of soft drinks, it could be sugar content. We can then construct an index to measure this feature. Each point on the index, ranging from low to high acceleration capacity, low to high sugar content, or whatever, represents a different product variety. Some consumers will prefer a car that accelerates rapidly or a very sweet beverage, while others will favor cars that

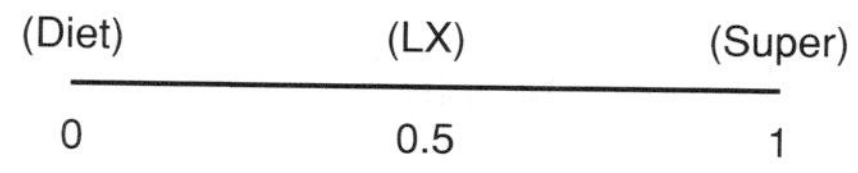

(Diet)	(LX)	(Super)
0	0.5	1

Figure 4.2 Location of cola products along the sugar content line

are easier to drive because they are capable of less acceleration or beverages with very low sugar content.

As an example, imagine a soft-drink company considering the marketing of three versions of its basic cola: (1) Diet or sugar free; (2) Super, with full sugar content; and (3) LX, an intermediate cola with just half the sugar content of Super. In this case, the distinctive feature separating each product type is sugar content, and so we want to construct an index of sugar content. It is customary to normalize such an index so that it ranges from 0 to 1. The spectrum of products for our imaginary company, therefore, ranges from Diet, located at point 0 on our index, to Super, located at point 1, with LX positioned, let's say squarely in the middle at point 0.5. This is illustrated in Figure 4.2.

The spectrum shown in Figure 4.2 may be alternatively regarded as a street. In turn, we may regard consumers as being located at different "addresses" on this street. Consumers who really like sugar will have addresses close to the Super product line. In contrast, consumers who really need to watch their calorie intake will have addresses near the Diet product line. Similarly, consumers who favor more than a medium amount of sugar but not quite so much as that contained in the Super variety, will have addresses somewhere between the LX and Super points.

It is reasonable to suppose that scope economies will exist for a firm producing different varieties of a common good, such as the various soft drink products just described. Such scope economies have become stronger in recent decades following the introduction of new manufacturing techniques, referred to as flexible manufacturing systems. They can be defined as "production unit(s) capable of producing a range of discrete products with a minimum of manual intervention" (U.S. Office of Technology Assessment, 1984, p. 60). The idea here is that production processes should be capable of switching easily from one variant of a product to another without a significant cost penalty.

A common example of a flexible manufacturing system is found in the popular clothing manufacturer, Benetton. Almost everyone is familiar with Benetton's advertisements and its array of brightly colored sweaters, T-shirts, and jeans. In fact, the coloring process is a distinctive feature of Benetton's manufacturing technology. The dyeing of the goods is done at the last moment just before shipment to the stores. Using computer-programmable equipment, Benetton is able to shift from one color-specific order to another with minimal adjustment costs. In other words, Benetton's extensive use of computer-assisted-design/computer-assisted-manufacturing (CAD/CAM) technology allows it to produce a wide array of differentiated (by color) products. In recent years, other firms have been similarly aided by CAD/CAM technology. Benjamin Moore paints and Toyota cars are just two of many companies that have used this technology to offer a wide range of choices within the same basic product line.

If scope economies exist, firms have a strong incentive to exploit them. Doing so will lower the firm's costs, possibly permit the firm to exploit multiproduct scale economies, and allow it to obtain a closer match between the products that are offered and those desired by specific customers. Eaton and Schmitt (1994) show that this is exactly what happens in a formal model of flexible manufacturing in which there are k possible versions of the good. They show that

Reality Checkpoint
Flexible Manufacturing at Lands' End

In October of 2000, Lands' End started to offer custom-made pants on its website. Customers interested in buying shirts, blouses, chinos, or jeans can simply go to the firm's website and type in measurements such as weight and height, and the characterization of the proportions of their bust, hips, and general body shape. Customers can also choose the fabric and color, and stylistic features such as cuffs, hemming, pocket dimensions, and so forth. A computer program then analyzes the information, calculates the precise design, and sends the information to a manufacturing plant in Mexico. At the plant, a computerized cutting machine creates the pattern and the item is cut and sewn and shipped to customers two to four weeks later depending on the volume of orders.

The price in 2007 for a customized pair of traditional fit men's ringspun denim jeans was $70. This compared to a price of about $40 for a comparable non-customized pair of jeans at the same website. Shipping was $6 in both cases. Lands' End can charge so much more for the customized jeans because consumers are getting exactly what they want in these products. Indeed, within a year of launching the customized service, the percentage of jeans sold at the Lands' End website that were customized rose from 0 to 40. The custom service also helped Lands' End to reduce the amount of unwanted merchandize in its warehouse at the end of each season. In turn, this reduced carrying costs and further raised the profit per item, in part because fewer clothes were sold at clearance.

Source: B. Tedeschi, "E-Commerce Report: A Lands' End Experiment in Selling Custom-made Pants Is A Success, Leaving Its Rivals to Play Catch-Up," *The New York Times*, September 30, 2002, p. C3.

when scope economies are very strong, it will be natural for each firm in the industry to produce the entire range of k products. In addition, the presence of strong scope economies also tends to give rise to important multiproduct scale economies, and this suggests that the industry will be concentrated. Moreover, even weak scope economies may be sufficient to imply that it is less costly to organize production in a smaller number of firms. That is, it will be less costly to have fewer firms producing a range of products rather than to have a firm producing each product separately. In short, the presence of scope economies in the production of differentiated products tends to increase market concentration in such industries.[8]

4.4 NONCOST DETERMINANTS OF INDUSTRY STRUCTURE

So far, we have focused on the role of cost relationships, especially scale and scope economies, as being the main determinants of firm size and industry structure. There are, however, other factors that can play an important role. Here, we mention three factors

---

[8] See Panzar (1989) for a good discussion of cost issues in general. See Evans and Heckman (1986) and Roller (1990) for evidence of scope economies in the telephone industry; Cohn et al. (1989) and DeGroot et al. (1991) for evidence of scope economies in higher education; and Gilligan et al. (1984) and Pulley and Braunstein (1992) for evidence of scope economies in finance.

specifically. These are: (1) the size of the market; (2) the presence of network externalities on the demand side; and (3) the role of government policy.

4.4.1   Market Size and Competitive Industry

The influence of market size on industry structure has been extensively investigated by Sutton (1991, 2001). The fact that a firm must be large to reach the minimum efficient scale of operations does not necessarily imply a highly concentrated structure if the market in question is large enough to accommodate many such firms. Similarly, the fact that it is cheaper to produce many different products (or many versions of the same product) in one firm rather than in several firms does not necessarily imply a market dominated by a few firms. Most farms produce more than one crop. Yet farming is a very competitively structured industry in part because the market for agricultural products is so extensive.

Just how big does a market have to be in order to avoid domination by a few firms? The answer: it depends. When scale economies are extensive, for example, when sunk or fixed costs associated with indivisible inputs are relatively large, the market will need to be greater to accommodate more firms. Thus, the relationship between market structure and market size will vary according to the specific market being examined.

If scale economies are exhausted at some point and if sunk entry costs do not rise with the size of the market then we ought to see that concentration declines as market size grows sufficiently large. Some direct evidence of this effect is provided by Bresnahan and Reiss (1991). They gathered data on a number of professions and services from over 200 towns scattered across the western United States. They find that a town of about 800 or 900 will support just one doctor. As the town grows to a population of roughly 3,500, a second doctor will typically enter. It takes a town of over 9,000 people to generate an industry of five doctors. The same positive relationship between market size and the number of firms is also found in other professions. For tire dealers, for example, Bresnahan and Reiss find that a town of only 500 people is needed to support one tire dealer and that five tire dealers will emerge when the town reaches a population of 6,000. The smaller market requirements needed to support a given number of tire dealers instead of doctors probably reflects, among other things, the fact that doctors have higher fixed/sunk costs than do the tire dealers.

Sutton (1991, 2001) however, provides an important qualification to the idea that concentration will decline with the size of the market, for example, as implied by equation (4.4). He notes that such a relationship does not appear to hold in a number of industries, particularly in industries that compete heavily using either advertising, such as processed foods, or R&D, such as pharmaceuticals. Sutton argues that these expenditures are not only sunk but also endogenous. They are sunk in that once the expenditures for a promotional campaign or product design have been incurred, they cannot be recovered. They are endogenous in that in these kinds of industries, sunk cost F is not fixed but in fact increases as the market size grows.

The logic of the Sutton argument can be seen by focusing on the sunk entry cost term F in equation (4.4). Assume that this term reflects advertising and/or R&D expenditures. However, rather than simply assuming that such expenditures are equal to some exogenous level F, assume instead that they are related to market size. For example, we may assume a linear relationship of the form:

$$F = K + \beta(AE) \tag{4.6}$$

Where recall that A is a constant and E is aggregate consumer expenditure in the industry.

Using (4.6) equation (4.4) now may be written as:

$$N^e = \left[\cfrac{1}{\left(\cfrac{K}{AE}\right) + \beta} \right]^{\frac{1}{1+\alpha}} \tag{4.7}$$

Equation (4.7) says that the equilibrium number of firms in the industry will grow as market size AE grows but that this process has an asymptotic limit. Specifically, the number of firms will never exceed $(1/\beta)^{1/(1+\alpha)}$ no matter how large the market gets. For example, suppose that $\alpha = 1$ and $\beta = 0.0625$. If this is the case, then the equilibrium number of firms in the industry will never exceed four, regardless of market size.[9]

Somewhat similarly, our initial derivation of equation (4.4) assumed that price-cost margins declined as a result of an increase in the number of firms as described by: $(P - c)/P = A/N^\alpha$. However, there may be systematic differences between industries in the relationship between the price-cost margin and the population of firms. In particular, markets in which firms sell a homogeneous product and in which they can quickly alter production to meet demand may have very small price-cost margins. This is because in such homogeneous good markets, the firm with the lowest price gets all the customers, especially if it can readily adjust output to meet that demand. Algebraically, this means that the parameter α above will differ across markets. It will be larger in those markets in which competition is naturally more intense. In such markets, the equilibrium number of firms will be correspondingly smaller.

4.4.2 Network Externalities and Market Structure

It's not news to anyone reading the recent press that there is basically only one firm producing operating systems for personal computers and that firm is *Microsoft*. For more than a decade the *Microsoft Corporation* has supplied about 90 percent of the market for operating systems for the personal computer market. Similarly, *Microsoft Word* and *Microsoft Excel* have nearly as great a share of the word-processing and spreadsheet software business. Scale and scope economies are undoubtedly part of the explanation for the highly concentrated nature of these markets. After all, once the costs have been sunk to design the basic program for the operating systems or application software, the cost of reproducing the product many times over is quite trivial. It is also highly likely that there will be a large common component to these design costs.

However, as many witnesses testified at the *Microsoft* antitrust case of 1999–2000, scale and scope economies are not the only reasons behind the dominance of this high-technology firm. A particularly important factor explaining the high concentration in this market is the presence of a demand factor known as *network externalities*. Network externalities refer to the phenomenon by which a consumer's willingness to pay for a good or service increases as the number of other consumers buying the product rises.

Telecommunications is an area in which network externalities are particularly strong. Consider the telephone for example. The usefulness or value of a single consumer connecting to a

---

[9] See Baldwin (1995) for some evidence on this point.

telephone system is essentially nil. If no one else is connected, the telephone cannot be used to make even one call. However, as more people sign on to the system, the number of potential calls and hence the utility of owning a phone increases as well. That is, each customer's individual decision to join the system confers benefits to the other customers—benefits that are therefore external to the consumer who is signing on. This is what we mean by a network externality. When market demand exhibits such an externality, there is a strong incentive for a firm to try to get a large number of consumers signed on to its network. To put it another way, any telephone system without a large number of customers would not be able to survive because it would not be very valuable to the few customers it does have.

We address the topic of network externalities more extensively in Chapter 24. However, from the brief discussion above, it should be relatively easy to see that markets with important network externalities are likely to be ones populated by a few very large firms. In other words, they are likely to have a highly concentrated structure—even if scale economies are not present on the cost side. Indeed, many analysts view network externalities as a case of scale economies that exist on the demand side of the market.

4.4.3   The Role of Government Policy

From 1934 to 1988—a period of 54 years—the number of medallions authorizing legal ownership of a taxicab in Boston was fixed at 1,525. Not a single additional medallion was issued in all that time despite the fact that the regional population increased by over 50 percent and the level of income and economic activity doubled several times over. Costs and technology were not the source of this fixed industrial structure. The primary reason for the limited entry into the Boston taxi industry was government policy. City and state officials deliberately limited the number of taxi medallions, largely at the request of those lucky taxi owners who obtained the first batch of medallions. Even in recent years with a court order to issue 300 new medallions outstanding for nearly five years, only a few additional ones have actually been issued as officials have again tried to slow the creation of additional legal taxi operators as much as possible.

A similar phenomenon prevailed from the 1930s through the 1970s when the number of so-called trunk airlines flying interstate routes never exceeded 16 and fell to 10 by the end of the 1970s. Not only was the total number of airlines small on a national scale, it was even smaller for individual city-pair markets. Many of these were often served by only one or two carriers. Here again, the primary cause was government policy. In this case, that policy was implemented by the Civil Aeronautics Board (CAB), the federal agency established in 1938 as the economic regulator of the airline industry. Throughout its existence, the CAB deliberately limited entry and sustained a high concentration level in the U.S. domestic airline industry. Indeed, this 40-year period witnessed numerous applications by freight and charter airlines to be granted the right to offer scheduled passenger services, as well as frequent applications of existing airlines to enter new city-pair markets. Virtually all of these requests were turned down. The CAB argued that this policy was necessary to promote the stability and healthy development of the airline industry. Whether it achieved its perceived goals, or whether such goals were appropriate, is a question to be answered elsewhere. The central point illustrated by both the taxicab and airline example is that explicit government policies often play an important role in determining market structure.

More often than not, the role of government policy has been to increase market concentration as both of the examples above illustrate. However, some government policies do work to increase the number of firms in an industry. The Robinson–Patman Act that prohibits price discounts to large firms if such discounts are deemed anticompetitive reflects a conscious effort to keep independent retailers in business. These are typically small firms who otherwise would have been driven out of the market by the large retail chains. Similarly, the decision of the U.S. government after the Second World War to force the Alcoa Company to sell some of its wartime aluminum plants to the Kaiser and Reynolds corporations was clearly an effort to promote a more competitive structure. Perhaps most obviously, antitrust policies that lead either the Federal Trade Commission or the Justice Department to block mergers also increase the equilibrium number of firms in an industry.

4.5   EMPIRICAL APPLICATION
Cost Function Estimation—Scale and Scope Economies

Since the underlying technology and associated cost implications are central determinants of industrial structure, economists have been interested in getting evidence on cost relationships for a long time. Unfortunately, we rarely have direct evidence on the production technology. Hence, estimating firm cost functions can be a tricky business. However, application of basic microeconomic theory can greatly facilitate the process.

To see this let us suppose that production is generated from capital K and labor L inputs using a Cobb–Douglas production function of the form:

$$Q = K^{\alpha}L^{\beta} \tag{4.8}$$

Total cost is simply the cost of the inputs. If r is the rental price of capital and w is the wage rate of labor, then total cost $C = rK + wL$. Cost minimization requires choosing the capital and labor inputs that minimize cost for achieving a given level of output. If we denote the target output level as $\bar{Q}$, the firm's problem then becomes:

$$\text{Minimize } C = rK + wL \text{ subject to } \bar{Q} = K^{\alpha}L^{\beta} \tag{4.9}$$

While there are many ways to solve this minimization problem, one way is to use the production requirement to substitute out the labor input. That is, the production constraint implies: $L = \bar{Q}^{\frac{1}{\beta}}K^{-\frac{\alpha}{\beta}}$. The cost function then becomes $C = rK + w\bar{Q}^{\frac{1}{\beta}}K^{-\frac{\alpha}{\beta}}$. If we hold output $\bar{Q}$ constant at the target level, we can minimize this expression with respect to the capital input by setting its derivative with respect to K equal to zero. Solving for K yields:

$$K = \left(\frac{\alpha}{\beta}\frac{w}{r}\right)^{\frac{\beta}{\alpha+\beta}} \bar{Q}^{\frac{1}{\alpha+\beta}} \tag{4.10}$$

If we now substitute the above value for K into the labor requirement implied by the production constraint, we may then solve for the optimal or cost minimizing labor input and we obtain:

$$L = \left(\frac{\beta}{\alpha}\frac{r}{w}\right)^{\frac{\alpha}{\alpha+\beta}} \bar{Q}^{\frac{1}{\alpha+\beta}} \tag{4.11}$$

Together, expressions (4.10) and (4.11) imply that the minimal cost for producing any given level of output $\bar{Q}$ is:

$$
C = w \left(\frac{\beta}{\alpha} \frac{r}{w} \right)^{\frac{\alpha}{\alpha+\beta}} \bar{Q}^{\frac{1}{\alpha+\beta}} + r \left(\frac{\alpha}{\beta} \frac{w}{r} \right)^{\frac{\beta}{\alpha+\beta}} \bar{Q}^{\frac{1}{\alpha+\beta}} = \left[\left(\frac{\alpha}{\beta} \right)^{\frac{\beta}{\alpha+\beta}} + \left(\frac{\beta}{\alpha} \right)^{\frac{\alpha}{\alpha+\beta}} \right] r^{\frac{\alpha}{\alpha+\beta}} w^{\frac{\beta}{\alpha+\beta}} \bar{Q}^{\frac{1}{\alpha+\beta}} \quad (4.12)
$$

Apart from the fact that we have now expressed total costs as a function of input prices and the level of output, certain features of the final expression above are important to recognize. First, note that the partial derivative of the cost function with respect to either the rental cost r or the wage w is positive. In other words, if input prices rise, it becomes more costly to produce a given output. Second, observe that the exponents for each factor price, r and w, in fact sum to unity. This means that if all factor prices increase by, say, 10 percent, the minimal cost of producing a given output will also increase by 10 percent. In economics jargon, the cost function is homogeneous of degree one in factor prices. Also, the exponent on the output level is $1/(\alpha + \beta)$. If $\alpha + \beta = 1$, then total costs will rise proportionately with output, i.e., there will be constant returns to scale. If, however, $\alpha + \beta > 1$, then costs will rise less rapidly than output so that there will be scale economies. It follows that if $\alpha + \beta < 1$, there will be scale diseconomies. Finally, note that while costs are homogeneous of degree one in both input prices, they rise less than proportionately with any one input price. That is, the coefficient on either r or w alone is less than one. This reflects the fact that as one factor's price rises, the firm will substitute out of that input and into the less expensive one.

It is convenient to write the cost equation above in logarithmic form. Hence, we have:

$$
\ln C = \ln \left[\left(\frac{\alpha}{\beta} \right)^{\frac{\beta}{\alpha+\beta}} + \left(\frac{\beta}{\alpha} \right)^{\frac{\alpha}{\alpha+\beta}} \right] + \left(\frac{\alpha}{\alpha + \beta} \right) \ln r + \left(\frac{\beta}{\alpha + \beta} \right) \ln w + \left(\frac{1}{\alpha + \beta} \right) \ln \bar{Q} \quad (4.13)
$$

For estimation purposes, this can easily be translated into:

$$
\ln C = \text{Constant} + \delta_1 \ln r + \delta_2 \ln w + \delta_3 \ln Q \quad (4.14)
$$

With observations on input prices and output levels, we may estimate the above equation and then use the estimated coefficients δ_i to recover the underlying production parameters, α and β. The properties of a well-behaved cost function discussed above suggest that both δ_1 and δ_2 should be positive, less than one separately, but sum to one together. Further, since changes in logarithms translate into proportional changes in the underlying variable, e.g., $\Delta \ln C \approx \Delta C/C$, a measure of the elasticity of costs with respect to output or η_C is provided by $\partial \ln C / \partial \ln Q$, which in this case, is reflected in the estimate of δ_3. Thus, our measure of scale economies derived earlier is: $S = 1 \Big/ \dfrac{\partial \ln C}{\partial \ln Q} = 1/\delta_3$.

However, the above derivation is based on the assumption that the underlying production technology is of the Cobb–Douglas type. Because that may be a rather strong assumption, empirical analyses often use a more flexible cost specification that permits a much wider array of underlying technologies including, as a special case, the Cobb–Douglas specification above. One such flexible specification is the translog cost function. For the basic, two-input case above, this function has the form:

$$
\begin{aligned}
\ln C = {} & \text{Constant} + \delta_1 \ln r + \delta_2 \ln w + 0.5[\delta_{11}(\ln r)^2 + \delta_{12}(\ln w)(\ln r) \\
& + \delta_{21}(\ln w)(\ln r) + \delta_{22}(\ln w)^2] + \delta_3 \ln Q + \delta_{31}(\ln Q)(\ln r) \\
& + \delta_{32}(\ln Q)(\ln w) + 0.5\delta_{33}(\ln Q)^2
\end{aligned}
\tag{4.15}
$$

As before, we expect δ_1 and δ_2 to be positive fractions that sum to unity. However, our measure of scale economies $S = 1 \left/ \dfrac{\partial \ln C}{\partial \ln Q} \right.$ is now no longer necessarily constant but instead can depend on the level of output. That is we now have: $S = 1 \left/ \dfrac{\partial \ln C}{\partial \ln Q} \right. = 1/(\delta_3 + \delta_{33} \ln Q +$ $\delta_{31} \ln r + \delta_{32} \ln w)$. Only if $\delta_{31} = \delta_{32} = \delta_{33} = 0$, will the index of scale economies be independent of the level of Q. This is a restriction that one can test. Indeed, use of a translog function such as (4.15) above allows the researcher to test numerous restrictions. For example, if $\delta_{31} = \delta_{32} = 0$ but $\delta_{33} \neq 0$, then while the technology is not homogeneous, the mix of capital and labor inputs does not change as output expands and the production technology exhibits what economists call homotheticity.

One of the earliest papers estimating a translog cost function is also one of the most illustrative. Christensen and Greene (1976) applied the translog approach to the electric power-generating industry adding fuel as a basic input along with labor and capital. Denoting the price of fuel as F, their estimation led to an equation with a constant and nine input price terms and five output terms. The five output variables are the pure output term $\ln Q$, the three interaction terms between the output term and each of the input price terms, and the $(\ln Q)^2$ term. Here we focus on these five terms because these are the ones that will indicate the extent of any economies of scale. The Christensen and Greene (1976) estimates for these terms are shown in Table 4.2.

Note that the interaction terms are virtually all statistically significant indicating that these interaction effects belong in the equation. Indeed, when Christensen and Greene (1976) estimate the cost equation with only the first term $\ln Q$ included, as would be implied by a Cobb–Douglas technology, they obtain a coefficient estimate on the order of 0.8. This would yield a scale economy index of $S = 1/0.8 = 1.25$ and indicate substantial unexploited scale economies for all firms. Including the additional terms permits the scale effect to vary by firm size as measured by the volume of output. On this basis, they then find that few firms operate with $S > 1.17$. Further, fully half of the electrical power was generated by firms that were sufficiently large that no further scale economies were present.

Table 4.2 Christensen and Greene (1976) cost function estimates and scale economies in electric power generation

Variable	Coefficient	t-statistic
$(\ln Q)$	0.587	20.87
$(\ln Q)(\ln r)$	−0.003	−1.23
$(\ln Q)(\ln w)$	−0.018	−8.25
$(\ln Q)(\ln F)$	0.021	6.64
$(\ln Q)^2$	0.049	12.94

It is relatively straightforward to adapt the translog cost function to the case of multiproduct firms. If, for example, we continue to assume just two inputs with prices r and w, but now instead assume two outputs, Q_1 and Q_2, the function has the form:

$$\ln C = \text{Constant} + \delta_1 \ln r + \delta_2 \ln w + 0.5[\delta_{11}(\ln r)^2 + \delta_{12}(\ln w)(\ln r)$$
$$+ \delta_{21}(\ln w)(\ln r) + \delta_{22}(\ln w)^2] + \delta_3 \ln Q_1 + \delta_{31}(\ln Q_1)(\ln r)$$
$$+ \delta_{32}(\ln Q_1)(\ln w) + 0.5\delta_{33}(\ln Q_1)^2 + \delta_4 \ln Q_2 + \delta_{41}(\ln Q_2)(\ln r)$$
$$+ \delta_{42}(\ln Q_2)(\ln w) + 0.5\delta_{44}(\ln Q_2)^2 + \delta_5(\ln Q_1)(\ln Q_2) \qquad (4.16)$$

However, in applying equation (4.16) to data gathered from many firms, there is a real possibility that some of the firms will be single-product enterprises for which either Q_1 or Q_2 is zero. This creates a serious problem in estimating the cost relationships because the logarithm of zero is not well defined. Hence, when multiple outputs are considered, many researchers follow the suggestion of Caves, Christensen, and Tretheway (1980) and use what is known as a Box–Cox transformation of the output variables. Under this transformation, the log of the level of good i production is replaced with the term $(Q_i^\theta - 1)/\theta$, where θ is estimated along with other parameters. Note that the limit of $(Q_i^\theta - 1)/\theta$ as θ approaches zero is in fact $\ln Q_i$.

Once the multiproduct cost function has been estimated, it is straightforward to derive the scale economy and scope economy measures described in the text. DeGroot, McMahon, and Volkwein (1991) use this translog approach to model the cost structure of American research universities, assuming three university outputs: (1) undergraduate education; (2) graduate education; and (3) research. They find that for the product mix of the typical university there were significant unexploited scale economies (declining Ray Average Cost). However, this was not true for the less student-intensive product mix of the top private schools for which they found little if any scale economies. They also found significant scope economies between graduate and undergraduate education but, somewhat surprisingly, little scope economies between graduate education and research.

Summary

This chapter has focused on technology and key cost concepts and the implications they have for industrial structure. Scale economies tend to increase market concentration. Economies of scope have a similar effect of concentrating the production of different products within a single firm. Scope economies also typically give rise to important multiproduct scale economies. This is particularly the case when the various products are not truly different goods but, instead, different versions of the same goods. In such product-differentiated markets, the presence of scope and scale economies will again imply a more concentrated structure.

Other factors influence market structure as well. One of these is market size. Because a large market has room for a number of firms, even if each firm is of considerable size, larger markets tend to be less concentrated than small ones. However, increasing market size does not lead to less concentration in markets in which sunk costs also increase with size. These are typically markets in which advertising or research and development costs play a major role.

Another important determinant of market structure comes from the demand side of the market in the form of network externalities. Network externalities imply that the value of a product to any one consumer increases as other consumers use it. Such externalities act much like scale economies on the demand side and they foster increased market concentration. Careful application of economic theory can generate clear implications for the statistical measurement of cost relationships. Such work has been extremely useful in identifying scale and scope economies. For example, regression analyses based on the theory of production costs have found significant scale economies in electric power generation and important economies of scope between graduate and undergraduate education.

Finally, government policy is also a very important determinant of market structure. Regulations such as those long applied to local taxi markets and the airline industry typically reduce the ability of new firms to enter the market. Antitrust policy can raise the number of firms in a market by blocking a proposed merger.

Problems

1. Let the cost function be $C = 100 + 4q + 4q^2$. Derive an expression for average cost. Derive an expression for marginal cost. Is there any range of production characterized by scale economies? At what production level are scale economies exhausted?

2. An urban rapid-transit line runs crowded trains (200 passengers per car) at rush hours, but nearly empty trains (10 passengers per car) at off-peak hours. A management consultant argues that the cost of running a car for one trip on this line is about $50 regardless of the number of passengers. Hence, the consultant concludes that the per passenger cost is about 25 cents at rush hour but rises to $5 in off-peak hours. Consequently, we had better discourage the off-peak business. Is the consultant a good economist? Why or why not?

3. Consider the following cost relationships for a single-product firm:

$$C(q) = 50 + 0.5q \text{ for } q < 7$$
$$C(q) = 7q \text{ for } q > 7$$

   a. Derive average and marginal cost for all integer outputs less than or equal to 7.
   b. What are average and marginal cost for all outputs above 7?

4. In the problem above is there a minimum efficient scale of plant implied by these cost relationships? If so, what is it?

5. Let P be industry price and Q be total industry output. If the industry demand curve is $P = 84 - 0.5Q$ use the data in question 3 to determine what is the maximum number of efficient-sized firms that the industry can sustain.

6. How would your answer to 5 be changed if industry demand were instead $P = 14 - 0.5Q$? Explain.

7. Some estimates for the cement industry suggest the following relationship between capacity and average cost:

Capacity (thousands of tons)	Average cost
250	28.78
500	25.73
750	23.63
1,000	21.63
1,250	21.00
1,500	20.75
1,750	20.95
2,000	21.50

   a. At what production level are scale economies exhausted?
   b. Calculate the scale economy index for the production levels 500, 750, 1,000, 1,500, and 1,750.

8. A newspaper article (J. Peder Zane, "It Ain't for the Meat; It's for Lotion," *New York Times*, Sunday, May 5, 1996, p. E5) presented the following data for a cow brought to market:

Part	Use	Price/lb ($)
Horns	Gelatin Collagen	0.42
Cheek	Sausage Baloney	0.55
Adrenal gland	Steroids	2.85
Meat	Beef	1.05
Lips	Taco filling	0.19
Hide	Footwear Clothing	0.75

   Comment on the scope economies illustrated by this example. What is the source of such economies? What does the existence of such economies imply about the supply of such products as leather skins, beef, and gelatin powder?

References

Baldwin, John R. 1995. *The Dynamics of Industrial Competition: A North American Perspective*. Cambridge: Cambridge University Press.

Baumol, W. J., J. C. Panzar, and R. D. Willig. 1982. *Contestable Markets and the Theory of Industry Structure*. New York: Harcourt, Brace, Jovanovich.

Bolton, P. and A. Scharfstein. 1998. "Corporate Finance, the Theory of the Firm, and Organizations." *Journal of Economic Perspectives* 12 (Autumn): 95–114.

Bresnahan, T., and P. Reiss. 1991. "Entry and Competition in Concentrated Markets." *Journal of Political Economy* 99 (October): 977–1009.

Caves, D., L. Christensen, and M. W. Tretheway. 1980. "Flexible Cost Functions for Multiproduct Firms." *Review of Economics and Statistics* 62 (August): 477–81.

Chenery, H. 1949. "The Engineering Production Function." *Quarterly Journal of Economics* 63 (May): 507–31.

Christensen, L. and W. Greene. 1976. "Economies of Scale in U.S. Electric Power Generation." *Journal of Political Economy* 84 (August): 655–76.

Coase, R. H. 1937. "The Nature of the Firm." *Economica* 4 (March): 386–405.

Cohn, E., S. L. Rhine, and M. C. Santos. 1989. "Institutions of Higher Education as Multi-Product Firms: Economies of Scale and Scope." *Review of Economics and Statistics* 71 (May): 284–90.

De Groot, H., W. McMahon, and J. F. Volkwein. 1991. "The Cost Structure of American Research Universities." *Review of Economics and Statistics* 73 (August): 424–31.

Dunne, T., M. J. Roberts, and L. Samuelson. 1988. "Patterns of Firm Entry in U.S. Manufacturing Industries." *Rand Journal of Economics* 19 (Winter): 495–515.

Eaton, B. C., and N. Schmitt. 1994. "Flexible Manufacturing and Market Structure." *American Economic Review* 84 (September): 875–88.

Evans, D. and J. Heckman. 1986. "A Test for Subadditivity of the Cost Function with Application to the Bell System." *American Economic Review* 74 (September): 615–23.

Gale, I. 1994. "Price Competition in Non-cooperative Joint Ventures." *International Journal of Industrial Organization* 12 (March): 53–69.

Gilligan, T., M. Smirlock, and W. Marshall. 1984. "Scale and Scope Economies in the Multi-Product Banking Firm." *Journal of Monetary Economics* 13 (May): 393–405.

Hart, O. 1995. *Firms, Contracts, and Financial Structure*. New York: Oxford University Press.

Hart, O. and J. Moore. 1990. "Property Rights and the Nature of the Firm." *Journal of Political Economy* 98 (December): 1119–58.

Milgrom, P. and J. Roberts. 1992. *Economics, Organization, and Management*. Upper Saddle River, NJ: Prentice Hall.

Panzar, J. C. 1989. "Technological Determinants of Firm and Industry Structure." In R. Schmalensee and R. Willig, eds, *Handbook of Industrial Organization*. Vol. 1. Amsterdam: North-Holland, 3–60.

Pulley, L. B. and Y. M. Braunstein. 1992. "A Composite Cost Function for Multiproduct Firms with an Application to Economies of Scope in Banking." *Review of Economics and Statistics* 74 (May): 221–30.

Roller, L. 1990. "Proper Quadratic Cost Functions with Application to the Bell System." *Review of Economics and Statistics* 72 (May): 202–10.

Sutton, John. 1991. *Sunk Costs and Market Structure*. Cambridge, MA: MIT Press.

——— . 2001. *Technology and Market Structure*. Cambridge, MA: MIT Press.

Williamson, O. E. 1975. *Markets and Hierarchies: Analysis and Antitrust Implications*. New York: Free Press.

Part II

Monopoly Power in Theory and Practice

In Part II, we consider the pure monopoly problem in much more detail than the simple textbook case presented in Chapter 2. In particular, we consider a range of price and non-price tactics the might be used by firms that operate as a pure monopolist. There are two reasons to study such tactics. First, there are a number of special cases in which firms might actually have an effective monopoly. In many regions, for example, there is just one ski lift operator within a radius of 50 miles and only one amusement park serving an even greater area. Second, and more importantly, the tactics we discuss such as quantity discounts and bundling are also available to imperfect competitors who are not monopolists. However, because it is much easier to understand the role of such measures in this more competitive environment *after* seeing them used by a single firm with no strategically linked rival, we introduce these concepts here.

We consider three basic techniques that a firm with a downward-sloping demand curve may use to increase its product over that achieved by the standard, uniform-pricing monopolist. In Chapters 5 and 6, we explore various price discrimination schemes. This includes both linear (market segmentation) and nonlinear (two-part tariff and quantity discount) pricing strategies.

In Chapter 7 we introduce the idea of product design as a means of enhancing profit. Beyond demonstrating that design issues are important, this permits us to introduce the concept of horizontal differentiation and its spatial representation as first formalized by Hotelling (1929). It also permits us to introduce the alternative concept of vertical product differentiation along the lines initially presented by Mussa and Rosen (1978). Although these models are more technically demanding, they each have an accessible underlying intuition. More importantly, both horizontal and vertical differentiation are crucial concepts that we will employ repeatedly in the settings of strategic interaction among a small number of firms that form the framework for the later Chapters 9 to 25. Hence, giving those concepts a formal representation that can be applied in a wide variety of settings is an important building block for later work. Chapter 7 also includes an empirical application based on the study by Stavins (2001) of price-discrimination techniques in airline ticketing. Although we have introduced discriminatory practices in a monopoly setting, everyday experience offers considerable evidence that such tactics are not limited to the rare case of a pure monopolist. This study helps to clarify the role of price discrimination in more competitive settings and gives a more realistic understanding of such tactics.

Microsoft sells much of it software as a bundle, e.g., the package of programs including Word, Excel, and PowerPoint available in its Office package. Similarly, the owner of a Hewlett–Packard inkjet printer is required or tied in to also use a Hewlett–Packard inkjet printer cartridge. Such bundling and tying practices are the focus Chapter 8. We demonstrate how such practices may again be used to increase the firm's profit. Here again, however, everyday experience offers abundant evidence that these practices are not limited to pure or even near monopoly cases. Therefore, we again examine the role of such practices in more competitive environments.

5

Price Discrimination and Monopoly: Linear Pricing

A central part of the growing debate over U.S. healthcare policy has been the high price of prescription drugs. It was this concern that led to the expansion of Medicare to include coverage for prescription drugs starting in 2006. It is this same issue that has led many Americans to buy their prescription drugs in other countries, most notably Canada. Yet for that to happen legally requires additional legislation. The existing statutes—enacted during the Clinton Administration—only permit such imports if the Secretary of Health and Human Services certifies that the drug "pose no additional risk" to consumers, and no such certifications have been issued. As of this writing, legislation to remove the certification requirement has so far failed to win passage in both houses of the U.S. Congress.

Whatever the risk of Canadian prescriptions, it is indisputable that there are significant differences in prescription drug prices between the United States and Canada. Graham and Robson (2000) collected detailed 1999 price information for 45 brand name prescription drugs, collectively covering approximately 25 percent of the total prescriptions written in the United States. From this sample they calculated that Canadian retail prices were far less than American ones, with the median discount approximately 46 percent. For one drug in their sample, this discount was 95 percent. In a related study, Graham and Tabler (2001) analyzed the retail prices charged in 2001 by a randomly selected set of pharmacies for three patented drugs in three neighboring Canadian and American areas. The Canadian discount averaged 45 percent.

Table 5.1 provides summary information on brand name drug prices that further confirms that these are generally lower in Canada than in the United States, with normal discounts running in the range of 50 percent. At the same time, however, there is considerable evidence that generic drug prices are much lower in the U.S. than in Canada. Studies by both the U.S. Food and Drug Administration (FDA) and the Canadian Patented Medicine Prices Review Board (PMPRB) find that generic drugs sell in the U.S. at prices that are on average 35 percent less than the comparable charge in Canada.[1]

What explains this pattern of drug prices? This is an especially pressing question in the case of branded drugs because these are generally made by the same firms regardless of whether they are sold in the U.S. or Canada. What is it that makes it profitable for these firms to

---

[1] Patented Medicine Prices Review Board, "Canadian and Foreign Price Trends," http://www.pmprb-cepmb.gc.ca (July, 2006) and Food and Drug Administration, "Generic Drug Prices in the US Are Lower Than Prices in Canada," White Paper (November, 2003).

Table 5.1   Comparison of prescription drug prices (U.S. dollars)

	Celebrex® 200 mg		Lipitor® 40 mg		Paxil® 20 mg	
	Mean	Standard deviation	Mean	Standard deviation	Mean	Standard deviation
Washington	86.26	5.66	110.01	8.97	82.47	3.86
British Columbia	33.17	2.37	52.83	3.50	40.75	2.54
North Dakota and Minnesota	78.08	5.70	107.75	7.03	78.63	6.08
Manitoba	32.36	1.60	52.43	1.52	39.80	2.00
New York	88.57	7.59	117.69	5.44	85.06	4.39
Ontario	34.82	1.96	55.52	2.09	42.62	2.03

Source: Graham and Tabler (2001) *Prescription Drug Prices in Canada and the United States: Part 3 Retail Price Distribution*, Public Policy Sources no. 50, Fraser Institute

set higher prices in the U.S. market? And what makes it possible for this differential to be sustained?

These questions go to the heart of the analysis in this and the following two chapters. Charging different prices to different consumers for the same good is referred to as price discrimination. We want to know what makes this profitable and when it is feasible. Essentially we are asking what tactics firms can use to implement price discrimination in a way that increases profits relative to charging the same price to everyone. Remember though that any increased profit must come either from a reduction in consumer surplus, improved market efficiency, or some combination of the two. From a policy perspective, it matters a great deal as to which of these is the case. Hence, we will also want to explore the welfare implications of price discrimination. Finally, it is worthwhile noting that discriminatory prices can also affect market competition. This occurs when the buyers are not final consumers but instead, retailers such as drug stores. If large drug store chains are charged different wholesale prices than are small, independent pharmacies, then retail competition between these two groups will not be conducted on a level playing field. In these next three chapters, we address each of these issues in turn.

5.1   FEASIBILITY OF PRICE DISCRIMINATION

A firm with market power faces a downward sloping demand curve, so if the firm charges the same price to each consumer—the standard case of non-discriminatory pricing—the revenue it gets from selling an additional unit of output is less than the price charged. In order to sell the additional unit the firm must lower its price not only to the consumer who buys the additional unit, but to all its other consumers as well. Having to lower price to all its customers in order to gain an additional consumer limits the monopolist's incentive to serve more consumers. As a result the textbook monopoly undersupplies its product relative to the efficient outcome.

However, non-discriminatory pricing is not just a source of potential inefficiency. It is also a constraint on the firm's ability to extract consumer surplus, particularly from those consumers willing to pay a lot for its product. If we allow the monopolist to price discriminate we shall see that this is a powerful technique that permits the firm to earn considerably more profit. We will also find that in some cases price discrimination may induce the monopolist to sell more output and so come closer to the competitive market outcome. Price discrimination can sometimes make a monopolized market more efficient.

While a monopolist can increase profit through price discrimination, it is important to realize that price discrimination is not always easily accomplished. There is a reason why the standard textbook case assumes that each customer pays the same price. To discriminate successfully the monopolist must overcome two main obstacles. The first of these is identifying who is who on the demand curve. The second is the problem of arbitrage.

In considering the identification problem it is useful to recall a common assumption in the textbook monopoly model. This assumption is that the monopolist has somehow learned what is the quantity demanded at each price—otherwise it would not know its marginal revenue curve and, hence, would not be able to determine the profit-maximizing output. Let's examine more carefully just what this assumption means in practice.

For some products such as bicycles, TVs, DVD players, or haircuts a single consumer will purchase at most one unit of the good over a given period of time. The firm's demand curve is then an explicit ordering of consumers by their reservation prices—the top price each is willing to pay. For these goods, knowledge of the demand curve means that the monopoly firm knows that the top part of the demand curve is made up of those consumers willing to pay a relatively large amount for the one unit they will purchase whereas the bottom part of the demand curve is made up by those willing to pay only a little. For other products, however, such as movies, CDs, refreshments, and tennis lessons, what is happening on the demand curve is slightly more complex. This is because each individual consumer can be induced to purchase more than one unit of the good if the price is sufficiently low. Hence, for these goods the demand curve reflects not only differences in the willingness to pay across consumers but also differences in the willingness to pay as any one consumer buys more of the product. When the monopolist practices uniform pricing, these distinctions are not relevant. In that case the assumption that the firm knows its demand curve means only that it knows how willingness to pay for the good *in the overall market* varies with the quantity of the good sold.

To be able to practice price discrimination the monopolist must learn or know more information about consumers than is assumed in the standard model. The monopolist must know how the market demand curve has been constructed from the individual consumer demand curves. In other words, the monopolist must know how different kinds of consumers differ in their demands for its good. This is easier for some sellers than for others. For example, tax accountants effectively sell one unit of their services to each client in any given year. Further, they know exactly how much their clients earn and, more importantly, how much they save their clients by way of reduced tax liabilities. They can certainly use this information to identify the customers' willingness-to-pay. Similarly, a car dealer typically sells one car to a customer. The dealer may be able to identify those buyers with the greatest or least willingness to pay by asking potential buyers where they live or work or shop. The same is often true for realtors, dentists, and lawyers.

Sellers of retail merchandise, however, face a more anonymous market. Various schemes such as varying the price depending on time of purchase, "early-bird" specials or Saturday morning sales, or offering coupons that take time to collect, can help retailers identify "who's who" on their demand curve. Nevertheless, the identification problem is still difficult to overcome. Moreover, even if weekend sales or coupon schemes do successfully identify the firm's different consumers, such schemes may be too costly to implement.

Even when a monopolist can solve the identification problem, there is still a second obstacle to price discrimination, arbitrage. To discriminate successfully, the monopolist must be able to prevent those consumers who are offered a low price from reselling their purchases to other consumers to whom the monopolist wants to offer a high price. Again, this will be

---

Reality Checkpoint
Old Wines in a New Format

On May 16, 2005, the five-year struggle of two entrepreneurial women, Eleanor Heald of Michigan and Juanita Swedenburg of Virginia, finally came to a happy end. Eleanor Heald and her husband, Ray, are wine aficionados living in Troy, Michigan. They love to get together with friends at wine tasting parties, and they contributed numerous articles about wine and specific vintners to magazines such as *Practical Winery and Vineyard*. Juanita Swedenburg ran a small winery in Middleburg, Virginia, until her death in early 2004. She too had the active support of her husband, Wayne.

Since Ms. Heald is an avid wine consumer and Ms. Swedenburg was a producer, one might think that what brought them together was Ms. Heald's purchase of some of Ms. Swedenburg's output. Actually, the truth is almost the opposite. The reason is that prior to the Supreme Court ruling of that mid-May day, Ms. Heald was forbidden by Michigan law to order wine directly from any winery located outside of Michigan. Like New York, Massachusetts, and about 12 other states Michigan had laws that prohibited such shipments.

In general, wine in the United States is marketed via a three-tier system. There are the wineries themselves that produce the wine. Then there are the wholesalers who buy from the wineries. Finally, there are the retailers who purchase supplies from the distributors and sell to final consumers. The winery level has seen fantastic growth since the 1970s as Americans have increasingly turned to wine as a beverage of choice. There are now over 2,000 individual commercial wineries in the U.S. Many of these are, however, very small firms shipping only a few thousand cases of very

individualized wine per year. As a result of this small volume, it is cost prohibitive for these firms to sell indirectly through the wholesale and retail tiers—especially as wholesale market structure has become an increasingly concentrated one, which, in many regions, is dominated by just one or two firms. For these many small wineries the Internet has been a lifesaver allowing them to ship directly to consumers—at least in some states. Others prohibit all such direct buying. States like Michigan and New York permitted such shipments but only if the winery was located in the state. It was this discrimination against out-of-state wineries that upset both Ms. Heald and Ms. Swedenburg. Ms. Heald could not get wine from outside Michigan and Ms. Swedenburg could not ship her wine to some interested buyers in New York. The two filed separate lawsuits claiming that these two states were violating the constitution. The cases wound their way through the court system and were finally combined into one case by the Supreme Court. Of course, Michigan and New York—backed by their own wineries, retailers, and wholesalers—and the states with similar laws fought back. Their principal defense was that the laws were meant to prevent minors from getting easy access to alcohol. Yet since the laws did not prevent direct shipments from wineries within the state, the Supreme Court found this argument unpersuasive. On that fateful day, it struck down the Michigan and New York laws and, by implication, all similar ones in other states.

Source: K. McLaughlin, "Will Buying Wine Get Easier?" *Wall Street Journal*, May 17, 2005, p. A1; and *Granholm v. Heald*, 544 U.S. 460 (2005).

more easily accomplished for some goods and services than for others. Medical, legal, and educational services are not easily resold. One consumer can't sell her appendectomy to another! Similarly, a senior citizen cannot easily resell a discounted movie theater ticket to a teenager. For other markets, particularly consumer durables such as bicycles and automobiles, resale—or sale across different markets—is difficult to prevent. This is an important part of the drug pricing story noted at the start of this chapter. Pharmaceutical companies can only price discriminate successfully if they can keep the American and Canadian markets separate, in other words, only if they can prevent arbitrage.

To sum up, we expect firms with monopoly power to try to price discriminate. In turn, this implies that we should expect that these firms will want to identify the different types of consumers who buy their goods and to prevent resale or consumer arbitrage among them. The ability to do this and the best strategy for achieving price discrimination will vary from firm to firm and from market to market. We now turn to the practice of price discrimination and investigate some of the more popularly practiced techniques. The tradition in economics has been to classify these techniques into three broad classes: first-degree, second-degree, and third-degree price discrimination.[2] More recently, these types of pricing schemes have been referred to respectively as personalized pricing, menu pricing, and group pricing.[3] In this chapter we focus on third-degree price discrimination or group pricing.

5.2   THIRD-DEGREE PRICE DISCRIMINATION OR GROUP PRICING

Third-degree price discrimination or group pricing is defined by three key features. First, there is some easily observable characteristic such as age, income, geographic location, or education status by which the monopolist can group consumers in terms of their willingness to pay for its product. Second, the monopolist can prevent arbitrage across the different groups. In the prescription drug case with which we started this chapter the issue would be to prevent the re-importing of prescription drugs initially exported from the United States to Canada. Finally, third-degree price discrimination requires that the monopolist quotes the same price per unit to all consumers within a particular group and consumers in each group then decide how much to purchase at their quoted price.

Group pricing reflects price discrimination because for the same good the price quoted to one group of consumers is not the same as the price quoted to another group. This type of pricing policy is the one most commonly found in economics textbooks and is referred to in the industrial organization literature as *linear pricing*—hence the title of this chapter. Consumers within a group are free to buy as much as they like at the quoted price, so that the average price per unit paid by each consumer is the same as the marginal price for the last unit bought.

The world is full of examples of third-degree price discrimination. Senior discounts and "kids are free" programs are both examples. An interesting case that is particularly familiar

---

[2] Price discrimination is a fascinating topic and its interest to economists goes well beyond the field of industrial organization. The distinction between first-, second-, and third-degree discrimination follows the work of Pigou (1920). A more modern treatment appears in Phlips (1983). Varian (1989) offers an excellent summary.

[3] These terms were first coined by Shapiro and Varian (1999).

Table 5.2 Schedule of annual membership fees for the American Economic Association (U.S. dollars)

Regular members with annual incomes of $47,000 or less	64
Regular members with annual incomes above $47,000 but no more than $62,000	77
Regular members with annual incomes above $62,000	90
Junior members (available to registered students—student status must be certified)	32
Family member (persons living at the same address as a regular member, additional membership without a subscription to AEA publications)	13

to economists is the fee schedule for membership in the American Economic Association, the major professional organization for economists in the United States. Payment of the fee entitles a member to receive professional announcements, newsletters, and three very important professional journals, the *American Economic Review*, the *Journal of Economic Perspectives*, and the *Journal of Economic Literature*, each of which is published quarterly.

The 2006 fee schedule is shown in Table 5.2. As can readily be seen, the aim is to price discriminate on the basis of income. A particularly interesting feature of this scheme is that the Association makes no attempt to check the veracity of the income declared by a prospective member. What they appear to rely upon is that economists will be either honest or even boastful in reporting their income. In addition, the Association must also hope to avoid the arbitrage problem whereby junior faculty members who pay a low subscription fee resell to senior faculty members who pay a high one. Here again, we can only report on casual observation, and on this basis, such reselling actually appears to be rare so that the arbitrage problem seems to be effectively non-existent.

The practice of the American Economic Association is not unique. Many academic journals charge a different price to institutions such as university libraries than to individuals. A subscription rate to the *Journal of Economics and Management Strategy*, for example, is $45 for an individual but $115 for an institution.

Airlines are particularly adept at applying third-degree price discrimination. It has sometimes been suggested that the number of different fares charged to economy class passengers on a particular flight is approximately equal to the number of passengers! A common feature of this type of price discrimination is that it is implemented by restrictions on the characteristics of the ticket. These include constraints upon the time in advance by which the flight must be booked, whether flights can be changed, the number of days between departure and return, whether the trip involves staying over a Saturday night and so on. We return to the airline case later in this chapter.

Other examples of third-degree price discrimination are restaurant "early bird specials" and supermarket discounts to shoppers who clip coupons. Similarly, department stores that lower their apparel prices at the end of the season are attempting to charge a different price based on the observable characteristic of the time of purchase.[4] Segmenting consumers by time of purchase is also evident in other markets. Consumers typically pay more to see a

---

[4] Discounting over time in a systematic fashion runs the risk that if consumers know prices will fall in the future, they will delay their purchases. If the number of customers that postpones is "too" large, seasonal discounts will not be a very good strategy.

film at a first-run theater when the film is newly released than to see it at a later date at a second-run cinema or, still later, as a rented DVD at home.

An essential feature of all third-degree price discrimination schemes is that the monopolist has some easily observed characteristic that serves as a good proxy for differences in consumer willingness to pay. This characteristic can be used effectively to divide the market into two or more groups, each of which will be charged a different price. The monopolist must next be able to ensure that resale of the product by those who are offered a low price to those who are offered a high one is not feasible. Consider the airlines again. The requirement to stay over a Saturday night effectively discriminates between those consumers who are traveling on business and those who are not.

Once the different consumer groups have been identified and separated, the general rule that characterizes third-degree price discrimination is easily stated. *Consumers for whom the elasticity of demand is low should be charged a higher price than consumers for whom the elasticity of demand is relatively high.*

5.3   IMPLEMENTING THIRD-DEGREE PRICE DISCRIMINATION OR GROUP PRICING

The logic underlying our pricing rule is fairly straightforward. Here, we illustrate it with a simple example and defer formal presentation of the general case to a Derivation Checkpoint (Discriminatory and Nondiscriminatory Pricing) later in the chapter. Suppose then that the publishers of J. K Rowling's final volume in the Harry Potter series, *Harry Potter and the Deathly Hallows*, estimate that inverse demand for this book in the United States is $P_U = 36 - 4Q_U$ and in Europe is $P_E = 24 - 4Q_E$. In each case, prices are measured in dollars and quantities in millions of books sold at publication of the first edition of the book. Marginal cost is assumed to be the same in each market and equal to $4 per book. The publisher also incurs other costs such as cover design and promotion, but we treat these as fixed and independent of sales volume. Therefore, we can ignore them in our current analysis.

As a first case, assume that the publisher treats the two markets as a single, integrated market. To work out the profit maximizing price, the publisher will first need to calculate aggregate market demand at any price P. This means that they will need to add the two market demand curves horizontally. In the United States we have $P = 36 - 4Q_U$ which can be inverted to give $Q_U = 9 - P/4$ provided, of course, that $P \leq \$36$. In Europe we have $P = 24 - 4Q_E$ so that $Q_E = 6 - P/4$. This gives us the aggregate demand equation:

$$Q = Q_U + Q_E = 9 - P/4 \qquad \text{for } \$36 \geq P \geq \$24$$
$$Q = Q_U + Q_E = 15 - P/2 \qquad \text{for } P < \$24$$
(5.1)

We can write this in the more normal inverse form as:

$$P = 36 - 4Q \qquad \text{for } \$36 \geq P \geq \$24$$
$$P = 30 - 2Q \qquad \text{for } P < \$24$$
(5.2)

This demand relationship is illustrated in Figure 5.1. The kink in the aggregate demand function at a price of $24 and a quantity of 3 million arises because at any price above $24 books will be sold only in the United States whereas once the price drops below $24 both

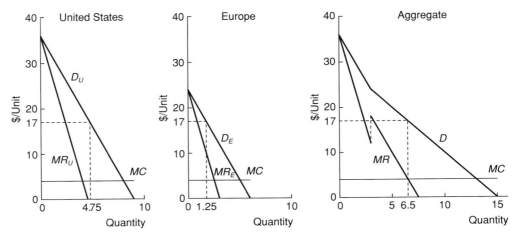

Figure 5.1   Non-discriminatory pricing: constant marginal cost
The firm identifies aggregate demand and the associated marginal revenue. It chooses total output where marginal revenue equals marginal cost and the non-discriminatory price from the aggregate demand function. Output in each market is the market clearing output.

markets are active. The marginal revenue function associated with this demand function satisfies the usual "twice as steep" rule:

$$MR = 36 - 8Q \qquad \text{for } Q \leq 3$$
$$MR = 30 - 4Q \qquad \text{for } Q > 3$$

(5.3)

This is also illustrated in Figure 5.1. The jump in the marginal revenue function at a quantity of 3 million arises because when price falls from just above $24 to just below $24 the inactive European market becomes active. That is, when the price falls to just below $24, it brings in a new set of consumers.

We are now is a position to calculate the profit maximizing price, aggregate quantity and quantity in each market. Equating marginal revenue with marginal cost assuming that both markets are active we have $30 - 4Q = 4$ so that $Q^* = 6.5$ million. From the aggregate demand curve this gives a price of $P^* = \$17$. It follows that 4.75 million books will be sold in the United States and 1.75 million books in Europe. Aggregate profit (ignoring all the fixed and other set-up costs) is $(17 - 4)*6.5 = \$84.5$ million.

That this pricing strategy is not the best that the monopolist can adopt is actually clear from Figure 5.1. At the equilibrium we have just calculated, the marginal revenue on the last book sold in Europe is greater than marginal cost whereas marginal revenue on the last book sold in the United States is less than marginal cost. Transferring some of the books sold in the United States to the European market will, therefore, lead to an increase in profit.

Let us be more explicit. A necessary condition for profit maximization under third-degree price discrimination is that marginal revenue must equal marginal cost in *each* market that the monopolist serves. If this were not the case in a particular market, then the last unit sold in that market would be generating either more or less in cost than it is earning in revenue. Cutting back or increasing total production in that market would therefore raise profits. If marginal cost in serving each market is identical, as in our case, then the rule implies that

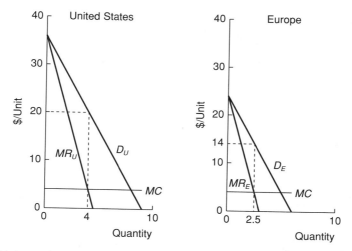

Figure 5.2   Third-degree price discrimination or group pricing: constant marginal cost
The firm sets output where marginal revenue equals marginal cost in each market and sets the market clearing price in each market.

marginal revenue be the same on the last unit sold in each market. If this condition does not hold, the monopolist can raise revenue and profit with no increase in production (and hence, no increase in costs), simply by shifting sales from the low marginal revenue market to the high one.

The application of these rules to our example is illustrated in Figure 5.2. Recall that demand in the United States market is $P_U = 36 - 4Q_U$ and in Europe is $P_E = 24 - 4Q_E$. This means that marginal revenue in the United States is $MR_U = 36 - 8Q_U$ and in Europe is $MR_E = 24 - 8Q_E$. Now apply the rule that marginal revenue equals marginal cost in each market. This gives a profit maximizing output in the United States of $Q_U^* = 4$ million books at a price of $P_U^* = \$20$ and in Europe a profit-maximizing output of $Q_E^* = 2.5$ million books at a price of $P_E^* = \$14$. Profit from sales in the Unites States is \$64 million and in Europe is \$25 million, giving aggregate profit (again ignoring all the fixed and other set-up costs) of \$89 million, an increase of \$4.5 million over the non-discriminatory profit.

How does this outcome relate to the elasticity rule that we presented above? An important property of linear demand curves is that the elasticity of demand falls smoothly from infinity to zero as we move down the demand curve. This means that, for any price less than \$24 (and greater than zero) the elasticity of demand in the United States market is lower than in the European market. (You can check this by evaluating the demand elasticity in the two markets at this or any other particular price.) Our rule then states that we should find a higher price in the United States than in Europe. This, of course, is precisely the result that our example gave.

How would our analysis be affected if marginal cost were not constant? The same basic principles apply with one important change. If marginal production costs are not constant, we cannot treat the two markets independently since whatever output the monopolist chooses to supply to the United States, for example, affects the marginal cost of supplying Europe. So the different markets have to be looked at together. Nevertheless, we still have simple rules that guide the monopolist's pricing decisions in these markets.

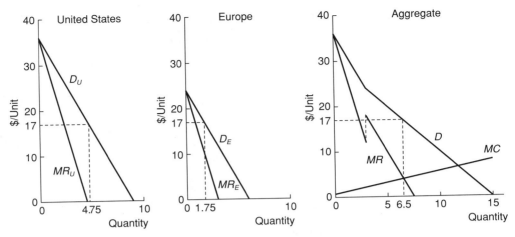

Figure 5.3   Non-discriminatory pricing with non-constant marginal cost

The firm identifies aggregate demand and the associated marginal revenue. It chooses total output where marginal revenue equals marginal cost and the non-discriminatory price from the aggregate demand function. Output in each market is the market clearing output.

To illustrate this point, suppose that the publisher of *Harry Potter and the Deathly Hallows* has a single printing facility that produces books for both the United States and European markets and that marginal cost is given by $MC = 0.75 + Q/2$, where Q is the total number of books printed.

Figure 5.3 illustrates the profit-maximizing behavior if the monopolist chooses not to price discriminate. The basic analytical steps in this process are as follows:

1. Calculate aggregate market demand as above.
2. Identify the marginal revenue function for this aggregate demand function. From our example, if $Q > 3$ so that both markets are active, this is $MR = 30 - 4Q$.
3. Equate marginal revenue with marginal cost to determine aggregate output. So we have $0.75 + Q/2 = 30 - 4Q$ giving $Q^* = 6.5$ million books.
4. Identify the equilibrium price from the aggregate demand function. Since both markets are active, the relevant part of the aggregate demand function is $P = 30 - 2Q$, giving an equilibrium price of $P^* = \$17$.
5. Calculate demand in each market at this price: 4.75 million books in the United States and 1.75 million books in Europe.

Now suppose that the monopolist chooses to price discriminate. This outcome is illustrated in Figure 5.4. The underlying process is clearly different, and the steps in implementing profit maximizing price discrimination are as follows:

1. Derive marginal revenue in each market and add these *horizontally* to yield an allocation of output across the two markets with the same marginal revenue. Marginal revenue in the United States is $MR = 36 - 8Q_U$ for any marginal revenue less than \$36 and in Europe is $MR = 24 - 8Q_E$ for any marginal revenue below \$24. Inverting these gives $Q_U = 4.5 - MR/8$ and $Q_E = 3 - MR/8$. Summing these gives an aggregated marginal revenue:

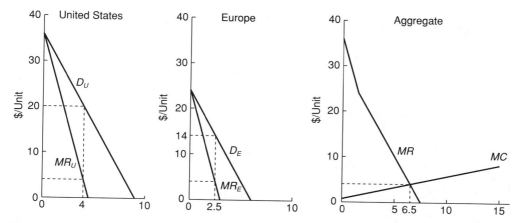

Figure 5.4   Third-degree price discrimination or group pricing with non-constant marginal cost
The firm calculates aggregate marginal revenue and equates this with marginal cost. Output in each market equates marginal revenue with aggregate marginal cost. Price in each market is the market-clearing price.

$$Q = Q_U + Q_E = 4.5 - MR/8 \qquad \text{for } Q \leq 1.5$$
$$Q = Q_U + Q_E = 7.5 - MR/4 \qquad \text{for } Q > 1.5 \tag{5.4}$$

This can be inverted to give aggregate marginal revenue its more usual form

$$MR = 36 - 8Q \qquad \text{for } Q \leq 1.5$$
$$MR = 30 - 4Q \qquad \text{for } Q > 1.5 \tag{5.5}$$

Note how this step differs from the non-discriminatory case. In the latter both markets are treated as one, so we start with aggregate demand and derive its associated marginal revenue. In the discriminatory pricing case, by contrast, the markets are supplied separately, with the profit maximizing condition that $MC = MR$ in both markets so we need aggregate marginal revenue, not aggregate demand.

2. Equate aggregate marginal revenue with marginal cost to identify the equilibrium aggregate quantity *and* marginal revenue. So we have $30 - 4Q = 0.75 + 2/Q$ giving $Q^* = 6.5$. As a result, the equilibrium marginal revenue is $4, which is equal to the marginal cost of the last unit produced.

3. Identify the equilibrium quantities in each market by equating individual market marginal revenue with the equilibrium marginal revenue and marginal cost. In the United States this gives $36 - 8Q_U = 4$ or $Q_U^* = 4$ million books and in Europe $24 - 8Q_U = 4$ or $Q_E^* = 2.5$ million books.

4. Identify the equilibrium price in each market from the individual market demand functions, giving a price of $20 in the United States and $14 in Europe.

The foregoing procedure is again derived from two simple rules that guide the monopolist's pricing decisions with third-degree price discrimination. These rules apply no matter the shape of the monopolist's marginal cost function. The rules are:

Derivation Checkpoint

Discriminatory and Non-discriminatory Pricing

Suppose that a monopolist supplies two groups of consumers with inverse demand for each group given by:

$$P_1 = A_1 - B_1 Q_1; \; P_2 = A_2 - B_2 Q_2$$

In these demand functions we assume that $A_1 > A_2$ so that group 1 is the "high demand" group whose demand is the less elastic at any given price. Inverting the inverse demands gives the direct demands at some price P:

$$Q_1 = (A_1 - P)/B_1; \; Q_2 = (A_2 - P)/B_2$$

and so aggregate demand is:

$$Q = Q_1 + Q_2 = \frac{A_1 B_2 + A_2 B_1}{B_1 B_2} - \frac{B_1 + B_2}{B_1 B_2} P$$

Of course, this holds only for any price less that A_2. Invert this to get the aggregate inverse demand for the two groups, again for any price less than A_2 yielding:

$$P = \frac{A_1 B_2 + A_2 B_1}{B_1 + B_2} - \frac{B_1 B_2}{B_1 + B_2} Q$$

The marginal revenue associated with this aggregate demand is:

$$MR = \frac{A_1 B_2 + A_2 B_1}{B_1 + B_2} - 2 \frac{B_1 B_2}{B_1 + B_2} Q$$

We can simplify matters a bit by assuming, without loss of generality, that marginal cost is zero. So solving $MR = 0$ for Q gives the equilibrium aggregate output with uniform pricing:

$$Q^U = \frac{A_1 B_2 + A_2 B_1}{2 B_1 B_2}$$

Substituting Q^U into the price equation gives the equilibrium uniform price

$$P^U = \frac{A_1 B_2 + A_2 B_1}{2(B_1 + B_2)}$$

Substituting this price into the individual demands then gives equilibrium output in each market

$$Q_1^U = \frac{(2A_1 - A_2)B_1 + A_1 B_2}{2B_1(B_1 + B_2)}; Q_2^U = \frac{(2A_2 - A_1)B_2 + A_2 B_1}{2B_2(B_1 + B_2)}$$

With third-degree price discrimination the firm sets marginal revenue equal to marginal cost for each group. From the demand curves, we know that the marginal revenues are:

$$MR_1 = A_1 - 2B_1 Q_1; \; MR_2 = A_1 - 2B_2 Q_2$$

It follows immediately that the equilibrium outputs for each group are

$$Q_1^D = \frac{A_1}{2B_1}; Q_2^D = \frac{A_2}{2B_2}$$

Comparison then confirms that $Q_1^D \le Q_1^U$ and $Q_2^D \ge Q_2^U$. In other words, third-degree price discrimination diverts output from the high-demand market to the low-demand market increasing price in the former and lowering price in the latter. You can also confirm that $Q_1^D + Q_2^D = Q^U$. In other words, when demands are linear *aggregate output is identical with uniform pricing and with third-degree price discrimination or group pricing.*

1. Marginal revenue must be equalized in each market.
2. Marginal revenue must equal marginal cost, where marginal cost is measured at the *aggregate* output level.

There is one further interesting point that is worth noting regarding the contrast between uniform pricing (no price discrimination) and third-degree price discrimination. When demand is linear and both markets are active under both pricing schemes *aggregate demand is identical with the two pricing policies.* This is proved formally in the Derivation Checkpoint: Discriminatory and Nondiscriminatory Pricing. The intuition is simple to see. When both markets are active aggregate marginal revenue is identical with the two pricing policies (we are below the discontinuity in *MR* in Figure 5.3). So equating aggregate marginal revenue with aggregate marginal cost must give the same aggregate output. The reason that third-degree price discrimination is more profitable in this case is because the aggregate output is allocated more profitably across the two markets—to ensure that marginal revenue on the last unit sold in each market is equal.

We complete our discussion of third-degree price discrimination in this section by making explicit the relationship between the price set and the elasticity of demand in any specific market segment. Our review of monopoly and market power in Chapters 2 and 3 explained how we could express the firm's marginal revenue in any market in terms of price and the point elasticity of demand at that price. Specifically, marginal revenue in market i is given

by $MR_i = P_i \left(1 - \dfrac{1}{\eta_i} \right)$ where η_i is (the negative of) the elasticity of firm i's demand. (See

Derivation Checkpoint: The Calculus of Competition, and Problem 4, both in Chapter 2.) The larger is η_i the more elastic is demand in this market. Now recall that third-degree price discrimination requires that the profit-maximizing aggregate output must be allocated such that marginal revenue is equalized across each market (and, of course, equal to marginal cost). For example, if there are two markets this says that $MR_1 = MR_2$. Substituting from the equations above, we then know that

$$MR_1 = P_1 \left(1 - \frac{1}{\eta_1} \right) = MR_2 = P_2 \left(1 - \frac{1}{\eta_2} \right).$$

We can solve this for the ratio of the two prices to give:

$$\frac{P_1}{P_2} = \frac{(1 - 1/\eta_2)}{(1 - 1/\eta_1)} = \frac{\eta_1 \eta_2 - \eta_1}{\eta_1 \eta_2 - \eta_2}. \qquad (5.6)$$

From this it is clear that price will indeed be lower in the market with the higher elasticity of demand. The intuition is that prices must be lower in those markets in which consumers are sensitive to price. Such price sensitivity means that raising the price will lose too many customers and this loss more than offsets any gain in surplus per customer. To put it differently, when consumers are price sensitive the strategy of lowering price can actually raise the monopolist's total surplus because it brings in many additional purchases. We encourage you to reinterpret the various examples with which we motivated our analysis in terms of demand elasticities. For example, is it reasonable to think that business travelers will have a lower elasticity of demand for air travel at a particular time than vacation travelers?

Practice Problem

The manager of a local movie theater believes that demand for a film depends on when the movie is shown. Early moviegoers who go to films before 5 p.m. are more sensitive to price than are evening moviegoers. With some market research the manager discovers that the demand curves for daytime (D) and evening (E) moviegoers are $Q_D = 100 - 10P_D$ and $Q_E = 140 - 10P_E$ respectively. The marginal cost of showing a movie is constant and equal to $3 per customer no matter when the movie is shown. This includes the costs of ticketing and cleaning.

a.   What is the profit maximizing pricing policy if the manager charges the same price for daytime and evening attendance? What is attendance in each showing and what is aggregate profit per day?

b.   Now suppose that the manager adopts a third-degree price discrimination scheme, setting a different day and evening price. What are the profit maximizing prices? What is attendance at each session? Confirm that aggregate attendance is as in a. What is aggregate profit per day?

5.4   PRODUCT VARIETY AND THIRD-DEGREE PRICE DISCRIMINATION OR GROUP PRICING

We have thus far defined price discrimination as occurring whenever a firm sells an identical product to two or more buyers at different prices. But what if the products are not identical? Ford, for example, offers several hundred (perhaps even several thousand) varieties of the Ford Taurus with slightly different features. Procter & Gamble offers a wide range of toothpastes in different tastes, colors, and claimed medicinal qualities. Kellogg offers dozens of breakfast cereals that vary in terms of grain, taste, consistency, and color.

Many examples of what looks like third-degree price discrimination or group pricing arise when the seller offers such *differentiated* products. For example, books are first released as expensive hardcover editions and only later as cheap paperbacks. Hotels in a ski area are more expensive in winter than in summer. First class air travel costs more than coach. The common theme of these examples is that they all involve variations of a basic product. This is a phenomenon that we meet every day in buying restaurant meals, refrigerators, haircuts, and many other goods and services. In each of these situations, what we observe is a firm selling different varieties of the same good—distinguished by color, or material, or design. As a brief reflection on the typical restaurant menu will reveal, what we also usually observe is that the different varieties are aimed at different groups and sell at different prices.

In considering these as applications of price discrimination we have to be careful. After all, the cost incurred in producing goods of different types, such as hardback and paperback books, or first class versus coach flights, is different. Phlips (1983) provides perhaps the best definition of third-degree price discrimination or group pricing once we allow for product differentiation:

> Price discrimination should be defined as implying that two varieties of a commodity are sold [by the same seller] to two buyers at different *net* prices, the net price being the price (paid by the buyer) corrected for the cost associated with the product differentiation. (Phlips, 1983, p. 6)

Using this definition, it would not be discriminatory to charge $750 extra for a car with antilock brakes if it costs $750 extra to assemble a car with such brakes. By contrast, the difference in price between a coach class fare of $450 and a first class fare of $8,000 for service between Boston and London must be seen as almost entirely reflecting price discrimination because the additional cost of providing first class service per passenger is well below the $7,550 difference in price. In other words, price discrimination among different versions of the same good exists only if the difference in prices is not justified by differences in underlying costs: which is what Phlips means by the *net price*.

Consideration of product variety leads to a very important question. Does offering different varieties of a product enhance the monopolist's ability to charge different net prices? That is, does a firm with market power increase its ability to price discriminate by offering different versions of its product? As we shall see, the general answer is, yes.

We can obtain at least some insight into this issue by recalling the two problems that successful discrimination must overcome, namely, identification and arbitrage. In order to price discriminate, the firm must determine who is who on its demand curve and then be able to prevent resale between separate consumers. By offering different versions or models of its

---

Reality Checkpoint

"Seventeen Tickets for *Seven Guitars*: Price Discrimination on Broadway"

In New York, about 25,000 people, on average, attend Broadway shows each night. As avid theatergoers know, prices for these tickets have been rising inexorably. The top price for Broadway shows has risen 31 percent since 1998. However, due to various discounts offered through coupons, two-for-one deals, special student prices, and the TKTS booth in Times Square, the actual price paid has gone up by only 24 percent.

Why so much discounting? The value of a seat in a theater, like a seat on an airplane, is highly perishable. Once the show starts or the plane takes off, a seat is worth next to nothing. So, it's better to fill the seat at a low price than not fill it at all.

Stanford economist, Phillip Leslie, investigated Broadway ticket price discrimination using detailed data for a 1996 Broadway play, *Seven Guitars*. Over 140,000 people saw this play, and they bought tickets in 17 price categories. While some of the difference was due to seat quality—opera versus mezzanine versus balcony—a large amount of price differentials remained even after quality adjustments. The

average difference of two tickets chosen at random on a given night was about 40 percent of the average price. This is comparable to the price variation in airline tickets.

Leslie used advanced econometric techniques to estimate the values that different income groups put on the various categories of tickets. He found that Broadway producers do a pretty good job, in general, at maximizing revenue. He found the average price set for *Seven Guitars* was about $55 while, according to Mr. Leslie's estimates, the value that would maximize profit was a very close $60. His data also indicated that the optimal uniform price would be a little over $50. Again, price discrimination is less about the average price charged and more about varying the price in line with the consumer's willingness to pay. In this connection, Leslie found that optimal price discrimination drew in over 6 percent more patrons than would optimal uniform pricing.

Source: P. Leslie "Price Discrimination in Broadway Theatre," *Rand Journal of Economics*, 35 (Autumn, 2004), 520–41.

product the monopolist may be able to solve these two problems. Different consumer types may buy different versions of a product and therefore reveal who they are through their purchase decision. Moreover, since different customers are purchasing different varieties, the problem of resale is considerably reduced.

As an example of the potential for product differentiation to enhance profit, consider an airline that we will call Northwest Airlines (NA), operating direct passenger flights between Boston and Amsterdam. NA knows that there are three types of customers for these flights: those who prefer to travel first class; those who wish to travel business class; and those who are reconciled to having to travel coach. One part of the arbitrage problem is easily solved of course: in order to sit in a first class seat you need a first class ticket. However, there is another aspect to this problem. If the difference in price is great enough relative to the valuation a consumer places on a higher class of travel, a business class traveler, for example, might choose to fly coach. For simplicity, we assume that this arbitrage, or self-selection problem does not arise. That is, we assume that first class passengers prefer not to travel rather than sit in business or coach and business class passengers similarly will not consider coach travel—they place sufficiently high values on the differences in quality between the types of seat that they will not trade down. (See end-of-chapter problem 5 for an example of this case.)[5]

NA's market research indicates that daily demand for first class travel on this route is $P_F = 18,500 - 1,000Q_F$, for business class travel is $P_B = 9,200 - 250Q_B$ and for coach travel is $P_C = 1,500 - 5Q_C$. The marginal cost is estimated to be $100 for a coach passenger, $200 for a business class passenger and $500 for a first class passenger.

The profit maximizing third-degree price discrimination scheme for differentiated products of this type satisfies essentially the same rules as for homogeneous products. Simply put, NA should identify the quantity that equates marginal revenue with marginal cost for each class of seat and then identify the equilibrium price from the relevant demand function. For first class passengers this requires $MR_F = 18,500 - 2,000Q_F = 500$, or $Q_F^* = 9$. The resulting first class fare is $P_F^* = \$9,500$. In business class we have $MR_B = 9,200 - 500Q_B = 200$, or $Q_B^* = 18$ and $P_B^* = \$4,700$. Finally, in coach we have $1,500 - 10Q_C = 100$, giving $Q_C^* = 140$ and $P_C^* = \$800$.

The example we have just presented resolved the arbitrage problem by assuming that different types of travelers are committed to particular classes of travel. Of course, this may not always be the case. For example, the downturn in economic activity through 2003 encouraged many businesses to seek ways to cut costs. In particular, business travelers are increasingly required by their companies to fly coach. It remains the case that these types of are travelers willing to pay more (though not as much more as before) for air travel than casual or vacation travelers. Now, however, the airline's ability to exploit the difference in willingness to pay faces a potentially severe arbitrage problem.

To see this more clearly, let's simplify the problem and suppose that the airline has just two types of customers, business people and vacationers. Business people are known to have a high reservation price, or willingness to pay, for a return ticket, which we will denote as V^B. Vacationers, by contrast, have a low reservation price, denoted as V^V. By assumption, $V^B > V^V$, and the airline would obviously like to exploit this difference by charging business customers a high price and vacationers a low one. However, the airline cannot simply

---

[5]   There is also the possibility that coach or business travelers would want to trade up. The equilibrium prices that we derive in the example preclude such a possibility.

impose this distinction. A policy of explicitly charging business customers more than vaca-tioners would quickly lead to every customer claiming to be on holiday and not on business. To be sure, the airline could try to identify which passengers really are on holiday, but this would be costly and likely to alienate customers.

If this were the end of our story, it would appear that the airline has no choice but to sell its tickets at a single, uniform price. It would then face the usual textbook monopoly dilemma. A high price will earn a large surplus from every customer that buys a ticket but clearly leads to a smaller, mostly business set of passengers. In contrast, a low price will encour-age many more people to fly but, unfortunately, leave the company with little surplus from any one consumer.

Suppose, however, that business and holiday travelers differ in another respect as well as in their motives for flying. To be specific, suppose that business travelers want to complete their trip and return home within three days, whereas vacationers want to be away for at least one week. Suppose also that the airline learns (through surveys and other market research) that business travelers would pay a premium beyond a normal ticket price if they could be guaranteed a return flight within their preferred three-day span. In this case, product differ-entiation by means of offering two differentiated tickets—one with a minimum time away of a week and another with no minimum stay—will enable the airline to extract consider-able surplus from each type of consumer.

The complete strategy would be as follows: first, set a low price of V^V for tickets requir-ing a minimum of one week before returning. Since holiday travelers do not mind staying away seven days, and since the ticket price does not exceed their reservation price, they will willingly purchase this ticket. Since such travelers are paying their reservation price, the airline has extracted their entire consumer surplus and converted it into profit for itself.[6]

Second, the airline should set a price as close to V^B as possible for flights with no minimum stay. The limit on its ability to do this will be such factors as the cost of paying for a hotel for extra nights, the price of alternative transportation capable of returning individuals in three days and related considerations. Denote the dollar value of these other factors as M. Business people wanting to return quickly will gladly pay a premium over the one-week price V^V up to the value of M, so long as their total fare is less than V^B. (The precise condition is $V^V + M < V^B$.) Using such a scheme enables the airline to extract considerable surplus from business customers, while simultaneously extracting the entire surplus from vacationers.

In short, even if the airline cannot squeeze out the entire consumer surplus from the mar-ket, it can nevertheless improve its profits greatly by offering two kinds of tickets. This is undoubtedly the reason that the practice just described is so common among airlines and other transportation companies (see inset). Such companies offer different varieties of their product as a means of having their customers self-select into different groups. Automobile and appliance manufacturers utilize a similar strategy—offering different product lines meant to appeal to consumers of different incomes or otherwise different willingness to pay. Stiglitz (1977) labels such mechanisms as *screening devices* because they screen or separate customers precisely along the relevant dimension of willingness to pay.

---

[6] An alternative and frequently used distinction is to require that the traveler stay over a Saturday night in order to qualify for a cheap fare. Presumably a corporation will not want to finance the lodgings of its employees when they are not on company business. Further, business travelers will typically want to spend weekends with family and loved ones. On both counts, the Saturday night requirement works as a self-separating device.

Reality Checkpoint
You Can't Go Before You Come Back

It is not uncommon to find that a coach fare to fly out on Tuesday and return quickly on Thursday costs well over twice the coach fare to fly out on Tuesday and return a week later. So, for travelers wanting to return in two days, an obvious strategy is to buy two round-trip tickets—one say that departs on Thursday the 10th and returns on Thursday the 17th, and another that departs on Tuesday the 15th and returns on Tuesday the 22nd. The passenger can use the outgoing half of the first ticket on Tuesday the 15th and then fly back on the return flight of the second ticket that flies on the 17th. Unfortunately for such savvy travelers—and for

the students and other needy consumers who could use the unused portions of each flight— the airlines are alert to such practices. In particular, when a passenger checks in for a flight, the airline checks to see if the passenger has an unused portion of a return flight. If so, the fee is automatically adjusted to the higher fare. The airlines have a great incentive to make sure that those who are willing to pay a substantial premium to return in two days really do pay it.

Source: "Why It Doesn't Pay to Change Planes or Plans," *London Daily Telegraph*, March 11, 2000, p. 27.

A rather curious kind of screening is illustrated by Wolfram Research, manufacturers of the *Mathematica®* software package. In making their student version of the software, Wolfram disables a number of functions that are available in the full academic or commercial versions. In 2007 Wolfram offered the full version of *Mathematica®* at around $2,495, the academic version at around $1,095 and the student version at around $140. There is little doubt that this is a case involving substantial differences in net prices.

The motivation behind this screening by means of product differentiation seems equally clear. Wolfram realizes that some customers do not need—or at least do not want to pay very much for—the full version of their software. Wolfram markets the low-priced version of *Mathematica®* for these consumers, and then sells the extended version to customers with a high willingness to pay for the improved product. Note that the two products must really differ in some important respect (to consumers at least). If Wolfram did not reduce the capabilities of the student version it would have to worry about arbitrage between the two customer groups, with students buying for their professors!

The Wolfram example just described is a type of screening referred to by marketing experts as "crimping the product." Deneckere and McAffee (1996) argue that crimping, or deliberately damaging a product to enhance the ability to price discriminate, has been a frequent practice of manufacturers throughout history. Among the examples that they cite are (1) IBM's Laser Printer E, an intentionally slower version of the company's higher-priced top-of-the-line laser printer and (2) simple cooking wine, which is ordinary table wine with so much salt added that it is undrinkable. Some people have even argued that the U.S. Post Office deliberately reduces the quality of its standard, first class service so as to raise demand for its two-day priority and overnight mail services.

Each of these examples is a clear case of a difference in net prices. The lower-quality product sells for a lower price, yet—because it starts as a high-quality product and then requires the further cost of crimping—the lower-quality product is actually more expensive to make.

Why do firms crimp a high-quality product to produce a low-quality one instead of simply producing a low-quality one in the first place? The most obvious answer relates to costs of production. Given that a firm with monopoly power such as Wolfram knows that there are consumers of different types willing to buy different varieties of its product, the firm must decide how these consumer types can be supplied with products "close" to those that they most want at least cost. It may well be cheaper to produce the student version of *Mathematica®* by crimping the full version rather than to set up a separate production line dedicated to manufacturing different versions of the software package.

The final type of product differentiation that we consider in this chapter is differentiation by *location of sale*.[7] In many cases a product for sale in one location is not the same as the otherwise identical product for sale in another location. A prescription drug such as Lipitor® for sale in Wisconsin is not identical to the same prescription drug for sale in New York State. Even with the advent of sophisticated Internet search engines, a new automobile for sale in one state is not identical to the same new automobile for sale in another state because consumers care about the location of the seller.

To illustrate why this type of product differentiation can lead to price discrimination, suppose that there is a company, Boston Sea Foods (BSF), which sells a proprietary brand of clam chowder. BSF knows that demand for its chowder in Boston is $P_B = A - BQ_B$ and in Manhattan is $P_M = A - BQ_M$ where quantities are measured in thousands of pints. In other words, the firm believes that these two markets have identical demands. BSF has constant marginal costs of c per thousand pints of chowder. Transport costs to reach the Boston market are negligible but it costs BSF an amount t to transport a thousand pints of chowder to Manhattan.

How does BSF maximize its profits from these two markets, given that BSF employs linear pricing? BSF should apply the rules that we have already developed. It should equate marginal revenue with marginal cost in each market. In the Boston market this requires that $A - 2BQ_B = c$, so that $Q_B^* = (A - c)/2B$ and the Boston price is $P_B^* = (A + c)/2$. In the Manhattan market we have, by contrast, $A - 2BQ_M = c + t$, so that $Q_M^* = (A - c - t)/2B$ and the Manhattan price is $P_M^* = (A + c + t)/2$.

Why is this outcome an example of third-degree price discrimination? Recall our definition of price discrimination with differentiated products. For there to be *no* such discrimination any difference in price should be equal to the difference in the costs of product differentiation. In our BSF example it costs BSF t per thousand pints to send chowder from Boston to Manhattan but the difference in price in the two markets is only $t/2$. In other words, BSF is price discriminating by absorbing 50 percent of the transport costs of sending its chowder to Manhattan.

What about the arbitrage problem in the BSF example? Manhattanites might want to buy their chowder directly in the Boston market but it is economic for them to do so only if they have access to a transport technology that is at least 50 percent cheaper than that employed by BSF, a very tall order other than for those who choose to vacation in Boston.

Returning to our prescription drug example in Table 5.1, one possible explanation for the difference in prices in the three United States regions might be differences in costs of supplying these three regions. Another, of course, would be differences in demands in the three regions arising from differences in these regions' demographics or incomes.

---

[7] We return to spatial differentiation in more detail in Chapter 7.

NonLegal Seafoods (NS) sells its excellent clam chowder in Boston, New York, and Washington. NS has estimated that the demands in these three markets are respectively $Q_B = 10{,}000 - 1{,}000P_B$, $Q_{NY} = 20{,}000 - 2{,}000P_{NY}$ and $Q_W = 15{,}000 - 1{,}500P_W$ where quantities are pints of clam chowder per day. The marginal cost of making a pint of clam chowder in their Boston facility is $1. In addition it costs $1 per pint to ship the chowder to New York and $2 per pint to ship to Washington.

a.   What are the profit maximizing prices that NS should set in these three markets? How much chowder is sold per day in each market?
b.   What profit does NS make in each market?

5.5   THIRD-DEGREE PRICE DISCRIMINATION OR GROUP PRICING AND SOCIAL WELFARE

The term "price discrimination" suggests inequity and, from a social perspective, sounds like a "bad thing." Is it? To answer this question we must recall the economist's approach to social welfare and the problem raised by the standard monopoly model. Economists view arrangements as less than socially optimal whenever there are potential trades that could make both parties better off. This is the reason that a standard monopoly is sub-optimal. The textbook monopolist practicing uniform pricing restricts output. At the margin, consumers value the product *more* than it costs the monopolist to produce it. A potentially mutually beneficial trade exists but under uniform pricing such a trade will not occur.

The question that arises with third-degree price discrimination is whether such discrimination worsens or reduces this monopoly distortion. The intuitive reason why third-degree discrimination may reduce efficiency relative to the uniform pricing case is essentially that such a policy amounts to uniform pricing within two or more separate markets. It thus runs the risks of compounding the output-reducing effects of monopoly power.

We can be more specific regarding the welfare effects of third-degree price discrimination by drawing on the work of Schmalensee (1981). This is illustrated for the case of two markets in Figure 5.5. In this Figure, P_1 and P_2 are the profit maximizing discriminatory prices—obtained by equating marginal revenue with marginal cost in each market—while P_U is the optimal non-discriminatory price. Market 2 is referred to as the strong market since the discriminatory price is higher than the uniform price while market 1 is the weak market. ΔQ_1 and ΔQ_2 are respectively the difference between the discriminatory output and the non-discriminatory output in the weak and the strong market. It follows, of course, that $\Delta Q_1 > 0$ and $\Delta Q_2 < 0$.

Our normal definition of welfare is the sum of consumer plus producer surplus. Using this definition, an upper limit on the increase in surplus that follows from third-degree price discrimination in Figure 5.5 is the area G minus the area L. This gives us the following equation. (In writing equation (5.7) we have used the property that $\Delta Q_2 < 0$.)

$$\Delta W \le G - L = (P_U - MC)\Delta Q_1 + (P_U - MC)\Delta Q_2 = (P_U - MC)(\Delta Q_1 + \Delta Q_2) \tag{5.7}$$

Extending this analysis to n markets, we have

$$\Delta W \le (P_U - MC)\sum_{i=1}^{n} \Delta Q_i \tag{5.8}$$

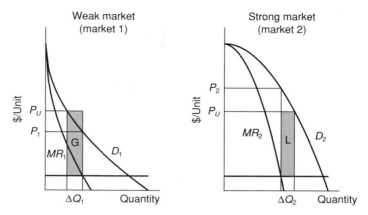

Figure 5.5   Welfare effects of third-degree price discrimination or group pricing
The upper limit on the welfare gain is area G and the lower limit on welfare loss is area L. The upper limit of the net welfare impact is $G - L$ and is positive only if aggregate output is greater with discriminatory pricing than with non-discriminatory pricing.

It follows from equation (5.8) that for $\Delta W \geq 0$ it is necessary that $\sum_{i=1}^{n} \Delta Q_i \geq 0$. In other words, a necessary condition for third-degree price discrimination to increase welfare is that it increases total output.

We know from the Harry Potter example and from the more general Derivation Checkpoint (see inset) that when demands in the various markets are linear total output is identical with discriminatory and non-discriminatory pricing. It follows that with linear demands third-degree price discrimination reduces total welfare. The increase in profit is more than offset by the reduction in consumer surplus. Schmalensee then states:

> If one thinks that demand curves are about as likely to be concave as convex . . . [this] . . . might lead one to the conclusion that monopolistic third-degree price discrimination should be out-lawed. (1981, p. 246)

However, before jumping to the suggested conclusion, we need to note an important *caveat*. The qualification is that our analysis implicitly assumes that the same markets are served with and without price discrimination. This may very well not be the case. In particular, one property of price discrimination is that it can make it profitable to serve markets that would not be served with non-discriminatory prices. If this is the case, then the additional welfare from the new markets that third-degree price discrimination introduces more than offsets any loss of welfare in the markets that were previously being served.[8]

A simple example serves to make this point. Suppose that monthly demand for a patented AIDS treatment is $P_N = 100 - Q_N$ in North America but $P_S = \alpha 100 - Q_S$ in Sub-Saharan Africa with $\alpha < 1$, on the assumption that African consumers have a lower demand because their income is much smaller. We also assume that the marginal cost of producing a month's treatment is constant at $c = 20$ per unit and that transport costs to the African market are negligible.

---

[8]   See also Shih et al. (1988) for a formal discussion of output effects under third-degree price discrimination.

Now assume that the patent holder either does not or cannot price discriminate across the two markets. As before, we start by inverting the demand functions to give $Q_N = 100 - P$ and $Q_S = \alpha100 - P$. If the price is low enough to attract buyers in both markets then aggregate demand is: $Q = (1 + \alpha)100 - 2P$ or $P = (1 + \alpha)50 - Q/2$, and marginal revenue is $MR = (1 + \alpha)50 - Q$. Equating marginal revenue with marginal cost $c = 20$, gives the equilibrium output, $Q = (1 + \alpha)50 - 20 = 30 + \alpha50$, and price $P = 35 + 25\alpha$.

Now recall our assumption that both markets are active without price discrimination. For this assumption to hold it must be that the equilibrium price when there is no discrimination is less than the maximum price—$\alpha100$—that Sub-Saharan African consumers are willing and able to pay. That is, for our assumption to hold it must be the case that $35 + 25\alpha < \alpha100$. In turn, this implies that for both markets to be active with no price discrimination it is necessary that $\alpha > 35/75$ or $\alpha > 0.466$. In other words, for the Sub-Saharan African market to be served it is necessary that the maximum willingness to pay for AIDS drugs in that market be about 47 percent of the maximum willingness to pay in North America.

Moreover, even if $\alpha > 0.466$ the Sub-Saharan African market may not be served. From the patent-holding firm's perspective, it is not quite enough that the maximum willingness to pay exceeds the price charged *if* it serves both markets. This is because the monopolist always has the option of choosing a higher price and serving only the North American market. In the end-of-chapter problem 6, you are asked to show that $\alpha > 0.531$ for it to be profitable for the firm to serve both markets when price discrimination is for some reason prohibited.

5.3

Return to practice problem 5.1 and confirm that total welfare is greater with non-discriminatory pricing than with third-degree price discrimination.

Practice Problem

Summary

We started this chapter with a discussion of prescription drug price differentials that seem not to be related to costs. In a well-functioning market, such differentials can only occur if there is something that separates the two groups of consumers buying at different prices. We showed that a firm with monopoly power that supplies consumers of different types can increase its profits if the firm can figure out a way to separate its consumers into these types and charge different prices to the different types. Our analysis has concentrated on third-degree price discrimination or group pricing, in which the firm offers different prices to different groups of consumer, but leaves it up to the consumers to determine how much they will purchase at the quoted prices. This is often referred to as linear pricing.

In order to implement third-degree price discrimination the firm has to solve two problems. First, it needs some observable characteristic by which it can identify the different groups of

consumers: the identification problem. Secondly, the firm must be able to prevent consumers who pay a low price from selling to consumers offered a high price: the arbitrage problem. Provided that both problems can be overcome, there is then a simple principle that guides the monopolist in setting prices. Set a high price in markets in which elasticity of demand is low and a low price in markets in which elasticity of demand is high. When the firm makes a single homogeneous product this implies that different groups of consumers will be paying different prices for the same good. If the firm sells differentiated products, it implies that the prices of different varieties will vary by something other than the difference in their marginal production costs.

While third-degree price discrimination or group pricing is undoubtedly profitable, it is less clear that it is socially desirable. Again there is a simple principle that can guide us. For third-degree price discrimination to increase social welfare it is necessary, but not sufficient, that it lead to an increase in output. This makes intuitive sense. After all, we know that under uniform pricing or non-discrimination a monopolist makes profit by restricting output. If price discrimination leads to increased output it might reduce the monopoly distortion. This is, however, a tall order, usually requiring some very restrictive conditions regarding the shapes of the demand functions in the different markets. For example, it is a condition that is *never* satisfied when demands are linear and the same markets are served with and without price discrimination.

The qualification regarding the same markets being served is, however, quite important. In particular, group price discrimination has the beneficial effect of encouraging the monopolist to serve markets that would otherwise have been left unserved. For example, markets populated by very low-income groups might not be supplied if the monopolist were not able to set discriminatory prices. When price discrimination leads the monopolist to serve additional markets, the likelihood that it increases social welfare is greatly increased.

We conclude by noting one limitation of focusing on third-degree price discrimination. Restricting the monopolist to simple, linear forms of price discrimination is qualitatively the same as allowing it to charge a monopoly price in each of its separable markets. Yet we know that in any given market, charging a monopoly price reduces the surplus. The monopolist knows this too and therefore, cannot help but wonder if a more complicated, i.e., a non-linear pricing strategy might permit the monopolist to capture more of the potential surplus as profit. It is to this question that we turn in the next chapter.

Problems

1. *True* or *false*: Price discrimination always increases economic efficiency, relative to what would be achieved by a single, uniform monopoly price.

2. A nearby pizza parlor offers pizzas in three sizes: small, medium, and large. Its corresponding price schedule is: $6, $8, and $10. Do these data indicate that the firm is price discriminating? Why or why not?

3. A monopolist has two sets of customers. The inverse demand for one set may be described by $P = 200 - X$. For the other set, the inverse demand is $P = 100 - 2X$. The monopolist faces constant marginal cost of 40.
   a. Show that the monopolist's total demand, if the two markets are treated as one is:

   $X = 0;$ $\quad\quad\quad\quad\quad P \geq 200$
   $X = 200 - P;$ $\quad\quad 100 < P \leq 200$
   $X = 300 - (3/2)P;$ $\quad 0 \leq P \leq 100$

   b. Show that the monopolist's profit maximizing price is $P = 120$ if both groups are to be charged the same price. At this price, how much is sold to members of Group 1 and how much to members of Group 2? What is the consumer surplus of each group? What are total profits?

4. Now suppose that the monopolist in #3 can separate the two groups and charge separate, profit-maximizing prices to each group.
   a. What will these prices be? What is consumer surplus? What are total profits?
   b. If total surplus is consumer surplus plus profit, how has price discrimination affected total surplus?

5. Suppose that Coca-Cola uses a new type of vending machine that charges a price according to the outside temperature. On "hot" days —defined as days in which the outside temperature is 25 degrees Celsius or higher— demand for vending machine soft drinks is: $Q = 300 - 2P$. On "cool" days—when the outside temperature is below 25 degrees Celsius —demand is: $Q = 200 - 2P$. The marginal cost of a tinned soft drink is 20 cents.
   a. What price should the machine charge for a soft drink on "hot" days? What price should it charge on "cool" days?
   b. Suppose that half of the days are "hot" and the other half are "cool." If Coca-Cola uses a traditional machine that is programmed to charge the same price regardless of the weather, what price should it set?
   c. Compare Coca-Cola's profit from a weather-sensitive machine to the traditional, uniform pricing machine.

6. Return to the final example of section 5.4, in which the demand for AIDS drugs was $Q_N = 100 - P$ in North America and $Q_S = \alpha 100 - P$ in Sub-Saharan Africa. Show that with marginal cost = 20 for such drugs, it must be the case that $\alpha > 0.531$ if the drug manufacturer is to serve both markets while charging the same price in each market. (*Hint*: Calculate the total profit if it serves only North America and then calculate the total profit if it serves both markets. Then determine the value of α for which the profit from serving both markets is at least as large.)

7. Frank Buckley sells his famous bad tasting but very effective cough medicine in Toronto and Montreal. The demand functions in these two urban areas, respectively, are: $P_T = 18 - Q_T$ and $P_M = 14 - Q_M$. Buckley's plant is located in Kingston, Ontario, which is roughly midway between the two cities. As a result, the cost of producing and delivering cough syrup to each town is: $2 + 3Q_i$ where $i = T, M$.
   a. Compute the optimal price of Buckley's cough medicine in Toronto and Montreal if the two markets are separate.
   b. Compute the optimal price of Buckley's medicine if Toronto and Montreal are treated as a common market.

8. The Mount Sunburn Athletic Club has two kinds of tennis players, Acers and Netters, in its membership. A typical Ace has a weekly demand for hours of: $Q_A = 6 - P$. A typical Netter has a weekly demand of: $Q_N = 3 - P/2$. The marginal cost of a court is zero and there are one thousand players of each type. If the MSAB charges the same price per hour regardless of who plays, what price should it charge if it wishes to maximize club revenue?

References

Deneckere, R. and R. P. McAffee. 1996. "Damaged Goods." *Journal of Economics and Management Strategy* 5 (Summer): 149–74.

Graham, J. and B. Robson. 2000. "Prescription Drug Prices in Canada and the United States—Part 1: A Comparative Survey." *Public Policy Sources* 22. Fraser Institute.

Graham, J. and T. Tabler. 2001. "Prescription Drug Prices in Canada and the United States—Part 3: Retail Price Distribution." *Public Policy Sources* 50. Fraser Institute

Leslie, P. 2004. "Price Discrimination in Broadway Theatre." *Rand Journal of Economics* 35 (Autumn): 520–41.

Phlips, L. 1983. *The Economics of Price Discrimination.* Cambridge: Cambridge University Press.

Pigou, A. C., 1920. *The Economics of Welfare.* London: Macmillan.

Schmalensee, R. 1981. "Output and Welfare Implications of Monopolistic Third-degree Price Discrimination." *American Economic Review* 71 (March): 242–7.

Shapiro, C. and H. R. Varian. 1999. *Information Rules.* Boston: Harvard Business School Press.

Shih, J., and C. Mai, and J. Liu. 1988. "A General Analysis of the Output Effect under Third-degree Price Discrimination." *Economic Journal* 98 (March): 149–58.

Varian, H. 1989. "Price Discrimination." In R. Schmalansee and R. Willig, eds, *The Handbook of Industrial Organization. Vol. 1.* Amsterdam: North-Holland, 597–654.

6

Price Discrimination and Monopoly: Non-linear Pricing

If you buy the *New Yorker* magazine at the newsstand you will pay $4.60 per issue, or $216.20 if you buy all 47 issues. If instead you purchase an annual subscription you will pay $47 for 47 issues—a saving of nearly 80 percent over the newsstand price. Similarly, if you are a baseball fan you will find out that the price per ticket on a season pass is much less than the price per ticket on a game-by-game basis. Likewise, when you go grocery shopping you will discover that a 24-pack of Coca-Cola costs less on a price per can basis than a six-pack or than a single can. These are all examples of price discrimination that reflect quantity discounts—the more you buy the cheaper it is on a per unit basis.

Quantity discounting is really a way of saying that the pricing is non-linear. The price per unit is not constant but varies with some feature of the buying arrangement depending, perhaps, on the consumer's income, value of time, the quantity bought, or other characteristics. Such a pricing strategy is different from the linear price discrimination methods discussed in Chapter 5. Yet, similar to linear price discrimination, the goal of nonlinear pricing techniques is again to capture as much of the individual consumer's willingness to pay in the seller's revenues and profits. We shall see that such techniques are generally more profitable than third-degree price discrimination or linear pricing, precisely because they permit the seller to set a price closer to willingness to pay *of each consumer*. As a result, nonlinear pricing can help the monopolist earn more profit.

The design and implementation of nonlinear pricing strategies are the focus of this chapter. We shall explore how a firm with monopoly power can implement such pricing schemes to a greater or lesser extent, along with the welfare implications of such pricing. Traditionally, non-linear pricing is divided into two general categories called first-degree price discrimination and second-degree price discrimination or, as Shapiro and Varian (1999) categorize them, personalized pricing and menu pricing.

6.1 FIRST-DEGREE PRICE DISCRIMINATION OR PERSONALIZED PRICING

First-degree or perfect price discrimination is practiced when the monopolist is able to charge the maximum price each consumer is willing to pay for *each* unit of the product sold. Suppose that you just inherited five antique cars, each a classic Ford Model T, and you want to sell them to finance your college education. They are of no other value to you. Your own market research tells you that there are several collectors interested in buying a Model T. When you rank these collectors in terms of their willingness to pay for a car, you estimate that the keenest collector is willing to pay up to $10,000, the second up to $8,000, the third up to $6,000, the fourth $4,000 and the fifth $2,000. First-degree price discrimination means that you are able sell the first car for $10,000, the second for $8,000, the third for $6,000, the fourth for $4,000 and the fifth car for $2,000. The revenue from such a discriminatory pricing policy will be $30,000. Not surprisingly this strategy is also called personalized pricing.

What if, on the other hand, you chose to sell all your cars at the same, uniform price? It is easy to calculate that the best you can do is to set a price of $6,000 at which you will sell three cars for a total revenue (and profit) of $18,000. Any higher or lower price generates lower revenues. In short, under uniform pricing your highest possible revenue is $18,000 while successful first-degree price discrimination yields much higher revenue of $30,000. Simply put, first-degree price discrimination enables you to extract the entire surplus that selling your car generates. No consumer surplus remains if you can successfully discriminate to this extent whereas with a uniform price the keenest buyer has consumer surplus of $4,000 and the second keenest buyer has consumer surplus of $2,000.

Since first-degree price discrimination or personalized pricing redirects surplus from consumers to the firm it should be expected to raise the incentive for the monopolist to produce. In fact, under first-degree price discrimination, the monopolist chooses the same socially efficient amount that would be achieved under perfect competition. In our Model T example no mutually beneficial trades are left unmade: all five cars are sold. By contrast, with uniform pricing only three cars are sold leaving two of the cars in the "wrong" hands.

The same is true in more general cases. For a monopolist able to practice first-degree price discrimination, selling an additional unit never requires lowering the price on other units. Each additional unit sold generates revenue exactly equal to the price at which it is bought. Hence, with first-degree price discrimination marginal revenue is equal to price. Accordingly, for such a monopolist, the profit maximizing rule that marginal revenue equals marginal cost yields an output level at which price equals marginal cost as well. As we know, this is the output level that would be generated by a competitive industry.

6.1

Practice Problem

Suppose that a monopoly seller knows that her demand curve is linear, and knows that at a price of $40, she sells five units, while at a price of $25, she sells 10 units.

a.   If each potential consumer buys only one unit, what is the reservation price of the consumer with the greatest willingness to pay?

b.   Suppose that the monopolist discovers that the demand curve just worked out applies only to the first unit a consumer buys and that, in fact, each consumer will also buy a second unit at a price $8 below the price at which they purchase just one. How many units will be sold at a price of $33?

At first glance it might seem that first-degree discrimination is little more than a theoretical curiosity. How could a monopolist ever have sufficient information about potential buyers and the ability to prevent arbitrage so as to implement effectively a pricing scheme in which a different, personalized price is charged to each buyer and for each unit bought?

Reality Checkpoint
The More *You* Shop the More *They* Know

Internet shopping has undoubtedly brought with it considerable convenience in shopping for books, DVDs, wine, and gourmet foods. At the same time, however, it has provided e-commerce retailers such as Amazon.com and Wine.com the ability to track your purchases. The result is that companies such as these are able to tailor special offers to each individual consumer based on their predictions of the books, wines, condiments, and so on that the consumer is most likely to find attractive. In other words, the Internet has made possible a kind of personalized marketing that is not feasible through more traditional media.

Source: C. Shapiro and H. R. Varian, *Information Rules: A Strategic Guide to the Internet Economy*, Harvard Business School Press, Boston, 1999.

The problems of identification and arbitrage prevention seem insurmountable. However, in some cases the monopolist seller may have the ability to achieve the personalized pricing outcome. Think, for example, of the tax accountant who knows the financial situation of his or her clients. Another example, perhaps closer to home, can be found in the students who apply to any of the (expensive) private universities in the United States. When they apply for financial aid they are required to complete a detailed statement of financial means. The universities of course can use this information, as well as SAT scores and other data, to determine the aid that will be granted and so the net tuition that each prospective student will be required to pay. Look around you. If one breaks down the total tuition on a per class basis, chances are that many of your classmates are paying a different fee for this class than you are!

Of course, the accountant or university example may be somewhat special because often the fee is set *after* the customer has contracted to purchase the service. What we now want to consider is whether there are pricing strategies that will permit the seller to achieve the same effect even when she must announce her fees in advance. The answer, to a greater or lesser extent, is yes. One such strategy is a *two-part pricing* scheme and another is *block pricing*. We discuss each in turn.

6.1.1   Two-Part Pricing

A two-part pricing scheme is a pricing strategy that consists of: 1) a fee, such as a membership fee, that entitles the consumer to buy the good; and 2) a price or usage fee charged for each unit the consumer actually buys. Many clubs use such two-part pricing. They charge a flat annual fee for membership in the club (which is sometimes differentiated by age or some other member characteristic), and additional user fees to use particular facilities or buy particular goods or services. Country clubs, athletic clubs, and discount shopping clubs are all good examples of clubs that use this kind of pricing. A related example of two-part pricing is that used by theme parks under which a flat fee is charged to enter the park and additional fees (sometimes set to zero) are charged on a per ride or per amusement basis.[1]

---

[1]   Versions of such a scheme are used, for example, at parks such as Disney World. See Oi (1971) for the seminal discussion. As Ekelund (1970) notes, much modern analysis was anticipated by the work of nineteenth-century French economist and engineer, Jules Dupuit. Varian (1989) provides a thorough survey of the price discrimination tactics discussed in this chapter.

Reality Checkpoint

Call Options

Nonlinear pricing is an increasingly common feature of everyday life. Consider the packages available for cell phone service offered by the four major providers in the U.S., AT&T/ Cingular, Verizon, Sprint/Nexus, and T-Mobile. Virtually all of these involve some variant of two-part pricing and quantity discount. Family plans, for example, offer two lines for a fixed monthly fee. After that, each minute of calling is free up to a specified maximum. Low-level plans offer something like 700 minutes for free at a monthly fee of, say, $70, while higher-use plans offer roughly twice as many free monthly minutes for a fee of about $90. There is also a 3,000-minute plan that usually sells

for about $150. Additional phones can be added to a family plan at a fee of $10 per month. There are also single line plans and even pay-as-you-go plans. The latter are essentially calling-card plans that sell say, 30 minutes or 90 minutes of phone time for $15 or $25, respectively. They are clearly for those who cannot be induced to make more than a few calls even with a hefty discount.

Sources: L. Magid, "BASICS: Plain Cellphones Can Overachiever, With A Little Help," *New York Times*, January 25, 2007, p. c14; and "The Bottom Line on Calling Plans," *Consumer Reports, February*, 2004, pp. 11–18.

To see how two-part pricing can work to achieve first-degree price discrimination, let us consider a jazz club where people meet for drinks and music. Assume that the club's customers are of two types: old and young (but both above the legal drinking age), and that there are just as many old members as young ones. A typical old consumer's inverse demand curve for the club's services is:

$$P = V_o - Q_o \tag{6.1}$$

While each young customer has the inverse demand curve:

$$P = V_y - Q_y \tag{6.2}$$

where Q_i is the number of drinks consumed in an evening by a customer of type i (O or Y), P is the price per drink and V_i is the maximum amount a consumer of type i will pay for just one drink. We shall assume that old customers are willing to pay more for a given number of drinks than young customers, i.e., $V_O > V_Y$. We further assume that the jazz club owner incurs a cost of c dollars per drink served plus a fixed cost F of operating the club each night. That is, the cost function for the club is:

$$C(Q) = F + cQ \tag{6.3}$$

This example is illustrated in Figure 6.1. The demand curve for a typical consumer starts at V_i and declines with slope -1 until it hits the quantity axis. The constant marginal cost curve is a horizontal line through the value c.

Suppose that the jazz club owner is a "traditional" monopolist who employs simple linear pricing. Entry to the club is free, the club owner sets a price per drink and customers decide how many drinks to buy at that price. The jazz club owner would like to employ

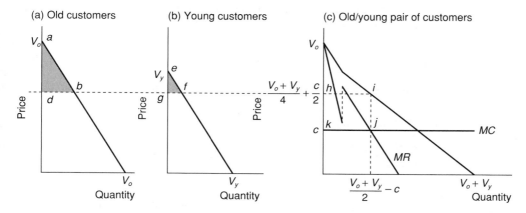

Figure 6.1   No price discrimination
No price discrimination leaves both types of consumer with consumer surplus that the monopolist would like to convert to profit.

third-degree price discrimination, charging old customers more per drink than young customers. While the identification problem is easily resolved, by carding the customers, the arbitrage problem is not. Each old customer could ask (or bribe) a young customer to buy his drinks. So, the best that the traditional linear pricing monopolist can do is to set a uniform price for drinks to customers of both types. Inverting (6.1) and (6.2) and adding gives the aggregate demand for each pair of customers consisting of one old and one young customer[2]

$$Q = Q_o + Q_y = (V_o + V_y) - 2P \tag{6.4}$$

Solving this demand curve for the price variable P to get the aggregate inverse demand for each old/young pair, assuming that both types of customer are allowed into the club, yields:

$$P = (V_o + V_y)/2 - Q/2 \tag{6.5}$$

The jazz club monopolist maximizes profit by identifying the quantity, in this case the number of drinks, at which marginal cost equals marginal revenue and then identifying the price at which this quantity can be sold. Given the straight-line demand curve of equation (6.5) it is clear that the marginal revenue curve for each old/young pair is:

$$MR = (V_o + V_y)/2 - Q \tag{6.6}$$

Setting marginal revenue equal to marginal cost c requires that $(V_o + V_y)/2 - Q = c$, which gives the profit-maximizing output—number of drinks sold to each old/young pair:

$$Q_U = (V_o + V_y)/2 - c \tag{6.7}$$

---

[2]   We can do this because we have assumed that there are equal numbers of each type of customer. With different numbers of each type we need a slightly different approach. See the end-of-chapter problems.

where the subscript U denotes uniform pricing. Substituting this into the demand function gives the profit-maximizing price per drink:

$$P_U = (V_o + V_y)/4 + c/2 \tag{6.8}$$

Each old customer buys $Q_o = V_o - P_U = (3V_o - V_y)/4 - c/2$ drinks and each young customer buys $Q_y = V_y - P_U = (3V_y - V_o)/4 - c/2$ drinks. The monopolist earns a surplus π_U from each pair of old and young customers of:

$$\pi_U = (P_U - c)Q_U = \frac{1}{8}(V_o + V_y - 2c)^2 \tag{6.9}$$

which is the area $hijk$ in Figure 6.1(c). If there are n customers of each type per evening, the jazz-club owner's profit, Π_U is:

$$\Pi_U = n\pi_U - F = \frac{n}{8}(V_o + V_y - 2c)^2 - F \tag{6.10}$$

For example, if V_o is \$16, V_y is \$12 and c is \$4, then the optimal uniform price is \$9 per drink. Old customers each buy 7 drinks and young customers each buy 3 drinks. Under this strategy, the club owner earns a profit of $(\$9 - \$4)*10 = \$50$ for serving an old and a young customer. [Note that this is what we obtain when substituting the values for V_o, V_y and c, respectively, in equation (6.10).] If there were 100 old and 100 young customers per evening, the jazz club owner would earn a profit of \$5,000 each night less any fixed costs F that are incurred. To see that the jazz club owner can improve on this outcome, first note that at the uniform price $P_U = \$9$ every customer of the jazz club enjoys some consumer surplus. Each old customer has consumer surplus given by the shaded triangle abd in Figure 6.1(a) and each young customer has consumer surplus given by area efg in Figure 6.1(b). These areas are, by standard geometric techniques, $CS_o^U = \frac{1}{2}(V_o - P_U) \cdot Q_o = \frac{1}{2}(Q_o)^2 = \frac{1}{2}\left(\frac{3V_o - V_y}{4} - \frac{c}{2}\right)^2$

for each old customer and $CS_y^U = \frac{1}{2}(V_y - P_U) \cdot Q_y = \frac{1}{2}(Q_y)^2 = \frac{1}{2}\left(\frac{3V_y - V_o}{4} - \frac{c}{2}\right)^2$ for each

young customer. In our numerical example, each old customer has consumer surplus of \$24.50 and each young customer has consumer surplus of \$4.50. This is a measure of the surplus that the club owner has failed to extract. He will clearly prefer any pricing scheme that appropriates at least some, or even better, the entire surplus.

One possibility is for the jazz club owner to switch to a non-linear pricing scheme that has two parts—a cover charge just to enter the club and an additional charge for every drink consumed. This pricing design is often referred to as a two-part tariff. The old customer is charged a cover or entry fee $E_o = \frac{1}{2}\left(\frac{3V_o - V_y}{4} - \frac{c}{2}\right)^2$, whereas the young customer is

charged a cover fee $E_y = \frac{1}{2}\left(\frac{3V_y - V_o}{4} - \frac{c}{2}\right)^2$. The cover charge is the first part of the tariff.

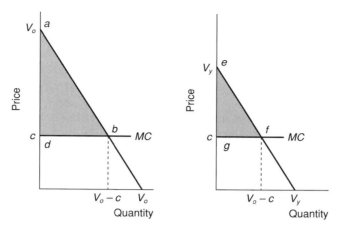

Figure 6.2   First-degree price discrimination with a two-part tariff
The monopolist sets a unit price to each type of consumer equal to marginal cost. It then charges each consumer an entry or membership fee equal to the resulting consumer surplus.

The second part is the charge of a price per drink of P_U. In our numerical example, each old customer is charged a cover of $24.50 and each young customer is charged a cover of $4.50 for entry, while drinks are priced at $9 each. Checking IDs at the door easily solves both arbitrage and identification problems.[3] Moreover, the customers will still be willing to patronize the club. Paying the entry fee reduces their surplus to zero but does not make it negative. The surplus is a measure of their willingness to pay. Finally, since the entry fee is independent of the amount the customer actually drinks, each customer will also continue to buy the same number of drinks as before. Because the entry fee is equal to the consumer surplus each customer previously enjoyed under the uniform pricing policy, the immediate effect of this two-part tariff is to extract the entire consumer surplus and to convert it into profit for the club owner. This implies a profit increase of E_o per old customer and E_y per young customer. Again, in our example, this yields a profit increase of $24.50 per old customer and $4.50 per young one.

However, the club owner can do better still. By *reducing* the price per drink the club-owner can increase the potential consumer surplus each consumer could have. In turn, this permits him to increase the entry fees, which enables him to extract that additional surplus and further increase his profit. The profit-maximizing two-part pricing scheme is illustrated in Figure 6.2. It has the following properties[4]:

---

[3]   We assume that the expense of serious facelifts, hair coloring, and falsifying IDs is more than the surplus older consumers lose by paying the higher price.

[4]   To see why these properties hold, denote the fixed portion of the two-part tariff for a particular type of consumer as T and the user charge as p. Express the demand curve for this type of consumer in inverse form, $p = D(q)$ and assume that the firm's total cost function is $C(q)$. The monopolist's problem is to choose the production level for this type of consumer, q^*, implying a price $p^* = D(q^*)$, that maximizes profits, $\Pi(q)$, where $\Pi(q)$ is given by: $\Pi(q) = \int_0^q D(x)dx - C(q)$. Standard calculus then reveals that maximizing this profit always requires setting a price or user charge equal to marginal cost, and a fixed charge T equal to the consumer surplus generated at that price.

1.   Set the price per unit (drink) equal to marginal cost c.
2.   Set the entry fee for each type of customer equal to that customer's consumer surplus.

In our jazz club case the price per drink is set at c. The area of the triangles abd and efg describe the consumer surplus at this price for old customers and for young customers respectively. These areas are $CS_o = \frac{1}{2}(V_o - c)^2$ and $CS_y = \frac{1}{2}(V_y - c)^2$. As a result, the jazz-club owner can now increase the entry fee to CS_0 for old customers and CS_y for young customers.

Under this optimal pricing scheme, the profit per drink from each consumer is zero, since drinks are sold at cost. This pricing strategy has the advantage of encouraging consumers to purchase many drinks, thereby yielding more consumer surplus. In turn, the jazz club owner can appropriate that surplus for himself by imposing the optimal cover charge. Since the funds claimed by the entry fees *are* profit, total profit has, therefore, been increased to:

$$\Pi_f = \frac{n}{2}((V_0 - c)^2 + (V_y - c)^2) - F \qquad (6.11)$$

In our example, profit per old customer is now \$72 while it is \$32 per young customer instead of the \$24.50 and \$4.50 earned from each when the cover charge was associated with a \$9 drink price. This is a hefty profit increase.[5]

While the increase in profit is sizable and important, the two-part tariff has had another result that is equally significant. Note that each customer is now buying the quantity of drinks, $V_o - c$ for the typical old customer and $V_y - c$ for the typical young one, that each would have bought if the drinks had been priced competitively. The ability to practice first-degree price discrimination leads the monopolist to expand output to the competitive level. That is, the market outcome is now efficient. The total surplus is maximized—and that total surplus is claimed entirely by the monopolist.

Practice Problem

6.2

Consider an amusement park operating as a monopoly. Figure 6.3 shows the demand curve of a typical consumer at the park. There are no fixed costs. The marginal cost associated with each ride is constant. It is comprised of two parts, each also a constant. There is the cost per ride of labor and equipment, k, and there is the cost per ride of printing and collecting tickets, c. A management consultant has suggested two alternative pricing policies for the park. Policy A: charge a fixed admission fee, T, and a fee per ride of r. Policy B: simply charge a fixed admission fee, say T', and a zero fee per ride.

a.   For pricing policy A, show on the graph the admission fee, T, and the per ride price, p, that will maximize profits.
b.   For pricing policy B, show on the graph the single admission fee, T', that will maximize profits.
c.   Compare the two policies. What are the relative advantages of each policy? What determines which policy leads to higher profits?

---

[5]   It is also easy to show that the jazz club owner's profit would be smaller than that achieved by the two-part tariff if he could somehow engage in third-degree price discrimination by somehow charging a different drink price for each group. We invite you to work this out for yourselves.

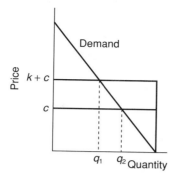

Figure 6.3 Diagram for the amusement park problem

6.1.2 Block Pricing

There is a second non-linear pricing scheme by which the jazz club owner can achieve the same level of profit. This scheme is often called block pricing. Using this type of pricing a seller *bundles* the quantity that he is willing to sell with the total charge that he wishes to set for that quantity. In our jazz club example, the owner sets a pricing policy of the form "Entry plus X drinks for Y dollars." In order to earn maximum profit and appropriate all potential consumer surplus, two simple rules determine the optimal block pricing strategy:

1. Set the quantity offered to each consumer type equal to the amount that type of consumer would buy at competitive pricing, i.e., the quantity bought at a price equal to marginal cost.
2. Set a fixed charge for each consumer type at the total willingness to pay for the quantity identified above.

Let's examine how this would work in our jazz club example. Applying rule 1, we know that each old customer will buy $V_o - c$ drinks and each young customer will buy $V_y - c$ drinks if the drinks are priced at marginal cost. The total willingness to pay for these quantities by old and young customers respectively is the area under the relevant demand curve at these quantities. In the case of old and young customers, respectively, this is:

$$WTP_o = \frac{1}{2}(V_o - c)^2 + (V_o - c)c = \frac{1}{2}(V_o^2 - c^2) \tag{6.12a}$$

$$WTP_y = \frac{1}{2}(V_y - c)^2 + (V_y - c)c = \frac{1}{2}(V_y^2 - c^2) \tag{6.12b}$$

Applying rule 2 we then have the following pricing policy. Offer each old customer entry plus $V_o - c$ drinks for a total charge of $\frac{1}{2}(V_o^2 - c^2)$ dollars and each young customer entry plus $V_y - c$ drinks for a total charge of $\frac{1}{2}(V_y^2 - c^2)$ dollars.

How would we implement this strategy in our jazz club example? One way would be to card the customers at the door and then to give each customer the appropriate number of tokens that can be exchanged (at no additional charge) for drinks. Profit from a customer of type i is the charge WTP_i minus the cost of the drinks, $c(V_i - c)$, or $\frac{1}{2}(V_o - c)^2$ or \$72 from each old customer and $\frac{1}{2}(V_y - c)^2$ or \$32 from each young customer, exactly as in the two-part pricing system.

Before leaving this section, we wish to point out a further interesting feature of both types of first-degree price discrimination that we have discussed. Both the two-part tariff and the block pricing schemes result in the jazz club owner serving each old customer entry plus 12 drinks for a total charge of \$120 and each young customer entry plus 8 drinks for a total charge of \$64. Therefore, in each case, the average price paid by an old customer is $\frac{1}{2}(V_o^2 - c^2)/(V_o - c) = \frac{1}{2}(V_o + c)$ or \$10. Similarly, each young customer pays an average price per drink of $\frac{1}{2}(V_y + c) = \$8$. You can easily check that these are exactly the same prices per drink that would be levied if the club owner were able to apply third-degree price discrimination. Yet the profit outcome is different.

The reason that first-degree and third-degree price discrimination lead to very different profits, despite the fact that the average price is the same in each case, lies in the very different nature of the two pricing schemes. Recall that a demand function measures the marginal benefit that a consumer obtains from the last unit consumed. The quantity demanded equates marginal benefit with the marginal cost to the consumer of buying the last unit where, of course, marginal cost to the consumer is just the price for that last unit. With third-degree price discrimination or linear pricing, there is no difference between the price paid for the first unit and the price paid for the last unit. Hence, average price and marginal price are the same. By contrast, the non-linear scheme pricing permits the club owner effectively to charge an old person \$16 for the first drink, \$15 for the second and so on, while charging a young person \$12 for the first drink, then \$11, etc. With the linear pricing scheme, the old person would pay \$10 for each drink, from the first to the last, while a young person would pay \$8. The average price to each type of customer is the same under either first- or third-degree price discrimination. Yet the non-linear pricing of first-degree price discrimination so lowers the price of the last unit purchased, that consumers are willing to buy (many) more units. Effectively this permits the owner to charge very high prices on the first few drinks purchased. As a result, the average price under first-degree discrimination is just as high as it is under third-degree discrimination. Yet since first-degree discrimination so greatly increases sales at that average price, and since that average price is greater than the firm's marginal cost, such non-linear pricing generates considerably more profit.

6.2   SECOND-DEGREE PRICE DISCRIMINATION OR MENU PRICING

First-degree price discrimination, or personalized pricing, is possible for the jazz club owner for two reasons. First, the club's different types of customers could be distinguishable by means of a simple, observable characteristic. Second, the club has the ability to deny access to those not paying the entry charge that was designed for them. Not all services can be marketed in this way. For example, if instead of a jazz club the monopoly seller is a refreshment stand located in a campus center then limiting access by means of a cover charge is not feasible.

Even in the jazz club case, first-degree discrimination by means of a two-part tariff would not be possible if the difference in consumer willingness to pay was attributable to some characteristic that the jazz club owner could not observe. For example, suppose that what differentiates high demand and low demand customers is not age but income. The club will now find that any attempt to implement the first-degree price discrimination scheme of charging high-income patrons an entry fee of $72 and low-income patrons an entry fee of $32 is not likely to succeed. Every customer could claim to have low income in order to pay the lower entry charge and there is no obvious (or legal) method by which the club owner can enforce the higher fee.

What about the block pricing strategy of offering entry plus 12 drinks for $120 and entry plus 8 drinks for $64? Will that work? Again, the answer is no. It is easy to show that high income customers are willing to pay up to $96 for entry plus 8 drinks. So they derive $32 of consumer surplus from the (8 drinks, $64) package but no consumer surplus from the (12 drinks, $120) package. They will prefer to pretend to be low income in order to pay the lower charge and enjoy some surplus rather than confess to being high income.

The monopolist could, of course, decide to limit entry only to high-income customers by setting the entry charge at $72 or offering only the (12 drinks, $120) package but this loses business (and profit) from low-income customers. Suppose, for instance, that there are N_o older customers and N_y younger customers. The profit from selling to only the older customers is $72N_o$. Setting the lower entry fee or offering only the (8 drinks, $64) package in order to attract both types of customer gives profit of $32(N_y + N_o)$. Clearly, the latter strategy is more profitable if $32N_y > 40N_o$. In other words, if the ratio of low-income to high-income customers is more than 1.25:1 (the ratio of the difference in the entry fees to the low entry fee) the policy of setting the higher entry fee or offering only the (12 drinks, $120) package will generate less profit than offering just the lower entry fee or the (8 drinks, $64) package to all customers.

The point is that once we reduce either the seller's ability to identify different customers or to prevent arbitrage among them (or both), complete surplus extraction by means of perfect price discrimination is no longer possible. Both the two-part and block pricing mechanisms can still be used to raise profit above that earned by uniform pricing but they cannot earn as much as they did previously. Solving the identification and arbitrage problem has now become costly. It is still possible that the monopolist can design a pricing scheme that will induce customers to reveal who they are and keep them separated by their purchases, but now the only way to do this incurs some cost—a cost reflected in less surplus extraction. Such a pricing scheme is called second-degree price discrimination or menu pricing.

Second-degree price discrimination is most usually implemented by offering quantity discounts targeted to different consumer types. To see how it works, let's continue with our jazz club example illustrated in Figure 6.4. Again, the high demand customers have (inverse) demand $P_h = 16 - Q_h$ and the low demand customers have (inverse) demand $P_l = 12 - Q_l$. Now, however, the jazz club owner has no means of distinguishing who is who because the source of the difference between consumers is inherently unobservable. All the owner knows is that two such different types of consumer exist and they both frequent the club.

Any attempt to implement a differentiated two-part tariff will not work in this case. Both types of customer will claim to be low demand types when entering the club in order to pay

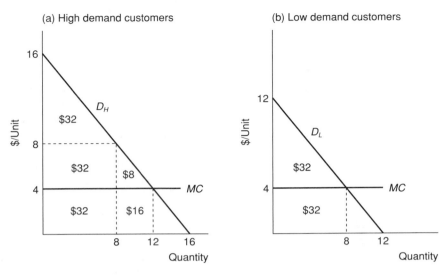

Figure 6.4 Second-degree price discrimination
Low demand customers are willing to pay $64 for entry plus 8 drinks. High demand customers are willing to pay up to $96 for entry plus 8 drinks, and so get $32 surplus from the 8-drinks, $64-package. They will therefore be willing to buy a 12-drinks, $88-package, which also gives them a $32 surplus.

the lower entry fee of $32. Only *after* they are in the club will the different consumers reveal who they are. Since the price per drink is set at marginal cost of $4, the high demand customers will buy 12 drinks and reveal themselves to be high demanders whereas the low demand customers will buy 8 drinks and reveal themselves as such.

You might be tempted to think that the club owner could implement first-degree price discrimination using the following strategy. When entering the club, patrons are given tickets that allow them to buy drinks. If they pay an entry charge of $32 they will be given 8 tickets while if they pay $72 they will be given 12 tickets. Yet this approach will not work either and for the same reason that the block pricing strategy of offering (12 drinks, $120) and (8 drinks, $64) packages failed. High demand customers again have every reason to pretend to be low demand customers and pay an entry charge of only $32, thereby getting 8 tickets and buying 8 drinks at $4 each for a total expenditure of $64. Because, as can be seen from Figure 6.4(a), their total willingness to pay for the 8 drinks is $96, high demand consumers will enjoy a surplus of $32 from this deception. By contrast, they will enjoy no surplus if they pay the entry charge of $72 and get 12 tickets because their total expenditure will be then $120, which exactly equals their willingness to pay for 12 drinks. As a result, it remains the case that the high demand customers are better off by pretending to be low demand even though this constrains the number of drinks that they can buy.

Yet, while unsuccessful, the idea of offering different price and drink combinations as different packages does contain the hint of a strategy that the jazz club owner can use to increase his profit. The point is to employ a variant on the *block pricing* strategy described earlier. The difference is that, since there is no easy way to identify and separate the different types of customers, the block pricing itself must be designed to achieve this purpose. This imposes a new constraint or cost on the owner and so will not yield as much profit as first-degree price discrimination. However, it will substantially improve on simply offering all customers a (8 drinks, $64) package that yields a profit of $32 from each.

To see how one might use block pricing to achieve the identification and separation necessary for price discrimination let us start with the low demand customers. The jazz club owner knows that these customers are willing to pay a total of $64 for 8 drinks. We know that the jazz club owner can offer a package of entry plus 8 drinks at a price of $64 for the package. This package will be attractive to low demand customers, effectively extracting the $32 surplus from each low demand consumer. The problem is that high demand customers will also be willing to buy this package because their willingness to pay for entry and 8 drinks is $96. While the club owner also gets $32 in profit from the high-demand customers buying this package, those customers themselves still enjoy a surplus of $96 − $64 = $32.

The club owner's optimal strategy at this point is to offer a second package targeted to high demand consumers. He knows that the high demand customers are willing to pay a total of $120 for 12 drinks. Yet he also knows that he cannot charge $120 for 12 drinks because the high demand customers will not be willing to pay this much, given that they can buy the (8 drinks, $64) package and enjoy consumer surplus of $32. For an alternative package to be attractive to high demand consumers it has to be what economists call *incentive compatible* with the (8 drinks, $64) package. This means that any alternative package must also allow the high demand customers to enjoy a surplus of at least $32.

A package that meets this requirement but that also generates some additional profit for the club owner is a package of entry plus 12 drinks for a total charge of $88. We know that the high demand customers value entry plus 12 drinks at $120. By offering this deal at a price of $88, the club owner permits these customers to get $32 of surplus when they buy this package, just enough to get them to switch from the (8 drinks, $64) package.[6] And while the high demand consumers get a $32 surplus on this package, the club owner's profit is also higher than it is on the (8 drinks, $64) package. On the latter, the owner earns $32, but on the new package, the owner earns $88 − ($4 × 12) = $40. Of course, the low demand customers will not buy the (12 drinks, $88) package since their maximum willingness to pay for 12 drinks is only $72. Nevertheless, the club owner still earns $32 from these consumers by continuing to sell them the (8 drinks, $64) package. So, the club owner's total profit is increased.

The two menu options have been carefully designed to solve the identification and arbitrage problems by inducing the customers themselves to reveal who they are through the purchases they make. The club owner now offers a menu of options, 8 drinks for $64 or 12 drinks for $88 designed to separate out the different types of customers that he serves. For this reason, this strategy is often referred to as *menu pricing*. It has one very important feature. Note that as before, the average price per drink of the (8 drinks, $64) package is $8. However, the average price per drink of the (12 drinks, $88) package is $7.33. The second package thus offers a *quantity discount* relative to the first.

Quantity discounts are common. Movie theaters, restaurants, concert halls, sports teams, and supermarkets all make use of them. It is cheaper to buy one huge container of popcorn than many small ones. Wine sold by the glass is more expensive per unit than wine sold by

---

[6]   We are working in round numbers to keep things neat. What the jazz club owner might actually do is price the package of entry plus 12 drinks at $87.99 to ensure that the high demand customers will strictly prefer this to the (8 drinks, $64) package.

the bottle. A 24-pack of Coca-Cola is cheaper than 24 individual bottles. It is cheaper per ticket to buy a season's subscription to your favorite football team's home games than to buy tickets to each game individually. A full-day pass at a ski resort will reflect a lower price per run than will a half-day lift ticket. In these and many other cases, the sellers are using a quantity discount to woo the high demand consumers.

There is another twist to consider. What if the club owner now decides to offer a lower number of drinks, say 7, in the package designed for the low demand customers? The maximum willingness to pay for entry plus 7 drinks by a low demand customer is $59.50 so this new package will be (7 drinks, $59.50). The profit it generates from each customer is $31.50, which is 50 cents less than the (8 drinks, $64) package. But now consider the high demand customers. Their maximum willingness to pay for 7 drinks is $87.50, so buying this new package gives them consumer surplus of $28. As a result, the jazz club owner can increase the price of the 12-drink package. Rather than pricing it so that it gives the high demand customers $32 of consumer surplus, he can now price it so that it gives them only $28 of surplus. In other words, he can now raise the price of the second package (entry plus 12 drinks) to be $120 − 28 = $92, increasing his profit from each such package to $44.

The example illustrates the importance of the incentive compatibility constraint. Any package designed to attract low demand customers constrains the ability of the monopolist to extract surplus from high demand customers. Again, this is because the high demand customers cannot be prevented from buying the package designed for low demand customers, and thus will always enjoy some consumer surplus from doing so. As a result, the monopolist will find it more profitable to reduce the number of units offered to low demand customers since this will allow him to increase the price he charges for the package targeted to the high demand customers. There may even be circumstances in which the monopolist would prefer to push this logic to the extreme and not serve low demand customers at all because of the constraint serving them imposes on the prices that can be charged to other customers. Whether or not the monopolist has an incentive to serve the low demand consumers will depend on the number of low demand consumers relative to high demand ones. The fewer low demand consumers there are relative to high demand ones, the less desirable it is to serve low demand consumers since any effort to do so imposes an incentive compatibility constraint on the extraction of surplus from high demand ones.

For a general case of more than two types of consumers the profit-maximizing second-degree price discrimination or menu pricing scheme will exhibit some key features. In particular, if consumer willingness to pay can be unambiguously ranked by type then any optimal second-degree price discrimination scheme will:

1. extract the entire consumer surplus of the lowest demand type served but leave some consumer surplus for all other types;
2. contain a quantity that is less than the socially optimal quantity for all consumer types other than the highest-demand type;
3. exhibit quantity discounting.

Second-degree discrimination enhances the ability of the monopolist to convert consumer surplus into profit, but does so less effectively than first-degree discrimination. With no costless way to distinguish the different types of consumers, the monopolist must rely on some sort of block pricing scheme to solve the identification and arbitrage problems. However, the incentive compatibility constraints that such a scheme must satisfy restrict the firm's ability to extract the entire consumer surplus. Instead, the firm is forced to make a compromise between setting a high charge that loses sales to low demand buyers, and a low charge that forgoes the significant surplus that can be earned from the high demand buyers. And contrary to what many consumers may think, the lower price charged for a larger quantity is entirely unrelated to scale economies. In our example the jazz club owner has no fixed costs and thus no economies of scale, nevertheless the owner finds it profitable to offer a quantity discount to high demand customers.

6.3

Practice Problem

Assume that a monopolist knows that his customers are of two types, low demand customers whose inverse demand is $P_l = 12 - Q_l$ and high demand customers whose demand is $P_h = 16 - Q_h$. However, he does not know which type of customer is which. His production costs are $4 per unit.

a. Complete the following table for this example.

Low demand customers			High demand customers			
Number of units in the package	Charge for the package*	Profit per package	Consumer surplus from low demand package	Maximum willingness to pay for 12 units	Charge for package of 12 units	Profit from each package of 12 units
0	0	0	0	$120.00		$72.00
1	$11.50		$4.00	$120.00	$116.00	
2		$14.00	$8.00	$120.00		$64.00
3						
4	$40.00	$24.00		$120.00		
5	$47.50	$27.50	$20.00	$120.00	$100.00	$52.00
6	$54.00			$120.00		$48.00
7	$59.50	$31.50	$28.00	$120.00	$92.00	$44.00
8	$64.00	$32.00	$32.00	$120.00	$88.00	$40.00
9						
10	$70.00	$30.00	$40.00	$120.00		
11						
12	$72.00		$48.00	$120.00	$72.00	

*This is the low-demand customer's maximum willingness to pay for the number of units in the package.

b. Assume that there are the same numbers of high demand and low demand customers. What is the profit-maximizing number of units that should be offered in the package aimed at the low demand customers?

c. Now assume that there are twice as many low demand customers as high demand customers. What is the profit-maximizing pair of packages for the monopolist?

d. The monopolist is considering offering two packages, one containing 6 units and the other 12 units. What are the charges at which these packages will be offered? What is the ratio of high demand to low demand customers above which it will be better for the monopolist to supply only the high demand customers?

6.3   SOCIAL WELFARE WITH FIRST- AND SECOND-DEGREE PRICE DISCRIMINATION

One way to understand the welfare effects of price discrimination is to consider a particular consumer group i. Suppose each consumer in this group has inverse demand:

$$P = P_i(Q) \tag{6.13}$$

Assume also that the monopolist has constant marginal costs of c per unit. Now let the quantity that each consumer in group i is offered with a particular pricing policy be Q_i. Then the total surplus—consumer surplus plus profit—generated for each consumer under this pricing policy is just the area between the inverse demand function and the marginal cost function up to the quantity Q_i, as illustrated in Figure 6.5.

The pricing policy chosen by the firm affects the quantity offered to each type of consumer, and also alters the distribution of total surplus between profit and consumer surplus. The first effect has an impact on welfare, whereas the second effect does not imply a change in total welfare, but rather a transfer of surplus between consumers and producers. As a result, *price discrimination increases (decreases) the social welfare of consumer group i if it increases (decreases) the quantity offered to that group.*

It follows immediately that first-degree price discrimination always increases social welfare even though it extracts all consumer surplus. With this pricing policy we have seen that the monopoly seller supplies each consumer group with the socially efficient quantity (the quantity that would be chosen if price were set to marginal cost). Hence first-degree discrimination always increases the total quantity to a level [$Q_i(c)$ in Figure 6.5] that exceeds that which would have been sold under uniform pricing.

With second-degree price discrimination matters are not so straightforward. As we have seen, this type of price discrimination leads to high demand groups being supplied with quantities "near to" the socially efficient level. However, we have also seen that the seller will

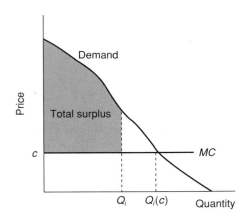

Figure 6.5   Total surplus
When the total quantity consumed is Q_i total surplus is given by the shaded area. Total surplus is maximized at quantity $Q_i(c)$.

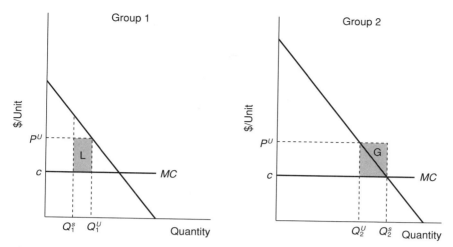

Figure 6.6   Impact of second-degree price discrimination on welfare
An upper limit on the change in total surplus that arises from second-degree price discrimination is the upper limit on the gain, G, minus the lower limit on the loss, L.

want to restrict the quantity supplied to lower demand groups and, in some cases, not supply these groups at all. The net effect on output is therefore not clear a priori.

The impact on social welfare of second-degree price discrimination can nevertheless be derived using much the same techniques that we used in Chapter 5. By way of illustration, suppose that there are two consumer groups with demands as illustrated in Figure 6.6 (i.e., Group 2 is the high-demand group). In this figure P^U is the non-discriminatory uniform price, and Q_1^U and Q_2^U are the quantities sold to each consumer in the relevant group at this price. By contrast, Q_1^s and Q_2^s are the quantities supplied to the two groups with second-degree price discrimination.[7] We define the terms:

$$\Delta Q_1 = Q_1^s - Q_1^U;\ \Delta Q_2 = Q_2^s - Q_1^U \qquad (6.14)$$

In the case illustrated we have $\Delta Q_1 < 0$ and $\Delta Q_2 > 0$. This tells us that an upper limit on the increase in total surplus that follows from second-degree price discrimination is the area G minus the area L. This gives us the equation:

$$\Delta W \le G - L = (P_U - MC)\Delta Q_1 + (P_U - MC)\Delta Q_2 = (P_U - MC)(\Delta Q_1 + \Delta Q_2) \qquad (6.15)$$

Extending the analysis to n markets, we then have:

$$\Delta W \le (P_U - MC)\sum\nolimits_{i=1}^{n} \Delta Q_i \qquad (6.16)$$

It follows that for $\Delta W \ge 0$ it is necessary that $\sum\nolimits_{i=1}^{n} \Delta Q_i \ge 0$. In other words, a necessary condition for second-degree price discrimination to increase welfare is that it increases total output.

---

[7]   Since group 2 is the high demand group, we know that $Q_2^s = Q_2(c)$.

We know from last chapter that this requirement is generally not met in the case of third-degree price discrimination and linear demands because then the monopolist supplies the same total quantity as with uniform pricing, so third-degree price discrimination does not increase welfare. By contrast, it could be the case that second-degree price discrimination leads to an increase in the quantity supplied to both markets and this would increase social welfare. In the jazz club owner case, for example, this will be the case if there are an equal number of high-demand and low-demand customers. (You are asked to consider this point in the end-of-chapter problem 7.)

Summary

In this chapter we have extended our analysis of price discrimination to cases in which firms employ more sophisticated, non-linear pricing schemes. Our focus has been on commonly observed examples of such non-linear pricing schemes. These are: (1) two-part pricing in which the firm charges a fixed fee plus a price per unit; and (2) block pricing in which the firm bundles the quantity being offered with the total charge for that quantity. Both schemes have the same objective, to increase the monopolist's profit either by increasing the surplus on existing sales or by extending sales to new markets, or both.

The most perfect form of price discrimination, first-degree price discrimination or personalized pricing, can only be practiced when the firm can costlessly solve the identification and arbitrage problems. The firm needs to be able to identify the different types of consumers and must also be able to keep them apart. If this is possible, then two-part tariffs and block pricing can, in principle, convert *all* consumer surplus into profit for the firm. The positive side to this is that the firm supplies the socially efficient level of output to each consumer type. The negative side is that there are potentially severe distributional inequities in that all social surplus takes the form of profit.

If the requirements necessary to practice perfect price discrimination are not met, then the monopoly seller cannot achieve such a large profit. The monopolist may then rely on second-degree price discrimination or menu pricing, another form of non-linear pricing. Second-degree price discrimination differs from both first- and third-degree, however, in that it relies on the pricing mechanism itself—usually some form of quantity discount—to induce consumers to *self-select* into groups that reveal their identity or who they are on the demand curve.

The use of a quantity discount to sort or screen consumers must always satisfy an *incentive compatibility* constraint across the different consumer types. This constraint affects in a negative way the monopolist's ability to extract consumer surplus. Because the incentive compatibility constraint adversely affects profits, the monopolist may choose to avoid it by refusing to serve low demand markets, with the result that the low demand type consumers are clearly worse off. As a consequence, the welfare effects of second degree price discrimination are not clear. Yet unlike the case of third degree discrimination (with linear demand curves at least), second degree pricing strategies do have some positive probability of making things better.

Problems

1. Many universities allocate financial aid to undergraduate students on the basis of some measure of need. Does this practice reflect pure charity or price discrimination? If it reflects price discrimination, do you think it lies closer to first-degree discrimination or third-degree discrimination?

2. A food co-op sells a homogenous good called groceries denoted g. The co-op's cost function is described by: $C(g) = F + cg$; where F denotes fixed cost and c is the constant per unit variable cost. At a meeting of the co-op board, a young economist proposes the following marketing strategy: Set a fixed membership fee M and a price per unit of groceries p_M that members pay. In addition, set a price per unit of groceries p_N higher than p_M at which the co-op will sell groceries to non-members.

a. What must be true about the demand of different customers for this strategy to work?

b. What kinds of price discrimination does this strategy employ?

3. At Starbuck's Coffee Shops, coffee drinkers have the option of sipping their lattes and cappuccinos while surfing the Internet on their laptops. These connections are made via a connection typically provided by a wireless firm such as T-Mobile. Using a credit card, customers can buy Internet time in various packages. A one-hour package currently goes for an average price of $6. A day pass that is good for any time in the next 24 hours sells for $10. A seven-day pass sells for about $40. Briefly describe the pricing tactics reflected in these options.

4. A nightclub owner has both student and adult customers. The demand for drinks by a typical student is: $Q^S = 18 - 3P$. The demand for drinks by a typical adult is: $Q^A = 10 - 2P$. There are equal numbers of students and adults. The marginal cost of each drink is $2.

a. What price will the club owner set if he cannot discriminate at all between the two groups? What will his total profit be at this price?

b. If the club owner could separate the groups and practice third-degree price discrimination what price per drink would be charged to members of each group? What would be the club owner's profit in this case?

5. If the club owner in #4 can "card" patrons and determine who among them is a student and who is not and, in turn, can serve each group by offering a cover charge and a number of drink tokens to each group, what will the cover charge and number of tokens be for students? What will be the cover charge and number of tokens given to adults? What is the club owner's profit under this regime?

6. A local phone company has three family plans for its wireless service. Under each of these plans, the family gets two lines (phones) and can make local and long distance (within the U.S. and Canada) for free so long as the total number of minutes used per month does not exceed the plan maximum. The price and maximum minutes per month for each plan are: plan 1: 500 minutes for $50; plan 2: 750 minutes for $62.50; and plan 3: 1,000 minutes for $75.00. Assuming that there are equal numbers of consumers in each group and that the value of a marginal minute for each group declines at the rate of $0.0004 per minute used, work out the demand curves consistent with this pricing. What surplus will each consumer group enjoy?

7. Now return to our club owner in the text in which low demand consumers have an inverse demand of: $P = 12 - Q$; while high demand consumers have an inverse demand of: $P = 16 - Q$. Marginal cost per drink is again $4. Assume that there are N_h high demand customers and N_l low demand customers. Show that under these circumstances the firm will only serve low demand customers, i.e., will only offer both packages if there are at least as many low demand consumers as high demand ones. In other words, $\dfrac{N_h}{N_l} \leq 1$ in order for low consumers to be served.

References

Ekelund, R. 1970. "Price Discrimination and Product Differentiation in Economic Theory: An Early Analysis." *Quarterly Journal of Economics* 84 (February): 268–78.

Oi, W. 1971. "A Disneyland Dilemma: Two-part Tariffs for a Mickey Mouse Monopoly." *Quarterly Journal of Economics* 85 (February): 77–96.

Shapiro, C. and H. R. Varian, 1999. *Information Rules: A Strategic Guide to the Internet Economy.* Boston: Harvard Business School Press.

Varian, H. 1989. "Price Discrimination." In R. Schmalansee and R. Willig, eds, *The Handbook of Industrial Organization.* Vol. 1. Amsterdam: North-Holland, 597–654.

7

Product Variety and Quality Under Monopoly

Most firms sell more than one product. Microsoft offers not only an operating system and an Internet browser but also a number of other products, most notably, the word-processing package *Word*, the spreadsheet software *Excel*, and the presentation package *PowerPoint*. Photographic firms such as Eastman Kodak sell both cameras and film, and in each case in a wide range of varieties. The telecommunications giant Comcast now offers telephone service, high-speed Internet service, and cable TV. A newer giant in the same field, AOL-Time Warner offers a combination of Internet access and entertainment programming. Fashion designers such as Ralph Lauren offer a broad range of apparel from sportswear to haute couture for both women and men.

The multiproduct firm is likely to be the norm. This leads us to the question of exactly how much variety a firm should aim to offer. Take a company such as Kellogg. Is there any flavor, color or texture of breakfast cereal that they do not market? Or take Procter & Gamble. Should this consumer product company offer more than a dozen varieties of their Head and Shoulders shampoo and even more varieties of their Crest toothpaste? Indeed Procter & Gamble asked itself the same question when it reexamined its product strategy in the early 1990s. By 1996 the company had reduced their list of products by one-third as compared with 1991.

A firm's incentive to offer many varieties of what is essentially the same product—breakfast foods, hair or tooth care—is simple enough to understand. It is a way for the firm to reach and sell to consumers with very different tastes. Because consumers often differ regarding their most preferred color, or flavor, or texture, selling successfully to many consumers requires offering something a little different to each of them. Specifically, to induce a consumer to make a purchase the firm must market a product that is reasonably close to the version that the consumer prefers. When a firm offers a variety of products in response to different consumer tastes, it is called *horizontal product differentiation*.

However, with respect to certain product features consumers often agree on what makes for a good product. For example, all consumers likely agree that a car with antilock brakes is better than one without such a stopping mechanism. Similarly, all probably agree that while the X-type Jaguar is an attractive car, it pales in comparison to the XJ. Everyone is likely to agree that flying from Boston to San Francisco first class is better than flying coach. Where consumers differ in these examples is not in what features they consider desirable but, instead, in how much a desired feature is worth to them, i.e., how much they are willing to pay for antilock brakes, a better Jaguar, or first class airfare. When a firm responds to differing consumer willingness to pay for a product's quality by offering different qualities of the same product it is called *vertical product differentiation*.

In this chapter we analyze the horizontal and vertical product differentiation strategies of a monopoly firm. We examine how product differentiation may be used by the firm to increase profitability. We also consider the welfare properties of these strategies.

7.1 A SPATIAL APPROACH TO HORIZONTAL PRODUCT DIFFERENTIATION

There are many situations in which individual consumers have their own preferred brand or variety of product, whether this is breakfast cereal, hair treatment, or an automobile. We begin by considering a market in which consumers differ regarding the features that make the product attractive to them. However, they are more or less alike in terms of their basic willingness to pay for one of these products. For example, all consumers might be willing to pay the same price for a product, a margherita pizza, if it is sold at a shop close to their home. However, not all consumers will be equidistant from the shop. Some will be close and some will be far away. Given the time and effort required to travel, the willingness to pay of those who live far from the shop will be lower. Alternatively, those who live close— and who therefore do not have to incur travel expenses—will be willing to pay a higher price. The fact that a product sold close to home is different from one that is sold far away is a good example of what is referred to as horizontal product differentiation. Such differentiation is characterized by the property that each consumer has her own preferred location of the shop or product, namely, one close to the consumer's own address.

When the consumer market is differentiated by geographic location, a firm can vary its product strategy through its choice of where the product is sold. The firm may choose to sell its product only in one central location to which all shoppers must come: Giorgio Armani, for example, does this. Alternatively, it may decide to offer the product at many locations spaced throughout the city: McDonald's, Dunkin' Donuts and Subway are obvious examples. Customers are not indifferent between these alternative strategies. If the firm sells only at one central location, those who do not live in the middle of town have to incur travel costs to come to the store. These costs are greatest for those living farthest from the center. The alternative strategy of selling at many different locations allows more consumers to purchase the good without going too far out of their way.

When geography is taken into account and traveling is costly, consumers are willing to pay more for a product marketed close to their own geographic location. In this case products are differentiated by the locations at which they are sold. This setting is known as the spatial model of product differentiation, pioneered by Hotelling (1929).[1] Before presenting the model formally, there is an additional point worth emphasizing. While the model is easiest to present in terms of a geographic representation it can easily be more broadly interpreted. With just a little imagination, geographic space can be transformed into a "product" or, more properly "characteristics space." In such a space, each consumer's "location" reflects her most preferred set of product characteristics such as color, style, or other features. Recall our earlier discussion in Chapter 4 of a soft-drink firm offering a product line differing in terms of sugar content. This example made use of precisely this type of horizontal or spatial differentiation.

---

[1] Hotelling (1929) was concerned with analyzing competition between two stores whereas we consider here the case in which the stores are owned by the same firm and so act cooperatively.

The travel cost of the geographic model can be understood as a psychic or utility cost that the consumer incurs if she must purchase a good whose characteristics are "distant" from her most preferred type. Just as consumers prefer to go to video stores close to their home, so they prefer to buy clothes that are "close" to their individual preferred style, or soft drinks close to their preferred amount of sugar content. In fact Hotelling suggested just this interpretation in his seminal article. As he wrote:

> Distance, as we have used it for illustration, is only a figurative term for a great congeries of qualities. Instead of sellers of an identical commodity separated geographically we might have considered two . . . cider merchants . . . one selling a sweeter liquid than the other. If consumers of cider are thought of as varying by infinitesimal degrees in the sourness they desire, we have much the same situation as before. The measure of sourness now represents distance, while instead of transportation costs there are degrees of disutility resulting from the consumer getting cider more or less different from what he wants. (1929, p. 54)

7.2   MONOPOLY AND HORIZONTAL DIFFERENTIATION

Assume that there is a town spread out along a single road; call it Main Street, of say one mile in length. There are N consumers who live spaced evenly along this road from one end of town to the other. A firm that has a monopoly in, for example, fast food, must decide how to serve these consumers at the greatest profit. What this means is that the monopolist must choose the number of retail outlets, or shops, that it will operate, where these should be located on Main Street, and what prices they should charge. In the product differentiation analogy to drinks of different sweetness, the monopolist has to decide how many different drinks it should offer, what their precise degrees of sweetness should be, and what their prices should be. More generally, what range of products should the monopolist bring to the market and how should they be priced? In what follows we use for clarity the geographic interpretation of the model, but we again emphasize that you should always bear in mind its much wider interpretation.

In this section we consider cases in which the monopolist does not price discriminate among the consumers that are served. Consumers travel to a retail outlet in order to buy the product, and they incur transport costs. We assume that the transportation cost is t per unit of distance (there-and-back) traveled. Except for their addresses or their locations, consumers are identical to each other. We assume that in each period each consumer is willing to buy exactly one unit of the product sold by the monopolist provided that the price paid, including transport costs, which we shall call the *full price*, is less than her reservation price, which we denote by V.

Suppose that the monopolist decides to operate only a single retail outlet. Then it makes sense to locate this outlet at the center of Main Street. Now consider the monopolist's pricing decision. The essentials of the analysis are illustrated in Figure 7.1. The westernmost resident (residing at the left end of the diagram) has an address of $z = 0$. The easternmost resident has an address of $z = 1$ and the shop is located at $z = 1/2$.

The vertical axis in Figure 7.1 is, as usual, a measure of price. The value V in this diagram is the reservation price for each consumer. The full price that each consumer pays is comprised of two parts. First, there is the price p_1 actually set by the monopolist. Second, there is the additional cost consumers incur in getting to the shop (and back home). Measured per unit of distance there and back, the *full price* actually paid by a consumer who lives a distance x from the center of town is the monopolist's price plus the transport cost

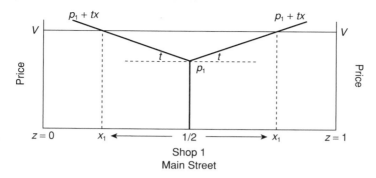

Figure 7.1 The full price at the shop on Main Street
The full price, including transport cost, rises as consumers live farther from the shop.

or $p_1 + tx$. This full price is indicated by the Y-shaped set of lines in Figure 7.1. It indicates that the full price paid by a consumer at the center of town—one who incurs no transport cost—is just p_1. However, as the branches of the Y indicate, the full price rises steadily beyond p_1 for consumers both east and west of the town center. So long as distance from the shop is less than x_1, the consumer's reservation price V exceeds the full price $p_1 + tx$ and such a consumer buys the monopolist's product. However, for distances beyond x_1 the full price exceeds V and these consumers do not buy the product. In other words, the monopolist serves all those who live within x_1 units of the town center. How is the distance x_1 determined? Consumers who reside distance x_1 from the shop are just indifferent between buying the product and not buying it at all. For them, the full price $p_1 + tx_1$ is equal to V so we have:

$$p_1 + tx_1 = V \text{ which implies that } x_1 = \frac{V - p_1}{t} \tag{7.1}$$

Now x_1 is really just a fraction. Since the town is one mile long, x_1 is a fraction of a mile and the retail outlet sells to a fraction $2x_1$ of the whole town—since it sells to consumers to the left and to the right of the market center so long as they live no further than x_1 from the shop. Moreover, there are N consumers evenly distributed over Main Street. Accordingly, there are $2x_1N$ consumers who each are willing to buy one unit of the product if it is priced at p_1. By substituting the expression for x_1 from equation (7.1) into the number of customers served by the monopolist, $2x_1N$ at price p_1, we find that the total demand for the monopolist's product given that it operates just one shop is:

$$Q(p_1, 1) = 2x_1N = \frac{2N}{t}(V - p_1) \tag{7.2}$$

Equation (7.2) says something interesting. Despite our assumption that each consumer buys exactly one unit or none of the monopolist's product, the demand function in the equation shows that aggregate demand increases as the monopolist lowers the price. The reason is illustrated in Figure 7.2. When the shop price is reduced from p_1 to p_2 demand increases because *more consumers are willing to buy the product at the lower price*. Now all consumers within distance x_2 of the shop buy the product.

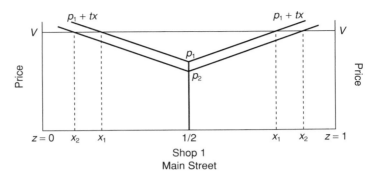

Figure 7.2 Lowering the price at the shop on Main Street
A fall in the shop price brings additional customers from both east and west.

Suppose that the monopolist wants to sell to every customer in town. What is the *highest* price that the monopolist can set and still be able to sell to all N consumers? The answer must be the price at which the consumers who live furthest from the shop, i.e., those who are half a mile away, are just willing to buy. At a shop price p these consumers pay a full price of $p + t/2$ and so will buy only if $p + t/2 \leq V$. What this tells us is that with a single retail outlet at the market center the maximum price that the monopolist can charge and still supply the entire market of N consumers with its one store is $p(N, 1)$ given by:

$$p(N, 1) = V - \frac{t}{2} \tag{7.3}$$

Let the monopolist's costs be c per unit sold and assume that there are set-up costs of F for each retail outlet. These set-up costs could be associated with the cost of buying a site, commissioning the building and so on. In the product differentiation analogy, the set-up costs might be the costs of designing and marketing the new product. Whatever the framework, the monopolist's profit with a single retail outlet that supplies the entire market is:

$$\pi(N, 1) = N[p(N, 1) - c] - F = N\left(V - \frac{t}{2} - c\right) - F \tag{7.4}$$

We are now ready to investigate why this single shop should be located in the center of town. The reason why this is the best location is that makes it easiest to reach all the customers. At the price $p = V - \frac{t}{2}$, a move a little to the east will not gain any new customers on the east end of town (there are no more to gain) but will lose some of those at the extreme west end of town. In other words, if the firm moves from the center, the only way it can continue to serve the entire town is by cutting its price below $V - \frac{t}{2}$. Only by keeping its single location at the center can it reach all customers with a price as high as $V - \frac{t}{2}$.

Now we wish to consider what happens when there are two, or three, or n outlets along Main Street. As before, we continue to assume that unit cost at each shop is c per unit sold

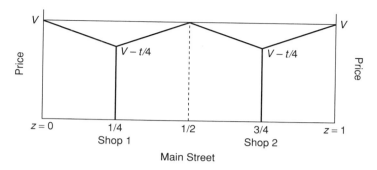

Figure 7.3 Opening two shops on Main Street
The maximum price is higher with two shops than it is with one.

and that the set-up cost for each outlet is F. In other words there are no scope economies from operating multiple outlets. We start by asking what happens if the number of retail outlets is increased to two. Because each segment of the market along Main Street is the same and each shop has the same costs the monopolist will choose to set the same price at each shop. Moreover, the monopolist will want to coordinate the locations of these two shops so as to maximize the price charged at a shop while still reaching the entire market. In fact, the same intuition that justifies a central location with just one firm can be used to show that the optimal location strategy is to locate one of the two shops 1/4 mile from the left-hand end and the other 1/4 mile from the right-hand end of Main Street as in Figure 7.3.[2]

Consider the maximum price that the monopolist can now charge while still supplying the entire market. The maximum distance that any consumer has to travel to a shop is 1/4 mile— much less than the 1/2 mile when there is only one retail outlet. As a result, the highest price that the monopolist can charge and supply the entire market is:

$$p(N, 2) = V - \frac{t}{4} \tag{7.5}$$

which is higher than the price with a single retail outlet. The monopolist's profit is now:

$$\pi(N, 2) = N\left(V - \frac{t}{4} - c\right) - 2F \tag{7.6}$$

What happens if the monopolist decides to operate three shops? By exactly the same argument as above, these shops should be located symmetrically at 1/6, 1/2, and 5/6 miles from the left-hand end of the market so that each supplies 1/3 of the market, as illustrated in Figure 7.4. The maximum distance that any consumer has to travel now is 1/6 mile, so the price at each shop (again assuming, of course, that all consumers are to be served) is:

$$p(N, 3) = V - \frac{t}{6} \tag{7.7}$$

---

[2] For the interested reader a formal proof of this result is given in Appendix A to this chapter. Appendix B extends the analysis to include the possibility that the two shops have different costs.

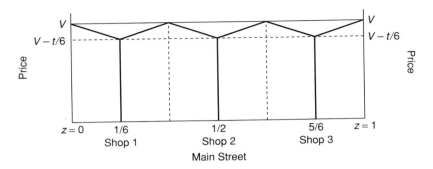

Figure 7.4   Opening three shops on Main Street

While profit is now

$$\pi(N, 3) = N\left(V - \frac{t}{6} - c\right) - 3F \tag{7.8}$$

There is, in fact, a general rule emerging. If the monopolist has n shops to serve the entire market, they will be located symmetrically at distances $1/2n$, $3/2n$, $5/2n$, ..., $(2i - 1)/2n$, ..., $(2n - 1)/2n$ from the left-hand end of the market. The maximum distance that any consumer has to travel to a shop is $1/2n$ miles, so the price that the monopolist can charge at each shop while supplying the entire market is

$$p(N, n) = V - \frac{t}{2n} \tag{7.9}$$

At this price, its profit is

$$\pi(N, n) = N\left(V - \frac{t}{2n} - c\right) - nF \tag{7.10}$$

The important feature that emerges from this analysis is that as the number of retail outlets n increases the monopolist's price at each shop gets closer and closer to the consumer's reservation price V. In other words, by increasing the number of shops the monopolist is able to charge each consumer a price much closer to her maximum willingness to pay, V, and thereby appropriate a much greater proportion of consumer surplus.

The moral of the foregoing analysis is clear—especially when we remember to interpret the geographic space of Main Street as a more general product space. Even if no scope economies are present, a monopolist has an incentive to offer many varieties of a good. Doing so allows the monopolist to exploit the wide variety of consumer tastes, charging each consumer a high price because each is being offered a variety that is very close to her most preferred type. It is not surprising, therefore, that we see such extensive product proliferation in real-world markets such as those for cars, soft drinks, toothpastes, hair shampoos, cameras and so on.[3]

---

[3]   See Shapiro and Varian (1999) for a similar argument regarding product variety in e-commerce markets.

However, there must be some factor limiting this proliferation of varieties or outlets. We do not observe a McDonald's on every street corner, or individually tailored Levis, or each person's custom-designed breakfast cereals or soft drinks! We therefore need to think about what constrains the monopolist from adding more and more retail outlets or product variants. Equation (7.10) gives the clue. Admittedly, adding additional retail outlets allows the monopolist to increase its prices. However, the establishment of each new shop or new product variant also incurs the set-up cost. If, for example, the monopolist decides to operate $n + 1$ retail outlets its profit is

$$\pi(N, n + 1) = N\left(V - \frac{t}{2(n + 1)} - c\right) - (n + 1)F \tag{7.11}$$

This additional shop, or variety of drink, or new product variant increases profit only if $\pi(N, n + 1) > \pi(N, n)$, which requires that:

$$\frac{t}{2n}N - \frac{t}{2(n + 1)}N - F > 0$$

This simplifies to:

$$n(n + 1) < \frac{tN}{2F} \tag{7.12}$$

Suppose, for example, that there are five million consumers in the market so that $N = 5{,}000{,}000$ and that there is a fixed cost $F = \$50{,}000$ associated with each shop. Suppose further that the transport cost $t = \$1$. Hence, $tN/2F = 50$. Then if n is less than or equal to 6, equation (7.12) indicates that it is profitable to add a further shop. However, once the monopolist sets up $n = 7$ shops equation (7.12) indicates that it is not worthwhile to add any more. (You can easily check that the monopolist should operate exactly 7 shops for any value of $tN/2F$ greater than 42 but less than 56.)

Equation (7.12) actually has a simple and appealing intuition. The monopolist has to balance the increase in price and revenues that results from increased product variety against the additional set-up costs that offering increased variety entails. What this tells us is that we would expect to find greater product variety in markets where there are many consumers (N is large), or where the set-up costs of increasing product variety are low (F is small), or where consumers have strong and distinct preferences regarding product characteristics (t is large).

The first two conditions should be obvious. It tells us why there are many more retail outlets in Chicago than in Peoria; why we see many franchise outlets of the same fast-food chain but not of a gourmet restaurant; and why we see many more Subway outlets in a city than Marriott hotels. What does the third condition mean? For a given number of n shops, equation (7.12) tells us that an additional $(n + 1)$ shop will be increasingly desirable as the transportation cost t becomes greater. Thus, as t increases so will the monopolist's optimal number of outlets or degree of product variety.

The interpretation is that when t is high consumers incur very large costs if they are not being offered their most preferred brand. That is, a large value of t implies that consumers are very strongly attached to their preferred product type or location and are unwilling to purchase products that deviate significantly from this type—or travel very far to buy the

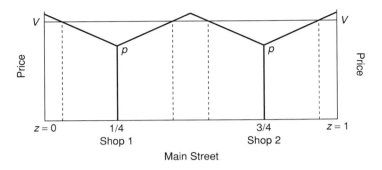

Figure 7.5   Stand-alone retail shops on Main Street

product. If the monopolist is to continue to attract consumers it must tailor its products more closely to each consumer's unique demand, which requires that it offers a wider range of product variants—or operates more retail outlets.

In this kind of market, adding a new shop does not necessarily mean increasing the total supply of the good. Instead, it means replacing some of an existing variety with an alternative variety that more closely matches the specific tastes of some customers. As we have seen, this also allows the firm to charge a higher price. Yet this advantage does not come free. The firm must incur the set-up cost F for each new shop.

However, we have not actually checked whether or not it makes sense and profit for the monopolist to serve the entire market. We need to identify the condition that determines whether the monopolist will prefer to supply only part of the market rather than the whole market. If only part of the market is served then each retail outlet is effectively a "stand-alone" shop whose market area does not touch that of the remaining outlets as in Figure 7.5. We show in the inset that the profit-maximizing price when only part of the market is served is $p^* = (V + c)/2$, which does not depend on the number of shops the monopolist has. This leads to a simple rule that determines whether or not the entire market is to be served. Suppose that there are n retail outlets. Then we know from equation (7.9) that the price at which the entire market can be served is $p(N, n) = V - t/2n$. Serving the entire market is therefore better than supplying only part of the market provided:

$$p(N, n) > p^* \text{ which implies } V - \frac{t}{2n} > \frac{V + c}{2} \text{ which implies } V > c + \frac{t}{n} \tag{7.13}$$

We can put this rule another way. What equation (7.13) tells us is that the monopolist's optimal pricing policy can be described as follows:

1. If marginal production cost plus per unit transport cost divided by the number of retail outlets, $c + t/n$, is greater than the consumers' reservation price V, the monopolist should set a price at each shop of $p^* = (V + c)/2$ and supply only part of the market.
2. If marginal production plus per unit transport cost divided by the number of retail outlets, $c + t/n$, is less than the consumers' reservation price V, the monopolist should set a price at each shop of $p(n) = V - t/2n$ and supply the entire market.

Derivation Checkpoint
Optimal Partial Market Price

Assume that the left-hand shop is located at $1/4$ mile. At a price p this shop sells to consumers located within distance r on each side such that $p + tr = V$, or $r = (V - p)/t$. Total demand for this shop is therefore $2rN$. Profit to this shop is therefore:

$$\pi = 2N(p - c)(V - p)/t$$

Differentiating with respect to p gives the first order condition:

$$\frac{\partial \pi}{\partial p} = \frac{2N}{t}(V - 2p + c) = 0$$

Solving for the optimal price p^* then yields

$$p^* = (V + c)/2$$

At this price, profit is:

$$\pi = \frac{N}{2t}(V - c)^2$$

The intuition behind this rule is relatively straightforward. When the consumer reservation price is low relative to production and transportation costs and when there are few outlets, trying to supply the entire market gives the monopolist a very low margin over operating costs and could even lead to selling at a loss. By contrast, when the consumer reservation price is high relative to the cost of production and transportation and there are many outlets, a price that allows the monopolist to supply the entire market offers a reasonable margin over costs. In these latter circumstances, the monopolist will not wish to set a high price that sacrifices any sales. Since the marginal revenue of every unit sold significantly exceeds the production cost, the monopolist will wish to sell all the units it can.

7.3   IS THERE TOO MUCH PRODUCT VARIETY?

The profit-maximizing firm with market power may have an incentive to create a large number of outlets or product varieties so as to provide each consumer with something close to her most preferred location and thereby extract a high price. It is easy to think of real-world firms that, while not pure monopolists, have substantial market power and employ this strategy. For instance, automobile manufacturers market many varieties of compact, midsize, and large, luxury class cars. Franchise operations such as McDonald's or Subway grant exclusive geographic rights so as to space their outlets evenly over an area and avoid competition between neighboring franchises. Telephones come in an increasingly wide variety of styles and colors. Soft drink, cereal, and ice cream companies offer a wide array of minimally differentiated goods.

The sometimes overwhelming degree of product variety that we frequently observe raises the question whether the incentive to offer a variety of product types could be too strong. Alternatively, does the monopolist provide the degree of product variety consistent with maximizing social welfare? Or are the incentives so strong that the monopolist provides too much product variety? To answer this question, we first need to describe the socially optimal degree of product variety. Although the argument can be made in general terms, it is easiest to see the answer for the case in which the entire market is served.

We use the efficiency criterion to determine the optimality of the variety of products offered. This requires that we maximize the total net surplus, i.e., consumer valuation minus cost. In this light, note that once the entire market is served, the total value to consumers of the output is unchanged no matter how many shops the monopolist operates. That is, once all N consumers are buying the product, the total value placed by consumers on this production is NV no matter how many shops, or product variants, there are. Similarly, once all N consumers are served, the total variable production cost is constant at cN, again regardless of the number of outlets.

Once all N consumers are served, only two factors change as more stores or product varieties are added. One of these is the transport cost incurred by a typical or average consumer. Clearly, as more shops are added more consumers find themselves closer to a store and this cost falls. That's the good news. The bad news is that adding more shops also incurs the additional set-up cost of F per shop. Our question about whether the monopolist provides too many (or too few) shops thus comes down to determining whether it is the good news or the bad news that dominates. More formally, when all consumers are served, the total surplus is the total value NV minus the total production cost cN minus the total transportation and set-up costs. Since the first two terms are fixed independent of the number of shops, maximizing the net social surplus is equivalent to minimizing the sum of transportation and set-up costs. Does the monopolist's strategy achieve this result?

One feature of the monopoly outcome makes answering this question a little easier. It is the fact that the monopolist always spaces its shops evenly along Main Street no matter how many it operates. That is, a single shop is located at the center; two shops are located at 1/4 and 3/4, and so on. This feature greatly facilitates the calculation of total transportation cost that consumers incur for any number of shops n.

Consider Figure 7.6 which shows both the full price and the transportation cost paid by those consumers buying from a particular outlet, shop i. As before, the top Y-shaped figure shows that a consumer located right next to the store has no transport cost and pays a price

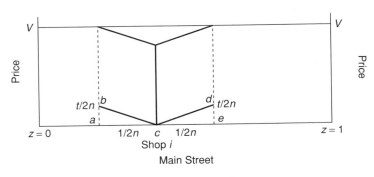

Figure 7.6   Cost of serving customers when there are n shops

of $p = V - \dfrac{t}{2n}$. As we consider consumers farther from the shop, the branches of the Y show that the full price rises because these consumers incur greater and greater transportation costs. The lower branches in the figure provide a direct measurement of this transportation cost for each such consumer. Again, the transportation cost for a consumer located right next to the store is zero. It rises gradually to $t/2n$—the transportation cost paid by a consumer who lives the maximum distance from the shop. Total transportation cost for the consumers of shop i is the sum of the individual transportation cost of each consumer.

This is indicated by the areas of the symmetric triangles abc and cde in Figure 7.6. Each of these triangles extends to a height of $t/2n$. Each also has a base $1/2n$. Hence, the area of each is $t/8n^2$. Remember though that the base reflects the fraction of the total N consumers that shop i serves in either direction. This means that to translate this area into actual dollars of transportation costs that the consumers of shop i pay we have to multiply through by N. The result is that the customers who patronize shop i from the east pay a total transportation cost of $tN/8n^2$ as do those who patronize it from the west. The total transportation costs incurred by all consumers of shop i is therefore the sum of these two amounts or $tN/4n^2$. If we now multiply this by the number of shops n, we find that the total transportation costs associated with all n shops is simply $tN/4n$. The same exercise tells us that the total set-up cost for all n shops is nF. Accordingly, the transportation plus set-up costs associated with serving all N customers and operating n shops is:

$$C(N, n) = \frac{tN}{4n} + nF \tag{7.14}$$

By the same argument, total transportation plus set-up costs with $(n + 1)$ shops are

$$C(N, n + 1) = \frac{tN}{4(n + 1)} + (n + 1)F \tag{7.15}$$

Recall that our goal is to minimize this total cost. Therefore, we will always wish to add an additional shop so long as total costs fall. Comparison of equations (7.15) and (7.14) indicates that this will be the case, i.e., $C(n + 1) < C(n)$, if:

$$\frac{tN}{4n} - \frac{tN}{4(n + 1)} > F \tag{7.16}$$

Simplification of this inequality reveals that it will be socially beneficial to add one more shop or one more product variant beyond the n existing ones so long as:

$$n(n + 1) < \frac{tN}{4F} \tag{7.17}$$

Now compare this condition with that of equation (7.12), which describes the condition under which the monopolist will wish to add an additional shop. The denominator of the right-hand-side term is $2F$ in equation (7.12) while it is $4F$ in (7.17). This means that it is less likely for an additional shop to meet the requirement of equation (7.17) and be socially desirable than it is for it to meet the requirement of equation (7.12) and enhance the monopolist's profit. In other words, the monopolist has an incentive to expand product variety even when the social gains from doing so have been exhausted. The monopolist chooses too great a degree of product variety.

Taking the same example that we had earlier in which $t = \$1$, $N = 5,000,000$, and $F = \$50,000$, we have that $tN/4F = 25$. In this case, equation (7.17) implies that the socially optimal number of shops is five. However, we have already shown that the monopolist would like to operate seven shops or offer seven product varieties in this market. In short, the monopolist offers too much product variety.

Casual evidence supports the "too much variety" hypothesis. Look at the myriad of ready-to-eat breakfast cereals offered by the major cereal firms, the multitude of options available on automobiles, and the vast array of finely distinguished perfumes and lipsticks available at department stores around the country. Admittedly, the producers of these goods are not pure monopolists but they do exercise considerable market power and so they are likely to be subject to many of the same influences that we have just been considering.

The basic reason that a monopolist offers too much variety is because the firm maximizes profit, not total surplus. When deciding to add another shop, the monopolist balances the additional set-up cost against the additional revenues that it can earn from being able to increase prices. However, from the viewpoint of efficiency this additional revenue is not a net gain. It is just a transfer of surplus from consumers to the monopolist. The true social optimum would balance the set-up cost of an extra shop against the reduction in transportation costs that results. Clearly, this criterion will lead to the establishment of fewer shops than will the criterion used by the monopolist.

Operating additional shops is attractive to the monopolist because it permits charging a high price to distant consumers. The monopolist operating just one shop at the center of Main Street could otherwise only sell to those distant consumers by offering a steep price cut that must be extended to all customers. Some variety is good. That is why the optimum in our

---

Reality Checkpoint
You Will Soon be able to Buy a Sandwich Anywhere

McDonald's has for many years been the model of a successful franchise operation. Approximately 85 percent of McDonald's outlets are operated by franchisees who have also been responsible for more than 60 percent of their annual revenues. Despite some recent problems that have led McDonald's to close more than 700 under-performing restaurants, the company still has some 30,000 outlets worldwide making it one of the largest owners of retail property in the world. There is, however, a threat looming on the horizon. An increased demand for healthier fast-food options has diverted demand to newer restaurant chains offering an alternative to the fat-rich traditional hamburger and fries. For the eleventh time in 15 years *Entrepreneur* magazine has named Subway as the number one franchise opportunity. Subway now has more than 18,000 locations in 72 countries and has more restaurants than McDonald's in the United States and Canada. Subway aims to open a further 2,000 outlets in the United States this year as well as expanding in the United Kingdom, Eastern Europe, and India.

Sources: *Financial Times*, June 4, 2003 "Healthier Options are in Demand"; "Landmark 18,000th Subway Restaurant Opens" http://www.prnewswire.com.

example is five shops. The monopolist goes beyond this point because while it reduces total surplus it grabs much more of that reduced total for the firm.[4]

Our discussion of excess variety raises another issue that takes us back to the discussion in Chapters 5 and 6. If somehow the firm could charge a price to distant consumers that they are willing to pay *without* lowering the price to nearby ones then reaching these distant consumers from just a few shops or with just a few varieties would be more attractive. That is, if the monopolist could price discriminate her tendency to oversupply variety might be much less strong. We now examine this possibility.

7.4 MONOPOLY AND HORIZONTAL DIFFERENTIATION WITH PRICE DISCRIMINATION

Our discussion so far has assumed that the monopolist does not price discriminate between its customers. This makes sense when customers travel to the shop to purchase the good and so do not reveal their addresses, or who they are to the monopolist. Suppose instead that the monopolist controls delivery of the product, and so will know who is who by their address in the market. What pricing policy might we expect the monopoly firm to adopt?

First, it should be clear that when the monopolist makes the delivery it will charge every consumer the consumer's reservation price V. This is a pricing policy known as *uniform delivered pricing*. A firm adopting such a pricing policy charges all consumers the same prices and absorbs the transportation costs in delivering the product to them. This is discriminatory pricing because even though consumers pay the same price, this price does not reflect the true costs of supplying consumers in different locations. By way of analogy, charging a consumer in San Francisco the same price as a consumer in New York for a product manufactured in New York is just as much discriminatory pricing as charging a different price for this product to two different New York residents.

As in the no-price-discrimination case, we should check whether the monopoly firm actually wants to supply every consumer. Suppose that, as before, the firm operates n retail outlets evenly spaced along Main Street. Then the transportation and production costs that the firm incurs in supplying the consumers located furthest away from a retail outlet are $c + t/2n$. There is profit to be made from such sales provided that:

$$V > c + t/2n \tag{7.18}$$

Notice that this is a weaker condition than equation (7.13) without price discrimination. This is another example of a typical property of price discrimination. It allows the monopolist to serve consumers who might otherwise be left unserved.

Now consider how many shops (or product varieties) the price-discriminating monopolist would choose to operate. Given that the firm is supplying the entire market and is charging every consumer the consumer's reservation price of V, the firm's total revenue is fixed at NV. Total costs are variable production costs, which are fixed at cN, plus the transport costs that the firm absorbs and the set-up costs nF. These two latter costs are just the costs $C(N, n)$ from equation (7.14). So the profit of the price-discriminating monopolist is:

---

[4] Spence (1976) is a classic analysis of optimal product variety.

$$\pi(N, n) = NV - cN - \left(\frac{tN}{4n} + nF\right) \tag{7.19}$$

How does the monopolist maximize profit in this case? Here, profit maximization is achieved by minimizing the costs $C(N, n)$ since total revenue and production costs are fixed. But this means that *the discriminating monopolist will choose to offer the socially efficient degree of product variety.*

If you recall our discussion of price discrimination in Chapter 5 you should not find this too surprising. We saw in that chapter that a monopolist who engages in first-degree price discrimination will extract all consumer surplus and therefore will want to produce the efficient amount of output. The result just obtained extends that finding to the case of a product differentiated market. In such a market, a firm that can achieve first-degree price discrimination will not only produce the socially efficient output but also the socially efficient amount of variety. With price discrimination the firm can reach far away customers by means of a price reduction (i.e., the firm pays a relatively high delivery charge) rather than by adding on an extra variety. Hence, the incentive to go beyond the socially optimal amount of variety does not exist.

Price discrimination in a geographic spatial model has a clear interpretation—the monopoly firm incurs the delivery cost and doing so charges different net prices for the same good. How do we interpret price discrimination in a product characteristics space rather than a geographic one? Alternatively, how can a monopolist control "delivery" of products that are differentiated by characteristics rather than by location? MacLeod, Norman, and Thisse (1988) provide the analogy:

> In the context of product differentiation, price discrimination arises when the producer begins with a "base product" and then redesigns this product to the customers' specifications. This means that the firm now produces a *band* of horizontally differentiated products . . . instead of a single product . . . Transport cost is no longer interpreted as a utility loss, but as an additional cost incurred by the firm in adapting its product to the customers' requirements . . . [So] long as product design is under the control of the producer—equivalent to the producer controlling transportation—he need not charge the full cost of design change. (1988, pp. 442–3)

Consider, for example, buying a Ford Taurus. On the one hand, you might choose one of the standard variants. Alternatively, the salesperson might persuade you into taking a different sound system, different wheels, an attractive stripe along the side that makes the car sportier, and so on. Effectively, what he is doing is making you reveal your actual "address" through the options you choose with perhaps the intention of also separating you from more of your money.

But how easy is it for firms to offer this type of product customization? After all, customization would seem to imply the sacrifice of economies of scale and so increased costs. You might be surprised to learn that it is becoming easier and less costly by the day. The ability to offer this type of product range is what distinguishes *flexible manufacturing systems*, defined as "production units capable of producing a range of discrete products with a minimum of manual intervention" (U.S. Office of Technology Assessment, 1984, p. 60). We discussed the properties of these types of manufacturing processes in Chapter 4, and they are becoming increasingly common. Companies such as Levi Strauss, Custom Shoe, Italian ceramic tile manufacturers, Ford, Mitsubishi, and Hitachi all operate flexible manufacturing systems. Any of you who regularly use web-retailers such as Amazon.com will have noticed that the initial page you see on entering the site changes over time to reflect your buying habits. You eventually have your very own, customized entry page resulting in your very own, customized prices.[5]

Henry Shortchap is the only blacksmith in the small village of Chestnut Tree. The village is comprised of 21 households evenly distributed one-tenth of a mile apart along the main street of the town. Each such household uses at most 1 unit of smithing services per month. In addition, each household incurs a there-and-back-again transport cost of $.50 for every tenth of a mile it lives from Shortchap's smithery. The reservation price of each household for such services is $10. Henry's cost of providing smithing services is $2 per unit. However, he can operate only one shop at most. Where should Henry locate his shop and what price should he charge? Suppose instead that Henry could operate a mobile smithy that allowed him to offer his services at his customers' homes. However, it would cost him $.75 there-and-back-again transport costs for every tenth of a mile he has to move his smithy. Should he switch to this mobile service?

7.5   VERTICAL PRODUCT DIFFERENTIATION

The distinguishing feature of horizontal product differentiation is that consumers do not agree on what is the preferred variety of product, and so if two different varieties are offered at the same price some consumers are likely to buy one variety and other consumers will buy the other. *Vertical differentiation* is different. In this case all consumers agree on what is the preferred or best product, the next to best product, and so on. If a high and a low quality good are offered at the same price, all consumers will buy the high quality good. Lower-quality goods will find a market only if they are offered at sufficiently lower prices. A Chevrolet costs much less than a Cadillac. No-frills airlines such as JetBlue and SouthWest attract customers because their flights are offered at large discounts relative to the larger carriers such as United and American. The Peninsula Hotel in New York charges much less than the Waldorf Astoria. However, while all consumers agree in their ranking of products from highest to lowest quality, they differ in their willingness to pay for quality. This may occur because consumers have very different incomes or simply because they have different attitudes regarding what quality is worth.

We would like to understand the incentives a monopoly firm has to offer different qualities of a product and the prices that it will charge for them. The analysis we use for this purpose is a simplified one. Nevertheless, it captures much of the flavor of more general treatments.[6]

7.5.1   Price and Quality Choice with Just One Product

We first consider how changes in quality affect consumer demand when the firm offers just one product and each consumer buys at most one unit of the good. This will give us some

---

[5]   A clear if brief expression of the view that e-commerce firms greatly facilitate price discrimination may be found in P. Krugman, "Reckonings: What Price Fairness," *New York Times*, October 4, 2000, p. A16.

[6]   The first and classic treatment of this problem is Mussa and Rosen (1978). Unfortunately, this is also a rather complex analysis.

idea of how quality or product design can be used to enhance a firm's profit. Then we will examine how the firm might increase its profit by offering more than one quality of a product. The firm knows that there is some feature, or set of features, that can be used to measure the product quality valued by consumers. The firm's ability to choose these features means that it can choose the quality of the product as well as its price.

The firm knows that each consumer is willing to pay something extra to get a higher quality product, but the precise amount extra varies across consumers. Some consumers place a high value on quality and will gladly pay a considerable premium for a quality improvement. Others are less concerned with quality and, unless the accompanying price increase is minimal, such consumers would not buy a high priced better quality good. In other words, each consumer examines the price and quality of the product and the utility she obtains from consuming it. If the consumer places a value on the quality of product offered greater than the price being charged, she purchases the good—say a CD player. If not, she simply refrains from buying altogether.

The demand curve facing the monopolist will depend on precisely what is the quality of the product being marketed. This is reflected in the inverse demand function, denoted by $P = P(Q, z)$, where the market clearing price P will depend not only on how much the firm produces Q but also on the quality z of these units. To put it somewhat differently, an increase in quality z will raise the market-clearing price for any given quantity, Q. The demand curve shifts out (or up) as product quality z increases.

It is useful to distinguish between two different ways an increase in quality can shift the inverse demand curve $P(Q, z)$. Each is illustrated in Figure 7.7. To better understand this diagram note that, since consumers vary in terms of their willingness to pay for a good of given quality z, and since each consumer buys at most one unit of the good, the demand curve really reflects a ranking of consumers in terms of their reservation price for a good of a specific quality z. The reservation price of the consumer most willing to pay for the good is the intercept term. The reservation price of the consumer next most willing to pay is the next point on the demand curve as we move to the right, and so on. In both Figures 7.7(a) and 7.7(b), the initial quantity produced is Q_1 and the initial quality is z_1. The market-clearing price for this quantity–quality combination is P_1. From what we have just said, this price must be the willingness to pay or reservation price of the Q_1th consumer. At price P_1, this consumer is just indifferent between buying the good and not buying it at all given that

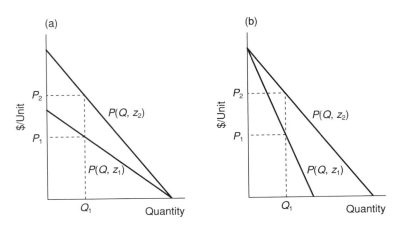

Figure 7.7 Impact of quality on demand

it is of quality z_1. This consumer is called the marginal consumer. Consumers to her left—those consumers who also buy the product—are called *infra*marginal consumers.

Figure 7.7(a) shows how the inverse demand curve shifts when there is an increase in quality that raises the willingness to pay of the inframarginal consumers by more than it raises the willingness to pay of the marginal consumer. An increase in quality from z_1 to z_2 raises the price at which the quantity Q_1 sells from P_1 to P_2. However, the increase in the reservation price is greatest for consumers who were already purchasing the product so that the demand curve shifts by "sliding along" the price axis. Figure 7.7(b) illustrates the alternative case. Here, the increase in quality from z_1 to z_2 increases the willingness to pay of the Q_1th or marginal consumer by proportionately more than it raises the reservation price of the inframarginal consumers. Once again, this quality increase will raise the market price of quantity Q_1 from P_1 to P_2. However, the demand curve now shifts by "sliding along" the quantity axis.[7]

Whether demand is described by Figure 7.7(a) or 7.7(b), we can see that for the monopolist the choice of quality really amounts to a decision as to which demand curve it will face. Increases in quality are attractive because they rotate the demand curve and so increase the firm's revenue at any given price. However, it is normally costly to increase product quality. So what the monopolist has to do is balance the benefits in increased revenue that improved quality generates against the increased costs that increased quality incurs. More precisely, the monopolist choosing quality should think through the profit-maximizing calculus in a way similar to that used when choosing output or price. For any given choice of output, the monopolist should choose the level of quality at which the marginal revenue from increasing quality equals the marginal cost of increasing quality. In other words, the monopolist who controls both quality and quantity of product has *two* profit maximizing conditions to satisfy. These are:

1. For a given choice of quality, the marginal revenue from the last unit sold should equal the marginal cost of making that unit at that quality.
2. For a given choice of quantity, the marginal revenue from increasing quality of each unit of output should equal the additional (marginal) cost of increasing the quality of that quantity of output.

Let us illustrate the quality or product design choice by assuming that demand is of the type shown in Figure 7.7(a). More specifically, let us assume that the demand function is given by the equation:

$$P = z(50 - Q) \tag{7.20}$$

Equation (7.20) says that regardless of the quality of the product, at a price of zero a total of 50 units will be sold but increased quality causes the demand function to rotate clockwise about the point $Q = 50$.

Let us also keep the example simple by assuming that the cost of improving quality is a sunk design cost so that marginal *production* cost is independent of the quality of the product. A better film or software package may require say, more expensive script or

---

[7] For models based on the case illustrated in Figure 7.7(b), some care must be taken to limit the ultimate size of the market. That is, quality increases cannot indefinitely expand the quantity demanded at a given price.

programming, respectively, but the actual costs of showing the film or printing the CD are independent of how good it is. To make matters even simpler, let us further assume that production costs are not only constant but also zero. Design costs, however, rise with the quality level chosen. Specifically, we shall assume that:

$$F(z) = 5z^2 \tag{7.21}$$

which implies that the marginal cost of increasing product quality is $10z$ (see inset). We can now write the firm's profit to be:

$$\pi(Q, z) = P(Q, z)Q - F(z) = z(50 - Q)Q - 5z^2 \tag{7.22}$$

Consider first the profit-maximizing choice of output. This turns out to be very simple in this case. As usual, marginal revenue has the same intercept as the demand function

---

Derivation Checkpoint
Optimal Choice of Output and Quality

Demand and costs are given respectively by:

$$P = z(\theta - Q) \text{ and } C(Q, z) = \alpha z^2$$

Hence the profit function is:

$$\pi(Q, z) = PQ - C(Q, z) = z(\theta - Q)Q - \alpha z^2$$

Differentiating this with respect to Q gives the first-order condition:

$$\frac{\partial \pi(Q, z)}{\partial Q} = z(\theta - 2Q) = 0$$

Solving for the optimal output $Q*$ then yields:

$$Q* = \theta/2$$

Now differentiate profit with respect to quality choice z to obtain the first-order condition:

$$\frac{\partial \pi(Q, z)}{\partial z} = (\theta - Q)Q - 2\alpha z = 0$$

Substitution of $Q*$ for Q in this last equation then implies:

$$2\alpha z = \theta^2/4$$

Solving this last expression for the optimal quality $z*$, then yields:

$$z* = \theta^2/8\alpha$$

In the text example, $\theta = 50$ and $\alpha = 5$. Hence, $Q* = 25$ and $z* = 62.5$.

but twice the slope. So with the demand function $P = 50z - zQ$ we know that marginal revenue is $MR = 50z - 2zQ = z(50 - 2Q)$. Equating this with marginal cost gives the profit-maximizing output condition: $z(50 - 2Q) = 0$. Hence, the profit-maximizing output is: $Q^* = 50/2 = 25$.

In this simple example the monopolist's choice regarding the quantity is independent of the choice of quality. The profit-maximizing output remains constant at $Q^* = 25$ no matter the choice of quality. Going back to the demand function, the profit-maximizing price is given by $P^* = z(50 - Q^*)$ so that the optimal price is: $P^* = 50z/2$. Unlike output, the profit-maximizing price is affected by the choice of quality. Moreover, the quality choice will also affect the firm's design costs. A higher quality design z permits the monopolist to raise price and earn more revenue but it also raises the firm's costs. This is the tradeoff that the monopolist must evaluate.

To choose the profit-maximizing quality the monopolist must compare the additional revenue resulting from an increase in z with the increase in design cost that the higher quality requires. Because the quantity sold is constant at $Q^* = 25$, the additional revenue of an increase in quality is just this output level times the difference in price that can be charged following the rise in quality. In our example, we can see from equation (7.20) that the firm's revenue PQ at product quality z when it charges the profit-maximizing price $P^* = 50z/2$, is:

$$P^*Q^* = \frac{50z}{2} \cdot \frac{50}{2} = \frac{2,500}{4} z = 625z \tag{7.23}$$

Increasing product quality by one "unit" increases revenue by $625, which is therefore the marginal revenue from increased quality. We know also from equation (7.21) that the marginal cost of increased quality is $10z$. Equating marginal revenue with marginal cost then gives the profit-maximizing quality choice:

$$z^* = 625/10 = 62.5 \tag{7.24}$$

An interesting question that arises in connection with the monopoly firm's choice of quality is how that choice compares with the socially optimal one. Does the monopolist produce too high or too low a quality of good? Looking at Figure 7.7(a) you might be able to work out that in this case the monopolist's quality choice will be too low. The reason is straightforward. An increase in z rotates the demand curve upward and increases the total surplus earned from the 25 units that are always sold. The social optimum requires that quality be increased so long as this gain in the total surplus exceeds the extra design cost. However, the monopolist only gets to keep the increase in producer surplus that a quality increase generates. As a result, profit maximization will lead the monopoly firm to increase quality only so long as the extra producer surplus covers the additional design cost. Since the producer surplus is less than the total surplus, the monopolist will stop short of producing the socially optimal quality. Of course, the monopolist holds quantity below the optimal amount, too.[8]

Our primary objective is not to determine whether firms with monopoly power choose to market products of either too low or too much quality. The main point is to show that for such firms the quality choice matters. By carefully choosing product quality jointly with product price, the monopolist can again extract further surplus from the market.

---

[8] Our results regarding the monopolist's quality choice might have been different had we instead assumed that quality affects demand as in Figure 7.7(b).

7.2

Will Barret is the only lawyer in the small country town of Percyville. The weekly demand for his legal services depends on the quality of service he provides as reflected by his inverse demand curve: $P = 4 - Q/z$. Here, P is the price per case; Q is the number of cases or clients; and z is the quality of service Will provides. Will's costs are independent of how many cases he actually takes. But they do rise with quality. More specifically, Will's costs are given by: $C = z^2$.

a.   Draw Will's demand curve for a given quality, z. How do increases in z affect the demand curve?

b.   Consider the three options: $z = 1$, $z = 2$, and $z = 3$. Derive the profit-maximizing output for each of these choices.

c.   Compute the market price and profit—net of quality costs—for each of the three choices above. Which quality choice leads to the highest profits?

Reality Checkpoint

Room Service? We'd Like a Baby and a Bottle of Your Best Champagne!

Although hospitals are always under pressure to rein in costs, they are also always on the lookout for ways to raise quality—at least for those who are willing to pay for it. Nowhere is this more apparent than in the recent splurge in spending on deluxe maternity wards. Moms-to-be who are willing to pay a little more can get private suites, whirlpool baths, Internet access, and top culinary food. For an extra fee, St. Vincent's Hospital in Indianapolis throws in a massage and the services of a professional photographer. Robert Wood Johnson Hospital in New Jersey allows patients to order from a restaurant-style menu and serves a "high tea" daily at 3:00 p.m. Offering such services is part of trend that started some years ago as a means to attract customers, especially wealthy ones. Matilda Hospital in Hong Kong is one of a number of hospitals that particularly courts those interested in a luxury hospital stay. Their three-day maternity package includes four-star cuisine meal service with champagne while staying in a beautiful private room with molding-trimmed high ceilings, cherry finished wood floors, and balcony that overlooks the sea far down below. Talk about vertical differentiation!

Sources: J. Barshay, "Luxury Rooms Are Latest Fads for Private Hospitals in Asia," *Wall Street Journal*, January 26, 2001, p. A1; and P. Davies, "Hospitals Build Deluxe Wings for New Moms," *Wall Street Journal*, February 8, 2005.

7.5.2   Offering More Than One Product in a Vertically Differentiated Market

Now that we have worked through the basics of how product quality can affect market demand, let's consider a multi-product strategy. To make it simple, suppose the monopolist knows there are only two types of consumers, distinguished by their willingness to pay for quality. Each consumer type buys at most one unit of the firm's product per period. In deciding which quality of product to buy the consumer buys the quality of product yielding the greatest consumer surplus. For consumer type i the indirect utility obtained from consuming a product of quality z at price p is:

$$V_i = \theta_i(z - \underline{z}_i) - p \qquad (i = 1, 2) \tag{7.25}$$

In this equation θ_i is a measure of the value that consumers type i place on quality and $\underline{z}_i$ is the lower bound on quality below which a consumer type i would not buy a product. We assume that $\theta_1 > \theta_2$. That is, type 1 consumers place a higher value on quality than type 2 consumers, perhaps because type 1 consumers have higher incomes than type 2 consumers or more generally because they have more intense preferences for quality. We also assume that $\underline{z}_1 > \underline{z}_2 = 0$. In other words, type 1 consumers will not buy the monopolist's product unless it is at least of quality $\underline{z}_1$. These are consumers who "wouldn't be seen dead" flying in coach, eating in fast-food outlets or shopping in discount stores. By contrast, type 2 consumers are willing to buy the monopolist's product of any quality provided, of course, that consumer surplus is non-negative.

Unfortunately for the firm, while it knows that these different consumer types exist it has no objective measure by which it can distinguish the different types. Similar to second-degree price discrimination, the monopolist would like to choose a product line that makes the consumers reveal their true types. The monopolist would like to induce type 1 consumers to buy a product of high quality z_1 at a high price while simultaneously inducing type 2 consumers to purchase a product of low quality z_2 at a lower price. As in second-degree price discrimination, the type 2 consumers will be charged a price that is equal to their willingness to pay for the low quality product.

Suppose that the firm is able to produce any quality in the quality range $[\underline{z}, \bar{z}]$. For simplicity we also assume that the marginal costs of production are constant and identical across all qualities of product and are equal to zero.[9] Finally, we make the following important assumption (we explain why below):

Assumption 1: $\bar{z} > \dfrac{\theta_1 \underline{z}_1}{(\theta_1 - \theta_2)}$.

Note that Assumption 1 is most easily satisfied when the difference between θ_1 and θ_2 is relatively large.

Let's look first at a consumer of type 2, the one with a low willingness to pay for quality. What the firm will do is charge this consumer a price that is just low enough for her to be willing to purchase the low quality product. From equation (7.25), and given that $\underline{z}_2 = 0$, consumer type 2 will buy z_2 if:

$$p_2 = \theta_2 z_2 \tag{7.26}$$

Now consider a consumer of type 1 with a stronger preference for quality. This consumer can, of course, buy the low quality product. So, in pricing the high quality product the firm faces the same type of *incentive compatibility constraint* that we met when discussing second-degree price discrimination. (There is also the incentive compatibility constraint, of course,

---

[9] It might be, for example, that the majority of the firm's costs are set-up costs and that crimping higher quality products makes lower quality products. Relaxing this assumption doesn't change much. Having it makes the analysis a bit easier.

that the type 2 consumers do, indeed, buy the low rather than the high quality product. We return to this below.) For a type 1 consumer to buy the high quality product it is necessary that:

$$\theta_1(z_1 - \underline{z}_1) - p_1 \geq \theta_1(z_2 - \underline{z}_1) - p_2$$
$$\theta_1(z_1 - \underline{z}_1) - p_1 \geq 0 \qquad\qquad (7.27)$$

The expressions in equation (7.27) say that the consumer surplus that a type 1 consumer obtains from buying the high quality product must be non-negative and greater than or equal to the consumer surplus that could be obtained if the type 1 consumer bought the low quality good. Substituting $p_2 = \theta_2 z_2$ from equation (7.26) into the first expression in equation (7.27) we find that:

$$p_1 \leq \theta_1 z_1 - (\theta_1 - \theta_2)z_2 \qquad\qquad (7.28)$$

Equation (7.28) says that the maximum price p_1 that can be charged for the high quality product is $p_1 = \theta_1 z_1 - (\theta_1 - \theta_2)z_2$. The price is greater the higher are the values θ_1 and θ_2 that the two types of consumers place on quality, and the higher is the quality differential between z_1 and z_2. That is, quality can be priced more highly when it is valued more highly by all consumers. And because by offering two products of different qualities the monopolist is effectively competing with itself, increasing the quality differential between the products, the monopolist raises profit by making the two goods more differentiated. The monopolist thereby weakens the competition between products and allows the firm to increase the price of its high quality product. Note that when $p_1 = \theta_1 z_1 - (\theta_1 - \theta_2)z_2$ the condition that consumers of type 1 receive non-negative surplus when they buy the high quality good can now be written as $\theta_1(z_1 - \underline{z}_1) - p_1 \geq 0 \Rightarrow (\theta_1 - \theta_2)z_2 - \theta_1 \underline{z}_1 \geq 0$. This explains why we need Assumption 1 $\bar{z} > \dfrac{\theta_1 \underline{z}_1}{(\theta_1 - \theta_2)}$. Given that this assumption holds, the condition that type 1 consumers have non-negative surplus can always be satisfied by some $z_2 \leq \bar{z}$.

It is easy to check that the incentive compatibility constraint is always satisfied for type 2 consumers. For this type of consumer *not* to want to buy the high quality product it must be the case that $\theta_2 z_1 - p_1 < 0$ which given that $p_1 = \theta_1 z_1 - (\theta_1 - \theta_2)z_2$ implies $-(\theta_1 - \theta_2)z_1 + (\theta_1 - \theta_2)z_2 < 0$. Since $z_1 > z_2$ and $\theta_1 > \theta_2$ this must be true. In other words, the prices given by equations (7.26) and (7.28) guarantee that type 1 consumers buy the high quality product and type 2 consumers buy the low quality product.

Now assume that there are N_i consumers of each type. Furthermore, suppose that variable costs of production do not depend on quality and so for simplicity we set the unit production costs of each good $c_1 = c_2 = 0$. Again for simplicity assume that there are no fixed costs as well. Given that $p_1 = \theta_1 z_1 - (\theta_1 - \theta_2)z_2$ and $p_2 = \theta_2 z_2$ the firm's total profit is:

$$\Pi = N_1 p_1 + N_2 p_2 = N_1 \theta_1 z_1 - (N_1 \theta_1 - (N_1 + N_2)\theta_2)z_2 \qquad\qquad (7.29)$$

The issue that we want to address now is what quality of goods, z_1 and z_2, will maximize the firm's profit.

In this respect, it is clear from equation (7.29) that the coefficient on z_1 is positive and, given by $N_1 \theta_1$. That is, profit rises as z_1 rises. As a result, the firm should set z_1 as high as possible; that is:

$$z_1^* = \bar{z} \qquad\qquad (7.30)$$

The firm should set the quality of its highest quality product at the maximum quality level possible.

For z_2 matters are not quite as straightforward. Equation (7.29) tells us that the impact of z_2 upon the monopolist's profit depends upon the sign of the coefficient, $N_1\theta_1 - (N_1 + N_2)\theta_2$. When this term is positive, the monopolist's profit decreases as z_2 increases. When it is negative profit increases as z_2 increases. We need to examine these two cases separately.

Case 1: $N_1\theta_1 > (N_1 + N_2)\theta_2$

From equation (7.29) it is clear that in this case profit is decreasing in z_2 and so the firm has an incentive to offer two qualities that are as differentiated as possible. The firm will choose $z_1^* = \bar{z}$, and set z_2 as low as is feasible. This does not mean, however, that z_2 can be reduced to its minimum of $\underline{z}$. Remember that we must also satisfy the constraint that type 1 consumers receive non-negative consumer surplus from buying the high quality good $\bar{z}$. That is,

$$\theta_1(z_1 - \underline{z}_1) - p_1 \geq 0 \Rightarrow (\theta_1 - \theta_2)z_2 - \theta_1\underline{z}_1 \geq 0 \Rightarrow z_2 \geq \frac{\theta_1\underline{z}_1}{\theta_1 - \theta_2}.$$ It follows that the monopolist will choose:

$$z_2^* = \frac{\theta_1\underline{z}_1}{\theta_1 - \theta_2} \tag{7.31}$$

It is here that we see the impact of the assumption that the monopolist cannot distinguish the two consumer types. The monopolist would like to set z_2 even lower than implied by equation (7.31) but cannot do so if she is to offer products that make the consumers self-select into their true types.

We can now work out the profit-maximizing prices for the two goods. Substituting equation (7.31) in (7.26) we find $p_2^* = \frac{\theta_2\theta_1\underline{z}_1}{\theta_1 - \theta_2}$. Similarly substituting equation (7.31) and $z_1^* = \bar{z}$ into $p_1 = \theta_1 z_1 - (\theta_1 - \theta_2)z_2$, we find that $p_1 = \theta_1(\bar{z} - \underline{z}_1)$. In other words, type 1 consumers are charged their maximum willingness to pay for the highest quality possible, $\bar{z}$, and type 2 consumers are charged their maximum willingness to pay for the lower quality $\frac{\theta_1\underline{z}_1}{\theta_1 - \theta_2}$.

Aggregate profit is:

$$\Pi = N_1(\bar{z} - \underline{z}_1)\theta_1 + N_2\frac{\theta_2\theta_1\underline{z}_1}{\theta_1 - \theta_2} \tag{7.32}$$

Case 2: $N_1\theta_1 < (N_1 + N_2)\theta_2$

If $N_1\theta_1 < (N_1 + N_2)\theta_2$ then it follows from equation (7.29) that profit is increasing in z_2. In this case the firm should set $z_2^* = z_1^* = \bar{z}$. In other words, the firm should offer only one product and that product should be of the highest possible quality.

It is, perhaps, easier to see the intuition behind this result by rewriting the inequality $N_1\theta_1 < (N_1 + N_2)\theta_2$ as

$$\frac{N_1}{N_1 + N_2} < \frac{\theta_2}{\theta_1} < 1 \tag{7.33}$$

Thus, what we are saying is that if there are not too many type 1 consumers, those who really like quality, or if their willingness to pay for quality is very high relative to that of type 2 consumers, then the firm should only offer one type of good. The intuition is that whenever the monopolist offers two products, the low quality product tends to cannibalize sales from the high quality product.

To be precise, we can see from equation (7.28) that offering both a high quality and a low quality product costs the firm $(\theta_1 - \theta_2)z_2$ in forgone revenue from each type 1 consumer. Accordingly, when there are a lot of type 1 consumers and/or when the difference between θ_1 and θ_2 is large, the firm will want to minimize this cost by offering a second good that is very low in quality so that it does not compete too vigorously with the high quality product. On the other hand, when there are roughly equal numbers of consumers of the two types and/or when preferences do not differ greatly across different consumer types the monopolist should offer a single high quality good.

There remains the question of whether the firm in this case should price the high quality product to sell to both types of consumer or price it to sell only to type 1 consumers.

Selling to both types of consumer requires that the product be priced low at $p = \theta_1 \bar{z}$. Assumption 1 then ensures that both consumer types receive non-negative surplus from purchasing the high quality good $\bar{z}$. The firm earns a total profit of $(N_1 + N_2)\theta_2 \bar{z}$. On the other hand, selling the high quality good $\bar{z}$ to only type 1 consumers means that the product can be priced at $\theta_1(\bar{z}_1 - z_1)$ giving the firm a total profit of $N_1\theta_1(\bar{z}_1 - z_1)$. Comparing these two profit levels reveals that selling to both types of consumer is more profitable if:

$$N_1\theta_1(\bar{z} - z_1) < (N_1 + N_2)\theta_2\bar{z} \Rightarrow N_1\theta_1 < (N_1 + N_2)\theta_2 \frac{\bar{z}}{(\bar{z} - z_1)} \tag{7.34}$$

A close look at equation (7.34) reveals that for this second case in which we have assumed that $N_1\theta_1 < (N_1 + N_2)\theta_2$ the condition in the equation must hold true. Therefore, the monopolist has an incentive in this case to price the product to sell to both consumer types.[10]

7.3

General Foods is a monopolist and knows that its market for Bran Flakes contains two types of consumers. Type A consumers have indirect utility functions $V_a = 20(z - z_1)$ while type B consumers have indirect utility functions $V_b = 10z$. In each case z is a measure of product quality, which can be chosen from the interval [0,2]. There are N consumers in the market, of which General Foods knows that a fraction η is of type A and the remainder is of type B. Assume marginal cost is $C = 0$.

a. Suppose that General Foods can tell the different consumer types apart and so can charge them different prices for the same quality of breakfast cereal. What is the profit maximizing strategy for General Foods?

Now suppose that General Foods does not know which type of consumer is which.

b. Show how its profit maximizing strategy is determined by η.
c. What is the profit maximizing strategy when $z_1 = 0$?

---

[10] Unlike the result in section 7.5.1, the monopolist here chooses the highest quality because there is no cost to increasing z.

7.6   EMPIRICAL APPLICATION
Price Discrimination, Product Variety, and Monopoly versus Competition

We have set our discussion of price discrimination and product variety over the last few chapters in the framework of a monopolized market. Nevertheless the strategies that we have described such as tying and quantity discounts are often practiced by firms that are far from a perfect monopoly. Competitive pressure and price discrimination often go hand-in-hand for at least two reasons. We will show formally in Chapter 14 that when rival firms practice price discrimination it tends to intensify the price competition between them. Moreover, imperfectly competitive firms also have an incentive to pursue discriminatory pricing strategies, as Borenstein (1985) was one of the first to emphasize.

Consider our two-store model from section 7.2. Let us now modify that example in a couple of significant ways. First, we will assume that while consumers have specific locations, they do not have transport costs, i.e., $t = 0$. Second, we will assume that there are two types of consumers both of which number N in total. For each group, the maximum willingness to pay is V. The difference is that the first type of consumers always shops at the store that is closest, no matter what the price at the alternative store. The second group is just the opposite. These consumers always shop wherever the price is lowest.

A little economic reasoning should convince you that a monopolist serving this market will set a price of V and serve all the $2N$ customers, half at each store. Clearly the price cannot be higher than this or no customer will buy the product. However, there is no need to reduce the price. The first set of consumers will not consider the price at any location other than the closest. The second group will consider alternative prices but, since the price is V at each spot, this group also splits evenly between the two stores. The monopolist would then make a total profit of $2(V - c)N$ divided evenly between the two stores. No amount of price discrimination can increase this value.

Now consider what would happen if the two stores were instead owned by two different firms, firm 1 and firm 2. If there were just the first type of consumers who are totally brand loyal to the nearest store, then each of these firms could again charge a price of V. Imagine that they are doing this. Now consider the second group of consumers who always shop where the price is cheapest. At the current price V, these consumers would also be split evenly between the two shops. Each firm would then earn a profit of $(V - c)N$ just as did each of the monopolist's two stores. However, this outcome cannot be an equilibrium. A slight cut in firm 1's price would lose very little profit from its existing customers. Yet because its price would now be less than firm 2's price, it would gain all of the $N/2$ consumers currently at firm 2 who always shop where the price is lowest. Of course, if firm 1 cuts its price, firm 2 will respond with price cut, too. Unfortunately, this brings the price down to all consumers, including the brand loyal ones who do not care about the price. Indeed, at any common price $p_1 = p_2 > c$, each firm will have a strong incentive to cut price to attract the $N/2$ price-sensitive consumer currently shopping at the rival's store. The result will be that prices are driven very close to the marginal cost c and each store's profit will be very low. In such a setting, we can easily see the incentives that each firm has to implement price discriminatory policies that permit it to cut the price to price-sensitive consumers while still charging V or at least a high price to the brand loyal ones.

The foregoing simple example provides the basic intuition as to why we might observe price discrimination in more price competitive markets. Price discrimination permits competing actively for those consumers who perceive alternatives to the firm's product while still charging a high price to those that do not. If there was only one other brand only a few customers might be tempted to try it. As more brands are available, however, more of the firm's customers are likely to consider an alternative product. Being able to fight for these customers without lowering the price to the cadre of brand loyal buyers then becomes all the more valuable.

The foregoing insight lies at the heart of the paper by Stavins (2001), which examines the influence of competition on the use of discriminatory pricing in the airline industry. For this purpose, she looked at price and other information for 5,804 tickets over 12 different routes on a specific Thursday in September, 1995. Selecting a single day is useful because it eliminates any price differentials due to flying on other days of the week, especially weekend days. A September choice also avoids both peak summer and winter demand periods. The key characteristics that Stavins (2001) looks at are: 1) whether a Saturday night stay-over was required; and 2) whether a 14-day advance purchase was required.

As discussed in Chapter 5, each of these restrictions serves as a means for airlines to identify and separate customers based on how they value their time and their need for flexibility. Prices for tickets requiring a Saturday night stay over or that had to be purchased 14 days prior to departure should sell for less than other tickets. The hypothesis to be tested is that the price discount on these restricted tickets gets bigger the more competition there is on the route. Stavins (2001) constructs a Herfindahl–Hirschman Index (*HHI*) for each route to serve as a rough measure of that market's competitive pressure.

To test this hypothesis, Stavins (2001) runs two sets of regressions. The first of these serves to confirm that ticket restrictions do indeed translate into discriminatory price differentials. It takes the basic form:

$$p_{ijk} = \beta_0 + \beta_1 R_{ijk} + \beta_2 HHI_i + \beta_3 S_{ij} + \beta_4 First_{ijk} + \beta_5 Days_{ijk} + \beta_6 Z_i + \varepsilon_{ijk} \tag{7.35}$$

Here, p_{ijk} is the (log of) the price of the kth ticket sold by airline j in city-pair market i. R_{ijk} is a dummy variable equal to 1 if there was a restriction on the flight (Saturday night stay-over or pre-purchase requirement) and 0 otherwise. HHI_i is the Herfindahl–Hirschman Index for the ith market. S_{ij} is the market share of airline j in market i. $First_{ijk}$ is a dummy variable equal to 1 if the ticket was for first-class fare and 0 otherwise. $Days_{ijk}$ is the number of days prior to departure that the fare for that ticket was last offered. Z_i is a vector of other market i characteristics such as average income and population. The error term ε_{ijk} is assumed to be normally distributed with a mean of 0.

If ticket restrictions serve as a means of implementing price discrimination then the coefficient β_1 on R_{ijk} should be negative. This would imply that passengers flying the same flight on the same airline paid lower prices if they accepted a requirement that they stay over Saturday night or that they purchase the ticket in advance.

However, simply finding that β_1 is negative only shows that price discrimination occurs. It does not tell us if there is any connection between the extent of such discrimination and the degree of competition in the market. To test this hypothesis, Stavins (2001) runs regressions of the basic form:

$$p_{ijk} = \beta_0 + \beta_1 R_{ijk} + \beta_2 HHI_i + \beta_3 (HHI_i \times R_{ijk}) + \beta_4 S_{ij} + \beta_5 First_{ijk} + \beta_6 Days_{ijk} + \beta_7 Z_i + \varepsilon_{ijk} \tag{7.36}$$

This is exactly the same as the previous regression except that it now includes the interactive term ($HHI_i \times R_{ijk}$), the product of the concentration index and the restricted travel

Table 7.1   Ticket restrictions and air fares

Variable	Coefficient	t-Statistic	Coefficient	t-Statistic	Coefficient	t-Statistic	Coefficient	t-Statistic
Saturday night stay-over required	−0.249	−2.50	—	—	−0.408	−4.05	—	—
Saturday night stay-over × HHI	—	—	—	—	0.792	3.39	—	—
Advance purchase requirement	—	—	−0.007	−2.16	—	—	−0.023	−5.53
Advance purchase requirement × HHI	—	—	—	—	—	—	0.098	8.38

variables. If the coefficient on this term is positive, it says that the discount associated with, say, a Saturday night stay-over requirement declines as the level of concentration rises. Stavins' (2001) results are shown in Table 7.1.

The first four columns indicate that passengers do indeed pay different prices depending on the restrictions applied to their tickets. These effects are both statistically significant and economically substantial. For example, passengers who accepted the requirement that they not return until after Saturday night paid 25 percent less on average than those who did not accept this restriction even though they were otherwise getting the same flight service.

However, the real issue is how these discounts vary as the extent of competition in the market as measured by *HHI* varies. This is where the next four columns become relevant as they show what happens when the term interacting competition or concentration and ticket restrictions is included. In both cases, the estimated coefficient on the interaction term is positive. This indicates that while ticket restrictions still lead to price reductions, this effect diminishes as the airline route becomes less competitive or has high concentration.

Given the range of *HHI* values observed over the 12 routes Stavins (2001) studies, she estimates that in the most competitive markets, a Saturday night stay-over requirement led to a price reduction of about $253, whereas in the least competitive ones the same restriction led to a price reduction of only $165. Likewise, an advance purchase requirement was associated with a price reduction of $111 in the most competitive markets but a cut of only $41 in the least competitive markets.

Summary

This chapter has investigated product-differentiated strategies that a monopolist may use when it sells to consumers with diverse tastes. By offering a line of products the firm can better appropriate consumer surplus and increase profit. First we considered horizontal product differentiation. In this scenario, consumers differ in their preferences for specific product characteristics. Some prefer yellow, some black, some soft, some hard, some sweet and some sour. By selling different varieties of the product, the monopolist expands its market and simultaneously enhances its ability to charge customers higher prices in return for selling a variety of product that is close to their most preferred flavor, color, or design.

A feature of this kind of market is that the monopolist tends to offer too much variety—a prediction for which there is a good bit of supportive casual evidence. However, the monopolist's incentive to over-supply variety is mitigated if the firm is able to price discriminate. Indeed, perfect or first-degree price discrimination encourages the firm to offer consumers the socially optimal product variety.

We also investigated the monopolist's strategy when products are vertically differentiated. In this case, all consumers agree that more quality is better, where quality is measured by some feature, or set of features of the product. Consumers, however, differ in their willingness to pay for quality. In the case where the monopolist offers only one type of product and quality is costly we found that the monopolist may choose too low a quality. The monopolist may also have an incentive in the vertically differentiated case to offer a range of different qualities in order to exploit the differences in consumers' preferences. In doing so, however, the firm faces an incentive compatibility constraint and must choose quality and price such that the different types of consumer will purchase the

quality targeted to their type. These incentive compatibility constraints are similar to those that affect second-degree price discrimination schemes, as discussed in the previous chapter.

Finally, while we have cast our theoretical discussion mainly in the context of monopoly, the practices we have described are often employed by firms that are far from a perfect monopolist without any significant rivals. This reflects the fact that imperfectly competitive firms often have a very powerful incentive to price discriminate as well. Such discrimination permits them to compete fiercely for price-sensitive consumers who are not brand loyal and who may easily choose an alternative brand while maintaining a high price to those less likely to buy from a competitor. Stavins (2001) offers empirical evidence of this phenomenon in the airline industry.

Problems

1. A monopolist faces the following inverse demand curve: $P = (36 - 2Q)z$; where P is price; Q is her total output; and z is the quality of product she sells. Quality z can take on only one of two values. The monopolist can choose to market a low quality product for which $z = 1$. Alternatively, she can choose to market a high quality product for which $z = 2$. Marginal cost is independent of quality and is constant at zero. Fixed cost, however, depends on the product design and increases with the quality chosen. Specifically, fixed cost is equal to $65z^2$.

    a. Find the monopolist's profits if she maximizes profits *and* chooses a low quality design.

    b. Find the monopolist's profits when she maximizes profits *and* chooses a high quality design.

    c. Comparing your answers to 1a and 1b, what quality choice should the monopolist make?

2. In the early 1970s, the six largest manufacturers of ready-to-eat breakfast cereals shared 95 percent of the market. Over the preceding 20 years, these same manufacturers introduced over 80 new varieties of cereals. How would you evaluate this strategy from the viewpoint of the Hotelling spatial model described earlier in the chapter?

3. Crepe Creations is considering franchising its unique brand of crepes to stall-holders on Hermoza Beach, which is five miles long. CC estimates that on an average day there are 1,000 sunbathers evenly spread along the beach and that each sunbather will buy one crepe per day provided that the price plus any disutility cost does not exceed $5. Each sunbather incurs a disutility cost of getting up from resting to get a crepe and returning to their beach spot of 25 cents for every $^1/_4$ mile the sunbather has to walk to get to the CC stall. Each crepe costs $0.50 to make and CC incurs a $40 overhead cost per day to operate a stall. How many franchises should CC award given that it determines the prices the stall-holders can charge and that it will have a profit-sharing royalty scheme with the stall-holders? What will be the price of a crepe at each stall?

4. Return to problem 3 above. Suppose now that CC requires that each stall-holder deliver the crepes in its own designated territory. How many franchises should now be awarded, if we make the standard assumption that the effort costs of the stall-holders are the same as those of the sunbathers? How would your answer change if the stall-holders instead incurred effort costs half as much as those of the sunbathers, i.e., if their costs were 12.5 cents for every $^1/_4$ mile of distance?

5. Imagine that Dell is considering two versions of a new laptop. One version will meet high performance standards. The other will only meet medium performance standards. To make the second, Dell uses cheaper materials and then crimps the keyboard of the high performance machine with the result that the marginal cost of each product is an identical $500. There are two types of consumers for the new laptop. "Techies" have the (indirect) utility function $V_t = 2000(z - 1)$. "Norms" have the (indirect) utility function: $V_n = 1000z$, where z is a measure of product quality. Dell can choose the quality level z for each machine from the interval $(1,3)$, subject only to the restriction that the medium performance machine has a lower z quality than the high performance machine. If Dell knows that there are N_t Techies and N_n Norms and if Dell also can identify which type any consumer is, what is its optimum price and product quality strategy?

6. Return to problem 5, above. Assume now that Dell cannot identify each customer but only knows the number of each type. Show that Dell's profit-maximizing strategy is determined by the relative numbers of each type.

7. A monopolist faces an inverse demand curve given by: $P = 22 - Q/100z$, where z is an index of quality. The monopolist incurs a cost per unit of: $c = 2 + z^2$.

    a. How do increases in product quality z affect demand?

    b. Imagine that the firm must choose one of three quality levels: $z = 1$; $z = 2$; and $z = 3$. Which quality choice will maximize the firm's profit? What profit-maximizing output and price are associated with this profit-maximizing quality level?

8. Return to problem 7, above. What is the quality choice that will maximize the social welfare? If the monopolist were constrained to produce this socially optimal quality, what price would she charge?

References

Borenstein, S. 1985. "Price Discrimination in Free-entry Markets." *Rand Journal Economics* 16 (Autumn): 380–97.

Hotelling, H. 1929. "Stability in Competition." *Economic Journal* 39 (January): 41–57.

Macleod, W. B., G. Norman, and J. F. Thisse. 1988. "Price Discrimination and Equilibrium in Monopolistic Competition." *International Journal of Industrial Organization* 6 (December): 429–46.

Mussa, M. and S. Rosen. 1978. "Monopoly and Product Quality." *Journal of Economic Theory* 18: 301–17.

Shapiro, C. and H. R. Varian. 1999. *Information Rules*. Boston: Harvard Business School Press.

Stavins, J. 2001. "Price Discrimination in the Airline Market: The Effect of Market Concentration." *Review of Economics and Statistics* 83 (February): 200–2.

Spence, A. M. 1976. "Product Differentiation and Welfare." *American Economic Review* 66 (June): 407–14.

Appendix A

Location Choice with Two Shops

We assume in this case that the shops have identical costs. Therefore, the monopolist locates them symmetrically, some distance d from each end of the market.

1. $d \leq 1/4$: Suppose that d is less than $1/4$. Then the maximum full price that can be charged if all consumers are to be served is determined by the consumers at the market center.

These consumers can be charged a price p such that when transport costs are included, they pay a full price equal to their reservation price V. In other words, since a consumer located at $x = 1/2$ dictates the highest price that can be charged for any value $d \leq 1/4$, the maximum price the firm can charge and still serve all consumers is:

$$p(d) + t\left(\frac{1}{2} - d\right) = V \quad \Rightarrow \quad p(d) = V - t\left(\frac{1}{2} - d\right) \tag{7.10A1}$$

Aggregate profit at this price is also a function of d and is given by:

$$\pi(d) = [p(d) - c]N = \left(V + td - \frac{t}{2} - c\right)N \tag{7.10A2}$$

This profit increases as d gets larger. Thus, if d is less than 1/4, the firm can increase its profit by making d larger until $d = 1/4$. Hence, d should never be less than 1/4.

2. $d > 1/4$. Suppose now that d is greater than 1/4. Then the maximum price that can be charged if all consumers are to be served is determined by consumers at the endpoints of the market. They will pay a full price equal to their reservation price, so that the maximum price the monopolist can charge is now determined by

$$p(d) + td = V \quad \Rightarrow \quad p(d) = V - td \tag{7.10A3}$$

Aggregate profit is now

$$\pi(d) = [p(d) - c]N = (V - td - c)N \tag{7.10A4}$$

This is decreasing in d. If d is greater than 1/4, then the firm can raise profit by making d smaller until $d = 1/4$. Hence, d should never exceed 1/4. Since we have already shown that d should also never be less than 1/4, it follows that profit maximization implies that $d = 1/4$ exactly. The shops should be located symmetrically 1/4 of the total length from each market endpoint. In this way, no consumer will ever travel more than 1/4 of that length to reach a store.

Appendix B

The Monopolist's Choice of Price When Her Shops Have Different Costs

Assume that shop 1 has marginal cost c_1 and shop 2 has marginal cost c_2. Once again, we have to distinguish between the case in which the monopolist chooses to supply only part of the market and the case in which she chooses to supply the entire market.

1.   Supply only part of the market

Consider shop 1. At a price p_1 this shop will supply a fraction x_1 of the market, where x_1 is given by $p_1 + tx_1 = V$, which implies $x_1 = (V - p_1)/t$. Profit to this shop is then

$$\pi_1 = (p_1 - c_1)x_1N = (p_1 - c_1)(V - p_1)N/t \tag{7.11B1}$$

Differentiating with respect to p_1 gives the first-order condition

$$(V - 2p_1 + c_1)N/t = 0 \tag{7.11B2}$$

The profit-maximizing price for shop 1 is therefore

$$p_1^* = (V + c_1)/2 \tag{7.11B3}$$

It follows immediately that the profit-maximizing price for shop 2 is

$$p_2^* = (V + c_2)/2 \tag{7.11B4}$$

2.   Supply the entire market

Consider the marginal consumer—the consumer who is indifferent between buying from shop 1 and shop 2. If the entire market is to be served, then this marginal consumer will be charged a full price just equal to his reservation price. If prices are set any lower, profits can always be increased by increasing the price at both shops since there will be no loss of sales. So we know that if the marginal consumer is distance x' from shop 1, $p_1 + tx' = V$, which implies that $x' = (V - p_1)/t$. Also, $p_2 + t(1 - x') = V$. Substituting for x' gives

$$p_2 = V - t(1 - x') = V = t[1 - (V - p_1)/t - 2V - t - p_1] \tag{7.11B5}$$

In other words, the prices at the two shops are connected. Increasing the price at shop 1 requires that the price at shop 2 be reduced if the entire market is to be served and the price charged to the marginal consumer is to be as high as possible.

Profit to the monopolist is

$$\pi = (p_1 - c_1)x'N + (p_2 - c_2)(1 - x')N \tag{7.11B6}$$

Substituting for x' and p_2 gives

$$\pi(p_1) = N\left[(p_1 - c_1)\frac{(V - p_1)}{t} + (2V - p_1 - t - c_2)\left(1 - \frac{(V - p_1)}{t}\right)\right] \tag{7.11B7}$$

Since the monopolist must coordinate the prices at the two shops, profits are fully determined by the price at shop 1. Differentiating profit with respect to p_1 gives

$$\frac{\partial \pi}{\partial p_1} = N\left[\frac{1}{t}(V - 2p_1 + c_1) - \left(1 - \frac{V - p_1}{t}\right) + \frac{1}{t}(2V - p_1 - t - c_2)\right] \tag{7.11B8}$$

Collecting terms gives the first-order condition

$$\frac{N}{t}(4V - 4p_1 + c_1 - c_2 - 2t) = 0 \tag{7.11B9}$$

This gives the optimal price at shop 1:

$$p_1^{**} = V + \frac{(c_1 - c_2 - 2t)}{4} \tag{7.11B10}$$

You can confirm that this is the solution in the text when there are two shops and $c_1 = c_2$. Substituting into the equation for p_2 gives the price at shop 2:

$$p_2^{**} = V + \frac{(c_2 - c_1 - 2t)}{4} \tag{7.11B11}$$

The final question is under what circumstances it is better for the monopolist to serve only part of the market. For this to hold, it must be the case that, for example, $p_1^* > p_1^{**}$. This requires that

$$\frac{V + c_1}{2} < V + \frac{(c_1 - c_2 - 2t)}{4} \quad \Rightarrow \quad V < \frac{c_1 + c_2}{2} + t = \bar{c} + t \tag{7.11B12}$$

where $\bar{c}$ is the mean of the marginal production costs of the two shops. So we have a rule that is nearly identical to that in the text:

1. Serve the entire market if the consumer reservation price is greater than the sum of transport costs plus the mean of the shops' marginal costs.
2. Serve only part of the market if the consumer reservation price is less than the sum of transport costs plus the mean of the shops' marginal costs.

The intuition behind this result is exactly the same as that presented in the main body of the chapter.

8

Commodity Bundling and Tie-in Sales

On November 5, 1999, Judge Thomas Penfield Jackson issued his "Findings of Fact" in the Microsoft antitrust trial—findings that served as the basis for Judge Jackson's guilty verdict in the trial five months later on April 3, 2000. Among other things, Judge Jackson concluded that Microsoft's *Windows* operating system and its *Internet Explorer* web browser constituted separate products that could, in principle, stand alone but that Microsoft had bundled together as one package. Judge Jackson's focus was on the use of such bundling as an illegal tying of the two products aimed at extending Microsoft's operating systems monopoly to the browser market. Any defense against this charge must offer an explanation for such bundling that is not related to extending monopoly power. The truth is that most firms —both those with market power and those without it—do sell more than one good and bundling or tying between a firm's different products is frequently observed. What are the possible gains to the firm from tying together the sale of its products apart from the anti-competitive effects that worried Judge Jackson? Does bundling raise both profit and efficiency, or does it earn profit at the expense of efficiency? Do consumers win or lose from these bundling and tying tactics? These are the questions we investigate in this chapter.

That consumers might actually gain from bundling seems possible when we examine the prices that Microsoft charges, not for its *Windows* operating system but for its software applications. The Microsoft *Office* suite is one of the most popular applications packages. *Office XP Professional* contains the *Word, Excel, Outlook, PowerPoint* and *Access* programs. In April, 2007 this package was priced at $400. You could also buy the individual components separately, *Word, Excel, PowerPoint* and *Access* selling for $200 each and *Outlook* for $95, a total of $695. In other words, there is a bundle discount of nearly $300. The question then becomes what incentive Microsoft has to engage in such bundling? How does offering the *Office* bundle help raise Microsoft's profit?

Before proceeding further it is helpful to make our discussion a bit more precise. In some cases, firms like Microsoft market two or more products as an explicit bundle comprised of fixed amounts of the individual components. Thus, the *Office* suite contains exactly one copy of each of the constituent programs just as a fixed-price menu at a restaurant contains one of each of the included courses. Similarly, a holiday travel package might specify one return flight to London, five nights' accommodation, and three West End plays.

There is though an alternative to bundling, more frequently known as tying. Under this strategy a firm *ties* the sale of one product to the purchase of another but does not control the proportions in which the two products are consumed. Under a tying strategy the purchase of some amount of one good (the tying good) is conditional upon the purchase of a second product (the tied good). For example, in the early days of business machines and computers IBM sold its machines only under the requirement that the buyer also use IBM-produced tabulating cards. In other words, the purchase of the machine was tied to the additional purchase of IBM cards.[1] We differentiate this from commodity bundling because IBM did not specify the number of cards that the consumer had to purchase.

More recent examples of tied sales are not difficult to find. Whenever you buy a computer printer, you are also committing yourself to buying the ink cartridges that fit into that printer. Hewlett-Packard cartridges do not fit Canon printers and vice versa. Similarly, Sony's Play Station games do not work on either a Nintendo *Wii* or a Microsoft *Xbox* system. What is tied in all these cases is just the brand of the associated product, not its quantity. You can always reduce your demand for Hewlett-Packard ink cartridges by being very strict with yourself on how many drafts of a term paper you actually print out! These modern examples of tie-in sales are *technology* based rather than *contractual* as in the IBM case. Yet, whether contractual or technical, the issues we wish to address are the motivations for and the implications of both tying and bundling practices. It is to a more formal analysis of these questions that we now turn.

8.1   COMMODITY BUNDLING AND PRICE DISCRIMINATION

We begin with a story told almost 30 years ago by Nobel laureate, George Stigler, who was one of the first to understand bundling as a mechanism for price discrimination.[2] At the time that he published his brief analysis he was responding to a recent Supreme Court case involving the movie industry. Throughout the 1950s and 1960s, airing older Hollywood films was a substantial part of television fare. Film distributors who owned the rights to the films would sell presentation rights for a fee to local television stations. However, they rarely sold films individually. Instead, they sold them in packages typically combining screen gems such as *Casablanca* and *Treasure of the Sierra Madre* with such "grade B" losers as *Gorilla Man* and *Tear Gas Squad*.[3] Stigler's insight was to recognize that while every television station would value the first two films (or others of similar quality) more than the last two films, the relative valuation of the two types of movies would vary from station to station. Such differences could provide a motive for the observed bundling.

A modified version of Stigler's example goes as follows. Suppose that there are two films, X and Y, and two stations (located in different cities), A and B. Each station's reservation prices for the two films are as follows:

	Maximum willingness to pay for film X	Maximum willingness to pay for film Y
Station A	$8,000	$2,500
Station B	$7,000	$3,000

---

[1]   See *International Business Machines v. U.S.*, 298 U.S. 131 (1936). Similar charges arose repeatedly in the many private antitrust suits against IBM in the following decades.
[2]   Stigler (1968).
[3]   See *United States v. Loew's Inc.*, 371 U.S. 38 (1962).

Successful price discrimination must surmount the twin problems of identifying which station is which and then avoiding arbitrage between stations. If this is not possible and the distributor is forced to charge a uniform price for each film, its best bet is to charge $7,000 for film X and $2,500 for film Y. At these prices, both stations will buy both films, and the distributor's total revenue will be $19,000.

Bundling, however, permits further revenues to be earned. Instead of selling the two films separately, suppose that the distributor offers the films in a bundle to the two stations for a combined price of $10,000. Since both stations value the bundle at least this highly, the distributor will sell both films to both stations. Its revenue now rises to $20,000.

The reason that bundling raises revenue is straightforward. Offering the films unbundled means that, if both stations are going to buy both films, the highest price that can be charged for any specific film is the minimum reservation price either station would pay for that film—$7,000 for film X and $2,500 for film Y. When the products are bundled, the highest bundle price that can be charged is the minimum of the sums of each station's reservation prices. This permits additional surplus extraction from both stations. Bundling extracts more from station A because it permits the distributor to circumvent the low value that station A places on film Y and to exploit its relatively high valuation of film X. Similarly, bundling avoids the need to charge a low price for film X in order to induce station B to buy it by exploiting that station's relatively high willingness to pay for film Y.

Stigler's insight into bundling as a way to price discriminate was surely valid. However, his analysis was incomplete on two fronts. First, his model included no discussion of production costs. The movie seller and television station example treats the distributor's costs as either sunk or nonexistent. The second limitation of Stigler's model was that it failed to consider the strategy of *mixed bundling*; that is, selling both products individually as well as in a bundle. Adams and Yellen (1976) address these issues and their paper has become the standard piece on commodity bundling. We now turn to a presentation of their paper.

Assume that there are two goods, labeled 1 and 2. Each of these goods is produced with constant marginal (and average) cost, denoted by c_1 and c_2, respectively. In other words, we assume that there are no cost advantages of multiproduct production. In particular, there are no scope economies of the type discussed in Chapter 4. Accordingly, the cost of producing a bundle or a package consisting of one unit of each good is $c_B = c_1 + c_2$.

We will also assume that a consumer buys exactly one unit of each good per unit of time provided that the price charged is less than his or her reservation price for that good. The consumer's reservation price or maximum willingness to pay for good 1 is R_1 and for good 2 is R_2. Finally, we assume that the consumer's reservation price for a commodity bundle consisting of one unit of each good is $R_B = R_1 + R_2$. This final assumption, that the reservation price for the bundle is the sum of the reservation prices for the individual goods, is a common one (and one made by Stigler as well). Yet the assumption is, at least in some circumstances, restrictive. If the two goods are complementary goods, such as nuts and bolts, the assumption is almost certainly false. We expect that the willingness to pay for bolts would be quite low in the absence of any nuts and vice versa. For complementary goods, the reservation price for the bundle would likely be higher than the sum of the separate reservation prices for each good consumed separately. Yet while the assumption that $R_B = R_1 + R_2$ is restrictive, it is also useful. It permits us to focus explicitly on the price discrimination motive for bundling. We return to the case of complementary goods in section 8.3.

Suppose that consumers differ in their separate valuations of the two goods—that is, the values of R_1, R_2, and R_B vary across consumers. Some consumers have a high R_1 and a low R_2; for others just the reverse is true. Some place a high value on both goods. For others,

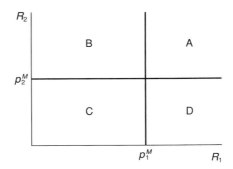

Figure 8.1   Consumers' reservation prices for goods 1 and 2 and simple monopoly pricing
At monopoly prices p_1^M and p_2^M, group A buys both goods; group B buys good 2; group D buys good 1; and group C buys neither good.

R_1 and R_2 are both quite low. If we draw a quadrant with R_1 on the horizontal axis and R_2 on the vertical axis as in Figure 8.1, then our assumptions allow us to describe each consumer's reservation prices by a point in the (R_1, R_2) quadrant.

It might be helpful to use a specific example, such as a restaurant menu. We are all familiar with restaurants that offer an à la carte menu from which we can pick individual items and a set menu that contains perhaps an appetizer and an entrée or an entrée and a dessert sold as a bundle. Figure 8.1 illustrates the simplest pricing strategy for the monopolist offering two goods. Sell the two products separately at their monopoly prices, p_1^M and p_2^M. (We leave aside for the moment just how these monopoly prices might be identified.) This could be a restaurant that sells soup at price p_1^M and a sandwich at price p_2^M. Buying both goods costs $p_1^M + p_2^M$. Facing these prices, consumers are partitioned into four groups. Consumers in group A have reservation prices for both goods that are greater than the prices being charged and therefore purchase one unit of each product. Consumers in group B have reservation prices for good 2 that are higher than its price, p_2^M and so buy good 2. However, their reservation prices for good 1 are lower than the price p_1^M and so they do not buy good 1. Similarly, consumers in group D have reservation prices for good 1 that are higher than its price, so they buy good 1. However, they do not buy good 2. Consumers in group C have reservation prices for both goods that are lower than the prices being charged and so do not purchase either product.

Now suppose that the monopolist adopts a *pure bundling* strategy in which the two goods can be purchased only as a bundle at a fixed price of p_B. In our restaurant setting, this would mean that the only deal on offer is soup plus a sandwich at a fixed price of p_B. The goods cannot be purchased separately at individual prices, p_1 and p_2.

The bundle price is illustrated in Figure 8.2 as a straight line with intercept on each axis of p_B and so with slope of −1. Now consumers are partitioned into two groups. Each consumer in group E has reservation prices for the two goods the sum of which is greater than p_B and so will buy the package. By contrast, each consumer in group F has reservation prices for the two goods the sum of which is less than p_B and so will not buy the package.

Figure 8.2 illustrates an interesting feature of the pure bundling strategy. There are consumers who, as a result of the two goods being offered as a bundle, are able to buy one of the goods even though their reservation prices for that good are less than its marginal production cost. This is true in the case of good 1 for all consumers in group E whose

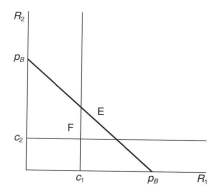

Figure 8.2   Monopoly pricing of a pure bundle of goods 1 and 2
At the bundle price p_B, consumers in group E buy the bundle.

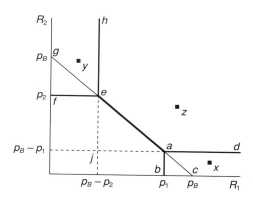

Figure 8.3   Monopoly pricing under mixed bundling of goods 1 and 2
The firm sets prices p_1 for good 1; p_2 for good 2; and $p_B < p_1 + p_2$ for the bundle.

reservation price for good 1 is less than c_1, and in the case of good 2 for all consumers in group E whose reservation prices for good 2 are less than c_2.

The third case is that of *mixed bundling*. Here, the monopolist offers to sell the two goods separately at specified prices, respectively, of p_1 and p_2 (which are not necessarily the monopoly prices) and also sells them as a bundle at price p_B (again not necessarily the pure bundle price). Of course, for this to make sense it must again be the case that $p_B < p_1 + p_2$. Figure 8.3 illustrates such a strategy. The restaurant offers the possibility of buying either soup or a sandwich individually at the stated prices or buying them as a set meal at price p_B.

Once again, we find that consumers are partitioned by this strategy into four groups. The determinants of these groups are, however, slightly different from those considered previously. What we need to do is to determine whether a consumer will prefer to buy only one of the two goods or the bundle or nothing.

Clearly, anyone who values good 1 at more than p_1 and good 2 at more than p_2, that is, anyone who is willing to buy both goods at the individual prices, will buy the bundle since its price is less than the sum of the individual prices. Consider now a consumer whose reservation price for good 2 is less than p_2. If this consumer buys anything, she will buy either the bundle or only good 1. Of course, she will make the choice that gives her the greatest consumer surplus. Suppose then that her reservation prices are R_1 for good 1 and R_2 for good 2. If she buys the bundle, then she pays p_B and gets consumer surplus of $CS_B = R_1 + R_2 - p_B$. If she buys only good 1, she gets consumer surplus of $CS_1 = R_1 - p_1$.

This type of consumer will buy only good 1 if two conditions are satisfied. First, $CS_1 > CS_B$, which requires that $R_2 < p_B - p_1$. Second, $CS_1 > 0$, which requires that $R_1 > p_1$.

The difference $p_B - p_1$ is easily illustrated in Figure 8.3. Since the line $p_B p_B$ has a slope of -1, the distance ab is equal to the distance bc, which is equal to $p_B - p_1$. So all points below the line jad represent consumers whose reservation prices for good 2 are such that $R_2 < p_B - p_1$ and, of course, all points to the right of ab represent consumers for whom $R_1 > p_1$. So all consumers with reservation prices in the region dab, such as consumer x, buy only good 1.

By exactly the same argument a consumer will buy only good 2 if two conditions are satisfied: first, $R_1 < p_B - p_2$ and second, $R_2 > p_2$. The difference $p_B - p_2$ is illustrated in Figure 8.3 by the line jeh and all points above fe represent consumers for whom $R_2 > p_2$. Therefore, all consumers with reservation prices in the region feh, such as consumer y, will buy only good 2.

Now consider a consumer for whom $R_2 > p_B - p_1$ and $R_1 > p_B - p_2$. This is a consumer whose reservation price for good 1 is to the right of jeh and for good 2 is above jad. If such a consumer buys anything at all she will buy the bundle since this gives more consumer surplus than either only good 1 or only good 2. For this consumer to buy the bundle it is then necessary that $R_1 + R_2 > p_B$, which means that her reservation prices must put her above the line $caeg$ in Figure 8.3. In other words, all consumers in the region $daeh$, such as consumer z, will buy the bundle.

This leaves only the region $feab$. What will be the choice of these types of consumers? Their reservation prices are less than the individual prices of the two goods, so they will not buy either good individually. In addition, the sums of their reservation prices are less than the bundle price, so they will not buy the bundle. Consumers in $feab$ do not buy anything.

When we compare either pure or mixed bundling with simple monopoly pricing, it is clear that mixed bundling always increases the monopolist's sales. What is less clear is whether bundling will increase the monopolist's profits. What we should expect is that the profit impact of commodity bundling will depend upon the distribution of consumer preferences for the goods being offered and the costs of making those goods. An example will serve to illustrate this and some of the other ideas introduced so far.

Assume that the monopolist knows that it has four consumers, A, B, C, and D, each interested in buying the two goods, 1 and 2. The marginal cost of good 1 is $c_1 = \$100$ and of good 2 is $c_2 = \$150$. Each consumer has reservation prices for these two goods as given in Table 8.1 and buys exactly one unit of either good in any period so long as its price is less than her reservation price for that good. Each consumer will consider buying the goods as a bundle provided that the bundle price is less than the sum of her reservation prices.

Suppose that the monopolist decides to sell the goods unbundled and adopt simple monopoly pricing. Table 8.2 allows us to identify the profit-maximizing monopoly prices for the two goods. Profit from good 1 is maximized at $450 by setting a price of $250 and selling to consumers B, C, and D. Profit from good 2 is maximized at $300 by setting a price of $450 and selling only to consumer A. Total profit from simple monopoly pricing is, therefore, $750.

Table 8.1   Consumer reservation prices (U.S. dollars)

Consumer	Reservation price for good 1	Reservation price for good 2	Sum of reservation prices
A	50	450	500
B	250	275	525
C	300	220	520
D	450	50	500

Table 8.2   Determination of simple monopoly prices

Price	Quantity demanded	Total revenue ($)	Profit ($)	Price	Quantity demanded	Total revenue ($)	Profit ($)
450	1	450	350	450	1	450	300
300	2	600	400	275	2	550	250
250	3	750	450	220	3	660	210
50	4	200	−200	50	4	200	−400

Now consider the pure bundling strategy. The firm can: (1) choose a bundle price of $525, which will attract only consumer B; (2) choose a bundle price of $520, which will attract consumers B and C; or (3) choose a bundle price of $500, which will attract all four consumers. The third strategy is preferable because it yields a total profit of 4($500 − $100 − $150), or $1,000. Pure bundling is, in this case, preferable to simple monopoly pricing. However, under bundling, consumer A is able to consume good 1 and consumer D is able to consume good 2 even though they each value the relevant good at less than its marginal production costs.

Can a mixed bundling strategy do better? Suppose, for example, that the monopolist merely combines the simple monopoly and pure bundling strategies. That is, the firm sets a price of $250 for good 1, $450 for good 2, and $500 for the bundle. How will consumers respond to this pricing and product offering? Consumer A will not buy just good 1, and is indifferent between buying the bundle or only good 2 because in either case, she earns zero surplus. However, the firm is definitely not indifferent. The firm makes a profit of $300 if consumer A buys just good 2 but only $250 if consumer A buys the bundle. Hence, the firm would like to find a way to encourage consumer A to opt only for good 2. Consumer B will not buy just good 2, earns no consumer surplus if she buys only good 1 and $25 consumer surplus if she buys the bundle so she will buy the bundle, giving the monopolist a profit of $250. Consumer C will not buy good 2, earns $50 consumer surplus if she buys only good 1 and $20 consumer surplus if she buys the bundle. She will buy only good 1 giving the monopolist profit of $150. Finally, consumer D earns the greatest surplus if she buys only good 1, in which case her consumer surplus is $200. Therefore, she will buy only good 1 and the profit to the monopolist from that sale will be $150. In this consumer's case, the monopolist would actually prefer that she buy the bundle at $500 from which the monopolist earns a profit of $250.

Adding up the sales and related profits, we find that the proposed mixed bundling strategy gives the monopolist a total profit of $800 or $850 depending upon whether consumer A buys the bundle or only good 2. This is certainly better than simple monopoly pricing profit derived earlier of $750. However, it is not as good as the profit of $1,000 earned in the pure bundling case of selling only the bundle at a price of $500.

These results assume that in employing mixed bundling the monopolist uses the same price as for no bundling or pure bundling. There is no reason to believe that this is the best strategy. With a little thought, it is easy to see how the monopolist could alter the current mixed bundling strategy to raise profits further. The insight is to change the prices to sort customers into different purchase choices. We have already noted that consumer A is indifferent between buying just good 2 or the bundle at the current prices. A slight rise in the bundle price say, to $520 will definitely tilt this consumer to purchasing just good 2. Suppose that in addition the firm also raises the price of good 1 to $450, so that the new price configuration is: $p_B = \$520$; $p_1 = \$450$; and $p_2 = \$450$. Consumer A will now buy good 2. Consumer D will continue to buy good 1 and consumers B and C will continue to buy the bundle. However, the price increases for these good 1 and the bundle, respectively will now let the monopolist earn an additional profit of $200 on its sale of good 1 to consumer D, and $40 on its two bundle sales to consumers B and C. Total profit is $300 + $270 + $270 + $350 = $1,190, which *does* exceed our pure bundling maximum.

This is actually the best that the monopolist can do in this case. The monopolist has extracted the entire consumer surplus of consumers A, C, and D and all but $5 of the consumer surplus of consumer B. In other words, the monopolist has done nearly as well as it would have done if it had been able to adopt first-degree price discrimination.

Mixed bundling (in which the bundle price is less than the price of buying each component separately) is always at least as profitable as pure bundling. The reason is simple enough to see. The worst that a mixed bundling strategy can do is to replicate the pure bundling strategy—by setting arbitrarily high individual prices and a bundle price equal to the pure bundle price. However, it will usually be possible to improve on this by setting individual component prices that are sufficiently low to attract those who really just want the one item but high enough to earn more profit than can be earned from the bundle.

We should note though that while mixed bundling must always improve profits relative to pure bundling, it is not always the case that some sort of bundling is more profitable than no bundling at all. A drawback to bundling—one illustrated in the previous example—is that it can lead to an outcome in which some of the consumers who buy the bundle actually have a reservation price for one of the goods that is less than marginal production cost. This is inefficient and so the firm would prefer a different pricing scheme. Our example also demonstrates that any bundling is likely to be profitable only when the variation in consumer valuations of the goods is significant. In our example, consumers A and D—who buy a single good—have very different valuations of the individual goods. In contrast, consumers B and C—who buy the bundled good—have very similar valuations. Adams and Yellen (1976) made clear that the gains from bundling arise from the differences in consumer valuations.

> Some people may value an appetizer relatively highly (soup on a cold day), others may value dessert relatively higher (Baked Alaska, unavailable at home), but all may wish to pay roughly the same amount for a complete dinner. The à la carte menu is designed to capture consumer surplus from those gastronomes with extremely high valuations of particular dishes, while the complete dinner is designed to retain those with lower variance. (p. 488)

We can see the same basic point in the context of the Stigler example above. If station A valued both movies at $8,000, and station B valued both at $3,500, the differences in the relative valuation of the products would vanish. In that case, bundling would no longer be a profitable strategy.

It is because the bundle price p_B is less than the sum of the individual prices $p_1 + p_2$ that commodity bundling may be viewed as discriminatory pricing. The lower bundle price serves to attract consumers who place a relatively low value on either of the two goods but are willing to pay a reasonable sum for the bundle. The two separate prices serve to extract surplus from those customers who have a great willingness to pay for only one of the products. We would, therefore, expect most multiproduct firms with monopoly power to engage in some sort of mixed bundling.

Mixed bundling is in fact a common practice. Restaurants serve combination platters and also offer items individually. Resorts often offer food and lodging both separately and as a package. Software companies sell individual products but also offer packages consisting of several applications, such as Microsoft's *Office* package. Some of this surely reflects price discrimination efforts.

Reality Checkpoint
All Bundled Up in the Vatican

These are hard times for traditional travel agents. Direct ticketing by airlines and the proliferation of discount Internet sites that permit customers to shop comparatively for the cheapest travel and lodging accommodations have taken their toll. But now the agents are fighting back with a new tool called "insider travel."

Many popular sites make it either difficult or impossible for tourists to get what they really want. Those who visit the Sistine Chapel will often stand in hours-long lines to get a glimpse of Michelangelo's masterpiece. Similarly, Queen Nefertari's tomb in Egypt can only be seen if one gets permission from the country's Supreme Council of Antiquities. Travel agents are increasingly doing the legwork to offer tourists these special features as part of a package. Select Italy will arrange a special, after-hours tour for tourists to see the Sistine Chapel artwork face-to-face. Los Angeles-based Destinations & Adventures International will likewise obtain the necessary permission to view the fabulous wall paintings in the tomb of the ancient Egyptian Queen Nefertari for an appropriate fee.

That fee can of course be intimidating. It can cost a fixed charge of $4,000 for a small group to take advantage of these opportunities and the fee rises if the group exceeds ten. However, by agreeing to stay at a hotel recommended by the agent or to use other agent-suggested services, tourists can often reduce these fees by anywhere from $400 to $1,000. In return, travelers get a personalized trip that can be truly memorable and for which they are willing to pay a lot. One of the larger tour operators, Abercrombie & Kent, claims that packaging a customized event with travel and lodging now makes up half of its business and earns some of the heftiest margins.

Source: C. Jackson, "VIP Travel on the Cheap," *Wall Street Journal*, May 17, 2006, p. D1.

8.1

Practice Problem

A cable company has two services. One service is the Basic Service channel. The other is the Walt Disney Movie channel. The potential subscribers for the services—students, families, hotels, schools, young adults, and pensioners—regard the two services as separate alternatives, that is, not as complementary products. So, the demands for the two services are completely unrelated for each and every consumer. Each buyer is characterized by a pair of reservation prices as shown in the following table:

Reservation prices for each cable service by type of subscriber:

	Basic Service ($)	Disney Channel ($)
Students	5	15
Families	11	9
Hotels	14	6
Schools	4	16
Young adults	0	17
Pensioners	17	0

The marginal cost of each service is $3. Assume there are equal numbers of consumers in each category.

a. If the services are sold separately and not offered as a bundle, what price should the cable operator set for each service? What profits will she earn? Which consumers will subscribe to which service?

b. Suppose that the operator decides to pursue a mixed bundling strategy. What price should be set for the bundled service? What price should she set for each service if purchased individually? Which consumers buy which options, and what are the cable operator's profits?

c. How would your answers to the first two questions be changed if the marginal cost of producing each service had been $10 instead of $3?

8.2   REQUIRED TIE-IN SALES

Tie-in sale arrangements differ from bundling in that they tie together the purchase of two or more products without prescribing the amount that must be bought. A further difference commonly but not always observed is that the tied goods typically exhibit a complementary relationship with each other whereas bundled goods need not. We now turn to a somewhat magical example to illustrate why tying is often an effective marketing strategy.

Consider an imaginary product called a *Magicam* that is produced by only one firm, Rowling Corp. A *Magicam* is much like an ordinary camera with one exception—the figures in a *Magicam* photograph can actually move and even wave back at the picture viewer because of Rowling's patented, magical method of placing the images on film. In all other respects, however, the *Magicam* is essentially identical to a typical real-world camera. In particular, both a *Magicam* and a regular camera can be used to make anywhere from one to a very large number of pictures per day or per month. It is up to the owner to decide how many pictures to take per period of time.

This fact does not mean that every consumer who has a *Magicam* will take a huge number of snapshots. After all, they have to pay for the film cartridge and spend time in taking snaps rather than doing other things. Presumably, consumers differ in this regard. Suppose that there are 1,000 low-demand consumers each with a monthly demand for pictures described by $Q = 12 - P$, and 1,000 high-demand consumers each with a monthly demand for pictures given by $Q = 16 - P$. In other words, if cartridges of film were free the first group of consumers would each take 12 pictures per month and the second group 16 pictures. Unfortunately, Rowling Corp. has no way, magical or otherwise, of identifying these different types.

Because of the sensitive nature of the technology incorporated in *Magicams* we assume that Rowling Corp. does not sell the cameras but rather uses its monopoly power to offer them on monthly lease agreements that include servicing the camera to maintain its magical properties.[4] Given that the lease fee is set such that each of the 2,000 consumers will lease a *Magicam* the manufacturing costs of the cameras become effectively fixed costs for Rowling Corp. The same is not the true for the camera film. Suppose that film production takes place under competitive conditions and that the marginal cost of producing film is $2 per photograph that the film can take. This means, of course, that film will be priced at the competitive price of $2 per picture. Now consider Rowling Corp.'s potential strategies for leasing its cameras.

If a *Magicam* and camera film are all that is needed for producing the wonderful pictures, Rowling Corp. might find the situation somewhat frustrating. Because the firm cannot tell one type of consumer from another, the firm cannot easily lease its *Magicams* at different prices to each type. About the best that Rowling Corp. can do is to charge a monthly rental rate of $50. Why? Because this is the consumer surplus earned by a low-demand consumer faced with a film price of $2 per picture and Rowling Corp. cannot price discriminate across the two consumer types. (You should check that this is indeed the consumer surplus for a low-demand consumer when film is priced at $2 per picture.)

Both types of consumer will lease the camera. High-demand consumers will use it to take 14 pictures per month while the low-demand consumers will take 10 pictures per month. Rowling earns a monthly profit of $50 on each of the 2,000 cameras leased—1,000 to the low-demand and 1,000 to the high-demand types—or $100,000 per month.

The situation is not desperate but like any good profit-maximizer, Rowling wonders if somehow the firm can do better. After thinking a bit, Rowling management realizes that with a bit of redesign of the camera and some clever marketing it can tie the lease of a *Magicam* to the use of its own *Magifilm*. This gives Rowling an idea. Why not implement a tying strategy and sell *Magifilm* cartridges at $4 per exposure?

Both low- and high-demand consumers now pay $4 at the margin for a picture. The low-demand consumers will therefore reduce their monthly demand for *Magicam* photos to just eight. And if low-demand consumers pay the $4 per picture price of *Magifilm*, they will enjoy a surplus of $32. So this surplus is the rental rate at which Rowling can lease the *Magicam*. (Notice the connection between this and our discussion of two-part pricing in Chapter 6.) As a result, Rowling earns $32 from each of the 1,000 low-demand consumers in camera rentals and $16 from each in cartridge sales, giving a total profit of $48,000 from the low-demand customers.

---

[4]   This is actually the strategy that IBM, Kodak, and Xerox used initially with their machines.

High-demand consumers will also lease the *Magicam* at $32. However, at $4 per picture in film costs, these consumers will shoot 12 photos per month. Hence, Rowling earns a profit of $32 on cameras and $24 on film cartridges from each of the 1,000 high-demand customers, giving a total profit from this group of $56,000. In total, Rowling now earns a combined profit of $104,000—greater than the $100,000 it earned without the tie-in. It has achieved this profit increase by exploiting its ability to *tie* the use of its camera to the use of its film.

To understand the way that tying helps Rowling, first note that high-demand consumers receive a quantity discount under either of the two regimes. When the *Magicam* is leased for $50 and the film is purchased competitively at $2 per photo, high-demand consumers take 14 photos and pay only $5.57 per shot, while low-demand consumers take 10 pictures and pay $7 for each. Under the tied film arrangement, high-demand consumers pay a total charge of $80 for 12 pictures or $6.67 per photo. By contrast, low-demand consumers pay a total of $64 and take only eight pictures per month or $8 per photo. Thus, the tied sale is not attractive solely because it permits a quantity discount.

What tying does accomplish is to permit Rowling to solve the identification and arbitrage problems by exploiting its post-lease position as the monopoly seller of *Magifilm*. Now, the high-demand consumers are revealed by their film purchases to Rowling and the quantity discount is put to work in a profit-increasing way. Nor is arbitrage capable of undoing the discrimination. After all, both the camera and the film are readily available to all consumers at the same prices. Given that a single *Magicam* can serve either a low-demand consumer or a high-demand consumer equally well, solving the identification and arbitrage problems can only be achieved by tying its use to another product whose volume does change depending on the consumer's type. No consumer will ever lease more than one *Magicam*, but they will differ in terms of how much *Magifilm* they purchase.

Now let's take Rowling's case one step further. The low- and high-demand functions we have used may look familiar to you. They are the same ones we used in Chapter 6 in our discussion of quantity discounts with second-degree price discrimination. In fact, if you want to look back at that earlier example you may get an idea of how Rowling can redesign and package the camera to do even better. For example, suppose that Rowling redesigns the *Magicam* so that the cartridge of *Magifilm* becomes an integral part of the camera that only Rowling's film developers can take out without destroying the camera.

Rowling can then design two varieties of its new, integrated *Magicam*, one of which has a 10-shot capacity and the other a 14-shot capacity.[5] The firm can offer to lease the 10-shot *Magicam* for $70 per month and the 14-shot *Magicam* for $88 per month. In both cases, the lease agreement also offers free developing as well as the free replacement of the cartridge. From our analysis in Chapter 6, we know what will happen in this case. Low-demand consumers will lease the 10-shot *Magicam* while high-demand consumers will lease the 14-shot *Magicam*. Rowling will then earn an even greater profit of $50,000 + $58,000 = $108,000. We also know from Chapter 6 that Rowling can do even better. If she designs a 14-shot and a 6-shot camera she can lease the 14-shot camera for $102 per month and the 6-shot camera for $54 per month, increasing her profit to $116,000. This technological integration plus the monthly leasing agreement has enabled Rowling to identify and separate the different customers even more profitably.

---

[5]   With marginal film costs of $2, these are the socially efficient quantities to offer.

Consider the *Magicam* story in the text. Again, let there be 1,000 high-demand and 1,000 low-demand consumers and let them have inverse demand functions of $P = 16 - Q$ and $P = 12 - Q$, respectively. Show that the price of \$4 per photo is, indeed, the profit-maximizing price for *Magifilm* when the film is sold separately from the camera. Now suppose that Rowling Corp. produces the integrated camera plus film cartridge in 8-shot and 14-shot varieties. What rental rates will be charged for the two varieties? What are Rowling Corp.'s profits? Finally, suppose that there are 1,000 low-demand consumers and N_h high-demand consumers. How many high-demand consumers would there have to be for Rowling to wish to manufacture only the 14-shot variety of integrated Magicam given that the other variety is

a.   10-shot;
b.   8-shot.

We have seen that, like bundling, tie-ins can be used to implement price discrimination schemes. This is no doubt one reason that tie-ins are frequently used, especially in situations where one of the components, like our fictitious *Magicam*, is capable of different intensities of use covering a very large range. Some tying is contractual, as in the case of IBM requiring the use of its punch cards for users of its punch card machines in the early days of computing. Some tying is technologically forced as in the *Magicam* and *Magifilm* example, or in the real-world case where Polaroid instant picture cameras used only Polaroid film. Nintendo's Wii uses only Nintendo or Nintendo-licensed games. The leading maker of computer printers, Hewlett-Packard, designs its printers so that they use only Hewlett-Packard cartridges. Again, these can be very useful product design strategies for extracting surplus from the market.

Price discrimination is not the only reason, however, that we may observe bundling and tying practices. As Judge Stevens made clear, an additional reason is that such practices may enhance monopoly power. At the same time, we also need to recognize that bundling and tying based on actual cost considerations will be observed in relatively competitive markets where they have little to do with discriminatory practices. We turn to these issues shortly, after first considering some aspects of complementary goods pricing.

8.3   COMPLEMENTARY GOODS, NETWORK EXTERNALITIES, AND MONOPOLY PRICING

The *Magicam* and *Magifilm* are, like real-life cameras and film, complementary goods. There is no point in buying a camera—magical or otherwise—unless one also buys some film (at least until the advent of digital cameras). Likewise, there is little point in owning a CD player without also purchasing CDs; or a PC without also buying some software applications; or in buying bolts without buying nuts. In passenger airline manufacture it is necessary to have both engines and avionics equipment.

Sometimes the market for at least one of the complementary goods is reasonably competitive. Other times, the same firm may control both goods. However, there is a third possibility. This is that each of the complementary goods is produced by a different monopolist. There might be just one camera corporation and one, separate film company. As the French mathematical economist, Augustin Cournot, recognized over a hundred and fifty years ago, this last situation may have particularly bad implications for both profit and efficiency.

Cournot's basic argument can be demonstrated fairly simply. For this purpose, let us assume that the two complementary goods in question are nuts and bolts. A separate monopoly firm produces each and, to keep things simple, marginal production cost for each firm is zero. (We provide in the inset an alternative solution in which we allow the two firms to have different marginal costs.) The two goods are perfect complements. A consumer who wants to purchase 100 bolts also wishes to buy 100 nuts. In other words, the two goods are always consumed in the fixed proportion of one-to-one. For this reason, consumers care only about the combined price, $P_B + P_N$, in determining their demand. As you can see, the demand for the two products are clearly interrelated. The price of bolts will affect the demand for nuts and vice versa.

Suppose that the demand for nut and bolt pairs is given by the demand function

$$Q = 12 - (P_B + P_N) \tag{8.1}$$

Since consumers always buy the two goods together—one nut for every bolt—equation (8.1) also describes the separate demand facing each monopolist. That is, the bolt producer and the nut producer each face demand curves

$$Q_B = 12 - (P_B + P_N) \quad \text{Bolt demand curve}$$
$$Q_N = 12 - (P_B + P_N) \quad \text{Nut demand curve} \tag{8.2}$$

The problem with separate production is easy to see. The nut producer's pricing decision affects the bolt producer's demand curve, and vice versa. A change in the price of nuts not only changes the quantity demanded in the nut market but also in the bolt market. This implies that any one firm's pricing decision has profit implications not just for itself but for the other firm as well. In other words, the pricing policy of either of the two firms imposes an externality on the other firm. In this situation, we might reasonably expect that a merger or creation of a business network to coordinate the pricing decisions of the two firms will offer significant advantages for them by at least partially correcting the market failure associated with the externality. Less obviously but, as we shall see nonetheless true, it is also possible that consumers will gain from such coordination.

Let's calculate the profit-maximizing decisions of the two firms, first without and then with coordination between them. We can rewrite the demand curves of equation (8.2) in inverse form.

$$P_B = (12 - P_N) - Q_B \quad \text{Inverse demand curve for bolts}$$
$$P_N = (12 - P_B) - Q_N \quad \text{Inverse demand curve for nuts} \tag{8.3}$$

From this we know that the marginal revenue curve facing each firm is

$$MR_B = (12 - P_N) - 2Q_B \quad \text{Bolt marginal revenue}$$
$$MR_N = (12 - P_B) - 2Q_N \quad \text{Nut marginal revenue} \tag{8.4}$$

Not surprisingly, just as each firm's demand curve depends on the other firm's price, so each firm's marginal revenue is affected by the other firm's price decision. When each firm

Derivation Checkpoint

Firms with Complementary Goods and Nonzero Marginal Costs

Assume that demand for nuts and bolts is given respectively by: $Q_N = Q_B = A - P_N - P_B$. Suppose now that the marginal cost of the nut producer is c_N, while that of the bolt producer is c_B. Then, with separate production, profit of the nut producer is: $\pi_N = (P_N - c_N)Q_N = (P_N - c_N)(A - P_N - P_B)$. Differentiate this with respect to P_N to obtain the necessary first-order condition for profit maximization:

$$\frac{\partial \pi_N}{\partial P_N} = (A - P_B - 2P_N + c_N) = 0$$

This gives the nut-pricing rule as:

$$P_N = (A + c_N - P_B)/2$$

By symmetry, it follows immediately that the profit-maximizing bolt-pricing rule is:

$$P_B = (A + c_B - P_N)/2$$

Solving these two equations for P_N gives:

$$P_N = \frac{1}{2}\left[A + c_N - \frac{1}{2}(A + c_B - P_N)\right].$$

This then simplifies to: $P_N = \dfrac{A + 2c_N - c_B}{3}$. In turn, this implies: $P_B = \dfrac{A + 2c_B - c_N}{3}$.

If the two firms merge, their joint profit is:

$$\pi_M = (P - c_B - c_N)(A - P).$$

The first-order condition necessary for profit maximization is:

$$\frac{\partial \pi_M}{\partial P} = A - 2P + c_B + c_N = 0.$$

Hence, the coordinated price for the nut-and-bolt combination after merger is:

$$P = \frac{A + c_B + c_N}{2}.$$

Comparison of this price with the sum of the nut and bolt prices under separate firms makes it clear that this price is lower by an amount $\dfrac{A - c_B - c_N}{6}$. Prices are lower as a result of the merger, while profits are higher. Both consumers and producers gain from coordinating the prices of these two complementary goods.

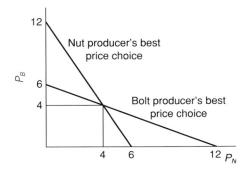

Figure 8.4   Pricing of complementary goods: the nuts and bolts case

independently maximizes its profit then each firm will choose an output where marginal revenue equals marginal cost, here assumed to be zero. So, setting each of the equations in (8.4) to zero and solving for Q_B and Q_N gives

$$Q_B = (12 - P_N)/2 \qquad \text{Bolt production}$$
$$Q_N = (12 - P_B)/2 \qquad \text{Nut production} \tag{8.5}$$

If we now substitute these outputs into the individual demand curves we obtain each firm's optimal price as a function of the other firm's price, as follows:

$$P_B = (12 - P_N)/2 \qquad \text{Bolt price rule}$$
$$P_N = (12 - P_B)/2 \qquad \text{Nut price rule} \tag{8.6}$$

These equations show that each producer's profit-maximizing price depends on the price set by the other firm. Alternatively, the equations identify what is the firm's best or profit-maximizing choice of price given the price of the other firm's good. Whatever price is being charged by the nut firm is communicated to the bolt firm through the effect on the demand curve facing the bolt producer. If nut prices are high, then bolt demand will be low. On the other hand, if nut prices are low, bolt demand will be strong. Taking the demand curve as given, the bolt producer simply picks the price–quantity combination that maximizes profits using the familiar profit-maximizing $MR = MC$ rule.

We can identify what the price equilibrium in the two markets will be by graphing equations (8.6) in a diagram with the two prices P_B and P_N on the axes. This is done in Figure 8.4. The more gently sloped line gives the bolt company's best choice of P_B for every alternate nut price, P_N. For example, if the nuts were given away free or the nut price were zero the profit-maximizing bolt price would be $6. If the nut price rises to somewhere near $12, the profit-maximizing bolt price falls to near zero. Higher nut prices reduce bolt demand and lower the bolt firm's profit-maximizing price. The more steeply sloped line describes the same strategic choices from the perspective of the nut company. This line describes the profit-maximizing choice of P_N for every choice of P_B.

Equilibrium occurs at the intersection. At this point, each firm has selected a price that is best given the price choice of the other firm. Accordingly, neither has an incentive to change.

In order to identify this equilibrium, we substitute the equation for the nut price, for example, into the equation for the bolt price. This gives

$$P_B = \frac{1}{2}(12 - P_N) = \frac{1}{2}\left(12 - \frac{1}{2}(12 - P_B)\right) = \frac{12}{4} + \frac{P_B}{4} \text{ so that } \frac{3P_B}{4} = 3 \text{ or } P_B = 4 \qquad (8.7)$$

This tells us that the profit-maximizing bolt price is $P_B = \$4$. Substituting into equation (8.6) also gives the profit-maximizing nut price as $P_N = \$4$. As a result, the combined nut/bolt price is $P_B + P_N = \$8$, and from the demand equation (8.1), the number of bolt and nut pairs sold is 4. The bolt firm makes profits of $P_B Q_B = \$16$, as does the nut producer.

Now consider what happens if the two firms merge and the newly combined firm markets a single, bundled "nut-and-bolt" product. Such a firm faces the joint demand curve of equation (8.1) and so recognizes that the relevant price to customers is the sum of individual bolt and nut prices, or the total price paid for the bundled nut-and-bolt product. The marginal revenue curve associated with the demand curve of equation (8.1) is $MR = 12 - 2Q$, where Q is the number of nut-and-bolt pairs sold. Equating marginal revenue with marginal cost identifies the optimal quantity of nut-and-bolt pairs to sell. Since we have assumed that marginal cost is zero, it is easy to see that the optimal quantity of nut-and-bolt pairs that the merged monopolist should offer for sale is $Q^* = 6$. The demand function then tells us that each pair can be sold at a combined price of $P^* = \$6$ (or separate prices of $3 each). The merged firm's total profit is $P^* Q^* = \$36$.

Comparing these values with those obtained when the firms set their prices independently of each other shows that a merger of the two firms leads to lower prices and more output than when the two firms act separately. This is because the merged firm understands the interaction of demands between the two products. As a result of coordinating nut and bolt production and pricing, consumers are made better off by this merger. Moreover, the profit of the combined firm exceeds the sum of profits earned by the two separate firms. This was Cournot's basic point.[6] By internalizing the interdependence of the two firms, both consumers and producers gain.

Merger is not the only way to achieve this outcome. Alternative means of coordinating the separate decisions of the two firms exist. For example, they could decide to form a product network. Examples include automatic teller machine (ATM) networks, airline computerized reservation systems (CRS), real estate multiple-listing services (MLS), markets for interactive components such as computer CPUs and peripherals, and long-distance and local telephone services. Where they exist, such networks have been created by the joint action of many firms with the aim of taking better account of the interactions between the demands for the firms' complementary products.

Alternatively, we might hope for one or both markets to become competitive. If this happened in only one of the two markets, say bolts, then the bolt price would fall to marginal cost, which in this case was assumed equal to zero. Each firm in the bolt market would be so small that it could not possibly impose any external effects on the nut-producing monopoly. Given a zero price for bolts, equations (8.6) imply that the profit-maximizing price for nuts —and therefore of a nut-and-bolt combination—would be $6. Accordingly, this outcome would duplicate that which occurs under merger. If both markets were to become competitive, the

---

[6]   Allen (1938) made the same point with regard to the price-reducing effects of merging two complementary-goods monopolies. A calculus-based presentation of our analysis is provided in the Appendix.

bolt price and the nut price would each fall to marginal cost. This, of course, would yield the maximum total surplus and all of that surplus would accrue to consumers.

There is a factor that can work against the emergence of competition in markets for complementary goods. This is the presence of network externalities. For some goods and services, there is a scale economy effect that operates on the demand side of the market. For example, the more consumers that are connected to a phone system, the more valuable the phone system is to existing and new consumers. Each consumer who connects to the phone system generates an external benefit to all those already connected and makes the system more attractive to potential consumers. Sometimes this feature is described as a positive feedback.

Product complementarities of the sort we have been discussing here can also give rise to a positive feedback. Consider the Microsoft case. Microsoft's operating system *Windows* serves as the platform from which software applications such as word-processing packages, computer games, and graphic arts programs can be launched. A technical aspect of this relationship is that the code for a particular application must include an applications program interface (API) in order to work with the operating system. Typically, the API that works with one operating system will not work with another. In other words, applications such as *Harvard Graphics* or *Mathematica* are usually written to work on a specific operating system such as *Windows*. The two products, the applications and the operating system, are therefore complements.

Two additional features of the design and production of applications programs are also important. First, such production exhibits substantial scale economies. The cost is almost entirely in the design phase. Once the underlying source code is written, the program can be put on CD-ROMs (or websites) and sold (or downloaded) to millions of consumers almost costlessly. Second, there is a network externality in that the more people who use the application, the more consumers will want to use it. It is convenient to know that I can put my presentation graphics on a memory stick or in an e-mail attachment and have it read by a colleague miles away because we both use the same graphics software. For both of these reasons, firms that make these software applications have an incentive to design them to work with the most widely used operating system because this permits the firms to exploit these supply-side and demand-side scale economies more effectively.

By exactly the same reasoning, the operating system that consumers will want the most is the one for which there are the most applications. The complementary relationship between applications and operating system has resulted in a very favorable positive feedback for Microsoft's *Windows*. As Windows has become the dominant operating system, applications are increasingly written to run on it. In turn, this ever-expanding menu of applications has greatly fortified the position of *Windows* as the dominant system. This interaction is sometimes called the *applications barrier to entry*. The idea is that any would-be rival operating system will have a great deal of difficulty entering the market. Applications producers will not have an incentive to design their products to run on the alternative system until it has a significant market share. Yet the system will never get any sizable market share unless applications are written for it.

We have a countervailing force to the benefits from closer coordination in the production and marketing of complementary products. Although it is generally true that coordination is profitable, and as our nut and bolt example indicates, is beneficial for consumers when there is monopoly power in the production of the complementary goods, the network effects and the positive feedback that they generate means that monopoly power can be enhanced. This is one way in which monopoly power in one product line could be extended or leveraged to others.

8.4 ANTITRUST, BUNDLING, AND TIE-IN SALES

We are now in a better position to consider the antitrust issues raised by bundling and tie-ins. The main question is whether such practices may be used by firms with significant market power either to sustain or to extend that power against competitors or potential competitors. We illustrate these issues first with a review of the Microsoft case with which we opened this chapter. We then briefly discuss other cases and legal developments in this area.

8.4.1 Bundling and the Microsoft Case

A central issue in the government's case against Microsoft was the claim that Microsoft had integrated or bundled its browser, *Internet Explorer*, directly into its operating system *Windows* as a means to eliminate the rival browser, Netscape's *Navigator*, from the market. The argument was that since Microsoft had monopoly power in the operating systems market, every consumer of *Windows* would now find *Internet Explorer* as her default browser thereby eliminating or greatly reducing Netscape's market share. To prove its claim and demonstrate a violation of the antitrust laws, the government would have to show: (1) that Microsoft did possess monopoly power; (2) that an operating system and a browser were two related but distinct products that did not need to be tightly bundled; and (3) that Microsoft's practices constituted an abuse of its power motivated by the firm's desire to maintain or extend its dominant position.

In light of the foregoing, it is worthwhile recalling Judge Jackson's three key findings of fact. First, the judge found that Microsoft is indeed a monopoly in the sense of the Sherman Act. The evidence for this finding appears reasonably strong. At the time of the trial, *Windows* had over 90 percent of the operating systems market and had maintained that share of the market for well over a decade. Additionally, Microsoft's use of mixed bundling and other price discriminatory practices provided further evidence of something less than a competitive market. Both the structural and behavioral evidence provided some support to Judge Jackson's finding that Microsoft possessed monopoly power.

The judge's second finding was that an operating system and an Internet browser are two separate albeit complementary products. Microsoft had argued that a browser was really just an integrated part of a modern operating system. Just as flash bulbs that used to be sold separately had become technologically embedded in cameras, Microsoft claimed that similar technological developments had led it to make its browser, *Internet Explorer*, an integral part of its *Windows* operating system. Microsoft further alleged that separation of the two could not be achieved without damaging at least one of them. However, the fact remained that Netscape still marketed its *Navigator* browser independently suggesting that consumers did not demand an integrated operating system and browsing experience. In addition, evidence was presented at the trial showing that it was relatively easy to separate Internet Explorer from the operating system with which Microsoft had bundled it, without harming either product. So, Judge Jackson's finding that *Windows* and *Internet Explorer* are separate products could also be justified.

In light of these first two findings, Microsoft's only remaining defense is that even though it possesses monopoly power, its practice of bundling its distinct operating system and browser products did not amount to "acting badly." In other words, arguing that its integration of *Windows* and *Internet Explorer* was not done with a view to hurt competition but instead to help consumers might avoid a finding that it had violated the antitrust laws. One way to make such a defense would be to pursue the coordination argument that we discussed above. That is, Microsoft might argue that the complementarity between an operating system and a browser requires coordination of the marketing of the two products in order to ensure that consumers receive both goods at low prices. Microsoft could then make a case that its behavior was in fact pro consumer.

As we saw in the previous section, the existence of a complementary relationship between two products can lead to serious inefficiencies if each product is produced by a separate monopoly. This was arguably the case in the software industry. Microsoft's Windows controlled the lion's share of the operating systems market and Netscape's *Navigator* dominated the complementary browser market. There was a good case to be made that some mechanism for coordinating the marketing of these two products was desirable. One way to achieve this coordination is by means of a merger of the two firms.[7] What happens, however, if one of the firms does not want to merge?

For example, suppose that Netscape feels that, as a much smaller company, any merger would amount to its being swallowed up by Microsoft and losing all its managerial independence. Its management might then decide to reject a merger proposal and to continue the separate marketing of its browser. In these circumstances we can imagine that Microsoft might decide to create its own browser and bundle it with its operating system.

We can illustrate how the market outcome might evolve, again using our simple nut/bolt example. Suppose that the demand by consumers who want both an operating system and a web browser is given by

$$Q = 12 - (P_O + P_B). \tag{8.8}$$

where the subscripts "O" and "B" now indicate operating system and browser, respectively. Again, let us simplify by assuming that marginal costs for both products are zero. (We noted earlier that for software, this assumption is actually quite realistic.)

Our nut/bolt example above tells us that, when operating independently, Microsoft will sell its operating systems at $P_O = \$4$ and Netscape will sell its browser at $P_B = \$4$, so that the price of a combined operating system and browser service is $8. We also know that this is an inefficient outcome. If the two firms coordinate or become one firm, the price of a combined system falls to $6. Total profit of the two firms would simultaneously rise.

If a merger with Netscape is rejected, Microsoft might then develop its own browser, which we also assume can be produced at a marginal cost of zero. It would then appear that Microsoft could offer the operating system at $3 and the browser at $3, or a package price of $6. However, this ignores the competition from Netscape. If Microsoft proceeds with this plan, Netscape can no longer offer its browser at a price of $4. It could, however, offer to sell its browser at a price of $2. After all, this is still well above marginal cost. Moreover, this price is sufficiently low that consumers would then be attracted to the Netscape browser while still buying Microsoft's operating system at the price of $3. Of course, Microsoft would then want to reduce the price of its browser, perhaps to $1.95. Netscape would then respond by selling its browser at perhaps $1.80 and so on.

What we have just described is an outbreak of price competition in the browser market. The ultimate effect of this price competition will be to drive the browser price to marginal

---

[7]   In June of 1995, Microsoft did in fact offer to work cooperatively with Netscape in the browser market and, allegedly, even suggested a merger—a proposal that was rejected by Netscape.

cost—in this case to zero. This is certainly bad news for Netscape. What about Microsoft? A review of its optimal pricing strategy as given by equations (8.6) implies that when the browser price falls to zero, Microsoft's optimal price for operating systems rises to $6. Further, a browser price of zero implies that $6 is also the best price for a combined operating system and browser package—exactly as would occur if the two firms merged. Moreover, the profit increase that a merger would bring is also realized, although it now goes entirely to Microsoft. In other words, a merger is not the only way to solve the coordination problem. Competition in one of the markets will remove the inefficiency that would otherwise result when each market is monopolized and the monopolists fail to coordinate their pricing. Prices are lower and both consumer and producer surplus have increased.

It is insightful to note that the outcome of the "browser war" just described involves a final browser price of zero. That is, in equilibrium Microsoft sells its operating system for $6 and then throws in its browser for free. This looks very much like bundling, the only complicating factor being that Netscape is also offering a free browser and so can be expected to retain a share of the browser market.

Review of the foregoing scenario should make clear that the accusation that Microsoft bundled its browser with its operating system to exploit its monopoly power and harm competitors can be challenged. Microsoft could legitimately argue that it has simply acted in a way that promotes price competition and that the lower browser prices are just a reflection of this fact. In this view, Microsoft's actions have been pro-competitive not anti-competitive.

There is, however, an additional aspect to the case that we must consider. This involves the interaction between complementary products and network externalities. The complementarity between operating systems and the applications written for them has created a substantial positive feedback loop for Microsoft. Because *Windows* has a monopoly in operating systems, the majority of applications are written to run on *Windows*. In turn, because most applications are written for *Windows*, no other operating system can challenge the *Windows* dominance. Internet browsers, however, offer a potential way around this problem. The advent of the JAVA programming language developed by Sun Microsystems and other technical advances make it possible to run applications on an Internet browser. The browser itself therefore can serve as a platform from which to launch applications.

If Navigator can serve as an applications platform, then even after the development of *Internet Explorer Navigator* would be expected to retain a reasonable share of the browser market. In turn, the existence of this alternative platform with a substantial market share means that design firms could begin to write their applications to run on an alternative to *Windows*. As this happened, Navigator would benefit from the same positive feedback that *Windows* enjoyed. As more applications could be run from the browser, the browser would become more popular and still more applications would be written for it. Clearly, such a development would strike at the core of Microsoft's success by leading to fierce competition in the platform market. Testimony at the trial revealed that Microsoft management was both aware and fearful of this development.

In light of the foregoing, Microsoft's explicit bundling of *Internet Explorer* with its *Windows* operating system takes on a different light. Instead of a competitive act that reduces a coordination inefficiency between complementary products, Microsoft's bundling can also be viewed as a deliberate effort to reduce Netscape's share of the browser market so that the Netscape browser becomes an unattractive alternative to applications designers. In turn, this would eliminate Netscape as a threat to Microsoft's operating system monopoly. Indeed, Microsoft initially required that PC manufacturers such as Compaq and Dell, who installed *Windows* as their operating system also install *Internet Explorer* as the default browser appearing on the *Windows* desktop. They did this presumably on the supposition that most consumers want only one browser even if a second can be obtained for free. The subsequent integration of *Internet Explorer* into the *Windows* software could be viewed as an attempt to replace contractual bundling with technological bundling.

Whatever the type of bundling, however, the foregoing analysis sees the motive as the same—namely the prevention of Netscape developing a viable competitor to Microsoft. This alternative interpretation of Microsoft's behavior does imply a violation of the antitrust laws because it alleges that Microsoft abused its power primarily to sustain its monopoly, i.e., to hurt competition. In support of this argument, the Justice Department offered much suggestive evidence only a portion of which we can summarize here.

First, there were internal Microsoft documents revealing management's concern over the potential threat that Netscape might pose to the dominance of *Windows* as the applications platform. Second, some additional evidence of malicious intent was that in addition to its bundling strategy that effectively required Windows users to acquire *Internet Explorer* as their default browser, Microsoft also pressured Macintosh to support *Internet Explorer* as its default browser. It did so by refusing to develop applications, such as its Office products, for the Macintosh computers unless Macintosh complied. Since Macintosh computers do not use the *Windows* operating system, this action was hard to justify as reflecting a technical improvement to *Windows* in the way that an internal flash device was an improvement to cameras. Finally, and perhaps even more damaging was the fact that Microsoft actually paid Internet service providers such as America-On-Line (AOL) to adopt its browser and even gave AOL a space on the *Windows* desktop. Since AOL competes directly with Microsoft's own Internet service, this action is again hard to understand except as a way to foreclose the AOL market to Netscape.

Ultimately, Judge Jackson found the evidence compelling that Microsoft had abused its market power to bundle separate goods as a means to extend its dominance to the browser market. To some extent, it is what the appellate court later found as well. However, that court differed strongly with Judge Jackson that the appropriate remedy for violation was to break up Microsoft into separate companies much as John D. Rockefeller's Standard Oil was broken up 90 years earlier. Instead, the court remanded the case to Judge Colleen Kollar-Kotelly to work out a less drastic remedy that would be based on restrictions on Microsoft's actions and on monitoring to insure that those restrictions are enforced. [8] These arrangements appear to have been worked out and the case is over as a legal matter (at least in the U.S.). As we noted in Chapter 1, however, Microsoft has continued to be sanctioned and fined in Europe for anti-competitive bundling practices, most notably, in connection with its audio-visual software, *Media Player*. This is simply further evidence that in an age of complementarities and "interconnectedness," such issues are unlikely to disappear.

8.4.2   Antitrust Policy, Bundling, and Tying: Additional Developments

The issues raised in the Microsoft case are not new. The fear that large, established firms could abuse their market power and prevent or eliminate competition is what lies at the heart of antitrust policy. As noted in Chapter 1, Section 1 of the Sherman Act explicitly proscribes

---

[8]   For the legal record, see *U.S. v. Microsoft*, 253 F.3d 34 (D.C. Cir., 2001) and *U.S. v. Microsoft*, 231 F. Supp. 2d 144 (D.D.C. 2002). For further discussion see Economides and Salop (1992), Shapiro and Varian (1999), and Rubinfeld (2003).

monopoly power whenever its exercise weakens competition. Moreover, the subsequent Clayton Act speaks rather directly to the issue of bundling or tying: "It shall be unlawful . . . to lease (or sell) goods . . . on the condition, agreement, or understanding that the lessee or purchaser thereof shall not use or deal in the goods . . . of a competitor or competitors of the lessor or seller, where the effect . . . may be *to substantially lessen competition or tend to create a monopoly in any line of commerce* [emphasis added]." We defer until Chapters 12 and 13 a detailed formal discussion of anti-competitive or predatory practices. However, now is a good time to examine further the evolution of antitrust policy towards bundling and more specifically, tying.

Two key cases established a very clear legal presumption against tie-in requirements. The first was the *United Shoe* case of 1922. As a result of over 50 mergers, the United Shoe company had emerged as the dominant maker of shoe-manufacturing machinery in the early twentieth century with a market share on the order of 80 to 90 percent. Shoe-making uses a number of machines, however, and United Shoe faced competition in at least some of these lines. In leasing its machines to shoe manufacturers it stipulated that the manufacturers could not use any United Shoe machines in combination with those of other rival manufacturers and also that the shoe manufacturers had to buy certain supplies exclusively from United Shoe. Twenty-five years later, the court confronted a similar case with the International Salt Company. That company refused to lease its salt processing machines unless the lessee also agreed to purchase all its salt from International Salt. In this case, the court inferred International Salt's monopoly power largely from the fact that the company had a patent on its machines. The court found that both the United Shoe and International Salt tying requirements violated the antitrust statutes. [9] In these cases and others (including one involving IBM), the court emphasized the defendant firm's monopoly power in the tying good. As a result, the conventional legal wisdom was that tying requirements imposed by large, dominant firms would almost constitute a *per se* violation of the antitrust laws.

Over the years, the court's views on tying mellowed. In part, this was the result of an important insight of the Chicago School. This insight was that tying contracts as a means of leveraging a firm's power in one market to power in another would make little sense in a wide class of cases. Recall our nut-and-bolt example. Assume that bolts are monopolized but nuts are competitive. As we showed earlier, the bolt monopolist would then set a price of $6 and earn a profit of $36. Suppose now that this monopoly bolt firm uses a tying clause to require the use of its own nuts and thereby extends its monopoly power to this second market, as well. We know that this would allow the firm to raise the price of nuts to say, $2. However, if it does this, the firm will need to lower the bolt price to $4 because what consumers really want is the nut-and-bolt combination and the profit-maximizing price for that combination is still $6, and the maximum profit earned is still $36. The point of this Chicago School argument is that there is a potential maximum monopoly profit in these two markets and the monopolist can get all of the profit in the bolt market if the nut market is competitive, thereby removing any incentive to extend its monopoly to nuts via a tying requirement.

As the Microsoft case shows, however, there is a qualification to this argument. Generally speaking, when the market for the tied good involves substantial scale or scope economies, tying (and bundling) and leveraging power from one market into another can be profitable.

---

[9] *United Shoe Machinery Corp. v. United States*, 258 U.S. 451; *International Salt Co. v. United States*, 332 U.S. 392 (1947). Peterman (1979) argues that the fact that firms were allowed to use salt from producers other than International Salt if it was cheaper suggests that the real purpose of the tying was to reveal to International Salt the pricing practices of its rivals.

The volume of profit in these cases depends positively on the scale of operations. By requiring tied purchases, the monopolist in say operating systems can deny those scale economies to rivals in web browsers—thereby making them unprofitable—and enhance its own profits by reaping those scale economies for itself.

Recognition that the leverage of market power may sometimes be anti-competitive has led the court to move cautiously in relaxing its earlier strict rules against tying and bundling. In 1960, the Supreme Court accepted the use of a tied-sales clause in a case involving Jerrold Electronics Corporation, a pioneer in cable television systems and the community antenna television (CATV) industry, because it felt that this was a legitimate way of guaranteeing quality performance of a service in the early, developmental stage of an industry.[10] More recently, in the 1984 *Jefferson Parish* case, the Supreme Court attempted to articulate a clear set of guidelines under which any such arrangement would be *per se* illegal. The case involved a requirement by the Jefferson Parish Hospital that to use its surgical services it was necessary to use the group of anesthesiologists with whom the hospital had an exclusive contract. In its decision, which found for the hospital, the court stated three conditions, all of which would have to be met for the tie-in to violate antitrust laws.[11] These are:

1.   the existence of two distinct products, the tying product and the tied one;
2.   the firm tying the products must have sufficient monopoly power in the tying market to force the purchase of the tied good; and
3.   the tying arrangement must foreclose, or have the potential to foreclose, a substantial volume of trade.

The logic behind these conditions is clear enough. It would be wrong, for example, to consider a computer and its power cord as two separate products and then claim illegal tying. Likewise, the anti-competitive abuse of market power is only plausible if a firm has such power in the first place, and must be substantial to constitute a violation of the antitrust laws. Yet the result of these efforts in practice has been a curious mixture of *per se* and rule of reason standards. On the one hand, the *Jefferson Parish* conditions are meant to establish conditions under which bundling and tying are *per se* illegal. On the other hand, the interpretation of those standards is open to enough variation that a sort of rule of reason has emerged about whether they apply.

One troubling feature of the foregoing judicial history is that so little attention has been paid to cost-based reasons for bundling and tying. Yet there can be little doubt that such cost-efficiencies are present. This is because we see bundling and tying requirements in many competitive situations where neither price discrimination nor the extension of monopoly power can be the motive. This point has been particularly emphasized in a series of recent papers by Evans and Salinger (2005) and Evans (2006).

To understand the intuition of the Evans and Salinger (2005) argument, consider the case of head cold remedies. Some cold sufferers primarily endure headaches and sore throats. For these consumers, the main treatment they want is pain relief. Others, however, find sinus congestion and irritation to be the main aggravating symptom. These consumers want a decongestant in their cold remedy. Of course, there is also a third group that wants both a pain reliever and a decongestant.

---

[10]   *United States v. Jerrold Corporation*, 187 F. Supp. 545 (1960), affirmed *per curiam* at 363 U.S. 567 (1961).

[11]   *Hyde v. Jefferson Parish Hospital District No. 2, et al.*, 466 U.S. 2, 15–18 (1984).

Table 8.3   Pure bundling as the sustainable equilibrium

Demand volume	Product		
	Pain relief 50	Decongestant 50	Bundle 100
Costs			
Fixed cost	$300	$300	$300
Marginal cost	$4	$4	$7
Possible prices under:			
Separate goods	$6	$6	—
Pure bundling	—	—	$8.5
Mixed bundling	$10	$10	$10
Bundle and good 1	$10	—	$9
Bundle and good 2	—	$10	$9

As a specific example, let us assume that there are 50 people in each of the first two groups and 100 in the third. Members of each group have a sufficiently high reservation price that they will always buy the product. Let us also assume that to produce, package, and market each cold remedy drug for this market incurs a fixed cost of $300. Further, assume that the marginal cost of producing and packaging either a bottle of pain relief medicine or a package of decongestants is $4, but that there are some marginal cost savings in putting the two in one pill so that the marginal cost of a combined pain reliever and decongestant product is just $7. Finally, rather than assume a perfectly competitive market, we will assume that there is just one firm. However, we will also assume that entry is easy and costless so that that firm is constrained to offer products at prices that just permit it to break even. Table 8.3 shows the possible product offerings and the associated zero-profit prices.

Let's first think about our firm just offering the pain reliever and the decongestant separately. The first group of consumers will buy the pain reliever, the second will buy the decongestant and the third group will want to buy both products. So, demand for each product is 150 implying an average fixed cost for each drug of $300/150 = $2. When added to the marginal cost of $4, the break-even price is $6. However, this outcome is not an equilibrium. Any firm could enter the market and sell just the bundle for $10.00. This would attract all of the 100 consumers who want a combined medication, since they currently pay $6 + $6 = $12 to get both types of relief. In turn, the loss of these customers would make the continued offering of the two separate products at a price of $6 impossible as the average cost of each of these would now rise to $10. Indeed, since this price is the same as the bundle price, we might imagine that some of these consumers will actually buy the bundle as it gives them the relief they want plus a little something extra. As this happens, however, the bundle price falls further due to additional fixed cost savings while the individual prices must rise further. This will push all 200 customers to buy the bundle at which point the break-even price for the bundle drops to $8.50. This is, in fact, the only sustainable price and product combination. It is therefore the equilibrium in this imperfectly competitive but contestable market.[12]

---

[12]   A review of Table 8.3 will make it clear why either mixed bundling or offering a bundle and one good separately also cannot be an equilibrium

The scenario just described is worth some reflection. Competitive pressures police the market and force prices to equal costs. Even so, the firm in the market offers only the two goods, pain reliever and decongestant, together in one package. No consumer can buy this firm's pain relief medicine without also buying its decongestant. This is definitely a case of tying. Yet the tying is not done either to price discriminate or to extend monopoly power. It is simply another result of the competitive pressure to offer low-cost medication.

The idea that competition underlies much of the tying and bundling we observe is precisely the point that Evans and Salinger (2005) and Evans (2006) make. In their view, these practices are far too common to be explained either by price discrimination or monopolization motives. They note as well that even when price discrimination is the cause, the market outcome does not merit policy intervention. Hence, the only time that tying or bundling is definitely harmful is when it is used for leveraging market power. Given that some large scale and possibly scope economies are required to make the leveraging argument powerful, these authors and others have argued that all attempts at a *per se* illegal rule is misguided. Instead, they call for an explicit use of a rule of reason with a general presumption that the tying is legal unless the intent and ability to extend market power is explicitly shown.

Summary

In this chapter we have shown that a firm with monopoly power in more than one product line may have additional opportunities to price discriminate. By bundling its two goods together as a package or, more generally, by tying the sale of one good to the purchase of the other, the firm can induce customers to sort themselves out by their purchase decisions and *ex post* identify who is who. This permits charging a higher net price to those consumers with a greater willingness to pay.

In the case of two complementary products for which a fall in the price of one good raises the quantity demanded of both, sales coordination may occur for reasons other than price discrimination. In the absence of such coordination through a merger or a business network, for example, the separate production and marketing of two complementary products will typically raise prices, reduce output, and reduce profits. By taking account of the interrelationship between the demands for each product, coordination potentially offers benefits to both consumers and firms alike.

There can, however, be a downside to both bundling and tie-in sales. In cases in which large scale economies are present, these strategies may enable a firm to extend its market power in one product to another product line. This was the charge against Microsoft, and it is the central issue in antitrust cases involving tie-in requirements. However, it is worthwhile recognizing that some fairly strong market conditions have to be met for this outcome to prevail. It is equally worthwhile to remember that much of the tying and bundling occurs in fairly competitive markets. In such cases, there is some presumption that the practices are cost efficient. It follows that when we observe firms with market power using the same tactics, the goal of cost minimization may again be the reason.

So far, our analysis has focused on the strategic choices of a monopoly firm either acting alone or interacting in a second market that is also monopolized. The next step is to consider firms' strategies in the context of imperfect competition where neither one nor many firms but just a few firms interact. In such a setting, a firm can no longer simply address the issue of how to extract greater surplus from consumers. Each firm must now also consider how its production and pricing strategies affect not just consumers but the other, rival firms. This is the stuff of game theory and it is to this topic that we turn next.

Problems

1. A university has determined that its students fall into two categories when it comes to room and board demand. University planners call these two types, Sleepers and Eaters. The reservation prices for a dormitory room and the basic meal plan of the two types are as follows:

	Sleepers	Eaters
Dorm room	$5,500	$3,000
Meal plan	$2,500	$6,000

Currently, the university offers students the option of selecting just the dorm room at $3,000, just the meal plan at $2,500, or both for a total price of $5,500. An economic consultant advises the university to stop offering the two goods separately and, instead, to sell them only as a single, combined room and board package. Explain the consultant's strategy and determine what price the university should set for the combined product.

2. Bundling is not always superior to non-bundling. To see this, consider a telecommunications firm that offers both phone service and a high-speed modem service. It has two types of consumers who differ in their willingness to pay a monthly rental fee for either service.

	Talkers	Hackers
Phone service	$30	$a
High-speed connection	$16	$24

Determine for what values of a bundling would be more profitable than not bundling.

3. Many years ago, the major alternative to xerography in copying was the Electrofax copying process. Electrofax machines used a special paper coated with a heavy wax film. Like Xerox, the Electrofax companies charged a low price for the use of the machine but set a paper price per page of 4 cents. The actual and marginal cost of manufacturing the paper was, in fact, only 1 cent per page.
   a. Explain the pricing policy of the Electrofax producers.
   b. The high markup on Electrofax paper soon attracted new firms offering to supply the paper at a much lower price than the Electrofax producers. How do you think Electrofax will respond to this competition?

4. Computer software, S, and hardware, H, are complementary products used to produce computer services. Customers make a one-time purchase of hardware, but buy various amounts of software. That is, once the hardware is purchased, the price of additional computer services is P_S, the price of a unit of software. The software market is competitive. However, the hardware market is monopolized by the firm, HAL, Inc. The cost of producing software and hardware is c_S and c_H, respectively:
   a. Assume that all users of computer services are alike, that is, have the same demand curve for computer services. Use a graph to describe the profit-maximizing price HAL can charge.
   b. Would HAL gain anything by buying software at the competitive price, branding it as its own, and then selling its hardware only to customers who use the HAL-brand software?

5. LRW runs a railroad line from New York to Philadelphia, the LRW line. At present, fixed costs are reasonably large making it difficult for others to enter the market. Later, Nat Skape discovers that there is a market for travel from Philadelphia to Washington that is sufficiently large to permit offering passenger service between these two cities. His service is called the NSRR. Over time, both the LRW Line and the NSRR learn that many, though not all, of the customers riding from Philadelphia to Washington are actually passengers who originated in New York.
   a. What pricing issues arise between the LRW Line and the NSRR?
   b. Imagine that once it has incurred the sunk costs of setting up the Philadelphia to Washington line, it is possible that with a little experience, NSRR may be able to enter successfully the New York to Philadelphia market. Imagine further that before such entry occurs, the LRW Line builds an extension to Washington and offers riders from New York the advantage of service to Washington without the need to change trains. How should antitrust policy makers respond to this development?

6. Return to Table 8.3. What would be the equilibrium product offering and associate prices if:
    a. All values were unchanged except that there are now 100 consumers in each of the first two groups and only 50 in the group that wants both a pain reliever and a decongestant?
    b. All values were unchanged except that there are now 100 consumers who want pain relief, and 100 who want both pain relief and a decongestant, but only 50 who want only a decongestant?

References

Adams, W. J., and J. Yellen. 1976. "Commodity Bundling and the Burden of Monopoly." *Quarterly Journal of Economics* 475 (May): 475–98.

Allen, R. G. D. 1938. *Mathematical Analysis for Economists*. New York: St. Martin's Press.

Economides, N. and S. Salop. 1992. "Competition and Integration among Complements, and Network Market Structure." *Journal of Industrial Economics* 40 (March): 105–23.

Evans, D. 2006. "Tying: The Poster Child for Antitrust Modernization." In R. Hahn, ed., *Antitrust Policy and Vertical Restraints*. Washington, DC: Brookings Institution Press, 65–88.

Evans, D. and M. Salinger. 2005. "Why Do Firms Bundle and Tie? Evidence from Competitive Markets and Implications For Tying Law." *Yale Journal on Regulation* 22 (Winter): 38–89.

Peterman, J. 1979. "The International Salt Case." *Journal of Law and Economics* 22 (October): 351–64.

Rubinfeld, Daniel. 2003. "Maintenance of Monopoly: *U.S. v. Microsoft* (2001)." In J. E. Kwoka, Jr. and L. J. White, eds, *The Antitrust Revolution: Economics, Competition, and Policy*. 4th edition. Oxford, Oxford University Press.

Stigler, G. 1968. "A Note on Block Booking." In *The Organization of Industry*. Homewood, IL: Irwin.

Shapiro, C. and H. R. Varian. 1999. *Information Rules*. Boston: Harvard Business School Press.

Appendix

Formal Proof of the Inefficiency Induced by the Marketing of Complementary Goods by Separate Monopolists

Assume that the products of two monopolists, A and B, are complementary goods. Consumers require one unit of good B for every unit of good A consumed. The price charged by each firm will be denoted as P_A and P_B, respectively. However, since consumers only buy the two goods together in a one-to-one proportion, the price of concern to either firm's customers is the sum of P_A and P_B, denoted here as S.

Total demand Q for the composite product or AB pair is described as:

$$Q = D(S); \text{ where } D' = \partial Q / \partial S < 0; \text{ and } S = P_A + P_B \tag{8A.1}$$

We simplify further by assuming that each firm has a constant marginal cost of production equal to zero. Hence, revenue maximization is equivalent to profit maximization. Firm A's profit and Firm B's profit Π^A and Π^B, respectively, are therefore given by:

$$\Pi^A (P_A, P_B) = P_A D(S)$$
$$\Pi^B (P_A, P_B) = P_B D(S) \tag{8A.2}$$

Individual profit maximization at each firm implies choosing a price such that the derivative of its profit, $\Pi^A(P_A, P_B)$ or $\Pi^B(P_A, P_B)$, with respect to its own price is zero. That is:

$$\frac{\partial\Pi^A(P_A, P_B)}{\partial P_A} = P_A D'(S) + D(S) = 0$$

$$\frac{\partial\Pi^B(P_A, P_B)}{\partial P_B} = P_B D'(S) + D(S) = 0$$

(8A.3)

Since each firm will always set its price so as to maximize profits, equations (8A.3) must always hold. Denote the resultant equilibrium value of S as S^e. We obtain some insight into the value of S^e by first summing the two equations in (8A.3) to obtain:

$$S^e D'(S^e) + 2D(S^e) = 0$$

(8A.4)

where we have made use of the fact that $S^e = P_A^e + P_B^e$. Subtracting $D(S^e)$ from each side of equation (8A.4) then yields:

$$S^e D'(S^e) + D(S^e) = -D(S^e) < 0$$

(8A.5)

Now consider the strategy of a firm M that markets both goods as a single, composite product selling at the price S^M. Its profit Π^M is given by:

$$\Pi^M(S^M) = S^M D(S^M)$$

(8A.6)

Profit maximization for this firm therefore requires:

$$\frac{\partial\Pi^M(S^M)}{\partial S^M} = S^M D'(S^M) + D(S^M) = 0$$

(8A.7)

If instead of choosing the optimal price S^M, firm M chose the price S^e chosen by the two separate firms A and B, it clearly would not be at a point where the derivative in equation (8A.7) is zero. Indeed, we can determine precisely what the sign of that derivative evaluated at S^e would be.

$$\frac{\partial\Pi^M(S^e)}{\partial S^e} = S^e D'(S^e) + D(S^e)$$

(8A.8)

It is clear from comparison with equation (8A.5) that the value of the derivative in equation (8A.8) must be negative. That is, if the single, two-product firm priced at the aggregate level that the two rival firms did individually, an increase in that total price would tend to reduce its profit while a decrease would tend to raise it. The two rival firms thus set prices P^A and P^B that exceed the optimal price of a single firm marketing both products. Starting from that price, the single, two-product firm could raise profit by lowering the price further. Such a price reduction would not only raise producer surplus. It would also raise consumer surplus.

Part III
Oligopoly and Strategic Interaction

Part III starts our analysis of markets populated by more than one but still just a few firms, i.e., oligopolies. In such a setting, the actions of any one firm can change the market environment, e.g., the market price, not just for itself but for all firms. Hence, such actions will induce reactions that will in turn prompt further actions and so on. This interaction is, of course, recognized by each firm and plays a crucial role in determining each firm's strategic choice. In short, we now enter the world of strategic interaction for which the standard analytical tool is game theory. Accordingly, the next three chapters present formal models of oligopoly behavior each of which is rooted in game theory principles and, in particular, yields a market equilibrium consistent with the Nash (1951) concept.

Chapter 9 begins with a brief presentation of game theory and the basic Nash equilibrium solution. We then consider the earliest formal model of oligopoly, namely, the Cournot model. Although conceived a century before Nash's seminal work, the Cournot equilibrium outcome has all the features of the Nash solution and has become a workhorse in economic theory.

An important insight of game theory is that the outcome of any game is heavily dependent on the rules of the game. In the Cournot model, a key rule or assumption is that the firms compete in quantities or production levels. In contrast, the Bertrand model of Chapter 10 assumes that the firms compete in prices. Because price competition can be particularly fierce when firms compete in homogeneous goods, the Bertrand assumption gives firms an important motivation for differentiating their products. Hotelling's (1929) spatial model is a useful approach to modeling product differentiation. Therefore, we return to that model here and use it to understand what happens when firms compete vigorously in prices in a product-differentiated industry. Of course, products may be differentiated vertically as well as horizontally. Which sort of differentiation is relevant depends on the nature of consumer preferences. We explore the implications of this point with an empirical study of gasoline prices in southern California in the 1990s.

Finally, in Chapter 11, we consider a different alteration of the Cournot analysis, namely, the order of play. Both the Cournot and Bertand models assume that firms move simultaneously—choosing either production levels or prices at the same time. In contrast, the Stackelberg model of Chapter 11 retains the Cournot assumption of quantity competition but now assumes that one firm plays first, i.e., chooses its production level before its rivals. This permits consideration of the benefits of incumbency and first mover advantages, more generally.

The analysis in the next three chapters is central to all that follows in the rest of the text. Whether the topic is collusion, mergers, advertising or innovation, all modern industrial economics builds on the game theoretic models described in Chapters 9 through 11. Therefore, it is essential to understand this material before proceeding further.

9

Static Games and Cournot Competition

One of the most successful companies in the history of business is Coca-Cola. Indeed, "Coca-Cola" is said to be the second most well-known phrase in the world, the first being "okay."[1] Yet despite its iconic status in American popular culture Coca-Cola is not a monopoly. Coca-Cola shares the carbonated soft drink market with its archrival PepsiCo. An ongoing battle for market share has engaged these two companies for around a hundred years. The cola wars have been fought with a number of strategies, one of which is the frequent introduction of new soft drink products. Pepsi launched Pepsi Vanilla in the summer of 2003 in response to the year-earlier introduction of Vanilla Coke. In 2006, Coke initiated its biggest new brand campaign in 22 years for its new diet drink, Coke Zero. This followed Pepsi's revitalization of its Pepsi One brand made with Splenda sweetener instead of Aspartame.

In fighting these cola wars each company must identify and implement the strategy that it believes is best suited to gaining a competitive advantage in the soft drink industry. If Coca-Cola were a monopoly, it would not have to worry about the entry of Pepsi products. Life is simpler when you do not have to worry about how rivals will react to your decisions. The simpler life is a feature common to both monopoly and perfect competition. When either a monopoly or a competitive firm chooses how much output to produce, neither has to worry about how that decision affects others. In a pure monopoly there *are* no other firms. In a perfectly competitive market, there are other firms but no one firm needs to be concerned about the effect its output decision will have on the others. Each firm is so small that its output decision will not even cause a ripple in the industry.

The truth is, however, that Coke, Pepsi, and many other firms are neither monopolists nor perfect competitors. These firms, perhaps the majority of corporations, live in the middle ground of *oligopoly* where firms have visible rivals with whom strategic interaction is a fact of life. Each firm is aware that its actions affect others, and therefore, prompt *reactions*. Each firm must, therefore, take these interactions into account when making a decision about prices, or output, or other business actions. Decisions in such an interactive setting are called *strategic* decisions, and *game theory* is the branch of social science that formally analyzes and models strategic decisions. As a result, it is not surprising that game theory and the study

---

[1] "Coca-cola is okay" has been claimed to be understood in more places by more people than any other sentence, Tedlow (1996).

of oligopoly are closely intertwined. A central goal of this chapter is to introduce some basic game theoretic analysis and to show how it may be used to understand oligopoly markets.

Game theory itself is divided into two branches: *noncooperative* and *cooperative* game theory.[2] The essential difference between these two branches is that in noncooperative games, the unit of analysis is the individual decision-maker or player, e.g., the firm. By contrast, cooperative game theory takes the unit of analysis to be a group or a coalition of players, e.g., a group of firms. We will focus almost exclusively on noncooperative game theory. The individual player will be the firm. The *rules of the game* will define how competition between the different players, or firms, takes place. The noncooperative setting means that each player is concerned only with doing as well as possible for herself, subject to the rules of the game. The player is not interested in advancing a more general group interest. As we shall see though, such noncooperative behavior can sometimes look very much like cooperative behavior because cooperation sometimes turns out to maximize the well-being of each individual player as well.

Two basic assumptions underlie the application of noncooperative game theory to oligopoly. The first is that *firms are rational*. They pursue well-defined goals, principally profit maximization. The second basic assumption is that firms apply their rationality to the process of *reasoning strategically*. That is, in making its decisions, each firm uses all the knowledge it has to form expectations regarding how other firms will behave. The motivation behind these assumptions is just to understand and predict how real firms will act. We assume that firms are rational and reason strategically because we suspect that real firms do precisely this or will be forced to do so by market pressures. Hence, understanding what rational and strategic behavior implies ought to be useful for understanding and predicting real-world outcomes.

There is one caution that any introduction to the study of oligopoly must include. It is that, unlike the textbook competition and monopoly cases, there is no single, standard oligopoly model. Differences in the rules of the game, the information available to the various players, and the timing of each player's actions all conspire to yield a number of possible scenarios. Yet while there is not a single theory or model of oligopoly, common themes and insights from the various models of oligopoly do emerge. Understanding these broad concepts is our goal for the next three chapters. Moreover, we should add that the lack of one single oligopoly model is not entirely a disadvantage. Rather, it means that one has a rich assortment of models from which to choose for any particular investigation. One model will be appropriate for some settings, a different model for other settings. Because the real business world environment is quite diverse, it is useful to have a variety of analyses on which to draw. We will present three different oligopoly models. In this chapter we introduce the Cournot model of oligopoly, in the next chapter the Bertrand model, and then in Chapter 11 the Stackelberg model.

9.1   STRATEGIC INTERACTION: INTRODUCTION TO GAME THEORY

In game theory, each player's decision or plan of action is called a *strategy*. A list of strategies showing one particular strategy choice for each player is called a *strategy combination*.

---

[2]   A good textbook that offers a more formal treatment of game theory and its applications to economics is Rasmusen (2007).

Any given strategy combination determines the *outcome* of the game that describes the pay-offs or final gains earned by each player. In the context of oligopoly theory, these payoffs are naturally interpreted as each firm's profit.

For a game to be interesting, at least one player must be able to choose from more than one strategy so that there will be more than one possible *strategy combination*, and more than one possible outcome to the game. Yet while there may be many possible outcomes, not all of these will be *equilibrium* outcomes. By equilibrium we mean a *strategy combination* such that no firm has an incentive to *change* the strategy it is currently using given that no other firm changes its current strategy. If this holds for each firm, then the combination of strategies across firms will remain unaltered since no one is changing her behavior. The market or game will come to rest. Nobel laureate John Nash developed this notion of an equilibrium strategy combination for a noncooperative game. In his honor, it is commonly referred to as the Nash equilibrium concept.[3]

In the oligopoly models studied in the next three chapters, a firm's strategy focuses on either its price choice or its output choice. Each firm chooses either the price it will set for its product or how much of that product to produce. A corresponding Nash equilibrium will, therefore, be either a set of prices, one for each firm, or, a set of production levels, again one for each firm, for which no firm wishes to change its price (quantity) decision given those of all the other firms.

We note parenthetically here that, unlike the monopoly case, the price strategy outcome differs from the quantity strategy outcome in oligopoly models. For a monopolist, the choice of price implies—via the market demand curve—a unique output. In other words, the monopolist will achieve the same market outcome whether he picks the profit-maximizing price or the profit-maximizing output.[4] Matters are different in an oligopoly setting. When firms interact strategically, the market outcome obtained when each firm chooses price will usually differ from the outcome obtained when each firm chooses the best output level. The fact that the outcome depends on whether the rules of the game specify a price strategy or a quantity one is just one of the reasons that the study of oligopoly does not yield a unique set of theoretical predictions.

Since interaction is the central fact of life for an oligopolist, rational strategic action requires that such interaction be recognized. For example, when one firm in an oligopoly market lowers its price, the effect will be noticed by its rivals as they lose customers to the price-cutter. If these firms then lower their price too, they may win back their original customers. Because prices have fallen throughout the industry, the quantity demanded at each firm may well increase. However, each firm will now be meeting that demand at a lower price that earns a lower mark-up. Our assumption that the oligopoly firm is a rational strategic actor means that the firm understands and anticipates this chain of events *and* that the firm will include this information in making the decision whether or not to lower her price in the first place.

Our opening story about carbonated beverages is an example of such interaction except that instead of a price decision, Coca-Cola and Pepsi were making product design choices.

---

[3]   Nash shared the 1994 prize with two other game theorists, R. Selten and J. Harsanyi. The award to the three game theorists served as widely publicized recognition of the importance game theory has achieved as a way of thinking in economic analysis.

[4]   Competitive firms have no option as to which choice variable—price or quantity—to select. Competitive firms by definition cannot make a price choice. They are price-takers and can only choose the quantity of output they sell.

In doing so, each forms some idea as to how its rival will react. It would be *irrational* for Coke to anticipate no reaction from Pepsi, when, in fact, Coke understands that not reacting is not in Pepsi's interest. Similarly, if Coke lowers the price of its soft drinks it doesn't make sense for Coke to hope that Pepsi will continue to charge a high price if Coke knows that Pepsi would do better to match its price reduction.

How can an oligopolist anticipate what the response of its rivals will be to any specific action? The best way to make such a prediction is to have information regarding the structure of the market and the strategy choices available to other firms. In a symmetric situation, where all firms are identical, such information is readily available. Any one firm can proceed by asking itself, "What would I do if I were the other player?" Sometimes, even when firms are not symmetric, they will still have enough experience or business "savvy" or other information to be fairly confident regarding their rivals' behavior. As we shall see later, precisely what information firms have about each other is a crucial element determining the final outcome of the game.

Another crucial element in determining the outcome of the game is the time-dimension of the strategic interaction. In a two-firm oligopoly or *duopoly*, like Coca-Cola and Pepsi, we can imagine that one firm, say Coca-Cola, makes its choice—and introduces Vanilla Coke first. Then in the next period, the other firm, Pepsi, follows with its choice. In that case, the strategic interaction is *sequential*. Each firm moves in order and each, when its turn comes, must think strategically about how the course of action it is about to choose will affect the future action of the other firm and how those reactions will then feed back on its own future choices. Chess and Checkers are each a classic example of a two-person, sequential game. Sequential games are often called dynamic games.

Alternatively, both players might make their choices *simultaneously*, thereby acting without knowledge as to what the other player has actually done.[5] Yet even though the other player's choice is unknown, knowledge of the strategy choices available to the other player permits a player to think rationally and strategically about what other players will choose. The childhood game, "Rock–Scissors–Paper" is an example of a simultaneous two-person game. Such simultaneous games are often called static games.

Whether the game is sequential or simultaneous, the requirement that the strategic firm rationally predicts the choices of its rivals is the same. Given its prediction, the firm chooses what action is in its own best interest. In other words, being rational means that the firm's choice of strategy is the optimal (profit-maximizing) choice against the anticipated actions of its rivals. When each firm does this, and when each has, as a result of rational strategizing, correctly predicted the choice of the others; we will obtain a Nash equilibrium. In this chapter we focus on solving for Nash equilibria in simultaneous or static games.

9.2   DOMINANT AND DOMINATED STRATEGIES

Sometimes Nash equilibria are rather easy to determine. This is because some of a firm's possible strategies may be *dominated*. For example, suppose that we have two firms, A and B, in a market and that one of A's strategies is such that it is *never* a profit-maximizing strategy regardless of the choice made by B. That is, there is always an alternative strategy for

---

[5]   The important aspect of simultaneous games is not that the firms involved actually make their decisions at the same time. Rather, it is that no firm can *observe* any other firm's choice before making its own. This lack of information makes the actions of each firm effectively simultaneous.

firm A that yields higher profits than does the strategy in question. Then we say that the strategy in question is dominated: rationally speaking, it will never be chosen. Player A would never choose a dominated strategy since to do so would be to guarantee that A's profit was not maximized. No matter what B does, the dominated strategy does worse for A than one of A's other strategies. In turn, this means that in determining the game's equilibrium, we do not have to worry about any strategy combinations that include the dominated strategy. Since these will never occur, they cannot possibly be part of the equilibrium outcome.

Dominated strategies can be eliminated one by one. Once the dominated strategies for one firm have been eliminated, we can turn to the other firms to see if any of their strategies are dominated given the strategies still remaining for the first firm that we examined. We can proceed firm-by-firm eliminating all dominated strategies until only non-dominated ones remain available to each player. Often, but not always, this iterative procedure of eliminating dominated strategies leaves one or more players with only one strategy choice remaining.[6] It is then a simple matter to determine the game's outcome since, for such firms, their course of action is clear.

As an example, consider the case of two airlines, Delta and American, each offering a daily flight from Boston to Budapest. We assume that each firm has already set a price for the flight but that the departure time is still undecided. Departure time is the strategy choice in this game. We also assume that the two firms choose departure times simultaneously. Neither can observe the departure time selected by the other before it makes its own departure time selection. Managers for each airline do realize, however, that at the very time American's managers are meeting to make their choice, Delta's managers are too. The two firms are engaged in a strategic game of simultaneous moves.

In part, the choice of departure time will depend upon consumer preferences. Suppose that market research has shown that 70 percent of the potential clientele for the flight would prefer to leave Boston in the evening and arrive in Budapest the next morning. The remaining 30 percent prefer a morning Boston departure and arrival in Budapest late in the evening of the same day. Both firms know this distribution of consumer preferences. Both also know that, if the two airlines choose the same flight time, they split the market. Profits at each carrier are directly proportional to the number of passengers carried so that each wishes to maximize its share of the market.

If they are rational and strategic, Delta's managers will reason as follows: If American flies in the morning, then we at Delta can either fly at night and serve 70 percent of the market or, like American, depart in the morning in which case we (Delta) will serve 15 percent of the market (half of the 30 percent served by the two carriers in total). On the other hand, if American chooses an evening flight time, then we at Delta may choose either a night departure as well, and serve 35 percent (half of 70 percent) of the market or, instead, offer a morning flight and fly 30 percent of the market.

A little reflection will make clear that Delta does better by scheduling an evening flight *no matter which departure time American chooses*. In other words, choosing a *morning* departure time is a dominated strategy. If Delta is interested in maximizing profits, it will never select the morning flight option. But of course, American's managers will reason similarly. They will recognize that flying at night is their best choice regardless of Delta's selection. So, it seems clear that the only equilibrium outcome for this game is to have both airlines choose an evening departure time.

---

[6]   If the process continues until only one strategy remains for each player then we have found an iterated dominance equilibrium.

Table 9.1   Strategy combinations and firm payoffs in the flight departure game

		American	
		Morning	Evening
Delta	Morning	(15, 15)	(30, 70)
	Evening	(70, 30)	(35, 35)

Table 9.1 illustrates the logic just described and the reasons as to why the outcome in which both Delta and American choose the evening flight must be the equilibrium. The table shows four entries, each consisting of a pair of values. These entries describe the payoffs or market shares associated with the four feasible strategy combinations of the game. American's strategy choices are shown as the columns, while Delta's choices are shown as the rows. The pair of values at each row–column intersection gives the payoffs to each carrier if that particular strategy combination occurs. The first (left-hand) value of each pair is the payoff—the percent of the total potential passenger market—that goes to Delta. The second (right-hand) value is the payoff to American.

When we put ourselves in the shoes of Delta's managers we ask first what Delta should do if American chooses a morning flight. The answer is obvious. If Delta also chooses a morning flight then Delta's market share will be 15 percent whereas if Delta chooses an evening flight its market share will be 70 percent. The evening flight is clearly the better choice. Now consider Delta's response should American choose an evening flight. If Delta opts for a morning departure its market share is 30 percent whereas if it goes for an evening departure its market share is 35 percent. Once again, the evening departure is the better choice. In other words, no matter what American does, Delta will never choose to depart in the morning. Whatever the equilibrium outcome is, it must involve Delta choosing an evening flight.

If we now place ourselves in American's shoes, a similar result obtains. Again we start by considering American's best response should Delta choose a morning flight. The answer is that American should choose an evening flight to gain 70 percent of the market as compared to the 15 percent that a morning departure would generate. Similarly, should Delta choose an evening departure, American should do likewise since this will give it 35 percent of the market as against the 30 percent that a morning departure would give. As in Delta's case, we discover that flying in the morning is a dominated strategy for American since it never does as well as flying in the evening no matter what Delta does. Hence, just like Delta, American will always choose the evening departure time.

The outcome of the game is now fully determined. Both carriers will choose an evening departure and share equally the 70 percent of the potential Boston-to-Budapest flyers who prefer that time. That this is a Nash equilibrium is easy to see by virtue of the dominated strategy argument. Clearly, neither carrier has an incentive to change its choice from evening to morning since neither carrier would ever choose a morning flight time in any case.

Solving the flight departure game was easy because each carrier had only two strategies and for each player one of the strategies—the morning flight—was dominated. To put it another way, we might refer to the evening departure strategy as *dominant*. A dominant strategy is one that outperforms all of a firm's other strategies *no matter what its rivals do*. That is, it leads to higher profits (or sales, or growth, or whatever the objective is) than any other strategy the firm might pursue regardless of the strategies selected by the firm's rivals. This does not imply that a dominant strategy will lead a firm to earn higher profits than its competitors. It only means that the firm will do the best it possibly can if it chooses such a strategy. Whether its payoff is as good as, or better than the payoffs obtained by its rivals depends on the structure of the game.

Except when the number of strategy choices is two, a firm may have some *dominated* strategies, or choices which are never good ones because better ones are available—but not have any *dominant* strategy, or a choice that always yields better results than all others. Sometimes, a firm will have neither a dominant nor a dominated strategy. But for a firm that has a dominant strategy, the choice is clear. Use it! Such a firm really does not have to think very much about what other firms do.

Let's rework the departure time game so that at least one firm has no dominated strategies (and so, since the number of strategies is just two, has no dominant strategy). To do this, we will now suppose that because of a frequent flyer program, some of the potential Boston-to-Budapest flyers prefer Delta even if the two carriers fly at the same time. Specifically, assume now that departing at the same time does not yield an even split of customers between the two carriers. Instead, whenever the two carriers schedule identical departure times, Delta gets 60 percent of the passengers and American gets only 40 percent. Table 9.2 depicts the new payoffs for each strategy combination.

As can be seen from the table, a morning flight is still a dominated strategy for Delta. It always carries more passengers by choosing an evening flight than it would by choosing a morning flight, regardless of what American does. However, American's strategy choices are no longer so clear. If Delta chooses a morning flight, American should fly at night. But if Delta chooses an evening departure time, American does better by flying in the morning.

It may appear that American cannot easily determine its own best course without knowing Delta's choice. Yet this is not the case. There is a self-evident way for American to make a selection even without waiting to see what Delta does. This is because each carrier knows the payoff structure shown in Table 9.2. Accordingly, American can readily determine that its rival, Delta, is never going to select a morning flight. Since a morning flight is a dominated strategy for Delta, there is no question of this strategy ever being that carrier's choice. Knowing that Delta will never choose the morning departure, it is then an easy matter for American to select a morning departure as its best response since it knows that Delta will choose an evening departure. The equilibrium outcome for this modified departure time game is therefore just as clear as that for the earlier version. In this case, the equilibrium involves Delta choosing an evening flight and American opting to fly in the morning. Again, it is easily verified that this equilibrium satisfies the Nash criteria.

Table 9.2   Strategy combinations and firm payoffs in the modified flight departure game

		American	
		Morning	Evening
Delta	Morning	(18, 12)	(30, 70)
	Evening	(70, 30)	(42, 28)

In solving both the previous games, we made extensive use of the ability to rule out dominated strategies and, when possible, to focus on dominant ones.[7] We showed that the outcomes obtained by this process were Nash equilibrium outcomes. However, in many games no dominated or dominant strategies can be found. In such cases, the Nash equilibrium concept becomes more than just a criterion to check our analysis. It becomes part of the solution procedure itself. This is because rational, strategic firms will use the Nash concept to determine the reactions of their rivals to their own strategic choice. In the modified departure time game just described, for instance, Delta can work out that if it selects an evening departure, then its rival American will choose a morning flight. Delta can infer that the strategy combination of both carriers flying at night can never be an equilibrium—in the Nash sense—because if that outcome occurred, American would have a clear incentive to change its choice.

9.3   NASH EQUILIBRIUM AS A SOLUTION CONCEPT

In order to understand how to use the Nash equilibrium concept to solve a game, let's change the Boston-to-Budapest game one more time. This time we will change the decision variable from the choice of flight time to one regarding the ticket price. We assume now that consumers are indifferent about the time of departure and, instead, care only about the price they pay for the flight. Specifically, we will suppose that there are 60 consumers with a reservation price of $500 for the flight, and another 120 with the lower reservation price of $220. If the two carriers set a common price, they share equally all those customers willing to pay that fare. On the cost side, we will suppose that the unit cost of serving a single passenger for either airline is $200 whether the flight leaves in the morning or the evening. Let us also assume that each airline is flying a plane with a 200-seat capacity.

Although many price strategies are available to each firm, let's limit ourselves to just two. One is to set a high price of $500. Another is to set a low price of $220. So, as before, each firm has two strategies and there are four possible strategy combinations. Each such strategy combination will have associated with it a set of profits. If both Delta and American set the high price of $500, then each airline will serve half of the 60 passengers willing to pay that fare, or 30 passengers. Because each such passenger involves a cost of $200, each airline will earn profits of ($500 − $200) × 30 = $9,000. On the other hand, if each sets a price of $220, they will each share equally in a market of 180 customers and therefore carry 90 passengers apiece. Because of the smaller price–cost margin profits to each firm are only ($220 − $200) × 90 = $1,800.

What happens if one airline sets a high price and the other a low one? If say, Delta sets a fare of $500 and American sets a fare of $220, Delta will carry *no* passengers. All 180 consumers willing to pay the fare of $220 or higher will choose American. Delta's profits will be zero. American's profits will be given by ($220 − $200) × 180 = $3,600. Obviously, just the reverse will occur if instead American sets the high price and Delta sets the low one.

---

[7] Some care needs to be taken in ruling out dominated strategies. While one can eliminate *strictly* dominated strategies as a rational choice, *weakly* dominated strategies cannot be so ruled out. A strategy is *weakly* dominated if there exists some other strategy, which is possibly better but never worse, yielding a higher payoff in some strategy combinations and never yielding a lower payoff. The Nash equilibrium may be affected by the order of exclusion of *weakly* dominated strategies. See Mas-Colell et al. (1995), pp. 238−41.

Table 9.3   Payoff matrix for the airfare game

		American	
		$P_H = \$500$	$P_L = \$220$
Delta	$P_H = \$500$	($9,000, $9,000)	($0, $3,600)
	$P_L = \$220$	($3,600, $0)	($1,800, $1,800)

The payoff matrix for the new airfare game is shown in Table 9.3. As before, the entries in each row–column intersection show the profit to each firm associated with that strategy combination, with Delta's profit listed as the first entry in each case.

The first thing to notice is that there is no dominant or dominated strategy for either firm. If American selects a high price, Delta should also select a high price. But if American selects a low price, Delta's best bet is to match this price reduction. So we cannot rely on eliminating dominated strategies to identify the outcome of the game. What can we do? Again, we can place ourselves in the shoes of each company's managers. We'll start with Delta. The managers of Delta will look at the payoff matrix of Table 9.3 and reason, as we just did, that their best bet is to choose the same fare as American does. The issue then becomes one of predicting what American will do. Let us suppose that Delta's managers expect American to set a low fare. Then their best choice is to also set the low fare of $220. But when would this expectation make sense? It will only do so if Delta also believes that American's management team is likewise persuaded that it, i.e., Delta, is going to set a low fare. Delta can go a small step further and reason that if this is in fact the expectation of American, then it may as well go ahead and set the low fare because that is exactly what American is going to do. In other words, Delta's expectation that American will set a low fare because American, in turn, expects Delta to do so will in fact induce Delta to set a low fare. The low fare strategy is Delta's *best response* to its prediction of American's strategy, and that predicted strategy is also the *best response* to Delta's *best response* to that predicted strategy.

In the language of game theory, the strategy combination (*low fare, low fare*) is a Nash equilibrium. If each firm chooses the low fare strategy then neither firm will have any incentive to change its behavior given that the other firm does not change. Each will be pursuing its best course of action given what the other is doing. However, in the airfare game of Table 9.3 there are *two* such equilibria. Following precisely the same reasoning as above, we can work out that the strategy combination (*high fare, high fare*) is also a Nash equilibrium. This game does not have a unique Nash equilibrium.

As we shall see, the existence of more than one Nash equilibrium for a game is not uncommon. But the fact that a unique Nash equilibrium does not always exist does not diminish the usefulness of the concept. To begin with, even if focusing on Nash equilibria does not completely solve the game it certainly narrows the list of potential outcomes. In the airfare game just described, the requirement that the solution be a Nash equilibrium has permitted us to eliminate two, i.e., half of the possible strategy combinations from consideration. Moreover, there are often good, largely intuitive means for determining *which* Nash equilibrium is most likely. The book by Nobel laureate, Thomas Schelling, *The Strategy of Conflict*, offers much guidance in this respect.

Consider the airfare game once more. We want to know which Nash equilibrium (*low fare, low fare*) or (*high fare, high fare*) is more likely to be the outcome. As Schelling observed, taking account of other factors such as the past experience and learning of each firm's managers may be helpful. If the managers of both sides are "old pros" who have dealt with each other for many years, they may be able to avoid the "price war" outcome and coordinate to achieve the more profitable (*high fare, high fare*) outcome. But if the management of either or both sides is new and inexperienced, it will be harder to determine which Nash equilibrium will occur.[8]

We should note that the foregoing analysis of Nash equilibria is relevant to *pure* strategy equilibria. In game theory, a strategy choice is *pure* if a player picks it with certainty, e.g., always calls "heads" in a coin toss. Such pure strategies should be distinguished from *mixed* strategies in which the player uses a probabilistically weighted mixture of two or more strategies, e.g., calling "heads" half the time and "tails" the other half. In some games, mixed strategies or randomizing among strategies makes the most sense. However, we focus primarily on market games in which the only sensible Nash equilibria are those involving pure strategies.

Practice Problem

9.1

Firm 1 and firm 2 are movie producers. Each has the option of producing a blockbuster romance or a blockbuster suspense film. The payoff matrix displaying the payoffs for each of the four possible strategy combinations (in thousands) is shown below, with firm 1's payoff listed first. Each firm chooses without knowing its rival's choice. Find the Nash equilibrium.

		Firm 2	
		Romance	Suspense
Firm 1	Romance	($900, $900)	($400, $1,000)
	Suspense	($1,000 $400)	($750, $750)

9.4   STATIC MODELS OF OLIGOPOLY: THE COURNOT MODEL

All the games of the previous section are single period or static. Delta and American, for example, are assumed to choose either their departure times or their airfares simultaneously and without regard to the possibility that, at some later date, they might play the game again. This is a feature of earlier work on modeling oligopoly markets. Firms in these models "meet only once" and the market clears once-and-for-all. There is no sequential movement over time and no repetition of the interaction. These may be limitations. Yet the analysis is still

---

[8]   Alternatively, we might think about the "regret" either player would feel if she plays the wrong strategy. If, for example, Delta chooses P_H expecting American will, too only to discover that American actually chooses P_L, it will earn zero. But if it chooses P_L expecting American also to set a low price and then discovers that American chooses P_H, Delta will earn a profit of $3,600. In other words, Delta will have much less regret when it assumes the Nash equilibrium will be (P_L, P_L) than when it assumes it will be (P_H, P_H). The same is of course true for American. This thinking suggests that the low price Nash equilibrium will prevail.

capable of generating important insights. Moreover, studying such static models is a good preparation for later examining more complex dynamic models.

The most well known static oligopoly models are the Cournot and Bertrand models, each named after its respective author who did their work in the late nineteenth century. Interestingly enough, these models incorporate modern game theoretic elements. The solution proposed by each author implies the concept of a Nash equilibrium, even though the two models were developed well before the formal development of game theory. In the Cournot model the choice or strategic variable which firms choose when they compete is the quantity of output, whereas in the Bertrand model, the strategic variable chosen is price. We now turn to a presentation of the Cournot model, leaving the Bertrand analysis to Chapter 10.

The work of Augustin Cournot, a French mathematician in the mid-nineteenth century, is now understood as a cornerstone of modern industrial organization theory despite the fact that it went largely unrecognized for about one hundred years after its publication in 1836. The Cournot duopoly model anticipates Nash's concept of an equilibrium, and so not surprisingly, Cournot's work is regarded as a classic in game theoretic analysis.

The story that Cournot told to motivate his analysis went as follows. Assume a single firm wishes to enter a market currently supplied by a monopoly. The entrant is able to offer a product that is identical in all respects to that of the incumbent monopolist and to produce it at the same unit cost. Entry is attractive because under the assumption of constant and identical costs, we know that the monopolist is producing where price is greater than marginal cost, which means that the price also exceeds the marginal cost of the would-be entrant. Hence, the entrant firm will see that it can profitably sell some amount in this market. However, the new entrant will, Cournot reasoned, choose an output level that maximizes its profit, *after taking account of the output being sold by the monopolist.*

Of course, if entry occurred and the new firm produced its chosen output, the monopolist would react. Before entry, the monopolist chose a profit-maximizing output assuming no other rivals. Now, the former monopolist will have to re-optimize and choose a new level. In so doing, the monopolist will (as did the new entrant previously) choose an output level that maximizes profits *given the output sold by the new rival firm.*

This process of each firm choosing an output conditional on the other's output choice is to be repeated—at least as a mental exercise. For every output choice by the incumbent, firm 1, the entrant, firm 2, is shown to have a unique, profit-maximizing response and vise-versa. Cournot called the graph representations of these responses Reaction Curves. Each firm has its own Reaction Curve that can be graphed in the $q_1 q_2$ quadrant. That Cournot anticipated Nash is evidenced by the fact that he described the equilibrium outcome of this process as that pair of output levels at which each firm's output choice is the profit-maximizing response to the other's quantity. Otherwise, Cournot reasoned, at least one firm would wish to change its production level. A further appealing aspect of Cournot's duopoly model is that the equilibrium price resulting from the output choices of the two firms is below that of the pure monopoly outcome. Yet it is also greater than that which would occur if there were not two firms but many firms and pure competition prevailed.

To present Cournot's analysis more formally we assume that the industry *inverse* demand curve[9] is linear, and can be described by:

$$P = A - BQ = A - B(q_1 + q_2) \tag{9.1}$$

[9] By an inverse demand curve we mean a demand curve in which price is expressed as a function of quantity rather than quantity being expressed as a function of price.

where Q is the sum of each firm's production, i.e., the total amount sold on the market, q_1 is the amount of output chosen by firm 1, the incumbent firm, and q_2 is the amount of output chosen by firm 2, the new competitor. As noted earlier, we shall also assume that each firm faces the same, constant marginal cost of production, c.

If we now consider firm 2, alone, and take firm 1's output, q_1, as given, the inverse demand curve, facing firm 2 is:

$$P = A - Bq_1 - Bq_2 \tag{9.2}$$

which is formally identical to equation (9.1). However, from firm 2's perspective, the first two terms on the right-hand side are not part of its decision-making, and can be taken as given. In other words, those two terms together form the intercept of firm 2's perceived demand curve so that firm 2 understands that the only impact *its* output choice has on price is given by the last term of the equation, namely, $-Bq_2$. Note, however, that any change in the anticipated output choice of firm 1 would be communicated to firm 2 by means of a shift in firm 2's perceived demand curve. Figure 9.1 illustrates this point.

As we can see from Figure 9.1, a different choice of output by firm 1 will imply a different demand curve for firm 2 and, correspondingly, a different profit-maximizing output for firm 2. Thus, for each choice of q_1 there will be a different optimal level of q_2. We can solve for this relationship algebraically, as follows. Associated with each demand curve illustrated in Figure 9.1 there is a marginal revenue curve that is twice as steeply sloped: this was discussed in Chapter 2, and is adapted to the present model in the inset. That is, firm 2's marginal revenue curve is also a function of q_1 given by:

$$MR_2 = (A - Bq_1) - 2Bq_2 \tag{9.3}$$

Marginal cost for each firm is constant at c. Setting marginal revenue MR_2 equal to marginal cost c, as required for profit-maximization, and solving for q_2^* yields firm 2's Reaction Curve. So we have $MR_2 = c$, which implies that $A - Bq_1 - 2Bq_2^* = c$ or $2Bq_2^* = A - c - Bq_1$. Further simplification then gives the Reaction Function for firm 2:

Derivation Checkpoint
Review of Marginal Revenue and Demand

Assume that the inverse demand curve facing firm 2 is:

$$P = A - Bq_1 - Bq_2$$

Then total revenue is:

$$TR_2 = (A - Bq_1 - Bq_2)q_2 = Aq_2 - Bq_1q_2 - Bq_2^2.$$

Marginal revenue is the differential of total revenue with respect to output, so that:

$$MR_2 = \partial TR_2 / \partial q_2 = A - Bq_1 - 2Bq_2$$

This has the same price intercept as the inverse demand function but twice the slope.

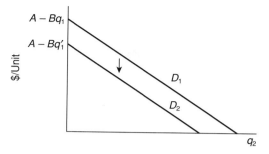

Figure 9.1 Firm 2's demand curve in the Cournot duopoly game depends on firm 1's output
An increase in q_1 to q_1' shifts D_2, the demand curve facing firm 2, downwards.

$$q_2^* = \frac{(A-c)}{2B} - \frac{q_1}{2} \tag{9.4}$$

Equation 9.4 describes firm 2's best output choice, q_2^*, for every choice of q_1.[10] Note that the relationship is a negative one. Every increase in firm 1's output lowers firm 2's demand and marginal revenue curves and, with a constant marginal cost, also lowers firm 2's profit-maximizing output.

Of course, matters work both ways. We may symmetrically re-work the industry demand curve to show that firm 1's individual demand depends similarly on firm 2's choice of output, so that as q_2 changes, so does the profit-maximizing choice of q_1. Then, we may analogously derive firm 1's Reaction Curve giving its best choice of q_1 for each alternative possible value of q_2. By symmetry with firm 2, this is given by:

$$q_1^* = \frac{(A-c)}{2B} - \frac{q_2}{2} \tag{9.5}$$

As was the case for firm 2, firm 1's profit-maximizing output level q_1^* falls as q_2 increases. The Reaction Curve for each firm is shown in Figure 9.2 in which the strategic variable, output level, of firm 1 and firm 2 is measured along the horizontal and vertical axis, respectively.

Consider first, the Reaction Curve of firm 1, the initial monopolist. This curve says that if firm 2 produces nothing, then firm 1 should optimally produce quantity $\frac{(A-c)}{2B}$, which is, in fact, the pure monopoly level, that we assumed firm 1 was producing in the first place. Now consider the Reaction Curve for firm 2. That curve shows that if firm 1 were producing at the assumed level of $\frac{(A-c)}{2B}$, then firm 2's best bet is to produce at level $\frac{(A-c)}{4B}$, that is, firm 2 should enter the market. However, if firm 2 does choose that level then firm

---

[10] We could alternatively solve for q_2^* by writing firm 2's profit function, Π^2, as revenue less cost, or: $\Pi^2(q_1, q_2) = (A - Bq_1 - Bq_2)q_2 - cq_2 = (A - Bq_1 - c)q_2 - Bq_2^2$. When we differentiate this expression with respect to q_2 and set the result equal to 0 (first order condition for maximization), and then solve for q_2^* we get the same result as equation (9.4). A similar procedure may be used to obtain q_1^*.

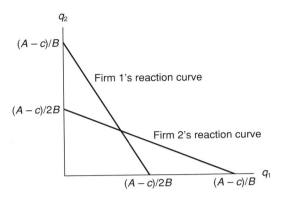

Figure 9.2   Best-response (reaction) curves for the Cournot duopoly model

1 will no longer do best by producing the monopoly level. Instead, firm 1 will maximize profits by selecting quantity $q_1 = \dfrac{3(A - c)}{8B}$.

As Cournot understood, none of the output or strategy combinations just described corresponds to an equilibrium outcome. In each case, the reaction of one firm is based upon a choice of output for the other firm that is not, itself, that other firm's best reaction. For the outcome to be an equilibrium, it must be the case that each firm is responding optimally to the (optimal) choice of its rival. We want each firm to choose a reaction based upon a prediction about what the other firm will produce and, in equilibrium, we want each firm's prediction to be correct. Put more simply, equilibrium requires that *both* firms be on their respective Reaction Curves. This happens at only one point in Figure 9.2, namely, the intersection of the two Reaction Curves.

To see how this works, recall the Reaction Function for firm 2: $q_2^* = \dfrac{(A - c)}{2B} - \dfrac{q_1}{2}$.

We know, and firm 2 knows, that in an equilibrium, firm 1 must also be on its Reaction Function, or that $q_1^* = \dfrac{(A - c)}{2B} - \dfrac{q_2}{2}$. Substituting this into firm 2's Reaction Function allows firm 2 (and also us) to solve for: $q_2^* = \dfrac{A - c}{2B} - \dfrac{1}{2}\left(\dfrac{A - c}{2B} - \dfrac{q_2^*}{2} \right) = \dfrac{A - c}{4B} + \dfrac{q_2^*}{4}$ so that

$\dfrac{3q_2^*}{4} = \dfrac{A - c}{4B}$. In turn, this implies: $q_2^* = \dfrac{(A - c)}{3B}$. Symmetry implies that $q_1^* = \dfrac{(A - c)}{3B}$ as well. We leave it as an end-of-chapter exercise for the reader to verify that this equilibrium also satisfies the Nash criterion.

Total output is for the market is $Q^* = \dfrac{2(A - c)}{3B}$. Substituting this into the demand function gives the equilibrium price: $P = A - BQ = \dfrac{A + 2c}{3}$. Profit for each firm is total revenue less total cost, which can be solved as $\pi_i = \dfrac{(A - c)^2}{9B}$.

As Figure 9.2 makes clear, the Cournot duopoly model just presented has a unique Nash equilibrium. Hence, in terms of our earlier discussion regarding the game solution concepts, we can solve the Cournot duopoly game simply by focusing on its Nash equilibrium. Since there is only one Nash equilibrium this must be the outcome of the game. The importance of this insight is difficult to overstate.

To see the power of the Nash concept, let us briefly reflect on the initial Cournot setup. We had two firms, each choosing quantity as its strategic variable. If, as also postulated, each knows the industry demand curve and the fact that each has an identical constant marginal cost, how should each firm act? Our discussion of Reaction Curves borrowed from Cournot suggests a kind of trial-by-learning process by which the two firms act and react until the equilibrium is achieved. But the power of the Nash equilibrium is that it makes such an iterative procedure played out in real time unnecessary. Recall the basic game theory assumptions that firms are rational and strategic. In choosing its own production level, firm 1 *must anticipate* that firm 2 will do whatever maximizes firm 2's profits. An expectation, for instance, by firm 1 that firm 2 will produce 0 and that therefore firm 1 should choose the monopoly output would *not* be rational because the reaction curve tells us that 0 is not firm 2's best response to that situation. Hence firm 1 would never predict 0 as firm 2's output choice. Similarly, firm 1 also ought never to predict $q_2 = \dfrac{(A - c)}{4B}$. Here, such a prediction would lead to an inconsistency because it would imply firm 1 choosing a profit-maximizing output $q_1^* = \dfrac{3(A - c)}{8B}$, for which the predicted value of $q_2 = \dfrac{(A - c)}{4B}$ is again not optimal. In short, there is only one prediction for q_2 that firm 1 can possibly make if it is to act rationally. This prediction is that $q_2 = \dfrac{(A - c)}{3B}$ the value of q_2 in the Nash equilibrium. This is the only prediction, which, if made, will actually induce the behavior consistent with that expectation being fulfilled. If firm 1 expects q_2 to be equal to $\dfrac{(A - c)}{3B}$, then firm 1 will *optimally* choose that output level, too. In turn, this output choice by firm 1 is such that firm 2 should indeed produce at the level of $\dfrac{(A - c)}{3B}$ if it wishes to maximize its profits.

To put it another way, what we are saying is that rational and strategic firms can work through the Cournot model as a pure thought experiment, without any time-consuming real world trials and errors. When they do, such firms will quickly realize that the only sensible prediction is that each will produce the unique Nash equilibrium output value, $q_i^* = \dfrac{(A - c)}{3B}$. It is only when each firm makes and acts upon that particular expectation that each firm will find that its prediction comes true.

Many economists, including us, prefer to use the term "*best response function*" instead of "Reaction Curve." The point is to emphasize that the correct interpretation of the Cournot model is one of *simultaneous* and *not sequential* output choice. The Cournot equilibrium is one in which each seller's predictions are consistent both with profit maximization and with the actual market outcome.[11]

---

[11] Friedman (1977) includes a brief discussion of these issues, particularly valuable to those interested in the history of economic thought. He notes that Cournot's fate was not quite one of total obscurity owing to his friendship with the father of the French economist Walras. The English economist Marshall apparently was also well aware of and influenced by Cournot's work.

As a numeric example, consider two firms, Untel and Cyrox, who supply the market for computer chips for toaster ovens. Untel's chips are perfect substitutes for Cyrox's chips and vice versa. Market demand for chips is estimated to be $P = 120 - 20Q$, where Q is the total quantity (in millions) of chips bought. Both firms have a constant marginal cost equal to 20 per unit of output. Untel and Cyrox independently choose what quantity of output to produce. The price then adjusts to clear the market of the total quantity of chips produced. What quantity of output will Untel produce? What quantity of output will Cyrox produce? What will be the price of computer chips and how much profit will each firm make?

Let's put ourselves on the management team at Untel to see the problem from its perspective. The demand curve that Untel faces can be written as $P = 120 - 20q_c - 20q_u$, where q_c is the output of Cyrox and q_u is the output of Untel. Untel's marginal revenue curve is $MR_u = 120 - 20q_c - 40q_u$. To maximize profit Untel chooses a quantity of output q_u^* such that its marginal revenue is equal to marginal cost. That is, $120 - 20q_c - 40q_u^* = 20$. This condition for profit maximization implies that:

$$q_u^* = \frac{120 - 20}{40} - \frac{20}{40}q_c \ or \ q_u^* = \frac{5}{2} - \frac{1}{2}q_c. \tag{9.6}$$

This is Untel's Reaction Function for any given level of output by Cyrox. In other words, Untel knows that its profit-maximizing choice of output depends on what its rival, Cyrox, chooses to produce. Untel wants to predict what Cryox is going to do, and then respond to it in a way that maximizes Untel's profit. Of course, Untel knows that Cyrox is also a profit maximizer, and so Untel anticipates that Cyrox will want to produce q_c^* to satisfy the condition for profit maximization at Cyrox. By precisely the same argument that we have just gone through, Untel knows that Cyrox's Reaction Function is $q_c^* = \frac{120 - 20}{40} - \frac{20}{40}q_u \ or \ q_c^* = \frac{5}{2} - \frac{1}{2}q_u.$ Untel can recognize that Cyrox's choice of output depends on Untel's. Untel also knows that Cyrox knows that Untel is a profit-maximizer, and that Cyrox will anticipate that Untel will choose a profit-maximizing level of output q_u^*. Therefore, Untel predicts that Cyrox will choose $q_c^* = \frac{5}{2} - \frac{1}{2}q_u^*.$ Substituting this prediction into Untel's Reaction Curve, equation (9.6), leads Untel to produce

$$q_u^* = \frac{5}{2} - \frac{1}{2}q_c^* = \frac{5}{2} - \frac{1}{2}\left(\frac{5}{2} - \frac{1}{2}q_u^*\right) \Rightarrow q_u^* = \frac{5}{3}.$$

Now let's put ourselves on the management team at Cyrox and repeat the exercise. Because the two firms are *identical* there is no reason why Cyrox would do anything different from Untel, and so we can quickly jump to the conclusion that Cyrox will also produce $q_c^* = \frac{5}{3}.$

Note that when Untel produces $\frac{5}{3}$, Cyrox's best response is to produce $q_c^* = \frac{5}{3}$, and similarly when Cyrox produces $\frac{5}{3}$, Untel's best response is to produce $q_u^* = \frac{5}{3}.$

Aggregate market output is $Q^* = \frac{10}{3}$, and so the price that clears the market is

$P^* = 120 - 20\left(\frac{10}{3}\right) = \$53.33$. For each firm the margin of price over unit cost is \$33.33 so that each firm makes a profit of \$55.55 million.

Assume that there are two identical firms serving a market in which the inverse demand function is given by $P = 100 - 2Q$. The marginal costs of each firm are \$10 per unit. Calculate the Cournot equilibrium outputs for each firm, the product price and the profits of each firm.

Cournot's model is insightful in its treatment of the interaction among firms and remarkably modern in its approach. Yet these are not its only strengths. Cournot's analysis has the further advantage that the results also blend well with economic intuition. In the simple Cournot duopoly model described above each firm produces its Nash equilibrium output of $\dfrac{(A - c)}{3B}$, implying that total industry output is $\dfrac{2(A - c)}{3B}$. This is clearly greater than the monopoly output for the industry, which would be $Q^M = \dfrac{(A - c)}{2B}$. Yet it is also less than the perfectly competitive output, $Q^C = \dfrac{(A - c)}{B}$, where price equals marginal cost. Accordingly, the market-clearing price in Cournot's model $P = \dfrac{(A + 2c)}{3}$ is less than the monopoly price $P^M = \dfrac{(A + c)}{2}$ but it is higher than the competitive price, c, which is equal to marginal cost. That is, Cournot's duopoly model has the intuitively plausible result that the interaction of two firms yields more industry output at a lower price than would occur under a monopoly, but not as much as the output produced under perfect competition.

9.5 VARIATIONS ON THE COURNOT THEME: MANY FIRMS AND DIFFERENT COSTS

Cournot's model can be enriched in several ways. One attractive feature of the model is its prediction that the addition of a second firm moves the industry outcome away from the monopoly result and toward that which obtains under perfect competition. A natural question then arises. Would introducing a third firm bring the industry still closer to the competitive ideal? What about a fourth? Or a fifth? Is the Cournot analysis consistent with the notion that when there are many firms the price converges to marginal cost?

To explore the Cournot model's implications when we vary the number of competing firms, let us work with the general case of N firms. These firms are, as before, assumed to be identical. Each produces the same homogeneous good and each has the same, constant marginal cost c. Industry demand is again given by $P = A - BQ$ where Q is aggregate output. However, now we have that $Q = q_1 + q_2 + \ldots + q_N = \displaystyle\sum_{i=1}^{N} q_i$ so that $P = A - B \displaystyle\sum_{i=1}^{N} q_i$, where q_i is the output of the ith firm. In turn, this means that we can write the demand curve facing just a single firm, say firm 1, as: $P = (A - Bq_2 - Bq_3 - \ldots - Bq_N) - Bq_1$. The parenthetical expression reflects the fact that for firm 1, this term is beyond its control and merely appears as the intercept in firm 1's demand curve. It is conventional to use the notation Q_{-1} as a shorthand method of denoting the sum of all industry output *except* that of firm 1's. Using this notation, we can write firm 1's demand curve even more simply as: $P = A - BQ_{-1} - Bq_1$.

Clearly, firm 1's profits depend on both Q_{-1}, over which it has no control, and its own production level, q_1, which it is free to choose. Given its constant unit cost of c, firm 1's profits Π^1 can be written as: $\Pi^1(Q_{-1}, q_1) = (A - BQ_{-1} - Bq_1)q_1 - cq_1$.

Profit maximization requires that firm 1 chooses its output level where marginal revenue equals marginal cost. Since marginal revenue is given by a curve with the same intercept but twice as steeply sloped as firm 1's demand curve, the condition for profit maximization at firm 1 is:

$$(A - BQ_{-1}) - 2Bq_1^* = c \tag{9.7}$$

Solving this equation for q_1^* gives us the Reaction Curve or what we will now call the *best response* function for firm 1 of:

$$q_1^* = \frac{(A - c)}{2B} - \frac{Q_{-1}}{2} \tag{9.8}$$

Since all firms are identical, we can extend this same logic to develop the best response function for any firm. Using the same shorthand notation, we can use Q_{-i} to mean the total industry production *excluding that of firm i*. This means that the demand function for firm i, taking the output of all other firms as given, is:

$$P = (A - BQ_{-i}) - Bq_i$$

The associated marginal revenue function of firm i is

$$MR_i = (A - BQ_{-i}) - 2Bq_i.$$

Equating marginal revenue with marginal cost gives the *best response function* for firm i:

$$q_i^* = \frac{(A - c)}{2B} - \frac{Q_{-i}}{2} \tag{9.9}$$

In a Nash equilibrium, each firm i chooses a best response, q_i^* that reflects a correct prediction of the outputs that the other $N - 1$ firms will choose. Denote by Q_{-i}^* the sum of all the outputs excluding q_i^* when each element in that sum is *each firm's best output response decision*. Then an algebraic representation of the Nash equilibrium is:

$$q_i^* = \frac{(A - c)}{2B} - \frac{Q_{-i}^*}{2}; \quad \text{for } i = 1, 2, \dots N \tag{9.10}$$

Recall however that the N firms are identical. They each produce the *same* good at the *same* unit marginal cost, c. From this it follows that, in equilibrium, each will produce the *same* output, i.e., $q_1^* = q_2^* = \dots = q_N^*$, or just q^* for short. So, noting that $Q_{-i}^* = (N - 1)q^*$, we can rewrite equation (9.10) as:

$$q^* = \frac{(A - c)}{2B} - \frac{(N - 1)q^*}{2} \tag{9.11}$$

from which it follows that the equilibrium output for each firm, what we refer to as the *Cournot–Nash* equilibrium output, is:

$$q^* = \frac{(A - c)}{(N + 1)B} \tag{9.12}$$

There are N firms each producing q^* as given by equation (9.12). From this we may derive both the Cournot–Nash equilibrium industry output, $Q^* = Nq^*$, and the Cournot–Nash equilibrium industry price, $P^* = A - BQ^*$, as:

$$Q^* = \frac{N(A - c)}{(N + 1)B}; \; P^* = \frac{A}{(N + 1)} + \frac{N}{(N + 1)}c. \tag{9.13}$$

Examine the two equations in (9.13) carefully. When $N = 1$, industry output is $\frac{(A - c)}{2B}$ and the corresponding price is $\frac{(A + c)}{2}$. But this is just the monopoly outcome, as of course it should be. When N increases to two we obtain the duopoly output and price levels derived in our earlier analysis. What happens when the number of firms rises above two? In particular, what happens when N gets very large?

Consider first the Cournot–Nash equilibrium price, P^*. As N gets larger and larger, the term $\frac{A}{(N + 1)}$ gets closer and closer to zero and, in the limit, vanishes. Similarly, as N increases the term $\frac{N}{(N + 1)}$ becomes arbitrarily close to 1. Thus, equation (9.13) says that when the number of industry firms gets very large, the industry equilibrium price, P^*, converges to marginal cost, c. But this is just the perfectly competitive result! Confirmation of this result is further obtained by noting that total industry output (the first part of equation 9.13) is similarly close to the competitive output of $\frac{(A - c)}{B}$ when N is large.

Consider the following numerical example, if the inverse demand curve is: $P = 100 - 2Q$, so that $A = 100$, and $B = 2$; and if the unit cost $c = 4$, then the monopoly output Q^M and price P^M are: $Q^M = 24$ and $P^M = 52$. Moving from a monopoly to a duopoly raises the equilibrium output, $Q^D = 32$, and lowers the price to $P^D = 36$. If the number of firms increases to 99 then the price falls to $P^{99} = \frac{100}{100} + \frac{99}{100} \times 4 = \$4.96$. As we increase the number of firms selling in the market the Cournot equilibrium market output continues to rise and the price continues to fall until, with many firms, we approximate the competitive equilibrium with $Q = 48$ and $P = 4$.

In short, the Cournot model implies that as the number of *identical* firms in the market grows, the industry equilibrium gets closer and closer to that prevailing under perfect competition. Of course, this result seems quite natural since, as N increases, each Cournot firm becomes smaller relative to the market. It is an appealing feature of Cournot's analysis that it predicts a plausible relationship between market structure and market performance. Market outcomes improve as market concentration falls and the competitive standard is approached.

What if the firms competing in the market are not identical? Specifically, what if each firm has a different marginal cost? We first handle this question for the case of two firms. Assume that the marginal costs of firm 1 are c_1 and of firm 2 are c_2. We use the same approach as before with the duopoly model, starting with the demand function for firm 1, which we can write as:

$$P = (A - Bq_2) - Bq_1$$

The associated marginal revenue function is

$$MR_1 = (A - Bq_2) - 2Bq_1.$$

As before, firm 1 maximizes profit by equating marginal revenue with marginal cost. So setting $MR_1 = c_1$ and solving for q_1 gives the best response function for firm 1 as:

$$q_1^* = \frac{(A - c_1)}{2B} - \frac{q_2}{2} \tag{9.14a}$$

By an exactly symmetric argument, the best response function for firm 2 is:

$$q_2^* = \frac{(A - c_2)}{2B} - \frac{q_1}{2} \tag{9.14b}$$

Notice that the only difference from our initial analysis of the Cournot model is that now each firm's best response function reflects its own specific marginal cost.

An important feature of these best response functions that is obscured when the firms are identical is that the *position* of each firm's best response function is affected by its marginal cost. For example, if the marginal cost of firm 2 increases from say, c_2 to c_2', its best response curve will shift inwards.

Figure 9.3 illustrates this point. It shows the best response function for each firm assuming initially that each firm has identical costs as in Figure 9.2. It then shows what happens when firm 2's unit cost rises. As equation (9.14b) makes clear, this cost increase *lowers* firm

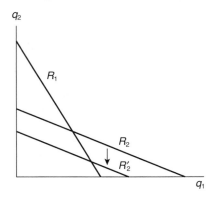

Figure 9.3   The Cournot duopoly model with different costs across firms
A rise in firm 2's unit cost shifts the firm 2 best response function downward from R_2 to R_2'. In the new equilibrium, firm 1 produces more and firm 2 produces less than previously.

2's best output response for any given level of q_1. That is, it shifts firm 2's best response curve inward. This change in firm 2's best response function affects the equilibrium outputs that the two firms will choose. As you can see from the diagram, an increase in firm 2's marginal cost leads to a new equilibrium in which firm 1 produces more than it did in the initial equilibrium and firm 2 produces less. This makes intuitive sense. We should expect that low-cost firms will generally produce more than high-cost firms. The changes are not offsetting, however. Firm 2's output falls by more than firm 1's production rises so that the new equilibrium is characterized by less output in total than was the original equilibrium. (Can you say why?)

The Cournot–Nash equilibrium can be obtained as before by substituting the expression for q_2^* into firm 1's best response to solve for q_1^*. Then we may use this value to solve for q_2^*. In other words, we have:

$$q_1^* = \frac{(A - c_1)}{2B} - \frac{1}{2}\left(\frac{(A - c_2)}{2B} - \frac{q_1^*}{2}\right)$$

which can be solved for q_1 to give the equilibrium:

$$q_1^* = \frac{(A + c_2 - 2c_1)}{3B} \tag{9.15a}$$

By an exactly symmetric argument, the equilibrium output for firm 2 is:

$$q_2^* = \frac{(A + c_1 - 2c_2)}{3B} \tag{9.15b}$$

It is easy to check that the relative outputs of these two firms are determined by the relative magnitudes of their marginal costs. The firm with the lower marginal costs will have the higher output.

Let's return to our Untel and Cyrox example of the two firms who produce computer chips for toaster ovens but now change this story a bit. While we still assume that Untel's chips are perfect substitutes for Cyrox's chips and vice versa, we no longer assume that they have identical costs. Instead, we now assume that Untel is the low cost firm with a constant unit cost of 20, and Cyrox is the high cost producer with a constant unit cost of 40. Market demand for chips is still estimated to be $P = 120 - 20Q$, where Q is the total quantity (in millions) of chips bought. What now happens when Untel and Cyrox independently choose the quantity of output to produce? What quantity of output will Untel produce? What quantity of output will Cyrox produce?

Again we put ourselves on the management team at Untel to see the problem from Untel's perspective. The demand curve that Untel faces is still $P = 120 - 20q_c - 20q_u$, where q_c is the output of Cyrox and q_u is the output of Untel. Untel's marginal revenue is again $MR_u = 120 - 20q_c - 40q_u$. To maximize profit Untel should sell a quantity of output q_u^* such that at that quantity marginal revenue is equal to marginal cost. That is, $120 - 20q_c - 40q_u^* = 20$, and so the condition for profit maximization implies that:

$$q_u^* = \frac{5}{2} - \frac{1}{2}q_c. \tag{9.16}$$

Untel's profit-maximizing choice of output still depends on the output that the higher cost rival, Cyrox, chooses to produce. Equally importantly, comparison of equation (9.16) with (9.6) indicates that Untel's best response function is unaffected by the assumed increase in Cryox's marginal cost. What about Cryox? By the same argument, the demand curve that Cryox faces is $P = 120 - 20q_u - 20q_c$ and its marginal revenue curve is $MR_c = 120 - 20q_u - 40q_c$. Equating this with marginal cost of 40 and solving for q_c gives the best response function for Cryox of $q_c^* = \dfrac{120 - 40}{40} - \dfrac{20}{40}q_u$ or $q_c^* = 2 - \dfrac{1}{2}q_u$. As we expected, the best response function for Cryox is shifted downward by the assumed increase in its marginal cost.

Untel knows that higher cost Cyrox is also a profit-maximizer and therefore anticipates that Cyrox will want to produce q_c^* that maximizes its profit. It is also the case, as it was before, that Untel knows that Cyrox knows that Untel is a profit-maximizer, and so knows that Cyrox will anticipate that Untel will choose a profit-maximizing level of output q_u^*.

All of this implies that Untel predicts that Cyrox will choose $q_c^* = 2 - \dfrac{1}{2}q_u^*$. Substituting this new prediction into Untel's best response function leads Untel to produce

$$q_u^* = \frac{5}{2} - \frac{1}{2}q_c^* = \frac{5}{2} - \frac{1}{2}\left(2 - \frac{1}{2}q_u^*\right) \Rightarrow q_u^* = 2.$$

Now we put ourselves on the management team at Cyrox and repeat the exercise. To cut to the chase, we know that Cyrox's best response is $q_c^* = 2 - \dfrac{1}{2}q_u$. Moreover, we know that Cyrox will predict that Untel will produce a best response that is based on a prediction that Cyrox will also produce a best response. That is, Cryrox predicts that Untel will produce $q_u^* = \dfrac{5}{2} - \dfrac{1}{2}q_c^*$. Substituting this prediction into Cyrox's best response function leads to:

$$q_c^* = 2 - \frac{1}{2}q_u^* = 2 - \frac{1}{2}\left(\frac{5}{2} - \frac{1}{2}q_c^*\right) \Rightarrow q_c^* = 1.$$ Again note that when Untel produces 2, Cyrox's best response is to produce $q_c^* = 1$, and similarly when Cyrox produces 1, Untel's best response is to produce $q_u^* = 2$.

Although the foregoing analysis is limited to just two firms, it still yields important insights. One of these is that in the Cournot model, firms with higher costs have smaller market shares and smaller profits. This means that a Cournot firm benefits when its rival's costs go up, as in our example above. Moreover, when costs vary across firms, the equilibrium Cournot output Q^* is not only too low (i.e., less than the competitive level), it is also produced inefficiently. As we know from Chapter 4, efficient production among two or more firms would allocate output such that, in the final configuration, each firm's marginal cost is the same. This would be the outcome, for example, if the industry were comprised of a single, profit-maximizing, multi-plant monopolist. It will also obtain under perfect competition. However, as we have just seen, the Cournot–Nash equilibrium does not require that firms' marginal costs be equalized.[12] Hence, output allocation in a Cournot equilibrium with different costs between firms is not an efficient one.

---

[12]   Our example assumed constant but different marginal costs across firms. The same insight could be easily obtained for the more general presentation in which the marginal cost of firm i, c_i, is a general function of its output, q_i, as in $c_i = c_i(q_i)$.

What is aggregate output, market price, Untel's profit and Cyrox's profit for the above case in which Untel is the low-cost producer and Cyrox the high-cost one? Compare your answers to the ones you work out when the two firms are identical and have a constant unit cost of 20.

9.6   CONCENTRATION AND PROFITABILITY IN THE COURNOT MODEL

Let us now try to combine the case of many firms together with the assumption of *non-identical* costs. That is, let us analyze the Cournot model with N firms, each with its own (constant) marginal cost such that the marginal cost of firm i is c_i. We can use the first order condition for profit maximization for each firm i, equation (9.7), and substitute c_i for c in this equation. This gives us the following:

$$A - BQ_{-i} - 2Bq_i^* - c_i = 0 \tag{9.17}$$

where Q_{-i} again is shorthand for the industry production accounted for by all firms other than the ith one.

In a Nash equilibrium, the equilibrium output q_i^* *for each firm i* must satisfy the first-order profit-maximizing condition. Hence, in the Nash equilibrium, the term Q_{-i} must be the sum of the *optimal* outputs q_j^* for each of the "not i" firms. Denote this equilibrium sum as Q_{-i}^*. Then we can re-write equation (9.17) as:

$$A - BQ_{-i}^* - 2Bq_i^* - c_i = 0 \tag{9.18}$$

By definition, the total equilibrium output, Q^*, equals the sum of Q_{-i}^* and q_i^*. Hence, equation (9.18) implies that

$$A - B(Q^* - q_i^*) - 2Bq_i^* - c_i = 0$$

Which can be reorganized to give:

$$A - BQ^* - c_i = Bq_i^* \tag{9.19}$$

We also know that the Nash equilibrium price, P^*, is obtained by substituting the Nash equilibrium output into the industry demand curve yielding, $P^* = A - BQ^*$. Substitution into equation (9.19) then yields:

$$P^* - c_i = Bq_i^* \tag{9.20}$$

Dividing both sides of equation (9.20) by P^*, and multiplying the *right-hand side* by $\dfrac{Q^*}{Q^*}$, we obtain:

$$\frac{P^* - c_i}{P^*} = \frac{BQ^*}{P^*} s_i^* \qquad (9.21)$$

where $s_i^* = \dfrac{q_i^*}{Q^*}$ is the ith firm's market share in equilibrium.

Let us consider equation (9.21) step-by-step. The left-hand side term is the difference between price and firm i's marginal cost as a proportion of market price. This is just the *Lerner Index of Monopoly Power* that we met in Chapter 3. The notion is that the greater firm i's market power, the greater its ability to keep price above marginal cost.

The right-hand side of equation (9.21) has two terms. The first is the slope of industry demand curve times the ratio of industry output to price. But the slope is just $B = dP/dQ$ so that we have $\frac{BQ^*}{P^*} = \frac{dP}{dQ} \cdot \frac{Q^*}{P^*}$. Recall the definition of the price elasticity of demand: $\eta = \frac{dQ}{dP} \cdot \frac{P}{Q}$. So the first term on the right-hand side of equation (9.21) is just the inverse of the price elasticity of demand. The second term is just the market share of the ith firm, i.e., its output relative to total industry output. Hence, equation (9.21) may be rewritten as:

$$\frac{P^* - c_i}{P^*} = \frac{s_i^*}{\eta} \qquad (9.22)$$

where η is the price elasticity of industry demand.

Equation (9.22) is a further implication of the Cournot model, now extended to allow for many firms with differing costs. What it says is this: a firm that produces in an industry where demand is relatively inelastic and where it has a relatively large market share will

Reality Checkpoint

Cournot Theory and Public Policy: The 1982 Merger Guidelines

In our review of antitrust policy in Chapter 1, we noted the dramatic change in policy regarding the treatment of mergers that occurred in 1982. In that year, the Department of Justice issued a new version of its *Horizontal Merger Guidelines*. This version replaced the original guidelines issued in 1968. Like that first set of guidelines, the 1982 document specified the conditions under which the government would challenge horizontal mergers. Unlike their predecessor, however, the new guidelines were based explicitly on the Herfindahl Index. Specifically, they stated that a merger would not be challenged if the industry Herfindahl Index was less than 1,000. A merger would also not be challenged if the index was over 1,000 but less than 1,800 *and* if the merger did not raise the Herfindahl Index by over 100 points. If the Herfindahl Index exceeded 1,800 points, then any merger that raised the index by over 50 points would cause concern and likely be challenged.

We will discuss these guidelines and their more recent modifications again in Chapter 16. For now, the point to note is that the explicit use of the Herfindahl Index may be viewed as a bow to the Cournot model which, as shown in the text, directly connects that index to the price–cost margin measure of monopoly power.

Source: Department of Justice, *Horizontal Merger Guidelines* (1982, 1984).

also be a firm with a substantial degree of market power as measured by the Lerner Index or the firm's price–marginal cost distortion.

The relationship described in equation (9.22) tells us about market power at the level of the firm. In Chapter 3, we discussed the structure–conduct–performance (SCP) paradigm in industrial organization that linked market power, as measured by the Lerner Index, to the structure of the *industry*. The question that remains is whether we can extend the relationship in equation (9.22) at the firm level to the level of the entire industry.

To see how let us first multiply each side of equation (9.22) by the firm's market share, s_i^*. Then add together the modified equation for firm 1 with that for firm 2 and that for firm 3 and so on until we add together all N modified (9.22) equations. The left-hand side of this sum of N equations is:

$$\sum_{i=1}^{N} s_i^* \left(\frac{P^* - c_i}{P^*} \right) = \frac{\left(\sum_{i=1}^{N} s_i^* P^* - \sum_{i=1}^{N} s_i^* c_i \right)}{P^*} = \frac{P^* - \bar{c}}{P^*}$$

where $\bar{c}$ is the weighted average unit cost of production, the weights being the market shares of the firms in the industry. The right-hand side of the summed N equations is:

$$\frac{\sum_{i=1}^{N} (s_i^*)^2}{\eta} = \frac{H}{\eta}$$

where H is the Herfindahl Index that we defined as a measure of concentration in Chapter 4 (here expressed using fractional shares, e.g., a 10 percent share is recorded as $s_i = 0.10$. Therefore, equation (9.22) aggregated at the level of the industry implies that:

$$\frac{(P^* - \bar{c})}{P^*} = \frac{H}{\eta} \tag{9.23}$$

Our generalized Cournot model thus gives theoretical support for the view that as concentration (here measured by the industry's Herfindahl Index) increases, prices also rise farther and farther above marginal cost.

A variant of the relationship in equation (9.23) was tested in Marion, Mueller, Cotterill, Geithmann, and Schmelzer (1979) for food products. They collected price data for a basket of 94 grocery products, and market share data for 36 firms operating in 32 U.S. Standard Metropolitan Statistical Areas, and found that price is significantly higher in markets with a higher Herfindahl Index. Likewise Marvel (1989) found that for 22 U.S. cities, concentration in the retail market for gasoline, as measured by the Herfindahl Index, had a significant impact on the average price of gasoline.

Summary

For industries populated by a relatively small number of firms, strategic interaction is a fact of life. Each firm is aware of the fact that its decisions have a significant impact on its rivals. Each firm will want to take account of the anticipated response of its rivals when determining its course of action. It is reasonable to believe that firms' anticipations or expectations are rational.

Game theory is the modern formal technique for studying rational strategic interaction. Each player in a game has a set of strategies to choose from. A strategy combination is a set of strategies— one for each player. Each such strategy combination implies a particular payoff or final outcome for each player. A Nash equilibrium is a strategy combination such that each player is maximizing her payoff *given* the strategies chosen by all other players. In a Nash equilibrium, no player has an incentive to change his behavior unilaterally.

In this chapter we presented the well-known Cournot model of competition. It is a static or single market period model of oligopoly. Although this model was developed prior to the formal development of game theory, the outcome proposed by Cournot captures basic game theoretic principles, specifically the Nash equilibrium solution.

The Cournot model makes clear the importance of firms recognizing and understanding their interdependence. The model also has the nice intuitive implication that the degree of departure from competitive pricing may be directly linked to the structure of the industry as measured by the Herfindahl Index. However, as pointed out before in Chapter 4, market structure is endogenous. Strategies that generate above normal profits for existing firms will induce new firms to enter. At the same time, incumbent firms may be able to take actions that deter such entry. We need to extend our analysis in ways that allow us to examine these issues.

The Cournot model studied in this chapter has firms interacting only once. The reality, of course, is that firms are involved in strategic interactions repeatedly. In such a setting, issues such as learning, establishing a reputation, and credibility can become quite important. We turn to a consideration of how the nature of strategic interaction over time affects market structure in Chapters 11–13.

Problems

1. Harrison and Tyler are two students who met by chance the last day of exams before the end of the spring semester and the beginning of summer. Fortunately, they liked each other very much. Unfortunately, they forgot to exchange addresses. Fortunately, each remembers that they spoke of attending a campus party that night. Unfortunately, there are two such parties. One party is small. If each attends this party, they will certainly meet. The other party is huge. If each attends this one, there is a chance they will not meet because of the crowd. Of course, they will certainly not meet if they attend separate parties. Payoffs to each depending on the combined choice of parties are shown below, with Tyler's payoffs listed first.

		Harrison	
		Go to small party	Go to large party
Tyler	Go to small party	(1,000, 1,000)	(0, 0)
	Go to large party	(0, 0)	(500, 500)

a. Identify the Nash equilibria for this problem.
b. Identify the Pareto optimal outcome for this "two party" system.

2. Suppose that the small party of Problem 1 is hosted by the "Outcasts," 20 men and women students trying to organize alternatives to the existing campus party establishment. All 20 Outcasts will attend the party. But many other students—not unlike Harrison and Tyler—only go to a party to which others (no one in particular, just people in general) are expected to come. As a result, total attendance A at the small party depends on just how many people X everyone *expects* to show up. Let the relationship between A and X be given by: $A = 20 + 0.6X$.

a. Explain this equation. Why is the intercept 20? Why is the relation between A and X positive?
b. If the equilibrium requires that partygoers' expectations be correct, what is the equilibrium attendance at the Outcasts' party?

3. A game known well to both academics and teenage boys is "Chicken." Two players each drive their car down the center of a road in opposite directions. Each chooses either *Stay*

or *Swerve*. Staying wins adolescent admiration and a big payoff *if* the other player chooses *Swerve*. Swerving loses face and has a low payoff when the other player stays. Bad as that is, it is still better than the payoff when both players choose *Stay* in which case they each are badly hurt. These outcomes are described below with player A's payoffs listed first.

		Player B	
		Stay	Swerve
Player A	Stay	(−6, −6)	(2, −2)
	Swerve	(−2, 2)	(1, 1)

a. Find the Nash equilibria in this game.
b. This is a good game to introduce mixed strategies. If player A adopts the strategy, *Stay* one-fifth of the time, and *Swerve* four-fifths of the time, show that player B will then be indifferent between either strategy, *Stay* or *Swerve*.
c. If *both* players use this probability mix, what is the chance that they will both be badly hurt?

4. You are a manager of a small "widget"-producing firm. There are only two firms including yours that produce "widgets." Moreover your company and your competitor's are identical. You produce the same good and face the same costs of production described by the following total cost function: total cost = $1,500 + 8q$ where q is the output of an individual firm. The market-clearing price, at which you can sell your widgets to the public, depends on how many widgets both you and your rival choose to produce. A market research company has found that market demand for widgets can be described as: $P = 200 - 2Q$ where $Q = q_1 + q_2$, where q_1 is your output and q_2 is your rivals. The board of directors has directed you to choose an output level that will *maximize* the firm's profit. How many widgets should your firm produce in order to achieve the profit-maximizing goal? Moreover, you must present your strategy to the board of directors and explain to them why producing this amount of widgets is the profit-maximizing strategy.

5. You are still a manager of a small widget-producing firm. Now however there are 14 such firms (including yours) in the industry. Each firm is identical; each one produces the same product and has the same costs of production. Your firm, as well as each one of the other firms, has the same total cost function, namely: total cost = $200 + 50q$ where q is the output of an individual firm. The price at which you can sell your widgets is determined by market demand, which has been estimated as: $P = 290 - \frac{1}{3}Q$ where Q is the sum of all the individual firms producing in this industry. So, for example, if 120 widgets are produced in the industry then the market-clearing price will be 250, whereas if 300 widgets are produced then the market-clearing price will be 190. The Board of Directors has directed you to choose an output level that maximizes the firm's profit. You have an incentive to maximize profits because your job and salary depend upon the profit performance of this company. Moreover, you should also be able to present your profit-maximizing strategy to the Board of Directors and explain to them why producing this amount maximizes the firm's profit.

6. The inverse market demand for fax paper is given by $P = 400 - 2Q$. There are two firms who produce fax paper. Each firm has a unit cost of production equal to 40, and they compete in the market in quantities. That is, they can choose any quantity to produce, and they make their quantity choices simultaneously.
a. Show how to derive the Cournot–Nash equilibrium to this game. What are firms' profits in equilibrium?
b. What is the monopoly output, i.e., the one that maximizes total industry profit? Why isn't producing one half the monopoly output a Nash equilibrium outcome?

7. Return to problem 6, but suppose now that firm 1 has a cost advantage. Its unit cost is constant and equal to 25 whereas firm 2 still has a unit cost of 40. What is the Cournot outcome now? What are the profits for each firm?

8. We can use the Cournot model to derive an equilibrium industry structure. For this purpose, we will define an equilibrium as that structure

in which no firm has an incentive to leave or enter the industry. If a firm leaves the industry, it enters an alternative competitive market in which case it earns zero (economic) profit. If an additional firm enters the industry when there are already n firms in it, the new firm's profit is determined by the Cournot equilibrium with $n + 1$ firms. For this problem,

assume that each firm has the cost function: $C(q) = 256 + 20q$. Assume further that market demand is described by: $P = 100 - Q$.

a. Find the long-run equilibrium number of firms in this industry.

b. What industry output, price, and firm profit levels will characterize the long-run equilibrium?

References

Cournot, A. 1836. *Researches into the Mathematical Principles of the Theory of Wealth.* Paris: Hachette (English Translation by N. T. Bacon, New York: Macmillan, 1897).

Friedman, J. 1977. *Oligopoly Theory.* Amsterdam: North-Holland.

Marion, B. W., W. F. Mueller, R. W. Cotterill, F. E. Geithman, and J. R. Schmelzer. 1979. *The Food Retailing Industry Market Structure, Profits and Prices.* New York: Praeger.

Marvel, H. 1989. "Concentration and Price in Gasoline Retailing." In Leonard Weiss, ed., *Concentration and Price.* Cambridge, MA: MIT Press.

Mas-Colell, A., M. D. Whinston, and J. Green. 1995. *Microeconomic Theory.* New York: Oxford University Press.

Rasmusen, E. 2007. *Games and Information: An Introduction to Game Theory.* 4th edition. Cambridge: Blackwell.

Schelling, T. 1960. *The Strategy of Conflict.* Cambridge, MA: Harvard University Press.

Tedlow, R. 1996. *New and Improved: The Story of Mass Marketing in America.* 2nd edition. Boston: Harvard Business School Press.

10

Price Competition

The two largest makers of x86-based microprocessors for use in computers are Intel and Advanced Micro Devices (AMD). While Intel is far larger with nearly 75 percent of the market, AMD's roughly 25 percent share gives it ample market clout and both firms are keenly aware of each other's presence. The strategic interaction that results often appears as a price war in which each firm tries to win customers from the other by offering steep price cuts. The latest such event was played out in 2006 and into 2007. AMD fired the first shot in May 2006, when it dropped the price of its dual-core Athlon 64 X2 5,000+ to $301 from $696. In July of that year, AMD then cut the price of the Athlon 64 X2 4,600+ by 57 percent to $240 from $558. A few days later, Intel marked down the price of its Intel Pentium D processor 960 by 40 percent to $316. Intel also cut prices on many older processors from 50 to 60 percent. Modest price cuts by both firms followed until April of 2007. In that month, AMD slashed prices on its Athlon processors by 20 to 50 percent in anticipation of coming Intel price reductions. Those anticipations were realized later that month when Intel launched its new Core 2 Duo processor line with discounts of 40 to 50 percent.

In the market for high-speed processors the major buyers are computer producers such as Dell, Compaq, and Gateway. These are savvy consumers who know quality and who, if the product is good, will buy from the lowest-priced provider. Intel and AMD post their prices and then try to adjust their production to the demand those prices elicit. This is the way competition works in many markets, including restaurants, electricians, moving companies, consulting firms, and financial services. However, it is quite different from the way competition works in the Cournot model. There each competing firm independently produces an amount of output so that production occurs before the consumer makes a purchase. It is only afterwards that the price adjusts so that consumers will buy the total output that the firms produced. This is what is meant by the phrase "the price adjusts so that the market clears," and it is perhaps an apt description of how the market works in the automobile, aircraft, and other manufacturing industries.

In a monopolized market, it would of course make no difference whether the firm initially set a price and then produced whatever amount consumers demanded at that price or, instead, first chose its production and let the price settle at whatever level was necessary to sell that output. When a profit-maximizing monopolist optimally sets price, that choice will imply, via the demand curve, an output level, which is precisely the same amount the monopolist would have chosen if instead it had initially chosen the profit-maximizing amount to produce.

However, once we leave the world of monopoly the equivalence of price and output strategies vanishes. In oligopolistic markets it matters very much whether firms compete in terms of quantities, as in Cournot, or like the high-speed Internet providers, in terms of price. The nature of the competition is markedly different. To understand these differences we begin by turning the Cournot model on its head, and look at the same market in which two firms produce identical products but now compete by first setting prices instead of production levels. This is known as the Bertrand model. Later in the chapter we allow the products to be less than perfect substitutes, or to be differentiated. As in Chapter 9, we focus on static or simultaneous models of price competition limited to a single market period.

10.1   THE BERTRAND DUOPOLY MODEL

The standard Cournot duopoly model, recast in terms of price strategies rather than quantity strategies, is typically referred to as the Bertrand model. Joseph Bertrand was a French mathematician who in 1883 reviewed and critiqued Cournot's work nearly 50 years after its publication in an article in the *Journal des Savants*. Bertrand was critical of mathematical modeling in economics, and to prove his point he analyzed the Cournot model in terms of prices rather than quantities. The legacy of Bertrand is not, however, his criticism of what he termed "pseudo-mathematics" in economics. Instead, Bertrand's contribution was the recognition that using price as a strategic variable is different from using quantity as the strategic variable, and that this difference is worth investigating.

Let us rework the Cournot duopoly model with each firm choosing the price it will charge rather than the quantity it will produce. Otherwise, the model and the assumptions are exactly the same as before. There are two firms who choose their strategies simultaneously. Each produces the identical good at the same, constant marginal cost c. Each firm knows the structure of market demand. In the Cournot model we described demand by a linear inverse demand function $P = A - BQ$. When firms choose prices, rather than quantities, it is more convenient to rewrite the demand function and have total output as the dependent variable.[1] Therefore, we have:

$$Q = a - bP; \quad \text{where } a = \frac{A}{B} \text{ and } b = \frac{1}{B} \tag{10.1}$$

Consider the pricing problem first from firm 2's perspective. In order to determine its best price response to its rival firm 1, firm 2 must first work out the demand for its product *conditional* on both its own price, denoted by p_2, and firm 1's price, denoted by p_1. Rationally speaking, firm 2's reasoning would go as follows. If $p_2 > p_1$, firm 2 will sell no output. The product is homogeneous so that consumers always buy from the cheapest source. Setting a price above that of firm 1 therefore means that firm 2 will serve no customers. The opposite is true if $p_2 < p_1$. When firm 2 sets the lower price, it will supply the entire market, and firm 1 will sell nothing. Finally, if $p_2 = p_1$, the two firms will split the market evenly. When both firms charge identical prices the same number of customers patronizes both producers.

---

[1]   When firms choose quantities (as in Cournot's model) it is often easier to work with the inverse demand curve and treat price as the dependent variable. When firms select prices, as in Bertrand's analysis, it is often best to let quantity be the dependent variable.

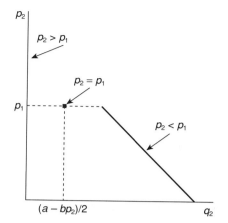

Figure 10.1   Firm 2's demand curve in the Bertrand model
Industry demand equal to $a - bp_2$ is the same as firm 2's demand for all p_2 less than p_1. If $p_2 = p_1$, then the two firms share equally the total demand. For $p_2 > p_1$, Firm 2's demand falls to zero.

The foregoing reasoning tells us that demand for firm 2's output, q_2, may be described as follows:

$$q_2 = 0 \qquad \text{if } p_2 > p_1$$

$$q_2 = \frac{a - bp_2}{2} \qquad \text{if } p_2 = p_1$$

$$q_2 = a - bp_2 \qquad \text{if } p_2 < p_1$$

As Figure 10.1 shows, this demand function is *not* continuous. For any p_2 greater than p_1, demand for q_2 is zero. But when p_2 falls and becomes exactly equal to p_1, demand jumps from zero to $\frac{a - bp_2}{2}$. When p_2 then falls still further so that it is below p_1, demand then jumps again to $a - bp_2$.

This discontinuity in firm 2's demand curve was not present in the quantity version of the Cournot model, and it turns out to make a crucial difference in terms of firms' strategies. The discontinuity in demand carries over into a discontinuity in profits. Firm 2's profit, Π_2, as a function of p_1 and p_2 is

$$\Pi_2(p_1, p_2) = 0 \qquad \text{if } p_2 > p_1$$

$$\Pi_2(p_1, p_2) = (p_2 - c)\frac{a - bp_2}{2} \qquad \text{if } p_2 = p_1$$

$$\Pi_2(p_1, p_2) = (p_2 - c)(a - bp_2) \qquad \text{if } p_2 < p_1$$

To find firm 2's *best response* function, we need to find the price p_2 that maximizes firm 2's profits $\Pi_2(p_1, p_2)$ for any given choice of p_1. For example, suppose firm 1 chooses a very

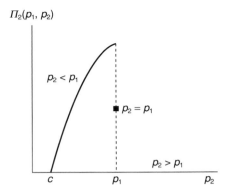

Figure 10.2   Firm 2's profits as a function of p_2 when firm 1 prices above cost but below the pure monopoly price

Firm 2's profits rise continuously as its price rises from the level of marginal cost, c, to just below firm 1's price. When p_2 equals p_1, firm 2's profits fall relative to those earned when p_2 is just below p_1. For p_2 greater than p_1, firm 2 earns zero profits.

high price—higher even than the pure monopoly price, which in this case is $p^M = \dfrac{a + bc}{2b}$.[2]

Since firm 2 could capture the entire market by selecting any price lower than p_1, its best response would be to choose the pure monopoly price p^M, and thereby earn the pure monopoly profits.

Conversely, what if firm 1 set a very low price, say one below its unit cost c? This would be an unusual choice, but if we wish to construct a complete *best response* function for firm 2, we must determine its value for *all* the possible values p_1 can take. If $p_1 < c$, firm 2 is best setting its price at some level above p_1. This will mean that firm 2 will sell nothing and earn zero profits. The alternative of setting $p_2 < p_1 < c$ will lead to *negative* profits: firm 2 sells a positive amount of output, but at a price below unit cost so that firm 2 will lose money on each unit sold.

What about the more likely case in which firm 1 sets its price above marginal cost c but either equal to or below the pure monopoly price p^M? How should firm 2 optimally respond in these circumstances? The simple answer is that it should set a price *just a bit less than* p_1. The intuition behind this strategy is illustrated in Figure 10.2, which shows firm 2's profit given a price p_1, satisfying the relationship $\dfrac{a + bc}{2b} \geq p_1 > c$.

Note that firm 2's profits rise continuously as p_2 rises from c to just below p_1. Whenever p_2 is less than p_1, firm 2 is the only company that any consumer buys from. However, when p_1 is less than or equal to p^M, the monopoly power that firm 2 obtains from undercutting p_1 is constrained. In particular, the firm cannot sell at the pure monopoly price, p^M and earn the associated profit because at that price, firm 2 would lose all its customers. Still, the firm will wish to get as close to that result as possible. It could, of course, just match firm 1's price exactly. But whenever it does so it shares the market equally with its rival. If, instead of

---

[2]   This is, of course, the same monopoly price as we showed in Chapter 8 for the quantity version of the model with the notational change that $a = A/B$, and $b = 1/B$.

setting $p_2 = p_1$, firm 2 just *slightly* reduces its price below the p_1 level, it will double its sales while incurring only an infinitesimal decline in its profit margin per unit sold. This is a trade well worth the making as Figure 10.2 makes clear. In turn, the implication is that for any p_1 such that $p^M \geq p_1 > c$, firm 2's best response is to set $p_2^* = p_1 - \varepsilon$, where ε is an arbitrarily small amount.

The last case to consider is the case in which firm 1 prices at cost so that $p_1 = c$. Clearly, firm 2 has no incentive to undercut this value of p_1. To do so, would only lead to losses for firm 2. Instead, firm 2 will do best to set p_2 either equal to or above p_1. If it prices above p_1, firm 2 will sell nothing and earn zero profits. If it matches p_1, it will enjoy positive sales but break even on every unit sold. Accordingly, firm 2 will earn zero profits in this latter case, too. Thus, when $p_1 = c$, firm 2's *best response* is to set p_2 either greater than or equal to p_1.

Our preceding discussion may be summarized with the following description of firm 2's best price response

$$p_2^* = \frac{a + bc}{2b} \quad \text{if } p_1 > \frac{a + bc}{2b}$$

$$p_2^* = p_1 - \varepsilon \quad \text{if } c < p_1 \leq \frac{a + bc}{2b}$$

$$p_2^* \geq p_1 \quad \text{if } c = p_1$$

$$p_2^* > p_1 \quad \text{if } c > p_1 \geq 0$$

By similar reasoning, firm 1's best response p_1^* for any given value of p_2 would be given by:

$$p_1^* = \frac{a + bc}{2b} \quad \text{if } p_2 > \frac{a + bc}{2b}$$

$$p_1^* = p_2 - \varepsilon \quad \text{if } c < p_2 \leq \frac{a + bc}{2b}$$

$$p_1^* \geq p_2 \quad \text{if } c = p_2$$

$$p_1^* > p_2 \quad \text{if } c > p_2 \geq 0$$

We may now determine the Nash equilibrium for the duopoly game when played in prices. We know that a Nash equilibrium is one in which neither firm has an incentive to change its strategy. For example, the strategy combination $[p_1 = \frac{a + bc}{2b}, p_2 = \frac{a + bc}{2b} - \varepsilon]$ *cannot* be an equilibrium. This is because in that combination, firm 2 undercuts firm 1's price and sells at a price just below the monopoly level. However, in such a case, firm 1 would have no customers and earn zero profit. Since firm 1 could earn substantial profit by lowering its price to just below that set by firm 2, it would wish to do so. Accordingly, this strategy cannot be a Nash equilibrium. To put it another way, firm 2 could never expect firm 1 to set the monopoly price of $p_1 = (a + bc)/2b$ precisely because firm 1 would know that so doing would lead to zero profit as firm 2 would undercut that price by a small amount ε and steal all firm 1's customers.

Reality Checkpoint

Flat Screens and Flatter Prices

Perhaps one of the most dramatic examples of Bertrand competition comes from the market for flat screen TVs. Such screens use one of three basic technologies. These are: liquid crystal display (LCD), digital light processing (DLP), and plasma. Initially, the technologies were such that LCD worked best on small screens, plasma worked best on medium-sized screens, and DLP worked best with large screens. In addition, DLP screens were not as flat. However, over time, the differences between the three types have diminished. The result has been the eruption of a severe price war. From mid-2003 to mid-2005, prices for new TVs based on these technologies fell by an average of 25 percent per year. Fifty-inch plasma TVs that sold for $20,000 in 2000 were selling for $4,000 in 2005. Nor has this pressure let up. In November 2006, Syntax-Brillian cut the price on its 32-inch LCD TV by 40 percent. Sony and other premium brands were forced to follow suit. Prices on all models fell further. Indeed, when Sony was rumored to be thinking of further reducing its 50-inch price to $3,000, James Li, the chief executive of Syntax-Brillian, was quoted as saying, "If they go to $3,000, I will go to $2,999." Bertrand would have been proud.

Source: D. Darlin, "Falling Costs of Big-Screen TV's to Keep Falling" and "The No-Name Brand Behind the Latest Flat-Panel Price War," *New York Times*, August 20, 2005, p. C1 and February 12, 2007, p. C1.

As it turns out, there is one and only one Nash equilibrium for the Bertrand duopoly game described above. It is the price pair, $(p_1^* = c, p_2^* = c)$.[3] If firm 1 sets this price in the expectation that firm 2 will do so, and if firm 2 acts in precisely the same manner, neither will have an incentive to change. Hence, the outcome of the Bertrand duopoly game is that the market price equals marginal cost. This is, of course, exactly what occurs under perfect competition. The only difference is that here, instead of many small firms, we have just two firms each of which is large relative to the market.

It is no wonder that Bertrand made note of the different outcome obtained when price replaces quantity as the strategic variable. Far from being a cosmetic or minor change, this alternative specification has dramatic impact. It is useful, therefore, to explore the nature and the source of this powerful effect more closely.

10.1

Let the market demand for carbonated water be given by $Q^D = 100 - 5P$. Let there be two firms producing carbonated water, each with a constant marginal cost of 2.

a. What is the market equilibrium price and quantity when each firm behaves as a Cournot duopolist choosing quantities? What are firms' profits?
b. What is the market equilibrium price and quantity when each firm behaves as a Bertrand duopolist choosing price? What are firms' profits?

Practice Problem

---

[3] If prices cannot be set continuously but only in say whole dollar amounts, then, another possible Nash equilibrium exists. Both firms set a price $p^* = c + 1$. There are two equilibria in this case: $(p_1^* = c, p_2^* = c)$ and: $(p_1^* = c + 1, p_2^* = c + 1)$.

10.2 BERTRAND RECONSIDERED

Like its Cournot cousin, the Bertrand analysis of a duopoly market is not without its critics. One chief source of criticism of the Bertrand model is its assumption that *any* price deviation between the two firms leads to an immediate and complete loss of demand for the firm charging the higher price. It is, of course, this assumption that gives rise to the discontinuity in both firms' demand and profit functions. It is also this assumption that underlies our derivation of each firm's best response function.

There are two very sound reasons why a firm's decision to charge a price higher than its rival would not result in the complete loss of all its customers. One reason is that typically the rival firm does not have the capacity to serve all of the customers who demand the product or service at its low price.[4] The second is that consumers many not view the two products as perfect substitutes.

To see the importance of capacity constraints, consider the fictional case of a small New England area with two ski resorts, Pepall Ridge and Snow Richards, each located on different sides of Mount Norman. Skiers regard the services at these resorts to be the same and will choose when possible to ski at the resort that quotes the lowest lift ticket price. Pepall Ridge is a small resort that can accommodate 1,000 skiers per day. Snow Richards is slightly bigger and can handle 1,400 skiers a day. Skiing on Mount Norman has this year become extremely popular. The demand for skiing services on Mount Norman is estimated to be $Q = 6,000 - 60P$, where P is the price of a daily lift ticket and Q is number of skiers per day.

The two resorts compete in price. Suppose that the marginal cost of providing lift services is the same at each resort and is equal to $10 per skier. However, the outcome in which each resort sets a price equal to marginal cost *cannot* be a Nash equilibrium. Demand when the price of a lift ticket is equal to $10 would be equal to 5,400 skiers, far exceeding the total capacity of the two resorts. To be sure, if each resort had understood the extent of demand, each might have built additional lifts, ski runs, and parking facilities and had greater capacity. Nevertheless, it is still not likely that the Nash equilibrium will end up with each resort setting its price of lift ticket equal to the marginal cost of $10 per skier. Why? Think of it this way. If Pepall Ridge sets a price of $11, does it make sense for Snow Richards to set a price of $10.90? This makes sense only if Snow Richards can serve all the skiers who would come at this lower price and it cannot! Should it try and build that much capacity? That would be fairly short-sighted behavior for Snow Richards. For if Pepall Ridge is serving no skiers at a price of $11 while Snow Richards is serving all the skiers at a price of $10.90, Pepall Ridge will have an incentive to lower its price to $10.80 and get back as many customers as it can. However, to serve all the customers Pepall Ridge would also need an increased capacity.

This reasoning suggests that the pressure for each resort, Pepall Ridge and Snow Richards, to cut price to marginal cost rests on each having sufficient capacity to serve the entire market demand at the competitive price. However, if each had that capacity then in equilibrium when each charges the competitive price of $10, the market is split and each serves only 2,700. It is unlikely that each resort would want to build capacity of 5,400 if each will only serve 2,700 in equilibrium. If that is the case, there is little pressure on price to fall to the marginal cost of $10.

---

[4] Edgeworth (1897) was one of the first economists to investigate the impact of capacity constraints on the Bertrand analysis.

More generally, denote as Q^C, the competitive output or the total demand when price is equal to marginal cost, i.e., $Q^C = a - bc$. If neither firm has the capacity to produce Q^C but instead each can produce only a smaller amount, then the Bertrand outcome with $p_1 = p_2 = c$ will *not* be the Nash equilibrium. In a Nash equilibrium, it must be the case that each firm's choice is a *best response* to the strategy of the other. Consider the original Bertrand solution with prices equal to marginal cost c and profit at each firm equal to zero. When there is a capacity constraint so that neither firm can serve the *entire* market at the competitive price, firm 2 can contemplate *raising* its price. If firm 2 sets p_2 above marginal cost, and hence above p_1, it would surely lose some of its customers. But it would not lose all of them. Firm 1 *does not have the capacity* to serve them. Some customers would remain with firm 2. Yet firm 2 is now earning some profit from each such customer ($p_2 > c$) implying that its total profit is now positive whereas before it was zero. It is evident, therefore, that $p_2 = c$, is not a best response to $p_1 = c$. Accordingly, the strategy combination ($p_1 = c, p_2 = c$) cannot be a Nash equilibrium if there are capacity constraints.

When capacity constraints come into play, the game between the two firms really becomes a two-stage one. In the first stage, the two firms choose capacity levels. In the second, they then compete in price. Examining the outcomes corresponding to the strategic combinations in such games is tricky. However, neither firm is likely to acquire enough capacity in stage one to serve the entire market when pricing at marginal cost in stage two. Yet if neither acquires that large amount of capacity then the Bertrand solution of each charging a price equal to marginal cost *cannot* be a Nash equilibrium. We will return to the issue of capacity choice in Chapter 12. It is worth noting at this point that the equilibrium in a model of price competition *with* capacity constraints takes us away from the simple Bertrand outcome, and closer in fact to the outcome in the Cournot model.[5]

To see this point more clearly let's return to the ski resort competition between Pepall Ridge and Snow Richards. We assume that at any price at which a resort has demand beyond its maximum capacity, the skiers that the resort serves are those skiers who are the most eager and who have the highest willingness to pay. For example, if each resort sets a lift price of $50, total market demand is 3,000. This is beyond the total capacity of 2,400 and, therefore, each resort will need somehow to ration or choose which skiers will actually ski. Our assumption, sometimes called the efficient rationing assumption, is that the resorts will do this by serving customers in order of their willingness to pay. Pepall Ridge will choose those 1,000 potential skiers with the 1,000 highest willingesses to pay. Given efficient rationing we can derive the residual demand curve facing Snow Richards at any price.

A price of particular interest is $60. Suppose then that both resorts have set $p_1 = p_2 = $60. At these prices, total demand is equal to 2,400, which is just equal to the total capacity of the two resorts. Is this a Nash equilibrium? We can answer this question by using the logic above to determine the demand function facing Snow Richards when Pepall Ridge sets a price equal to $60. Under our assumption of efficient rationing, this is shown in Figure 10.3. It is the original demand curve shifted to the left by 1,000 units, i.e. it is $Q = 5,000 - 60P$ (or, in inverse form, $P = 83.333 - Q/60$). The marginal revenue curve facing Snow Richards when Pepall Ridges charges a price of $60 is also shown there.

Note though that while changes in its price also change its quantity demanded, Snow Richards is always constrained to serve no more than its capacity of 1,400. In this light, consider again, the situation in which Snow Richards sets a price just equal to the $60 that Pepall Ridge is

5   This result is formally modeled in a two-stage game in Kreps and Scheinkman (1983).

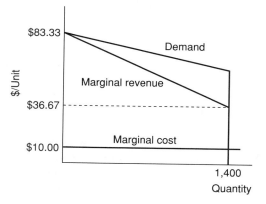

Figure 10.3   Snow Richards residual demand curve

charging. Is this a best response? We check this by asking whether Snow Richards has an incentive to change its price. The answer is no. Lowering its price will not lead to any more customers since Snow Richards is at capacity. Yet raising its price is not an attractive option either. This will lower its demand below capacity of 1,400. Since marginal revenue exceeds marginal cost, losing customers also loses profit. Accordingly, Snow Richards has no incentive either to lower or to raise its price from $60, assuming that Pepall Ridge is also setting that price. By a similar logic, we can also show that Pepall Ridge has no incentive to change its price from $60 given that Snow Richards is charging that amount. Therefore, $p_1 = p_2 = \$60$ is the Nash equilibrium for this game.

As noted earlier, the logic of the above example is quite general. Firms competing in prices selling identical products will rarely choose the capacity necessary to serve the total market demand forthcoming at competitive prices. As a result, both output and capacity will be less than the competitive level. In turn, this implies that prices must rise to a level at which demand equals the total industry capacity—a level that is necessarily above marginal cost. Thus, the efficiency property of the Bertrand solution can break down when firms are capacity constrained.

10.2

Suppose now market demand for skiing increases to $Q^D = 9{,}000 - 60P$. However, because of environmental regulation the two resorts cannot increase their capacities and serve more skiers. What is the Nash equilibrium outcome for this case? That is, what are the profit-maximizing prices set by Pepall Ridge and Snow Richards?

Practice Problem

10.3   BERTRAND IN A SPATIAL SETTING

There is a second reason why the simple Bertrand efficient outcome of price equal to marginal cost may not occur. The two firms often do not, as Bertrand assumed, produce identical products. Think of hair salons, for example. No two hair stylists cut and style hair in exactly the same way. Nor will the salons have exactly the same sort of equipment or furnishings. Also, so long as the two firms are not side-by-side, they will differ in their locations. As we saw in Chapter 7, this is often sufficient by itself to generate a preference by some consumers for one salon or the other even when different prices are charged. In short, differences in locations, furnishings, or cutting styles can each be sufficient to permit one salon to price somewhat higher than its rival without immediately losing all of its customers.

We presented a spatial model of product differentiation in Chapter 7. There our aim was to understand the use of such differentiation by a monopoly firm to extract additional surplus from its customers. The same model, however, may also be used to understand the nature of price competition when competing firms market differentiated products. Let's review the basic set-up presented earlier. There is a line of unit length (say one mile) along which consumers are uniformly distributed. This market is supplied by two stores. This time though, the same company does not operate the two stores. Rival firms operate them. One firm—located at the west end of town—has the address $x = 0$. The other—located at the east end of town—has the location, $x = 1$. Each of the firms has the same, constant unit cost of production c.

We define a consumer's "location" in this market to be that consumer's most preferred product, or style. Thus "consumer x" is located distance x from the left-hand end of the market, where distance may be geographic in a spatial model or measured in terms of characteristics in a more general product differentiation sense. While consumers differ regarding which variant or location of the good they consider to be the best, or their ideal product, they are identical in their reservation price V for their most preferred product. We assume that V is substantially greater than the unit cost of production c. Each consumer is assumed to buy at most one unit of the product. If consumer x purchases a good that is not her ideal product she incurs a utility loss. Specifically, consumer x incurs the cost $t.x$ if she consumes good 1 (located at $x = 0$), and the cost $t(1 - x)$ if she consumes good 2 (located at $x = 1$). If she buys good 1 at price p_1 she enjoys consumer surplus $V - p_1 - t.x$ and if she buys good 2 at price p_2 she enjoys consumer surplus $V - p_2 - t(1 - x_2)$. Of course, she will purchase the good that offers her the greater consumer surplus provided that this is greater than zero. Figure 10.4 describes this market setting.

It bears emphasizing that the concept of location that we have introduced here serves as a metaphor for all manner of qualitative differences between products. Instead of having two stores geographically separated we can think of two products marketed by two different firms that are differentiated by some characteristic, such as sugar content in the case of soft drinks, or fat content in the case of fast food, or fuel efficiency in the case of automobiles. Our unit line in each case represents the spectrum of products differentiated by this characteristic and each consumer has a most preferred product specification on this line. For the case of soft drinks our two firms could be Pepsi and Coca-Cola. For the case of fast food, our two firms could be McDonald's and Burger King, whereas for automobiles our two firms could be Ford and GM.

As in the simple Bertrand model, the two firms compete for customers by setting prices p_1 and p_2, respectively. These are chosen simultaneously, and we want to solve for a Nash equilibrium solution to the game. If $V > c$ then in equilibrium it must be the case that both firms have a positive market share—otherwise it would mean that at least one firm's price was set so high that it had zero market share and, therefore, zero profits. But a firm could

Firm 1 x Firm 2

Figure 10.4   The Main Street spatial model once again

always obtain positive profits by cutting its price. Thus, the zero market share situation cannot be part of a Nash equilibrium. We focus here on the Nash equilibrium outcome when the entire market is served. That is, when the market outcome is such that every consumer buys exactly one unit of the product from either firm 1 or firm 2.[6] The entire market will be served so long as each consumer's reservation price V is sufficiently large. When V is large, firms have an incentive to sell to as many customers as possible because such a high willingness-to-pay implies that each customer can be charged a price sufficiently high to make each such sale profitable.

When the entire market is served then it must be the case that there is some consumer, called the marginal consumer x^m, who is indifferent between buying from either firm 1 or firm 2. That is, she enjoys the same consumer surplus either way. Algebraically, this means that for consumer x^m:

$$V - p_1 - tx^m = V - p_2 - t(1 - x^m) \tag{10.2}$$

Equation 10.2 may be solved to find the address or the location of the marginal consumer, x^m. This is:

$$x^m(p_1, p_2) = \frac{(p_2 - p_1 + t)}{2t} \tag{10.3}$$

At any set of prices, p_1 and p_2, all consumers to the left of x^m buy from firm 1. All those to the right of x^m buy from firm 2. In other words, x^m is the fraction of the market that buys from firm 1 and $(1 - x^m)$ is the fraction that buys from firm 2. If the total number of consumers is N and they are uniformly distributed over the market space the demand function facing firm 1 at any price combination, (p_1, p_2) in which the entire market is served is[7]:

$$D^1(p_1, p_2) = x^m(p_1, p_2) = \frac{(p_2 - p_1 + t)}{2t} N \tag{10.4}$$

Similarly, firm 2's demand function is:

$$D^2(p_1, p_2) = (1 - x^m(p_1, p_2)) = \frac{(p_1 - p_2 + t)}{2t} N \tag{10.5}$$

These demand functions make sense in that each firm's demand is decreasing in its own price but increasing in its competitor's price. Notice also that, unlike the simple Bertrand duopoly model in section 10.1, the demand function facing either firm here is continuous in both p_1 and p_2. This is because when goods are differentiated, a decision by say firm 1 to set p_1 a little higher than its rival's price p_2 does not cause firm 1 to lose all of its customers. Some of its customers still prefer to buy good 1 even at the higher price simply because they prefer that version of the good to the style (or location) marketed by firm 2.[8]

---

[6] Refer to Figure 7.3 in Chapter 7 for a discussion of this point.

[7] We are using N here to refer to the *number of consumers* in the market.

[8] Our assumption that the equilibrium is one in which the entire market is served is critical to the continuity result.

The continuity in demand functions carries over into the profit functions. Firm 1's profit function is:

$$\Pi^1(p_1, p_2) = (p_1 - c)\frac{(p_2 - p_1 + t)}{2t} N \tag{10.6}$$

Similarly, firm 2's profits are given by:

$$\Pi^2(p_1, p_2) = (p_2 - c)\frac{(p_1 - p_2 + t)}{2t} N \tag{10.7}$$

In order to work out firm 1's best response pricing strategy we need to work out how firm 1's profit changes as the firm varies price p_1 in response to a given price p_2 set by firm 2. The most straightforward way to do this is to take the derivative of the profit function (10.6) with respect to p_1. When we set the derivative equal to zero we can then solve for the firm's best response price p_1^* to a given price p_2 set by firm 2.[9]

However, careful application of the alternative solution method of converting firm 1's demand curve into its inverse form and solving for the point at which marginal revenue equals marginal cost will also work. From equation (10.4), we can write firm 1's inverse demand curve for a given value of firm 2's price p_2 as $p_1 = p_2 + t - \frac{2t}{N} q_1$. Hence firm 1's marginal revenue curve is $MR_1 = p_2 + t - \frac{4t}{N} q_1$. Equating firm 1's marginal revenue with its marginal cost gives the first-order condition for profit maximization, $p_2 + t - \frac{4t}{N} q_1^* = c$. Solving for the optimal value of firm 1's output, again given the price chosen by firm 2, we then obtain:

$$q_1^* = \frac{N}{4t}(p_2 + t - c) \tag{10.8}$$

When we substitute the value of q_1^* from equation (10.8) into firm 1's inverse demand curve, we find the optimal price for firm 1 to set given the value of the price set by firm 2. This is by definition firm 1's best response function:

$$p_1^* = \frac{p_2 + c + t}{2} \tag{10.9}$$

where t is the per unit distance transportation or utility cost incurred by a consumer. Of course, we can replicate this procedure for firm 2. Because the firms are symmetric, the best response function of each firm is the mirror image of that of its rival. Hence, firm 2's best price response function is:

$$p_2^* = \frac{p_1 + c + t}{2} \tag{10.10}$$

---

[9]   Setting $\partial \Pi^1(p_1^*, p_2)/\partial p_1 = 0$ in equation (5.31) yields immediately: $p_1^* = (p_2 + c + t)/2$.

The best response functions described in (10.9) and (10.10) for the two firms are illustrated in Figure 10.5. They are upward sloping. The (Bertrand–)Nash equilibrium set of prices is, of course, where these best response functions intersect. In other words, the Nash equilibrium is a pair of prices (p_1^*, p_2^*) such that p_1^* is firm 1's best response to p_2^*, and p_2^* is firm 2's best response to p_1^*. Thus, we may replace p_1 and p_2 on the right-hand side of the equations in (10.9) and (10.10) with p_1^* and p_2^*, respectively. Solving jointly for the Nash equilibrium pair (p_1^*, p_2^*) yields:

$$p_1^* = p_2^* = c + t \qquad\qquad\qquad (10.11)$$

In equilibrium, each firm charges a price that is equal to the unit production cost *plus* an amount t, the utility cost per unit of distance a consumer incurs in buying a good that is at some distance from her preferred good. At these prices, the firms split the market. The marginal consumer is located at the address $x = 1/2$. The profit earned by each firm is the same and equal to $(p_i^* - c)N/2 = tN/2$.

Consider the two hair salons located one mile apart on Main Street. All the potential customers live along this stretch of Main Street and they are uniformly spread out. Each consumer is willing to pay at most $50 for a haircut done at the consumer's home. However if a consumer has to travel to get her haircut she incurs a round-trip travel cost of $5 per mile. Each of the hair salons can cut hair at a constant unit cost of $10 per cut, and each wants to set a price per haircut that maximizes the salon's profit. Our model predicts that the equilibrium price of a haircut in this town will be $15, a price that is greater than the marginal cost of a haircut.

Two points are worth making in connection with these results. First, note the role that the parameter t plays. It is a measure of the value each consumer places on obtaining her most preferred version of the product. The greater is t, the less willing the consumer is to buy a product "far away" from her favorite location or product or style. That is, a high t value indicates consumers have strong preferences for their most desired product and incur a high utility loss from having to consume a product that is less than ideal. The result is that neither firm has much to worry about when charging a high price because consumers prefer to pay that price rather than buy a low-price alternative that is "far away" from their preferred style. When t is large, the price competition between the two firms is softened. In other words, a large value of t means that product differentiation makes price competition much less intense.

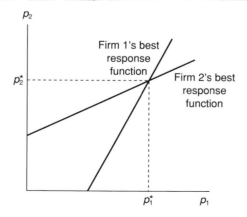

Figure 10.5   Best-reponse functions for price competition with imperfect substitutes.

Reality Checkpoint
Unfriendly Skies: Price Wars in Airlines Markets

Following general deregulation in 1977, the profitability of the passenger airline industry has generally deteriorated and also become much more volatile. An important source of these developments has been the continued outbreak of price wars. Morrison and Winston (1996) define such conflicts as any city-pair route market in which the average airfare declines by 2 percent or more within a single quarter. Based on this definition, they estimate that over 81 percent of airline city-pair routes experienced such wars in the 1979–95 time period. In the wars so identified, the average fare in fact typically falls by over 37 percent and sometimes falls by as much as 79 percent. These wars appear to be triggered by unexpected movements in demand and the entrance of new airlines on a route, especially low-cost airlines like Southwest. Morrison and Winston (1996) also find that the effect of such fare wars

on industry profits is important. On average, they estimate that the intense price competition cost airlines $300 million in forgone profits in each of the first 16 years following deregulation. This amounts to over 20 percent of total net income over these same years. Of course, to the extent that this profit loss simply reflects movement toward the Bertrand outcome of marginal cost pricing it shows up as a gain to consumers and a net improvement in efficiency. Judging from their comments in the press, however, airline executives appear to take little comfort in such gains.

Sources: S. Morrison and C. Winston, "Causes and Consequences of Airline Fare Wars," *Brookings Papers on Economic Activity, Microeconomics, 1996* (1996), 85–124; M. Maynard, "Yes, It Was a Dismal Year for Airlines: Now for the Bad News," *New York Times*, December 16, 2002, p. C2.

However, as t falls consumers place less value on obtaining their most preferred styles, but rather are attracted by lower prices. This intensifies price competition. In the limit, when $t = 0$, product differentiation is of no value to consumers. They treat all goods as essentially identical. Price competition becomes fierce and, in the limit, drives prices to marginal cost just as in the original Bertrand model.

The second point concerns the location of the firms. We simply assumed that the two firms were located at either end of town. However, the location or product design of the firm is also part of a firm's strategy. Allowing the two firms to choose simultaneously *both* their price and their location strategies makes the model too complicated to solve here. Still, the intuition behind location choice is instructive. There are two opposing forces affecting the choice of price and location. On the one hand, the two firms will wish to avoid locating at the same point because to do so eliminates all differences between the two products. Price competition in this case will be fierce as in the original Bertrand model. On the other hand, each firm also has some incentive to locate near the center of town. This enables a firm to reach as large a market as possible. Evaluating the balance of these two forces is what makes the solution of the equilibrium outcome so difficult.[10]

---

[10]   There is a wealth of literature on this topic with the outcome often depending on the precise functional forms assumed. See, for example, Eaton (1976), D'Aspremont et al. (1979), Novshek (1980), and Economides (1989).

Imagine that the two hair salons located on Main Street no longer have the same unit cost. In particular, one salon has a constant unit cost of $10 whereas the other salon has a constant unit cost of $20. The low-cost salon, call it Cheap-Cuts, is located at the east end of town, $x = 0$. The high-cost salon, The Ritz, is located at the west end, $x = 1$. There are 100 potential customers who live along the mile stretch, and they are uniformly spread out along the mile. Consumers are willing to pay $50 for a haircut done at their home. If a consumer has to travel to get a haircut then a travel cost of $5 per mile is incurred. Each salon wants to set a price for a haircut that maximizes the salon's profit.

a. The demand functions facing the two salons are not affected by the fact that now one salon is high-cost and the other is low-cost. However the salons' best response functions are affected. Compute the best response function for each salon. How does an increase in the unit cost of one salon affect the other salon's best response?

b. Work out the Nash equilibrium in prices for this model. Compare these prices to the ones derived in the text for the case when the two salons had the same unit cost equal to $10. Explain why prices changed in the way they did. It may be helpful in your explanation to draw the best response functions when the salons are identical and compare them to those when the salons have different costs.

10.4 STRATEGIC COMPLEMENTS AND SUBSTITUTES

Best response functions in simultaneous-move games are extremely useful tools for understanding what we mean by a Nash equilibrium outcome. But an analysis of such functions also serves other useful purposes. In particular, examining the properties of best response functions can aid our understanding of how strategic interaction works and how that interaction can be made "more" or "less" competitive.

Figure 10.6 shows both the best response functions for the standard Cournot duopoly model and the best response functions for the Bertrand duopoly model with differentiated products. One feature in the diagram is immediately apparent. The best response functions for the Cournot

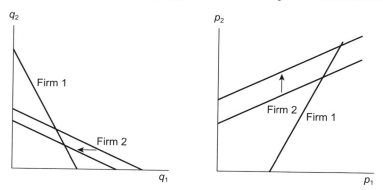

Figure 10.6 Best-response functions for the Cournot (quantity) case and the Bertrand (price) case
A rise in firm 2's cost shifts its response function inwards in the Cournot model but outwards in the Bertrand model. Firm 1 reacts aggressively to increase its market share in the Cournot case. It reacts mildly in the Bertrand price by *raising* its price.

quantity model are *negatively* sloped—firm 1's best response to an increase in q_2 is to *decrease* q_1. But the best response functions in the Bertrand price model are *positively* sloped. Firm 1's best response to an increase in p_2 is to increase p_1, as well.

Whether the best response functions are negatively or positively sloped is quite important. The slope reveals much about the nature of competition in the product market. To see this, consider the impact of an increase in firm 2's unit cost c_2. Our analysis of the Cournot model indicated that the effect of a rise in c_2 would be to shift *inward* firm 2's best response curve. As Figure 10.6 indicates, this leads to a new Nash equilibrium in which firm 2 produces less and firm 1 produces more than each did before c_2 rose. That is, in the Cournot quantity model, firm 1's response to firm 2's bad luck is a rather aggressive one in which it seizes the opportunity to expand its market share at the expense of firm 2.

Consider now the impact of a rise in c_2 in the context of the differentiated goods Bertrand model. The rise in this case shifts firm 2's best response function *upwards*. Given the rise in its cost, firm 2 will choose to set a higher p_2 than it did previously in response to any given value of p_1. How does firm 1 respond? Unlike the Cournot case, firm 1's reaction is less aggressive. Firm 1—seeing that firm 2 is now less able to set a low price—realizes that the price competition from firm 2 is now less intense. Hence, firm 1 now reacts by raising p_1.

When the best response functions are upward sloping, we say that the strategies (prices in the Bertrand case) are *strategic complements*. When we have the alternative case of downward sloping best response functions, we say that the strategies (quantities in the Cournot case) are *strategic substitutes*. This terminology comes from Bulow, Geanakopolos, and Klemperer (1985) and reflects similar terminology in consumer demand theory. When a consumer reacts to a rise (fall) in the price of one product by buying less (more) of it and more (less) of another, we say that the two goods are substitutes. When a consumer reacts to a change in the price of one good by buying either more or less of *both* that good and another product, we say that the two goods are complements. This is the source of the similarity. Quantities in Cournot analysis are strategic substitutes because a rise in c_2 induces a fall in q_2 but a rise in q_1. Prices in a Bertrand model are strategic complements because a rise in c_2 induces an increase in p_2 and also in p_1.

The different nature of the strategic interaction and the different equilibria makes clear that the choice of whether to use price or quantity as the strategic variable to model market competition is an important one. What factors influence this choice? In those industries in which firms set their production schedules far in advance of putting the goods on the market for sale, there is a good case to assume that firms compete in quantities. Examples include the world energy market, coffee-growers, and automobile producers. In many service industries, such as banking, insurance, and air travel, it is much more natural to think in terms of price competition. In certain manufacturing industries, such as cereal and detergents, the price competition for customers is a stronger factor then the setting of production schedules, and so Bertrand price competition may be the more appropriate model.

10.5   EMPIRICAL APPLICATION
Brand Competition and Consumer Preferences—Evidence from the California Retail Gasoline Market

Gasoline is typically produced by refiners and then shipped to a central distribution point. The gasoline is then bought either by an unbranded independent retailer such as RaceTrac, or by service stations selling a branded product such as an Exxon or a Chevron station. In the latter case, a special additive unique to the brand has to be added. For example, to sell "Chevron" gasoline, a station has to have added Techronas™ to the fuel. Thus, each specific brand is differentiated by the use of its own additive. Independent stations, however, simply sell the basic gasoline without any additive. Here, we briefly describe a paper by Justine Hastings (2004) that examines the nature of price competition in the retail gasoline market in the southern California.

The background to the study is as follows. In June of 1997, the Atlantic Richfield Company (ARCO), a well-known refiner and retail brand, acquired control of about 260 gasoline stations that formerly had been operated by the independent retailer, Thrifty, in and around Los Angeles and San Diego. ARCO then converted these to ARCO stations—a process that was essentially completed by September of that same year. Thus, the ARCO–Thrifty acquisition resulted in the exit of a large number of independent service stations in southern California as these were replaced by ARCO sellers.

Hastings (2004) asks what effect the ARCO–Thrifty deal had on retail gasoline prices. In principle, the effect could be either positive or negative, depending on consumer preferences. If consumers identify brands with higher quality and independents with lower quality, then conversion of the unbranded (low-quality) stations to the ARCO brand would mean that these stations now sell a closer substitute to the other branded products. This would intensify price competition and *lower* branded gasoline prices. However, if a large pool of consumers is unresponsive to brand labels because their willingness to pay for higher quality is limited and they only want to buy gasoline as cheaply as possible, then the loss of the Thrifty stations removes this low-cost alternative and *raises* gasoline prices.

To isolate the effect of the ARCO–Thrifty merger, Hastings (2004) looked at how prices charged by gasoline stations in the Los Angeles and San Diego areas differed depending on whether they competed with a Thrifty or not. Her data cover the prices charged by 699 stations measured at four different times: February 1997, June 1997, October 1997, and December 1997. Notice that the first two dates are for prices before the conversion while the last two dates are for prices after the conversion. She then defines submarkets in which each station's competitors are all the other stations within one mile's driving distance. A simple regression that might capture the effect of the merger would be:

$$p_{it} = Constant + \alpha_i + \beta_1 X_{it} + \beta_2 Z_{it} + e_{it} \tag{10.12}$$

where p_{it} is the price charged by station i at time t; α_i is a firm-specific dummy that lets the intercept be different for each service station; X_{it} is a dummy variable that has the value 1 if station i competes with an independent (Thrifty) at time t and 0 otherwise; likewise Z_{it} is 1 if a competitor of station i has become a station that is owned by a major brand as opposed to a station that operates as a franchisee or lessee of a major brand, and 0 otherwise. This last variable, Z_{it} is meant to capture the impact of any differential effects depending on the contractual relationship between a major brand and the station that sells that brand. The key variable of interest however is X_{it}. We want to know whether the estimated coefficient β_1 is negative, which would indicate that having independent rivals generally leads to lower prices— or is positive, which would indicate that the presence of independents softens competition and raises prices.

However, there is a potentially serious problem with estimating equation (10.12). The problem is that over the course of 1997, gasoline prices were rising generally throughout southern California. Equation (10.12) does not allow for this general rising trend. Consider our key variable X_{it}. In the data, this will be 1 for a lot more stations before the merger in

February and June, than it will be in October and December. As a result, the coefficient β_1 will likely be negative because prices were lower in February and June (when there were a lot more independents) than in September and December (after the merger removed the Thrifty stations). That is, β_1 will be biased because it will pick up time effects as well as the effects of independents.

In order to isolate the price effects that are purely due to independent rivals alone, Hastings (2004) puts in location specific time dummies for February, June, and September. (The effect of December is of course captured in the regression constant.) That is, she estimates an equation something like:

$$p_{it} = Constant + \alpha_i + \beta_1 X_{it} + \beta_2 Z_{it} + \beta_3 T_i + e_{it} \tag{10.13}$$

where T_i or time is captured not as a continuous variable but, again, by time-specific dummies. Her results, both with and without the time dummies (but suppressing the firm specific intercepts) are shown in Table 10.1.

Consider first the column of results for the equation that includes the location-time dummies. Here, the estimate of β_1, the coefficient on having a Thrifty or independent rival in a station's local market, implies that this led the station to lower its price by about five cents per gallon. The standard error on this estimate is very small, so we can be very confident of this measure. Note too how this contrasts with the effect measured in the regression results shown in the first column that leaves out the time effects. That estimate suggests a much larger effect of ten cents per gallon decline when a station has independent rivals. Again, this is because in leaving out the time effects, the regression erroneously attributes the general rise in gasoline prices throughout the region to the merger when in fact prices were clearly rising for other reasons as well. We should also note that the coefficient estimate for β_2 is not significant in either equation. So, the type of ownership by a major brand does not seem to be important for retail gasoline prices.

One picture is often worth a large number of words. Figure 10.7 illustrates the behavior of southern California gasoline prices over the period covered by Hastings's data for each of two groups: (1) the treatment group that competed with a Thrifty station; and (2) the control group of stations that did not.

Table 10.1 Brand competition and gasoline prices

Variable	Without location-time dummies Coefficient (standard error)	With location-time dummies Coefficient (standard error)
Constant	1.3465 (0.0415)	1.3617 (0.0287)
X_{it}	−0.1013 (0.0178)	−0.0500 (0.0122)
Z_{it}	−0.0033 (0.0143)	−0.0033 (0.0101)
LA*February		0.0180 (0.0065)
LA*June		0.0243 (0.0065)
LA*December		0.1390 (0.0064)
SD*February		−0.0851 (0.0036)
SD*June		−0.0304 (0.0036)
SD*December		0.0545 (0.0545)
R^2	0.3953	0.7181

Dependent variable = price per gallon of regular unleaded

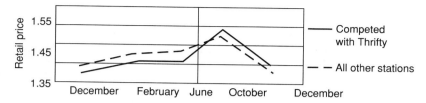

Figure 10.7 "Thrifty" competition and gasoline prices in southern California

Notice the general rise in prices in both groups through October. Clearly, this is a phenomenon common to the gasoline market in general and not the result of the merger *per se*. However, a close look at the data does reveal that the merger did have some impact. In the months before the merger, stations that competed with a Thrifty had prices that were two to three cents *lower* than those in the control group. Starting about the time of the merger in June, however, and continuing afterwards, these same stations had prices two to three cents *higher* than those in the control group. It is this roughly five-cent effect that is being picked up in the final column of the preceding table. For both groups, those that initially competed with a Thrifty prior to the merger and those that did not, prices differ between the beginning of 1997 and the end. To isolate the effects of the merger, we need to look at how these differences over time were different between the two groups. If we recall that for the treatment group stations $X_{it} = 1$, at first but 0 after the merger, while it is always zero firms in the control group, the price behavior for the two groups is:

	Before merger	*After merger*	*Difference*
Treatment group:	$\alpha_i + \beta_1$	α_i + time effects	$-\beta_1$ + time effects
Control group:	α_j	α_j + time effects	time effects

Thus, β_1 in our regression reflects the difference between the difference over time in the treatment group and that in the control group. For this reason, β_1 is often referred to as a *difference-in-differences* estimator.

Summary

In the Bertrand model firms compete in prices. In the simple model of Bertrand competition, prices are pushed to marginal cost even if there are just two firms. By contrast, when there is quantity or Cournot competition, prices remain substantially above marginal cost so long as the number of firms is not large. High-cost firms can survive in Cournot competition. However, high-cost firms cannot survive Bertrand competition against a firm with lower costs. In short, the simplest Bertrand model predicts competitive and efficient market outcomes even when the number of firms is quite small.

However, the efficient outcomes predicted by the simple Bertrand model depend upon two key assumptions. The first is that firms have extensive capacity so that it is possible to serve all a rival's customers after undercutting the rival's price. The second key assumption is that the firms produce identical products so that relative price is all that matters to consumers when choosing between brands. If either of these assumptions is relaxed, the efficiency outcomes of the simple Bertrand model no longer obtain. If firms must choose production capacities in advance, the outcome with Bertrand price competition becomes closer to what occurs in the Cournot model. If products are differentiated, prices are again likely to remain above marginal cost. Indeed, given the fierceness of price competition, firms have a real incentive to differentiate their products.

A useful model of product differentiation is the Hotelling (1929) spatial model, which we first introduced in Chapter 4. This model uses geographic location as a metaphor for more general distinctions between different versions of the same product. It thereby makes it possible to consider price competition between firms selling differentiated products. The model makes it clear that Bertrand competition with differentiated products does not result in efficient marginal cost pricing. It also makes clear that the deviation from such pricing depends on how much consumers value variety. The greater value that the typical consumer places on getting her most preferred brand or version of the product, the higher prices will rise above marginal cost.

Ultimately, the differences between Cournot and Bertrand competition reflect underlying differences between quantities and prices as strategic variables. The quantities chosen by Cournot firms are strategic substitutes—increases in one firm's production lead to decreases in the rival's output. In contrast, the prices chosen by Bertrand competitors are strategic complements. A rise in one firm's price permits its rival to raise price, too.

Models of price competition based on the spatial model have provided an extremely useful framework for empirical work. Many policy makers are interested in investigating how a change in market structure—through entry or mergers or regulatory policy—will affect price competition. One key underlying issue in price competition is how it is affected by consumer preferences for the different brands. The spatial model of differentiation captures consumers' preferences for both variety (horizontal product differentiation) and quality (vertical product differentiation) and is used extensively in empirical work on competition policy. In this respect, it is important to identify which type of differentiation applies. Depending on the nature of consumer preferences, a merger between a high-quality and low-quality firm that results in the transformation of the low-quality firm outlets to high-quality ones could either weaken competition because it removes a low-quality competitor or intensify competition because it adds to the high-quality supply.

Problems

1. Suppose firm 1 and firm 2 each produce the same product and face a market demand curve described by $Q = 5,000 - 200P$. Firm 1 has a unit cost of production c_1 equal to 6 whereas firm 2 has a higher unit cost of production c_2 equal to 10.

   a. What is the Bertrand–Nash equilibrium outcome?

   b. What are the profits of each firm?

   c. Is this outcome efficient?

2. Suppose that market demand for golf balls is described by $Q = 90 - 3P$, where Q is measured in kilos of balls. There are two firms that supply the market. Firm 1 can produce a kilo of balls at a constant unit cost of $15 whereas firm 2 has a constant unit cost equal to $10.

   a. Suppose firms compete in quantities. How much does each firm sell in a Cournot equilibrium? What is the market price and what are firms' profits?

   b. Suppose firms compete in price. How much does each firm sell in a Bertrand

equilibrium. What is market price and what are firms' profits?

3. a. Would your answer in 2b change if there were three firms, one with unit cost = $20 and two with unit cost = $10? Explain why or why not.

   b. Would your answer in 2b change if firm 1's golf balls were green and endorsed by Tiger Woods, whereas firm 2's are plain and white? Explain why or why not.

4. In Tuftsville everyone lives along Main Street that is 10 miles long. There are 1,000 people uniformly spread up and down Main Street, and each day they each buy a fruit smoothie from one of the two stores located at either end of Main Street. Customers ride their motor scooters to and from the store and the motor scooters use $0.50 worth of gas per mile. Customers buy their smoothies from the store offering the lowest price, which is the store's price plus the customer's travel expenses getting to and from the store. Ben owns the store at the west end of Main Street

and Will owns the store at the east end of Main Streets.

a. If both Ben and Will charge $1 per smoothie how many will each of them sell in a day? If Ben charges $1 per smoothie and Will charges $1.40 how many smoothies will each sell in a day?

b. If Ben charges $3 per smoothie what price would enable Will to sell 250 smoothies per day? 500 smoothies per day? 750 smoothies per day? 1,000 smoothies per day?

c. If Ben charges p_1 and Will charges p_2 what is the location of the customer who is indifferent between going to Ben's and going to Will's? How many customers go to Will's store and how many go to Ben's store? What are the demand functions that Ben and Will face?

d. Rewrite Ben's demand function with p_1 on the left-hand side. What is Ben's marginal revenue function?

e. Assume that the marginal cost of a smoothie is constant and equal to $1 for both Ben and Will. In addition each of them pays Tuftsville $250 per day for the right to sell smoothies. Find the equilibrium prices, quantities sold and profits.

5. Return to Main Street in Tuftsville. Now suppose that George would like to open another store at the midpoint of Main Street. He too is willing to pay Tuftsville $250 a day for the right to sell smoothies.

a. If Ben and Will do not change their prices what is the best price for George to charge? How much profit would he earn?

b. What do you think would happen if George did open another store in the middle of Main Street? Would Ben and Will have an incentive to change their prices? Their locations? Would one or both leave the market?

6. Suppose that there are two firms, firm B and firm N, producing complementary goods, say bolts and nuts. The demand curve for each firm is described as follows:

$$Q_B = Z - P_B - P_N \text{ and } Q_N = Z - P_N - P_B$$

For simplicity, assume further that each firm faces a constant unit cost of production, $c = 0$.

a. Show that the profits of each firm may be expressed as $\Pi^B = (P_B)(Z - P_B - P_N)$ and $\Pi^N = P_N(Z - P_B - P_N)$.

b. Show that each firm's optimal price depends on the price chosen by the other as given by the optimal response functions: $P_B^* = (Z - P_N)/2$ and $P_N^* = (Z - P_B)/2$.

c. Graph these functions. Show that the Nash equilibrium prices are: $P_B = P_N = Z/3$.

d. Describe the interaction between two monopolists selling separate but complementary goods, which we presented in Chapter 9 as a game.

7. Assume that two firms sell differentiated products and face the following demand curves:

$$q_1 = 15 - p_1 + 0.5p_2 \text{ and } q_2 = 15 - p_2 + 0.5p_1$$

a. Derive the best response function for each firm. Do these indicate that prices are strategic substitutes or strategic complements?

b. What is the equilibrium set of prices in this market? What profits are earned at those prices?

References

Bertrand, J. 1883. "Review." *Journal des Savants* 68: 499–508. Reprinted in English translation by James Friedman. In A. F. Daughety, ed., 1988, *Cournot Oligopoly*. Cambridge: Cambridge University Press.

Bulow, J., J. Geanakopolos, and P. Klemperer, 1985. "Multimarket Oligopoly: Strategic Substitutes and Complements." *Journal of Political Economy* 93 (June): 488–511.

D'Aspremont, C., J. Gabszewicz, and J. Thisse, 1979. "On Hotelling's Stability in Competition." *Econometrica* 47 (September): 1145–50.

Eaton, B. C. 1976. "Free Entry in One-dimensional Models: Pure Profits and Multiple Equilibrium." *Journal of Regional Science* 16 (January): 21–33.

Economides, N. 1989. "Symmetric Equilibrium Existence and Optimality in Differentiated

Products Markets." *Journal of Economic Theory* 27 (February): 178–94.

Edgeworth, F. Y. 1897. "The Pure Theory of Monopoly." *Giorni degli Economisti* 10 (June): 110.42.

Hastings, J. 2004. "Vertical Relationships and Competition in Retail Gasoline Markets: Empirical Evidence From Contract Changes in Southern California." *American Economic Review* 94 (March): 317–28.

Hotelling, H. 1929. "Stability in Competition." *Economic Journal* 39 (January): 41–57.

Kreps, D. and J. Scheinkman. 1983. "Quantity Precommitment and Bertrand Competition Yield Cournot Outcomes." *Bell Journal of Economics* 14 (Autumn): 326–37.

Morrison, S. and C. Winston. 1996. "Causes and Consequences of Airline Fare Wars." *Brookings Papers on Economic Activity: Microeconomics*, 85–131.

Novshek, W., 1980. "Equilibrium in Simple Spatial (or Differentiated Products) Models." *Journal of Economic Theory* 22 (June): 313–26.

11

Dynamic Games and First and Second Movers

Since its introduction in the 1970s, Boeing's 416-seat 747 jet aircraft has dominated the jumbo jet market. Like McDonnell–Douglas before it, Airbus has for some time sought to develop a challenge to this long-reigning champion. After many delays and disappointments, Airbus may have finally come up with such a challenge. Its new A380 plane with anything between 555 and 800 seats is scheduled to make its regular passenger service debut in 2007 for Singapore Airlines. Whether the plane will win the market share and profit that Airbus hopes for remains unclear. What is clear is that Airbus made a deliberate and careful decision to respond to Boeing's earlier move.

The strategic interaction between the production decisions of the world's two principal manufacturers of commercial aircraft is sequential. First Boeing took an action, and then after that action was taken and observed Airbus chose its action. This is quite different from the static or simultaneous games that we studied in the previous two chapters. Games in which the players take their actions sequentially are dynamic games, and dynamic games are the focus of this chapter. In principle, these games can have many rounds of play, which are often called stages. Here, we concentrate mostly on games with just two stages and, for convenience, just two firms. Typically, one firm will play in the first round, the first mover, and the other will play in the second round, the second mover.

Popular business literature is replete with stories about first mover advantages and often gives advice as to how firms can establish a leadership position by moving first.[1] A classic example of first mover advantage is found in the prepared soup industry. In the late nineteenth century, Campbell was the first entrant into the prepared soup market in the U.S. In the early twentieth century, Heinz was the first entrant in the U.K. market. Campbell entered the U.K. market after Heinz, and similarly Heinz entered the U.S. market after Campbell. Yet the first mover in each market continues to dominate. Campbell has roughly 63% of the US market, but only 9% of the U.K. market, whereas Heinz has a 41% market share in the U.K. and a relatively minor market share in the U.S.[2]

The observation that early entry into a market can confer substantial advantages relative to later entrants raises a further possibility of great interest to industrial economists. The issue

---

[1] Lieberman and Montgomery (1988).
[2] See, for example, Sutton (1991).

is whether the initial entrant's advantages are so great that it would be impossible for any subsequent firm to enter at all. Remember, entry is a key part of the competitive market's success story as an allocative mechanism. Entry is the policing mechanism that ensures a market will return to competitive pricing whenever firms in an industry are earning substantial economic profits. If entry does not occur then the market may not be working very well.

In the next two chapters, we explore the entry process in detail when the firms—the entrants and the incumbents—are strategic players in the market place. This is an important part of oligopoly. At this juncture, the point to realize is that entry is a sequential process— some firms enter early and some enter late. So, developing an understanding of dynamic games is good groundwork for our later investigation of entry and entry deterrence in oligopoly markets.

We first examine quantity and price competition when firms move sequentially rather than simultaneously. We will discover again that price and quantity competition are different, and depending on the kind of competition, there can be first mover or second mover advantages. This raises the interesting question of whether and how a firm can become either a first or second mover. Often the key to achieving the desired position and the associated higher profits is the ability of the firm to make a credible commitment to its strategy when the market opens for trade. We examine what credibility means in game theory and how it affects our equilibrium solution concept for dynamic models.

Simultaneous games, such as the traditional Cournot or Bertrand model, describe a once-and-for-all market interaction between the rival firms. In some sequential games as well there is only one market period where trade takes place, although this might occur in several stages. However, the more likely scenario is that rival firms interact and trade today in the market and then interact again in the future. Moreover, the competing firms understand the likelihood of future interaction today. Repeating the market interaction over and over again gives rise to a somewhat different type of dynamic game, usually called a repeated game. We defer our discussion of repeated games until Chapter 14.

11.1   THE STACKELBERG MODEL OF QUANTITY COMPETITION

The duopoly model of Stackelberg (1934) is similar to the Cournot model except for one critically important difference. Both firms choose quantities but now they do so *sequentially* rather than *simultaneously*. The firm, which moves first and chooses its output level, first, is the leader firm. The firm that moves second is the follower firm. The sequential choice of output is what makes the game dynamic. However, the firms trade their goods on the market only once and their interaction yields a "once-and-for-all" market-clearing outcome.

Let market demand again be represented by a linear inverse demand function $P = A - BQ$. Firm 1 is the leader who moves first and firm 2 is the follower who chooses its output *after* the choice of the leader is made. Each firm has the same constant unit cost of production c. Total industry output Q equals the sum of the outputs of each firm, $Q = q_1 + q_2$.

Firm 1 acts first and chooses q_1. How should it make this choice? Both firms are rational and strategic and both firms know this, and know that each other knows this. As a result, firm 1 will make its choice taking into account its best guess as to firm 2's rational response to its choice of q_1. In other words, firm 1 will work out firm 2's best response to each value of q_1, incorporate that best response into its own decision-making and then choose the q_1 option which, given firm 2's best response, maximizes firm 1's profit.

We can solve for firm 2's best response function q_2^* exactly as we did in the Cournot model in Chapter 9. For any choice of output q_1, firm 2 faces the inverse demand and marginal revenue curves:

$$P = (A - Bq_1) - Bq_2$$
$$MR_2 = (A - Bq_1) - 2Bq_2 \tag{11.1}$$

Setting marginal revenue equal to marginal cost, yields firm 2's best response q_2^* as the solution to the first-order condition:

$$A - Bq_1 - 2Bq_2^* = c \tag{11.2}$$

From which we obtain:

$$q_2^* = \frac{(A - c)}{2B} - \frac{q_1}{2} \tag{11.3}$$

If firm 1 is rational, firm 1 will understand that equation (11.3) describes what firm 2 will do in response to each choice of q_1 that firm 1 might make. We can summarize equation (11.3) by $q_2^*(q_1)$. Anticipating this behavior by firm 2, firm 1 can substitute $q_2^*(q_1)$ for q_2 in its demand function so that its inverse demand function may be written as:

$$P = A - Bq_2^*(q_1) - Bq_1 = \frac{A + c}{2} - \frac{B}{2}q_1, \tag{11.4}$$

In turn, this implies that its profit function is:

$$\Pi_1(q_1, q_2^*(q_1)) = \left(\frac{A + c}{2} - \frac{B}{2}q_1 - c\right)q_1 = \left(\frac{A - c}{2} - \frac{B}{2}q_1\right)q_1 \tag{11.5}$$

Note that this substitution results in firm 1's demand and profits being dependent only on its own output choice, q_1. This is because firm 1 effectively sets q_2 as well, by virtue of the fact that q_2 is chosen by firm 2 in response to q_1 according to firm 2's best response function, *and firm 1 anticipates this*. In other words, the first mover correctly predicts the second mover's best response and incorporates this prediction into its decision-making calculus.

To solve for firm 1's profit-maximizing output q_1^* we find the marginal revenue curve associated with firm 1's demand curve in equation (11.4), that is, $MR_1 = \frac{A + c}{2} - Bq_1$, and find the output q_1^* at which marginal revenue is equal to marginal cost. Alternatively, we could derive and solve the first-order condition for profit maximization of equation (11.5), using the calculus technique of differentiation, setting $\frac{d\Pi_1(q_1^*, q_2^*(q_1^*))}{dq_1} = 0$, and solving for q_1^*. Either way we find that:

$$q_1^* = \frac{(A - c)}{2B} \tag{11.6}$$

Given this output choice by firm 1, firm 2 selects its best response as given by equation (11.3), which yields:

$$q_2^* = \frac{(A - c)}{4B} \tag{11.7}$$

Together, equations (11.6) and (11.7) describe the Stackelberg–Nash equilibrium production levels of each firm. Note that the leader's output is exactly equal to the level of output chosen by a simple uniform-pricing monopolist. This is a well-known feature of the Stackelberg model when demand is linear and costs are constant.

The total industry production is, of course, the sum of the two outputs shown in equations (11.6) and (11.7). This sum is: $Q^S = \frac{3(A - c)}{4B}$. Compare this market output with the earlier Cournot–Nash equilibrium industry output $Q^C = \frac{2(A - c)}{3B}$. Clearly, the Stackelberg model yields a greater industry output. Accordingly, the equilibrium price is lower in the Stackelberg model than it is in the Cournot model. The price and output results are illustrated in Figure 11.1.

A central feature of the Stackelberg model is the difference in the relative outcome of the two firms. Recall that from the standpoint of both consumer preferences and production techniques, the firms are identical. They produce identical goods and do so at the same, constant unit cost. Yet, because one firm moves first, the outcome for the two firms is different. Comparing q_1^* and q_2^* reveals that the leader gets a far larger market share and earns a much larger profit than does the follower. Moving first clearly has advantages. Alternatively, entering the market late has its disadvantages.

An interesting additional aspect of the disadvantaged outcome for firm 2 in the Stackelberg model is that this outcome occurs even though firm 2 has full information regarding the output choice of q_1. Indeed, firm 2 actually observes that choice before selecting q_2. In the Cournot duopoly model, firm 2 did not have such concrete information. Because the Cournot model is based upon simultaneous moves, each firm could only make a (rational) guess as to its rival's output choice. Paradoxically, firm 2 does worse when it has complete

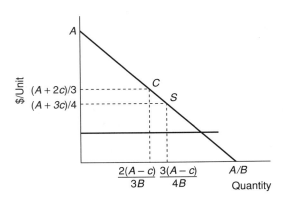

Figure 11.1 The Cournot and Stackelberg outcomes compared
C = Cournot equilibrium; S = Stackelberg equilibrium.

information about firm 1's choice (the Stackelberg case) than it does when its information is less than perfect (the Cournot case). This is because saying the information is complete amounts to saying that firm 1's choice—at the time that firm 2 observes it—is irreversible. In the Stackelberg model, by the time firm 2 moves, firm 1 is already fully committed to $q_1 = \dfrac{(A - c)}{2B}$. In the Cournot context $q_1 = \dfrac{(A - c)}{2B}$ is *not* a best response to the choice $q_2 = \dfrac{(A - c)}{4B}$ and so firm 2 would not anticipate that firm 1 would produce that quantity. In contrast, in the Stackelberg model we do not derive firm 1's choice as a best response to $q_2 = \dfrac{(A - c)}{4B}$. Instead, we derived firm 1's output choice as the profit-maximizing output when firm 1 correctly anticipates that firm 2's decision rule is to choose its best value of q_2 *conditional* upon the output choice already made by firm 1. It is this fact, which reflects the underlying assumption of sequential moves that distinguishes the Stackelberg model.

Stackelberg's modification to the basic Cournot model is important. It is a useful way to capture the observed phenomenon that one firm often has a dominant or leadership position in a market. The Stackelberg model reveals that moving first can have its advantage and therefore could be an important aspect of strategic interaction.

Consider the following game. Firm 1, the leader, selects an output q_1, after which firm 2, the follower, observes the choice of q_1 and then selects its own output q_2. The resulting price is one satisfying the industry demand curve $P = 200 - q_1 - q_2$. Both firms have zero fixed costs and a constant marginal cost of 60.

a. Derive the equation for the follower firm's best response function. Draw this equation on a graph with q_2 on the vertical axis and q_1 on the horizontal axis. Indicate the vertical intercept, horizontal intercept, and slope of the best response function.

b. Determine the equilibrium output of each firm in the leader–follower game. Show that this equilibrium lies on firm 2's best response function. What are firm 1's profits in the equilibrium?

c. Now let the two firms choose their outputs simultaneously. Compute the Cournot equilibrium outputs and industry price. Who loses and who gains when the firms play a Cournot game instead of the Stackelberg one?

11.2   SEQUENTIAL PRICE COMPETITION

What if the two firms, the leader and follower, in this dynamic game competed in price instead of quantity? If the firms are identical, that is, they produce the same product at the same costs then the outcome to the sequential price-setting game is not much different from the simultaneous price game of the previous chapter. Prices again fall to marginal cost.

To see this, let us rework the Stackelberg quantity-setting model with instead each firm choosing the price it will charge. Firm 1 is again the leader and sets its price first and firm 2 is the follower setting its price second. Otherwise, the model is exactly the same as before. Each firm produces an identical good at the same, constant marginal cost, c, and consumers will purchase the good at the lower priced firm. If they set the same prices then each firm will serve half the market.

In setting its price, firm 1 must of course anticipate firm 2's best response. Clearly firm 2 will have an incentive to price slightly below firm 1's price whenever firm 1 sets a price greater than unit cost c and less than or equal to the monopoly price. In that case, by under-cutting, firm 2 will serve the entire market and earn all the potential profits. On the other hand, if firm 1 sets a price less than unit cost c, then firm 2 will not match or undercut firm 1's price because firm 2 has no interest in making any sales when each unit sold loses money. Finally, if firm 1 sets a price equal to unit cost c firm 2's best response is to match it. The anticipated behavior of firm 2 in stage 2 puts firm 1 in a tight bind. Any price greater than unit cost c results in zero sales and there is no sense in setting a price less than c. The best firm 1 can do then is set a price equal to unit cost c. Firm 2's best response in the next stage is to match firm 1's price.

Matters are very different, however, if the two firms are not selling identical products. In this case, not all consumers buy from the lower priced firm. Product differentiation changes the outcome of price competition quite a bit. To illustrate the nature of price competition with differentiated products, recall the spatial model of product differentiation that we developed previously. The setup is the following. There is a product spectrum of unit length along which consumers are uniformly distributed. Two firms supply this market. One firm has the address or product design $x = 0$, on the line whereas the other has location, $x = 1$. Each of the firms has the same constant unit cost of production c.

A consumer's location in this market is that consumer's most preferred product, or style. "Consumer x" is located distance x from the left-hand end of the market. Consumers differ regarding which variant or location of the good they consider to be the best, or their ideal product, but are identical in their reservation price V for their most preferred product and we assume that the reservation price V is substantially greater than the unit cost of production c. Each consumer buys at most one unit of the product. If consumer x purchases a good that is not her ideal product she incurs a utility loss of tx if she consumes good 1 (located at $x = 0$), and $t(1 - x)$ if she consumes good 2 (located at $x = 1$).

The two firms compete for customers by setting prices, p_1 and p_2, respectively. However, unlike the simple Bertrand model, firm 1 sets its price p_1 first, and then firm 2 follows by setting p_2. In order to find the demand facing the firms at prices p_1, and p_2 we proceed as in the previous chapter by identifying the marginal consumer x^m, who is indifferent between buying from either firm 1 or firm 2. Indifference means that the consumer x^m gets the same consumer surplus from either product and so satisfies the condition:

$$V - p_1 - tx^m = V - p_2 - t(1 - x^m) \tag{11.8}$$

From equation (11.8) we find that the address of the marginal consumer x^m is:

$$x^m(p_1, p_2) = \frac{(p_2 - p_1 + t)}{2t} \tag{11.9}$$

At any set of prices, p_1 and p_2, all consumers to the left of x^m buy from firm 1, and all those to the right of x^m buy from firm 2. In other words, x^m is the fraction of the market buying from firm 1 and $(1 - x^m)$ is the fraction buying from firm 2. If the total number of consumers is denoted by N and they are uniformly distributed over the product spectrum the demand function facing firm 1 at any price combination (p_1, p_2) is:

$$D^1(p_1, p_2) = x^m(p_1, p_2) = \frac{(p_2 - p_1 + t)}{2t} N \tag{11.10}$$

Similarly, firm 2's demand function is:

$$D^2(p_1, p_2) = (1 - x^m(p_1, p_2)) = \frac{(p_1 - p_2 + t)}{2t} N \tag{11.11}$$

Firm 1 acts first and sets its price p_1. In doing so, firm 1 anticipates firm 2's best response to the price p_1 that firm 1 sets. In other words, firm 1 works out firm 2's best response to each possible price p_1, and then chooses its profit-maximizing price p_1 given firm 2's best response to that price. We can solve for firm 2's best response function p_2^* exactly as we did in section 4 of Chapter 11. It is

$$p_2^* = \frac{p_1 + c + t}{2} \qquad \text{\textit{deriv of profit function}} \tag{11.12}$$

Firm 1 knows that equation (11.12) describes what firm 2 will do in response to each price p_1 that firm 1 could set. We can summarize equation (11.12) by $p_2^*(p_1)$. Firm 1 knows that if it sets first a price p_1 then firm 2 will set a price $p_2^*(p_1)$. As a result, firm 1's demand (11.10) becomes:

$$D^1(p_1, p_2^*(p_1)) = \frac{(p_2^*(p_1) - p_1 + t)}{2t} N = \frac{N}{4t}(c + 3t - p_1) \tag{11.13}$$

In turn, this implies that firm 1's profit can be described by:

$$\Pi^1(p_1, p_2^*(p_1)) = \frac{N}{4t}(p_1 - c)(c + 3t - p_1) \tag{11.14}$$

In order to solve for firm 1's optimal price we need to work out how firm 1's profit changes as the firm varies its price p_1. The most straightforward way to do this is to take the derivative of the profit function (11.14) with respect to p_1 and set the derivative equal to zero. That is, solving $\dfrac{d\Pi(p_1^*, p_2^*(p_1^*))}{dp_1} = 0$ leads us to:

$$p_1^* = c + \frac{3t}{2} \tag{11.15}$$

Given this choice of price by firm 1, firm 2 selects its best response as given by equation (11.12), which yields:

$$p_2^* = c + \frac{5t}{4} \tag{11.16}$$

The profit-maximizing prices in equations (11.15) and (11.16) for the sequential price game differ in important ways from the prices that we found for the simultaneous price game in

Figure 11.2   Sequential price competition: firm 1 sets its price first anticipating that firm 2 will price below firm 1's price

section 10.3 from the last chapter. One difference is that prices now are higher. In the simultaneous price game the two firms set the same prices $p_1^* = p_2^* = c + t$, whereas in the sequential game firm 1 sets a price in stage 1 that is greater than $c + t$, and firm 2 responds by setting a slightly lower price, but still higher than $c + t$.

A second difference is that the two firms in the sequential price game have different market shares and earn different profits. In the simultaneous price-setting game, each firm served one half the market and earned the same profit equal to $Nt/2$. In the sequential game, on the other hand, firm 1 serves 3/8 of the market, and earns a profit equal to $18Nt/32$, whereas firm 2 serves 5/8 of the market and earns a profit equal to $25Nt/32$. This outcome is described in Figure 11.2.

Finally, note that unlike the Stackelberg output game, the sequential price game just described presents a clear *second* mover advantage. Firm 2 enjoys a larger market share and higher profit than firm 1. Both are better off than in the simultaneous game but firm 2, the second mover, is even better off than firm 1. However, this advantage diminishes as consumer preference for differentiation, as measured in our example by the parameter t, decreases. When the goods are perfect substitutes there is no second mover advantage.

11.2

Practice Problem

Let there be two hair salons located on Main Street, which is 1 mile long. One is located at the east end of town, $x = 0$, and the other is located at the west end, $x = 1$. There are 100 potential customers who live along the mile stretch, and they are uniformly spread out along the mile. Consumers are willing to pay $50 for a haircut done at their home. If a consumer has to travel there and back to get a haircut then a travel cost of $5 per mile is incurred. Each salon has the same unit cost equal to $10 per haircut.

a.   Suppose the east end salon posts its price for a haircut first and then the west end salon posts its price for a haircut. What prices will the two salons set? How many customers does each salon serve? What are the profits?

b.   Compare the prices to the ones we found when the two salons set their prices simultaneously (see Chapter 10). Explain why prices changed in the way they did. ʿ

Firms generally seem to do better when they compete sequentially in prices than when they compete sequentially in output. The average price is higher and both firms earn higher profits when price competition is sequential rather than simultaneous. In contrast, the industry price falls and only one firm earns higher profit when quantity competition becomes sequential rather than simultaneous. This difference is related to another distinction. Whereas it is the first mover who has the clear advantage in the quantity game, in the price game, it is the firm who moves last that does best.

The fact that one firm has an advantage over the other firm in either the quantity or the price sequential game is due largely to the fact that the first mover's initial play is irrevocable by the time the second player moves. This may make some sense in the output game if the first mover has actually completed its production and incurred its costs before firm 2

Reality Checkpoint

First Mover Advantage in the TV Market: More Dishes and Higher Prices

When a firm markets a new good or service its consumers are likely to be aware of the fact that it may not work that well. In particular, it may take time to learn how to use the good properly or to use it in such a way that one gets full use of all the features that the product or service contains. Think, for example, of such goods and services as personal computers, personal digital assistants, cellular phones, DVD players, online auctions. It takes experience using a Palm Pilot or an Apple Computer or purchasing a product on e-Bay before one really can get the most out of these modern products. Gabszewicz, Pepall, and Thisse (GPT) (1992) build on this idea to show how consumer learning may confer a first-mover advantage to the first firm to market a new product. Imagine a simple two-stage model. Firm 1 introduces its version of the new product and a rival enters in the second stage with its own, differentiated version of the same good. GPT argue that those consumers who bought firm 1's product in stage 1 will know how it works but they will not know that for firm 2's new product. As a result, they will tend to prefer firm 1's good even if firm 2 sells at a lower price.

Indeed, GPT show that the pricing implications can be quite novel. When firm 1 introduces its product in stage 1, it foresees the later entry of firm 2. Firm 1 will have an incentive to price very low in the first stage so as to induce a lot of consumers to try and to become experienced with its product before firm 2 enters. This will create a large group of captive consumers for firm 1 who will be willing to pay a higher price for its product in stage 2 now that they know how the product works. Thus when firm 2 enters, firm 1 actually raises its price and still retains a larger number of consumers because they do not want to learn how to work with firm 2's imperfect substitute. The first mover may not only have a large market share but we may actually see that firm raise its prices at the very time that new competition emerges—exactly the opposite of what simple textbook analysis often implies.

Evidence of the first-mover advantage suggested by GPT may come from the television market. Here, the initial new product was cable TV, which has rapidly spread so that now 70 percent of American homes receive cable service. The Telecommunications Act of 1996 essentially deregulated the cable TV industry hoping that new firms, especially telephone companies, would provide competition to the local cable franchises. By and large, however, competition from alternative cable providers has remained weak. Instead, the major competition to cable that has emerged is from direct broadcast satellite (DBS) TV that consumers receive through a satellite dish. Textbook analysis would suggest that DBS competition would lead to lower cable prices. However, Goolsbee and Petrin (2003) find that, to the contrary, penetration of the market by DBS has led, on average, to an increase in the annual cable fee of about $34.68. The ability of cable firms to raise price as new rivals appear may reflect precisely the first-mover advantage noted by Gabszewicz, Pepall, and Thisse.

Source: Gabszewicz, J., L. Pepall, and J.-F. Thisse, "Sequential Entry with Brand Loyalty Caused by Consumer Learning-by-doing," *Journal of Industrial Economics*, 60 (December 1992), 397–416; and A. Goolsbee and A. Petrin, "The Consumer Gains from Direct Broadcast Satellite and Competition with Cable TV," *Econometrica*, 72 (March 2004), 351–81.

selects its output. For the price game, however, it seems less plausible. Rather than settle for a second best profit, what is to stop the firm 1 from taking an additional move and trying to undercut the price of firm 2? If it is possible that when the market opens firm 1 can still undercut firm 2's price, then it is also clear that firm 2 will anticipate such a price cut by firm 1 and will want to cut its price still further. Yet if firm 1 anticipates that behavior, it will wish to reduce its price even more. Very quickly, this reasoning brings us back to the simultaneous price setting game. In other words, the sequential aspect of the price game requires that firm 1 *not* be able to change its price after it is set. Instead, firm 1 must be committed to that price. In turn, this raises the question as to how firm 1 can commit to its initial price in a manner that is *credible* to firm 2.

The issue of making a *credible commitment* is also crucial in the quantity setting Stackelberg game. If the first mover actually incurs the cost and produces the output before the follower moves then its production decision is irreversible and the credibility question is resolved. Talk on the other hand is cheap. If the leader simply announces an intention to produce the monopoly output, the follower would have good reason to doubt that the firm will follow through with this announcement. The monopoly output is not what firm 1 would choose to produce in response to the output firm 2 would choose if firm 1 produces the monopoly output.

The bottom line is that while dynamic games yield different results than those played simultaneously, those results depend crucially on the credibility of firms' strategies. Since credibility is so important, we should expect that the firms playing dynamic games will also distinguish between credible strategies and non-credible ones. So, we need to understand what makes strategies credible in dynamic games.

In the next section we explore what credibility means in a dynamic game. We do so in the context of dynamic game that has been of great interest to industrial organization economists. It is a market entry game. The firm to move first is a potential entrant to a monopolized market. The firm that moves second is the incumbent firm and the interest here is whether the incumbent can choose a strategy that deters the entrant from entering its profitable market. Before making its initial move, the entrant anticipates the incumbent's subsequent reaction. The question is what reactions are credible ones.

11.3   CREDIBILITY OF THREATS AND NASH EQUILIBRIA FOR DYNAMIC GAMES

We begin by introducing a concept that is critical to all dynamic games, namely, that of a subgame. A subgame is a part of an entire game that can stand alone as a game in itself. A proper subgame is a game within a game. Simultaneous games cannot have subgames, but dynamic games can. An example of a subgame in a two-period model is the competition in the second period, which is a one-shot game within the larger two-period game.

Closely related to the notion of subgame is the concept of subgame perfection, first introduced by Nobel Prize winner Reinhard Selten (1978). It is the concept of subgame perfection that permits us to understand whether a firm's strategy is credible in a dynamic game. The term sounds very technical but it is actually quite simple. Basically, subgame perfection means that if a strategy chosen at the start of a game is optimal, it must be optimal to stick with that strategy at every subsequent juncture of the game.

It is easier to understand the concept of subgame perfection by seeing its application in practice. Imagine a dynamic game between two software firms, one a giant called Microhard who is the incumbent firm in the market and the other an upstart firm, Newvel, who wishes to enter the market. In this game the potential entrant, Newvel, moves first choosing either to enter Microhard's market or stay out. If Newvel stays out it earns a normal profit from being somewhere else in the economy, say $\Pi = 1$, and Microhard continues to earn a monopoly profit in the software market, say $\Pi = 5$. If Newvel enters the market then Microhard can choose either to accommodate the new entrant and share the market or to fight the new entrant by slashing prices. If Microhard accommodates Newvel's entry then each firm earns a profit $\Pi = 2$. If, on the other hand, Microhard fights then neither firm makes any profit so each firm earns $\Pi = 0$.

Dynamic games with moves in sequence require more care in presentation than single-period, simultaneous games. In a simultaneous game, a firm moves once and simultaneously and so its *action* is the same as its *strategy*. For a dynamic game, a firm's strategy is a complete set of instructions that tell the firm what *actions* to pick at every conceivable situation in the game. Nevertheless, for this simple dynamic game between Microhard and Newvel we can use a payoff matrix of the type introduced in Chapter 9 to gain insight into which strategy pairs yield a Nash equilibrium to this game.

		Microhard	
		Fight	Accommodate
Newvel	Enter	(0, 0)	(2, 2)
	Stay out	(1, 5)	(1, 5)

Start with the combination (Enter, Fight). This *cannot* correspond to an equilibrium. Enter will lead Newvel to come into the market. If Microhard has adopted the Fight strategy, it must respond to such entry very aggressively. Yet, as the payoff matrix makes clear, such an aggressive action is not Microhard's best response to entry by Newvel. Now try (Enter, Accommodate). This *is* a Nash equilibrium in strategies. If Newvel chooses to Enter, and if Microhard has adopted the strategy, Accommodate, the associated outcome is a best response for both Newvel and Microhard. That is, if Microhard has adopted a strategy to Accommodate, then Enter is the best response for Newvel and if Newvel enters accommodating is a best response for Microhard. So, the combination (Enter, Accommodate) is a Nash equilibrium.

What about the combination (Stay Out, Fight)? It also satisfies the Nash definition. If Newvel chooses Stay Out, then the Fight strategy is a best response for Microhard, while if Microhard has chosen its Fight strategy, then Stay Out is a best response for Newvel. Therefore, (Stay Out, Fight) is also a Nash equilibrium in strategies. We leave it for the reader to show that the strategy combination (Stay Out, Accommodate) is not a Nash equilibrium.

Again, it is important to understand that a Nash equilibrium is defined in terms of strategies that are best responses to each other. In the second Nash equilibrium (Stay Out, Fight), Microhard never actually takes or implements a fighting action. Instead, it relies fully on the *threat* to do so as a device to deter Newvel from entering. The Nash equilibrium concept is not based on what actions are actually observed in the market place, but rather upon what thinking or strategizing underlies what we observe. This is what is meant when we say we need to define a Nash equilibrium in terms of firms' strategies.

There are two Nash equilibria to this game. There is, however, something troubling about one of these, namely, the Nash equilibrium (Stay Out, Fight). It is true that if Microhard has fully committed itself to the strategy, "Fight", then Newvel's best strategy is "Stay Out". But Newvel might question whether such a commitment is really possible. By adopting the Fight strategy, Microhard's essentially says to Newvel, "I am going to price high so long as you stay out but, if you enter my market, I will cut my price and smash you." The problem is that this threat suffers a serious *credibility* problem. We already know that once Newvel has entered the market, taking action to fight back is not in Microhard's best interest. It does much better by accommodating such entry. Consequently, Microhard does not have an incentive to carry out its threat. So, why should Newvel believe that threat in the first place?

What we have really just discovered is that any Nash equilibrium strategy combination based on non-credible threats is not very satisfactory. This means that we need to strengthen our definition of Nash equilibrium to rule out such strategy combinations. This is where the notion of subgame perfection, or a subgame perfect Nash equilibrium, becomes important. If Microhard adopts a strategy that includes the threat of a fight if entry occurs then if the strategy is subgame perfect it must be optimal for Microhard to fight in the event that Newvel enters. However, this is not the case. Accordingly, the Fight strategy is not subgame perfect.

A Nash equilibrium is said to be subgame perfect or perfect if at that point in the game when a player is called upon to make good on a promise or a threat, doing exactly that and fulfilling the promise or threat is what would be the player's best response. In other words, if any promises or threats are made in one period, carrying them out is still part of a Nash equilibrium in a later period should the occasion arise to do so.

The reason we originally found two Nash equilibria in the game above is that we did not apply this notion of subgame perfection. Strategies that employ threats over future actions can be more difficult to identify in the matrix representation of the game and hence it is more difficult to test for subgame perfection using this representation of the game. It is for this reason that for dynamic games we prefer instead to use an extensive or tree representation of the game.

The extensive form of a game is comprised of dots, branches and vectors of payoffs. The dots are called nodes and describe where we are in the game. They are labeled by which firm makes the move at that position—N for Newvel and M for Microhard, in our case. The branches that are drawn from a node represent the choice of actions available to the player at that node. Each branch points either to another node, where further action takes place, or to a vector of payoffs (Newvel's payoff shown first), which means that this particular choice of action has ended the game. Finally, at any node players know about the course of play that has led to that node. The extensive form of the Microhard–Newvel game is shown in Figure 11.3.

When we represent a sequential game in extensive form it is easy to identify a subgame. A subgame is defined as a single node and all the actions that flow from that node. In the extensive game illustrated in Figure 11.3, there are two subgames. There is the full game

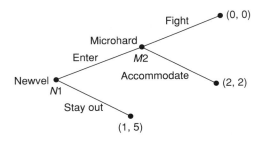

Figure 11.3   The extensive form of the Microhard–Newvel game

starting from node N1 (the full game is always a subgame). Then there is the subgame starting at node M2, and including all subsequent actions that flow from this node. A strategy combination is subgame perfect if the strategy for each player is a best response against the strategies of the other players for every subgame of the entire game. In the case at hand, it is readily apparent that for the subgame beginning at node 2, the best response strategy for Microhard is Accommodate and *not* Fight. Hence, the strategy combination (Stay Out, Fight) cannot correspond to a subgame perfect equilibrium. The only such equilibrium in this case is that of (Enter, Accommodate).

There is an important technique for solving dynamic games with a finite number of nodes. In such games, the simplest way to identify the subgame perfect equilibria is to work backwards from the end nodes of the game. This takes advantage of the property that a subgame perfect equilibrium strategy combination must be a Nash equilibrium in each subgame, including the subgames, which define the end of the game. Using this method in our example, we first calculate the Nash equilibrium for the subgame starting at node M2. This gives the unique Nash equilibrium (Accommodate) with the associated payoffs (2,2). We can therefore eliminate the "Fight" branch, leaving only the single "Accommodate" branch from node M2.

Now pass down the tree to node N1. At this juncture, Newvel understands that Stay Out leads to a payoff of 1, while Enter leads to M2 and to Accommodate by Microhard. Of course, this response results in a payoff for Newvel of 2. Accordingly, the Stay Out branch can be eliminated. The game tree now has a single branch from N1 and a single branch from M2, so we have solved the game. Newvel chooses Enter and Microhard chooses to Accommodate. In other words, this procedure has eliminated the combination (Stay Out, Fight) as a perfect Nash equilibrium.

11.3

Practice Problem

Centipede is a well-known variant of games involving a chance to "grab a dollar." The game is played as between two players, as follows. A neutral third party, call it Nature, puts $1 on the table. Player 1 can either "grab" this dollar or "wait." If player 1 takes the dollar, the game is over and player 1 gets $1 and player 2 obviously gets nothing. However, it is completely understood that, if player 1 waits, Nature will *triple* the amount on the table to $3. At that point, it becomes player 2's turn to move. Her options are as follows. She can either take the entire $3 for herself or, share the money equally with player 1.

a. Construct the 2×2 payoff matrix for this game taking player 1's actions to be either Grab, or Wait, and player 2's actions to be either Grab (the whole $3), or Share. Assume the payoffs are equal to the amount of money the player receives.
b. Draw the game in its extensive form.
c. Suppose that player 2 promises player 1 that she will take the action, Share, if player 1 waits. Is this promise credible? Why or why not?

11.4   THE CHAIN STORE PARADOX

In the Microhard and Newvel game there is just one market and one potential entrant, and fighting the entrant was not an optimal response to entry. However, what if Microhard faced more than one entrant? Perhaps fighting one entrant builds a reputation for aggressive behavior that will scare off later entrants. The consideration of the reputational effects of fighting may change Microhard's optimal strategy. Taking predatory action against a rival—costly though it is—could be useful *if* it serves to make the threat credible against *other* rivals, either those in other markets or those who may appear later in time. If we introduce this possibility into our example, could Microhard's threat to fight become credible because the subsequent gains in other markets from establishing a reputation as a fighter are sufficiently large? In other words, could reputation effects make Fight credible and the strategy combination (Stay Out, Fight) subgame perfect?

The fact that extension of the above game to many markets (distributed over time or space) and to other rivals may *not* lead to a different outcome is a famous result dubbed by Selten as *The Chain Store Paradox*.[3] To see the logic of this puzzling result, consider a situation in which Microhard has established operating units in each of 20 markets, perhaps 20 different cities. In each city, Microhard faces potential entry by a single, small competitor. At the moment, none of these potential competitors has the capital to start operations. However, as time goes on, one after another will raise the necessary funds. To make matters simple, assume that the payoffs in each of the 20 markets are just as in the payoff matrix of the previous section. The question facing Microhard is how to react to this sequence of potential entrants. In particular, should Microhard adopt an aggressive response to the first entrant and drive it out of business? Will this tactic earn Microhard a reputation for ruthlessness such that subsequent entrants in its other markets will get the message and choose not to enter?

Again, working backwards can help us identify a subgame perfect strategy. So, let's start with one possible scenario in which Microhard is facing the last potential entrant in the final, twentieth market. It is possible that Microhard has followed through on its threat to cut price and drive out any entrant not just in the first market, but also in all previous 19 markets. This is a possible path in the game and we are interested if such an aggressive response to entry can convince the last potential entrant to stay out, so that Microhard would be spared a fight in this final case.

However, consider the viewpoint of the entrant to the twentieth market. This firm will realize that because there are no subsequent entrants, it is playing a game that is exactly the one-period game we discussed in the previous section. So, using the argument of the previous section, this last entrant will understand that Microhard has an incentive to accommodate its entry. Microhard's profit is greater if it follows a "live and let live" strategy in this last case[4] because it cannot gain from any further demonstration of its ruthlessness. There are no other entrants left to impress! Since Microhard's only possible reason to respond to entry with aggressive price cutting is to establish a reputation for toughness, and because, after the twentieth market battle, having such a reputation does it absolutely no good, Microhard will accommodate the entrant in this last market. The entrant will understand this and of course enter. Note that the threat to fight in the twentieth market is *not* credible even though

---

[3]   Selten (1978). We have obviously limited ourselves here to consideration of finitely repeated games only. Infinitely repeated games are considered in the next chapter.

[4]   Implicit here is the presumption that accommodating an entrant is in the short run more profitable than engaging in a price war.

Microhard could have already done so in 19 prior cases! The threat to fight is made no more credible by fighting only in 18 markets, or 17, or just one. If a record of 19 previous rounds of aggressive price-cutting does not convince the final entrant, nothing will.

One might think that this simply implies that Microhard cannot credibly threaten the potential entrant in its final market because there are no more entrants, but it is still possible to deter the entry of earlier rivals by means of a threat. To see why this is not possible, consider the potential entrant in the nineteenth rather than the twentieth market. Once again, let's take the extreme case in which Microhard has taken predatory or fighting action in the prior 18 markets. Now the potential entrant in the nineteenth market can reason as well as we can. As a result, this firm will work out the logic of the preceding case and rightfully conclude that Microhard will not fight in the twentieth market. The entrant in the nineteenth or next-to-last market will then reason as follows: "Microhard will let the last rival firm survive because it is pointless to cut price at that point to gain a tough reputation. Since I know that the entry of the last rival will not be challenged, there is, in fact, no reason for Microhard to act tough on me. Its only reason to do so would be to convince the entrant in the next market. Since this is not possible, the only justification for fighting in market nineteen has been removed." Once again, Microhard's promise to fight if entry occurs is not credible. It gains Microhard nothing by way of a demonstration to the next rival. Absent such a reputation effect, Microhard's best response to entry in the nineteenth market is again to accommodate. Knowing this, the potential entrant in market nineteen will enter.

We can continue in this fashion repeatedly, bringing us back all the way to the initial market. At every stage, we will find that a strategy to fight after entry occurs is not subgame perfect and accordingly not credible. This will be just as true in the first market as in the last. There is no way for the incumbent to threaten credibly an aggressive low-price response to entry.

At this point the only subgame perfect Nash strategy equilibrium is one in which entry occurs and fighting never happens. If this were the end of the story, our interest in the predatory conduct would certainly be very low. Why should we worry about an event that presumably never occurs? The answer is that there may be ways to make the threat to fight credible other than actual fighting, itself. A firm's predatory efforts, no matter what form it takes, will work only if they are *credible* to actual and potential rivals and so influence their beliefs about competing in the market.[5] Predatory conduct that is credible is what we will investigate in the next two chapters.

Summary

Sequential market games are different from simultaneous ones. Moreover, the effect of changing from simultaneous to sequential play differs depending on whether the strategic variable of choice is quantity or price. The basic sequential quantity game, typically referred to as the Stackelberg model, confers a large advantage to the firm that chooses production first. In the linear demand and cost case, the first mover in a Stackelberg game produces the monopoly output. The follower produces only half this much. Prices are lower than in the basic Cournot model but the large market share of the first mover gives that firm an increase in profit over what it would earn in the simultaneous production game.

In contrast, a sequential price game with differentiated products yields higher profits for both firms than either would earn if prices were set simultaneously. Moreover, in this case, it is the firm that sets price last that does best. Sequential price games can confer a second mover as opposed to a first mover advantage. This advantage to the

---

[5]   Schelling (1960) contains early and lasting contributions to developing equilibrium notions for dynamic games. See also Tirole (1988) and Rasmusen (2007).

second mover diminishes as the products become closer substitutes for each other.

Crucial to any sequential game is the issue of commitment. How do firms establish themselves as leaders or followers? How can a firm commit to its initial choice of output or price in a way that a rival finds credible? This issue is best explored by considering the game in its extended form and identifying strategy combinations that are subgame perfect, i.e., strategies that call for actions at later points in the game in which those actions continue to be optimal when the time comes to

take them given the history of play up to that date.

Threats and promises of later punishments and rewards are particularly important in games in which one firm is trying to prevent another from entering its market (or perhaps trying to induce it to leave). The question again is whether such threats and promises can be made credible. If they can then incumbent firms may be able to maintain their dominant position in an industry and not fear competitive entry. This is the subject of our next chapter.

Problems

1. Consider a Stackleberg game of quantity competition between two firms. Firm 1 is the leader and firm 2 is the follower. Market demand is described by the inverse demand function $P = 1,000 - 4Q$. Each firm has a constant unit cost of production equal to 20.
   a. Solve for Nash equilibrium outcome.
   b. Suppose firm 2's unit cost of production is $c < 20$. What value would c have so that in the Nash equilibrium the two firms, leader and follower, had the same market share?

2. Let's return to Tuftsville (Chapter 10) where everyone lives along Main Street, which is 10 miles long. There are 1,000 people uniformly spread up and down Main Street, and each day they each buy a fruit smoothie from one of the two stores located at either end of Main Street. Customers ride their motor scooters to and from the store and the motor scooters use $0.50 worth of gas per mile. Customers buy their smoothies from the store offering the lowest price, which is the store's price plus the customer's travel expenses getting to and from the store. Ben owns the store at the west end of Main Street and Will owns the store at the east end of Main Street. The marginal cost of a smoothie is constant and equal to $1 for both Ben and Will. In addition, each of them pays Tuftsville $250 per day for the right to sell smoothies.
   a. Ben sets his price p_1 first and then Will sets his price p_2. After the prices are posted consumers get on their scooters and buy from the store with the lowest price

including travel expenses. What prices will Ben and Will set?
   b. How many customers does each store serve and what are their profits?

3. In Centipede[6] there are two players. Player 1 moves first, player 2 moves second. After at most two moves, the game ends. The game begins with $1 sitting on a table. Player 1 can either take the $1 or wait. If player 1 takes the $1 the game is over, and player 1 gets to keep the $1. If player 1 waits the $1 quadruples to $4. Now it is player 2's turn. Player 2 can either take the entire $4 or split the $4 evenly with player 1.
   a. Draw the extensive form for the game of Centipede.
   b. What is the equilibrium to this game? Can player 2's strategy of splitting the money ever be a part of an equilibrium outcome to the game?
   c. Now suppose that Centipede has three moves. Player 2 can now either wait, split the money or take the $4. If player 2 waits then the money on the table quadruples again and player 1 can either take it all or split it. Draw the extensive form for the new game and solve for the equilibrium outcome.

4. Dry Gulch has two water suppliers. One is Northern Springs whose water is crystal clear but not carbonated. The other is Southern Pelligrino whose water is naturally carbonated but also somewhat "hard." The marketing department of each firm has worked out the following profit matrix depending on the

---

6   This game was first introduced by Rosenthal (1982).

price per 2-gallon container charged by each firm. Southern Pelligrino's profits are shown as the first entry in each pair.

		Northern Springs' price			
		3	4	5	6
Southern Pelligrino's price	3	24,24	30,25	36,20	42,12
	4	25,30	32,32	41,30	48,24
	5	20,36	30,41	40,40	50,36
	6	12,42	24,48	36,50	48,48

a. What is the Nash equilibrium if the two firms set prices simultaneously?

b. What is the Nash equilibrium if Northern Springs must set its price first, and stick with it, and Southern Pelligrino is free to respond as best it can to Northern Springs' price?

c. Show that choosing *price* first is a disadvantage for Northern Springs? Why is this the case?

5. Suppose that firm 1 can choose to produce either good *A* or good *B* or both goods or *nothing*. Firm 2, on the other hand, can produce only good *C* or *nothing*. Firms' profits corresponding to each possible scenario of goods for sale are described in the following table:

Product selection	Firm 1's profit	Firm 2's profit
A	20	0
A,B	18	0
A,B,C	2	−2
B,C	−3	−3
C	0	10
A,C	8	8
B	11	0

a. Set up the normal form game for when the two firms simultaneously choose their product sets. What is the Nash equilibrium (or equilibria)?

b. Now suppose that firm 1 can commit to its product choice before firm 2. Draw the extensive form of this game and identify its subgame perfect Nash equilibrium. Compare your answer to (a) and explain.

c. The game is like the one in (b) only now suppose that firm 1 can reverse its decision after observing firm 2's choice and this possibility is common knowledge. Does this affect the game? If so, explain the new outcome? If not, explain why not.

6. Find three examples of different ways individual firms or industries can make the strategy "This offer is good for a limited time only" a credible strategy.

7. The Gizmo Company has a monopoly on the production of gizmos. Market demand is described as follows: at a price of $1,000 per gizmo 25,000 units will be sold whereas at a price of $600 30,000 will be sold. The only costs of production are the initial sunk costs of building a plant. Gizmo Co. has already invested in capacity to produce up to 25,000 units.

a. Suppose an entrant to this industry could capture 50% of the market if it invested in $10 million to construct a plant. Would the firm enter? Why or why not?

b. Suppose Gizmo could invest $5 million to expand its capacity to produce 40,000 gizmos. Would this strategy be a profitable way to deter entry?

References

Gabszewicz, J., L. Pepall, and J.-F. Thisse. 1992. "Sequential Entry with Brand Loyalty Caused by Consumer Learning-By-Doing." *Journal of Industrial Economics* 60 (December): 397–416.

Goolsbee, A. and A. Petrin. 2004. "The Consumer Gains from Direct Broadcast Satellite and Competition with Cable TV." *Econometrica* 72 (March): 351–81.

Lieberman, Marvin B. and David B. Montgomery. 1998. "First Mover Advantages."

Strategic Management Journal 19 (December): 1111–25.

Rasmusen, E. 2007. *Games and Information*. 4th edition. Cambridge, MA: Blackwell.

Rosenthal, R. W. 1981. "Games of Perfect Information, Predatory Pricing, and the Chain Store Paradox." *Journal of Economic Theory* 25 (August): 92–100.

Schelling, T., 1960. *The Strategy of Conflict*. Cambridge, MA: Harvard University Press.

Selten, R. 1978. "The Chain Store Paradox." *Theory and Decision* 9 (April): 127–59.

Stackelberg, H. von 1934. *Marktform und Gleichgewicht*. Berlin and Vienna. English translation by A. T. Peacock, 1952, London: William Hodge.

Sutton, J. 1991. *Sunk Cost and Market Structure*. Cambridge, MA: MIT Press.

Tirole, J. 1988. *The Theory of Industrial Organization*. Cambridge, MA: MIT Press.

Part IV
Anticompetitive Strategies

Part IV builds on the game theoretic analysis of the previous three chapters to explore the tactics that firms can employ to blunt competitive pressures and thereby earn supracompetitive profits. In the Stackelberg setting, the first mover has to worry about later entry or expansion by rivals. In the Cournot model and, to an even greater extent, in the Bertrand model the competition among firms prevents them from maximizing their joint profit. It is natural therefore to consider what strategies incumbent firms may use to prevent rival entry, and to investigate the potential for existing firms to suppress their competition by colluding and thereby achieving something closer to the monopoly profit.

Chapters 12 and 13 focus on the use of market power by an incumbent firm either to keep potential rivals from entering or to drive existing rivals from the market. Such predation, as it is usually called, has been at the core of antitrust policy and antitrust cases ever since the antitrust laws were passed. Standard Oil, Microsoft, and American Airlines are just some of the firms that have been accused of predatory practices. Chapter 12 focuses primarily on price tactics by which the dominant incumbent prices below cost in an effort to exclude rivals from the market. In Chapter 13, we consider contractual and other non-price strategies that achieve this same purpose. We also present an empirical analysis of possible predatory advertising behavior in the pharmaceutical industry.

Chapters 14 and 15 then turn to a consideration of the ability of firms to cooperate and suppress competitive pressures. Such collusion amounts to what is popularly called price-fixing and it is also a major concern of the antitrust laws. Indeed, the period since the 1990s has witnessed the successful prosecution of a record number of price-fixing cartels. In Chapter 14 we present the obstacles to successful collusion and the well-known Folk theorem describing the conditions under which those obstacles can be overcome. We also present an empirical examination of such collusion in the real estate market.

In Chapter 15 we return to a historical consideration of price-fixing cases and what these tell us about how such agreements can be uncovered by authorities. Many believe that an important element in the recent string of successful cartel prosecutions has been the adoption of a leniency policy that typically drops any criminal charges against the first member of a cartel to confess to the authorities. Therefore, this chapter concludes with an exploration of antitrust policy towards cartels and the role of such leniency provisions. This includes an analysis of a game theory experiment designed to simulate cartel behavior when there is a positive probability of detection and when the first member of the cartel that confesses goes free.

12

Limit Pricing and Entry Deterrence

For most of the twentieth century, Campbell's accounted for 70 percent or more of canned soup sales in the U.S. For at least two decades, the American firm, Sotheby's, and the British firm, Christie's, have together controlled roughly 90 percent of the world auction market while each has more than half of its own domestic auction market. The semiconductor firm Intel has accounted for 75 percent or more of the market for PC processors for some two decades. Over that same period, Microsoft has maintained control of over 90 percent of the market for operating systems software.[1] There can be little doubt that each of these firms has substantial market power. Some appear almost to be pure monopolies. Accordingly, we must expect that such dominant firms are able to exercise their market power and earn supra-competitive profits.

The Microsoft, Intel, and other examples of sustained market power just described are not isolated cases. Analyses by Baldwin (1995) and Geroski and Toker (1996) find that, on average, the number one firm in an industry retains that rank for somewhere between 17 and 28 years. The fact that continued market power is so common does, however, raise the question as to how such firms can sustain this profit-winning position. Why don't new rivals emerge to compete away that market share and profit? Are there strategies that the dominant firms can adopt to prevent this from happening? If so, what are these strategies and what are their implications for market outcomes?

The questions just raised are the focus of this chapter and the next one. They continue our theme of strategic interaction. Here, the interaction is between an existing dominant firm and potential or actual entrants. We emphasize at the outset that this issue is of much more than mere academic interest. The question of whether large incumbent firms can eliminate or prevent the entry of rivals goes to the heart of many concerns that inspired the creation of the antitrust laws and have remained central in antitrust cases ever since. This concern lay at the crux of the Microsoft antitrust case.[2] Section 2 of the Sherman Act deems it illegal to "monopolize or attempt to monopolize . . . any part of the trade or commerce." Enforcement of this provision requires an understanding of what a firm can do in order to "monopolize" the market.

---

[1] See, "Squeeze Gently," *Economist*, November 30, 1996, pp. 65–6.
[2] Indeed, each of the firms mentioned has been accused of unfair practices and has been the subject of antitrust scrutiny.

Strategies that are designed to deter rival firms from competing in a market are what economists call *predatory* conduct.[3] A firm engaging in predatory conduct wants to influence the behavior of its rivals—either those currently in the market or those thinking of entering it. Predatory conduct often involves the making of threats and, if necessary, actually implementing the threats in a way that ensures such threats are *credible*. Credibility is absolutely essential for predatory conduct to be successful. After all, as we learned from the Chain Store Paradox in the last chapter "talk is cheap." A threat aimed at dissuading a rival from entering one's market will only have the desired effect if it is credible. Such threats work when the rival or prey believes that the predator really "means business" and will pursue the predatory conduct *when the rival chooses to ignore the threat*.

In this chapter we investigate predatory conduct that is designed to deter rivals from entering an incumbent's market. In doing so, we limit ourselves to cases of certainty or complete information. We defer the examination of predatory conduct under uncertainty or incomplete information until the next chapter.

Considerable care is required in an investigation of predatory conduct. For example, we must be careful not to characterize actions by a firm either to improve its cost-efficiency or to promote its product as predatory, even if such actions have the effect of enhancing the firm's market position. For a firm's conduct to be predatory or anti-competitive it must be the case that the firm's action is profitable *only if* it causes a rival firm to exit, or deters a potential rival from entering the market in the first place. This is in keeping with the spirit of the antitrust provisions themselves, which focus on efforts "to monopolize . . . any part of the trade or commerce" and to "materially reduce competition."[4] The basis for this legislative concern is, of course, the fear that with existing rivals and the threat of entry removed, a dominant firm will pursue monopoly practices that reduce efficiency.

12.1   MONOPOLY POWER AND MARKET STRUCTURE OVER TIME: SOME BASIC FACTS

The evolution of an industry's structure, whether into one of persistent monopoly, concentrated oligopoly, or more competitive configurations, depends on a number of factors. One of these is the relationship between a firm's size and its growth rate. An early finding in this respect is known as the Law of Proportionate Effect or, more commonly, Gibrat's Law after its originator Robert Gibrat (1931). Gibrat asked what would happen if, starting with a population of say 100 equally sized firms, each firm in each period was randomly assigned a growth rate drawn from a distribution with a constant average growth rate and variance of growth rates over time. The answer is perhaps surprising. Even though the firms in the industry all start at the same size and even though each has the same chance for growth in every period thereafter, it is still the case that over time the industry becomes more and more concentrated. In particular, the distribution of firm sizes approaches a log normal one in which the logarithm of firm sizes approaches a normal distribution. Gibrat (1931) and later others, e.g., Kalecki (1945) produced some evidence that was very supportive of this natural concentrating tendency.

The Gibrat hypothesis has been enormously influential. To a large extent, this influence has been for what Gibrat's analysis leaves out rather than what it keeps in. This is because

---

[3]   See, e.g., Fisher (1991).
[4]   Our definition is also similar to that of Ordover and Willig (1981).

Derivation Checkpoint
The Gibrat Logic

Let x_t denote a firm's size at time t, where size might be measured in sales or assets or employees. Similarly, denote the firm's size in period $t - 1$ as x_{t-1}. Now let ε_t be the rate of growth of the firm from time $t - 1$ to time t, where growth is measured as the rate of proportional change, i.e., a growth rate of 4 percent is expressed as $\varepsilon_t = 0.04$. This growth factor is a random variable drawn each period from a normal distribution with constant mean and variance, and that is the same for all firms. It then follows that the firm's size from time $t - 1$ to time t evolves according to the equation:

$$x_t = (1 + \varepsilon_t)x_{t-1}$$

Next, take the log of both sides. If the time interval between t and $t - 1$ is short, then the random growth term ε_t is small. This permits us to use the approximation that $\log(1 + \varepsilon_t) \approx \varepsilon_t$. With this approximation we may now write:

$$\log x_t = \log x_{t-1} + \varepsilon_t.$$

In turn, this implies that we may also write

$$\log x_{t-1} = \log x_{t-2} + \varepsilon_{t-1}$$

By repeated substitution, we then obtain:

$$\log x_t = \log x_0 + \varepsilon_t + \varepsilon_{t-1} + \varepsilon_{t-2} + \varepsilon_{t-3} + \ldots + \varepsilon_0$$

This last equation says that the logarithm of the firm's size at time t will just be a random variable reflecting the accumulation of all the random growth shocks it has experienced up to that time. Since each shock is assumed to be a random variable drawn from the normal distribution, the sum over time of all those accumulated shocks is also a normal random variable. Recall however that logarithms reflect exponential power. As the log of a firm's assets doubles the actual volume of those assets is squared. So, although the log of firm size may be normally distributed, the distribution of actual firm sizes will be skewed. Those firms with above average values for the log of firm size will have way above average values when size is measured without logs. Hence, if firm sizes evolve so that each firm is generated by the process described above, the industry will eventually become quite heavily concentrated.

as originally presented, Gibrat's process is very mechanistic. There is no talk of research and cost-saving innovations. There is no consideration of mergers and firm combinations over time. Perhaps most relevant for our present purpose, there is no discussion of new firms entering an industry or older firms leaving; or what strategic interaction may lie behind such entry and exit. Subsequent research has tried to remedy these omissions and to develop theoretical models of industry evolution that build in these features (see, for example, Jovanovic 1982; Nelson and Winter 1982; Sutton 1997; and Klepper 2002).

Of course, any theoretical model must ultimately confront the real-world facts. On this front, too, however, there was a need for much work. In the 1950s and 1960s, we knew precious little regarding the lifecycle of firms, their births (entry) and their deaths (exit). Since the 1980s, however, economists have worked hard to review the data and to document any empirical regularities or stylized facts that appear. Any valid theory must be consistent with these facts.

There are four stylized facts worth noting. The first is that *entry is common*. Dunne, Roberts, and Samuelson (1988, 1989), using U.S. census data between 1963 and 1982, computed rates of entry in a wide cross-section of two-digit SIC manufacturing industries. Their estimate of the average entry rate in manufacturing—defined as the number of *new* firms over a five-year period relative to the number of incumbent firms at the start of that period—ranged between 41.4 percent and 51.8 percent (about 8 percent to 10 percent on an annual basis). For the U.K., Geroski (1995) estimated somewhat smaller but still significant annual rates of entry for a sample of 87 three-digit manufacturing industries. These ranged between 2.5 percent and 14.5 percent over the period 1974 to 1979. Cable and Schwalbach (1991) show that similar rates of entry obtain across a wide range of developed countries. More recently, Jarmin, Klimek, and Miranda (2004) show that rates of entry are even higher in the retail sector and may reach well over 60 percent, especially during periods of economic prosperity.[5]

The second stylized fact is that when entry occurs it is, by and large, *small-scale entry*. The studies by Dunne, Roberts, and Samuelson (1988, 1989) showed that the collective market share of entrants in an industry ranged between 13.9 percent and 18.8 percent again over a five-year interval.[6] Similarly, in Geroski's (1995) U.K. study, the market share of entrants was found to be quite modest, ranging from 1.45 percent to 6.35 percent. In the U.S., Cable and Schwalbach (1991) find that while new entrants typically constitute 7.7 percent of an industry's firms in any year, they account for only 3.2 percent of its output. The typical share of entrants in retailing is noticeably larger, say closer to 25 percent according to Jarmin, Klimek, and Miranda (2004) but they also find that this value has been declining over recent years.

The third stylized fact is that the *survival rate is relatively low*. Dunne, Roberts, and Samuelson (1988, 1989) find that roughly 61.5 percent of all entrant firms exited within five years of entry and 79.6 percent exited within ten years. The corresponding exit rates found in retailing by Jarmin, Klimek, and Miranda (2004) are very similar, between 59 percent and 82 percent. Birch (1987) used Dun and Bradstreet data for all sectors in the U.S. including, but not limited to, manufacturing and found that about 50 percent of all new entrant firms fail within the first five years.

Our final stylized fact that appears to hold in every study is that while rates of entry and exit vary across industries, *industries with high entry rates also have high exit rates*. In other words, entry and exit rates are strongly correlated. To take just one clear example, Cable and Schwalbach (1991) find that corresponding to an entry rate of 7.7 percent accounting for 3.2 percent of industry output, the exit rate is 7.0 percent and similarly it accounts for 3.3 percent of industry output. This finding is a little surprising because it does not appear consistent with the hypothesis that entry occurs in response to above-normal profit or that exit reflects a below-normal profit. If profit is high, and therefore entry attractive, there is no reason for firms to leave. Similarly, if profit is so low that firms are induced to leave the industry, there ought to be little incentive for new entrants to emerge.

---

[5]   The Dunne et al. (1988, 1989) entry (and exit) estimates are generally higher than those obtained by other researchers owing to the fact that they explicitly recognize the multiproduct and multiplant nature of firms.

[6]   Dunne et al. (1988) do find that existing firms who enter a new market through diversification typically enter at a larger scale than new, or *de novo*, entrants do.

Taken together, the stylized facts reported above can be read as suggesting a sort of revolving-door setting in which mostly small firms enter, eventually fail and exit, only to be replaced by a new cohort of small-scale entrants. In this view, the major difference across industries would be the pace at which this entry–fail–exit cycle proceeds. One interpretation of this evidence is that it reflects repeated attempts and, just as often, repeated failures of small firms to penetrate the markets dominated by large incumbents. This may help explain the correlation between entry and exit rates. Incumbents in markets that may seem the most tempting entry targets may for that very reason fight the hardest against new entrants.

More formal support for this revolving door interpretation is offered by Urban, Carter, Gaskin, and Mucha (1984) on the benefits of incumbency. They studied 129 frequently purchased brands of consumer products in 12 U.S. markets and found that market shares were a decreasing function of the order of entry of the brand. Earlier entrants enjoyed larger market shares, all else being equal. Similar results have been found by Lambkin (1988), Mitchell (1991), and Brown and Lattin (1994).[7] Generally, this finding probably reflects the fact that early (and surviving) entrants possess superior cost efficiency and more favorable locations (either in geographic or product space). However, it is frequently alleged (especially by the failed entrants) that the ability of early entrants to sustain a dominant industry position also reflects predatory behavior aimed at driving new entrants out. This is the primary issue addressed in this and the subsequent chapter.

12.2   PREDATORY CONDUCT AND LIMIT PRICING

Economists define predatory conduct to be actions taken by a firm that are profitable *only if* they drive existing rivals out of the market or deter potential rivals from coming in to the market. Predatory conduct is some costly action for which the only justification is the reduction in competition that such action is designed to achieve. If there is no cost to the firm to engage in some conduct, then that behavior could simply be part of profit-maximizing strategy and, hence, not explicitly "anti-competitive." To put it somewhat loosely, predatory conduct must appear on the surface to reduce the predator firm's profit and seem to be "irrational." The rationality for such conduct would be the additional profit the predator earns if the conduct is successful.

When a firm charges an "irrationally" low price so that other rival firms cannot compete it is called *predatory pricing*. Historically, predatory pricing refers to cases where rival firms are driven out of the market. However, setting a low price that deters firms from entering the market is also predatory. The low price with the purpose of deterring entry is known as the *limit price*. In truth, actual litigation rarely involves limit pricing. Instead, the courts and policy makers have focused on cases in which existing firms are forced to leave the market.

It is not difficult to understand how and why there is this legal bias in predation law. Predatory pricing cases in which existing firms are driven from the market have no *habeas corpus* problem. There is an actual victim or victims. As a result, there is a supply of plaintiffs ready to press charges against the alleged predator. Moreover, the existence of a "body" can serve as powerful evidence to persuade a judge or a jury that a crime has been committed. In contrast, the victims of limit pricing are typically *potential* competitors. Here, no

---

[7]   As Caves (1998) notes though, there is regression toward the mean in firm growth rates. That is, really large firms tend to grow more slowly than do small ones. This feature blunts the ever-increasing concentration tendency implied by Gibrat's law.

firm actually dies, some are just prevented from ever being born. Such cases are difficult to prosecute.

However, economic theory can proceed even where lawyers fear to tread. Accordingly, we start the important work of this chapter by reviewing two approaches to limit pricing. The first one is an earlier approach predating the advent of a game theoretic treatment of the subject. The second approach takes the insight of the first and investigates the entry deterrent effect in a dynamic game between the incumbent and the entrant.

12.2.1   An Informal Model of Entry Deterrence

The traditional limit-pricing story of entry deterrence is told in the work of Bain (1956) and later modeled in Sylos-Labini (1962). These earlier industrial organization economists were shrewd observers of everyday business practices and had reasons to believe that predatory pricing and entry-deterring behavior occurred. We can illustrate the essence of the limit-pricing strategy using a simple variant of the Stackelberg model. Recall from the previous chapter that the strategic variable in the Stackelberg model is quantity. So, the analysis we present might more properly be labeled a limit output model, rather than a limit price one. Yet the basic idea of setting the strategic variable so as to deter entry is the same in either case—especially since the dominant firm's output choice will greatly influence the industry price. That is, we might regard the resulting price in our model as the limit price.

Figure 12.1 illustrates the essential features of the model.[8] The incumbent firm is the Stackelberg leader and is allowed to choose its output first. We begin by making a simple and yet strong assumption that whatever this choice is, the entrant believes that its own entry into the market will not alter the leader's choice of output. That is, the entrant regards the incumbent as irrevocably committed to its output choice. A further crucial assumption is that the entrant's average cost declines over at least the initial range of low levels of production. When both of these assumptions hold then, by the correct choice of its pre-entry output level, the incumbent can manipulate the entrant's profit calculation and discourage entry.

In Figure 12.1, the appropriate production level to which the incumbent must commit to deter entry is $\bar{Q}$. If the entrant stays out, this implies a market price $\bar{P}$. What would happen to market price if the entrant now produced any positive output? The answer is also shown

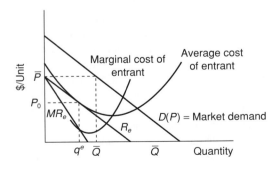

Figure 12.1   The limit output model
By producing at $\bar{Q}$, the incumbent can preclude profitable entry.

---

[8]   This presentation borrows heavily from that of Gilbert (1989).

in Figure 12.1. Because the entrant believes that the incumbent will maintain $\bar{Q}$, the demand the new entrant faces at any price P is the total quantity that is demanded at that price, $D(P)$, less $\bar{Q}$. That is, the entrant faces a *residual demand curve* R^e which, in this case, is simply the market demand curve $D(P)$ shifted inward along the horizontal axis by the amount $\bar{Q}$. Corresponding to this residual demand curve is the entrant's marginal revenue curve MR^e. The entrant maximizes its profit by selecting output q^e at which its marginal revenue just equals its marginal cost. As shown in Figure 12.1, this output is such that when it is added to the output $\bar{Q}$ of the incumbent firm market price becomes P_0 and this price barely covers the entrant's average cost. In other words, by committing to the output $\bar{Q}$, the incumbent firm removes any profit incentive for the entrant to actually participate in the market.

12.1

Practice Problem

Suppose that market demand is described by $P = 100 - (Q + q)$, where P is the market price, Q is the output of the incumbent firm and q is the output of a potential entrant to the market. The incumbent firm's total cost function is $TC(Q) = 40Q$, whereas the cost function of the entrant is $C(q) = 100 + 40q$, where 100 is a sunk cost incurred to enter the market.

a. If the entrant observes the incumbent producing $\bar{Q}$ units of output and expects this output level to be maintained, write down the equation for the residual demand curve that the entrant firm faces.
b. If the entrant firm maximizes profit given the residual demand curve in a) what output q^e will the entrant produce? (Your answer should be a function of $\bar{Q}$.)
c. How much output would the incumbent firm have to produce to just keep the entrant out of the market? That is, solve for the limit output $\bar{Q}_L$. At what price will the incumbent sell the limit output?

It should be clear that successful predation of the type just described depends crucially on the entrant's belief that the incumbent is truly committed to its action. In the language of the last chapter, the strategy must be subgame perfect. The issue then becomes whether this is possible. Can the incumbent truly commit to produce output $\bar{Q}$ even if the entrant enters the market?

Earlier scholars such as Bain (1956) and Sylos-Labini (1962) did not make use of the formal model just described. Nevertheless, they appear to have understood that in order to deter entry the incumbent firm had to commit or "lock in" to the predatory behavior. They assumed that such commitment was achieved by further supposing that the incumbent's output $\bar{Q}$ was "very" costly to adjust. Hence, the potential entrant was correct to assume that the incumbent's output would remain at $\bar{Q}$ because it was too costly to change. In other words, the presence of adjustment costs once the incumbent is already producing at a particular level acted as a mechanism to commit the incumbent to the output $\bar{Q}$ even in the face of entry.

The idea sounds plausible and may well be true. Unfortunately, as stated, it is a little *ad hoc*. Without a full specification of how such costs are generated and how they fit into a complete analysis of strategic interaction between the two firms, the adjustment cost story amounts to little more than a statement that the incumbent's output is given because it is given. Producing $\bar{Q}$ is a credible action only if $\bar{Q}$ is the incumbent's best response to the entrant coming into the market and choosing an output level to produce. Limit pricing can only work if the incumbent firm can commit to producing the limit output even if entry occurs.

12.2.2   Capacity Expansion as a Credible Entry-deterring Commitment

In a key article, Spence (1977) recognized that what may make limit pricing a credible deterrent strategy is the incumbent firm's ability to make a prior and irrevocable investment in production capacity, and specifically an investment in the *capacity* to produce the limit output $\bar{Q}$. Spence did not work out the underlying logic of this approach in a complete manner. He did make it clear that if the entrant believes that the incumbent will, after entry, produce at its pre-entry capacity, then the incumbent firm has an incentive to invest in a capacity level that keeps the potential entrant at bay. What was still required, however, was an analysis demonstrating that in the post-entry game between the incumbent and the new entrant the entrant's belief that the incumbent's post-entry output is equal to its pre-entry capacity is reasonable, i.e., subgame perfect. This was the contribution of Dixit (1980). Dixit modeled the post-entry game between the two firms. We present the essentials of his model below. We warn the reader in advance that this model is hard work. While no one piece of the analysis is difficult, considerable care is required in putting all the pieces together.

The game Dixit posits between the two firms is a dynamic, two-stage one. In the first stage, the incumbent firm moves first and chooses a capacity level $\bar{K}_1$ at a cost $r\bar{K}_1$. This capacity is measured in terms of output, and the cost r is the constant cost of one unit of capacity. By investing in capacity $\bar{K}_1$ in the first stage of the game, the incumbent firm has the capability of producing any output less than or equal to $\bar{K}_1$ when the second stage of the game begins. The incumbent's capacity can be further increased in stage two of the game. However, it cannot be reduced. One may think of the capacity investment as the construction of say, a uranium processing plant, a plant for which any other industry has little use. If so, the plant cannot be resold if the firm decides it no longer needs it. In this sense, the $r\bar{K}_1$ spent on capacity investment in stage one is an irrevocable or sunk cost.

The potential entrant is assumed to observe the incumbent's choice of capacity in stage one. It is only after that observation that the potential entrant makes its entry decision in stage two. If entry does occur then, in the second stage of the game, the two firms play a Cournot game in output. Market demand for the product in stage two is described by $P = A - B(q_1 + q_2)$. It is very important to note that the two firms simultaneously choose both their outputs (q_1, q_2) and their capacity levels (K_1, K_2) in stage two. For the incumbent, the capacity choice is constrained because its capacity in the second stage cannot be less than the capacity chosen in the first stage, i.e., $K_1 \geq \bar{K}_1$. The incumbent firm can increase its capacity in stage two but not decrease it.

We will denote any sunk costs incurred by the incumbent other than those associated with its capacity choice $\bar{K}_1$ as F_1. For simplicity, we will further assume that every unit produced requires the input of one unit of labor as well as a unit of capacity. If labor can be hired at the wage w, then the incumbent's marginal cost of production in stage two for output $q_1 \leq \bar{K}_1$ is just wq_1. However, if the incumbent wishes to produce an output greater than $\bar{K}_1$ then it must hire additional capacity, again at the price of r per unit. That is, for every unit of output above $\bar{K}_1$ the incumbent must hire one unit of labor at price w and one unit of capital at price r. Hence, the marginal cost of production for output greater than $\bar{K}_1$ is $w + r$. These relationships are reflected in the following description of the incumbent's cost function in stage two of the game:

$$\begin{aligned} C_1(q_1, q_2; \bar{K}_1) &= F_1 + wq_1 + r\bar{K}_1, \quad \text{for } q_1 \leq \bar{K}_1; \text{ Marginal Cost} = w \\ &= F_1 + (w + r)q_1, \quad \text{for } q_1 > \bar{K}_1; \text{ Marginal Cost} = w + r \end{aligned} \tag{12.1}$$

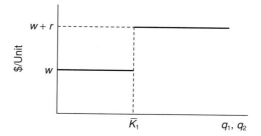

Figure 12.2 The effect of previously acquired capacity on current marginal cost
The incumbent has previously acquired capacity $\bar{K}_1$ and therefore incurs a marginal cost of only w up to this level of production. For greater levels, its marginal cost is $w + r$. The entrant has no previously acquired capacity. Its marginal cost is $w + r$ for all production levels.

The only difference between the entrant and the incumbent is that the entrant cannot invest in capacity in stage one. Instead, the entrant must hire both labor and capital as they are needed to produce whatever output it selects during the second stage. Thus, the entrant's marginal cost is always $w + r$ no matter what output it chooses. If we denote any sunk cost the entrant incurs as result of participating in the market as F_2, its cost function in stage two is:

$$C_2(q_2) = F_2 + (w + r)q_2; \text{ Marginal cost} = w + r \tag{12.2}$$

It is important to note that the two firms face different *marginal* costs of production in stage two of the game. For the incumbent firm, the marginal cost of producing any output q_1 is equal to w so long as it is within its initial capacity, or so long as $q_1 \leq \bar{K}_1$. However, because the entrant does not enjoy the first mover advantage of having already invested in capacity in stage one, it faces a marginal cost of production equal to $(w + r)$ for all output levels. This difference is reflected in Figure 12.2 where we draw the marginal cost curve for both firms. The diagram suggests why investment in capacity can have a commitment value. The incumbent's commitment to produce at least as much as $\bar{K}_1$ is made more believable by the fact that up to that production level, its marginal cost is *relatively* low.

In a sequential game, we begin by working out what happens in the last stage in order to work out the incumbent firm's optimal move in the first stage. To solve for a subgame perfect equilibrium strategy for the incumbent firm, we need to determine how the incumbent's choice of capacity in stage one affects the market outcome when the two firms compete in stage two. So, we start by working out what happens in stage two for any particular level of capacity chosen in stage one. We determine what happens in stage one by choosing the capacity that maximizes the incumbent's profits in stage two.

In stage two the firms are playing a Cournot game in quantities. The incumbent firm's profit will be:

$$\pi_1(q_1, q_2, \bar{K}_1) = \text{Revenue} - \text{Cost} = [A - B(q_1 + q_2)]q_1 - [wq_1 - F_1] \quad \text{for } q_1 \leq \bar{K}_1$$
$$\pi_1(q_1, q_2, \bar{K}_1) = \text{Revenue} - \text{Cost} = [A - B(q_1 + q_2)]q_1 - [(w + r)q_1 - F_1] \tag{12.3}$$
$$\text{for } q_1 > \bar{K}_1$$

From equation 12.3, we can see that the marginal revenue to the incumbent associated with an incremental unit of q_1 is always given by $MR_1 = A - 2Bq_1 - Bq_2$. However, its marginal cost will change depending on whether or not the firm decides to add capacity. When the incumbent firm's best response q_1^* to the entrant's choice of output q_2 is such that it does not need to add capacity, i.e., when $q_1^* \leq \bar{K}_1$, the incumbent's marginal cost is just w. But if the incumbent's best response q_1^* is such that it needs additional capacity $q_1^* > \bar{K}_1$, its marginal cost becomes $(w + r)$. Accordingly, equating the incumbent's marginal revenue and marginal cost and solving for its optimal output in stage two, thus leads to a best response function with two parts. These are:

$$q_1^* = \frac{(A - w)}{2B} - \frac{q_2}{2} \qquad \text{when } q_1^* \leq \bar{K}_1; \text{ and}$$

$$q_1^* = \frac{(A - w - r)}{2B} - \frac{q_2}{2} \qquad \text{when } q_1^* > \bar{K}_1 \tag{12.4}$$

This means that the incumbent firm's best response function jumps at the output level $q_1^* = \bar{K}_1$. We can see the jump more clearly when we draw the reaction function for the incumbent firm in the second stage of the game. We do this in Figure 12.3. Again, $\bar{K}_1$ is the incumbent's capacity that is given in stage two but chosen in stage one of the game. For output levels $q_1^* \leq \bar{K}_1$, the incumbent firm's reaction function is the solid line described by $L'L$, whereas for output levels $q_1^* > \bar{K}_1$ the reaction function jumps to the lower solid line described by $N'N$.

Now consider the situation facing the entrant in stage two. Profits for the entrant firm are, as always, the difference between its revenue and its cost, which implies:

$$\pi_2(q_1, q_2, \bar{K}_1) = \text{Revenue} - \text{Cost} = [A - B(q_1 + q_2)]q_2 - [(w + r)q_2 - F_2] \tag{12.5}$$

The requirement that marginal revenue equals marginal cost implies that the entrant firm's best response function is:

$$q_2^* = \frac{(A - w - r)}{2B} - \frac{q_1}{2}. \tag{12.6}$$

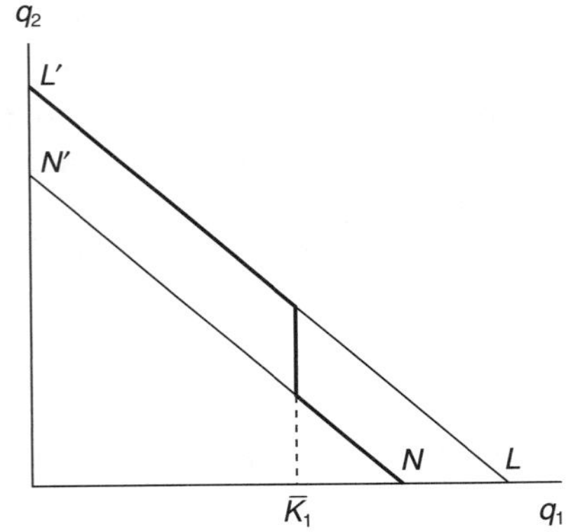

Figure 12.3 The best response function of the incumbent firm depends on its first stage choice of capacity

For output less than $\bar{K}_1$, the incumbent will have a low marginal cost and operate on the higher response function $L'L$. For output greater than $\bar{K}_1$, the incumbent will have a high marginal cost and operate on the lower best response function $N'N$.

Derivation Checkpoint

The Calculus of Predation: Limit Output/Price and Capacity Commitment

In the Stackelberg limit output model, inverse market demand is given by: $P = A - BQ$. Once the dominant firm commits to a specific output q^F, the entrant's residual demand is: $P = A - B(q^F + q)$, where q is the amount produced by the entrant. The entrant's marginal revenue curve is then described by: $MR = A - Bq^F - 2Bq$. Setting this equal to the entrant's marginal cost then yields the entrant's optimal output, q^*. The incumbent's limit output is that choice of Q^F such the entrant's residual demand curve is just tangent to its average cost curve at the output choice, q^*.

The Dixit model of capacity commitment to deter entry relies on the fact that while the capacity can be installed in varying amounts it is, once made, a sunk cost. Because the incumbent firm will not want to let installed capacity stand idle, its ability to build capacity prior to any entrant allows it to transform the structure—but not the total amount—of its costs. The incumbent's marginal cost will be w for output less than or equal to its capacity choice $\bar{K}_1$, but $w + r$ for all outputs greater than that amount. In contrast, the entrant's marginal cost is always $w + r$. Competition is of the Cournot or quantity type. The industry inverse demand function is: $P = A - BQ = A - B(q_1 + q_2)$, where q_1 and q_2 are the outputs of the incumbent and entrant firm, respectively. This implies a profit function of: $\pi_1 = [A - B(q_1+q_2)]q_1 - wq_1 - r\bar{K}_1 - F_1$ if output is less than $\bar{K}_1$, and $\pi_1 = [A - B(q_1 + q_2)]q_1 - (w + r)q_1 - F_1$ if output is greater than $\bar{K}_1$. Setting the derivative with respect to q_1 equal to zero in each case then yields the incumbent's two possible reaction functions. For output less than or equal to $\bar{K}_1$, the incumbent's optimal response curve is:

$q_1 = \dfrac{A - w}{2B} - \dfrac{q_2}{2}$. For output above $\bar{K}_1$, its optimal response is: $q_1 = \dfrac{A - (w + r)}{2B} - \dfrac{q_2}{2}$. Firm 2's best response function is the same as firm 1's for $q_1 > \bar{K}_1$.

We may simultaneously solve for q_1 and q_2 using the best response curve of each firm. If both firms follow the response function, $q_i = \dfrac{A - (w + r)}{2B} - \dfrac{q_j}{2}$, each firm will produce $q_i = \dfrac{A - (w + r)}{3B}$. This corresponds to the outputs at point T in Figure 12.3. If the entrant has the response function $q_2 = \dfrac{A - (w + r)}{2B} - \dfrac{q_1}{2}$, but the incumbent has the response function, $q_1 = \dfrac{A - w}{2B} - \dfrac{q_2}{2}$, the incumbent will produce at level $q_1 = \dfrac{A - w}{3B} + \dfrac{r}{3B}$. In this case, the entrant will produce at level $q_2 = \dfrac{A - w}{3B} - \dfrac{2r}{3B}$. This combination corresponds to point V in Figure 12.3. The monopoly or Stackelberg leader output is $q_1 = \dfrac{A - (w + r)}{2B}$. The equilibrium must be one in which firm 1 produces between the monopoly output and V_1. In the example in the text, $A = 120$, $B = 1$, and $w = r = 30$. The incumbent's output as a Stackelberg leader is therefore: $q_1 = 30$. The intersection of the best response functions corresponding to point V is one at which $q_1 = 40$ and $q_2 = 10$. The final outcome must lie within the interval defined by these two points.

One point worth stressing before going further is that equation (12.6) is the entrant's best response function *given* that it chooses to produce a positive level of output at all, i.e., so long as it is the case that the entrant's profit at that output will be nonnegative. The best response function is derived using the marginal conditions and therefore does *not* take account of the sunk cost F_2 that the potential entrant incurs should it actually decide to enter. The intercept of equation (12.6) with the q_2 axis, $(A - w - r)/2B$, is the entrant's optimal output if the incumbent somehow decided to produce nothing. That would correspond to the entrant being a monopoly and would almost certainly imply positive profits (otherwise we could rule out entry from the start). However, as one moves from left to right along the best response function, the entrant's output becomes successively smaller as it adjusts to larger and larger output choices by the incumbent. This decline limits the volume over which the entrant's fixed cost may be spread. As a result, firm 2's average total cost rises as its output falls. It is quite possible that, at some point where the incumbent's output q_1 is sufficiently large, the market price implied by the combined output of both firms will not cover the entrant's average cost *at the production level implied by its best response curve*. Accordingly, the entrant will lose money if it actually produces that output once the fixed cost F_2 is taken into account. Recall, however, that the entrant always has the option of **not** producing at all, instead staying out of the market and thereby earning a zero profit. If, at the output implied by equation (12.6), the entrant's profit would in fact be negative, it will not produce that level but simply refrain from entering the market. We will return to this point below.

We know that the Nash equilibrium in stage two will occur at the intersection of the incumbent's best response function and the best response function of the potential entrant providing, as just noted, that the latter earns a nonnegative profit. This brings us back to the first stage. Understanding how competition works out in stage two, the incumbent firm also understands that it can manipulate this intersection by its choice of $\bar{K}_1$ in stage one. Naturally, the incumbent firm will choose $\bar{K}_1$ in the first stage to give itself the maximum profit possible in stage two. Let us now investigate this choice and whether or not it implies the possibility that the incumbent firm will choose $\bar{K}_1$ to deter the second firm from entering.

We begin by drawing a diagram that describes all the possible equilibria for stage two of the game. In Figure 12.4 we draw the two reaction functions for firm 1, one corresponding to the low marginal cost of production w labeled $L'L$, and the other reaction function corresponding to the higher marginal cost of production $(w + r)$ labeled $N'N$. We then add the reaction function for firm 2, labeled $R'R$. We denote the point where firm 2's reaction function meets $N'N$ by T. This point corresponds to stage two outputs for the incumbent and entrant of T_1 and T_2, respectively. Similarly; the point where $R'R$ meets $L'L$ is labeled V and corresponds to respective outputs of V_1 and V_2.

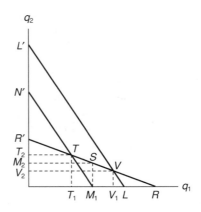

Figure 12.4   The rational bounds on the incumbent's initial choice of capacity, K_1
The incumbent will choose an initial capacity investment somewhere in the interval from T_1 to V_1.

In the second stage, firm 2 is either going to enter or stay out. Consider what happens if firm 2 does enter. In this case, the Nash equilibrium must lie somewhere between points T and V on firm 2's best response function $R'R$. The actual point will depend on the capacity choice of the incumbent and, in particular, on the output level at which the incumbent shifts from response function $L'L$ to $N'N$. The minimum amount that firm 1 will produce if its rival enters is T_1 and the maximum amount it will produce is V_1. Accordingly, firm 1 would never wish to choose a capacity level less than T_1 or larger than V_1 if it foresaw that firm 2 was definitely going to enter.

What if firm 2 does not enter? First, think of what this means. If firm 2 does not enter it must be because entry is not profitable. This could happen if firm 2 is unable to make a positive profit even in its most favorable Nash equilibrium, namely, the one at T. At T, firm 2 produces its highest equilibrium output T_2. If it cannot break even at this volume then it surely cannot break even at any smaller output level such as that at V_2. However, if this is the case, and if firm 1 understands this fact, then firm 1 will recognize that it will be a monopolist in stage two. A monopoly firm in this market would of course produce at production level M_1. The marginal cost of producing any output that fully utilizes capacity is $(w + r)$. Equating this amount with its marginal revenue gives the pure monopolist's profit-maximizing output, and it is the production level M_1, corresponding to firm 1's optimal output when firm 2 produces zero. Firm 1 would choose in this case a capacity equal to M_1.

Even at this early stage of our analysis then we have obtained some useful results. First, the incumbent's choice of capacity in stage one must lie in the interval ranging from T_1 to V_1. Second, if the entrant cannot break even at output T_2, the incumbent's best choice within this interval is M_1, namely the output chosen by a pure monopolist with marginal cost $(w + r)$ which is precisely what the incumbent will be.

What we need to do now is to determine the incumbent's best initial choice of capacity when the entrant *can* at least break even at output T_2. In this regard, the capacity level of M_1 is again relevant because it is not only the monopoly output but, as just noted, also the output of a Stackelberg leader. Because only the incumbent gets to choose capacity in stage one, we might expect that even if the entrant can operate at levels of output below T_2, the incumbent still ought to be able to achieve the market share and profit of a Stackelberg leader. In other words, we should expect that the incumbent will never choose an initial capacity less than M_1. Note though that if this presumption is true, we have then reduced the set of sensible initial capacity choices from the broad range of T_1 to V_1, to the much narrower range of M_1 to V_1. In fact, we will soon see that this conjecture is quite correct. The incumbent's profit-maximizing initial capacity choice will always lie within the M_1 to V_1 range.

To see why the incumbent will do best by choosing initial capacity in the M_1 to V_1 range, and also to determine precisely what point within that range is best we proceed as follows. We denote by the point B the output level at which the entrant, firm 2, ceases to make a profit, i.e., when the revenue from the entrant's best output response just covers both its variable and its fixed cost so that $\pi_2 = 0$. By definition, the relevant range of B lies somewhere on the entrant's response function, RR'. Indeed, B must lie on RR' somewhere to the left of where that response curve intersects the q_1 axis, since with a sunk cost of F_2, the entrant cannot break even if it enters but produces nothing ($q_2 = 0$).

The incumbent firm's best choice of its initial capacity $\bar{K}_1$, which again determines both where the jump occurs in its reaction function and the location of the stage two equilibrium, depends on just where the point B lies. Figure 12.5 shows four possibilities. For example, suppose that because of a relatively high sunk cost F_2, firm 2's profit is negative when it produces T_2 and firm 1 produces T_1, or $\pi_2(T_1, T_2) < 0$. In other words, B is at a point like B_L

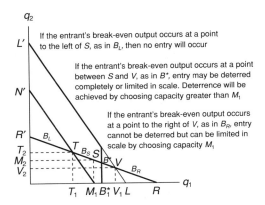

Figure 12.5   Possible locations of the entrant's break-even point

to the left of **T**. This is the case that we have already discussed. Here, entry by firm 2 is not profitable under any condition and will not occur. The incumbent firm understands at the time of its first stage investment that it will be a monopoly in stage 2, and therefore will choose the pure monopoly capacity level M_1. It will then produce at output $q_1 = M_1$ in stage two.

What if **B** is at a point such as B_S? This means that the entrant can break even at a production level below T_2 so long as it is above M_2. What is the incumbent's best choice now? In Figure 12.5 we have designated the output combination (M_1, M_2) by **S**. The reason for this notation is that as noted above, M_1 is not only the incumbent's pure monopoly output but also the output chosen by the Stackelberg leader. The key point here is that even if the entrant can break even at output levels less than T_2, so long as it cannot cover its costs at output levels M_2 or less, then M_1 remains the optimal capacity choice by the incumbent.[9] If the entrant cannot profitably enter when the incumbent produces the pure monopoly output M_1, then by selecting that capacity the incumbent guarantees that entry will not occur. In turn, this will justify the incumbent's decision to build capacity M_1 in the first place. Using Bain's (1956) terminology, this is a case of blockaded entry. It is not really predatory conduct, however. The firm is producing and pricing like the monopolist that it is. It is not engaging in any action that is solely profitable by virtue of its entry deterring effect.

We now consider a third possibility at the other end of firm 2's reaction function. Here we consider a break-even point **B** that lies to the right of V as is the case at B_H. This means that firm 2's costs are such that its profit is still positive at (V_1, V_2), where it produces the relatively small amount V_2 and firm 1 produces the much larger quantity V_1. As we noted above, this implies that firm 2 will definitely find it profitable to enter the market. Not only is entry not blockaded in the sense of Bain (1956), it is in fact inevitable.

Think a bit about what this really means. The incumbent knows that entry is inevitable. It simply cannot maintain a monopoly position. Yet if entry cannot be prevented it may at least be limited. Since the incumbent can see that it will have an active rival in stage 2, it may as well take actions in stage one that give the incumbent the best possible profit potential when competing with firm 2. The obvious choice in this regard is to play the Stackelberg leader. In this linear model the pure monopoly output choice is the same as the Stackelberg

---

[9]   Strictly speaking, when the entrant's break-even output lies between T_2 and M_2, the incumbent would be indifferent between choosing M_1 or a smaller capacity just sufficient to preclude entry and then expanding output in stage two to the level of $\boldsymbol{M_1}$.

leader's, and so again the incumbent has an incentive to install an initial capacity equal to M_1. True enough, this will no longer lead to an equilibrium in which the incumbent is a monopoly in stage 2. Entry will occur and output will rise above the monopoly level while the market price will decline. Yet the installation of capacity equal to M_1 will force the entrant to enter on the limited scale of a Stackelberg follower producing only M_2. To install less than M_1, forgoes some of the incumbent's first mover advantage. To install more would further limit the scale of the entrant's production but this gain would be more than offset by the negative price effect that the extra production would exert. M_1 is then the best choice. Entry is not deterred but it is limited or, to use Bain's (1956) terminology, is "ineffectively impeded."

What we have just shown is that so long as the point B lies to the left of S, such as in the cases of B_L or B_S, or to the right of V, as in the case of B_R, the incumbent's optimal choice of initial capacity $\bar{K}_1$ is to set $\bar{K}_1 = M_1$. These possibilities cover the case in which entry is blockaded and the entrant cannot break even at any output M_2 or less, and the case in which entry is certain and the best that the incumbent can do is to limit the entrant's scale.

The remaining and perhaps the most interesting case to consider is what happens when firm 2's costs of production are such that firm 2's profit, as we move down its reaction function, is positive at M_2 but negative at V_2. This implies that the B where firm 2 just breaks even lies between S and V, such as B^*. In this case, firm 1 has a choice to make. On the one hand, it can continue to play the Stackelberg leader by initially installing capacity M_1 and producing at that level in stage two. Firm 2 will then choose its optimal response of producing M_2. On the other hand, firm 1 can expand its initial capacity choice to the level B_1^*. This will require that it produce more output which lowers the industry price, but it is also enough to prevent firm 2 from entering, preserving the incumbent's monopoly in the market. The latter strategy may well prove the more profitable one. This case is where entry deterrence is a real possibility. If the incumbent earns less profit when sharing the market at S than it earns when it deters entry by choosing in stage one capacity B_1^*, it will act so as to preclude entry altogether. This outcome corresponds to what Bain (1956) describes as the case in which entry is effectively impeded. We emphasize that this will not always be the case. Even if B lies at B^* so that the output at which the entrant breaks even lies between M_2 and V_2, the incumbent may still better exploit its first mover advantage by acting as a Stackelberg leader. Yet credible deterrence by a capacity choice greater than M_1 is now a real possibility. Moreover, even when absolute deterrence does not occur, the incumbent can still limit the scale of entry by playing the Stackelberg leader. Practice Problem 12.2 provides a numerical example of these calculations.

12.2

Practice Problem

Suppose that the inverse demand function is described by: $P = 120 - (q_1 + q_2)$, where q_1 is the output of the incumbent firm and q_2 is the output of the entrant. Let both the labor cost and capital cost per unit be 30, i.e., $w = r = 30$. In addition, let each firm have a fixed cost of $F_1 = F_2 = 200$.

a. Suppose that in stage one the incumbent invests in capacity $\bar{K}_1$. Show that in stage two the incumbent's best response function is $q_1 = 45 - \dfrac{1}{2}q_2$ when $q_1 \leq \bar{K}_1$ and $q_1 = 30 - \dfrac{1}{2}q_2$ when $q_1 > \bar{K}_1$.

b. Show that the entrant's best response function in stage two is $q_2 = 30 - \dfrac{1}{2}q_1$.

c. Show that the monopoly or Stackelberg leader's output is equal to 30. If the incumbent commits to a production capacity of $\bar{K}_1 = 30$ show that in stage two the entrant will come in and produce an output equal to 15. Show that in this case firm 2, the entrant, earns a profit equal to \$25, whereas the incumbent earns a profit of \$250.

d. Show that if the incumbent instead commits in stage one to a production capacity $\bar{K}_1 = 40$ then in stage two the entrant's best response to this choice is to produce $q_2 = 10$. However, in this case the entrant does not earn sufficient revenue to cover its total cost. Specifically the entrant earns -100.

e. Now show that if the incumbent chooses a $\bar{K}_1 = 32$ in stage one then the entrant in stage two can not earn a positive profit if it enters the market. In this case the incumbent produces slightly more output than the monopolist and earns a profit equal to \$632, which is far greater than the profit earned in part (c). Compare your analysis with that described in Figure 12.6.

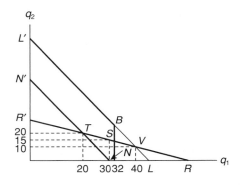

Figure 12.6   An example of entry deterrence
By initially investing in capacity of 32 in stage one, the incumbent firm insures that it will operate on the response function $L'L$ up to this output level in stage two. It also signals the potential entrant that the incumbent will produce an output of $q_1 \geq 32$ in this later stage. The entrant's best response to this production level is to set $q_2 = 14$. However, the entrant will not cover its cost even with this best response. Therefore, by committing to an output of $q_1 = 32$, the incumbent deters any actual entry.

In sum, entry may well not occur. This can happen because the entrant's costs are so high that it cannot profitably enter even if the incumbent produces and prices non-strategically as a pure monopolist. It can also happen when entry might otherwise be profitable except that the incumbent, foreseeing this, acts strategically and deters entry by investing in enough capacity to produce beyond the output of a pure monopoly. Even if entry cannot be profitably deterred the incumbent still retains the lion's share of the market because it acts as a Stackelberg leader.

The Dixit model makes clear that the incumbent firm has an advantage. More importantly, the model reveals precisely the source of that advantage. It is the incumbent's ability to commit credibly to a particular output level in stage two by means of its choice of capacity in stage one. Effectively, the incumbent commits to producing at least as much as the initial capacity it installs because to produce any less amounts to throwing away some of that investment, which is costly. In this respect, two further aspects of the model are worth noting. First, when the incumbent deters entry it does so by deliberately *over* investing in initial capacity. That is, installing an initial capacity greater than M_1 would not be profitable

Reality Checkpoint
Take-Or-Pay . . . And Win!

Firms typically have contracts with their key suppliers that stipulate the amount of the input to be bought and the price to be paid for the coming year. A common additional feature of such contracts, especially for supplies of natural gas, electricity, and commodity raw materials, is a "take-or-pay" clause. A contract that includes a take-or-pay clause requires that the purchasing firm either uses all the amount of the input initially contracted or, that if it orders less than that amount, it still pays some amount, usually less than the full contract price, for the additional amount remaining.

Take-or-pay contracts stabilize both the production schedule and the revenues of supplier firms. However, as you should recognize, they also serve another purpose. They are a straightforward way to implement the Dixit entry deterrence strategy.

For example, Corning is one of the leading manufacturers of fiber optic cables. One of its key suppliers is Praxair, a major producer of specialty gases. Suppose that Corning signs a contract with Praxair that calls for Corning to purchase 1,000,000 cubic feet of helium (which is used as a coolant in the production of fiber optic cable) at $400 per 1,000 cubic feet. The contract also includes a take-or-pay contract where Corning has to pay $300 per 1,000 cubic feet for any amount of the 1,000,000 that it does not use. What this does is effectively transform the structure of Corning's costs. If Corning orders all of the 1,000,000 cubic feet its helium bill will be: ($400/1,000) × 1,000,000 = $400,000. Suppose though that

Corning only uses 900,000 cubic feet of helium (perhaps because a new rival steals some Corning customers). Because of the take-or-pay clause, it will still pay $300 per 1,000 cubic feet for the 100,000 cubic feet that it did not order. Hence, Corning's total helium cost in this case will be: ($400/1,000) × 900,000 + ($300/1,000) × 100,000 = $390,000. In other words, using the last 100,000 cubic feet of helium only raises Corning's total helium bill by $10,000. Effectively, the contract has changed the marginal cost of helium for Corning from $400 to $100 per 1,000 cubic feet. Note that it has not changed the total cost of using one million cubic feet of helium. The contract has simply transformed some of those costs into fixed costs so that up to the one million volume, Corning has a very low marginal cost.

There is, of course, a downside to the take-or-pay contract. This occurs when another large rival, e.g., the British fiber optic producer Marconi, already exists and both firms sign take-or-pay contracts with their helium suppliers, the industry could find itself in a nasty price war in which prices fall to the low levels of marginal cost via Bertrand competition. Some believe that this is part of what happened in the fiber optic market following the burst of the telecommunications bubble.

Sources: A. M. Brandenburger and B. J. Nalebuff, *Co-opetition*, New York: Doubleday, 1996; and F. Norris, "Disaster at Corning: At Least the Balance Sheet is Strong," *New York Times*, July 13, 2001, p. C2.

were it not for the fact that doing so eliminates the competition. Therefore, such capacity expansion is predatory in the usual sense of the word. Such a choice is illustrated in the practice problem, where the incumbent's strategy to increase capacity to $\bar{K} = 32$ *is* predatory. If the entrant could break even at low levels of output, the incumbent would not have an incentive to choose capacity $\bar{K} = 32$ to deter entry. In other words this investment is only profitable because it keeps the entrant from the market altogether so that the incumbent can sell its 32 units at a very high price.

Second, note that capacity expansion is credible as a deterrent strategy only to the extent that capacity, once in place, is a sunk cost. If unused plant capacity can be sold for a per unit fee r, then capacity is truly flexible and acquiring it does not reflect any real commitment on the part of the firm. When such flexibility is not possible, which is often the case, then capacity investment is a much more effective way to deter entry than simply a promise to set a low price. A price commitment is much less credible precisely because it may easily be changed.

Now think back to the empirical evidence on entry that we reviewed at the beginning of the chapter. Two of the stylized facts are: (1) entry is commonly observed in a wide cross-section of industries; and (2) market penetration as measured by market share is relatively low for the entrants. These stylized facts are consistent with this model. The incumbent has a strategic advantage in being the first to invest in capacity, and can use this advantage to strategically limit the impact of entry into its market—perhaps eliminating it altogether.

Practice Problem

12.3

The extensive form for a dynamic game between an incumbent and an entrant firm is described in Figure 12.7. The incumbent firm moves first and chooses whether or not to spend C as a means of enhancing its ability to be aggressive. The entrant moves next and decides whether or not to enter the market. If the entrant enters then the incumbent decides whether to accommodate its new rival or to fight. If the entrant does not enter, the incumbent earns $8 - C$ if it has made that expenditure, and 8 if it has not. If the entrant does enter, the incumbent's payoffs depend on whether it fights or accommodates. Fighting when the expenditure C has been sunk yields a payoff of 3. Fighting is bloodier when the incumbent has not spent C. Accommodation when C has been spent wastes that investment. The final payoffs are described in parentheses, the first being the incumbent's payoff and the second the entrant's.

a. Show that for C greater than or equal to 1, the incumbent will always fight *if* it has invested in the capacity to do so, i.e., if it has initially made the expenditure, C.
b. Show that for C greater than or equal to 3.5, the incumbent will not make the initial investment, C.

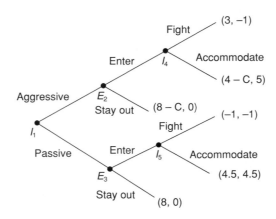

Figure 12.7 Extensive form for Practice Problem 12.3

Nodes labeled I indicate that it is the incumbent's turn to move. Nodes labeled E indicate that it is the entrant's turn to move.

12.3   PREEMPTION AND THE PERSISTENCE OF MONOPOLY

The scale of a plant or plant capacity is rarely a continuous variable. Instead, it comes in discrete sizes, say one efficient scale corresponding to the U-shaped average cost curve. This means, for example, that one plant may be the most efficient way to supply an industry even if that plant is operating at a volume beyond the point of minimum average cost. Because a second plant cannot be built to operate at an arbitrarily small scale but must, instead, be of the same size as the first, it pays to operate just one plant at a high volume and some-what high average cost rather than to build an additional establishment. Only when market demand has expanded sufficiently to operate a second plant at close to the minimum aver-age cost will building that plant be worthwhile.

In this setting, the possibility arises for an incumbent firm to take actions that are similar to but logically distinct from the predatory investment of the Spence and Dixit models. In particular, the first mover advantage of the incumbent is to *preempt* the entry of a rival firm by investing before that entry is on the horizon. The distinction between this and the invest-ment stories told earlier is subtle. Here, we are essentially talking about *timing* with the issue being who will build the next plant first. Will it be the entrant as the expanding market offers the entrant an opportunity to participate or, will it be the incumbent rushing ahead of the entrant and thereby eliminating the entrant's opportunity?

Rather than work out a formal model[10] we will simply sketch out the intuition behind the basic notion. So, imagine a market in which one firm is operating and earning a monopoly profit π^M. Everyone knows, however, that demand is about to grow. In particular, everyone can see that next period the market demand at any price will double. It will then stay at this higher level for every period thereafter. If entry were not a problem, the monopolist would expand its plant at the start of the next period, pay the cost of such expansion F, and earn $2\pi^M$ thereafter provided that present value of the profit increment $\pi^M R/(1 - R)$ of doing so exceeds present value of the cost RF, where R is the monopolist's discount factor.[11]

Recall, though, that there is a potential entrant lurking on the sidelines. Should this entrant come in, it will share the market with the incumbent and each will earn the Cournot profit. This is π^C in the first period and $2\pi^C$ for every period afterwards when the market is twice as big. For the second firm to enter, however, it must build a new plant just as the monopolist does when it expands. So the entrant would also incur a cost of F if it builds the next plant.

The point is that the entrant has a choice about *when* it enters as well as *if* it enters. That is, the entrant can come into the market now or wait until next period when the market is bigger. Consider then, the consequences of each choice. If the entrant builds its plant in the first period, it will earn π^C for one period and $2\pi^C$ thereafter. Using the discount techniques, presented in Chapter 2, the present value of this profit stream is $\pi^C + 2\pi^C R/(1 - R)$, where we assume that the entrant has the same discount factor as the incumbent. So, the net pre-sent value of entering the market now is $\pi^C + 2\pi^C R/(1 - R) - F$. If, on the other hand, the entrant delays entering until the start of next period, and *if the incumbent does not build a second plant before then*, the entrant can look forward to a net income stream whose present value is $2\pi^C R/(1 - R) - R.F$. We will assume that this is positive. This ensures that the entrant would like to enter next period, assuming, of course, no action by the

---

[10]   See Gilbert and Harris (1984).

[11]   In evaluating the present value of the profit stream we use the discounting techniques of Chapter 2.

incumbent. Let us now also make the further assumption that it is more profitable for the second firm to enter next period rather than today. In other words, we assume that the second of the two net present value streams above is the larger one.[12]

Of course, the incumbent can work all this out, too. When it does, the incumbent will understand that unless it does something right now, firm 2 will enter at the start of the next period and take away its monopoly position. The only way that the incumbent can stop this from happening is if it decides to build a second plant today. Yet, this means that it incurs the cost F right away instead of being able to put it off. However, it also means that when the next period arrives, there is no room for a new entrant. The incumbent is ready to meet the market growth fully with supply from its own factories.

Will the above strategy be in the incumbent's interest? Quite possibly, yes. If the incumbent waits and lets the entry occur next period it will only earn $2\pi^C$ in every subsequent period. The present value of its profit is $2\pi^C R/(1 - R)$ (since it does not need to add any more capacity). If, however, the incumbent invests now, it precludes later entry and so will earn $2\pi^M$ next period and indefinitely into the future. The present value of investing this period then is $2\pi^M R/(1 - R) - F$. Recall that the discount factor $R = 1/(1 + r)$. Therefore, so long as $2(\pi^M - \pi^C)/r > F$ the incumbent will invest today and thereby, preclude subsequent entry. The left-hand side is the present value of the additional profit that the incumbent makes by maintaining its monopoly. The right-hand side is the cost of installing the additional capacity necessary to preempt entry and maintain its monopoly.

Why is it that that investing in a new plant right away is more likely to be profitable for the incumbent than it is for the entrant? The reason is that the incumbent's gain is the maintenance of its monopoly position and the monopoly income π^M. By contrast, the best that the entrant can do is to get a share of a Cournot duopoly and earn π^C. Since $\pi^M > \pi^C$, the incumbent's incentive to invest right now exceeds the entrant's incentive.

12.4   EVIDENCE ON PREDATORY CAPACITY EXPANSION

Both the Dixit–Spence and the preemption models discussed in the preceding sections suggest that we may observe dominant firms expanding capacity rapidly as a means to deter entry. Is this a serious concern? Is there any evidence that such capacity investment actually occurs?

To begin with there is the stylized fact noted at the start of this chapter that the same firms continue to dominate their industries and earn superior profit for long periods of time. However, this could happen for a lot of reasons, including superior management or cost efficiency at such firms. The specific question is whether there is evidence of the maintenance of such market power explicitly by means of capacity expansion or preemptive investment.

Since investment commitment strategies are more likely to occur in more capital-intensive industries, one might expect profitability to be higher in such industries, all else being equal, if preemptive expansion is the norm. An early study by Caves and Ghemawat (1986) does not find support for this result. Yet if preemptive expansion is not the norm, there does seem to be clear historic instances of its practice. The Alcoa case (see inset) is perhaps the best known example, but there are others.

---

[12]   Recall, $R = 1/(1 + r)$. The necessary condition is that $rF > (1 + r)\pi^C$. Roughly speaking, the interest payments on the fixed sum invested in the plant are not covered by the first-period Cournot profit.

Reality Checkpoint

The Alcoa Case: Do It First, Do It Right, . . . and Keep On Doing It

In 1945, a U.S. Court of Appeals for the Second Circuit, under the direction of Judge Learned Hand. rendered one of the most famous decisions in U.S. antitrust history. The case involved the charge against the Aluminum Co. of America (Alcoa) that it had unlawfully monopolized the domestic market for aluminum and aluminum products. Alcoa had previously been involved in an antitrust case in 1912. At that time it was found guilty of restrictive and anticompetitive practices, including: (1) signing contracts with electric power companies to obtain the large amount of electricity needed to process raw alumina and including in those contracts covenants that prohibited the power companies from selling electricity to any other aluminum manufacturer; and (2) forming a cartel with foreign manufactures to divide the world aluminum market into regions and restrict sales in any one region to primarily one member of the cartel. In part, the 1945 case was based on the allegation that these practices had continued despite the 1912 settlement. However, the court's decision against Alcoa this time was predicated primarily on the view that Alcoa expanded capacity to keep out competitors. The court noted that Alcoa increased its capacity eight-fold between 1912 and 1934. It noted that there had been "one or two abortive attempts to enter the industry, but Alcoa effectively anticipated and forestalled all competition." The court continued, saying that "we can think of no more effective exclusion than . . . to face every newcomer with new capacity already geared into a great organization".

Of course, much as the Microsoft case revealed 55 years later, the finding that a firm has illegally abused its market power does not make clear what the remedy to such abuse should be. Even a serious fine may seem too weak a penalty because it leaves the firm intact and able perhaps to resume its illegal practices. Yet breaking up a successful organization as was done in the Standard Oil case may seem overly harsh. In the Alcoa case, the government was fortunate to have an alternative remedy. The case was decided in the immediate aftermath of the Second World War. During that war, the government had operated a number of aluminum plants. The decision was made to sell these plants to two new firms, Kaiser and Reynolds, and thereby create a more competitive market structure.

Source: *U.S. v. Aluminum Co. of America*, 148 F. 2d 416 (1945).

Weiman and Levin (1994) find that preemptive investment was an explicit tactic of Southern Bell Telephone (SBT) in its effort to monopolize the local phone service market in the central southern and eastern southern regions of the U.S. Those markets had become intensely competitive after the expiration of the Bell patents so that by 1902, independent firms accounted for 60 percent of the local phone service in the region from Virginia to Alabama and Florida. Company archival records reveal that SBT's leader, Edward J. Hall, launched an aggressive capital expansion program to build a regional toll network in anticipation of market development and with the explicit goal of preempting rivals. Within four years, SBT had increased the geographic reach of its system from 2,000 to 8,600 pole miles. Even more impressively, its calling capacity as measured by toll wires grew from 5,000 to over 55,000 miles. All this was accompanied by an aggressive price-cutting campaign both in markets where it faced competition and those where it expected it. Among other features, this had the effect of restricting the investment funds available to competitors for their own expansion whereas SBT was able to rely on heavy financing from its parent firm, AT&T. The plan worked. By 1912, SBT had virtually complete control of the southern local telephone market.

A more recent example is set in the town of Edmonton, Alberta during the 1960s and early 1970s. The major retail grocer in Edmonton at that time was Safeway. However, in the early 1960s a number of other grocery stores from other regions began to enter the Edmonton market. These included two Ontario firms, Loblaws and Dominion, and one Western Canada firm, Tom Boy. Between 1960 and 1963, these three firms opened 12 new stores in the Edmonton area. By 1964, they were operating a total of 21 stores—not far behind Safeway's then total of 25. Safeway could clearly see that continued entry by these and other firms was a real possibility and it rapidly responded. It opened four new stores in 1963–4, another four new stores in 1965–6, and then added five new stores in 1968. Moreover, Safeway chose the locations of these new stores quite carefully. It located them in areas where due to increasing population and the fact that no other store was currently close by, it looked like a site of potential entry. In addition, just to drive home the seriousness of its intentions, Safeway also located some of its new stores almost right next to locations where its rivals also had a store. The strategy worked. By 1973, Safeway was operating 35 stores in the Edmonton area whereas, due to closings, its three major rivals were operating just 10. Indeed, Safeway had so effectively established its credibility as a preemptive competitor that whenever its major rivals or even fringe firms opened up a new store, they typically located near each other rather than in neighborhoods already served by Safeway but sufficiently densely populated to permit room for a second store.[13]

Our final anecdote comes from the market for titanium dioxide. This is a chemical additive used as a whitener in such products as paint, paper, and plastics. It can be produced by three processes. One of these is a sulfate procedure that uses ilmenite ore. Another technique is a chloride process that uses rutile ore. Both of these processes are known and available to all producers. The third process, however, is a special chloride process that because of legal restrictions is known and available for use only by DuPont. Like the sulfate process, DuPont's procedure uses ilmenite ore. Yet like the generic chloride process, DuPont's method emits little pollution. This is not the case with the sulfate procedure, which has bad pollution affects.

Seven domestic firms were active in the titanium dioxide market during the 1970s. DuPont was the largest of these with about 34 percent of the market, but NL Industries—which used the sulfate procedure—was a close second. Then, two events happened in the early 1970s that gave DuPont a decided advantage. First, rutile ore became more expensive, implying that other producers using the generic chloride technique might have to cut back. Second, strict pollution controls were imposed that made the sulfate process very expensive, too. Suddenly, DuPont's proprietary chloride technique based on ilmenite ore gave the company an edge with respect to costs. A strategic firm would lose no time in exploiting that edge. It would know that those producers using sulfate were not likely to expand. It might also recognize that rutile could someday become cheap again (it did). If in addition the firm expected, as did all participants in the titanium oxide market, that demand would grow, a firm in DuPont's position might wish to expand capacity immediately. This would preclude

---

[13]   Safeway was charged with monopolizing the Edmonton market in 1972 and, in late 1973, signed a consent decree that, among other things, prohibited it from expanding its total square footage in Edmonton for three and a half years. See Von Hohenbalken and West (1986).

those rivals using the rutile-based technique from expanding production when and if rutile prices dropped and thus, permit the firm to capture the gap caused by market growth and the declining sulfate-based production entirely for itself.

In point of fact, DuPont increased its capacity by over 60 percent in the next five years while the industry, in general, stagnated. By 1977, DuPont's market share had risen to 46 percent. Moreover, when rival Kerr-McGee began to construct a new plant in 1974, just before DuPont got its planned expansion going, DuPont reacted by trumpeting its plans to the whole industry. This likely precluded any further entry beyond that of Kerr-McGee's.[14]

In short, there is much anecdotal evidence that supports the use of capacity expansion to overcome the Chain-Store Paradox and thereby maintain market power. We should note that such evidence may be even greater when we use a spatial interpretation of expansion along the lines of the Hotelling "Main Street" model that we discussed in Chapter 10. Indeed, it is often claimed that General Motors' strategy of offering many different automobile varieties, and the ready-to-eat breakfast cereal manufacturers' strategy of selling a wide assortment of cereals both reflect attempts to "crowd out" any would be rival by leaving it no market niche into which it can profitably enter.

Summary

This chapter has investigated the ability of firms to maintain a dominant market position in their industry for a prolonged period of time. Both anecdotal and formal evidence indicate that such sustained market power is a widespread feature. In turn, this implies that the entry of new rivals who can compete away an incumbent firm's profits is not as powerful in the real world as it is suggested to be in basic microeconomic texts. Something permits an incumbent to preserve its market position and successfully defend itself against rival entry.

There are good reasons to believe that market structures may evolve toward increasing concentration over time. The Law of Proportionate Effects or Gibrat's Law is a random growth process that generates such an outcome. Richer theoretical models such as Klepper's (2002), in which innovation becomes easier as firms get larger and more experienced also yield oligopoly as their equilibrium outcome. Thus, the fact that many industries are long-dominated by one or two firms does not necessarily imply that those firms have obtained and kept that dominance by predatory means. Yet the clear concerns that motivated the antitrust laws, as well as numerous court cases, also imply that predatory entry deter-rence is a common concern. An important question in this respect is whether economic theory can shed light on that concern.

The proper analytical framework for studying entry deterrence is a dynamic game of sequential moves. Here, the key issue is credibility. Broadly speaking, the question is whether the incumbent dominant firm can persuade a would-be rival that it is committed to a price or output level that, if maintained, would make entry unprofitable. Capacity expansion and preemption may be ways to achieve such a commitment. There is reason to believe that such tactics have been used by real-world firms in specific cases, but often it is difficult to distinguish such predation from normal competitive behavior.

In both theory and practice, there is a distinction between preventing entry of new firms and driving existing ones out of business. In this chapter we have focused on the issue of entry deterrence or predatory conduct in a setting of complete information. However, it is important to recognize that often firms do not have complete information about each other and so are only able to guess at a rival's likely response to any action. We examine predation in the context of incomplete information in the next chapter.

---

[14]   See Ghemawat (1984). See also, Hall (1990) for evidence that DuPont's action was consistent with the Dixit model.

Problems

1. Let the domestic market for small, specialized calculators and similar office equipment be currently served by one firm, called firm I. The firm has the following cost schedules: $TC(q_I) = 0.025q_I^2$ and $MC(q_I) = .05q_I$. Market demand is $P = 50 - 0.1Q$, and right now q is equal to q_I because the only firm in the market is the incumbent firm I.

   a. If the incumbent acts as a simple monopolist what price will it charge and what level of output will it produce?

   b. Suppose now that a foreign producer of calculators is considering exporting to the U.S. market. Because of transportation costs and tariffs this foreign firm faces some cost disadvantage vis-à-vis the domestic incumbent. Specifically the foreign firm's cost schedules are: $TC(q_E) = 10q_E + 0.025q_E^2$ and $MC(q_E) = 10 + .05q_E$. Suppose that the incumbent firm is committed to the monopoly level of output. What is the demand curve faced by the potential entrant? Write it down. Facing this demand what level of output will the foreign firm actually export to the domestic market? What will be the new industry price?

   c. To what level of output would the incumbent firm have to commit in order to deter the foreign firm from entering the market? (Hint: you must solve for output level q^* with the property that if the entrant believes that the incumbent will produce q^* then the entrant's profit-maximizing response will be to produce q_E^* such that $\Pi^E(q_E^*, q^*) = 0$.) What is the incumbent firm's profit?

2. Return to problem 1. Suppose that the incumbent and the entrant instead will play a Cournot game if and when the entrant enters. What are firms' profits in this case? Is it reasonable to believe that the incumbent will try and commit to q^* in order to deter entry? Why?

3. Suppose that the inverse demand function is described by: $P = 100 - 2(q_1 + q_2)$, where q_1 is the output of the incumbent firm and q_2 is the output of the entrant. Let the labor cost per unit be $w = 20$ and capital cost per unit

be $r = 20$. In addition, let each firm have a fixed cost of $F_1 = F_2 = \$100$.

   a. Suppose that in stage one the incumbent invests in capacity $\bar{K}_1$. Show that in stage two the incumbent's best response function is $q_1 = 20 - \frac{1}{2}q_2$ when $q_1 \le \bar{K}_1$ and $q_1 = 15 - \frac{1}{2}q_2$ when $q_1 > \bar{K}_1$.

   b. Show that the entrant's best response function in stage two is $q_2 = 15 - \frac{1}{2}q_1$.

4. Return to Problem 3. Now show that if the incumbent commits to a production capacity of $\bar{K}_1 = 15$, the entrant will do best by producing 7.5 and earn a profit of \$12.5, while the incumbent earns a profit of \$125.

   a. Show that if the incumbent instead commits in stage one to a production capacity $\bar{K}_1 = 16$ then the entrant's best stage two response is to produce $q_2 = 7$, at which output the entrant does not earn a positive profit.

   b. In light of your answer to 4a, show that committing to a production capacity of $\bar{K}_1 = 16$, gives the incumbent a profit of \$348.

5. Two firms, firm 1 and 2, must decide whether to enter a new industry. Industry demand is described by $P = 900 - Q$, where $Q = q_1 + q_2$, $q_j \ge 0$. To enter the industry a firm must build a production facility of one of two types: small or large. A small facility requires an investment of \$50,000 and allows the firm to produce as many as 100 units of the good at a unit production cost of zero. Alternatively, the firm can pay \$175,000 to construct a large facility that will allow the firm to produce any number of units of output at zero unit cost. A firm with a small production facility is capacity constrained whereas a firm with a large facility is not. Firm 1 makes the entry decision first. It must choose whether to enter and, if it enters, what kind of production facility to build. After observing firm 1's action, firm 2 chooses from the same set of alternatives. If only one firm enters the industry then it selects a quantity of output and sells it at the

corresponding price. If both firms are in the industry they compete as Cournot firms. All output decisions in the market stage are subject to the capacity constraints of the production facilities. The market lasts for only one period.

   a. Draw the extensive tree that represents the entry game being played between firm 1 and firm 2.

   b. What is the outcome? Does firm 1 enter and at what size? Does firm 2 enter and at what size?

6. Let the demand for hand-blown glass vases be given by $q = 70{,}000 - 2{,}000P$, where q is the quantity of glass vases consumed per year and P is the dollar price of a vase. Suppose that there are 1,000 identical small sellers of these glass vases. The marginal cost function of such a seller is $MC(q) = q + 5$, where q is the firm's output

   a. Assuming that each small seller acts as a price taker in this market derive the market supply curve, the equilibrium price, and quantity traded.

   b. Suppose that a new mechanized technique of producing vases is discovered and monopolized by some firm, call it firm B for "BIG". Using this technique, vases can be produced at a constant average and marginal cost of \$15 per vase. Consumers cannot tell the difference between vases produced by the old and the new technique. Given the existence

of the fringe of small sellers what is the demand curve facing firm B?

   c. Facing this demand curve what is the profit-maximizing quantity produced by firm B? What is the price that it sets and the overall amount of vases traded in the market?

7. Suppose that two firms are in a race to enter a new market. For each firm, there is an advantage to taking time and perfecting its product because then consumers will pay more for it and it will be more profitable. However, there is also a disadvantage in waiting in that this has an interest opportunity cost of r. Let the time to enter t vary from 0 to 1 (year), and denote the choice of firm 1's entry and firm 2's entry be t_1 and t_2, respectively. The (symmetric) profit functions are:

$$\pi^1(t_1, t_2) = \begin{cases} e^{(1-r)t_1}; & \text{if } t_1 < t_2 \\ e^{\left(\frac{1}{2} - rt_1\right)}; & \text{if } t_1 = t_2 \\ e^{(1-t_2)-rt_1}; & \text{if } t_1 > t_2 \end{cases}$$

$$\pi^2(t_1, t_2) = \begin{cases} e^{(1-r)t_2}; & \text{if } t_2 < t_1 \\ e^{\left(\frac{1}{2} - rt_2\right)}; & \text{if } t_2 = t_1 \\ e^{(1-t_1)-rt_2}; & \text{if } t_2 > t_1 \end{cases}$$

Show that the Nash equilibrium entry times are $t_1 = t_2 = 1/2$.

References

Bain, J. 1956. *Barriers to New Competition: Their Character and Consequences in Manufacturing Industries.* Cambridge, MA: Harvard University Press.

Baldwin, J. 1995. *The Dynamics of Industrial Competition.* Cambridge: Cambridge University Press.

Birch, D. 1987. *Job Creation in America: How Our Smallest Companies Put the Most People to Work.* New York: Macmillan, Free Press.

Brandenburger, A. B. and B. J. Nalebuff. 1996. *Co-opetition.* New York: Doubleday.

Brown, C. and J. Lattin. 1994. "Investigating the Relationship Between Time in Market and Pioneering Advantage." *Management Science* 40 (October): 1361–9.

Cable, J. and J. Schwalbach. 1991. "International Comparisons of Entry and Exit." In P. Geroski and J. Schwalbach, eds, *Entry and Market Contestability.* Oxford: Blackwell.

Caves, R. E. 1998. "Industrial Organization and New Finding on the Turnover and Mobility of Firms." *Journal of Economic Literature* 36 (December): 1947–82.

Caves, R. E. and P. Ghemawat. 1986. "Capital Commitment and Profitability: An Empirical Investigation." *Oxford Economic Papers* 38 (July): 94–110.

Dixit, A. 1980. "The Role of Investment in Entry Deterrence." *Economic Journal* 90 (January): 95–106.

Dunne, T., M. J. Roberts, and L. Samuelson. 1988. "Patterns of Firm Entry and Exit in U.S. Manufacturing Industries." *Rand Journal of Economics* 19 (Winter): 495–515.

——. 1989. "The Growth and Failure of U.S. Manufacturing Plants." *Quarterly Journal of Economics* 104 (November): 671–98.

Fisher, F. 1991. *Industrial Organization, Economics and the Law.* Cambridge MA: MIT Press.

Kalecki, M. 1945. "On the Gibrat Distribution." *Econometrica* 13 (April): 161–70.

Geroski, P. A. 1995. "What Do We Know about Entry?" *International Journal of Industrial Organization* 13 (December): 421–40.

Geroski, P. A. and S. Toker. 1996. "The Turnover of Market Leaders in UK Manufacturing Industries, 1979–86." *International Journal of Industrial Organization* 14 (June): 141–58.

Ghemawat, P. 1984. "Capacity Expansion in the Titanium Dioxide Industry." *Journal of Industrial Economics* 33 (December): 145–63.

Gibrat, P. 1931. *Les inegalities economiques; applications: aux inegalities des richesses, a la concentration des enterprises, aux populations des villes, aux statistiques des familles, etc., d'une loi nouvelle, la loi de l'effet proportionnel.* Paris: Librairie du Recueill Sirey.

Gilbert, R. 1989. "Mobility Barriers and the Value of Incumbency." In R. Schmalansee and R. Willig, eds., *Handbook of Industrial Organization, Vol. 1.* Amsterdam: North-Holland.

Gilbert, R. and R. Harris. 1984. "Competition with Lumpy Investment." *Rand Journal of Economics* 15 (Summer): 197–212.

Hall, E. A. 1990. "An Analysis of Preemptive Behavior in the Titanium Dioxide Industry." *International Journal of Industrial Organization* 8 (September): 469–84.

Jarmin, R. S., S. D. Klimek, and J. Miranda. 2004. "Firm Entry and Exit in the U.S. Retail Sector: 1977–1997." Working Paper 04-17.

Center for Economic Studies, Bureau of the Census.

Jovanovic, B. 1982. "Selection and the Evolution of Industry." *Econometrica* 50 (May): 649–70.

Klepper, S. 2002. "Firms Survival and the Evolution of Oligopoly." *Rand Journal of Economics* 33 (Summer): 37–61.

Lambkin, M. 1988. "Order of Entry and Performance in New Markets." *Management Science* 9 (Summer): 127–40.

Mitchell, W. 1991. "Dual Clocks: Entry Order Influences on Incumbent and Newcomer Market Share and Survival When Specialized Assets Retain Their Value." *Strategic Management Journal* 12 (February): 85–100.

Nelson, R. and S. G. Winter. 1982. *An Evolutionary Theory of Economic Change.* Cambridge, MA: Harvard University Press.

Ordover, J. and R. Willig. 1981. "An Economic Definition of Predation: Pricing and Product Innovation." *Yale Law Journal* 91 (November): 8–53.

Spence, A. M. 1977. "Entry, Investment, and Oligopolistic Pricing." *Bell Journal of Economics* 8 (Fall): 534–44.

Sylos-Labini, P. 1962. *Oligopoly and Technical Progress.* Cambridge, MA: Harvard University Press.

Sutton, J. 1997. "Gibrat's Legacy." *Journal of Economic Literature*, 35 (March): 40–59.

Urban, G., T. Carter, S. Gaskin, and Z. Mucha, 1984. "Market Share Rewards to Pioneering Brands." *Management Science* 32 (June): 645–59.

Von Hohenbalken, B. and D. West. 1986. "Empirical Tests for Predatory Reputation." *Canadian Journal of Economics* 19 (February): 160–78.

Weiman, D. and R. C. Levin. 1994. "Preying for Monopoly? The Case of Southern Bell Telephone Company, 1894–1912." *Journal of Political Economy* 102 (February): 103–26.

Yergin, D. 1991. *The Prize.* New York: Simon and Schuster.

13

Predatory Conduct: More Recent Developments

The central issue in the antitrust suit against Microsoft was the government's contention—eventually upheld by the courts—that Microsoft had abused its market power in an effort to stifle competition. Microsoft was accused of a variety of anticompetitive actions, including the bundling of its web browser, Internet Explorer, with its Windows operating system in an effort to drive Netscape's Navigator out of the market.

Fears of predatory behavior are not new. To the contrary, they lie at the heart at the foundation of the antitrust laws. It was precisely such a fear that led to the first major "trust-busting" in the *Standard Oil* case. The belief that large firms could drive out competitors by pricing low today with a view tomorrow to raising prices to monopoly level was given forceful expression by Supreme Court Justice Louis Brandeis, a member of the *Standard Oil* court. Brandeis warned in 1913 that: "Americans should be under no illusion as to the value of price-cutting. It is the most potent weapon of monopoly—a means of killing the small rival to which the great trusts have resorted most frequently. Far-seeing organized capital secures by this means the cooperation of the shortsighted consumer to his own undoing. Thoughtless or weak, he yields to the temptation of trifling immediate gain; and selling his birthright for a mess of pottage, becomes himself an instrument of monopoly."[1]

In the previous chapter, we focused on predatory practices aimed at keeping potential entrants out. In this chapter we explore some modern variations on that theme. However, we start by addressing the much more common charge of predatory actions aimed at driving out existing rivals as in the *Microsoft* case. That this sometimes happens there can be little doubt. In the late nineteenth and early twentieth century, the Mogul Steamship Company appears to have maintained its market power in trade with China by quoting shipping rates so low that rivals were forced from the business.[2] The *Sugar Trust* case (see Reality Checkpoint) offers another example of predatory action. Whether more recent similar charges against modern firms such as Wal-Mart,[3] AT&T,[4] Toyota and Mazda,[5] and American Airlines are equally warranted remains in question. But the issue of predatory conduct is real.

[1]   L. Brandeis, Cutthroat Prices—The Competition That Kills," *Harpers Weekly*, 15 (November 1913), pp. 10–12.
[2]   This case is discussed in Yamey (1972) and more recently in Scott Morton (1997).
[3]   *Economist*, "Slinging Pebbles at Wal-Mart," 10-23-93.
[4]   *Wall Street Journal*, "AT&T Discounts Signal a National Price War," 5-80-96, B1
[5]   Note though that the International Trade Commission subsequently ruled that U.S. auto makers were not in fact harmed by the pricing policies of Toyota and Mazda.

At the same time, it must be recognized that while predatory attacks happen, they may not be as common as alleged. The logic of the dynamic games in the last two chapters implies that it takes some work to make a plausible charge of explicit predation and of predatory pricing, in particular. The predator's rival must somehow be convinced of the predator's commitment to pursue the tactic in order to induce the rival to exit. Even if the rival does leave,

---

Reality Checkpoint

Sweet (Sugar) and Low (Price): Predation in the Sugar Refining Industry

In the late nineteenth and early twentieth centuries, the American Sugar Refining Company, originally the U.S. Sugar Trust, dominated U.S. sugar refining. The company was first formed in 1887 as a consolidation of 18 firms that then controlled 80 percent of the domestic market for refined sugar. The consolidation was quickly followed by a rationalization in which the 20 plants brought together by the merger were reduced to only 10, and the price of refined sugar rose by 16 percent. However, many owners of the plants that were bought and also other entrepreneurs each then began to operate a new plant so that a growing number of small sugar refineries emerged. Consistent with our earlier observations on entry, these new firms were small—each about 1/50th the size of ASRC. Some succeeded but most failed, though not as a result of any obvious predation by ASRC.

The first attempt at large-scale entry was made by Claus Spreckels, Senior, a West Coast refiner. Spreckels opened a new refinery on the East Coast with a capacity twice that of the largest of the small refiners and with an announcement of plans to double capacity shortly. This threat did invoke an aggressive ASRC response. A price war soon erupted in which the difference between the prices of refined and raw sugar—which had been about 70 cents per 100 pounds before the Spreckels plant opened—quickly fell to between 19 and 31 cents. Given the costs of other inputs besides raw sugar, this price decline implied prices well below marginal cost. Industry trade publications of that time estimated that ASRC and its rivals were losing about 10 cents per 100 pounds of refined sugar, which implied substantial losses in total. The price war ended when Spreckels exited the market by selling his plants to ASRC.

Several years later, two new large entrants emerged. The Arbuckle Brothers who also controlled a large segment of the U.S. coffee roasting market operated one. The other was the Doschler company. Each firm opened up a plant of roughly the same size as the earlier Spreckels plant so that together, the two possessed the capacity that Spreckels had claimed as his short-run goal. Once again a price war emerged in which it is again generally agreed that prices fell below short-run marginal cost and all firms were losing money. The war came to an end when Doschler merged with two other small firms in a deal arranged by ASRC. One possible motive for this action was that ASRC feared that with the end of the war, Doschler would start to use its profits to expand capacity. When this was added to the existing industry capacity, it would exert downward pressure on prices. However, if Doschler expanded by purchasing existing plants, no net increase in industrial capacity would arise. Of course, the price war also worked to limit such expansion by eliminating the profits of both Arbuckle and Doschler. Estimates suggest that the profits ASRC secured by limiting entry were probably sufficient to justify the losses incurred in the price wars.

Source: D. Genesove and W. Mullin, "Testing Static Oligopoly Models: Conduct and Cost in the Sugar Industry, 1890–1914," *Rand Journal of Economics*, 14 (Summer, 1998), 355–77.

then what? Any attempt by the predator to raise price may well attract new rivals negating the whole purpose of the predation.

In this chapter, we investigate the logic of predation more deeply. We focus on the credible commitment that predation requires and the role of information in making that commitment possible. As it turns out, information, specifically "who knows what" plays a key role in predatory behavior. To understand predatory strategies, it is important to examine very carefully the information that each player has about the other players and about the market.

The logic of predation requires at least two periods—the first period to get or keep the rival out and the second to reap the benefit. Often it is assumed that the transactions an incumbent firm has with its customers are simple ones. The incumbent sets the price for its product in each period and consumers buy at that price in that period. This can be too simplistic. There may be an advantage to the incumbent firm from having a longer-term contract with its customers that binds them to a contract to buy its product in both periods. In turn, this raises the possibility that such a long-term contract might lock out rivals from the market. Later in this chapter, we explore possible predatory strategies based on the use of long-term contracts. Lastly, we examine alleged cases of predatory behavior and the role of public policy.

13.1 PREDATORY PRICING: MYTH OR REALITY?

For many economists, the term predatory pricing conjures up the image of John Rockefeller and Standard Oil. The famed antitrust case against Standard Oil occurred at the turn of the century. Between the years 1870 and 1899 Standard Oil built a dominant 90 percent market share in the U.S. petroleum refining industry. It did this by acquiring more than 120 rival companies. The conventional story is that Rockefeller would first make an offer to acquire a rival refiner and, when rebuffed, would cut prices until the rival exited the market.[6] After achieving its market dominance in oil refining capacity and distribution, Standard raised prices to oil producers. This eventually led to its federal prosecution and dissolution in 1911 under the Sherman Antitrust Act of 1890.

On the face of it there seems little doubt that Standard Oil did engage in fierce price competition with its rivals and that rival firms in the refining business did leave the market. There is some doubt, however, whether this is in fact evidence of *predatory* pricing. Such doubt has foundations in both theory and evidence.

There are two arguments that imply predatory pricing is not an optimal strategy and therefore we should not expect a firm to practice it. The first argument is basically that predatory pricing as in the Chain Store Paradox is not subgame perfect.

To understand the power of this argument we will review the Microhard–Newvel game that we introduced in Chapter 12. However, we will add some new twists that make the game more like the real-world setting facing a dominant incumbent firm, such as Standard Oil, and a smaller rival. The game is again a two-period one. In the first period, Newvel, the new firm has already entered the market. Microhard is the long-established incumbent who has the first move and must decide whether or not to engage in predatory practices. One important new twist is that now we assume that each firm incurs a fixed cost of $115 million in

---

[6] There is an extensive literature on the varied business practices used by Standard Oil during this period. Other practices include securing discriminatory rail freight rates and rebates, foreclosing crude oil supplies to competitors by buying up local pipelines and allegedly blowing up competing pipelines. See Yergin (1991).

each market period. This amount must be paid up front at the start of each period. Unlike Microhard, which has internal retained earnings from its long track record in the market, Newvel has no internal funds. Therefore, Newvel must borrow such funds from a competitive banking sector.

Next we introduce some uncertainty into the market. Independent of Microhard's actions, there is a 50 percent chance in any period that Newvel will be successful and enjoy a high operating profit of $200 million. There is also a 50 percent chance that it will not be successful and earn a lower profit of $100 million. In the former case, Newvel's net profit for the period is $200 million less what it must pay to the bank for its loan. In the second case, Newvel does not earn enough to repay even the principal, equal to $115 million, of the loan. As a result, Newvel will simply default and turn over the $100 million it earned to the bank.

Since the banking sector is competitive any bank should expect to earn roughly zero profit on the loan it makes to Newvel. We assume that the discount factor R between periods is equal to one (the interest rate $r = 0$). To earn zero profit the bank, or more generally the investor, must ask for a repayment of $130 million when Newvel's operating profit is high and $100 million when its profit is low. With such a contract, the bank will be paid $130 million half the time and $100 million the other half of the time when Newvel defaults. On average, such a contract would result in the bank earning $115 million and hence, just covering its loan. To give the bank some incentive to take on the risk, it may need to do a bit better than this. So, we assume that it can demand a repayment of $132.5 million in the event that Newvel's operating profit is high. This gives the bank an expected net return of $0.5[\$132.5 + \$100] - \$115 = \$1.25$ million each period. In contrast, Newvel will either net ($200 - $132.5) = $67.5 million with probability 0.5 or nothing, also with probability 0.5. Hence, Newvel's expected net income in any period is $33.75 million.

Now consider the incumbent Microhard. Suppose that in any period that Newvel is in the market Microhard earns an operating profit of $150 million, but that it would earn a monopoly profit of $325 million if Newvel exits. Suppose further that by cutting prices and sacrificing $30 million of profit in any period, Microhard could raise the probability to 70 percent that Newvel is not successful and hence would earn only $100 million in that same period. Will Microhard have an incentive to cut prices and worsen Newvel's chances?

Let's begin by analyzing the second period of the game. First, Microhard will not engage in predation and cut prices in period two. As there is no "next period" this would only sacrifice profit with no prospect of recovering the loss at a later date. Hence, if Newvel stays after the first round, the outcome in the last period has to be a duopoly in which each earns an expected $150 million in operating or gross profit. Thus, regardless of what happened in the first period, Newvel will be able to get a loan for its fixed cost at the start of the second period. Even if Newvel defaulted in the first period, and the bank lost $15 million, Newvel and the bank would still have an incentive to renegotiate another loan for the second period. Because Microhard will not engage in predation the bank has an expectation of earning $1.25 million, which will at least help a little in covering its first period loss. Similarly, Newvel can expect to earn $33.75 million.

Will Microhard engage in predation and try to drive Newvel out of the market in the first period? Again the answer is no. No matter what happens in the first period, we know that Newvel will want to stay for the second period. Hence, no amount of predation by Microhard in the first period can prevent Newvel from operating in the second. Microhard will recognize that Newvel is here to stay in which case there is no reason to pursue predatory pricing and lose revenue in the first period. Predation will not occur.

Suppose that Newvel's chance of success worsens and the probability that it will earn a high operating profit of $200 million falls to 40 percent. For a loan of $115 million what would be the contingent contract demanded by a bank in a competitive banking sector? In other words how much repayment would the bank demand when operating profits were high and when they were low? Does the worsening of Newvel's prospects affect Microhard's incentive to price low in the first period? Explain why or why not.

If the foregoing scenario is close to capturing the reality of the corporate battlefield, then predatory tactics such as selling below cost don't seem to make sense, and so should not be observed in practice. The argument is even stronger than that just presented because we simply assumed that if Microhard were somehow successful in driving out Newvel then it would then enjoy full monopoly power. Yet there is no reason to believe that a new rival would not emerge at that time. If such later entry is a possibility, then there is even less for Microhard to gain from predation.

Beyond the reasoning that predation is not a subgame perfect strategy, there is a second argument implying that predatory strategies should not be used. This argument is due to the economist John McGee (1958, 1980) who reviewed the *Standard Oil* case extensively and argued that the firm was *not* engaged in predation. In his classic 1958 article, "Predatory Price Cutting: The Standard Oil Case," McGee argued that predatory pricing only makes sense if two conditions are met. The first is that the increase in post-predatory profit (in present value terms) is sufficient to compensate the predator for the loss incurred during the predatory price war. This amounts, of course, to a requirement that the predation be subgame perfect. However, if this requirement were met, McGee also noted that there was a second requirement that a predation strategy would have to meet. This is that there is *no more profitable strategy* to achieve the same outcome. It was this second point that drew McGee's attention. He argued that a merger is always more profitable than predatory pricing. Hence, predatory pricing should not occur.

McGee's reasoning is straightforward and can be understood in a game theoretic framework. Basically the point is that predatory pricing is a dominated strategy and hence, one that will never be used. We can illustrate this point using the Stackelberg model. The Stackleberg leader is the potential predator, and the follower is the intended prey. Suppose that each firm has a constant average and marginal cost c. The inverse market demand curve is: $P = A - BQ = A - B(q_L + q_F)$. Here, q_L is the output of the Stackelberg leader and q_F is the output of the follower. In Chapter 11 we found that the Nash equilibrium outcome is $q_L = (A - c)/2B$, and $q_F = (A - c)/4B$, which leads to an industry price $p = (A + 3c)/4$. At this price, each firm earns a positive profit. The leader earns the profit $(A - c)^2/8B$, while the follower earns half this amount. Large as it may be, however, the leader's profit is still less than that earned by a pure monopolist, namely, $(A - c)^2/4B$.

The leader would obviously prefer to be alone in the market. Let's now allow for two market periods, thus giving scope to the leader to engage in predatory behavior. All we need do is imagine that for the first market period, the leader is fully committed to producing an output so large that it can only all be sold at a price just equal to its average cost of c. Since the follower can only sell additional units by driving the market price below c, and therefore losing money, the follower will exit or not enter. If we suppose that this experience is enough to keep the follower out forever it will mean that, in the second market period, the leader is now a monopolist and can set the monopoly price and earn the monopoly profit, $(A - c)^2/4B$.

Apart from the issue of subgame perfection, the trouble with this strategy, as McGee pointed out, is that a better one is available. Under the predatory strategy just described, the leader or predator earns a stream of profit of 0 in the first market period and then $(A - c)^2/4B$ in the second. The follower or victim can look forward to a stream of 0 profit in both periods. McGee's point is that it would be more profitable for the leader to buy out or merge with the follower at the start of the first period. The merged firms can then act as a monopoly and earn the monopoly profit $(A - c)^2/4B$ in both market periods. Even if the leader has to share this first period profit with the follower, say on a 50–50 basis, *both* firms still do better than they did under predation when both the predator and prey earned a zero profit in period one. Since the second period profit is unchanged by the merger, it seems clear that the merger strategy dominates the predatory one.

There are some weaknesses in the McGee (1958) argument that merging is a preferred strategy to predatory pricing. To begin with, any such merger between rival firms is a public event. The antitrust authorities, who may easily disapprove and prevent the merger, will know about it. The authorities may, in fact, be more concerned about such a merger than they would be about predatory pricing since the merger would eliminate even the short, predatory period in which consumer prices are low. Second, and perhaps most importantly, the logic of McGee's merging strategy begins to weaken when we extend the analysis to include additional potential entrants. Once a dominant firm such as Standard Oil is seen as willing to buy out any rival, it will likely face a stream of entrants who enter just for the profitability of being purchased.[7] That is, the merger tactic may actually encourage entry—the last thing the dominant firm wishes to do. In this light, predatory pricing may be more attractive because it not only encourages existing rivals to exit but can deter subsequent entrants as well.[8]

13.2

Suppose that there are two firms in a market. One firm is a dominant firm and behaves like a Stackelberg leader. The other rival firm is the follower. The firms compete in quantities and face market demand described by $P = 100 - Q$. Assume that marginal production cost is constant and equal to 10.

a. Solve for the single-market period equilibrium outcome; that is, the quantity produced by each firm and the firms' respective profits.

b. Now consider a two-market period game. One possibility is that the two firms play the Stackelberg game twice, once in each market period. The other possibility is that the dominant firm chooses an output level so great in the first market period that the rival firm exits the market or sells zero output. In the second market period the dominant firm is alone in the market and acts like a monopoly. Solve for the dominant firm's first and second market period output choices under this scenario, and the firm's overall profit.

c. Suppose that we allow the dominant firm the option of making an offer at the beginning of the first market period to the rival firm to buy it out. What is the maximum amount the dominant firm will have to pay the rival firm to buy it out? Show that the dominant firm is better off buying out its rival in the first period and monopolizing the market through merging than through predation.

---

[7] Rasmusen (2007) explores this possibility.

[8] This point was made by Yamey (1972): "the aggressor will, moreover, be looking beyond the immediate problem of dealing with its current rival. Alternative strategies for dealing with that rival may have different effects on the flow of future rivals."

Reality Checkpoint

Getting to the Heart of the Matter: McGee on Drugs

Millions of Americans, including Vice-President Dick Cheney, suffer from hypertension (high blood pressure) and coronary heart disease or angina. Two major prescription drugs used to treat these conditions are Cardizem CD, produced by Aventis (formerly Hoechst Marion Roussel) and Hytrin, produced by Abbott Laboratories. These drugs are protected by patents and therefore protected from competition by generic or unbranded substitutes. However, the Hatch-Waxman Act of 1984 does provide some conditions under which a firm is permitted to market a generic substitute to a patented drug even before the patent expires. The generic producer must claim either that the new substitute does not really infringe on the patent or that the patent was not really valid in the first place. If the patent holder challenges this claim, then entry of the generic drug is automatically delayed for 30 months to decide the issues. Such delay clearly makes life more difficult for the generics. As partial compensation aimed at promoting generic entry, the Hatch-Waxman Act has another provision. The *first* generic to enter obtains, after entry, a 180-day immunity against all other generics. That is, once one firm is granted the right to sell a generic substitute to the patented product, no other firm is allowed to do so for at least 180 days.

In the mid-1990s, the pharmaceutical firm, Andrx, applied for permission to market a generic substitute for Cardizem CD. Another firm, Geneva (a division of Novartis), requested authorization to market a generic substitute for Hytrin. Both Aventis and Abbott challenged these applications and the automatic 30-month delay began. As the end of the 30 months drew near and with the cases still not resolved, each incumbent was faced with the imminent entry of a rival. Presumably, each firm could have pursued predatory pricing to deter such entry. But each instead went the route proposed by McGee. They bought out the potential competitor.

Aventis forged an agreement to pay Andrx $10 million per quarter in return for *not* entering the Cardizem market starting in July, 1998

when Andrx gained FDA approval. Aventis also agreed to pay an additional $60 million per year from 1998 until the end of the ongoing patent trial if Andrx eventually won that litigation. A similar agreement between Abbott and Geneva required that Abbott pay $4.5 million per month in return for Geneva agreeing to stay out of the Hytrin market. A common feature of both agreements was that Andrx and Geneva each also agreed not to transfer their 180-day immunity to any other firm. Since no other generic could enter the relevant market until 180 days after Andrx or Geneva entered, and since each of these two firms had agreed not to enter at all, these agreements had the effect of blocking all generic entry in these markets. Thus, neither Aventis nor Andrx had to face the prospect of paying off an endless stream of entrants.

A somewhat related case involves Mylan laboratories, the maker of two major anti-anxiety drugs, Lorazepam and Clorazepate. Both drugs use a key ingredient produced by a European firm, Cambrex. Starting in 1998, Mylan paid Cambrex not to sell this ingredient to any other firm. As a result, no other firm could compete with Mylan. Once in effect, Mylan raised the price of its drugs on the order of 2,000 percent to 3,000 percent.

Pursuant to a complaint filed by the FTC, Abbott agreed to terminate its agreement with Geneva. Mylan also settled with the FTC and agreed to pay $100 million into a fund designed to reimburse those who paid the exorbitant prices. Aventis pursued the matter in the courts but both a federal district court and an appellate court found its agreement with Andrx to be a violation of the antitrust laws. It has so far paid out over $200 million in settlements with drug wholesalers and individual states.

Sources: J. Guidera and R. T. King, Jr., "Abbott Labs, Novartis Unit Near Pact with FTC Over Agreement on Hytrin," *Wall Street Journal*, March 14, 2000, p. B6; M. Schroeder, "Mylan to Pay $100 Million to Settle Price-Fix Case," *Wall Street Journal*, July 13, 2000, p. A4. See also various press releases at the FTC website, www.ftc.gov.

Although there are some qualifications to the McGee's reasoning, the existence of a less costly alternative means of eliminating rivals and doubt about the credibility of predatory pricing are two good reasons to be suspicious of rivals alleging predatory pricing by a dominant firm. There is also a third reason. Business is tough and it will inevitably be the case that some firms lose market share or even to go out of business entirely. Such outcomes may simply reflect vigorous competition and not "cutthroat" pricing. Vigorous prosecution of predation allegations may lead to the prosecution of a competent firm on behalf of inefficient ones.

For example, consider the famous *Utah Pie*[9] case decided by the U.S. Supreme Court in 1967. Utah Pie was a producer of frozen dessert pies operating out of Salt Lake City and selling to supermarkets in Utah and surrounding states. In 1957, it had over two-thirds of the Salt Lake City market. However, three national firms, Continental Bakeries, Pet, and Carnation all began to compete vigorously in the Salt Lake City area. Over the next three years, this resulted in a prices falling by over a third and Utah Pie's market share declining to as low as 33 percent, though it later climbed to nearly 45 percent. Utah Pie filed suit arguing that the three national firms were selling at prices in the Salt Lake City market below those that they charged in other cities and that the three firms were therefore engaged in illegal price discrimination with a predatory objective.

However, Utah Pie's sales grew steadily throughout the period of alleged predation as did its net worth. Moreover, except for the first year of the intensified competition, Utah Pie also continued to earn a positive net income. To many economists, it appeared that Utah Pie's real complaint was more about preserving its initial near monopoly position and the high prices that monopoly power permitted, than it was about predatory tactics. In the end, however, the Supreme Court found in favor of Utah Pie in a decision that was widely decried and since, largely repudiated. Yet the point remains. Company officials will inevitably wish to claim that the source of their profit and market share decline is illegal activity by rivals who are "not playing fairly" rather than confess to their own inefficiencies. For that reason, charges of predatory pricing must be taken with at least a few grains of salt.

The deep skepticism that predation—especially predatory pricing—ever occurs is a view closely associated with the Chicago School. This view has had a profound effect on both public policy and court judgments regarding predatory pricing cases. However, since the 1990s, a new view—sometimes called the Post-Chicago School—has emerged. In this alternative view, predatory tactics are not seen as a theoretical impossibility and real-world predation is not an idle threat.

13.2   PREDATION AND IMPERFECT INFORMATION

Much of the Post-Chicago literature on the topic of predation is based on two-period games in which one firm knows something and the other firm does not, and both firms are aware of this asymmetry in information.[10] In this section, we present two important models that build on this feature of asymmetric information. The first is due to Bolton and Scharfstein (1990) and focuses on the informational asymmetry between the new rival, such as Newvel, and the bank from which it borrows. The second is due to Milgrom and Roberts

---

[9]   *Utah Pie Co. v. Continental Baking Co. et al.*, 386 U.S. 685 (1967).
[10]   Early important papers in this vein included Milgrom and Roberts (1982), Benoit (1984), and Fudenberg and Tirole (1988).

(1982) and focuses on the information asymmetry between the new rival, in our case Newvel and the dominant incumbent rival, Microhard.

13.2.1   Predatory Pricing and Financial Constraints

Recall the two-period model above in which Microhard is the incumbent and Newvel is the new firm that must borrow $115 million at the start of each period in order to operate. Following Bolton and Schaferstein (1990) we make one fundamentally important change. We now assume that at the end of any period *only* Newvel, and *not* its bank or lender, knows whether Newvel's operating profit is $100 million or $200 million. To make clear how this informational asymmetry affects both Newvel's incentives in its dealing with the bank and the bank's incentive to lend to Newvel we introduce the bank as an explicit player in the game. Figure 13.1 illustrates the interaction between the bank and Newvel for just a single-market period. The bank first makes a loan. Then Nature chooses whether Newvel's profit is high or low. Subsequently, Newvel chooses whether to report high or low operating profit. For each outcome, both the net profit to the bank and to Newvel are shown; since the bank moved first its payoff is shown first.

Focusing on the game for just one period is insightful because, as Figure 13.1 makes clear, the bank would never lend Newvel the required $115 million if the game were only one period long. The reason is straightforward. At the end of the period, only Newvel knows what its profit is. Accordingly, it has every incentive to say that it was only $100 million, pay that amount to the bank and default on any remaining amount. Obviously, if operating profit really was $100 million this is all Newvel can do. However, if actual profit was $200 million, lying and reporting that profit was only $100 million allows Newvel to walk away with $100 million for itself. In other words, because only Newvel know the truth it has an incentive to exploit this informational asymmetry to its own advantage. Anticipating this, however, the bank would realize that in a one-period setting it would never get more than $100 million in return for the $115 million that it lent. Therefore, it would never agree to the loan.

The one-period analysis carries two immediate insights for a two-period model. The first is that whatever repayment R the bank gets at the end of the first period, it can never get more than $100 million at the end of the second period. When the second period comes about, it will simply be a replay of the one-period game just described. The other and related insight is that if the bank is actually to make a loan, it will have to write a contract that extends

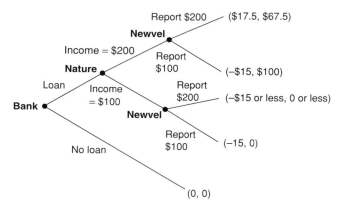

Figure 13.1   The bank and Newvel for just one period

over both periods. Two one-period contracts will just run into the same problem twice. Somehow, the bank and Newvel will have to agree on a contract that links the repayment over both market periods.

Bolton and Scharfstein (1990) show that the optimal contract has the following terms. First, recognizing that it will never get paid more than $100 million at the end of period two, the bank will contract for a high repayment at the end of period one. Second, to give Newvel an incentive to report a high income at the end of the first period, the bank will cut funding, i.e., refuse to make a loan for the second period if Newvel reports low first-period income. Since Newvel will only ever pay $100 million to the bank at the end of the second period, it can therefore expect to earn $150 − $100 = $50 million at that time, and this contractual feature gives Newvel a real interest in making sure that the second period happens.

In our example the lending contract might look as follows. The bank loans the required $115 million at the start of the first period. At the end of that period, if Newvel reports the higher profit of $200 million, then it is required to repay $150 million—its average profit. When it does so the bank will lend the $115 million necessary to operate in the second period. At the end of that second period, the bank is paid $100 million whatever happens by virtue of our earlier argument about a one-period loan. Alternatively, if at the end of the first period Newvel reports only the lower profit of $100 million, the bank is paid that amount but *no* further loans are made. Newvel in this case does not survive into the second period.

Figure 13.2 describes the nature of the loan contract. After the bank makes an initial loan, Nature's choice of profit outcome occurs. This is not shown in the diagram because at the end of the first period Newvel's incentive is to report Nature's draw accurately, and the bank understands this. If it is low, the loan is terminated and Newvel exits. If it is high, the loan is extended for a second period, after which Nature again draws a profit outcome. As we know, at the end of the second period Newvel has an incentive always to report a low profit. The payoff pair shows the total payoff for the bank and Newvel over the two periods, with the bank's shown first.

Note that both parties do well with this contract. Consider the bank. If first period profits are low, Newvel is liquidated and the bank walks away with only $100 million for a loss of $15 million. If, on the other hand, first period profits are high, the bank is paid $150 million, thereby netting $35 million. However, it is then obligated to lend out $115 million for a second time. At the end of the second period the bank receives only $100 million because at that point, Newvel never reports a high income. Because good luck and bad luck happen with equal probability, the bank's expected profit from the two-period contract is:

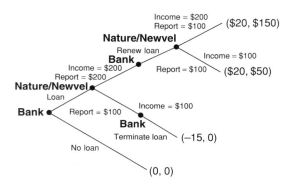

Figure 13.2   The decision tree in the two-period loan contract

0.5[$100 − $115] + 0.5[($150 − $115) + ($100 − $115)] = $2.5 million. Note that this is exactly the profit the bank earned with two, one-period contracts when it was fully informed of Newvel's income.

Newvel also earns a positive expected profit. With probability 0.5, it receives a net payment of [$200 − $150] million at the end of the first period, and with equal probability it receives nothing. Similarly, at the end of the second period, Newvel receives a net payment of either [$200 − $100] million or again zero, each with probability 0.5. Thus, the firm's expected profit under the contract is $50 million.

Yet while both players earn profit under the contract, there is a flaw. Half the time, Newvel fails after the first period and no second period loan is made. This is inefficient because that investment does have an expected profit of $35 million. Again, such inefficiency is the result of the asymmetric information that characterizes the relationship between the bank and Newvel. The only way to prevent Newvel from exploiting its informational advantage is to include a promise to stop funding Newvel should it perform badly in the first period.

Now let's think about adding Microhard to the game. Suppose again that Microhard's duopoly profit is $150 million, its monopoly profit is $325 million and by preying and cutting prices its profit is reduced by $30 million. By cutting prices low Microhard can raise the probability that Newvel fails from 50 to 70 percent. Since now Newvel exits whenever it fails to earn a first period profit of $200 million, predation results in raising Microhard's chance of being a monopolist in the second period by 20 percent. Its expected profit then rises from 0.5 × $150 million + 0.5 × $325 million = $237.5 to 0.3 × $150 + 0.7 × $325 = $272.5, a gain of $35 million—more than enough to cover the $30 million cost of predation. Unlike our earlier case, predation is now rational and therefore should be expected to occur.[11]

The intuition as to why the outcome is different with asymmetric information from what it was in our earlier analysis is straightforward. Newvel can report low first period profits for one of two reasons. Either profits really are low because it has had bad luck including being a possible victim of predation or, profits are really high but Newvel's management has hidden them by spending them on lavish offices, expensive business trips, and excessive compensation. In the absence of a contract like the one described, the lender cannot easily know the truth. If it simply believes whatever Newvel says, the lender will quickly find that Newvel constantly reports low profits in every period and blames this on bad luck and predation—leaving the lender holding the bag at a cost of ($115 − $100) or $15 million each time. The only way to prevent deception by Newvel's management is to write a two-period contract that, among other things, cuts off second-period funding in the wake of a poor first-period profit. Yet while such a contract removes the potential for dishonesty, it increases the likelihood that predation will be successful and therefore raises the incentive for Microhard to engage in predatory tactics.

It is worth repeating that "pulling the plug" and killing Newvel at the start of the second period is inefficient. Because Microhard will never predate in the second period, Newvel's expected profit in that period is $150 million. This is more than enough to pay off the needed loan of $115 million. Yet the optimal contract is a two-period one that cannot look at the second period alone and that in order to keep Newvel honest must call for Newvel's premature death if it reports low profit.

---

[11]   The predation story told here is closely related to "long purse" or "deep pockets" models. See, e.g., Phlips (1995).

In the above example it is worthwhile for Microhard to engage in predatory behavior because such behavior increases the odds of Newvel failing in the market from 50 to 70 percent, an increase of 20 percent. What is the lowest increase in unfavorable odds that will induce Microhard to engage in predatory behavior?

13.2.2   Asymmetric Information and Limit Pricing

In the Bolton and Scharfstein (1990) model, the upstart rival firm, Newvel, knows a lot about the market. Newvel knows not only its own profitability but it understands the profits and incentives facing Microhard as well. In reality, this is often unlikely to be the case. A new firm can typically only guess at the profits and costs of the rival incumbent. In their classic paper, Milgrom and Roberts (1982) present a model in which the assumption that the rival entrant firm is perfectly informed is relaxed. Specifically they assume that the rival entrant firm does not know the incumbent firm's cost of production. In this context charging a low price to keep the entrant out may no longer be an empty bluff. We now turn to the classic Milgrom and Roberts (1982) limit pricing model, noting that in this model we return to strategies aimed at preventing the entry of a rival and not ones aimed at eliminating an existing rival.

The setting is again a two period game in which there is a long-standing incumbent and a *potential* entrant. At the risk of repetition, let's again call the incumbent Microhard and the potential entrant, Newvel. There is no lender or other player. Microhard is alone in the market in the first period. During that time, Newvel observes Microhard's behavior, specifically the price that Microhard chooses to set for that period, and then Newvel decides whether or not to enter the market in the second period. As before, we assume the interest rate is zero so that we do not have to worry about discounting future profits.

Newvel knows its own unit cost and the market demand in each period, but Newvel does not know Microhard's unit cost. Microhard, on the other hand, knows its unit cost, Newvel's unit cost as well as market demand in each period. Both firms also know that all of this is understood by both of them. From Newvel's perspective Microhard's unit cost could be either high or low, depending on factors such as the expertise of management, the quality of equipment, or the input prices that Microhard has negotiated with its suppliers. These are all features of production costs that are in fact not easily ascertained by outsiders. And while Newvel does not know Microhard's unit cost, it does know something about how likely it is that Micohard is a high-cost or low-cost type. Specifically Newvel knows that there is a probability ρ that Microhard has a low cost and a probability $(1 - \rho)$ that it has a high cost.

In the interest of making the model easier to understand, we will work through a specific numeric example. Let's assume that when Microhard has low costs and acts like a profit-maximizing monopoly in the first period, it sets a relatively low price but, because of its low costs, earns a profit equal to $100 million. In contrast, if it were a less efficient high-cost monopoly Microhard's profit-maximizing price would be higher but, again due to its cost inefficiency, it would earn less profit at that price, namely, $60 million. Finally, we assume that if Microhard were a high-cost firm but, nevertheless, chose the price that is optimal for a low-cost incumbent, its profit would fall still further to $40 million.

Microhard's second period profits depend both on its unit cost and on whether or not Newvel comes into the market. We will assume that if Microhard is alone in the second period, it simply sets the monopoly price appropriate for its cost structure since entry is no longer a worry. It then earns either $100 million (low-cost monopoly profit) or $60 million (high-cost monopoly profit) in the second period when no entry occurs. We also assume that the potential entrant, Newvel, earns a profit of 0, whenever it stays out of the market.

If entry occurs in the second period, Microhard's profit suffers. If it is a low-cost firm, it earns only $50 million in the second period when Newvel is present. If Microhard is a high-cost firm, it is less able to compete and earns only $20 million. If Newvel enters and competes against an inefficient, high-cost incumbent, it earns a positive profit of $20 million. But if the incumbent turns out to be a low-cost type, then entry results in a *loss* of $20 million for Newvel.

The extensive form for this example of the entry game is shown in Figure 13.3. Newvel's uncertainty about Microhard's cost is modeled by introducing the player Nature who moves first and chooses the cost of the incumbent firm. With probability ρ Nature chooses a low-cost incumbent and with probability $(1 - \rho)$ Nature chooses a high-cost incumbent. Microhard moves next and sets either a high or low price when it sells output in the first period. Then Newvel decides whether to enter and to compete in period two or to stay out. At the end of each path, we show the total payoffs for each firm over the two periods depending on the choices about prices and entering. Microhard's total profit is the sum of its profit in each period. Newvel's profit is just that which it earns in the market for the final period.

Figure 13.3 shows three possibilities for Microhard. The first is that it is a high-cost firm and sets a first-period monopoly price that corresponds to being high cost. The second possibility is that it is again a high-cost firm but now chooses to set the lower price appropriate for a more cost-efficient firm. Finally, the third possibility is that Microhard is truly a low-cost firm and sets the lower monopoly price corresponding to being low cost. Note that we have ruled out the possibility of a low-cost Microhard charging the high-cost monopoly price. We will see in a moment that a low cost Microhard has no incentive to do so. One important point to understand is that we have captured the asymmetry of information or who knows what by circling together the nodes E_2 and E_3. This is meant to indicate that when the entrant Newvel observes a low price in the first period it does not know whether that corresponds to node E_2 or to E_3, and Microhard, the incumbent knows that the entrant firm does not know at which node it is.

You may ask at this point why a high-cost incumbent firm would ever set a sub-optimally low price that would lead to a lower level of profit. The answer is that this may influence

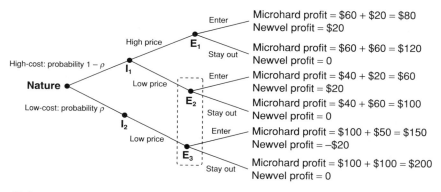

Figure 13.3   Extensive form of the Sequential Entry game with asymmetric information on cost

the entrant's decision to enter in period 2. Newvel might, for instance, reason as follows: "If Microhard charges a high price during the first period, it must be an inefficient, high-cost firm and I will enter. However, if Microhard charges a low price, it must be a cost-efficient firm and I am best to stay out of the market." In this setting, there is a considerable incentive for a high-cost incumbent initially to play against type and set the low monopoly price in period 1. True, this will mean that it earns only a profit of $40 million instead of the $60 million during the first period. Yet given the entrant firm's reasoning, this sacrifice pays off in the second period because it deters entry and thereby permits Microhard to earn a profit then of $60 million rather than the $20 million it would have earned had it initially set a high price that would have encouraged entry.

This same reasoning helps explain our assertion above that a low-cost incumbent firm will never initially set the high-cost monopoly price. Such a choice is not profit-maximizing in the short run and, in addition, serves to attract entry.

Our analysis so far makes clear that what happens in this game is sensitive to the nature of the beliefs that Newvel holds based on the behavior of Microhard observed in the first period. What we have just said above is that if the Newvel believes "low price means low-cost, high price means high-cost" its entry decision will be easily manipulated by Microhard. Accordingly, this may not be a very reasonable sort of belief for Newvel to hold. We should therefore expect that Newvel will also realize this and will adopt an alternative way to inter-pret the evidence observed in the first period.

The important question here is what beliefs are reasonable. Suppose that Newvel—recognizing the foregoing argument—thinks in a different way. Since Newvel understands that it is possible for both a high-cost and a low-cost type firm to play a low price strategy, it reasons that observing a low first-period price really gives no useful information as to the type of incumbent it is facing. Instead, when Newvel observes a low initial price it simply uses what it knows about the probabilities associated with different cost types. Specifically, when Newvel observes a low price it simply concludes that Microhard is a low-cost firm with probability ρ and a high-cost one with probability, $(1 - \rho)$. However, because a low-cost firm never has an incentive to charge a high price, Newvel does continue to believe that a high price in the first period means that.

Microhard has high costs. In other words, Newvel's conditional inferences are as follows:

If Microhard sets a low price in period 1, it has a low unit cost with probability ρ and a high unit cost with probability $1 - \rho$. Accordingly, second period entry will yield an expected profit of $[(1 - \rho)\$20 - \rho\$20]$ million.

If Microhard sets a high price in period 1, it has a high unit cost. Second-period entry will yield a certain profit of $20 million.

The foregoing beliefs are rational. Note, however, that they imply that if Newvel observes a low first-period price and then enters, its *expected profit* when it enters is: $-\$20\rho + \$20(1 - \rho)$ $= 2 - 4\rho$ (in millions). If Nature's draw or the probability that Microhard is a low-cost firm is high enough, in our example, if $\rho > 1/2$, then Newvel's *expected profit* from entering is negative. Consequently, it will not enter if it observes a low price. Microhard can work this out, too. It will therefore recognize that if the probability of being a low-cost firm $\rho > 1/2$, it will do better by pretending to be a low-cost firm and setting a low price in the first period even if, in reality, it is a high-cost firm. Once again, this will lead to a profit of $40 million initially and then, in the second period when the firm is a secure monopoly, a profit of

$60 million, for a total profit of $100 million. This is better than the alternative strategy of initially charging a high price which would reveal its type to the potential entrant, invite entry, and lead to the lower total profit of $80 million. That is, when $\rho > 1/2$, a high-cost Microhard will set a limit price—one lower than its true profit-maximizing price—in order to deter an imperfectly informed entrant from entering the market. This is, of course, predatory conduct.[12]

In sum, both the Bolton and Scharfstein (1990) and the Milgrom and Roberts (1982) models show how predatory pricing can be rational or, more formally, part of a subgame perfect strategy in a dynamic game. When the players, either investors or rivals, have incomplete information, the incumbents may find that predation can be an effective tool to eliminate rival firms.

The incentive for strategic low pricing can also be shown to improve the terms of a takeover, as in Saloner (1987) in a premerger game that is somewhat similar to the Bolton and Scharfstein (1990) model.

A study of the business practices of American Tobacco from 1891 to 1906 by Burns (1986) supports this idea that predatory pricing can be used to improve the terms of a takeover. During the period of study, American Tobacco acquired some 43 rival firms. The strategy used by American Tobacco was to identify the target rival that it wished to buy and introduce a competing brand at a low price in the target's market. The resultant drop in the target firm's profit would induce it to settle for a lower acquisition price. Burns (1986) estimates that such a predatory episode preceding a takeover bid lowered the acquisition costs by about 25 percent.[13]

13.3   CONTRACTS AS A BARRIER TO ENTRY

Our discussion of the Microsoft antitrust trial has focused mostly on Microsoft's practice of bundling its *Windows* operating system with its *Internet Explorer* web browser as a means

---

[12]   We can complicate the story by introducing uncertainty on both sides of the game. Suppose, for instance, that Newvel does not know what Microhard's payoff is from fighting an entrant, and Microhard does not know a potential entrant's payoff from entering. Specifically, from an entrant's point of view, Microhard can be one of two types: with probability p^0 Microhard is believed to be "tough" (i.e., low-cost), which means that its payoffs are such that it will always fight in every market; and with probability $1 - p^0$ Microhard is believed to be "weak" (high-cost) and more accommodating of entry. Similarly, each potential entrant is believed by Microhard to be "tough" with probability q^0, in which case the entrant's will always enter no matter what Microhard does; and to be "weak" with probability $1 - q^0$, in which case the entrant's payoffs are as in the current example. The "tough" version of Microhard always fights and so is of no interest to us. What *is* of interest is that a Microhard that knows itself to be "weak" will, as before, still have an incentive to fight entry in order to develop a reputation in the minds of potential entrants that it might, in fact, be "tough." The willingness of a "weak" incumbent to fight is an increasing function of p^0 and a decreasing function of q^0. More generally, the greater the number of markets there are the lower is the probability p^0 necessary for entry to be deterred. Simply put, a "weak" incumbent is more likely to fight entry if there are "many" of its markets remaining in which entry has not taken place than if there are "few."

[13]   In 1911, immediately following the *Standard Oil* decision, the Supreme Court found American Tobacco guilty of monopolizing the cigarette and tobacco product market, and cited predation to induce rivals to sell out as evidence of illegal monopolistic intent. A district court ordered that American Tobacco be dissolved and reconstituted as separate firms, the big three being American Tobacco, Ligget, and Myers and Lorillard.

of pushing Netscape out of the browser market. While such behavior might well have been predatory it was not, however, the only predatory practice of which Microsoft was accused. Another crucial question in the case was whether or not Microsoft was able through its contracts with PC makers to foreclose other rivals from entering the operating systems market in which Microsoft had a virtual monopoly.

The idea that formal agreements, which impose penalties for breach of contract, between a monopoly firm and its buyers can be a predatory instrument to deter other firms from competing with the monopolist has an important place in antitrust history. It underlies the reasoning of Judge Wyzanksi in the famous United Shoe Machinery Corporation antitrust case in the early 1950s. At that time, United Shoe controlled about 85 percent of the shoe-making equipment market, and it leased its machinery to shoe manufacturers. These leasing contracts were binding and were viewed by the court as a way to foreclose effectively the market for shoe machinery.

Perhaps not surprisingly, the Chicago School has traditionally been skeptical of the use of contracts as a predatory device. The simple logic of this counter-argument is well expressed by prominent antitrust scholars Bork (1978) and Posner (1976). Buyers do not have an incentive to sign contracts that disadvantage them with respect to a monopolist. Any contract signed must give not just the supplier but also the buyer some benefit—say by way of increased service or repair—and therefore a step toward greater efficiency. These proponents of the Chicago School emphasize the efficiency grounds for observed contracts rather than the predatory motive. Again, however, more recent theory has provided consistent arguments supporting the view that predation can occur in this rational world.

13.3.1   Long-term Exclusive Contracts as Predatory Instruments

Two basic analyses have been advanced to show that buyers may voluntarily sign contracts with suppliers that, in fact, are predatory and inefficient. The first is due to Aghion and Bolton (1987). The second is due to Rasmussen, Ramseyer, and Wiley (1991). We briefly present each model in turn.

Aghion and Bolton (1987) consider a market for some essential intermediate good that extends over two periods. In the first period, there is an incumbent monopoly seller of the good whose unit cost is $50. Each buyer of this good uses exactly one unit of the input per period and is willing to pay up to $100 for the product. In the second period there is the possible arrival of a new entrant. This is recognized by all parties at the start of the first period. However, neither a buyer in the second period nor the monopoly seller initially in the market knows the unit cost c of this second period potential entrant. All that these initial participants know is that c is distributed randomly but uniformly on the interval between $0 and $100.

We begin by considering matters from the viewpoint of a buyer looking forward to the second period. We assume that if the entrant actually enters the market at that time, Bertrand or price competition will emerge between the initial monopoly supplier and the new rival. If the entrant's unit cost c exceeds $50, however, it will lose this competition. With $c > \$50$, the incumbent can always underbid the entrant. The entrant obviously knows this. Hence, if the entrant finds that its cost $c > \$50$, no entry will occur. In this case, which by our assumption happens with probability 1/2, the incumbent remains a monopolist and can charge a buyer its full reservation price of $100 for the good.

However, if $c \leq \$50$, then entry will occur. In this case, the competition between the entrant and the incumbent will bid the price down to $50 at which point the incumbent will drop out. Once this happens, however, the entrant is under no additional pressure to lower its price so a buyer will end up paying $50 for the good for any case in which $c \leq \$50$. This too happens with probability 1/2. Notice that once again, there is an element of uncertainty as well as some asymmetry. For $0 \leq c \leq 50$, only the entrant will know its true cost as the buyer will be charged $50 whatever that is.

One of the two scenarios just outlined must happen. Therefore, in the absence of any contract obligating a buyer to purchase from the initial incumbent, the buyer's expected price for the intermediate good in the second period is:

$$\tfrac{1}{2} \times \$50 + \tfrac{1}{2} \times \$100 = \$75 \tag{13.1}$$

Note that equation (13.1) also implies that since a buyer values the product at $100, it should expect a surplus of $25 in the absence of any contract with the initial monopolist supplier. To put it another way, any contract that the incumbent offers to the buyer must promise the buyer an expected surplus of at least $25 in the second period, or the buyer will not sign it. The question then is whether the monopolist can and will offer such a contract. If it will, we would also like to know the efficiency aspects of such an arrangement.

One long-term contract that a buyer might find attractive is the following. In the first period, the buyer agrees to make its second-period purchase of the good from the incumbent at a price of $75 with only one possible exception. The exception is that buyer can instead make its second-period purchase from the new entrant so long as it pays the initial incumbent a $50 breach-of-contract fee.

There are several features of this proposed contract that deserve emphasis. First, observe that the entrant will now only enter the market if its cost $c \leq \$25$. The reason is that in the second period, a buyer can either buy from the incumbent for $75 or from the entrant at some price p plus the breach-of-contract fee of $50. Hence, a buyer will prefer to fulfill the contract rather than switch to the alternative supplier unless that supplier charges a price of $25 or less. However, the only way that the entrant can do this is when cost $c \leq \$25$. Accordingly, the entrant will only enter the market when $c \leq \$25$. Notice that this also implies that the contract restricts entry. Without the contract, entry occurred with probability 1/2. With the contract, entry will only occur when $c \leq \$25$, which happens only with probability 1/4.

Will the buyer actually sign the proposed contract? This is where the second noteworthy feature of the agreement becomes relevant. The contract is such that no matter what happens, the buyer will pay $75 for the good. Three-fourths of the time, the potential rival will not enter and the buyer will pay the stipulated $75 to the initial incumbent. One-fourth of the time, the rival will have a cost $c \leq \$25$. In this case, it will enter and charge the buyer the highest price it can while still making a sale, namely, $25 (or just a penny less). A buyer will then switch and purchase the good from the new entrant at $25 but, in addition, pay a $50 breach-of-contract fee to the initial incumbent. Again, the buyer's total payment is $75, leaving it a surplus of $25. Thus, a buyer's expected (in fact guaranteed) surplus with this contract is $25. Since this is also its expected profit or surplus without the contract, a buyer will be willing to sign the agreement.

The next question is whether or not the incumbent monopoly seller will actually find it worthwhile to offer the agreement. Here again, the answer is yes. To see this, we now need to consider the monopoly seller's expected profit both without and with the contract.

In the absence of any agreement, the incumbent monopolist will sell to a buyer at a price of $100 half the time. The other half it will be underbid by the new entrant. When it does

Reality Checkpoint
Coke Takes Out a Contract on Texas Rivals

Dangerfield, Texas gets awfully hot. The summertime temperature can regularly top 100 degrees Fahrenheit and shade is hard to find. That's probably one reason that Dangerfield residents and their neighbors drink a lot of soft drinks every year. Indeed, for convenience stores in the area, it is estimated that as much as half of their sales are from beverages. In the years just before 1992, the stores received their soft drink supplies from a number of small, soft drink firms and bottlers, as well as from Coca-Cola and Pepsi. However, that all began to change after 1992.

Bruce Hackett, a former Coke employee and owner of Hackett Beverages, supplied ice-filled barrels to a number of stores that were also stocked with his soft drink bottles. The barrels were usually displayed just outside the cash register line so that customers could easily grab a cold beverage and pay for it on the way out. However, starting in 1992, Hackett found more and more of his barrels turned upside down and left at the side of the road. In four years, he went from having barrels in 52 stores to barrels in just two. Other independent bottlers and small beverage firms had similar experiences. They found stores abandoning the refrigerator units they gave them to display their products, dumping their fresh soda dispensing and vending machines, and even refusing them any shelf space.

The reason for these changes was easy to find. Coca Cola had started an aggressive marketing campaign in which it paid store owners to display its products *exclusively* and refused to give them access even to non-Coke drinks handled by Coca-Cola bottlers if they did not.

Thus, one contract offered a bonus of $2 million to a regional supermarket chain, Brookshire's, in return for just selling Coke products alone. Another contract required that "Coca Cola products will occupy a minimum of 100 percent of total soft-drink space" in the store.

The case went to trial before a Texas court in 2003. Coke's defense was that the stores wanted the contract deals that it was offering. They argued that the stores felt they had little to offer in the soft drink category unless they offered the national Coke brand at the best terms possible. Coke argued that the contracts it offered, allowed the stores to do just that. However, it was indisputable that as the smaller firms were driven from the market, Coke prices went up. At Nu-Way, a popular Dangerfield convenience store that still offers Royal Crown Cola, a 20-ounce container of the Royal Crown product sells for 69 cents while the same size container of Coke sells for 92 cents. However, at another convenience store, E. Z. Mart, a short distance away, there is no Royal Crown alternative and Coke sells for $1.09. Whether this was a case of predation or not is a question of judgment. However, a comment by Coca-Cola spokesperson, Polly Howes, probably did not help Coke's cause. In a widely distributed statement, Ms. Howes said that far from "a lack of competition. There was too much competition." The Texas jury found Coca-Cola guilty of violating the antitrust laws.

Source: C. Hays, "How Coke Pushed Rivals Off the Shelf," *New York Times*, August 6, 2003, section 3, p. 1.

sell at $100, the incumbent makes a profit of $50. Since this happens with probability 1/2, the monopoly seller's expected profit in the second period without the contract is $1/2 \times \$50$ = $25 per customer.

With the contract, the calculation of the incumbent's profit is slightly more complicated. With probability 3/4, the monopolist will still sell to the buyer at the pre-specified price of $75. Since the monopolist has a unit cost of $50, such a sale generates a profit of $25. With probability 1/4, however, the monopolist makes no sale because the buyer breaks the contract and switches to the new entrant. This is not bad news, however. The switch means that the monopolist no longer has to incur the $50 unit production cost. Moreover, the buyer's breach of contract entitles the seller to a $50 fee in the one-fourth of the time that the contract is broken. In short, the contract offers the initial incumbent seller an expected surplus in period two of:

$$^3/_4 \times (\$75 - \$50) + {}^1/_4 \times \$50 = \$31.25 > \$25 \tag{13.2}$$

As equation (13.2) makes clear, the monopoly seller's expected profit with the contract is $31.25, an amount that definitely exceeds its expected profit of $25 without the contract. Moreover, we have already shown that a typical buyer's expected surplus is the same whether the agreement is in force or not. In other words, the incumbent monopolist is made better off and the buyer is made no worse off by the contract. Accordingly, with one party desiring the contract and the other indifferent, we expect that the contract will be offered and signed.

From a social viewpoint, however, the contract is inefficient. To be sure, it does increase the expected surplus of the buyer and seller together from $50 (= $25 + $25) to $56.25 (= $25 + $31.25) for a net gain of $6.25. However, it reduces the entrant's expected surplus by more than this amount. Why?

Without the contract, the entrant will stay out of the market half the time and enter the other half. When it does enter, the entrant will sell at a price of $50 per unit. In such cases, the entrant's unit cost c will range from 0 to $50 or $25 on average. This implies that the entrant has an expected profit of $^1/_2 \times (\$50 - \$25) = \$12.50$ when there is no contract. When the incumbent binds a second-period buyer with a contract the potential rival only enters the market with probability 1/4 and sells at a price of only $25. Its unit cost in such cases will range from 0 to $25 or, $12.50, on average. So, once the contract is signed, the potential rival's expected profit is only $1/4 \times (\$25 - \$12.50) = \$3.13$. From this, we can see that the issuance of a contract reduces the potential entrant's expected surplus from $12.50 to $3.13 or by $9.37. As noted, this reduction exceeds the joint gains to the buyer and seller ($6.25), so the total social surplus is less with the contract than without it.

The intuition behind the foregoing result, however, is subtle. From the buyer's perspective, the problem is that without the contract, the new entrant will never sell at a price less than $50—even if it has a cost of $0. Ideally, the buyer would like to benefit more in such cases where the entrant has such a particularly low cost. Yet, in the absence of the contract, nothing compels the new entrant to engage in such sharing. Once the price falls to $50, the initial incumbent drops out of the market and the entrant faces no further pressure to reduce its price. By offering the contract, the incumbent monopolist effectively enables the buyer to force the seller to never charge a price above $25. The buyer is, as just noted, willing to pay for this service. The point is that even though a contract may bring benefits to a monopoly supplier and its buyers, the contract is still inefficient if it achieves these gains only by reducing the surplus of the new entrant by an even greater amount. The inefficiency reflects the fact that under the contract regime some desirable entry is prevented. Specifically, entry does not occur when the new rival has a cost c satisfying $\$25 < c \leq \$50$ despite the fact that within this range, the entrant is more efficient than the initial monopoly seller. Because of the breach-of-contract clause in the long-term contract, the entrant cannot break into the market.

The Rasmusen, Ramseyer, and Wiley (1991) model differs from the above in so far as it focuses on an externality in the contract rather than on an uncertainty. Suppose again that there is one supplier with a unit cost of $50, and, say, three buyers. As before, each buyer will pay up to $100 for one unit of the input. There is also an entrant with a unit cost of $40 waiting to enter the market next period. However, the entrant also has a sunk cost—say due to market research or promotional activities—of $60. Hence, to underbid the incumbent and cover its sunk cost, the entrant has to serve at least two customers. If the new entrant serves three customers, it can charge each a price as low as $60. The $20 in operating profit that it makes on all three customers combined will then give it enough extra to cover its overhead. If it serves two customers, the entrant can still underbid the incumbent but it must now charge a price no lower than $70. If it serves only one customer, the entrant must charge a price of $100 to acquire the $60 needed to cover its sunk cost. In this case, of course, the entrant will not enter.

The incumbent can, of course, match any of the entrant's price offers in the second period. Still, the incumbent has to recognize that if the entrant comes in at a price of $70 and the incumbent has to match that price, the incumbent's profit will fall to $60 even if it keeps all three customers. The incumbent therefore has some incentive to stop the entrant from acquiring two or more clients with a long-term contract. To sell this contract, the incumbent engages in the following tactic. It tells two customers that each will be able to buy the input at $70 if, and only if, she signs an exclusive contract promising not to buy from any other supplier. Why might this work?

Each buyer who is offered an exclusive contract with a purchase price of $70 has to worry about what the other buyers will do. Once two sign the contract, no offer needs to be made to the third because once two buyers are bound to the incumbent, the entrant cannot profitably underbid the incumbent's price. Therefore, the third buyer may well face a price of $100 once the other two have signed. In an effort to avoid such an outcome, each buyer will rush to sign the contract. In fact, by playing buyers off against each other in this way, the incumbent may be able to sign exclusive deals even if it offers a small price reduction to only $90.

Here again the contract inefficiently blocks entry. The potential entrant is a more efficient producer. The problem is that each buyer looks only to the effect that the contract has on the buyer's profit. Each ignores the impact that signing the contract has on overall competition and the profitability of other buyers (perhaps some of whom are rivals to the buyer in the downstream market).

13.3.2   Tying as a Predatory Contract

In the contracting scenarios described above, the mechanism that blocks entry is a contract that extends over two periods, i.e., a long-term contract. The contract is written in the first period, before a potential second entrant arrives and extends into the next period. When the rival does arrive in period two, it finds that potential customers are hard to come by because they have already been contractually bound to the initial monopolist.

Rather than extending a contract over two or perhaps more periods, one might instead consider extending a contract to two or more markets. That is, an incumbent seller in one market might be able to contract with its customers in a manner that effectively binds them to that same seller in a second market. This is what generally happens with a tying arrangement. As we saw in the *Magicam* and *Magifilm* parable of Chapter 8, a primary motivation for tying is the implementation of effective price discrimination—not predation. In that story, the Rowling Corp. markets a *Magicam* camera that only works with its own *Magifilm*. Tying can enable Rowling to price discriminate among its consumers.

If the *Magicam* worked equally well with film cartridges made by any firm, Rowling would still enjoy a monopoly in the *Magicam*, but its ability to extract additional surplus by means of price discrimination would be very limited. Tying the two goods together is therefore good for Rowling Corp. Indeed, it may even be good for consumers because, as we know, price discrimination often works to expand the market and increase the social surplus. This price discrimination motive was not part of the long-term contract models that we described above and, in this respect, the two contractual arrangements are not equivalent.

Even though Rowling's motive for the tying of *Magicam* and *Magifilm* is to price discriminate more effectively, the other makers of film cartridges will nonetheless find that this practice causes them to lose customers. Once again, this raises the fear that the tie-in may permit Rowling Corp. to extend its *Magicam* monopoly into the film market. This will be particularly true if, for instance, there are significant scale economies in film production so that loss of part of the market makes it more difficult for a rival maker of film to produce at minimum average cost.

Reality Checkpoint
Tied Up on the Rock

Roughly 1,500 inmates were interred in Alcatraz or "the Rock" as it was sometimes called during the 30 years of its use as a federal penitentiary from 1934 to 1963. Born in the Depression Era, the prison was envisioned as a necessary response to the violence that first, Prohibition, and later, severe economic dislocation brought to America. Law enforcement officials including J. Edgar Hoover sought to build a special institution in which the most violent and hardened criminals such as George "Machine Gun" Kelly, would be kept securely. The prison's location on an island in the middle of San Francisco harbor also made it ideal as a place to incarcerate gang leaders such as Al Capone in a manner that made it difficult for such criminals to maintain any control of their still-active criminal organizations. The prospect of imprisonment with such a hardened crew of inmates and in such an isolated place led many, if not all, prisoners to dream of escape. Indeed, many risked life and limb in such attempts. Yet no successful break out has ever been documented. Escape was impossible.

These days, getting to the island, which is now operated as a tourist attraction, is almost as difficult as escape used to be. The National Park Service issues 4,200 daily tickets to visit the tiny island and all are typically bought.

Pursuant to an exclusive contract, these tickets are issued to Blue and Gold Fleet Cruise Lines, the only tour boat company operator permitted to transport visitors to the island. The contract also permits Blue and Gold, if it so desires, to sell 1,800 of the Alcatraz tickets to travel agents and others who put together vacation and excursion packages. Because of the strong demand for such tickets, those operators who receive them find that they are very popular with vacationers. In turn, this gives Blue and Gold considerable leverage with the tour operators. Indeed, soon after it first received the exclusive rights, the cruise company exploited this leverage by requiring that any tour operator receiving Alcatraz tickets must also use Blue and Gold for its harbor cruises and other boating excursions. In other words, Blue and Gold tied the sale of Alcatraz tickets to the mandatory use of its other services. Of course, the other boating companies who lost customers to Blue and Gold were unhappy. Several complaints were filed with the California Attorney General's Office. In a settlement with these officials, Blue and Gold agreed to terminate its tying practices.

Source: A. Chiu, "San Francisco Tourboat Antitrust Case is Settled," *San Jose Mercury News*, September 13, 2000, p. A1.

Whether or not Rowling or any other firm has an incentive to extend its monopoly in the manner just described is, however, far from clear. After all, consumers are ultimately interested in *Magicam* pictures—not the *Magicam* or the *Magifilm* itself. From this perspective, a higher price for say, *Magifilm*, requires a lower price for the *Magicam*. To put it another way, Rowling has little incentive to monopolize the *Magifilm* market solely as a means to raise the price of *Magifilm* since this will reduce the demand for its *Magicam* product.

There are other factors that may affect the incentive for tying. Suppose for instance that there are economies of scope between film and camera production. Then by extending its monopoly from the *Magicam* market to that of *Magifilm*, Rowling may prevent other manufacturers from realizing such scope economies. In turn, this may prevent other firms from developing their own *Magicam* product. That is, the extension of the Rowling monopoly from one product line to another may be a means of protecting its core monopoly.

It is for this reason that whenever a firm possesses substantial market power in a tying product, and coerces the buyer to take the tied product as a condition to obtaining the desired good, the arrangement is almost always found to be a violation of the antitrust laws (see inset).

13.4   PREDATORY CONDUCT AND PUBLIC POLICY

Should there be public policies that restrain the conduct of firms who have acquired or are likely to acquire a dominant position in the marketplace? The answer to this question rests largely on three issues. The first of these is whether or not predation is a rational strategy. The second is the empirical issue as to whether there is any actual evidence of predatory behavior. The third is whether the public policy can itself be made workable. It is not too much of an exaggeration to say that little attention was paid to either of the first two issues (and possibly the third) in the years immediately following the passage of the Robinson–Patman Act in 1936, and its condemnation of discriminatory prices. For a number of years thereafter, price cuts by large firms that had the effect of severely reducing or eliminating the market share of small ones were almost routinely regarded as predatory if the prices reflected any degree of discrimination, i.e., if the large firm sold at a lower price in more competitive markets. The culmination of this period of stringent prosecution of even vague charges of predatory pricing was the *Utah Pie* case that we discussed above.

Against a history of cases such as *Utah Pie*, the work of McGee (1958, 1980), Koller (1971), Posner (1976), Bork (1978), and Easterbrook (1984), and others of the Chicago School reflected a necessary corrective. Many firms achieve dominance not because of predation but because of their superior competitive skill. Hence, policies that constrain "bigness" would have adverse incentive effects on competitive behavior. A corollary to this view is that market dominance will not persist if it is due to any factor not related to superior skill or efficiency. Indeed, these very arguments were made by Microsoft during its 1998–2001 trial and appeal.

As a result of the force of these arguments, the Chicago School perspective on predatory behavior became increasingly influential. It received an official blessing in the 1986 *Matsushita* case when the Supreme Court wrote "For this reason, there is a consensus among commentators that predatory pricing schemes are rarely tried, and even more rarely successful."[14] A few

---

[14]   See *Matsuhita Electronic Industrial Co., Ltd v Zenith Radio Corporation et al.*, 475 U.S. 574 (1986).

years later, in the *Brooke* case of 1993, the Court went even further and outlined stringent evidentiary standards that had to be met before a predation claim would be supported.[15]

The Brooke Group (also known as Ligget) was a small cigarette manufacturer that began selling a generic brand in 1980, at prices well below those of the major brands. When consumers responded favorably to the introduction of these cheap cigarettes, Brown & Williamson and other large tobacco companies responded with vigorous price cuts. In its effort to undersell Brooke, it seems clear that Brown cut prices so low that it sustained millions of dollars of losses over a period as long as a year or more. Ultimately, however, Brooke could not keep pace. It raised the price on its cigarettes. Almost immediately thereafter, Brown & Williamson and other cigarette manufacturers did the same.

The Supreme Court did not find the foregoing evidence conclusive. As noted, the court had moved to a view that there was an economics consensus that predatory pricing was irrational. The court then established two broad requirements for a successful prosecution of a predatory pricing case. The first was evidence of selling below some measure of cost. The second, and really new element introduced by the court was evidence that the predator had a reasonable expectation of recouping the losses endured during the predatory period. Just how strong the new requirements were can be seen in the fact that there was not one successful prosecution of predatory action in the first 40 cases that followed the Brooke decision. It was not until the important case of Microsoft that a finding of guilty was made.

The consensus to which the Supreme Court referred in *Matsuhita* no longer exists—if it ever did. Commitment via capacity expansion, asymmetric information, and contractual exclusions are all features that can be combined to make a coherent argument for the rationality of predatory actions. Moreover, with respect to recoupment, it is important to recognize that successful predation has important reputation effects. Once a firm is successful in eliminating one rival, it sends a message to all other potential competitors. Thus, in measuring the ability of a firm to recover its losses, one has to include in the calculations all the profits secured by the deterrent effect that the firm's reputation has on other would-be entrants.

However, the court's statement of necessary evidence does speak to an important issue. The recognition that predation can be rational and can happen does not carry any clear policy implications unless we have a clear standard by which predatory actions can be identified and distinguished from conduct that is truly procompetitive. Any entry will generally evoke some reaction from the incumbent firms. Typically, this may come in the form of lower prices or other expanded consumer benefits. Most such responses are not predatory in nature. To the contrary, they are exactly the conduct that we expect and hope that markets will promote. Similarly, when any firm, large or small, first comes into a market as a new entrant, it may want to set a low initial price, lower than the short-term, profit-maximizing one, as a way to induce consumers to forgo their usual brand and try the entrant's relatively unknown product. Once established the firm may then raise prices. Clearly, the intent of this kind of promotional pricing is not to drive a rival from the market. Yet, it may be difficult empirically to distinguish this pricing strategy from predatory pricing.

In other words, to the extent that antitrust enforcement seeks to prevent predatory practices, policy makers need to create workable legal standards that are able to distinguish procompetitive from anticompetitive conduct. Ideally, we would like such policy to be governed by a simple rule that could be used to detect the presence of predation. This would

---

[15] *Brooke Group v. Brown & Williamson Tobacco*, 509 U.S. 209 (1993). Interestingly enough, Brooke actually won the initial jury trial but lost in subsequent appeals to the federal courts.

permit all parties to understand just what is and what is not legal. Yet in the area of predation simple rules rarely work.

Of the various rules that have been proposed, the most famous is that of Areeda and Turner (1975), which essentially finds any price to be predatory if it is below the firm's short-run average variable cost standing in as a proxy for marginal cost. Unfortunately, it is not a very good proxy. In actual practice, average variable cost can be significantly less than short-run marginal cost so that a firm could set a price below its current marginal cost yet still above its average cost. In so doing, the firm would be acting within the legal range permitted by the Areeda and Turner rule even though a price below short-run marginal cost would likely be judged as predatory by many economists. Hence, as Scherer (1976) was quick to point out, the use of the average cost standard could still permit serious predation.[16] Moreover, if there are important learning curve effects so that average cost falls with a firm's cumulative production over time (as opposed to scale economies in which average cost falls with the volume of production per unit of time), predation can occur by means of a vigorous output expansion without prices ever falling below cost.[17]

Another problem is that the rule ignores the strategic aspect of predatory pricing. To take a simple example, consider a market in which there is one firm operating as a monopoly. Suppose that if a new firm enters it will produce an identical good to that of the monopolist and that the game is one of Bertrand or price competition. As we saw in Chapter 10 the equilibrium of this game is price equal to unit cost. Prices fall immediately to their marginal cost. By Areeda and Turner's rule, this would not be predatory. Yet if the entrant foresees this outcome, the existence of any sunk entry cost will be enough to induce it to stay out. Here again, the Areeda and Turner rule might permit entry-deterring behavior. Whenever the threat of "cutthroat pricing" is sufficiently credible that it is never actually used, the evidence Areeda and Turner look for will not be found.

Despite its shortcomings, the Areeda and Turner rule has been applied in many U.S. antitrust cases. It has been frequently relied upon by Supreme Court Justice, Stephen Breyer.[18] It was also used to exonerate IBM against predatory price-cutting charges in *California Computer Products, Inc., et al. v. International Business Machines* [613 F. 2d 727 (9th Cir. 1979)]. Perhaps the clearest statement is that of Judge Kaufman who, in *Northeastern Telephone Company v. American Telephone and Telegraph Company et al.,* [651 F. 2d 76 (2nd Cir. 1981)], wrote: "We agree with Areeda and Turner that in the general case, at least, the relationship between a firm's prices and its marginal costs provides the best single determinant of predatory pricing."

Yet despite its frequent use, the weaknesses in the Areeda and Turner rule have led many economists to propose modified alternatives. Some of these are like the Areeda and Turner approach in that they focus essentially on the behavior of a single variable. Baumol (1979), for example, focuses primarily on the behavior of the incumbent's price before entry and after exit of a rival. Essentially, this rule requires that any price reduction by a dominant firm in the face of entry be required to be "quasi-permanent," say for a period of five years. If the price reduction that entry induced is quickly reversed following the entrant's exit, Baumol's (1979) rule would find the pricing behavior predatory.

---

[16] See Scherer's (1976) exchange with Areeda and Turner (1976) on this and other points.
[17] See Cabral and Riordan (1997) for an elaboration of this point.
[18] See, for example, his decision in *Barry Wright Corporation v. ITT Grinnell Corporation, et al.,* 724F. 2d 227 (1st Cir. 1983).

In a recent updating of this work, Baumol (1996) also suggests comparing the predator's price with a measure of average avoidable cost (AAC). AAC is a measure of the cost that the alleged predator could have avoided had it not engaged in the predatory increase in output. Thus, if the predatory action lasted for a year, AAC would be the total amount of extra costs incurred in that year divided by the extra quantity produced.

In contrast, Williamson (1977) suggests looking at the incumbent's *output* before and after entry. The idea is that a rapid expansion of output after entry would be a sign of possible predation. This rule has two advantages. First, because of the prohibition against expansion after entry, the incumbent might well expand output earlier. In turn, this eliminates some of the monopoly distortion that would otherwise occur when the incumbent is alone in the market. Second, Williamson's rule may also prevent capacity expansion as an entry-deterring strategy by making the threat to expand after entry no longer credible.

While both the Baumol (1979) and Williamson (1977) rules are insightful, both are also limited by focusing on a single variable to indicate predation. As we have emphasized, predatory conduct is part of an often complicated corporate strategy. As a result, it is unlikely to be reflected accurately in the behavior of a single variable. The Dixit (1980) model of capacity deterrence does not involve pricing at all and so would go undetected by both the Areeda–Turner and the Baumol tests. Similarly, Williamson's test would not prevent deterrence by preemption. None of these tests involve any consideration as to whether the strategic environment actually permits predation.

Joskow and Klevorick (1979) were among the first to suggest a more complete assessment of alleged predation within a strategic framework. Their rule combines the separate criteria mentioned above—below-cost pricing, output expansion, and price reversal—but requires as well that there be evidence that such actions were or at least could have been conceived as part of an overall strategy. In particular, Joskow and Klevorick (1979) propose to examine company documents to determine whether or not a firm was intentionally pursuing the aggressive policies. These authors would also examine the industry's structural features to see whether the conditions for predatory pricing exist.

Ordover and Willig (1981) and Bolton, Brodley, and Riordan (2001) also try to present a comprehensive framework for evaluating predatory accusations. The Ordover and Willig (1981) paper is important for its clear and modern definition of predatory conduct as any action for which the profitability is dependent on driving the rival out or preventing it from entering in the first place. In this view, predatory pricing is but one of a number of predation tactics. Both papers argue that an important first step is to check the market structure for the preconditions necessary to make predation worthwhile. The structural conditions so identified are that the accused predator really has significant market power and that entry be difficult so that if a rival is forced to exit it is not subsequently replaced. Bolton, Brodley, and Riordan (2001) also argue that recoupment can be demonstrated by relating the predator's actions to a clear and evidence-supported strategy of predation. In the case of predatory pricing, these authors would rely on an Average Avoidable Cost measure as a benchmark.

None of the proposed predatory standards is simple or easily translated into a courtroom proceeding. The difficulty of distinguishing between good, fierce competition, on the one hand, and predatory efforts, on the other, is substantial. Moreover, as tough as this distinction is to make in the case of pricing, it may be even more difficult to achieve in considering other actions.

For example, consider predatory product innovation which was alleged in two well-known cases, *Telex v. IBM*, and *Berkey v. Kodak*. In the former, the issue at hand was the claim by

Reality Checkpoint
Cut-rate or Cut-throat Fares?

In 1994, Sun Jet Airlines began offering service between Dallas-Fort Worth airport and a select few other cities including Tampa, Florida, and Long Beach, California. Its entry was subsequently followed by that of Vanguard Airlines flying between Dallas and Kansas City, and Western Pacific offering flights between Dallas and Colorado Springs. All three airlines are small startup carriers whose operating costs are widely recognized to be well below those of the major, established airlines. Indeed, it was this cost advantage that gave these small startups their only hope of surviving in the Dallas-Fort Worth market. This is because the Dallas-Fort Worth airport is a central hub for American Airlines. American carries 70 percent of all the passengers who travel from any city nonstop to Dallas and 77 percent of all those nonstop passengers originating in Dallas. It has concessions from local businesses and has already sunk the costs necessary to operate its gates, ticketing desks, and so on. Internal documents obtained from American by the Justice Department reveal that these and other advantages made the firm confident that its dominance would not be challenged by another major airline. However, those same documents suggest that American was concerned about the entry of low cost startups, especially after observing how much market share such firms had taken from other major carriers at their hub airports.

American responded aggressively to the three startups. It greatly expanded its flight offerings in the challenged markets and lowered its fares. In each of the three markets shown, this strategy ultimately led the startups to exit the market. Immediately thereafter, American cut its flights and raised fares back to or above earlier levels. This is shown for the case of three markets in the table below.

	Before entry Daily flights	Price	During conflict Daily flights	Price	After exit Daily flights	Price
Kansas City	8	$108	14	$80	11	$147
Long Beach	0	—	3	$86	0	—
Colorado Springs	5	$150	7	$81	6	$137

Was this a case of predatory pricing? The Justice Department thought so. It claimed that during the battle with the startups, American lost money on each flight. The actual losses are claimed to be even greater because to offer the additional flights, aircraft were diverted from profitable routes to these unprofitable ones. American won an initial decision in district court. In July 2003, a three-judge Appeals Court upheld the lower court's decision.

Source: D. Carney and W. Zellner, "Caveat Predator: The Justice Department is Cracking Down on Predatory Pricing," *Business Week*, May 22, 2000, p. 116.

Telex (and others) that IBM, which at the time admittedly controlled the market for mainframe computers but faced serious competition in markets for peripheral equipment, began to develop new equipment designs so that only new IBM peripherals were compatible with IBM mainframes (a tying arrangement). In the *Berkey* case, Berkey was a photo-finisher and camera manufacturer who claimed that Kodak should have given it advance notice of Kodak's introduction of a new 110 camera so as to permit Berkey to redesign its cameras and remain viable in the market. In both cases, the courts eventually ruled against the plaintiffs and in favor of IBM and Kodak, respectively. There is perhaps good reason to believe that the technological alterations reflected in these two cases truly were motivated by predatory considerations. However, there is also a legitimate fear that punishing such actions could have a chilling effect on all innovation.

13.5   EMPIRICAL APPLICATION
Entry Deterrence in the Pharmaceutical Industry

While legal cases and anecdotal examples of entry deterrence can be easily found, empirical work testing systematic entry deterrence has been limited. The reason for this is that the data requirements necessary to identify consistently any systematic predatory behavior across a set of market data points are fairly demanding. For example, in a paper on shipping cartels, Scott Morton (1997) finds some supportive evidence that established cartels in the late nineteenth and early twentieth century engaged in predatory pricing to deter new shipping entrants, especially when the entrants were small and/or had poor financial resources. However, in an another paper (Scott Morton 2000), finds little evidence that pharmaceutical firms successfully use advertising to deter generic entry as the end of the incumbent's patent nears.

One reason that econometric work on predation is so tricky is that such work must somehow identify cases where an incumbent both regarded entry as a real threat *and* felt that there was a way to prevent it. Suppose for instance that the data set includes two kinds of markets. One type is characterized by a high likelihood of entry by several new firms and that by taking a costly action X the incumbent can reduce the number of entrants. The second market type is characterized by a very low probability of entry and by at most one new rival. Finally, suppose that post-entry competition is Cournot so that the fewer new entrants the better from the viewpoint of the incumbent.

In such a setting, we may find that incumbents only take action X in the first type of market because entry is so unlikely in the second kind of market that incurring the cost of action X is not worthwhile. If this is so, the data will be divided into two groups. In one set of cases, the incumbent takes action X and there is some entry (though less than otherwise would have been the case). In the other set of cases, the incumbent does not take action X, yet there is no entry. Thus, on balance, the data will show that there is *more* entry when the predatory tactic X is used than when it is not. Unless care is taken to identify such markets a priori, it will be hard to conclude from such data that predation is a serious threat.

Another difficulty that the researcher must overcome is identifying the entry-deterring strategy. This too is trickier than it may at first appear. Consider the first-mover, consumer learning-by-doing model of Gabszewicz, Pepall, and Thisse (1992) discussed in Chapter 11. Recall that in the first period of that model when the incumbent is alone, the incumbent prices low to "buy up" a cohort of customers who will be loyal to its product after the second-period entry of a rival because these customers have learned how to work with the incumbent's brand. On the one hand then, such aggressive pricing may seem as if it deters entry because it limits the number of customers for whom the later entrant can compete. On the other hand, however, the fact that it has such a loyal, and price-insensitive cohort encourages the incumbent to charge a high price when entry occurs and this allows the entrant to gain more consumers at a high price as well. Of course, this latter effect makes entry more likely.

A recent paper that tries to sort all these issues out is Ellison and Ellison (2006). They look at the advertising and pricing behavior of pharmaceutical companies in the case of 64 drugs about to lose their patents over the years 1986–92. They first do a simple regression to determine which markets are most vulnerable to entry. For this purpose, they code each market as to whether or not there was any generic entry within three years after the expiration of the incumbent's patent. This procedure creates a 1, 0 variable for each market called Entry, where the variable is 1 if there was entry and 0 if there was not. Ellison and Ellison (2006) then try to explain this entry variable with an equation that includes three right-hand side variables that should be related to entry. These are: Rev_i, the average annual revenue earned by the incumbent over the three years prior to patent expiration; $Hosp_i$, the fraction of revenues from the drug due to hospital sales in the year prior to patent expiration; and Chronic/Acute$_i$, which takes on the value 0 if the drug treats an acute condition but 1 if it treats a chronic condition. Their estimated equation then is:

$$Entry_i = constant + \beta_1 Rev_i + \beta_2 Hosp_i + \beta_3 Chronic/Acute_i + \varepsilon_i \qquad (13.3)$$

where ε_i represents random factors that may affect entry in the ith market.

Because the dependent variable is not continuous but instead, either 1 or 0, equation (13.3) cannot be efficiently estimated by ordinary least squares (OLS) regression. The linear feature of OLS means that it is quite likely that for plausible values of the independent variables the OLS estimates of the β_k coefficients will predict a value for entry outside the 0–1 interval.

Instead, Ellison and Ellison (2006) use an alternative regression procedure called Probit. This procedure effectively transforms the data so that for any value of the right-hand side variables, the coefficient estimates give rise to a value for Entry$_i$ that lies between 0 and 1. This predicted value is then a measure of the probability of entry given the market features. In turn, this allows them to classify each of their 64 markets as one of three types: (1) low probability of entry; (2) intermediate probability of entry; and (3) high probability of entry.

Ellison and Ellison (2006) next consider the strategic use of advertising to deter entry in these markets. They start by noting that in these cases, advertising by one firm has considerable spillover to the products of another. In particular, advertising by an incumbent calls attention to the specific functions of the drug, its potential benefits, its proper use, and so on, in a way that is likely to inform consumers of the benefit of later generic rivals. This is particularly the case with drugs since doctors are smart enough to realize that the active ingredients in branded medications and generics are chemically identical. It is even more the case in those states in which pharmacies are required by law to fill a prescription with a cheaper generic medication if one is available and the doctor has not explicitly forbidden it. In other words, Ellison and Ellison (2006) assume that advertising by an incumbent today will *help* tomorrow's generic entrant. Hence, if incumbents wish to deter entry, they should *reduce* advertising in the period prior to the expected emergence of a rival.

Of course, whether or not incumbents will wish to deter entry will depend in part on how likely entry is. A key insight of the Ellison and Ellison (2006) paper is that the relationship between the probability of entry and strategic deterrence efforts is likely to be nonmonotonic. This is because entry deterrence is probably not worth the cost either in markets where entry is highly probable or in ones where it is very unlikely. In the first case, no amount of deterrence is likely to prevent entry. In the second case, no deterrence is really necessary. Thus, Ellison and Ellison (2006) predict that deterrence efforts will first rise (relative to what they would otherwise be) as the probability of entry rises from a low value to an intermediate one, and then fall, as the probability of entry rises still further to a high value. In terms of advertising, this means that incumbents will *lower* their advertising in those markets that their Probit regression results characterize as having an intermediate probability of entry

Table 13.1   Detail advertising trend by category of entry probability, 64 pharmaceutical markets

Coefficient	Estimated value	Standard error
β_1	−0.007	0.013
β_2	−0.032	0.009
β_3	0.009	0.007

but exhibit no advertising response to the threat of entry in either low or high probability of entry markets. Again, this is because Ellison and Ellison (2006) assume that advertising by the incumbent also has strong benefits for the generic entrant. Reducing advertising prior to the period of potential entry can then make that entry less likely. To some extent, this is precisely what they find.

Consider so-called detail advertising. By this we mean the promotional efforts of pharmaceuticals to influence physicians' prescribing practices by visiting doctors and health care providers and making direct presentations in their offices. Ellison and Ellison (2006) look at the time trend in the value of detail advertising relative to its average in the three years prior to patent expiration for each month starting 36 months before that expiration and continuing for 12 months after by estimating the regression equation:

$$\frac{Advertising_{it}}{Average\ Advertising_i} - 1 = (\beta_1 LowEntry_i + \beta_2 IntermedEntry_i + \beta_3 HighEntry_i)Time + \varepsilon_{it}$$
$$(13.4)$$

The *Time* variable is just a trend term that increases by one as one moves a month closer to expiration date. The dependent variable is the ratio of advertising in the ith market in month t relative to average monthly detail advertising in that market. *LowEntry*, *IntermedEntry*, and *HighEntry* are each a 1,0 dummy variable indicating what entry category market i is in. The hypothesis is that β_2 will be significantly less than either β_1 or β_3, reflecting the efforts of incumbents in these markets to reduce advertising as a means of deterring entry. The estimated results are shown in the Table 13.1.

As you can see, the estimate of β_2 is noticeably smaller (algebraically) than either of the other two coefficients. That is, the results imply that while the incumbent's detail advertising declines by less than 1 percent per month relative to the norm in high entry markets (β_1) and actually rises a bit in low entry markets (β_3), it falls by over 3 percent per month in markets with an intermediate chance of entry. Thus, Ellison and Ellison (2006) provide some interesting evidence of strategic deterrence efforts in U.S. pharmaceutical markets in the late 1980s.

Summary

Allegations of pricing below cost to drive out a competitor and other comparable predatory strategies have been met in the last part of the twentieth century with increasing skepticism by the courts. This reflects the Chicago School view that predation is irrational. In the language of game theory, the Chicago view is that predation is neither a subgame perfect strategy nor a dominant strategy. Accordingly, few charges of predatory activity have been successfully prosecuted since the 1980s. The *Microsoft* case is, however, a notable exception in this regard.

At the same time, there appear to be clear cases of actual predatory conduct. As a result, an important question in contemporary industrial organization theory has been whether we can construct plausible models in which predatory actions are rational. The answer turns out to be yes and numerous game theoretic models have now been developed that overturn the logic of the Chain Store Paradox.

An important common feature in many of these models is asymmetric information. Asymmetries between a lender and a firm regarding the firm's true profitability, or between an established firm and an upstart regarding the incumbent's cost can make predation a feasible and attractive strategy. Even without such uncertainty, long-term and/or tying contracts can also be used to deny rivals a market. Yet while the viability of predation in both theory and practice seems clear, the proper role of public policy remains clouded.

The principal problem is one of distinguishing aggressive pricing and other competitive strategies from ones that are truly predatory—profitable only if they succeed in driving a rival out of business. Some antitrust enforcement—especially those cases prosecuted under the Robinson–Patman Act in the first 35 years after it was passed—appear to have been misguided efforts to protect competitors and not competition. Both economists and the courts continue to struggle with the implementation of a workable definition of predation. Empirical work testing systematic entry deterrence has been challenged by the data requirements necessary to identify predatory behavior across a set of market data points. Nevertheless, this is an active research area in empirical industrial organization, holding promise for policy makers seeking to implement and enforce antitrust laws on predatory behavior.

Problems

1. Return to the Microhard Newvel game as discussed in section 13.1. Suppose now that Newvel's fixed costs are only $80 million per period. What would be the loan contract that a bank in a competitive banking industry would accept to loan Newvel $80 million in each period? Now suppose that the worst case scenario facing Newvel worsens. Specifically there is a 50 percent chance of earning $200 million and a 50 percent chance of earning only $40 million. Fixed costs are $80 million per period. Now what would be the loan contract that a bank in a competitive banking industry would accept to loan Newvel $80 million in each period?

2. An incumbent firm operates in a local computer market, which is a natural monopoly. That is, there is room for only one firm to sell profitably in this market. Market demand for the good is estimated to be $Q^D = 100 - P$. Another firm would like to enter this market, but only if the incumbent firm has a higher unit cost than it does. Specifically, there is a 25 percent chance that the incumbent is a low-cost firm, with a unit cost equal to 20, and there is a 75 percent chance that the incumbent is a high-cost firm with a unit cost of 30. The entrant's unit cost is 25. The entrant knows its costs but not that of the incumbent. The incumbent does know its unit cost. Market demand is common knowledge to both firms. The entrant, however, does get to observe the current or pre-entry market price at which the incumbent sells its good. If the entrant decides to enter the market it incurs a set-up cost of $1,000. Does the high-cost firm have an incentive to set a low price in order to masquerade as a low-cost firm?

3. Suppose a buyer is willing to pay up to 200 for one unit of some good. There is currently only one supplier of the good and the cost of supplying one unit of the good is 100. Next period a rival supplier may appear in the market. The rival's cost of supplying the good is not known. It is assumed to be uniformly distributed on the interval [50, 150]. Describe a long-term contract that the current supplier can offer the buyer that will be attractive to the buyer and that at the same time will strengthen the monopoly power of the current supplier.

4. An incumbent firm has a cost function: $C_I = 100 + 1.5q_I^2$. Hence, its marginal cost is given by: $MC_I = 3q_I$. Recently, an upstart firm has entered the market. The upstart has the cost function: $C_U = 100 + 75q_U$. Suppose the incumbent sets a price of 74 and meets all the demand at that price. Demand is given by: $P = 100 - Q$.
   a. Does the incumbent's behavior violate the Areeda–Turner rule of selling below marginal cost?
   b. Does the incumbent's behavior violate the Areeda–Turner rule when average variable cost is used as a proxy for marginal cost?

References

Aghion, P. and P. Bolton. 1987. "Contracts as a Barrier to Entry." *American Economic Review* 77 (June): 388–401.

Areeda, P. E. and D. F. Turner. 1975. "Predatory Pricing and Related Practices under Section 2 of the Sherman Act." *Harvard Law Review* 88 (February): 697–733.

——. 1976. "Scherer on Predatory Pricing: A Reply." *Harvard Law Review* 89 (March): 891–900.

Baumol, W. J. 1979. "Quasi-permanence of Price Reductions: A Policy for Prevention of Predatory Pricing." *Yale Law Journal* 89, 1–26.

——. 1996. "Predation and the Logic of the Average Variable Cost Test." *Journal of Law & Economics* 39 (April): 49–72.

Benoit, J. P. 1984. "Financially Constrained Entry in a Game with Incomplete Information." *Rand Journal of Economics* 15 (Winter): 490–9.

Bolton, P. and D. Scharfstein. 1990. "A Theory of Predation Based on Agency Problems in Financial Contracting." *American Economic Review* 80 (March): 93–106.

Bork, R. 1978. *The Antitrust Paradox*. New York: Basic Books.

Brandeis, Louis. 1913. "Cutthroat Prices: The Competition That Kills." *Harpers Weekly* (15 November): 10–12.

Brodley, J., P. Bolton, and M. Riordan. 2001. "Predatory Pricing: Strategic Theory and Legal Policy." *Georgetown Law Review* 88 (August): 2239–330.

Burns, M. R. 1986. "Predatory Pricing and the Acquisition Cost of Competitors." *Journal of Political Economy* 94, (April): 266–96.

Cabral, L. M. B. and M. J. Riordan. 1997. "The Learning Curve, Predation, Antitrust, and Welfare." *Journal of Industrial Economics* 45 (June): 155–69.

Dixit, A. 1980. "The Role of Investment in Entry Deterrence." *Economic Journal* 90 (March): 95–106.

Easterbrook, F. H. 1984. "The Limits of Antitrust." *Texas Law Review* 63 (January): 1–40.

Ellison, G. and S. Ellison. 2006. "Strategic Entry Deterrence and the Behavior of Pharmaceutical Incumbents Prior to Patent Expiration." Working Paper, MIT Economics Department.

Fudenberg, D. and J. Tirole. 1986. "A Signal-jamming Theory of Predation." *Rand Journal of Economics* 17 (Autumn): 366–76.

Gabszewicz, J., L. Pepall, and J.-F. Thisse. 1992. "Sequential Entry with Brand Loyalty Caused by Consumer Entry-By-Doing." *Journal of Industrial Economics* 60 (December): 397–416.

Genesove, D. and W. Mullin. 1998. "Testing Static Oligopoly Models: Conduct and Cost in the Sugar Industry, 1890–1914." *Rand Journal of Economics* 14 (Summer): 355–77.

Gilbert, R. 1989. "Mobility Barriers and the Value of Incumbency." In R. Schamalansee and R. Willig, eds, *Handbook of Industrial Organization, Vol. 1.* Amsterdam: North-Holland.

Joskow, P. L. and A. K. Klevorick. 1979. "A Framework for Analyzing Predatory Pricing Policy." *Yale Law Journal* 89 (December): 213–70.

Koller, R. H. II. 1971. "The Myth of Predatory Pricing: An Empirical Study." *Antitrust Law & Economics Review* 4 (Summer): 105–43.

McGee, J. S., 1958. "Predatory Price Cutting: The Standard Oil (N.J.) Case." *Journal of Law and Economics* 1 (April): 137–69.

——. 1980. "Predatory Pricing Revisited." *Journal of Law and Economics* 23 (October): 289–330.

Milgrom, P. and J. Roberts. 1982. "Limit Pricing and Entry under Incomplete Information: An Equilibrium Analysis." *Econometrica* 50 (March): 443–60.

Ordover, J. A. and G. Saloner, 1989. "Predation, Monopolization and Antitrust." In R. Schmalansee and R. Willig, eds, *Handbook of Industrial Organization. Vol. 1.* Amsterdam: North-Holland, 537–95.

Ordover, J. A. and R. Willig. 1981. "An Economic Definition of Predation: Pricing and Product Innovation." *Yale Law Journal* 91 (November): 8–53.

Posner, R. 1976. *Antitrust Law: An Economic Perspective*. Chicago: University of Chicago Press.

Phlips, L. 1995. *Competition Policy: A Game Theoretic Analysis*. Cambridge: Cambridge University Press.

Rasmusen, E. 2007. *Games and Information*. 4th edition. Cambridge, MA: Blackwell.

Rasmusen, E., J. M. Ramseyer, and J. Wiley. 1991. "Naked Exclusion." *American Economic Review* 81 (December): 1137–45.

Saloner, G. 1987. "Predation, Mergers And Incomplete Information." *Rand Journal of Economics* 18 (Summer): 165–86.

Scherer, F. M. 1976. "Predatory Pricing and the Sherman Act: A Comment." *Harvard Law Review* 89 (March): 869–90.

Scott Morton, F. 1997. "Entry and Predation: British Shipping Cartels, 1879–1929." *Journal of Economics and Management Strategy* 6 (Winter): 679–724.

——. 2000. "Barriers to Entry, Brand Advertising, and Generic Entry in the U.S. Pharmaceutical Industry." *International Journal of Industrial Organization* 18 (October): 1085–124.

Tirole, J. 1988. *The Theory of Industrial Organization*. Cambridge. MA: MIT Press.

Williamson, O. E. 1977. "Predatory Pricing: A Strategic and Welfare Analysis." *Yale Law Journal* 87 (December): 284–340.

Yamey, Basil, S. 1972. "Predatory Price Cutting: Notes and Comments." *Journal of Law and Economics* 15 (April): 129–42.

Yergin, D. 1991. *The Prize*. New York: Simon and Schuster.

14

Price Fixing and Repeated Games

In February 2007, the European Union Competition Directorate imposed their largest-ever fines on companies found guilty of colluding to fix prices. Five elevator manufacturers were fined a total of €992 million (approximately $1.4 billion) for operating a cartel that controlled prices in Germany, Belgium, Luxembourg, and the Netherlands. ThuysenKrupp received the heaviest fine, more than €479 million, since it was judged to be a "repeat offender" by the Commission. Otis was fined €225 million, Schindler €144 million, Kone €142 million, and Mitsubishi's Dutch subsidiary €1.8 million.[1]

The elevator case came just one month after another case involving gas insulated switch-gear projects in which the Commission imposed fines totally €750 million on 11 companies for their parts in a price-fixing cartel. In this case, the largest fine of €396.5 million was imposed on Siemens, Germany. This case is particularly interesting because it was broken open largely as a result of the Commission's leniency policy. Under that policy, the first firm in a conspiracy to confess and "fink" on its co-conspirators gets a much reduced penalty. In fact, the finking firm in the switch-gear case, ABB Switzerland, was granted full immunity and paid no penalties in return for its confession and provision of information to the authorities. That reflects a considerable savings from the €215 million it would otherwise have had to pay as a repeat offender.

Action to curb the activities of cartels has been equally active in the United States.[2] The Department of Justice has recently imposed a total of more than $732 million on companies operating a cartel to control the pricing of dynamic random access memory (DRAM). This includes a fine of $300 million imposed in 2005 on Samsung, the second-largest fine ever imposed on a single firm. The largest fine remains the $500 million penalty imposed in 1999 on Swiss pharmaceutical company Hoffman-LaRoche for its role in running a decade-long conspiracy to restrict competition and fix vitamin prices worldwide.

Table 14.1 shows the firms and products involved in the more than two dozen price-fixing cases this century in which the fine exceeded $10 million. Figure 14.1 shows the sharp increase in fines that has accompanied antitrust enforcement in recent years.

---

[1] Details of the European Union cases can be obtained at http://ec.europa.eu/comm/competition/antitrust/cases/index.html.

[2] Details can be found at http://www.usdoj.gov/atr.

Table 14.1 Violations yielding a corporate fine of $10 million or more since 2000

Firm	Year	Product	Fine (U.S. dollars, millions)
Samsung Electronics Company, Ltd. and Samsung Semiconductor, Inc.	2006	DRAM	300
Hynix Semiconductor, Inc.	2005	DRAM	185
Infineon Technologies AG	2004	DRAM	160
Mitsubishi Corp.	2001	Graphite Electrodes	134
Elpida Memory, Inc.	2006	DRAM	84
Dupont Dow Elastomers L.L.C.	2005	Chloroprene Rubber	84
Bayer AG	2004	Rubber Chemicals	66
Bilhar International Establishment	2002	Construction	54
Daicel Chemical Industries, Ltd.	2000	Sorbates	53
ABB Middle East & Africa Participations AG	2001	Construction	53
Crompton	2004	Rubber Chemicals	50
Sotheby's Holdings, Inc.	2001	Fine Arts Auctions	45
Odfjell Seachem AS	2003	Parcel Tanker Shipping	43
Bayer Corporation	2004	Polyester Polyols	33
Philipp Holzmann AG	2000	Construction	30
Irving Materials, Inc.	2005	Ready Mix Concrete	29
Arteva Specialties	2003	Polyester Staple	29
Jo Tankers, B.V.	2004	Parcel Tanker Shipping	20
Merck KgaA	2000	Vitamins	14
Degussa-Huls AG	2000	Vitamins	13
Akzo Nobel Chemicals, BV	2001	Monochloracetic Acid	12
Hoechst Aktiengesellschaft	2003	Monochloracetic Acid	12
Ueno Fine Chemicals Industry, Ltd.	2001	Sorbates	11
Zeon Chemicals L.P.	2005	NBR	11
De Beers Centenary AG	2004	Industrial Diamonds	10
Morganite, Inc.	2003	Carbon Products	10

Source: U.S. Department of Justice, Antitrust Division, www.usdoj.gov/atr

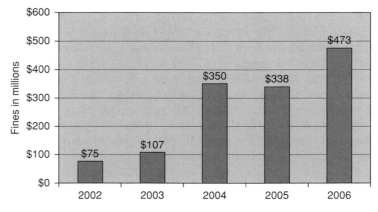

Figure 14.1 Criminal antitrust fines for fiscal years 2002–6
Source: U.S. Department of Justice, Antitrust Division, www.usdoj.gov/atr

As both Table 14.1 and Figure 14.1 illustrate, the foregoing examples are just a few of the many cartels that have been successfully prosecuted over the past few years. Together, these cases and the supporting data illustrate two important points. First, it is clear that cartels happen. There appears to be no shortage of firms that enter into collusive agreements to fix prices and avoid competition. This is so despite the many difficulties conspiring firms must overcome in order to implement such collusion. Perhaps more tellingly, firms appear to enter price-fixing agreements frequently despite the fact that both the antitrust laws of the United States and the legal framework established in Europe's Treaty of Rome, as well as the laws of most other nations, are explicit in making such collusion illegal.[3]

The second fact revealed by Table 14.1 and Figure 14.1 is that government agencies can and sometimes do catch the culprits. The recent historical experience in both Europe and the United States suggests that the ability of legal authorities to uncover and prosecute cartel conspirators successfully has been greatly enhanced by the use of leniency programs that offer either a reduced penalty or amnesty to the first cartel member that cooperates with officials. Of course, we do not know how many cartels remain undetected. The record of the last several years, however, must surely be regarded as encouraging.

The obvious reason why firms choose to break the law and enter into collusive price fixing arrangements, risking fines and even imprisonment, is profit. Competing firms recognize that by limiting competition they may be able to replicate the monopoly outcome and maximize their joint profits. However, the cooperative monopoly outcome is rarely if ever the Nash equilibrium outcome of strategic interaction between two or more firms. This means that achieving a cooperative monopoly outcome requires overcoming the fact of life that cooperating is not a best response.

To be specific, in any collusive price-fixing agreement each member must resist the strong temptation to cheat on the agreement. Why is that temptation so strong? To begin with, when all other firms are charging a high price, any one firm cannot help but realize that it can reap enormous profits by charging a somewhat lower price that will attract lots of customers from the high-priced conspirators. Further, each firm will not only recognize this opportunity for itself but also understand that other cartel members face the same temptation. The fear that others will cheat also acts as a powerful incentive for a cartel member to deviate from the agreement before others do.

If the agreement to collude was a legally enforceable contract, cheating would not be much of a problem. However, in the language of U.S. antitrust law, price-fixing agreements are *per se* illegal. Essentially, there is no acceptable defense. The firms cannot argue that there is some "reasonable explanation" for the collusion or that price fixing is necessary to prevent ruinous competition that would lead to the industry being monopolized.[4] Hence, cartel members cannot call on the courts to enforce their agreements. This then raises the question of how firms effectively enforce and execute any collusive agreement that they make. Given the temptation that members have to cheat, some sort of enforcement is likely to be necessary for a collusive agreement to hold. The fact that a formal contract is not enforceable does, however, have one small plus for the conspirators. It means that no such written contract is ever created, and this makes life more difficult for the antitrust authorities. In the absence of such a document the existence of the crime can be hard to prove.

---

[3]   If anything, the language of European Union law is even stronger in that it also treats "concerted practices" based upon a "concordance of wills" as *per se* illegal. In practice, however, the U.S. and European policy is nearly identical.

[4]   This argument was tried but rejected in the *Trans-Missouri* case, 166, U.S. 290 (1897).

In this chapter and the next, we explore the balance between the various forces just described. Specifically, we investigate the incentives to form cartels, the temptations of cartel members to cheat on the price-fixing agreement, the enforcement mechanisms that cartels may use to prevent such cheating, and the ability of the antitrust authorities to deter cartel formation. For the most part, we focus on the underlying theory in this chapter and reserve for the next one a discussion of the collusion in practice.

14.1   THE CARTEL'S DILEMMA

The motivation to form a price-fixing cartel is obvious. The profit of a monopolist is the maximum profit the industry can earn. By acting as "one," the cartel members hope to achieve that monopoly profit as a group. Since that is the maximum industry profit it follows that there is, in principle, some way to share that profit so that all firms (though not consumers) are better off with the cartel than without it. However, the challenge the firms face in forming a cartel to increase prices *and sustain the increased prices* is equally clear. At the price set by the cartel, each firm's price–cost margin is relatively large, with price significantly in excess of marginal cost. This gives each individual firm a strong profit incentive to sell a little more output—to cheat on the agreement. Yet if every firm acts on this incentive and chisels on the agreement by selling a little more, the extra output on the market will not be a little but a lot. Market price will fall and the price-fixing agreement will break down.

Another factor that complicates price-fixing is the fear of discovery and legal prosecution. Most antitrust law makes collusive behavior illegal. In the United States, the courts have consistently refused to consider any mitigating circumstances that might justify collusion.

Reality Checkpoint

School for Scandal—Bid Rigging by Suppliers to New York City Schools

On June 1, 2000 almost all of the companies that supply food to New York City's schoolchildren were charged in a bid-rigging scheme that overcharged the city at least $21 million for frozen goods and fresh produce. Twelve of the officials and six of the companies involved immediately pleaded guilty. Some of these defendants were also charged with rigging the bids to supply schools in Newark as well. The defendants reportedly designated which of the companies would be the low bidder on several contracts with the New York Board of Education. The system of schools supervised by the Board services a student population of nearly 1.1 million and serves about 640,000 lunches and 150,000 breakfasts every day.

The school board buys more food than any other single U.S. customer except the Defense Department. The conspirators allegedly agreed on prices to bid for supplying such standard items as French fries, meat, and fish sticks. One firm would be designated as the low bidder and all others would either refrain from bidding or submit intentionally high or complementary bids on the contracts. The cartel also allegedly paid potential suppliers not to bid competitively, including a payment of $100,000 to one produce company.

Source: A. Smith, "N.Y. Schools' Food Suppliers Accused of Bid-rigging," *Washington Post*, June 2, 2000, p. A8.

That is, there is no defense[5] and the firms that are party to the agreement face potentially heavy legal penalties.[6] As a result, any cartel-like agreements that the firms make must necessarily be kept secret—covert as opposed to overt—so as to reduce the likelihood of being caught. Yet the more secretive the agreement is—the more hidden the firms' actions are—the more opportunities arise for firms to cheat on the agreement and sell more output without being caught. This, of course, undermines the cartel still further.

Some international cartels such as OPEC are, on the other hand, overt. Here, the members come from different countries at least some of which have governments that support the cartel. The diamond cartel De Beers is another example in this regard. While such cartels violate the antitrust laws of the U.S. and other nations, prosecution of these international cartels is difficult because it requires that one country reach into the sovereign affairs of others.[7] Nevertheless, even overt international cartels have to worry about members cheating or breaking the agreement because there is no supranational authority to enforce the agreement. Here too, the cartel is faced with the problem of how to implement its agreements.

Stories of cheating and agreement breakdown have accompanied virtually all of the major cartels such as the electrical conspiracy of the 1950s, OPEC, and the NASDAQ pricing agreement (see Chapter 15). In order to understand how cartels might work, we can begin by understanding why they might not and identify the sources of conflict between cartel members.[8]

A good place to begin is with the simple Cournot duopoly model that we introduced in section 9.3 in Chapter 9. There we had two identical firms, each producing the same good and facing the same costs of production. Suppose, for example, that the inverse market demand curve for this duopoly market is described by the linear function, $P = 150 - Q$, where Q is total industry output and $Q = q_1 + q_2$ is the sum of outputs produced by firms 1 and 2, respectively. Assume also that the marginal cost of production is the same for each firm and constant at \$30 per unit.

When the firms act noncooperatively, each firm maximizes profit by choosing an output on its best response function. Given this demand function, we know that firm 1's best response function is $q_1^* = 60 - q_2/2$, and firm 2's is $q_2^* = 60 - q_1/2$. From these best response functions it is easy to confirm that in a Cournot–Nash equilibrium each firm chooses to produce an output level $q_1^* = q_2^* = 40$, which leads to an aggregate market output of $Q^C = 80$ and to a market-clearing price $P^C = \$70$. In this Cournot–Nash equilibrium each firm earns profit of $\pi_i^C = \$1,600$.

How do matters change if instead the firms cooperate with each other and form a cartel? Ideally, the cartel will act like a pure monopolist, in which case it agrees on a joint output of $Q^M = 60$, with each firm producing a share $q_i^M = 30$. As a result, the market-clearing price rises to $P^M = \$90$, giving the aggregate cartel or industry profit of $\pi^M = \$3,600$. Dividing this equally between the two firms, gives each a profit of $\pi_i^M = \$1,800$ which is greater than the profit earned in the Cournot–Nash noncooperative outcome.

[5] See Chapter 1 for a brief history of earlier antitrust cases and a discussion of how price-fixing agreements have been viewed by the courts as *per se* violations of Section 1 of the Sherman Act and hence have been uniformly condemned.

[6] Posner (1970) found that cartels were more active when the regulatory authorities were relatively lax in their enforcement of antitrust legislation.

[7] It is worth noting, however, that the United Sates has become increasingly active in pursuing international cartels.

[8] A terrific guide to the intuition underlying the cartel problem and, indeed, all of game theory is Schelling (1960).

Cooperation obviously pays but the cartel solution has one problem: the temptation that both firms have to cheat on their agreement. We know this for one very simple reason. The cooperative output levels of $q_1^M = q_2^M = 30$ do not constitute a pair of best responses. That is, 30 is not firm 1's best response to firm 2's production of 30, and similarly, 30 is not firm 2's best response to firm 1's production of 30. If firm 1 believes that firm 2 is going to stick to their agreement, then firm 1's best course of action is to produce an output q_1^d where the superscript d denotes defecting from the agreement and q_1^d is a best response to $q_2^M = 30$. From firm 1's best response function we can see that $q_1^d = 60 - q_2^M/2 = 45$. With firm 1 producing 45 and firm 2 producing 30, total output will then be $Q^d = 75$, which leads to a price of $P^d = \$75$. As a result, the profit to firm 1 is now $\pi_1 = \$2,025$, noticeably higher than the $1,800 it earned by acting cooperatively. Thus, firm 1 has a real incentive to break the agreement. Of course, when it does, it drives down the profit at firm 2 to $\pi_2 = \$1,350$. But firm 1 did not go into business to make firm 2 rich. Firm 1's management cares only about firm 1's profit and if firm 2 is really going to produce 30 units, then firm 1 maximizes its profit by producing 45 units.

The non-cooperative Cournot–Nash solution $q_1^* = q_2^* = 40$ is, of course, a pair of best responses. And for this example, the Cournot outcome is the only Nash equilibrium. This is made clear by the payoff matrix of Table 14.2(a). The unfortunate fact of life for the would-be colluding firms is that the collusive outcome $q_1 = q_2 = 30$ cannot be supported by any equilibrium strategies available to these firms. Each firm has a stronger profit incentive to defect or to cheat upon the cooperative agreement than to stick with it.[9]

What if the two firms compete in prices rather than in quantities? Now we have the Bertrand duopoly case. We know from our discussion of the Bertrand model in section 10.1, Chapter 10, that when the two firms act noncooperatively competition for customers drives price down to marginal cost. In our example, the Bertrand outcome has both firms setting a price of $30. Aggregate demand is $Q^B = 120$, which will be shared equally by the two firms. Both firms break even with profit to each firm of $\pi_i^B = 0$.

If the firms enter into a price-fixing agreement they will earn maximum industry profit by agreeing to set the monopoly price. So each firm sets a price of $90, aggregate demand is 60 units, again shared equally between the two firms, and each firm earns a profit of $\pi_i^M = \$1,800$. The temptation to cheat is, if anything, even stronger in the Bertrand case. Suppose that firm 1 believes that firm 2 will set a price of $90. Then firm 1 knows that it can win the entire market by just undercutting firm 2, perhaps by setting a price of $89.50. Aggregate demand at this price is 60.5 units. Firm 1's profit is approximately $3,600 while firm 2 sells nothing and so makes nothing.

Of course, firm 2 can make the same calculations, as a result of which we obtain the payoff matrix of Table 14.2(b). As in the Cournot case, the only Nash equilibrium to this game has both firms cheating on their agreement and charging a price that is arbitrarily close to marginal cost and making a profit that is arbitrarily close to zero rather than the significantly greater returns they would both make if they could only enforce their agreement.

The games we have just described and illustrate in Table 14.2 are examples of many games in which players share possibilities for mutual gain that cannot be realized because

---

[9]   Throughout this and succeeding chapters we restrict our analysis to pure strategies. The reader should be aware, however, that the analysis can be extended, with some qualifications, to include mixed strategies: see, for example, Harsanyi (1973).

Table 14.2a Payoffs (U.S. dollars, thousands) to cooperation (*M*) and defection (*D*) in the Cournot duopoly game

		Strategy for firm 2	
		Cooperate (*M*)	Defect (*D*)
Strategy for firm 1	Cooperate (*M*)	($1.8, $1.8)	($1.35, $2.025)
	Defect (*D*)	($2.025, $1.35)	($1.6, $1.6)

Table 14.2b Payoffs (U.S. dollars, thousands) to cooperation (*M*) and defection (*D*) in the Bertrand duopoly game

		Strategy for firm 2	
		Cooperate (*M*)	Defect (*D*)
Strategy for firm 1	Cooperate (*M*)	($1.8, $1.8)	($0, $3.6)
	Defect (*D*)	($3.6, $0)	(ε, ε)

of a conflict of interest. Such games are often referred to as "prisoners' dilemma" games because one of the earliest illustrations of this case involved dealings between a prosecutor and two suspects (see Practice Problem 14.1, below).

Each firm has a mutual interest in cooperating and achieving the monopoly outcome. However, there is also a conflict. If one firm cooperates and sticks to the agreement, then the other firm can do much better for itself in terms of profit by deviating from the cooperative agreement and producing more output in the Cournot case, or lowering price in the Bertrand case. In deciding whether to cooperate or not each firm must take this conflict of interest into account. In so doing, each firm could reason as follows: "If I cooperate and the other firm cooperates, then we share the monopoly profit. However, if the other firm does not cooperate while I do, then I lose a lot of profit. If, on the other hand, I don't cooperate and the other firm does, then I make a lot of money; and if the other firm does not cooperate, then it's as if we were playing noncooperatively anyway. No matter what the other firm does, I am better off not cooperating."

If both firms follow the logic just described, we will not observe cooperation. Such is the prisoners' dilemma. Together, both firms are worse off not cooperating than if they cooperate. Individually, however, each firm gains by not cooperating. Unless there is some way to overcome this conflict, it would appear that antitrust policy need not be terribly worried about cartels because logically they should not happen. But cartels do happen. The evidence is compelling that collusive agreements are not uncommon and firms do pursue cooperative strategies. The prisoner's dilemma argument cannot be the full story. There must be some way that firms can create incentives that will sustain cartel agreements among them.

14.1

Jacoby and Myers are two attorneys suspected of mail fraud in the small principality of Zenda. In an effort to obtain a confession, Sergeant First Brigadier Morse has had the two suspects brought in and subjected to separate questioning. Each is given the following options: (1) Confess (and implicate the other); or (2) Do not confess. Morse indicates to each suspect that if only one suspect confesses that one will be released in return for providing evidence against the other and spends no time in jail. The one not confessing in this case will "have the book thrown at her" and do ten years. If both confess, Morse indicates that he will be a bit more lenient and each will spend six years behind bars. When asked what will happen if neither confesses, Morse responds that he will find some small charge that he knows will stick, so that, in this case, each will do at least one year.

Using Confess and Do not confess as the possible actions of either Jacoby or Myers, derive the payoff matrix and Nash equilibrium for the game between these prisoners of Zenda.

Since the 1970s, economists have come to understand that there is a clear way around the logic of the prisoner's dilemma. The way around requires that firms look at their strategic interaction from a somewhat different perspective than that described in the static Cournot and Bertrand models. Specifically, the different perspective is not found in a single-period framework in which the colluding firms interact only once but rather a dynamic one in which the strategic interaction is repeated over time. This, of course, is a quite reasonable change. The firms considering the formation of a cartel are very likely to have been competing with each other for some time—otherwise how did they meet in the first place? More importantly, they are likely to believe that their market interactions will continue or repeat into the future.

Recognizing this "shadow of the future" fundamentally alters the incentives that firms have to defect on collusive agreements. When market interaction is repeated over and over again it is possible for the firms that are party to a collusive agreement to reward "good" behavior by sticking with the agreement and to punish "bad" behavior by guaranteeing a breakdown in the cartel. In order to work out such a strategy we need to analyze what is called a repeated game. Repeated games are dynamic games in which a simultaneous market interaction is repeated in each stage of the dynamic game. By moving from one period to many, we are changing the rules of the game. The appropriate strategies therefore also change. How and why the firms' strategic choices change in the dynamic setting of repeated games is the subject matter of the next section.

14.2 REPEATED GAMES

Let's return to the game of Table 14.2(a). Collusion between the two firms to produce the monopoly output is unsustainable in that it is not a Nash equilibrium to the single-period game. Now suppose that firm 2 for example thinks forward a bit, knowing that its interactions with firm 1 are going to occur several, perhaps many, times. Then firm 2's calculations may go very differently. Firm 2 might calculate as follows: "If I cheat on the cartel my profits go up to $2,025 and I gain a one-off increase in profits of $225. But then the cartel falls apart, and we revert to the non-cooperative, Cournot, equilibrium with profits to me of $1,600 per period, so that I earn $200 less per period than if I had not cheated in the first place. Is it worth my while to cheat?"

The foregoing reasoning suggests that if firm 2's horizon is sufficiently long and if firm 2 does not discount the future too heavily, then contrary to our earlier analysis, firm 2 may decide not to leave the cartel. The short, one-period gain of $225 may be offset by the loss of $200 every period thereafter. Whether or not this is in fact the case—whether or not firm 2's calculations are fully reasonable—remains to be seen. Nevertheless, one can see that moving from a static one-period game to a repeated game may alter a firm's thinking in a manner that dramatically raises the profitability of cooperative, cartel behavior.

The reason that repetition makes successful collusion more likely is that when the market interaction among firms extends over a number of periods, there is the real possibility that cartel members are able to retaliate against defectors. Because potential defectors will rationally anticipate such retaliation, punishment can act as a deterrent—stopping the non-cooperative behavior before it starts.

The formal description of a strategy for a repeated game is quite complicated because current and future actions are now conditional on past actions. That is, a firm's action today depends critically on what has happened in previous plays of the game. To get some idea of how rapidly the complexity grows, consider the simple Cournot game in Table 14.2(a). Suppose that this game, which we will call the stage game, is played 3 times in succession. At the end of the first round there are 4 possible outcomes, that is, 4 possible histories. At the end of the second round, we have 16 possible game histories—four second-round outcomes for each of the first-round results. By the third round, 64 game histories are possible—and this assumes that there are only 2 players with 2 possible actions to take in each round. Since, formally speaking, a strategy must define how a player acts at each round of play depending on the precise history of the game to that point, the complexity introduced by considering repeated games is formidable.

There are, fortunately, a few mental shortcuts available to us. The critical concept in this regard is the familiar one of Nash equilibrium. We know that resolving the outcome of any game requires identifying the game's Nash equilibrium (or equilibria). The same holds true in repeated games. It is possible to identify the Nash equilibrium or equilibria for a repeated game relatively quickly if one keeps a few key principles clearly in mind. We can best illustrate these by working through our Cournot example.

Recall that when this game is played once its only equilibrium is that both firms defect. This is referred to as the "one-shot" equilibrium. Our interest is to see what happens when the firms interact with each other over and over again. We shall show that the key factor is whether the interaction is repeated over a finite (though perhaps large) number of periods or whether it goes on forever indefinitely. In other words, we can separate repeated games into two classes: (1) those in which the number of repetitions is finite *and known to the potentially colluding firms*, and (2) those in which the number of repetitions is infinite.

14.2.1   Finitely Repeated Games

When is it reasonable to assume that the number of times that the firms interact is finite *and known to both firms*? At least three situations come to mind. First, it may be that the firms exploit an exhaustible and non-renewable resource such as oil or natural gas. Secondly, the firms might operate in a market with proprietary knowledge protected by patents. All patents are awarded for a finite period—in the United States, the duration is 20 years dated from the filing of the application. Once the patent expires a market protected from entry suddenly becomes competitive. For example, as the patents on serotonin-based antidepressants, Prozac, Zoloft, and Paxil, expire the manufacturers of these drugs can expect a major increase in the number of competitors in this market, ending the market interaction of the original three firms that had previously prevailed. Finally, while we conventionally equate the players in the game with firms, the truth is that it is ultimately individuals who make the output or price decisions. The same management teams can be expected to be around for only a finite number of years. When there is a major change in management at one or more of the firms the game is likely to end. Often this end can be foreseen.

It turns out that what happens in a one-shot or stage game gives us a very good clue to what is likely to happen in a repeated game when the number of repetitions is finite. After all, a one-period game is just one that is very finite. Consider a simple extension of our Cournot game from one-period to two and determine what the equilibrium will be in this limited but nonetheless repeated setting.[10] When we do this we find that the two-period repeated game will have the same non-cooperative outcome in each round as the one-shot game. To see why, consider the following alternative strategy for firm 1:

First play: Cooperate.
Second play: Cooperate if firm 2 cooperated in the first play, otherwise Defect.

The idea behind this strategy is clear enough. Start off on a friendly footing. If this results in cooperation in the first round, then in the second round firm 1 promises to continue to cooperate. However, should firm 2 fail to reciprocate firm 1's initial cooperation in the first round then in the second round firm 1 will "take the gloves off" and fight back.

The problem with this strategy is that it suffers from the same basic credibility problem that afflicted many of the predatory threats that we discussed in the preceding chapters. To see why, suppose firm 2 chooses to cooperate in the first round. Now think of firm 2's position at the start of its second and last interaction with firm 1. The history of play to that point is one in which both firms adopted cooperative behavior in the first round. Further, firm 2 has a promise from firm 1 that, because firm 2 cooperated in the first round, firm 1 will continue to do so in the second. However, this promise is worthless. When firm 2 considers the payoff matrix for the last round, the firm cannot fail to note that—regardless of firm 1's promise—the dominant strategy for firm 1 in the last round is not to cooperate. This breaks firm 1's promise, but there is nothing firm 2 can subsequently do to punish firm 1 for breaking its promise. There is no third round in which to implement such punishment. Firm 2 should rationally anticipate that firm 1 will adopt the noncooperative behavior in the last round.

Firm 2 has just discovered that any strategy for firm 1 that involves playing the cooperative strategy in the final round is not credible, i.e., it is not subgame perfect. The last round of the game is a subgame of the complete game, and a strategy that calls for firm 1 to cooperate in this last period cannot be part of a Nash equilibrium in that period. No matter what has transpired in the first round, firm 1 can be counted upon to adopt noncooperative behavior in the final period of play. Of course, the same is true when viewed from firm 1's perspective. Firm 2's strategy in the last round is likewise not to cooperate. In short, both firms realize that the only rational outcome in the second round is the noncooperative equilibrium in which each earns a profit of $1,600.

---

[10]   Even though the game lasts for two market periods we will keep things simple and assume that profits in the second period are not discounted. In other words we will assume that the discount factor $R = 1$ or, equivalently, the interest rate $r = 0\%$. See the discussion of discounting in Chapter 2.

The fact that we have identified the equilibrium in the final round may seem like only a small part of the solution that we were originally seeking—especially if the game has 10 or 100 rounds instead of just 2. However, as you may recall from the Chain Store Paradox in section 11.4, Chapter 11, the outcome for the terminal round can lead directly to a solution of the entire game. Consider again our two-period repeated game. In the first round firm 1 will see that firm 2's first-round strategy is not to cooperate. The only hope that firm 1 has of dissuading firm 2 from such noncooperative action in the first round is to promise cooperation in the future if firm 2 cooperates today. Yet such a promise is not credible. No matter how passionately firm 1 promises to cooperate tomorrow in return for cooperation today, firm 2 will recognize that when tomorrow actually comes, firm 1 will not cooperate. It follows that the only hope firm 1 had of dissuading firm 2 from noncooperative action in the first round is gone.

Again symmetry implies the same reasoning holds true for any hope firm 2 had of inducing cooperation from firm 1. Hence, we have identified the subgame perfect equilibrium for the entire game. Both firms adopt strategies that call for noncooperative behavior in *both* period one and period two. In other words, running the game for two periods produces outcomes identical to that observed by playing it as a one-period game.

14.2

Consider our first example but now assume that the interaction between the firms extends to three periods. What will be the outcome in the final period? What does this imply about the incentive to cooperate in period two? If both firms believe that there will be no cooperation in either period two or period three, will either cooperate in period one?

Practice Problem

We have identified the subgame perfect equilibrium for our example when the game is played for two periods. However, as Practice Problem 14.2 illustrates, our reasoning also extends to a solution for the game whether it is played two, three, or any finite number of periods, T. In all such cases, no strategy that calls for cooperation in the final period is subgame perfect. Therefore, no such strategy can be part of the final equilibrium. In the last period, each firm always chooses not to cooperate regardless of the history of the game to that point. But this means that the same noncooperative behavior must also characterize the penultimate, or $T - 1$, period. The only possible gain that might induce either firm 1 or firm 2 to cooperate in period $T - 1$ is the promise of continued cooperation from its rival in the future. Since such a promise is not credible, both firms adopt noncooperative behavior in both period $T - 1$ and period T. In other words, any strategy that calls for cooperative behavior in either of the last two periods can also be ruled out as part of the final equilibrium. An immediate implication is that a three-period game must be one in which the players simply repeat the one-shot Nash equilibrium three times.

We can reiterate this logic for larger and larger values of T. The outcome will always be the same Nash equilibrium as in our first example no matter how many times it is played, so long as that number is finite and known. The one-shot Nash equilibrium is just repeated T times, with each firm taking noncooperative action in every period.

The foregoing result is by no means a special case. Rather, the foregoing analysis is an example of a general theorem first proved by Nobel Prize winner Reinhard Selten (1973).

Selten's theorem: If a game with a unique equilibrium is played finitely many times, its solution is that equilibrium played each and every time. Finitely repeated play of a unique Nash equilibrium is the Nash equilibrium of the repeated game.[11]

Introducing repetition into a game theoretic framework adds history as an element to the analysis. When players face each other over and over again, they can adopt strategies that base today's action on the behavior of their rivals in previous periods. This is what rewards and punishments are all about. What Selten's theorem demonstrates is that history, or rewards and punishments, really do not play a role in a finitely repeated game in which the one-shot or stage game has a unique Nash equilibrium.

Nevertheless, we know that effective collusion does occur in the real world. So, there must be some way to escape the logic of Selten's theorem. In fact, the "solution" is suggested by the theorem itself. We have so far limited our analysis to finitely repeated games in which the firms understand exactly when their interaction together will end. If firms think that their interactions will be repeated over and over, indefinitely, it turns out that the outcome can be radically different.

14.2.2   Infinitely or Indefinitely Repeated Games

There are situations in which the assumption of finite repetition makes a great deal of sense. However, for many, and perhaps most, situations it does not. Firms may be regarded as having an infinite or, more precisely, an indefinite life. General Motors may not last forever but nobody inside or outside the giant automaker works on the assumption that there is some known date T periods from now at which GM will cease to exist. Our assumption that everyone knows the final period with certainty is probably far too strong. The more likely situation is that after any given period, the players see some positive probability that the game will continue one more round. So, while firms may understand that the game will not last forever, they cannot look ahead to any particular period as the last. Alternatively, as long as there is some chance of continuing on it makes sense to treat General Motors and other firms as if they will continue indefinitely

Why is this important? Recall the argument that we used to show that finite repetition will not lead to cooperation in a Cournot, or Bertrand game. Cooperation is not an equilibrium in the final period T, and so is not an equilibrium in $T - 1$, and so in $T - 2$ and so on. With infinite or indefinite repetition of the game this argument fails *because there is no known final period*. So long as the probability of continuing into another round of play is positive, there is, probabilistically speaking, reason to hope that the next round will be played cooperatively and so reason to cooperate in the present. Whether that motivation is strong enough to overcome the short-run gains of defection, or can be made so by means of some reward-and-punishment strategy will depend on certain key factors that we discuss below. We will see that once we permit the possibility that strategic interaction will continue indefinitely, the possibility of successful collusion becomes a good bit more real.

In developing the formal analysis of an infinitely repeated game we must first consider how a firm values a profit stream of infinite duration. The answer is simply that it will apply the discount factor R to the expected cash flow in any period. Suppose that a firm knows that its profits are going to be π in each play of the game. Suppose also that the firm knows that in each period there is a probability p that the market interaction will continue into the

---

[11]   A formal proof can be found, for example, in Eichberger (1993).

next period. Then starting from an initial period 0, the probability of reaching period 1 is p, the probability of reaching period 2 is p^2, of reaching period 3 is p^3, ... of reaching period t is p^t and so on. Accordingly, the profit stream that the firm actually expects to receive in period t is $p^t \pi$.

Now assume the firm's discount factor, R. The expected present value of this profit stream is given by:

$$V(\pi) = \pi + pR\pi + (pR)^2\pi + (pR)^3\pi + \ldots + (pR)^t\pi + \ldots \tag{14.1}$$

To evaluate $V(\pi)$ we use a simple trick. Rewrite equation (14.1) as:

$$V(\pi) = \pi + pR(\pi + pR\pi + (pR)^2\pi + (pR)^3\pi \ldots + (pR)^t\pi + \ldots) \tag{14.2}$$

Now note that the term in brackets is just $V(\pi)$ as given by equation (14.1) so (14.2) can be rewritten:

$$V(\pi) = \pi + pRV(\pi)$$

Solving this for $V(\pi)$ then gives:

$$V(\pi) = \frac{\pi}{1 - pR} = \frac{\pi}{1 - \rho} \tag{14.3}$$

where $\rho = pR$ can be thought of as a "probability-adjusted" discount factor. It is the product of the discount factor reflecting the interest rate and the belief the firm holds regarding the probability that the market will continue to operate from period to period.

At first sight, consideration of games that are infinite or indefinitely repeated, which are often referred to as supergames, may seem hopeless. Repetition allows history to figure in strategy making and with infinitely repeated play the number of possible histories also becomes infinite. Once again, however, we have a shortcut available to us. It turns out that the actual strategies on which firms rely to secure compliance with cartel policy can be made remarkably simple. The type of strategy that will work is called a *trigger strategy*. A player will play the cooperative action upon which the players have agreed as long as all the players have always stuck to the agreement. However, if any player should deviate from the agreement then the player will revert to the Nash equilibrium forever.

To see how a trigger strategy might work, consider a simple duopoly example.[12] Suppose that the firms formulate a price-fixing agreement that gives them both profits of π^M. Each firm knows that if it deviates optimally from this agreement it will earn in that period of deviation a profit of π^D. Finally, the Nash equilibrium profit to each firm is π^N. Common sense and our Cournot and Bertrand examples of Table 14.2 tell us that $\pi^D > \pi^M > \pi^N$.

Now consider the following trigger strategy:

Period 0: Cooperate.
Period $t \geq 1$: Cooperate if both firms have cooperated in every previous period. Switch to the Nash equilibrium forever if either player has defected in any previous period.

It should be clear why strategies of this type are called trigger strategies. Firm 1's switch to the Nash equilibrium is triggered by a deviation from the agreement by firm 2. The promise

---

[12]   Our analysis generalizes to an *n*-firm oligopoly as we note below.

or threat to make this move, that is, to punish firm 2, is credible precisely because it simply requires that firm 1 moves to the noncooperative Nash equilibrium.

To identify the conditions under which the adoption of this trigger strategy by both firms can work to achieve an equilibrium that is different from the one-shot noncooperative Nash equilibrium, consider again our duopoly example. Assume that at the beginning of the game both firms announce the trigger strategy just described. Now consider a possible deviation from the agreement by firm 2. We already understand the temptation to deviate. If firm 1 sticks by the cooperative agreement in any period then firm 2 can increase its profit in that period to π^D by defecting.

However, that gain lasts for only one period, given that firm 1 has adopted the trigger strategy. In the next period following firm 2's deviation, firm 1 retaliates by switching to the Nash equilibrium. Since firm 2's best response is to do the same, the result of its initial defection is that the one period of higher profit π^D is followed by an endless number of periods in which its profit is only π^N. This represents a real cost to firm 2 since, had it not broken the agreement, it could have enjoyed its share of the cartel profit, π^M indefinitely. In short, firm 1's adoption of the trigger strategy means that firm 2 realizes both a gain and a loss if it breaks the cartel agreement. The gain is an immediate, but only one-period rise in profit. The loss is a delayed, but permanent fall in profit in every period that the game continues thereafter.

The only way to compare the gain with the loss is in terms of present values. The present value of profits from sticking to the agreement is, using equation (14.3):

$$V^C = \pi^M + \rho\pi^M + \rho^2\pi^M + \ldots = \frac{\pi^M}{1 - \rho} \tag{14.4}$$

Now consider the present value of the profits that firm 2 makes if it deviates. We can always number the period in which firm 2 deviates as period 0 (today). Its profit stream from deviation is then:

$$V^D = \pi^D + \rho\pi^N + \rho^2\pi^N + \rho^2\pi^N + \ldots$$

$$= \pi^D + \rho[\pi^N + \rho\pi^N + \rho^2\pi^N + \ldots] = \pi^D + \frac{\rho\pi^N}{1 - \rho} \tag{14.5}$$

Cheating on the cartel is not profitable, and so the cartel is *self-sustaining* provided that $V^C > V^D$, which requires that:

$$\frac{\pi^M}{1 - \rho} > \pi^D + \frac{\rho\pi^N}{1 - \rho} \tag{14.6}$$

Multiplying both sides by $(1 - \rho)$ and simplifying gives:

$$V^C > V^D \Rightarrow \pi^M > (1 - \rho)\pi^D + \rho\pi^N \Rightarrow \rho(\pi^D - \pi^N) > \pi^D - \pi^M$$

In other words, the critical value of ρ above which defection on the cartel does not pay and so firms will voluntarily stick by the cartel agreement is:

$$\rho > \rho* = \frac{\pi^D - \pi^M}{\pi^D - \pi^N} \tag{14.7}$$

Equation (14.7) has a simple underlying intuition. Cheating on the cartel yields an immediate, one period gain of $\pi^D - \pi^M$. However, starting the next period and continuing through every period thereafter, the punishment for cheating is a loss of profit of $\pi^M - \pi^N$. The present value of that loss starting next period is $(\pi^M - \pi^N)/(1 - p)$. Its present value as of today when the profit from cheating is realized is $p(\pi^M - \pi^N)/(1 - p)$. Cheating will be deterred if the gain is less than the cost when both are measured in present value terms, i.e., if $\pi^D - \pi^M < p(\pi^M - \pi^N)/(1 - p)$. It is easy to show that this condition is identical to that in equation (14.7). Because $\pi^D > \pi^M > \pi^N$ it follows that $p^* < 1$. Hence, *there is always a probability-adjusted discount factor above which a cartel is self-sustaining.*

Consider our two examples in Table 14.2. In the Cournot case we have $\pi^D = 2{,}025$, $\pi^M = 1{,}800$ and $\pi^N = 1{,}600$. Substituting into equation (14.7) the critical probability adjusted discount factor above which our Cournot duopolists can sustain their cartel is $p_C^* = 0.529$. In the Bertrand case $\pi^D = 3{,}600$, $\pi^M = 1{,}800$ and $\pi^N = 0$. The critical probability adjusted discount factor above which our Bertrand duopolists can sustain their cartel is $p_B^* = 0.5$. Practice Problem 14.3 below asks you to prove that these critical discount factors hold for *any* Cournot or Bertrand duopoly with linear demand and constant, equal marginal costs.

Suppose that both firms playing the Cournot game believe that their interaction will always be repeated with certainty, so that $p = 1$. Then the critical probability adjusted discount factor p_C^* corresponds to a pure discount factor of $R = 0.529$. That is, if $p = 1$, neither firm will deviate so long as the firm's interest rate r does not exceed 89 percent. Now suppose instead that both firms perceive only a 60 percent probability that their interaction lasts from one period to the next, i.e., $p = 0.6$. Now the cartel agreement is self-sustaining only when the pure discount factor $R > 0.529/0.6 = 0.882$. That is, successful collusion now requires that the interest rate r does not exceed 14.4 percent, which is a more restrictive requirement. This example points to a general result. An indefinitely lived cartel is more sustainable the greater is the probability that the firms will continue to interact and the lower is the interest rate.

Assume a duopoly and let demand be given by $P = A - BQ$. In addition, let both firms have the same marginal cost c. Show that:

14.3

a. If the firms compete in quantities, the probability adjusted discount factor must satisfy $p_C^* \geq 0.529$ for collusion to be sustained; and
b. If the firms compete in prices, the probability adjusted discount factor must satisfy $p_B^* \geq 0.5$ for collusion to be sustained.

Practice Problem

14.2.3 Some Extensions

Our analysis easily extends to cases where the number of firms is more than two. All we need do is to identify the three-firm level profits $\pi^D > \pi^M > \pi^N$ for each firm and substitute these values into equation (14.7) to identify the critical probability-adjusted discount factor for each firm.

However, there are two objections to trigger strategies. First, these strategies are based on the assumption that cheating on the cartel agreement is detected quickly and that punishment is swift. What if, as seems likely, it takes time for cartel members to discover a firm that is cheating and additional time to retaliate?

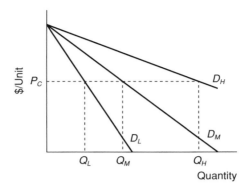

Figure 14.2   Cartel maintenance with uncertain demand
If demand is uncertain and varies between D_L and D_H with a mean of D_M, cartel members will not be able to tell whether a variation in their output is the result of normal variation in the market or cheating by other cartel members.

The fact that detection and punishment of cheaters takes time certainly makes sustaining the cartel more difficult. Delay allows the culprit to enjoy the gains for more periods and this raises the incentive to engage in cheating behavior. Nevertheless, this does not necessarily make collusion impossible. Trigger strategies can still work even if detection of cheating on the agreement takes more than one period, and even if it takes the remaining cartel members some time to agree on the proper punishment.

A second and related objection to the trigger strategy is that it is harsh and unforgiving because it does not permit mistakes. For example, suppose that market demand fluctuates within some known bounds, as shown in Figure 14.2, and that the cartel has agreed to set a price P^C or has agreed to production quotas that lead to that market price. In this setting, a cartel firm that observes a decline in its sales cannot tell whether this reduction is due to cheating by one of its partners or to an unanticipated reduction in demand. Yet under the simple trigger strategies we have been discussing, the firm is required quickly and permanently to move to the retaliatory behavior. Clearly, this will lead to some regret if the firm later discovers that its partners were innocent and that it has needlessly unleashed a damaging price war.[13]

This objection too can be overcome. The trick is to adopt a modified trigger strategy. For instance, the firm might only take retaliatory action if sales, or price fall outside some agreed range. The firm refrains from retaliation against minor infractions. A different modification would impose punishment swiftly after any deviation from the cartel agreement is observed but limit the period of punishment to a finite period of time. Thus, we can envision a trigger strategy of the form "I will switch to the Nash equilibrium for $\tau \geq 1$ periods if you deviate from our agreement but will then revert to our agreed cooperative strategies." This approach may mistakenly punish innocent cartel members, but by limiting the period of such punishment, it permits reestablishment of the cartel at a later date.

The point is that in an infinitely repeated game there are many trigger strategies that allow a cartel agreement to be sustained. Indeed, in some ways, there are almost too many. This

---

[13]   Two different views of oligopolistic behavior with uncertain demand that makes detection difficult may be found in Green and Porter (1984), and Rotemberg and Saloner (1986).

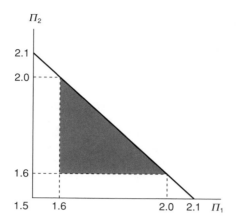

Figure 14.3 The Folk theorem
Any distribution of profits in the shaded area can be supported by a trigger strategy for some discount factor sufficiently close to unity.

point is made clear by what is known as the *Folk theorem* for infinitely repeated games (Friedman 1971):[14]

> *Folk theorem*: Suppose that an infinitely repeated game has a set of payoffs that exceed the one-shot Nash equilibrium payoffs for each and every firm. Then any set of feasible payoffs that are preferred by all firms to the Nash equilibrium payoffs can be supported as subgame perfect equilibria for the repeated game for some discount rate sufficiently close to unity.

We can illustrate the folk theorem using our first example. If the two firms collude to maximize their joint profits, they share aggregate profits of $3,600. If they act noncooperatively they each earn $1,600. The Folk theorem says that any cartel agreement in which each firm earns more than $1,600 and in which total profit does not exceed $3,600 can, at least in principle, be sustained as a subgame perfect equilibrium of the infinitely repeated game. The shaded region of Figure 14.3 shows the range of profits for this example that can be earned by each firm in a sustainable cartel.

A qualifying note should be added here. The Folk theorem does not say that firms can always achieve a total industry profit equal to that earned by a monopoly. It simply says that firms can do better than the noncooperative, Cournot–Nash or Bertrand–Nash equilibrium. The reason that exact duplication of monopoly may not be possible is that the monopoly outcome always results in the highest possible price relative to marginal cost. At such a high price, any cartel member can earn substantial short-term profit with even a small deviation from the cartel agreement. Consequently, duplicating the monopoly outcome gives members a tremendous incentive to cheat unless the probability adjusted discount factor is fairly large. Yet the incentive to deviate and break the monopoly agreement does not mean that no cartel can be sustained. Firms can still earn profits higher than the noncooperative equilibrium by means of a sustainable cartel agreement, even if they cannot earn the highest possible profits that the industry could yield. This is what the Folk theorem says.

---

[14] The term "Folk theorem" derives from the fact that this theorem was part of the "folklore" or oral tradition in game theory for years before Friedman wrote down a formal proof.

Reality Checkpoint

Was It to Their Credit That Visa and MasterCard Cooperated?

Together, the two major credit card companies, Visa and MasterCard, process 75 percent of the dollar volume of credit card transactions, with the split being two-thirds Visa and one-third MasterCard. Historically, both companies have operated as "membership corporations." Here, the members are banks that sit on the board of directors, choose the management, and serve on policy-making committees. The card companies issue cards to consumers and businesses, provide merchants with access to credit-processing networks, and allow banks to issue credit cards with access to their network. Before 1970, different banks controlled Visa and MasterCard. However, starting in the mid-1970s, Visa and MasterCard began to allow their member banks to join each other, a practice known in the industry as "duality." The result has been that the same set of banks controls both credit card networks.

In 1996, Wal-Mart Stores filed suit against Visa and MasterCard, alleging that the two networks were illegally tying their credit and debit products. They were later joined by several other retailers in a class action suit. Their complaint was that because of their common control, Visa and MasterCard did not compete against each other. In turn, it was argued that this lack of competition allowed the firms to impose harmful tying requirements that required a retailer to accept any bank debit card if it accepted the Visa or MasterCard. Wal-Mart and others had wanted to issue their own debit cards and felt the collusion between Visa and MasterCard prevented them from doing so. They further claimed that MasterCard and Visa charged $1.50 for a $100 debit card transaction while similar ATM networks charged only 14 to 30 cents. In 2003, Visa and MasterCard settled the case, agreeing to pay $3 billion to merchants over the next ten years, to lower their transaction fees, and to stop tying credit and debit card acceptance. Almost immediately, Wal-Mart and other retailers began to issue debit and credit cards of their own.

In 1998, almost simultaneously with these events, the Department of Justice filed suit against Visa and MasterCard charging a conspiracy in violation of the Sherman Act. The government charged that the duality arrangement itself was a conspiracy violation. It further argued that in cooperating with each other the two networks had consciously conspired to prevent the emergence of strong credit card rivals. In particular, both Visa and MasterCard prohibited their member banks from issuing American Express ("Amex") or Discover cards. The government provided quotes from company officials and internal records such as this 1992 quote from the Executive Vice President of Visa International that "it is very difficult for us to take a step, an aggressive step that hurts MasterCard because the same banks who sit there on the board, who are in Visa are also in MasterCard." There was also this 1997 quote from the President of MasterCard International U.S. Region that: "It is clear that because of duality today you don't see MasterCard and Visa in the marketplace attacking each other."

With respect to blocking entry, the government noted that processing transactions involves transmitting transaction data from a merchant's terminal to a central computer that directs the information to the appropriate card network for authorization and settlement. Visa and MasterCard permit banks to process transactions for both networks through a single merchant terminal, enhancing the ability of both networks to convince merchants to accept their cards. In response, both American Express and Discover developed their own acceptance terminals. Initially, they also entered into agreements with some Visa and MasterCard banks that each would allow the other to use their respective terminals. Very shortly, however, a number of other Visa and MasterCard banks complained that this was hurting their business. Soon afterwards, Visa and

MasterCard issued regulations preventing such sharing by their member banks. The government provided many similar examples of what appeared to be deliberate and coordinated efforts by Visa and MasterCard to prevent the emergence of strong rivals.

In October, 2004, after a very short, 34-day trial, the district court issued its finding that Visa and MasterCard were guilty of Sherman Act violations, mainly those that prevented the emergence of rivals. The decision was later upheld by an Appellate Court and the Supreme Court declined to question that judgment. Again, market reaction was swift. Banks belonging to the Visa and MasterCard networks immediately began to accept other cards. Competition seemed to be emerging as American Express quickly raised its market share by 3 percentage points.

Sources: *United States v. Visa U.S.A., Inc.*, 163 F.Supp.2d 322; and J. Kingston, "Credit Card Issuers Adjust to Open Field," *New York Times*, March 26, 2005, p. C4.

In sum, once we consider a framework of infinitely or indefinitely repeated interaction between firms, there is a real possibility for sustainable collusive behavior among these firms so long as the interest rate is not too high and the probability of their continued interaction is not too low. Indeed, the examples noted at the start of this chapter offer ample evidence that this is the case.

We have focused our attention on identifying conditions under which cartels are self-sustaining, but there are in addition other explicit actions that help cartel members sustain collusive agreements. There is ample evidence that cartel members engage in a whole series of actions to monitor compliance with the cartel agreement. Regular strategy meetings, usually in plush hotels and resorts, explicit checking on compliance by lower level executives, the formation of trade associations are all mechanisms that firms have used to sustain cartel agreements.[15] There appears then to be good reasons for the Justice Department and other antitrust authorities to worry about collusion.

14.3   COLLUSION: THE ROLE OF THE ANTITRUST AUTHORITIES

The Folk theorem teaches that authorities should not rely on cartels failing of their own accord as a result of cheating by cartel members. In a recent survey Levenstein and Suslow comment: "in many case studies, authors asserted that cheating was simply not a problem for the cartel." (2006, p. 78). Explicit action is needed to search for and prosecute cartels if they are to be apprehended. Such action will do more than simply disrupt existing cartels. Because of its deterrent effect, the prosecution of price-fixing arrangements should also lead fewer collusive agreements to emerge in the first place.[16] We now present a simple model that captures the impact of enforcement on cartels.

Suppose that a cartel has been formed and that it satisfies equation (14.7) so that it is potentially self-sustaining. Now introduce an antitrust authority, which is charged with looking for and attempting to prosecute cartels. In any given period assume that there is a

---

[15]   *The Informant* (2000) by Kurt Eichenwald provides an informative and amusing illustration of how the lysine cartel that operated in the 1990s was sustained and also eventually prosecuted.

[16]   The approach that we take in this section is simplified and adapted from Motta and Polo (2003).

probability a that the authority will investigate our cartel. If no investigation is instituted the cartel continues to the next year. The investigation takes one period and we assume that there is a probability s that it leads to successful prosecution, in which case the cartel members are subjected to a fine of F and the cartel breaks down.[17] If, by contrast, the investigation is unsuccessful the cartel continues.

We denote the expected present value of the profits that each cartel member receives as V^C. To evaluate this expected value we need to consider three possibilities:

(1)   No investigation in period 0, which has probability $1 - a$: the cartel continues and expected profit is:

$$V_1 = (1 - a)(\pi^M + \rho V^C) \tag{14.8}$$

The first term in the second bracket is profit in the current period given that the cartel is active. The second term uses the same reasoning as we used to derive equation (14.3). Given that there is no investigation the "cartel game" begins again in period 1 and so has expected profit V^C, which has to be discounted one period.

(2)   Unsuccessful investigation in period 0, which has probability $a(1 - s)$: the cartel continues and expected profit is:

$$V_2 = a(1 - s)(\pi^M + \rho V^C) \tag{14.9}$$

Similar to equation (14.8) the second term in the second bracket reflects the fact that the cartel game begins again in period 1 after an unsuccessful prosecution.

(3)   Successful prosecution, which has probability as: each cartel member is fined and the cartel collapses after the prosecution. Expected profit is:

$$V_3 = as\left(\pi^M - F + \frac{\rho}{1 - \rho}\pi^N\right) \tag{14.10}$$

The assumption that the cartel continues during an investigation deserves some comment. As we show in the next chapter, firms may stop colluding before an actual indictment is issued or while an investigation is still under way. However, this does not mean that they stop colluding as soon as an investigation begins. In the first place, the firms may not actually know that they are being investigated for some considerable amount of time. In the second place, they may continue to collude even after they discover that they are under suspicion because a sudden change in their behavior could be interpreted by the authorities as a sure sign that their behavior to date is not innocent of all wrongdoing. For these and other reasons, firms may continue to collude for some time after an investigation into their operations has begun, leading to our assumption here that they collude while being investigated.

---

[17]   Motta and Polo (2003) assume that the cartel begins again after one period of punishment. We prefer our approach since, in the former case, the antitrust authority, having once found a cartel, could simply keep on investigating the same firms. We are aware, of course, that the evidence does show that there are repeat offenders.

Putting together all the possibilities in equations (14.8), (14.9) and (14.10) gives us the expected present value of profit for a cartel member, $V^C = V_1 + V_2 + V_3$:

$$V^C = (1 - a)\pi^M + a(1 - s)\pi^M + as\pi^M - asF + \frac{as\rho}{1 - \rho}\pi^N$$

$$+ (1 - a)\rho V^C + a(1 - s)\rho V^C \tag{14.11}$$

$$= \pi^M - asF + \frac{as\rho}{1 - \rho}\pi^N + (1 - as)\rho V^C$$

Solving for V^C gives the expected profit of each firm in the cartel:

$$V^C = \frac{\pi^M - asF + \dfrac{as\rho}{1 - \rho}\pi^N}{1 - \rho(1 - as)} \tag{14.12}$$

Comparing equation (14.12) with (14.4) confirms, as we would have expected, that the introduction of an antitrust authority reduces the expected profit from cartel formation, even if the authority merely breaks up the cartel while imposing no fines.

It should be clear from equation (14.12) that antitrust policy has two major tools. The first and most obvious tool is the fine F. As F increases the expression in equation (14.12) decreases for any positive values of a and s. Even with small detection probabilities, a large enough fine would deter cartel formation. The second tool is the probability of investigation and successful prosecution as. As this term increases, the expression in equation (14.12) becomes smaller. In the extreme case of $as = 1$, the expression becomes $\pi^M - F + [\rho/(1 - \rho)]\pi^N$. For this expected profit to exceed the gains from cheating on a collusive agreement, or $\pi^D + [\rho/(1 - \rho)]\pi^N$, requires that $\pi^M - F > \pi^D$, which, of course, is not possible even if the fine F is zero. In other words, a sufficiently high rate of successful cartel discovery and prosecution would end cartel formation even if there were no penalty. For the case of a zero fine, a bit of manipulation (see the Derivation Checkpoint) of equations (14.5) and (14.12) indicates that the critical probability adjusted discount factor ρ^A for this case is:

$$\rho > \rho^A = \frac{\pi^D - \pi^M}{(1 - as)(\pi^D - \pi^N)} \tag{14.13}$$

Comparison of equations (14.13) and (14.7) confirms that $\rho^A > \rho^*$ and that ρ^A rises as either a or s increases. The underlying reason is that there are now two forces that can cause the cartel to fail. One of these is the ever-present pursuit of self-interest that induces individual cartel members to cheat on the agreement. The other is the newly introduced force stemming from the possibility of successful prosecution by the authorities.

Take our Bertrand example. We know that $\pi^M = 1,800$, $\pi^D = 3,600$ and $\pi^N = 0$. Substituting into equation (14.13) we find that the critical probability adjusted discount factor for this cartel to be self-sustaining despite the presence of an antitrust authority (which causes cartel breakdown but does not impose a penalty) is $\rho^A = 1/2(1 - as)$. If there had been no investigative effort ($as = 0$), then ρ need only be greater than 1/2 for the cartel to be self-sustaining. However, as a or s rises, the likelihood that the cartel can survive declines. For $as \geq 1/2$, no cartel can be self-sustaining.

Derivation Checkpoint

Probability-adjusted Discount Factor When There Are No Fines

In the absence of fines, the cartel will be self-sustaining if the expected gains from staying in the cartel exceed the net benefits obtained by cheating on the cartel and earning profit π^D for one period but then earning just the noncooperative Nash profit π^N every period thereafter. That is, the requirement for the cartel to be self-sustaining is:

$$\frac{\pi^M + \frac{as\rho}{1-\rho}\pi^N}{1 - \rho(1 - as)} > \pi^D + \frac{\rho\pi^N}{(1 - \rho)}$$

This may be rewritten as:

$$\frac{(1 - \rho)\pi^M + as\rho\pi^N}{1 - \rho(1 - as)} > (1 - \rho)\pi^D + \rho\pi^N$$

In turn, this implies:

$$(1 - p)\pi^M + as\rho\pi^N > [1 - \rho(1 - as)](1 - \rho)\pi^D + [1 - \rho(1 - as)]\rho\pi^N$$

Rearranging yields:

$$as\rho\pi^N - [1 - \rho(1 - as)]\rho\pi^N + \rho(1 - as)(1 - \rho)\pi^D > [1 - \rho(1 - as)]\pi^D + (1 - \rho)(\pi^D - \pi^M)$$

or

$$(1 - \rho)\rho(1 - as)(\pi^D - \pi^N) > (1 - \rho)(\pi^D - \pi^M)$$

or

$$\rho > \rho^A = \frac{\pi^D - \pi^M}{(1 - as)(\pi^D - \pi^N)}$$

It is self-evident that the hurdle for ρ rises as the probability of investigation and successful prosecution as rises. Again, this is the probability-adjusted discount factor when the fine F is zero. It will, of course, be an even higher hurdle if the fine is positive.

Which tool—fines or increased probability of apprehension and conviction—should the authorities use? Uncovering and prosecuting price-fixing conspiracies requires careful surveillance and legal work, which is expensive. In contrast, fines may be imposed rather costlessly. This suggests that a heavy reliance on substantial punishment is likely to be the more cost-effective strategy. In turn, this helps to explain why the law imposes treble damages in private antitrust lawsuits. However, unlike detection efforts, fines can never be used by themselves as part of a deterrence strategy. The reason is simple. If either a or s is zero, then the probability of getting caught and paying the fine is also zero. In that case, a fine will have no deterrent effect no matter how large it is. It is also true that judges and juries are sometimes reluctant to find a party guilty if they suspect that the finding will lead to an incredibly harsh penalty. The general rule is that some reliance on both detection and fines is appropriate, though the latter may play the dominant role.

One point to make in considering equation (14.13) is that whether the authorities rely on investigations or fines, much of what antitrust enforcement is about is deterrence. The policy works by preventing cartels from forming in the first place and not just by breaking them up once they have been uncovered. Such deterrence means that we may have difficulty in evaluating the full impact of antitrust efforts because we cannot easily measure the number of cartels that would have formed were it not for these deterrent effects. Here again, the extreme case is insightful. Suppose that because of a combination of investigative efforts and punishments, as and F are set such that firms never find it worthwhile to form a cartel. Because no cartels are ever observed, it may seem to an outsider that price-fixing penalties are not necessary and that the funds spent on detection (as) are wasted. Yet in fact, it is precisely because of those expenditures and punishment policies that cartels have been eliminated.

Our analysis suggests that it is possible for active antitrust policy to deter cartels from forming. However these agencies have limited resources. Since they cannot patrol every industry and every market, they must focus on those settings where collusion is most likely to occur. Furthermore, they must develop methods to detect such collusion if and when it occurs or to encourage firms to turn themselves in if they fear prosecution. These are the subjects to which we turn in the next chapter.

14.4   EMPIRICAL APPLICATION
Estimating the Effects of Price-fixing

In assessing the fines to be imposed on cartel members after a successful prosecution often the antitrust authorities must estimate the damage that the cartel has caused. This requires that the authorities, or more properly their expert econometric witnesses, estimate four numbers: the duration of the cartel, the price(s) charged and quantity (or quantities) sold by the cartel during the period the cartel is active, and the price(s) that the cartel would have charged if there had been no cartel—the "but for" price(s).

Of these, undoubtedly the most challenging is the last: estimating an inherently unobservable price. Several approaches have been suggested for estimating the "but-for" price. First, we could base the estimate on the Cournot model of competition in section 9.5 of Chapter 9, and solve for the "but for" price using the industry measure of concentration, costs, and demand elasticity. Second, and related, we could solve for the price using the Lerner Index in combination with data on capacity utilization, fixed and marginal costs. Third, we could use a before-and-after approach. That is, identify a period during which the cartel was not active and generate a measure of the prices charged in that period. Fourth, we could specify and estimate a reduced-form, time-series econometric model to estimate demand and supply interactions in the market and include a dummy or other variable to capture the impact of the cartel. Of these the third and fourth are the most commonly used.[18]

---

[18]   Connor (2001) provides a detailed discussion of the use of the before-and-after method in estimating the impact of the lysine cartel.

The econometric method is typically applied[19] by estimating a reduced-form price equation of the form:

$$P_{it} = \alpha + \beta y_{it} + \gamma w_{it} + \delta s_{it} + \lambda D_{it} + \varepsilon_{it} \tag{14.14}$$

Here, P_{it} is price in region i at time t, y_{it} is a vector of variables that affect demand (income, prices of other goods), w_{it} is a vector of variables that affect supply (factor prices), s_{it} is a vector of market structure variables (concentration, some measure of the strength of economies of scale), D_{it} is a vector of dummy variables intended to capture the impact of the cartel and ε_{it} is an error term. This is referred to as a reduced form equation since it is derived from an equilibrium condition equating demand and supply functions, which are functions themselves of underlying structural parameters that are not directly estimated.

A potential drawback of this approach is, of course, that it is very demanding on data. There needs to be sufficient "before-and-after" the cartel observations to give reliable estimates of the dummy variables and some of the variables in w_{it} such as factor costs can only be obtained with the consent of the firms that are accused of being parties to the cartel. There will often be problems with endogeneity of the right-hand side variables requiring an instrumental-variables estimation technique, with the "correct" choice of instruments.

There are, however, examples where a variant of the econometric technique has been used with great effect. One such example is Kwoka (1997) who estimated the price impact of a long-running cartel to rig prices in a particular set of real estate auctions held in the District of Columbia.

The auctions related to properties that were either foreclosed as a result of mortgage default or were being sold under court supervision: the latter are referred to as nisi auctions. The cartel members constituted a relatively small and stable set of real estate investors who specialized in the purchase and subsequent resale of this type of property. They operated the cartel by designating a bidder who would submit an agreed winning bid at the auction while the other cartel members either did not bid or deliberately bid low. A non-cartel member who turned up at such an auction was discouraged in various ways. For example, the cartel members might make negative remarks about the property, or the non-member might be paid not to bid or might be allowed to purchase one property. One measure of the success of this cartel at deterring entry and sustaining the cartel is that the cartel appears to have operated successfully for roughly 14 years, from January 1976 to August 1990.

At the end of the public auction the cartel members then conducted a second, private, "knock-out" auction among themselves to determine the final ownership of the property. Since this auction was conducted as a normal ascending bid auction, the property went to the high bidder: presumably the cartel member who valued the property most highly. The winner of the public auction would then be reimbursed for the price that she had paid and the remaining difference between the public auction price and the knockout auction price would be distributed as side payments to the members of the bidding ring.

To see how this collusive arrangement works among N members in the bidding ring we denote the true value of the property by V, the public auction-winning bid by P, and the knockout auction bid by K. Only P and K are observable. There are $N - 1$ losing bidders who each receive a payoff of S where

$$S = \frac{K - P}{N - 1} \tag{14.15}$$

---

[19]   Baker and Rubinfeld (1999) discuss the use of this method.

Every member of the ring knows that she will be paid at least S if she loses in the knock-out auction. The winner of the knock out gets $V - K$ and so in equilibrium $S = V - K$. In other words, the true value of the property is $V = K + S$. Using equation (14.15) this condition implies:

$$V = K + \frac{K - P}{N - 1} = \frac{N}{(N - 1)}K - \frac{P}{(N - 1)} = P + \frac{N}{(N - 1)}(K - P) \qquad (14.16)$$

Kwoka adds a bit more structure to the model by assuming that the fixed public auction price P on which the bidding ring agreed was a "constant fraction of a property's competitive valuation." If this fraction is m then $m = V/P$. Substituting $V = mP$ in (14.16) and solving for K we have the reduced form equation to be estimated:

$$K = P + (m - 1)P\frac{(N - 1)}{N} \qquad (14.17)$$

where the independent variables in the regression are P and $P(N - 1)/N$ and m is to be estimated.

Members of the cartel kept detailed records of the identities of all the bidders in each auction and the payoffs that were made to each losing bidder. These records were central to the eventual prosecution of the cartel and are also essential to the estimation of the cartel's impact on prices. However, of the 12 individuals that were charged with Sherman Act violations, 10 pleaded guilty before trial and so no data are available for these cases. This left Kwoka with data for 30 of the 680 properties affected by the cartel, all of which were auctioned between 1980 and 1988.

Summary statistics for these auctions are reported in Table 14.3. The average number of bidders was 4.6 and ranged from 2 to 9. The average knockout price was 28 percent in excess of the public auction price, or alternatively the rigged public auction price was on average 22 percent less than the knockout price.

This is not, however, the full impact of the cartel, since we know that $V = K + S$. Moreover, it can be seen from Table 14.3 that there is considerable variance in K/P. Kwoka, therefore, estimated equation (14.17) directly, obtaining the results in column (a) of Table 14.4.

In the first regression in column (a) observe that the coefficients on the two terms P and $P(N - 1)/N$ are significant and have the expected signs and the fit is remarkable. In addition, the coefficient on P is (just) insignificantly different from unity, as required by equation (14.17). The coefficient on $P(N - 1)/N$ is an estimate of $m - 1$, giving $m = 1.86$. Since $P/V = 1/m$ this tells us that $P/V = 0.54$. In other words, the cartel results in public bid prices 46 percent lower than the true valuation of the properties being auctioned.

Table 14.3 Summary statistics for the auction cartel

	Mean	Minimum	Maximum
P	$25,800	$8,800	$44,800
K	$30,500	$10,800	$47,300
N	4.63	2	9
K/P	1.28	1.02	2.46

Table 14.4 Regression results

	(a)	(b)	(c)
P	0.519	0.520	0.703
	(2.18)	(2.15)	(4.47)
$P(N-1)/N$	0.860	0.879	0.481
	(2.58)	(2.58)	(2.01)
$DP(N-1)/N$		−0.045	0.014
		(0.51)	(0.23)
UNEQUAL			3,501
			(3.08)
R^2	0.979	0.980	0.995
S	667	433	694

Kwoka then estimated two refinements on the simple model of equation (14.17). First, of the 30 properties in his sample, 19 were foreclosure auctions and 11 were nisi auctions. Since the latter are held under court supervision it is possible that the cartel members would be more careful in their public auction bidding. Suppose, therefore, that on nisi actions we have that $V/P = m - d$. Introduce a dummy variable D that takes the value of unity for nisi auctions and zero otherwise. Then the reduced form to be estimated becomes:

$$K = P + (m-1)P\frac{(N-1)}{N} - dDP\frac{(N-1)}{N}$$ (14.18)

The results are given in column (b) of Table 14.4. The coefficient on $DP(N-1)/N$ is the estimate of d. It has the correct sign (negative) but is statistically insignificant.

The second refinement modifies the mechanism by which losing bidders in the cartel were compensated. In some auctions losing bidders were compensated equally while in others the compensation was based on each losing bidder's final but losing bid. The impact of unequal compensation is potentially ambiguous. On the one hand, it might make bidders more aggressive to secure them a higher share. On the other hand, aggressive bidding might result in a bidder winning an auction that she did not want to win. To test for this impact, Kwoka added a dummy variable UNEQUAL to equation (14.18) and ran the regression for the 18 auctions in which it was possible to distinguish the compensation mechanism.

The results are given in column (c) of Table 14.4. The coefficient on UNEQUAL is positive and significant, implying that unequal compensation increased the subsequent knockout price. Moreover, the coefficient on $P(N-1)/N$ gives a revised estimate for m of 1.48, implying that the cartel rigged the public auction prices to 32.5 percent below the true property values. From this and the rest of Kwoka's (1997) results, this cartel is seen to have had an unambiguous and significant impact on the prices at which these properties were traded in the public auctions lowering prices some 30 to 45 percent below their true value.

Summary

At least since the time of Adam Smith, there has been the fear that firms in the same industry may try to collude and set a price close to the monopoly price rather than vigorously compete. The good news since the 1990s is that a large number of such collusive cartels have been caught and successfully prosecuted in the courts both in Europe and North America. The bad news is that this same evidence also reveals that collusion remains a real problem. Somehow firms are able to work out and implement cooperative strategies rather than noncooperative ones. So, while the competition authorities can feel good about the cartels that have been broken, they must also worry that there are many other price-fixing agreements that they have not uncovered.

It is the repetition of corporate interaction that makes cartels possible. Firms rarely meet on the corporate battlefield just once. Instead, they can expect to meet many times, and perhaps in many other markets as well. When a game is played only once, each firm has a strong incentive to cheat on the collusive agreement. Since the agreement is not legally enforceable, there is little any firm can do to deter others from cheating. However, when the game is played repeatedly over a number of periods, the scope for cooperation widens considerably. This is because a firm can threaten to "punish" any cheating on the collusive agreement in one period by being more aggressive in the subsequent periods.

While repetition of the game is necessary for firms to collude successfully, it is not by itself sufficient. In addition to the game being repeated it must have an indefinite end point. That is, in any given period, there is always a positive probability that the game will be played one more time. Absent these conditions, Selten's theorem makes clear that a finitely repeated game with a unique Nash equilibrium will simply result in that Nash equilibrium being the outcome in each period. However, for repeated games that go on indefinitely, the Folk theorem makes clear that collusion that allows for all firms to gain relative to the one-shot Nash equilibrium is possible.

We have further shown that an active antitrust policy reduces the likelihood of a cartel being self-sustaining. However, this by no means guarantees that cartels will not be formed. Based on the recent historical experience, it appears that the conditions for successful collusion are often met. Antitrust concern with price-fixing agreements is then justified. Empirical work on assessing the welfare impact of collusive pricing is a rich and growing field in industrial organization. Designing and implementing antitrust policy to punish price-fixing agreements is increasingly based on econometric work that identifies what would have happened had the cartel not been in operation. As we saw in section 14.4 there is sound empirical evidence that pricing rigging in auctions has a sizable impact on prices.

Problems

1. Suppose that two firms compete in quantities (Cournot) in a market in which demand is described by: $P = 260 - 2Q$. Each firm incurs no fixed cost but has a marginal cost of 20.
   a. What is the one-period Nash equilibrium market price? What is the output and profit of each firm in this equilibrium?
   b. What is the output of each firm if they collude to produce the monopoly output? What profit does each firm earn with such collusion?

2. Return to the cartel in problem 1. Suppose that after the cartel is established, one firm decides to cheat on the collusion, assuming that the other firm will continue to produce its half of the monopoly output.
   a. Given the deviating firm's assumption, how much will it produce?
   b. If the deviating firm's assumption is correct, what will be the industry price and the deviating firm's profit in this case?

3. Suppose that the market game described in problems 1 and 2 is now repeated indefinitely. Show that the collusive agreement can be maintained so long as the probability adjusted discount factor, $\rho R > 0.53$.

4. Suppose again that market demand is given by: $P = 260 - 2Q$ and that firms again have a constant marginal cost of 20, while incurring no fixed cost. Now, however, assume that firms compete in prices (Bertrand) and have unlimited capacity.
    a. What is the one-period Nash equilibrium price? Assuming that firms share the market evenly any time they charge the same price, what is the output and profit of each firm in this market equilibrium?
    b. What will be the equilibrium output and profit of each firm if each agrees to charge the monopoly price?

5. Return to problem 4. Assume that the cartel is established at the monopoly price. Suppose one firm now deviates from the agreement assuming that its rival continues to charge the monopoly price.
    a. Given the deviating firm's assumption, what price will maximize its profit of the other firm?
    b. If its assumption is correct, how much will the profit of the cheating firm be? How much will be the profit of its non-cheating rival?

6. Return again to the cartel in problems 4 and 5. Now suppose that the market game is repeated indefinitely. What probability adjusted discount factor is necessary now in order to maintain the collusive agreement?

7. Compare your answers in problems 3 and 6. Based on this comparison, which market setting do you think is more amenable to cartel formation, one of Cournot competition or one of Bertrand competition?

8. Once again, assume Cournot competition in an industry in which market demand is described by: $P = 260 - 2Q$ and in which each firm has a marginal cost of 20. However, instead of two firms let there now be four.
    a. What is the one-period Nash equilibrium market price? What is the output and profit of each firm in this equilibrium?
    b. What is the output of each firm if they collude to produce the monopoly output? What profit does each firm earn with such collusion?

9. Return to problem 8. Suppose that one firm decides to cheat on the collusion, assuming that each of the three other firms continue to produce one-fourth of the monopoly output.
    a. Given the deviating firm's assumption, how much will it produce?
    b. Assuming that its assumption is correct, what will be the industry price and the deviating firm's profit?

10. Consider again your results in problems 8 and 9. Suppose that the market game is repeated indefinitely. Show that the collusive agreement can be maintained so long as the probability adjusted discount factor, $\rho R > 0.610$.

11. Compare your answers in problems 10 and 3. Based on this comparison, what do you infer about the ability of firms to sustain a collusive agreement as the number of firms in the industry expands?

12. Imagine that in the 1990s, the market demand for the food additive, lysine, had a price elasticity of 1.55. The structure of that market and the (assumed constant) marginal cost per pound for each firm are shown below:

Firm	Market share (%)	Marginal cost
Ajinomoto	32	$0.70
Archer Daniels Midland	32	$0.70
Kiyowa Hakko	14	$0.80
Sewon/Miwon	14	$0.80
Cheil Sugar	4	$0.85
Cargill	4	$0.85

    a. Use elasticity, market share, and cost data above to determine the weighted average industry equilibrium price if the firms are competing in quantities.
    b. During the 1990s, the lysine producers formed a (now famous) cartel that maintained the shares shown in part a. Under the cartel, the world price of lysine rose to an average of $1.12 per pound. Total world production at this time was about 100,000 metric tons per year. A metric ton = 2,200 pounds.
    c. Focusing on Archer Daniels Midland (ADM), and assuming market shares are the same in the Cournot and collusive settings, use the above and what you know about the Cournot equilibrium from Chapter 9 to determine:
        (i)   ADM's profits in the Cournot equilibrium; and
        (ii) ADM's profits under the cartel.

References

Baker, J. B. and D. L. Rubinfeld. 1999. "Empirical Methods in Antitrust Litigation: Review and Evidence." *American Law and Economics Review* 1 (Fall): 386–435.

Connor, J. M. 2001. *Global Price Fixing: Our Customers Are the Enemy*. Boston: Kluwer Academic.

Eichberger, J. 1993. *Game Theory for Economics*. New York: Academic Press.

Eichenwald, K. 2000. *The Informant*. New York: Random House.

Friedman, J. 1971. "A Non-Cooperative Equilibrium for Supergames." *Review of Economic Studies* 38 (January): 1–12.

Green, E. J. and R. Porter. 1984. "Noncooperative Collusion under Imperfect Price Information." *Econometrica* 52 (January): 87–100.

Harsanyi, J. C. 1973. "Games with Randomly Distributed Payoffs: A New Rationale for Mixed Strategy Equilibrium Points." *International Journal of Game Theory* 2 (December): 1–23.

Kwoka, J. 1997. "The Price Effect of Bidding Conspiracies: Evidence from Real Estate 'Knockouts'." *Antitrust Bulletin* 42 (Summer): 503–16.

Motta, M. and M. Polo. 2003. "Leniency Programs and Cartel Prosecution." *International Journal of Industrial Organization* 21 (March): 347–9.

Posner, R. 1970. "A Statistical Study of Cartel Enforcement." *Journal of Law and Economics* 13 (October): 365–419.

Rotemberg, J. and G. Saloner. 1986. "A Supergame Theoretic Model of Price Wars During Booms." *American Economic Review* 76 (June): 390–407.

Schelling, T. 1960. *The Strategy of Conflict*. Cambridge, MA: Harvard University Press.

Selten, R. 1973. "A Simple Model of Imperfect Competition Where 4 Are Few and 6 Are Many." *International Journal of Game Theory* 2 (December): 141–201. Reprinted in R. Selten, *Models of Strategic Rationality*. Amsterdam: Kluwer Academic, 1988.

15

Collusion: Detection and Public Policy

The formation and sustained operation of cartels by means of repeated interaction among colluding firms is not only a theoretical possibility but a real phenomenon. Illegal cartels continue to emerge in practice even though explicit price fixing is illegal in the U.S., the European Union, and many other developed countries. If the price-increasing effects of these cartels were relatively small, their persistence might not warrant much concern. However, the evidence is clear that cartels raise prices by a substantial amount. For example, Froeb, Koyak, and Werden (1993) found that a price-rigging scheme involved in supplying frozen fish to the U.S. military raised prices by 23 to 30 percent. Connor (2001) found that the lysine cartel raised the market price by 17 percent, while Morse and Hyde (2000) argue the effect was a twice-as-high 34 percent. In the most exhaustive and complete review of the evidence that we have seen, Connor and Lande (2005) find that the median cartel price effect over all time periods and across all cartel types is 22 percent. They estimate that this effect is 18 percent for domestic cartels and 32 percent for international cartels.[1]

The twin facts of continued cartel formation and the consequent impact of substantially higher prices imply a clear need for an active antitrust authority charged with finding and prosecuting cartels. In a recent statement, Thomas Barnett, Assistant Attorney General of the U.S. Antitrust Division stated[2]: "The detection, prosecution and deterrence of cartel offences—such as price fixing, bid rigging and market allocation—continue to be the highest priority of the Antitrust Division." The same concern with the detection and prosecution of cartels can be found in Europe. Since Neelie Kroes was appointed European Union competition commissioner in 2004 she has adopted a "zero tolerance" approach to cartels and has been instrumental in markedly increasing the fines that have been imposed on cartel members.

Moreover, in recent years, the antitrust authorities' detection efforts have been quite successful. In fiscal year 2006 the U.S. Antitrust Division secured over $473 million in fines

---

[1] One of the few contrary studies is Sproul (1993) who finds that industry prices typically rise slightly *after* an indictment, which he interprets as evidence that cartels work to keep costs low. However, apart from notable data problems, Sproul's (1993) analysis suffers from the difficulty that indictments only come after a long investigation. If, as many suspect, the investigation itself triggers a breakdown in the cartel, then prices will fall to competitive levels long before any announced indictment. What happens at that date then gives little guidance as to the actual cartel price effect.

[2] The full text of the statement can be viewed at http://www.usdoj.gov/atr/public/testimony/221777.htm.

(one of the highest totals ever) and imposed 5,383 jail days on executives found guilty of active participation in these cartels. By early March of fiscal year 2007, 18 individuals had been sentenced to a total of 12,890 days in jail. In Europe, the Commission secured cartel fines of €1.85 billion (nearly $2.5 billion) in 2006 and by the end of March 2007 had secured fines of an additional €1.74 billion ($2.3 billion). There are further cases in the pipeline in both the U.S. and in Europe (some of them involving companies thought to be members of international cartels operating in both regions) making it likely that 2007 will be another record-breaking year.

Given that enforcement of the laws against price-fixing is important, the immediate question becomes how the authorities should allocate their scarce resources (time and money) in detecting cartels. Without detailed information on the costs facing each firm and on industry demand, the authorities must develop a sense of where such illegal behavior is most likely to occur, and then police those areas more heavily. In this respect, being a good antitrust economist is like being a good detective. One has to look for clues about which firms have the motive, the means, and the opportunity to commit the crime.

Of course, identifying likely cartel behavior is not enough in itself. The real trick is uncovering evidence that will satisfy the courts. It is here that the power of recent leniency programs is revealed. While these programs may make cartel formation somewhat more likely, the main impact, one hopes, is to make cartel detection easier by encouraging finking by cartel members once they suspect an investigation is underway. It is difficult to imagine stronger evidence of the existence of a cartel than the sworn testimony of a co-conspirator.

15.1   THE CARTEL PROBLEM

In principle, collusive behavior can occur in almost any market. However, one suspects that it is more likely to occur in some markets rather than others. In order to identify the market features that facilitate collusion we first consider a central problem that colluding firms have to surmount.

Figure 15.1 presents the basic problem facing any cartel, here illustrated in the case of a duopoly. The curve $\pi_1^* \pi_2^*$ describes the *profit–possibility frontier* for two firms, 1 and 2. This frontier defines the maximum profit firm 2 can achieve for any specific profit level assigned to firm 1. The profit levels at M and other points on the frontier are achieved by an appropriate choice of output at each firm. Thus, if firm 2 is assigned zero profit (zero output), the maximum profit possible for firm 1 is π_1^*. Similarly, if firm 1 is assigned zero profit or zero output, the maximum amount of profit firm 2 can earn is π_2^*. The underlying example for this figure assumes that marginal costs are increasing for both firms but that firm 2's costs rise more rapidly than firm 1's. The problem of collusion is more interesting when costs are asymmetric between colluding firms.

There is one point on the profit frontier that generates the highest total profit for both firms. This is point M. It is identified by the fact that a straight line with slope -1, i.e., the line $\pi_m \pi_m$ is just tangent to the frontier at this point. This implies that at M a small change in the allocation of production would not affect total industry profit. Production has been allocated such that marginal cost is equal at both firms and this constant marginal cost is equal to industry marginal revenue. At M, firm 1 earns profit π_1^m, and firm 2 earns π_2^m, which is the most that it can earn given that firm 1 earns π_1^m. The sum of these two profit levels is just π_m.

Because it has a slope of -1, all points on the line $\pi_m \pi_m$ have the same *total* profit level π_m. Note that neither firm can earn this profit level by itself. That is, both π_1^* and π_2^* are

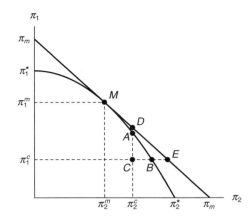

Figure 15.1   A collusive agreement between firms with different costs

The maximum joint profit that the two firms can generate is π_m, and this would give the distribution of profits at point M. the Cournot–Nash equlibrium is point C. Hence, point M is unattainable. However, a side payment from firm 1 to firm 2 could get the cartel somewhere on DE. In the absence of side payments though, the best the two firms can do is attain a point on AB.

less than π_m. This is because of our assumption of rising marginal cost. If firm 1 were to do all the production by itself, marginal cost would rise to a sufficiently high level that it could not earn π_m. The same is true for firm 2. The two firms need each other if they are to achieve the joint maximum at M.

The point C identifies the profit to each firm in the Cournot–Nash equilibrium. Notice that it does not lie on the curve $\pi_1^* \pi_2^*$. The Cournot outcome is a noncooperative one. Each firm tries to maximize its own profit, not the combined profit of the industry. As a result, each ignores the fact that an increase in its own production lowers the rival's profit. Suppose, as illustrated, that C lies below and to the right of M. What this means is that firm 2 earns more profit in the Cournot–Nash equilibrium than it does producing the output it would produce at M and earning the profit π_2^m. This creates a real conflict in achieving the cartel goal of M.

This conflict can be overcome but doing so requires that the firm 2 be persuaded to act cooperatively and produce the output associated with M. One obvious way to do this is by means of side payments from firm 1 to firm 2. Under such an arrangement, both firms produce the outputs necessary to achieve the industry maximum at M. Then, to make this acceptable to firm 2, firm 1 gives up some of the large profit it makes at M, and pays it to firm 2. This transfer allows the firms to move along the $\pi_m \pi_m$ line and to end up somewhere on the interval DE.

If side payments are not possible, the best that the cartel can do is to reach some point on the arc AB. Total industry profit is not maximized, but at least both firm 2 and firm 1 earn a level of profit as least as great as their respective Cournot–Nash levels. However, while side payments are not necessary to achieve this outcome, some cooperation is. We know this because we know that the noncooperative Cournot solution lies inside the frontier.

Figure 15.1 thus illustrates a central dilemma facing all oligopolists. With sufficient asymmetry across firms, achieving the point on the profit–possibility frontier that actually maximizes industry profit not only requires cooperation but also typically requires side payments in order for this to be profitable for both firms. Efficient side payments require that the cooperating firms report their costs honestly, but each firm has a clear incentive to misrepresent their costs in order to secure a greater side payment.

Despite these complications, firms can achieve at least some degree of cooperation. The question that remains is when such cooperation is most likely. That is, what industry characteristics are most conducive to firms achieving a cooperative outcome? This question has been the focus of considerable theoretical and empirical research.[3] The broad findings of that research now seem clear. Successful collusion is more likely when there is a sufficiently strong profit motive and when there are easily understood methods by which firms can reach and enforce a collusive agreement.

In identifying the market features that seem to be necessary for collusive behavior we will use the Bertrand model as a benchmark case. This model is very convenient for this purpose because if the firms collude they share the monopoly profit π_m, while if the cartel breaks down they earn a competitive profit of zero.

15.2   FACTORS THAT FACILITATE COLLUSION[4]

What factors make collusion easier and therefore more likely? Any factor that facilitates collusion must do one of two things. It must either reduce the critical probability-adjusted discount factor ρ^* (see Chapter 14) above which the cartel is potentially self-sustaining, or it must reduce the likelihood of profitable cheating by cartel members. We examine specific industry features to see whether and how they meet these criteria.

15.2.1   High Industry Concentration

We are more likely to find collusion in more concentrated markets for at least two reasons. First, increased concentration typically reduces the critical probability-adjusted discount factor ρ^*. Take our Bertrand model[5] and assume that there are n identical firms in the market. Each has profit π_m/n per period if it participates in the cartel and one-off total monopoly profit π_m if it deviates. Deviation is not profitable, therefore, if

$$\frac{\pi_m}{n}(1 + \rho + \rho^2 + \dots) = \frac{\pi_m}{n(1 - \rho)} > \pi_m \Rightarrow \frac{1}{n} > 1 - \rho \Rightarrow \rho(n) > 1 - \frac{1}{n} \tag{15.1}$$

Note that if $n = 2$, equation (15.1) gives the critical probability adjusted discount factor $\rho^*(2) = 0.5$ as we found in Chapter 14. If, by contrast, $n = 4$ we have $\rho^*(4) = 0.75$ and if $n = 10$ we have $\rho^*(10) = 0.9$. The intuition is easy to see. A firm in the cartel has to share the cartel's profits with other cartel members. As a result, the returns to collusion fall as the number of cartel members increases. By contrast, the returns to deviation typically do not decrease with n. Deviation is, in other words, more profitable as industry concentration falls, i.e., as n increases.

Industry concentration affects the ability to collude for other reasons as well. We noted in discussing Figure 15.1 that it is not always easy for duopolists to arrive at a collusive

---

[3]   Stigler (1964) is a classic in this field.
[4]   Motta (2004) provides an excellent and detailed discussion of these factors.
[5]   In the exercises you are asked to conduct the same analysis for Cournot competitors.

Table 15.1   Cartels and industry concentration

Number of conspirators	2	3	4	5	6	7	8	9	10	11–15	16–20	21–25	>25	Total
Number of cases	1	7	8	4	10	4	3	5	7	5	2	–	6	62
Trade associations	–	–	1	–	4	1	–	1	3	1	1	–	6	18

	Concentration ratios				
Concentration (%)	0–25	25–50	51–75	76–100	Total
Number of cases	3	9	17	21	50

Source: Hay and Kelley (1974)

agreement if they have asymmetric costs. Matters are even more complicated when we increase the number of firms involved in the negotiations over prices and market shares. In addition, in "real life" markets with imperfect information, it may not be easy in a large-numbers cartel to detect whether and who is deviating from the agreement. Even if deviation is discovered it may be difficult for the non-deviating members to agree and implement punishment of the deviator.

Hay and Kelley (1974) provide compelling support for this proposition in their analysis of successful prosecutions of 62 cartels by the U.S. Department of Justice from 1963–1972. Table 15.1 summarizes the size distribution of these cartels.[6]

15.2.2   Significant Entry Barriers

Easy entry undermines collusion. Suppose that an entrant does not join the cartel. Ease of entry weakens the ability of the cartel to maintain its goal of higher profit. Suppose, alternatively, that the entrant joins the cartel. Then our analysis above applies: there are now more cartel members making the cartel harder to sustain. Moreover, such accommodation is likely to attract even more new entrants! Levenstein and Suslow (2006) note that "the most common cause of cartel breakdown in (their) nineteen case studies was entry" (p. 76). We can put this another way. For a cartel to succeed, it will need either to create strategic barriers to entry or to have structural ones in place.

15.2.3   Frequent and Regular Orders

An industry in which firms receive infrequent and irregularly timed orders will not be one conducive to price fixing. The critical discount factor ρ^* is a per period discount factor (day, week, month . . .) that can be converted into an annual discount factor if we know the relevant time period. The longer the time between orders, the higher the annual discount factor. Suppose, for example, that orders are monthly and $\rho^* = 0.9$. This is equivalent to an annual discount factor of $0.9^{12} = 0.28$. If, by contrast, the period between orders is six months, then the annual discount factor is $0.9^2 = 0.81$. Simply put, with infrequent orders it takes longer to punish a firm that cheats on the cartel agreement, making cheating more attractive.

---

[6]   Concentration ratios were available for only 50 of these cartels. We comment on the importance of trade associations below.

Reality Checkpoint
The Guild Trip

European guilds first appeared in the eleventh century as a result of growing commercial activity and urbanization. Merchants from the same city traveling to distant markets protected themselves by banding together in a caravan, called a *gilde* or *hansa* in the Germanic countries and a *caritas* or *fraternitas* in Latin-speaking ones. Caravan members had specific duties for defense if the caravan were attacked, and were also required to support each other in any legal disputes. Since the members of a hansa or fraternitas remained in touch with each other when they returned to their home city, they also began to assume rights and privileges in regard to trade within their local community—rights often supported by the authorities. This led in time to the merchant guilds monopolizing all of the industry and commerce of the city; nonguild members were only permitted to sell goods at wholesale.

Guilds based on specialized crafts replaced the earlier merchant guilds by the fourteenth century. The members of the craft guilds were all those engaged in any particular craft. They monopolized the making and selling of a particular commodity within the cities in which they were organized.

They did this in two ways: (1) by preventing goods from other cities being imported; and (2) by controlling local entry to membership in the craft guild. All those fortunate enough to be accepted as members were required to establish both uniform hours for all shops making the same commodity and uniform wages for workers in the same industry. Similarly, the number of people to be employed in each shop, the tools to be used, and the prices to be charged were all strictly regulated and enforced by close supervision. No advertising was allowed and improvements in techniques of production, which might give one artisan a cost advantage, were also prohibited. Both the merchant and craft guilds were based in the cities of their day. These were small by our standards. This size coupled with the "everyone knows everyone else's business" aspect of medieval life meant that the setting was one of frequent, repeated encounters extending over an indefinite future.

The decline of the crafts guilds came in the sixteenth century with the emergence of capitalist methods of production. This made possible the manufacture of goods on a larger scale at one point and shipping them to many others. Competition came now not from one's fellow local craftsmen but from anonymous sources further away. Policing and enforcement became impossible and the new, more efficient production methods gradually forced the craft guilds out of existence.

Source: M. Weber, *General Economic History*, Collier, New York, 1961.

That regular orders aid collusive efforts is also easily illustrated. Take our Bertrand case but suppose that in the current period ($t = 0$) a large order is received that has profit $\lambda \pi_m$, with $\lambda > 1$, while all later profits are expected to return to π_m per period. A slightly altered equation (15.1) gives the condition for the cartel to be self-sustaining in the face of this large order:

$$\frac{\pi_m}{n}(\lambda + \rho + \rho^2 + \ldots) = \frac{\pi_m}{n}\left(\lambda + \frac{\rho}{(1-\rho)}\right) > \lambda \pi_m \Rightarrow \lambda + \frac{\rho}{(1-\rho)} > \lambda n \qquad (15.2)$$

Solving this for ρ gives the critical probability-adjusted discount factor

$$\rho(\lambda, n) = \frac{\lambda(n-1)}{1 + \lambda(n-1)} \qquad (15.3)$$

Suppose that $n = 2$ and $\lambda = 1$ (no large orders). Then we have the familiar Bertrand condition that the probability-adjusted discount factor necessary for collusion must exceed $\rho(1, 2) = 0.5$. If, by contrast, $n = 2$ and $\lambda = 2$, then the critical discount factor necessary for collusion is $\rho > \rho(2, 2) = 2/3$. More generally, it is easy to show that $\rho(\lambda, n)$ is increasing in the parameter λ. In other words, the temptation to "steal" the profits from a one-time increase in demand can be sufficiently great to undermine the cartel. The same argument can be applied in analyzing random shocks to expected demand.[7] A positive demand shock "looks like" a large unexpected order and we have just shown that this makes the cartel harder to sustain. By contrast, a negative demand shock can provide an incentive for the cartel to stick together.

15.2.4   Rapid Market Growth

Cartels are more likely to be sustainable in growing markets and more likely to be unstable in declining markets. Once again, the intuition is simple to see. Take the case where the market is expected to grow over time. Deviation "early" in the market's growth generates profits as usual but now runs the risk of sacrificing the larger profits that the cartel will generate as the market grows. The opposite argument applies, of course, if the market is expected to decline over time. In this case, there is a stronger temptation to cheat and get out now while the gains from doing so are reasonably good.

Again we can illustrate the foregoing point using our basic Bertrand case. Suppose that the market is forecast to grow at a rate g per period. In other words, aggregate profit in period t is forecast to be $\pi_m \cdot g^t$. For the cartel to be self-sustaining it is necessary that:

$$\frac{\pi_m}{n}(1 + g\rho + g^2\rho^2 + \ldots) = \frac{\pi_m}{n(1 - g\rho)} > \pi_m \Rightarrow \frac{1}{n} > 1 - g\rho \Rightarrow \rho(g, n) > \frac{1}{g}\left(1 - \frac{1}{n}\right) \quad (15.4)$$

Clearly, $\rho(g, n)$ is decreasing in g. We can take $g = 1$ as our base case. With the market forecast to be unchanging over time, $\rho(1, n) = 1 - 1/n$ as in equation (15.1). However, when $g < 1$, so that the market is forecast to decline, we have that $\rho(g, n) > \rho(1, n)$ and the cartel is harder to sustain. By contrast, when $g > 1$ we have $\rho(g, n) < \rho(1, n)$ and the cartel is easier to sustain.

15.2.5   Technological or Cost Symmetry

Symmetry among industry firms in terms of technology and costs is another market feature that can support cartel formation. Our analysis in section 15.1 suggests one reason why this should be the case. When two firms have different costs it will be more difficult to formulate a collusive agreement that they both find satisfactory. A firm is more able to formulate a collusive agreement with a firm that "looks like" it does rather than one that does not. In addition, detailed negotiations over prices and market shares are much more straightforward when firms are similar.

Collusion is more likely to be sustainable when the colluding firms are of roughly equal size, as they will tend to be when they have similar production capabilities. Once again, the Bertrand model provides a useful means by which this can be illustrated. Suppose that there are n firms in the cartel and that the profit share of firm i is s_i. For convenience we number

---

[7]   Rotemberg and Saloner (1986) provide a more formal analysis.

the firms in decreasing order of their profit shares, so that $s_1 \geq s_2 \geq s_3 \geq \ldots \geq s_i \geq \ldots \geq s_n$ with, of course, $s_1 + s_2 + \ldots + s_n = 1$. For firm i to be willing to remain in the cartel the condition is:

$$s_i \pi_m (1 + \rho + \rho^2 + \ldots) = \frac{s_i \pi_m}{(1 - \rho)} > \pi_m \Rightarrow s_i > 1 - \rho \Rightarrow \rho(s_i) > 1 - s_i \qquad (15.5)$$

If all the firms have equal profit shares $s_i = 1/n$ this simplifies to our "standard" Bertrand case of equation (15.1). By contrast, when profit shares are different, the firm with the lowest profit share determines the binding probability-adjusted discount factor used in equation (15.5). The smaller the share of the smallest firm, the higher that discount factor has to be for collusion to be sustainable.

15.2.6   Multi-market Contact

The fact that the same firms in an industry meet many times, i.e., the fact that the game is repeated, is perhaps the crucial element facilitating collusion. It is, therefore, tempting to suspect that a similar force is at work when rival firms compete in several distinct markets. That is, competing against the same set of rivals in many markets at one point in time is similar in some respects to competing against the same set of rivals in one market over several periods. Cheating in one period risks punishment and the loss of cartel profits in many subsequent periods, whereas cheating in one market could risk punishment and the loss of cartel profits in the other markets. This intuition would suggest that multi-market contact should again be a feature that facilitates collusion.

Unfortunately, the foregoing intuition is somewhat misleading because time is in fact different from space. In the multi-market case a firm can cheat on all of its collusive arrangements across different markets at one point of time. However, it requires the passage of time to cheat across different time periods. Nevertheless our intuition may well be correct when the colluding firms have asymmetric market shares in the different markets in which they compete.[8]

For example, suppose that two firms A and B each operate in two markets 1 and 2. Aggregate cartel profits in each market we assume to be π_m per period. The profit share for firm A in each of these markets is respectively s_{A1} and s_{A2} and we assume that $s_{A1} > 1/2$ while $s_{A2} < 1/2$. Of course, we have that $s_{B1} = 1 - s_{A1} < 1/2$ and $s_{B2} = 1 - s_{A2} > 1/2$. In other words, firm A is the "large" firm in market 1 and firm B is the "large" firm in market 2. As an example, A might be a U.S. firm and B a European firm with market 1 being the U.S. and market 2 being the EU. To keep matters simple, further assume that the two firms have the same time preferences and the same discount rates. In other words, they have the same probability-adjusted discount factors.

If we treat the two markets separately, we know from our discussion in the previous section that collusion is sustainable in market 1 only if the probability-adjusted discount factor for each firm is greater than $1 - s_{B1} > 1/2$ and in market 2 only if the probability-adjusted discount factor for each firm is greater than $1 - s_{A2} > 1/2$. Now consider the two markets together. Take firm A. Firm A knows that if it deviates from the collusive agreement in either market then it will be punished in both. So if firm A is contemplating deviation it

---

[8]   See Bernheim and Whinston (1990) for a more complete analysis of this insight.

should deviate in both markets. In these circumstances, for deviation *not* to be profitable it must be that:

$$(s_{A1} + s_{A2})\pi_m(1 + \rho + \rho^2 + \ldots) = \frac{(s_{A1} + s_{A2})\pi_m}{(1 - \rho)} \geq 2\pi_m$$

$$\Rightarrow (s_{A1} + s_{A2}) > 2(1 - \rho) \Rightarrow \rho(s_{A1}, s_{A2}) \geq 1 - \frac{(s_{A1} + s_{A2})}{2}$$

(15.6)

The analogous result applies for firm B: $\rho(s_{B1}, s_{B2}) \geq 1 - \frac{(s_{B1} + s_{B2})}{2}$.

To see the point about multi-market contact let's make it simple and suppose that firm A has profit share s in market 1 and $1 - s$ in market 2, with $s > 1/2$ to reflect asymmetric positions. Analogously firm B has profit share $1 - s$ in market 1 and s in market 2. From equation (15.6) the cartel between firms A and B is sustainable when they operate in both markets for any probability-adjusted discount factor greater than or equal to 1/2 (which is the standard Bertrand result again). However, the probability-adjusted discount factor would have to be greater than s, which by assumption is greater than 1/2, if the firms collaborate in only one market. Multi-market contact can then support cooperation. What is necessary is first, that the colluding firms have asymmetric positions in the markets in which they jointly operate and second, that the asymmetry is reduced when all the markets in which they compete are considered. In our example, each firm had a share in excess of 1/2 in any one market. However, aggregated across both markets each firm has a share of 1/2.

15.2.7   Product Homogeneity

The empirical evidence reported in Hay and Kelley (1974) and the conventional wisdom of government authorities and the courts is that collusion is easier to sustain when the cartel members produce homogeneous or nearly homogeneous products. Again, there is an intuitive basis for this finding that stems from the complexity of the cartel agreement. First, with homogeneous products a price-fixing cartel, in principle, has to set and monitor only one price, while by contrast, collusion in pricing-differentiated products requires agreeing and monitoring a different price for each product. This raises a second issue. Setting such a set of distinct prices requires that the cartel members agree on the degree to which their products are differentiated. This is a far from simple matter especially as its resolution will largely determine each firm's share of the cartel profits. Third, punishment of deviation becomes more complex in a differentiated products context. Should all non-deviating firms punish a deviant or should punishment be imposed by those whose products are the closest substitutes to the deviant's product? If the latter, can punishment be targeted to affect only the deviant firm or will there be spillover effects to other members of the cartel?

It should be noted, however, that there is a potential advantage to product differentiation for cartel sustainability. When the cartel members sell differentiated brands, each of which has substantial brand loyalty, then the temptation to cheat falls. If consumers exhibit considerable loyalty to their favorite brand then a deviant firm will find it hard to win much business even when it secretly cuts its price. However, the weight of the evidence suggests that cartels will be more successful—and therefore more likely—when they offer fairly homogeneous products.

15.2.8   Other Factors

Several other important factors facilitate the formation and continuation of cartel agreements. Monitoring the cartel agreement is easier when prices are *observable*. This is the reason often cited for the use of *basing-point pricing*, a somewhat unusual method of pricing products that are going to be transported at some cost to the consumer. The common sense way to account for the cost of delivery is for the firm to charge a uniform price at the plant, called a mill price, and then vary the price paid by each customer depending on how much it costs to deliver the product to the customer's doorstep. This scheme is usually referred to as *free-on-board* or *fob* pricing. With basing-point pricing by contrast, one or at most, a few plant locations are picked as a basing point. All delivered prices are quoted as the mill or factory price plus the delivery cost *from the basing point*. For example, for the first twenty years of the last century, Pittsburgh was the basing point in pricing U.S.-produced steel. A consumer in Columbus, for example, paid the same price for delivered steel—the mill price plus the transportation cost *from Pittsburgh*—whether the delivery actually came from Pittsburgh or from Birmingham, Alabama.

The advantages of basing-point pricing in sustaining collusion are twofold. First, it ensures that all producers, no matter where they are located, quote the same delivered price to customers at any specific location. This is not the case with fob pricing, in which the delivered price to a given spot depends on the location of the producer. Thus, basing-point pricing considerably simplifies collusion by streamlining the price structure and making it easier to detect cheaters.

The basing-point system also weakens the incentive to cheat. Suppose that there are just two steel plants—one in Pittsburgh and one in Birmingham—and that the two firms aim to set a cooperative monopoly price. Under fob pricing, prices are set at the mill. If one firm cheats, retaliation by the other firm requires a reduction in that firm's mill price. This reduces its profit on sales to *all customers* and so imposes a considerable cost, making the threat of retaliation less credible. With basing-point pricing, however, a price cut can be made by shading the delivered price to just the area or areas in which the noncooperative firm violated the agreement. As a result, the retaliation can be more surgically precise and, most importantly, less costly, discouraging cheating in the first place. It is little surprise that basing-point pricing schemes have now been declared illegal in the United States.

Factors that facilitate a cartel's task of monitoring its members and responding to transgressions swiftly favor collusion. Regulations that require government agencies to publish the bids they have received assist price monitoring by bid-rigging cartels. On private sector contracts, a *trade association* among the companies can help to facilitate collusive bidding behavior. The Hay and Kelley study noted above (Table 15.1) provides evidence of the importance of such trade associations in sustaining "large number" cartels.

In many consumer product markets *most-favored-customer* and *meet-the-competition clauses* can help to maintain a price-fixing agreement among firms.[9] *Most-favored-customer clauses* guarantee that if the seller offers the same product to another buyer at a lower price, the first buyer will receive a rebate equal to the difference in the two prices, whereas *meet-the-competition clauses* guarantee that a firm will match any lower price offered by another seller. It might seem surprising to think of these clauses as being anti- rather than pro-competitive but a moment's thought should indicate how they each can work to maintain cartel discipline.

---

[9]   See Salop (1986) for more details on these competition clauses.

Reality Checkpoint

Most Favored Customer Policy Was a Bad Prescription for Medicaid

The Omnibus Budget Reconciliation Act of 1990 (OBRA 90) contained a most-favored-customer clause that applied to reimbursement for pharmaceuticals purchased under Medicaid. Medicaid is a very large program that accounts for nearly 15 percent of the prescription drug market sales in the U.S. The drug companies routinely offered other large buyers of drugs, such as HMOs and drug store chains, quantity discounts. However, because Medicaid did not purchase the drugs directly in bulk itself but, instead, reimbursed hospitals and pharmacies on an individual basis, it never received these discounts.

OBRA 90 included a number of steps that Congress hoped would alleviate this problem. On the one hand, it required that the drug price charged to Medicaid had to be no more than 12.5 percent *less* than the average price charged to all customers. Moreover, a most-favored-customer clause further required that if a firm charged any customer a price more than 12.5 percent below the average, that same price had to be extended to all Medicaid customers.

The theory outlined in this and the preceding chapter implies that these well-intentioned regulations may well have backfired. The most-favored-customer clause tends to soften price competition. If, a firm tries to cut its price in one market to gain competitive advantage there, the most-favored-customer clause requires that it will have to cut its price in all other markets, too. This acts as a disincentive to aggressive price competition. Indeed, the legislation also required that the Office of Inspector General monitor all firms so that there would be no secret price discounts that were not passed on to Medicaid. Of course, this meant no secret price discounts at all and, as a result, a further weakening of price competition.

Economist Fiona Scott Morton (1997) studied the impact of OBRA 90 on cardiovascular drug prices in the two years starting with January 1, 1991—the date that the regulations went into effect. She found that prices for well-known brand drugs that had been facing tough price competition from generic substitutes, actually rose by over 4 percent. This finding supports the view that most-favored-customer clauses, like meet-the-competition clauses, facilitate collusive behavior aimed at reducing price competition.

Source: Fiona Scott Morton, "The Strategic Response by Pharmaceutical Firms to the Medicaid Most Favored Customer Rules," *Rand Journal of Economics*, 28 (Summer, 1997), 269–90.

The *most-favored-customer clause* severely restricts the temptation of any seller to reduce its price since the price reduction has to be offered to all previous buyers as well. Similarly, *meet-the-competition clauses* make the process of detecting cheating particularly effective, since now the firms offering these guarantees have vast numbers of unpaid market watchers in the person of every consumer who has bought the product. At the same time, such clauses effectively bind the hands of the firms that offer them.

If meet-the-competition clauses have anticompetitive effects why are consumers lured by such guarantees? A price-matching clause is valuable to any one buyer who is assured of getting the very best deal possible. However, because that buyer then becomes implicitly a monitor of prices on behalf of the colluding firms, there is an externality to the buyer's purchase of which she may be unaware. Moreover, such monitoring will lead to prices being set higher (albeit identical) for all consumers. So, in fact, the equilibrium outcome will be one in which all buyers are worse off.

Table 15.2 Payoff matrix for a 2 × 2 pricing game

		Strategy for firm 2	
		Price high	Price low
Strategy for firm 1	Price high	(12, 12)	(5, 14)
	Price low	(14, 5)	(6, 6)

Meet the competition clauses can also strengthen the trigger strategies that support collusive behavior among firms. To get some idea as to just how powerful this effect can be, consider a simple one-period pricing game between two firms. The payoff matrix shown in Table 15.2 describes this prisoners' dilemma game. The one-shot nature of the game leads the firms to the only Nash equilibrium in which both firms price low. Now consider what happens when we permit both firms to publish meet-the-competition guarantees that are legally and instantaneously binding.[10] These guarantees render the off-diagonal price pairs in Table 15.2 unattainable. There is no opportunity to undercut one's cartel partner when each firm has announced a meet-the-competition policy that goes into effect immediately. Because the combinations of one firm pricing low and the other firm pricing high are unattainable, neither firm has any incentive to deviate from the price high policy. The cartel works even in this simple one-period setting.

Stable market conditions also facilitate the detection and punishment of cheating on the cooperative agreement. When demand or production costs are uncertain and subject to random shocks it is easy to make mistakes and punish rivals wrongly suspected of cheating on the cartel. For this reason, the simple trigger strategy of punishing suspected cheating with a permanent reversion to noncooperative play is too harsh. But a modified trigger strategy that punishes the defector only for a number of periods is not as potent a deterrent as a trigger strategy that retaliates forever. Moreover, with uncertain demand, the kinds of strategies that work to sustain collusion often do so only by establishing a market price well below that of a pure monopoly.

One way for a cartel in an unstable market to reinforce the trigger strategy is to establish a *centralized sales agency*, as in the De Beers diamond cartel, or a trade association. Either institutional arrangement can monitor and report upon both market conditions and individual firm performance. Monitoring may be further facilitated by agreements to divide the market explicitly, say by percentage of total sales or by geographic territory.

To summarize, cooperative price-fixing agreements are facilitated when an industry exhibits characteristics that make the detection and the deterrence of cheating easier. Such factors include the presence of only a few firms, selling homogeneous products on a reasonably frequent basis and relatively stable market conditions. All of these factors have been found to be present in the prosecution of numerous recent international cartels.[11] Agreements on market division, whether by geography or sales, also make it easier to

---

[10] This is perfectly legal since the price-matching guarantees are offered to buyers rather than communicated to other sellers.

[11] See Connor (2001) for a detailed and very readable analysis of these cartels.

monitor the behavior of cartel members. The potential for punishment, in some cases, violence, is greatly enhanced by such features and should never be understated.[12]

15.3   AN ILLUSTRATION: COLLUSION ON THE NASDAQ EXCHANGE

Empirical evidence suggests that price-fixing arrangements are not unusual and that their impact can be large. Experience clearly shows that not all of the characteristics listed above need to be present for collusion to occur. It can occur even in conditions that seem on the surface to be quite competitive. We illustrate this point with the well-known case of collusion in the National Association of Securities Dealers Automated Quotations (NASDAQ) market.

Started in 1971, the NASDAQ was the world's first electronic stock market. Since that date it has grown rapidly and now vies with the New York Stock Exchange for position as the largest stock market in the United States. In March 2007 alone more than 33 billion shares were traded with a dollar volume of more than $822 billion.[13] NASDAQ trading is made online and for any given stock there are multiple traders.

The traders post two quotes for each stock in which they deal—an "ask" price at which they will sell the stock and a "bid" price at which they will buy the stock. By convention ask and bid prices used to be quoted in increments of eighths of a dollar. Traders make profits by quoting ask prices that are greater than bid prices but compete with each other through the ask and bid prices they quote. Market prices are determined by the lowest ask price and the highest bid price—called the *inside prices*—the difference between the lowest ask and highest bid being referred to as the *inside spread*.

Because the number of dealers trading a particular stock on the NASDAQ market can be large (sometimes as many as 60) and because entry is relatively easy, this market would seem to be pretty close to satisfying the competitive market ideal. However, other conditions favorable to cooperation are present. Play is repeated frequently and on a regular basis. The traded items (shares) are basically homogeneous. Firms have very similar costs and technical abilities. Are these conditions enough to overcome the procompetitive effects of low concentration and relatively easy entry?

The work of two economists, Christie and Schultz, suggests that the answer to that question is, yes. They found that in the 1990s NASDAQ was not the competitive market it seemed.[14] The evidence came to light when Christie and Schultz constructed a matched sample of securities on the NASDAQ and on the NYSE/AMEX exchanges and compared the distribution of inside spreads. Figure 15.2 reports their results. They concluded that a much higher proportion of NASDAQ stocks had inside spreads of even eighths—2/8 or 4/8—than did similar stocks on NYSE/AMEX.

You might wonder why this should matter. After all, what is an eighth of a dollar between friends? However, given a share volume of around 1.5 billion shares per day, an additional spread of 1/8 is equivalent to additional profits of $187.5 million *per day*, a gift that most friends would be delighted to receive. Christie and Schultz suggested that collusion among NASDAQ dealers could explain the higher proportion of even eighths. The argument goes

---

[12]   A number of cartels in New York City have used violence to enforce their market power.

[13]   For further details visit the NASDAQ website at http://www.nasdaq.com.

[14]   "Why do NASDAQ market makers avoid odd-eighth quotes?," *Journal of Finance*, December, 1994, pp. 1813–49.

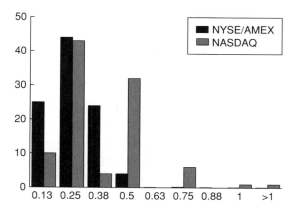

Figure 15.2   The distribution of inside spreads on NYSE/AMEX and NASDAQ
Source: W. G. Christie and P. Schultz, "Why Do NASDAQ Market Makers Avoid Odd Eighth Quotes?,"
Journal of Finance, 49 (December, 1994): 1813–49

Reality Checkpoint

"I Am the Broker, You Are the Brokee!"

Once upon a time, two economists named Paul Schultz (of Ohio State) and William Christie (of Vanderbilt) were talking about stock prices for trades in the over-the-counter market quoted by the National Association of Securities Dealers Automated Quotation (NASDAQ) system. As described in the text, this is a computerized market in which dealers list the prices at which they will buy (the "bid" price) and sell (the "ask" price) various stocks. The difference between the bid and ask prices is the "spread," and it is a major source of dealer profits. Over time, the two economists noticed something odd. The spread was rarely less than 75 cents and always expressed as a multiplier of 25 cents, even though stocks themselves are priced in odd eighths (e.g., 20 and 3/8, or 24 and 5/8). The two economists subsequently published a research paper suggesting that NASDAQ prices could only come about as a result of a price-fixing agreement.

The paper caused an immediate stir and, ultimately, led to an investigation by the antitrust division of the Justice Department. Some time later, the Justice Department filed a civil complaint against two dozen securities dealers. The complaint documented the earlier findings of Schultz and Christie. It also showed that cheating was a potential problem that the dealers dealt with by harassment and verbal assault of the culprit. For example, consider this recorded conversation of one dealer complaining to a second dealer that the latter employed a trader who was not maintaining a spread divisible by 25.

> *First trader*: "He's trading it at one-eighths and embarrassing your firm."
> *Second trader*: "I understand."
> *First trader*: "You know, I would tell him to straighten up his act, stop being a (expletive deleted) moron!"

The agreement did not require the two dozen dealers involved to admit guilt or pay a fine. But it did require the dealers to cease and desist the practice and to tape randomly 3.5 percent of all trader conversations to ensure compliance.

Source: D. Lohse and A. Raghavan, "Will NASDAQ Accord Lead to Better Prices," *Wall Street Journal*, July 18, 1996, p. C1.

as follows. Essentially the NASDAQ dealers are engaged in an infinitely repeated game. When the dealers collude in their bid and ask prices then under certain conditions a dealer will earn more profit by sticking to the collusive agreement than she would earn if she defected from the agreement and undercut the other traders' inside spreads.

Let's investigate under what conditions collusion is possible. Suppose that there are N dealers in a particular stock?[15] Dealer i quotes an ask price of a_i and a bid price of b_i, both measured by convention in eighths of a dollar. The inside ask is defined as $a = \min_i a_i$, the lowest ask price, and the inside bid is defined as $b = \max_i b_i$, the highest bid price. The inside spread is, of course, $a - b$. The demand for shares of this stock by members of the public who wish to purchase at price a is denoted $D(a)$, while the supply of shares by members of the public who wish to sell at price b is denoted $S(b)$. To be specific, we will assume that:

$$D(a) = 200 - 10a \tag{15.7}$$

$$S(b) = -120 + 10b \tag{15.8}$$

where, again by convention, quantities are measured in blocks of 10,000 shares.

We make two further simplifying assumptions. First, we assume that dealers set their bid and ask prices to equate expected demand with expected supply. That is, they do not buy for inventory. What this means is that dealer i quotes ask price a_i and bid price b_i such that $200 - 10a_i = -120 + 10b_i$ which implies that $b_i = 32 - a_i$. As Figure 15.3 shows, this assumption means that the only combinations of ask and bid prices that we need consider are $\{(20, 12), (19, 13), (18, 14), (17, 15), (16, 16)\}$. Second, we assume that any dealer who does not quote the inside spread gets no business while all market makers who quote the inside spread share the orders equally.

We define the value of this stock, v, as the price that equates public demand with public supply. You can easily confirm that, given our demand and supply functions, $v = 16$. In other words, the value of this stock is 16 (or in dollar terms $2.00) and at that price a quantity of 400,000 shares would be traded. Aggregate profit from trading in this stock is made up of

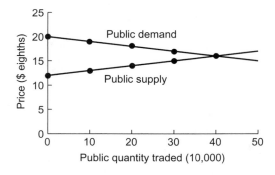

Figure 15.3 Demand and supply for a stock
The stock is traded in units of 10,000 shares and priced in increments of one-eighth of a dollar. Ask (demand) and bid (supply) prices are quoted to equate demand and supply.

---

[15]   For a more complete, but complex, analysis see Dhutta (1999) and Dhutta and Madhavan, (1997).

Table 15.3   Profits in the NASDAQ example

Ask price a	Bid price b = 32 − a	Volume of shares (10,000)	Aggregate profit ($000)
20	12	0	0
19	13	10	75
18	14	20	100
17	15	30	75
16	16	40	0

Table 15.4   Payoff matrix for the NASDAQ cartel game (U.S. dollars, thousands)

		Strategy for Millennial Securities (ask, bid) quotes		
		(18, 14)	*(17, 15)*	*(16, 16)*
Strategy for all other market makers (ask, bid) quotes	*(18, 14)*	$\left(\dfrac{100(N-1)}{N}, \dfrac{100}{N}\right)$	(0, 75)	(0, 0)
	(17, 15)	(75, 0)	$\left(\dfrac{75(N-1)}{N}, \dfrac{75}{N}\right)$	(0, 0)
	(16, 16)	(0, 0)	(0, 0)	(0, 0)

two components: revenues from selling at greater than v and revenues from buying at less than v. In other words,

$$\pi(a, b) = (a - v)D(a) + (v - b)S(b) \tag{15.9}$$

Given our specific demand and supply functions and the "no inventory" assumption, so that $b = 32 - a$ and $D(a) = S(b)$, this simplifies to:

$$\pi(a) = (a - b)(200 - 10a) = (2a - 32)(200 - 10a) = 20(a - 16)(20 - a) \tag{15.10}$$

Table 15.3 gives these profits at the five possible combinations of bid and ask prices.

Aggregate profit is maximized at an ask price of 18 (or $2.25) and a bid price of 14 (or $1.75) with a spread of 4 (or 50 cents) and a volume of 200,000 shares. The question is: can dealers sustain an agreement to quote these prices, or will one dealer defect and quote a lower ask and a higher bid price? Consider a particular dealer, Millennial Securities Inc. Table 15.4 gives her payoff matrix given that she quotes prices (a_m, b_m) while all other dealers quote prices (a_j, b_j).[16]

It would appear that there are two Nash equilibria to this game—(17, 15) and (16, 16). But this ignores one of the beauties of a convention to set prices in increments of eighths

---

[16]   We can confine ourselves to the three sets of prices (18, 14), (17, 15), and (16, 16) since no trader would wish to charge (19, 13) given an agreement to charge (18, 14).

of a dollar. The strategy (16, 16) is (weakly) dominated for Millennial Securities. She never does any worse and usually does better by quoting (17, 15). So we will eliminate the (16, 16) strategy. As a result, we are left with yet another prisoners' dilemma game. If this game were to be played between these market makers only once, the collusive agreement (18, 14) could not be sustained. It is not a Nash equilibrium. Millennial Securities, among others, has the incentive to undercut the agreed prices by quoting (17, 15).

What happens if this game is repeated indefinitely? Does Millennial Securities now have the incentive to stick with the collusive prices or will she still wish to undercut them? Let p be the probability that Millennial Securities will be competing with these dealers in the next period and R be the discount factor. Millennial's discounted profit from sticking to the collusive agreement is:

$$PV_\infty^M = \frac{100}{N} + \frac{100}{N} pR + \frac{100}{N} p^2 R^2 + \frac{100}{N} p^3 R^3 + \ldots = \frac{100}{N(1 - pR)} \tag{15.11}$$

If instead, Millennial undercuts the agreed spread she can expect rapid reaction. After all, as Christie and Schultz noted, all asks and bids are public knowledge with screen trading. So let us assume that the other dealers react to Millennial's undercutting in one period and that the collusive agreement breaks down forever. Then Millennial Securities' expected profit from cheating on the agreement is:

$$PV_\infty^D = 75 + \frac{75}{N} pR + \frac{75}{N} p^2 R^2 + \frac{75}{N} p^3 R^3 + \ldots = 75 + \frac{75pR}{N(1 - pR)}. \tag{15.12}$$

Cheating on the collusive agreement does not pay if $PV_\infty^M > PV_\infty^D$. Simple manipulation shows that for this to be the case the probability-adjusted discount factor must satisfy:

$$pR = \rho > \frac{3N - 4}{3N - 3} \tag{15.13}$$

At the time Christie and Schultz were doing their research, NASDAQ indicated that while there were sometimes as many as 60 dealers, there were, on average, only about 11 dealers for each stock. If $N = 11$ then the necessary value of pR in equation (15.13) is $pR > 0.966$. If $N = 15$, then pR must be as high as 0.976. Since $pR = \frac{p}{1 + r}$ collusion requires both a very high probability p of continued play and a very low interest rate. This, however, is where the frequency issue comes into play. The relevant time period between trades is probably not much more than an hour in any given trading day and market makers' memories carry over from day to day, if they ever go to sleep and stop trading! So the probability in any given period that a particular market maker will continue making a market in this specific stock one hour later is near unity, or $p \approx 1$. Moreover, since the relevant period is only an hour long, the interest rate that we use should also be measured on a per hour basis. A rate of 10 percent per year, for instance, implies a very small value for r per hour—less than 0.01 percent in fact. Hence, values for pR on the order of 0.99 are not at all unreasonable.

In short, the Christie and Schultz suggestion of NASDAQ dealer collusion is consistent with the conditions that economic theory predicts are necessary for such behavior. Moreover, NASDAQ's Preference Trade Rule acted very much like a "no price undercutting" guarantee. It specified that a dealer who did not post the inside spread could nevertheless receive preferenced orders provided he or she matched the best intermarket prices. Thus, not only did NASDAQ meet the basic conditions for successful collusion but also the dealers appeared to have implemented an effective enforcement mechanism. A firm like our Millennial Securities knew that deviating from the cartel price (18, 14) and pricing at (17, 15) would not win the market even for one period since all the other brokers were committed to match her.

Of course, the proof of any pudding is in the eating. The paper by Christie and Schultz served as a catalyst to an investigation of NASDAQ pricing by the Department of Justice and the Securities and Exchange Commission (SEC). The eventual outcome shows that academic research can, in fact, directly lead to the detection of a cartel.[17] The investigation produced convincing evidence of collusion and the case was settled with an agreement by NASDAQ to change its practices. Dealers were required to record at least 3.5 percent of their traders' telephone conversations with other traders and to report any violations. In addition, NASDAQ introduced a *limit order display*. This allows investors to compete directly with dealers by specifying a price and quantity at which they are willing to buy or sell a stock. If the current inside bid on a particular stock is $20^7/_8$ and a private investor specifies a limit order, for example, to buy 10,000 shares of this stock at $21, then the market makers must raise their bids to $21. The result appears to have been a considerable narrowing in spreads.

Finally, for a variety of reasons including the above analysis, the SEC required NASDAQ and other markets to change their pricing practices by moving to decimal quotations in dollars (SEC order, June 2000) beginning "on or before September 5, 2000."[18] Interestingly enough, NASDAQ accompanied this move by a press release on the NASDAQ website citing the "increased savings potential for investors if decimal pricing leads to smaller price increments and narrower bid-ask spreads."

15.4   DETECTING COLLUSION AMONG FIRMS

In the preceding sections we have offered some guiding principles on where the authorities should watch most closely for collusive arrangements. Just watching, however, can never be enough. Even if the authorities are looking in the right place they may not detect price-fixing behavior. Some idea as to how difficult it is for the government to detect collusive behavior may be inferred from the fact that the majority of cartels that have been uncovered have only been disclosed through "finking." Sometimes the disclosure has been made by firms in the industry who have been unhappy either with the shares that they have been allocated in the cartel or because they have been excluded altogether. Sometimes it has been former employees of cartel members who have blown the whistle after losing their jobs.[19]

---

[17]   For details see the Department of Justice press release at http://www.usdoj.gov/atr/public/press_releases/1996/343.html.

[18]   To view this order go to http://www.sec.gov/rules/othern/34-42914.htm.

[19]   A classic example of this is the garbage-hauling business in New York, which was controlled by a trade association between firms who carved up the city between them. If a firm in the cartel took business away from another member, then the association forced the offending company to pay compensation amounting to "up to forty times the monthly pickup charge." Any firm attempting to enter the industry was met by arson and physical violence. Ex-mobsters who had been the victims of the financial penalties and violence provided some of the evidence necessary to break the cartel. (S. Raab, "To Prosecutors, Breakthrough after 5 Years of Scrutiny," *New York Times*, June 23, 1995, p. 3.)

Legally proving the existence of the cartel to the satisfaction of the courts has not been easy in many of these cases. Where successful, such prosecution has almost always been the result of the cartel members being careless. For example, they have spoken on telephones that have been tapped, or have kept permanent records of their agreements—on paper, or hard-drives on computers, and in one spectacular case inadvertently sending a copy of the agreement to a buyer along with the bid documents!

Without such evidence it is remarkably difficult for the authorities to prove, legally, the existence of a cartel. Moreover, even if uncovering a cartel is possible, there is a huge difference between detection and successful legal prosecution. The conspiring firms are entitled to their "day in court" and they have both the incentive and the ability to put up a strong defense. The cartel members have an informational advantage over any government agency, namely, the fact that they are the ones who know the nature of market demand as well as the costs of production and transportation. The best the authorities can do is to infer this information from data provided by the very same firms who are being investigated. In these circumstances, counsel for the defense can make the proof of collusion extremely difficult by making a collusive outcome appear to be competitive. This problem has been termed the *indistinguishability theorem* by Harstad and Phlips (1990).[20]

To show the indistinguishability theorem in action, we consider a case in which the European Commission ultimately rendered a verdict against ICI and Solvay, the two firms that control the European market for soda ash, which is a raw material used in glass manufacture. ICI and Solvay had operated a number of cartel agreements for many years. Solvay supplied continental Europe while ICI supplied the U.K., Ireland, and the British Commonwealth. These explicit agreements terminated in 1972, but there was no subsequent market interpenetration by the two producers. In the 1980s prices in the U.K. rose some 15 to 20 percent above those in continental Europe, which the Commission argued was greater than the transport costs across the English Channel. The Commission judged that the lack of market invasion by either firm into the other's historic regional market—especially in the face of such price differentials—was strong evidence of continued tacit collusion by the two firms.

While the Commission's judgment may appear to be sound there is a counter-argument. If each firm has the same marginal cost schedule and if each sets its price equal to marginal cost plus the cost of transportation across the Channel no cross-market penetration will ever occur. Such pricing behavior would reflect true rivalry, would lead to prices well below the collusive level, and yet there would be no market invasion of one firm by the other. Unless the regulatory agency has independent data on transportation costs, the nature of demand on each side of the Channel, and also on production costs, it cannot make a definitive case that the continued market segmentation of the market is the result of collusive action.

Similar considerations apply when defending companies who are being charged with collusion because of evidence that they changed their prices in parallel. MacLeod (1985) shows that when firms' profit functions are not known to each other then there is no systematic difference in the way that collusive and noncollusive equilibrium prices change in response to exogenous shocks. This is relevant to a 1984 judgment by the European Commission against a number of North American, Finnish, and Swedish companies who exported wood pulp to Europe for use by paper manufacturers. The Commission determined that these companies had to pay fines of between 50,000 and 500,000 ECU because they had announced and enforced parallel seasonal price changes. The judgment was thrown out on appeal in 1993 to the European

---

[20] For a much more detailed exposition of the indistinguishability theorem see Phlips (1995a). See also LaCasse (1995).

Court of Justice because, as the MacLeod (1985) analysis suggests, such common price responses do not necessarily imply collusion.

The situation facing government authorities is not hopeless. Sometimes a bit of good detective work can find the necessary evidence. The studies by Porter and Zona (1993, 1999) are good illustrations of the kind of hard and thoughtful work that is necessary. Porter and Zona (1999) studied school milk procurement auctions in which a cartel was active, but in which there were also non-cartel members bidding in the auctions. They were able to show that the bidding characteristics of the cartel members were very different from those of the non-cartel members. While non-cartel members' bids increased with distance from the firm to the school district as would be expected, cartel members' bids often decreased with distance. The explanation is that the cartel members were bidding competitively in distant districts not covered by the cartel but cooperatively in proximate districts they controlled.

In their 1993 study, Porter and Zona reviewed bidding on highway paving projects on Long Island in the early 1980s. They note that since the Department of Transportation specified exactly what was to be built, the product of each firm was effectively identical. They also note that while not all firms bid on any given contract, each firm that bid knew precisely who the others were. In addition, the winning firm and its bid were publicly announced. Hence, detection of any cheating on a cartel agreement would be easy. The market outcome was concentrated. Of the 76 largest contracts, half went to one of just four firms. Finally, there were active trade associations and union groups through which the firms communicated. In short, the highway construction industry on Long Island exhibited many of the characteristics necessary for successful collusion. Perhaps it is not surprising that in 1984 one of the largest firms in this industry was convicted of price-fixing along with four other unindicted co-conspirators. The other four later faced charges in other suits. The conviction came as the result of a confession by one executive.

In their study of this market Porter and Zona (1993) ranked separately the cartel firms and the non-cartel firm by order of their unit costs. They then compared this ranking with the ranking of the submitted bids. For the non-cartel firms, the ranking of bids and costs are similar. The lower a firm's cost, the lower its bid. This is not the case for the cartel firms. For these firms, there is little relationship between their cost and bid ranks. Again, this makes intuitive sense. The choice by the cartel firms as to who among them will be the low bidder has little to do with cost: the bid is designed to generate profit. Once that firm and that bid are chosen, all the others need to do is to bid a bit higher whether their costs are a little higher or a lot.

Porter and Zona's (1993, 1999) work is insightful, but it has the advantage of working backwards. Members of the cartels had already been convicted by the time that Porter and Zona began their work. That is, they knew that a cartel was there and the only remaining question was what kind of evidence forensic economics might uncover that would further verify the collusive arrangement. While such analysis is helpful in prosecuting alleged price-fixing conspirators, the question from a policy perspective is whether this sort of work is also helpful in uncovering collusion in the first place. If the bidders on the Long Island projects had known in advance that the authorities would examine the relationship, or lack of it, between bids and firms' costs, then all they needed to do to defeat the test was to ensure that non-winning bids were ranked by costs.[21]

---

[21]   In a related piece, Hendricks and Porter (1988) examine bids for offshore oil and gas leases. They find that firms with tracts adjacent to the tract being auctioned often lose to non-neighboring firms even though the latter are, presumably less well informed and, therefore, should bid more cautiously. This suggests that neighboring firms are colluding to keep bids low.

Table 15.5 The great salt duopoly

	1980	1981	1982	1983	1984
BS profit	7,065	7,622	10,489	10,150	10,882
WP profit	7,273	7,527	6,841	6,297	6,204
BS profit per unit of capacity	8.6	9.3	12.7	12.3	13.2
WP profit per unit of capacity	6.6	6.9	6.3	5.8	5.7
Industry capacity/total UK sales	1.5	1.7	1.7	1.9	1.9

Osborne and Pitchik (1987) propose another test for detecting collusion. Recall our discussion in section 12.2.2 of the Spence (1977) and Dixit (1980) models in which a large firm invests in extra capacity as a means to discipline a new rival. Osborne and Pitchik argue that extra capacity may play a similar disciplinary role in cartels.[22] For example, we know that Bertrand price competition cannot yield the competitive outcome unless each firm has the capacity to serve the entire market. In the case of a cartel, however, acquiring such large capacity affords the firm the means to threaten the other firms with the competitive outcome if either one cheats on the collusive agreement. Osborne and Pitchik (1987) show that in this case cartel members have an incentive to acquire a larger amount of capacity.

However, it is likely that the firms choose their capacities before the collusive agreement is implemented and so the collusive agreement covers only their pricing behavior. Because the capacity choice is made noncooperatively, it is unlikely that each will choose exactly the same amount of capacity. Accordingly, when collusion subsequently begins, the price marginal cost distinction may be the same for each firm but the profit per unit of capacity will be greater for the firm with the smaller amount of capacity. Not only will the smaller firm have a higher profit per unit of capacity but Osborne and Pitchik (1987) also show that this difference will increase as the total amount of excess capacity grows. By contrast, if there is no collusion the profits per capacity unit will be identical across firms.

Phlips (1995b) shows how this analysis can be used to examine the behavior of the two British producers of white salt, British Salt and ICI Weston Point. Many analysts suspected these two firms of collusion even after they abandoned an earlier explicit price agreement when the U.K. adopted its Restrictive Practices Act in 1956. Phlips claims that:

> Throughout the period under investigation, both British Salt (BS) and ICI Weston Point (WP) had excess capacity. BS had a given capacity of 824 kilotons, WP had a given capacity of 1095 kilotons. All I had to do was to divide the yearly profits by the capacities and to divide the sum of the capacities by total sales, to find the ... numbers [shown in Table 15.5]. Not only was BS's profit per unit of capacity larger than WP's: it also increased relative to WP's as their joint capacity increased relative to market demand. None of these numbers is disputable ... This beats the indistinguishability theorem: I wish more such tests were available. (Phlips, 1995b, p. 15)

15.5 CARTEL LENIENCY (AMNESTY) PROGRAMS

While our discussion in the previous section implies that the regulatory authorities face severe problems in detecting and prosecuting cartels, all is not lost. An increasing number of regulatory authorities have enacted leniency programs as a way of combating cartels. While

---

[22] Davidson and Deneckere (1990) offer a similar analysis.

the actual programs enacted in different regions differ in their details, they typically have the form: "The first member of a cartel to provide evidence that leads to successful prosecution of the cartel receives lenient treatment. Everybody else is subject to heavy fines." Even if an investigation has been started, a lighter sentence or even total amnesty might still be offered to the first firm coming forward with evidence if this evidence proves central to successful prosecution of the cartel.[23] This new program has been wildly successful in aiding the prosecution of cartels. As the Antitrust Division of the U.S. Department of Justice has said:

> Today, the Amnesty Program is the Division's most effective generator of large cases, and it is the Department's most successful leniency program. Amnesty applications over the past year have been coming in at the rate of approximately two per month—a more than *twenty-fold increase* as compared to the rate of applications under the old Amnesty Program. Given this remarkable rate of amnesty applications, it certainly appears that the message has been communicated. (http://www.usdoj.gov/atr/public/speeches/2247.htm)

Why has granting amnesty proven so successful in breaking cartels? One reason is that such a program encourages finking by cartel members if they believe that an investigation has been started. Leniency programs put the prisoners' dilemma to work. However, as Motta and Polo (1999) and Spagnolo (2004) among others have pointed out, that explanation cannot be the whole story. For while leniency encourages confessions once an investigation is under way, it also raises the possibility of getting out of the cartel free of prosecution and thereby increases the expected net gains from starting a cartel in the first place. Indeed, the apparent evidence that more cartels are being successfully prosecuted since the advent of leniency programs might simply be the result of more cartels being formed so that with the same or even lower detection rate more conspiracies are caught!

Initiation of a leniency program involves a complicated trade-off. In order to illustrate how this trade-off might play out we use the duopoly model presented in section 14.3. Our notation is as follows. A price-fixing agreement gives a cartel member profit π^M, while optimal deviation from the agreement gives profit π^D. The noncooperative Nash equilibrium profit to each firm is π^N. Both firms have probability-adjusted discount factors of ρ. Now consider the following game.[24] Each firm can adopt one of three strategies:

(1) (*Collude, not reveal*): Form a cartel and do not reveal evidence of the existence of the cartel if it is investigated. This is the strategy that we analyzed in section 14.3. We know from equation (14.12) that the value V_{NR}^C of expected profit is:

$$V_{NR}^C = \frac{\pi^M - asF + \dfrac{as\rho}{1-\rho}\pi^N}{1 - \rho(1 - as)} \tag{15.14}$$

where a is the probability that the antitrust authorities launch an investigation; s is the probability that the investigation leads to successful prosecution given that the members of the cartel do not provide evidence of the cartel's existence; and F is the maximum legal fine that can be levied on successful prosecution.

---

[23] For further details of the precise conditions under which amnesty might be granted see the speech by the Deputy Assistant Attorney General at http://www.usdoj.gov/atr/public/speeches/2247.htm.

[24] This game is a highly simplified version of the game presented in Motta and Polo (2003): see also Motta (2004) pp. 195ff.

(2)   (*Collude, reveal*): Form a cartel but reveal its existence once an investigation has been started. Now we assume that the investigation takes one period and that the cartel firms maintain the cartel until the investigation is "nearly" complete. Each firm earns the cartel profit for one period but then both confess and the cartel collapses. To evaluate expected profit V_R^C for this strategy we consider two possibilities:

a.   No investigation is initiated in period 0, which has probability $1 - a$. In this case, the cartel continues and expected profit is:

$$V_1 = (1 - a)(\pi^M + \rho V_R^C) \tag{15.15}$$

The first term in the second bracket is cartel profit in the current year, after which the "game" with the authorities resumes with expected profit V_R^C discounted by one period.

b.   An investigation is initiated in period 0, which has probability a. The cartel continues until the investigation is nearing completion, at which point the firms confess and pay a reduced fine of $0 \leq R < F$. The cartel then collapses. Expected profit is:

$$V_2 = a\left(\pi^M - R + \frac{\rho}{1 - \rho} \pi^N \right) \tag{15.16}$$

Summing equations (15.15) and (15.16) gives the expected profit from the strategy (collude, reveal) $V_R^C = V_1 + V_2$.

Solving for V_R^C gives:

$$V_R^C = \frac{\pi^M - aR + \dfrac{a\rho\pi^N}{1 - \rho}}{1 - (1 - a)\rho} \tag{15.17}$$

Equation (15.17) reveals the potential downside of a leniency program. Expected profit is decreasing in the fine R. In other words, the more generous the leniency program—the smaller is R—the more profitable is (collude, reveal) and so the more likely it is that a cartel will be formed.

(3)   *Defect* on the cartel in period $t = 0$, in which case, of course, the cartel breaks down or, more accurately, is never effectively formed. We know from equation (14.5) that the value of expected profit in this case is:

$$V^D = \pi^D + \frac{\rho\pi^N}{1 - \rho} \tag{15.18}$$

We need some further assumptions to complete the analysis. If both firms defect then no cartel is ever formed and each firm has profit $V^N = \pi^N/(1 - \rho)$. If one firm defects while the other does not the defecting firm earns V^D while the non-defecting firm makes "very low" profits V^L. If one firm reveals while the other does not, the revealing firm earns V_R^C as above while the non-revealing firm earns $V_R^C - D$ where $D > 0$ can be calculated by substituting F for R in equation (15.17). This gives the payoff matrix of Table 15.6 in which Firm 1's payoffs are listed first.

Inspection of Table 15.6 reveals that it has potentially a number of possible Nash equilibria. (*Defect, defect*) is, of course, one of these. The noncooperative Nash equilibrium to

Table 15.6   Payoff matrix with a leniency program

		Strategy for firm 2		
		Defect	Collude, reveal	Collude, not reveal
Strategy for firm 1	Defect	(V^N, V^N)	(V^D, V^L)	(V^D, V^L)
	Collude, reveal	(V^L, V^D)	(V_R^C, V_R^C)	$(V_R^C, V_R^C - D)$
	Collude, not reveal	(V^L, V^D)	$(V_R^C - D, V_R^C)$	(V_{NR}^C, V_{NR}^C)

the one-shot game repeated over and over is always one of the potential equilibria to the repeated game. As Table 15.6 shows, however, there are also other and more interesting equilibrium possibilities. In particular:

1. (*Collude, reveal*) for both players is an equilibrium provided that $V_R^C > V^D$;
2. (*Collude, not reveal*) for both players is an equilibrium provided that $V_{NR}^C > \max\{V_R^C, V^D\}$

Indeed, an interesting feature of this game is that if $V_{NR}^C > V_R^C > V^D$, then there are actually three equilibria. These are: both defect, both play (collude, reveal) and both play (collude, not reveal). It seems reasonable to assume that if the firms are able to agree on forming a cartel, then they will also be able to agree to choose the most profitable strategy combination for the cartel, which in this case would be (collude, not reveal).

To make matters more concrete, we now illustrate the impact of the leniency program using the Bertrand example of section 14.3. Recall that in this example, we have: $\pi^M = 1,800$, $\pi^D = 3,600$ and $\pi^N = 0$. In the context of the model above, this yields:

$$V_R^C = \frac{1,800 - aR}{1 - (1-a)\rho}; \ V_{NR}^C = \frac{1,800 - asF}{1 - (1-as)\rho}; \ V^D = 3,600 \qquad (15.19)$$

We also assume that the antitrust authority can use its scarce resources to affect three parameters in our model. These are: (1) the probability a that an investigation is initiated; (2) the probability s that the investigation is successful in identifying the cartel; and (3) R, the strength of the leniency program. The maximum penalty F paid in litigation that results in a conviction is, on the other hand, determined by the courts. We set this at $F = \$3,600$ or twice the per period excess cartel profit. (Recall that private antitrust lawsuits pay treble damages to successful plaintiffs.) Given that we know F and ρ we can illustrate how the parameters a and s determine the equilibrium for a given value of R. Finally, for convenience and without being too unrealistic, we set $\rho = 0.8$.

Table 15.7 gives the profits for each of the three strategies for any values of a and s, and for two values of R, namely, $R = 0$ (complete amnesty); and $R = \$600$ (one-third of the cartel profits). From Table 15.7 we have:

(1) $V_R^C > V^D$ if $a < a_{CR}(R) = 3/8$ if $R = 0$ and $= 9/29$ if $R = 600$;
(2) $V_{NR}^C > V^D$ if $a < a_{CNR}(s) = 1/6s$;
(3) $V_{NR}^C > V_R^C$ if $a < a_{ES}(R, s) = (2 - 3s)/4s$ if $R = 0$ and $(13 - 18s)/20s$ if $R = 600$.

Table 15.7   Profits for the leniency program game

	$R = 0$	$R = 600$
V_R^C	$\dfrac{9{,}000}{1 + 4a}$	$\dfrac{3{,}000(3 - a)}{1 + 4a}$
V_{NR}^C	$\dfrac{9{,}000(1 - 2as)}{1 + 4as}$	$\dfrac{9{,}000(1 - 2as)}{1 + 4as}$
V^D	$3{,}600$	$3{,}600$

The subscript ES in (3) stands for "equilibrium selection" when both (Collude, reveal) and (Collude, not reveal) are Nash equilibria. Given our equilibrium selection assumption, (Collude, reveal) is the equilibrium for $a \in [a_{ES}(R, s), a_{CR}(R)]$, (Collude, not reveal) is the equilibrium for $a < \min\{a_{ES}(R, s), a_{CNR}(s)\}$ and no cartel is formed otherwise.

These outcomes are illustrated in Figure 15.4 and allow us to highlight the conflicting effects of the leniency program. Look first at Figure 15.4(a), which assumes that the leniency program offers compete amnesty or $R = 0$. If no leniency program exists a cartel

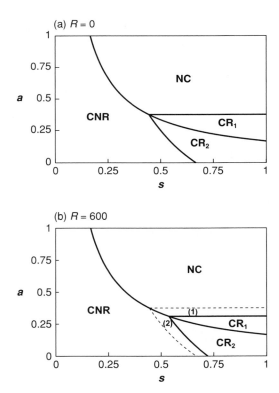

Figure 15.4   Equilibria with a leniency program

Reality Checkpoint
Leniency Program Succeeds—Only Too Well

The Competition Directorate of the European Commission introduced its leniency program in 2002 and updated the program in December 2006. The new program guidelines include the following provisions:

- Fines are up to 30 percent of the sales value affected by the cartel, multiplied by the number of years over which the cartel operated.
- Cartel members will also be fined an "entry fee" for joining the cartel, which will be between 15 and 25 percent of annual sales in the sectors affected by the cartel.
- Repeat offenders can have their fines doubled for a second offence, tripled for a third offence and so on.
- Fines can be further increased for companies that do not cooperate with the Commission's investigation and for the ring-leader in the cartel.
- Fines can be decreased if a company fully cooperates with the cartel investigation.
- Companies that "blow the whistle" on the cartel receive full immunity from punishment.

The problem is that this policy appears to be almost too successful. The lure of immunity has generated more than 200 applications since 2002. While this has led to a series of high-profile successes, it also runs the risk of over-whelming the 70 specialist investigators. Even with evidence provided by immunity appli-cants, cartel investigations currently take at least three years to complete. The flood of immunity applications threatens to drag this out even more. In response, the competition com-missioner Neelie Kroes has floated the idea of offering "direct settlements": reduced fines in return for cooperation with the cartel investi-gation and the promise not to appeal the Commission's final ruling. However, this pro-posal faces many practical and legal obstacles, so for the time being it looks as if the investi-gators will have to soldier on with their increased workload unless, of course, some of the rapidly growing revenues from fines are used to hire additional investigators!

Source: "Cartels Feel Pain of Kroes Crusade," *Financial Times*, Companies International, Thursday, March 29, 2007.

will be formed only if the probability of an investigation $a < a_{CNR}(s)$ and these cartels will not reveal evidence if they are investigated. There is no incentive to do so if there is no hope of leniency.

The leniency program extends the parameter region in which cartels form. If a and s lie in region CR_1 cartels form using the strategy (collude, reveal) whereas without the leniency program no cartels form in this region. On the other hand, cartels in the region CR_2 that follow the policy (collude, not reveal) in the absence of a leniency program now switch to (collude, reveal), potentially making the antitrust authorities' detection problems somewhat easier. In other words, the leniency program encourages the creation of more cartels but also makes them easier to find and prosecute.

The same conflict arises when we compare the generous leniency program of Figure 15.4(a) with the less generous program of Figure 15.4(b), in which $R = 600$. In region (1) cartels that would form with the generous program do not form with the less generous program. On the other hand, in region (2) cartels that would adopt (collude, reveal) with the generous program adopt (collude, not reveal) with the less generous program. A less generous leni-ency program creates fewer cartels but makes them harder to find.

15.6   EMPIRICAL APPLICATION
An Experimental Investigation of Leniency Programs

The observation that many more cartels have been uncovered since the adoption of leniency programs has not yet yielded a large number of efforts to test the effect of such programs empirically. In part, this reflects the difficulty that attends the fact that the only cartel evidence we can ever have relates to cartels that have been successfully prosecuted rather than to those that successfully avoided detection. This creates a serious problem in using statistical evidence from actual data to evaluate the effectiveness of leniency programs. We have used statistical evidence and more specifically, formal regression analysis, in many other chapters in this text, and it is probably clear from these that in some real world cases, such analysis is difficult at best. In recent years economists have turned to an alternative source of economic data—namely, using individuals to conduct laboratory simulations of actual economic interactions. While such controlled experiments are contrived, when done carefully they can nonetheless offer important insight into real-world settings.

In this section we report on an experiment designed by Hinloopen and Soetevent (2006) (HS hereafter) in which they assess the impact of leniency programs on cartel formation, effectiveness and duration.[25] The experiment consists of volunteer subjects playing a repeated Bertrand game against each other. Four different treatments or settings are examined, each played by different groups of respondents. The *Benchmark* case is just the Bertrand pricing game without communication between players. *Communication* is the same game except that players are allowed to communicate before setting prices via computer screens. *Antitrust* introduces a 15 percent probability in each period that any cartel or communication that is formed is detected. Finally, *Leniency* gives cartel members the option of reporting the cartel in return for a reduced penalty.

In each treatment each subject is randomly assigned to a group of three without knowing who the other two group members are. Throughout the experiment all communications between players take place through computer screens. The subjects play a repeated discrete price Bertrand game against the other players in their group. All groups play independently.

The precise play of the game is that in each period, each of the three subjects acts like a firm and sets price by choosing an integer in the range 101–110. Those members of a group who set the lowest price p receive net earnings of $\pi = (p - 100)/L$ where L is the number of group members setting the lowest price. All other group members earn nothing. In each treatment or setting, the game is played for at least 20 periods and this is known from the start. The subjects are informed that after period 19 each next period would be the last one with probability 20 percent: this is intended to attenuate end-period effects.

The one-shot equilibrium for this pricing game is for all players to set a price of 101. The indefinitely repeated equilibrium is for all players to set a price equal to 110 provided that players' are sufficiently patient (HS provide a formal proof of these results).

In each round of play, the subjects in the *Leniency* treatment have the most steps. There are seven steps as follows:[26]

---

[25]   Jeroen Hinloopen and Adriaan R. Soetevent, "Trust and Recidivism: The Partial Success of Corporate Leniency Programs in the Laboratory," Tinbergen Institute Discussion Paper TI 2006-067/1, 2006, available at http://www.tinbergen.nl.

[26]   Detailed descriptions of subject instructions are provided in the Hinloopen and Soetevent (2006) paper.

Step 1: Decide whether or not to communicate with the other group members. If all three choose to communicate move to step 2, otherwise move to step 3.

Step 2: Communicate by suggesting minimum and maximum prices. Players have one minute to reach an agreement through repeated iteration on these prices.

Step 3: Each player in the group sets a market price. This need not be the price agreed in step 2, since agreements are non-enforceable, giving players the option to defect on an agreement.

Step 4: Market price is revealed. Market price is equal to the minimum price submitted by the three group members in step 3.

Step 5: If a cartel is formed in step 1 players are given the option of reporting the cartel. Reporting costs one point. The first player to report receives full amnesty, the second a 50 percent reduction in the fine and the third no reduction. The point deduction for non-reporting group members (or the third member to report) is 10 percent of gross earnings for the relevant period.

Step 6: If no report is submitted in step 5 there is a 15 percent probability that the cartel is detected, in which case all players pay the full point deduction.

Step 7: Close of the game for this period, when players are notified of their earnings (points) for this period, whether a reporting decision was made and how many players in the group reported.

In contrast to the Leniency group, those in the Benchmark treatment are restricted to only three steps: steps 3, 4 and 7. Those in the Communication treatment have five steps omitting steps 5 and 6, while those in the Antitrust treatment have six steps, omitting step 5.

In all treatment groups, the subjects can at any time, review the entire history of their rivals' play on a scrollable screen. At the end of the experiment, the profit points accumulated by a player are converted into euros at an exchange rate of one point for €0.25.

The experiment was conducted over the period June 13–17, 2005 at the University of Amsterdam, with subjects drawn from a large pool of undergraduates across all subject fields. There were approximately 40 subjects in each treatment. This allows running that scenario with different sets of players. Remember that the players in this game are just people like you! They are not actual firms. However, they do have a monetary incentive and they do understand the rules of the game. So, their behavior should tell us something about real-world cartel formation.

Table 15.8 summarizes the overall intention to form a cartel among players in each of the three settings in which formation is possible. (Recall that in the Benchmark group, no communication is allowed.) The first row shows the average fraction of players in that treatment

Table 15.8 Cartel formation

	Communication	*Antitrust*	*Leniency*
Cartel intention	78.08	64.74	62.26
Always	30.77	20.51	23.81
Never	0.00	0.00	9.52
Cartel formation	47.31	27.31	12.86

group who wanted to form a cartel in any given period. The next two rows show the fraction of players in a treatment group who either: (a) always wanted to form a cartel in every period; or (b) never wanted to form a cartel in any period. The final row shows the average number of cartels formed for each group.

On average 78 percent of those who had the opportunity to collude on price without fear of any antitrust prosecution were interested in forming a cartel. This falls to 65 percent when an antitrust authority with a 15 percent detection rate is introduced. Perhaps somewhat surprisingly, introducing a leniency program does not noticeably reduce this willingness any further.

Since unanimity is an important element in a cartel's success, the actual number of cartels formed is much less than the average fraction of players interested in forming one. In this experiment not only does the presence of an active antitrust agency cut cartel formation by 20 percentage points, but the augmentation of that agency's policy to include a leniency program reduces cartel formation by a further 15 percentage points. Thus, this initial evidence suggests that fears that leniency works to encourage cartel formation may be overstated. Moreover, with leniency there is a small group of subjects that is persistent in their unwillingness to participate in a cartel at all, which the authors interpret as the first indication that the leniency program is working to break down trust among potential cartel members.

Of course, the fact that cartel formation declines with the emergence of a leniency program does not necessarily give us a complete description of the effect of that program. It may be that even though there are fewer cartels, the ones that form are more aggressive in that they set a higher cartel price. Evidence on this point is provided in Tables 15.9 and 15.10. A quick inspection of the first of these indicates, however, that there is no significant difference across treatments in the average agreed-upon price. A similarly quick inspection of Table 15.10 indicates that the average market price actually established is somewhat lower with a leniency program. There is in this experiment little evidence that the beneficial effect of a leniency program in reducing cartel formation is offset by higher prices in those instances in which cartels are actually formed. If anything, the leniency program seems to have a procompetitive effect on prices. In addition, the average defection size—the difference between

Table 15.9   Agreed-upon prices

	Mean	*Median*	*Minimum*	*Maximum*
Communication	109.40	110	102	110
Antitrust	109.12	110	103	110
Leniency	109.60	110	105	110

Table 15.10   Average market prices

	Benchmark	*Communication*	*Antitrust*	*Leniency*
All	103.24	103.31	103.04	101.38
Cartels	—	105.43	104.82	103.39
Non-Cartels	103.24	101.40	102.38	101.08

Table 15.11   Cartel breakdown

	Fraction of cartels			Fraction of cartel members	
	Defection	*Detection*	*Reporting*	*Defection*	*Reporting*
Communication	0.67	—	—	0.52	—
Antitrust	0.68	0.17	—	0.50	—
Leniency	0.94	0.03	0.78	0.72	0.40

the agreed-upon price and the market price—is greatest in the Leniency treatment. It would appear that in this treatment defectors want to be more certain of capturing the entire market, a second indication that the leniency program is working to undermine trust between cartel members.

We now return to the question about the role of leniency or amnesty programs in detection of price-fixing agreements. Table 15.11 presents the HS results regarding cartel breakdowns using as a unit of analysis both cartels themselves and also actual cartel members. The evidence indicates that a large fraction of cartels—roughly two-thirds—suffer at least a temporary break down and as many as 94 percent of cartels break down. The HS evidence also shows that when a leniency program exists, a sizable percentage of cartel defection is accompanied by members reporting to the antitrust authorities in order to take advantage of the leniency offer. If by detection we also mean finking, this evidence suggests that leniency programs actually do enhance the discovery of illegal cartels. In turn, their findings suggest that another reason for the high rate of defection when leniency is introduced is that leniency leads cartel members to defect before they can be reported, a third indication that the leniency program undermines trust among cartel members.

HS conclude that the evidence from their experiments imply that leniency programs lower prices for three reasons. These are:

1. Cartel formation is made more difficult.
2. Defection is more likely and more frequent.
3. Defection is more severe in so far as there is a greater difference between the agreed-upon price and the undercutting price.

In effect, leniency programs undermine trust among potential cartel members.

HS also use statistical analysis to illuminate the dynamics of prices over the course of a cartel. As Sproul (1993) found in a number of real-world cartel cases, HS find that their laboratory generated cartel prices tend to rise at the moment of detection. The reason for this in the HS generated data is equally clear. Because in the basic Antitrust treatment group, there is a constant 15 percent chance of detection in any period, the cartels most likely to be caught are those that are most successful and last the greatest number of periods. However, these are precisely the ones in which the price is likely to be highest. The statistical data may show a correlation between cartel detection and high prices but this should not necessarily lead to the inference made by Sproul (1973) that cartels work to keep costs and, therefore, prices down. That correlation is present in the HS simulations even though it is clear from the way the experiment is set up that the only role of cartels in this setting is to raise prices.

Summary

Collusion, both explicit and tacit is a topic of great interest and importance to both industrial economists and antitrust authorities. Uncovering and prosecuting cartels is a major policy goal. This is because the vast bulk of evidence and experience reveals not only that cartels happen but that, when they do, the effect on price is substantial—on the order of 20 or 30 percent above the price that would have prevailed in the absence of collusion. To pursue their goal of detection and successful prosecution efficiently, antitrust authorities need to use economic theory and evidence so as to focus on those markets in which cartel formation is most likely and will do the greatest harm.

Theory suggests that markets in which collusive agreements are likely to succeed are ones with just a few firms in total or at least where just a few firms account for most of the output. Such markets will also typically exhibit a low elasticity of demand, substantial barriers to new entry, relatively homogeneous products, similar cost functions across firms, and relatively stable market conditions. Virtually all cartels that have been uncovered have occurred in industries that meet these conditions.

Just knowing where to look for cartel arrangements, however, is not enough. Authorities must have the additional ability to identify collusion accurately and to prosecute it successfully. Yet obtaining compelling evidence of price-fixing is difficult, particularly since the authorities often have to rely on the very same firms it is investigating to obtain the incriminating information. This is no doubt why so many cartels have been uncovered only as a result of revelations by rivals, suppliers, employees, or customers of the firms involved. In this light, Phlips' call for the development of more tests to discriminate between collusion and non-collusion is well noted. Whether economists will be able to answer that call remains to be seen.

In the meantime, the antitrust authorities are probably doing the best they can by using leniency programs. As we have shown, however, these may not be the simple panacea that some analysts hoped they would be. On the one hand, they certainly make cartel detection easier since evidence provided by a cartel member attesting to the operations of the cartel is undoubtedly compelling. On the other hand, the prospect of a "free walk" may reduce the costs of joining a cartel, potentially encouraging cartel formation that would otherwise not have occurred. Experimental evidence suggests, however, that leniency programs ultimately lead to lower prices because there is an overall adverse effect on cartel formation.

Problems

1. Explain why collusion is more likely to occur in industries with higher concentration.

2. Repeat the proofs of sections 15.2.1 and 15.2.3 for the Cournot model of Chapter 14.

3. Suppose that fence companies submit sealed bids for government contracts to put guard rail on highways. Devise a method for submitting bids that spreads the work evenly among the companies.

4. When highway departments receive bids from guard rail and other construction firms, they regularly open the sealed bid tenders and announce the identity and the bid of the winning bidder. Do you think that this practice facilitates or hinders collusion among the construction firms?

5. List the features of the NASDAQ market that facilitate collusion. What features would make collusion in this market difficult? How should this affect policy?

6. Why has the OPEC oil cartel been successful in raising prices, while the CIPEC copper cartel has not?

7. Suppose that a cartel has just been created and it includes both large and small firms, each having different average and marginal costs curves. The cartel agreement is for each member to reduce its output by 20 percent from the current level. Suppose that the current level of industry output approximates the competitive output level. Will this 20 percent reduction rule maximize the cartel's profit? Explain why or why not.

8. It has been often noted that cartel firms often maintain excessive capacity. This is true for example in the case of OPEC (especially for

Saudi Arabia). It was also true in the electric turbine conspiracy of the 1950s and, more recently, the international lysine conspiracy of the 1990s, among others. One explanation of this is that the success of the cartel inevitably leads the members to reinvest their profits in new capacity. In this view, the cartel sews the seeds of its own destruction. Based on the analysis of this chapter, can you give an alternative explanation? What implications does your explanation have for the long-run viability of the cartel?

9. Show how Figure 15.4 is affected if:
    a. the fine that is imposed is decreased to 1,800; or
    b. each firm's probability-adjusted discount factor is increased to $\rho = 0.9$. Interpret your answers.

References

Bernheim, B. D. and M. D. Whinston. 1990. "Multimarket Contact and Collusive Behavior." *Rand Journal of Economics* 21 (Spring): 1–26.

Christie, W. G. and P. Schultz. 1994. "Why Do NASDAQ Market Makers Avoid Odd Eighth Quotes?," *Journal of Finance* 49 (December): 1813–49.

Connor, J. M. 2001. *Global Price Fixing: Our Customers Are the Enemy*. Boston: Kluwer Academic.

Connor, J. M. and Lande, Robert H. 2005. "How High Do Cartels Raise Prices? Implications for Reform of the Antitrust Sentencing Guidelines." American Antitrust Institute Working Paper, April 20. Available at SSRN: http://ssrn.com/abstract=787907.

Davidson, C. and R. Deneckere. 1990. "Excess Capacity and Collusion." *International Economic Review* 31 (August): 521–42.

Dhutta, P. K. 1999. *Strategies and Games: Theory and Practice*. Cambridge, MA: MIT Press.

Dhutta, P. K. and A. Madhavan. 1997. "Competition and Collusion in Dealer Markets." *Journal of Finance* 25 (May): 245–76.

Dixit, A. 1980. "The Role of Investment in Entry Deterrence." *Economic Journal* 90 (January): 95–106.

Froeb, L., R. Koyak, and G. Werden. 1993. "What Is the Effect of Bid Rigging On Prices?," *Economics Letters* 42 (April): 419–23.

Harstad, R. M. and L. Phlips. 1990. "Perfect Equilibria of Speculative Futures Markets." In R. Selten, ed., *Game Equilibrium Analysis*. Vol. 2. Berlin: Springer, 289–307.

Hay, G. and D. Kelley. 1974. "An Empirical Survey of Price-fixing Conspiracies." *Journal of Law and Economics* 17 (April): 13–38.

Hendricks, K. and R. H. Porter. 1988. "An Empirical Study of an Auction with Asymmetric Information." *American Economic Review* 78 (December): 865–83.

Hinloopen, J. and A. R. Soetevent. 2006. "Trust and Recidivism: The Partial Success of Corporate Leniency Programs in the Laboratory." Tinbergen Institute Discussion Paper, 06-067/1.

LaCasse, C. 1995. "Bid Rigging and the Threat of Government Prosecution." *Rand Journal of Economics* 26 (Autumn): 398–417.

MacLeod, W. B. 1985. "A Theory of Conscious Parallelism." *European Economic Review* 27 (February): 25–44.

Morse, B. A. and J. Hyde. 2000. "Estimation of Cartel Overcharges: The Case of Archer Daniels Midland and the Market for Lysine." Purdue University, Department of Agricultural Economics, Staff Paper 00-8.

Motta, Massimo and M. Polo. 1999. "Leniency Programs and Cartel Prosecution." IGIER Working Paper 150, May. Available at SSRN: http://ssrn.com/abstract=165688.

———. 2004. *Competition Policy: Theory and Practice*. Cambridge: Cambridge University Press.

Osborne, M. J. and C. Pitchik. 1987. "Cartels, Profits, and Excess Capacity." *International Economic Review* 28 (June): 413–28.

Phlips, L. 1995a. *Competition Policy: A Game-theoretic Perspective*. Cambridge: Cambridge University Press.

———. 1995b. "On the Detection of Collusion and Predation." EUI Working Papers in Economics 95/35, Florence, Italy: European University Institute.

Porter, R. H. and J. D. Zona. 1993. "Detection of Bid Rigging in Procurement Auctions." *Journal of Political Economy* 101 (June): 518–38.

———. 1999. "Ohio School Milk Markets: An Analysis of Bidding." *Rand Journal of Economics* 30 (Summer): 263–88.

Rotemberg, J. and G. Saloner. 1986. "A Supergame-theoretic Model of Pricing Wars During Booms." *American Economic Review* 76 (June): 390–407.

Salop, S. 1986. "Practices That (Credibly) Facilitate Oligopoly Coordination." In J. Stiglitz and F. G. Mathewson, eds, *New Developments in the Analysis of Market Structure*. Cambridge: MIT Press, 265–90.

Scott Morton, F. 1997. "The Strategic Response by Pharmaceutical Firms to the Medicaid Most Favored Customer Rules." *Rand Journal of Economics* 28 (Summer): 269–90.

Spagnolo, G. 2004. "Divide et Impera: Optimal Deterrence Mechanisms Against Cartels and Organized Crime." CEPR Discussion Paper 4840.

Spence, A. M. 1977. "Entry, Investment, and Oligopolistic Pricing." *Bell Journal of Economics* 8 (Spring): 1–19.

Sproul, M. 1993. "Antitrust and Prices." *Journal of Political Economy* 101 (August): 741–54.

Stigler, G. 1964. "A Theory of Oligopoly." *Journal of Political Economy* 72 (February): 44–61.

Part V
Contractual Relations Between Firms

In this part we examine the various ways in which firms may interact that involve formal and legally enforceable contracts. Such formal relationships employ strategic considerations just as much as do the pricing and production decisions considered in the last several chapters. However, the manifestation of these tactical issues is more subtle because, by its very nature, a formal contract involves some elements of cooperation as well as the usual ingredient of self-interest.

Chapters 16 and 17 explore the implications of the most binding of all contracts, the marriage agreement. The corporate term for marriage, however, is merger (or acquisition). Chapter 16 explores the issues surrounding the merger of two firms that formerly competed against each other in the same product market, a horizontal merger. Mergers happen with a frequency that is difficult to justify with formal economic analysis. We examine models that aim to resolve this difficulty and, in particular, that help to explain why one merger in an industry often leads to others so that mergers often come in waves. Of course, a merger between two former rivals runs the risk of weakening competition. Therefore, the antitrust authorities and the courts must often evaluate such mergers and try to forecast the post-merger market outcome. Increasingly, such evaluations have made use of econometric data on market demand conditions to build computer models that are then used to simulate the post-merger equilibrium. Chapter 16 includes an extensive description of this process and the difficulties it can involve as illustrated by the well-known proposed merger of Staples and Office Depot. In Chapter 17 we then turn to consider a merger not between two former competitors but, instead, between an upstream firm, such as a manufacturer, and a downstream firm, such as a retailer. Here again, an important goal is to explain why such mergers occur and what anticompetitive issues they may raise. Vertical mergers can increase efficiency and so raise both firm profit and consumer welfare. However, they can also disadvantage non-merged firms and reduce competitive pressures. We present some evidence on these issues based on a recent empirical investigation of vertical integration in the ready-mixed concrete industry.

Firms may use formal contracts that stop short of a merger in order to harmonize their interests. Chapter 18 focuses on contracts between an upstream and a downstream firm that are primarily concerned with the price charged to the final consumer. Chapter 19 focuses on other vertical contracts, such as those that grant a franchise or exclusive dealing rights. We also examine the public policy concerns raised by all vertical constraints. An empirical study of exclusive dealing in the U.S. beer industry illustrates how one might obtain evidence on these important questions.

16

Horizontal Mergers

The merger mania that transformed much of corporate America through the 1990s largely disappeared in the wake of the terrorist attack of September 11, 2001, the corporate scandals at Enron, Tyco, HealthSouth, and WorldCom, and the bursting of the dot.com bubble. However, after quieting down for a few years, merger activity bounced back sharply in 2004, when over 10,000 deals were transacted in the U.S. for a total value of $746.3 billion. 2005 followed with another 10,000-plus deals with a total value of over $1 trillion. In 2006, the number of mergers rose still further to over 11,000 and the value increased to $1.23 trillion.[1] The urge to merge is back.

The organization and reorganization of firms brought about by mergers and acquisitions raises several issues. Perhaps the most central of these is the question, why? What is the motivation behind the marriage of two (or more) firms? One possible answer is that a merger creates cost savings by eliminating wasteful duplication or by improving information flows within the merged organization. Similarly, a merger may lead to more efficient pricing and/or improved services to customers. This can happen for example when two firms producing complementary goods such as nuts and bolts merge.[2]

To the extent that reducing cost or rationalizing complementary production is the primary motivation for mergers, the mergers are likely to be beneficial to society as well as to the merging firms and ought not to be discouraged. However, mergers can also be an attempt to create legal cartels. The merged firms come under common ownership and control. Hence, the new corporate entity will coordinate what were formerly separate actions with a view to achieving the joint profit-maximizing outcome. By placing such coordination within the boundaries of one firm a merger legitimizes precisely the kind of behavior that would have been illegal had the two firms remained separate. Viewed in this light, mergers are an undesirable attempt to create and exploit monopoly power in a market.

Mergers pose a difficult challenge for antitrust policy because policy makers need to be able to distinguish between anticompetitive mergers, on the one hand, and those that are not injurious to competition, on the other. This tension is openly acknowledged in the overview to the *Merger Guidelines*: "While challenging competitively harmful mergers, the Agency

---

[1]   *Mergerstat Review*, January 2006 and 2007.
[2]   See section 8.3, Chapter 8.

seeks to avoid unnecessary interference within the larger universe of mergers that are either competitively beneficial or neutral."[3]

We explore these issues in this chapter and the next. We examine what economic theory can tell us about the profit rationale for mergers and whether the enhanced profit stems from greater efficiency or from enhanced monopoly power. While the relevant theory is mainly an extension of the Cournot and Bertrand models, we warn the reader in advance that it is nevertheless somewhat difficult. The rewards of a deeper understanding of mergers and merger policy justify, we hope, the necessary extra work.

Before proceeding further, it is useful to classify merger types because all mergers are not alike. An important source of distinction is the nature of the relationship that existed between the merging firms prior to their combination. This gives rise to three different kinds of mergers. First, there are horizontal mergers. These occur when the firms joining together in the merger were formerly competitors in the same product market. A horizontal merger involves two or more firms that, so far as their buyers are concerned, market substitute products. The 2006 merger of the telecommunications software firms, Alcatel and Lucent, is one example of a horizontal merger.

Vertical mergers are the second type. These typically involve firms at different stages in the vertical production chain. Consider the purchase by the Disney Company of Capital Cities/ABC. Here, a major producer of films and television programs has acquired a major distributor and network that airs this material. The 2006 purchase of Murphy Farms, a major hog farming enterprise by Smithfield Foods, the largest pork company in the world is a similar vertical combination. Vertical mergers include more than mergers between upstream–downstream firms. They include as well any combination of firms that, prior to the merger, produced complementary goods. The merger between Hewlett-Packard, primarily a producer of software, printers, and scanners, and Compaq, a major personal computer firm also could fall in the vertical category. The merger of CSX and Conrail, two large freight rail companies in the eastern United States provides another example because, for the most part, the rail lines of the two firms did not overlap but instead served adjacent regions, i.e., the southeast and the northeast United States. Thus, the two firms together offered complementary services to customers who wish to transport goods across both regions.

Finally, conglomerate mergers involve the combination of firms without either a clear substitute or a clear complementary relationship. General Electric, a firm that produces aircraft engines, electric products, financial services, and through its subsidiary NBC television programming, is one of the world's most successful conglomerate firms. Recent examples of conglomerate mergers include: (1) the purchase of Duracell Batteries by Gillette, (2) the purchase of Snapple (iced tea) and Gatorade (a sports drink) by Quaker Oats, and (3) the merger of CUC International, a health and home-shopping company with HFS, a major hotel firm.

In this chapter we focus on horizontal mergers. Since these reflect combinations of two or more firms in the same industry, they raise the most obvious antitrust concerns. Vertical and conglomerate mergers are discussed in Chapter 17.

---

[3] The Department of Justice/Federal Trade Commission *Merger Guidelines* can be read at http://www.ftc.gov/bc/docs/horizmer.htm. Section 2 on the potential adverse effects of mergers is particularly relevant.

16.1   HORIZONTAL MERGERS AND THE MERGER PARADOX

Horizontal mergers replace two or more former competitors with a single firm. The merger of two firms in a three-firm market changes the industry to a duopoly. The merger of two duopolists creates a monopolist. The potential for a merger to create monopoly power is therefore clearly an issue in the horizontal case. Our first order of business is, therefore, rather surprising. It is to discuss a phenomenon known as the *merger paradox*. The paradox is that it is, in fact, quite difficult to construct a simple economic model in which there are sizable gains for firms participating in a horizontal merger *that is not a merger to monopoly*.[4] We illustrate the paradox using the Cournot model of section 9.4.[5]

Let's start with a simple example. Suppose we have three firms, each with a constant marginal cost of $c = \$30$ and jointly facing an industry demand curve described by: $P = 150 - Q$. The Cournot equilibrium results in each firm producing one-fourth of the competitive output or 30 so that total output is 90. The price therefore is $P = \$60$ and each firm earns a profit of $30(\$60 - \$30) = \$900$.

What happens if two of these firms merge? In the wake of a two-firm merger, the industry will become one with two firms, each of which will produce one-third of the competitive output or 40 so that total output now falls to 80. The price will then rise to $70 and each of the two remaining firms will earn a profit of $1,600.

We may now evaluate the impact of the merger. First, note that the merger is bad for consumers. Output falls and the price rises. Second, the merger is good news for the firm that did not merge. It now expands its output to 40 units and sells these at a higher price than previously so that it enjoys a profit increase of $1,600 - \$900 = \$700$. Finally, we come to the central element in the merger paradox. For the two firms that merged, the merger did not pay off. Previously, each firm produced 30 units and earned a profit of $900 for a combined pre-merger output and profit of 60 units and $1,800, respectively. In the post-merger market, however, these two firms have a combined output of only 40 and a total profit of $1,600. The merger has hurt the firms that merged and brought benefits to their rival. If this example is reflective of a more general result, then we ought not to observe many mergers. Of course, the paradox is that we do observe mergers all the time.

The fact of the matter is that the foregoing example is not a special case. It is in fact easy to show that a merger will almost certainly be unprofitable in the basic Cournot model whether it is between two firms or even more so long as the merger does not create a monopoly. To see this more general result, start by assuming a market of N > 2 firms, each of which produces a homogeneous product and acts as a Cournot competitor. The firms have identical costs given by the total cost function

$$C(q_i) = cq_i \text{ for } i = 1, \ldots, N, \tag{16.1}$$

where q_i is output of firm i. Market demand is linear and, in inverse form, is given by the equation

$$P = A - BQ = A - B(q_i + Q_{-i}), \tag{16.2}$$

---

[4]   A merger to monopoly is when all the firms in an industry combine into a single monopoly producer.
[5]   The paradox was first formalized in a slightly different form by Salant et al. (1983).

where Q is aggregate output produced by the N firms and Q_{-i} is the aggregate output of all firms except firm i; that is,

$$Q_{-i} = Q - q_i$$

The profit function for firm i can then be written as

$$\pi_i(q_i, Q_{-i}) = q_i[A - B(q_i + Q_{-i}) - c]. \tag{16.3}$$

In a Cournot game, firms choose their output levels simultaneously to maximize profit. The resulting profit to each firm in a Cournot equilibrium is

$$\pi_i^C = \frac{(A - c)^2}{B(N + 1)^2} \tag{16.4}$$

Suppose now that $M \geq 2$ of these firms decide to merge. In order to exclude the case of merger to monopoly we assume that $M < N$. Such a merger leads to an industry in which there are now $N - M + 1$ firms competing in the industry. Since all firms are the same, we can think of the merged firm as comprised of firms 1 through M.

The new merged firm picks its output q_m to maximize profit, which is given by

$$\pi_m(q_m, Q_{-m}) = q_m[A - B(q_m + Q_{-m}) - c] \tag{16.5}$$

where $Q_{-m} = q_{m+1} + q_{m+2} + \ldots + q_N$ denotes the aggregate output of the $N - M$ firms that have not merged.

Each of the nonmerged firms chooses its output to maximize profit given, as before, by

$$\pi_i(q_i, Q_{-i}) = q_i[A - B(q_i + Q_{-i}) - c]. \tag{16.6}$$

In this case the term Q_{-i} now denotes the sum of the outputs q_j of each of the $N - M$ nonmerging firms excluding firm i, plus the output of the merged firm q_m.

The only difference between equations (16.5) and (16.6) is that in the former we have a subscript m while in the latter we have a subscript i. In other words, a crucial implication of equations (16.5) and (16.6) is that, after the merger, *the merged firm becomes just like any one of the other firms in the industry*. This means that all of these $N - M + 1$ firms, each having identical costs and producing the same product, must in equilibrium produce the same amount of output and therefore earn the same profit. In other words, in the post-merger Cournot equilibrium, it must be the case that the output and profit of the merged firm, q_m^C and π_m^C, are the same as the output and profit of each nonmerged firm. Using the Cournot output and profit equations for a market with $N - M + 1$ firms, these are, respectively:

$$q_m^C = q_{nm}^C = \frac{A - c}{B(N - M + 2)} \quad \text{and} \quad \pi_m^C = \pi_{nm}^C = \frac{(A - c)^2}{B(N - M + 2)^2} \tag{16.7}$$

where the subscript m denotes the merged firm and nm a nonmerged firm.

Equations (16.4) and (16.7) allow us to compare the profit of the nonmerging firms before and after the merger. The first point to note is the free-riding opportunity afforded to the non-merging firms when other firms merge. We know that in the Cournot model as the number of firms decreases industry output falls (and price rises). Of course, a merger does just that. It reduces the number of firms. So the price rises for all firms, including those that did not merge. Moreover, the merger allows those firms to gain market share while also benefiting from an increase in the market price.

What about the merging firms? There are M of these and, prior to the merger, each one earned the profit shown in equation (16.4). Hence, the aggregate profit of these firms taken together is M times that amount. After the merger, the profit of the merged firm is the profit shown in equation (16.7). Is the profit of the merged firm greater than the aggregate profit earned by the M firms before the merger? In order for the answer to be yes, it must be the case that

$$\frac{(A - c)^2}{B(N - M + 2)^2} \geq M \frac{(A - c)^2}{B(N + 1)^2} \tag{16.8}$$

This requires

$$(N + 1)^2 \geq M(N - M + 2)^2 \tag{16.9}$$

Note that equation (16.9) does not include any of the demand parameters or the firms' marginal costs. In other words, equation (16.9) tells us about the profitability of any M-firm merger. All that is required is that demand is linear and that the firms each have the same, constant marginal costs.

In our example in which the number of firms is $N = 3$, and the number of firms merging is $M = 2$, it's easy to see then that the inequality in equation (16.9) is not satisfied. In other words, in a three-firm market satisfying our demand and cost assumptions *no two-firm merger is profitable*.

Condition (16.9) is a general condition that turns out to be very difficult to satisfy even when more than two-firms merge as long as the merger does not result in a monopoly. To see this, suppose that we substitute $M = aN$ in equation (16.9), with $0 < a < 1$. That is, a is the fraction of firms in the industry that merge. We can then work out how large a has to be for the merger to be profitable. A little manipulation of condition (16.9) shows that for a merger to be profitable, we must have $a > a(N)$ where[6]:

$$a(N) = \frac{3 + 2N - \sqrt{5 + 4N}}{2N} \tag{16.10}$$

Table 16.1 gives $a(N)$ and the associated minimum number of firms $\underline{M}$ that have to merge for the merger to be profitable for a range of values of N, the number of firms in the industry.

Table 16.1   Necessary condition for profitable merger

N	5	10	15	20	25
a(N)	80%	81.5%	83.1%	84.5%	85.5%
$\underline{M}$	4	9	13	17	22

---

[6]   You can check this equation by direct substitution of $a(N)$ in equation (16.9).

Equation (16.10) and Table 16.1 illustrate what has come to be termed the 80 percent rule. For a merger to be profitable in our simple Cournot world of linear demand and identical constant costs, it is necessary that at least 80 percent of the firms in the market merge. The problem is that a merger of this magnitude would almost never be allowed by the antitrust authorities.

16.1

Suppose that demand for carpet-cleaning services in Dirtville is described by $P = 130 - Q$. There are currently 20 identical firms that clean carpets in the area. The unit cost of cleaning a carpet is constant and equal to $30. Firms in this industry compete in quantities.

a. Show that in a Cournot–Nash equilibrium the profit of each firm is $\pi = 22.67$.
b. Now suppose that six firms in the industry merge. Show that the profit of each firm in the post-merger Cournot game is $\pi = 39.06$. Show that the profit earned by the merged firm is insufficient to compensate all the shareholders/owners who owned the six original firms and earned profit from them in the pre-merger market game.
c. Show that if fewer than 17 firms merge, the profit of the merged firm is not great enough to buy out the shareholders/owners of the firms who merge.

The merger paradox is that many, if not most, horizontal mergers are unprofitable when viewed through the lens of our standard Cournot model. Yet, as the events of the 1990s and more recent years tell us, horizontal mergers appear to happen all the time. What aspect of real-world mergers has the simple Cournot model failed to capture? Alternatively, what aspect of the Cournot model is responsible for this prediction that seems at odds with reality?

The critical aspect of the Cournot model that gives rise to the merger paradox is not difficult to find. When firms merge in the Cournot model, the new combined firm behaves after the merger just like any of the remaining firms that did not merge. Thus, if two firms in a three-firm industry merge, the new firm competes as a duopolist. The nonmerging firm in this case has, after the merger, equal status to the merged firm even though it now faces the combined strength of both of its previous rivals.

One cannot help but suspect that, for a merger of any substantial size, either the newly merged firm is different in some material sense from its unmerged rivals, or the overall market has changed in a way that alters rivals' behavior. In the next three sections, we explore such possible modifications while staying within the basic Cournot framework. Subsequently, we consider mergers in a market with differentiated products.

16.2 MERGERS AND COST SYNERGIES

In developing the merger paradox we assumed that all firms in the market have identical costs and that there are no fixed costs. What happens if we relax these assumptions? It seems reasonable to suppose that if a merger creates sufficiently large cost savings it should be profitable. In this section we develop an example to show that this can indeed be the case.[7]

---

[7]   This is a special case of a much more sophisticated analysis by Farrell and Shapiro (1990) who show in a general setting that for consumers to benefit from a profitable horizontal merger of Cournot firms the merger has to create substantial cost synergies.

Suppose that the market contains three Cournot firms. Consumer demand is given by

$$P = 150 - Q \tag{16.11}$$

where Q is aggregate output, which pre-merger is $q_1 + q_2 + q_3$. Two of these firms are low-cost firms with a marginal cost of 30 so that total costs at each are given by

$$C_1(q_1) = f + 30q_1; \ C_2(q_2) = f + 30q_2 \tag{16.12}$$

The third firm is potentially high-cost with total costs given by

$$C_3(q_3) = f + 30bq_3 \tag{16.13}$$

where $b \geq 1$ is a measure of the cost disadvantage from which firm 3 suffers. In these cost functions f represents fixed costs associated with overhead expenses such as those for marketing or for maintaining corporate headquarters. We now consider the effect of a merger of firms 2 and 3.

16.2.1   The Merger Reduces Fixed Costs

Consider first the case in which $b = 1$ so that all firms have the same marginal cost of 30. Suppose, however, that after the merger the merged firm has fixed costs af with $1 \leq a \leq 2$. What this means is that the merger allows the merged firms to economize on overhead costs, for example, by combining the headquarters of the two firms, eliminating unnecessary overlap, combining R&D functions and economizing on duplicated marketing efforts. These are, in fact, typical cost savings that most firms state that they expect to result from a merger.

Because the merger leaves marginal costs unaffected, this is similar to our first example only now firms also have fixed costs. Accordingly, we know that in the pre-merger market each firm earns a profit of $900 - f$. In the post-merger market with just two firms, one earns a profit of $1,600 - f$ while the merged firm earns $1,600 - af$. Hence, for this merger to be profitable, it must be the case that $1,600 - af > 1,800 - 2f$ which requires that $a < 2 - 200/f$. What this says is that a merger is more likely to be profitable when fixed costs are relatively high and the merger gives the merged firm the ability to make "substantial" savings in these costs. Note, however, that even if the merger is profitable for the merging firms, consumers are actually worse off as a result of the higher equilibrium price. That same higher price also raises the profit of the nonmerged firm. Moreover, it is still the case that the merged firm loses market share post-merger.

16.2.2   The Merger Reduces Variable Costs

Now consider the case in which the source of the cost savings is not a reduction in fixed costs but instead a reduction in variable costs which we capture by assuming that $b > 1$. In other words, firm 3 is a high variable cost firm. It follows that after a merger of firms 2 and 3, production will be rationalized and the high-cost operations will be shut down (or redesigned to have the low-cost technology). To make matters as simple as possible we will now assume that there are no fixed costs ($f = 0$).

Once again we assume a Cournot framework. The outputs and profits of the three firms prior to the merger are:

$$q_1^C = q_2^C = \frac{90 + 30b}{4}; q_3^C = \frac{210 - 90b}{4} \text{ and } \pi_1^C = \pi_2^C = \frac{(90 + 30b)^2}{16}; \pi_3^C = \frac{(210 - 90b)^2}{16}$$

$$(16.14)$$

The equilibrium pre-merger price is[8] $P^C = \dfrac{210 + 30b}{4}$. Total output is $Q = \dfrac{390 - 30b}{4}$ with each of the low-cost firms, 1 and 2, producing a greater amount than their high-cost rival, firm 3.

Now, as before, suppose that firms 2 and 3 merge. Since for any $b > 1$, it is always more expensive to produce a unit of output at firm 3 than it is at firm 2, all production will be transferred to firm 2's technology. The result is that the market now contains two identical firms, 1 and 2, each with marginal costs of $30. Accordingly, in the post-merger industry, each firm produces 40 units, the product price is $70 and each firm earns $1,600.

Is this a profitable merger? For the merger to increase aggregate profit of the merged firms it must be the case that

$$1600 - \left(\frac{(90 + 30b)^2}{16} + \frac{(210 - 90b)^2}{16} \right) > 0 \qquad (16.15)$$

You can check that this simplifies to

$$\frac{25}{2}(7 - 3b)(15b - 19) > 0 \qquad (16.16)$$

The first bracketed term in equation (16.16) has to be positive for firm 3 to have been in the market in the first place (see footnote 8). So the merger is profitable provided that the second bracket is also positive, which requires that $b > 19/15$. In other words, *a merger between a high-cost and a low-cost firm will be profitable provided that the cost disadvantage of the high-cost firm prior to the merger is "large enough."* In the case at hand, large enough means that firm 3's unit cost is at least 25 percent greater than firm 2's unit cost. However, as we have already demonstrated, whether the merger is profitable or not, the price rises and consumers are made worse off.

Together, our analysis of a merger that generates fixed cost savings and one that generates variable cost savings makes clear that mergers can be profitable when the cost savings are great enough. However, there is no guarantee that consumers gain from such a merger. Admittedly, the merger removes a relatively inefficient firm technology but it also reduces competitive pressures between the remaining firms. Farrell and Shapiro (1990) demonstrate that in the Cournot setting used here, the cost savings necessary to generate a gain for consumers are much larger than those needed simply to make the merger profitable. In turn, this suggests that we should be skeptical of cost savings as a justification of the benefits to consumers of horizontal mergers.

---

[8]   Note that this equilibrium only exists only if there is a limit on the disadvantage b for firm 3. Specifically, firm 3's pre-merger output will be positive only if $b < 210/90 = 7/3$, otherwise it will not operate in this market in the first place.

Research by both Lichtenberg and Siegel (1992) and Maksimovic and Phillips (2001) finds that merger related productivity gains and therefore marginal cost savings, while real, are typically no more than 1 to 2 percent. Salinger (2005) expresses even more doubt that fixed cost savings are substantial. Beyond all this it is also worth noting that even with cost savings, part of our initial paradox still remains since large profit gains continue to accrue to the firms that do not merge. Why should a firm incur the headaches of merging if it can enjoy many of the same benefits by free-riding on other mergers?[9]

16.2

Practice Problem

Return to the market for carpet-cleaning services in Dirtville, now described by the demand function $P = 180 - Q$. Suppose that there are currently three firms that clean carpets in the area. The unit cost of cleaning a carpet is constant and equal to $30 for two firms and is $30b$ for the third firm, where $b \geq 1$. In addition, all firms have fixed overhead costs of $900. Firms in this industry compete in quantities.

a. What is the Cournot–Nash equilibrium price and what are the outputs and profits of each firm? What is the upper limit on b for the third firm to be able to survive?
b. Now suppose that a low-cost firm merges with the high-cost firm. In doing so, the fixed costs of the merged firm become $900a$ with $1 \leq a \leq 2$. What is the post-merger equilibrium price? What are the outputs of the nonmerged and the merged firms?
c. Derive a relationship between a and b that is necessary to guarantee that the profit earned by the merged firm is sufficient to compensate all the shareholders/owners who owned the two original firms and earned profit from them in the pre-merger market game. Graph this relationship and comment on it.

16.3   THE MERGED FIRM AS A STACKELBERG LEADER

If cost efficiencies are not a likely way to resolve the merger paradox, then perhaps a resolution can be found in some other change that gives the merged firm an advantage. One possibility is that merged firms become Stackelberg leaders in the post-merger market.[10] Recall from our discussion in section 11.1 that the source of a Stackelberg leader firm's advantage is its ability to commit to an output before output decisions are taken by the follower firms. This permits a leader to choose an output that takes into account the reactions of the followers.

Let us assume that a merged firm acquires a leadership role and see whether this assumption can help resolve the merger paradox. Certainly, such a role seems plausible. After all, the new firm has a combined capacity twice that of any of its nonmerged rivals, and so might well be able to act as a Stackelberg leader. Will this be enough to make a merger profitable? If so, what will be the response of other firms? Will they also have an incentive to merge? If they do, will their merging undo the profitability of the first merger and thereby, if firms are foresighted, discourage them from merging in the first place?

---

[9] Perry and Porter (1985) assume that each firm's cost schedule declines with the total amount of capital it owns. Hence, by merging and gaining more capital, a firm lowers its costs. The scarcity of capital makes it difficult for other firms to do this and, because of rising costs, to free-ride as much on the merger of rivals.

[10] This analysis draws on the work of A. F. Daughety (1990) who suggested this role for the merged firms.

Suppose that demand is of the usual linear form: $P = A - BQ$. There are $N + 1$ firms in the industry and each of the $N + 1$ firms has a constant marginal cost of c. Again from section 9.4 we know that the equilibrium is described by the following equations:

$$q_i = \frac{A - c}{(N + 2)B} \Rightarrow Q = \frac{(N + 1)(A - c)}{(N + 2)B} \text{ and } P = \frac{A + (N + 1)c}{N + 2} \tag{16.17}$$

The profit of each firm, $(P - c)q_i$ is therefore:

$$\pi_i = \frac{(A - c)^2}{B(N + 2)^2} \tag{16.18}$$

Suppose now that two of these firms merge and, as a result, become a Stackelberg leader. There will then be F, which is equal to $N - 1$, follower firms and one leader firm so that we now have N firms in total. Of course, the Stackelberg leader is able to choose its output first in a two-stage game. In stage one, the leader chooses its output Q^L. In the second stage, the follower firms independently choose their outputs in response to that chosen by the leader.

To find the equilibrium, we work through the game backwards. Accordingly, we consider the second stage of the game in which the follower nonmerged firms make their output decisions in response to the output choice Q^L of the leader or merged firm. We use the notation Q_{F-f} to denote the aggregate output of the follower firms *other than f*, and denote the output of follower firm f by q_f. Aggregate output of *all* firms is $Q = Q^L + Q_{F-f} + q_f$. Moreover, the residual demand for firm f, which is the demand left after taking into account the outputs of the leader and the followers other than firm f is:

$$P = [A - B(Q^L + Q_{F-f})] - Bq_f \tag{16.19}$$

Marginal revenue for firm f is, therefore,

$$MR_f = [A - B(Q^L + Q_{F-f})] - 2Bq_f. \tag{16.20}$$

Equating this with marginal cost gives the best response function for firm f:

$$A - 2Bq_f - BQ^L - BQ_{F-f} = c \Rightarrow q_f^* = \frac{A - c}{2B} - \frac{Q^L}{2} - \frac{Q_{F-f}}{2} \tag{16.21}$$

Equation (16.21) is the best response of a follower firm to both the output of the leader and the output of all the other follower firms. Since all follower firms are identical, symmetry demands that in equilibrium the output of each of the follower firms must be identical. The group of followers excluding the firm f has $F - 1 = N - 2$ firms. Therefore, $Q_{F-f}^* = (N - 2)q_f^*$. Substituting this into equation (16.21) and simplifying gives the optimal output for each non-merged follower firm as a function of the aggregate output of the leader comprised of the now merged firms:

$$q_f^* = \frac{A - c}{BN} - \frac{Q^L}{N} \tag{16.22}$$

The aggregate output of all followers as a function of the output of the leader is then

$$Q^F = (N - 1)q_f^* = \frac{(N - 1)(A - c)}{BN} - \frac{(N - 1)Q^L}{N} \tag{16.23}$$

We can use the same basic technique to determine the output for the leader firm in stage one of the game. The residual inverse demand function for the leader firm is dependent upon the output of all the other firms, which is given in equation (16.23). So, the demand function facing leader firm l:

$$\begin{aligned} P = A - B(Q^F + Q^L) &= A - B\left[\frac{(N - 1)(A - c)}{BN} - \frac{(N - 1)Q^L}{N}\right] - BQ^L \\ &= A - \frac{(N - 1)(A - c)}{N} - \frac{B}{N}Q^L \end{aligned} \tag{16.24}$$

Its associated marginal revenue function is

$$MR_L = A - \frac{(N - 1)(A - c)}{N} - \frac{2B}{N}Q^L \tag{16.25}$$

Equating this marginal revenue with marginal cost allows us to solve for the leader firm's optimal output:

$$MR_l = c \Rightarrow Q^L = \frac{A - c}{2B} \tag{16.26}$$

You will by now recognize that the output level in equation (16.26) is just the output level chosen by a uniform-pricing monopolist. This is, of course, a standard result for a single leader model with linear demand and constant costs. In turn, this implies the following industry equilibrium values:

$$q_f^* = \frac{A - c}{2BN}; Q^F = \frac{(N - 1)(A - c)}{2BN}; Q = Q^L + Q^F = \frac{(2N - 1)(A - c)}{2BN}; \text{ and}$$

$$P = \frac{A + (2N - 1)c}{2N} \tag{16.27}$$

Profits for the leader and for each follower firm are then:

$$\pi^L = \frac{(A - c)^2}{4BN} \text{ and } \pi^F = \frac{(A - c)^2}{4BN^2} \tag{16.28}$$

A comparison of equation (16.28) with (16.18) reveals that for any industry initially comprised of three or more firms and characterized by symmetric Cournot competition, a two-firm merger that creates a Stackelberg leader will be profitable. This seems to resolve the merger paradox. However, equations (16.28) and (16.18) also show that the unmerged firms who have become followers are definitely worse off as a result of the merger. We may therefore expect some response from these firms.

Furthermore, if we compare the market price and output in equation (16.17) with that in equation (16.27), we find that while the merger has raised the profit of the merging parties, it also has lowered price. Hence, the merger is good for consumers. We seem to have replaced one paradox with another. We now have a model in which a merger is profitable, but that model also removes a principal reason why the antitrust authorities should object to such a merger.

However, we also need to consider the response of other firms to the merger. Since leadership confers additional profit, they, too, will have an incentive to merge and try to become a leader. This raises the question as to what happens if there is a second or third two-firm merger. Daughety's (1990) model answers this question by assuming that there can be more than one leader firm and that merging is the ticket to entry into the club of such leaders. That is, imagine a market that may be divided into two groups of firms: followers and leaders. The first of these groups acts just as the followers did in the preceding analysis. They compete as Cournot rivals over the demand remaining after the leaders make their output decisions. The group of leaders understands this reaction. They compete as Cournot rivals with the knowledge that they act first and the followers will take their production decisions as given.

To analyze this two-stage competition, we can use the model derived above. In particular, instead of assuming N firms with one leader and $N - 1$ followers, let us assume N firms with L leaders and $N - L = F$ followers. Since followers simply take their cue from the total leader output Q^L regardless of whether it is produced by one firm or many, equation (16.21) still describes the best response of the typical follower firm. Since there are $N - L$ such firms, a little algebra quickly reveals that total follower output Q^F is then:

$$Q^F = (N - L) q_f^* = \frac{(N - L)(A - c)}{B(N - L + 1)} - \frac{(N - L)Q^L}{(N - L + 1)} \tag{16.29}$$

Let us denote the output of any one leader firm as q^l and that of all the leaders *other than* firm l, Q_{L-l}. The residual demand function for firm l is then:

$$P = [A - B(Q^F + Q_{L-l})] - Bq_l \tag{16.30}$$

Substituting for total follower output Q^F from equation (16.29) and re-arranging yields the typical leader's demand:

$$P = \frac{A + (N - L)c - BQ_{L-l}}{(N - L + 1)} - \frac{B}{(N - L + 1)} q_l \tag{16.31}$$

Hence, the associated marginal revenue function is

$$MR_l = \frac{A + (N - L)c - BQ_{L-l}}{(N - L + 1)} - \frac{2B}{(N - L + 1)} q_l \tag{16.32}$$

Equating this marginal revenue with marginal cost gives the leader firm l's best output response to the output produced by all the other leader firms, Q_{L-l}:

$$MR_l = \frac{A + (N - L)c - BQ_{L-l}}{(N - L + 1)} - \frac{2B}{(N - L + 1)} q_l = c \Rightarrow q_l^* = \frac{A - c}{2B} - \frac{Q_{L-l}}{2} \tag{16.33}$$

Once again, we can take advantage of the fact that since all of the leader firms have the same costs they will each produce the same level of output in equilibrium. Because there are $L - 1$ leaders other than firm l, this gives the symmetry condition $Q_{L-l}^* = (L - 1)q_l^*$ which when substituted into equation (16.33) allows us to solve for the output chosen in stage one by each merged firm in the leader group:

$$q_l^* = \frac{A - c}{2B} - \frac{(L - 1)}{2}q_l^* \Rightarrow q_l^* = \frac{A - c}{B(L + 1)} \text{ and } Q^L = Lq_l^* = \frac{L(A - c)}{B(L + 1)} \qquad (16.34)$$

Substituting the value for Q^L into equation (16.29) we can then find total follower output Q^F and individual output for each follower $q_f^* = Q^F/(N - L)$. These are:

$$q_f^* = \frac{A - c}{B(L + 1)(N - L + 1)} \text{ and } Q^F = \frac{(N - L)(A - c)}{B(L + 1)(N - L + 1)} \qquad (16.35)$$

Finally, summing Q^L and Q^F together yields total market output Q and, via the demand curve, the equilibrium price P:

$$Q^T = Q^L + Q^F = \frac{(N + NL - L^2)(A - c)}{B(L + 1)(N - L + 1)} \text{ and } P = \frac{A + (N + NL - L^2)c}{(L + 1)(N - L + 1)} \qquad (16.36)$$

In turn, the price and output equations imply that in an industry comprised of N firms in total, L of which are leaders, the price-cost margin $(P - c)$ and the profits for the typical leader firm $(P - c)q_l^*$ and typical follower firm $(P - c)q_f^*$ are:

$$P - c = \frac{A - c}{(L + 1)(N - L + 1)}; \; \pi^L(N, L) = \frac{(A - c)^2}{B(L + 1)^2(N - L + 1)}; \text{ and}$$

$$\pi^F(N, L) = \frac{(A - c)^2}{B(L + 1)^2(N - L + 1)^2} \qquad (16.37)$$

You can readily confirm that the profit values shown in equation (16.37) for the general case of N total firms with L leaders, yields the same profits as those given in equation (16.28) for the special case of N firms and $L = 1$ leader.

It is clear from the profit equations in (16.37) that the leader firms are more profitable than the nonmerged followers. Yet that is not the real issue facing two firms that are contemplating merger. The question is whether *one more merger* is profitable, given that there will then be one more leader, two fewer followers, and one less firm in total. This is why we have written the profit expressions as functions of N and L. The point is that an additional merger creates two countervailing forces. On the one hand, there are fewer firms in total, which ought to increase profits, but there are also more leaders, which ought to decrease the profits of the leaders. Which force is greater?

Suppose there is an additional merger of two followers, so that the newly merged firm and all other leaders earn profit given by equation (16.37) with N replaced by $N - 1$ and L replaced by $L + 1$ to give $\pi_l^L(N - 1, L + 1)$. For there to be an incentive to merge, this profit must exceed the combined profit earned by the two follower firms prior to the merger.

Table 16.2   Profit effect of two follower firms merging to become a leader, given N followers and L leaders prior to the merger

Original number of leaders L	Original number of firms N									
	5	10	15	20	25	30	35	40	45	50
2	80	505	1,380	2,705	4,480	6,705	9,380	12,505	16,080	20,105
4		865	2,880	6,145	10,660	16,425	23,440	31,705	41,220	51,985
6		841	3,876	9,361	17,296	27,681	40,516	55,801	73,536	93,721
8		529	3,984	11,489	23,044	38,649	58,304	82,009	109,764	141,569
10			3,204	12,049	26,944	47,889	74,884	107,929	147,024	192,169
12			1,920	10,945	28,420	54,345	88,720	131,545	182,820	242,545
14				8,465	27,280	57,345	98,660	151,225	215,040	290,105
16				5,281	23,716	56,601	103,936	165,721	241,956	332,641
18				2,449	18,304	52,209	104,164	174,169	262,224	368,329
20					12,004	44,649	99,344	176,089	274,884	395,729
22					6,160	34,785	89,860	171,385	279,360	413,785
24						23,865	76,480	160,345	275,460	421,825

This latter profit is $2\pi_f^F(N, L)$. So, the merger will be profitable if the following condition is satisfied:

$$\pi^L(N - 1, L + 1) = \frac{(A - c)^2}{B(L + 2)^2(N - L - 1)} > 2\pi^F(N, L) = \frac{2(A - c)^2}{B(L + 1)^2(N - L + 1)^2}$$

(16.38)

This simplifies to the condition

$$(L + 1)^2(N - L + 1)^2 - 2(L + 2)^2(N - L - 1) > 0$$

(16.39)

Note that this condition does not include the demand parameters A and B or the marginal cost c. In other words, the profitability or otherwise of this type of merger depends only on the number of leaders and followers, not on the precise demand and cost conditions.

As turns out, the condition in equation (16.39) is always met. This is shown in Table 16.2 where we have calculated the left-hand side of equation (16.39) for any two-firm merger for a range of values of N and L. In other words, starting from any configuration of leaders and followers, *an additional two follower firms always wish to merge*.

This result is encouraging. It says that our model offers one way to resolve the merger paradox. A merger raises the profit of the two merging firms by allowing them to take a position as one of, perhaps several, industry leaders. Moreover, the fact that such a merger is always profitable also helps us to understand better the domino effect so often observed within an industry. Once one firm merges and becomes a leader, the remaining firms will wish to do the same rather than watch their output and their profits be squeezed.

Return again to the town of Dirtville where the inverse demand for carpet-cleaning services is described by $P = 130 - Q$. Once again assume that there are 20 identical firms that clean carpets in the area, and the unit cost of cleaning a carpet is constant and equal to $30. Firms in this industry compete in quantities.

a. Show that in a Cournot equilibrium the aggregate number of carpets cleaned is $Q = 95.24$. What is the equilibrium price?

b. Suppose that five two-firm mergers occur, that these five merged firms become leader firms, and the remaining 10 nonmerged firms are followers. Now there are 15 firms in the industry. Work through the model just described and show that in the two-stage game a leader firm cleans 16.67 carpets and each follower firm cleans 1.51 carpets. Leadership certainly has its benefits! Show that the total industry output in this case will be $Q = 98.45$. What is the equilibrium price now?

c. If after the five two-firm mergers took place there were no leadership advantage conferred to the merged firms, then we would have 15 firms competing like Cournot firms in the market. Show that in this case aggregate output is $Q = 93.75$.

While the Daughety model can resolve the merger paradox it does leave unanswered the question as to whether such mergers are in the public interest. Is there some point at which further mergers are harmful to consumers? The answer to this question can be most easily derived from the price-cost relation $P - c$ shown in equation (16.36). Since marginal cost c is constant, any rise or fall in P will be reflected in a rise or fall of $P - c$.

With L leader merged firms and $N - L$ follower nonmerged firms the price–cost differential is $\dfrac{A - c}{(L + 1)(N - L + 1)}$. An additional two-firm merger increases L to $L + 1$ and decreases N to $N - 1$, so that the price–cost margin is now $\dfrac{A - c}{(L + 2)(N - L - 1)}$. So for this additional merger to benefit consumers it must be the case that:

$$\frac{A - c}{(L + 2)(N - L - 1)} < \frac{A - c}{(L + 1)(N - L + 1)} \tag{16.40}$$

$$\Rightarrow (L + 1)(N - L + 1) < (L + 2)(N - L - 1) \Rightarrow N - 3(L + 1) > 0$$

What this tells us is that an additional two-firm merger benefits consumers only if $N > 3(L + 1)$ or, equivalently, $L < N/3 - 1$. In other words, *a two-firm merger that increases the number of leaders benefits consumers only if the current group of leaders contains fewer than a third of the total number of firms in the industry*. We know from Table 16.2 that a two-firm merger that creates a leader will always be profitable. Yet, as also just shown, such a merger will be harmful to consumers once the leader group includes one-third or more of the industry's firms. In other words, some mergers are bad—at least for consumers. Accordingly, we now have a model that both resolves the merger paradox and explains why the antitrust authorities are correct to worry about anticompetitive mergers.

For example, return to Practice Problem 16.3 in which we had five leader firms and 10 follower firms cleaning carpets in Dirtville. In that scenario we know that the equilibrium

Reality Checkpoint

It's a Gusher! Merger Mania in the Oil Industry

In August of 1998, British Petroleum (BP) announced plans to merge with Amoco another large oil firm although not quite as large as BP. The price tag was $48.2 billion making it, at the time, the biggest industrial merger ever. The new BP-Amoco would control more oil and gas production within North America than any other firm. It would also be the third-largest publicly traded oil firm in the world. (The largest firm of all, Saudi Aramco, is not publicly traded.)

Reaction from the rest of the oil industry came swiftly. Within a year, Exxon and Mobil merged in a deal worth $73.7 billion to become the largest publicly traded firm on earth. That was quickly followed by the merger of Phillips Petroleum and Conoco. Almost simultaneously, Paris-based Total acquired both PetroFina and Elf to create TotalFinaElf. Soon after, Chevron acquired Texaco for $36 billion. BP then went a step further and acquired Arco for $27 billion. The oil merger wave subsided with the economic decline of 2000–1 but even then, did not die altogether. Chevron acquired Unocal in 2005.

This wave of merger activity concentrated oil and gas refining and marketing into the hands of a noticeably smaller number of firms relative to the situation prior to BP's purchase of Amoco. The BP-Amoco merger was then the catalyst for a major wave of mergers and consolidations. In turn, this suggests that a common motive must be behind all these mergers.

Yet whether this common factor was the naked pursuit of market power or simply the profit-maximizing response of firms to similar problems is difficult to say. The mergers were taken at a time when energy prices were quite low. Oil, for example, was selling at less than $12 per barrel in 1998. Indeed, this low price —and the low energy company profits that went with it—is probably the reason that none of the mergers was seriously challenged by antitrust authorities. However, oil prices and profits have risen dramatically since that time. This could reflect the demand growth driven by a rising world economy coupled with improved cost efficiency that the mergers generated. However, it could also reflect the exploitation of newly enhanced market power. In this connection, a recent study by the Government Accounting Office (GAO) found that increased concentration could account for only a few cents of the large rise in wholesale gasoline prices. The rest appeared to be demand and cost pressures. If this view is correct, lower oil and gas prices are only likely if conservation measures reduce energy demand.

Sources: Jim Wells, "Energy Markets: Factors Contributing to Higher Gasoline Prices," Statement of Director of Natural Resources and Environment, General Accounting Office, to U.S. Senate Judiciary Committee, February 1, 2006; and B. Bahree, C. Cooper, and S. Liesman, "BP to Buy Amoco in Biggest Industrial Merger Ever," *Wall Street Journal*, August 12, 1998, p. A1.

price for cleaning a carpet is $31.55. Now suppose that two additional firms merge to join the leadership group. We then have a market structure of six leaders and eight followers. In this case, the equilibrium price for cleaning a carpet is $31.60. This merger harms the consumers in Dirtville.

Daughety's (1990) model solves the merger paradox and gives rise to a merger wave by assuming an asymmetry between newly merged firms and their remaining unmerged rivals. The former gain membership in the club of industry leaders. However, this is a rather strong assumption. While some mergers may create corporate giants with an ability to commit to large production levels, it is far from obvious that every two-firm merger should have this leadership role regardless of which two firms are joined and irrespective of the number of leaders already present. In principle, Daughety's (1990) model implies that in an industry of 10 firms there could be, say, eight leaders. It seems odd though to imagine a configuration with so many leaders and so few followers. Moreover, it leaves unanswered the question as to what happens if two leaders merge. Does this merger create a super-leader?

It is also worth noting that while production is sequential in Daughety's (1990) model, merging is not. While leader firms choose production first, it is not accurate to describe the decision to merge in a sequential way. The model simply says that for any market configuration, if a two-firm merger creates an industry leader, all follower firm pairs will wish to merge as well. One pair does not merge only after it sees another pair merge. Instead, at any single point in time, merging is a dominant strategy and, absent any antitrust intervention, all follower firms will pursue it. Again, this is not because of any new cost savings or product development. It is simply because merging confers leadership status. Thus, Daughety's (1990) model does not give rise to the sporadic merger waves that we often see as much as it suggests an ever-present tendency for the industry to become more concentrated.

To capture the idea that merger decisions may be explicitly sequential, i.e., that the decision of one firm pair to merge is a catalyst for another pair to do the same, a number of papers including Nilssen and Sørgaard (1998), Fauli-Oller (2000), and Salvo (2006) have recently presented models in which a sudden change in cost or product qualities give rise to merger opportunities that are only profitable if other mergers also occur. It is difficult for this to happen in a simultaneous game because each potential merger pair cannot be sure if others will also merge. However, in a sequential game, some firms get to make their merger decision knowing for certain that others have already merged. This greatly enhances the likelihood of a successful merger.

We illustrate the sequential merger model with a simplification of the Fauli-Oller (2000) model. Consider a four-firm industry characterized by Cournot competition. Initially, all of these firms are high-cost firms with constant unit cost $c^h = c$. Suppose that two firms have had a technical breakthrough that allows them to become low-cost firms with low constant unit cost $c^l = 0$. Industry demand is described by: $P = A - Q$.

Using the Cournot model in section 9.4, it is easy to show that the initial, post-innovation equilibrium is described as follows:

$$q_i^h = \frac{A - 3c}{5}; i = 1,2 \quad q_j^l = \frac{A + 2c}{5}; j = 1,2 \quad \Rightarrow \quad Q = \frac{4A - 2c}{5}; P = \frac{A + 2c}{5} \quad (16.41)$$

As a result, each firm earns a profit π of

$$\pi_i^h = \left(\frac{A - 3c}{5}\right)^2; i = 1,2 \quad \text{and} \quad \pi_j^l = \left(\frac{A + 2c}{5}\right)^2; j = 1,2 \quad (16.42)$$

Now consider two possible mergers. In each merger, a low-cost firm buys a high-cost firm and the two then operate as a single low-cost producer. The merger permits the transfer of production from the high-cost plant to the low-cost one. If both of these mergers happen, there will be just two low-cost firms and the industry equilibrium will have the following features:

$$q_j^l = \frac{A}{3}; j = 1, 2 \quad \Rightarrow \quad Q = \frac{2A}{3}; P = \frac{A}{3}; \quad \text{and} \quad \pi_j^l = \left(\frac{A}{3}\right)^2; j = 1, 2 \quad (16.43)$$

Observe that we must have $A > 3c$ for the pre-merger equilibrium to involve any positive output for the high-cost firms. In turn, this means that the expression for π_j^l in equation (16.43) will always exceed the sum of π_i^h and π_j^l from (16.42). That is, a merger between one pair of high- and low-cost firms will be profitable so long as the other pair also merges.

For example, suppose that $A = 100$ and $c = 10$. Then in the pre-merger equilibrium, high-cost firms each earn $196 in profit and low-cost firms each earn $576 in profit. So, the pre-merger profit of any low-cost and high-cost pair is $772. If both such pairs merge, however, the profit of each merged firm rises to $1,111.11. Clearly, this is the preferable outcome from the viewpoint of the two firms.

A potential problem is that one merger will be unprofitable just as the merger paradox suggests. If only one low-cost and high-cost pair merges, the new equilibrium will be:

$$q_1^h = \frac{A - 3c}{4}; \ q_j^l = \frac{A + c}{4}; \ j = 1, 2 \ \Rightarrow \ Q = \frac{3A - c}{4}; \ P = \frac{A + c}{4} \tag{16.44}$$

The profit of the remaining high-cost firm and of each of the two low-cost firms, respectively, will be:

$$\pi_i^h = \left(\frac{A - 3c}{4}\right)^2; \ i = 1, 2 \quad \text{and} \quad \pi_j^l = \left(\frac{A + c}{4}\right)^2; \ j = 1, 2 \tag{16.45}$$

Thus, in our numerical example, the remaining high-cost firm will benefit from the price increase the merger causes and see its profit rise to $306.25. The same is true for the unmerged low-cost firm whose profit will rise to $756.25. The merged firm will also now earn $756.25 as it transfers production from the acquired high-cost plants to the more efficient low-cost ones. However, this is less than the $772 earned as two separate companies in the pre-merger equilibrium. Therefore, no one pair has an incentive to merge on its own. As a result, it seems difficult to reach the two-merger equilibrium outcome even though this would raise profits for all involved.

Let us now introduce a sequential structure to the game, where firms do not make the merger decision simultaneously but, instead, sequentially. Thus, the second merger pair gets to make its decision *after* the first pair. Moreover, the first pair knows this. The rules of the game—in this case, simultaneous versus sequential play—matter a lot for the outcome.

Consider again the outcome when only one pair merges as given by equation (16.45). In our numerical example, this results in the remaining high-cost firm earning $306.25 in profit while the merged firm and its low-cost rival each earn $756.25. Knowing that one merger has already taken place, the second merger pair now has a choice of either staying in this equilibrium or merging themselves in which case the market outcome would have two, low-cost firms as described by equation (16.43). If they merge, this second merged new firm will earn a profit of $1,111.11, which is an increase over the $1,062.50 in combined profit that the two firms will earn if they do not merge. Conditional on the first merger taking place then, the second merger *is* profitable. In effect, the sequential nature of the game allows the first pair to commit credibly to merging. In turn, that means that the second merger pair does not have to worry that in merging they may be acting alone.

The first pair of merging firms can work through the foregoing logic as well as we can. These firms will therefore understand that their merger will also not be the only one but, instead, be followed by another in which case they too will see their combined profits rise to \$1,111.11. As a result, we can expect a merger wave in which first one pair merges and then the second pair merges. Suppose that in this wave, mergers are motivated by a low-cost firm buying a high-cost firm. Since the profit forgone by a high-cost firm is \$306.25 and that forgone by a low-cost firm is \$756.25 when each is part of the second merger, and since the order of mergers is arbitrary, there will be a sequence of mergers in which the acquisition price is somewhere between \$306.25 and \$354.86 (= \$1,111.11 − \$756.25), and the industry will end up with just two, low-cost firms. The merger wave is not, however, desirable for consumers. The industry price rises from \$24 to \$33.33.

The foregoing story is not limited to just two mergers or to models of Cournot competition. Once cost asymmetries or product quality differences are introduced, we can construct sequential merger models that lead to merger waves for a large number of firms in a variety of settings, e.g., Nilssen and Sørgaard (1998) and Salvo (2006), and these mergers are also anticompetitive. This approach offers another resolution to the merger paradox not simply because it demonstrates why mergers may happen but, in addition, why they often happen in sequential waves. As with Daughety's (1990) model, these models also justify concern over the impact that mergers may have on consumer prices.

16.4   HORIZONTAL MERGERS AND PRODUCT DIFFERENTIATION

Our analysis of mergers has so far been set in the Cournot framework of identical products and quantity competition. However, many firms expend considerable effort differentiating their products and this differentiation gives them some latitude in setting their price. Accordingly, we also need to consider the incentives for and the impact of mergers in industries in which firms produce and market differentiated products.

It is particularly important to explore the merger phenomenon in differentiated product markets because often firms are price setters in such markets and the nature of competition is different with price competition than with quantity competition. In quantity competition firms' best response functions are downward sloping, i.e., quantities are strategic substitutes. Thus, when merging occurs, the nonmerged firms want to *increase* their outputs in response to the lower output produced by the merger. This response undermines the effectiveness of the merger. By contrast, with price competition best response functions are upward sloping: prices are strategic complements. A merger leading to an increase in the merged firms' price(s) will encourage the nonmerged firms also to increase their prices, potentially strengthening the effectiveness of the merger.

We develop this intuition more explicitly using two different approaches to product differentiation. The first approach is to extend our standard linear demand representation of consumer preferences to incorporate product differentiation. The second is to adopt the spatial model of horizontal differentiation, which we first introduced in Chapter 4 and then revisited in Chapter 10.[11]

---

[11]   The spatial model was first formulated in Hotelling (1929), and subsequently extended in Schmalensee (1978) and Salop (1979). We saw in Chapters 4, 7, and 10 that this sort of spatial model has proven insightful in analyzing a variety of topics in industrial organization, including brand proliferation in the ready-to-eat breakfast cereal industry, Schmalensee (1978), and the effects of deregulation of transport services such as airlines or passenger buses, Greenhut et al. (1991). It is not surprising that the spatial model is also useful in analyzing mergers of firms selling differentiated products.

16.4.1   Bertrand Competition and Merger with Linear Demand Systems

Suppose that there are three firms in the market, each producing a single differentiated product.[12] Inverse demand for each of the three products is assumed to be given by:

$$p_1 = A - Bq_1 - s(q_2 + q_3)$$
$$p_2 = A - Bq_2 - s(q_1 + q_3) \qquad (s \in [0, B)) \tag{16.46}$$
$$p_3 = A - Bq_3 - s(q_1 + q_2)$$

In these inverse demand functions the parameter s, where $0 \leq s \leq B$, measures how similar the three products are to each other. If $s = 0$ the products are totally differentiated. In this case, each firm is effectively a monopolist. By contrast, as s approaches B the three products become increasingly identical, moving us closer to the homogeneous product case. We will also assume that the three firms have identical marginal costs of c per unit. Finally, assume that the three firms are Bertrand competitors, i.e., they compete in prices and set their prices simultaneously.

We show in Appendix A to this chapter that when these firms compete they each set a price of $p_{nm}^* = \dfrac{A(B - s) + c(B + s)}{2B}$ and each sell quantity $q_{nm}^* = \dfrac{(A - c)(B + s)}{2B(B + 2s)}$. Profit of each firm is then

$$\pi_{nm}^* = \frac{(A - c)^2(B - s)(B + s)}{4B^2(B + 2s)} \tag{16.47}$$

Now suppose that firms 1 and 2 merge but that the merged and nonmerged firms continue to set their prices simultaneously. The two previously independent, single-product firms are now product divisions of a two-product merged firm, coordinating their prices to maximize the joint profit of the two divisions. The result is that the merged firm sets its product prices to $p_1^m = p_2^m = \dfrac{A(2B + 3s)(B - s) + c(2B + s)(B + s)}{2(2B^2 + 2Bs - s^2)}$ while the remaining nonmerged firm 3 sets its product price as $p_3^{nm} = \dfrac{A(B + s)(B - s) + cB(B + 2s)}{(2B^2 + 2Bs - s^2)}$.

It is straightforward to confirm that the merger increases the prices of all three products, as we might have expected since the merger reduces competitive pressures in the market. However, there remains the question of the merger's profitability. The profits of each product division of the merged firm, and of the independent nonmerged firm are:

$$\pi_1^m = \pi_2^m = \frac{(A - c)^2 B(B - s)(2B + 3s)^2}{4(B + 2s)(2B^2 + 2Bs - s^2)^2} \; ; \; \pi_3^m = \frac{(A - c)^2(B - s)(B + s)^3}{(B + 2s)(2B^2 + 2Bs - s^2)^2} \tag{16.48}$$

In comparing equations (16.47) and (16.48) we can simplify matters by normalizing $A - c = 1$ and $B = 1$, so that profits are functions solely of the degree of product differentiation s. It is then easy to confirm that this two-firm merger is profitable for the merged firm

---

[12]   An excellent example of the full analysis can be found in Davidson and Deneckere (1986).

and for the nonmerged firm. More generally, Davidson and Deneckere (1986) show that in a market containing N firms any merger of $M \geq 2$ firms is profitable for the merged firms and for the nonmerged firms. This simple framework of price setting in a product differentiated market avoids the merger paradox, suggesting that mergers are both profitable and of potential concern to antitrust authorities unless accompanied by cost efficiencies.

16.4.2   Mergers in a Spatial Market

In the spatial model, a merger between two firms may well bring increased profit for reasons similar to those in the previous section. Although merging means that the firms lose their separate identity, they do not lose the ownership or control of the product varieties they can offer. For example, the merger of two major banks, Bank of America and Fleet Bank, results in a single new corporate entity. Yet it does not require that the new firm give up any of the locations at which either Bank of America or Fleet currently operate—or that it lose control over the choice of moving some of those locations. Similarly, the acquisition some years ago of American Motors by Chrysler did not mean that the Jeep product line disappeared.

When we consider a firm's product lines, there is a second source of potential profit increase. The merged firms can now coordinate not just the prices but also the design of their product line, or in the context of the spatial model, their location choices. Chrysler can redesign the Jeep line to fit better in its overall range of models. Similarly, Bank of America and Fleet can change the locations of their branches in those areas where each formerly operated an outlet quite close to the other.

To investigate the impact of a merger in the spatial model we begin by recalling the basic setup of the model.[13] There is a group of consumers who are uniformly distributed over a linear market of length L. Again, we can think of this as Main Street in Littlesville. However, one small problem with the Main Street analogy is that outlets at either end of the market can only reach consumers on one side. This restriction introduces an asymmetry in the model, which we would like to avoid. To make the product differentiated market symmetric we can bend the ends of the line around until they touch each other, and replace our straight line of length L with a circle of circumference L. If we use the spatial model to represent departure times in the differentiated airline market, the circle represents the 24 hours of the day about which consumers differ in terms of their most preferred time of departure. In all other respects, the spatial model remains as before.

Each consumer has an "address" indicating her location on the circle and, hence, her most preferred product type. Each consumer is also willing to buy at most one unit of a particular good. The consumer's reservation price for her most preferred good is denoted by V. Different varieties of the good are offered by the firms that are also located on Main Street— or, more appropriately, Main Circle.[14] A consumer buys from the firm that offers the product to her at the lowest price, taking into account the costs of transporting the good from the firm's address to the consumer's. We assume that these transport costs are linear in distance. If the distance between a firm and a consumer is d, the transport costs from the firm to the consumer is td, i.e., t is the transport cost per unit distance. Recall that in the nongeographic interpretation of the model, transport costs become the consumer's valuation of

---

[13]   A more general, but much more complicated version of this analysis can be found in Brito (2003).

[14]   It bears repeating that the spatial or geographic interpretation of this model is only the most obvious one. See the discussion in Chapter 10.

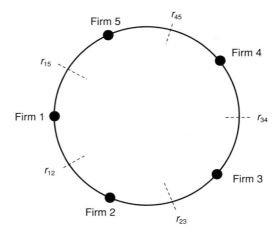

Figure 16.1   Product differentiation: no price discrimination

the loss of utility incurred by consuming a product with characteristics that are not the consumer's most preferred features.

Suppose that there are five firms selling to a group of N consumers who are distributed evenly around the circle of circumference L. A firm is differentiated only by its location on the circle, and we assume that the distance between any two neighboring firms is the same and equal to $L/5$. Each firm has identical costs given by $C(q) = F + cq$, where F is fixed cost and c is (constant) marginal cost. In contrast to our earlier merger analysis, we do not set F, the fixed cost, equal to zero, but instead set unit cost $c = 0$. This simplifies the analysis without losing any generality. What it does do is make it easy to talk about the price–cost margin, which is now just price, denoted by m for mill price.[15]

No price discrimination

We start by considering the case in which firms do not engage in price discrimination. This means that each firm sets a single mill price m that consumers pay at the firm's store or mill location. The consumer then pays the fee for transporting the product back to her location. The full price paid by a consumer who buys from firm i is $m_i + td_i$, where m_i is firm i's mill price and td_i is the consumer's transport cost (or the utility lost by this consumer in buying a product that is not "ideal"). Since marginal cost is zero, the net revenue or profit margin earned by firm i on every such sale is m_i. Consumers buy from the firm offering the product at the lowest full price. As a result, for any set of mill prices across our five hypothetical firms $(m_1, m_2, m_3, m_4, m_5)$ the market is divided between the firms as illustrated in Figure 16.1. The dotted lines indicate the market division between the firms. Firm 1, for example, supplies all consumers in the region (r_{15}, r_{12}).

When the firms set their prices noncooperatively and the maximum willingness to pay V is relatively large, the market is completely covered. That is, every consumer buys from some firm. Hence, the marginal consumer for any firm is the one who is just indifferent between

[15]   If the reader is interested in working out the outcome for the case of $c \neq 0$, then we note here that in each case that we examine, the equilibrium price m^* that we derive should be replaced by $c + m^*$.

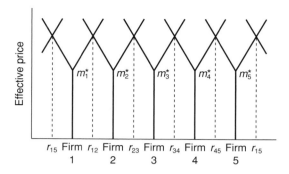

Figure 16.2   Price equilibrium without a merger

buying from that firm and buying from one of the firm's neighbors.[16] We show in Appendix B to this chapter that in equilibrium the mill price set by each firm is $m_i^* = tL/5$. At this price, the profit earned by each firm is

$$\pi_i^* = \frac{NtL^2}{25} - F \tag{16.49}$$

The market outcome is illustrated in Figure 16.2 in which we have "flattened out" the circular market to simplify the geometry; that is, firm 1 is to the right of firm 5 and firm 5 is to the left of firm 1. In Figure 16.2, the vertical distance is the effective price—mill price plus transport cost—that each buyer pays. The sloped lines show how this price rises for consumers who live farther from a firm.

Now consider a merger between some subset of these firms. The first point to note is that, taking store locations or product choice as given, *such a merger will have no effect unless it is made between neighboring firms.* A merger, for example, between firms 2 and 4 leaves prices and market shares unaffected. More generally, this suggests that a merger has no effect on the market outcome unless the market areas of the merging firms have a common boundary. The reason is straightforward. The merging firms hope to gain by softening price competition between them. This will happen only if, prior to the merger, they actually competed for some of the same consumers. For example, the merger of the two investment firms Dean Witter and Morgan Stanley was not for the most part regarded as anticompetitive because the two firms market their services to different, or non-neighboring customers of households and businesses.

Mergers between neighboring firms, however, *do* alter the market outcome. Consider a merger between firms 2 and 3. Suppose that after the merger, the firms do not change either the locations of their existing products or the number of products they offer. Acting now as a single corporate firm with stores in two locations, the merged firm has an incentive to set prices to maximize the joint profits of both products 2 and 3, while the remaining firms continue to price noncooperatively. Of course, firms 1, 4, and 5 also take account of the fact that the merger has taken place. Since firms 2 and 3 are now cooperating divisions of the merged firm they no longer compete for the consumers located between them and so have

---

[16]   We assume no firm prices so low as to lure buyers from beyond its two immediate neighbors. See Appendix to this chapter.

an incentive to raise the prices of products 2 and 3.[17] This will likely lead to the loss of some consumers, namely, those just on the boundaries identified by the points r_{12} and r_{34}. But provided that the merged firm does not raise prices too much the loss of market share will be more than offset by the increased profit margins on their "captive" consumers—the consumers between the two merging firms. Moreover, the increased prices set by the merged firm will induce a similar increase in prices set by firms 1, 4, and 5. Such a response reduces the loss of market share that the merged firm actually suffers making the price increase all the more profitable.

Again we show in Appendix B that the merger leads to a new equilibrium with the following prices:

$$m_2^* = m_3^* = \frac{19tL}{60}; \; m_1^* = m_4^* = \frac{14tL}{60}; \; m_5^* = \frac{13tL}{60} \qquad (16.50)$$

Profits to each product are

$$\pi_2^* = \pi_3^* = \frac{361NtL^2}{7,200} - F; \; \pi_1^* = \pi_4^* = \frac{49NtL^2}{900} - F; \; \pi_5^* = \frac{169NtL^2}{3,600} - F \qquad (16.51)$$

This equilibrium is illustrated in Figure 16.3. Comparison with equation (16.37) confirms that this merger is profitable for the merging firms.

The equilibrium we have identified is based upon the assumption that the merged firms leave their product lines unchanged after the merger. What do we expect to happen if we relax this assumption? It turns out that the answer to this question depends upon the precise nature of transport costs. Consider the product location choice facing the newly merged firm 2 and firm 3. The firm faces a trade-off. On the one hand, relocating products 2 and 3 nearer to products 1 and 4, respectively gives the merged firm two advantages. First, it softens the competition between the merged firm's own two product lines, so that when the firm tries to reach out to customers near the boundary with a lower price there is less of a fear of simply "robbing Peter to pay Paul." Second, the move also makes it easier for the firm to steal some customers away from its true rivals, firms 1 and 4.[18] On the other hand, relocating

---

[17] If the merger leaves products 2 and 3 under the control of separate, competing product divisions, prices will not change. It is important, in other words, that the merged firms take advantage of the opportunity they now have to coordinate their prices.

[18] There is one complication that we have ignored in this discussion. Judd (1985) argues that a merger that creates a multiproduct firm, as for example a merger of firms 2 and 3, may not be sustainable. The intuition is as follows: Assume that an entrant comes in exactly at firm 3's location after the merger of firms 2 and 3. Price competition will drive the price for this product down to marginal cost, in which case the entrant and the incumbent earn zero profits at this location (ignoring fixed costs). But the merged firm also loses money at the neighboring location 2 since the price war with the new entrant forces it to reduce the price there as well. If the merged firm were to close down its location 3 product, the entrant will raise price above marginal cost, and so the merged firm can raise the price at location 2. There is, in other words, a stronger incentive for the merged firm to exit location 3 than for the entrant to do so. Hence, this kind of multiproduct merger may not be sustainable because it is not credible. This argument turns, however, on two important assumptions: that entry costs are not recovered on exit and that the merged firm has no incentive to try to develop a reputation for toughness. If only part of the entry costs are sunk (unrecoverable costs), or if reputation is important, the merged firm can sustain the multiproduct configuration.

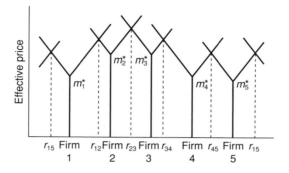

Figure 16.3 Price equilibrium after merger of firms 2 and 3

products 2 and 3 further from products 1 and 4 offers potential advantages. Admittedly this gives up market share to the rivals but such a move also softens price competition, leading to increased prices by all firms. In our example with linear transport costs it turns out that the merged firm will wish to relocate its products closer to its nearby rivals. On the other hand, if transport costs were quadratic, of the form td_i^2 the merged firms would actually want to relocate *further* from their rivals.[19]

A merger between two firms in our spatial market is clearly advantageous to the merging firms but is disadvantageous to consumers because a merger tends to raise prices throughout the industry. Both merged and unmerged firms enjoy greater profit and consumers obtain less surplus. There is a possible gain that could benefit consumers: when the merger leads to cost savings that permit lower prices. Remember that the two products, while not identical, are close substitutes. They might be, for example, low-sugar and high-sugar versions of a soft drink. We might expect there to be some cost complementarities in the production of these products. If so, then production of both goods by one firm will be cheaper than production of both by two separate firms. In short, we should not be surprised if in a product-differentiated market, production of many closely related product lines exhibits economies of scope.[20]

Scope economies provide a strong incentive to merge. The merger allows the new firm to operate as a multiproduct company and thereby exploit the cost-savings opportunities this generates. These savings may be reflected in a reduction in fixed costs. For example, the firms can combine their headquarters, research and development, marketing, accounting, and distribution operations. If in addition the merger leads to a reduction in variable costs of production, then this change will be reflected in lower prices. Moreover, even if scope economies are not present, it is still possible that one of the merging firms has a more effective purchasing division or a superior production technology that, following the merger, will be extended to its new partners. The greater are such cost synergies, the more likely it is that consumers will benefit from the merger.

Price discrimination

Firms that operate in a spatial or product-differentiated setting clearly have some monopoly power. Yet if firms have monopoly power, we might expect them to use discriminatory pricing strategies to exploit this power. In particular, we might expect these firms to adopt

---

[19] A formal proof for the case of three firms is provided by Posada and Straume (2004).
[20] Refer to section 4.3, Chapter 4 for a definition and explanation of economies of scope.

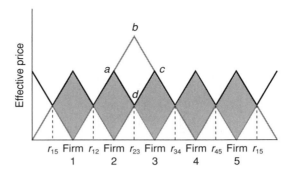

Figure 16.4   Price equilibrium with price discrimination

some of the price discrimination strategies that we developed in earlier chapters. We now turn to the analysis of how price discrimination affects the incentives for and the impact of mergers in a product differentiated market.

Suppose that firms adopt first-degree or personalized discriminatory pricing policies (section 6.1, Chapter 6) but maintain at the same time all the remaining assumptions of our spatial model in the no-price-discrimination case. The noncooperative price equilibrium is then easy to identify. Remember that firms compete in prices for customers. Accordingly, they set the price as low as need be—at the margin—to attract customers, so long as that price covers their marginal cost. As a result, the equilibrium must be characterized by the following condition. Suppose that firm i is the firm that can supply consumer location s at the lowest unit cost, say $c + ts$ (the marginal production cost plus transport fee), and that firm j is the firm that can supply this location at the next cheapest unit cost, $c + ts + e$, where e is a measure of how much closer the consumer is to firm i than it is to firm j. The Bertrand–Nash equilibrium price to consumer s will be for firm i to charge one cent or epsilon less than the cost of firm j to supply consumer s; that is, to charge just less than $c + ts + e$.

The heavy shaded line in Figure 16.4 illustrates this price equilibrium. Firm 2 is the lowest-cost supplier (including transport cost) for all consumers in the region (r_{12}, r_{23}). Therefore, firm 2 supplies all consumers in this market region, charging its consumers on the left one cent less than firm 1's costs of supplying them, and its consumers to the right one cent less than firm 3's costs of supplying these consumers. By adopting this pricing strategy, each firm earns a gross profit (profit before deducting fixed cost) given by the shaded areas for their market regions in Figure 16.4.

An interesting feature of the set of discriminatory prices is that the highest price now paid by any consumer is $c + tL/5$. This was the *lowest* price paid by any consumer when firms did not practice price discrimination! Price discrimination in this oligopolistic market unambiguously benefits consumers. Why is this?[21] With nondiscriminatory pricing, when a firm reduces the price to one consumer, it has to reduce the price to every consumer—an expensive prospect. With discriminatory pricing, by contrast, a firm can lower price in one location

---

[21]   This is discussed in Norman and Thisse (1996). They show that with a given number of firms, discriminatory pricing always benefits consumers. They also show, however, that the much more competitive environment of discriminatory pricing may cause enough firms to want to leave the market that prices actually increase for some consumers. In our example, there is no incentive to exit the market. See also Reitzes and Levy (1995).

without having to lower its prices elsewhere. But this means that price discrimination weakens each firm's ability to commit to a set of higher prices, making price competition between the firms much fiercer and so leading to the lower prices that we have just identified.

Now consider the effect on this equilibrium of a merger between two of these firms, say firms 2 and 3, as before. Two points should be clear. First, as in the no-price discrimination case, a merger of non-neighboring firms has no effect. Second, the merged firm's ability to coordinate the formerly separate pricing strategies is particularly valuable in this discriminatory setting. This is because prior to the merger these firms were engaged in what is nearly cutthroat price competition. By merging, the two firms can avoid this expensive conflict, at least with respect to each other.[22] From the perspective of the merged firm, the nearest competitor for consumers in the region between firm 2's location and r_{23} is now firm 1. Similarly, for consumers in the region between firm 3's location and r_{23}, the nearest competitor is now firm 4. As a result, the merged firm can raise prices to all consumers located between firms 2 and 3, as indicated by the line *abc* in Figure 16.4. A merger of firm 2 and firm 3 increases the profits of the merging firms by an amount given by the area *abcd*. One further effect of this type of merger, which is not quite so intuitive, is that when firms practice price discrimination the merger only benefits the merging firms. Prices and profit increase only for those consumers who were served by the merged firm prior to the merger. All other prices are unaffected, and so the profits of the nonmerging firms are unaffected by the merger.

We could also consider issues regarding the merged firm's product location strategies, but the basic point has been made. Prices to consumers rise and the merging firms are more profitable. There is absolutely no paradox about merging in this price discrimination case. Our conclusions for the no-price discrimination case hold all the more strongly when firms engage in discriminatory pricing practices.

There is one final point to emphasize. Why is it that mergers with price competition in a product-differentiated market do not run into the merger paradox that so bedeviled our earlier analysis with homogeneous products and quantity-setting firms? The first part of the answer has already been suggested. Prices are strategic complements whereas quantities are strategic substitutes. With price competition, therefore, the strategic responses of non-merged firms are potentially beneficial to the merged firms whereas with quantity competition they are potentially harmful.

The second part of the answer is equally important and is related to the notion of credible commitment discussed in section 11.3, Chapter 11. The reason why mergers are profitable in the spatial or differentiated products context is that the merged firms can credibly commit to produce some particular *range* of products—that is, the commitment required in the spatial context is a commitment to particular locations or to continue marketing the products of the previously independent firms. By contrast, the commitment necessary with homogeneous products and quantity competition must be in terms of production *levels*. The merging firms must be able to commit to a high volume of output following the merger. Generally, this is not credible because such a high volume of production is not the merged firm's best response to a Cournot output decision by the other firms. If, however, the merged firm becomes a Stackelberg leader then the commitment to a high level of post-merger output is credible.

---

[22] In this type of merger the potential problems discussed in footnote 15 cannot arise if firms charge discriminatory prices. Consider, for example, entry at product 3's location. This yields the price equilibrium in Figure 6a whether or not the merged firm exits this location. A potential entrant can correctly anticipate that there is no benefit to the merged firm exiting and so entry will not occur.

16.5   PUBLIC POLICY TOWARD HORIZONTAL MERGERS

American public policy with respect to horizontal mergers has changed dramatically over the last 40 years. To a large extent, this change is reflected in the differences between the first Merger Guidelines issued by the Justice Department in 1968 and the Merger Guidelines currently in force. While it is tempting to summarize these differences as a move from a very strict regime to a more permissive one, it is more accurate to describe the evolution of merger policy as one that has increasingly become more sophisticated and that gives greater recognition to the complexity of corporate organizations in the real world.

The 1968 Merger Guidelines relied heavily on market structure—particularly the four-firm concentration ratio[23]—to determine the legality of a proposed merger. Mergers would be challenged in any industry in which the four-firm concentration ratio exceeded 75 percent and the merging firms each had a market share of as little as 4 percent. In markets with a four-firm ratio below 75 percent, mergers would be challenged if the two firms each had market shares of 5 percent or more. Thus, under the 1968 Guidelines, a combined share of as little as 10 percent would be sufficient in many cases for the government to challenge a merger.

The approach taken in 1968 reflected many years of empirical work within the SCP framework. We described economists' increasing discomfort with that framework in Chapter 1. By the mid-1960s, economists were also increasingly concerned with the rigidity with which the courts seemed to apply the SCP learning. Perhaps nowhere was this more apparent than in the controversial merger case, *U.S. v. Von's Grocery* (1966), in which the Supreme Court upheld the government's prohibition of a merger between two grocery store chains in Los Angeles that, in combination, had less than 10 percent of the market.

Ironically, courts began to deviate from the rigid, structure-based Guidelines of 1968 almost as soon as they were adopted. One early such case was the acquisition by General Dynamics of another coal producer, which was ultimately allowed by the Supreme Court in 1974 despite the fact that the combined market shares of the two firms clearly exceeded the permissible levels set forth by the then 1968 Merger Guidelines. As the courts permitted a number of similar mergers it soon became clear that the 1968 Guidelines were no longer compelling. This eventually led to the Justice Department issuing a new set of Merger Guidelines in 1982.

Under the new rules, reliance on the four-firm concentration ratio was abandoned in favor of the Herfindahl–Hirschman Index (HHI).[24] The threshold for intervention now became an HHI of 1,800 (a little more concentrated than an industry comprised of six, equally large firms). Mergers in less concentrated industries would only be challenged if they raised the HHI by more than one hundred points and even then, only if the industry HHI already exceeded one thousand. Subsequent amendments to the Guidelines in 1984, 1992, and 1997 relaxed even more the constraints on mergers by specifying and enlarging the ability of merger-generated cost efficiencies as a merger justification.

Underlying these developments was an increasing awareness of modern industrial organization theory as well as a growing body of empirical data that suggested many mergers did

[23]   Refer to section 3.1, Chapter 3 for a discussion of concentration ratios.
[24]   For a discussion of HHI again refer to section 3.1, Chapter 3.

Reality Checkpoint
Baby, Baby, Where Did that Brand Go?

Cost savings have always been a possible justification for horizontal mergers. Such efficiencies took on increased importance after 1997 when the U.S. Federal Trade Commission (FTC) and Department of Justice amended their well-known merger guidelines to give greater weight to such cost efficiencies as a rationale for what otherwise might be a questionable merger. The intuition is that while there may be potential harm to consumers from the monopoly power that the merger creates, this will often be offset by the lower prices that result from the lower costs that the merger makes possible.

Evaluation of the cost-efficiency defense is therefore important. It is also tricky. Besides the question of how real the cost savings may be, there is the further question as to whether the cost savings will be passed on to consumers in the form of lower prices.

Consider the proposed acquisition of Beech-Nut Baby Food by Heinz in 2001. Along with Gerber, these two companies controlled the bulk of the jarred or prepared baby food market. Gerber was the industry giant with a market share between 65 and 70 percent. The remaining 30 to 35 percent was split fairly evenly between Heinz and Beech-Nut.

The FTC sought to block the merger arguing that it would significantly decrease competition in the baby food industry. Heinz and Beech-Nut responded that the merger would actually increase competition. Their analysis relied heavily on cost savings. In brief, the merging parties argued that Beech-Nut has a superior brand image but very old and costly production techniques relative to Heinz. They further argued that the merger would permit the two firms to offer a single product of the higher Beech-Nut quality but at the lower Heinz cost. As a result, this product would enable the merged firm to really put pressure on the industry giant, Gerber. Given Gerber's large size, and market share, a fall in its price would bring large gains to consumers.

Heinz and Beech-Nut backed up their claims with statistical evidence. Using a model of the baby food industry that is similar in spirit to the circular spatial model used here, they provided simulations of the post-merger market that implied a fall in baby food prices. These simulations took the assumptions of a 15 percent cost savings as given and suggested that between 50 and 100 percent of these savings would be passed through to consumers as lower prices.

The claim that much of the cost savings would be passed on to consumers depends critically on the nature of competition in the post-merger market. As noted, Heinz and Beech-Nut assumed that that market could be described as a spatial one of the type used in this chapter. Horizontal differentiation is not the only type of product differentiation that we observe, however. An alternative approach is to view the market as vertically differentiated (Chapter 7) with each brand representing a different level of quality and consumers differing in how much they are willing to pay for quality. Gerber would be the highest quality, Beech-Nut the next highest, and Heinz (well known as the discount brand) would be the least highest. In this set-up it is the Beech-Nut quality that directly competes with the Gerber premium brand. If this is the case, then Heinz and Beech-Nut have a strong incentive to discontinue the Beech-Nut brand after the merger. This would allow the firms post-merger to soften price competition in the market by producing the brand that is maximally differentiated (furthest) from Gerber. If so, consumers could be hurt in two ways. Not only would prices rise but consumers would also suffer a loss in choice as one brand was removed from the market. Moreover, removal of a brand in the post-merger market means that the demand estimates made for the pre-merger market (the ones relied on by Heinz and Beech-Nut in their simulations) might not be relevant.

Norman, Pepall, and Richards (2002) show that the foregoing concern is very real. Indeed, they show that no matter what the cost savings, a merger of two lower quality brands will always lead to the removal of the higher quality one and a rise in consumer prices on the remaining brands. They show that this is true even when there is potential competition from a later entrant.

Sources: G. Norman, L. Pepall, and D. Richards, "Product Differentiation, Cost-Reducing Mergers, and

Consumer Welfare," *Canadian Journal of Economics*, 38 (November, 2005), 1204–23. See also, J. Baker "Efficiencies and High Concentration: Heinz Proposes to Acquire Beech-Nut (2001)," in J. Kwoka and L. White, eds., *The Antitrust Revolution*, Oxford University Press, Oxford, 2004, 150–69; and Gandhi, *et al.* (2007), "Post-Merger Product Repositioning," forthcoming, *Journal of Industrial Economics*.

not threaten competition as much as the SCP paradigm implied. Moreover the evidence on profitability of mergers was mixed as well. Quite a long list of studies including Mueller (1985), Ravenscraft and Scherer (1987), Lichtenberg and Siegel (1992), Loughran and A. Vijh (1997), Andrade, Mitchell, and Stafford (2001), and Maskimovic and Phillips (2001) have found that mergers are not terribly profitable—especially for the acquiring firm. Indeed, many acquisitions are later reversed by "spin-offs."[25]

The change in attitude reflected by the 1982 Guidelines has led to many more mergers being permitted. These have included such major consolidations as Union Pacific and Southern Pacific (railroads), AOL and Time Warner (telecommunications), Chase Manhattan and J. P. Morgan (finance), Exxon and Mobil and also British Petroleum and Amoco (both petroleum mergers), Westinghouse and Infinity Broadcasting (radio), Aetna and U.S. Healthcare (health services), MCI and WorldCom (telecommunications), and Maytag and Whirlpool (laundry machines) among others. Many of these mergers were controversial and virtually all raised some competitive concerns. Yet these and other mergers were nevertheless approved.

Public policy on mergers has increasingly made use of sophisticated empirical techniques to estimate key market parameters and then to use these parameters to model the most likely post-merger scenario. We briefly describe this process of merger simulation in the next section. As developed by Werden and Froeb (1994, 2002) and extended by Epstein and Rubinfeld (2002), among others, merger simulation has become an important, albeit somewhat controversial tool in merger policy. (See Slade (2007).)

In addition to a greater reliance on econometric evidence and economic modeling, policy makers have taken two additional steps that permit horizontal mergers to be approved despite some clear antitrust concerns. First, the antitrust authorities have increasingly used a "fix-it-first" approach regarding proposed mergers. This procedure usually centers on divestiture of some of the assets of the merging parties to another, third firm so as to ensure that competitive pressures are maintained. If, for example, the two firms operate in several towns across the country, but in one town they are the only two such suppliers, then the government may permit the merger so long as one of the firms sells off its operations in the town in question to a new, rival entrant firm. This principle was applied in both of the petroleum mergers mentioned above and it is often used in the case of media mergers where

---

[25] Note though that these findings also raise doubts about any cost savings that mergers are alleged to generate.

newspaper and broadcasting firms have been required to sell their operations in certain locations before being permitted to conclude a merger.

Divestiture does have some problems. Cabral (2003) notes that divestiture allows the merging firms to dictate the entry position for new rivals. If we think of the circle spatial model described above, if two firms merge but sell the location of some of their stores to a formerly excluded entrant, it means that entrant enters at the same location at which the initial stores existed rather than at other locations on the circle that would be better for consumers. Further, firms can act strategically to reduce the competitive threat presented by divested stores. This occurred in 1995 when Schnucks Markets, a supermarket chain, acquired National Food Markets, which was the major competitor of Schnucks in the St. Louis area. The merger was approved when Schnucks agreed to divest 24 supermarkets in the St. Louis area over the next year. However, no immediate buyer was named. Schnucks then took the stores to be divested and proceeded to run them into the ground. It closed departments. It kept the stores understaffed, and referred customers to the other Schnucks stores that were not being divested. Soon sales at the divesting stores had declined by about one-third and, as a result, they posed less of a competitive threat to the stores that the new Schnucks/National firm continued to operate. It was partly a response to this case that led the FTC to now require that the buyer of the divested plants be named in advance and that the firm be one that has the industry knowledge to be an effective competitor. This remedy does not, however, correct for the problems identified by Cabral (2003).

A second, alternative procedure has been to approve mergers subject to behavioral constraints on the merging firms, and then to follow this agreement with active monitoring by government agents. Typically, these consent agreements require the firms to take specific actions and to avoid engaging in certain practices. In monitoring these agreements, the regulatory agencies can always count on a reliable source of outside help, namely, the competitors of the merged firms and other parties who opposed the merger. They are always quick to report violations of the consent agreement. Since 1992, the number of consent decrees issued by the FTC and the Justice Department has dramatically increased.

In addition to these procedural changes, the FTC and the Justice Department have also continued to adjust the merger guidelines themselves. In this connection, an important recent modification is the 1997 expansion of section 4 of the Guidelines to permit greater reliance on documented cost savings as a justification of a merger. With this change, the antitrust authorities have indicated an increased willingness to judge a merger to be pro-competitive if it generates cost savings that are likely to translate into lower consumer prices. As we have already noted, however, most analysis finds that the cost savings necessary to generate lower prices are substantial. This may be why the proposed acquisition of Beech-Nut baby food by the Heinz Corporation (see inset) was ultimately denied. Hence, the full implication of the 1997 cost efficiencies amendment is yet to be seen.

We should also note that merger-generated cost efficiencies are not necessarily completely beneficial once entry possibilities are considered. If a merger generates lower marginal costs, then any potential entrant will know that *if it enters* price competition will be relatively fierce. If the entrant has fixed costs, this will mean that the market will need to be larger for entry to be profitable. In other words, for a given market size, merger-generated cost efficiencies make post-merger entry less likely. Thus, cost savings can have two price effects. One is the downward pressure on prices exerted by lower costs while the other is the upward pressure exerted by the reduced likelihood of rival entry. Cabral (2003) shows that it is possible that the former outweighs the latter.

Reality Checkpoint
Whose Welfare Is It, Anyway?

In January 2003, a Canadian federal court upheld the decision of that country's Competition Tribunal to permit the merger of Superior Propane and IGC Propane, the two major producers in Canada's propane gas market, both based in Calgary. This was the final act in a five-year case in which the Tribunal and, ultimately, the courts, rejected the argument of the Canadian Competition Bureau, Canada's major antitrust enforcement agency, that the merger should be blocked.

The issue that kept the Superior/IGC case alive through so many rounds of litigation was the question of the proper standard for evaluating mergers. Section 96 of the Canadian Competition Act says that mergers should be allowed if they result in cost efficiencies "that will be greater than, and will offset, the effects of any prevention or lessening of competition" that the merger might create. Effectively, this clause appears to state that mergers ought to be judged on the basis of their impact on the total, producer plus consumer, surplus. This stands in sharp contrast to the U.S. (and European) approaches that give primary emphasis to a merger's impact on consumer surplus, alone. In either setting, merger-generated cost efficiencies may help justify a merger but in the U.S. those efficiencies must be passed on to consumers, whereas the Canadian framework only requires that the cost savings be verified. Whether they result in greater profits or greater consumer surplus is irrelevant in this view.

The relevant surplus question was particularly crucial to the Superior-IGC case because there was no question that the merger conferred substantial market power on the two merging companies. Together, the two would control more than 70 percent of the propane market. Moreover, there was widespread agreement that this power would translate into price increases on the order of 9 percent. The estimated deadweight loss resulting from this price increase was about $3 million. However, this loss was dwarfed by an estimated gain in profit for the two firms of $29 million. Thus, it was crucial to determine whether the Act's apparent endorsement of a total surplus standard was, in fact, the proper interpretation of the law. As indicated above, the tribunal's decision, with the court's support, endorsed that view.

It is probably fair to say that many economists support the total surplus criterion. It is rooted in the economic definition of efficiency and can be presented with clarity and certainty to all parties involved in a merger case. What justification can there be then for the U.S. (and European) approaches that focus primarily on just consumer surplus?

Apart from distributional concerns, there are at least two arguments in support of a consumer surplus only standard. First, as noted in the text, merging firms may well exaggerate the cost efficiencies stemming from the merger. Focusing on consumer surplus alone will diminish the incentives to do this since the profits that result from such cost savings will not help to justify the merger. Since consumers are not well represented at these proceedings, there may be merit in giving less weight to the claims of producers. Second, even when total surplus is the real goal, focusing on consumer surplus may still prove a useful selection criterion. Suppose that a firm is considering two different mergers. Each will raise total surplus by X. However, the first will raise producer surplus by $X + e$ while reducing consumer surplus by e. In contrast, the second merger will raise both producer and consumer surplus by $X/2$. Under a total surplus standard, the firm will choose the first merger. Under a consumer surplus alone standard, it will choose the second. In short, a consumer surplus criterion may serve as a useful instrument to guide firms' choice of merger possibilities even when total surplus is the real target.

Source: T. Ross and R. Winter, "Canadian Merger Policy following *Superior Propane*," *Canadian Competition Record* (2003).

16.6   EMPIRICAL APPLICATION
Evaluating the Impact of Mergers with Computer Simulation

In recent years the important new tool of merger simulation has emerged to assist with the evaluation of mergers. Merger simulation basically works in two steps. The first is to obtain relevant information on such variables as firms' costs, prices, and demand elasticities, among others. This is usually accomplished with the aid of modern econometric techniques. The second step is then to use this evidence to run computer-simulated models of the market in question both before and after a proposed merger. In effect then, merger simulation allows economists to conduct laboratory experiments to examine a merger's likely effects. While not necessarily conclusive, such experiments can be very helpful as an evaluative tool.

   To understand merger simulation better, consider an industry with four firms each of which produces a differentiated product and which competes in prices against its rivals. For any one firm, the first-order condition for profit maximization is effectively the Lerner condition, as first identified in section 3.2, Chapter 3. That is,

$$\frac{p_i - c}{p_i} + \frac{1}{\eta_{ii}} = 0 \quad i = 1 \text{ to } 4 \tag{16.52}$$

Here, η_{ii} is the (negative of) the elasticity of the firm i's demand with respect to its own price. If we denote the price-cost margin term as μ_i; firm i's market share as s_i; and then multiply through by the product of the firm's market share s_i and the own price elasticity of demand η_{ii} (16.52) becomes:

$$s_i + s_i \eta_{ii} \mu_i = 0 \tag{16.53}$$

If two firms merge, however, the first-order condition will change as we saw in section 16.5. Now, the merged firm will coordinate the prices of its two separate products by taking account of the cross-demand effects between the two products. Specifically, assume that firms 1 and 2 merge. Then it is straightforward to show that for the merged firm, the first-order condition is:

$$s_1 + s_1 \eta_{11} \mu_1 + s_2 \mu_2 \eta_{21} = 0$$
$$s_2 + s_2 \eta_{22} \mu_2 + s_1 \mu_2 \eta_{12} = 0 \tag{16.54}$$

Where η_{ij} is the cross-elasticity of good i with respect to the price of good j. It is clear from equations (16.53) and (16.54) that measures of the own and cross-price elasticities for each good are critical to estimating the impact of a proposed merger. Indeed, once these elasticities are known, it is relatively straightforward to work out the implied post-merger equilibrium and, therefore, the post-merger prices.

   In order to estimate the elasticities, one needs a model of market demand. One commonly used such model is derived from what is referred to as the Almost Ideal Demand System (AIDS) as first described by Deaton and Mulbauer (1980). Essentially, such a system describes the demand facing each firm as a function of its own price and the prices charged by other firms, similar to the linear demand that we used to describe our initial model of Bertrand competition with differentiated products. In the case of our four-firm example above, a conventional approach would be to describe market demand with a system of equations something like the following:

$$s_1 = a_1 + b_{11} \ln p_1 + b_{12} \ln p_2 + b_{13} \ln p_3 + b_{14} \ln p_4$$
$$s_2 = a_2 + b_{21} \ln p_1 + b_{22} \ln p_2 + b_{23} \ln p_3 + b_{24} \ln p_4$$
$$s_3 = a_3 + b_{31} \ln p_1 + b_{32} \ln p_2 + b_{33} \ln p_3 + b_{34} \ln p_4 \qquad (16.55)$$
$$s_4 = a_4 + b_{41} \ln p_1 + b_{42} \ln p_2 + b_{43} \ln p_3 + b_{44} \ln p_4$$

The b_{ij} coefficients in the above system are directly linked to the demand elasticities needed to run the merger simulation. Thus, econometric estimation of those coefficients is the first step in obtaining a simulated outcome.

Not counting the a_i coefficients or intercepts, this still leaves 16 b_{ij} coefficients to estimate even in our small four-product example. In general, unless some restrictions are imposed on the nature of the own and cross-price effects, there will be on the order of n^2 coefficients to estimate in a general n-product demand system of the type illustrated above. This is a rather large number of estimates to make with any degree of precision. To simplify matters, it is common to impose restrictions that reduce the number of parameters to be estimated directly.

For example, suppose that our four-firm case is characterized by $q_1 = 250$; $q_2 = 100$; $q_3 = 100$; and $q_4 = 50$, or $s_1 = 50$ percent; $s_2 = s_3 = 20$ percent; and $s_4 = 10$ percent. One way to proceed is to calibrate the model under the assumption of proportionality. As developed by Epstein and Rubinfeld (2002) Proportionally Calibrated AIDS (PCAIDS) assumes that the output loss for good 1 caused by an increase in p_1 will be allocated to the other products in proportion to their market shares. Suppose that the overall elasticity of market demand $\eta = -2$ and the own price elasticity of good 1 is $\eta_{11} = -4$. If we think of the overall industry price as the share-weighted average price across the four firms, then a 1 percent increase in firm 1's price p_1 translates into a 0.5 percent increase in the industry price, all else being equal. Firm 1's price increase will then reduce industry output by one-half of 2 percent, or by 1 percent, which in this case is five units. Firm 1's own output will fall by 4 percent, or ten units. Thus, five of these ten units will be picked up in the demand for the other firms if the net industry demand decline is to be just five units. The proportionality assumption is that $[0.2/(0.2 + 0.2 + 0.1)] \times 5$ or 2 units will be diverted to each of firms 2 and 3, while the remaining one unit will be diverted to firm 4. Note that this implies that a 1 percent increase in firm 1's price will raise the demand at each of the other firms by 2 percent, i.e., the cross-elasticities η_{21}, η_{31}, and η_{41} are -2 in each case.

What we have just shown is that with the proportionality restriction, the knowledge of just the market demand elasticity and firm 1's own price elasticity has permitted us to deduce three other of the elasticity measures needed for simulation. As it turns out, we can go much farther. In fact, the proportionality assumption permits the complete derivation of all the relevant elasticities once the elasticity is known for the market and for one firm. To put it slightly differently, knowing the market elasticity and own-price elasticity of one firm permits complete calculation of all the b_{ij} coefficients in equation (16.55). The proportionality assumption reduces the number of parameters to be estimated from n^2 to just 2. Once that estimation is complete, we may use the resulting elasticity and market share data to solve the first-order conditions in equations (16.53) and (16.54) for both the pre-merger and post-merger market. We can then evaluate the price effects of the merger.

Of course, proportionality is a strong assumption. Other techniques for simplifying the estimation procedure also exist. Unfortunately, which technique is chosen can affect the predicted post-merger price change by a very large amount, as Slade (2007) in particular, has emphasized. Moreover, even if proportionality is assumed there still remain two elasticity parameters to be estimated. There is ultimately no way to avoid the use of some econometric analysis in the merger evaluation process.

Efforts to estimate the relevant parameters from a demand system such as the one in equation (16.55) are tricky at best. Even if only a few parameters are required, there remain difficult measurement questions. And while the specification in equation (16.55) is common it is not the only way to structure market demand. Alternative specifications will imply different functional forms and cross-product elasticity restrictions that in turn will have different effects on the post-merger equilibrium. For example, the linear demand function that we use in most of the examples in this text implies that demand becomes more elastic as prices rise. This imposes a constraint on post-merger prices even if a merger raises market power because it means that consumers become increasingly sensitive to such price increases. In contrast, a log-linear demand function implies a constant price elasticity of demand that will yield a notably higher price rise for the same market power increase. Yet it is often far from clear what precise specification is most appropriate.

A firm's market share will depend heavily on the definition of the market employed. Yet as we can see from the first-order conditions (16.52–16.54), these share values are crucial to understanding market dynamics. Indeed, they are crucial to understanding whether or not the merger raises antitrust concerns in the first place.

The difficulties posed by the econometrics in merger analysis were dramatically illustrated by the proposed 1996 merger of two office superstore chains, Staples and Office Depot.[26] Along with Office Max, the merging firms dominated the office superstore retail market. Of course, these three firms are not the only retailers of office supplies. While Staples and Office Depot had between 70 and 75 percent of the market defined by office superstores alone, their combined share of the retail sales of office supplies by all stores, including large discounters such as Wal-Mart, drug store chains, and stationery stores, was probably under 10 percent. Accordingly, the question of whether the merger even crossed the threshold of concern established by the Merger Guidelines had to be addressed.

Moreover, even within the category of office superstores, market definition remains problematic. In the *Staples* case, it was widely agreed that there was not one national market but many local ones. In principle, this means that estimation of a demand structure like that in equation (16.55) would have to take the specific nature of each localized market into account. That is, account would need to be taken of variation across locations in the extent of competition. How should this variation be modeled?

The government argued that the local market boundaries were those of the Metropolitan Statistical Area (MSA) used by the Census Bureau. For any Staples store, competitors included all other Office Depot and Office Max stores in the same MSA. In contrast, the merging firms argued that there was a difference within an MSA depending on the actual distance between rivals. That is, an Office Depot store exerted greater price pressure on a Staples store if it were only 5 miles away than if it were 10, or 20 miles away. Again, these seemingly small changes in specifying the competitive interaction can (and did) have a large effect on the results. Just this one alteration led to more than a three-percentage point difference between the firms' prediction that the merger would raise prices by about 0.8 percent and the government's estimate of a rise of 4.1 percent. Together these and other modest econometric modifications meant that the range in predicted price increases varied from less than 1 percent to almost 10 percent.

---

[26] For a more complete discussion of the econometric evidence in this case, see Ashenfelter et al. (2004).

In short, simulating merger effects inevitably requires different estimation techniques and structural demand assumptions that vary according to the conceptualization of the market environment. Assumptions to ease the estimation burden do not alleviate other measurement and econometric issues. We can expect self-interest to lead each side in a merger case to choose the framework and associated econometric technique that yield parameter values and other evidence most favorable to its own objective. Unfortunately, it is typically the case that each approach has some objective justification. It becomes very difficult even for economists to separate the truth from the self-interest in interpreting the results. It is even more difficult for the courts to resolve such debates. One of the striking features of the *Staples* case is that the final court decision never mentions the econometric evidence despite the fact that this case probably involved more econometric presentation than virtually any other merger litigation.

Summary

Horizontal mergers are combinations of firms that are rivals within the same industry. Because they result in the joining of firms that were previously competitors, horizontal mergers raise obvious antitrust concerns. Such mergers may, in fact, be a means to create a legal cartel. One major puzzle in economic analysis is the merger paradox. This paradox reflects the fact that many commonly used economic models suggest that merger is not profitable for the merging firms and that the true beneficiaries of a merger are the non-merging firms.

The clue to resolving the merger paradox is to find some means of credibly committing the newly merged firm to a profit-enhancing strategy. One way to do this in quantity-setting models is to permit the merged firm to take on the role of Stackelberg leader whose increased production is credible. Another way is to consider merger decisions sequentially. Either of these approaches is capable of generating profitable mergers that also have adverse consequences for consumers. The sequential merger approach can also help explain the "domino effect," often observed, by which a merger of two firms in an industry is quickly followed by similar marriages among other firms in the same industry.

The merger paradox does not arise in markets where firms offer differentiated products and compete in price for customers. In these markets the merging firms can more easily make a true commitment to specific locations or product designs—namely, those used by the firms before they merged. The ability to make such a commitment is sufficient to make merger profitable.

The ambiguous effects of mergers found in economic theory are also found in empirical analysis. To date, there is little clear evidence that mergers have resulted in legalized cartels with significant monopoly power. Instead, what is clear is that the combination of theoretical and empirical ambiguity has led the legal authorities to take a much less aggressive and much less rigid stand against proposed mergers, a point to which we return in the policy discussion of the next chapter.

Policy also increasingly includes formal attempts to model the post-merger market and to evaluate mergers on a case-by-case basis. The theory behind this approach builds on the first-order conditions for profit maximization and using these along the estimates of the relevant price elasticities to analyze the optimal pricing decisions of the merged firm and its rivals in the post-merger market. In practice, this is hard work and typically requires a number of simplifying assumptions to identify the needed parameters. However, there appears to be little alternative.

In sum, there is no general rule regarding the impact of mergers. The merger paradox suggests that only mergers that are associated with large cost efficiencies will be profitable. Since firms do not pursue unprofitable opportunities, this suggests that any proposed merger must have very large cost efficiencies and, perhaps, should be approved. On the other hand, we know if merged firms can acquire the ability to commit to a production level before others, then the merger can be profitable without cost savings and thus, would be anticompetitive. Antitrust authorities cannot rely solely on economic theory to determine whether or not a specific merger should be challenged. This is an area where empirical work based on advanced econometrics necessarily play a more complicated role.

Problems

For problems 1, 2, 3 and 4 consider a market containing four identical firms each of which makes an identical product. The inverse demand for this product is $P = 100 - Q$, where P is price and Q is aggregate output. The production costs for firms 1, 2, and 3 are identical and given by $C(q_i) = 20q_i$; ($i = 1, 2, 3$), where q_i is the output of firm i. This means that for each of these firms, variable costs are constant at $20 per unit. The production costs for firm 4 are $C(q_4) = (20 + \gamma)q_4$, where γ is some constant. Note that if $\gamma > 0$, then firm 4 is a high-cost firm, while if $\gamma < 0$, firm 4 is a low-cost firm ($|\gamma| < 20$). Note also that $Q = \sum_{i=1}^{4} q_i$

1. Assume that the firms each choose their outputs to maximize profits given that they each act as Cournot competitors.
    a. Identify the Cournot equilibrium output for each firm, the product price, and the profits of the four firms. For this to be a "true" equilibrium, all of the firms must at least be covering their variable costs. Identify the constraint that γ must satisfy for this to be the case.
    b. Assume that firms 1 and 2 merge and that all firms continue to act as Cournot competitors after the merger. Confirm that this merger is unprofitable.
    c. Now assume that firms 1 and 4 merge. Can this merger be profitable if γ is positive so that firm 4 is a high-cost firm? What has happened to the profits of firm 2 as a result of this merger?

2. Now assume that each firm incurs fixed costs of F in addition to the variable costs noted above. When two firms merge the merged firm has fixed costs of bF where $1 \le b \le 2$.
    a. Suppose that firms 1 and 2 merge and that $\gamma \ge 0$. Derive a condition on b, F and γ for this merger to be profitable. Give an intuitive interpretation of this condition.
    b. Suppose by contrast that firms 1 and 4 merge. Repeat your analysis in a.
    c. Compare the conditions derived in a. and b. What does this tell you about mergers that create cost savings?

3. Assume that if two firms merge, the merged firm will be able to act as an industry leader,

making its output decision before the non-merged firms make theirs. Further assume that $\gamma = 0$ so that the firms are of equal efficiency.
    a. Confirm that a merger between firms 1 and 2 will now be profitable. What has happened to the profits of the nonmerged firms and to the product price as a result of this merger?
    b. Confirm that the two remaining firms will also want to merge and join the leader group given that the leaders act as Cournot competitors with respect to each other (hint: this merger will create a leader group containing two firms and a follower group containing none). What does this second merger do to the market price?

4. Continue with the conditions of question 3 but now suppose that for a merger to be undertaken, the merging firms each have to incur a fixed cost, f (this might include costs of identifying a merger partner, negotiating the terms of the merger, legal fees, and so on).
    a. How high must f be for the merger between firms 1 and 2 to be unprofitable?
    b. How high must f be for the subsequent merger between firms 3 and 4 to be unprofitable?

5. In the chapter it was shown that for a two-firm merger to be profitable, the following condition must be satisfied:

$$\pi_l^L(N - 1, L + 1) = \frac{(A - c)^2}{B(L + 2)^2(N - L - 1)}$$
$$> 2.\pi_f^F(N, L)$$
$$= 2\frac{(A - c)^2}{B(L + 1)^2(N - L + 1)^2}$$

Assume as in questions 1 and 2 that $A = 100$, $B = 1$, $c = 20$. Further assume that $\gamma = 0$.
    a. Assume that the number of firms in the market is ten, that is, $N = 10$, and that, as in question 4, a two-firm merger requires that each of the merging firms incurs a fixed cost of f prior to the merger. Derive a relationship, $f(L)$,

between f and the size of the leader group, L, such that if $f > f(L)$, the two-firm merger will be unprofitable. Calculate $f(L)$ for $L = 1, 2, 3, 4,$ and 5 to confirm that $f(L)$ is decreasing in L. Interpret this result.

b. Now assume that there are eight firms in the market, that is, $N = 8$. Repeat your calculations in part (a) to show that the function $f(L)$ rises as N falls. Interpret this result.

6. Normansville consists of a single High Street that is 1 mile long and has 100 residents uniformly located along it. There are three independent video rental stores located in the town at distances 1/6, 1/2 and 5/6 of a mile from the left-hand edge of Normansville. Each resident rents one video per day provided that the price charged is no more than \$5. If a consumer is located s miles from a store the transport costs in getting a video from that store is \$0.50s.

Suppose first that the two stores do not price discriminate.

a. What rental charge will the three stores set given that they act as price competitors?

b. What profits do they earn?

7. Suppose that two neighboring stores in Normansville merge.

a. What does this do to prices and profits?

b. Recalculate your answers to 7a assuming that the stores can perfectly price discriminate.

8. Recall that the first-order condition for maximizing profit may be written as: $p = \dfrac{\varepsilon - 1}{\varepsilon} c$; where ε is the absolute value of the firm's elasticity. Show that this result implies that, as an approximation, the proportional change in a firm's price as a result of a merger can be written as: $\dfrac{\Delta p}{p} = \dfrac{\Delta h}{h} + \dfrac{\Delta c}{c}$; where $h = \dfrac{\varepsilon - 1}{\varepsilon}$. Suppose that as a result of a merger and decline in competitive pressure, a firm's demand elasticity falls by the proportion δ, i.e., $\varepsilon' = (1 - \delta)\varepsilon$. Show that we may write $\dfrac{\Delta h}{h} = \dfrac{\delta}{(1 - \delta)\varepsilon - 1}$.

9. Use your results in question 9, to determine the necessary degree of cost efficiencies (i.e., the value of $\dfrac{\Delta c}{c}$), for the firm's price not to rise if its initial elasticity is $\varepsilon = 2$, and if as a result of a merger, its demand elasticity falls by 10 percent, i.e., $\delta = 0.1$. That is, by what proportion will costs have to decline in this case to keep p constant?

References

Andrade, G., M. Mitchell, and E. Stafford. 2001. "New Evidence and Perspectives on Mergers." *Journal of Economic Perspectives* 15 (Spring): 103–20

Ashenfelter, O., D. Ashmore, J. Baker, S. Gleason, and D. Hosken. 2004. "Econometric Methods in *Staples*." *Princeton Law & Public Affairs Paper* 04–007.

Baker, J. 2004. "Efficiencies and High Concentration: Heinz Proposes to Acquire Beech-Nut (2001)." In J. Kwoka and L. White, eds, *The Antitrust Revolution*. Oxford: Oxford University Press, 150–69.

Brito, D. 2003. "Preemptive Mergers under Spatial Competition." Working Paper, FCT, Universidade Nova de Lisboa.

Cabral, L. 2003. "Horizontal Mergers with Free Entry: Why Cost Efficiencies May Be a Weak Defense and Assets Sales A Poor Remedy." *International Journal of Industrial Organization* 21 (May): 607–23.

Daughety, A. F. 1990. "Beneficial Concentration." *American Economic Review* 80 (December): 1231–7.

Davidson, C. and R. Deneckere. 1986. "Long-run Competition in Capacity, Short-run Competition in Price, and the Cournot Model." *Rand Journal of Economics* 17 (Autumn): 404–15.

Deaton, A. and J. Mulbauer. 1980. "An Almost Ideal Demand System." *American Economic Review* 70 (June): 312–26.

Epstein, R. and D. Rubinfeld. 2002. "Merger Simulation: A Simplified Approach with New Applications." *Antitrust Law Journal* 69 (December): 883–920.

Fauli-Oller, R. 2000. "Takeover Waves." *Journal of Economics and Management Strategy* 9 (Summer): 189–210.

Farrell, J. and C. S. Shapiro. 1990. "Horizontal Mergers: An Equilibrium Analysis." *American Economic Review* 80 (March): 107–26.

Gandhi, A., L. Froeb, S. Tschantz, and G. Werden. 2007. "Post-merger Product Repositioning." *Journal of Industrial Economics.*

Greenhut, J., G. Norman, and M. L. Greenhut. 1991. "Aspects of Airline Deregulation." *International Journal of Transport Economics* 18 (January): 3–30.

Hotelling, H. 1929. "Stability in Competition." *Economic Journal* 39 (January): 31–47.

Judd, K. 1985. "Credible Spatial Preemption." *Rand Journal of Economics* 16 (Summer): 153–66.

Lichtenberg, F. and D. Siegel. 1992. "Takeovers and Corporate Overhead." In F. Lichtenberg, ed., *Corporate Takeovers and Productivity.* Cambridge, MA: MIT Press.

Maskimovic, V. and G. Phillips. 2001. "The Market for Corporate Assets: Who Engages in Mergers and Assets Sales and Are There Efficiency Gains?" *Journal of Finance* 56 (December): 2019–65.

Mueller, D. C. 1985. "Mergers and Market Share." *Review of Economics and Statistics* 67 (May): 259–67.

Nilssen, T. and L. Sørgaard. 1998. "Sequential Horizontal Mergers." *European Economic Review* 42 (November): 1683–702.

Norman, G. and J. F. Thisse. 1996. "Product Variety and Welfare under Soft and Tough Pricing Regimes: *Economic Journal* 106 (January): 76–91.

Norman, G., L. Pepall, and D. Richards. 2005. "Product Differentiation, Cost-reducing Mergers, and Consumer Welfare." *Canadian Journal of Economics* 38 (November): 1204–23.

Perry, M. and R. Porter. 1985. "Oligopoly and the Incentive for Horizontal Merger." *American Economic Review* 75 (January): 219–27.

Posada, P. and O. D. Straume. 2004. "Merger, Partial Collusions and Relocation." *Journal of Economics* 83 (December): 243–65.

Ravenscraft, D. J. and F. M. Scherer. 1989. "The Profitability of Mergers." *International Journal of Industrial Organization* (Special Issue), (March): 101–16.

Reitzes, J. D. and D. T. Levy. 1995. "Price Discrimination and Mergers." *Canadian Journal of Economics* 28 (May): 427–36.

Ross, T. and R. Winter. 2003. "Canadian Merger Policy following *Superior Propane.*" *Canadian Competition Record* (May): 7–23.

Salant, S., S. Switzer, and R. Reynolds. 1983. "Losses from Horizontal Merger: The Effects of an Exogenous Change in Industry Structure on Cournot–Nash Equilibrium." *Quarterly Journal of Economics* 98 (May): 185–213.

Salinger, M. 2005. "Four Questions about Horizontal Merger Enforcement." Remarks to ABA Economic Committee of Antitrust Section, September 14.

Salop, S. C. 1979. "Monopolistic Competition with Outside Goods." *Bell Journal of Economics* 10 (Spring): 141–56.

Salvo, A. 2006. "Sequential Cross-border Mergers in Models of Oligopoly." Mimeo (August). Northwestern University.

Schmalensee, R. 1978. "Entry Deterrence in the Ready-to-eat Breakfast Cereal Industry." *Bell Journal of Economics* 9 (Autumn): 305–27.

Slade, M. 2007. Merger Simulations of Unilateral Effects: What Can We Learn from the U.K. Brewing Industry?," In B. Lyons, ed., *Cases in European Competition Policy: The Economic Analysis.* Cambridge: Cambridge University Press.

Werden, G. and L. Froeb. 1994. "The Effects of Mergers in Differentiated Products Industries: Logit Demand and Merger Policy." *Journal of Law, Economics, and Organizations* 10 (October): 407–26.

——. 2002. "The Antitrust Logit Model for Predicting Unilateral Competitive Effects." *Antitrust Law Journal* 70: 257–60.

Appendix A

Bertrand Competition in a Simple Linear Demand System

Start with the inverse demand system of equation (16.46):

$$p_1 = A - Bq_1 - s(q_2 + q_3)$$
$$p_2 = A - Bq_2 - s(q_1 + q_3) \qquad (s \in [0, B)) \qquad \text{(16.A1)}$$
$$p_3 = A - Bq_3 - s(q_1 + q_2)$$

In order to identify the Bertrand–Nash equilibrium prices we first need to invert this demand system to get the direct demands. Some simple manipulation gives these demands as:

$$q_1 = \frac{A(B - s) - (B + s)p_1 + s(p_2 + p_3)}{(B - s)(B + 2s)}$$

$$q_2 = \frac{A(B - s) - (B + s)p_2 + s(p_1 + p_3)}{(B - s)(B + 2s)} \qquad (s \in [0, B)) \qquad \text{(16.A2)}$$

$$q_3 = \frac{A(B - s) - (B + s)p_3 + s(p_1 + p_2)}{(B - s)(B + 2s)}$$

Note that these make intuitive sense: demand for each firm is decreasing in the firm's own price and increasing in its rivals' prices.

THE PRE-MERGER CASE

We begin by identifying the equilibrium when each firm acts independently. Profit to firm 1 is

$$\pi_1 = (p_1 - c)q_1 = (p_1 - c)\left[\frac{A(B - s) - (B + s)p_1 + s(p_2 + p_3)}{(B - s)(B + 2s)}\right] \qquad \text{(16.A3)}$$

Differentiating with respect to p_1 and simplifying gives the first-order condition for firm 1:

$$\frac{\partial \pi_1}{\partial p_1} = \frac{A(B - s) - 2(B + s)p_1 + s(p_2 + p_3) + c(B + s)}{(B - s)(B + 2s)} = 0 \qquad \text{(16.A4)}$$

There are similar best response functions for firms 2 and 3. Rather than use these to identify the equilibrium, we can take advantage of the knowledge that this equilibrium will be symmetric, i.e., in equilibrium $p_1^* = p_2^* = p_3^* = p_{nm}^*$. Substituting this into the best response function (16.A4) gives: $\dfrac{A(B - s) - 2Bp_{nm}^* + c(B + s)}{(B - s)(B + 2s)} = 0.$

Solving for the equilibrium price gives

$$p_{nm}^* = \frac{A(B - s) + c(B + s)}{2B} \tag{16.A5}$$

Substituting these prices into the direct demand functions (16.A2) gives the equilibrium output for each firm of $q_{nm}^* = \dfrac{(A - c)(B + s)}{2B(B + 2s)}$ and substituting into the profit functions (16.A3) gives the no-merger profit for each firm of

$$\pi_{nm}^* = \frac{(A - c)^2(B - s)(B + s)}{4B^2(B + 2s)} \tag{16.A6}$$

MERGER OF FIRMS 1 AND 2

Now assume that firms 1 and 2 merge. Post-merger, the merged firm chooses its prices p_1 and p_2 to maximize its aggregate profit $\pi_1 + \pi_2$ while the non-merged firm chooses p_3 to maximize its profit π_3. This gives the first-order conditions:

$$\frac{\partial(\pi_1 + \pi_2)}{\partial p_1} = \frac{A(B - s) - 2(B + s)p_1 + 2sp_2 + sp_3 + cB}{(B - s)(B + 2s)} = 0$$

$$\frac{\partial(\pi_1 + \pi_2)}{\partial p_2} = \frac{A(B - s) - 2(B + s)p_2 + 2sp_3 + sp_3 + cB}{(B - s)(B + 2s)} = 0 \tag{16.A7}$$

$$\frac{\partial\pi_3}{\partial p_3} = \frac{A(B - s) - 2(B + s)p_3 + s(p_1 + p_2) + c(B + s)}{(B - s)(B + 2s)} = 0$$

Solving these for the equilibrium prices gives $p_1^m = p_2^m = \dfrac{A(2B + 3s)(B - s) + c(2B + s)(B + s)}{2(2B^2 + 2Bs - s^2)}$ for the merged firm and $p_3^{nm} = \dfrac{A(B + s)(B - s) + cB(B + 2s)}{(2B^2 + 2Bs - s^2)}$ for the non-merged firm. Substituting these prices into the profit equations (16.A3) gives the profits of equation (16.48):

$$\pi_1^m = \pi_2^m = \frac{B(A - c)^2(B - s)(2B + 3s)^2}{4(B + 2s)(2B^2 + 2Bs - s^2)^2}; \quad \pi_3^m = \frac{(A - c)^2(B - s)(B + s)^3}{(B + 2s)(2B^2 + 2Bs - s^2)^2} \tag{16.A8}$$

COMPARISON OF THE PRE-MERGER AND POST-MERGER CASES

Comparison of the pre- and post-merger profits looks on first sight to be difficult. However, if we define $\sigma = s/B$, where σ lies in the interval [0, 1) since we have that $0 \leq s < B$, then we can write the non-merged profit as:

$$\pi_{nm}^* = \frac{(A - c)^2(B - s)(B + s)}{4B^2(B + 2s)} = \frac{(A - c)^2 B^2(1 - \sigma)(1 + \sigma)}{4B^3(1 + 2\sigma)} = \frac{(A - c)^2(1 - \sigma^2)}{4B(1 + 2\sigma)} \tag{16.A9}$$

and we can write profit of each division of the merged firm as:

$$\pi_1^m = \pi_2^m = \frac{B(A-c)^2(B-s)(2B+3s)^2}{4(B+2s)(2B^2+2Bs-s^2)^2} = \frac{B^4(A-c)^2(1-\sigma)(2+3\sigma)^2}{4B^5(1+2\sigma)(2+2\sigma-\sigma^2)^2}$$

$$= \frac{(A-c)^2(1-\sigma)(2+3\sigma)^2}{4B(1+2\sigma)(2+2\sigma-\sigma^2)^2} \qquad (16.A10)$$

Note that both profit equations (and post-merger the profit of firm 3) have the term $(A-c)^2/B$ in common. As a result, in comparing pre- and post-merger profits no generality is lost if we normalize this term to unity. The result is that profits are function solely of σ and can be compared by plotting (16.A8) and (16.A9) in the interval $\sigma \in [0, 1)$. Doing so confirms that the merger increases the profits of the merged firm—and of the non-merged firm.

Appendix B

Equilibrium Prices in the Spatial Model without a Merger

We can take any one of the five firms as typical of the others. So consider firm 3. Demand for this firm from consumers to its left is Nr_{23}, where r_{23} is the marginal consumer given by

$$m_3 + tr_{23} = m_2 + t\left(\frac{L}{5} = r_{23}\right) \Rightarrow r_{23} = \frac{m_2 - m_3}{2t} + \frac{L}{10} \qquad (16.B1)$$

Similarly, demand from consumers to the right of firm 3 is Nr_{34}, where r_{34} is

$$r_{34} = \frac{m_4 - m_3}{2t} + \frac{L}{10} \qquad (16.B2)$$

Firm 3's profit is, therefore,

$$\pi_3 = Nm_3(r_{23} + r_{34}) = Nm_3\left(\frac{m_2 - m_3}{2t} + \frac{m_4 - m_3}{2t} + \frac{L}{5}\right) \qquad (16.B3)$$

Differentiating this with respect to m_3 to give the first-order condition for firm 3:

$$\frac{\partial \pi_3}{\partial m_3} = N\left(\frac{m_2 + m_4}{2t} - \frac{2m_3}{t} + \frac{L}{5}\right) = 0 \qquad (16.B4)$$

Since the five firms are identical, in equilibrium we must have $m_3 = m_2 = m_4$. Substituting this into (16.B4) then gives the Bertrand–Nash equilibrium price:

$$m^* = tL/5 \qquad (16.B5)$$

Appendix C

Equilibrium Prices in the Spatial Model after Firms 2 and 3 Merge

Profit for each firm is easily identified by changing the firms' "labels" in equation (16.B3), so that we have

$$\pi_1 = Nm_1 \left(\frac{m_5 - m_1}{2t} + \frac{m_2 - m_1}{2t} + \frac{L}{5} \right)$$

$$\pi_2 = Nm_2 \left(\frac{m_1 - m_2}{2t} + \frac{m_3 - m_2}{2t} + \frac{L}{5} \right)$$

$$\pi_3 = Nm_3 \left(\frac{m_2 - m_3}{2t} + \frac{m_4 - m_3}{2t} + \frac{L}{5} \right) \qquad (16.C1)$$

$$\pi_4 = Nm_4 \left(\frac{m_3 - m_4}{2t} + \frac{m_5 - m_4}{2t} + \frac{L}{5} \right)$$

$$\pi_5 = Nm_5 \left(\frac{m_4 - m_5}{2t} + \frac{m_1 - m_5}{2t} + \frac{L}{5} \right)$$

After the merger, the merged firm chooses m_2 and m_3 to maximize aggregate profit $\pi_2 + \pi_3$, while the remaining firms choose their prices to maximize their individual profits. This means there are five first-order conditions to solve:

$$\frac{\partial \pi_1}{\partial m_1} = N \left(\frac{m_5 + m_2}{2t} - \frac{2m_1}{t} + \frac{L}{5} \right) = 0$$

$$\frac{\partial (\pi_2 + \pi_3)}{\partial m_2} = N \left(\frac{m_1 + m_3}{2t} - \frac{2m_2}{t} + \frac{L}{5} \right) + N \frac{m_3}{2t} = 0$$

$$\frac{\partial (\pi_2 + \pi_3)}{\partial m_3} = N \left(\frac{m_2 + m_4}{2t} - \frac{2m_3}{t} + \frac{L}{5} \right) + N \frac{m_2}{2t} = 0 \qquad (16.C2)$$

$$\frac{\partial \pi_4}{\partial m_4} = N \left(\frac{m_3 + m_5}{2t} - \frac{2m_4}{t} + \frac{L}{5} \right) = 0$$

$$\frac{\partial \pi_5}{\partial m_5} = N \left(\frac{m_4 + m_1}{2t} - \frac{2m_5}{t} + \frac{L}{5} \right) = 0$$

Solving these equations simultaneously gives the prices in the text. In determining this equilibrium, we assume that no firm i ever finds it profitable to price so low that it actually competes with firms beyond $i - 1$ and $i + 1$.

17

Vertical and Conglomerate Mergers

In the fall of 2000, General Electric (GE) and Honeywell International announced that the two companies would merge with GE acquiring Honeywell. GE is, of course, a very well known firm with annual revenues well over $100 billion. Its businesses are involved in everything from lighting and appliances to television programming (it owns NBC) and financial services. GE is also a major supplier of jet engines for commercial aircraft for which its chief competitors are Rolls Royce and Pratt-Whitney. Honeywell was originally a leader in temperature and environmental controls but has, over time, developed into a major aerospace firm whose products included electric lighting, ventilation units, and braking systems for aircraft and also starter motors for aircraft engines of the type GE builds. The deal was approved in the United States. However, in July 2001, the European Commission following the recommendation of Competition Commissioner, Mario Monti, blocked the merger.

The proposed GE–Honeywell merger was a marriage of complementary products. The more aircraft engines GE sells the more starter motors and other related aircraft items Honeywell could sell. A merger of GE and Honeywell is a vertical merger. Often vertical mergers are comprised of firms operating at different levels of the production chain, say, a wholesaler and a retailer. However, the connection between an upstream and a downstream firm is qualitatively the same as the relation between Honeywell and GE, or that between computer hardware and software, or nuts and bolds or zinc and copper, which are combined to make brass. In all of these cases, two or more products are combined to yield the final good or service. Because an upstream–downstream relationship is just one of the many types of complementary relationships that may exist between firms, the term vertical merger has come to have the more general interpretation of a merger between any two firms that produce complementary products.

We showed in Chapter 8, section 8.3, that the separate production of complementary goods—each one produced by a firm with monopoly power—reduces the joint profit of the two firms and imposes an efficiency loss on both firms and consumers. The intuition behind this result is straightforward. Each firm's pricing decision imposes an externality on the other firm. A high price for computer hardware reduces demand for PCs. It also reduces demand for programs and operating systems. The hardware manufacturer takes the first effect into account, but not the second. The same is true, of course, in reverse. The software manufacturer does not take into account the impact its price choice has on the demand for hardware. In the noncooperative Nash equilibrium, the prices of both goods are too high. If, say, the hardware firm were to cut its price, this would generate additional demand and additional profit for the software firm. However, since the hardware firm does not receive any of this additional profit, its incentive to reduce price is weakened. This suggests that, with cooperation, both firms would lower their prices and be better off. Consumers, too, would gain as a result of lower prices and expanded output.

One way to achieve the profit and efficiency gains of cooperation is for the two firms to merge. Such a merger creates a single decision-making entity and, therefore, permits the externality to be internalized. The combined hardware and software firm will maximize its total profit by reducing the prices of both complementary goods so as to maximize the joint profit from each. Whenever firms with monopoly power produce complementary products, they have a strong incentive either to merge or to devise some other method to ensure cooperative production and pricing of the complementary goods.

Precisely the same issues of cooperation arise when the the complementarities affect the fact that the firms occupy different levels in the vertical production chain. This is important because it sheds light on how vertical mergers affect competition and so consumer welfare. In the 1980s the realization that vertical mergers can generate efficiency gains led to something of a revolution in antitrust policy related to vertical mergers. In the decades prior to 1980, vertical mergers were often seen as anticompetitive because of the fear that such mergers they would facilitate foreclosure. That is, the upstream merger partner would, after the merger, refuse to supply its product to other downstream firms and thereby either drive them out of the market or create barriers to entry adversely affecting them.

Economists primarily associated with the Chicago School challenged this negative view of vertical mergers. They argued that vertical mergers could also be seen as ways to achieve complementary efficiencies and that "vertical integration was most likely procompetitive or competitively neutral" (Riordan, 1998, p. 1232). By the 1980s, the Chicago School approach began to gain in the courts and vertical mergers were treated increasingly favorably by the antitrust authorities. However, by the mid-1990s the pendulum once more began to swing the other way. A Post-Chicago approach has now emerged that employs game theoretic tools to build new and logically consistent models of vertical mergers in which once again the potential for consumer harm is real. This counter-revolution has led to a detailed scrutiny of a number of vertical combinations including, for instance, the GE and Honeywell merger.

We begin this chapter by developing an analysis of vertical mergers based on the proposition that these are procompetitive and correct market inefficiencies. In section 2, we consider some of the more recent analysis suggesting that such mergers might adversely affect competition in final product markets. Section 3 presents a simple formal model to illustrate this phenomenon.

Section 4 turns to the third and final type of mergers. These are conglomerate mergers involving the combination of firms without either a clear substitute or a clear complementary relationship. Examples include the purchase of Duracell Batteries by Gillette, the purchase of Snapple (iced tea) and Gatorade (a sports drink) by Quaker Oats, and the series of acquisitions in 1986 by Daimler-Benz, a luxury car and truck manufacturer, which turned it into Germany's largest industrial concern, producing aerospace to household goods. Finally, section 5 presents a brief overview of antitrust policy with respect to different types of mergers.

17.1 PROCOMPETITIVE VERTICAL MERGERS

When firms occupy different stages of the production stream the convention is to label those firms farthest from the final consumer of the product as upstream and those closest to that consumer as downstream. Film companies and movie theaters are an example. In this case, the film company is the upstream firm and the theater that shows the film is the downstream firm. Manufacturers and retailers have a similar upstream–downstream relation. All such relationships can be usefully viewed through the lens of complementarity. Each firm in the vertical chain provides an essential service to other firms in the chain. Vertical relationships between two firms—each with monopoly power—leads to a loss of economic efficiency in the absence of some mechanism to coordinate the decisions of the two firms. In the case of vertically related firms, this is referred to as the problem of *double marginalization*. We now give a formal illustration of this problem.

Suppose that we have a single upstream supplier, the manufacturer, who sells a unique product to a single downstream firm, the retailer. The manufacturer produces the good at constant unit cost, c, and sells it to the retailer at a wholesale price, r. The retailer resells the product to consumers at the market-clearing price, P. For simplicity, we assume that the retailer has no retailing cost. Consumer demand for the good is described by our familiar linear inverse demand function $P = A - BQ$, and we assume of course that $c < A$.

Given that the retailer purchases Q units from the manufacturer at wholesale price r and resells these Q units to consumers at price $P = A - BQ$ the retailer's profit is

$$\Pi^D(Q, r) = (P - r)Q = (A - BQ)Q - rQ \tag{17.1}$$

The retailer maximizes profit by equating marginal revenue with marginal cost. Marginal revenue is $MR = A - 2BQ$ and marginal cost is r. Equating these two terms yields the optimal downstream output,

$$Q^D = (A - r)/2B \tag{17.2}$$

Substituting this expression into the demand function gives the market-clearing retail price $P^D = (A + r)/2$. From equation (17.1) the retailer's profit is, therefore, $\Pi^D = (A - r)^2/4B$. Figure 17.1 illustrates these results.

What about the manufacturer? What wholesale price should be charged? It is clear from equation (17.2) that the wholesale price determines the number of units the upstream

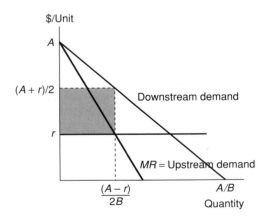

Figure 17.1   Independent retailer's optimum pricing as a function of manufacturer's wholesale price, r

At wholesale price r the retailer will set retail price $P = (A + r)/2$ to maximize profit. Total retail profit is indicated by the shaded region.

supplier is able to sell to the retailer. At the wholesale price r the retailer chooses to sell $Q^D = (A - r)/2B$ units. The retailer must purchase this number of units from the manufacturer. In other words, $Q = (A - r)/2B$ is the demand curve which the upstream manufacturer faces. It describes the relationship between the wholesale price r set by the manufacturer and the quantity of his product demanded by the retailer. But this means that *when the retailer has no marginal costs other than the input price charged by the manufacturer the inverse demand facing the upstream manufacturer at wholesale price r is r = A − 2BQ, which is also the marginal revenue function facing the retailer.*[1]

17.1

The inverse market demand curve facing a monopoly retailer of gold bracelets is described by $P = 3,000 - Q/2$. The retailer buys gold bracelets at a wholesale price, r, set by the manufacturer and has no other costs. Show that the inverse demand curve facing the manufacturer is $r = 3,000 - Q$. Suppose instead that the retailer has additional marginal costs (labor etc.) of c^U. Show that the inverse demand curve facing the manufacturer is $r = (3,000 - c^U) - Q$.

Practice Problem

We can now derive the profit-maximizing price that the manufacturer charges for its product. Very simply, the manufacturer equates marginal cost with marginal revenue. The inverse demand curve for the manufacturer is $r = A - 2BQ$, so the marginal revenue curve for the manufacturer is $MR = A - 4BQ$. Equating this with marginal cost, c, yields the profit-maximizing output and wholesale price. These are, respectively,

$$Q^U = \frac{A - c}{4B} \text{ and } r^U = \frac{A + c}{2} \tag{17.3}$$

This analysis is illustrated in Figure 17.2. When the upstream manufacturer sets the price $r^U = (A + c)/2$, the downstream retailer charges a price $P^D = (A + r^U)/2 = (3A + c)/4$. The retailer sells $Q^D = (A - c)/4B$ units, which is, of course, precisely the amount the upstream manufacturer anticipated it would sell when it set its upstream price $r^U = (A + c)/2$ in the first place. The profit of the manufacturer, shown in Figure 17.2 as the lightly shaded area $wrgv$, is $\Pi^U = (A - c)^2/8B$. The profit of the retailer, shown as the darkly shaded area *refg*, is $\Pi^D = (A - c)^2/16B$. The combined profit of the two firms is, of course, just the sum of these two areas, $3(A - c)^2/16B$.

Suppose now that the two firms merge so that the manufacturer becomes the upstream division of an integrated firm, selling its output to the downstream retail division of the same parent company. The manufactured good is still produced at constant marginal cost, c. This effectively transforms the integrated firm into a simple monopoly whose goal is to maximize monopoly profit through its choice of retail price P. This profit is just total revenue PQ minus total cost cQ, which is $\Pi^I = (A - BQ) - cQ$.

The marginal revenue curve of the integrated firm is just the marginal revenue curve of the nonintegrated retailer, $MR^I = A - 2BQ$. Equating this with marginal cost c gives the

---

[1]   If, by contrast, the retailer has additional marginal costs of c^U then the inverse demand facing the manufacturer is $(A - c^U) - 2BQ$: see Practice Problem 17.1.

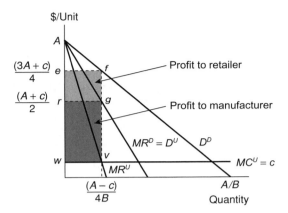

Figure 17.2 Upstream and downstream profit maximization without vertical integration
The retailer's marginal revenue curve MR^D is the manufacturer's demand curve D^U. Double marginalization results when the manufacturer sets its optimal wholesale price $r = (A + c)/2$ above marginal cost c, after which, the retailer adds a further markup by setting retail price $P = (3A + c)/4$. Retail profit is area $refg$. The manufacturer's profit is area $wrgv$.

profit-maximizing output of the integrated firm, $Q^I = (A - c)/2B$. Substitution of this into the inverse demand curve then gives the retail price to consumers, $P^I = (A + c)/2$.

The merger of the manufacturer and retailer results in consumers being charged a lower price. As a result, the merged firm sells more of the product than did the two independent firms. But is this merger profitable? Yes! The profit earned by the integrated firm is $\Pi^I = (A - c)^2/4B$. This is 12.5 percent greater than the aggregate pre-merger profit of the manufacturer and the retailer, which we saw was $3(A - c)^2/16B$. From a social welfare point of view, *integrating the two monopoly firms has benefited everyone*. Total profit is increased *and* consumer surplus is increased with more of the good being sold at a lower price.

The gains from this vertical merger are illustrated in Figure 17.3. The retailer's pre-merger profit, area *refg*, is redistributed to consumers as surplus. In addition, consumers gain the

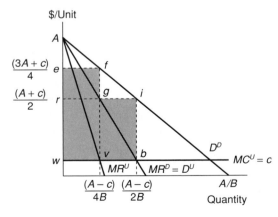

Figure 17.3 Upstream and downstream profit maximization with vertical integration
An integrated manufacturer–retailer sets a retail price to consumers at $P = (A + c)/2$. The area *refg* that would have been profit for a non-integrated retailer now becomes part of consumer surplus. However, the increased sales volume generates a more than offsetting profit gain of area *gjbv*. Total profit for the integrated firm is *rjbw*.

area *fgi*. The manufacturer's profit has doubled from area *wrgv* to *wrib* and this more than offsets the loss of the retailer's profit.

Merger of vertically related firms generates an all round efficiency gain because it allows the separate but related activities to be coordinated and, thereby, to internalize the externality that each imposes on the other. In the absence of coordination, the final product price reflects a double marginalization. The independent manufacturer marks up its price to the retailer who then compounds that price–cost distortion by adding a further markup in setting a price to the consumer. This is the basis of the old saying, "What is worse than a monopoly? A chain of monopolies!"

17.2

Practice Problem

Suppose that the downstream market for widgets is characterized by the inverse demand curve $P = 100 - Q$. Widget retailing is controlled by the monopolist WR Inc., which obtains its widgets from the monopoly wholesaler WW Inc. at a wholesale price of w_w per widget. WW Inc. obtains the widgets in turn from the monopoly manufacturer WM Ltd. at a manufacturing price of w_m per widget. WM Inc. incurs marginal costs of $10 per unit in making widgets. WW and WR each incur marginal costs of $5 in addition to the prices that they have to pay for widgets.

a. What is the equilibrium widget price to consumers, P, the equilibrium wholesale price w_w and the equilibrium manufacturing price w_r? What is the profit earned by each firm at these prices?

b. Show that vertical integration by any two of these firms increases profit and benefits consumers.

c. Show that integration of all three firms is even more beneficial.

There are, of course, several qualifications that we should mention. Some are noted in the accompanying Reality Checkpoint. In addition it is important to note that the benefits of vertical merger just described assume that the downstream firm uses a fixed amount of the upstream firm's product for every unit of output that the downstream firm sells. In our example of a manufacturer and a downstream retailer, this assumption makes sense. The retailer has to have one unit of the manufacturer's product for every unit it sells to its customers. But in other situations this assumption could be too strong. For example, if the upstream firm is a steel producer and the downstream firm is an automobile manufacturer, the steel firm's decision to charge the car manufacturer a price *r* that includes a high markup may induce the automaker to reduce its use of steel in favor of aluminum or perhaps fiberglass. In such a case, the potential gains of the car manufacturer integrating backwards into the steel market are less clear-cut.

In summary, vertical integration of a chain of producers, each of which has monopoly power, is likely to benefit both firms and consumers by correcting the market failure associated with double (and triple and quadruple . . .) marginalization. These benefits are more likely to arise when the technology operated by downstream firms offers limited opportunities for substitution into other inputs.

Reality Checkpoint

Vertical Disintegration in the Automobile Industry

Our analysis of vertical integration has stressed the gains of eliminating "the middle man" and the problem of double marginalization. If this were all there were to it, we would see much more vertical integration and very little outsourcing. Quite to the contrary, however, the business news since the 1990s has been filled with stories of outsourcing and vertical *dis*integration as firms have spun off their former internal divisions. Nowhere has this phenomenon been more dramatic than in the U.S. automobile industry.

Consider the General Motors Corporation. GM founder W. C. Durant and his protégé Alfred Sloan, were devoted to vertically integrating the firm. Their logic was the same as we have presented here. GM could capture more of the surplus its automobiles generated if more of that generation took place within GM. As a result, GM and the U.S. automotive industry in general became models of vertically integrated firms, controlling engine production, body assembly, parts supplies, and extending down to official dealerships.

Over the years, however, problems with this organizational strategy emerged, the major one of which concerns incentives. Since GM bought virtually all its parts internally, the parts division did not face outside competition to spur its efficiency. Often, buyers at the automaking divisions did not even know the names of alternative suppliers. To be sure, buyers would sometimes solicit bids from outside suppliers as a means to check the quotes from the internal sources but the outsiders typically knew that they were just being used as a measuring stick—the order would ultimately go to the GM parts division—and were reluctant to make serious bids. At the same time, devising internal schemes to promote efficiency is difficult. Those outside the parts division cannot specify parts prices because they lack the needed cost knowledge. An obvious alternative to asking the division to supply parts at minimal cost is to give it a budget and ask it to supply parts subject to that budget. However, this scheme has problems, too. To begin with, the parts division shares some costs with other divisions and it is difficult to know how to apportion these costs. Further, if the budget is too tight, the parts division may meet this constraint by skimping on quality. In the end, the problems of high costs and/or uncertain quality proved too much. GM spun off its parts division as the independent part firm, Delphi Automotive Systems, in 1999. Ford followed quickly and spun off its parts division as Visteon Corporation.

Source: J. Schnapp, "Lesser Than the Sum of Its Parts," *Wall Street Journal* (Tuesday, April 4, 2006), p. 18.

17.2   POSSIBLE ANTICOMPETITIVE EFFECTS OF VERTICAL MERGERS

The merger analysis of the previous section suggests that the antitrust authorities should be less concerned about the welfare impact of vertical mergers than the impact of horizontal mergers. However, the analysis is based upon important assumptions that underlie the results. In particular, we have assumed that there is a single market in which the final output is sold and that there is monopoly at each stage in the vertical chain. Before coming to the general conclusion that "vertical mergers are good for firms and consumers" we should check on the effects of relaxing these assumptions.

17.2.1   Vertical Merger to Facilitate Price Discrimination

While life is good for a monopolist, it is even better for a monopolist who price discriminates. This is equally true for an upstream monopolist selling to a number of downstream firms. Moreover, there are many cases in which those downstream firms differ in their willingness to pay for the upstream firm's product. Examples include a wholesaler supplying retailers in different cities, a manufacturer of motor car parts supplying automakers in different countries, a consultant advising different firms in different industries, and so on. In these circumstances, the upstream firm would like to charge a high price for its product or service to those firms whose demand is inelastic and a low price to those whose demand is elastic.

Our earlier discussion of price discrimination showed, however, that successful price discrimination has two requirements. First, the firm must be able to identify which buyers have elastic and which have inelastic demand. Second, the firm must somehow prevent resale of its product among its buyers. Such arbitrage would clearly undo any price discrimination efforts. We will assume that the firm has somehow solved the identification problem. The question then becomes, what strategies can the firm use to surmount the arbitrage problem?

The simplest approach would be for the upstream firm to write a no-resale contract with its buyers. In many circumstances, however, such contracts are unenforceable—for example, when the client firms are in different legal jurisdictions—in which case some other approach is necessary. One such approach is for the upstream firm to merge with some or all of its downstream customers.

Suppose that the upstream firm supplies a series of downstream firms and that, because of financial constraints, the upstream firm can integrate forwards with only some of the downstream firms. Then, as Practice Problem 17.3 shows, the firm needs to act strategically in determining the market into which it will integrate. By merging with the retailer facing more elastic demand the upstream firm can lower price where demand is responsive and raise price to the less elastic market. Is such a merger pro- or anticompetitive? Successful price discrimination can improve economic efficiency. When success is achieved by means of a vertical merger the effect on economic efficiency is, however, ambiguous. The reason is that while the merger increases profits and removes double marginalization in one group of markets, the merger also leads to increased prices in the remaining markets. In other words, some consumers gain and others lose from the vertical merger. The overall effect is uncertain and can be resolved only when we have more information on the precise nature of demand in the various markets.

17.3

Practice Problem

Assume that Widget International supplies widgets to Gizmo Inc. in Boston, where the demand for gizmos is $P_{gb} = 1 - Q_{gb}$, and TruGizmo Inc. of New York, where demand for gizmos is $P_{gn} = 0.5 - 0.2Q_{gn}$. Assume that WI's marginal costs of supplying both markets is $0.1 per widget and that both Gizmo Inc. and TruGizmo Inc. need exactly one widget for every gizmo they sell. Both gizmo dealers have other costs of production that amount to $0.1 per gizmo.

a. What are the profit-maximizing prices for widgets and gizmos in these two markets if Widget International cannot price discriminate? What are the profits of the three firms?

b. What are the profit-maximizing prices for widgets and gizmos in these two markets if Widget International can price discriminate? What are the profits of the three firms?

c. Show that if WI can merge with either Gizmo Inc. or TruGizmo Inc., it prefers to merge with TruGizmo Inc.

d. What is the effect of the merger on consumer prices and consumer surplus when WI (i) cannot and (ii) can price discriminate pre-merger?

17.2.2   Vertical Merger, Oligopoly, and Market Foreclosure

Now consider the second important assumption underlying the analysis in section 17.1. The gains from the merger hinge crucially on the fact that prior to the merger there was monopoly at both levels of activity, manufacture and retail. Suppose, instead, that we had started with either a competitive manufacturing sector upstream selling to a monopoly downstream, or a monopoly upstream selling to a competitive retail sector. Price competition upstream among manufacturers leads to a wholesale price equal to marginal cost. Alternatively, competition among retailers downstream brings the retail price equal to the upstream price P^U plus downstream marginal cost r. In either case, no double marginalization can occur, and there is no efficiency gain to vertical integration.

It could be argued, of course, that assuming perfect competition rather than monopoly in either the upstream or downstream market merely replaces one extreme assumption by another. We now turn, therefore, to the more realistic case in which both upstream and downstream markets are oligopolies. This raises another important issue that needs to be considered explicitly. Beyond the desire to reduce or eliminate double marginalization, there is an additional motive for vertical integration that is more clearly anticompetitive. The motive is the possibility of *market foreclosure*. That is, the merger of vertically related firms might result in an upstream–downstream company that can either deny downstream rivals a source of inputs, or upstream competitors a market for their products.

Consider a hypothetical case in which two suppliers of computer chips compete for sales to two downstream computer manufacturers who in turn sell to the general public. The chips of the two upstream firms are identical so that, if the two suppliers compete in price, they must sell at marginal cost. Hence, only the two downstream firms earn any economic profit. Suppose now that one of the chip manufacturers and one of the computer firms merge. The argument that this merger may be anticompetitive goes roughly as follows. The upstream chip division of the newly merged firm will no longer offer to sell any chips to the remaining independent computer firm, that is, it may foreclose sales of its product to this downstream rival. Why? The answer is that such foreclosure leaves the independent computer firm with only one supplier, namely, the remaining independent chip firm. That independent chip producer will have monopoly power vis-à-vis the independent computer firm and, accordingly, set a monopoly wholesale price for its chips. In turn, this will raise the costs of the independent computer firm relative to the pre-merger situation and make it less able to compete with the downstream computer division of the integrated firm. This will permit the merged firm to raise the price of its computers and earn more profit. Because the upstream market was initially competitive there was no double-marginalization and since there are no other cost savings as a result of the merger, this vertical integration is clearly anticompetitive.[2] The merger raises the cost of the nonintegrated rivals on the supply side and thereby leaves them at a disadvantage relative to the integrated firm.

The telecommunications industry is one in which foreclosure concerns have been quite real for regulatory authorities in both the United States and in Europe. In this industry, the local telephone network has generally been monopolized by a firm that also competes in the more competitive long-distance market. Since a long-distance provider, such as Sprint Nextel has to gain access to its potential customers by connecting to the local network, the local network provider has the potential to price its long-distance competitors out of the

---

[2]   For a description of the many ways in which an integrated firm can impose a cost squeeze see Krattenmaker and Salop (1986).

market by charging them a very high price for network access or, in an extreme case, denying them access to the network at all. Accordingly, a major concern of the regulatory authorities has been the prices that suppliers of local telephone networks are allowed to charge for access to the local network.

Alcoa has been accused of subjecting its rivals to a similar price squeeze—both by making contractual arrangements with power companies to prevent them from supplying vital electricity to competing aluminum producers, and by charging very high prices for aluminum ingots that were used by rivals that competed with Alcoa in downstream markets such as the aluminum sheet market. In short, foreclosure arguments suggest that monopoly power in one, say upstream, market may be leveraged into power in another, downstream market.

17.4

Suppose that the downstream market for widgets is perfectly competitive and characterized by the inverse demand curve $P = 100 - Q$. Retailers have zero production costs, but do incur a fee, r, for every unit sold. This fee is the payment that retailers must pay to the only manufacturer of widgets, the monopolist Widget International (WI). WI bears no fixed cost. It does, however, have a constant marginal cost of $10.

a. What is the equilibrium price to consumers, P, and fee to retailers, r? What is the profit earned by retailers and WI at these prices?
b. Show that vertical integration by which WI becomes the single producer and retailer of widgets does not raise WI's profit and does not lower the price to consumers.
c. What is the price to consumers if both widget manufacturing and retailing are competitive?

Practice Problem

17.3   FORMAL OLIGOPOLY MODELS OF VERTICAL INTEGRATION

The conventional foreclosure argument just described is somewhat compelling especially when buttressed by the accompanying examples. However, there are also some clear weaknesses in the argument that need to be confronted. The local phone network and Alcoa examples are different from our hypothetical computer chip story in that the real-world cases begin with something less than competition in the upstream market. We have not identified why this may be the case. Apart from this practical consideration, the logic of the argument is still incomplete. We have not explained why the integrated firm will definitely stop selling chips to the independent downstream computer firm. Nor have we considered an obvious response by the remaining independent firms, namely, to merge and similarly enjoy the benefits of vertical integration. In the next section, we describe two models of foreclosure through vertical integration that address these concerns. One is due to Salinger (1988) and is based on Cournot competition. The other is due to Ordover, Saloner, and Salop (1990) and is rooted in price competition.

17.3.1   Vertical Integration and Foreclosure in a Cournot Model

To illustrate Salinger's (1988) contribution we return to our basic Cournot model except that we now assume that there is Cournot competition both in an upstream market populated by two firms and in a downstream market, also with two firms. The upstream firms produce a homogeneous intermediate good that is used by the downstream firms to make a good for final consumption. One unit of downstream output requires exactly one unit of the intermediate product. Each upstream firm has constant marginal costs of c^U per unit and each downstream firm has constant marginal costs, excluding the cost of the intermediate good, of c^D per unit. Inverse demand for the final consumption good is:

$$P = A - BQ = A - B(q_1 + q_2) \tag{17.4}$$

The market game has two stages. In the first stage the two upstream firms compete in quantities, generating a price P^U for the intermediate product. In the second stage the downstream firms compete in quantities taking the upstream price P^U as given. We consider first what happens when there is no vertical merger and then compare this outcome with what happens when there is vertical merger. Such a comparison is easier to make when we have a specific numerical example and so for purposes of illustration we shall assume: $A = 100$; $B = 1$; and $c^U = c^D = 23$.

No vertical mergers

Cournot competition upstream in the first stage leads to a market-clearing intermediate product price of P^U so that each downstream firm in the second stage faces marginal cost $P^U + c^D$. Cournot competition downstream leads each downstream firm to produce[3]:

$$q_1^D = q_2^D = \frac{A - P^U - c^D}{3B} \tag{17.5}$$

and to earn a downstream profit of

$$\pi_1^D = \pi_2^D = \frac{(A - P^U - c^D)^2}{9B} \tag{17.6}$$

We can use equation (17.5) to identify the *derived demand* that the upstream firms face. Aggregate downstream output is $Q^D = 2(A - P^U - c^D)/3B$. Since each unit of final product output requires one unit of the intermediate product, this is also the aggregate demand, $Q^U = Q^D$ for the intermediate product, which we can write in inverse form as:

$$P^U = (A - c^D) - \frac{3B}{2} Q^U \tag{17.7}$$

This is in the standard linear form $P = a - bQ$, where $a = A - c^D$ and $b = 3B/2$. As a result, we know that in the first stage of the game the Cournot equilibrium output of each upstream firm is:

$$q_1^U = q_2^U = \frac{a - c^U}{3b} = \frac{(A - c^D) - c^U}{9B/2} = \frac{2(A - c^U - c^D)}{9B} \tag{17.8}$$

---

[3]   See section 9.4 Chapter 9 for the derivation of the Cournot equilibrium.

It follows that aggregate output in the upstream market is $Q^U = 4(A - c^U - c^D)/9B$. Substituting this into the upstream demand in equation (17.7) gives the equilibrium upstream price for the intermediate product:

$$P^U = (A - c^D) - \frac{3B}{2} \cdot \frac{4(A - c^U - c^D)}{9B} = \frac{(A - c^D + 2c^U)}{3} \tag{17.9}$$

Profit of each upstream supplier is $(P^U - c^U)q_i^U$, which from equations (17.8) and (17.9) gives

$$\pi_1^U = \pi_2^U = \frac{2(A - c^U - c^D)^2}{27B} \tag{17.10}$$

Finally, substituting the upstream price into equations (17.7) and (17.8) gives the equilibrium output and profit for each downstream firm:

$$q_1^D = q_2^D = \frac{2(A - c^U - c^D)}{9B} \tag{17.11}$$

$$\pi_1^D = \pi_2^D = \frac{4(A - c^U - c^D)^2}{81B} \tag{17.12}$$

It is easy to check that, as we would expect, aggregate downstream demand equals aggregate upstream output. Using the numbers from our specific example, total output is 24 units. The wholesale price is \$41 and the price to consumers is \$76. Each upstream firm earns \$216 in profit and each downstream firm earns \$144.

Vertical integration of an upstream and downstream firm

Now consider what happens if one of the downstream firms $D1$ and one of the upstream firms $U1$ merge. Assume for the moment that this newly merged firm refuses to supply the independent downstream firm at all. Hence, the downstream firm $D2$ has to turn to the remaining independent wholesaler $U1$ for its input supply. Suppose that $U2$ sets a price P^U for its intermediate product. Then we know that $D2$ has marginal cost $P^U + c^D$ while $D1$ has marginal cost $c^U + c^D$. In other words, the integrated firm has removed the double markup in its pricing. As a result, it now competes in the downstream market as a low-cost competitor vis-à-vis $D2$. Applying the standard Cournot equations we know that the post-merger equilibrium outputs of the two firms downstream are:

$$q_1^D = \frac{A - 2(c^U + c^D) + (P^U + c^D)}{3B} = \frac{A - 2c^U - c^D + P^U}{3B}$$

$$q_2^D = \frac{A - 2(P^U + c^D) + (c^U + c^D)}{3B} = \frac{A - 2P^U - c^D + c^U}{3B} \tag{17.13}$$

and their equilibrium profits are:

$$\pi_1^D = \frac{(A - 2(c^U + c^D) + (P^U + c^D))^2}{9B} = \frac{(A - 2c^U - c^D + P^U)^2}{9B}$$

$$\pi_2^D = \frac{(A - 2(P^U + c^D) + (c^U + c^D))^2}{9B} = \frac{(A - 2P^U - c^D + c^U)^2}{9B} \tag{17.14}$$

Because of our foreclosure assumption that the integrated firm $D1$ will not sell its upstream good to the non-integrated downstream firm $D2$, it follows that the upstream firm $U2$ has monopoly power and will set a price to $D2$ of $P^U > c^U$. Equation (17.13) then confirms that, under our foreclosure assumption, the downstream division of the integrated firm has a greater output than its non-integrated rival.

We can in fact use equation (17.13) to identify the derived demand, $q_2^U = q_2^D$ facing the independent upstream firm. Again writing this in inverse form we have

$$P^U = \frac{A - c^D + c^U}{2} - \frac{3B}{2} q_2^U \tag{17.15}$$

This is in the form $P = a - bq$ and we know that with this demand function the monopoly output is $(a - c^U)/2b$; where $a = (A - c^D + c^U)/2$ and $b = 3B/2$. This then gives the equilibrium output for upstream firm 2:

$$q_2^U = \frac{A - c^U - c^D}{6B} \tag{17.16}$$

The equilibrium price for the intermediate product is, therefore

$$P^U = \frac{A - c^D + c^U}{2} - \frac{3B}{2} \cdot \frac{(A - c^U - c^D)}{6B} = \frac{(A + 3c^U - c^D)}{4} \tag{17.17}$$

Profit of the independent upstream firm is $(P^U - c^U)q_2^U$, which from equations (17.16) and (17.17) is

$$\pi_2^U = \frac{(A - c^U - c^D)^2}{24B} \tag{17.18}$$

Finally, we can substitute the equilibrium intermediate product price into equations (17.13) and (17.14) to identify the equilibrium outputs, prices, and profits in the downstream market:

$$q_1^D = \frac{5(A - c^U - c^D)}{12B}$$

$$q_2^D = \frac{(A - c^D - c^U)}{6B} \tag{17.19}$$

$$P^D = \frac{5A + 7c^U + 7c^D}{12} \tag{17.20}$$

$$\pi_1^D = \frac{25(A - c^U - c^D)^2}{144B}$$

$$\pi_2^D = \frac{(A - c^D - c^U)^2}{36B} \tag{17.21}$$

The downstream division of the integrated firm is noticeably larger and more profitable than its independent downstream rival. This is the result of the foreclosure of supply to $D2$, which has given monopoly power to $U2$ that it has exploited in setting a high upstream price. Again, using our specific numbers, the upstream price to $D2$ is $36.5. Since the integrated retailer buys its input at cost, it sells 22.5 units downstream while its independent rival sells just nine units. The resulting retail price is $68.5. Prior to the merger, $D2$ earned a profit of $144. That has now been reduced to $81. The merging firms, however, have benefited. Their combined profit before the merger was $360. It has risen through integration to $506.25.

Two points need to be considered. First, does our assumption of foreclosure make sense? Is it profit-maximizing for the integrated firm not to sell any inputs to its independent downstream rival? This is where Salinger's (1988) argument comes into play. The integrated firm has a total input cost of $c^U + c^D$. It therefore earns $P^D - (c^U + c^D)$ on each unit that it sells downstream. Further, we know that for the rival $D2$ to be in business, it must be the case that $P^D > (P^U + c^D)$. Suppose that the integrated firm did sell one unit of its intermediate good to its independent rival $D2$ at price P^U. What would happen if instead it withdrew this unit and sold it internally to the downstream division so that the total output and, therefore, the price in the downstream market remain unchanged? In withdrawing the unit originally sold to $D2$, the integrated firm loses the profit $P^U - c^U$. However, it then gains the profit $P^D - (c^U + c^D)$ that it makes on every internal sale. It will, therefore, be profitable to stop selling to the downstream rival or to foreclose if $P^D - (c^U + c^D) > P^U - c^U$. This condition is in fact identical to $P^D > (P^U + c^D)$, which we know has to hold given that the downstream rival is in business. In other words, if the integrated firm were selling to $D2$ then it could always do better by withdrawing those units and, instead sell them internally to increase its own downstream production. In our numerical example, the integrated firm ultimately earns $68.5 - 23 - 23 = 22.5 for every upstream unit sold internally. By contrast, it would earn only $36.5 - 23 = 13.5 on upstream sales to $D2$. So, foreclosure of sales to downstream rivals does seem to be optimal.

The second feature worth noting is that the vertical merger brings benefits to consumers despite the foreclosure that also accompanies it. In our numerical example, the vertical integration of firms $U1$ and $D1$ causes the price in the downstream market to fall from $76 to $68.5. The elimination of double marginalization by the integrating firms benefits consumers. Salinger (1988) shows, however, that this need not be the case. The competitive impact of a vertical merger is determined by the balance between two forces. On the one hand, vertical merger and market foreclosure reduces the number of independent upstream suppliers and so reduces competitive pressure on upstream—and downstream—prices. On the other hand, vertical merger eliminates double marginalization for the merged firms and, by reducing their input costs, makes them fiercer competitors in the downstream market, tending to reduce consumer prices. It is difficult to predict how this will play out. What is likely to be the case is that the anticompetitive effect will be weak if the number of independent upstream competitors remains large.

Moreover, there is an important strategic issue that is not addressed by the Salinger (1988) model. The independent downstream firms that are foreclosed upon may well have an incentive to react to integrated rivals by merging with an upstream firm themselves. If vertical integration brings business advantages, then all firms should have an incentive to pursue them. Policy should not penalize any one firm because it happens to be first in line in this process. To address this point, as well as to explore other features of vertical mergers, we now consider the model of Ordover, Saloner, and Salop (1990) (OSS).

17.3.2   Vertical Integration and Foreclosure in a Model with Differentiated Products

To understand the OSS model, we again consider an industry in which there are two upstream firms and two downstream firms. The upstream firms produce a homogeneous product one unit of which is needed for every unit of downstream production. Firms compete in prices in both markets. Since the upstream firms supply a homogeneous product, price in that market prior to any integration must be marginal cost, which is again denoted by c^U. However, in this model, the downstream products are differentiated. We capture this feature by letting the demand for either downstream product be:

$$q_i^D = A - p_i - B(p_i^D - p_j^D); \ i = 1,2 \text{ and } 0 < B < \infty \tag{17.22}$$

The fact that B is finite means that neither downstream firm loses all its customers when its rival undercuts its price. As in our discussion of the Salinger (1988) model, we will find it useful to have a specific numeric example. For this purpose, we assume that the constant marginal upstream is $c^U = 10$; that any additional downstream cost c^D is zero; and that $A = 100$ and $B = 2$.

We describe first the outcome in the absence of any vertical integration. Price competition in a homogeneous upstream product means that the upstream price $P^U = c^U$. Our assumption that there are no additional retailing costs in turn implies that each downstream firm i will set a downstream price p_i^D to maximize profit:

$$\pi_i^D = (p_i^D - P^U)[A - p_i^D - B(p_i^D - p_j^D)];$$

where $i = 1,2$ and $P^U = c^U$. This gives rise to the best response functions:

$$p_1^D = \frac{A + (1 + B)c^U}{2(1 + B)} + \frac{B}{2(1 + B)} p_2^D$$

$$p_2^D = \frac{A + (1 + B)c^U}{2(1 + B)} + \frac{B}{2(1 + B)} p_1^D \tag{17.23}$$

The downstream equilibrium prices, outputs, and profits are therefore:

$$p_1^D = \frac{A + (1 + B)c^U}{2 + B}$$

$$p_2^D = \frac{A + (1 + B)c^U}{2 + B} \tag{17.24}$$

$$q_1^D = \frac{(1 + B)(A - c^U)}{2 + B}$$

$$q_1^D = \frac{(1 + B)(A - c^U)}{2 + B} \tag{17.25}$$

$$\pi_1^D = \frac{(1 + B)(A - c^U)^2}{(2 + B)^2}$$

$$\pi_2^D = \frac{(1 + B)(A - c^U)^2}{(2 + B)^2} \tag{17.26}$$

For our numerical example, we have $p_1^D = p_2^D = \$32.5$; $q_1^D = q_2^D = 67.5$; and each downstream firm earns a profit of $\pi_1^D = \pi_2^D = \$1518.75$. The upstream price is $10 and upstream profits are zero. Because of the upstream competition there is no double marginalization. Any and all profits are earned at the retail level. This also means that the profit earned by a downstream firm in this case is, all else being equal, the same profit as that earned by an integrated firm, which sells its final product for more than the true marginal cost upstream.

Now what happens if upstream firm $U1$ and downstream firm $D1$ vertically merge? As in the Cournot case, we will suppose that the integrated firm can refuse to supply the independent downstream firm $D2$. Once again this means that upstream firm $U2$ becomes a monopoly supplier to $D2$ and so these two firms will independently set prices that reflect the familiar double marginalization problem. Specifically, let W be the wholesale price $U2$ now charges $D2$. Then the best response functions for the downstream rivals are now:

$$p_1^D = \frac{A + (1 + B)c^U}{2(1 + B)} + \frac{B}{2(1 + B)}p_2^D$$

$$p_2^D = \frac{A + (1 + B)W}{2(1 + B)} + \frac{B}{2(1 + B)}p_1^D \tag{17.27}$$

This yields a downstream equilibrium set of prices, conditional on W of:

$$p_1^D = \frac{(2 + 3B)A + 2(1 + B)^2 c^U + B(1 + B)W}{(2 + B)(2 + 3B)}$$

$$p_2^D = \frac{(2 + 3B)A + B(1 + B)c^U + 2(1 + B)^2 W}{(2 + B)(2 + 3B)} \tag{17.28}$$

From equation (17.28) we can check that p_2^D will exceed p_1^D for any upstream price W greater than c^U. Substitution of the prices in equation (17.28) yield downstream firm $D2$'s output q_2^D as a function of the wholesale price W set by upstream independent $U2$.

$$q_2^D = \frac{(1 + B)(2 + 3B)A + (1 + B)^2 Bc^U}{(2 + B)(2 + 3B)} - (1 + B)\frac{[2(1 + B) + B(2 + B)]}{(2 + B)(2 + 3B)}W \tag{17.29}$$

Equation (17.29) is the demand curve now facing upstream firm $U2$. Given its constant marginal cost of c^U the upstream firm $U2$ maximizes profit by setting a price W^*:

$$W^* = \frac{(2 + 3B)A + (2 + B)(1 + 2B)c^U}{2[2(1 + B) + B(2 + B)]} \tag{17.30}$$

It is straightforward to show that $W^* > c^U$ for any $A > c^U$, which must hold for the downstream market to be viable. In our numerical example, $W^* = \$35.7143$, far above the $10 input cost paid by $D1$. Hence, as in the Salinger (1988) model, vertical integration has disadvantaged the independent downstream firm. It now has a higher input cost than its integrated rival and, therefore, charges a higher price losing both customers and profits as a result. Moreover, because p_2^D has increased, the integrated firm can now raise p_1^D. In our numerical example, the new prices are: $p_1^D = \$37.321$ and $p_2^D = \$46.964$. Since $D1$ still buys at marginal cost, its post-merger profit is higher. However, the increase in all retail prices means that consumers are worse off.

As OSS point out, however, the foregoing need not be the end of the story. From the perspective of the independent firms, their problem lies as much in their own non-cooperative behavior as in the integration of their rivals. $U2$ must charge a wholesale price $W^* > c^U$ if it is to make any profit. Since $D2$ must in turn set a retail price $p_2^D > W^*$ if it is to make profit, the two firms suffer together the problem of double marginalization. An obvious solution would be that $U2$ and $D2$ mimic their rivals and merge themselves. In this way, $D2$ could buy at cost from its upstream division and compete against $D1$ on an even playing ground.

We already know what the outcome will be if both pairs of firms merge. Recall that the upstream firms were forced by competition to sell at marginal cost in the pre-merger world. Since these same firms also sell at marginal cost after they become divisions of an integrated firm, downstream prices and outputs must be the same when both pairs of firms vertically integrate as they were when neither was integrated. There does seem to be an easy remedy to the anticompetitive effects of the vertical merger of $D1$ and $U1$ and that is $D2$ and $U2$ should also merge. Since they have every incentive to do this, this remedy should happen.

Of course, a merger of $U2$ and $D2$ will undo the advantage of the already integrated firm. Is there anything the integrated firm can do to prevent this? OSS say yes. Perhaps somewhat surprisingly, the integrated firm has a strategy that will prevent the vertical merger of its independent rivals. Rather than withdraw its supply from $D2$ altogether, the integrated firm can instead commit to selling it to $D2$ at some price $\bar{W}$ above marginal cost, so that $D2$ is disadvantaged, but less disadvantaged than when it was paying W^*.

What is the advantage of this strategy? The commitment of the integrated firm serves to check the monopoly power of $U2$. If the independent upstream producer $U2$ wishes to sell any positive output, it must do so at a price of $\bar{W}$ or less. Because $\bar{W} < W^*$, the independent downstream firm $D2$ will sell more and earn more profit. For the integrated firm, this is the bad news. However, there is good news. There will always be values of $\bar{W}$ satisfying $c^U < \bar{W} < W^*$ such that the combined profits of the two independent firms, $U2$ and $D2$, are greater than they would be in the case in which all firms become integrated. By constraining the wholesale price that $U2$ can charge, the integrated firm creates a situation in which these two firms earn at least as much total profit as they would if they merged. Hence, this strategy removes the merger incentive for $U2$ and $D2$ and the risk of returning to the prices set in the initial equilibrium.

The underlying intuition in OSS is relatively clear. Although $D2$ has to raise its price and lose some customers when its input price W rises, the nature of price competition downstream is that $D1$ takes this as an opportunity to raise its own price as well. In turn, this softens the blow for non-integrated firms because their own price increase will now not lose as many customers. The rise in W lessens the intensity of downstream price competition. As long as W does not rise too much, firms $U2$ and $D2$ will prefer this softened downstream price competition to merging and returning to the market outcome, prices and profits, prior to any integration.

Table 17.1 illustrates the model for our numerical example where $A = 100$; $B = 2$; and $c^U = 10$. The first row indicates the market equilibrium before any vertical mergers. In this case,

Table 17.1 Vertical integration, foreclosure, and strategic commitment

	Wholesale price W	D1s downstream price p_1^D	D2s downstream price p_2^D	D1s quantity q_1^D	D2s quantity q_2^D	Combined profit of U1 and D1	Combined profit of U2 and D2
No vertical integration	10	32.5	32.5	67.5	67.5	1,518.75	1,518.75
U1 and D1 integrate	35.71	37.32	46.96	81.96	33.75	2,239.38	1,247.54
U1 and D1 integrate and U2 and D2 integrate	10	32.5	32.5	67.5	67.5	1,518.75	1,518.75
U1 and D1 integrate and commit to maximimum W	21.43	34.64	38.93	73.93	52.50	1,821.71	1,518.78

the wholesale price set by U2 is just equal to marginal cost. The downstream firms compete symmetrically and each makes a profit of $1518.75. Since the upstream firms earn no profit, this is also the combined profit of each upstream and downstream pair. The second row illustrates the outcome after U1 and D1 merge and withdraw all supply from D2. The monopoly power that this confers on U2 then allows it to set a wholesale price of $35.71. This forces independent retailer D2 to raise its price to $46.96. In turn, this allows the integrated firm to raise its downstream price to $37.32 even though its own input costs are still $10. Total profit for the merged firms rises to $2,239.38. However, total profit for the independents now falls to $1,247.54, with some of this profit being earned by upstream firm U2. The third row shows what happens if firms U2 and D2 vertically merge just as their rivals did. This move restores the original price equilibrium with the one difference that both upstream firms are no longer independent but are now divisions of vertically integrated companies. Finally, the fourth row illustrates what happens if, instead of foreclosing supply to D2 altogether, the integrated firm U1 – D1 now strategically commits to selling supplies to D2 at a maximum price $\bar{W}$ equal in this case to $21.43. Faced with such a prospect, the upstream independent U2 can no longer charge a wholesale price of $W* = $35.71. Instead, it has to match or slightly undercut this price ceiling. This hurts U2 but helps D2 and, together, they earn just as much as they would if they fully integrated. This strategy, therefore, removes the incentive these remaining independent firms have to merge. Of course, this is precisely the point. Had U2 and D2 merged, prices and the profit of integrated firm U1 – D1 would have fallen back to their original, pre-merger level. Committing to $\bar{W} = $21.43 prevents this, albeit at some cost.

Another vertical merger is not a viable remedy in the OSS model to the anticompetitive impact that a first vertical merger can have. The integrated firm can prevent such mergers from being attractive by offering to sell inputs to its independent downstream rival. This means, of course, abandoning a strict foreclosure strategy. However, as Chen (2001) points out, such foreclosure seems to be a rarity in practice as we often see integrated firms selling to independent downstream rivals. Chen (2001) takes the OSS model one step further. He notes that whenever the wholesale price offered by the integrated firm and independent producer U2 are the same, the independent downstream firm D2 will prefer to buy from the integrated producer. Why? Because in so doing, D2 gives the integrated firm another source of profit—a source that rises as D2 sells more downstream. As a result of selling to D2, the integrated firm will price less aggressively in the downstream market because this would cut into its profit on input sales to D2. Of course, less aggressive downstream pricing also helps D2 and that is precisely why D2 would prefer to buy from the integrated firm rather than from U2. Indeed, Chen (2001) suggests that if there are cost efficiencies associated with the vertical merger so that c^U falls at the integrated firm, the merger could lead to a different sort of foreclosure altogether. Instead of cutting off independent downstream firms from a source of supply, the vertical merger may leave independent upstream firms without any customers.[4]

17.3.3   Reappraisal and Application: The GE–Honeywell Merger

Let us return to the GE–Honeywell merger described at the start of this chapter. As noted, the European Commission eventually ruled against the merger. Their reasoning is summarized in the following extract from the Commission's report (paragraph 355):

> Because of their lack of ability to match the bundle offer . . . [independent] suppliers will lose market shares to the benefit of the merged entity and experience an immediate damaging profit shrinkage. As a result, the merger is likely to lead to market foreclosure on the existing aircraft platforms and subsequently to the elimination of competition in these areas.[5]

There are several points to make in regard to this judgment. First, the "bundling" and unfair competitive advantage that the Commission feared would give GE–Honeywell a competitive advantage is nothing more than the elimination of the double marginalization that we have described above. Eliminating double marginalization gave a similar advantage to the integrated firms in the oligopoly models that we have studied in this chapter. Packaging jet engines with engine starter motors is economically equivalent to combining the upstream manufacturing with the retail services of a downstream dealer. Thus, there is some legitimacy in the Commission's fear that GE–Honeywell would gain some advantage over independent rivals.

Whether the merger would lead to foreclosure and whether, if it did, this would raise prices is another matter. In part, that would depend on the nature of initial competition. If the market were very competitive with lots of jet engine firms and avionics companies, then the merger could have very little anticompetitive impact. The nature of competition in both the upstream and the downstream affects the likelihood of foreclosure and its ultimate impact. In short, some understanding of the real-world marketplace is necessary to make an informed judgment regarding this merger.

It is fair to say that neither pre-merger market was competitively structured. Estimates of GE's share of the jet engine market for large commercial aircraft range from 28 to 52 percent, and it had just two major rivals, the Pratt-Whitney division of United Technologies and the Rolls-Royce Group. Likewise, Honeywell's share of the avionics market was on the order of 50 percent, and it had just three rivals: Rockwell Collins (25 percent); Thales (15 percent); and Smiths Industries (5 percent). In reaching its decision, the European Commission appears to have been persuaded that the preeminence of GE and Honeywell made subsequent integration by their rivals impossible. As a result, and as the quote above makes clear, the Commission feared foreclosure of GE's competitors and the ultimate loss of competition in the jet engine market.

The Commission is implicitly claiming that rivals could not integrate as well and this would need to be documented. More importantly, we should in this case show that even with foreclosure, the resulting market outcome would be worse than the pre-merger case. This was *not* the case in our numerical example of the Salinger (1988) model. In that example, integration by one firm did lead to foreclosure of its rival. Nevertheless, the post-merger

---

[4]   Pepall and Norman (2001) offer a similar analysis to Chen (2001) in which vertical foreclosure is never an equilibrium precisely because, again, this leads to competition between multiple vertically integrated firms.

[5]   The full decision is available at http://ec.europa.eu/comm/competition/mergers/cases/decisions/m2220_en.pdf.

Reality Checkpoint
Going Whole Hog on Vertical Integration

Nowhere have the strategic advantages of vertical integration been more aggressively pursued in recent times than in meat and poultry markets. Firms in these markets have made a concerted effort to control all aspects of production from the farm to the store counter or, as they say in the pork business, from "birth to bacon and squeal to meal."

The largest pork producer in both the U.S. and the world is Smithfield Industries. It controls 26 percent of the U.S. market—and control is the right word. Smithfield has either ownership or decision-making rights over every single stage of the production chain up until the product is displayed in a local store. It owns the DNA line for the hogs that it uses and the feed that they eat. It directly owns hundreds of mega hog farms. In addition, thousands of farms work as Smithfield contractors in which case Smithfield still owns the hogs if not the farms themselves.

The advantages of such control are clear. By directing insemination and breeding, Smithfield can maintain a supply of new, and bigger litters that allow it to slaughter more hogs each year without threatening the sustainability of its herds. Feed and genetic control give the firm a tight grip on the leanness and other key features of its pigs. Contracts and ownership also permit Smithfield to design the warehouse barns in which the hogs are raised. This has the added virtue of ensuring that the hogs will mature on schedule and be ready for transport to the pork processing plant in a timely fashion. This is important because the plants are designed to operate efficiently at a particular level of use and even small deviations from this capacity utilization rate can lead to rapidly escalating costs.

Thus, vertical integration has permitted standardization, quality control and, of course, the elimination of double marginalization. As a result, Smithfield has become the world's largest pork producer, annually slaughtering close to 20 million hogs to turn out over 5 billion pounds of pork. Nor is Smithfield the only meat processor that has pursued this strategy. Tyson, which with its poultry, beef, and pork operations is even bigger than Smithfield and is, in fact, the world's largest meat producer, is also highly integrated. In fact, it was Tyson that introduced such large-scale integration to farming when it began to reorganize its poultry business. Other pork firms such as ConAgra and Swift have also organized their operations in this same, vertical manner. It's the swine of the times.

Sources: S. Kilman, "Smithfield to Buy Hog Farmer Premium Standard," *Wall Street Journal*, Tuesday, September 19, 2006, p. A4; and S. Martinez, "A Comparison of Vertical Coordination in the U.S. Poultry, Egg, and Pork Industries," *Current Issues in Economics of Food Markets*, Agriculture Information Bulletin, AIB-747-05 (May, 2002).

downstream price of $68.5 was still well below the pre-merger price of $76. As a review of that example will quickly reveal, even if the foreclosure eventually led the integrated firm to enjoy a complete downstream monopoly, the retail price would still decline to $73. This is, of course, a stylized example. Nevertheless, it reveals just how large the inefficiencies of double-marginalization could be, and perhaps why many economists thought the ruling a mistake.[6]

---

[6] For a similar analysis of the GE–Honeywell case, but one that is set in a framework of differentiated products see, Nalebuff (2004). To be fair, the Commission also expressed other fears besides foreclosure. One of these was that GE already had an unfair advantage in that its large financial operations allowed it to package financing with jet aircraft in a way that Pratt-Whitney and Rolls-Royce could not. In addition, there was a horizontal element to the case in that GE and Honeywell were the only two suppliers of engines for large regional jets.

17.4   CONGLOMERATE MERGERS

The final type of merger to consider is a conglomerate merger. Such mergers bring under common control firms whose products are neither direct substitutes nor complements. The outcome is a set of firms producing a diversified range of products with little or nothing in common. While conglomerate companies have been with us for some time, the U.S. merger wave starting in the 1960s and continuing into the early 1980s is, particularly in the earlier years, when many of the conglomerates that we see today were formed. The question is whether we can develop a convincing economic rationale for these mergers. If not, then we should think of conglomerates as an accident of history that are being gradually corrected through corporate downsizing and the focus on "core businesses," strategies that appear to characterize corporate change as we move into the new millennium. A number of reasons have, however, been advanced to support the emergence of conglomerate firms. We examine these in turn.

17.4.1   Possible Economies Associated with Conglomeration

Scope economies and saving on transactions costs are two possible advantages that may accrue to conglomerate firms. By scope economies we mean that a variety of products or services are more cheaply produced by one firm than by two or more firms. By transaction costs we mean the costs that are incurred by firms when they use external markets in order to exchange goods and services.[7] These include, for example, the costs of searching for the desired inputs, negotiating supply contracts, monitoring and enforcing these contracts and the risk associated with unforeseen changes in supply conditions.

Scope economies derive primarily from the ability of the firm to exploit common inputs in the manufacture of a range of products. The same production line can be used for several products, marketing efforts can promote the whole range of goods a firm produces, and the fruits of research and development may extend to a number of diverse products. Advertising and promotional activities also frequently exhibit scope economies across a variety of activities. This line of argument implies that for scope economies to be an important element in conglomerate mergers it is necessary that the firms that merge are related in some respect. Either they sell in similar markets or they have similar production technologies. The data on conglomerates do not appear to be consistent with this hypothesis. A detailed study by Nathanson and Cassano (1982) concludes that there are at least as many conglomerate firms that produce goods with little in common, whether this be technology or the markets at which they are targeted, as there are firms that have relatively low product and market diversity.

Transactions costs are particularly significant when specialized or knowledge-intensive assets are traded. Consider a specialized asset, such as a sophisticated machine that is specifically designed to produce two goods, A and B. Let us also suppose that the markets for A and B are highly concentrated with a small number of producers, and that the owner of the machine has spare capacity if the machine is used only to produce A. This might arise, for example, if demand for A is limited relative to the productive capacity of the machine. If such spare capacity exists, the owner of the machine may wish to use it to produce B goods as well. A conglomerate merger or the machine owner merging together A and B

---

[7]   For an excellent discussion of transactions costs, see Besanko et al. (2007).

production is one way that this can happen. However, as Teece (1982) and others have argued, conglomeration is not strictly necessary. The machine owner, a producer of A, can instead simply lease the spare capacity to B producers.

There is a potential problem with the leasing arrangement, however. Because the number of B producers is small, each will have some monopoly power in bargaining over the terms of the lease. As a result, the machine owner may find that the costs and risks associated with the negotiations between the interested parties are large as each side tries to get the best possible deal. Conglomeration may be a means of avoiding such costs. By using the machine to produce both A and B within the same firm, the machine owner avoids all the bargaining hassles. There is no longer any conflict over how to divide the gains from using the machine because those gains all go to the same owner.

Transaction cost problems are particularly important when the asset involved is knowledge or information intensive. The knowledge of such matters as organizational routines or specialized customer needs is generally embodied in specific individuals or teams employed by the company. It is difficult to envision contracts to "lease" such personnel.

In short, the effort to minimize the transaction costs associated with contracting between firms may explain conglomerate mergers to some extent. Nevertheless this motivation seems unlikely to be the major factor behind such mergers. The reason is that here again, we are talking about some asset that is common to all the lines of production operated by the conglomerate, and such commonality in productive assets does not seem to be a feature of actual conglomerate firms.

17.4.2   Managerial Motives

The skepticism surrounding the explanations based on scope economies, transaction cost savings, and other arguments why conglomerate mergers improve production efficiency has led some to postulate a different, less benign motivation. The motive for conglomeration may be that it is in the interest of management even if it is not in the interest of shareholders. Because management calls the shots, it is the managerial interest that prevails.

In any reasonably large public company, ownership, which essentially resides with the shareholders, may be separated from control, which essentially resides with the management team. This separation would not matter too much if management performance could be perfectly observed and monitored by shareholders. Yet perfect monitoring is rare, and absent such monitoring, management can pursue its own agenda at least to some extent. This would not matter so long as the best interests of management are served by maximizing shareholder wealth. It is precisely the attempt to secure this harmony of interest that lies behind the use of performance-related clauses and payment in stock options in many executive compensation schemes. Still, the match between the interests of shareholders and management is rarely perfect, leaving management with at least some ability to pursue goals other than maximization of shareholders' returns.

Suppose that management compensation is based upon company growth.[8] Growth is far from easy to generate internally. It requires that market share be won from competitors who can hardly be expected to sit passively by when they lose customers. Nor is it easy to buy growth through horizontal merger since this is the kind of acquisition that is watched by the antitrust authorities. In these circumstances, we should not be surprised to find management supporting a conglomerate merger, even if this is not necessarily in the

---

[8]   This analysis is treated in detail in Mueller (1969).

Reality Checkpoint

A Conglomerate of Errors: Cendant Corporation

In the early 1970s, Walter Forbes, a recent graduate of Harvard Business School and a business consultant, was convinced of the eventual triumph of home shopping using computers and credit cards. His faith in this market led him to launch a new company, Comp-U-Card, designed to build on this idea. Home computers were a rarity in those days and the new firm struggled until it finally hit on a discount telephone shopping club service called Shopper's Advantage. After paying a fee of about $40, members could call a toll free number to purchase hundreds of goods at a discount. Even this might not have been enough to win success if it had not been that the credit card business was in a competitive boom and, to attract members, credit card firms began to seek arrangements with other companies, such as airlines, in order to attract members. Shopper's Advantage was one of those companies. Credit card firms competed for customers in part by offering a membership in the home shopping club. Soon the Comp-U-Card was CUC International and owned many shopping clubs for travel, dining, and health services along with financial interests such as Benefit Consultants, an insurance firm. It suffered in 1989–90 when the firm had to acknowledge some sloppiness in its accounting systems that overstated its profits. However, growth resumed in 1994, as CUC bought NetMarket Company to help bring its shopping services to the Internet. In 1996, it diversified further by purchasing computer software firms, Sierra On-Line and Davidson & Associates.

HFS was formed in 1990 to exploit undervalued brand names. Under the leadership of Henry Silverman, it quickly focused on hotel brands and quickly bought the rights to both the Howard Johnson and Ramada (U.S.) hotel chains. Overnight, it had become a major player in the U.S. lodging industry. These purchases were soon followed by the acquisition of the Day's Inn and Super 8 Motel chains. In 1993, HFS surpassed Holiday Inn as the world's largest hotel operator. As the buying spree continued, HFS diversified into real estate by acquiring Century 21, Coldwell Banker, and ERA as well as into car rental services, acquiring Avis and Budget in 1996. Like CUC, analysts also raised questions about HFS and, in particular, its heavy reliance on debt to finance its numerous acquisitions.

In 1997, CUC and HFS surprised everyone by merging to form the Cendant Corporation. The deal was completed in December of that year. By April 1998, the share price of Cendant had climbed 25 percent. Then disaster struck. Cendant was forced to admit that its earnings, especially those generated by the former CUC, were vastly overstated. The share price fell from $41 to $11 within a few months. It fell below $10 within a year as shareholders filed a lawsuit for accounting fraud.

The conglomerate came to an end over the course of 2005–6. The firm broke into four separate companies: (1) Travelport took over all travel related services, including the recently acquired Orbitz; (2) Realogy took control of Cendant's former real estate businesses; (3) Wyndham now operates the hotel chains; and (4) Cendant Car Rental Group now controls the Avis and Budget car rental firms. The longevity of management at CUC, HFS, and later Cendant despite continued accounting problems suggests that management entrenchment and self-enrichment is a problem at conglomerate firms.

Sources: G. Morgenson, "Market Watch: A Fanfare for the Vanities of 1998," *New York Times*, Sunday December 27, 1998, p. D1; *Wall Street Journal*, September 19, 2006, p. A4; and R. Chittum and I. McDonald, "Cendant to Test Appeal of Spinoffs," *Wall Street Journal*, Tuesday May 30, 2006, p. C2.

best long-term interests of shareholders. Such a merger offers management the desired growth while avoiding antitrust problems. In this light it is, perhaps, significant that the greatest wave of conglomerate mergers in the United States coincided with a period in which the antitrust authorities were particularly fierce in their examination of mergers between related companies.

Management may also pursue conglomeration as a means to minimize risk. When a firm is involved in many distinct markets it avoids putting "all its eggs in one basket." Such diversification may be important to management.[9] Shareholders often use compensation schemes that closely tie management's pay to the firm's profit performance.[10] Yet while these practices work to ally management's interest more closely to that of the stockholders, they also increase the risk that management faces. As profits go up and down, management's compensation rises and falls irrespective of whether the profit results were management's fault or not. To protect against such fluctuations, management may seek to diversify the sources of the firm's income by pursuing conglomeration. This smoothes the firm's income stream because with many product lines operating, positive and negative shocks tend to cancel each other out. The derived income stream of the firm's executives is also smoother. Even shareholders might prefer this approach if, in the absence of such diversification, the firm would have to pay its executives higher salaries to compensate them for the greater risk. This may be particularly true for managers who are heavily invested in the firms so that not only their labor income but also their capital income is subject to the same risk.

Some evidence in support of diversification as a means of diversifying managerial risk is found in studies by Ahimud and Lev (1981) and by May (1995). The first of these studies finds that when no shareholder owns 10 percent or more of the stock and management control is high, firms tend to be more diversified. May (1995) finds that a comparison of CEOs in terms of the proportion of their wealth invested in the firm reveals that as this proportion rises, CEO's tend to favor conglomeration.

There are also less attractive or more self-serving managerial goals that may be pursued through conglomeration. These include entrenchment and rent-seeking. It may be more difficult to replace managers who run more complicated firms. Obvious candidates to replace the existing CEO and other executives may be hard to find when the firm is a complex conglomerate. Similarly, the more complex the organization, the more difficult it is for shareholders to monitor management and to guard against managers skimming off profits to their own benefit. These problems are sufficiently real that shares in a conglomerate are often considered low-priced and subject to a conglomerate discount (Aggarwal and Samwick 2003).

17.5   A BRIEF DIGRESSION ON MERGERS AND THE THEORY OF THE FIRM

A merger involves the acquisition of one company by another. As a result of that purchase, the acquiring firm gets the physical capital—buildings, equipment, and land—and perhaps certain intangible assets, such as reputation or brand name, that formerly belonged to the acquired company. The ultimate question raised by any merger is, what does the change in ownership permit the merged firm to do that could not be done before?

---

[9] For a detailed discussion of these ideas, see Ahimud and Lev (1981).

[10] For example, Boeing Corp. linked its annual award of stock options to its 1,500 top executives to the performance of the company's share price over the next five years. See F. M. Biddle, "Boeing Links Managers' Stock Options to Five-year Performance of Shares," *Wall Street Journal*, February 26, 1998, p. B12.

In the case of a horizontal merger, the possibility of enhanced market power is clearly part of the motivation. Yet we often see horizontal mergers in which such an increase in market power does not occur. The merger paradox discussed in the last chapter suggests that increases in market power as the result of a merger could be rare. In the case of a vertical merger, the market power motivation is even more suspect. If the upstream and downstream firm each had 5 percent of their respective markets before the merger, little seems changed by moving the ownership of those market shares from two different firms to two different divisions of the same firm.

With upstream–downstream firms there is the issue of double marginalization. We have suggested a vertical merger as a response to that problem. It is not the only response, however. Various contracts between two vertically related firms can be written to overcome the problem of double marginalization, and these contracts do not require integrating the two firms into one. We will examine such contracts in depth in the next chapter. Here we simply want to raise the question as to why firms merge rather than make use of such contracts. Alternatively, why don't more firms merge? What in fact limits the size of a firm? What stops firms from merging into bigger and bigger firms?

This question is really about what determines the boundaries of a firm. What is the difference between organizing the production of a commodity through many independent companies, on the one hand, and organizing that production through many divisions of the same company, on the other? Viewing the matter in this light makes transparent that what determines the boundaries of the firm is an important question for industrial organization theory.

Many alternative theories of the firm have been developed since the last 1970s. There is sufficient work in this area now to comprise a course, or a field in itself. Our aim here is not to cover this material in depth. Instead, we wish simply to offer a brief discussion of the limits on firm size. Now seems a particularly appropriate point to raise this topic since a merger, by definition, is a transaction that increases those limits.

Neoclassical theory does not tell us much as to what such a transaction gains for the parties. Nor does it tell us why firms operate internal divisions rather than "spinning them off" into individual companies. However, neoclassical theory is not alone in this regard. Other approaches to the theory of the firm also fall short of a complete answer. Take, for instance, the agency view of the firm. Under this view, a firm is an organization designed to generate the proper incentives when the various parties engaged in the production process have different and private information. For example, a supplier of glass may contract with an automobile producer to provide windshields of a particular quantity and quality according to a particular schedule. Obviously, the actual quality of such windshields is beyond the complete control of the glass supplier but the supplier does know whether it gave its full effort to supplying the specified quality. The automaker, though, is not so well informed. It cannot be sure whether a batch of low-quality glass is due to bad luck or, instead, bad faith on the part of its supplier. Agency theory has generated extremely useful insights into the types of contracts that might be used to surmount such informational problems and provide the proper incentives for both parties to live up to their contractual obligations. Yet it does not tell us whether such contracts must be between two separate firms, as in the automaker and the glass supplier of our story, or whether the contract could simply be the incentive scheme offered to the windshield division of a giant car manufacturer.

Similar problems arise with the transaction cost approach to the firm. Under that approach, the firm is viewed as an organization designed to minimize the costs of negotiating, interpreting, enforcing, and renegotiating contracts. However, the precise mechanism by which this cost reduction is achieved is not typically spelled out. There is no reason, a priori, to assume that haggling is less a problem between two divisions within one firm than between two separate firms.

The issue of corporate mergers reveals a weakness in economic theory regarding the limits or boundaries of a firm's activities. Why is it that we observe General Motors supplying auto bodies internally rather than purchasing them from an independent supplier? What advantages are gained and then lost when these divisions are instead independent firms?

One answer is provided in the work of Hart (1995) and centers on the issue of ownership. A merger changes the ownership of assets and ownership gives control. The carmaker that owns its own windshield supply unit is in a position to resolve, by itself, any dispute between its assembly line and the glass unit. This does not necessarily minimize the cost of haggling. However, common ownership may permit investments that increase efficiency that would be less likely to occur otherwise.

Suppose that there is specific machinery that can be used to produce, inexpensively, windshields of a quality and style unique to the automaker in question. An independent glass company might not invest in such equipment because it ties the glassmaker too closely to supplying the particular auto firm. If the glass supplier did make the investment, its bargaining position in disputes with the automaker would be weak because it has no other buyer for the one product that this machinery permits it to make. From the perspective of the glass supplier, it is less risky to use more general equipment that makes it easy to produce glass products for other firms as well. This is true even though the use of such generic processes requires the firm to incur an extra cost to mold the windshield to the specific dimensions specified by the carmaker.

A merger or acquisition of the glass company by the automaker offers a way out. By operating windshield production as a unit within its own firm, the automaker removes the potential conflict. Now, the specialized machinery can be bought and the windshields produced at lower cost because there is no longer any friction over how the gains from this investment will be shared. They all go to the one, common owner of the assets.

In other words, common ownership is desirable whenever there are complementarities— or synergies—between different assets. As a result, we should expect firms to combine whenever such complementarities are present—and to split apart if such complementarities vanish. Since technological changes are ever present, and since such innovations are constantly altering the extent of production complementarities, we should also expect a constant fluctuation in the size and organization of firms. This approach may help explain the recent wave of mergers in the telecommunications industry where rapid innovations have greatly altered the production technology.

17.6   EMPIRICAL APPLICATION
Vertical Integration in the Ready-mixed Concrete Industry

Ready-mixed concrete is one of the most widely used construction materials. It is comprised mainly of cement, water, and aggregates such as sand and gravel. Of these, cement is clearly crucial as the binding agent that hardens the aggregates into a solid mass. Almost invariably, cement comprises 12 percent of the concrete mixture by weight. Hence, cement and ready-mixed concrete match the assumptions of the Salinger (1988) and Ordover, Saloner, and Salop (1990) models in that cement is an upstream product used in fixed proportion per

Table 17.2   Vertical integration in cement/ready-mixed concrete market

Year	1963	1967	1972	1977	1982	1987	1992	1997
Fraction of cement sales accounted for by vertically integrated firms	25.2	51.2	48.4	41.0	49.5	51.3	75.1	55.4

unit of the downstream product, ready-mixed concrete. This makes it an ideal industry in which to study the effects of vertical integration.[11]

Ali Hortaçsu and Chad Syverson (2006) point out that there is a further aspect of the concrete business that makes studying vertical integration in that industry interesting. This is the fact that the different phases of antitrust policy over the late twentieth century were very much evidenced in the ready-mixed concrete market. In the 1960s, cement makers were interested in integrating forward into ready-mixed concrete and the percentage of vertically integrated plants rose steadily throughout the decade. Fearing that these consolidations would lead to foreclosure and anticompetitive price squeezes, the Justice Department filed 15 antitrust cases in this industry and each one led to divestiture. This vigorous policy also deterred further mergers with the result that during the 1970s, the fraction of cement firms that were vertically integrated fell noticeably. Then came the 1980s and rise of the "Chicago School" approach to antitrust policy, which viewed vertical integration much more favorably. There was a new wave of mergers that again sharply increased the extent of vertical integration in the concrete market. Finally, in the 1990s, the "post-Chicago" school began to make its influence felt and antitrust policy became less lenient. Vertical integration in concrete again declined. This pattern is shown in Table 17.2.

Of course, transport costs are far too high for there to be one, national market for ready-mixed concrete. Using Commerce Department data, Hortaçsu and Syverson (2006) identify 348 local markets over the years 1963 to 1997. They then use this data to determine whether the differences in ready-mixed concrete prices across markets are systematically related to the extent of vertical integration in those markets. A simple regression aimed at answering this question might have the form: $P_{it} = A + \beta VI_{it} + e_{it}$, where P_{it} is the average concrete price (measured in logs) in market i in year t; A is an intercept term; VI_{it} is the market share of output accounted for by vertically integrated firms in market i in year t, and e_{it} is a random error term centered on zero. Such a simple model though leaves out many other variables that are likely to be important in determining concrete prices in any given market-year and, therefore, would lead to a biased estimate of the coefficient β.

To begin with, the average price over time might be different in each market. There might be something about the Chicago market, for example, that makes its price of cement always relatively high. This effect can be handled by letting the intercept term vary across each market. Then too, industrial organization theory suggests that market structure, as measured by the Herfindahl Index (HI), could also be important for the behavior of prices, as might be the level of demand coming from the local construction industry in that year. In fact, given our discussion of antitrust policy, we might also think that the precise year is important as well because firms might try to keep prices low in years when antitrust pressure is more

---

[11]   See Chipty (2001) for a study of vertical integration in cable television.

Table 17.3   Results for regressions explaining ready-mixed concrete prices in the U.S.

Independent variable	Dependent variable: weighted average market price (log)	Dependent variable: weighted average market price (log)	Dependent variable: weighted average market price (log)
Market share of vertically integrated firms	−0.090[a] (0.041)	−0.086[a] (0.041)	−0.043 (0.039)
Market share of multiple plant firms	—	−0.015 (0.022)	0.001 (0.024)
Weighted average total factor productivity	—	—	−0.293 (0.054)
R^2	0.433	0.434	0.573

[a] Significant at 5% level.

intense than in years when it is lenient. We need to control for such time-specific factors and the many other forces that could affect concrete prices if we are to isolate the influence of changes in vertical integration alone. The easiest way to do this is to include measures of concentration and local demand and put in a dummy variable for each market and each year.

Hortaçsu and Syverson (2006) make the foregoing adjustments and some others as well to estimate regressions explaining the variation in concrete prices across markets and time. Their central results are shown in Table 17.3.

In the tables here, results for the time and market dummies are suppressed, as are those for the HI and construction demand, which are never significant. The first column shows the results when, apart from the control variables just mentioned, the only explanatory variable is the extent of vertical integration in the local market. This effect is both negative and statistically significant. It is also economically meaningful. For their entire sample, Hortaçsu and Syverson (2006) find that on average, vertically integrated firms account for 31.5 percent of the typical market. The estimated coefficient shown in the first column then implies that ready-mixed concrete prices would be 4 percent lower in such a market than they would be in a market with no vertically integrated firms. Thus, this result suggests that the efficiency results of vertical integration typically outweigh any anticompetitive effects so that consumers benefit.

The next two columns test additional variables that may be important for concrete prices. In column 2, a second independent variable is added for the fraction of firms that operate more than one plant. This includes all the vertically integrated firms plus all those that operate multiple plants horizontally. Including this variable is a means of testing whether the vertically integrated variable is really capturing efficiencies that come from coordinating different plants, e.g., better-timed production, lower transport costs, rather than from vertical integration per se. However this variable is insignificant and does not materially affect the results in column 1.

The third column is perhaps the most interesting. Here, Hortaçsu and Syverson (2006) include as an additional regressor a measure of average productivity in the local market. This is clearly an important variable. Including it reduces the magnitude of the effects of vertical integration and eliminates their statistical significance. What are the implications of this finding?

First, it makes intuitive sense that concrete prices will be lower in markets where firms are more productive. In this sense, the results in column 3 are not surprising. Second, we should recall that vertical integration has potentially two effects, a price-reducing effect due to greater efficiency and a price-increasing effect due to foreclosure-type forces. Including the productivity variable should control for any efficiency effects so that the vertical integration term now picks up only the price-increasing impact of vertical mergers. The findings in column 3 suggest that once this control for efficiency effects is included, the price-increasing effects appear very weak. Finally, Hortaçsu and Syverson (2006) produce other evidence to show that vertically integrated firms have higher productivity. If vertical integration in this industry has an impact on prices it does so through the efficiency effect. Overall, these results imply that vertical integration has been welfare-enhancing and good for consumers, at least in the ready-mixed concrete business.

Summary

We have considered two broad types of merger in this chapter: vertical and conglomerate. A vertical merger typically involves the merging of companies operating at different stages of production in the same product line. A conglomerate merger is when two firms merge that have little or no common markets or products.

Vertical mergers raise complicated issues. On the one hand, such mergers can benefit firms and consumers by eliminating the practice of double marginalization. On the other hand, they may be a means to foreclose either upstream or downstream markets to rivals, and to facilitate price discrimination. There is no simple way of determining which of these forces is likely to be the stronger. Some argue that the negative impact of potential vertical foreclosure itself sets up a countervailing force that will induce remaining independent companies to integrate as well. If so, this can reduce inefficiencies still further. However, we have seen that the vertically integrated firm may have both the means and the motive to prevent such subsequent mergers. Resolution of these issues in any particular case must, as always, depend on careful evaluation of the realities of the specific situation.

It is worth noting however that even when foreclosure and a price squeeze for independent rivals do happen, it may nonetheless be the case that final consumers are made better off with the vertical merger. Policy makers should therefore not be too hasty in condemning a vertical merger simply because it disadvantages rival firms. The goal of antitrust policy is to preserve the benefits of competition, not the fortunes of competitors.

Conglomerate mergers probably raise the fewest problems from an antitrust perspective. However, for this very reason, the motivation for such mergers can be difficult to identify. They may reflect an attempt to minimize risk either for stockholders or managers. But there would seem to be other means to achieve these same ends.

The ambiguous effects of mergers that characterize our economic models are also found in empirical analysis. To date, there is little clear evidence that vertical mergers have led to significant increases in monopoly power. A recent study of the ready-mixed concrete industry suggests that such vertical integration tends to bring greater productive efficiency and lower consumer prices. The combination of ambiguity in the theory and, if anything, favorable empirical evidence has led the legal authorities to take a much less aggressive and much less rigid stand against proposed vertical mergers. Today these are inevitably handled on a case-by-case approach. In the absence of definitive results—either from economic theory or economic data—this is the best approach to follow.

Problems

1. Norman International has a monopoly in the manufacture of *whatsits*. Each *whatsit* requires exactly one *richet* as an input and incurs other variable costs of $5 per unit.

   Richets are made by PepRich Inc., which is also a monopoly. The variable costs of manufacturing *richets* are $5 per unit. Assume that the inverse demand for *whatsits* is: $p_w = 50 - q_w$ where p_w is the price of *whatsits* in dollars per unit and q_w is the quantity of *whatsits* offered for sale by Norman International.

a. Write down the profit function for Norman International assuming that the two monopolists act as independent profit-maximizing companies, with Norman International setting a price p_w for *whatsits* and PepRich setting a price p_r for *richets*. Hence, derive the profit-maximizing price for *whatsits* as a function of the price of *richets*, and use this function to obtain the derived demand for *richets*.

b. Use your answer in (a) to write down the profit function for PepRich. Hence, derive the profit-maximizing price of *richets*. Use this to derive the profit-maximizing price of *whatsits*. Calculate the sales of *whatsits* (and so of *richets*) and calculate the profits of the two firms.

2. Now assume that these two firms merge to form NPR International.

a. Write down the profit function for NPR given that it sets a price p_w for *whatsits*. Hence, calculate the post-merger profit-maximizing price for *whatsits*, sales of *whatsits*, and the profits of NPR.

b. Confirm that this merger has increased the joint profits of the two firms while reducing the price charged to consumers. By how much has consumer surplus been increased by the merger in the market for *whatsits*?

c. Assume that the two firms expect to last forever and that the discount factor R is 0.9. What is the largest sum that PepRich would be willing to pay the owners of Norman International to take over Norman International? What is the lowest sum that the owners of Norman International would be willing to accept? (Hint: calculate the present value of the profit streams of the two firms before and after the merger, and notice that neither firm will want to be worse off with the takeover than without it.)

3. Now assume that PepRich gets the opportunity to sell to an overseas market for *whatsits*, controlled by a monopolist FC Hu Inc.,

which has the same operating costs in making *whatsits* as Norman International. PepRich knows that it will have to pay transport costs of $2 per *richet* to supply the overseas market. Inverse demand for *whatsits* in this market is: $p_w = 40 - q_w/2$.

a. Repeat your calculations for question 1a.

b. The authorities in the overseas market are contemplating taking an antidumping action, accusing PepRich of dumping *richets* into its market. They calculate that by doing so, they will induce PepRich to offer to take over FC Hu. Assume that PepRich has limited access to funds, so that it can take over only one of the two firms Norman International and FC Hu. Are the overseas authorities correct in their calculations? (Hint: compare the maximum amounts that PepRich would be willing to pay for Norman International and FC Hu.)

4. Go back to the conditions of question 1, so that PepRich is supplying only Norman International. But now assume that the manufacture of each *whatsit* requires exactly one *richet* and one *zabit*. Zabits are made by ZabCor, another monopolist, whose variable costs are $2.50 per *zabit*.

a. Assume that the three firms act independently to maximize profit. Calculate the resulting prices of *richets*, *zabits*, and *whatsits* and the profits of the three firms.

b. Assume an infinite life for all three firms and a discount factor $R = 0.9$. PepRich and ZabCor are each contemplating a takeover of Norman International. Which of these two companies would win the bidding for Norman International? What will be the effect of the winning takeover on consumer surplus in the market for *whatsits*?

5. As an alternative to buying Norman International, the owners of PepRich and ZabCor contemplate merging to form PRZ, which will control the manufacture of both *richets* and *zabits*.

a. Calculate the impact of this merger on (1) the prices of *richets*, *zabits*, and *whatsits*, (2) the profits of these firms, and (3) consumer surplus in the *whatsit* market.

b. Which merger will be preferred
    (i)   by consumers of *whatsits*?
    (ii) by the owners of PepRich and ZabCorp.?
    (iii) by the owners of Norman International?

6. (More difficult) Ginvir and Sipep are Bertrand competitors selling differentiated products in the carbonated drinks market. The demands for the products of the two firms being given by the inverse demand functions:

$$p_G = 25 - q_G - q_S \text{ for Ginvir and}$$
$$p_S = 25 - q_S - q_G \text{ for Sipep.}$$

Both companies need syrup to make their drinks that is supplied by two competing companies, NorSyr and BenRup. These companies incur costs of $5 per unit in making the syrup. Both Ginvir and Sipep can use the syrup of either supplier.

a. Confirm that competition between NorSyr and BenRup leads to the syrup being priced at $5 per unit.
b. What are the resulting equilibrium prices for Ginvir and Sipep and what are their profits?

7. Now suppose that Ginvir and NorSyr merge and that NorSyr no longer competes for Sipep's business.

a. What price will BenRup now charge Sipep for the syrup?
b. What are the resulting profits to the three post-merger companies?
c. Do BenRup and Sipep have an incentive also to merge?

8. Return to the model of Cournot competition presented in section 17.3. Show that when both pairs of upstream–downstream firms vertically integrate, total industry profit falls below what it was with no vertical integration.

9. (Hart and Tirole 1990.) Consider a monopolist upstream supplier $U1$ selling to two downstream producers $D1$ and $D2$ engaged in Cournot competition. Downstream demand is described by: $P = 100 - Q$ and marginal cost is zero at both the upstream and downstream level.

a. Show that the monopoly level of output is 50 and that monopoly profit is $2,500.
b. Imagine a contract by which $U1$ sells 25 units as a package to each of $D1$ and $D2$ at a price of $1,250. Each firm can either accept the package or reject it. Show that if decisions are made simultaneously, and each firm has full information about the other's actions, the Nash equilibrium is for each to accept this offer.

10. Imagine now that deals between $U1$ and $U2$ are done in secret. This can be thought of as raising the possibility that one player goes first. If that player accepts 25 units at a package price of $1,250, $U1$ can then offer a second package to the other retailer.

a. Show that in a sequential setting the first downstream firm will never accept the $U1$'s offer.
b. Show that by vertically integrating with one of the downstream firms and foreclosing the other, $U1$ can earn the monopoly profit of $2,500.

References

Aggarwal, R. K. and A. Samwick. 2003. "Why Do Managers Diversify Their Firms? Agency Reconsidered." *Journal of Finance* 58 (February): 71–118.

Ahimud, Y. and Lev, B. 1981. "Risk Reduction as a Managerial Motive for Conglomerate Mergers." *Bell Journal of Economics* 12 (Autumn): 605–17.

Besanko, D., D. Dranove, S. Schaefer, and M. Shanley. 1996. *Economics of Strategy*. 4th edn. New York: John Wiley and Sons.

Chen, Y. 2001. "On Vertical Measures and Their Competitive Effects." *Rand Journal of Economics* 32 (Winter): 667–85.

Chipty, T. 2001. "Vertical Integration, Market Foreclosure, and Consumer Welfare in the Cable Television Industry." *American Economic Review* 91 (June): 428–53.

Hart, O. 1995. *Firms, Contracts, and Financial Structure*. Oxford: Oxford University Press.

Hart, O. and J. Tirole. 1990. "Vertical Integration and Market Foreclosure." *Brookings Papers on*

Economic Activity (Special Issue), (February): 205–76.

Hortaçsu, Ali and Chad Syverson. 2006. "Cementing Relationships: Vertical Integration, Foreclosure, Productivity, and Prices." Working Paper, University of Chicago.

Krattenmaker, T. and S. Salop. 1986. "Anticompetitive Exclusion: Raising Rivals' Costs to Achieve Power over Price." *Yale Law Journal* 96 (December): 209–95.

May, D. O. 1995. "Do Managerial Motives Influence Firm Risk-reduction Strategies?" *Journal of Finance* 50 (November): 1291–308.

Mueller, D. C. 1969. "A Theory of Conglomerate Mergers." *Quarterly Journal of Economics* 83 (November): 643–59.

Nalebuff, B. 2004. "Bundling: GE–Honeywell." In J. Kwoka and L. White, eds, *The Antitrust Revolution*. 4th edn. Oxford: Oxford University Press, 388–412.

Nathanson, D. A. and J. Cassano. 1982. "What Happens to Profits When a Company Diversifies?," *Wharton Magazine* 24 (Summer): 19–26.

Ordover, J. A., G. Saloner, and S. Salop. 1990. "Equilibrium Vertical Foreclosure." *American Economic Review* 80 (March): 127–42.

Pepall, L. and G. Norman. 2001. "Product Differentiation and Upstream Downstream Relations." *Journal of Economics and Management Strategy* 10 (Summer): 201–33.

Riordan, M. 1998. "Anticompetitive Vertical Integration by a Dominant Firm." *American Economic Review* 88 (December): 1232–48.

Salinger, M. A. 1988. "Vertical Mergers and Market Foreclosure." *Quarterly Journal of Economics* 103 (May): 345–56.

Salop, S. C. 1979. "Monopolistic Competition with Outside Goods." *Bell Journal of Economics* 10 (Spring): 141–56.

Teece, D. 1982. "Towards an Economic Theory of the Multiproduct Firm." *Journal of Economic Behavior and Organization* 3 (March): 39–63.

18

Vertical Price Restraints

When the holiday season approaches, you will likely want to make some purchases. These could include asked-for books, apparel, jewelry, or perhaps some toys for your younger siblings or relatives. Suppose that buying a toy is your top priority. Once in the market for toys, you must decide what brand of toy, say Lego, Playmobile, or Fisher–Price, is your best buy. You may realize that the same Fisher–Price toy is available at both Wal-Mart and Toys "R" Us, but that you can find the customized Lego train set only at the small toyshop on your college town's Main Street. The decisions of what toy to buy and where to buy it are affected by two different levels of competition. One level is the competition between the different manufacturers of toys or what we might call brand competition. The other level is competition between the different retailers who sell toys to customers, that is, retail competition.

Let's continue with the story a bit further. After deciding what and where to buy your holiday presents, you will then need to get back home. Suppose you want to drive home. This will put you in the market for a car if you do not already have one. (Remember that this is the holiday season, traditionally a time of big spending.) When you begin to shop for a new automobile, you will quickly discover that you cannot buy one at Sears or at any other large department store. For instance, to buy a Ford Taurus you will need to go to a Ford dealership, to buy a Toyota Corolla you will have to visit a Toyota dealership, and so on.

Even after the purchase of the car, there still remain some shopping decisions. On your drive home, you will likely need to purchase some fuel. You will discover that you can only get Mobil gasoline at a Mobil station, British Petroleum gasoline at a BP station, and Sunoco gasoline at a Sunoco station. This may or may not strike you as terribly odd. Yet it is certainly different from when you bought some Cheerios to eat as a healthy, low-sugar snack during the drive. To make that purchase you did not have to worry about finding a General Mills dealership. Almost every grocery store from your local corner convenience store to the discount supermarket chain carries that brand of cereal.

Now the fact that you are reading this book clearly shows that you are a bright and inquisitive student. So, at some point in your trip home—perhaps as the tedium of driving builds—you will likely ask yourself, "What's going on, here? What makes the retailing of cars, toys, gasoline, and cereal so different?" "What is the relationship between manufacturers, on the one hand, and retailers, on the other?" "What sorts of agreements exist between manufacturers and retailers that lead to this wide array of retailing options?"

These questions lie at the heart of the next two chapters. Our goal is to understand what explains the variety of relationships between manufacturers and retailers. Toy stores and super-markets sell the products of many different manufacturers. Gasoline stations and auto dealers sell the products of only one or, at most, a few manufacturers. These different arrangements must reflect the various contractual agreements made between manufacturers and retailers, each of whom accepts some restraints on their behavior. In some cases the contractual arrange-ment restricts the price at which the retailer can sell the manufacturer's product.

If you do decide to buy a car then you will probably find that a new car has a sticker on it indicating the Manufacturer's Suggested Retail Price. This is the price at which the car-maker "suggests" that the dealer should sell to you. It is only a suggested price but it does serve as a reference point for the dealer's pricing decision and probably restrains the dealer's behavior in some way. More broadly, it indicates the general nature of vertical price restric-tions. Replace the word "suggested" with the word "required" and you have what is called resale price maintenance (RPM). Because of the great attention historically given to vertical price agreements they are the focus of this chapter.

Other aspects of the contractual agreements between manufacturers and retailers can restrict who the manufacturer sells to, or who the retailer buys from, or can set the level of pro-motional and support services each party is expected to provide, and so on. These are called non-price vertical restraints and are the topic of the next chapter. There may be sound eco-nomic reasons for vertical restraints and in this chapter we consider arguments that suggest RPM agreements may actually be pro-competitive.

18.1   RESALE PRICE MAINTENANCE: SOME HISTORICAL BACKGROUND

In the United States, RPM agreements were initially considered to be a form of price-fixing outlawed under the Sherman antitrust act and were therefore considered illegal per se. The view—first enunciated in the 1911 decision of the Supreme Court in the *Dr. Miles* case[1]— was that since the Sherman Act clearly outlawed any arrangement for different retailers to collude on a common price, the attempt by a manufacturer to achieve the same outcome by means of an agreement with a retailer should also be prohibited. Moreover, this view was applied to RPM agreements that set retail price ceilings as well as price floors. Such restric-tions, according to the courts, could not be justified either by arguing that the economic envir-onment in which the agreement was made was special or by arguing that the agreement would actually lower prices to consumers.

Since the *Dr. Miles* case the legal framework in which RPM agreements have been evalu-ated has, however, grown increasingly permissive, although that growth has been sporadic. The first important development was the *Colgate* case of 1919 in which the Supreme Court ruled that a unilateral decision by a producer to stop supplying a specific price-cutting dealer was legitimate, so long as this was not part of an RPM involving many separate dealers.[2] This permissive attitude was expanded in the wake of the Great Depression by the Miller-Tydings Act of 1937, which explicitly exempted RPM agreements from antitrust prosecution. At that time, RPM agreements became legal. Moreover, their use was greatly strengthened by the 1952 McGuire Act, which permitted the enforcement of an RPM agreement even on

---

[1]   *Dr. Miles Co. v. John D. Park and Sons, Co.*, 220 U.S. 373 (1911).
[2]   *United States v. Colgate & Co.*, 250 U.S. 300 (1919).

Reality Checkpoint
Yesterday's News

Resale price maintenance contracts have both a variety of motivations and a variable legal history. One clear motivation, however, is to resolve the double marginalization problem and, in particular, to insure that retailers do not set downstream prices too high. The important case of *Albrecht v. The Herald Co.*, settled in 1968, nicely illustrates this point.

The Herald Co. was a newspaper firm publishing, among others, the St. Louis *Globe Democrat*. In turn, the company hired various carriers to deliver the morning paper to subscribers. Each carrier was given an exclusive territory from which all other carriers were excluded. On the newspaper itself, Herald printed its suggested retail price for the *Globe Democrat*.

Albrecht was one of the carriers hired by the newspaper who served about 1,200 customers. In 1961, Albrecht began charging his customers a newspaper price above that recommended by Herald. The company quickly objected. When its several requests that Albrecht lower the price back to the suggested retail charge were rejected by Albrecht, Herald took decisive action. It contacted Albrecht's customers and offered to deliver the paper to them itself at the lower price. Subsequently, it contracted with an alternative carrier to "invade" Albrecht's exclusive territory, again, delivering the paper at the lower recommended price. Albrecht's response was thoroughly American. The firm sued Herald for breach of contract and for attempting to fix prices in violation of the Sherman Act.

In its 1968 decision, the U.S. Supreme Court found in Albrecht's favor. The decision found that Herald's efforts to force a specific price on Albrecht amounted to price-fixing and was therefore per se illegal in keeping with the court's treatment of all price-setting agreements. Thus, once it was determined that Herald was in fact trying to enforce a price restraint there was no defense. The *Albrecht* case did not sit well with many economists and others who recognized the double-marginalization problem and, more broadly, the possibility that some vertical price arrangements might actually be

good for consumers as well as for firms. Gradually, this learning spread to the courts as well. The *Sharp* case of 1988 expanded the *Colgate* exception to the per se ruling. However, the major break came with the court's ruling in *State Oil v. Khan*.

Barkat Khan was a midwestern gasoline dealer supplied by State Oil. The oil firm required that all dealers who set a markup of more than 3.25 cents per gallon would have to rebate the excess markup to the company, itself. Much like Albrecht, Khan began to exceed this maximum and when State Oil complained, Khan filed suit. As the case progressed to the Supreme Court, it generated enormous interest. Newspapers, auto manufacturers, and the U.S. Department of Justice were among the many urging the court to reverse the *Albrecht* decision and eliminate the per se status of vertical price agreements. On the other side, associations representing auto dealers and service station owners, as well as 33 states' attorney generals filed briefs urging the court to hold to the *Albrecht* finding.

The court's decision was dramatic. Not only did it find in favor of State Oil, but it also made an explicit statement that vertical price agreements stipulating *maximum* prices would no longer be per se illegal. This is not to say they would be automatically legal. However, they would be subject to a rule of reason and therefore permitted if it could be shown that there was a legitimate justification for their use and if they did not substantially lessen competition. What made the decision particularly compelling was that it was unanimous—a rarity in Supreme Court cases. However, while the court opened the door to resale price arrangements that limited *maximum* prices, the per se illegality of agreements setting *minimum* prices was maintained. The court was not quite ready to address that question in 1997.

Sources: *Albrecht v. The Herald Co.*, 390 U.S. 150 (1968), and *State Oil v. Khan*, 522 U.S. 3 (1997). See also, L. Greenhouse, "High Court, in Antitrust Ruling, Says Price Ceilings Are Allowed," *New York Times*, November 5, 1997, p. A1.

firms who had not signed on to the arrangement, provided at least one retailer and manufacturer had agreed to it.

The one loophole in the Miller-Tydings and McGuire legislation was that it required participation by state legislatures to make it effective. Some states, however, continued to prohibit RPM agreements so that in these states, RPM agreements did not become legal. Over time, this led to considerable discounting of prices in these states relative to those with pro-RPM legislation. Consumers willing to drive across the state line, or just willing to deal with a mail-order firm, were able to gain access to discount stores with lower prices. Such competition put tremendous pressure on firms participating in RPM agreements. In 1975, in the wake of the substantial inflation induced by OPEC's four-fold increase in the price of crude oil, both the Miller-Tydings and the McGuire Acts were repealed. This reestablished the presumed illegality of RPM agreements, but it did not remove the ability of manufacturers to cut off discount dealers established by the *Colgate* decision.

Three subsequent legal cases have expanded the ability of manufacturers to impose retail price restrictions. In the *Sharp Electronics* case,[3] the Court broadened its *Colgate* exception by allowing a manufacturer to terminate a discount dealer even if this was the result of other dealers' complaints. Then, in the 1997 *State Oil v. Khan* case, the Court moved to renounce explicitly any per se illegality for RPM agreements establishing a maximum price or a price ceiling. Recently, in the *Leegin* case of 2007, the court reversed the *Dr. Miles* per se ruling and held that all resale price agreements, maximum or minimum, should be subject to a rule of reason test.

The fear underlying the resistance to any legal justification for RPM agreements is, of course, that such agreements amount to either explicit or implicit collusion. There are two main ways in which this could happen. First, and most obviously, RPM agreements restrict price competition between retailers and so may foster retailer price-fixing conspiracies. What makes an RPM particularly attractive in this view is that it puts responsibility for the implementation and the enforcement of the cartel on the manufacturers, thereby protecting the retailers from any prosecution. Further, if the RPM extends automatically to new entrants, then it may also work to protect incumbent retailers from price-cutting entrants.

Alternatively, RPM agreements may foster collusion among manufacturers. In the first instance, a manufacturers' cartel would collude on wholesale prices. However, cartels can only survive if they can prevent cheating on the cartel agreement. If the cartel members can agree on a minimum price that each will impose on their retailers, then cheating becomes less likely. No member manufacturer could increase its sales by defecting from the cartel and charging a lower wholesale price because, given the stipulated retail price, consumer demand would not change. Moreover, if such a defecting manufacturer also lowered the minimum retail price at which it required retailers to sell, its cheating would very quickly be caught by the other manufacturers.

It is important to understand manufacturers' and retailers' incentives to restrict price, and of course the effect of such restrictions on consumer welfare. In this light the historical record is helpful. It is noteworthy that most of the political support for legislation such as the Miller-Tydings and McGuire Acts did not come from upstream manufacturers, but rather from downstream retailers. The retail lobby has consistently led the fight to legalize and enforce RPM agreements at both the federal and state levels. In addition, as documented by both Overstreet (1983) and Steiner (1985), the vast majority of RPM legal cases have been ones in which the issue was the setting of a minimum retail price, not a maximum price. Similar evidence for the United Kingdom has been presented by Pickering (1966). This record strongly

[3]   *Business Electronics Corp. v. Sharp Electronics Corp.* 488 U.S. 717 (1988).

Reality Checkpoint
Leather Cuts All Too Deep

On December 7, 2006, the United States Supreme Court agreed to hear the case, *Leegin Creative Leather Products, Inc. v. PSKS, Inc.*, No. 06A179. In accepting this case, the court signaled that is was ready to review its century-old policy on resale price maintenance. The court's decision in the case could give manufacturers and franchisors considerably more leeway in controlling the retail prices paid by consumers.

Leegin is a manufacturer of a line of women's accessories. In 1997, it initiated a new marketing policy designed to encourage retailers to promote its brand in a separate section of their stores. In order to participate in this program, retailers had to pledge to adhere to Leegin's suggested prices at all times. One of those retailers was PSKS. However, while it initially agreed to participate in Leegin's marketing initiative, PSKS found in mid-2002 that the product was not selling as hoped. Therefore, it placed its entire line of Leegin's products on sale. On discovering this, Leegin suspended its shipments of product to PSKS.

PSKS demonstrated at trial that its sales and profits decreased substantially as a result of Leegin's action. It argued that it was not bound by Leegin's promotion agreement and, specifically, by that part of the agreement that required that it not price below Leegin's stipulated minimum because such agreements are per se unlawful. While the *Colgate* decision would allow Leegin's not to supply PSKS,

the per se rule makes the agreement invalid. Under that rule, once the conduct is proven, liability is found without the need to show an adverse impact on competition. The jury agreed with PSKS and awarded the firm $1.2 million in damages, which was then trebled, plus attorneys' fees of approximately $350,000.

On appeal, Leegin did not contest the finding that there had been an unlawful agreement. Rather, it challenged the application of the per se rule to vertical minimum resale price maintenance. However, the United States Court of Appeals for the Fifth Circuit affirmed the district court's decision. The case then went to the Supreme Court.

As noted in the text, the Supreme Court decided that *maximum* resale price agreements would no longer be subject to the per se rule but, instead, be evaluated under the rule of reason. That decision, however, left intact the per se unlawful status of *minimum* resale price agreements. On June 28, the Supreme Court issued its decision. In *Leegin Creative Leather Products, Inc. v. PSKS, Inc.*, 551 U.S. _____(2007) the court overturned the century-old *Miles* case precedent. The ruling meant that now minimum as well as maximum resale price maintenance agreements would be subject to a rule of reason test.

Source: S. LaBaton, "Century-Old Ban Lifted on Minimum Retail Pricing," *New York Times*, June 29, 2007, p. A1.

suggests that if RPM agreements have been anti-competitive, it has been retail competition that has been suppressed.

18.2   VERTICAL PRICE RESTRAINTS AS A RESPONSE TO DOUBLE-MARGINALIZATION

One reason that a manufacturer may wish to restrict the pricing discretion of a downstream retailer is to remedy the double-marginalization problem. Let us review that argument first. Consider the simple case of a monopoly manufacturer selling to a single or monopoly retailer.

The manufacturer produces the good at constant unit cost c and sells it to the retailer at a wholesale price r. The retailer then resells the product to consumers at price P. For simplicity, we will assume for now that the retailer has no retailing cost. Consumer demand for the good is described by the linear demand function $P = A - BQ$. Hence, marginal revenue in the downstream market is $MR = A - 2BQ$. Equating marginal revenue and marginal cost downstream yields the optimal downstream output, $Q^D = (A - r)/2B$. Substituting this into the demand function then implies that the associated optimal downstream or retail price, P^D is:

$$P^D = \frac{A + r}{2} \qquad\qquad (18.1)$$

This will yield a maximum downstream profit, $\Pi^D = (A - r)^2/4B$.

At the downstream price, $P^D = (A + r)/2$, the retailer sells $Q^D = (A - r)/2B$ units of the good, which must also be the amount sold by the upstream supplier. Accordingly, $Q^D = (A - r)/2B$ describes the demand facing the upstream firm given any price it charges r. The inverse demand function confronting the upstream firm is thus $r = A - 2BQ$. This implies a marginal revenue curve upstream of $MR = A - 4BQ$. Equating this with the manufacturer's marginal cost c, then yields the upstream manufacturer's profit-maximizing output, Q^U, and, by implication, its optimal wholesale price, r^U. These are

$$Q^U = (A - c)/4B, \text{ and} \qquad\qquad (18.2)$$
$$r^U = (A + c)/2.$$

An integrated firm resulting from a merger of the downstream and upstream companies will earn greater profit and set a lower retail price because the merger eliminates the double-marginalization inherent in the preceding analysis. Such a merger transforms the two firms into a simple monopoly whose goal is to maximize total profit from manufacturing and retailing. The final price to consumers under integration is $p^I = (A + c)/2$ and output is $Q^I = (A - c)/2$.

For example, if consumer demand (in inverse form) is described by $P = 100 - 2Q$, then the monopoly retailer's marginal revenue is $MR^D = 100 - 4Q$. Profit maximization at the retail level requires that this be equated to whatever wholesale price r the manufacturer sets. In turn, this implies that the manufacturer's demand curve is $r = 100 - 4Q$. Hence, his marginal revenue curve is $MR^U = 100 - 8Q$. Accordingly, if the manufacturer incurs a constant production cost of $12 per unit, he will produce 11 units. These will be sold to the retailer at a wholesale price of $r = $56. The goods will then retail at a price of $78. Total profit is $242 for the retailer and $484 for the manufacturer. By contrast, an integrated firm facing the same demand curve will set the retail price at $p^I = $56, at which it will sell $Q = 22$ units. It will earn a total profit of $968, which clearly exceeds the total combined profit of the separate manufacturer and retailing firms ($968 > $242 + $484). Consumer surplus also increases under integration since consumers now get more of the product at a lower price.

This simple example suggests that there are gains from having the manufacturer restrict the retailer's price decision. Specifically, the manufacturer may impose a retail price agreement that requires that the retailer never charge a price above $56. With this restriction in place, the manufacturer would then set a wholesale price also equal to $56. The retailer would then have to charge that price as well. By the terms of the contract, the retailer cannot set a higher price and has no interest to set a lower one. By imposing a maximum price at which the retailer can sell, the manufacturer can achieve an outcome in which the retail price is the one that maximizes the total combined profit and which, moreover, transfers all of that profit to the manufacturer itself.

18.1

Practice Problem

Tiger-el is an upstream manufacturer of electric trains that sells wholesale to The Great Toy Store, the only such store in the area. Demand for the trains at the retail store level in inverse form is $P = 1,000 - 2Q$, where Q is the total number of trains sold. The Great Toy Store incurs no service cost in selling the train. Its only cost is the wholesale price it pays for each train. Tiger-el incurs a production cost of \$40 per train.

a.   What wholesale price should Tiger-el charge for its trains? What price will these trains sell for at retail? How many trains will be sold?

b.   What profit will the toy store and the retailer earn under the pricing choices found in part (a)?

c.   What would be the retail price and the quantity sold if Tiger-el sold the trains to the toy store at cost but received a 66.67 percent sales royalty on every train sold? What would each firm's profit now be?

We have shown that one motivation for the manufacturer to restrain the pricing of the retailer is the double-marginalization problem. In such a setting, an RPM agreement acts as a ceiling on the price consumers pay. As the *Albrecht* and *Khan* cases (see inset) illustrate, this motivation is clearly one of the forces that leads manufacturing firms to seek such restraints. However, double-marginalization cannot be the sole explanation for vertical price restriction. The issue in double-marginalization is that in the absence of an RPM agreement, the retail price will be too high. Yet much of the support for vertical price restraints reflects the view that without them retail prices will be too low.

No double-marginalization issue will occur if either the upstream market or the downstream market is competitive. If the manufacturer competes with other producers to sell to a single retailer, then the wholesale price will fall to marginal cost c, or \$12 in our earlier example. Equating marginal revenue with marginal cost, the retailer will then set a price to consumers of $(A + c)/2$ which, of course, is the same as the integrated price. Thus, in our example, competition in the upstream market will result in a retail price of $(\$100 + \$12)/2 = \$56$. A similar result will obtain if the retail market is competitive. In this case, the manufacturer will find that the retail price will be the same as the wholesale price r. As a result, all the manufacturer need do is set the wholesale price at \$56 to each retailer. With competition at either the wholesale or retail level, only one segment adds a markup. Therefore, no double markup will occur.

If neither the wholesale nor retail sector is competitive then, of course, the double-marginalization problem is potentially a real one. However, there are solutions other than the establishment of an RPM agreement. One solution for the upstream manufacturer is to adopt a nonlinear pricing strategy. In particular, it can adopt a two-part tariff pricing strategy. The manufacturer specifies that the retailer first pay a lump sum amount T and only after that be permitted to buy as much of the product as it wishes at the price r per unit. The optimal pricing strategy in such a two-part scheme calls for the per unit fee r to be set equal to marginal cost c. With a wholesale price of c, the retailer maximizes profit by setting a price of $(A + c)/2$ just as in the case in which the manufacturing market is competitive. Selling at this price the retailer will earn the maximum total profit of

$$\pi^D(c, T) = \frac{(A - c)^2}{4B} - T \tag{18.3}$$

Once again using the numerical values from our earlier example in which the market inverse demand curve was given by $P = 100 - 2Q$, and $c = \$12$, we find that the retailer's profit will be $\$968 - T$. The role of the fixed fee T is now clear. It is this fee that permits the manufacturer to claim some of the total profit generated by its product. Presumably, the manufacturer would set T no less than $\$616$ since this is the amount he could earn without the agreement. By the same logic, T could be no greater than $\$726$, since values above this amount would leave the retailer with less than the $\$242$ that she could earn in the absence of the agreement. Accordingly, we would expect T to lie somewhere between $\$616$ and $\$726$, depending on the outcome of negotiations between the two parties. Whatever value is chosen for T, the point is that this somewhat more complicated vertical arrangement solves the double-marginalization problem without recourse to an RPM agreement.

We hasten to add that the two-part pricing arrangement just described is not merely a theoretical curiosity. It is precisely the agreement specified in many franchising contracts. Franchising is a vertical relationship under which an upstream company gives a downstream firm, or franchisee, the exclusive right to market and sell its product. Franchise contracts typically involve the franchisee paying a lump sum amount up front to the franchiser for the right to carry the product. In our discussion, T corresponds to this franchising fee.[4]

In sum, double-marginalization can be a real problem that reduces profit at both the manufacturing and retailing levels when both manufacturer and retailer possess market power. RPM agreements that put a ceiling on the retail price can solve this issue. Yet the double-marginalization problem cannot be the only reason that we observe such agreements. There are at least three reasons why. First, many RPM contracts are motivated by a desire to establish a floor and not a ceiling on the retail price. Second, the double-marginalization problem does not arise when either the upstream retail market or the downstream manufacturing market is competitive. Finally, even when double-marginalization is a legitimate concern, firms can and do use alternative arrangements to remedy the problem. We now consider other possible explanations for the use of RPM agreements.

18.3   RPM AGREEMENTS AND RETAIL PRICE DISCRIMINATION

If a retailer can figure out "who is who" on its demand curve and separate consumers into different groups the retailer will find it profitable to charge the different groups different prices for the same good. In particular, the retailer will wish to charge a higher price to those customers with less elastic demand. Coupons, quantity discounts, variations in quality in which the price difference does not match the cost difference, and market segmentation are all mechanisms by which a retailer may price discriminate. However, while such price discrimination can enhance retail profits, it can make life difficult for the upstream manufacturer.

---

[4]   See O'Brien and Schaffer (1994) for further theoretical analysis. See Lafontaine (1992, 1993, and 1995) for evidence on this point.

To see how retail price discrimination can raise problems for the manufacturer, we return to our example to illustrate the issue. Suppose now that the retailer actually serves two separate markets. In each market, retail demand is characterized by $P = 100 - 2Q$ and, again, the only retail cost is the wholesale price r set by the manufacturer. In one market, the retailer is a monopolist. In the other, the retailer faces competition from a potential rival who will buy from the manufacturer and sell at the retail cost r if the retailer ever charges a price greater than r. In the first market, the retailer can add a markup to the wholesale price r, but in the second, potential competition forces the retailer to sell at a retail price exactly equal to r. Again we assume that the manufacturer's unit cost is $c = \$12$.

Although the retailer sells in two markets, there is just one contract covering all its purchases from the manufacturer. Following our logic from above, we will allow this contract to specify both a wholesale price r and an upfront franchise fee, T. The manufacturer's problem is to choose T and r to maximize its total profit. We know that each market is capable of generating \$968 in total profit and that to achieve this profit it is necessary to set a retail price of $P = \$56$. Again, however, the manufacturer cannot sign a separate contract with this retailer for the goods sold in each market separately. Instead, the manufacturer must sign a single contract that covers the total amount of goods sold by the retailer in both markets.

Without an RPM agreement the manufacturer's dilemma should now be clear. To achieve a retail price of \$56 in the competitive market, it needs to set the wholesale price r also equal to \$56. This will lead to 22 units being sold and ($56 - \$12) = \$44$ being earned on each for the desired total of \$968 in this segment. However, if the manufacturer specifies a wholesale price of $r = \$56$, then in the monopolized market, the retailer will set a price of \$78 and sell only 11 units, leading to a total profit in this market of only ($78 - \$12) \times 11 = \$616$. Although the manufacturer may be able to capture part or even all of this profit by means of the franchise fee, it is still well below the potential maximum of \$968. Of course, the manufacturer could lower the wholesale price r. Yet as we know, to realize the maximum profit of \$968 in the monopolized market requires that the wholesale price fall all the way to cost, i.e., to \$12. At this price, the profit in the monopolized segment will be maximized but the profit in the competitive segment will fall to zero because in that segment, competition always forces the retail price to equal r.

With a single contract covering all the retailer's wholesale purchases, the manufacturer faces a painful tradeoff if the retailer can price discriminate. In order to capture profit from customers with less elastic demand (those in the monopolized market) the wholesale price should be close to marginal cost. However, to capture profit from customers with more elastic demand (those in the competitive market), requires a wholesale price well above marginal cost.

In the Appendix to this chapter, we show that, without an RPM agreement, the best that the manufacturer can do in this case is to set a wholesale price of \$47.20 which results in a combined profit from both markets of \$1,742.40. The retail prices in the monopolized and competitive market are then, respectively, \$73.60 and \$47.20. Relative to the profit maximizing retail price of \$56 in each market, the price is too high in the monopolized segment and too low in the competitive segment.

An RPM agreement, however, can solve the manufacturer's problem. One solution is to set a wholesale price of $r = \$56$ and to impose an RPM agreement that the retail price can never exceed this amount. Alternatively, one could set a wholesale price of \$12 and impose an RPM requirement that the retail price never fall below \$56. In the first case, the retailer will sell at cost equal to \$56 in the competitive segment and, because of the RPM price ceiling, also sell at \$56 in the monopolized segment. In the second case, the retailer will markup the wholesale cost to a retail price of \$56. This will also be the price in the competitive market by virtue of the RPM price floor. In either case, the manufacturer will attempt to extract some or all of the downstream profit by means of a franchise fee, T.

There are many reasons why a retailer may be able to successfully price discriminate. While the two-market story told above is somewhat contrived, it nonetheless serves as a useful illustration of a general principle. Whatever the source of a retailer's ability to discriminate in prices, such discrimination makes it difficult for the upstream manufacturer to establish a wholesale contract that maximizes the total, manufacturing and retail profit unless that agreement includes an RPM provision. Without an RPM agreement, there will be a tendency for the retail price to be too low to consumers with more elastic demand and too high to those whose demand is less elastic.[5]

In the *State Oil v. Khan* case the Supreme Court removed the *per se* presumption against RPM agreements specifying a maximum price. In this case, State Oil Co. had imposed a maximum retail price on its distributors, one of whom, Barkat Khan, tried to exceed that price. However, Khan's actual pricing strategy was more complex. He did want to raise the price to premium buyers, but he wanted to lower the price to consumers of regular grade fuel. That is, Khan wanted to price discriminate. The RPM agreement subsequently legitimized by the Supreme Court appears to have been motivated in part by State Oil's need to prevent such price discrimination. In turn, this suggests that this motivation may well be important in promoting RPM contracts more generally.

18.4   RPM AGREEMENTS TO ENSURE THE PROVISION OF RETAIL SERVICES

In the preceding two sections, we have treated retailing as simply an extra stage that occurs between production and final consumption. This approach has allowed us to gain some important insights into the downstream pricing issues that the retailing stage raises. However, our modeling of retailing to date has failed to incorporate any actual positive role for retailers. Retailers such as supermarkets, discount chains, and department stores form the crucial link between those who make goods and those who use them, and these retailers provide many services that are valuable to the manufacturers. Not only do they gather information about customer satisfaction and desired changes in the manufacturer's product, but they also provide such valuable services as the provision of desirable shelf space, large displays, advertising, and product demonstration. These services can be crucial to the marketing and sales of the manufacturer's product.

Consider the magazine industry. Supermarkets and discount chains presently account for over 55 percent of single-copy sales of U.S. magazines. Because such sales are made at the full, nonsubscription price, they are profitable and quite important to publishing firms. Yet the publishers must rely heavily on the efforts of the retailers to sell their magazines. A prominent display near the checkout register, for example, can greatly increase sales. So can advertising, or a promotional visit to the store by a celebrity. Publishers have a deep interest in making sure that the retailers undertake such efforts. In recent years, publishers of *People* and other magazines, such as *Cosmopolitan* and *Harper's Bazaar*, have had tense

---

[5]   See Chen (1999).

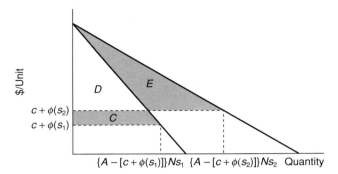

Figure 18.1   The effect of services on demand, costs, and the social surplus

Demand is given by $P = A - Q/sN$. This means that as the level of services rises from s_1 to s_2 the demand curve rotates up and to the right. At service level s_1, marginal cost $= c + \phi(s_1)$. If price equals marginal cost, total demand is $\{A - [c + \phi(s_1)]\}Ns_1$, and social surplus is the sum of areas C and D. At service level s_2, marginal cost $= c + \phi(s_2)$. In this case, equality of price and marginal cost implies that total output $= \{A - [c + \phi(s_2)]\}Ns_2$, and the social surplus is $D + E$.

negotiations with retailers such as Wal-Mart and Winn Dixie supermarkets over the display and promotion of various issues of these publications.[6]

The relationship between a manufacturer and its retailers should address the upstream manufacturer's interest in the provision of retail services, and the motivation for the retailer to incur the expense of such services. Promotion, product demonstration, and simply providing a pleasant place to shop are costly. Moreover, it is extremely difficult for the manufacturer to monitor the provision of such services. Taken together, these two facts mean that a manufacturer cannot simply specify the level of retail services that it wants for its product and assume that they will be provided. What is required is an enforceable contract that specifies the obligations of both the manufacturer and the retailer. It is this aspect of the vertical contract—that pertaining to the provision of retail services—that we now wish to examine.

Let us begin by describing how demand is affected by retail services. Denote by $D(p, s)$ the amount of the good demanded at price p with retail service level s. Increases in the level of services s raise the quantity demanded at any price or, alternatively, raise the willingness to pay of each consumer. We assume that this effect takes the form shown in Figure 18.1. In this case an increase in the service level from say s_1 to s_2 raises most the willingness to pay of the marginal consumer. An example of a demand curve that captures this effect is $Q(p, s) = s(A - p)N$, where N is the number of consumers in the market. In inverse form this is: $p = A - Q/sN$. The top price anyone is willing to pay for the product is \$$A$, no matter the service level, s, and more is bought as s rises.

Providing retail services is costly. Let the cost of supplying s retail services per unit of the good sold be described by a function $\phi(s)$. We will assume that the provision of retail services is subject to diminishing returns so that raising the service level s raises the cost of providing such services and does so at an ever-increasing rate. [In calculus terms,

---

[6]   G. Knecht, "Big Retail Chains Get Special Advance Looks at Magazine Contents," *Wall Street Journal*, October 22, 1997, p. A1.

this means that both $\phi'(s)$ and $\phi''(s)$ exceed zero.] For a given level of services, s, the retailer's marginal cost of selling the manufacturer's product is $r + \phi(s)$. This is the sum of the wholesale price paid to the manufacturer r plus the cost of providing s retail services per unit sold, $\phi(s)$.

We now consider the provision of retail services under a variety of circumstances. We point out in advance that this presentation is a little advanced. For those who wish to skip this section, our main result is that, in the absence of vertical price restraints, it is unlikely that a retailer will provide the manufacturer's preferred level of service. The intuition behind this argument is straightforward. The manufacturer wants a high level of service because this will raise the price consumers are willing to pay and, hence, the manufacturer's profit. Yet while the profit gain of better service flows at least in part to the manufacturer, the cost of providing such service falls entirely on the retailer. Accordingly, the retailer's incentive to offer such service is reduced. Vertical restrictions such as a resale price maintenance agreement may be a way to overcome this difficulty, at least in part.

18.4.1   Optimal Provision of Retail Services

Let's start by figuring out what is the efficient level of services from the viewpoint of society overall, i.e., the level that would maximize the combined consumer and producer surplus. Recall that efficiency in a market requires that price equal marginal cost. Because marginal cost for a given level of services is constant we have that $p = c + \phi(s)$, which means that there is no producer surplus. As shown in Figure 18.1, the social surplus at any price equal to $c + \phi(s)$ is just the triangular area above the cost line but below the demand curve. Accordingly, the optimal choice of service level s is the level of s that maximizes the area of this triangle. By definition, this area is given by $\{A - [c + \phi(s)]\}^2(Ns)/2$. To find the surplus maximizing value of services, denoted by s^*, we take the derivative of this expression with respect to s, and set it equal to zero. This yields:

$$\{A - [c + \phi(s^*)]\}^2 N/2 - Ns^*\{A - [c + \phi(s^*)]\}\phi'(s^*) = 0. \tag{18.4}$$

In turn, this implies that s^* must satisfy:

$$(A - c)/2 = \phi(s^*)/2 + \phi'(s^*)s^*. \tag{18.5}$$

Suppose for instance that $N = 100$, $c = 5$, $A = 10$, and that $\phi(s) = s^2$. Then a small bit of algebra will reveal that the social optimum calls for a service level of $s^* = 1$. (Remember, s is an index and so it is measured in some arbitrary unit.) At this level of service, optimality would require that the price be equal to $c + \phi(s^*) = \$6$.

Now consider what the outcome would be if the monopolist could operate as a vertically integrated manufacturing and retailing business. Certainly, the price will be higher. The monopolist will not make a profit at a price equal to cost. Yet what about the integrated firm's choice of service level s? How would this compare to the optimum described in equation (18.5)?

The profit of the integrated firm depends upon the price it sets and the service level it provides, and is:

$$\pi(p, s) = p(A - p)Ns - [c + \phi(s)](A - p)Ns \tag{18.6}$$

To maximize profit, the firm must choose both the profit-maximizing price p and the service level s. We take the derivative of the profit function with respect to each of these variables and set it equal to zero yielding:

$$\frac{\partial \pi(p, s)}{\partial p} = (A - 2p)Ns + [c + \phi(s)]Ns = 0 \tag{18.7}$$

and

$$\frac{\partial \pi(p, s)}{\partial s} = p(A - p)N - [c + \phi(s)](A - p)N - Ns\phi'(s)(A - p) = 0 \tag{18.8}$$

Equation (18.7) may be simplified to read:

$$p^I = [A + c + \phi(s)]/2 \tag{18.9}$$

Here, p^I is the firm's optimal price conditional upon a given service level s. Equation (18.9) implies that, as usual, the integrated monopolist will set a price of obtaining a unit of the good along with a given service level that exceeds the marginal cost of providing the good and the associated service cost $c + \phi(s)$. This is shown in Figure 18.2.

The next step is straightforward. Substitute the optimal price value from equation (18.9) into the profit-maximizing service level shown in equation (18.8). Simplification then yields the following necessary condition for the profit-maximizing service level s^I:

$$(A - c)/2 = \phi(s^I)/2 + \phi'(s^I)s^I \tag{18.10}$$

Comparing equations (18.5) and (18.10), it is clear that they are the same. Although the integrated monopoly firm sets too high a price, the service level s^I that it chooses is the same as the socially optimal service level s^*. As it turns out, this specific result reflects the particular demand and cost relationships that we assumed and is not fully general. Nevertheless, the result is useful because it does show that the manufacturer's interest in providing retail services is often in harmony with the public interest as well. As we shall shortly see, this is why vertical price restrictions can play a potentially welfare enhancing role.

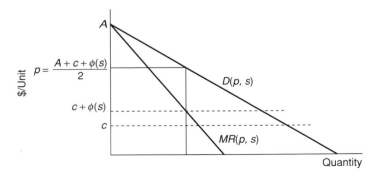

Figure 18.2   The integrated firm's optimal price as a functon of the service level, s

18.4.2 The Case of a Monopoly Retailer and a Monopoly Manufacturer

Let us next examine the case where the retailing of the good is done by an independent monopoly downstream retailer. The manufacturer sells the product to the monopoly retailer at price r, after which the retailer sells the good to final consumers at retail price p^M and provides s^M retail services. Keeping with the values of our earlier example, the retailer's profit downstream is:

$$\Pi^D(p^M, s^M, r) = [p^M - r - \phi(s^M)]D(p^M, s^M) = [p^M - r - \phi(s^M)]s^M N(A - p^M). \quad (18.11)$$

As in the case of the integrated firm, the retailer must choose the two strategic variables, price p and the level of services s. The retailer in this case has exactly the same profit-maximizing problem as did the integrated firm of the previous discussion, except that the retailer faces a marginal cost r that may differ from the true production cost c, depending on the upstream firm's price choice. So, we can work out the monopoly retailer's choices just by replacing c with r in equations (18.6) and (18.10). This yields the choices p^M and s^M satisfying

$$p^M = \frac{A + r + \phi(s^M)}{2} \quad (18.12)$$

and

$$(A - r)/2 = \phi(s^M)/2 + \phi'(s^M)s^M. \quad (18.13)$$

Because $r > c$, the price implied by equation (18.12) exceeds that implied by equation (18.9). This is simply the double-marginalization problem again. At any given service level, the monopoly retailer adds her markup to the markup already reflected in the manufacturer's wholesale price. Yet as a comparison of equations (18.10) and (18.13) also makes clear, having $r > c$ means that this double-markup is now compounded by a further problem, namely, a suboptimally low level of retail services. A careful examination of these two equations reveals that when $r > c$ then the level of retail services chosen by the retailer s^M is less than the level $s*$ that is optimal from the viewpoint of both society and the upstream manufacturer. The intuition behind this outcome is straightforward. Providing retail services is costly and this, along with the fact that the manufacturer charges a wholesale price r above marginal production cost, puts the squeeze on the retailer's profit. In response, the retailer tries to recapture some of her surplus by cutting back on services.

18.2

Assume as in the example in the text that $c = 5$ while $\phi(s) = s^2$, so that $\phi'(s) = 2s$. Assume that the manufacturer sells through a monopoly retailer and initially sets a wholesale price, r equal to $6. Assume that retail demand is $Q(p, s) = s(10 - p)100$.

a. What will be the retail service level and the retail price? How much output will be sold at this price and service level combination? What will be the manufacturer's profit?

b. Would the manufacturer's profit rise or fall if it raised its wholesale price to $7? At this price, how does the profit of the manufacturer selling through the retailer compare with the profit of the integrated manufacturer?

Practice Problem

The failure to coordinate the actions of the manufacturer and the retailer leads to a less than desirable outcome—both for the firms and for consumers. Clearly, the manufacturer will not be happy with this situation. From his perspective, the retail firm is charging too high a price and offering too few retail services. Both of these actions reduce the final consumer demand facing the retailer and the profit to the manufacturer. Coordination of the upstream and downstream operations would result in lower prices and better services, increasing the joint profits of the two firms and making consumers better off. In the absence of vertical integration, what can be done to improve the outcome for both manufacturer and retailer?

As with the double-marginalization problem, we consider two possible solutions. The first is an RPM agreement. The second is a two-part pricing strategy comprised of a fixed franchise fee T and a constant wholesale price r charged to the monopoly retailer.

In general, resale price maintenance will not solve the upstream manufacturer's problem. It is true that under an RPM agreement, the manufacturer can require the retailer to sell the product at the price p^* and thereby solve the double-marginalization problem. However, since there is no franchise fee, the manufacturer will only make a profit by charging a wholesale price r to the retailer that is greater than marginal cost c. Thus, referring to our earlier example, the RPM agreement could set a retail price of \$8, which as you can verify is the integrated firm's choice. In order to make a profit though the manufacturer must set a wholesale price $r > c$, that is, above the \$5 wholesale price charged in the two-part tariff scheme. With the retail price capped at \$8, this means that the retailer now has a smaller margin of price over wholesale cost. Because the contract still leaves the retailer free to choose the level of services s the retailer will react to this profit squeeze by cutting its service provision below s^*. Of course, this is precisely what the manufacturer wishes to avoid.

What happens if the manufacturer adopts a two-part pricing mechanism? To begin with we know that the manufacturer will set r equal to marginal production cost, or $r = c$. Only when r is equal to c is it possible for the retailer's final retail price and level of services to be exactly the same as those chosen by the integrated firm. Accordingly, the manufacturer must set a wholesale price equal to c.

Faced with a wholesale price of $r = c$, however, the retailer is in exactly the same position as our integrated firm was earlier. Hence, it will make the identical choices regarding the price to consumers p^I and the service level s^I. The retailer's profit Π^R prior to paying any franchise fee T will therefore be

$$\Pi^R = [p^I - c - \phi(s^I)]s^I(A - p^I)N \tag{18.14}$$

where p^I and s^I now take on those values that maximize the joint profit of the manufacturer and retailer together, namely, the values described by equations (18.9) and (18.10). Of course, if $r = c$, the manufacturer earns nothing and all profit goes to the retailer. As usual, this is where the franchise fee T comes in. By setting a fee equal to the integrated firm's profit, the manufacturer can capture all that profit for itself. In our earlier example in which $c = \$5$ and demand is $Q = s(10 - p)100$, the manufacturer should set its wholesale price $r = \$5$. The retailer will then find it optimal to set a retail price of \$8 and to provide a service level $s = 1$. This will generate the maximum profit of \$400, which the manufacturer can appropriate by means of a franchise fee T. Of course, if the retailer is truly a monopoly without which the manufacturer cannot bring its good to market, then the retailer is unlikely to agree to such a high franchise fee. Some profit sharing would have to occur. Again, however, the point is that this arrangement can yield the optimal service outcome.

The foregoing argument suggests that franchising agreements are superior to an RPM agreement as a means to achieve the provision of retail services. However, this argument rests critically on our assumption that the downstream retail market is monopolized. As we show below, matters change greatly if there is retail competition.

18.4.3   The Case of Competitive Retailing

Let's now consider the case of a competitive retailing sector. This is often the more realistic case. It is also a market structure that should work to the manufacturer's benefit. When there is only one retailer, the manufacturer's reach into the retail market is limited, as is its bargaining power with respect to claiming any of the additional profit that coordination yields. When there are many retailers, both the manufacturer's reach and bargaining power are enhanced. Competition among the retailers downstream will bring the retail price–cost margin to zero and, therefore, minimize the problem of double-marginalization. The issue of the provision of promotional or retail services though still remains. We want to determine the level of services s^c provided by a competitive retail sector and compare that level with the manufacturer's preferred amount, s^*.

We assume that all the downstream retailers are identical. Each buys the manufacturer's product at a wholesale price r and incurs the cost $\phi(s)$ per unit of output for retail service s. A little thinking leads us to two quick results. First, we know that retail competition will drive the retail price down to marginal cost. In other words, the price to final consumers will have to be $p = r + \phi(s)$. Second, that same competitive pressure will also force every retailer to offer at that price, the level of services most preferred by consumers. Any retailer who offered a lower service level would quickly lose all his customers. Accordingly, competitive pressure will lead each and every retailer to offer the same retail price and the same service package. The competitive retail price will be $p^C = r + \phi(s^C)$, and the competitive service level s^C will be the level that maximizes consumer surplus given the price p^C. In section 18.4.1 we showed that when the price of the good is equal to its true marginal cost, i.e., when $p = c + \phi(s)$, consumer surplus is $\{A - [c + \phi(s)]\}^2 Ns/2$. It follows that when price $p = r + \phi(s)$ consumer surplus is just $\{A - [r + \phi(s)]\}^2 Ns/2$. Maximizing this with respect to s yields the service level under competitive retailing, s^C

$$(A - r)/2 = \phi(s^C)/2 + \phi'(s^C)s^C \tag{18.15}$$

Comparison of the value s^c that satisfies equation (18.15) with the manufacturer's or the efficient level of services [s^* in equation (18.5) or s^I in equation (18.10)] reveals that the competitive outcome will again provide too low a level of services so long as the wholesale price r exceeds the production cost c. Since the manufacturer can only earn a profit if $r > c$, we once again have the problem that from the manufacturer's point of view the retail sector— now organized competitively—will provide too low a level of retail services. As always, the source of the problem is that the profit that results from providing increased service flows to the upstream manufacturer. As a result, each competitive retailer focuses only on the cost of services and ignores the extra profit that they bring to the upstream manufacturer.

Is there a solution to this problem of suboptimal service provision in the case of a competitive retail sector? If there is, it will not be reached by means of the two-part tariff strategy that worked before. The reason for this is straightforward. Competition among retailers drives the price–cost margin to zero. Consequently, there is no profit margin in the retail sector from which the manufacturer can extract the lump sum fee T. The only way that the manufacturer can earn any profit is to set $r > c$. However, unless it takes some additional steps, this will raise retailing costs and thereby create an incentive to cut services further.

The solution is to impose a carefully designed RPM agreement by working backwards from the desired outcomes. The manufacturer wants a retail price equal to the integrated price of p^I. Hence, it should impose an RPM agreement that stipulates p^I at the retail level. The manufacturer also wants a level of services equal to the integrated level of s^I. If the retail price is p^I, then the wholesale price r should be set less than p^I by just enough to cover the cost of providing the desired service level, s^I. In an effort to win consumers, retailers will provide as much service as they can afford given the difference between p^I and r. By setting $p^I - r = \phi(s^I)$, the manufacturer can count on retail competition in services to result in service provision at the desired level s^I. Again, continuing with our numerical example, with $c = \$5$, $A = 10$, and $N = 100$, we have a preferred service level of $s^I = 1$ and an optimal retail price of $p^I = \$8$. The cost of providing this service level $\phi(s) = s^2 = 1$. The manufacturer should impose an RPM agreement with each retailer requiring a retail price of $8 and sell at a wholesale price of $7. This will give retailers exactly $1 of revenue above cost which retailers will then compete away by providing the optimal service level of $s^I = 1$.

18.4.4 Free-riding and the Provision of Retail Services

We have just shown that once there is competition in the retail market, an RPM agreement may become a better arrangement to ensure the provision of retail services than a two-part tariff scheme. There is in fact another reason why this may be the case. It is often difficult for a retailer to obtain a higher price when it provides more services. Services that are provided by one retailer, particularly informational services, such as service demonstrations on the strengths and weaknesses of different brands of digital cameras, can be consumed freely by consumers prior to buying, but then consumers may buy the camera at a different—perhaps discount—store. This creates the potential for a serious free-riding problem in the retail sector.

Think about it for a moment. A consumer electronics shop may keep experts on hand to assist a customer in choosing the digital camera that best meets her needs in terms of portability and convenience, works most effectively with her computer and other peripherals, and fits best within her budget. Similarly, wine shops may employ personnel to advise customers regarding the quality of a particular vintage or the food that best accompanies a given wine.

Providing such presale or point of sale services is costly. Unfortunately, there is no obligation for the consumer, once educated by the store's expert staff, to buy from that specific establishment. Quite to the contrary, once fully informed, the consumer has a strong incentive to go to the "no frills" electronics shop down the street or to the discount wine shop around the corner and purchase what she now knows to be the proper digital camera and the appropriate wine at a lower price. Even worse, she is free to share her information with friends who can then use this knowledge to bypass the specialty shops altogether and go directly to the low-price, low-service outlets.

The problem is that information is a public good and, therefore, hard to deny even to those who do not pay for it. The low-price discount dealers in our two simple examples are "free-riding" on the specialty shops. We call this behavior free-riding because the discounter benefits from the activities of the specialty shop but does not pay for them. The scenarios above indicate the likely outcome of this problem. Specialty shops that incur the cost of providing in-store demonstrations and consultations will lose market share to the "no frills" discount stores.

As such stores come to dominate the retail market, the outcome will be one in which few retail services are provided.

It is important to emphasize that the source of this underprovision of services is, in this setting, somewhat different from the cause of underprovision in our earlier examples. In the analysis of the previous sections, retailers tended to overprice and underservice the products of a monopoly manufacturer because the impact on the manufacturing firm's profit is ignored in setting the retail price and service level. This was true whether the retail sector was monopolized or competitive. In the current case though, we are talking about a problem that is explicitly related to the presence of retail competition. If retailing were monopolized, then no free-riding would be possible because there would be no potential free-riders. While we already had reason to believe that retail services would be undersupplied—at least from the viewpoint of the monopoly manufacturer—the argument just presented implies that this result is all the more likely once we take into account the public good aspect of presale services and the presence of retail competition. To put it another way, the first externality with which we dealt was a vertical one between the downstream and upstream firms. The externality that we now introduce is a horizontal one between the different retail firms.

Yet while the source of the problem is new, the effect from the manufacturer's point of view is the same. When retail competition leads to an undersupply of customer services, the manufacturer suffers because this adversely affects the overall demand for the manufacturer's product and reduces the manufacturer's profit. In the present case, however, we do not need to assume anything specific about demand or cost conditions to obtain the result that the undersupply of services will hurt both the manufacturer and consumers. Competitive markets generally do undersupply goods with beneficial externalities, such as the retail services described above. Accordingly, if the resultant losses are sufficiently severe, the extension of monopoly power by means of some sort of vertical restraint may be in the public interest. One such possible restraint is an RPM agreement.

At this point, the advantage of an RPM agreement should be clear. It prevents one retailer from undercutting another and, hence, stifles the emergence of discount stores. In turn, this implies that consumers will visit the retailer who provides the best services since they will not find a lower price elsewhere. By putting a freeze on price discounting, the effect of an RPM agreement is to foreclose discount outlets, resulting in a possibly higher average retail price. Yet this price effect and the loss it imposes on consumers may be offset by the gains that the provision of retail services generate, not only for consumers but for the manufacturer as well.

The view that RPM contracts enhance efficiency by restoring incentives to provide valued retail services, first articulated by Telser (1960), is associated with the Chicago School economists who strongly advocate the efficiency-enhancing role of vertical relationships among firms.[7] The free-riding argument, which endorses the efficiency effect of resale price maintenance, is more or less limited to presale services, such as advertising or instructional demonstrations. Other services, such as warranty service, can easily be provided and, more importantly, charged for by any retailer. In fact, Telser's argument was frequently criticized[8] because it was applied to many goods for which presale informational services play a limited role. In the case of fashion apparel, for example, consumers can go to the store and examine clothes for style and appropriate fit for themselves with little assistance from store personnel.

[7] See also Bork (1966). For a somewhat different view, see Mathewson and Winter (1983 and 1998).
[8] See, e.g., Steiner (1985).

Yet even in these cases, the Chicago School has a rejoinder. The free-riding justification for RPM might still be valid in this alternative setting because such stores play a screening or certification role. One of the services provided by top stores such as Bloomingdales, Neiman-Marcus, and Bergdorf Goodman is to identify and then sell "what's hot" or in fashion. Here again, providing this service is not cheap. Prestigious retail stores must spend considerable resources to build up their reputation for being on the "cutting edge" of fashion trends. When the store carries a manufacturer's fashion line, the store's reputations stands behind the quality or fashionability of the garment. Proponents of RPM agreements argue that if a consumer can go window shopping at a prestigious store to find out "what's in" this season and then buy the apparel at a discount store, we again have the problem of free-riding. The discount store free-rides on the market research and quality certification of the prestigious store. This problem could become sufficiently severe that, absent RPM protection, no store would find it worthwhile to screen and identify the fashionability and quality of products.[9]

18.5   RETAIL PRICE MAINTENANCE AND UNCERTAIN DEMAND

We have been discussing in the preceding two sections the way in which competitive pressures in the retail market can reduce the profit of the manufacturer and the welfare of consumers by creating disincentives to provide customer services. However, retail competition can be destructive in other ways as well. Consider the case of Nintendo, one of the dominant players in the video games market. When Nintendo first introduced its video game players and cartridges in the late 1980s, it faced one very serious obstacle. This was the recent history of the video game market. Led by Atari, that market grew from $200 million in 1978 to over $3 billion in 1982. However, the market then crashed even more rapidly, with sales falling to just $100 million in 1983. In that year, retailers found themselves with greatly excessive inventories and cut prices drastically in order to liquidate this stock. Atari itself went bankrupt.

The boom-and-bust cycle of the video game market in the early 1980s, and especially the sizable losses incurred in 1983, made retailing firms highly skeptical about the prospects for any new video game product. Nintendo representatives found that department and toy stores were almost totally unwilling to talk to them about their product. Nobody wanted to buy Nintendo's games and risk getting caught with an inventory that could only be sold at distressed prices as in the previous video game cycle. Eventually, of course, Nintendo prevailed. Along with Sony and Microsoft it is a dominant player in the video game market, earning a generous profit as a result. However, that victory was not guaranteed. Nintendo's product—so obviously valued by consumers—might never have survived had it not been for Nintendo's pricing strategy.

The Nintendo story was used by Deneckere, Marvel, and Peck (1997) to offer another explanation for RPM agreements when retailing is competitive. Their argument is based on

---

[9]   Matthewson and Winter (1983) make a similar argument that resale price maintenance can benefit consumers by economizing on consumer search costs since consumers will no longer spend time trying to find out which retailer sells at the lowest price. This argument assumes, however, that no other means is available to inform consumers about retail prices.

the simple fact that retail demand for any product is uncertain. Like many of the examples of vertical restrictions offered earlier, this case also raises the possibility that both producers and consumers will benefit from the imposition of an RPM agreement.[10]

When demand is uncertain, a retailer faces a dilemma in determining how much output to stock for sale to final consumers. On the one hand, the retailer will wish to have the amount on hand necessary for profit maximization during periods when demand is strong. On the other hand, if demand is weak, retailers with a lot of stock will have to do one of two things. Either they must throw away the extra output to keep the price high, or they can sell the extra output, thereby lowering the price and perhaps even driving it to zero.[11]

It is in this situation that the behavior of the monopolist and the competitive firm will differ. Faced with weak demand, the monopolist will tend to throw away a good bit of its excess inventory because the monopolist recognizes that every extra unit sold lowers the price on all units. A firm in a competitive retail sector, however, will do the opposite. Under competition, each retailer perceives that its own sales have no or little effect on the market price. Accordingly, each such competitive retailer will try to sell all of its stock. After all, it has already paid for it and it may as well try to get something for it rather than throw any of it away. The problem is that if all retailers act this way the market the price will fall, possibly quite far.

The fact that competition induces sharp price-cutting during periods of weak demand has two implications. First, a manufacturer selling through a competitive retail sector will not earn the profit of an integrated firm. Second, as Nintendo discovered, the manufacturer will also find it difficult to induce retailers to hold any sizable inventory. An RPM agreement that establishes a minimum retail price can solve the manufacturer's problem. The reason is straightforward. Setting a minimum price at which the good can be sold ensures that in periods of low demand, retailers will deal with excess inventory exactly the way that an integrated manufacturer would choose. They will throw away the amount that cannot be sold at the specified retail price.

We illustrate the essential insight of the Deneckere, Marvel, and Peck argument in Figure 18.3. The figure shows the price and profit outcome for an integrated monopolist manufacturer facing variable demand. As usual, we assume a constant unit cost, c. With

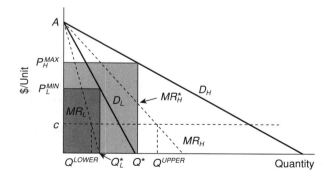

Figure 18.3   Resale price maintenance and variable demand

[10]   See also Marvel and McCafferty (1984).
[11]   We assume that inventories cannot be stored. Either they physically perish or become worthless due to introduction of new goods.

probability one-half, demand is strong and the demand curve is D_H. Similarly, with probability one-half, demand is weak and the demand curve is D_L. The integrated monopolist then faces a two-stage problem. In stage one, the firm must choose how much to produce, Q. Once the firm has produced this amount, it will have incurred a cost, which is now sunk, equal to cQ. Afterwards, demand will be either strong or weak, D_H or D_L. At that point, the firm will have no additional cost and will simply have to choose how much of the output in its inventory that it actually wants to sell. Of course, the integrated firm can sell no more than it originally produced, Q. Subject to this constraint, however, it will simply sell the amount that maximizes its revenue conditional upon demand. Since all its costs are sunk, revenue maximization and profit maximization amount to the same thing in the second stage.

The integrated firm will never initially produce more than the amount that would maximize profit if it knew for sure that demand would be high. This is an amount at which the marginal revenue when demand is D_H equals marginal production cost, c. It is shown as Q^{UPPER} in Figure 18.3. To produce more than this level would guarantee that the firm earns a marginal revenue below its production cost even in the best of demand conditions. Similarly, the firm will never produce for inventory an amount less than Q^{LOWER}, the amount it would produce if it were certain demand would be low. To do so would guarantee too little inventory even in the weakest of markets. The firm must produce somewhere between Q^{LOWER} and Q^{UPPER}. Within this interval, optimization requires that it choose an amount whereby its marginal cost c equals its expected marginal revenue, or one-half times the marginal revenue in a high-demand state plus one-half times the marginal revenue in a low-demand state.

As we have drawn Figure 18.3, the optimal amount of initial production is Q^*. Note that in this figure, demand is quite variable. As a result, in order to come even close to the true profit-maximizing level in a high-demand state, the amount produced for inventory Q^* would be enough to drive the price to zero if it is all sold in a weak-demand state.

If demand is strong, the firm will sell the entire amount Q^* at the price P_H^{MAX}. If demand is weak, an inventory of Q^* is excessive. Since the integrated firm has already incurred its production cost, all it can do then is maximize its revenue. It will do this by selling the amount Q_L^* at the price, P_L^{MIN}. This is an output at which marginal revenue is zero. Weak demand does not lead the firm to try to liquidate its entire inventory, as such an action would drive the price to zero. Instead, the firm throws away the amount $Q^* - Q_L^*$. When demand is weak, the firm drives its marginal revenue to zero. However, because this occurs where the price is still positive, the firm's total revenue remains greater than zero even in the face of weak demand. Its marginal revenue when demand is strong is the marginal revenue at Q^*, shown here as MR_H^*. Its expected marginal revenue is therefore $MR_H^*/2$ which is an amount just equal to c.

The integrated monopolist firm will expect to earn a positive profit in this story. Its total cost is cQ. Its revenue in a low-demand period is $P_L^{MIN}Q_L^*$. This is the lightly shaded rectangle in Figure 18.3. Its revenue in a high-demand period is $P_H^{MAX}Q^*$. This is the sum of the lightly shaded rectangle and the darkly shaded region in the figure. The expected profit for the integrated firm, Π_I^e is therefore

$$\Pi_I^e = \frac{1}{2} P_H^{MAX} Q^* + \frac{1}{2} P_L^{MIN} Q_L^* - cQ^*. \tag{18.16}$$

Now consider what happens under competitive retailing. If competitive retailers stocked the optimal amount Q^*, they would earn less total profit than that shown in equation (18.16).

The reason is the nature of competition. In a low-demand period, the integrated firm sells only up to the point where its marginal revenue is zero. However, competitive firms holding a total inventory of $Q*$ will sell more than this amount. Each such firm perceives price and marginal revenue to be the same. Hence, having already sunk the cost of acquiring its inventory, each such firm will continue to sell its inventory so long as the price is positive. Yet if demand is weak, the amount $Q*$ can only be sold by driving the retail price—and not just the marginal revenue—to zero. This means that a competitive retail sector with an inventory equal to $Q*$ will earn no revenue when demand is low. Of course, when demand is high, retailers will sell the entire stock $Q*$ for the price P_H^{MAX} and generate exactly the same revenue as would an integrated monopolist. However, because the competitive outcome during a low-demand period is a zero price, competitive retailers will always generate less total profit from the optimal inventory stock, $Q*$, than would an integrated monopolist whose revenue remains positive even when demand is weak.

In short, unfettered competition during a period of weak demand dramatically reduces the revenue retailers can expect to earn. Accordingly, a manufacturer can only persuade retailers to stock the optimal amount $Q*$ by selling to them at a sufficiently low wholesale price P_W, so that retailers can still expect to break even. Since retailers only earn positive revenue when demand is high, $P_W Q*$ must equal the revenue earned by retailers in a high-demand period, times the probability that such a period occurs. Therefore, $P_W Q*$ must equal $P_H^{MAX} Q*/2$, implying that $P_W = P_H^{MAX}/2$. In turn, this implies an expected profit, Π^e, for the manufacturer without an RPM agreement of

$$\Pi^e = \left(\frac{1}{2} P_H^{MAX} - c\right) Q*. \tag{18.17}$$

A comparison of equations (18.16) and (18.17) shows that the profit of the manufacturer in this case will be less than that earned by its integrated counterpart by an amount equal to $P_L^{MIN} Q_L^*/2$. However, an RPM agreement can save the day. The necessary features of such an agreement are suggested by Figure 18.3. That figure shows that the integrated firm never sells at a price below P_L^{MIN}. So, the nonintegrated manufacturer should negotiate an RPM agreement that likewise prohibits anyone from selling below this price. In addition, it should charge a wholesale price P_W^*, satisfying

$$P_W^* Q* = \frac{1}{2} P_H^{MAX} Q* + \frac{1}{2} P_L^{MIN} Q_L^*. \tag{18.18}$$

In turn, this implies that

$$P_W^* = \frac{1}{2} P_H^{MAX} + \frac{1}{2} P_L^{MIN} \frac{Q_L^*}{Q*}. \tag{18.19}$$

At this wholesale price, the competitive retail sector will in fact buy and inventory the optimal amount, $Q*$. Why? When they buy this amount, retailers know that their expected revenue, $P_H^{MAX} Q*/2 + P_L^{MIN} Q_L^*/2$, just equals their expected cost, $P_W^* Q*$. Hence, the inventory of $Q*$ is exactly the amount that leads to an expected profit of zero for retailers. This of course is the equilibrium requirement for a competitive retail sector. Moreover, since retailers buy the amount Q^* at this wholesale price, the manufacturer's expected profit, Π_{RPM}^e, with an RPM is

$$\Pi_{RPM}^e = P_W Q^* - cQ = \frac{1}{2} P_H^{MAX} Q^* + \frac{1}{2} P_L^{MIN} Q_L^* - cQ^* \qquad (18.20)$$

A comparison of equations (18.16) and (18.20) quickly reveals that this RPM agreement permits the manufacturer in this case to earn the same profit as that earned by an integrated firm.

Something like an RPM arrangement seems to have been the source of Nintendo's ultimate victory. It closely monitored inventories and cut off dealers who sold below Nintendo's suggested retail prices. Nintendo was forced in 1991 to sign a consent decree with the FTC under which it promised not to engage in any further implicit RPM behavior. By that time, however, Nintendo was well established in the video games market.

As the Nintendo example is meant to illustrate, it is not just the manufacturer who may benefit from the RPM agreement just described. Absent an RPM agreement, retailers may not be willing to offer the product to consumers at all. More formally, such an agreement can benefit consumers in the sense that it leads to a bigger expected consumer surplus. The intuition behind this result is that, depending on the nature of demand fluctuations, the equilibrium without an RPM agreement will result in retailers buying less than the amount they would purchase for inventory with such an agreement. As a result, the price during a period of strong demand will be higher without an RPM contract than it would be with one. This price increase hurts consumers and may more than offset the gains consumers enjoy from permitting prices to fall quite far when demand is weak. Hence, under uncertain demand in a competitive retail sector both the manufacturer and consumers can benefit from an RPM agreement.[12]

18.3

Practice Problem

Suppose that demand is either strong (with probability one-half) and described by $Q = (10 - p)100$, or weak (with probability one-half) and described by $Q = (10 - p)30$. To simplify further, assume that the manufacturer's unit cost is constant at $c = 0$.

a.   Show that the revenue-maximizing price is $5 regardless of whether demand is weak or strong.

b.   Assume that the firm produces 500 units prior to learning the strength of demand. How much of this will it sell when demand is strong? How much will it sell when demand is weak? What is the firm's expected profit?

c.   Suppose now that the firm sells the 500 units through a competitive retail sector. If retailers buy and stock the entire 500 units, what will be the retail price when demand is strong? What will be the retail price when demand is weak?

d.   In light of your answer to c, what wholesale price will induce the retailers to purchase initially an inventory of 500? What will be the manufacturer's profit at this price?

---

[12]   The manufacturer always gains from the specified RPM agreement. The outcome for consumers depends on just how variable is demand. If demand is highly variable, consumers are probably hurt by the agreement. However, if demand is only moderately variable, consumers may well benefit from the agreement.

Summary

Consumers buy most of their products from retailers such as department stores, supermarkets, automobile dealers, and gasoline stations. In these and many other cases, the retailer from which the consumer buys is not the firm that originally made the product. The manufacturer lies further upstream in the chain of production.

Because a manufacturer relies on retailers to get his goods to the market, the manufacturer must hope that the retailers will share his views about the appropriate price to consumers and the proper amount of promotional and other services to provide. Unfortunately, this is rarely the case. Double-marginalization and other problems lead to a divergence of interests between the manufacturer and the retailer. However, contractual agreements governing this vertical relationship can resolve some of these differences. Yet such agreements can also facilitate price collusion either among manufacturers or retailers. As a result, public policy regarding vertical restraints is complicated.

In this chapter we have focused on one particular type of vertical restraint—a resale price maintenance or RPM agreement. Such agreements may specify a maximum price above which a retailer may not charge, or a minimum price that the retailer cannot discount. For many years, RPM agreements were considered anticompetitive and treated as *per se* illegal. However, starting as early as 1919, the courts have chipped away at this strict view so that now RPM agreements and behavior that closely duplicates such a contract even when the contract itself does not formally specify a retail price, are subject to a more flexible rule of reason. This is particularly the case regarding those RPM agreements that stipulate a maximum retail price.

The reason that the courts have moved to a more lenient attitude toward RPM agreements is straightforward. Increasingly, economists and policy makers have understood that without such agreements, problems such as double-marginalization, ensuring the provision of services to consumers, and dealing with demand uncertainty, work against consumer as well as producer interests. This is not to say that the concern that vertical price restraints may be anticompetitive is unwarranted. The historical record is clear that the vast majority of support for RPM agreements has come from retailers. The fact that it has also been these same retailers who have supported legislation such as the Miller–Tydings and McGuire Acts suggests that retailers see RPM agreements, at least in part, as a means of suppressing competition that would otherwise emerge in the absence of legislative efforts. However, economic analysis makes it equally clear that the potential benefits of RPM restraints—for consumers as well as producers—are substantial. Viewed in this light, it would seem that a rule of reason approach rather than a *per se* illegal standard makes sense.

Problems

1. Suppose that a car dealer has a local monopoly in selling Volvos. It pays w to Volvo for each car that it sells, and charges each customer p. The demand curve that the dealer faces is best described by the linear function $Q = 30 - p$, where the price is in units of thousands of dollars.

   a. What is the profit-maximizing price for the dealer to set? At this price, how many Volvos will the dealer sell and what will the dealer's profit from selling the cars be?

   b. Now let us think about how the situation looks from the car manufacturer's point of view. If Volvo charges w per car to its dealer, calculate how many cars the dealer will buy from Volvo. In other words, what is the demand curve facing Volvo? Suppose that it costs Volvo $5,000 to produce each car. What is the profit-maximizing choice of w? What will Volvo's profits be? What price p will the dealer set and what profit will the dealer earn at Volvo's profit-maximizing choice of wholesale price w?

2. Now suppose in problem #1 Volvo operates the dealership and sells directly to its customers. What will be Volvo's profit-maximizing price p? What will Volvo's profit be? Compare your answer here to the answer you worked out in 1(b). Give an intuitive explanation for why the answers differ.

3. ABC, Inc. is a monopolist selling to competitive retailers. It faces a constant marginal cost of 10. Demand at the retail level is described by $P = 50 - Q$.

    a. What wholesale price will maximize ABC's profit? What retail price will this imply?

    b. What will be the value of consumer surplus if ABC sets a profit-maximizing wholesale price?

    c. What will be the value of ABC's maximum profit?

4. ABC is still a monopolist selling to competitive retailers but it now discovers that if retailers supply customer services, demand shifts to: $P = 90 - Q$. Each retailer can provide the required services at a total cost of $400.

    a. ABC decides now to implement an RPM agreement with retailers. Under this agreement, what retail price should ABC specify? How many units will retailers sell at this price?

    b. What is consumer surplus under the RPM agreement?

5. Under the RPM agreement and the price specified in 4(a), what is the maximum wholesale price that ABC can set? What will its profit at this wholesale price be? Did adoption of the RPM agreement improve social welfare?

6. A significant number of the resale price maintenance cases that have been the subject of antitrust policy involve the pricing of such simple consumer products as Russell Stover candy, Levi jeans, Arrow shirts, and Colgate toiletries. Who has the incentive for resale price maintenance for these products? Explain why.

7. In the antitrust case *Albrecht v. Herald Co.*, the successive monopoly problem was created by the publisher granting an exclusive territory to the distributor. Could the problem have been solved by opening up home delivery to competition among several distributors?

References

Bork, Robert. 1966. "The Rule of Reason and the Per Se Concept: Price Fixing and Market Division." *Yale Law Journal* 75 (January): 399–441.

Chen, Yongmin. 1999. "Oligopoly Price Discrimination and Resale Price Maintenance." *Rand Journal of Economics* 30: 441–55.

Deneckere, R., H. P. Marvel, and J. Peck. 1997. "Demand Uncertainty and Price Maintenance: Markdowns as Destructive Competition." *American Economic Review* 87 (September): 619–41.

Lafontaine, Francine. 1992. "Agency Theory and Franchising: Some Empirical Results." *Rand Journal of Economics* 23 (Summer): 263–83.

——. 1993. "Contractual Arrangements as Signaling Devices: Evidence from Franchising." *Journal of Law, Economics, and Organization* 9 (October): 256–89.

——. 1995. "Pricing Decisions in Franchised Chains: A Look at the Restaurant and Fast-food Industry." Mimeo, University of Michigan, April.

Marvel, H. and S. McCafferty. 1984. "Resale Price Maintenance and Quality Certification." *Rand Journal of Economics* 15 (Autumn): 346–59.

Mathewson, G. F. and R. A. Winter. 1983. "The Incentives for Resale Price Maintenance under Imperfect Information." *Economic Inquiry* 62 (June): 337–48.

——. 1998. "The Law and Economics of Resale Price Maintenance." *Review of Industrial Economics* 13 (April): 57–84.

O'Brien, D. P. and G. Schaffer. 1994. "The Welfare Effects of Forbidding Discriminatory Discounts: A Secondary Line Analysis of Robinson-Patman." *Journal of Law, Economics, and Organization* 10 (October): 296–318.

Overstreet, T. 1983. *Resale Price Maintenance: Economic Theories and Empirical Evidence.* Washington, DC: Federal Trade Commission Bureau of Economics Staff Report, November.

Pickering, J. F. 1966. *Resale Price Maintenance in Practice.* New York: August M. Kelley.

Steiner, Robert L. 1985. "The Nature of Vertical Restraints." *Antitrust Bulletin* (Spring): 143–97.

Telser, L. 1960. "Why Should Manufacturers Want Free Trade?" *Journal of Law and Economics* 3 (October): 86–105.

Appendix

Manufacturer's Optimal Wholesale Price When Retailer Discriminates between Two Markets

In this appendix, we derive the optimal wholesale price r and fixed fee T that a manufacturer should select to maximize total profit when the retailer sells in two identical markets, one of which is a monopoly but the other of which is constrained by potential entry to sell at a price equal to the wholesale price.

Demand in each market is given by: $P = A - BQ$. Manufacturing cost is c. No cost is incurred in retailing. In the monopolized market, profit maximization by the retailer will lead to an output of:

$$Q_M = \frac{A - r}{2B} \tag{18.A1}$$

and a price of

$$P_M = \frac{A + r}{2} \tag{18.A2}$$

The retailer's profit Π_M^R in this market will therefore be:

$$\Pi_M^R = \frac{(A - r)^2}{4B} \tag{18.A3}$$

Absent any franchise fee T, the manufacturer's profit Π_M^M derived from sales in the retailer's monopoly market will be:

$$\Pi_M^M = \frac{(r - c)(A - r)}{2B} \tag{18.A4}$$

In the entry-constrained market, the price to consumers will be r and the retailer will earn no profit. Output will be given by:

$$Q_C = \frac{A - r}{B} \tag{18.A5}$$

The manufacturer's profit Π_C^M from the retailer's sales in this competitive market will therefore be:

$$\Pi_C^M = \frac{(r - c)(A - r)}{B} \tag{18.A6}$$

For a given r at which the retailer buys goods to be sold in both its markets, total profit to the manufacturer and retailer combined is:

$$\Pi = \Pi_C^M + \Pi_M^M + \frac{(A - r)^2}{4B} = \frac{(r - c)(A - r)}{B} + \frac{(r - c)(A - r)}{2B} + \frac{(A - r)^2}{4B} \qquad (18.A7)$$

Maximizing this with respect to r yields the following necessary condition:

$$r = \frac{4A + 6c}{10} \qquad (18.A8)$$

With $A = 100$ and $c = 12$, this yields the value of $r = \$47.20$ reported in the text.

19

Nonprice Vertical Restraints

Bake sales, book fairs, and other events are commonly used as fundraising devices at hundreds of elementary and secondary schools throughout North America. The event organizers typically offer beverages at these events, sometimes giving drinks away for free. Yet these well-intentioned citizens may very well be breaching a contract. This is because many schools have exclusive sales agreements with a soft drink company. Under such a contract, the beverages of only one soft drink firm, e.g., Coca-Cola or Pepsi, may be sold by anyone on the school's premises. Most contracts specify that only milk and (at most) a few juices are allowed to be sold at school at all. Other restrictions are also common. The drinks of the permitted company are usually not to be offered at a discount price, let alone for free. School personnel are often required to keep the vending machines stocked, and so on.

Requiring the school to sell no other soft drink is known as an exclusive dealing requirement. Such contracts are common not just between soft drink makers and schools, but also between manufacturers of many products and their dealers. Lafontaine and Slade (2007) estimate that some such sort of exclusive dealing covers one-third of sales by independent retailers in the U.S. Other non-price vertical restraints such as exclusive territories are also common. For the most part these restraints create many of the same issues raised by the vertical price restrictions studied in the previous chapter. They have an obvious potential for weakening competition, yet they can also be useful arrangements that benefit both manufacturers and consumers.

19.1 UPSTREAM COMPETITION AND EXCLUSIVE DEALING

As the soft drink and school example above illustrates, exclusive dealing is a contractual agreement that restricts the behavior of the dealer. Essentially, the dealer is not allowed to buy (and then resell) brands that may compete with that of the manufacturer's. Justifications for exclusive dealing agreements are typically based on the presence of conflicting interests between the manufacturer and the dealer. Unless some vertical restrictions can be imposed, such conflicts may lead to outcomes that hurt consumers as well as manufacturers.

To understand this concern, we should first recognize that manufacturers often expend considerable resources promoting their products. Household products companies such as Procter

& Gamble, cosmetic manufacturers such as Revlon, and appliance firms such as Whirlpool/ Maytag, are just some of the many manufacturers that extensively advertise their products. Such advertisements may well increase demand for the manufacturer's brand. They may also increase demand for the product category in general.

Consider, for example, advertisements for Tylenol, the well-known non-aspirin pain reliever. Undoubtedly, such advertising helps raise the consuming public's awareness of both Tylenol, in particular, and of the benefits of non-aspirin pain relievers in general. Such advertising is expensive. To recover the cost of the advertising, Johnson & Johnson, Tylenol's manufacturer will have to raise Tylenol's price. We can easily imagine the following transaction between a pharmacy owner and a customer searching for Tylenol. When asked why she wants Tylenol, the consumer will say because she needs non-aspirin medication for pain and fever. The pharmacist may say that Tylenol will work fine but that he also can offer a lower-cost, unadvertised brand that is the chemical equivalent of Tylenol. The price of this alternative may not be a lot below the Tylenol price—just enough to persuade the customer to switch to this brand.

It is precisely because the pharmacist can sell the alternative non-aspirin pain reliever at a price relatively close to the price of Tylenol that the pharmacist has an incentive to inform the consumer of the alternative. From the perspective of Tylenol, however, the pharmacist is free-riding on Tylenol's advertising. Tylenol now makes no sale even though it was the Tylenol advertising that may have induced the customer to ask for a non-aspirin pain reliever in the first place.

An exclusive dealing agreement offers a solution to this problem because it permits the manufacturer to prevent the retailers of its product from making such substitutions.[1] This is particularly important in the case of goods in which the retailer plays a role something similar to that of a doctor whose recommendation acts like an informal guarantee of the product's quality. Many intermediate goods sold between firms, e.g., chemical products, may have this feature. At the retail consumer level, automobile dealers are among retailers who may serve this function.

From an antitrust perspective, however, exclusive dealing can also be a means of suppressing competition. We showed in section 13.3.1 Chapter 13 one way that this can happen. There we discussed the Rasmussen, Ramseyer, and Wiley (1991) model illustrating how exclusive dealing requirements can prevent entry when there are important scale economies in upstream production.[2] However, entry prevention is not the only way that exclusive dealing can limit competition. Such contracts can also be used to limit competition between existing manufacturers. By excluding a rival's product, the remaining manufacturer can enjoy more monopoly power.

The manufacturer will have to share the profit from that power with the retailer. In order to get the exclusive contract in the first place, a manufacturer will have to offer the retailer as much profit as its rival can offer. As Mathewson and Winter (1987) show, this consideration can greatly complicate the analysis of exclusive dealing. In particular, the manufacturer that gets the exclusive contract may only do so by offering to sell to the retailer at a very low wholesale price. In turn, this low wholesale price will translate into a low retail price. One issue is whether the fall in the retail price is sufficient to compensate consumers

---

[1]   Marvel (1982) is among those who have stressed this argument.

[2]   Strictly speaking, the long-term contract model of Aghion and Bolton (1987) is not an exclusive dealing contract though, practically speaking, it may have the same effect.

for the loss of the alternative product. In principle welfare could improve despite the fact that the exclusive deal eliminates one product line from the market.[3]

Exclusive dealing can serve to limit competition among retailers and manufactures, simultaneously. For example, suppose that there are two manufacturers selling to two retailers who are spatially separated but still operate within a given territory. Without any exclusive dealing, each retailer may offer both products. As a result, price competition between the two products or interbrand competition, will be quite fierce at each retail location. However, if each manufacturer signs one of the retailers to sell its product by means of an exclusive contract, then interbrand competition can be softened. Effectively, the exclusive dealing injects an element of spatial differentiation between the two goods that did not previously exist.[4]

19.2   EXCLUSIVE SELLING AND TERRITORIAL ARRANGEMENTS

We now turn to a different aspect of exclusive selling that relates to territorial restrictions. These cases differ from our soft drink and school example in two important respects. Whereas the restrictions in that example were aimed at limiting *interbrand* competition between rival soft drink companies, exclusive selling and territorial arrangements are aimed at limiting *intrabrand* competition between downstream dealers. In this case the manufacturer agrees not to sell his product to any other retailer in a defined geographical area. For example, under an exclusive selling agreement, Toyota may sign a contract with a Lexus dealership that prevents Toyota from selling Lexus automobiles to any other Lexus dealership within a certain radius. Similarly, in an exclusive territorial arrangement, Toyota may sign agreements with a number of Lexus dealers that require each dealer to agree that it will not open a new outlet in any region where one of the other dealers already operates. To some extent then, the territorial restraints have a more obvious horizontal element. They can be more easily interpreted as an agreement among dealers not to compete, i.e., an agreement to limit intrabrand competition.

We know that retail competition can help manufacturers in so far as it reduces or even eliminates the double-marginalization problem. We may well wonder then why a manufacturer would ever sign a contract that limits such retail competition. However, the rationale behind such restrictions is relatively intuitive.

Consider a simple case of a single manufacturer that sells to two, downstream retailers. In addition, we assume, not unreasonably that while the manufactured product is the same, the retailers are differentiated at least by location if by no other attribute. In other words, consumers do not view the purchase of the good at each retailer as perfect substitutes so that retail competition is not perfect.

In this context, two externalities emerge. The first of these is a pricing externality. If one retailer lowers its price, it will attract consumers and thereby reduce the profit of the other

---

[3]   The foreclosure argument has been a recurrent topic in industrial organization. Bernheim and Whinston (1990) show that when there are two brands produced by two upstream firms and a single retailer, there are no incentives to adopt exclusive dealing. The retailer will always be a common dealer of both products. In the case of several retailers, O'Brien and Schaffer (1994) and Besanko and Perry (1994) find that exclusive dealing is always adopted. However, in the last two models, foreclosure is explicitly ruled out as an option.

[4]   See Besanko and Perry (1994) for a model along these lines.

retailer. However, in deciding whether or not to lower its price, the retailer will consider only the impact of that decision on her own profit—not on the profit of its rival. Because each retailer fails to account for the impact that her pricing decisions have on her rival's profit, each tends to set its price too low or below the level that would maximize industry profit. This not only reduces retail profit but also lowers the profit that the manufacturer may claim through any two-part tariff or profit-sharing contract.

The second externality that plagues intrabrand competition is the service externality that we encountered in the last chapter. If one retailer incurs the expense of advertising or providing informational services, it benefits the other retailer as well. For example, if one Lexus dealer runs Lexus commercials on local TV, it potentially raises the demand for all Lexus dealers in the area. Similarly, if one camera store provides information to customers on how to get the best pictures with a Canon digital camera, those customers may then make their final camera purchase from a low-price retailer who does not offer such services. In short, there is a temptation for each retailer of a specific brand to free-ride on the services provided by other sellers of that brand. As a result, the level of such services will very likely be too low. Moreover, because consumers value such services, this externality not only reduces the profit available to the manufacturer and the retailer, but reduces consumer surplus, as well.[5]

It should be clear how exclusive selling and territorial agreements may remedy the foregoing externality problems. Effectively such contracts limit the number of sellers of the manufacturer's good to just one within any given region. As a result each retailer reaps all the benefits of any price and service decisions that it makes. There is no externality because there is no retailer external to the one in question. Hence, exclusive selling and territorial restrictions can serve to raise both the price and the service level associated with the manufacturer's good. This will definitely increase the profit available to the manufacturer and dealer jointly. The impact on consumers though is ambiguous. The reduction in intrabrand competition and resultant price increase lowers consumer welfare. The increase in the service level, however, benefits consumers.

Exclusive selling and territorial arrangements have two other potentially important effects in addition to those just described. Because these contracts result in a single dealer being the only seller of a specific product in its area, the dealer's willingness to dump its merchandise on the market when demand is weak is reduced. This effect can be important in getting dealers to stock an appropriate amount of the manufacturer's good in the first place.[6] The other effect is that an exclusive selling or territorial agreement creates in each region a monopoly upstream supplier selling to a monopoly downstream retailer. This makes the use of a two-part tariff or franchise fee attractive as a tool to prevent the double-marginalization and low service problems. Viewed in this light, it should not be surprising that we usually observe exclusive territories and franchise fees in the same contract.[7]

So far we have only considered exclusive selling and territorial arrangements in the context of a single manufacturer. When there is more than one upstream manufacturer, these contracts can be used to reduce interbrand competition—to the detriment of consumers. Suppose that there are two upstream manufacturers producing products that are imperfect substitutes.

[5]   This case differs from those considered in section 18.4.3 in Chapter 18 where downstream competition helped solve the double-marginalization problem. Here, the retailers are differentiated and so therefore are their products. The prices of such retailers are strategic complements and coordination of their price-setting can raise the profit of each firm.

[6]   See section 18.5 Chapter 18 for an analysis of uncertain demand and its suboptimal effect.

[7]   See section 18.4.2 and Lafontaine (1993).

Imagine as well that the two manufacturers sell to a competitive retail sector. If the two manufacturers have identical costs and symmetric demand, then they will set the same wholesale price w^C, which will also be the retail price because competition eliminates any retail markup. Hence, all downstream retailers will earn zero profit. More importantly, this means that every increase in the wholesale price will be one-for-one translated into an equivalent increase in the retail price.

Now, following Rey and Stiglitz (1995) let us imagine that the market for these products can be divided into regions or territories. Suppose further that each manufacturer grants an exclusive territory to a retailer in each territory giving that retailer the exclusive right to sell its product in that region. As a result, within any given territory each manufacturer's product will be sold by a retail monopoly. We know that selling to a monopoly retailer will give rise to the double-marginalization problem. Why then should the two manufacturers decide to do this? The answer, in part, is that it softens the intensity of the competition between the two brands. It does so because it weakens the link between the wholesale price and the retail price. From the perspective of each retailer, the wholesale price is a cost. Suppose then that one of the manufacturers raises its wholesale price. For the dealer selling this product, costs have risen. The dealer will want to pass on this increase by means of a higher retail price. Competition with the other retailer will limit how much the dealer can do this. However, now under exclusive territories prices are strategic complements. As the rival retailer sees the first dealer's price rising, the rival retailer will see an opportunity to raise price without losing customers even though its wholesale cost has not risen. Thus, when a manufacturer raises its wholesale price it will no longer lose as many customers as it did when there was competition without exclusive territories. Even though the rival manufacturer does not raise its wholesale price, the rival retailer does raise the retail price.

Of course, both manufacturers realize the foregoing logic. By each granting an exclusive territory, they weaken retail competition, which feeds back to weaker wholesale competition. As a result, the granting of exclusive territories will lead to higher prices at both the retail and the wholesale level. Whether the agreement will increase manufacturer profit is another question. It might not because even though wholesale prices are higher, the double-marginalization problem means that the quantity sold is lower than it would be if retailing remained competitive. However, if the double-marginalization problem is not too large (as would be the case if the two goods are fairly close substitutes) the exclusive territorial arrangement will also lead to higher upstream profits. If the manufacturing firms can also adopt a two-part tariff arrangement, the double-marginalization problem can be overcome altogether.[8]

It may even be possible to use exclusive selling arrangements to achieve monopoly profit in what would otherwise be a competitive industry. To see this, suppose that the products of the two manufacturers are perfect substitutes. With a competitive retail sector, neither manufacturers nor retailers will make any profit. However, suppose that the two manufacturers coordinate so that within any territory they give the exclusive rights to their products to the same retailer, each agreeing not to sell to other dealers in that region. The lucky retailer in any region is thereby transformed into a monopolist who can set the monopoly retail price. Since monopolies make extra profit, the lucky downstream retailer in any region will be happy with this scheme.

---

[8] The mechanism by which exclusive territories soften interbrand price competition described in Rey and Stiglitz (1995) is conceptually quite similar to the argument in Bonanno and Vickers (1988).

What about the manufacturers? To some extent, their situation is unchanged. Each still produces a good for which there is a very close substitute. Hence, competition between the two should still be fierce. Of course, if this happens, all the monopoly profit will accrue to the retailer. If competition is less than fierce then the manufacturers can extract some of that profit by means of a two-part tariff. In fact, manufacturers may be able to extract profit even without using two-part tariffs. For instance, manufacturers can offer an exclusive sales contract only if the retailer also agrees to purchase a minimum amount from the manufacturer even if that manufacturer charges a wholesale price higher than the rival's price. This technique—known as a quantity-forcing requirement—again has the effect of softening wholesale price competition. When each manufacturer does this, each can raise wholesale price above cost without fear of losing sales to the rival. As a result manufacturers now earn some

---

Reality Checkpoint

Trouble in Toyland: "It's Toys 'R' Us or Them!"

On September 30, 1997, an administrative law judge ruled against the toy retailer, Toys "R" Us, on a charge of anticompetitive exclusive dealing. Three years later, a U.S. Appeals court upheld this decision. The crux of the case was a government charge that Toys "R" Us had made informal agreements with America's leading toy makers, notably, Mattel and Hasbro. The nature of the agreement was that Toys "R" Us agreed to sell these manufacturers' products only if the manufacturers in turn refused to sell their products to large discount firms such as Sam's Club. This exclusive arrangement may have helped both Toys "R" Us and the toy makers by creating downstream profits that could be shared amongst them.

Toys "R" Us did not deny the charges. Indeed, at the time of the decision, it had already settled an earlier suit brought by 44 states by agreeing to stop the practice and paying a settlement fee of $50 million. Mattel and Hasbro also agreed to stop the practice and each had paid a fee of $5 million.

Instead of disputing the allegation, Toys "R" Us argued that the practice was "perfectly lawful" as the firm's lawyer, Michael Feldberg, said. Mr. Feldberg continued that "[We] simply posed a choice to the manufacturers: It's us or them. If you sell an item to the warehouse clubs, we may not buy it." The justification for this policy was that Toys "R" Us screened what toys were in high demand and did the bulk of the promotional work for these items. In this view, the discount stores simply used Toys "R" Us to identify the hottest products and free-rode on its advertising. There may be some merit to this contention as we have seen. However, the case had the additional unusual twist of horizontal collusion. Instead, of just offering an exclusive dealing contract to all toy firms, there was evidence that Toys "R" Us had worked to make the deal go through by coordinating with Mattel and Hasbro. In particular, it brokered a deal whereby Mattel agreed to the restriction of not selling to the discount clubs on condition that Hasbro would do the same (so that Mattel would not be disadvantaged). Likewise, Hasbro agreed to the restraint on condition that Mattel would, as well. As noted in the text, there are sound theoretical reasons to worry that vertical restrictions may facilitate horizontal collusion. The Toys "R" Us case suggests that those theoretical concerns also have some basis in fact.

Source: W. M. Bullkeley and J. R. Wilke, "Toys Loses a Warehouse-Club Ruling with Broad Marketing Implications," *Wall Street* Journal, October 1, 1997, p. B10; and T. Hall, "Toys 'R' Us Loses Ruling," *New York Times*, August 2, 2000. For further details, consult the Federal Trade Commission website at http://www.ftc.gov.

profit.[9] Of course, the higher wholesale prices will translate into higher retail prices. That is, this arrangement does not enhance efficiency. The profit gain of the manufacturers is more than offset by a reduction in retailer profit and a fall in consumer surplus. Thus, while vertical contracts can be socially beneficial there is a downside risk. Recognition of the type of upstream coordination orchestrated by the retailer that we have just described appears to have been an important element in the Toys "R" Us case described in the Reality Checkpoint.

19.3 AFTERMARKETS

The vertical restrictions that we have examined so far primarily reflect constraints on the sale of the same product as it moves through the chain from the upstream producer to the downstream dealer. In recent years, a different kind of vertical restriction has caught the interest of economists—one that is closely related to the tying arrangements that we considered in section 13.3.2, Chapter 13. This restriction effectively involves an exclusive selling arrangement in what are known as aftermarkets.

The key legal case in the aftermarkets debate is the *Kodak* case. The specifics of that case are as follows. Kodak was one of a number of manufacturers of micrographic equipment—used for creating, viewing, and printing microfilm and microfiche—and office copiers. This was the primary or foremarket. However, Kodak also provided repair parts and services to these machines through a nationwide network of technicians. Kodak advertised the quality of this network as a means of persuading consumers to buy its machines in the first place. Because no one needs micrographic or copier parts and services if they have not already purchased a micrographic machine or copier, the parts and services market is referred to as the aftermarket.

Just as in the foremarket, Kodak had competition in the aftermarket. There were many independent firms providing parts and services to firms using Kodak's office machines. However, to the extent that these independent firms needed replacement parts, they relied on Kodak to provide them. Kodak was happy enough to do so until it lost a service contract with Computer Service Corporation (CSC) to an independent firm, Image Technical Services (ITS). After that, Kodak announced a new policy of not providing replacement parts to any independent service provider. Effectively, Kodak agreed to an exclusive selling arrangement with its service network. It would only sell its repair parts to that group. As Kodak enforced the new policy more and more strictly, ITS and other independents filed a lawsuit contesting Kodak's action.

In court Kodak asked for a summary dismissal of the plaintiffs' case. Kodak's basic argument ran along the following lines. There were many other producers of photographic office equipment. Kodak faced competition in the foremarket. As a result, Kodak argued it could not possibly exert monopoly power in the aftermarket. Before making a purchase in the foremarket, consumers consider the full cost of, say, a copier—both the price at the initial time of purchase and the price of services later in time. If Kodak were to try to charge a high price in the aftermarket for services, it would only attract foremarket customers if it reduced its machine prices by a corresponding amount. Hence, Kodak argued that it could not impose monopoly pricing in the aftermarket. The Supreme Court rejected Kodak's contention. Later, a jury turned in a verdict against Kodak.

---

[9] Note that in the final equilibrium the quantity constraint does not need to be binding.

The Kodak case has been followed by a number of similar cases (see Reality Checkpoint). Again, the central issue is whether and how a firm can exercise monopoly power in the aftermarket if it does not have such power in the foremarket. It seems clear that this will not happen if buyers find it easy to switch service providers in the aftermarket in the face of any price increase by one such supplier. In other words, there must be some sort of lock-in or switching cost such that once a buyer has a Kodak copier, the buyer cannot easily switch to another copier by selling its Kodak machine in a used-machine market and buying an alternative machine for which no service companies are excluded from obtaining parts. This seems a reasonable assumption in many cases so long as the used machine market is not very well developed.

However, if buyers are forward looking, the presence of lock-in or switching cost effects may not be enough to permit the exercise of pricing power in an aftermarket. If buyers understand that buying a Kodak machine also means later buying expensive Kodak parts and

---

Reality Checkpoint

Aftermarkets After Kodak

The controversy over the aftermarkets issue raised in the Kodak case has continued to this day. Two cases subsequently decided by different circuit courts amply illustrate the continuing tension.

The case of *Allen-Myland v. IBM* 33 F.3d 194 (3rd Cir. 1994), involved a suit filed by an independent firm, Allen-Myland, that specialized in the maintenance and upgrading of IBM mainframe computers. The upgrade market was a substantial one—in some years as valuable as the mainframe market itself. At one point, Allen-Myland had half the upgrade market. Then IBM introduced a set of new policies. Specifically, IBM began to offer lower installation prices for firms that committed to use only IBM's upgrade services. Subsequently using an independent like Allen-Myland would then involve a financial penalty for breeching this contract. IBM also started to require customers to return used parts to them, thus drying up a potential alternative source of parts. Although the District Court originally ruled for IBM, the Appeals Court overturned the ruling noting that IBM could have substantial power in the upgrade market.

In *PSI v. Honeywell*, 104 F.3d 811 (6th Cir. 1997), the court considered the case of PSI Repair Services, Inc., an independent firm engaged in the repair of computer systems. PSI filed suit under the Sherman Act against the computer manufacturer Honeywell, Inc. The basis of the suit was the fact that Honeywell forced computer chip makers to refrain from selling parts unique to Honeywell computers to any independent repair services such as PSI and also to any Honeywell customers. PSI contended that this practice was precisely what was found to be illegal in the *Kodak* case.

After losing in the District Court PSI appealed to the Sixth Circuit U.S. Court of Appeals. That court also rejected PSI's claims citing two reasons. First, the court noted that unlike Kodak, Honeywell's refusal to deal was not a change in policy but something that it had always done. Second, the court rejected the assertion of aftermarket power based on "lock-ins." The court instead said that the relevant market was not the aftermarket for Honeywell parts but rather the equipment market shared by Honeywell and its competitors. Consumers were free to purchase computers from other sources with different servicing policies.

Sources: *Antitrust Litigation Reporter*, June 5, 1997; and G. Graham, "IBM Sent Back by Appeals Court to Face Retrial in Anti-Trust Suit," *Financial Times*, August 19, 1994, p. 6.

service, Kodak will only sell its machine by cutting its price below that of its rivals for whose machines cheaper service is available. Thus, Kodak and other companies as well have argued that they have no incentive to raise aftermarket prices because it will simply require that they lower the price in the primary market by an offsetting amount.

We think that there are at least two reasons to suspect that the lock-in effect may translate into the ability to raise price above cost in the aftermarket. The first is simply that buyers may not be so forward looking as to consider the machine and its subsequent service as one integral purchase. To do so would require that they acquire information regarding their future service needs and future service costs over many years in the future, and moreover that they do this across all machine brands. This is both difficult and expensive. Yet if buyers do not do this, then a firm with a lock-in technology can raise its aftermarket price without lowering its primary market price.

The second reason is more subtle. It is that firms such as Kodak may have no credible way to commit to a low service price far into the future because there are always some locked-in customers who have recently bought the machine and who can be exploited. To see this point in a simple context, consider the following scenario.

Imagine that there are two producers of copying machines. Each type of machine lasts potentially for two periods. A machine runs without problems in the first period but has a 50 percent chance of breaking down in the second period. When it breaks down, the buyer can have it repaired but only by using the repair service of the company that manufactured the machine. For simplicity, we will assume that the costs of producing the machine and also of repairing it are each zero.

Buyers are assumed to derive $50 of value from the machine for each period that it runs well. However, once a buyer buys a particular brand and integrates it into their production, the cost of switching to an alternative brand, setting up and reintegrating it into the buyer's operations midway through the machine's expected life is at least $50. In any given period, there are equal numbers of buyers who are in the market for new machines and buyers who have already owned a machine for one period.

If buyers are forward looking, they will be willing to pay $75 for a new machine. This is the expected surplus they will receive over the machine's two-period life. With 50 percent probability, the machine will run fine for two periods and generate $100 worth of value. With an equal probability, it will break down in the second period at which point switching to an alternative machine is not worthwhile given the switching cost.

Of course, the price of a new machine will be far less than $75. Indeed, competition between the two firms will likely lower this price quite close to cost. However, the price for repairs is another story. For those unlucky buyers who have bought a machine that has broken down after one period, they either have to do without a machine and lose $50 of value or get their machine fixed. As long as the cost of fixing the machine is less than $50, these buyers will be willing to pay for the repairs.

There is a time inconsistency in the firm–customer relationship in that buyer behavior changes once a machine is bought. By the second period, whatever price buyers paid for the machine initially becomes an irrelevant sunk cost. As a result, the firm always has some motivation to raise the repair price and extract some surplus from these buyers. Note that even if the repair price rises to close to $50, consumers with a broken machine will still be willing to pay to have it fixed since they get $50 of value from the machine working. In other words, even with that high a repair price, the expected value of a machine when it is first purchased remains at least at $75 so long as the price for repairs is less than $50. However, $50 is well above the cost of repairs. Thus, the equilibrium will be one in which the repair price exceeds marginal cost and everyone, including consumers, understands that this will be the case.

The model just used is a simple one. However, its basic point can be generalized in a more sophisticated model as Borenstein, Mackie-Mason, and Netz (2000) have shown. Work by Gabaix and Laibson (2006) suggests that the presence of some unsophisticated consumers can interact with the lock-in effects just described to make firms unwilling to announce low aftermarket prices even when they can and even when competition is strong.

Suppose that while most buyers are rational, there are a few unsophisticated ones who, if repairs are needed, do not look at the alternative of buying and integrating a new machine but just purchase the repairs as long as these cost $50 or less. Suppose however that unlike our earlier case the cost of switching to a new machine and integrating it with current operations is only $25. Rational or sophisticated buyers will foresee the possibility of machine failure and the need to switch. Competition may then lead to market entry until all profits are exhausted, implying that the price of machine and repairs *together* would have to be close to cost. This does not mean that the equilibrium prices of both the machine and repairs have to fall to their respective marginal costs, which are here assumed to be zero. Instead, the outcome is likely to be one in which each firm sells its machine below cost but sells repairs well above cost, say at $50. Firms will lose money on rational consumers because these consumers will buy the machine at a price below cost and, if it breaks down, pay $25 in switching costs. However, the firms will recoup these losses from unsophisticated consumers who pay $50 for repairs rather than switching.

What is particularly noteworthy about the above outcome is that each firm has little incentive to announce a low repair price. If it does, it will only lose the demand of forward-looking or sophisticated buyers. These buyers did not pay the high repair price in the first place. When they discover that the firm is lowering its repair fees, sophisticated buyers will recognize that this is only possible if the price for the initial machine is raised. As a result, at least some will switch their initial purchases to other firms. Even worse, the lower repair price will reduce the profits earned from unsophisticated buyers. For example, hotels often charge a low room price but set high fees for use of the phone and the mini-bar. Similarly, rental car firms may set a low rent for the car itself but charge hefty rates for insurance and gasoline. In neither case do the firms try to compete by announcing low prices in these associated aftermarkets. They really have no incentive to do so. Profits may be low overall but that is because the foremarket price is inefficiently too low and the aftermarket price is inefficiently too high.

19.4   PUBLIC POLICY TOWARD VERTICAL RESTRAINTS

Non-price vertical agreements can have both positive and negative effects. Accordingly, a "rule of reason" approach has dominated the legal cases in this area. The outcome in the courts typically reflects the court's balancing of the conflicting pro- and anti-competitive forces. Not all analysts agree on the wisdom of this approach. For some, such as Posner (1981), the potential efficiency gains of exclusive selling and territorial agreements are likely to be sufficiently large that all such vertical restrictions ought to be considered per se legal under the antitrust laws. The argument is essentially that vertical restrictions must at least benefit the upstream and downstream firms that have agreed to such restraints. They may, as we have seen, benefit consumers as well. Attempting to use a rule of reason and judge each situation on a case-by-case method will, in this view, be very difficult and produce a large number of inconsistent and quite possibly wrong decisions. Accordingly, the wisest course for antitrust policy is simply to let all vertical restrictions alone. The U.S. Justice Department came close to adopting such a view in its Vertical Restraints Guidelines of 1985, and there was little prosecution of vertical arrangements for the next several years. However, those guidelines were rejected in 1993 and the antitrust authorities have since taken a still tolerant but somewhat less generous attitude towards vertical restraints.

A similar fluctuation in policy has been observed in Europe. Up until the late 1990s, the approach taken by the European Union was one of condemnation for any type of non-price vertical restraint in general, coupled with broad exemptions for specific arrangements, especially franchise contracts. However, in 1999 as the economic integration became more complete, the European Union adopted its own Vertical Restraint Guidelines that applied a much more lenient treatment of vertical restraints again based on a rule-of-reason approach.

A good bit of tolerance toward non-price restrictions is probably warranted. While there are many well justified concerns about the potential for these restraints to exert anticompetitive effects, the large bulk of the empirical evidence is that such restraints are usually good for producers and have either positive or at least no negative consequences for consumers.[10] Moreover, when studies do find negative consequences for consumers, it is usually because they find a rise in retail prices. Yet this may occur for benign reasons. Recall the free-riding problem in our earlier Tylenol example. Because the cost of Tylenol's advertising is reflected in its price, the more free-riding is a serious problem, the more we would expect Johnson & Johnson to seek an exclusive dealing contract or other vertical restraint. In other words, it is likely that we will observe vertical restrictions most in precisely those markets where manufacturers have to make serious investments in advertising or quality improvement that need to be protected. Since the expense of those investments will be reflected in the product price, this also means that the use of those restrictions will be associated with higher prices. Yet the restriction is not the cause of the higher price and its use does not necessarily hurt consumers. When the possible endogeneity of vertical restraints is recognized, the accumulated empirical evidence implies even more strongly that the use of such restraints has generally been beneficial.

Sometimes non-price vertical restraints are imposed by the government and sometimes these restraints have a negative effect. For example, in many states independent opticians have been prohibited from fitting contact lenses. Instead, lens wearers have been required to see an ophthalmologist or optometrist, thereby effectively tying the purchase of lenses to the services of these professionals. Haas-Wilson (1987) found that such policies raised consumer prices without any improvement in quality. They also diminished the variety of consumer choices. Such findings are not unusual in the case of state-imposed vertical restrictions.[11]

The efforts of policy makers to balance anticompetitive effects such as entry deterrence against the efficiency gains that exclusive dealing can generate are illustrated by a U.S. case involving the two principal manufacturers of the water pumps used by fire engines. Hale Products, Inc. and Waterous Company, Inc. were the pump-makers in question. Each manufactured the water pump that is installed on fire trucks in the U.S. Each sold its pumps directly to the makers of such fire trucks through exclusive dealing contracts. Those fire truck manufacturers who bought from Hale agreed not to buy from any other pump-maker and

---

[10]   See Lafontaine and Slade (2007).

[11]   Occasionally, state governments also categorically block vertical restraints, as with laws that ban direct ownership of gasoline service stations by oil refineries. Such state intrusion into private organizational choices can also create difficulties. See, e.g., Blass and Carlton (2001).

likewise for those who agreed to purchase their pumps from Waterous. In determining the effect of these agreements, the FTC noted that together the two firms accounted for 90 percent of the U.S. market for water pumps and had done so for nearly fifty years, with the remainder accounted for by a small third firm, W. S. Darley & Company. During that time, no new entrant had come into the market. This was taken as evidence by the FTC that the exclusive dealing agreements had effectively blocked such entry. In addition, the FTC alleged that the agreements also worked to reduce competition between Hale and Waterous. Documents were presented indicating that each firm realized that so long as it dealt only with its half of the engine manufacturers, it did not need to fear competition from the other. Further, the FTC noted that neither pump-maker would wish to cheat on this tacit agreement because such cheating would be quickly detected. Waterous would know immediately if one of its customers ever stopped buying the Waterous pump. The same would be true for Hale. Ultimately, the FTC prevailed and the two firms agreed to cease the exclusive dealing arrangements.[12]

The above procedure illustrates how a rule of reason operates in practice. The threshold issue is the fraction of the market such agreements cover. Unless that fraction is large, the agreements are presumed not to weaken competition in any meaningful way and are therefore deemed legal. Even if the threshold is reached however, that merely sets the stage for subsequent investigation. The question then becomes whether the restrictions are substantially harmful to competition. Here, factors such as the history of entry, the behavior of prices, and the potential for free-riding problems need to be examined. This is a complicated process and the per se presumption of legality suggested by Posner (1981) is understandably tempting. Our view is that there are sufficient grounds for concern that the continued use of a rule of reason approach is warranted despite the difficulties that entails.

19.5   A BRIEF DISCUSSION OF FRANCHISING AND DIVISIONALIZATION

Our discussion of vertical relations has often included references to franchising. In fact, probably the bulk of vertical restrictions arise in the context of franchising agreements since these cover a large fraction of retail sales, roughly over a third. As a result, franchising warrants some individual attention on its own.

There are two basic types of franchising agreements. Under the traditional type observed with soft drinks, gasoline, and car dealerships, the upstream franchisor sells its branded product to the downstream franchisee who then resells this good either to other firms or consumers. More recently, a second type of franchising known as business format franchising has emerged. Here, the franchisee buys the right to a brand name and a complete business plan. Food establishments such as McDonald's and hotel chains such as Marriott are examples of this latter type. Business format franchising has grown rapidly and now accounts for over a quarter of all franchising.[13]

---

[12] See Federal Trade Commission, Decision and Order, In the Matter of Hale Products Inc., Docket No. C-3694, November 22, 1996, and Decision and Order, In the Matter of Waterous Company, Inc., Docket No. C-3694, November 22, 1996.

[13] See Lafontaine (1993), Lafontaine and Shaw (1999), and Blair and Lafontaine (2005).

The proliferation of franchised outlets reflects in part the scale economies that such outlets can enjoy in terms of advertising and the purchase of supplies. It also reflects the greatly increased mobility of households resulting in a need for recognizable brand names that reduce uncertainty about quality and save on shopping time. However, even after the decision to establish new outlets has been made, a franchisor still has an organizational choice to make. In particular, it has to determine whether it wishes to operate the outlet as a company-owned operation managed by a salaried employee or as an independent franchise run by a profit-maximizing owner.

There are two countervailing forces that affect this choice. On the one hand, a salaried employee running a company-owned outlet may not have strong incentives to put forth effort and maximize profit whereas the franchisee as residual claimant does have incentives much more closely aligned with those of the franchisor. On the other hand, the company-owned outlet can perhaps be more easily monitored and controlled to make sure that it works cooperatively with others in pursuit of the franchisor's goals. In contrast, while an independent franchise owner may have a strong incentive to innovate and earn the maximum profit since that means more for its owner, we need to recognize that maximizing the outlet's profit and maximizing the franchisor's profit can be two different matters. For example, an independent franchisee may not support the promotional and service efforts that maximize the joint profit of all the company's outlets but, instead, free-ride on the efforts of others. Of course, if all outlets do this, promotional and service levels may fall far below the level that maximizes joint profit.

We have seen that vertical restrictions such as exclusive territorial rights may help resolve the incentive conflicts between franchisors and franchisees. Further, by granting a local territorial monopoly, the franchisor may induce franchisee owners to pay a higher initial franchise fee. However, once that fee has been collected, a further potential conflict arises between franchisor and franchisee. The franchising firm may have an incentive to open additional outlets that crowd in on the territory of the initial franchisee.

There are at least three reasons for a franchisor to wish to have a large number of franchisees. From a spatial perspective, operating many outlets means that the franchisor is better able to meet the specific preferences of each individual customer. This enables the franchise operation to extract more surplus by charging each customer an amount much closer to his maximum willingness to pay for the customer's most preferred variety. In short, operating many outlets may enhance the franchisor's ability to price discriminate.

In addition, the operation of a large number of outlets may be a means for firms to overcome asymmetric information and attendant moral hazard problems. With just one outlet, the franchisor cannot tell whether a low-profit outcome is due to bad luck—which could happen to anyone—or to the outlet's poor management. With many outlets, it is less likely that they all will have bad luck at the same time. Hence, the average performance of a large number of outlets may serve as a benchmark against which to measure the performance of each franchise individually.

Both of these are perfectly plausible explanations for why franchising is a popular business model and also for why companies might wish to establish various operating divisions as independent profit centers. A third motivation is also possible, however. It is that, operating a large number of independent franchises (or divisions) may be a way for a firm to commit to a large total output. This is the approach taken by Baye, Crocker, and Ju (1996) who analyze the implications of this motive for franchising or divisionalization using a two-stage model. In the first stage, there are two independent franchisors, each of which chooses the number of independent franchises that it wishes to establish. In the second stage, the franchises from both franchisors compete in a Cournot quantity-setting game.[14]

Suppose that the franchises of both firms produce a homogeneous product at a constant marginal cost of c. The inverse demand for the product in the downstream market is described by our usual linear function, $P = A - BQ$, where Q is total market output.

In stage one of the game, let n_1 and n_2 denote the number of franchisees established by franchisors 1 and 2, respectively. A franchisor incurs a sunk cost K in the first stage when it sets up a franchise. In stage two, all of the franchisees act as independent players in a simultaneous-move Cournot game. By that we mean that each franchise acts like an independent profit-maximizer.

To solve this game we begin with the stage-two competition. Let q_{ij} denote the output chosen by the ith franchise of firm j, where i runs from 1 to n_j and j is equal to 1 or 2. Let Q_{-ij} describe the total output of all franchises except the ith franchise of firm j. The profit of this franchise π_{ij} can then be written as

$$\pi_{ij}(q_{ij}, Q_{-ij}) = [A - B(Q_{-ij} + q_{ij})]q_{ij} - cq_{ij} \tag{19.1}$$

where total market output Q is equal to $\sum_{j=1}^{2}\sum_{i=1}^{n_j} q_{ij}$.

The ith franchise of firm j chooses output q_{ij} to maximize its profit. This, of course, requires setting its marginal revenue to its marginal cost. This implies in turn that the optimal output of any franchise q_{ij}^* satisfies

$$A - BQ_{-ij} - 2Bq_{ij}^* = c \tag{19.2}$$

Since all franchises are identical, they must all choose the same optimal output in equilibrium—that is, $q_{ij}^* = q^*$ for all i, j. This greatly simplifies matters. Since there are $n_1 + n_2$ franchises in total, Q_{-ij} must equal $(n_1 + n_2 - 1)q^*$. Substitution into equation (19.2) then yields

$$q^* = \frac{A - c}{(n_1 + n_2 + 1)B} \tag{19.3}$$

from which it follows that the total industry output Q and associated market price P in stage two are

$$Q = \left(\frac{n_1 + n_2}{n_1 + n_2 + 1}\right)\left(\frac{A - c}{B}\right) \text{ and } P = \frac{A + (n_1 + n_2)c}{n_1 + n_2 + 1} \tag{19.4}$$

At this price, each franchise will earn a stage-two profit π_{ij} given by

$$\pi_{ij} = \frac{(A - c)^2}{B(n_1 + n_2 + 1)^2} \tag{19.5}$$

---

[14] Rather than franchises, these could be divisions of the company provided that the divisions are established as independent profit centers.

The two franchisors who anticipate competition among franchises in stage two along the lines just described must decide in stage one how many franchises to set up. Firm 1's profit can be written as $\pi_1 = \sum_{i=1}^{n_1} \pi_{i1} - Kn_1$ where π_{i1} is the stage two profit of the ith franchise of firm 1. Since equation (19.5) shows the profit earned by each of firm 1's n_1 franchises in stage two, we can rewrite firm 1's overall profit as

$$\Pi_1(n_1, n_2) = n_1 \frac{(A - c)^2}{B(n_1 + n_2 + 1)^2} - Kn_1 \tag{19.6}$$

Firm 1 chooses its total number of franchises n_1^* so as to maximize its profit $\Pi_1(n_1, n_2)$ when firm 2 has n_2 franchises of its own. In other words, firm 1 wants to choose a best response n_1^* to the number of franchises, n_2 that firm 2 has. It is straightforward to show that this best response function satisfies[15]

$$\frac{(A - c)^2}{B(1 + n_1^* + n_2)^2} \left(1 - \frac{2n_1^*}{(1 + n_1^* + n_2)} \right) - K = 0 \tag{19.7}$$

Since firm 2 is identical to firm 1, we have a symmetric condition for n_2^*. So, using the notation that $n_1^* = n_2^* = n^*$, and recognizing that this symmetry implies that $n_1^* + n_2^* = 2n^*$, we can solve for n^*. This solution is

$$n^* = \frac{1}{2} \left[\left(\frac{(A - c)^2}{BK} \right)^{1/3} - 1 \right] \tag{19.8}$$

Equation (19.8) shows that the greater is $(A - c)$ and/or the smaller is K, the greater is the number of franchises chosen by firm 1 and firm 2 in stage one of the game. Recall that the difference between price and cost is $(A - c)/2$ if the market is monopolized. One implication of this model is that firms will create more franchises the greater the price–cost differential would be under a monopoly. However, having more franchises is tantamount to having more Cournot-type units, and this brings us closer to the competitive equilibrium. Hence, the greater the possible markup under a monopoly, the greater the number of franchises the two firms operate, and the more closely they end up approximating the competitive equilibrium. The firms are locked in a "prisoners' dilemma" in which the best response of each firm acting separately is not optimal from the standpoint of the two firms collectively. The firms independently open up more franchises than they would if they cooperated or colluded.

There are many reasons behind the extensive growth of franchising. These include cost advantages and modern lifestyles in which households change geographic locales frequently and therefore prefer inter-regional brands to facilitate shopping decisions. An additional reason is that operating many franchises may be a natural outcome of competition between

---

[15]   The response function in equation (19.7) is derived by taking the derivative of the profit function (19.6) with respect to n_1 and setting it to zero. This technique assumes that we can ignore the constraint that n_1 be an integer.

Reality Checkpoint
Mail Boxes, Etc. Has Some Downs With UPS

In 2001, the shipping giant, United Parcel Service (UPS), acquired the small package delivery firm, Mail Boxes, Etc. Independent franchisees at Mail Boxes were at first ecstatic about the deal. They thought that UPS, widely known by its recognizable large vans and nicknamed "Brown," would bring them a sizable increase in volume and permit offering a wider range of services. UPS had been looking to expand its retail reach for some time and the feeling was that their decision to pursue Mail Boxes must reflect its view that this was an excellent match.

Now, a few years later, many of the former Mail Boxes franchisees have left. Hundreds of these have banded together to file a suit against UPS. What went wrong?

From the franchisees' perspective, the UPS business model imposed far too many vertical restraints. The first sign of this was UPS's decision to convert all the Mail Boxes outlets to UPS Stores. Not only did this take away a hard-won brand identity but it also required costly store makeovers that came largely at the franchisees' expense. By right of their previous contracts, franchisees had the right to keep the Mail Boxes name and look for a few years. However, those that did were told that UPS would stop promoting the Mail Boxes brand. Further, while volume did increase somewhat, extra franchisee profit failed to materialize. In addition to the makeover costs, this was partly due to the fact that UPS imposed a limit on the retail price as a means to limit double-marginalization. Moreover, while this limit might have been acceptable in principle, UPS set its maximum retail price on a national basis so that all prices were the same irrespective of regional cost differences. UPS also reduced the compensation franchisees received for handling pre-labeled packages right after it established a website where consumers could prepare their own labels. In addition, UPS imposed exclusive dealing restrictions so that franchisees could no longer deal with rival shippers such as FedEx. The result was that many franchisees felt they were basically being turned into mere drop-off points. Worst of all from the franchisees' perspective, UPS opened up a considerable number of additional UPS Stores, including many close to the original Mail Boxes establishments. This has been the biggest source of friction.

The theme of UPS ads for some years has been, "What can Brown do for you?." A number of its former unhappy franchisees see that ad and reply, "Stop competing with me."

Source: R. Gibson, "Small Business Report: Package Deal," *Wall Street Journal*, May 8, 2006, p. R13.

independent franchisors. The result will be that there are many more franchises than the number that would maximize industry profits. Moreover, while expanding the number of franchises may be hard on firm profits, it can be especially hard on the profits earned by each individual franchisee. This again reflects another aspect of the incentive conflicts that beset the franchisor–franchisee relationship.

While we have cast our example in terms of the operation of independent franchisees, it could equally well be cast in terms of operating independent divisions such as the different divisions run by major auto makers such as GM and Ford. Here again, the outcome may be too many divisions from the viewpoint of maximizing industry profits, but with no real way for any one car firm to reduce the number of divisions unilaterally.

Assume two firms confront each other in an industry in which the inverse demand is $P = 100 - Q$. Let marginal cost be constant at $c = 25$, and let the sunk cost of setting up a franchise be $K = 45$.

a. According to equation (19.8), how many franchises will each firm operate?
b. According to equation (19.6), what profit will each firm make if each operates the number of franchises derived in part (a)?
c. According to equations (19.4) and (19.5) what will be the industry price, P, and output, Q?
d. Calculate the industry output, price, and profit earned by a pure monopolist. Compare this with your answers in parts (b) and (c).

Practice Problem

19.6   EMPIRICAL APPLICATION
Exclusive Dealing in the U.S. Beer Industry

The impact of exclusive dealing and exclusive territorial contracts has been the subject of many studies. The emerging consensus from these studies is that such contracts are beneficial, both for firms and for consumers, when they are not mandated by the government but instead, the result of private negotiations. A study by Tim Sass (2005) on exclusive dealing in the U.S. domestic beer market is an example of the kind of analysis that finds support for private vertical contracts.

The U.S. has a three-tiered beer market. At one end of the stream, are the beer producers or breweries, such as Anheuser–Busch (AB), Miller, and Coors. In the case of a foreign beer, the domestic firm importing that beer plays the role of a producer. Besides producing the beer, brewers also engage in a good bit of advertising and product promotion.

The brewers sell to the next tier, which is comprised of distributors. These sales are usually made at a constant price per unit, i.e., they typically do not set franchise fees or use two-part tariffs. The distributors warehouse the product, do local advertising and promotion, and also monitor local beer quality. They sell to the third tier, the retailers from whom consumers make their purchases of beer. Again, sales to retailers usually employ linear pricing.

All of the major breweries have exclusive dealing contracts with at least some of their distributors. They also typically assign exclusive territories. The latter means that there is little *intra*brand competition among distributors. However, there is a fair bit of *inter*brand competition. It is very rare that a single distributor possesses a monopoly in a regional market.

Sass (2005) first tries to determine what factors lead to the use of exclusive contracts in the beer market. Data from a *1996/1997 Distributor Brand-Equity Survey* provides evidence on 381 distributor contracts, 69 of which include an exclusive dealing clause (most of these are AB distributors). If foreclosure is a motivation for such contracts, then they should become less likely as market size grows. This is because foreclosure basically works by denying the rival a sufficiently large sales base to permit exploiting scale economies, and this is harder to do when the market is large. Sass (2005) uses two variables to capture potential market size. One is the population (*POP*) of the distribution region. The other is the state-level market share (*MSD*) of the brewery that is the primary supplier of the distributor.

Another factor has to do with the local market information that the distributor has acquired. A distributor who has a lot of information about local consumer tastes and price responsiveness will likely be less willing to sign an exclusive dealing contract because this

Table 19.1   What explains the use of exclusive dealing in U.S. beer distributor contracts?

Explanatory variable	Estimated coefficient	t-statistic
POP	0.0001	(1.87)
MSD	0.0079	(2.79)
YRS	−0.0017	(−2.10)
ADS	−0.0002	(−0.38)
BAN	−0.0955	(−2.12)

limits that distributor's ability to profit from her information. Sass (2005) proxies this information by the number of years (*YRS*) that the distributor has been owned by the same family.

Finally, brewers may want to have exclusive dealing when they have large promotional expenses themselves that raise retail demand for beer in general but which, in the absence of an exclusive arrangement, the distributor might meet by selling an alternative brand. To capture the importance of such non-brand specific advertising, Sass (2005) uses the national advertising of the brewer's primary supplier (*ADS*) and a 1,0 variable indicating whether or not there is a state ban on billboard or sign advertising (*BAN*). If protecting its advertising against free-riding is a motivation for the brewer, the first should have a positive effect and the second should have a negative effect.

Since a contract is either classified as an exclusive deal or not, the independent variable in the econometric specification is a 1,0 variable and Sass (2005) estimates this regression using the Probit procedure that we described in the Empirical Application in Chapter 13 regarding the Ellison and Ellison (2006) study of entry into generic drug markets. This means that the estimated coefficients indicate how much a change in the explanatory variable would raise or lower the *probability* of using an exclusive contract. The results are shown in Table 19.1.

Overall, the evidence on the determinants of where exclusive dealing contracts are used in the U.S. beer market implies that these contracts are not used to harm competition. Instead, they appear to be used for the beneficial reason of protecting brewers' investments in their own product promotion. For example, increases in market size as measured by both *POP* and *MSD* raise the likelihood of an excusive dealing clause and the *t*-statistics indicate that both of these effects are statistically significant. This suggests that these contracts are not being used to foreclose markets to rivals. There is some evidence that the real motive is to protect the brewer's generalized advertising efforts against free-riding. While *ADS* is not statistically significant, the presence of a ban against beer advertising on billboards and signs does have a negative effect on exclusive dealing. When there is less promotion, there is less need to protect it with an exclusive dealing contract. Finally, there is also evidence that as distributors gain experience and knowledge of the local market, they are less willing to sign an exclusive dealing contract that might restrict their ability to profit from that information. The coefficient on *YRS* is negative and significant.

Having examined the factors that lead to exclusive dealing, Sass (2005) then turns to examining the market effects that such contracts have. He considers four possible variables that might be affected. These are: (1) the average price paid by the distributor to brewers, *PB*; (2) the price the distributor charges retailers for its primary brand, *PD*; (3) the quantity of the primary brand sold, *QPRIMARY*; and (4) the quantity of all brands sold, *QTOTAL*, each measured in logarithms.

Prices, of course, should reflect both supply (i.e., cost) and demand pressures. Assuming that production costs are roughly the same for the brewers, the cost differences in supplying a distributor will reflect shipping costs or the distance from the nearest plant *DIST*; the level of excise taxes *TAX*; and possibly, the presence of a ban on outside advertising *BAN*, which could raise promotional costs. If these variables affect the price paid by the distributor then they should also affect the price paid by the retailer. That price in turn should affect both sales of the primary brand and of all brands. Thus, these three variables belong in all four equations.

To capture demand effects, Sass (2005) uses three variables. These are: (1) per capita income in the distribution territory, *INC*; (2) population in the distribution territory, *POP*; and (3) the percent of the population that is of prime drinking age, *AGESHARE*. Of course, the primary variable of interest is whether or not the distributor in question operated under an exclusive dealing contract, *EXDEAL*. This is a binary variable equal to 1 if there was an exclusive dealing contract and 0 if there was not.

The four regressions suggested by the variables just described are:

$$PB = CONSTANT + a_1 EXDEAL + a_2 DIST + a_3 TAX + a_4 BAN + a_5 INC$$
$$+ a_6 POP + a_7 AGESHARE + \varepsilon_{PB}$$
$$PD = CONSTANT + b_1 EXDEAL + b_2 DIST + b_3 TAX + b_4 BAN + b_5 INC$$
$$+ b_6 POP + b_7 AGESHARE + \varepsilon_{PD}$$
$$QPRIMARY = CONSTANT + c_1 EXDEAL + c_2 DIST + c_3 TAX + c_4 BAN + c_5 INC$$
$$+ c_6 POP + c_7 AGESHARE + \varepsilon_{QPRIMARY}$$
$$QTOTAL = CONSTANT + d_1 EXDEAL + d_2 DIST + d_3 TAX + d_4 BAN + d_5 INC$$
$$+ d_6 POP + d_7 AGESHARE + \varepsilon_{TOTAL}$$

Basically, these are the regressions that Sass (2005) estimates. However, in both the first and the fourth equations, he also includes market share data for three of the major brands to see how the extent of their presence affects the brewer's price to the dealer and final total sales. Sass (2005) also recognizes that the distributor's costs and, therefore, price to retailers, may reflect both the distributor's business savvy as captured by the number of years the same family has owned the distributorship, and an additional cost factor based on the average number of retailing stops the distributor must stop at per week. Hence, Sass's final set of regressions are as follows:

$$PB = CONSTANT + a_1 EXDEAL + a_2 DIST + a_3 TAX + a_4 BAN + a_5 INC$$
$$+ a_6 POP + a_7 AGESHARE + MARKET\ SHARE\ EFFECTS + \varepsilon_{PB}$$
$$PD = CONSTANT + b_1 EXDEAL + b_2 DIST + b_3 TAX + b_4 BAN + b_5 INC$$
$$+ b_6 POP + b_7 AGESHARE + OTHER\ COST\ FACTORS + \varepsilon_{PD}$$
$$QPRIMARY = CONSTANT + c_1 EXDEAL + c_2 DIST + c_3 TAX + c_4 BAN + c_5 INC$$
$$+ c_6 POP + c_7 AGESHARE + \varepsilon_{QPRIMARY}$$
$$QTOTAL = CONSTANT + d_1 EXDEAL + d_2 DIST + d_3 TAX + d_4 BAN + d_5 INC$$
$$+ d_6 POP + d_7 AGESHARE + MARKET\ SHARE\ EFFECTS + \varepsilon_{TOTAL}$$

We are mainly interested in the impact of exclusive dealing. Before discussing that effect, however, it is worth noting two features of this system. These are reduced form equations. That is, they are not equations that describe the full supply and demand structure. Instead,

Table 19.2   Effect of exclusive dealing on market outcomes

PB		PD		QPRIMARY		QTOTAL	
EXDEAL Coefficient	t-statistic	EXDEAL Coefficient	t-statistic	EXDEAL Coefficient	t-statistic	EXDEAL Coefficient	t-statistic
0.0630	(2.73)	0.0368	(2.13)	0.3241	(3.09)	0.2816	(2.74)

they describe the outcome for the dependent variable in terms of the basic factors that underlie supply and demand. In each case, the final term represents the influence of random factors that may affect the brewer's price, the distributor's price, primary brand sales, or total brand sales.

In principle, each of these regressions could be run alone using ordinary least squares (OLS). However, it seems likely that the random factors that, say, raise total demand may also affect primary brand demand and, in turn, feed into prices. In other words, while the regressions may seem independent of each other, there is a correlation between the random forces affecting each one, i.e., ε_{PB}, ε_{PD}, $\varepsilon_{QPRIMARY}$, and ε_{TOTAL} may all be correlated. If they are, then information about the nature of this correlation can be used to estimate the regression coefficients more precisely. To do this, Sass (2005) employs a regression technique known as Seemingly Unrelated Regression. This approach estimates the four regressions simultaneously by applying an estimate of the correlation across the error terms to construct generalized least squares (GLS) estimates. The estimated effect of exclusive dealing in each of the four regressions is shown in Table 19.2.

In every case, the effect of an exclusive dealing clause is positive and highly significant. It raises the unit price set by brewers by about 6 percent and the price set by distributors by about 4 percent. Despite these increases, final sales of both the primary producer's brand and of all brands also rise under exclusive dealing. These effects are particularly large. Demand for the brewer's product rises by 32 percent as the result of exclusive dealing. Yet this does not come at the expense of other brands. Instead, their sales rise as well by over 28 percent. In further regressions, Sass (2005) finds that exclusive dealing by one brewer (AB, in particular) does not significantly decrease rival brewers' prices.

The implications of these findings are relatively straightforward. The fact that exclusive dealing rises with the size of the market seems inconsistent with the idea that it is used as an anticompetitive foreclosure device. This inference is strengthened by the finding that such restrictions also do not tend to force rivals to lower their prices. Instead, the fact that exclusive dealing restraints rise with both market size and the presence of restrictions on outdoor advertising is more consistent with the notion that such contracts are used to mitigate conflicts between the brewery and its distributors.

Since the price to the distributor and the distributor's price to the retailer rise and sales volume also rises, there is no doubt that the surplus of brewers and distributors is enhanced by exclusive dealing. What happens to retailers and consumers is less clear. However, the rise in sales volume is sufficiently large that there is a strong supposition that their surplus also goes up. In short, the results of Sass (2005) strongly indicate that exclusive dealing in the U.S. beer industry is welfare enhancing.

Summary

Contracts between manufacturers and the various retailers that sell the manufactured products directly to consumers include a variety of non-price restrictions. These may include an exclusive dealing restriction that prevents the retailer from selling the products of any other manufacturer, or exclusive selling and territorial arrangements that restrain the manufacturer from allowing any other retailer to sell its product. Because these restrictions so clearly have the appearance of a restraint on trade, they fall under suspicion as anticompetitive.

In reality, however, there may be many efficiency gains that lie behind such restrictions. Often they may serve to ensure adequate promotional activities and other consumer services. They may also be useful in creating an environment in which retailers can better handle demand shocks.

A particularly complicated vertical relationship arises in the context of so-called aftermarkets. For a number of technological goods, the firms that supply the initial equipment also compete in an aftermarket to provide repair services to those machines. Frequently, these firms impose vertical restrictions that require the machine owners to buy their repair services from the same firm from which they bought the machine initially. The effects of such lock-in effects are difficult to determine. They may again be a means of insuring quality. Yet there are good reasons to believe that these restrictions give firms an ability to charge supracompetitive prices in the aftermarket even when the primary market has lots of competition. This issue has still to be resolved fully.

For the most part, public policy towards vertical restraints has increasingly recognized their potential benefits. This largely reflects the accumulating empirical evidence that these restrictions generally help producers and may help, or at least not hurt consumers. However, the potential for the abuse of market power seems clear, especially when the restrictions apply to a large fraction of the existing market. For this reason, authorities have continued to take a rule-of-reason approach to non-price vertical restraints rather than a *per se* legal one.

Before concluding we note that, in many respects, the retailer acts as an agent on behalf of the manufacturer. It learns about consumer tastes, makes promotional and other service decisions, and, of course, sets the final consumer price. Consequently, the vertical relationship between the producer and the retailer is a principal–agent relationship akin to the relationship between a client and his lawyer, or between shareholders and management. The contractual issues that arise between manufacturer and retailer are, therefore, part of a broader set of questions that arise in connection with contracts that govern all principal–agent relationships. These are important issues in the theory of the firm. For example, what is the difference between a producer connected to its retailer by means of a formal contract and a producer that is simply fully integrated into the retail market; or, for that matter, a producer that operates a retail division? Why do firms choose one form of organization over another? We do not answer these questions here. However, we do want to acknowledge that the issue of vertical relationships is really part of a larger question regarding the boundaries and limits of the firm.

Problems

1. Most beer companies impose an exclusive dealing clause on the supermarkets that sell their products. Discuss whether you think this practice will yield efficient market outcomes.

2. General Motors, Ford and Daimler–Chrysler all operate many divisions of automobile lines, e.g., Chevrolet, Pontiac, Cadillac, and Buick. Discuss the motivation for this practice. Who do you think this practice benefits the most, automakers or consumers?

3. In Europe, automobile dealers have traditionally been granted exclusive territories. Do you think that this practice should be legal?

4. Review the model of Rasmussen, Ramseyer, and Wiley (1991) from Chapter 13. Why are scale economies important for this argument that exclusive dealing can deter entry?

5. Most McDonald's hamburger outlets are owned by individual entrepreneurs who pay franchise fees to McDonald's for the right to

use the McDonald's name and recipes. Recipes for food at least as good as McDonald's are easy to find and cost less than the fees these entrepreneurs pay to McDonald's. Given the lower cost of equally good products, why are franchise holders willing to pay so much money to the franchiser corporation?

6. Who would be willing to pay more for the right to use the McDonald's name—an outlet located in the center of Centerville, or one that would do the same amount of business at the interstate turnpike?

7. What are the incentives for McDonald's to require franchisees to buy hamburger buns, meat, napkins, and other supplies from it rather than from other, possibly lower-cost local suppliers, other than the incentive of removing double-marginalization?

References

Aghion, P. and P. Bolton. 1987. "Contracts as a Barrier to Entry." *American Economic Review* 77 (June): 388–401.

Baye, Michael, K. Crocker, and J. Ju. 1996. "Divisionalization, Franchising, and Divestiture Incentives in Oligopoly." *American Economic Review* 86 (March): 223–36.

Bernheim, B. D. and M. Whinston. 1990. "Multimarket Contact and Collusive Behavior." *Rand Journal of Economics* 21 (Spring): 1–26.

Besanko, D. and M. K. Perry. 1994. "Exclusive Dealing in a Spatial Model of Retail Competition." *International Journal of Industrial Organization* 12 (Fall): 297–329.

Blair, R. D. and F. Lafontaine. 2005. *The Economics of Franchising.* New York: Cambridge University Press.

Blass, A. A. and D. W. Carlton. 2001. "The Choice of Organizational Form in Gasoline Retailing and the Cost of Laws that Limit that Choice." *Journal of Law and Economics* 44 (October): 511–24.

Bonanno, G. and J. Vickers, 1988. "Vertical Separation." *Journal of Industrial Economics* 36 (March): 257–65.

Borenstein, S., J. Mackie-Mason, and J. Netz. 2000. "Exercising Market Power in Proprietary Aftermarkets." *Journal of Economics and Management Strategy* 9 (Summer): 157–88.

Ellison, G. and S. Ellison. 2006. "Strategic Entry Deterrence and the Behavior of Pharmaceutical Incumbents prior to Patent Expiration." Working Paper. MIT Economics Department.

Gabaix, X. and D. Laibson. 2006. "Shrouded Attributes, Consumer Myopeia, and Information Suppression in Competitive Markets." *Quarterly Journal of Economics* 121 (May): 461–504.

Hass-Wilson, D. 1987. "Tying Requirements in Markets with Many Sellers: The Contact Lens Industry." *Review of Economics and Statistics* 69 (February): 170–5.

Lafontaine, F. 1992. "Agency Theory and Franchising: Some Empirical Results." *Rand Journal of Economics* 23 (Summer): 263–83.

Lafontaine, F. and K. Shaw. 1993. "Contractual Arrangements as Signaling Devices: Evidence from Franchising." *Journal of Law, Economics, and Organization* 9 (October): 256–89.

——. 1999. "The Dynamics of Franchise Contracting: Evidence From Panel Data." *Journal of Political Economy* 107 (October): 1041–80.

Lafontaine, F. and M. Slade. 2007. "Exclusive Contracts and Vertical Restraints: Empirical Evidence and Public Policy." In P. Buccirossi, ed., *Handbook of Antitrust Economics.* Cambridge, MA: MIT Press.

Marvel, Howard. 1982. "Exclusive Dealing." *Journal of Law and Economics* 25 (April): 1–25.

Mathewson, G. F. and R. A. Winter. 1987. "The Competitive Effects of Vertical Agreements: Comment." *American Economic Review* 77 (December): 1057–62.

McAfee, Preston, J. McMillan, and M. D. Whinston. 1989. "Multiproduct Monopoly, Commodity Bundling, and Correlation of Values." *Quarterly Journal of Economics* 104 (May): 371–82.

O'Brien, D. P. and G. Schaffer. 1994. "The Welfare Effects of Forbidding Discriminatory Discounts: A Secondary Line Analysis of Robinson-Patman." *Journal of Law, Economics, and Organization* 10 (October): 296–318.

Posner, R. 1981. "The Next Step in the Antitrust Treatment of Restricted Distribution: Per se Legality." *University of Chicago Law Review* 48 (Winter): 6–26.

Rasmussen, E., J. Ramseyer, and J. Wiley, 1991. "Naked Exclusion." *American Economic Review* 81 (December): 1137–45.

Rey, P. and J. Stiglitz. 1995. "The Role of Exclusive Territories in Producer Competition." *Rand Journal of Economics* 26 (Autumn): 431–51.

Sass, T. 2005. "The Competitive Effects of Exclusive Dealing: Evidence from the U.S. Beer Industry." *International Journal of Industrial Organization* 23 (April): 203–25.

Steiner, Robert L. 1985. "The Nature of Vertical Restraints." *Antitrust Bulletin* (Spring): 143–97.

Whinston, Michael. 1990. "Tying, Foreclosure, and Exclusion." *American Economic Review* 80 (September): 837–59.

Part VI
Nonprice Competition

So far, most of our analysis has focused on inter-firm competition centered on quantity or price. However, firms compete in many other dimensions, as well. Two such competitive mechanisms are advertising and innovative effort. These are the topics addressed in Part VI.

The economic function of advertising has long been an issue of both academic and popular concern. Initially, economists focused on the use of advertising to build brand loyalty and thereby to soften price competition between different brands. However, subsequent analysis has focused on the informational role of advertising. By helping consumers learn what alternatives are available and at which prices; or by informing consumers about the appropriate uses of a new product and its overall quality; or in numerous other ways, advertising can play a useful role that improves the welfare of both producers and consumers. Our analysis of advertising considers both its potential use as a tactic to suppress competitive pressures as well as its use as an informational tool that may enhance competition. Indeed, we conclude our advertising analysis in Chapter 21 with a description of a recent empirical study that tries to separate the informational role of advertising from its role in conferring prestige and building brand loyalty.

We then turn in Chapters 22 and 23 to an analysis of research and development (R&D). Here we begin with a well-known set of propositions typically referred to jointly as the Schumpeterian hypothesis. This is that large firms and concentrated industries are necessary for technological innovation. Chapter 22 addresses explicitly the nature of R&D competition and precisely the sort of market structure that most encourages technical progress. We also explore the potential gains and losses when firms cooperate on R&D activity. This includes a detailed description of recent evidence on the spillover of benefits from technical research in one area to productivity growth in another.

In Chapter 23, we consider public policy designed to encourage R&D, especially patent policy. Such policy must walk a thin line between granting wide access to available technologies and yet also giving innovators the rights to restrict such access so as to earn a return on their inventions. We discuss recent patent policy developments and illustrate these issues with an empirical study of patent behavior in the semiconductor industry.

20

Advertising, Market Power, and Information

Large retail stores that sell many different kinds of goods and many different brands of each good are a relatively recent phenomenon in the history of commerce. A customer buying say, a pair of shoes in the early twentieth century would have faced a different shopping experience from the one faced today. She would have been restricted to making her purchase in a specialized shoe store carrying only one or at most two brands, or possibly a cobbler's shop that made its own shoes. In addition, the consumer of a hundred years ago would have had to consult with the store proprietor, and would not have been able to examine and compare the merchandise directly.

How different the modern shopping experience is from the practices of the not-so-distant past. Today's consumer can go to a shoe or department store and see a whole range of different brands. Once there, she can personally handle and inspect each different style without any need to deal with a store employee. Only when she decides actually to try a specific pair of shoes on will she require assistance from a store employee—and even that is not always necessary. Consumers now may choose directly from an even wider range of different brands and never deal with a sales representative when they purchase shoes over the web.

What has made this dramatic change in the nature of retailing possible? Our reference to the web provides a clue. The retailing revolution of the twentieth century owes much to the advent of mass media, specifically, radio and television. This technological change made it possible for manufacturers to reach their consumers en masse and promote their products directly to the public. Using wide-scale advertising, manufacturers themselves were able to promote the important features of their products to a wide target audience. As a result, the task of selling goods at the retail level required much less specialized expertise, and in turn this greatly facilitated the formation of large-scale retail establishments such as department stores and discount stores, selling several varieties of hundreds of different kinds of goods. As mass communication technology continued to evolve, these retailers were joined by large mail-order businesses and, more recently, by e-tailers. The advent of large-scale advertising by manufacturers has been the source of a major revolution in the way consumers learn about the products that are out there waiting for them to buy.[1]

---

[1] For a good discussion of this revolutionizing effect of modern advertising and other aspects of advertising and promotional activities see, D. Pope, *The Making of Modern Advertising* (1983).

Yet while it is clear that the emergence of large-scale advertising has played a crucial role in the development of retailing, the full nature of advertising's impact remains a puzzle. We do not know exactly how advertising affects the consumer's decision of whether to buy and if so, what brand to buy. Consider, for example, television ads for Nike shoes. These ads often say little about the nature of the shoes and instead just feature a collage of images accompanied by the Nike Company's famous "swoosh" logo. How does this affect a consumer's decision to buy? In some Nike ads the company expressly points out that it is a corporate sponsor and apparel provider for the U.S. Olympic team. How does this affect our consumer's decision of whether to purchase Nike shoes?

The question as to how ads like those run by Nike actually work is important for many reasons. To begin with, Nike is not alone. Its promotional efforts are typical of many firms marketing consumer products and these efforts are very costly. Advertising on network television for example can cost millions of dollars for a single minute of airtime. For the 2007 Super Bowl the average price of a 30-second spot was a record breaking $2.6 million. Yet Anheuser-Busch, Frito-Lay, Pepsi-Cola, Procter & Gamble and others all bought spots for that game. We would like to understand first how advertising works in order to understand the incentives for these firms to incur such costs. At that point we can examine the decisions of firms to promote their products and why firms in some industries do much more advertising than those in others. Understanding how advertising works allows us to move on to investigate how advertising affects the strategic interaction between firms, and what this means for the consumer.

Our goal in the next two chapters is to understand the role of advertising and the implications that this carries for strategic interaction in the market place and consumer welfare. Advertising is provided by both manufacturers, e.g., Nike, and by retailers, e.g., Target. As a result, the provision of promotional services involves many of the vertical incentive conflicts that we have discussed in the previous two chapters. For the most part, we will suppress this distinction and focus on how advertising affects consumer buying decisions and the strategic interaction among firms competing for the consumer's patronage. We are interested in how advertising works; what information or other feature advertising provides that induces consumers to buy the advertised brand; and what it costs to provide such information.

We also want to understand the effect of advertising on competition in order to evaluate it from a policy perspective. Advertising could be viewed as an integral element of competition among firms that sell different brands of the same good. In this case, high advertising could be considered a sign of good health—a way to increase consumer awareness of different brands and therefore a vital component of healthy competition. In contrast, advertising could be seen as a way to differentiate one manufacturer's brand from another and thereby weaken competition by making it more difficult for a consumer to switch brands. High advertising in this case would be a sign of market power. Our analysis should help us determine which, if either, of these two cases is more likely.

It is important to note that there is a long-standing policy concern that advertising expenditures overall could be socially wasteful—that is, that firms spend far too much on promotional activities that yield little net gain for anyone and too little on more important activities such as product development. Our analysis should help to address this issue. Gaining insight into whether there is too much or too little advertising requires that we learn the underlying economic logic behind advertising. Why do firms do it and how does it work?

20.1   THE EXTENT OF ADVERTISING

The phenomenon of advertising is something of a paradox. Promotional efforts such as TV commercials are often barely tolerated by social critics. More often than not, advertising is disparaged as something that is wrong with contemporary society—something that tricks us into wanting and even buying things we don't need. At the same time, advertising is ubiquitous. It airs on our television sets and radios, accounts for many of the pages in magazines and daily newspapers, dots the landscape and cityscape with billboards, and even shows up on our T-shirts and other apparel. However much one might be critical of advertising, it seems that we can hardly live without it.

The magnitude of the advertising phenomenon as reflected in total dollars of expenditure is staggering. In 2006 the total expenditure on advertising in the U.S. was $285.1 billion dollars. This amounted to nearly 2.2 percent of the gross domestic product that year.[2] This was not unusual. From the 1940s on, advertising expenditures in the U.S. have consistently claimed about 2 percent of the U.S. national income.

Roughly 58 percent of total advertising expenditure is measured media advertising. This includes spending on nationwide broadcast and cable television networks, radio networks, national magazines, newspapers, yellow pages and the Internet.[3] The other 42 percent is non-measured or only indirectly measured media spending. This category includes expenditures on direct mailings, promotions, coupons, catalogs, business publications, and the sponsorship of special events. Retail advertising is often more heavily concentrated in non-measured media spending.

Firms differ substantially in their advertising behavior. For many years, the number one advertiser in the U.S. was General Motors, a firm that spent $3.3 billion on advertising in 2006. However, that same year witnessed the beginning of a decline in GM's market share with the result that the consumer goods giant, Procter & Gamble, moved into first place, spending $4.9 billion on advertising. In contrast, the much smaller Mattel toy company incurred a 2006 advertising expense of only $391 million in the United States.

In order to compare firms advertising efforts across firms of different sizes we typically compute advertising expenditure as a percentage of sales revenue. Even looking at this fraction—the advertising-to-sales ratio—however, still leaves considerable variation among firms. In 2006, the ratio for GM was about 2.9 percent and this was roughly the same for other U.S. automakers. However, the advertising-to-sales ratio for Volkswagen in 2005 was 3.8 percent and for Mitsubishi, 5.8 percent. Variations in advertising-to-sales ratios across industries are even larger. For example, advertising expenditures claimed over 10 percent of Mattel's domestic sales revenue in 2005, and over 12 percent of Pfizer's revenue in that year.

What explains the variation we see in advertising expenditures across firms and industries? There is some evidence that the profitability of a consumer goods industry appears to be positively correlated with the advertising intensity in that same industry.[4] Consumer goods such as cereals, perfumes, soaps, and pharmaceutical drugs have traditionally been

[2]   Data on advertising expenditures are from Advertising Age Data Center, adage.com.
[3]   Expenditures on measured media is tracked by TNS Media Intelligence.
[4]   This is one of Schmalensee's (1989) nine stylized facts on U.S. industry profitability. It is based on the studies by Comanor and Wilson (1967, 1974). Their findings have been replicated by other studies done on U.S. data as well as on data from other countries.

characterized by their relatively high profit rates and also by high advertising expenditures relative to sales. In contrast, other consumer goods such as hats, carpets, and jewelry have both lower profit rates and lower advertising expenditures. We also know that consumer goods industries tend to advertise more than those selling producer or intermediate goods. The issue is how to interpret this empirical evidence. Does advertising make firms more profitable or do more profitable firms advertise more? What is it about consumer goods that makes it profitable for a firm to make extensive use of advertising? To answer these questions we develop an analytical framework that permits us to identify the role that advertising plays.

20.2   ADVERTISING, PRODUCT DIFFERENTIATION, AND MONOPOLY POWER

Economists have long been interested in understanding the role of advertising in the marketplace. Some of the earliest writings on advertising came in the 1950s and 1960s. Much of this work drew a fairly negative assessment that advertising is a socially wasteful way for firms to compete (Kaldor 1950; Galbraith 1958; Solow 1967). Essentially, these studies view advertising as an effort by the firm to alter consumer tastes and to persuade consumers that there are few if any substitutes for the firm's products. To the extent that this effort is successful with at least some consumers, the firm will then enjoy a degree of monopoly power because it will not lose its customers to a rival should the firm raise its price. Yet while beneficial for the firm, these efforts in persuasion are bad for consumers not only because of the monopoly power and resultant deadweight loss, but also because these advertising efforts are costly in themselves. Since the differentiation achieved by advertising is not considered to be "real" but instead an artificial distinction created in the consumer's mind, the resources expended in creating that differentiation were seen as wasted. Accordingly, they would be better used to produce real goods and services.[5]

The advent of widescale advertising in the second half of the twentieth century followed closely the advent of mass production technology or economies of scale in production. Advertising enabled manufacturing firms to expand their markets and sell more, and hence exploit economies of scale in production. This led naturally to the fear that there would inevitably be a much more concentrated industrial structure. Even worse, if advertising were simply persuasive it could deter potential competition and new entry even when there was no real product differentiation.

The well-known early industrial organization economist, Joe Bain, explicitly considered the advertising-to-sales ratio of an industry as a proxy for barriers to entry. Many other economists—particularly those working in the structure–conduct–performance framework—shared this view. The fear was that established firms with a history of advertising would possess a market identity for their products that any new entrant would find difficult to overcome. As a result, the incumbent firm would be more immune to competitive entry.

It is worth noting that the fear that advertising would confer monopoly power was not without empirical support. There is both anecdotal and formal evidence to support the hypothesis that wide-scale advertising enhances a firm's market power and its ability to raise price above cost. The casual evidence is readily obtainable from a trip to the local drug store or supermarket. Anyone who compares the price of a nationally advertised brand of pain reliever

---

[5]   Viewed in this light, advertising is much like rent-seeking behavior. See, for example, Posner (1975).

with that of its generic substitute will find that the national brand sells at a noticeable premium. The same is true for cola drinks, shampoos, laundry bleaches, and a host of other products. In these cases and others, there are substitutes available that are chemically identical or nearly identical to the nationally advertised brand. Hence, production costs should be roughly the same. In turn, this suggests that the higher price commanded by the national brand reflects an increase in the markup over cost that monopoly power makes possible.

Evidence along these lines has been provided by the many statistical studies that find a significant positive relationship between advertising and industry profitability across a wide range of consumer goods industries. The pioneering work in this regard is that of Comanor and Wilson (1967). Their basic finding that industries with high profitability are associated with high advertising-to-sales ratio has been replicated many times since both for different time periods and different countries.[6] Another early but very well-known study is that by Nichols (1951) of the American cigarette market. Nichols provides statistical evidence that the major brands relied heavily on advertising to differentiate their products and thereby insulate them from price competition, especially that of "penny cigarettes."

There are, however, reasons to be wary of the view that advertising strengthens market power and inhibits competition. To begin with, there is a fine line between persuasion and information. After all, persuasion doesn't work in a vacuum. Persuading the consumer often requires that some information be given. To the extent that advertising provides information it will play a useful role, and one that could promote competition. Telser (1964) was one of the earliest studies to challenge the idea that advertising fostered monopoly. He studied the relationship between firms' advertising expenditures and market shares in three consumer good industries: food; soap; and cosmetics. Telser found that market shares are less stable, i.e., more likely to change, the greater is the advertising in that industry. This finding contradicts the persuasive view. In that view, advertising would make consumers less likely to switch brands and so should promote market share stability. Instead, Telser's (1964) findings suggest advertising makes consumers less loyal or makes competition fiercer.

Second, in examining any link between advertising and market power we should try to identify what causes that relationship. It may be that monopoly power leads a firm to advertise more rather than that advertising leads a firm to have monopoly power. Finally, if advertising does change consumer tastes then calculating its effects requires that we think carefully about how it changes consumer tastes and what this implies for the benefits that consumers derive from the product.

20.3   THE MONOPOLY FIRM'S PROFIT-MAXIMIZING LEVEL OF ADVERTISING

Rational firms will only expend considerable resources on advertising if it is profitable to do so. Since advertising is costly, this means that it must generate revenue to cover those costs. In other words, advertising must affect demand. It is useful in this respect to recall that any firm with market power faces a downward sloping demand curve. The firm is interested in pushing its demand curve out and selling more at the same price rather than selling more by lowering its price and moving down along the existing demand curve. So, one

---

[6] See, for example, Lambin (1976), Geroski (1982), and Round (1983).

way of thinking of how advertising works is that advertising shifts the firm's demand curve. In other words, demand depends not only upon the price the firm sets but also upon the amount of advertising that the firm chooses. This can be described by the demand function $Q^D(P, \alpha)$ where P is the product price and α is the amount of advertising messages sent, measured, for example, as seconds of television or radio time, or perhaps as page space in newspapers or magazines per period. For a given level of advertising, the firm's demand is decreasing in price and for a given price the amount demanded is increasing in advertising. Alternatively we can write the firm's inverse demand function as $P(Q, \alpha)$ where, for a given level of advertising, the price consumers are willing to pay falls as quantity is increased and, for a given quantity, the price consumers are willing to pay increases with a given level of advertising.

The ability of advertising to increase demand is the "good news" of advertising. The "bad news" is that advertising is costly. Suppose that every unit of advertising or advertising message costs the firm T dollars.[7] Let us also assume that every unit of output costs c dollars to produce and that there are no economies of scale in either production or in advertising. We can now describe the decision problem confronting a monopoly firm. It must pick a level of advertising α, and a level of production Q (or price P), that together maximize profit. In particular this means that the firm needs to quantify the good news and bad news aspects of advertising and work out whether the benefit of sending out one more ad is greater than the incremental cost incurred T.

Let us first work out the profit-maximizing quantity of output to produce for a given number of advertising messages, α. Holding α constant, the firm's marginal revenue curve is:

$$MR(Q, \alpha) = P(Q, \alpha) + \frac{\partial P(Q, \alpha)}{\partial Q} Q. \tag{20.1}$$

Profit maximization implies choosing Q^* such that marginal revenue is equal to marginal cost or:

$$MR(Q^*, \alpha) = P(Q^*, \alpha) + \frac{\partial P(Q^*, \alpha)}{\partial Q} Q^* = c \tag{20.2}$$

We can rewrite the profit-maximizing condition (20.2) and express it in terms of the Lerner Index, which is the firm's price–cost margin as a percentage of price, or $\frac{P^* - c}{P^*}$, where $P^* = P(Q^*, \alpha)$.[8] If, for a given level of advertising α, the firm chooses to sell the profit-maximizing quantity Q^* at a price P^* the Lerner Index will satisfy:

$$\frac{P^* - c}{P^*} = \frac{1}{\eta_P} \tag{20.3}$$

---

[7]   This assumption may not always hold. Often there is considerable quantity discounting when air time, network time, or magazine space is purchased by a firm for advertising.

[8]   For a derivation of the Lerner Index see, section 3.2, Chapter 3.

where $\eta_p = \dfrac{dQ/Q}{dP/P} = \dfrac{P}{Q}\dfrac{\partial Q}{\partial P}$ is the price elasticity of demand evaluated at the firm's choice of output Q^* and corresponding price P^*.[9]

Now consider the monopoly firm's optimal amount of advertising, or α^*. At any output level Q the firm's corresponding price $P(Q, \alpha)$ will increase in the amount of advertising α. To maximize profit the firm should choose an amount of advertising α^* such that the marginal revenue from an additional unit of advertising is equal to its marginal cost T. In other words the firm should choose α^* such that:

$$\frac{\partial P(Q, \alpha^*)}{\partial \alpha}Q = T \tag{20.4}$$

We can rewrite condition (20.4) by multiplying each side by α and dividing each side by PQ so that we have:

$$\frac{\alpha^*}{P^*}\frac{\partial P(Q^*, \alpha^*)}{\partial \alpha} = \frac{\alpha^*T}{P^*Q^*} \tag{20.5}$$

Observe that the right-hand side of (20.5) is the optimal or profit-maximizing advertising expenditure-to-sales ratio for the firm. We can rewrite the left hand side of (20.5) by defining a new elasticity measure, the elasticity of demand with respect to advertising, or $\eta_\alpha = \dfrac{dQ/Q}{d\alpha/\alpha} = \dfrac{\alpha}{Q}\dfrac{\partial Q}{\partial \alpha}$. Now again recall the price elasticity of demand $\eta_p = \dfrac{dQ/Q}{dP/P} = \dfrac{P}{Q}\dfrac{\partial Q}{\partial P}$. Observe that the ratio of these two elasticities η_α/η_p is equal to the left-hand-side of (20.5). We now have a key result. The firm with market power maximizes profits by choosing a level of output (or price) and a level of advertising such that the ratio of advertising expenditure to sales is just equal to the ratio of the advertising elasticity of demand to the price elasticity of demand. That is, profits are maximized when:

$$\frac{Advertising\ Expenditure}{Sales\ Revenue} = \frac{\alpha^*T}{P^*Q^*} = \frac{\eta_\alpha}{\eta_P} \tag{20.6}$$

The condition in equation (20.6) is usually referred to as the Dorfman-Steiner condition after the pioneering paper on advertising written by Dorfman and Steiner in (1954).[10] It states that the monopoly firm maximizes profit by choosing to spend a proportion of its revenue on advertising that is just equal to the ratio of the advertising elasticity of demand to the price elasticity of demand. That is, the firm will advertise until the ratio of dollar advertising to dollar sales equals the ratio of the advertising elasticity of demand to the price elasticity of demand. The *less price elastic* is demand, or the smaller is η_P, the *more* the firm should spend on advertising, and the *more advertising elastic is* demand, or the greater η_α the *more* the firm should spend on advertising.

[9] Actually, η_P is the negative of the elasticity of demand as the actual elasticity is formally a negative value.

[10] Dorfman, R. and P. Steiner, "Optimal Advertising and Optimal Quality," *American Economic Review*, 44, pp. 826–36.

20.1

Suppose that a monopoly firm faces an inverse demand curve described by $P(Q, \alpha) = 100 - \dfrac{1}{\sqrt{\alpha}}Q$. The firm has a constant marginal production cost equal to 60. Each advertising message costs the firm $1.

a.   What is the slope of the demand curve when $\alpha = 100$? When $\alpha = 1,000$? Illustrate your answers.
b.   Suppose that firm decides to send $\alpha = 2,500$ advertising messages.
    (i)   What is the monopolist's marginal revenue curve?
    (ii)   What will be the monopolist's profit-maximizing price and output values?
    (iii)   What is the price elasticity of demand at this price and output combination?
c.   The demand function is such that the advertising elasticity of demand is constant at 1/2. Does the price and output combination derived in part b), satisfy the Dorfman–Steiner condition?

The Dorfman–Steiner condition is an extremely useful reference point in the analysis of advertising behavior. The condition helps us see the positive relationship observed between the firm's profit margin and the extent of advertising in a different light. This relationship has often been used as evidence to support the argument that advertising is a way for a firm to differentiate its product in the eyes of the consumer, and thereby achieve some market power, that is, advertising makes the firm's customers less likely to switch brands.

The Dorfman–Steiner condition in equation (20.6) does make it clear that advertising will be greater in a market where the demand elasticity is low. The profit margin, as measured by the Lerner Index, is inversely proportional to the elasticity of demand. In other words, the Dorfman-Steiner condition says that, all else equal, advertising will be more intense the more market power there is in the industry. But the causality here is different. Rather than the heavy advertising causing the market power, it is in fact the market power, or really the low price elasticity of demand, that induces the heavy advertising.

Think about it for a minute. A perfectly competitive firm faces an infinitely elastic demand curve. As a result, it has a price–cost margin of zero. Clearly, such a firm has little incentive to advertise. It can sell all it wants to at the current price without any additional promotional effort. Moreover, because its price just equals its cost, selling extra units does not bring in any additional profit. In contrast, a firm with market power has a smaller elasticity of demand and, accordingly, a positive price–cost margin. If such a firm can shift out its demand curve it can earn its margin on every additional unit sold. It clearly has an incentive to do this. If not, the firm can only make additional sales by cutting its price. In short, the Dorfman–Steiner condition makes clear that the frequent statement that high advertising and low price elasticity go together cannot be used to vindicate the view that advertising is used by firms to increase their market power. It is rather the market power already there that gives the firm a strong incentive to advertise.

A second insight of the Dorfman–Steiner condition is what it says about how the firm's advertising-to-sales ratio changes in response to changes in the cost of advertising. The condition in equation (20.6) shows that unless the change in cost alters the ratio of the two elasticities—the price elasticity of demand, and the advertising elasticity of demand—the profit maximizing advertising-to-sales ratio will be constant. Thus, even if the cost of advertising

Table 20.1 Estimated industry advertising-to-sales ratios, 2006

Industry	NAICS	$\dfrac{\alpha T}{PQ}$	Industry	NAICS	$\dfrac{\alpha T}{PQ}$
Amusement parks/arcades	713,110	10.5	Mobile homes (mfg.)	321,991	1.9
Soft drink beverages	312,111	10.2	Motor vehicles (mfg.)	336,111	3.5
Preserves (tin, jar, frozen)	311,421	5.4	Cosmetics (mfg.)	325,620	11.1
Radio and TV stores	443,112	3.2	Bedroom furniture (mfg.)	337,122	4.0
Passenger airlines	481,111	3.3	Tires (mfg.)	326,211	3.0
Hotels and motels	721,110	3.6	Legal services	541,110	6.4
Non-discount dept. stores	452,111	5.4	Tobacco products (mfg.)	312,229	5.7

Source: *Advertising Age* and *Outburst Advertising*

increases, the firm's advertising-to-sales ratio will not change if these elasticities are unaffected. This result suggests that the ratio of advertising expenditure to sales across industries will not be greatly affected by changes in the cost of advertising.

In Table 20.1 we report the advertising-to-sales ratio for a sample of industries products for the year 2006. The advertising-to-sales ratio for this small sample of industries range from 1.9 percent for motor homes to 11.1 percent for cosmetics. The Dorfman–Steiner condition suggests that the differences in advertising to sales ratios could be explained by differences in both the advertising and price elasticity of demand. A firm's price elasticity of demand is, of course, affected by the availability of substitute products, which in turn is affected by the number of rivals and the degree of product differentiation. Yet what determines a firm's advertising elasticity of demand? The magnitude of this elasticity reflects just how responsive consumer demand is to an increase in advertising. This begs the larger question to which we now turn. Why do consumers respond to advertising?

20.4   ADVERTISING AS CONSUMER INFORMATION

The traditional textbook model of consumer choice assumes that consumers are perfectly informed about the kinds of goods and services available and their prices. However, consumers typically do not know which brands of products are available, or how quality varies across brands, and which stores sell which brands at the lowest prices.

Certain consumer goods and services, such as cars, furniture, and legal services are relatively expensive items in the consumer's budget and they are products that tend to be rather infrequently purchased. These goods are called *shop* goods because consumers find it worthwhile to "shop around" and become informed about what is available before deciding which brand of good or service to buy. The time and effort spent by the consumer to become informed makes sense for goods that are costly for the consumer and that are bought infrequently.

On the other hand, there are many other consumer goods such as cosmetics, beverages, and perhaps tobacco products that are purchased with some frequency—perhaps once a week and certainly once a month. These goods are called *convenience* goods. For these goods, consumers might be expected to expend less time doing research on what is available and where.

We might expect advertising to be a more influential factor in the purchase of a convenience good than in the purchase of a shop good. Because consumers consider the buying decision for a shop good carefully they will want to seek out reliable information on their own. Advertising sent out by the party interested in selling is likely to be less influential than a trusted friend's endorsement. The opposite holds in the case of convenience goods. For these products, consumers simply want to know such things as what the product does—is Old Spice a deodorant or a food seasoning?—and where it can be bought. Advertising can provide this information quickly and cheaply. Hence, we would expect the advertising elasticity of demand to be greater for convenience goods than for shop goods. To the extent that advertising plays this informational role it serves an economically useful function for the consumer.

We can also take another step and distinguish within the categories of shop and convenience goods those products whose quality or performance cannot be known by consumers before being tried or consumed. For certain goods, it is relatively easy to ascertain the quality of any one brand relative to others. This may be because of widely available ratings guides or simply reflect any consumer's judgment ability. It may also be because there is little quality variation from one store to another. These goods are called *search* goods, indicating that the primary information issue confronting the consumer is one of searching out where the best deals on such goods are to be found. There are other goods, however, such as cars and cosmetic brands where the actual quality is difficult to know without consumers actually purchasing them and actually trying them out. Often this reflects the fact that quality is a matter of personal taste, as is the case with cosmetics, so that the consumer cannot be sure what she feels about the product until she has tried it. Sometimes, it will reflect the fact that quality can only be judged over an extended period of use, as in automobiles. Whatever the reason, we call these kinds of goods *experience* goods as it takes first-hand experience to know how good they are.

Of course, some shop goods will also be search goods while others will be experience goods. A similar division may be made for convenience goods. We might expect that consumers would be more responsive to advertising for convenience goods that are also experience goods. The ad is an inexpensive way for the consumer to learn whether she is likely to enjoy this relatively inexpensive experience good. In other words we might expect the advertising elasticity of demand to be greatest for goods that are both convenience and experience goods. Following the Dorfman–Steiner logic and for the moment, holding all else equal, this logic implies that we should expect a higher advertising expenditure-to-sales ratio for convenience goods that are also experience goods.

In Table 20.2 we have attempted to classify the sample of industries in Table 20.1 according to each of the four product categories just identified. Our grouping is admittedly somewhat arbitrary. Nevertheless, we think that it is roughly accurate. These data tend to support our conjecture that products that are both convenience goods and experience goods ought to

Table 20.2   Advertising expenditures as a % of sales by different categories of products

Convenience, search		Convenience, experience		Shop, search		Shop, experience	
Radio and TV stores	3.2	Soft drink beverages	10.2	Tires	3.0	Amusement parks	10.5
Passenger airlines	3.3	Cosmetics	11.1	Mobile homes	1.9	Motor vehicles	3.5
Hotels and motels	3.6	Preserves	5.4	Bedroom furniture	4.0	Legal services	6.4
Tobacco products	5.7	Department stores	5.4				

be among those most heavily advertised. The convenience good industries in our sample tend to have higher advertising-to-sales ratios, and these ratios are highest for the experience category. Of course, other factors such as the degree of competition in the market—because it affects the price elasticity of demand—are also important. Overall though, these data support the view that advertising plays, at least in part, a useful role of informing consumers about the function and availability of various goods.

To the extent advertising provides consumers with information on price, quality, and retail location advertising should strengthen competition rather than weaken it. Such ads make it difficult for a seller to sell a product at a high price when consumers are aware that a perfect or at least a good substitute is available nearby at a lower price. When viewed in this light, advertising or brand awareness is a highly useful and pro-competitive force that works to reduce the type of product differentiation that results because each consumer knows only a local store's offerings but lacks *information* about what products and prices are available elsewhere.

There is sound empirical evidence to support the view that advertising prices and retail locations intensify price competition. The classic study is that of Benham (1972) who showed that the average price of eyeglasses was significantly higher in states where advertising the prices and retail locations of opticians' services was prohibited. Similar price effects when advertising is restricted were found by Cady (1976) in the market for prescription drugs. The view that advertising promotes price competition may also explain why many professional associations, such as those of lawyers, doctors, and dentists, have long argued for legislation to restrict such price advertising in their professions.

We will consider in greater depth the role of advertising in promoting price competition in the next chapter. For now, we focus on the informational role of advertising in a setting in which firm rivalry is not important, i.e., a setting of monopoly power. A major point of contention concerns precisely what informational role advertising plays. Often the explicit information content seems surprisingly little. What information is provided by an ad in which Tony the Tiger says that sugar-frosted flakes are great? What do consumers learn from a Nissan auto commercial that simply focuses on the figure of a scantily clad woman as she rides in a car? If no useful information is provided by advertising, how then does it affect consumer purchases?

20.5   PERSUASIVE ADVERTISING

The Tony the Tiger and Nissan advertisements appear devoid of any useful information. Instead they aim at somehow persuading consumers that their corn flakes or cars, respectively, are special. Thus this kind of advertising raises the same issue as those raised in early analyses of advertising. These ads appear largely persuasive, and aimed at differentiating the firm's products so as to soften price competition. Yet, even if this view is true some important questions remain. In particular, we need to examine more carefully what it means to say that advertising convinces some consumers that a particular brand of good is superior and a bargain, even at a relatively high price.

If advertising messages devoid of any true information can persuade consumers to buy a product then advertising appears to be effectively *changing* consumer preferences. This presents a new and important twist in how we model consumer behavior. Typically, we assume that the consumer preferences that underlie consumer demand are given or exogenous. The utility function is a formal way to represent the consumer's set of tastes. The conventional textbook model of consumer decision-making describes how the consumer chooses a set of goods that reflect her tastes, i.e., that maximize her utility given her budget constraint.

If advertising does change consumer tastes and hence the consumer's utility function then we must take that into account when we evaluate the role of advertising. For example, suppose that without any advertising, consumers regard one unit of Good X to be worth about $10 at the margin and that firm X finds that it maximizes profit at a price of $10 per box. Now suppose that if the firm advertises it raises consumers' valuation of Good X from $10 to $20 per box and that the firm now finds it profitable to raise its price from $10 to $15 per box. In this scenario, advertising is purely persuasive but is it harmful? Consumer surplus on the marginal box sold rises from 0 to $5 even as the firm has become more profitable as well.[11]

Consumer tastes do change over time. In some sense, every taste is an acquired one developed in response to what we might call persuasive efforts. The training and experience to appreciate fully a classical symphony or an abstract painting or, for that matter, a baseball game can also be thought of as persuasive efforts. Similarly, children have to be taught or persuaded of the value of a healthy diet and adults often have to learn the value of regular exercise. We do not generally complain about efforts to persuade or encourage individuals to enjoy such activities, even though such efforts are an attempt to change an individual's tastes. Why then should we be concerned about promotional efforts to change consumer preferences among competing brands? But perhaps the real question here is *how* the cereal or Nissan ads change consumer tastes. How does the image of a friendly cartoon tiger or a scantily clad young woman on a car persuade a consumer to buy these products?

20.6   ADVERTISING AND SIGNALING

Persuasive advertising is viewed by many as a challenge to the basic tenet of "the invisible hand." According to the persuasive view of advertising it is not the invisible hand but rather visible advertising that convinces consumers what it is that they want and what they should buy. Perhaps not surprisingly, it was the Chicago School with its long intellectual heritage of defending free markets that took up this challenge to the invisible hand.[12] The very important contribution of these economists was to recognize that image advertising may be more informative than first meets the eye. But what sort of information can be inferred from the typical sort of commercials aired on television that seem almost entirely devoted to building a brand image? This was the question raised by the Chicago School economist Philip Nelson (1970, 1974) in two seminal articles written in the 1970s. Nelson began answering the question by first posing another. "What do consumers *know* about a product *before* they

---

[11]   Dixit and Norman (1978) proposed a way to evaluate welfare effects by using both pre-advertising demand and post-advertising consumer tastes. If on the basis of both sets of tastes one gets the same welfare effects then conclusions can be drawn about the effect of persuasive advertising on welfare. This approach was subsequently criticized in Fisher and McGowan (1979) because Dixit and Norman compare welfare before and after advertising using either one set of preferences or the other for both equilibrium outcomes. The comparison that should be made is a comparison of the pre-advertising equilibrium using pre-advertising tastes to the post-advertising equilibrium using post-advertising tastes. But this raises the familiar problem of interpersonal comparison of utility levels.

[12]   It is also important to point out the Chicago School's belief in the stability of consumer preferences. Since this assumption is the starting point of most economic models, there is a lot at stake in taking up this challenge.

purchase it?" Specifically, can consumers identify the quality or other characteristics of the product before they try it?

For certain goods, specifically the ones such as salt or dishes, that we defined as search goods Nelson argued that the answer is surely, yes. Consumers can more or less ascertain the quality of these goods before they decide to buy them. Nelson reasoned that it was in the other category goods, experience goods, such as cars, electrical appliances, wine, and health care products where there was a potential role for image-based advertising to play.

Nelson's argument is quite straightforward. The manufacturer of an experience good knows whether it is a high-quality or a low-quality product. The producer knows whether or not the consumer will be satisfied with the product after purchasing it. The problem is that the consumer does not have this information and can only acquire it by perhaps painful experience. How can the producer—particularly one who knows that he is selling a high-quality product—get this information across to potential customers? Advertising is the key.

The manufacturer of say, an analgesic, does not want the customer's business only once but also hopes to gain that patronage on a repeated basis. If the good is of high quality and works well then, once a consumer tries it, she will probably buy the product again. As long as experience with the pain reliever is satisfactory, the typical consumer will very likely continue to purchase that same product repeatedly rather than start all over searching for an alternative brand. This is not the case, though, for an ineffective pain relief product. The consumer who buys a low-quality product will, in all probability, switch to an alternative brand the next time she goes shopping. Accordingly, only makers of high-quality analgesics have any hope of earning repeat purchases.

Nelson's model combines the above intuition with the concept of discounting and present value of future profits that we discussed in section 2.2 in Chapter 2. Nelson argues that a firm's advertising expenditures are incurred up front. They can only be justified if the discounted value of the future stream of revenues generated by the advertising is sufficient to cover this sunk cost. Nelson's idea is that if a consumer tries an experience good and finds it to be a "good deal" then the consumer is likely to continue to buy it. Indeed, the "better the deal" the producer offers, the higher the probability of repeat purchase and, therefore, the greater the present value of the profits that the firm can expect from an ad that induces or persuades the consumer to try the good in the first place.

Only the maker of a good quality product can be confident that an additional customer lured to the store by an additional successful ad will come back for a second and third purchase. Hence, only the maker of a high-quality product can be sure that an advertisement will generate the extra income necessary to cover the initial expense. The better the quality of its product, the more customers will return in the future and the higher the price they will pay. Accordingly, the better the quality of its product, the more advertising the firm will wish to do to get that first purchase. Moreover, Nelson argued that consumers can recognize this logic, too. They will rationally conclude that if a firm does a lot of advertising it must be because the firm is offering a high-quality product at a reasonable price. This is true even though the explicit content of the advertising may simply be an image and little else. It is the fact of advertising and not its content that signals to the consumer the "good deal" that the firm is offering.

Nelson's dual insight was that in a world in which firms know the quality of their products, but consumers do not, the makers of good quality products would look for some technique to signal that quality, and advertising could be precisely that signaling device. Since the argument applies explicitly to experience goods, a natural test of Nelson's idea would be to examine whether or not the manufacturers of experience goods do more advertising than manufacturers of search goods. In fact, we saw that this seems to be the case with the data shown in Table 20.2. Nelson provided further statistical evidence that this relationship holds.

For the next 15 years Nelson's insight into advertising and signaling set the agenda for most of the theoretical work on advertising. An important early paper in this regard is Schmalensee (1978). That paper raises the point that Nelson's argument that a firm offering a "good deal" has a stronger incentive to advertise than a firm offering a "bad deal" depends quite a bit on the price–cost margin of a "good deal" relative to that of a "bad deal." Suppose, for example, that a high quality pain reliever can be produced at a cost of 10 cents per dosage while a worthless pain reliever, made from a commonly available extract of carrot roots, costs only a penny per dose to make. Then a firm offering the carrot root painkiller may find that it can earn a very high markup on each bottle sold. Even if no repeat purchases occur, the firm may earn enough on every first-time purchase to justify considerable advertising expense. Quite possibly, this expense will exceed the amount the maker of the high quality pain reliever will spend.

Yet despite Schmalensee's cautionary point, the signaling possibility raised by Nelson remained the subject of investigation and much additional work was done.[13] Among the more important papers in the signaling literature are those by Kihlstrom and Riordan (1984) and Milgrom and Roberts (1986). Kihlstrom and Riordan (1984) develop a two-period model in which a firm's advertising alone in the first period determines whether consumers believe the good to be a high- or low-quality product. Given consumer beliefs about quality, prices are then determined in a traditional demand and supply manner. The important result of the Kihlstrom and Riordan (1984) study is that they too find a strong incentive for high quality producers to lure "repeat buyers" by advertising heavily in the first period, just as Nelson (1970, 1974) found in his earlier and much simpler analysis. The contribution of Milgrom and Roberts (1986) is to show that pricing can serve as a quality signal as well as can advertising. Because both advertising and pricing can indicate product quality, the extent to which either is used is very complicated. Using a high price to signal quality is a cheaper alternative for the firm than advertising, with the result that the Milgrom and Roberts (1986) paper weakens the theoretical link between advertising and product quality. The Milgrom and Roberts signaling model is, however, a monopoly or single firm model. Fluet and Garella (2002) show instead that when the firm competes in price with other firms it may be necessary to use advertising, and not price, to signal quality.[14]

The large volume of papers on the signaling theory of advertising and prices has generated empirical research as well. In general, this research has tried to provide evidence on the extent to which the quality of a good is linked with the manufacturer's advertising-to-sales ratio, or price. Of course, one obvious issue is that the task of empirically measuring quality is far from easy. The truth is that quality has many dimensions and it is not clear how to combine the many dimensions into a single index. Nevertheless, broad rankings of product quality are regularly published by Consumers Union. An important early study using this data was done by Reisz (1978) on over 10,000 brands of 685 products. He found, however, only a weak correlation between price and product quality.

If high prices do not necessarily signal high quality, what about advertising? Kotowitz and Mathewson (1986) examined this relationship for both automobiles and whole-life

---

[13]   The interested reader can refer to Bagwell and Riordan (1991) and Schwartz and Wilde (1985).

[14]   Remember, we are assuming again that firms care about repeat business. If not, and if consumers always inferred that high quality meant high price, every producer would raise its price whether it made a high-quality or a low-quality product.

Table 20.3   Price and quality in the upright vacuum cleaner market

Brand/model	Model quality rating (0–100)	Price
Kenmore Progressive	74	$300
Hoover Wind Tunnel	69	$250
Eureka Boss	68	$150
Electrolux Oxygens	67	$400
Kirby Sentria	67	$1,350
Riccar Superlite	66	$350
Bissell Healthy	64	$300
Oreck XL21	63	$750
Panasonic MV-V7720	63	$200
Dyson DC 14	62	$550

insurance. They did not, however, find evidence that the higher the advertising the better the deal. Similarly, Archibald, Haulman, and Moody (1983) examined running shoes and again found that neither price nor advertising levels for 187 brands were strongly correlated with the quality rankings, which were published in the magazine *Runner's World*. However, these authors did find that the magazine's quality ratings, once publicized and circulated, were very positively correlated with the extent of advertising done *after* those rankings were published. Firms with a high ranking were anxious to let consumers know this fact, while those with a low ranking were less interested in displaying their product's deficiencies.[15]

A study of 196 different industries by Caves and Green (1996) finds few discernible tendencies in the relation between advertising and brand quality. For many industries, these authors find that the quality–advertising expenditure correlation approaches a negative one—the exact opposite of Nelson's prediction. They do, however, find a positive relationship between advertising and quality in the case of new or innovative goods. They also find a weaker but still positive correlation between advertising and the quality of those goods in their sample that might be called "experience goods." The Caves and Green evidence on Nelson's hypothesis may then be best described as mixed.

As a final but less formal bit of evidence on this issue we offer in Table 20.3 an analysis of upright vacuum cleaners recently reported by *Consumer Reports*.[16] The table lists the top ten models and their prices. It is quite clear that the correlation between price and quality is very weak. One of the lowest ranked brands, the Oreck XL21, sells for nearly $300 above the average of $460. A medium quality model, the Kirby Sentria, sells for nearly three times the average and four times the most highly ranked model. Moreover, while Kenmore and Hoover both advertise extensively, it is not clear that they advertise more than Eureka, Bissall, or Oreck.

While Nelson's insight that costly advertising might serve as signal for high product quality remains a valuable one, the theory has not held up well in empirical testing. There are as well other problems with the signaling theory of advertising. First, the basic idea that the

---

[15]   It is worthwhile noting as well that the magazine *Runner's World* does allow manufacturers to quote their rankings in advertisements whereas the magazine *Consumer Reports* does not.

[16]   Consumer Reports.org, Upright Vacuum Ratings, May, 2007.

more advertising the higher is the quality suggests that the firm has a clear incentive to let consumers know just how costly that ad campaign is. However, firms do not announce to consumers how much they spend on advertising.

Further difficulties with the view that advertising signals quality come from the assumption that the goods are experience goods. Some experience goods are sold to consumers while others are sold to businesses. The signaling approach would suggest that the type of buyer should not matter and hence, that the extent of advertising should not differ across these two type of experience goods. However, advertising expenditure-to-sales ratios are markedly higher for experience goods that are marketed to consumers than for those that are marketed instead to other firms, i.e., intermediate or producer goods. And even within the consumer goods category advertising expenditures are also relatively high for search goods as well as experience goods. For example, a Ralph Lauren Polo shirt or a pair of Calvin Klein jeans can be tried on and inspected before purchase. So, these are search goods. Yet Ralph Lauren, Calvin Klein, and the manufacturers of clothing apparel in general do a great deal of advertising. Here again, it is not clear how the signaling approach can explain this observation.

Finally, it should be noted that the signaling theory is only relevant for untried products. After many or most consumers have tried the good and experienced its quality, the underlying logic of the signaling approach suggests that there is little further role for advertising. Yet if this is the case, that approach cannot tell us why firms who market established and well-known brands, such as Coca-Cola, Miller-Lite, Chevrolet, and Rice Krispies, each continue to launch expensive advertising campaigns.

20.7   SUPPRESSED ADVERTISING CONTENT

An even-handed reading of the evidence to date is that while the signaling approach to advertising pioneered by Nelson (1970, 1974) is insightful, it cannot provide a complete explanation for all the advertising we observe. In trying to understand the low information content of many ads, we are left with the view that these ads are mostly efforts to manipulate consumer preferences or that the information or quality signals they convey cannot be easily deciphered. A somewhat related explanation is that these ads do contain information but there is a conscious attempt to limit that information. There may be a reason for a firm to offer some information about its products but not "too much." This is the approach taken by Anderson and Renault (2006). We explore their argument briefly, here.

The Anderson and Renault (2006) model begins with the recognition that once the consumer has traveled to the store that travel cost is sunk. This can lead to a so-called "hold-up" problem for consumers. You may remember the 1990s fad of Beanie Babies. Suppose consumers value the Beanie Babies differently. Some are willing to pay $25 for Crunch the Shark whereas others do not value Crunch at all. Instead, they prefer Chilly the Polar Bear. If there are any transport costs, a retailer that advertises that she has Crunch the Shark for sale will only attract the first group. The retailer may prefer simply to advertise that she has Beanie Babies in general and suppress the information that her inventory is Crunch in particular. The retailer also knows that anyone that does come to the store and asks for Crunch values Crunch at $25. Since the transport cost is sunk at that point, the retailer will have a strong incentive to "hold up" the consumer and charge them the full $25.

Somewhat more formally, let there be three consumer types, 1, 2, and 3, and three kinds of widgets, red, blue, and yellow. Consumer type 1 values red widgets at $40, yellow widgets at $20, and blue widgets at $15. Type 2 values red widgets at $15, yellow widgets at $40, and blue widgets at $20. For type 3, the respective valuations are $20, $15, and $40. These willingness to pay values for each consumer are shown in the following table.

		Consumer 1	Consumer 2	Consumer 3
		Consumer type		
	Red	$40	$15	$20
Widget type	Yellow	$20	$40	$15
	Blue	$15	$20	$40

Each consumer also incurs a transport cost of $5.01 to visit the store. Once a consumer actually visits a store, the transport cost is sunk. A store is equally likely to have either red, yellow, or blue widgets. If consumers know only that a store has widgets, they infer a probability of one third that the store has widgets of any specific color. The store incurs zero cost per widget.

Consider two advertising strategies for a store that has only red widgets. The store can advertise that it has red widgets or the store can advertise simply that it has widgets. Which strategy will the store prefer? First, observe that the store will never set a widget price below $15, the minimum valuation of any consumer. Now consider the first strategy of advertising that the store has only red widgets. If the retailer does this, consumer types 2 and 3 will not come to the store. The $5.01 in transport cost will mean that the effective price for them will never be less than $20.01. So, it is not worthwhile for either of these two types to come. Of course, the store knows this, too. So, if it advertises its "Red Widgets" alone, it knows that the only buyers who show up are type 1 consumers. Since, for these consumers, the $5.01 in transport cost is a sunk cost once they are at the store, the owner can then charge them their full willingness-to-pay of $40 for the widgets. Foreseeing this outcome, type 1 consumers will not respond to a red widget advertisement either. Advertising that the store only has red widgets will not attract customers.

However, if the shop announces that it simply has widgets in general, consumers can reason as follows. Faced with a crowd of all consumer types but not knowing who is who, the shopkeeper will set a price of $15 per widget. This will permit the store to sell one (red) widget to each type and earn profit of $45 from each threesome rather than set a price of $40 and sell only to one type or a price of $20 and sell to types 1 and 3 (each of which yields profit of $40 per threesome). Moreover, since consumers infer that the probability associated with each color is one-third, all three types will in fact respond to the ad by showing up at the store knowing that, in fact, when this happens, the store owner will keep the price at $15. Consumer *i* will work out that for a price of $15 and a transport cost of $5.01, she will receive either a red, yellow, or blue widget (each with probability 0.3333) whose value therefore is: $0.3333(\$40 + \$20 + 15) = \$25$, implying a net value of $5 regardless of what consumer *i*'s most preferred type is.

There are a number of features of the foregoing outcome worth noting. First, the store suppresses some information in its advertising. Specifically, it does not reveal that its inventory is just red widgets. The store also need not mention the price in its ads. Consumers can work out that the profit-maximizing price to set is $15. It is the presence of a variety of consumer types—due to precisely the vagueness of the advertisement—that supports this outcome. Because some of the consumers attracted to the store do not value red widgets very highly, the store-owner is motivated to keep the price low. We have a market outcome in which advertising deliberately does not mention either the specific attributes of the product for sale or its price.

Perhaps most surprising of all, the suppression of this informational content can raise welfare. To see this, observe that advertising red widgets led to a complete breakdown of the market whereas advertising widgets in general leads to trades from which everyone potentially can gain.[17] In other words, a law requiring full disclosure by the firm would make things worse.

Ellison and Ellison (2005) present a somewhat related argument regarding search engines on the web. In principle, search engines increase the competitive pressure on Internet firms. Moreover, the search engine can claim for itself some of the profit that would have gone to the firm in return for providing consumers with the relevant price information. Thus, an e-commerce company has some reason to thwart the search engine even though it may like the fact that the search engine or shopbot brings customers to its site. It can do this in a variety of ways. For example, it can list a low product price that the search engine sees but charge a very high transport price that the search engine does not see or similarly offer only very slow delivery. Again, once the consumer has invested in the search cost and arrived at the firm's website, the firm may find that it can charge the consumer a very high price for the product that she really wants, e.g., one with quick delivery. Here again, e-tailers are happy to list some information to entice the search engine but simultaneously to keep too much information from being revealed.

20.8   TRUTH VERSUS FRAUD IN ADVERTISING

Suppression of information borders closely on misrepresentation. We, therefore, conclude this chapter by considering briefly the issue of false advertising. Fraudulent or misleading product claims are a problem that is at least as old as alchemy. Sometimes, the harm in such activities is relatively minor, such as a claim that a particular toothpaste will leave one's teeth 30 percent whiter. Sometimes, however, fraudulent advertising claims have turned trusting consumers into unwilling victims. Often the main wounds suffered in these episodes are financial ones as individuals have parted with large sums of money to pursue "get rich quick" schemes or have fallen for other phony promises. However, in the case of health products and health care services, the victims of fraudulent claims of both ancient and modern "snake oil" salesmen have suffered pain, physical harm, and even death in addition to any monetary loss. It was in part such events that led Congress to include in the Federal Trade Commission Act a prohibition of methods of competition deemed unfair, including the practice of false or deceptive advertising.

Advertising is considered false by the FTC when it includes actual or implied claims about a product that are verifiably untrue. In addition, these claims must have affected the decision of a substantial number of consumers to buy the product before the FTC will take enforcement action. Omitting information about a product does not constitute false advertising unless the product is one for which the advertising is regulated by the Food and Drug Administration. Subjective claims, such as "this product can change your life," are almost nonverifiable by definition and so are not considered false advertising under current law. Illegal advertising consists of claims that are demonstrably false and that induce a large number of consumers to buy the product. Firms found guilty of such conduct are frequently required to compensate the customers who were deceived by the false advertisement.

---

[17]   Not counting (sunk) transport costs, all consumers and the seller are better off in the limited information equilibrium. Including sunk costs, type 2 consumers are (trivially) worse off but the gains for all other participants are enough that these consumers could be compensated while others would still be better off.

Popular culture is filled with images of dishonest promoters. The used car salesman tirelessly pushing his stock that he knows to be filled with "lemons," the real estate dealer selling the Brooklyn Bridge or some other phony property claim, and the "quack" medical expert promoting the latest miracle cure are all common, even stereotypical images. The widespread currency of such images, coupled with a general suspicion that Madison Avenue can manipulate consumer tastes at will, has focused the attention of both the public and the regulatory agencies on fraudulent or deceptive claims as perhaps the major issue in connection with advertising.

When we review the FTC case files regarding charges of illegal advertising over the past several years, what do we find? Broadly speaking, we find that most cases involve situations in which customers have little ability to pursue any compensation from the firm engaged in such advertising for either or both of two reasons. One is that the substance of the advertised claim—while verifiable in a laboratory or by individuals with specialized knowledge—is one that most consumers are ill equipped to monitor and verify. Thus, for example, Pizzeria Uno was asked to stop making the claim that its Thinzetta pizza line is low fat not because it is misleading but because it is virtually impossible for the consumer to evaluate. Similarly, the FTC stopped the frequent claim of weight-loss company Jenny Craig that nine out of ten clients would recommend Jenny Craig to a friend. This claim reflects a statement that can only be judged for accuracy by a formal statistical survey and not by most potential customers of Jenny Craig.

The second and perhaps more important reason the victims of false advertising may have difficulty pursuing their claims is that often the guilty firms are "fly-by-night" operations that disappear into thin air whenever an irate customer tries to track them down. Fly-by-night firms have little concern for repeat business. These firms know that the product or service they sell will fail, but only after the customer has paid up front. The "snake oil" medical quacks of the American Old West quickly left town after selling their wares. A more modern example of a fly-by-night firm using false advertising might be the New York City-based firm Student Aid Incorporated, which guaranteed each of its customers that in return for a fee of $97 the company would obtain for them a minimum of $1,000 in college scholarship funds. These examples effectively make the cautionary point first raised by Schmalensee (1978) regarding the signaling approach to advertising.

In light of the foregoing, we expect fraudulent advertising to be most prevalent in markets in which two conditions are satisfied. The first is that the firm is selling a product for which an actual purchase is necessary in order to evaluate the product's efficacy, or what we call experience goods. The second is that a customer who is dissatisfied with the product's performance cannot easily claim compensation from the firm. While the latter condition is most easily met by "fly-by-night" firms, we should recognize that it may be difficult for consumers to verify how well many modern products, such as medications, software, and automobile repair parts are working and to obtain compensation if they are not performing. More generally, different products will satisfy these two criteria to a greater or lesser extent.

This has implications well beyond the narrow issue of fraudulent advertising because consumers are smart too. Because they understand the settings in which advertising will be less honest, consumers' response to advertising will be equally strategic. Consumers will accept such promotional efforts as truthful only to the extent that they can verify the product's quality prior to purchase and even that criterion will be moderated by whether the consumer will be back in this product market for additional purchases later. Here again the way in which advertising affects consumers' decision to buy will vary across product markets. As a result, there will be no single role that advertising plays in consumer decision-making.

Reality Checkpoint

Taken for A Ride on the Internet Superhighway

The advent of mass media and the associated mass advertising made possible has greatly altered the selling of goods to final consumers. The advent of the Internet and worldwiide web is certainly part of this information revolution. At the same time, because it is easy for anyone to advertise on the web but difficult for the recipients of those ads to track down the location of the advertisers in real space, this medium has also prompted a wave of fraudulent claims. These deceptive practices have included promotions for products falsely alleged to help one lose weight without exercise or dieting; products to increase the size of sexual organs; and, perhaps most commonly, get-rich-quick schemes.

For example, Michael J. Gardner and Rebecca Dahl Gardner, operated several businesses that offered buyers the chance to make as much as $900 per week just working at home and using the specialized software that the Gardner's would provide to operate a billing service for a healthcare firm whose name would also be provided by the Gardners. In return, the customer had to pay the Gardner's an upfront fee ranging from $59 to $150. However, after paying the fee consumers found that they either never received the software or that if they did, it did not work properly. Nor were the customers ever given any healthcare firms as clients. Similarly, Gregory P. Roth and Peter W. Stolz, operated a company known as 30 Minute Mortgage that promised consumers incredibly low interest rate mortgages. Potential customers were asked for all kinds of sensitive private information such as names, addresses, phone numbers, social security numbers, employment information, income, first and second mortgage payments, and bank account balances. However, no mortgages were ever actually offered. Instead, the firm just sold this sensitive information to other firms who could then better target their own promotions.

Snake oil remedies also still sell. David L. Walker maintained a website and conducted seminars and personal consultations promoting his purported cancer cure, the "CWAT Treatment: BioResonance Therapy and Molecular Enhancer." The website claimed his treatments, for which he charged between $2,400 and $5,200, made surgery, chemotherapy, and other conventional cancer treatments unnecessary. However, there was no real evidence that Walker's BioResonance Therapy had any therapeutic effects.

All the firms mentioned above and others were caught and prosecuted by the Federal Trade Commission. Yet many other fraudulent promotions undoubtedly persist. As Schmalensee (1978) noted, when advertising is cheap and the gains from one sale are large, it matters little if dissatisfied customers make no repeat purchases and Nelson's (1970, 1974) hypotheses that advertising itself is a signal of quality breaks down.

Sources: Federal Trade Commission, various news releases, www.ftc.gov.

Summary

Large-scale advertising has played a pivotal role in shaping the modern shopping experience. The development of large retail outlets offering numerous brands of products is largely a result of the rise of mass media and the promotional efforts that have accompanied this rise. Yet from the beginning, advertising has had its critics. In particular, early economic analyses viewed advertising as a way to increase and protect monopoly power.

The evidence that firms with relatively high profit and in relatively concentrated industries tended to do relatively more advertising lent support to this view.

The view that advertising strengthens market power and weakens price competition is based, in part, on the empirical finding that advertising is most intense in industries where firms have considerable market power and in part on the belief that advertising is persuasive and changes consumer tastes in favor of the advertised brand. Yet from a purely economics perspective, such arguments must be viewed as, at best, incomplete. To begin with, the observed empirical correlation of market power and advertising may well result from the fact that the more inelastic is a firm's demand curve, the more it will find it worthwhile to use advertising to push that demand curve out rather than to try to sell more units by dropping the price. Firms with market power have a greater incentive to advertise than perfectly competitive firms.

Moreover, if consumers are rational, they are not likely to be duped by any artificial distinctions advertising tries to create. Alternatively, the preference for an advertised good may in fact reflect some real information that the advertising conveys. The most obvious kind of information that advertising could provide is about product characteristics and prices. Several empirical studies have documented cases where laws permitting various professional occupations and stores to advertise have led to lower prices and increased consumer welfare.

Many advertisements, however, do not seem to include much explicit information. Following the work of Nelson (1970, 1974), many economists have explored the possibility that important information is being conveyed just by the fact that the firm is advertising, regardless of whether that advertising mentions price or all the salient characteristics of its products. This literature focuses on the fact that a consumer can learn the true value of many goods only by a process of trial and error so that when a particular brand of a good is found

to be satisfactory, the consumer will likely continue to purchase that brand in the future. If good products enjoy a high likelihood of repeat business then the firms marketing good products have a strong incentive to advertise in order to get consumers to make an initial purchase. Rational consumers will recognize this and therefore infer that a product that is widely advertised must be of high quality—regardless of the content of the advertising message. Yet despite the theoretical appeal of this argument there does not seem to be a close connection in reality between product quality and advertising expense.

It may be the case that firms have an incentive to advertise but to do so in a way that in fact limits the amount of information transmitted. Offering some but not all information may be a means for a firm to commit to a low price since it means that the typical set of customers that it faces will include some who are not really willing to pay very much for the good. Suppressing information may also be a way to suppress price competition and to thwart the ability of a search engine or other mechanism to claim profits for itself at the expense of the firm.

In sum, advertising is a complex phenomenon. We need to be clear about the way advertising works to influence consumer demand in order to evaluate its impact and design appropriate public policy. Moreover, as our discussion of search engines suggests, a crucial aspect of the advertising issue is its impact on the strategic interaction among firms. In the next chapter, we examine advertising when firms compete with each other for customers.

Problems

1. You have been hired to market a new music recording that is expected to have target sales of $20 million for the coming year. The marketing department has estimated that a 1 percent increase in advertising the recording would increase the recordings sold by about 0.5 percent, and that a 1 percent increase in the price of the recording would reduce the number sold by about 2 percent. How much money should you commit to advertising the recording in the coming year?

2. Suppose that the demand for a new wrinkle cream is described by a nonlinear demand

function $Q(P, A) = P^{-1/2}A^{1/4}$, and so $\partial Q(P, A)/\partial P = -P^{-3/2}A^{1/4}/2$ and $\partial Q(P, A)/\partial A = P^{-1/2}A^{-3/4}/4$. Show that the price elasticity of demand is $\eta_P = 1/2$, and that the advertising elasticity of demand is $\eta_A = 1/4$.

   a. What do you predict the advertising-to-sales ratio would be in this industry?

   b. Does it depend on how costly it is to advertise for this product?

3. A firm has developed a new product for which it has a registered trademark. The firm's market research department has estimated that the demand for this product is

$Q(P, A) = 11,600 - 1,000P + 20A^{1/2}$, where Q is annual output, P is the price, and A the annual expenditure for advertising. The total cost of producing the new good is $C(Q) = .001Q^2 + 4Q$. This implies that the marginal cost of production is $MC(Q) = .002Q + 4$. The unit cost of advertising is constant and equal to one, or $T = 1$.

a. Find the inverse demand function $P(Q, A)$, and show that the marginal revenue from an additional dollar of advertising is $MR_A = QA^{-1/2}/100$.

b. Calculate the optimal output level Q^*, price P^*, and advertising level A^* for the firm.

c. What is firm profit if it follows this optimal strategy?

d. What is consumer surplus if the firm adopts this strategy?

4. Consider again the firm in question 3. Work out the firm's profit-maximizing output, price, and profit if the firm did not advertise. By how much does the use of advertising in this market change the firm's profit and consumer surplus for the customers of the firm?

5. How could you explain the different advertising-to-sales ratios of the following firms:

Firm	Main products	$\alpha T/PQ(\%)$
Philip Morris	Tobacco, food, beer	7.3
Procter & Gamble	Soaps, paper, food	5.3
General Motors	Autos	3.5
Kodak	Photo supplies	9.3
Johnson & Johnson	Pharmaceuticals	11.3
Pepsico	Soft drinks, snacks	5.2
Sears, Roebuck	Retailing	3.4
American Home Products	Pharmaceuticals	17.3

6. Imagine that there are 1,000 consumers. For each consumer, the willingness to pay for a widget is distributed uniformly over the interval $[0, 1]$ depending on the style of the widget. A retailer with a particular style of the good knows this distribution. Her costs are zero. Consumers do not know the style that the retailer has and incur a transport or search cost of $c = 0.125$. Once this cost is incurred it is sunk. At that point, a consumer in the retailer's store will purchase the product so long as her valuation is greater than or equal to the price charged by the retailer.

a. Show that faced with a random selection of customers, the retailer's profit maximizing price is $p = 0.5$

b. Show that with $c = 0.125$, all consumers will come to shop expecting and getting a price of 0.5. What would happen if $c = 0.15$?

7. Suppose that the retailer in question 6 could communicate in some way to those customers with valuations less than 0.5 of the style that she has in stock and tell them that it is not worthwhile coming. If the retailer keeps the price at 0.5, how large can the transport cost c now be before the market collapses? Will the retailer keep the price at $p = 0.5$?

References

Anderson, S. and R. Renault. 2006. "Advertising Content." *American Economic Review* 96 (March): 93–113.

Archibald, R., C. A. Haulman, and C. E. Moody. 1983. "Quality, Price, Advertising, Published Quality Ratings." *Journal of Consumer Research* 9 (March): 347–53.

Bagwell, K. and M. Riordan. 1991. "High and Declining Prices Signal Product Quality." *American Economic Review* 81 (March): 224–39.

Benham, L. 1972. "The Effects of Advertising on the Price of Eyeglasses." *Journal of Law and Economics* 15 (October): 337–52.

Cady, J. F. 1976. "An Estimate of the Price Effects of Restrictions on Drug Price Advertising." *Economic Inquiry* 14 (July): 493–510.

Caves, R. E. and D. P. Green. 1996. "Brands' Quality Levels, Prices, and Advertising Outlays: Empirical Evidence on Signals and Information Costs." *International Journal of Industrial Organization* 14 (February): 29–52.

Comanor, W. S. and T. A. Wilson. 1967. "Advertising Market Structure and Performance." *Review of Economics and Statistics* 49 (November): 423–40.

——. 1974. *Advertising and Market Power*. Cambridge, MA: Harvard University Press.

Dixit, A. and V. Norman. 1978. "Advertising and Welfare." *Bell Journal of Economics* 9 (Spring): 1–17.

Dorfman, R. and P. O. Steiner. 1954. "Optimal Advertising and Optimal Quality." *American Economic Review* 44 (December): 826–36.

Ellison, G. and S. Fisher Ellison. 2005. "Search, Obfuscation, and Price Elasticities on the Internet." Working Paper, MIT Department of Economics.

Fluet, C. and P. Garella. 2002. "Advertising and Prices as Signals of Quality in a Regime of Price Rivalry." *International Journal of Industrial Organization* 20 (September): 907–30.

Fisher, F. and J. J. McGowan. 1979. "Advertising and Welfare: Comment." *Bell Journal of Economics* 10 (Autumn): 726–7.

Galbraith, J. K. 1958. *The Affluent Society*. Boston: Houghton-Mifflin.

Geroski, P. 1982. "Simultaneous Equations Models of the Structure-Performance Paradigm." *European Economic Review* 19 (September): 145–58.

Kaldor, N. V. 1950. "The Economic Aspects of Advertising." *Review of Economic Studies* 18 (February): 1–27.

Kihlstrom, R. and M. Riordan. 1984. "Advertising as a Signal." *Journal of Political Economy* 92 (June): 427–50.

Kotowitz, Y. and G. F. Mathewson. 1986. "Advertising and Consumer Learning." In P. M. Ippolito and D. T. Schefman, eds, *Empirical Approaches to Consumer Protection Economics*. Washington, DC: Federal Trade Commission, U.S. Government Printing Office.

Lambin, J. J. 1976. *Advertising, Competition, and Market Conduct in Oligopoly over Time*. Amsterdam: North-Holland.

Milgrom, P. and J. Roberts. 1986. "Price and Advertising Signals of Product Quality." *Journal of Political Economy* 94 (August): 796–821.

Nelson, P. 1970. "Information and Consumer Behavior." *Journal of Political Economy* 78 (May): 311–29.

——. 1974. "Advertising as Information." *Journal of Political Economy* 82 (August): 729–54.

Nichols, W. H. 1951. *Price Policy in the Cigarette Industry*. Nashville: Vanderbilt University Press.

Pope, D. 1983. *The Making of Modern Advertising*. New York: Basic Books.

Posner, R. 1975. "The Social Cost of Monopoly and Regulation." *Journal of Political Economy* 83 (June): 807–38.

Reisz, P. 1978. "Price versus Quality in the Marketplace." *Journal of Retailing* 54 (Winter): 15–28.

Round, D. K. 1983. "Intertemporal Profit Margin Variability and Market Structure in Australian Manufacturing." *International Journal of Industrial Organization* 1 (June): 189–209.

Schmalensee, R. 1978. "A Model of Advertising and Product Quality." *Journal of Political Economy* 86 (June): 485–503.

——. 1989. "Inter-industry Studies of Structure and Performance." In R. Schmalensee and R. D. Willig, eds, *Handbook of Industrial Organization, Vol. 2*. Amsterdam: North-Holland.

Schwartz, A. and L. Wilde. 1985. "Product Quality and Imperfect Information." *Review of Economic Studies* 52 (April): 251–62.

Solow, R. M. 1967. "The New Industrial State or Son of Affluence." *Public Interest* 9 (Fall): 100–8.

Telser, L. 1964. "Advertising and Competition." *Journal of Political Economy* 72 (December): 537–62.

21

Advertising, Competition, and Brand Names

Many of the most memorable advertising campaigns promote a brand by emphasizing that it is different in some way from other leading brands in the market. The soft drink 7-Up was long touted as the Uncola Drink. Kellogg's Sugar-Frosted Flakes are uniquely identified with Tony the Tiger and his testimony that this cereal is Grrr-Great. Perhaps most famous of all is Coca-Cola's claim that "Coke is the real thing." These and other campaigns for countless other products tell consumers that the advertised brand is special and different from all others. Of course, sometimes the differences emphasized by the ads are real. Apple Computer does in fact offer a different product from Windows-operated PCs. Likewise, Apple's iPhone is different from most others. When the product differences across the brands are important to consumers, advertising can play an important and useful role in matching consumers to the brand that they prefer.

However, when the different brands of products do not appear to be actually very different, advertising by competing brands turns into a "capture-the-consumer" game. As such it has the potential to become a form of wasteful competition. The advertising expenditure on product promotions yields little useful information to consumers. This may be the case when it appears that it is advertising itself that is the chief source of differences among the brands.

In this chapter, we consider the role that advertising can play when, in contrast to the previous chapter, there are many firms competing for customers. Advertising and the creation of brand names are important strategies for a firm. When consumers have a preference for variety and product differentiation is important to them the creation of brand names can play an important matching role—directing consumers to the products that they prefer. Advertising is a key part of developing and promoting brand names. On the other hand, advertising can yield little additional information and be both wasteful and harmful to consumers. Which outcome obtains will depend on how one thinks advertising works when employed as a strategy by rival firms. This issue is the central focus of this chapter.

21.1 ADVERTISING AS WASTEFUL COMPETITION

One concern about advertising is that it allows firms a way to differentiate their products in the minds of consumers and thereby soften price competition. In other words, there is again the fear that advertising confers or strengthens monopoly power. There is added concern that advertising could be socially inefficient in markets with strategic interaction. Advertising expenditures in such markets may simply be a form of wasteful competition that does not even increase firm profitability.

This insight can be easily illustrated by means of a simple game. Suppose that ZIP Studios and Gamma Studios are both in the entertainment industry and they compete for customers of their films through advertising. The profit of each company depends on both its own advertising expenditure as well as that of its rival. To be specific, suppose that the profits of each studio are as follows:

$$ZIP \text{ profit} = (60 - A_G)A_Z - A_Z^2$$
$$Gamma \text{ profit} = (60 - A_Z)A_G - A_G^2 \tag{21.1}$$

where A_Z and A_G are the advertising expenditures of ZIP and Gamma, respectively. Each studio company seeks to maximize its profit through its choice of advertising expenditure. This leads to the following advertising best response functions:

$$R^Z: A_Z = 30 - A_G/2$$
$$R^G: A_G = 30 - A_Z/2 \tag{21.2}$$

Reality Checkpoint
The Brush War in Hog Heaven

A classic example of a "prisoner's dilemma" advertising war comes from the rivalry between Braun (owned by Gillette) and Optiva (owned by Philips), the two biggest makers of electric toothbrushes. For years the two firms engaged in a "no holds barred" PR war, each side taking extreme measures to convince households and dentists that its brush is best.

A most extraordinary round in this fight occurred in 1999. Optiva was vigorously pursuing market share for its Sonicare brand. It conducted tests purporting to show that Sonicare toothbrushes were both less abrasive to tooth enamel and far better at attacking bacteria below the gumline than Braun's Oral B Plaque Remover model. Under a Swiss dental scientist, researchers compared the two brushes by repeatedly brushing the teeth of 3,000 dead pigs. This was expensive. It required the purchase of pigs' heads from slaughterhouses and arranging for their transportation and refrigeration. Further expenses arose from ensuring that the tests were completed before decay set in.

Braun's response was quick and forceful. It sent a team of scientists to Kansas where it contracted with farmers to brush the teeth of a similarly large number of live pigs. For this, it not only had to pay the farmers but also arrange to sedate the swine, since hogs don't like their teeth cleaned electronically. Braun also had to pay its researchers extra to enter the sties and squat in the muck to brush the hogs' teeth. Unsurprisingly, Braun claimed the tests on live pigs demonstrated Oral B's superiority.

The whole affair was very expensive. It is hard to know how relevant the brushing of pigs' teeth is to human oral hygiene. Moreover, the resultant claims and counterclaims led to yet another court battle. Doubtless, both sides would have preferred a ceasefire to avoid these costs. Yet each found it difficult to halt its aggressive behavior unilaterally. It seems these tests yielded little gain for consumers. Since they also appear to be jointly unprofitable for producers, the advertising expenses must be considered largely wasteful—unless one thinks a hog's healthy smile is worth a lot, even if it's dead!

Source: M. Maremount, "Braun, Sonicare Brush Up on Their Legendary Feud," *Wall Street Journal*, April 30, 1999, p. A1.

Simple algebra confirms that the Nash equilibrium, that is, a pair of best responses for this game, is $A_Z^* = A_G^* = \$20$. Total advertising expenditure in the industry is \$40 and each studio earns a profit of \$400. However, it is also easy to show that each studio would be better off if they both advertised less. Specifically, the joint profit of the two firms is maximized when $A_Z = A_G = \$15$. In that case, total advertising in the industry is reduced to \$30 and each studio earns a profit of \$450.

The problem is that the two studios are caught in a "prisoners' dilemma" game spending extra resources on advertising in a futile struggle to steal consumers from each other. If advertising does not bring in additional consumers to the market, then the loss in producer surplus that results from this dilemma is not counterbalanced by any gain in surplus. Instead, each studio is led to advertise so as to avoid being the loser whose customers will be lured to the rival. However, the net result of such spending in total is that each studio ends up with basically the same number of customers it would have had if it and its rival had agreed not to advertise.

21.2   ADVERTISING AND INFORMATION IN PRODUCT-DIFFERENTIATED MARKETS

When the differences among the products sold in a market are relatively small, advertising strategies are often used to play a capture the consumer game, and as such can lead to wasteful competition. However, the game changes when the products marketed are different in some key dimension that is important to consumers. In this case advertising can play an important information role—matching consumers to brands. To investigate the role and impact of advertising in this context, we of course need to work in a setting of differentiated products, such as the now familiar Hotelling model of spatial competition. The set of different kinds of products potentially available is described by a unit line segment. Each point on the line represents a potential brand or variety of product. The total population of consumers in this market, again denoted by N, is uniformly distributed along the line. Each consumer is identified by a point on the line that corresponds to that consumer's most preferred version of the product. A consumer wants to buy at most one unit of the product and is willing to pay up to V for her most preferred brand.

Let us work out first the benchmark case when consumers are perfectly informed about products and there is no advertising in the market. If the consumer's most preferred brand is not being offered for sale, then the consumer must decide whether or not to purchase another brand at some distance x along the line from her most preferred brand. The consumer's willingness to pay for a brand at a distance x from her most preferred brand is $V - tx$, where the parameter t is, as usual, the cost incurred by the consumer per unit distance she travels from her most preferred brand. As t increases, consumer tastes in this market become more specialized. A high value of t implies that a consumer incurs a large cost when forced to buy a brand even a short distance removed from her most preferred type. In this case, we would regard consumer tastes to be very specialized. The preference for specialized varieties of goods is strong.

We assume that there are two firms, each located at the opposite ends of the line. Firm X markets brand x and is located at point 0, the leftmost or farthest westward location. Firm Y markets brand y and is located at point 1, the rightmost or most eastern end of the line. The unit cost of production of each brand, denoted by c, is constant and the same for the two firms. The benchmark model is one in which consumers are *perfectly informed* about the exact locations (i.e., characteristics) of the two brands and their prices, p_x and p_y. The decision of a consumer in this case is which brand to buy given that her most preferred brand is located at a distance d from brand x and a distance $1 - d$ from brand y. That consumer will buy the brand that gives her the most consumer surplus, provided of course that her surplus from buying is positive. In other words, this consumer will buy brand x if such a purchase yields a positive surplus,

$$V - td - p_x \geq 0 \qquad (21.3)$$

and if that surplus is greater than the surplus earned from buying the alternative good, y,

$$V - td - p_x > V - t(1 - d) - p_y. \qquad (21.4)$$

Let us suppose that V is sufficiently large or the prices of the brands, p_x and p_y, are sufficiently low so that all consumers find it worthwhile to buy one of the two brands and that both brands have positive market share at these prices. This means that there must be a consumer, whose preferred brand is located at some distance $\bar{d}$ from brand x, and who is indifferent between buying brand x at price p_x and buying brand y at price p_y. For a consumer to be indifferent to the two brands, the consumer gets the same consumer surplus from buying one or the other, or:

$$V - t\bar{d} - p_x = V - t(1 - \bar{d}) - p_y. \qquad (21.5)$$

The location of the marginal consumer, $\bar{d}$, the one who is indifferent between buying x and buying y, is affected by the prices that the two firms set for their brands. Specifically, we can solve equation (21.5) in terms of $\bar{d}$. Thus,

$$\bar{d} = \frac{1}{2t}(p_y + t - p_x) \qquad (21.6)$$

If the price p_x of brand x increases, then the location of consumer $\bar{d}$ moves to the left and the fraction of consumers who buy x falls. In contrast, if the price p_x decreases, then the location of consumer $\bar{d}$ moves to the right and the faction of consumers who buy x rises. In other words, $\bar{d}$ and $(1 - \bar{d})$ are the market shares of brands x and y, respectively. Recall that N is the total number of consumers evenly distributed from one end of the line to the other. Therefore, at any set of prices, p_x and p_y, consumer demand for brand x can be written as

$$q_x(p_x, p_y) = \bar{d}N = \frac{(p_y + t - p_x)}{2t}N \qquad (21.7)$$

Similarly, the demand for brand y is

$$q_y(p_x, p_y) = (1 - \bar{d})N = \frac{(p_x + t - p_y)}{2t}N \qquad (21.8)$$

Accordingly the profit from selling brand x is $\pi^x(p_x, p_y) = (p_x - c)(p_y - p_x + t)N/2t$, while the profit from selling brand y is $\pi^y(p_x, p_y) = (p_y - c)(p_x - p_y + t)N/2t$. We can now derive each firm's profit-maximizing best response function in prices and work out the Nash equilibrium in prices when consumers are perfectly informed about brands. The best response function for brand x is $p_x^* = (p_y + c + t)/2$, and the best response function for brand y is $p_y^* = (p_x + c + t)/2$.[1]

Our assumption that each firm has an identical unit cost of c implies that in a symmetric equilibrium each firm also has the same profit-maximizing price. This leads to equilibrium prices in the benchmark case that include a markup over cost equal to the measure of how specialized are consumer tastes, as represented by the parameter t. Hence, the equilibrium prices in the benchmark case are:

$$p_x^* = p_y^* = c + t \tag{21.9}$$

21.1

Consider two firms producing differentiated products and serving a market of 1,000 customers. Each firm has a unit cost, c, of \$5. Assume as well that the degree of specialization in consumer tastes is $t = \$4$.

a. What will be the equilibrium price of each firm according to equation (21.9)?
b. What market share will each firm have at these prices? What profit will they each earn?
c. Suppose that one firm lowered its price by \$1 below the equilibrium derived in part (a). What would happen to this firm's market share? What would happen to its profit?

It is worth emphasizing that the equilibrium prices in equation (21.9) and the underlying demand functions upon which they are based depend strongly on the assumption that all consumers in the market are perfectly informed about the availability of the two brands. In the absence of an airtight means to distribute that information to each and every potential customer, it is more likely that consumers are not well informed about the brands. Obviously, advertising can play an informational role here. Yet it is far from a foolproof technique to "get the word out" about one's product. Some consumers may remain uninformed about how many brands are on the market and the specific features of each brand even after an extensive advertising campaign.

In order to introduce advertising in the context of this model, we adopt an approach based on Grossman and Shapiro (1984).[2] In this model a consumer knows the important information about a brand (i.e., its location and price) only when the consumer receives an advertisement from the firm selling that brand. In addition, the probability that each consumer actually receives that message is less than one. This is not unreasonable. When a firm airs a commercial, it is quite likely that some consumers will not hear it, and so not every one is informed in this market.

Formally, we assume that consumers located along the segment have the same chance of receiving an advertisement about a brand. In particular, we assume that a proportion, θ_x, of

---

[1] The best response function for firm 1 is found by maximizing firm 1's profit with respect to its price p_1 given p_2.

[2] Our model is similar to that developed in Tirole (1988) as a simplification of the Grossman and Shapiro model (1984).

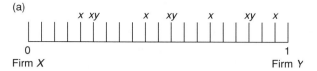

(a)

N customers are evenly distributed between the two firms. Those marked x have heard commercials about brand x. Those marked xy have heard commercials about both brand x and brand y.

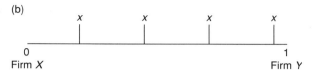

(b)

Those consumers who have heard only about brand x are also distributed uniformly but less densely than the full market of N consumers between firm X and firm Y. These consumers are assumed to buy one unit each of brand x.

(c)

The consumers who have received commercials from both brand x and brand y are distributed uniformly between firm X and firm Y as well but, again, less densely than the full market of N consumers. The two firms therefore must compete for these consumers in price. Given the uniform distribution of this group, we may use the same marginal consumer condition used earlier in the case with N fully informed consumers. Because there is no price discrimination, it is the set of prices established by this competition that is paid by every consumer both those who know of both brands and those who know of only one brand.

Figure 21.1   Advertising in a Hotelling spatial model

the total population of N consumers receives an advertisement about brand x.[3] Similarly, we assume that a proportion, θ_y, of all potential consumers receives an advertisement about brand y. The fraction θ_x that receives an advertisement for brand x may be further divided into two groups. One group is the proportion $\theta_x\theta_y$ who also received an advertisement for brand y, and the remaining group is the fraction $\theta_x(1 - \theta_y)$ who received the message from firm X but did not hear a commercial for brand y. There is also a fraction of consumers, $(1 - \theta_x)(1 - \theta_y)$, who receive no advertisement from either firm. We will assume that this last group of consumers simply does not participate in the market—that is, consumers who receive no commercial from either firm do not buy either brand x or brand y.

The situation is illustrated in Figure 21.1. Here, the top part of the figure shows the two firms and the distribution of the N potential customers along the line segment or "Main Street" between the addresses of 0 and 1. Of course, if each of these customers were perfectly informed this entire set of N customers would end up buying either brand x or brand y. However, the

[3]   This means that firms do not target their advertising to those most likely to buy their product. Firm X, for example, is assumed not to concentrate its advertising on the eastern side of town near its own location but, instead, to advertise over the entire market evenly. Television commercials that are aired to all viewers probably come close to this description, though even here we often observe some targeting, e.g., advertising for kids' cereals and toys is heaviest on Saturday mornings during the "cartoon hours."

illustration shows that in fact not all of these individuals are truly potential customers for each firm. From the viewpoint of firm X for instance, only two subsets of the original N customers may actually purchase the firm's product. The first group is comprised of that fraction of customers, $\theta_x(1 - \theta_y)N$, who heard only the commercial of firm X. These consumers are expected to be distributed uniformly between the two ends of the town, but less densely than the full population of N consumers. Whereas there is a customer at every vertical mark along the line segment between 0 and 1, those that are also marked with an x are the consumers who received ads only about brand x. If we draw a picture of this set of customers by themselves, it will look exactly like the picture of the original N customers except that there will be fewer people living less densely between the two town ends. This is what is shown in the middle illustration of Figure 21.1. We will assume that each of these consumers buys a unit of firm X's product; that is, firm X does not have to compete for their business but, instead, captures all these consumers for itself.

The other set of potential customers for the brand x version of the good are those who have heard the commercials of both firms. These consumers are also distributed between the addresses of 0 and 1, and are each indicated with an xy in the top illustration of Figure 21.1. A picture of this group—who are $\theta_x\theta_yN$ in number—is shown in the bottom illustration of the figure. Once again, this subset of customers is expected to be distributed uniformly along the line between the two ends of town. But again, they are distributed less densely than the total set of N consumers.

There is an important difference between this last group of consumers and those in the subset illustrated in the middle diagram of Figure 21.1. Unlike that former group who we assumed will buy only brand x, this latter group that has received both firms' commercials will potentially buy the product of either firm depending on which deal is more attractive. In other words, these $\theta_x\theta_yN$ consumers are perfectly informed just as in our earlier benchmark case. Hence, the two firms will compete in price for this subset of $\theta_x\theta_yN$ customers in exactly the same way as they competed for the full range of N customers in that previous case. This means that we can once again talk about a critical consumer with an address of $\bar{d} = (p_y + t - p_x)/2t$. The only difference is that this consumer now defines the dividing line between the two parts of the smaller market comprised only of the $\theta_x\theta_yN$ customers who have received the advertisements of both firms rather than the entire market of N consumers as in the perfect-information case.

The foregoing analysis implies that the demand for brand x is comprised of two parts. The first part is the $\theta_x(1 - \theta_y)N$ consumers who have heard only firm X's commercial and who we assume buy firm X's product. The second part comes from the $\theta_x\theta_yN$ consumers who have heard commercials for both products and for whose patronage the two firms must compete through the prices they set. What this tells us is that the demand for brand x, denoted by q_x, depends on the advertising efforts of each firm, θ_x and θ_y, and the prices each charge, p_x and p_y, as given by the equation:

$$q_x(\theta_x, \theta_y, p_x, p_y) = \theta_x(1 - \theta_y)N + \theta_x\theta_y\bar{d}N = \left(\theta_x(1 - \theta_y) + \theta_x\theta_y\frac{(p_y + t - p_x)}{2t}\right)N \quad (21.10)$$

where, as before, $\bar{d} = \dfrac{1}{2t}(p_y + t - p_x)$.

Equation (21.10) makes quite clear that firm X has an incentive to raise θ_x and to increase consumer demand for brand x. However, to increase θ_x or the likelihood that consumers will

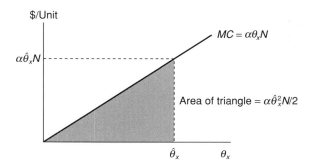

Figure 21.2   Marginal and total advertising cost assumed for the spatial competition model

The marginal cost is indicated by the upward-sloping line and is equal to $\alpha\theta_x N$. The upward slope indicates that the marginal cost rises as the firm tries to reach a greater fraction θ_x with its advertising. The total cost of reaching any specific fraction θ_x is given by the area of the triangle below the marginal cost line up to that fraction. Total cost of reaching θ_x of the N consumers is $\alpha\theta_x^2 N/2$.

know about brand x also requires that firm X increase its advertising expenditures. To put it differently, the expenses associated with airing advertisements for brand x will be larger as the fraction of consumers θ_x that the firm decides it wants to reach becomes greater.

We can write this formally by saying that a firm's advertising costs $T(\theta_x)N$ are a function of the total number of consumers that the firm tries to inform. It is reasonable to assume that this function is increasing in θ_x. As the firm tries to contact a greater fraction θ_x of consumers, its advertising expenses increase. Moreover, we will assume that this happens at an increasing rate. Thus, we will assume that advertising is subject to diminishing returns.

One way to obtain this feature is to assume that the additional cost incurred in raising θ_x—that is, the marginal cost of raising the fraction of consumers that hear about brand x, or what we will denote as T'—is given by the equation $T' = \alpha\theta_x N$. Such a function is illustrated in Figure 21.2. It is of course a simple linear relationship beginning at the origin and rising with slope α. The total cost of advertising for any given value of θ_x such as $\hat{\theta}_x$, is $T(\hat{\theta}_x)N$ and is just the sum of the marginal cost of each increment in θ_x up to the value $\hat{\theta}_x$. This is just the area of the triangle under the curve, which is equal to $\dfrac{\alpha}{2}\hat{\theta}_x^2 N$. Hence, our assumption that $T' = \alpha\theta_x N$ is equivalent to assuming that $T(\theta_x)N = \dfrac{\alpha}{2}\theta_x^2 N$. In other words, we are assuming that advertising costs rise with the square of the fraction of the market that the firm attempts to inform.[4]

Given its demand curve, firm X wants to choose a price, p_x, and an advertising strategy, θ_x, to maximize the profit from selling brand X. This profit is equal to the firm's revenue less its costs. Its revenue is equal to the price it sets times the amount demanded at that price. Its cost is the sum of its production cost—the unit cost, c, times the amount it sells—and its advertising cost, $T(\theta_x)N$. Formally, the firm wants to maximize its profit, θ_x:

$$\Pi_x(\theta_x, \theta_y, p_x, p_y) = (p_x - c_x)\,[\theta_x(1 - \theta_y)N + \theta_x\theta_y \bar{d}N] - \frac{1}{2}\alpha\theta_x^2 N \tag{21.11}$$

[4]   Recall that the area of a triangle is given by $bh/2$, where b is the length of the triangle's base and h is the triangle's height. In Figure 21.2, the base or b is θ_x, and the height is $\alpha\theta_x N$. Hence, the area of the triangle, or total cost of reaching the fraction θ_x of all N consumers, is $\alpha\theta_x^2 N/2$.

Maximization of this profit function requires that the firm's price and advertising choices jointly satisfy two profit-maximizing conditions. The first of these conditions is the familiar one that, given its advertising level, as well as the price and advertising level of its rival, the firm set its price to equate marginal revenue with marginal production cost. This condition can be solved to find the best response function in price for firm X:

$$p_x^* = \frac{p_y + t + c}{2} + \frac{(1 - \theta_y)}{\theta_y}t \qquad (21.12)$$

Equation (21.12) is firm X's best price response function given the price and advertising effort of firm Y. Note that it is made up of two terms. The first term is in fact the best price response function for firm X when all consumers are perfectly informed about both brands as in our benchmark case.[5] The second term describes the additional markup when consumers do not know about the competing brand y. The smaller the fraction of consumers who receive advertising about brand y, the higher is the profit-maximizing price for brand x.

The second necessary condition is also one that is familiar. This is the requirement that the marginal benefit of reaching additional consumers through increased advertising just equal the marginal cost of such advertising given the firm's price level and the actions of its rival. The marginal benefit of additional advertising is the increased number of customers it brings in times the price–cost margin that the firm earns on each of these additional sales. Since we have assumed that the marginal cost of such additional advertising message is $\alpha\theta_x N$, this condition can be written as:

$$(p_x - c)\left[(1 - \theta_y) + \theta_y\left(\frac{p_y - p_x + t}{2t}\right)\right]N = \alpha\theta_x^* N \qquad (21.13)$$

Similarly, we work out the corresponding profit-maximizing conditions for firm Y. To find the equilibrium outcome we can take a short cut. The firms are identical with respect to both costs and demand. Thus, we know that in equilibrium both $p_x^* = p_y^*$ and $\theta_x^* = \theta_y^*$ will hold. When we substitute these two equilibrium relationships into the two conditions (21.12) and (21.13), we obtain the equilibrium price p^* and advertising level θ^*, for each firm (see inset). These are

$$p^* = c + \sqrt{2\alpha t} \qquad (21.14)$$

and

$$\theta^* = \frac{2}{1 + \sqrt{\dfrac{2\alpha}{t}}} \qquad (21.15)$$

---

[5]   You can easily confirm this. Since the two firms are identical, the equilibrium must involve $p_x^* = p_y^*$. When the second term in equation (21.9) is omitted, imposing this condition then yields our initial, fully informed equilibrium, $p_x^* = p_y^* = c + t$.

Derivation Checkpoint

Optimal Advertising and Optimal Pricing in the Spatial Model

In the two-firm Hotelling model with advertising, we must now recognize that firms are optimizing on two fronts. They must choose both a profit-maximizing price and a profit-maximizing advertising effort. In turn, this requires that we differentiate the profit function of equation (21.11) with respect to both p_x and θ_x, and set each derivative equal to zero. The two resulting first-order equations may then be expressed as:

$$\left[\theta_x(1-\theta_y) + \theta_x\theta_y\left(\frac{p_y + t - p_x}{2t}\right)\right] = (p_x - c)\left[\frac{\theta_x\theta_y}{2t}\right] \quad \text{and}$$

$$(p_x - c)\left[(1-\theta_y) + \theta_Y\left(\frac{p_y + t - p_x}{2t}\right)\right] = \alpha\theta_x$$

Of course, similar necessary conditions also apply to firm Y. Multiplying through the first of the above equations by $2t$ and simplifying then yields firm X's best price response function shown in equation (21.12) and below:

$$p_x = \frac{p_y + t + c}{2} + \left(\frac{1-\theta_y}{\theta_y}\right)t$$

If we now invoke the symmetry requirement that, in equilibrium, $p_x = p_y = p^*$ and $\theta_x = \theta_y = \theta^*$, this condition may be rewritten to imply that in equilibrium:

$$p^* = t + c + 2\left(\frac{1-\theta^*}{\theta^*}\right)t \quad \Rightarrow \quad (p^* - c) = \left(\frac{2-\theta}{\theta}\right)t$$

From the second first-order condition, substitution also yields:

$$(p^* - c)\left(1 - \frac{\theta^*}{2}\right) = \alpha\theta^*$$

Substitution of the implied value for $p^* - c$ from the first condition into the second one then yields the equilibrium advertising effort shown in equation (21.15) and below:

$$\left(\frac{2-\theta^*}{\theta^*}\right)t\left(1 - \frac{\theta^*}{2}\right) = \alpha\theta^* \quad \Rightarrow \quad (2-\theta^*)^2 t = 2\alpha\theta^{*2} \quad \Rightarrow \quad \theta^* = \frac{2}{1 + \sqrt{\frac{2\alpha}{t}}}$$

Substitution of the solution for θ^* into the equilibrium pricing relationship then yields:

$$p^* = c + \sqrt{2\alpha t}$$

Remember that we assumed that some of the initial N consumers in the market remain uninformed.[6] In order for this to be the case, there must be some consumers who do not receive an ad from either firm. Therefore, it must be the case that the equilibrium value of each firm's advertising effort θ^* is less than one. To guarantee that $\theta^* < 1$ we assume that the cost of advertising, as measured by the parameter α, is not too low relative to consumers' preference for variety, as measured by t. Specifically we want $\alpha > t/2$ so that it is too costly for a firm to find it profitable to inform the entire consumer population about its brand.[7] When $\theta^* < 1$ we have in equilibrium a fraction $2\theta^*(1 - \theta^*)$ of consumers who know only about one brand, a fraction θ^{*2} who know about both brands, and a fraction $(1 - \theta^*)^2$ who do not know about either brand.

To make the foregoing a bit more concrete, consider a simple example in which there are $N = 1,000$ consumers, each with a reservation price of $V = 10$ and a taste parameter $t = 2$. The unit cost of production is $c = 2$, and the cost of advertising is such that $\alpha = 4$. The perfect information equilibrium or benchmark case for this example is one in which the two firms split the market with each charging a price of $c + t = 4$ by equation (21.9). How does this compare with the imperfectly informed equilibrium with advertising?

From equation (21.14), the price in the imperfectly informed equilibrium will be $p^* = 6$. From equation (21.15) the advertising effort by each firm will be $\theta^* = 2/3 = 0.67$. Note that the equilibrium price has increased from \$4 to \$6, or by a factor of 50 percent over its value in the fully informed benchmark case. Given the advertising efforts of the two firms, 22 percent $[\theta^*(1 - \theta^*)]$, or 222 of the 1,000 consumers, know about brand x only. Similarly, another 22 percent know only about brand y. In addition, 44 percent $(\theta^*\theta^*)$, or 444, know about both brands. The remaining 12 percent $[(1 - \theta^*)(1 - \theta^*)]$ do not know about either brand.

These data imply that each firm sells 444 units. Each sells 222 units to the consumers that know only its brand. In addition, the two firms split the market of 444 consumers who know about both brands. At a price of \$6, each firm therefore earns revenue of \$2,664. At a unit cost of \$2, the total production cost at each firm is \$888. In addition, each firm incurs a total advertising cost of $4000(2/3)^2/2 = \$888$. Total cost—production plus advertising cost—is therefore, \$1,776. Subtracted from each firm's total revenue, this leaves each firm with a net profit of \$888. Note that on a per unit basis, each firm incurs an advertising cost of \$2, which in this case is just as high as its per unit production cost. However, such advertising costs are necessary in this market for a firm to get its product known.

The market outcome that we have just derived yields a number of insights regarding advertising in product-differentiated markets where firms compete for consumers in price. First, note that our assumption that $\alpha > t/2$ implies that the equilibrium price will now be greater than $c + t$—the price that prevailed under the fully informed equilibrium (see equation (21.9). The higher price is necessary, in part, to fund the advertising that provides consumers with the information that they need in order to go shopping.

---

[6]   Indeed, it is this assumption—made rather implicitly—that explains why the equilibrium price shown in equation (21.11) does not converge to the equilibrium when one lets α take on the value $t/2$ necessary to make θ equal 1. Having derived the equilibrium under the assumption that $\theta < 1$ and the market is imperfectly informed, we cannot now impose on that equilibrium result the contrary assumption that $\theta = 1$ and the market is perfectly informed.

[7]   However, we do not want the cost of advertising to be so high that firms send out so few ads that there are too few consumers who know about both brands. In such circumstances firms find it not worthwhile to compete in price to attract these consumers.

The foregoing is not to say that the higher price only covers the cost of the advertising that takes place. That higher price also reflects the advantage that each firm now has with respect to an important fraction of its customers. This advantage is that some of those customers do not know about the rival brand. As a result, those consumers are willing to pay any price for, say, brand x that yields a positive surplus. Had they known about the existence of brand y, however, they would only be willing to pay a price for brand x that yielded no less a surplus than that obtained from buying the alternative brand. A real-life example may be consumers who purchase a high-priced national brand of pain relief because they are unaware that a generic substitute is available.

A further insight from our analysis is that an increase in the degree of specialization in consumer tastes—an increase in t—causes both price and advertising to increase. Prices are higher and advertising expenses are larger the more that differences in product brands do in fact matter to consumers. Here is yet another case in which it is important to understand that advertising does not play a causal role in these results. Advertising is not the force that causes consumers to have specialized tastes nor is it the factor that enables firms to set high prices. Instead, it is the fact that consumers have specialized tastes to begin with that both encourages firms to advertise extensively and that permits price to be set well above costs.

The final insight is the relationship implied between profitability and the cost of advertising. Substituting our results from equations (21.14) and (21.15) for the optimal price and advertising efforts into the profit function of equation (21.11), we find that, in equilibrium, each firm will earn a profit, π^*, equal to

$$\Pi^* = \frac{2\alpha}{\left(1 + \sqrt{2\alpha/t}\right)^2} N \qquad (21.16)$$

Inspection of equation (21.16) reveals that each firm's profit is increasing in the parameter α, which is a measure of the cost of advertising. How is it the case that making it more difficult for firms to inform consumers about their brands results in increased firm profitability? The reasoning is as follows: When α increases, it becomes more costly to advertise to consumers, and so firms reduce their advertising levels. As a result, consumers in the market are now less well informed about the alternatives that are available and so each firm can raise the price of its brand with less fear of losing customer to its rival. The increase in the price–cost margin outweighs the increase in the overall cost of advertising.

There is a well documented "stylized fact" that in a wide cross-section of consumer good industries higher advertising expenditures are associated with higher profitability. The pioneering work in this regard is that of Comanor and Wilson (1967). Their basic finding is that industries with high profitability are associated with high advertising-to-sales ratios, and the relationship between advertising and profitability has been found again and again both for different time periods and different countries. This model is consistent with the empirical evidence. As α increases both industry profitability and advertising expenditures increase.

Another insight is that public policy that attempts to restrict advertising efforts and thereby make it more costly to reach a given number of potential consumers could actually raise the profit of the industry's firms. Perhaps this helps to explain the recent agreement of the major American tobacco companies to abide by a proposed settlement that restricts advertising of tobacco products. A similar outcome could occur if regulations are enacted to restrict advertising in the alcoholic beverage industry.

We have already mentioned the increasing use of the Internet by firms as a medium in which to advertise their products by buying "space" on a firm's home page. Suppose we now project these developments a bit into the future and consider an economy linked by an information superhighway in which the worldwide web allows advertisers to reach hundreds of millions of potential customers. Within the model just developed, such an outcome would be reflected by a sharp fall in the parameter α. That is, because the web has no distribution or printing fees and because it reaches so many customers, the cost of reaching any potential consumer is sharply reduced.

a.   According to the spatial competition model just developed, what effect will a sharp fall in α have on the fraction of potential consumers who hear a firm's message?

b.   What does the model imply will be the impact of this sharp fall in α on the firm's price-cost margin, $p - c$? What effect will it have on firm profits? Explain.

21.3   WHAT'S IN A BRAND NAME?

Brand names like Fruit-Loops or Cheerios correspond to different kinds of cereals, and consumers seem to care about variety in the cereal market and making the right match. Often there is more to a brand name. Brand names like Coca-Cola in the soft drinks market, or Calvin Klein in the jeans market have a social or psychological edge that goes beyond our simple interpretation of matching or mapping consumers to brands. Consumers may prefer Coke to Pepsi not because of the taste but because of the brand name. Consumers may prefer to buy Calvin Klein jeans not because of the fit but because of the name. Recognizing that there is a "peer pressure" quality in brand names and their advertising points us back to the view of advertising as a persuasive message. However, such messages do not have to change consumer tastes in order to have an impact on consumer utility.

This subtle point is made clear in Becker and Murphy (1993). These authors take a different view of the persuasive role of advertising. They argue that yes, these image ads do stimulate wants but, no, such advertisements do not necessarily change consumer preferences. The reason why image advertising can affect the demand for goods *without necessarily changing the underlying preferences* of consumers is that this kind of advertising may be a complementary good to the product. In the same way that consumers place a greater value on lodging accommodations the better the surrounding landscape, or on iPods, the greater the availability of iTunes, they may also place greater value on a soft drink or an automobile or a pair of jeans the greater the advertising done by the soft drinks maker or auto maker or clothing firm, respectively.

There are several ways in which advertising can be thought of as a complement to the good being promoted. One is that some consumers may enjoy knowing that the brands of products that they buy are widely seen and recognized by lots of others on television, in the movies and on billboards. Advertising in this case enhances the consumption value of the product by making it more prestigious and desirable because that is how it is seen in the eyes of the consumer's friends and acquaintances.[8] This view of advertising is close in spirit

---

[8]   Clark and Horstmann (2005) show that if consumers care about wearing the "right" clothes or eating the "right" food then firms can use advertising to coordinate consumer purchases. Consumers believe that a firm advertising more will have more purchases and a more valued product. This builds on the Bagwell and Ramey (1994) idea that advertising is a coordinating mechanism.

to the traditional persuasive view. The subtle difference here is that consumers are not duped into believing that advertised goods are better. Rather the extensive advertising actually serves to make those goods better known and hence worth more to consumers who enjoy using brands that are widely known. This kind of advertising campaign is aimed at building brand value. Its goal is to make the product more desirable and to increase the willingness to pay of consumers.

At the same time, it seems clear that brand name advertising can also convey information, such as how to use the good or service more effectively. For example, the food-manufacturing giant, General Mills, operates a website for its brand name Betty Crocker. Among other offerings, this site includes a link to "Betty's Recipes—What's on Hand?" Here, the interested browser is asked to list the ingredients that are available for that night's meal. Then, the site provides a number of "Betty's Favorite Recipes" which utilize those very ingredients. The recipes include both preparation steps and nutritional information. However, when listing the ingredients necessary for each dish, the site always gives a plug for the General Mills brand of that product, e.g., Gold Medal all-purpose flour.

Clearly, this kind of advertising does play an informative role. Yet the information provided is not about the product's price, quality, or retail store location. Instead, the information is of the sort that will enable the consumer to use the advertised product more effectively and, thereby, to obtain greater benefits from it. This kind of campaign extends the reach of the brand and can expand the market by bringing in new consumers. Alternatively, consumers would be willing to pay for this kind of information—a cookbook, a software user's guide, a car owner's manual—if such information were not readily available. More often, however, the information is sold bundled with the good at one price. Brand name advertising that serves a similar "how to" role may be viewed similarly. The consumer buying the product pays for both the product and the information included in the advertising. This is not so very different from the consumer who buys a software package at a price, which also includes a software user's guide.

Whether advertising provides social appeal or complementary information or a combination of both, the result is that consumers value the joint consumption of the product and its advertising. This approach to advertising is different from the approach that lies at the heart of the signaling theory discussed in the last chapter. Signaling theory is based on the premise that advertising does not itself give utility to consumers but rather is a signal for what does give them utility. The view that advertising is a complement to the good advertised is, on the other hand, based on the premise that advertising itself is desired by consumers.

An important advantage of the complementary approach to advertising is that it is consistent with the fact that consumers who have already tried an experience good and know its quality continue to respond to advertising, and with why there is considerable advertising for goods that do not fit the experience good category. Viewing advertising as a way to make the product better known can also account for the observation—unexplained by the signaling approach—that advertising is much greater for experience goods sold to consumers than those sold to producers.

When advertising is viewed as a complement to the good being marketed firms can raise the demand for their good by increasing their advertising. Corresponding to our description above, we consider two ways that advertising, when viewed as a complementary good, can affect consumer demand. One way is by increasing the social value of brand name appeal that is closer in spirit to the persuasive role of advertising. The second way is by conveying information on how to better use the product that is closer to the more purely informational role of advertising. We first explore the complementary approach to advertising in the context of a monopoly. We then briefly outline its application in a competitive setting.

21.3.1 Advertising and Building Brand Value

Consider a firm that sells a product such as a car, or a new book, or a film video, or a spring coat, of which each consumer typically wishes to buy only one unit. There are N potential consumers of the product. Assume further that each consumer differs by how much utility he or she gets from consuming the product. Specifically, we assume that consumers can be ranked in terms of the utility each gets from consuming the good. Consumer utility ranges from a minimum value of 0 to a maximum value denoted by $\bar{V}$.[9] In the absence of advertising, the consumer least interested in the product receives a utility from consuming the product equal to 0. Such a consumer will not purchase the product unless it is given away for free. The next person obtains a utility equal to $\bar{V}/N$; the third least interested consumer obtains a utility equal to $2\bar{V}/N$; and so on all the way up to the most interested consumer who obtains a utility equal to $N\bar{V}/N = \bar{V}$ from consuming the product. We may thus think of each consumer as located along a line segment with the addresses on that line ranging from 1 to $N + 1$. If we refer to consumers by their addresses, consumer n will, in the absence of advertising, obtain a utility equal to $(n - 1)\bar{V}/N$ if she consumes the product, where n ranges from 1 to $N + 1$.[10]

Advertising enhances consumer utility from consuming the product. To be explicit, we assume that the effect of advertising is to increase consumer's utility multiplicatively by a factor, $v(\alpha)$, where α is the level of advertising services provided by the monopoly firm. Hence, the utility enjoyed by consumer n when she consumes the good with advertising α is now $v(\alpha)(n - 1)\bar{V}/N$. We assume that $v(0) = 1$, so that if the good is not advertised at all ($\alpha = 0$) then each consumer n merely obtains their base utility from consumption of the good. When the good is advertised and α is positive, then $v(\alpha)$ is greater than one and each consumer's utility from consumption is increased. Moreover, the scale factor $v(\alpha)$ increases as α does, or $v'(\alpha) > 0$.

Because advertising increases the overall utility derived from the consumption of the good, each consumer is willing to pay *more* for the good the *more* it is advertised. A consumer will buy the product whenever her utility level exceeds the product price; in other words, when consumer surplus is positive. Therefore, a consumer n will buy the product whenever:

$$v(\alpha)\left(\frac{n - 1}{N}\right)\bar{V} - P \geq 0.$$

We can now derive the demand curve facing the monopoly firm. Suppose that the firm decides to advertise an amount α and to sell the good at price P. How much of the good will the firm sell? To answer this question, assume that over the population of consumers, that is, over the range of addresses n that run from 1 to $N + 1$, there is, at these values of α and P, some consumer with address $\hat{n}$ who is just indifferent between buying and not buying. This consumer is called the marginal consumer. For this consumer $\hat{n}$ it will be the case

that $v(\alpha)\left(\dfrac{\hat{n} - 1}{N}\right)\bar{V} = P$. All consumers with lower addresses or lower values of n will not

buy the product. They do not value it highly enough. All the consumers with higher

---

[9] For example, if the good were a new cosmetic treatment and if utility were measured in dollars $\bar{V}$ could be equal to \$100, or for a new holiday package $\bar{V}$ could be \$1,000.

[10] We permit n to range as high as $N + 1$ in the numerator because we start at 0 as the lowest valuation of the product. In order to have N customers with N separate utilities, the first being 0, the addresses must range from $n = 1$ to $N + 1$.

addresses or higher values of n will buy the product. If we use the equality above to solve for the address of the marginal consumer, $\hat{n}$, we find that:

$$\hat{n} = \frac{NP}{v(\alpha)\bar{V}} + 1 \tag{21.17}$$

Recall that the minimum value of $\hat{n}$ is 1 and the maximum value is $N + 1$. When price P is near 0, or at very high levels of either $v(\alpha)$ or $\bar{V}$, all N consumers will wish to buy the good. At high levels of P or low levels of either $v(\alpha)$ or $\bar{V}$, no consumers will wish to buy the good. Hence, total demand when the firm advertises at level α and charges price P is the fraction of the N potential consumers whose address or n value exceeds $\hat{n}$. This is given by:

$$Q^D(P, \alpha) = \left[\frac{N + 1 - \hat{n}}{N} \right] N = \left[\frac{N - \frac{NP}{v(\alpha)\bar{V}}}{N} \right] N = \left[1 - \frac{P}{v(\alpha)\bar{V}} \right] N \tag{21.18}$$

The total demand for the firm's product is negatively related to the price it charges, P, but positively related to the extent of advertising, α. Note that the demand function is linear in price, and can be represented in what follows more simply by the form: $Q^D(P, \alpha) = a - \frac{b}{v(\alpha)} P$. As advertising or α increases, so does the factor $v(\alpha)$ and, hence, the demand curve rotates outward as shown in Figure 21.3.

When the amount of advertising is increased the demand function shifts out and so does consumer willingness to pay. Moreover the willingness to pay of those consumers who really like the good, that is, the relatively high V consumers, increases proportionately more. These consumers are called the inframarginal consumers. The rotation pictured in Figure 21.3 implies that when advertising is increased the inframarginal consumer's willingness to pay for the good goes up by proportionately more than does the marginal consumer's willingness to pay.

When brand names have a recognition or prestige value then consumers actually enjoy watching or reading advertisements. In this case, they should have an incentive to listen to

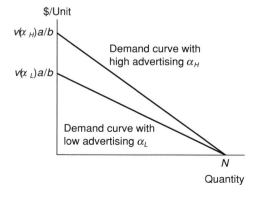

Figure 21.3   Effect of advertising services α on firm's demand when advertising raises brand value

all the advertising sent out by the firm.[11] However, this is less likely to be the case when advertising is purely informative. We all know individuals who, as soon as there is a commercial break in a television program, jump up to do something else. Not everyone consumes or cares about the advertising that a firm sends out. This means that there is a "hit or miss" problem of reaching consumers with advertising and this feature is not captured well in the above approach to brand names and advertising.

Suppose instead that unless a firm's potential customers hear or see a commercial message then they may not know that the product is available or alternatively they will not know how to use the product. The problem is that some consumers may not pay attention to the message when it is aired. Cellular phones are a case in point. It seems clear that many consumers are simply unaware of the easy availability of such technology or, perhaps, how to get any real use out of such devices. While this is bad enough for the uninformed consumer, it is especially disappointing to the firm who can only sell its products to consumers who know those products are there and who also understand how to work them. We now turn to an alternative view of advertising and building a brand name that captures this informational aspect of the firm's marketing problem.

21.3.2   Advertising and Extending the Reach

Suppose that if a firm did not advertise and build a brand name for its product then consumers would simply not know about the product, or know that they had a demand for it. This scenario could be appropriate to the marketing of cellular phones or a brand new pharmaceutical product. The essential point is that, in the absence of information about how best to use the product, consumers may not demand any of the good at all. The informational content of advertising is, in this case, complementary to the advertised product in so far as without it, the consumer will simply refrain from buying the product altogether. We will also suppose that when a firm sends out ads, not every potential customer will actually receive the ad. Some will miss it altogether. Others may see it but not really pay attention to its content. Consequently, advertising messages are received randomly by consumers. The issue that we want to explore is how advertising for brand recognition creates effective demand for the firm's product in this setting.[12]

Once again denote the number of potential consumers interested in buying this new product as N, which we assume to be a very large number. Furthermore, we suppose that all consumers are identical. Specifically let each consumer, once fully informed about the product, have a demand that is described by the function $q(P)$, which we assume is decreasing in price P. If all N consumers were in fact perfectly informed about the product, the monopolist's demand curve would be $Q(P) = Nq(P)$.

All consumers may not, however, be informed. To become informed, a consumer must receive, i.e., see and understand an advertisement. Some consumers may not truly hear the advertisement's message either because it never reaches them at all or because, if it does, they mentally "tune it out." We model this "hit or miss" aspect of advertising by assuming that if the monopolist sends out only *one* ad to the group of N potential customers, then each

---

[11]   On this point it is interesting to note that Becker and Murphy (1993) cite a study by several psychologists who did find that people who have recently purchased a new car were more likely to read ads for the same type of car than for other types.

[12]   This specification of advertising is based upon the model in Butters (1977).

such consumer has a probability $1/N$ of receiving it. Alternatively, each consumer has a probability of $\left(1 - \dfrac{1}{N}\right)$ of not receiving the one ad.

However, the monopolist can send out more than just one ad. Suppose that the monopolist sends out two ads. The probability that any one consumer receives *neither* message is then $\left(1 - \dfrac{1}{N}\right)^2$. By extension, if the monopolist sends out α messages, then the probability that a consumer does *not* receive any one of these α advertisements is $\left(1 - \dfrac{1}{N}\right)^\alpha$. When N is a large number, the probability that any one consumer *does not receive* an ad can be approximated by the function $e^{-\frac{\alpha}{N}}$, where e is the natural logarithm base, 2.7183. That is, the probability $\left(1 - \dfrac{1}{N}\right)^\alpha \approx e^{-\frac{\alpha}{N}}$. Since the probabilities of all possible events must sum to 1, this in turn means that the probability that any one consumer *does receive* an ad from the monopolist is $1 - e^{-\frac{\alpha}{N}}$.

Therefore, of the N potential consumers, the number of consumers the monopolist can actually expect to hear about the product when α ads are sent out is: $\left(1 - e^{-\frac{\alpha}{N}}\right)N$. Since each of these consumers will, when informed, exhibit a demand for the product equal to $q(P)$, the monopolist's expected demand is:

$$Q^D(P, \alpha) = \left(1 - e^{-\frac{\alpha}{N}}\right)Nq(P). \tag{21.19}$$

Assuming that the individual consumer demand function $q(P)$ is linear in price then the market demand function is also linear in price and can be more simply represented by:

$$Q^D(P, \alpha) = g(\alpha)(a - bP), \text{ where } g(\alpha) = \left(1 - e^{-\frac{\alpha}{N}}\right).$$

As in the previous case, increases in advertising or α will raise the expected demand at a given price. However, in this case the effect is to rotate the demand curve out in the way that we have shown in Figure 21.4. When the monopolist increases the amount of advertising the demand curve for the product again shifts out, but now the willingness to pay of the consumer who is on the margin of buying or not buying increases proportionately more than that of the inframarginal consumer.

21.3.3   Brand Name Advertising and Prices

The two cases just described are examples of the different ways advertising, or a brand name, can serve as a complementary good and thereby affect the demand for the advertised product. In both cases market demand is decreasing and linear in price and increasing in advertising. The way in which increases in advertising affect market demand is, however,

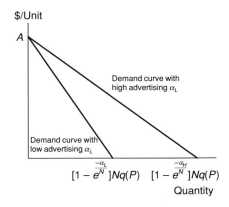

Figure 21.4   Effect of advertising services α on firm's demand when advertising extends reach

different for the two cases. Specifically, for the *building brand value* case the monopolist's demand function is represented by $Q^D(P, \alpha) = a - \dfrac{b}{v(\alpha)}P$, whereas for the *brand recognition* case the monopolist's demand function is given by $Q^D(P, \alpha) = g(\alpha)(a - bP)$. The fact that increases in advertising will *at a given price* increase demand for the monopolist's product is the "good news" of advertising. The "bad news" is of course that advertising is costly. We will assume that every unit of advertising costs T dollars.[13] We also assume that every unit of output costs c dollars to produce. The task confronting the firm is to pick a level of advertising, α, and a level of production Q, or price P that together maximize profit.

It is interesting to compare the effect of advertising on the firm's pricing strategies in the two cases. Consider first the *brand recognition* case. We find it more convenient to work with the *inverse* demand function, which for the *brand recognition* case, can be written as follows: $P(Q, \alpha) = A - \left[\dfrac{B}{g(\alpha)}\right]Q$. As illustrated in Figure 21.3, increases in advertising in the *brand recognition* case make the slope of the inverse demand function less negative. The firm wants to identify the profit-maximizing quantity of output and advertising to produce. Let us first work out the profit-maximizing quantity of output to produce at a given level of advertising services, α. With advertising α constant, and hence $g(\alpha)$ constant, the firm's marginal revenue curve is: $MR = A - \left[\dfrac{2B}{g(\alpha)}\right]Q$. Equating marginal revenue to marginal production cost, c, then yields the optimal quantity, Q^* and the corresponding optimal price, P^*. These are:

$$Q^* = \frac{(A - c)g(\alpha)}{2B} \quad \text{and} \quad P^* = \frac{A + c}{2} \tag{21.20}$$

Note that for the *brand recognition* case increases in advertising α lead to an increase in quantity sold, but not to an increase in price.

---

[13]   This assumption may not always hold. Often there is considerable quantity discounting when air time, network time, or magazine space is purchased by a firm for advertising.

On the other hand for the *building brand value* case we have the demand function $Q^D(P, \alpha) = a - \dfrac{b}{v(\alpha)} P$, which leads to an inverse demand function: $P(Q, \alpha) = v(\alpha)[A - BQ]$. Again, the firm wants to identify the profit-maximizing quantity of output and advertising to produce. The profit-maximizing quantity of output to produce at a given level of advertising services, α, is found by equating marginal revenue to marginal cost. That is: $MR = v(\alpha)[A - 2BQ] = c$ yields the optimal quantity, Q^* and the corresponding optimal price, P^*. In this case these are:

$$Q^* = \frac{Av(\alpha) - c}{2Bv(\alpha)} \quad \text{and} \quad P^* = \frac{Av(\alpha) + c}{2} \tag{21.21}$$

In contrast to the *brand recognition* case increases in advertising α in the *building brand value* case do lead to an increase price. However, if unit cost c is relatively small the effect on quantity sold of an increase in advertising in this case is relatively small. In the extreme when unit cost c is equal to zero then Q^* does not depend on advertising in the *building value* case. The two cases help us understand how advertising can have an ambiguous effect on prices depending in part on what is the value of the brand name to consumers. When the building value role predominates we could expect increased advertising and increased prices, but when the informative role predominates increased advertising should not lead to higher prices.

21.3

Practice Problem

Suppose a firm marketing styling gel faces an inverse demand curve $P(Q, \alpha) = \alpha^{1/2}[1 - Q]$ where Q is number of tubes sold per period, measured in millions, and α is advertising seconds on television per period. Currently the firm is advertising 100 seconds. The cost of advertising is \$10,000 per second. For simplicity suppose that the production cost of a tube of gel is constant and set to zero. There are no fixed costs.

a.   Calculate the firm's profit-maximizing quantity and price. Work out the firm's profit as well.
b.   Now suppose that the firm's marketing manager has struck a deal that if the firm advertises 625 seconds the cost of advertising falls to \$5,000 per second. Work out the firm's profit maximizing strategy and profits if it increases it advertising to 625 seconds.

21.4   TOO MUCH OR TOO LITTLE ADVERTISING: THE QUESTION REVISITED

A frequent complaint about network television in the United States is the abundant frequency of commercials. This feature is often cited as a key factor in the demand for both DVD's, premium cable channels, and TIVO all of which permit television viewing uninterrupted by commercials. Such anecdotes suggest that the market place somehow leads to too much advertising. Of course, we need to be precise. In economics, "too much" or "too little" advertising can only be interpreted as an amount of advertising that is either greater than or less than the efficient amount, where by efficient we mean that amount of advertising that maximizes the sum of consumer and producer surplus.

Because efficiency requires price equal to marginal cost, there does at first sight seem to be some logic to the charge of inefficiently excessive advertising. This is because advertising is available to consumers at a zero price, which is likely less than the marginal cost of advertising. Yet if advertising is considered to be *one* of two goods that consumers wish to consume together, then the relevant price is really the combined price of both the product and the commercial advertising it. If the good itself is sold by a firm with market power then the firm will maximize profit by restricting output and raising price somewhat. This would imply that the combined price of the product and the commercial together may not be below their marginal cost.[14]

It turns out that when advertising is a complement to the good being advertised it is possible to show that either too much or too little advertising could result. In general, because the firm chooses the advertising level to maximize profit, the firm does not consider any additional gain in consumer surplus that results from a change in advertising and so will not be induced to produce the efficient amount of advertising. But whether the firm's choice will be too large or too small is not *a priori* clear. A further examination of Figures 21.3 and 21.4 suggests why this is so. The firm's choice depends on how advertising affects the willingness to pay of the marginal consumers.

Figure 21.4 illustrates the case when the effect of advertising is to raise the marginal consumer's willingness to pay proportionately more than that of inframarginal consumers. Figure 21.3 illustrates the alternative case in which the effect of advertising is proportionately greater for inframarginal rather than marginal consumers. These figures are similar to those described in section 7.5.1 in Chapter 7 when we considered how product quality affects consumer demand. There we showed that the firm's choice of quality could be either too small, when the effect on demand is similar to Figure 21.3, or too large, when the effect on demand looks more like Figure 21.4.

What about the effect of competition and other firms' advertising strategies? There are several points to consider. When firms market a more or less homogenous product then advertising by any one of them increases overall market demand for the product to the benefit of all firms. In this case, a firm that incurs the cost of advertising would not appropriate the full benefit of its action. There would be a "free-rider" effect as firms that did not advertise would still benefit from the increased demand caused by the one firm's advertising. Consequently, the incentive to advertise by any one firm in the market would be considerably weakened—the more so the greater the number of firms. In turn, this would lead us to predict too little advertising when there are many firms and the industry looks more or less competitive. It is precisely this problem that leads to collaborative advertising efforts such as the dairy industry's "Got Milk" campaign. If any one firm paid for such advertising, that firm would earn very little return. By arranging for many firms to sponsor such commercials jointly, the dairy industry hopes to overcome such free-rider difficulties.

When the firms in the market sell differentiated as opposed to identical products matters change. If the advertisement is a complement to only the product of the firm sending out the ad, then the free-rider problem disappears and each firm appropriates the benefit from its advertising. However, because it is hard to "stand out in a crowd" we expect that this case will be more likely to hold in markets with relatively fewer firms. This suggests that we

---

[14]   This result is shown formally in Becker and Murphy (1993, pp. 957–8) for a more general model of advertising as a complementary good. In effect, the market for advertising is not cleared by price but, instead, rationed by the monopolist. Hence, the true marginal benefit to consumers may be either above or below the "price" for advertising that we actually observe.

should observe a negative relationship between industry advertising expenditure and the number of firms in the industry. The fewer the number of firms, or the more concentrated the industry, the greater should be the industry advertising-to-sales ratio.

John Sutton (1991) has offered additional analysis that further supports the foregoing prediction. His work builds on the stylized fact that the greater the extent of sunk costs in the industry, the higher the equilibrium concentration tends to be.[15] Advertising may be viewed as such a sunk cost. Once the ad campaign is mounted and waged, the associated expenses can never be recovered. Hence, Sutton argues that in industries in which such product differentiation through advertising is possible, advertising expenditures will be high. Such industries will therefore be characterized by both considerable sunk cost and a high degree of concentration.

Here again, it is important to note the source of the link between advertising and market structure. If Sutton is right, this link will be observed in those markets in which it is truly possible to differentiate one's product in the eyes of the consumer. More importantly, it is *not* the advertising that causes the concentration. It is the ability of advertising to differentiate products that leads jointly to both the large advertising expense and the concentrated industrial structure.[16]

There are numerous empirical studies linking advertising intensity to either profitability or concentration and the evidence on the relationship between advertising and concentration is quite mixed. Telser (1964) was one of the first studies to look for evidence of an advertising–concentration link. He found that, if anything, higher advertising was associated with *lower* industry concentration. Many other such studies soon followed. The findings of all these studies may be closely approximated by the summary statement that about half support Telser's original finding and half support the opposite view that advertising is positively associated with concentration. Moreover, as we have repeatedly emphasized, the interpretation of any such empirical findings is far from obvious. It may well be the monopoly power associated with highly concentrated industries that generates the heavy advertising expenditures, and not the high advertising expenditures that cause concentration to be high.

In light of the mixed empirical results on advertising and concentration, the case study evidence that Sutton (1991) provides seems the most compelling. Sutton finds that in those industries in which advertising might be reasonably expected to play a significant role in distinguishing one brand from another, such as breakfast cereals and frozen foods, advertising expenditures and the degree of concentration are both high. Perhaps the most interesting aspect of Sutton's argument is that, all else equal, the high advertising–high concentration link will likely be strongest precisely when price competition is the most intense. This is because, beyond the large sunk cost that the heavy advertising reflects, such fierce price rivalry further limits the number of firms that can profitably enter.[17]

---

[15] More precisely, the higher the *minimum* concentration ratio tends to be. This relationship is developed in section 4.2, Chapter 4.

[16] Schmalensee (1978) foreshadows this point. He considers a circular spatial model of product differentiation with a few incumbent firms. The firms suppress price competition but compete heavily in advertising. In turn, the heavy advertising makes it impossible for new firms to enter because the consumer density is not enough at any potential entry point to support such overhead expenditures. In other words, the price coordination leads to heavy advertising by incumbents such that there is no "room" left for a potential entrant.

[17] Robinson and Chiang (1996) also provide evidence in support of Sutton's basic analysis.

The famous *RealLemon* (1978) case is a good example supporting Sutton's argument.[18] Borden's RealLemon brand dominated the market for many years. When a rival firm, Golden Crown, entered the market with its own lemon juice product, which was chemically identical to RealLemon, it found itself at a real disadvantage relative to RealLemon, which had advertised heavily during the previous 10 years. Not only did Golden Crown have to sell at a 15 to 25 percent discount relative to RealLemon's price, but also substantial price competition broke out. The result was that RealLemon lowered its price and this in turn forced Golden Crown to do the same. Yet because of the price differential imposed on Golden Crown, it found that it could barely break even. Why? Because this was a product market in which consumers seemed particularly responsive to advertising, even though physical product differences were minimal. The heavy advertising in which the makers of RealLemon engaged gave rise to a very high market concentration. Because of the intense price competition there was a limit to the number of firms that could sustain the sunk costs of heavy advertising in this market.

The *Clorox* (1967) bleach case offers a further supporting example.[19] This case involved the proposed acquisition by Procter & Gamble of the Clorox bleach firm. Clorox was the dominant brand of household bleach accounting for nearly half of industry sales and selling for a substantial premium over rival brands despite the fact that all household bleaches are chemically indistinguishable. The courts found that Clorox's dominant position was due to its massive advertising. The Supreme Court considered such advertising to be a vital part of the market for household soaps, detergents, and cleansers. This view suggests that this was again a market in which differentiation by advertising was feasible and, hence, a market in which the equilibrium concentration level would be quite high, exactly as it was. Moreover, it appears again to be the case that this concentration was heightened as a result of the fierce price competition in the market. It was the fear of such intense price competition that led Procter & Gamble to prefer to enter this market by acquiring *Clorox* rather than by marketing its own brand.

21.5   COOPERATIVE ADVERTISING

Up until now we have focused on advertising as informational promotion of a firm's products with little concern about whether it is done by the manufacturer or the retailer. In fact, however, the provision of promotional services is one of the most crucial issues in the contractual link between these two parties. In recent years, new marketing arrangements broadly categorized as cooperative advertising agreements have emerged as a common feature of such promotional contracts. These practices are sufficiently novel and raise sufficient antitrust concerns that they are worth a separate investigation.

Cooperative advertising arrangements come in a variety of shapes and sizes. One type of agreement commonly used in book and music retailing is a simple one in which the manufacturer helps the retailer pay for advertising space in local media and also provides in-store displays and other promotional items. A closely related set of practices used frequently in the supermarket industry is the manufacturer's payment of "slotting allowances." These include

---

[18] *FTC v. Borden, Inc.*, 92 FTC 669 (1978). The FTC found Borden, the maker of the RealLemon brand guilty of monopolizing the reconstituted lemon juice market and that its successful differentiation of its product was the source of this monopoly power. The finding was later upheld by a U.S. Court of Appeals.

[19] *Federal Trade Commission v. Procter & Gamble Co.*, 386 U.S. 568 (1967).

a lump-sum payment just to have one's product on the shelf. Slotting allowances can also include additional payments for end-of-the-aisle display stands in which a manufacturer's product is shown at eye level, so-called "pay-to-stay" fees which are essentially a form of rent, and failure fees that the manufacturer must pay when a product fails to achieve a pre-specified sales volume over say, a six-month period.

The competitive effects of all of these arrangements are complicated. To a large extent, they can enhance both efficiency and competition. By directly involving the manufacturer in promotional activities, they may mitigate the tendency for retailers to under-provide such services.[20] In addition, slotting fees have the beneficial effect of allocating scarce shelf space to those manufacturers who value it most highly as well as providing an incentive for the expansion of the most efficient retailers over time. Further, by putting more of the risk on the manufacturer, the failure fees may help overcome the reluctance of dealers to stock new products. In general, cooperative advertising agreements all reflect efforts to resolve the conflicts of interest that characterize vertical relationships. However, they do raise antitrust issues, as illustrated by three cases from the 1990s.

Perhaps the most obvious way that a cooperative advertising arrangement can be anti-competitive is when it is used by a large manufacturer to foreclose retail outlets to a smaller rival. Suppose for instance that a dominant manufacturer earns a profit of $10 million currently but that entry by a rival will reduce total industry profit to $8 million half of which goes to the new entrant. The incumbent is therefore facing a reduction of its profit from $10 million to $4 million if entry occurs. As a result, it will be willing to spend up to $6 million in slotting fees to retailers in order to keep the rival off the dealers' shelves. Since the most that the rival can pay is $4 million, the incumbent has a clear ability to outbid the rival and thereby to prevent entry.

The threat of foreclosure was at the heart of the Federal Trade Commission case against McCormick & Company, the world's largest spice company. McCormick sells a full line of prepared spices and related products such as dry seasoning mixes to supermarkets under its own name and, in different local markets, under the name of subsidiary brands. While there are other spice companies they are all much smaller than McCormick. In fact, only one of these, Burns Philp Food, Inc., sold on a national level and actually offered a full line of spices. In the early 1990s, Burns Philp began to price its products quite aggressively and a price war erupted between the two firms.

McCormick's tactics in the price war included the offering of generous up-front fees that were essentially the equivalent of paying slotting allowances. In return, McCormick demanded that the recipient store devote the vast majority of its spice shelf space—sometimes 90 percent or more—to McCormick products alone. Because not all stores either agreed to McCormick's demands or received exactly the same payments, the net amount for McCormick's products actually paid by a store was different across supermarkets. For this reason, the FTC's initial complaint was couched in terms of illegal price discrimination. However, there can be little doubt that the predatory foreclosure effect of buying up shelf space played a central role in the FTC's decision. The FTC noted that Burns Philp fared quite badly in the price war and that the loss of access to shelf space played a role in this outcome. It also noted that other competitors were now keenly aware of the danger of taking on McCormick. In the end, McCormick's agreed to stop paying differential allowances and to charge all grocery stores the same net price. While this solution addressed the price

---

[20]   The under provision of retail services is discussed in section 18.4, Chapter 18.

discrimination issue, the question of foreclosure and what to do about it remained. However, this issue had become rather moot in the spice market by the time of the FTC's decision. By that time, Burns Philp had lost the price war.[21]

The FTC complaint against McCormick was largely couched in terms of illegal price discrimination that gave some grocery stores better terms than others. This is, in fact, the second way in which cooperative advertising agreements can be anticompetitive. This concern has been particularly strong in the book-selling market. Selling books is a tough business. There are over 150,000 books published each year. Even if the stock of each book is only a few thousand copies, these numbers imply a tremendous volume of books and a serious scarcity of shelf space at retail bookstores. This scarcity is obviously even more severe in the case of prime display locations at the front of the store, in the windows, and on the end of aisles. As this scarcity has intensified, shelf space and window displays have become prime real estate and publishers have paid fees ranging from $5,000 to $20,000 to have their books displayed in the window or on a popular shelf at consumer eye level.[22]

It is possible that payments for displays and for shelf space can be harmful when not all retailers are offered the same terms. This has been a persistent claim of independent bookstores. These outlets tend to be much smaller than the large discount chains. Hence, the "rent" a publisher will pay to such dealers for their top display spots is considerably less than that offered to the larger chain stores. Indeed, many small independent bookstores have complained that such cooperative advertising allowances are not available to them at all or that, if they are, the compensation they receive from publishers is lower and the reimbursement process is much more cumbersome. Accordingly, independent sellers have made repeated claims that the greater subsidization of the promotional costs at large chains allows the chains to sell their books at a lower price thereby giving the chains an unfair advantage.

If such price discrimination occurred and if it materially weakened competition it would, of course, be a violation of the Robinson–Patman Act. The difficulty with Robinson–Patman cases lies in distinguishing damage to competition from damage to individual competitors. That is, do the advertising subsidies damage the workings of the retail market or do they simply damage the small booksellers?

This question was the subject of both a lengthy investigation by the FTC and a number of lawsuits filed by the American Booksellers Association (representing over 4,500 independent bookstore owners) against the major publishing houses in the 1990s. In the end, the complaints were dismissed without any comment from the FTC on the legality of the practices. Instead, the FTC noted that the retailing of books was changing rapidly due to the rise of e-commerce giants like Amazon.com. The fierce rivalry that was emerging among electronic retailers made it difficult to argue that bookseller competition had been seriously threatened by publishers' cooperative advertising policies.[23] After the FTC ruling, the private lawsuits were quickly settled, usually with an agreement that each publisher make a small, lump sum payment to the independent booksellers and take modest steps to guarantee equal access of all bookstores to cooperative advertising.

---

[21] See "World's Largest Manufacturer of Spice and Seasoning Products Agrees to Settle Price Discrimination Charges," FTC News Release, March 8, 2000. See as well the case of *Avery Dennison Corp. v. Acco Brands, Inc.*, Case No. Cv 99-1877 (Mcx), United States District Court For The Central District Of California, 2000 U.S. Dist.

[22] From J. Hitt, "The Theory of Supermarkets," *New York Times Magazine*, March 10, 1996, p. 61.

[23] See "FTC Dismisses Case against Six Book Publishers," FTC News Release, September 21, 1996, http://www.ftc.gov.

A third way that cooperative advertising can raise troublesome antitrust issues is when it is used as a means to implement what is effectively a resale price maintenance agreement. This concern is illustrated by a well-known case in the recorded music industry. At the time, this industry was dominated by five major companies: Sony; TimeWarner; EMI; Bertelsman; and Universal. Together these firms accounted for about 85 percent of U.S. sales of pre-recorded music. The firms distributed their CDs and tapes through both specialized retailers such as Musicland, Tower Records and Sam Goody, and sometimes through generalized retailers such as department stores. In the early 1990s, large discount sellers such as Best Buy Corp., Circuit City, and Wal-Mart entered the market.

In order to gain market share and establish a market presence, the discount stores entered with very low promotional CD prices. For some popular CDs, the price reductions were as much as 50 percent resulting in retail prices of under $10. Each of the five producers responded to this fall in retail prices by adopting cooperative advertising agreements with virtually all retailers. These agreements included a Minimum Average Price (MAP) clause. The typical arrangement called for the manufacturer to help fund the retailer's advertisements that did *not* mention prices below those that the manufacturer suggested. At least initially, however, the retail firm was free to run ads that mentioned lower prices so long as it did so at its own expense. This is exactly what some retailers did, especially the discount houses. They used the cooperative advertising funds for general promotion and then used their own funds to advertise their price cuts. The result was that the price war continued.

As time passed and retail CD prices stayed low, the music producers began to receive requests for lower wholesale prices from the traditional outlets, e.g., Sam Goody. These retailers justified such requests with the claim that lower wholesale prices would enable them to meet the discount competition. Thus, from the perspective of the CD makers, the intense competition at the retail level was spilling over into competition at the wholesale level. The five producers each then revised their cooperative advertising contracts. Starting in 1995, the agreements required that the retailer not mention a lower-than-suggested price *in any advertisement*, even those completely paid for by the retailer. Violation of this clause led to suspension of *all* cooperative advertising funding for 60 to 90 days. The spread of these contracts appears to have quickly ended discounting and led to a rise in both retail and wholesale CD prices.

In light of the foregoing, it is hard to escape the conclusion that the MAP agreements were primarily meant to enforce minimum resale prices. Moreover, the underlying motive does not appear to be the desire to guarantee the provision of retail services. What seems more likely based on the observed pricing behavior and company documents is that the primary purpose behind the MAP contracts was to suppress retail competition as a means to prevent the spread of such competition to the level of the five CD producers. In other words, the cooperative advertising appears really to have been a vertical arrangement designed to foster horizontal collusion. This was in fact exactly the judgment of the FTC, which found the five music producers to be in violation of the antitrust laws and ordered a stop to the MAP agreements. The five companies quickly complied with this order but the potential for this difficulty to rise again in another context seems clear.[24]

---

[24] See J. R. Wilke and P. M. Reilly, "FTC Investigates Retail Pricing of CDs, Seeks Data From Recording Companies," *Wall Street Journal*, May 7, 1997, p. B1. See also "Record Companies Settle FTC Charges of Restraining Competition in CD Music Market," FTC News Release, May 10, 2000, http://www.ftc.gov.

In fact, as Shaffer (1991) shows, lump sum slotting fee payments may play a similar role to the MAP agreements in weakening wholesale price competition. The argument is simple. In order to pay the slotting fee, the manufacturer has to set a wholesale price above marginal cost. Therefore, at the downstream level, each retailer who signs the agreement is effectively signaling its intention to be less aggressive in its pricing because it is accepting the higher wholesale price. Even if other retailers are aggressive, the firm with the slotting fee is compensated by the lump sum payment. As a result, each retailer has an incentive to adopt the slotting fee arrangement. This is in fact what happens in the Nash equilibrium. In turn, the weaker retail competition and higher retail prices also spill over to higher prices at the wholesale level.

In sum, cooperative advertising such as slotting fees and similar arrangements are examples of vertical contractual agreements. Almost certainly, these arrangements reflect attempts to deal with incentive conflicts between manufacturers and retailers and, for the most part, are probably either pro-competitive or neutral. Yet as with all vertical practices, there is also the potential for such agreements to have anticompetitive effects. As a result, while the courts typically apply a fairly generous rule of reason in such cases, they have not yet been comfortable with any sort of *per se* legal approach.[25]

21.6   EMPIRICAL APPLICATION
Advertising, Information, and Prestige

There has been considerable debate over the role that advertising plays in influencing consumer demand. Advertising could offer basic information, signal quality, or provide a complementary aspect of social status or prestige to the advertised product. While important insights come from exploring each of these approaches, the question of advertising's actual role may be ultimately an empirical one. It is difficult, however, to come up with good clean empirical evidence that identifies the nature of advertising's role. A relatively recent paper by Daniel Ackerberg (2001) does offer some interesting and promising results.

Ackerberg's (2001) paper studies the introduction of a new yogurt product by Yoplait, the second largest yogurt firm in the U.S. In April of 1987, the company introduced Yoplait 150 as its first entry into the low-calorie and low-fat yogurt product line. This period falls within the time frame of data collected by the A. C. Nielsen Co. for just under 2,000 households split roughly evenly between Sioux Falls, South Dakota and Springfield, Missouri.

Scanner data was used to monitor the shopping trips and purchases of these households. They also had TV meters installed in their homes that allowed Nielsen to monitor their television viewing and, hence, their exposure to Yoplait 150 advertising over the 12 months starting three months after the Yoplait 150 introduction, i.e., from July of 1987 to July of 1988, Thus, the data are a panel of observations covering consumers in two cities at weekly intervals over a one-year period.

Ackerberg (2001) considers two broad effects that advertising could have. The first of these is an information effect. Advertising may either inform consumers of the good's existence as in Grossman and Shapiro (1984), or signal quality or other information about the product's attributes, as in Nelson (1970) and Kihlstrom and Riordan (1984). In contrast, the Becker and Murphy (1993) model of complementary advertising and the advertising as persuasion

---

[25]   See Klein and Wright (2007) for a recent discussion of these issues.

models suggest that the role of advertising is not informative but instead one that confers a separate recognition or prestige effect of its own. Ackerberg (2001) argues that if advertising plays an informational role then it should have little effect on experienced consumers. This is particularly the case if the relevant information is, as in Grossman and Shapiro (1984), simply about the existence and availability of the good. Once a consumer has used a good, she should know these facts so further advertising exposure will have no impact on them if, of course, this is the way advertising works.

This is also true but to a lesser extent if the information is about the quality of the product. Yoplait 150, for example, came out in many different flavors. It may take consumers a few tries to determine whether there is a flavor that they really like or not. In this case, advertising about alternative flavors will still have some effect on consumers over time, but one that should definitely diminish as they become more experienced with the product.

However, if advertising confers a prestige or recognition effect then there should be little distinction between its impact on experienced and inexperienced consumers. The complementary gains in consuming a well-recognized product should, on average, be the same whether a consumer is enjoying them for the first time or the tenth.

Ackerberg (2001) hopes to identify the role of advertising by distinguishing between its effects on experienced and inexperienced buyers. Two preliminary ordinary least squares (OLS) regressions suggest that this strategy may work. In these regressions, he looks at the total Yoplait 150 purchases over specific days in his sample and then divides these into two types. In one group are the sales that reflect first-time purchases. In the other group, are the sales that reflect repeat purchases, each measured as a fraction of the number of shopping trips that day. Ackerberg (2001) creates separate time series of first-time sales and repeat sales on specific market days over the 12-month period. For each of those making either a first or a repeat purchase, Ackerberg (2001) also has data on the average Yoplait 150 price for each market day (PRICE), and, for each purchase, the number of Yoplait 150 TV ads the buyer was exposed to in the last four days (ADS). Since Yoplait 150 generally sold much better in Springfield, he also includes a dummy variable (MARKET) equal to 1 if the data are from Springfield but 0 if they are from Sioux Falls. These preliminary results are shown in Table 21.1.

Observe first that the price effects are negative and statistically significant. Likewise, there is clearly a stronger preference for Yoplait 150 in Springfield than there is in Sioux Falls. Of most importance however, is the differential effect of advertising on the two types of expenditures. Recent advertising exposure has a far greater positive effect on first-time

Table 21.1 Effect of advertising and price on demand for new Yoplait product: preliminary results

| | Dependent variable | | | |
| | Initial purchases | | Repeat purchases | |
	Coefficient	Std. error	Coefficient	Std. error
PRICE	−0.038	(0.013)[a]	−0.029	(0.014)[a]
ADS	0.030	(0.015)[a]	0.014	(0.017)
MARKET	0.002	(0.001)[a]	0.006	(0.001)[a]

[a] Indicates significant at the five % level.

buyers of Yoplait 150. In fact, the effect on repeat purchases is not statistically significant from zero. Thus, this evidence gives rough support to the idea that advertising provides information in that it has little effect on experienced consumers who, presumably already know of the existence and quality (taste) of Yoplait 150.

To get a deeper understanding of the role that advertising plays, Ackerberg (2001) exploits more fully the panel nature of his data and the variation among consumers that this implies. His approach, with some simplification, is to first hypothesize that the propensity of consumer i in period t to purchase Yoplait 150 (y^*_{it}) is a linear function of k different exogenous variables X_{it} and a random factor ε_{it}. That is

$$y^*_{it} = \sum_{j=1}^{k} \beta_j x_{jit} + \varepsilon_{it}$$

However, one does not observe y^*_{it} directly. All one actually observes is whether consumer i at time t bought Yoplait 150 ($Y_{it} = 1$) or does not ($Y_{it} = 0$). The standard assumption in this case then is that we observe $Y_{it} = 1$ when $y^*_{it} \geq 0$, and $Y_{it} = 0$ when $y^*_{it} < 0$. This implies that the probability of observing a purchase $Y_{it} = 1$ is given by

$$\text{Prob}(Y_{it} = 1) = \text{Prob}\left[\sum_{j=1}^{k} \beta_j x_{jit} + \varepsilon_{it} \geq 0\right]$$

$$= \text{Prob}\left[\varepsilon_{it} > -\left(\sum_{j=1}^{k} \beta_j x_{jit}\right)\right] = 1 - F\left[-\left(\sum_{j=1}^{k} \beta_j x_{jit}\right)\right]$$

where $F()$ is the cumulative distribution of ε_{it}. It is convenient if $F()$ has a symmetric distribution so that $1 - F(-Z_{it}) = F(Z_{it})$. Then we have

$$\text{Prob}(Y_{it} = 1) = F\left(\sum_{j=1}^{k} \beta_j x_{jit}\right)$$

Clearly, much depends on the choice of the distribution of the random term ε_{it}. If ε_{it} is assumed to be distributed normally[26] one gets the Probit estimation procedure. A popular alternative is to assume instead that ε_{it} has a logistic cumulative distribution in which case:

$$F(Z_{it}) = \frac{e^{Z_{it}}}{1 + e^{Z_{it}}}$$

The reason for the popularity of this distribution is that this transformation implies that:

$$\ln\left[\frac{F(Z_{it})}{1 - F(Z_{it})}\right] = Z_{it}$$

---

[26]   This assumption was made in the empirical applications in Chapters 13 and 19.

In other words,

$$\ln\left[\frac{F\left(\sum_{j=1}^{k}\beta_j x_{jit}\right)}{1-F\left(\sum_{j=1}^{k}\beta_j x_{jit}\right)}\right]=\ln\frac{\text{Prob}(Y_{it}=1)}{\text{Prob}(Y_{it}=0)}=\sum_{j=1}^{k}\beta_j x_{jit}$$

The ratio of the probability $Y_{it}=1$ to the probability that $Y_{it}=0$ is known as the odds ratio. By assuming a logistic distribution for ε_{it}, the logit estimation procedure assumes that the log of the odds ratio is a linear function of the key exogenous variables. This is a very convenient feature for estimation purposes.

Ackerberg (2001) presents a number of regressions based on the above logit procedure. The independent variables X_{it} include: (1) the amount (in time) of Yoplait 150 advertising the household has seen up to that time divided by the total time spent watching television, ADS; (2) the price of Yoplait 150 in the relevant market at that time, OWN PRICE; (3) a comparable measure of the average competitor's price, RIVAL PRICE; (4) the number of times (possibly zero) the household had purchased Yoplait 150 previous to that time, NUMBER PREV; and (5) the key 1,0 variable indicating whether the household had any previous purchases of Yoplait 150, EXPERIENCED or INEXPERIENCED.[27] Some of his main results are summarized in Table 21.2 below.

Consider the first column results. Here advertising's effect is significant but only for those who have not yet tried the new product. Again, this implies that advertising mostly plays an informative role. Specifically, the coefficient on the interactive term, ADS* EXPERIENCED captures the impact of advertising on consumers who know the quality of Yoplait 150 and therefore should reflect only complementary prestige or recognition effects. This coefficient is not statistically different from zero. In contrast, the coefficient on

Table 21.2 Effect of advertising and price on demand for new Yoplait product: final (logit) results

Independent variable	Coefficient	Std. error	Coefficient	Std. error
ADS[a] INEXPERIENCED	2.306	(0.776)[a]	—	—
ADS[a] EXPERIENCED	0.433	(1.212)	—	—
ADS	—	—	2.014	(0.790)[a]
ADS[a] (NUMBER PREV)	—	—	−0.356	(0.108)[a]
NUMBER PREV	−0.267	(0.093)[a]	−0.270	(0.092)[a]
(NUMBER PREV)	0.009	(0.001)[a]	−0.001	(0.001)
OWN PRICE	−5.584	(0.350)[a]	−5.616	(0.356)[a]
RIVAL PRICE	0.761	(0.217)[a]	0.768	(0.219)[a]

Dependent variable: purchase (or not) of Yoplait 150 by household i at time t. [a] Indicates significant at 5% level

[27] Household size and income and, as before, a market dummy for Springfield households were also included. Ackerberg (2001) also includes a random, household-specific intercept to control for household heterogeneity in time-persistent preferences for the product.

ADS*INEXPERIENCED reflects both prestige and information effects. It *is* statistically different from zero and this suggests that the information effect is behind this since our estimate of prestige effects is not distinct from zero.[28]

The second regression tries to discriminate more between the two types of information that advertising provides. In the first regression, the assumption is that a household becomes fully informed after just one purchase of Yoplait 150. This would likely be the case if the important information provided by advertising were simply knowledge of the good's existence and availability. Once a household has bought the product, it presumably knows these features of the product. Learning brand characteristics such as taste, calories, and so on may take a little longer and may be facilitated by continuing advertisements. For this reason, the regression includes ADS alone as an independent regressor, but then also includes this variable in an interaction term with NUMBER PREV, the number of prior purchase of the Yoplaint 150. The idea is that the pure effect of advertising measured by ADS will decline as the consumer's experience grows. The more rapidly this decline occurs, the more likely it is that the primary information obtained from advertising is existence and availability. The more slowly it declines, the more likely that the information provided concerns product attributes that take time to learn. Sure enough, the coefficient on ADS*(NUMBER PREV) is negative but a relatively small -0.36. This implies that it takes 6 or 7 purchases of Yoplait 150 before the advertising information is no longer useful. As noted, this implies that part of the information provided concerns product attributes.

Are these coefficient estimates sensible? It is difficult to say immediately since the coefficients in the logit model relate to the effect of advertising on the *probability* of purchase and not directly to demand itself. However, there are some aspects of the results that give us confidence in the findings. First, in each case, the price of Yoplait 150 had a strong negative impact and the rival's price a strong positive effect on a household's purchase decision. Second, one can simulate the model to see what overall demand features the price and advertising coefficients imply. When Ackerberg (2001) conducts such simulations with the full model he finds that, taken at the mean, the own-price elasticity of demand is 2.8—a fairly elastic response. He also finds that the elasticity of demand with respect to advertising is 0.15. Taken together, the advertising and price elasticities would imply, by virtue of the Dorfman–Steiner condition, an advertising-to-sales ratio of $0.15/2.8 = 0.054$ or 5.4 percent. This is a quite reasonable result given that Yoplait's overall advertising-to-sales ratio was reported at the time to be about 7 percent. Overall then, Ackerberg's (2001) findings seem to be quite plausible.

In short, the evidence from Ackerberg (2001) is that the primary role of advertising is to provide consumers with information. Some of this information is simply making consumers aware of the product's availability, but some of it concerns educating consumers about the product's key features. There is little evidence that in this particular market advertising provides prestige or recognition effects. The data are based however on a perishable consumer food product purchased with some frequency. Whether it applies to other more durable consumer goods, or to goods such as medications that consumers buy less frequently, merits further investigation.

---

[28]   To be precise, the difference between the two coefficients, ADS*INEXPERIENCED and ADS* EXPERIENCED is a direct estimate of the pure information effects. Standard techniques yield a *t*-statistic for this difference of about 1.5.

Summary

Advertising by manufacturers can play a useful role in informing consumers of real differences in product attributes. For example, within the market for painkillers, some consumers can benefit from the anti-inflammatory effects of aspirin. Others find aspirin too abrasive to the lining of their stomachs. For these customers, knowing that aspirin alternatives are available such as Tylenol with acetaminophen and Advil with ibuprofen is important. In all markets in which consumers have a strong taste for variety, informative advertising improves the matching of consumers with the product types they most prefer.

There are also many goods such as films, clothes, cosmetics, watches, vacation packages and hiking shoes where promotional efforts may be useful because they serve as a complement to the product being advertised. For example, one's enjoyment of a new movie is often greatly enhanced if, after viewing it, one can talk about the film with friends who will at least know a bit about the film such as the plot and the star performers. The same is true for the purchase of designer clothes. There is little status in wearing clothes designed by Calvin Smith no matter how good they are. There is considerable crowd appeal in wearing those designed by Calvin Klein. By providing such complementary services, advertising can again enhance consumer welfare.

Advertising may improve social welfare and economic efficiency. Nevertheless, advertising still raises important public policy issues. There remains the question as to whether the market generates too little or too much advertising effort. A case can be made for either view. In addition, the advertising agreements between manufacturers and retailers could be used to suppress both retail and wholesale price competition. All of this is a way of saying that advertising raises complicated issues that do not give rise to broad general statements. This is not to say that the frustration of TV viewers, internet surfers, and others over advertising-induced interruptions of their activities are not real. What the analyses presented here do suggest though is that without any advertising at all there would likely be a different but equally real set of frustrations.

Problems

1. A recent survey by an advertising agency found that many consumers thought that there were too many different brands available for sale in certain product categories. For example, 70 percent of the consumers surveyed thought that there were too many brands of dry cereal, and 60 percent thought that there were too many brands of bar soap. Explain what is meant by the phrases "too many" or "too few" from the point of view of efficiency. Explain how the market could lead to "too many" brands of a product being produced.

2. There are the two hair salons located on Main Street, which is one mile long. The low-cost salon, Quick-Cuts, is located at the east end of town, at the address $x = 0$. It has a constant unit cost of $6 for a "haircut." The higher cost salon, Le Coupe, is located at the west end, or $x = 1$. The unit cost of a "haircut" at Le Coupe is $18. There are 1,000 potential customers distributed uniformly along Main Street. Consumers are willing to pay $50 for a "haircut" if it was done at their home. If a consumer has to travel to get a "haircut" then a travel cost of $$t$ per unit mile is incurred. Suppose that $t = \$12/\text{mile}$. Each salon wants to set a price for a "haircut" that maximizes the salon's profit.

   a. What is the demand function facing Quick-Cuts? What is the demand function facing Le Coupe?

   b. What are the equilibrium prices set by the two salons?

   c. What are the market shares of the two salons at these prices?

3. Return to problem 2, above.

   a. What happens to equilibrium prices and market shares if travel cost t increases from $12 to $20 per mile?

   b. What happens to equilibrium prices and market shares if the travel cost t decreases from $12 to $6 per mile?

4. Suppose now that consumers are not perfectly informed about where the salons are and what prices are charged for a "haircut."
   a. Which salon do you think has the greater incentive to advertise? Why?
   b. The incentive to advertise of course depends upon the cost of advertising. Let's suppose that Le Coupe is working with a more effective ad agency and so the cost of reaching consumers, as for example measured by the parameter α, is lower for Le Coupe than for Quick-Cuts. In particular suppose that the proportion of consumers along Main Street that are informed of a "haircut" at Quick-Cuts is $1/2$, whereas the proportion of consumers informed about Le Coupe is $3/4$. What happens to equilibrium prices?

5. Consider the following list of ad campaigns: evaluate them according to extending reach or building value:
   a. promoting a quicker braking for a specific type of tire;
   b. presentation of taste test data on French fries;
   c. presentation of sales data on a cola product;
   d. demonstration of a close shave by an attractive well-known athlete;
   e. a dog taking its owner to a particular car dealership;
   f. testimonials by adults who like a "kid's" cereal;
   g. laundry detergent commercial showing items washed by two different brands;
   h. liquid soap commercial showing celebrities lathering themselves;
   i. athletic apparel commercial showing big stars being provocative.

6. Consider again Practice Problem 21.3 only now the inverse demand curve is $P(Q, \alpha) = 1 - \alpha^{-1/2}Q$, where Q is number of tubes sold per period, measured in millions, and α is advertising seconds on television per period.

Currently the firm is advertising 100 seconds. The cost of advertising is $10,000 per second. The production cost of a tube of gel is constant and set to zero and there are no fixed costs.
   a. Calculate the firm's profit-maximizing quantity and price. Work out the firm's profit as well.
   b. Now suppose that the firm's marketing manager has struck a deal that if the firm advertises 625 seconds the cost of advertising falls to $5,000 per second. Work out what the firm's profit maximizing strategy and profits if it increases it advertising to 625 seconds.
   c. Compare your answer to that for the Practice Problem.

7. Let there be two firms, 1 and 2. Each firm sells a product of innate quality level 1 and each chooses its price, p_1 and p_2, respectively. However, firm 1 also gets to choose an advertising level a_1. Consumers perceive product quality to be the product's advertising level times its innate quality. In other words, consumers perceive product 1 to be of quality a_1 and product 2 to be of quality 1. Consumers are indexed by θ distributed continuously from zero to 1. θ_i is consumer i's willingness to pay for quality. Consumer i's net gain from consuming product 1 is $\theta_i a_1 - p_1$, while consuming product 2 generates a net gain of $\theta_i - p_2$. There is no production cost. However, firm 1 incurs advertising cost of $(a_1/2)^2$.
   a. Assume all N consumers always buy the product of either firm 1 or firm 2, i.e., the market is always covered. Show that the marginal consumer indexed by θ^m satisfies: $\theta^m a_1 - p_1 = \theta^m - p_2$.
   b. Derive the equilibrium values of p_1, p_2, and a_1.
   c. Suppose firm 2 is permitted now to advertise at any positive level a_2 between 0 and 0.5. What level of advertising will it choose if it takes firm 1's choice a_1 as given?

References

Ackerberg, D. 2001. "Empirically Distinguishing Informative and Prestige Effects of Advertising." *Rand Journal of Economics* 32 (Summer): 316–33.

Bagwell, K. and G. Ramey. 1994. "Coordination Economies, Advertising, and Search Behavior in Retail Markets." *American Economic Review* 84 (June): 498–517.

Becker, G., and K. Murphy. 1993. "A Simple Theory of Advertising as a Good or Bad." *Quarterly Journal of Economics* 108 (August): 941–64.

Butters, G. 1977. "Equilibrium Distribution of Sales and Advertising Prices." *Review of Economic Studies* 44 (June): 465–91.

Clark, C. and I. Horstmann. 2005. "Advertising and Coordination in Markets with Consumption Scale Effects." *Journal of Economics and Management Strategy* 14 (June): 377–401.

Comanor, W. S. and T. A. Wilson. 1967. "Advertising Market Structure and Performance." *Review of Economics and Statistics* 49 (November): 423–40.

——. 1974. *Advertising and Market Power.* Cambridge, MA: Harvard University Press.

Grossman, G. M. and C. Shapiro. 1984. "Informative Advertising with Differentiated Products." *Review of Economic Studies* 51 (February): 63–81.

Kihlstrom, R. and M. Riordan. 1984. "Advertising as a Signal." *Journal of Political Economy* 92 (June): 427–50.

Nelson, P. 1970. "Information and Consumer Behavior." *Journal of Political Economy* 78 (May): 311–29.

Robinson, W. T., and J. Chiang. 1996. "Are Sutton's Predictions Robust? Empirical Insights into Advertising, R&D, and Concentration." *Journal of Industrial Economics* 44 (December): 389–408.

Schmalensee, R. 1978. "Entry Deterrence in the Ready-to-eat Breakfast Cereal Industry." *Bell Journal of Economics* 9 (Autumn): 305–27.

Schwartz, A. and L. Wilde. 1985. "Product Quality and Imperfect Information." *Review of Economic Studies* 52 (April): 251–62.

Shaffer, G. 1991. "Slotting Allowances and Resale Price Maintenance: A Comparison of Facilitating Practices." *Rand Journal of Economics* 22 (Spring): 121–35.

Stigler, G. 1968. "Price and Non-price Competition." *Journal of Political Economy* 76 (February): 149–54.

Sutton, J. 1991. *Sunk Costs and Market Structure.* Cambridge, MA: MIT Press.

Telser, L. 1964. "Advertising and Competition." *Journal of Political Economy* 72 (December): 537–62.

Tirole, J. 1988. *The Theory of Industrial Organization.* Cambridge, MA: MIT Press.

Wright, J. and B. Klein. 2007. "The Economics of Slotting Contracts." *Journal of Law & Economics* 50 (August): 403–27.

22

Research and Development

The final results of the human genome project indicate that we humans are not as complicated as we thought we were. Rather than consisting of the approximately 100,000 genes
that were initially predicted, it appears that we have only 30,000 genes, not much more than
twice as many as the humble roundworm with its 19,098 genes.[1] This finding is important
for many reasons. From our perspective, there is an important economic aspect to this result.
It is well understood that genes are a crucial factor in predicting and curing many diseases.
Therefore, identifying and understanding the workings of each gene could lead to the creation
of a new family of custom-made drugs. The rough equation quoted by the pharmaceutical
companies was "one gene, one patent, one drug."[2] If, as initially expected, there were 100,000
genes then there was potentially a vast number of revenue-generating patents. The finding
that the actual number of genes is far less than 100,000 has suggested to many that genes
hold many fewer of the keys to the treatment of disease. As a result, understanding genes
and their functions may offer a much less lucrative source of new patentable treatments.

However, all is not lost. It is being suggested that much of human biology is determined
at the protein level rather than at the DNA level, and we have well over 1,000,000 different proteins in our bodies. So now we have a whole new science, proteomics—studying how
genes control proteins—as a method for creating tailored drugs. Proteomics is being pursued by an increasingly wide number of companies and institutions: Harvard University, for
example, has created a new Institute of Proteomics.

The race to understand the proteomic causes of diseases and to develop new drugs targeted at those diseases will not come as a surprise to anyone familiar with the popular business literature of the past 20 years. That literature is characterized by the dominant theme
that the most successful firms find new ways of doing things, or develop new products and
new markets.[3] The now prevalent view is that firms become industry leaders by conducting
research and development (R&D) leading to innovations in their production technologies or

---

[1] If you are interested, the complete human genome is available as a free download from http://
gdbwww.gdb.org/.
[2] "Scientists, Companies Look to the Next Step After Genes," *New York Times*, February 13, 2001.
[3] This is virtually the mantra in the best-selling book by Peters and Waterman, *In Search of Excellence:
Lessons from America's Best Run Companies* (1982). However, the argument is repeated frequently in
other business books, including, as noted herein, Porter's (1990) encyclopedic volume.

the products they provide. Michael Porter's *The Competitive Advantage of Nations* (1990) serves to make the point. Porter writes that any theory of competitive success:

> must start from the premise that competition is dynamic and evolving . . . Competition is a constantly changing landscape in which new products, new ways of marketing, new production processes, and whole new market segments emerge . . . [Economic] theory must make improvement and innovation in methods and technology a central element. (p. 20)

Porter's quote could almost have been taken verbatim from Joseph Schumpeter's classic work written almost 50 years earlier. Schumpeter was both an economist and a historian. He brought a historical perspective to his study of competition and the rise and fall of corporate empires. The following dramatic passage appears in his book *Capitalism, Socialism, and Democracy* first published in 1942.

> [I]t is not . . . [price] . . . competition which counts but competition from the new commodity, the new technology, the new source of supply, the new type of organization . . . competition which commands a decisive cost or quality advantage and which strikes not at the margins of the profits and outputs of existing firms but at their foundations and very lives. (p. 84)

Interest in the forces behind innovative activity is perhaps stronger today than it was when Schumpeter wrote.[4] An important issue, raised by Schumpeter, concerns the market environment most conducive to R&D activity. Schumpeter conjectured that R&D efforts are more likely to be undertaken by large firms than by small ones. He speculated secondly that monopolistic or oligopolistic firms would more aggressively pursue innovative activity than would firms with little or no market power. Accordingly, Schumpeter argued that the benefits of an economy comprised largely of competitive markets populated by small firms reflected the rather modest gains of allocating resources efficiently among a *given set of goods and services produced with given technologies*. In contrast, the benefits of markets dominated by large firms, each with sizable market power, stems from the much larger dynamic efficiency gains of developing new products and new technologies. As Schumpeter wrote, "a shocking suspicion dawns upon us that big business may have had more to do with creating (our) standard of life than with keeping it down" (p. 88).

The validity of Schumpeter's ideas—which have come to be jointly referred to as the Schumpeterian hypothesis—is the key issue addressed in this chapter. Do larger firms do more R&D? Does a concentrated market structure provide a better environment for the development of new innovations than a competitive structure? Table 22.1 lists the 10 companies awarded the most patents by the U.S. Patents and Trademark Office (USPTO) in 2006 as well as their ranks in 2005 and 2004. Each of these is a large company. Most operate in oligopolistic markets with only a few large competitors. Moreover, there is considerable stability in the rank ordering, at least over these three years. It is tempting to conclude on the basis of such data that Schumpeter was right and that large firms in concentrated markets are more innovative. However, great care is needed before reaching that conclusion. Rather than implying that large firms do more R&D, these results could imply that firms that do more R&D become large.

---

[4] For example, see the story by C. J. Whalen, "Today's Hottest Economist Died 50 Years Ago," *Business Week*, December 11, 2000. Ever since Solow's (1956) classic work, macroeconomists studying growth have also focused intensively on technological progress and innovation as the primary source of improved living standards over time. See, e.g., the books by Barro and Sala-I-Martin (1995) and Romer (2006).

Table 22.1   Top ten U.S. patent-receiving firms in 2006 and their rank in 2005 and 2004

Company	# of patents in 2006	Rank in 2005	Rank in 2004
International Business Machines	3,621	1	1
Samsung Electronics	2,451	5	3
Canon Kabushiki Kaisha	2,366	2	4
Matsushita Electric Industrial	2,229	4	2
Hewlett-Packard	2,099	3	6
Intel Corporation	1,959	7	5
Sony Corporation	1,771	12	7
Hitachi	1,732	8	8
Toshiba Corporation	1,672	9	9
Micron Technology	1,610	6	11

Source: USPTO

Table 22.2   Top ten patent-receiving industries in 2006 and cumulative patents to that year

Industry class	Patents granted in 2006	Cumulative patents granted
Semiconductor device manufacturing: process	4,467	50,224
Active solid-state devices (e.g., transistors, solid-state diodes)	4,287	42,436
Drug, bio-affecting and body treating compositions	2,784	73,234
Multiplex communications	2,754	25,157
Chemistry: molecular biology and microbiology	2,423	46,466
Telecommunications	2,271	20,624
Stock material or miscellaneous articles	2,263	54,326
Static information storage and retrieval	2,019	24,710
Optical: systems and elements	2,013	28,024
Computer graphics processing and selective visual display systems	2,004	22,507

Source: USPTO

The most active areas for research activity are likely to vary over time. Table 22.2 lists the top patent-receiving industries or research areas in 2006. It also shows the cumulative patents in that area up to that year. While there is some consistency across the two columns there is also considerable variation. Thus, while semiconductor and solid-state devices have led the patent parade in recent years, bio-science drugs and molecular chemistry have accounted for many more patents in total over time.

Introducing a new product can often undermine the marketability of the firm's existing products. Similarly, the development of a new production process requiring new equipment reduces the value of existing productive capacity. Because introducing new products or processes inevitably means the destruction of old ones, Schumpeter dubbed such competition by innovation "creative destruction." In addition, since some of the products and processes that are made obsolete may well be those of the innovating firm itself we can ask our central question in a somewhat different way. Why do firms undermine existing activities (including

Reality Checkpoint

Creative Destruction in the Pharmaceutical Industry: Will the Prozac Work if the Viagra Fails?

Perhaps no market offers better examples of Schumpeter's "creative destruction" than that for pharmaceuticals. Consider the market for antidepressants. For several years after its introduction in 1987 by Eli Lilly & Co., Prozac dominated this market. Originally envisioned as a treatment for high blood pressure and, when that failed, an anti-obesity drug, Lilly was pleasantly surprised when hospital tests on mildly depressed patients showed a marked and widespread positive effect. Lilly took its fluoxetine drug as it was then called, and asked Interbrand, one of the major branding companies in the world, to develop a new name and sales campaign. Prozac was born and soon it dominated the antidepressant market. By the early 1990s, Prozac accounted for nearly a quarter of Lilly's $10 billion revenue.

However, rivals were soon at work inventing around Lilly's patent. In 1992 Pfizer, Inc., introduced a rival Zoloft, which quickly jumped to a third of the market. This was shortly followed by SmikthKline Beecham's Paxil, which soon had 20 percent of the market. All three drugs increased the levels of the neurotransmitter, serotonin, in the brain. But all three had slightly different chemical bases and different side effects. Finally, in 2001, the Prozac patent expired. Within two weeks, prescriptions for generic fluoxetine exceeded those for brand-name Prozac. Within a year, Lilly had lost 90 percent of its Prozac prescriptions. Lilly countered with a new drug, duloxetine, with the brand name of Cymbalta that works on two neurotransmitters, serotonin and norepinephrine.

This brings us to the story of Viagra, the original drug to combat male impotence patented by Pfizer in 1996. Like Prozac, the drug originally known as sildenafil citrate, was originally envisioned as a treatment for high blood pressure and angina. Even though it failed in that regard, its many male users reported a dramatic increase in sexual function.

Pfizer received approval from the Food and Drug Administration (FDA) to market the drug as a treatment for erectile dysfunction and re-launched the drug under the name, Viagra, in 1998. Sales topped $1 billion within a year.

Once again, success brings competition. By 2003, two new drugs were approved by the FDA as treatments for male impotence. These were Levitra (made by Bayer and GlaxoSmithKline) and Cialis (developed by a small startup firm, ICOS, and marketed by Lilly). Both work in much the same way as Viagra but, again, there are important differences and side effects. Levitra penetrates cell walls in as little as 16 minutes rather than the 30 minutes minimum required for Viagra. Cialis works about as fast as Viagra but has a serum half life of nearly 18 hours. Hence, it can be effective for up to 36 hours or 9 times longer than the typical duration of Viagra. The relative efficacy of these two products has made them fierce competitors to Viagra. Within the U.S., the two drugs combined quickly for as much as 40 percent of the market. In countries such as Australia and France, Cialis alone claimed 40 percent of the market within its first year. Of course, the real competition will start in 2011 when the Viagra patent expires. If the Prozac experience is any guide, competition from generics will very quickly become fierce and Viagra sales will decline even as the general market rises. Drug firms like Lilly and Pfizer could then take a double hit as the change in lifestyles that may then occur may lead to a decline in the demand for antidepressants among both men and women.

Sources: R. Langreth, "High Anxiety: Rivals Threaten Prozac's Reign," *Wall Street Journal*, May 9, 1996, p. A4; A. Pollack, "Lilly Pays Bid Fee up Front to Share in Rival of Viagra," *New York Times*, October 2, 1998, p. C1; S. Carey, "Lilly Reports 22% Decline in Net Income as Generics Hurt Sales of Prozac," *Wall Street Journal*, April 16, 2002, p. C2; and "Viagra Rival Cialis Wins up to 40 Percent Market Share," *Reuters News Wire*, March 23, 2004.

their own ones) in this way? More generally, what are the incentives to engage in innovative activity and how do these vary with firm size and market structure?

Both the professional and the popular business literature have had much to say on the Schumpeterian hypothesis in recent years. In this chapter, we approach this topic using the tools of economic analysis and strategic interaction that we have built throughout the book. However, before we begin a more formal analysis we need to establish some definitions or classifications to which we can easily refer.

22.1   A TAXONOMY OF INNOVATIONS

Research and development consists of three related activities. The first is *basic research*. This includes studies that will not necessarily lead to specific applications but, instead, aim to improve our fundamental knowledge in a manner that may subsequently be helpful in a range of activities. The derivation and validation of the theory of laser technology is a good example. A second category is *applied research*. Such research generally involves substantial engineering input and is aimed at a more practical and specific usage than basic research. The creation of the first laser drill for dentistry would be an example of applied research. Finally, there is the *development* component of R&D. Here, the goal is to move from the creation of a prototype to a product that can be used by consumers and that is capable (to some extent at least) of mass production. To continue our analogy, the transformation of the first laser drill into a small, handheld product that is affordable and usable by a large number of dentists would be an example of the development stage. For the most part we shall be concerned with applied research rather than development, but we shall touch upon some of the important issues that characterize the decision to move from research to development.

In considering the output of R&D, it is common to distinguish between two kinds. *Process innovations* are discoveries of new, typically cheaper methods for producing existing goods. *Product innovations* are the creation of new goods. For the most part, we shall concentrate on process innovations, but we shall also present examples showing how the analysis can be extended to product innovations.

Finally, with respect to process innovations, there is a further distinction that can be made. This is the division of innovations into *drastic* or major innovations, and *nondrastic* or minor innovations. Roughly speaking, drastic innovations are ones that reduce a firm's unit cost to such an extent that even if it charges the profit-maximizing monopoly price associated with that low cost, it will still undercut all competitors. Hence, a drastic innovation creates a monopolist unconstrained by any fear of entry or price competition—at least for some time. By contrast, a firm making a nondrastic innovation may gain some cost advantage over its rivals but not one so large that the firm can price like a monopolist without fear of competition.

The formal distinction between drastic and nondrastic innovations is illustrated in Figure 22.1. Assume that demand for a particular product is given by $P = 120 - Q$ and that before the innovation all firms can produce the product at a constant marginal cost of $80. Assume also that the existing firms are Bertrand competitors so that the price is $80 and total output is 40 units.

Now suppose that one firm gains access to a process innovation that reduces its marginal costs to $20 as in Figure 22.1(a) and that, perhaps because of a patent, this firm is the only one able to use the new low-cost technology. If this innovator were alone in the market, it would set the monopoly price corresponding to its new, lower marginal costs of $20. Given our demand function we know that marginal revenue is $MR = 120 - 2Q$. Equating this with

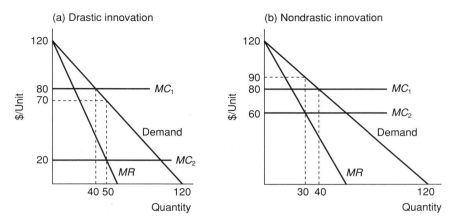

Figure 22.1   Drastic and nondrastic process innovations

marginal cost of $20 gives an output of 50 units and a monopoly price of $70. Setting this monopoly price forces all the other firms out of the market. The innovation is a drastic one because the reduction in cost is so great that the innovating firm can charge the full monopoly price associated with the new low cost and still be able to undercut the marginal costs of all other firms.

Suppose by contrast that the innovation reduces marginal costs to $60 as in Figure 22.1(b). By exactly the same argument as above, the innovating firm acting as a monopolist wants to produce an output of 30 units and set a price of $90. The problem is that this will not work. The remaining firms can profitably undercut this price. So the best that the innovating firm can do now is to set a price of $80 (more accurately, $79.99) and an output of 40 units. This still eliminates the other firms but only by the innovator lowering the price that it charges. Hence, this is a nondrastic innovation.

22.1

Assume that demand in a competitive market is given by the linear function: $P = 100 - Q$ and that current marginal cost of production is constant at $60. Now assume that there is a process innovation that reduces marginal cost to $28. Show that this is a nondrastic innovation. How much would the innovation have to lower marginal costs for it to be drastic?

Practice Problem

22.2   MARKET STRUCTURE AND THE INCENTIVE TO INNOVATE

We now turn to some of the basic questions economists have asked regarding how the incentives to spend on R&D are affected by market structure.[5] We assume the demand for a particular good is linear. Specifically, the inverse demand curve is again assumed to be given

---

[5]   This analysis owes much to Nobel Prize winner Kenneth Arrow's path-breaking work (1962).

by the equation $P = 120 - Q$. We also assume that each producer of the good has a marginal cost of \$80. Accordingly, if the market is competitive and there are many such producers, the current price is also \$80.

22.2.1   Competition and the Value of Innovation

Suppose that a research firm, not involved in the actual manufacture of this good, discovers a new production process by undertaking research at some cost K. Using the notation from above, we consider the case of a nondrastic process innovation that reduces the marginal production cost to \$60. We further assume that the innovation is protected by a patent of unlimited duration that cannot be "invented around" by other potential or actual firms. What benefits does the innovation bring, and does the market mechanism work to convey such incentives to the research firm?

Let us first consider how society as a whole values the innovation. Imagine a social planner whose goal is to maximize total social surplus (producer surplus plus consumer surplus) and, moreover, who has the power to command that prices be set at whatever level the planner requests. Such a benevolent dictator would reason as follows: With or without the innovation, optimality requires that price be set to marginal cost. The per-period value that the social planner places upon the innovation is the increase in consumer surplus when price equals (constant) marginal cost as then there is no producer surplus. Prior to the innovation, consumer surplus at a price of \$80 is \$800. After the innovation, when firms set the price equal to the new lower marginal cost of \$60, consumer surplus increases to \$1,800.[6] The increase in consumer surplus is \$1,000, the shaded area in Figure 22.2(a). This additional surplus will be realized not just in one period but also in all present and future periods following the innovation. Hence, using the discounting techniques discussed in section 2.2 Chapter 2, the total present value of the additional surplus created by the innovation is $V^p = 1,000/(1 - R)$ where $R = (1 + r)^{-1}$ and r is the interest rate. The more this value exceeds the cost K, that is, the more it exceeds the present value of the expenses associated with discovering the process, the more desirable is the innovation.

Of course, we don't have a dictator and if we did it is doubtful that her goal would be the maximization of social welfare. What we have are markets. The issue is how the structure of the market affects the realization of the value of this innovation. What is the incentive of a research firm to pursue the innovation if, when it is successful, it can auction the rights to the innovation to a competitive industry comprised of many firms.

Prior to the innovation all firms sell at a price equal to the marginal cost of \$80 and earn zero profit. Total output each period prior to the innovation is just 40 units. Now consider the behavior of a firm that has the rights to the innovation? Quite evidently, its best strategy is to undercut its erstwhile competitors just slightly, driving them out of the market and giving it an effective monopoly. The firm that wins the rights will set a price that is one cent less than the old competitive price, \$80. At this price, the industry's total output remains identical to what it was prior to the adoption of the innovation. Consequently, the firm will earn per-period profit of $\$(80 - 60) \times 40 = \$800$. This is illustrated by the shaded rectangle in Figure 22.2(b). The present value that a competitive firm places on the innovation is the maximum amount it willingly bids for the rights to it and

---

[6]   Given our demand function $P = 120 - Q$ and assuming that $P = MC$, consumer surplus is the area of a triangle with height $120 - MC$ and base $120 - MC$. That is, $CS = (120 - MC)^2/2$.

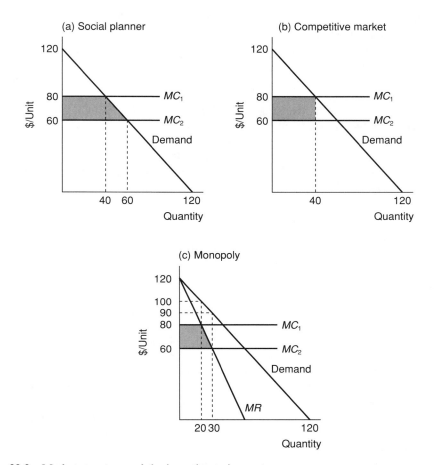

Figure 22.2   Market structure and the incentive to innovate

this is $V^c = 800/(1 - R)$. This is less than the social value of the innovation. The reason is simple: the competitive firm only considers the profit it can earn as a result of the innovation. It ignores the additional benefit from increased consumer surplus that the innovation brings.

Now consider the potential value when it is a monopolist who has the rights to the innovation and who faces no threat of entry. For such a firm, the gain from introducing the innovation is the additional profit it makes as a result of being able to produce at a lower marginal cost. Since the monopolist maximizes profit by setting marginal revenue equal to marginal cost, we can measure this gain by comparing the monopolist's per-period profit at its current marginal cost with its per-period profit at the lower marginal cost that the innovation permits. This is illustrated in Figure 22.2(c).

Given our demand function we know that marginal revenue is $MR = 120 - 2Q$. So, prior to the innovation, the monopolist produces an output of 20 units, sets a price of $100 and earns profit per period of $400. After the innovation output is increased to 30 units, price is reduced to $90 and per-period profits are $900. As a result, the per-period value placed by the monopolist on the innovation is $500—the difference between profits with and without the innovation. This is illustrated by the shaded area in Figure 22.2(c).[7] In turn, the total present value the monopolist places on the innovation is $V^m = 500/(1 - R)$.

From the foregoing analysis, it is obvious that $V^p > V^c > V^m$. Both the competitive firm and the monopolist undervalue the innovation relative to the social planner interested in maximizing total welfare. However, a competitive firm values the innovation more than the monopolist.

The reason that the value placed upon the innovation by the monopolist is less than its value to a competitive firm as well as its value to society is again easily explained. A competitive firm is just breaking even prior to adopting the innovation and so values the innovation at the full additional profits it will generate. By contrast, the monopolist is already earning a monopoly profit with its existing technology. Introducing the new process displaces and therefore undermines that investment, and as with the competitive firm, the monopolist ignores the increase in consumer surplus. This is often referred to as the *replacement effect* but the term is misleading. After all, society also values the innovation by comparing it to the technology that it is replacing. The important reason the monopolist undervalues the innovation is because the monopolist restricts output to less than the socially optimal level. To see why suppose, by contrast, that the monopolist could employ first-degree price discrimination. Then the monopolist's valuation of the innovation would exactly equal society's valuation.

While the comparison just drawn is between a monopolist and a firm in a perfectly competitive market, the results would be the same if we instead compare a monopolist with a firm in an oligopoly market characterized by Bertrand competition. (Why?) Moreover, the same qualitative result will be obtained in a comparison of a monopoly firm with firms engaged in Cournot competition. The basic reason remains. While the Cournot firm does enjoy some positive, pre-innovation profits, these are much smaller than those of a monopolist. Therefore, the Cournot competitor has much less to lose than does the monopolist from pursuing the innovation. While the case just described considered a nondrastic process innovation, the same ordering, $V^p > V^c > V^m$, holds for a drastic one. In other words, the social gain from a drastic innovation exceeds the gain to a firm engaged in Bertrand (or Cournot) competition, which in turn exceeds the gain to a monopolist. Finally, while our analysis assumes a specific linear demand, the same results are obtained for any demand function even if it is nonlinear.[8]

22.2

Practice Problem

Assume that demand for a homogeneous good is $P = 100 - Q$, where P is measured in dollars, and that a process innovation reduces marginal costs of production from \$75 to \$60 per unit. Assume that the discount factor is $R = 0.9$.

a. Confirm that this is a nondrastic innovation and that marginal costs would have to be reduced to less than \$50 per unit for the innovation to be drastic.

b. Calculate the maximum amount that a monopolist is willing to pay for the innovation.

---

[7] This is derived from the property that one way to represent the monopolist's profit is the area between the monopolist's *MR* and *MC* curves.

[8] Gilbert (2006) shows that our results generalize to any demand function.

Now assume that the market is served by Cournot duopolists who have identical marginal costs of \$75 prior to the innovation.

c.   Confirm that the pre-innovation price is \$83.33 and that at this price each firm has profits per period of \$69.44.
d.   Confirm that if one of these firms is granted use of the innovation, the price will fall to \$78.33.
e.   Show that this firm is willing to pay more for the innovation than the monopolist.

22.2.2   Preserving Monopoly Profit and the Efficiency Effect

The analysis in the previous section assumed that there was only one innovator, namely, a lab outside the industry. If that laboratory company does not innovate, no one does. This view does not truly capture the spirit of Schumpeter's contention. Instead, Schumpeter's point is precisely that firms compete by means of innovation. This means that firms have their own labs and that each firm is a potential innovator. As a result, even if one firm does not innovate, another might. This can reverse our previous results.[9]

Suppose that demand is given by $P = 120 - Q$ and that the current technology allows production at a marginal cost of \$60. An incumbent monopolist and a potential entrant play the following three-stage game. In stage 1 the incumbent decides whether or not to undertake R&D, which we assume reduces marginal cost to \$30. In stage 2 a potential entrant decides whether or not to enter. If the incumbent has not undertaken R&D, the entrant then chooses whether or not to undertake R&D. Without R&D the entrant's marginal cost is \$60 and with it marginal cost is \$30. No matter who innovates, the innovation is protected by a patent of unlimited duration that cannot be "invented around" by other potential or actual firms. If entry occurs then in stage 3 the entrant and the incumbent act as Cournot competitors. The extensive form of this game is illustrated in Figure 22.3.

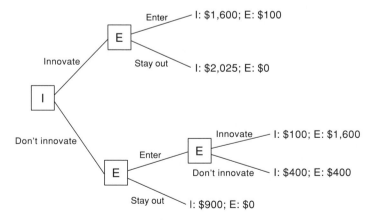

Figure 22.3   Extensive form for the Innovation and Entry game

---

[9]   The underlying analysis can be found in Gilbert and Newbery (1982). Reinganum (1983) shows, however, that this conclusion might not hold when the timing of the successful breakthrough is uncertain. The incumbent monopolist might delay innovation in order to enjoy its current profits. A potential entrant has no such incentive to delay its innovative activity.

As usual we solve this game "backwards." Suppose that the incumbent has undertaken R&D. Then the entrant will enter with a cost $60. The incumbent earns per period profit of $1,600 and the entrant earns per-period profit of $100. (This assumes, of course, that there are no sunk costs of entry. We return to this point below.) Now suppose that the incumbent does not innovate. The entrant will certainly enter. Innovation by the entrant gives the entrant per-period profit of $1,600 while no innovation leads to per-period profit of $400.

We can now calculate how much the innovation is worth to the incumbent and to the entrant. For the entrant, innovation increases per-period profit from $400 to $1,600. Accordingly the present value of the innovation to the entrant is $V^e = \$1,200/(1 - R)$. What about the incumbent? No innovation by the incumbent will lead to innovative entry provided only that the cost of the innovation is less than $\$1,200/(1 - R)$. In that case, the incumbent then earns per-period profit of $100. By contrast, if the incumbent innovates and pre-empts innovation by the entrant the incumbent earns per-period profit of $1,600. As a result, the value of the innovation to the incumbent is $V^i = \$1,500/(1 - R)$. Clearly this exceeds the value placed on the innovation by the entrant. Hence, the monopolist has the stronger incentive to innovate.

Our analysis illustrates the potential for innovation to deter entry, protecting the incumbent's monopoly position and profit. Suppose that sunk entry costs S are such that $\$100/(1 - R) < S < \$400/(1 - R)$. That is, imagine that sunk costs are greater than the profit that the entrant expects to make if the incumbent innovates but less than the profit that the entrant expects to make if neither entrant nor incumbent innovates. The value of the innovation to the entrant is unchanged at $\$1,200/(1 - R)$. This is not the case for the incumbent. Now innovation deters entry, allowing the incumbent to maintain her monopoly position with per-period profit of $2,025. Failure to innovate, by contrast, leads to innovative entry and per-period profit to the incumbent of $100. The value of the innovation to the incumbent is now even greater at $V^m = \$1,925/(1 - R)$.

The foregoing result is not peculiar to the numbers we have assumed. It is in fact quite general. Suppose first that innovation by the incumbent does not deter entry. Denote the per-period duopoly profit of the incumbent as $\pi_i^d(c_i, c_e)$ and of the entrant as $\pi_e^d(c_i, c_e)$, where c_i is marginal cost of the incumbent and c_e is marginal cost of the entrant. Innovation reduces marginal cost from c_h (high) to c_l (low). The incumbent knows that innovation gives per-period profit $\pi_i^d(c_l, c_h)$ while failure to innovate leads to innovative entry and profit $\pi_i^d(c_h, c_l)$. For the entrant, innovation is possible only if the incumbent has not innovated. Innovation then gives per-period profit of $\pi_e^d(c_h, c_l)$ while the failure to innovate gives per-period profit of $\pi_e^d(c_h, c_h)$. The per-period value of the innovation to the incumbent is $\pi_i^d(c_l, c_h) - \pi_i^d(c_h, c_l)$ while the per-period value of the innovation to the entrant is $\pi_e^d(c_h, c_l) - \pi_e^d(c_h, c_h)$.

Symmetry between the two firms tells us that $\pi_i^d(c_l, c_h) = \pi_e^d(c_h, c_l)$ and $\pi_e^d(c_h, c_h) = \pi_i^d(c_h, c_h)$. As a result, for the incumbent to place a higher value on the innovation than the entrant requires that $\pi_i^d(c_h, c_l) < \pi_i^d(c_h, c_h)$. This condition is always satisfied. The profit of the incumbent firm when it faces a low-cost rival is less than its profit when it faces a high-cost rival, no matter what the incumbent's marginal costs are.

Now suppose that innovation by the incumbent deters entry. The per-period value of the innovation to the entrant is unchanged. By contrast, the per-period value of the innovation to the monopolist is now $\pi^m(c_l) - \pi_i^d(c_h, c_l)$. This is clearly greater than the value of the innovation with entry since $\pi^m(c_l) > \pi_i^d(c_l, c_h)$. A low-cost incumbent always prefers monopoly to sharing the market, even when the sharing is with a high-cost rival.

To summarize, no matter whether innovation by an incumbent monopolist maintains that monopoly or not, the incumbent firm values the innovation more highly than a potential entrant. Replacing oneself is better than being replaced by a newcomer. This effect is called the *efficiency effect*.

22.3   A MORE COMPLETE MODEL OF COMPETITION VIA INNOVATION

What drives the efficiency effect is the fact that the cost of not innovating becomes higher once we recognize that it is precisely in this case that a rival may innovate. Such an increase in the opportunity cost of non-innovation makes the incumbent monopolist much more willing to pay for the innovation. Clearly, the strategic interaction from potential entry through innovation seems closer to the view Schumpeter (1942) presents.

We can get even closer to the Schumpeterian spirit by making the decision to spend on R&D an explicit part of a firm's strategy. The simplest model in this spirit is one due to Dasgupta and Stiglitz (1980). Their model is attractive both for its key insights and because it builds on the Cournot model developed in section 9.5 Chapter 9. We present the essentials of their analysis here.

Dasgupta and Stiglitz assume an industry comprised of n identical Cournot firms each of which has to determine the level of output, q_i it will produce and the amount, x_i, that it will spend on R&D. While R&D is costly, the benefit of R&D spending is that it lowers the firm's unit cost of production, c. Specifically, each firm's unit cost is a decreasing function of the amount it spends on R&D, $c_i = c(x_i)$ and $dc(x_i)/dx_i < 0$. Total net profit for any firm, π_i, is:

$$\pi_i = P(Q)q_i - c(x_i)q_i - x_i \tag{22.1}$$

Suppose that each firm spends a specific amount, x^*, on research. Each firm then has a unit cost of $c(x^*)$. Accordingly, if we know the value of x^*, we know each firm's unit cost, and we can work out the equilibrium output for the individual firm and the industry in total using the analysis from section 9.5.[10] In particular, we know that the outcome in this symmetric, n-firm Cournot model is an equilibrium price–cost margin, or Lerner Index, given by

$$\frac{(P - c(x^*))}{P} = \frac{s_i}{\eta} \tag{22.2}$$

Here, P is the industry price, s_i is the ith firm's share of industry output, η is the elasticity of market demand, and x^* is the amount that each firm spends on R&D in equilibrium. We have dispensed with the subscript on the term x^* because for identical firms the amount chosen is the same in equilibrium for each firm. We can simplify further by recognizing that since all firms are identical, s_i is just $1/n$. So, equation (22.2) can be written as

$$P\left(1 - \frac{1}{n\eta}\right) = c(x^*) \tag{22.3}$$

---

[10]   If we set the derivative of equation (22.1) with respect to q_i to zero, taking the production of all firms other than the ith, Q_{-i} as given, and then solve for q_i we obtain each firm's best response function.

Equation (22.3) does not by itself tell us the amount of R&D expenditure, x^*, that each firm will find optimal in the ultimate equilibrium. To determine that value we must add a second equilibrium condition indicating when a firm will know that it has spent the right amount on research activities. This is obtained by differentiating the profit equation (22.1) with respect to the R&D expenditures, x_i, to give the condition

$$\frac{\partial \pi_i}{\partial x_i} = -\frac{dc(x_i)}{dx_i} q_i - 1 = 0 \tag{22.4}$$

which can be simplified to the condition that in equilibrium we must have

$$-\frac{dc(x_i)}{dx_i} q_i = 1 \tag{22.5}$$

What does this mean? Remember that an increase in R&D expenditures reduces marginal cost $c(x_i)$, so that $dc(x_i)/dx_i$, the amount by which marginal cost changes as a result of an additional dollar of R&D expenditures, is negative. The left-hand side of equation (22.5) is, therefore, positive and is equal to the full marginal benefit of an extra dollar of R&D spending. The marginal cost of an extra dollar spent on R&D is simply \$1. At the equilibrium level of R&D expenditures, x^*, the marginal benefit of an extra dollar spent on R&D just equals its marginal cost.

What are the implications of the equilibrium conditions of equations (22.3) and (22.5)? The most obvious conclusion is that an increase in the number of firms in the industry will decrease the amount that each firm is willing to spend on R&D. The reason is that a fall in the number of firms decreases the amount that each firm will choose to produce. This is, actually, a direct implication of equation (22.3). But equation (22.5) makes clear that the marginal benefit of extra R&D spending is directly proportional to the volume of a firm's output. Hence, the reduction in a firm's output that results from increasing the number of firms also reduces the marginal benefit that R&D spending yields to an individual firm. It follows that the equilibrium level of such spending per firm, x^*, will fall as the number of firms rises.

This does not necessarily imply, however, that the total industry spending on R&D, which is nx^*, will also fall. It is perfectly possible that each firm spends less on R&D but total R&D spending increases. Dasgupta and Stiglitz show that aggregate spending on R&D may actually either increase or decrease as the number of firms in the industry increases. The key point is that for aggregate R&D spending to increase, the elasticity of market demand must be fairly large. When demand is relatively elastic, the expansion of industry output resulting from a greater number of firms will not decrease the price too much and, as a result, will not decrease the marginal revenue of equation (22.3) very much either. Since this difference between price and cost is what finances a firm's R&D expenditure, such expenditure can be expected to rise in total with the number of industry firms so long as η is relatively large. If, however, the elasticity of market demand declines as output expands (as is the case with linear demand curves), then increasing the number of firms will, beyond some point, lead to a reduction in total R&D efforts. Even for a relatively small number of firms in the market adding one more firm induces a decline in total R&D spending. Therefore, the Dasgupta and Stiglitz model may be taken as partial support for the Schumpeterian hypothesis that concentration fosters innovation.

The foregoing does not explain what determines the number of firms in an industry. Dasgupta and Stiglitz invoke a third equilibrium condition that, in the long run, free entry will lead to an increase in the number of firms until each firm makes zero profit. In other words, industry structure is determined endogenously by the firms' output and R&D expenditure decisions. The zero profit condition, when applied to equation (22.1) tells us that

$$P(Q^*)q^* - c(x^*)q^* - x^* = 0 \tag{22.6}$$

Aggregating this over the equilibrium number of firms in the industry, n^*, gives

$$P(Q^*)Q^* - c(x^*)Q^* - n^*x^* = 0 \tag{22.7}$$

which implies that $(P(Q^*) - c(x^*))Q^* = n^*x^*$. Now since each of the n firms is of the same size, each has a market share equal to $1/n$. By equation (22.2) we know that $P - c(x^*) = P/n^*\eta$. Using this substitution, the equilibrium R&D outcome derived by Dasgupta and Stiglitz is

$$\frac{n^*x^*}{P(Q^*)Q^*} = industry \ R\&D \ spending \ as \ a \ share \ of \ industry \ sales = \frac{1}{n^*\eta} \tag{22.8}$$

Comparing across industries, equation (22.8) suggests that the share of an industry's total sales revenue that will be devoted to R&D is likely to be smaller in less concentrated industries. In other words, those industries with a naturally more competitive structure will undertake less R&D effort, all else being equal. This may then be seen as offering fairly strong support for Schumpeter's basic claim that imperfect competition is good for technical progress and more imperfect competition is even better.

22.4 EVIDENCE ON THE SCHUMPETERIAN HYPOTHESIS

The debate over the Schumpeterian hypothesis cannot be resolved by an appeal to economic theory alone. We must also consider empirical evidence. To date, a number of statistical studies relating R&D effort to firm size and industry structure have been conducted. While these studies are far from uniform in their results, one general finding does emerge. R&D intensity does appear to increase with increases in industrial concentration but only up to a rather modest value after which R&D efforts appear to level off or even decline as a fraction of firm revenue.

Some of the earliest studies exploring the link between industry structure and R&D were those of Scherer (1965, 1967). His basic finding was that while firm size and concentration are each positively associated with the intensity of R&D spending, these correlations diminish beyond a relatively low threshold. That is, once firms reach a relatively small size and/or markets reach a relatively low level of concentration, any positive effects of firm size or market concentration on innovative activity tend to vanish. Subsequent studies, including those of Levin and Reiss (1984), Levin, Cohen, and Mowery (1985a, 1985b), Levin, Klevorick, Nelson, and Winter (1987), Lunn (1986), Scott (1990), Geroski (1990), Blundell, Griffith, and Van Reem (1995) have tended to confirm Scherer's (1965) basic finding.[11]

---

[11]   See Cohen and Levin (1989) for an early summary.

Reality Checkpoint
Some Little Inventors That Could

While the jury is still out on the Schumpeterian hypothesis that larger firms and/or concentrated markets spur technological progress, there is certainly a good bit of anecdotal evidence regarding the prowess of individual inventors and small firms to come up with the big breakthrough. The personal computer, for instance, was mainly introduced by a then-small firm called Apple. The phonograph and wireless telegraphy were developed by individuals, Edison in the first case and Marconi in the second. George Westinghouse was a young man of 22, working alone, when he patented his model for a compressed air braking system that was soon adopted by every train on both the Southern Pacific and Central Pacific railroads—and virtually all other U.S. trains within a few years.

The story does not end in the late nineteenth or early twentieth century. Xerox was a small firm called Haloid when it developed the Xerographic copying method. Intel, which now controls more than two-thirds of the microprocessor market, started out as a small firm packaging transistors on a sliver of silicon. More recently, small firms and entrepreneurs continue to be an active source of innovation. For example, two of the most heavily trafficked sites on the web, e-Bay and Amazon, were both the creation of small independent entrepreneurs. Genentech was just a tiny venture capitalist experiment when it launched the field of recombinant DNA. Larry Page and Sergey Brin were Stanford graduate students when they began collaboration on a search engine called BackRub that relied on a new kind of server environment using many low-end PCs instead of big, expensive machines. Within a few years BackRub became Google and Page and Brin were billionaires.

While it may be surprising that so many well-known inventions came from relatively small firms and entrepreneurs, what is perhaps even more surprising is how often larger firms turned their backs on those very innovations that later proved so successful. IBM for instance, totally ignored the PC market at its inception. Apple came out with the first personal digital assistant (PDA) but it was a little firm called Palm that solved the problem of making a connection between the PDA and the PC desktop. Edison himself, well after his firm had been established as the premier technical enterprise of its time, initially regarded his own invention of the motion picture camera as little more than a pleasant toy and his fights against the superior alternating current technology to provide the electricity for his light bulbs are famous.

The anecdotal record tempts one to suspect that the confidence that comes from being a large firm with market power easily crosses over to an arrogance that blinds the firm to major innovations. However, there is some rational explanation. First, as noted in the text, large firms based on existing goods and processes have much to fear from the replacement effect that innovations bring. Second, there may also be a natural division of effort in which small entrepreneurs introduce new technologies while large, established firms play the role of "fast second" that quickly capitalizes on the small-firm breakthroughs. The reason for this is that a large firm with many products may fear that any failure with a new good will in fact taint its entire product line. A new small firm focused on just a few goods does not have this risk.

Source: C. Markides and P. Geroski, *Fast Second: How Smart Companies Bypass Radical Innovations to Enter and Dominate New Markets*, Jossey-Bass, San Francisco, 2005.

In examining the influence of firm size and market structure on innovative activity, a number of important issues must be addressed. The first of these is that in comparing R&D efforts across markets, we should control for the "science-based" character of each industry: recall the very different patent activity by industry category noted in Table 22.2. Markets in which the member firms produce goods such as chemical products or computer hardware have such a strong technical base that general advances in scientific understanding can rapidly translate into either product or process innovations. Other markets, however, such as those for haircuts or hairstyling, will have more difficulty in making use of scientific breakthroughs and have less direct contact with universities and research laboratories. It turns out that measures of such technological opportunities tend to be highly correlated with the degree of industry concentration. In other words, while the simple correlation between concentration and innovation may be positive, this correlation reflects the positive effects on innovation that come with increases in an industry's opportunity for technical advances. The more recent studies cited above demonstrate that controlling for this factor is very important.

A second factor is the distinction between R&D expenditures and true innovations as perhaps measured by patents. While innovative effort can be measured by the ratio of R&D spending to sales this approach really measures the inputs to the innovative process. Presumably though, what we are really interested in are the outputs of that process—the true number of innovations as perhaps measured by the number of patents a firm acquires. Even though different firms do the same amount of R&D spending, the Schumpeterian hypothesis might be validated if size or concentration leads that spending to be more productive. The studies cited above do in fact look at the patent output of firms. Here again, however, little evidence is found in support of the Schumpeterian claims. Cohen and Klepper (1996) conclude that the general finding is that large firms do proportionately more R&D than smaller firms but get fewer innovations from these efforts. A notable exception in this regard, however, is Gayle (2002) who finds that firms in concentrated industries do generate many more patents when patents are not simply counted but, instead, are measured on a citation-weighted basis.[12]

Finally, a third issue is the endogeneity of market structure. Some firms, for example Alcoa or Microsoft, came to dominate their industry on the basis of a dramatic innovation. In the case of Alcoa, it was its unique process for refining aluminum. In the case of Microsoft, it was its unique Windows operating systems for personal computers. In these and other cases, the key technology that led to the firm's dominant position was associated with a number of patents. If this experience is pervasive, a naïve researcher may find that large, dominant firms are also firms with many patents and wrongly conclude that the Schumpeterian hypothesis is validated. In these cases it is the innovative activity that leads to market power and not the other way around. If the firms that come to dominate their markets start out as small operations and then grow on the basis of entrepreneurial skill and technical breakthroughs, the implication could be quite to the contrary of Schumpeter's model.[13]

---

[12]   When a patent application is filed, the applicant must cite all the prior patents related to the new process or product. It is plausible that the most important patents are those that are cited most frequently. Hence, in evaluating a firm's true innovative output, one may want to control for how often the firm's patents are cited.

[13]   Generally, market structure and innovative activity evolve together. For example, if experience raises R&D productivity then older firms will tend to do more innovation because it has a higher return for them, so that early entrants will tend to dominate an industry over time. See Klepper (2002) for an analysis along these lines.

22.5   R&D COOPERATION BETWEEN FIRMS

Our final topic in this chapter addresses the issue of cooperation on R&D efforts among firms. Two features of the innovative process make such efforts attractive from the viewpoint of economic efficiency. First, modern technology is very complicated and often draws on different areas of expertise and experience. Because it is doubtful that the scientists and engineers in one firm possess all this knowhow, it is desirable that firms share their experiences, experimental results, and design solutions with each other so as to realize fully the benefits from scientific study. Second, there is a potential for wasteful R&D spending as firms duplicate each other's efforts in a noncooperative R&D race.

We do have explicit evidence on this score. One of the most dynamic and creative groups of firms in the U.S. economy in recent years has been the American steel minimills. These firms rely on small-scale plants using electric arc furnaces to recycle scrap steel. They are widely regarded as world leaders and have outperformed even the Japanese steel firms once thought to be invincible. Through a series of interviews, von Hippel (1988) found that these firms regularly and routinely exchanged technical information with each other. In fact, sometimes workers of competing firms were trained (at no charge) by a rival company in the use of specific equipment. Such exchanges of information and expertise were made with the knowledge and approval of management even though they had the effect of strengthening a competitor.

To analyze the implications of research spillovers, we again make use of the Cournot duopoly model, similar to the Dasgupta and Stiglitz (1980) model except that we now explicitly permit one firm's research to benefit others.[14] We address three issues. First, how do technical spillovers affect the incentives firms have to undertake R&D? Second, what is the impact of such spillovers on the effects of R&D? Finally, what are the benefits to be gained from allowing firms to cooperate in their research, for example, by forming research joint ventures (RJVs)? Are these benefits worth the risk that cooperation in R&D might facilitate collusion between the same firms in the final product markets?

To begin, suppose that the demand for a homogeneous good is linear and given by $P = A - BQ$. Two firms, each of which has constant marginal costs of c per unit, manufacture the good. These costs can be reduced by research and development activity, but it is possible that the knowledge developed by one firm can spill over to its rival. This can happen, for example, because the firms fund common sources of basic research such as universities or research laboratories; or because the research direction that one firm is taking becomes known to its rival; or because some of the preliminary results of research effort leak out; or, of course, because of industrial espionage.

Specifically, if firm 1 undertakes R&D at intensity x_1 and firm 2 undertakes R&D at intensity x_2, the marginal production costs of the two firms become

$$c_1 = c - x_1 - \beta x_2$$
$$c_2 = c - x_2 - \beta x_1$$

(22.9)

---

[14]   The model is developed in d'Aspremont and Jacquemin (1988). A more general version of this type of investigation can be found in Kamien et al. (1992).

Here $0 \leq \beta \leq 1$ measures the degree to which the R&D activities of one firm spill over to the other firm.[15] If $\beta = 0$, there are no spillovers—firm 1's research effort x_1 yields benefits only to firm 1 itself. If $\beta = 1$, spillovers are perfect—every penny of cost reduction that x_1 brings to firm 1, it also brings to firm 2. For the intermediate case of $0 < \beta < 1$, spillovers are only partial—if firm 1's research lowers its own cost by one dollar per unit, it will lower firm 2's cost by some fraction of a dollar per unit.

Research is, of course, costly. Indeed, not only is it costly but we assume that R&D activity exhibits *diseconomies* of scale, i.e., it becomes more costly the more research the firm does. Specifically, we assume that research costs are the same for both firms and given by the research cost function

$$r(x_i) = \frac{x_i^2}{2}, \quad i = 1, 2. \tag{22.10}$$

Thus, if the R&D intensity is $x_i = 10$, then the research budget $r(x_i) = 10^2/2 = \$50$. If the R&D intensity doubles to $x_i = 20$, the budgetary expense climbs to $20^2/2 = \$200$. A doubling of R&D effort therefore leads to a quadrupling of the R&D cost. This is an example of what we mean by a scale diseconomy.

22.5.1   Noncooperative R&D: Profit, Prices, and Social Welfare

Consider first what happens when firms do not cooperate on research. Suppose that we have a two-stage game and in the first stage, each firm chooses its research intensity x_i. In the second stage, each firm acts as a Cournot competitor in choosing its output. As usual, this game is solved backwards. From section 9.4, we know the Cournot equilibrium outputs for given values of c_1 and c_2 are

$$q_1^C = \frac{(A - 2c_1 + c_2)}{3B}$$

$$q_2^C = \frac{(A - 2c_2 + c_1)}{3B} \tag{22.11}$$

and the firm profits after paying the research costs are

$$\pi_1^C = \frac{(A - 2c_1 + c_2)^2}{9B} - \frac{x_1^2}{2}$$

$$\pi_2^C = \frac{(A - 2c_2 + c_1)^2}{9B} - \frac{x_2^2}{2} \tag{22.12}$$

---

[15]   We confine our attention to the case in which the spillovers are positive. It is, however, possible that there might be negative spillovers. For example, firms might spread misinformation about their research or claim that they have made a breakthrough in order to discourage rivals from continuing with a particular line of research.

We know from equation (22.9) that $c_1 = c - x_1 - \beta x_2$ and $c_2 = c - x_2 - \beta x_1$. This allows us to express the final equilibrium outputs directly as a function of each firm's choice of R&D effort and the degree of spillover from one firm's findings to the other firm's costs. The resultant Cournot–Nash equilibrium outputs for each firm are

$$q_1^C = \frac{(A - c + x_1(2 - \beta) + x_2(2\beta - 1))}{3B}$$

$$q_2^C = \frac{(A - c + x_2(2 - \beta) + x_1(2\beta - 1))}{3B}$$

(22.13)

and their profits are

$$\pi_1^C = \frac{(A - c + x_1(2 - \beta) + x_2(2\beta - 1))^2}{9B} - \frac{x_1^2}{2}$$

$$\pi_2^C = \frac{(A - c + x_2(2 - \beta) + x_1(2\beta - 1))^2}{9B} - \frac{x_2^2}{2}$$

(22.14)

Equation (22.13) indicates that the output of each firm is an increasing function of its own R&D expenditures x_i. Such expenditures reduce a firm's costs and thereby make higher output more profitable. By contrast, the effect of the *rival's* R&D effort on a firm's production can go either way. Consider firm 1. On the one hand, the R&D activity of firm 2 spills over and lowers firm 1's costs, which has an expansionary effect on firm 1's own output. On the other hand, firm 2's R&D reduces firm 2's cost. This makes the firm 2 more competitive and permits it to expand its output leaving less market available to firm 1. The net result of these two countervailing forces is ambiguous. This ambiguity is reflected in the coefficient on x_2 in the q_1 equation and the coefficient of x_1 in the q_2 equation. In both cases, this coefficient, $2\beta - 1$, is positive only when the degree of spillover is large, that is, when $\beta > 0.5$. When spillovers are small, that is, when $\beta < 0.5$, a firm's output and profit are decreasing functions of the R&D expenditures of its rival. The same ambiguity appears in the profit equations (22.14).

We know that each firm will choose the level of research activity that maximizes its profit given the research effort of its rival. For every choice of effort that firm 2 makes, firm 1 will choose its own profit-maximizing response. The same is true for firm 2 in reverse. So we can in principle identify the best response or *research intensity reaction function* for each firm.

This is done mathematically in the inset to confirm an intuitive result that follows from our previous discussion. When research spillovers are low, the research intensity reaction functions for the two firms are downward sloping, indicating that the research expenditures of the two firms are *strategic substitutes*—more research by one firm reduces the amount done by the other. That is, research activity by one firm substitutes for research activity by the other. The intuition is that in this case the increased research effort by one firm, primarily reduces its costs and so gives it a competitive advantage with respect to the other rival firm. In turn, this results in a reduction in the profitability of the rival firm, which can be offset only by the rival reducing its expenditure on research.

By contrast, when spillovers are high, the research intensity reaction functions are upward sloping, meaning that the research expenditures of the two firms are *strategic complements*. When spillovers are this high, an increase in research intensity by one of the firms induces an increase in research intensity by the other. In this case the intuition is that if one firm

Derivation Checkpoint

Optimal Noncooperative R&D Effort in the Presence of Spillovers

Differentiation of the profit equation (22.14) with respect to research effort of firm i and setting the derivative equal to zero yields:

$$\frac{\partial \pi_i^C}{\partial x_i} = \frac{2(2 - \beta)[A - c + x_i(2 - \beta) + x_j(2\beta - 1)]}{9B} - x_i = 0$$

This result implies best response curves R_1 and R_2 for firm 1 and firm 2 of

$$R_1: x_1 = \frac{2(2 - \beta)[A - c + x_2(2\beta - 1)]}{[9B - 2(2 - \beta)^2]} \quad \text{and} \quad R_2: x_2 = \frac{2(2 - \beta)[A - c + x_1(2\beta - 1)]}{[9B - 2(2 - \beta)^2]}$$

Clearly these are upward sloping if $\beta > 0.5$ and downward sloping if $\beta < 0.5$. The equilibrium must be symmetric since the two firms have identical costs in the absence of R&D and face the same demand function. Thus in equilibrium $x_1 = x_2$. Substituting this into R_1, for example, and solving for x_1 gives the Nash equilibrium research intensity:

$$x_1^C = x_2^C = \frac{2(A - c)(2 - \beta)}{9B - 2(2 - \beta)(1 + \beta)}.$$

This is decreasing in β, implying that increased research spillovers decrease each firm's chosen research intensity. The solution for research effort x_i implies output levels and profits for the two firms of

$$q_1^C = q_2^C = \frac{3(A - c)}{9B - 2(2 - \beta)(1 + \beta)}$$

$$\pi_1^C = \pi_2^C = \frac{(A - c)^2 [9B - 2(2 - \beta)^2]}{[9B - 2(2 - \beta)(1 + \beta)]^2}.$$

opts for a high level of R&D effort, the benefits of that activity spill over to the other firm to such an extent that the other firm's profit increases, providing that firm with the funds and the incentive to increase its own R&D spending. Figure 22.4 illustrates typical research intensity reaction functions.

However, determining whether the reaction functions slope downward or upward—whether the two firms' R&D efforts are strategic substitutes or complements—does not tell us what the equilibrium level of R&D spending is. In particular, there can be no presumption that the presence of large R&D spillovers and hence the case of strategic complements will result in a higher equilibrium level of R&D spending than the case in which such spillovers are low. The Nash equilibrium occurs at the intersection of the two response functions, and the case in which this point is farthest from the origin is far from obvious.

In order to illustrate this last point we shall focus our remaining discussion on a numeric example.

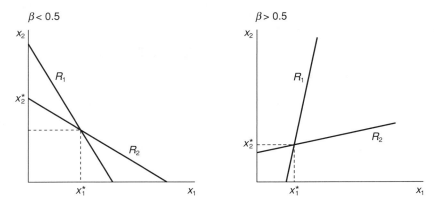

Figure 22.4   Best response functions for research intensity in the noncooperative R&D game

Let demand for the good be $P = 100 - 2Q$, and each firm's marginal production cost be currently \$60. The firms can choose two levels of research intensity: $x_i = 10$ or $x_i = 7.5$. Further, we assume that the degree of research spillover (which is outside the control of the two firms) takes one of two values: a low value of $\beta = 1/4$ or a high value of $\beta = 3/4$.

Consider first the low-spillover case and assume that firm 2 chooses the high research intensity of $x_2 = 10$. If firm 1 also chooses high research intensity, its output and profits will be, from equations (22.13) and (22.14)

$$q_1^C = \frac{(40 + 17.5 - 5)}{6} = 8.75; \ \pi_1^C = \frac{(40 + 17.5 - 5)^2}{18} - \frac{100}{2} = \$103.13$$

By contrast, if firm 1 chooses the low research intensity, its output and profits will be

$$q_1^C = \frac{(40 + 13.125 - 5)}{6} = 8.02; \ \pi_1^C = \frac{(40 + 13.125 - 5)^2}{18} - \frac{56.25}{2} = \$100.54$$

Now assume that firm 2 chooses the low research intensity of $x_2 = 7.5$. If firm 1 chooses the high research intensity, its output and profits will be

$$q_1^C = \frac{(40 + 17.5 - 3.75)}{6} = 8.96; \ \pi_1^C = \frac{(40 + 17.5 - 3.75)^2}{18} - \frac{100}{2} = \$110.50$$

By contrast, if firm 1 chooses the low research intensity, its output and profit will be

$$q_1^C = \frac{(40 + 13.125 - 3.75)}{6} = 8.23; \ \pi_1^C = \frac{(40 + 13.125 - 3.75)^2}{18} - \frac{56.25}{2} = \$107.31$$

The same calculations apply to firm 2. We then have the payoff matrix of Table 22.3(a). *The Nash equilibrium in this case of low spillovers is for both firms to adopt high research intensities.*

When the degree of R&D spillover is high, with $\beta = 0.75$, the same calculations lead to the payoff matrix of Table 22.3(b). *The Nash equilibrium in this case is for both firms to*

Table 22.3a   Payoff matrix with low R&D spillovers, $\beta = 0.25$

		Firm 2	
		Low research intensity	High research intensity
Firm 1	Low research intensity	\$107.31; \$107.31	\$100.54; \$110.50
	High research intensity	\$110.50; \$100.54	\$103.13; \$103.13

Table 22.3b   Payoff matrix with high R&D spillovers, $\beta = 0.75$

		Firm 2	
		Low research intensity	High research intensity
Firm 1	Low research intensity	\$128.67; \$128.67	\$136.13; \$125.78
	High research intensity	\$125.78; \$136.13	\$133.68; \$133.68

adopt low research intensities. An increase in the degree of R&D spillover causes the two firms to reduce their research intensities. Why? Consider first the case when R&D spillovers are weak. In this case the more firm 1 spends on R&D, the less firm 2 will spend because the primary effect of such spending is to strengthen the competitive position of firm 1. Yet somewhat paradoxically, this gives each firm an incentive to spend aggressively on R&D so as to avoid being the loser in this competition. If firm 1 spends a lot on R&D and firm 2 spends nothing, virtually all the benefits of firm 1's spending stay with firm 1. Firm 2 would find itself losing significant market share and profit to a much lower-cost competitor. When each firm tries to avoid falling behind in this manner, the net result can be a substantial amount of R&D effort, both at each firm and in total.

Just the opposite holds in the case of large spillovers. Yes, the more firm 1 spends on R&D, the more firm 2 is induced to spend by virtue of the strategic-complements setting, but this relation is a two-edged sword. Even if firm 1 spends only a little on R&D it knows that this will still induce firm 2 to do a fair bit of research activity. Moreover, the research activity at firm 2 will bring substantial benefits to firm 1 by virtue of the large spillovers. In this setting, the incentive for either firm to spend much on R&D can be quite small as each firm seeks to free ride on the other's efforts.

Where graphs fail to give clear results, algebra can often save the day. That this is true here is shown in the Derivation Checkpoint. We merely state the final result. The amount of research done by each firm *decreases* as β, the degree of R&D spillover, increases—the free-riding effect to which we have just referred.

22.5.2   Technology Cooperation

We now consider two alternative arrangements between the duopoly firms that can alter the outcome from that described above. The first possibility is that the two firms agree that while each will continue to do its own R&D, they will coordinate the extent of such research effort.

Derivation Checkpoint
Optimal R&D Effort with R&D Cooperation

With cooperation, each firm's optimal research intensity is the R&D effort that maximizes the sum of the two firms' profits, given that output is determined noncooperatively in the second-stage output game. From equation (22.14) we know that aggregate profit is:

$$\pi_1^C + \pi_2^C = \frac{[A - c + x_1(2 - \beta) + x_2(2\beta - 1)]^2}{9B} - \frac{x_1^2}{2}$$

$$+ \frac{[A - c + x_2(2 - \beta) + x_1(2\beta - 1)]^2}{9B} - \frac{x_2^2}{2}$$

Differentiating this with respect to x_1 gives the first-order condition:

$$\frac{\partial(\pi_1^C + \pi_2^C)}{\partial x_1} = \frac{2(2 - \beta)[A - c + x_1(2 - \beta) + x_2(2\beta - 1)]}{9B} - x_1$$

$$+ \frac{2(2\beta - 1)[A - c + x_2(2 - \beta) + x_1(2\beta - 1)]}{9B} = 0$$

A similar condition applies for firm 2 but we do not need this. Rather, we can take advantage of the fact that the equilibrium for these two firms will be symmetric. Substituting $x_1^c = x_2^c = x^{RC}$ (where the superscript RC denotes "R&D cooperation") and simplifying gives:

$$\frac{2(1 + \beta)[A - c + x^{RC}(1 + \beta)] - 9Bx^{RC}}{9B} = 0$$

which gives the equilibrium R&D intensity as:

$$x_1^{RC} = x_2^{RC} = \frac{2(A - c)(1 + \beta)}{9B - 2(1 + \beta)^2}.$$

This is increasing in β.

The Nash equilibrium outputs and profits for the two firms when they cooperate in R&D can be identified by substituting into equations (22.13) and (22.14). After simplification this gives:

$$q_1^{RC} = q_2^{RC} = \frac{3(A - c)}{9B - 2(1 + \beta)^2}$$

$$\pi_1^{RC} = \pi_2^{RC} = \frac{9B(A - c)^2}{[9B - 2(1 + \beta)^2]^2}.$$

Thus, the two firms now choose x_1 and x_2 to maximize their joint profit. They continue to recognize that they will compete as Cournot firms in the product market. The other alternative we consider is that the firms explicitly share their R&D activities by setting up a research joint venture (RJV). One way this scenario might work in practice would be for the two firms to jointly set up a laboratory for experimentation and analysis with all the discoveries made at that laboratory to be made fully available to both firms.

We introduce this RJV arrangement into the model by letting the two firms pick x_1 and x_2 cooperatively but by adding the further assumption that the degree of spillover is complete, that is, $\beta = 1$. Whatever is learned in the research lab—whether discovered by a firm 1 scientist or a firm 2 scientist—reduces the cost of both firms by the same amount.

We start with the simple coordination case. What we want to do is to pick the values of x_1 and x_2 that maximize the sum of the individual profit expressions shown in equation (22.14). The mathematical solution, as in the previous section, is shown in the Derivation Checkpoint.

We shall concentrate once again on our simplified example as given by the payoff matrices of Tables 22.3(a) and (b). When the firms coordinate their research efforts they choose the combination of R&D intensities that maximizes the sum of the profits in the cells of the relevant payoff matrix. *When R&D spillovers are low, coordination leads each of the firms to choose the low R&D intensity.* Cooperation then increases each firm's profits from \$103.13 to \$107.31. By contrast, *when the R&D spillover is high, coordination leads each firm to choose the high R&D intensity*, increasing their profits from \$128.67 to \$133.68.

What our example and the more detailed analysis of the inset show is the following: First, it is now the case that the higher is the level of R&D spillover—the larger is β—the more each firm spends on research. This is because the agreement between the two firms to set their R&D efforts jointly explicitly forces each firm to internalize the external benefits that such spending has upon its rival. In turn, this eliminates the free-riding problem that characterizes R&D competition when there are high spillovers. The ability to avoid this problem also means that the two firms will each enjoy a profit at least as great as that which they would have earned in the absence of such cooperation.[16]

The second point to note is that the outcome under the simple coordination plan may not necessarily be good for the consumer. In particular, consumers are hurt by the technology cooperation when $\beta < 0.5$ and the extent of spillover is small. The reason is straightforward. When β is small, then without cooperation each firm tends to do a fair bit of research. It does so because a low value of β means that most of the benefit from its innovative efforts will accrue to it alone and because it knows that its rival is proceeding along the same line of attack. From the viewpoint of consumers, this is great since there has been considerable cost reduction and therefore a sharp decline in the price they pay. If, in this setting, we now introduce a cooperative R&D agreement, the two firms realize that their best bet is to reduce R&D intensity, which otherwise simply makes competition tougher in the product market. By decreasing R&D intensity, the firms increase their profits. Unfortunately, the lower rate of innovation also implies a higher price to consumers.

By contrast, when the degree of R&D spillover is high ($\beta > 0.5$), both firms and consumers benefit from a cooperative R&D agreement. This happens because now the primary effect of the R&D cooperation is to correct a market failure. In the absence of cooperation, a large degree of spillover leads each firm to free ride on the R&D efforts of its rivals and to take no account of the beneficial effects its own R&D expenditures have on the costs and profits of other firms. R&D cooperation internalizes these effects because it forces the cooperating firms to look at the impact their R&D expenditures have on aggregate profit rather than merely on their individual profit.

---

[16] For $\beta = 0.5$ each firm earns exactly the same profit under uncoordinated R&D spending as each does with an R&D cartel. For all other values of β each firm's profit is higher with the R&D cartel.

Derivation Checkpoint

Optimal R&D Effort with a Research Joint Venture (RJV)

The third and final case that we consider is where the firms form an RJV to coordinate their research activities and ensure that these are fully shared. This case is easily dealt with. It amounts to the firms ensuring that the degree of R&D spillover is perfect, that is that $\beta = 1$.

The optimal degree of research intensity, outputs and profits are, therefore, identified by substituting $\beta = 1$ in the equations derived for R&D cooperation. Thus:

$$x_1^{RJV} = x_2^{RJV} = \frac{4(A - c)}{9B - 8} \quad q_1^{RJV} = q_2^{RJV} = \frac{3(A - c)}{9B - 8} \quad \pi_1^{RJV} = \pi_2^{RJV} = \frac{9(A - c)^2}{(9B - 8)^2}.$$

An RJV in which firms coordinate their research efforts to maximize their joint profits and share the results of their R&D activities dominates the other cases that we have considered in that it gives the highest per-firm profits and the lowest consumer prices.

What about a research joint venture? As noted, an RJV can be best thought of as a case in which the firms take actions not only to coordinate their research expenditures but also to ensure that the spillover from one firm's research to the other's is complete, that is, so that $\beta = 1$. A little thought should convince you that an RJV will likely yield the maximum benefits to both firms and consumers. As we just saw, coordination of R&D levels benefits both producers and consumers whenever $\beta > 0.5$. Moreover, the profit outcomes in Tables 22.3 indicate that if the firms could find some way of increasing the technology spillover from $\beta = 0.25$ to $\beta = 0.75$ they would both benefit at *any* research intensity. We can make this discussion even more general. The inset on R&D cooperation shows that an increase in the spillover parameter β increases the research intensity and the profits of each firm *and* increases the output that each firm brings to the market. In other words, *both firms and consumers benefit* from an increase in β. The RJV takes this to its logical conclusion by ensuring that $\beta = 1$, its highest possible value.

In our example the benefits of an RJV are easily confirmed. Consider the case in which both firms choose the high degree of research intensity. Thus, with perfect R&D spillover, the profits to each firm are $(40 + 10 + 10)^2/18 - 50 = \$150$, while if each chooses the low research intensity, the profits to each firm will be $(40 + 7.5 + 7.5)^2/18 - 56.25/2 = \$139.93$. Clearly, the RJV will go for the high research intensity leading to the lowest costs. In turn, this will translate into the lowest consumer prices that these Cournot firms will offer.

The intuition behind the foregoing analysis is as follows. First, by maximizing the extent of spillovers, the RJV also maximizes the benefits of R&D. Every discovery is spread instantly to all firms in the industry. Second, despite this extensive spillover, the free-riding problem is now avoided. Because the two firms have agreed to coordinate their research efforts they fully internalize the otherwise external effects of research. Thus, firms will pursue extensive research, which, partly because of the extensive spillover effect of sharing, will lead to a sizable reduction in costs for every firm. This substantial cost reduction translates into an equally impressive reduction in the price to consumers.[17] The policy implication of this is obvious and important. Research joint ventures should be encouraged because they benefit both consumers and producers so long as the antitrust authorities can ensure that such cooperation on research effort does not also extend to cooperation in production and prices, that is, to a price-fixing cartel.

The potentially large benefit from technology cooperation is undoubtedly the reason that research joint ventures—unlike price-fixing agreements—are not treated as *per se* violations by the antitrust authorities. Instead, they are evaluated on a rule of reason basis. Indeed, the U.S. Congress passed legislation in 1984 to require explicitly the application of a reasonability standard in the specific case of RJVs.

22.6   EMPIRICAL APPLICATION
R&D Spillovers in Practice

R&D spillovers suggest a diffusion-like process. The greater the spillover, the more rapid or the more complete is the diffusion of technological advances in one firm to the productivity of other firms. We might also suspect that a similar process is at work at a national and even international level. In particular, it seems likely that the R&D efforts of one country could spill over to enhance the productivity of its neighbors. Here again, the extent of such spillover is of interest. If technical advances in one country spread quickly to others, β will be high. In a world in which the international transfer of technical knowledge is weak, β will be low.

Wolfgang Keller (2002) explores the extent of international technical spillover by looking at data covering 12 broadly defined manufacturing industries from 14 countries over the years, 1970–95. To understand his basic approach, consider a simple Cobb–Douglas production function (see section 4.5) for industry i in country c.

$$Q_{ci} = K_{ci}^{1-\sigma} L_{ci}^{\sigma} \tag{22.15}$$

Here Q_{ci} is output (value added) and K_{ci} and L_{ci} are capital and labor inputs, respectively, in industry i in country c and σ is the share of costs accounted for by labor. Taking logarithms then yields:

$$\ln Q_{ci} = (1 - \sigma) \ln K_{ci} + \sigma \ln L_{ci} \tag{22.16}$$

For industry i, we define $\ln \bar{Q}_i$ to be the average log of output across all countries. Similarly, for industry i, let $\ln \bar{K}_i$ and $\ln \bar{L}_i$, be the average amount of capital and labor inputs (again in logs), respectively, across all countries. If we define total factor productivity, TFP_{ci} in industry i and country c as the difference between the log of output and the weighted average level of inputs, i.e., $TFP_{ci} = \ln Q_{ci} - (1 - \sigma) \ln K_{ci} + \sigma \ln L_{ci}$, then the *relative* (to the mean) factor productivity F_{ci} of industry i in country c at a point in time is:

$$F_{ci} = (\ln Q_{ci} - \ln \bar{Q}_i) - (1 - \sigma_{ci})(\ln K_{ci} - \ln \bar{K}_i) - \sigma_{ci}(\ln L_{ci} - \ln \bar{L}_i) \tag{22.17}$$

---

[17]   While we have derived this result for a duopoly, Kamien et al. (1992) show that it extends to an *n*-firm oligopoly.

where we now let the cost share of labor σ_{ci} vary across countries and industries. Equation (22.17) is a measure of the extent to which output in industry i in country c remains above average even after correcting for any above average use of inputs. It is thus a measure of the productivity advantage (or disadvantage) in industry i in country c at any point in time. This is why it is called *relative* productivity. Of course, this will probably change over time due to R&D and other factors. For this reason, Keller (2002) measures relative productivity for each year from 1970 to 1995. This means that for each of the 12 industries in each of the 14 countries, Keller (2002) has a measure of relative productivity in each year, 1970 to 1995. Because we are now measuring this term over time as well as over industries and across countries, relative factor productivity now has an additional time subscript, i.e., F_{cit}. It is this series of relative productivity measures that Keller seeks to explain.

Because, by construction, variations in the relative productivity measure F_{cit} reflect variations in factors other than capital and labor inputs it is natural to identify these remaining differences as those due to differences in technology. In turn, these technical differences ought to reflect differences in R&D. Keller's (2002) approach in this respect is to distinguish a difference between R&D done domestically in industry i and that done abroad. The first research question is whether foreign R&D spills over to domestic productivity. The second is whether these spillovers are greater for countries that are closer to each other.

The 14 countries in Keller's (2002) sample are Australia, Canada, Denmark, Finland, France, Germany, Italy, Japan, the Netherlands, Norway, Spain, Sweden, the United Kingdom, and the United States. Five of these countries—France, Germany, Japan, the United Kingdom, and the United States—account for over 92 percent of all the R&D in the sample. Hence, Keller (2002) treats these G5 countries as the potential engines of technical change and examines how their R&D affects productivity in the remaining nine. Specifically, he estimates the parameters of the following equation:

$$F_{cit} = \alpha_{ci} + \alpha_t + \lambda \ln \left[S_{cit} + \gamma \left(\sum_{g \in G5} S_{git} e^{-\delta D_{cg}} \right) \right] + \varepsilon_{cit} \qquad (22.18)$$

Here, F_{cit} is the relative productivity measure derived above for industry i in country c in year t, measured for each of the nine countries examined. The first term is a country and industry specific constant that permits for a time-independent productivity advantage or disadvantage for that sector in that country. The second is meant to pick up productivity increases over time that affect all firms in all countries in common. The key parameters are embedded in the next term. S_{cit} is a measure of the R&D done in industry i in country c up to time t. In contrast, S_{git} is a measure of R&D in that same industry but in one of the G5 countries and D_{cg} is the distance of that country from the domestic country in question. ($D = 1$ implies a distance of 235 kilometers.) Together, S_{cit} and the summation term for the G5 countries are meant to capture the R&D relevant to productivity in the domestic industry i at time t.

The effect of that combined industry-based R&D on productivity in that same industry in the domestic country is captured by the parameter λ. However, two adjustments are included to distinguish the impact of foreign from that of domestic R&D. To understand the first of these adjustments suppose that all G5 countries were right next to the domestic country in question ($D_{cg} = 0$). Then the contribution of their R&D on domestic productivity in industry i to total industry-relevant R&D, is adjusted by the parameter γ (taken to be same for all G5 countries). That is, if $\gamma < 1$, foreign R&D contributes less than the full effect of domestic R&D in adding to the knowledge relevant to a particular domestic industry's productivity. In many ways, then γ comparable to the β of our industry analysis above. However, Keller (2002) also introduces a second source of distinction between domestic and foreign research lies in the distance term, D_{cg}. As this distance grows, the contribution of that G5 country's R&D to domestic productivity diminishes further if the parameter δ is positive. In short, the specification permits both for the possibility that simply by being foreign R&D may contribute less to domestic technology than home-grown research, and also for the more complicated fact that spillovers from foreign R&D grow smaller as the source of that R&D is farther away. Of course, the error term ε_{cit} picks up any remaining random factors that affect productivity.

The specification in equation (22.18) assumes that the decay parameter δ is the same through-out the time period. Keller (2002) recognizes, however, that increased globalization over the 25 years of his sample suggests that δ will decline over this period. He therefore estimates an alternative specification given by:

$$F_{cit} = \alpha_{ci} + \alpha_t + \lambda \ln \left[S_{cit} + \sum_{g \in G5} \gamma_G \left(1 + \psi_F I_t \right) S_{git} e^{-\delta(1+\psi_D I_t)D_{cg}} \right] + \varepsilon_{cit} \qquad (22.19)$$

In this equation, I_t is a 1,0 dummy variable equal to zero over the first half of the sample to 1982 and then 1 in the 13 years thereafter. The coefficient ψ_F permits the effect of G5 R&D to have a different effect on domestic productivity in the second half of the sample than it does in the first, holding the distance between the domestic and G5 countries constant. Similarly, the coefficient ψ_D permits the extent to which spillovers decline with distance to change from the first half of the sample to the second half. Note too that this specification allows the effect of G5 R&D to differ across each G5 country by permitting a different coefficient γ_G for each one. This is reasonable as the different languages in these countries may affect the ease with which a technology can be transferred.

Because the contribution of foreign R&D to the total relevant measure of R&D depends on the parameters γ (or γ_G) and δ that are also to be estimated, equations (22.18) and (22.19) cannot be estimated by ordinary least squares. Instead, a nonlinear least squares estimation is required. In this procedure, we begin with a starting value for the nonlinear parameters and then estimate the regression with OLS. We may then use these estimates to reiterate the process until the coefficient estimates stop changing and converge to stable values. Table 22.4 shows the key parameter estimates and their standard errors that Keller (2002) obtains from this maximum likelihood process for both specifications.

The estimates in specification 1 suggest that technical spillovers are strongly localized. The cumulative productivity effect of overall R&D is to raise productivity by 7.8 percent. However, foreign (G5) R&D contributes only 84 percent to the technical base that domestic research does and that is only if the domestic country is right next to the G5 source nation so that $D = 0$. The estimate of $\delta = 1.05$ though, indicates that that contribution dies out rapidly. Half of it is gone when $D = 0.69$ or at a distance of 162 kilometers (100 miles), and the rest is virtually eliminated once the source country of the foreign R&D is more than 400 miles away.

However, the results from specification 2 qualify the foregoing findings. It is useful to first note that the estimate of ψ_F is insignificantly different from zero. Hence, correcting for distance and country of origin, the contribution of a G5 country's R&D on domestic technical know-how is pretty much the same throughout the sample years and, on average, not too different from the 84 percent found in specification 1 when the distance to the G5

Table 22.4 Regression estimates of international R&D spillovers

Parameter	Specification 1		Specification 2	
	Parameter estimate	Standard error	Parameter estimate	Standard error
λ	0.078	(0.013)	0.096	(0.008)
δ	1.005	(0.239)	0.384	(0.047)
γ	0.843	(0.059)	—	—
γ_J	—	—	1.000 (set)	set
γ_{US}	—	—	1.031	(0.059)
γ_{UK}	—	—	0.863	(0.060)
γ_{GER}	—	—	1.157	(0.060)
γ_F	—	—	1.011	(0.060)
ψ_D	—	—	−0.784	(0.068)
ψ_F	—	—	−0.061	(0.108)

country is $D = 0$. The real change comes in the extent to which the impact of G5 R&D declines with distance. Now the estimate of δ is a much smaller 0.384 indicating that the effect declines much more slowly with distance, even in the first half of the sample when $I_t = 0$. Over the latter half though when I_t is 1, the estimate of $\psi_D = -0.784$ indicates that this small rate of decline is even smaller from 1983 to 1995 than it was previously. Together, these estimates indicate that at least half of the effect that a G5 nation's R&D would have had if the domestic country had been right next to it ($D = 0$) is still there as far out as 424 kilometers (263 miles) from 1970 to 1982, and is felt as far out as 1,963 kilometers (1,217 miles) after 1983. This implies a larger and growing degree of technical spillovers between industries in different nations.

Because Keller's spillover estimates apply to whole sectors separated by national boundaries they may well be a lower bound for the extent of such spillovers between firms within the same domestic industry. If this is so, then these empirical estimates when taken together with our analysis of the noncooperative outcome with high spillovers, suggest that the market will likely be characterized by inefficiently low R&D. If that is the case, then the argument for permitting R&D cooperation and/or joint ventures becomes noticeably more compelling.

Summary

Research and development is the wellspring of technical advancement. Such advancement is the true source of the gain in per capita income and living standards that has characterized the developed economies for almost all of the last two centuries. It should be clear, however, that firms will only be willing to incur the heavy expenses and considerable risks associated with R&D if they can be reasonably assured that their efforts will be rewarded. Imitation by rivals has the social benefit of intensifying price competition after innovation occurs. However, it makes it less likely that the innovation will occur in the first place.

The tension between the gains from competition and the gains from innovation, i.e., the tension between the replacement effect and the efficiency effect is unavoidable. It has led economists to consider which market environment—competitive or monopolistic—will foster greater research and development. The Schumpeterian hypothesis is, broadly speaking, that oligopolistic market structures are best in this regard.

Both theory and empirical data give ambiguous evidence as to the market structure most conducive to R&D effort. Competitive markets can sometimes fail to be as innovative as their less competitive counterparts but a surprising number of key inventions have come from small firms. Policy has a role to play here, too. One role for policy is to encourage cooperation in research efforts. Empirical evidence suggests that we live in an increasingly interconnected world in which the benefits from one firm's R&D spill over to other firms including, in particular, its rivals. In such a world, the noncooperative outcome is likely to be one with too little R&D effort. Policy that fosters research cooperation among firms can be helpful

in this setting. Yet caution is also necessary. The trick is somehow to foster cooperation on R&D without simultaneously inducing collaboration on prices and product design.

A similar tension arises in the role of patent policy. Patents can enhance the incentives for firms to pursue technological innovations. Yet, by temporarily granting monopoly power, patents can also weaken competitive forces and reduce consumers' access to those breakthroughs. We consider patents and related policy issues in the next chapter.

Problems

1. Assume that inverse demand is given by the linear function $P = A - BQ$ and that current marginal costs of production are c.
   a. By how much would an innovation have to reduce marginal cost for it to be a drastic innovation?
   b. Use your answer to derive a condition on the parameters A, B and c that determines whether a drastic innovation is feasible. (Hint: costs cannot be negative.)

   For Problems 2 through 5 assume the following: Inverse demand is given by $P = 240 - Q$. The discount factor is 0.9. Marginal production costs are initially \$120:

2. Calculate the market equilibrium price, output, and profits (if any) on the assumption that the market is currently
   a. monopolized,
   b. a Bertrand duopoly,
   c. a Cournot duopoly.

3. Suppose that a research institute develops a new technology that reduces marginal costs to \$60.
   a. Confirm that this is not a drastic innovation in either the Bertrand or Cournot cases.
   b. Calculate the new market equilibrium price, output, and profits for the monopolist and each duopolist, given that in the duopoly case the innovation is made available to only one firm.
   c. How much will the monopolist and duopolist each be willing to pay for the innovation?

4. Now assume that there is a potential entrant in the monopolized case and that the research

institute is considering offering the innovation to this firm as well as to the monopolist. How does this affect the amount that the incumbent monopolist will be willing to pay for the innovation?

5. Now return to the duopoly case but assume that the research institute is considering whether it should actually sell the innovation to both firms. Will it wish to do so
   a. in the Bertrand duopoly?
   b. in the Cournot duopoly?

6. Consider a Cournot duopoly in which inverse demand is given by $P = 120 - Q$. Marginal cost of each firm is currently \$60.
   a. What is the Cournot equilibrium quantity for each firm, product price, and profit of each firm?

   Now assume that one of the firms develops a new technology that reduces marginal cost to \$30.
   b. If it keeps control of this innovation itself, what will be the new Cournot equilibrium outputs, product price, and profits of the two firms?
   c. If it licenses the innovation to its rival at some per unit fee r, calculate the innovator's profit as a function of r. What is the profit-maximizing value of r for the licensor?

7. Return to Problem 4, above. Assume now that the innovator licenses the innovation to its rival for a fixed fee of L. What is the maximum fee that it can charge? Will the innovator prefer to set a per-unit license fee or a fixed license fee? What kind of licensing arrangement would consumers prefer?

8. Consider the same Cournot duopoly as in question 9, but now assume that the research has been conducted by an outside research firm. Suppose that this firm agrees to license the technology at a per unit fee of r. What license fee will the research firm charge
   a. if it licenses to only one of the duopolists?
   b. if it licenses to both?
   c. How are your answers to a. and b. affected if the research firm chooses instead to charge a fixed fee of L for the license?

9. Consider the same Cournot duopoly as in question 9, but now assume that research takes the following form. It costs a firm $x^2/2$ to undertake research at intensity x. If this research is successful, it reduces the firm's marginal cost by x, but the research results spill over to its rival, reducing the rival's marginal cost by $\beta.x$. Research intensity can take one of two values, $x = 30$ or $x = 15$, and the degree of spillover can also take two values, $\beta = 1/3$ or $\beta = 2/3$.
   a. Determine whether the firms will prefer the low or the high research intensity for each value of the research spillover.
   b. Assume that the two firms agree to coordinate their research efforts to maximize their joint profits. This technology cooperation does not, however, extend to cooperation between the firms in the final output market. Which value of research intensity will the two firms prefer for each value of the research spillover? How are consumers affected by the technology cooperation?
   c. Now assume that the firms form a research joint venture to share the results of their research, so that we have $\beta = 1$. What research intensity will the joint venture choose? How are consumers affected by the research joint venture?

References

Arrow, Kenneth. 1962. "Economic Welfare and the Allocation of Resources for Inventions." In R. Nelson, ed., *The Rate and Direction of Inventive Activity: Economic and Social Factors*. Princeton: National Bureau of Economic Research, Princeton University Press.

Barro, R. and X. Sala-i-Martin. 1995. *Economic Growth*. New York: McGraw-Hill.

Blundell, R., R. Griffith, and J. Van Reenen. 1995. "Dynamic Count Data Models of Technological Innovation." *Economic Journal* 105 (March): 333–44.

Cohen, W. and R. Levin. 1989. "Empirical Studies of Innovation and Market Structure." In R. Schmalensee and R. Willig, eds, *Handbook of Industrial Organization. Vol. 2*. Amsterdam: North-Holland, 1059–98.

Cohen, W. and S. Klepper. 1996. "A Reprise of Size and R and D." *Economic Journal* 106 (July): 925–51.

Dasgupta, P. and J. Stiglitz. 1980. "Industrial Structure and the Nature of Innovative Activity." *Economic Journal* 90 (January): 266–93.

d'Aspremont, C. and A. Jacquemin, 1988. "Cooperative and Noncooperative R&D in Duopoly with Spillovers." *American Economic Review* 78 (September): 1133–7.

Gayle, P. 2002. "Market Structure and Product Innovation." Working Paper, Department of Economics, Kansas State University.

Geroski, P., 1990. "Innovation, Technology Opportunity and Market Structure," *Oxford Economic Papers* 42 (July): 586–602.

Gilbert, R. J. 2006. "Competition and Innovation," *Journal of Industrial Organization Education* 1 (1): Article 8. Available at: http://www.bepress.com/jioe/vol1/iss1/8

Gilbert, R. J. and D. M. G. Newbery. 1982. "Preemptive Patenting and the Persistence of Monopoly." *American Economic Review* 72 (June): 514–27.

Kamien, M. I., E. Muller, and I. Zang. 1992. "Research Joint Ventures and R&D Cartels." *American Economic Review* 82 (December): 1293–306.

Keller, W. 2002. "Geographic Localization of International Technology Transfer." *American Economic Review* 92 (March): 120–42.

Klepper, S. 2002. "Firm Survival and the Evolution of Oligopoly." *Rand Journal of Economics* 33 (Spring): 37–61.

Levin, R. and P. Reiss. 1984. "Tests of a Schumpeterian Model of R and D and Market Structure." In Z. Griliches, ed., *R and D,*

Patents and Productivity. Chicago: NBER University of Chicago Press.

Levin, R., W. Cohen, and D. C. Mowery. 1985a. "R and D Appropriability, Opportunity, and Market Structure: New Evidence on Some Schumpeterian Hypotheses." *American Economic Review, Papers and Proceedings* 75 (May): 20–4.

———. 1985b. "Firm Size and R&D Intensity: A Reexamination." *American Economic Review* 75 (June): 543–65.

Levin, R., A. Klevorick, R. Nelson, and S. Winter. 1987. "Appropriating the Returns from Industrial Research and Development." *Brookings Papers on Economic Activity: Microeconomics* 2: 783–822.

Lunn, J. 1986. "An Empirical Analysis of Process and Product Patenting: A Simultaneous Equation Framework." *Journal of Industrial Economics* 34 (February): 319–30.

Markides, C. and P. Geroski. 2005. *Fast Second: How Smart Companies Bypass Radical Innovations to Enter and Dominate New Markets.* San Francisco: Jossey-Bass.

Porter, M. 1990. *The Competitive Advantage of Nations.* New York: Free Press.

Romer, D. 2006. *Advanced Macroeconomics.* 3rd edition. New York: McGraw-Hill/Irwin.

Scherer, F. M. 1965. "Firm Size, Market Structure, Opportunity and the Output of Patented Innovations." *American Economic Review* 55 (September): 1097–125.

———. 1967. "Market Structure and the Employment of Scientists and Engineers." *American Economic Review* 57 (June): 524–31.

Schumpeter, J. A. 1942. *Capitalism, Socialism, and Democracy.* New York: Harper.

Scott, J. T. 1990. "Purposeful Diversification of R&D and Technological Advancement." In A. Link, ed., *Advances in Applied Micro-economics.* Vol. 5. Greenwich, CT, and London: JAI Press.

Solow, R. 1956. "A Contribution to the Theory of Economic Growth." *Quarterly Journal of Economics* 70 (February): 65–94.

von Hippel, E. 1988. *The Sources of Innovation,* New York: Oxford University Press.

23

Patents and Patent Policy

In 1769, an English inventor, Richard Arkwright, patented a spinning frame that would revolutionize the production of cotton cloth. Two years later, in 1771, Englishman James Hargreaves introduced another invention, the spinning jenny. With these inventions, Britain entered the Industrial Revolution. Equally important, the inventions allowed Arkwright and Hargreaves to establish a commanding position in the production of cloth and, more generally, textile products. This allowed the inventors to reap large profits and to sell at a high price in the American colonies even after these became independent states.

The British energetically protected their monopoly position. Westbound ships out of London were searched thoroughly to make sure that no passenger was a former Arkwright or Hargeaves employee or had a copy of the design plans for the Arkwright–Hargreaves machines that firms outside of Britain might copy. Such restrictions along with the very high price for British textiles vexed many Americans. Consumers did not like paying the monopoly prices and firms were eager to get some version of the machines that would permit them to compete with the British producers. Some firms offered "bounties" for English apprentices who would be able to obtain the necessary information. Finally, in 1789, an enterprising young Englishman and former Arkwright partner, Samuel Slater, responded to just such a bounty offer. After completely memorizing the engineering details of the Arkwright–Hargreaves machines, he disguised himself as a common laborer and set sail for America. Shortly thereafter, Slater arrived in Pawtucket, Massachusetts and established the first of many New England textile mills consolidating the region's manufacturing base and finally breaking the British monopoly.

The issues raised by Slater's entrepreneurship (what some might call theft) lie at the heart of this chapter. The central question is how strongly a firm's innovation should be protected from imitative competition. On the one hand, information about an innovation is a public good so that once the information is produced, efficiency requires that access to this information, i.e., new production techniques and new products, should be unrestricted to prevent the rise of monopoly. On the other hand, if the government does not protect innovators against imitation, there may be little incentive to do the hard work that led to the invention in the first place.

The patent system was designed to create incentives for innovative activity. Patents and copyrights confer ownership to new inventions, new designs, and new creative works. In turn, those property rights permit innovators to restrict the use of their ideas just as the British restricted the flow of information on their textile technology. The patent holder can act as a monopolist regarding its discovery and earn a monopoly profit as a result. Yet while that profit may create an incentive to undertake R&D efforts, the monopoly that generates the profit reduces the total surplus below what it could be given that the invention has occurred.

Getting this balance right is not easy. We can imagine just how much less productive the economy would be if the science behind electric lighting, the aerodynamics of airplanes, and semiconductors had never been developed. However, production would also suffer were those same technologies not widely available to all firms. At some point, policy must shift from a stance of protecting innovators from imitation to one of permitting the use of the innovation on as wide a basis as possible. The sixty-four-million-dollar question is, exactly where does that point arise? When has protection of the innovator extended sufficiently far that we ought to start thinking about protection of consumers?

The issue as to how far patent rights should extend has two dimensions. First, what is the length of time for which any patent rights ought to extend? Second, to what range of products should the patent apply? Should the developer of a new AIDS treatment based on a special combination of protease inhibitors be protected against a rival's later development of an alternative AIDS treatment based on a different combination of protease inhibitors? What about a new AIDS treatment that is not based on protease inhibitors? Or what if a protease inhibitor treatment originally created as a treatment for AIDS is now applied as a treatment for multiple sclerosis? These issues—typically referred to as patent length and patent breadth—are the central questions in patent policy.

23.1   OPTIMAL PATENT LENGTH

Current patent law establishes a patent duration that varies from country to country. In the United Kingdom and the United States patent law grants protection for 20 years from the date of filing the application. In both countries it is up to the patent holder to ensure that the patent is renewed during its life and to ensure that the patent is not infringed.

Economic theory can provide some insight as to whether that duration makes sense. The key is to find a balance between the innovator's ability to earn a return on its R&D investment and the benefits that will accrue to consumers once the patent expires and competition emerges. The basic model, which is due to Nordhaus (1969), is presented below.

Imagine a competitive industry in which each firm is pursuing a nondrastic innovation. Innovative efforts incur costs. Each firm's unit operating cost is currently c. If a firm invests in R&D at some intensity x, it expects to reduce its unit operating costs from c to $c - x$. The cost of undertaking R&D at intensity x is $r(x)$. We assume that such costs rise as the level of research intensity increases and that they do so at an increasing rate. Formally, this means that $dr(x)/dx > 0$ and $d^2r(x)/dx^2 > 0$. Thus, R&D is expensive to do and exhibits decreasing returns in that a doubling of research intensity will give less than double the reduction in operating costs.

Our assumption of a competitive market implies that price equals marginal cost, which means that the initial market price is c and that the output level is Q_0^C. This is shown in Figure 23.1. A successful innovator will be able either to produce at the lower unit cost of $c - x$ and drive out all its rivals by setting a price just one penny less than the current price, or to license its discovery to its competitors for a fee of $c - x$ per unit produced. Either way, the current market price and volume of output remain unchanged. The innovator, however, will earn a profit equal to area A in Figure 23.1. Assuming that the life of the innovator's patent is T years, this profit will last for T years as well.

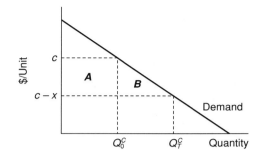

Figure 23.1   Innovation gains during period of patent protection (T years) and after patent protection
The innovator receives profit of area A for the T years that the patent is in effect. When the patent expires, competition lowers the price to $c - x$. Consumers gain the former profits A and also area B as consumer surplus.

When the patent expires, all firms will have access to the technology for free. Competition will reduce the price to $c - x$, and output will expand to Q_T^C. The profit that the innovator used to earn becomes consumer surplus. This is simply a transfer from a producer to consumers and so does not reflect a net gain. However, the expansion of industry output to the higher level Q_T^C does bring such a net benefit by virtue of the additional consumer surplus this generates. This additional surplus is shown in Figure 23.1 as area B.

The longer the duration of the patent (the higher is T), the longer is the time over which the innovator earns the profit A and the greater is the innovator's incentive to do costly R&D. Denote the per-period profit flow to the innovator (area A in Figure 23.1) as $\pi^m(x; T)$ and the discount factor as R. The present value of the innovator's profit from R&D is[1]

$$V_i(x; T) = \sum_{t=0}^{T-1} R^t \pi^m(x; T) = \frac{1 - R^T}{1 - R} \pi^m(x; T) \tag{23.1}$$

Therefore, the R&D has a net value to the innovator of

$$V_i(x; T) - r(x) \tag{23.2}$$

For a given value of T chosen by the patent office, the innovator will select a level of R&D activity, $x^*(T)$, that maximizes this expression. This choice will just balance the marginal gain of additional discounted profit against the marginal cost of doing more R&D work.

Of course, a rational patent office recognizes that its choice of patent life T affects the firm's choice of R&D effort. We suppose that the patent office can work out this relationship precisely. In other words, the patent office can determine the innovator's profit-maximizing research intensity, $x^*(T)$, as a function of T. To choose T optimally, the patent office will wish to pick the patent duration that maximizes the net social gain to both consumers and producers given how firms choose their research intensities. Let us denote by $ss(x, T)$ the per-period increase in social surplus that the innovation generates once it becomes freely

---

[1]   This result uses the following equation in calculating discounted value. Assume that a sum A is to be received each period for T periods, and recall from section 2.2 Chapter 2 that $R = (1 + r)^{-1}$ where r is the interest rate. Then the discounted value of these cash flows is $S = A + RA + R^2A + R^3A + \ldots + R^{T-1}A$ $= A(1 + R + R^2 + \ldots + R^{T-1}) = A(1 - R^T)/(1 - R)$.

available, relative to the surplus in the absence of any innovation (area $A + B$ in Figure 23.1). The present value of this increase in surplus is then

$$SS(x; T) = \sum_{t=T}^{\infty} R^t ss(x; T) = \frac{R^T}{1-R} ss(x; T) \qquad (23.3)$$

The total net social surplus from the innovation is

$$NS(x^*(T); T) = V_i(x^*(T); T) + SS(x^*(T); T) - r(x^*(T)) \qquad (23.4)$$

and the objective of the patent office is to choose the patent duration T^* that maximizes this net surplus. This is a complicated expression but we can develop an intuitive argument to support a very important proposition, namely, that *the optimal patent duration is finite*.

To see why, note that as the patent office initially increases patent duration it induces greater R&D effort and, at first, a greater discounted net surplus to producers and consumers. If patent duration is zero, the returns to an innovator are also zero since the results of the innovation will be imitated immediately. Accordingly, there will be no R&D and no change in the social surplus. If we now increase the patent length to a value $T > 0$, we will induce some innovation and, thereby, some increase in the total surplus. Beyond some point, however, continued increases in T will reduce net social surplus even though they lead to more R&D and therefore greater reductions in production cost. Two forces work to limit the optimal value of T. The first is our assumption of diminishing returns to R&D activity. Because it becomes progressively more expensive to lower production costs, it will take progressively greater increases in T to achieve a given additional cost saving. The second force limiting optimal patent duration is the fact of discounting. The consumer benefits shown as area B in Figure 23.1 will not be realized until after the patent expires. If the patent office chooses a very long duration time T the present value of those benefits will be very small indeed.

This is particularly important since it has sometimes been argued that innovation should be granted patent protection forever. Such a long patent duration puts far too heavy a value on the monopoly profits that patent protection generates and too little consideration on the additional consumer surplus that will emerge only after the patent protection has expired.[2]

23.1

Practice Problem

Let the inverse demand function for a particular product be $P = 100 - Q$, and let it be provided by a group of competitive firms, each with an identical marginal (and average) cost of $70 per unit.

a.   Show that the current market output and price are, respectively, $Q = 30$ and $P = \$70$.
b.   Imagine that one firm can conduct R&D at a pace x, at a cost of $r(x) = 15x^2$. Let the interest rate, r, be 10 percent so that the discount factor, R, is 0.9091. Show that a patent length of 25 years will induce the firm to pursue R&D at a level of approximately $x = 10$. Note that if $x = 10$, the firm's research activity will reduce the unit cost from $70 to $60.
c.   Will the firm's R&D effort increase or decrease if patent duration is reduced to 20 years?
d.   Will total social welfare increase or decrease if patent duration is reduced to 20 years?

---

[2]   Author Mark Helprin has similarly argued for an infinite copyright for creative works ("A Great Idea Lives Forever, Shouldn't Its Copyright?," *New York Times*, May 20, 2007. Note, the argument for an infinite patent life is moot if there is continual innovation that effectively limits the economic life of any one patent.

23.2   OPTIMAL PATENT BREADTH

The question of the optimal patent breadth is trickier than that of patent length, mainly because there is no universally accepted measure of breadth comparable to time as a measure of duration. Conceptually, the idea is to set a minimum amount by which a new innovation must differ from an existing process (or good) in order for the new one either to avoid infringement on an existing patent or to be itself patentable. The larger this required minimal degree of difference, the more difficult it is for other firms to "invent around" the patent and to cut into the inventor's profit. We could in principle work out the optimal patent breadth just as we worked out the optimal patent length. But the lack of a clear method for measuring breadth makes implementing this plan very difficult.

This lack of precision is reflected in the language of the patent office. Each application for a patent is required to specify all the "related" existing patents and to indicate not only how the patent being applied for is a discovery distinct from those already patented, but also to show that the discovery is "novel, nonobvious, useful." Such language leaves the patent office a lot of discretion regarding how it will rule in any particular case.

What makes the question of the optimal patent breadth even more difficult is that it cannot be divorced from the question of optimal duration. Patent policy must set both dimensions of patent protection. Typically, this amounts to choosing between a system in which patents should have a short duration but a broad coverage, the "short and fat" approach, or a long duration combined with a very narrow coverage, the "long and thin" solution. As always, these choices involve balancing the need to maintain the incentive to innovate against the need to distribute the benefits of innovation as widely as possible.

Unfortunately, introducing a second dimension of breadth into patent policy is more difficult than one might suspect, largely because breadth is less obviously defined. Consider for instance the analysis of Gilbert and Shapiro (1990). They define patent breadth in term of the extent to which the patent-holder can charge a price above marginal cost. Broader patents decrease consumer substitute options and permit a higher price–cost margin. This margin of course is the source of the patent-holder's profit. Suppose that we know the desired innovative effort level x, and hence the cost $r(x)$ necessary to achieve that effort. The trick then is to do this with a patent design that produces the necessary (discounted) profit at the lowest possible social cost. That is, we may frame the objective as choosing patent breadth and length so as to minimize the deadweight loss per unit of innovator profit subject to that profit level being sufficient to undertake the desired inventive activity.

Given the social objective and their definition of patent breadth, Gilbert and Shapiro (1990) then demonstrate that the optimal patent is to have very narrow but infinitely long patents. Why? The underlying intuition is as follows. If we think of time as a sequence of equally long intervals, then each interval may be thought of as a separate market. A standard condition for welfare maximization is that it should not be possible to raise welfare by shifting production from one market to another, i.e., the net marginal value of an extra unit should be the same in each market or, in our case, in each period. A finite patent though will not typically satisfy this condition. During the patent life, the price will be high due to the patent-holder's monopoly power. Once the patent has expired, however, the price will fall to marginal cost. The only way to avoid this discontinuity is to keep the price above marginal cost in all markets, i.e., for all time periods into the infinite future, while limiting the accompanying distortion that this brings by restricting the patent's breadth so that price is just enough above cost permanently that the necessary profit level is achieved. In other words, optimal patent policy induces small but equal price distortions for many periods rather that a few large distortions in some periods and none in others.

However, the Gilbert and Shapiro (1990) approach is not the only way to model patent breadth. Klemperer (1990), for example, offers an alternative that relates patent breadth more directly to product differentiation. If we think of a Hotelling line segment of finite length, Klemperer's view is that a useful definition of patent breadth is the fraction of the line segment that is covered by the patent. Again assuming that the goal is to minimize the ratio of social cost to innovator profit subject to covering desired innovation costs, Klemperer (1990) then shows that there will be cases in which optimal patent design is just the opposite of that implied by the Gilbert and Shapiro analysis. That is, it will now often be the case that the best patent design is one of broad patents that are short-lived.

To understand Klemperer's (1990) argument, consider a simple example. Suppose that the new good costs nothing to produce (all the costs are sunk design costs) and that there are 10 potential customers for the product. Assume further that each customer values the good at $10. If there were no other substitutes available, the monopolist firm would then simply set a price of $10, sell one unit to each of the 10 consumers and claim all of the $100 surplus from the market. There would be no consumer surplus but also no welfare loss. Total output would also have been 10 had the monopolist priced at marginal cost (= 0).

Now suppose that the transport cost of buying an alternative legal substitute is different for each of the 10 consumers. Specifically, let one consumer incur a transport cost of $1 per unit of distance the substitute is from the product; a second incur a transport cost $2 per unit; and so on. In this setting, patent breadth w is interpreted as how far consumers have to travel to obtain a legal alternative brand. A very wide breadth or high value for w effectively puts one back in the setting of no alternatives. Hence, if w is very broad, the market outcome will again be a price again of $10, and there will be no deadweight loss. Now, however, consider what happens if we limit the patent width to $w = 1$ (or just a bit less). In this case, at any price $p \geq \$1$, the patent holder will lose some customers. At a price of $1, he will lose one client. At a price of $2, he will lose a second and so on. His best bet (assuming whole-dollar prices) is then to set a price of $5, in which case he will sell five units and earn profit of $25. Now there is a deadweight loss. Real resources are being used to produce the less desired substitutes into which consumers are shifting. Consumers are now incurring transport costs, as well. Accordingly, the narrower patent results in the greater deadweight loss. Its length should then be set at the minimum necessary to achieve the desired innovative expenditure.

As noted, Klemperer's (1990) analysis also yields conditions under which a narrower but longer-lived patent is preferred. This occurs, for example, when, unlike the case above, it is the transport cost that is the same for all and the valuation that varies across consumers. However, the crucial result is that when consumer variation primarily reflects differences in transport cost or strength of preference for the brand of the new good and not in the basic valuation of that good, broad patents of relatively short derivation are preferred.

Gallini (1992) provides a further reason why short-lived broad patents may be best. She makes the important point that imitators can often get around patent protection if they spend enough money to imitate the product without infringement. They will be particularly encouraged to do so when patents are long because otherwise, entry into the market will be greatly delayed. When patents are short, imitation is less attractive because firms now find it cheaper simply to wait for the patent to expire than to engage in costly efforts to imitate legally now. In other words, Gallini (1992, 2002) makes the important point that costly imitation efforts need also to be accounted for in considering any welfare effects. If these imitation costs are sizeable, then broad but short-lived patents are preferable.

Denicolò (1996) synthesizes many of these features in a framework that also incorporates the extent of market competition. He finds that "Loosely speaking, the less efficient is the type of competition prevailing in the product market, the more likely it is that broad and short patents are socially optimal" (p. 264). By "efficient," Denicolò means roughly the extent to which competition drives firms close to the competitive ideal. Denicolò's statement implies that markets in which firms have a greater degree of monopoly power will do best with the "short and fat" approach, while markets characterized by a good bit of competition will do best with patents that are "long and thin."

As a policy recommendation, a major drawback of Denicolò's proposal is that it seems to suggest applying different standards to different innovators depending on the structure of the innovator's basic industry. In reality, the rule of law cannot be applied so selectively without risking serious inconsistency. Even apart from that consideration, there is a further difficulty in implementing any of the proposed standards. The problem again is that it is not always easy to make the concept of breadth operational. We do not have an easy way to translate real markets into a spatial representation and no obvious measure of distance. Indeed, as Scotchmer (2004) has noted, Klemperer's (1990) horizontal concept of breadth is itself too limiting. There is also a vertical component reflecting how much better (or how much worse) a rival's product has to be before it infringes on the patented good. Recognizing this second dimension of patent breadth makes its measurement all the more difficult from a practical perspective. While it is probably fair to say that we will not go too far wrong if we adopt a one-size-fits-all policy of granting patents with "reasonable" breadth but constrained length, precisely what this means in practice is a lot less clear.

23.3   PATENT RACES

Our discussion of market structure and innovative activity was largely motivated by Schumpeter's observation that innovation is a crucial and different kind of competition. The Schumpeter vision is one in which firms vie with each other by racing to develop new technologies or new goods and in which this sort of rivalry is potentially deadly for those who come up short. This is particularly true when innovations are eligible for patent protection. With patents, coming in first is all that matters whether one wins by several lengths or by just a nose. The first firm to discover a cure for male baldness or to engineer a successful system for producing "talking" pictures leaps far ahead of its rivals and stays there for some time by virtue of patent or copyright protection. Patent awards have a "winner-take-all" feature so that finishing second can be no better than finishing third or fourth or, for that matter, tenth.

Innovative competition can be regarded as a race in which one player's success is the other player's serious defeat. The loser of a patent race may see years of investment and hard work wiped out overnight when the rival announces its breakthrough. We now turn to some of the issues that arise when we consider the implications of a patent system for generating a race in which finishing first is all that matters. What are the consequences of such races? Do they lead to inefficient investment in R&D? Does the innovative activity generated by the race influence market structure?

Consider a patent race between two firms that can choose to invest in research with a view to developing a new product. The first to make the breakthrough wins the race and files a patent giving that firm exclusive rights to its invention. This is what gives the race its winner-take-all aspect. The loser walks away less than empty-handed, having expended resources on R&D with no return.

To be specific, assume two, quantity-competing firms, BMI and ECN, who are both considering doing the R&D necessary to create a new product. They each estimate that if the innovation is successful they can produce this new product at a marginal cost of c and that demand for the new good is $P = A - BQ$. They are also confident that the new product is a sufficiently radical departure that it will have a negligible impact on their existing business and so will not affect their existing profits—that is, there is no replacement effect.

The R&D effort by each firm requires a research division that will cost a fixed sum, K. This sum covers both the costs of research and of development if the research is successful and, once sunk, can never be recaptured. Given that such a division is established, the probability of a successful innovation is ρ. If only one firm is successful in its R&D efforts, we assume that the innovation is protected from imitation, perhaps by a patent or by some other means. If both are successful simultaneously, we assume that both firms can make the new product, in which case they will be involved in Cournot competition in selling it. To keep matters reasonably simple, we assume that both firms discount the future heavily—that is, the interest rate r is so large that the discount factor $R \approx 0$.

In order to identify the incentives each firm has to establish the research division, we need to identify their profits with and without a successful innovation. If neither firm attempts to develop the new product, neither firm will enter this new market. As a result, each will earn zero profit in this new market. Conversely, if both firms undertake R&D and are successful in making the innovation, we know that their profits, ignoring the cost of establishing the R&D division, will be the Cournot duopoly profits[3] at marginal costs $\underline{c}$:

$$\pi_b = \pi_e = \frac{(A - \underline{c})^2}{9B} \tag{23.5}$$

If one firm, say BMI, is successful in its R&D efforts but ECN is not, then BMI will be a monopolist in the new product market eanning the monopoly profits. ECN will earn nothing from the new market. The profits earned by BMI in this case, again ignoring the costs of establishing the R&D division, will become

$$\pi_b = \frac{(A - \underline{c})^2}{4B} \tag{23.6}$$

Of course, if ECN is successful but BMI is not, these profits will be reversed.

We can now calculate the expected profit for each firm depending on whether or not it establishes a research division. If neither firm sets up such a division, neither will innovate and each will earn zero profit in this new market. Now consider the expected profit if only one firm, say BMI, establishes an R&D division. For BMI expected profit is made up of two components:

1. profit if the R&D division is unsuccessful, which is zero and occurs with probability $(1 - \rho)$;
2. profit if the R&D division is successful, which is the monopoly profit $(A - \underline{c})^2/4B$ and occurs with probability ρ.

---

[3] See section 9.4 Chapter 9 for a derivation of Cournot profit.

As a result, the expected profit of BMI if it is the only firm to establish an R&D division is

$$\pi_b = \rho \frac{(A - \underline{c})^2}{4B} - K \tag{23.7}$$

Of course, the expected profit of ECN, given that only BMI has established an R&D division, is zero. By symmetry, we reverse these payoffs to get expected profits if ECN is instead the only firm to establish a research division.

If both firms establish R&D divisions, the expected profit to either firm is given by

1. profit if the firm's R&D division is successful and the rival's is not, which is $(A - \underline{c})^2/4B$ and occurs with probability $\rho(1 - \rho)$;
2. profit if both R&D divisions are successful, which is $(A - \underline{c})^2/9B$ and occurs with probability ρ^2.

Of course, if neither firm is successful in R&D they earn nothing from the new market. This means that the expected profit of each firm, given that they both operate R&D divisions, is

$$\pi_b = \pi_e = \rho(1 - \rho) \frac{(A - \underline{c})^2}{4B} + \rho^2 \frac{(A - \underline{c})^2}{9B} - K = \frac{(A - \underline{c})^2}{36B} \rho(9 - 5\rho) - K \tag{23.8}$$

Before we put these payoffs into a payoff matrix, we can do a bit of simplifying. The profit equations share a common expression, the monopoly profit, which we denote as $M = (A - \underline{c})^2/4B$. We can use this to define a parameter $S = K/M$, which is the share of the monopoly profits that are needed to establish the R&D division. With the substitution of S and M, the expected profits are summarized in the payoff matrix of Table 23.1. This matrix allows us to identify the possible Nash equilibria for this R&D game. As we shall see, these will be dependent upon the relative magnitudes of the two parameters, S and ρ.

There are three possibilities that have to be considered:

1. *Neither firm wishes to establish an R&D division.* For this to be a Nash equilibrium, the payoff to BMI, for example, from not having an R&D division, given that ECN also has no R&D division, must be greater than the expected profit from investing in R&D, again given that ECN does not. In other words, BMI expects to make more profit from the

Table 23.1   Payoff matrix for the Duopoly patent race

		ECN	
		No R&D Division	R&D Division
BMI	No R&D Division	0, 0	$0, M(\rho - S)$
	R&D Division	$M(\rho - S), 0$	$M\left(\dfrac{\rho(9 - 5\rho)}{9} - S\right), M\left(\dfrac{\rho(9 - 5\rho)}{9} - S\right)$

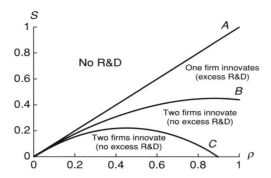

Figure 23.2   A patent race with a duopoly

strategy combination (No R&D, No R&D) than from the combination (No R&D, R&D). This requires that $M(\rho - S) < 0$, which implies that $S > \rho$, the probability of success is less than the fraction of monopoly profit required to fund the R&D. This expression is illustrated by the line 0A in Figure 23.2. All parameter combinations above 0A give the Nash equilibrium (No R&D, No R&D).

2. *Only one firm wishes to establish an R&D division.* Assume that the firm that establishes the R&D division is BMI. Then for the strategy (No R&D, R&D) to be a Nash equilibrium, two conditions must be satisfied:

(a)   BMI expects its expenditure on R&D to be profitable, given that ECN is not investing in R&D—that is, BMI expects to make more profit from the strategy combination (R&D, No R&D) than from the strategy combination (No R&D, No R&D). This is just the opposite of the expression derived in part 1. It requires that $S < \rho$.

(b)   ECN does not expect its expenditure on R&D to be profitable, given that BMI is investing in R&D—that is, ECN prefers the strategy combination (No R&D, R&D) to (R&D, R&D). For this to be the case, the following must be true:

$$M\left(\frac{\rho(9 - 5\rho)}{9} - S \right) \text{ which requires that } S > \frac{\rho(9 - 5\rho)}{9}$$

This relationship is illustrated by the curve 0B in Figure 23.2. All parameter combinations that lie between 0A and 0B are such that only one of the firms will establish an R&D division.

3. *Both Firms Wish to Establish an R&D Division.* For this to be a Nash equilibrium, the payoff to, for example, BMI from having an R&D division, given that ECN also has an R&D division, must be greater than the expected profit from not investing in R&D, again given that ECN does. In other words, BMI expects to make more profit from the strategy combination (R&D, R&D) than from the strategy combination (R&D, No R&D). For this to be the case we must have that

$$M\left(\frac{\rho(9 - 5\rho)}{9} - S \right) > 0 \text{ which requires that } S < \frac{\rho(9 - 5\rho)}{9}$$

Of course, exactly the same condition guarantees that ECN prefers the strategy combination (R&D, R&D) to the strategy combination (No R&D, R&D). Thus, all parameter combinations below 0B are such that both firms will establish an R&D division.

One question about patent races is whether the potential profit from successful innovation can lead the two firms to overinvest in R&D. Neither of the firms will establish an R&D division unless this division is expected to be profitable. For the strategies (R&D, No R&D), (No R&D, R&D), and (R&D, R&D) to be equilibria, they must each give positive expected profits to the two firms. This tells us that no equilibrium in which only one firm invests in R&D is characterized by "excessive" R&D in the sense that the firms would be better off without the R&D. The question that is left is whether there is "too much" R&D when both firms establish R&D divisions. Are there situations in which the strategy combination (R&D, R&D) is a Nash equilibrium but generates less aggregate profit than the strategy combinations (R&D, No R&D) or (No R&D, R&D)? For this to be the case it must be that

$$2M\left(\frac{\rho(9-5\rho)}{9} - S\right) < M(\rho - S) \text{ which requires that } S > \frac{\rho(9-10\rho)}{9}$$

This is illustrated by the curve 0C in Figure 23.2. All parameter combinations between 0C and 0B lead to excessive R&D as the two firms race to be first to discover and introduce the new product.

Our simple model delineates three distinct possibilities. First, neither firm will invest in R&D unless it is expected to be profitable. Hence R&D must have a reasonably low cost relative to the monopoly profits that it might generate (low S), or a reasonably high probability of success. Second, for any given probability of success, a larger number of firms will establish R&D facilities when there is a lower cost of R&D relative to the profit the innovation is expected to generate. Thus, for any given probability of success ρ, the equilibrium number of firms with R&D divisions increases from zero to one and finally to two as S is reduced. Third, there is an intermediate range of values for the cost of R&D in which there is excessive R&D in that both firms establish R&D divisions although this reduces their aggregate profits. In this range, the lure of profit from innovation involves the firms in a competitive R&D race that they would be better to avoid.

So far, we have only considered the gain that research brings in terms of the expected profit of the two firms. From a public policy perspective, however, increased profit is not the only potential benefit of innovation. We should also consider the gain in consumer surplus that development of this new product will generate. While we have just shown that the level of R&D activity can be excessive from the viewpoint of the firms' combined profits, we have not demonstrated that this is the case when viewed with the objective of maximizing the total gain of profit plus consumer surplus. The R&D which seems excessive to the firms may still be worthwhile to society overall if the additional consumer surplus more than offsets the reduction in aggregate profit. However, R&D can be excessive even when evaluated with this broader criterion, (see Practice Problem 23.2). The patent race can lead both firms to establish research divisions even when the total cost of such divisions is not justified by the sum of expected producer and consumer surplus.

Perhaps it is equally interesting that we can show that the possibility of too little R&D —as judged from a social welfare criterion—is also real. Consider the case in which neither firm does any R&D. As we know, this happens when $S > \rho$. Suppose that although this inequality holds, S is so close to ρ that one firm could almost expect to break even if it pursued the innovation (and its rival did not). If the sale of the product generates any significant consumer surplus at all, then it is socially desirable that the research takes place. The value of the expected consumer surplus more than provides the extra funds needed to ensure that the innovator breaks even. Yet, in the absence of some sort of government intervention, the fact that $S > \rho$ means that no such R&D efforts will occur.[4]

23.2

Consider the BMI–ECN example of a patent race. Assume that demand for the new good is $P = 100 - 2Q$, and that each firm believes that it will be able to produce this good at a unit cost of $c = \$50$. Assume further that the discount factor R is so small that each firm cares only about the one-period profit it will make. (Alternatively, assume that one period is of a very long duration, say, 30 years or more.) The probability that such a lab will be successful and actually produce a discovery is $\rho = 0.8$.

a. Show that if one firm is successful in introducing the product, it will have a monopoly price of $75, sell 12.5 units, and earn monopoly profits (before paying for the research) of $M = \$312.50$. Show also that consumer surplus is $156.25.
b. Show that if each firm sets up a lab and if each lab is successful, the Cournot equilibrium output for each firm will be 8.33 units, the price will be $66.67, and each firm will earn a profit (before paying for the research) of $138.89. Confirm that consumer surplus is now $277.78.
c. Now show that the expected profit (before paying for the research) to BMI (or ECN) if it is the only firm to establish an R&D division is $250 while the expected profit to each firm if they both establish R&D divisions (again before paying for the research) is $138.89. Use these results to construct the payoff matrix for this case, now including the cost, K, of establishing an R&D division.
d. Show that if K, the cost of setting up the research lab, is such that $K > \$250$, neither firm will set up a lab, while if $K < \$138.89$, both firms will set up a lab.
e. Show that expected social surplus ignoring research costs if one firm establishes a research lab is $375, and if two research labs are established, is $505.56. Hence, show that the second lab is socially desirable only if $K < \$130.56$.

Practice Problem

We have focused on the risk that patent races may yield either too much or too little R&D investment. Another issue to consider is the possibility that patent races will lead firms to pursue more risky innovations. The intuition behind this argument can be illustrated fairly simply. Suppose that firms can choose to invest either in a relatively safe R&D route that has an expected discovery time uniformly distributed between one and three years or a more risky route that has an expected time of discovery uniformly distributed between zero and four years. Both discoveries are equally costly, and both are expected to become redundant or worthless in five years' time. We will also assume that each discovery will generate the same profit of $1 million per period during the time that it is utilized and is protected from imitation by a patent.

Since the expected date of discovery is the same, namely two years for both routes, then assuming neither firm had any competition, a risk-neutral firm considering them would be

---

[4]   See Reinganum (1989) for a masterful survey of patent races and the timing of innovation, including the consequences for social welfare.

indifferent between the two options, and a risk-averse firm would go for the less risky route. However, when firms are involved in a patent race, competition between the firms may lead them to choose the more variable or risky route in which success can come anytime between zero and four years.[5] The reason is that again, when innovation is protected from imitation, all that matters is winning the race. The second-place firm loses the same amount no matter how close it is behind the winner. In our example, if my rival chooses the less risky R&D route, I have an incentive to choose the more risky route, since this offers the possibility of success and a quick victory right away. Similarly, if my rival adopts the risky strategy, I can see that unless I do the same there is a real possibility that I will be left behind in the race. Of course, my rival can work out all this too. The result is that both of us choose the more risky route.

23.4   MONOPOLY POWER AND "SLEEPING PATENTS"

Another way in which the patent system and innovative competition can interact to affect market structure is through "sleeping patents." Many students at first find it puzzling that a firm will hold a large number of patents all related to the same process or product, and some patents are never acted upon. (Return to Table 23.1 for some evidence on this point.) What possible reason can a firm have to earn patent rights to products and processes that it never uses, that is, what could be the rationale for a firm to create and hold what is called a "sleeping patent"?

The motivation behind a sleeping patent is to create a buffer of protection for the monopoly profits generated by the truly valuable patent. Legal history and economic analysis have both documented that the protection granted by a single patent is often very limited. Edwin Mansfield and his associates (1981) found in a study of 48 patented new products, that 60 percent were imitated within four years after their introduction. Firms often can and do "invent around" patent protection, as we discussed earlier in the case of pharmaceuticals. Frequently, there are several technical solutions to a particular problem such as is the case for the production of the whitening agent, titanium oxide. Each such alternative production technique is a threat to the firm holding a patent on a particular process or product. Hence, by patenting as many of these alternatives as it can, a firm increases the protection it has in using whatever process it actually decides upon.

Suppose, for example, that market demand is given by $P = 100 - Q$ and that the incumbent firm has a proprietary technology with a constant marginal cost of $c_I = \$20$. The firm has a patent that protects its technology. Let us also suppose that this technology is so efficient that entry is not possible, and thus the incumbent is free to set the monopoly price and earn a monopoly profit each period of $\pi^m(c_I = 20)$. To be precise, the monopolist will sell 40 units at a price of \$60 and earn a profit of \$1,600.

Assume now that there is also an alternative technology that the monopolist has discovered, which permits production at the higher constant marginal cost of $c_E = \$30$. Clearly, the monopolist has no incentive to switch to this technology. However, if \$30 is a low enough unit cost so that another firm could acquire this technology and enter the industry, then the incumbent's current monopoly would be eroded. The entrant would either be the high-cost member of a Cournot duopoly or, if Bertrand competition prevailed, the entrant's cost based on using this alternative technology would at least establish a clear upper bound of \$30 on the incumbent's price—one that we know (by construction of the example) is below the incumbent's current monopoly price.

---

[5]   This type of case is discussed in Klette and de Meza (1986).

It is easy to see that the incumbent has an incentive to patent the higher-cost technology as well as the lower-cost one, even though it will never use this alternative, higher-cost technology. By acquiring this patent and letting it lie dormant or sleep, the incumbent strengthens his hold on his monopoly position. The question that we need to ask is whether the incumbent's incentive to acquire the higher-cost technology is so strong that it actually exceeds the incentive of the entrant to acquire the technology and enter.

The surprising answer is yes. Acquiring a patent to the high-cost technology is worth more to the incumbent monopolist than to his potential rival. This is obvious in the case of Bertrand competition. In that case, the rival's entry with a high unit cost of $30 would provoke a price war in which the incumbent would have to lower his price from its current monopoly level to the marginal cost of the entrant, namely, $30. Of course, when this happens, the entrant earns nothing. The incumbent, however, because of his lower cost, will still earn $30 − $20 = $10 per unit. At this price, the incumbent will now sell 70 units and earn a profit of $700. This is less than what he earned previously but still better than nothing. From this it should be clear why the monopolist will place a greater value on discovering the alternative process than would the entrant. Under Bertrand competition, the entrant will never earn any money with this innovation. Hence, for the entrant, discovering the process is worthless. Yet, even though the entrant cannot make money with this higher-cost process, it can put pressure on the incumbent. Specifically, discovery of the process by the entrant imposes a ceiling of $30 on the incumbent's price. Hence, it is worth something to the monopolist to acquire the process first and thereby preclude the imposition of this price cap altogether.

The same basic result holds in a Cournot model. The gain to the monopolist from acquiring the second, sleeping patent on the high-cost process is the profit earned as a monopoly firm using the low-cost technology, $\pi^m(c_I = 20) = \$1,600$, less the profit earned as a duopoly firm with the low-cost technology facing a rival with the high-cost technology, or $\pi_I^d(c_I, c_E) = \pi_I^d(20, 30) = \$900$. So, the total net gain to the monopolist is $\pi^m(c_I = 20) - \pi_I^d(20, 30) = \$700$. In contrast, the gain to the potential entrant is the profit earned as the high-cost firm in a duopoly, $\pi_E^d(c_I, c_E) = \pi_E^d(20, 30) = \$400$ less his current profit, taken to be zero.[6] Therefore, the entrant's net gain from developing the technology is $400. Hence, in the Cournot case, the gain to the monopolist incumbent exceeds that of the potential entrant.

The reason that the incumbent monopolist is more willing than a potential rival to develop the high-cost process and patent it is now familiar. It is because the monopolist has a lot more at stake. If he wins the race, he gets to keep his current monopoly position. If the entrant wins the race, the best the entrant can hope for is to be the high-cost member of a duopoly. The incumbent acquires the patent on the high-cost process to make sure that nobody else will use it. Viewed in this light, acquiring "sleeping patents" amounts to broadening the patent's width.

The data in Table 23.2 provide some empirical support for this proposition. These data are drawn from a PatVal–EU survey of 9,017 patents issued by the European Patent Office between 1993 and 1997 to individuals located in France, Germany, Italy, the Netherlands, Spain and the United Kingdom.[7] The survey asked the inventors to rate the importance that they put on different motives for patenting.

---

[6] We leave it to the reader to show that the Cournot equilibrium has the incumbent producing 30 units and the entrant producing 20 units implying the profit amounts we have used here.

[7] For a detailed description and analysis of these data see Giuri and Mariani (2005) "Everything you Always Wanted to Know about Inventors (But Never Asked): Evidence from the PatVal-EU Survey," available at http://www.lem.sssup.it/WPLem/files/2005-20.pdf.

Table 23.2   Patent use by inventor's employer (%)

	Internal use	Licensing	Cross-licensing	Licensing and use	Blocking competitors	Sleeping patents
Large companies	50.0	3.0	3.0	3.2	21.7	19.1
Medium companies	65.6	5.4	1.2	3.6	13.9	10.3
Small companies	55.8	15.0	3.9	6.9	9.6	8.8

Source: Giuri et al. (2005, p. 20)

In Table 23.2 "blocking competitors" refers to sleeping patents that are used specifically for the strategic reasons we have been discussing in this section (what the researchers term sleeping patents are patents that, according to the respondents, were not used for any of the other six purposes identified in Table 23.2). As can be seen, large companies used fewer of their patents and used a higher proportion of patents for blocking purposes than did medium sized or small companies, consistent with our "protecting monopoly power" analysis.

Reality Checkpoint
The Light That Failed

Carlile Stevens, an inventor, and Bill Alling, his business partner, endured a legal odyssey of longer duration than the fabled 10 years of wandering suffered by Ulysses. The two men met in 1969 when they both worked for Singer Corporation. Mr. Stevens was a physicist then employed by Singer on a project to make traffic lights brighter. In the course of his work, he hit upon an idea for a solid-state electronic ballast to be used in fluorescent lamps. At that time, all ballasts were magnetic ones that wore out quickly, causing the fluorescent lights first to "hum" incessantly and, eventually, to fail. Mr. Stevens got together with Mr. Alling, who was then in Singer's marketing department. The two went out on their own and persuaded 175 investors to put up $3.6 million in seed money. By the late 1970s, they patented their product, which was shown not only to outlast the existing magnetic ballasts but also to offer a 50 to 70 percent improvement in energy efficiency. In 1982, Universal Manufacturing Corporation, which owned, Magnetek, one of the two major manufacturers of magnetic ballasts, approached Stevens and Alling about acquiring the rights to their new technology. The two entrepreneurs agreed in return for a share of the royalties Magnetek earned from licensing the process. By 1984, however, Stevens and Alling had received no royalties and became convinced that Magnetek had no intention of putting their new ballast on the market. Meanwhile, Motorola, a firm that had originally approached Stevens and Alling before Magnetek, was able to invent around the patent and introduce its own solid-state ballast.

Stevens and Alling filed a suit against Universal and Magnetek. They argued that Magnetek acquired the rights to the invention with no intention to use it but simply to protect their own magnetic ballast product. In 1996, two juries ruled in favor of Stevens and Alling and awarded them $96 million in damages. The awards were upheld by an appeals court in 1997. The saga of this sleeping patent finally came to rest.

Source: T. Riordan, "Patents: Two Investors Hope They Will Finally Win Compensation for a Device That Was Squelched," *New York Times*, July 21, 1997, p. D2; and A. Salpukas, "Award to Lighting Inventors Upheld On Appeal," *New York Times*, September 1, 1997, p. D32.

The Reality Checkpoint on the patent for solid-state ballast to be used in fluorescent lighting is one example of the use of sleeping patents. Other examples—all instances of an incumbent attempting to inhibit rival expansion—also exist. Alcoa achieved its dominant market position largely on the strength of Charles Martin Hall's electrolytic process for the reduction of aluminum bauxite ore. Fifteen years after it was formed, the company bought up the competing Bradley patents on an alternative reduction process—one that Alcoa never used. Similarly, Du Pont's patent of the synthetic fiber nylon was accompanied by the company's filing of literally hundreds of other patents all based on variants of the same molecule. Perhaps the best example of the use of sleeping patents comes from Hollywood. Film companies regularly buy the film rights to books, staged plays, and submitted screenplays knowing that many of these script ideas will never be turned into a final product. In part, each film company simply wants to make sure that a rival producer does not get the chance to make a film based on this material.

23.5   PATENT LICENSING

Efficiency requires that the existing stock of information should be available to all buyers at the marginal cost involved in sharing such knowledge. However, since this would imply a "price for information" of near zero, it would leave little incentive for anyone to produce new information as embodied in new goods or new technologies. Patent protection is an effort to cut a middle path between these two pressures. The firm receiving the patent is protected (to some extent) from sharing its discovery with others for free. In fact, it does not have to share it at all.

One interesting possibility is that an innovating firm might be willing to share its technical advance with other firms for a price. When this happens, it results in a licensing agreement between the patent owner and the patent user. Not sharing the patent at all can be interpreted as charging a very high (perhaps infinite) licensing fee. Actual licensing reflects a movement away from such a high fee and toward a price for information that is closer to—if still some way off—the efficient charge of near zero. In this sense, the licensing of a patent is unambiguously a good thing. The question is, does an innovating firm have a profit incentive to license its discovery?

The most obvious case in which a firm would prefer to license an innovation is if the licensee operates in a totally different market from the licensor. For example, a U.S. firm that has a patent on a particular product or process innovation may prefer to license a foreign firm to use this patent (for a fee, of course) rather than setting up a foreign subsidiary or exporting. About the only reasons for not licensing are, first, that the licensor may not be able to secure a satisfactory payment for the license except after extensive bargaining. If such negotiations will be prolonged, either or both parties may decide that it is simply not worthwhile. Second, the licensor may fear that, ultimately, the foreign licensee will produce in some market where it competes directly with the licensor. Finally, there is the fear that the licensee may—by acquiring rights to use the new process or product—improve its ability to develop the next generation of this technology by itself and thereby enhance its future ability to compete.

While these fears are undoubtedly real, there are considerable offsetting benefits to licensing agreements. Licensing gains revenue for the innovator today. Because the cost of sharing the information is low, any such revenue translates into profit.

What about cases though where the licensor and licensee are not separated by large geographic distance but instead are competitors in the same market? Will an innovating firm license its patented discovery for use by some or all of its rivals? The answer depends on market structure and the strength of competition in the market.

23.5.1   The Incentive for an Oligopolist to License a Nondrastic Innovation

Consider the toughest type of competition—price competition between firms making identical products. A firm that obtains a patent on a new technology that permits it to sell at a lower cost has little incentive to license the process to a competitor. Suppose, for example, that both firms are currently selling at a price equal to their (constant) marginal cost of $15 and that one firm has discovered a way to reduce this cost to $12. Without licensing its rival, the innovating firm can supply the entire market at $14.99 and drive its competitor from the market while earning a $2.99 profit on every unit sold. If it tries to sell a license to its rival, the only sensible royalty rate is $2.99 per unit. The rival firm will pay no higher royalty since then it will be unable to compete because its cost will be $12 plus the royalty, which is no better than its current cost of $15. At any lower royalty, the rival will force the innovating firm to lower its price below the current $14.99. But at a royalty of exactly $2.99, both firms will sell at $14.99 and split the market. The licensing firm loses $2.99 on those units it would have sold if it had not licensed but stayed a monopolist. It then gains the $2.99 back as a royalty payment on each of those same units now sold by its rival. In short, licensing gains the innovator nothing. Hence, the incentive to license is very small when the competition is Bertrand.[8]

By contrast, consider a market in which firms are Cournot competitors. In this case, a patent holder has a strong incentive to license, as a simple example shows. Assume that demand for the product in question is $P = 120 - Q$ and that there are three firms in the market, each with constant marginal costs of $60. Then we know from our earlier analysis that the Cournot equilibrium output of each firm is 15 units, total output is 45, the equilibrium price is $75, and each firm is making profits of $225.

Suppose now that one firm makes a nondrastic process innovation lowering its cost to $40 per unit, while the other two firms continue to produce at the higher value of $60 per unit. If the innovating firm does not license the innovation, then the Cournot–Nash equilibrium price falls to $70. The innovating firm increases its output to 30 units, while the other, high-cost firms reduce their outputs to 10 units. Profit to the innovating firm increases to $900 while profit to each of the other firms falls to $100.[9]

Now assume that the innovating firm agrees to license the innovation to its rivals at a fee of $10 per unit that each rival produces. This means that the innovator's costs are $40 per unit and the other firms' costs are $50 per unit. At the post-licensing equilibrium the

---

[8]   For the patent holder that is selling in a *differentiated products market*, the analysis is a bit more complicated. Here, each additional license has three effects. First, it adds licensing revenue. Second, however, it makes the market more competitive and hurts the patent holder in its product market. Third, and as a result of the second effect, each additional license sold drives down the market value of licenses in general. In other words, the demand curve for licenses will be downward sloping because the more that are sold, the more competitive is the market and therefore the less any licensee can afford to pay for a license. Because the patent holder is the monopoly supplier of such licenses, its marginal revenue curve for selling will lie below the demand curve for licenses.

[9]   These numbers come from simple application of the equations for the Cournot–Nash equilibrium that we have developed in previous chapters.

Derivation Checkpoint

Optimal License Price

Suppose that demand is $P = A - BQ$ and that the innovation gives marginal costs of c. Further suppose that the innovator charges a royalty of r per unit to its rivals. Then the innovator's profit is:

$$\pi = \frac{(A - Nc + (N - 1)(c + r))^2}{B(N + 1)^2} + r(N - 1)\frac{(A - Nc + (N - 1)(c + r))}{B(N + 1)}$$

The first term is profit from the innovator's sales and the second is revenue from the royalty agreement. Differentiating π with respect to r and simplifying confirms that the innovator's profit in increasing in the royalty price r. So the innovator should set as high a royalty price as is possible consistent with the non-innovator's being willing to pay the royalty price.

---

innovating firm's output is 25 units while the other firms produce 15 units each so that price is $65. The profit of the innovating firm is now $25 per unit on its own sales plus $10 per unit on the sales of its two rivals, giving a total profit of $925. For each non-innovating firm, profit is $15 per unit, giving each firm profit of $225.

Licensing is, indeed, potentially quite profitable. Moreover, the licensing fee of $10 that we have chosen is not even the best that the innovating firm can do.[10] We show (in the inset) that the innovator should actually push the license price as close as possible to the difference in costs that the innovation generates—in our example, as close as possible to $20. Suppose for example that the innovator charges a royalty rate of $20 per unit (more accurately, $19.99). This restores the equilibrium with the innovation but without licensing. The innovator produces 30 units and each non-innovating firm 10 units, giving a product price of $70. Profit of each non-innovating firm is, once again, $100 since their costs are $60 per unit. By contrast, profit of the licensing firm is $30 per unit on its own output and $20 per unit on the output of its rivals, giving the licensor a total profit of $1,300. The message then is clear. For a Cournot firm with a nondrastic innovation, licensing its discovery is very attractive.

23.5.2   Licensing, Drastic Innovations, and Monopoly Power

What if the innovation had been drastic? Or what if the industry had been a monopoly instead of an oligopoly? Consider each question in turn. If one firm in a Cournot oligopoly patents a drastic innovation, it will not want to license its discovery. Take the simple case of a duopoly. Without licensing, the innovating firm becomes a monopoly. The innovation offers such a dramatic reduction in cost that even when it sets the monopoly price associated with that cost, it still underprices its old duopolist rival, while earning considerable monopoly profit. Here, nothing can be gained by licensing. If the rival is permitted to compete, the market returns to being a duopoly except at lower cost. The most the rival would ever pay for the

---

[10]   For details see Katz and Shapiro (1985).

license is therefore its share of the duopoly profit. Combining this with the innovator's share would yield the innovator a total profit with licensing equal to the profit earned by two duopoly firms. Yet we know that—because the firms cannot collude—this is generally a smaller amount than the innovating firm could earn as a pure monopolist without licensing. Accordingly, a Cournot firm that makes a drastic innovation will not share its discovery with rivals even for a fee. Of course, this is also true for firms engaged in Bertrand competition. In all such cases, the oligopolist that makes a truly dramatic breakthrough may be expected to emerge as a monopolist driving his former competitors from the field.

Turning next to the case of monopoly in the first place, we now have to permit the innovation to take place at an outside firm or laboratory if we are to consider any licensing. (If the monopolist makes the innovation himself, there is no other firm to which he can license!) It should be clear that in such cases—whether the innovation is drastic or nondrastic—the innovating firm will license the monopolist. Since the patent holder is not active in the market himself, the only way he can obtain any revenue from his discovery is to sell or license it to the monopolist.

The interesting point in this case is the precise form that such a licensing contract should take. Should the licensor charge a royalty of X per unit? Or should he charge a fixed fee independent of output? Or should he use some combination of both? You should recognize that charging a per unit royalty—while it has the advantage that it relates revenue directly to usage—runs into the familiar problem of double marginalization (see Chapters 17 and 18). It raises the licensed firm's marginal cost so that—after that firm adds its markup—the price to the final consumer is doubly distorted and sales volume is restricted. In this light, it should not be surprising that the innovating lab will do best by using a two-part tariff. The principal part of this scheme will be a fixed fee (per month or per year). The second part will be a small royalty per unit reflecting any per unit cost the patent holder incurs in licensing his technology. For a transfer of pure information, this per unit charge will be zero. But if the patent holder needs to offer services or technical advice that increases with the frequency with which the technology is used, this fee will be positive. The licensing contract is much like a franchising contract. In principle, the inventor can appropriate all the increased profit that the invention brings if the contract is written correctly, that is, with a fixed fee exactly equal to that additional profit. In practice, however, the patent holder's bargaining position will usually not be strong enough to achieve this outcome. When the manufacturer has a monopoly in the product market, the inventor needs the manufacturer just as much as the manufacturer needs the inventor.

23.5.3 Patent Licensing, Social Welfare, and Public Policy

The foregoing cases indicate that most of the time an innovator has an interest in licensing his discovery. This is a reassuring result because our intuition is that licensing is typically a desirable outcome. Katz and Shapiro (1985) have provided a formal argument that licensing nearly always increases social welfare. Specifically, they show that licensing is socially desirable if total output increases as a result of the licensing activity. To see why, note that licensing will not take place unless both the licensor and the licensee can raise profit. The license agreement will not be signed unless the licensees see some benefit from it and will not be offered unless the licensor also sees some benefit from it. If, in addition to this mutual gain in profit, the license agreement increases total output, then the price will be lower and consumer surplus will be increased too. In other words, if the license agreement increases total output, both consumers and producers gain from the agreement, and so the agreement is socially desirable. Yet even if this fails to happen—even if the industry output is unchanged—licensing is still likely to be socially beneficial since the licensing revenue at least increases producer surplus. Somebody then, either a producer or a consumer or both, is made better off by licensing.

Moreover, licensing may have other beneficial effects. First, if a firm knows that it is going to gain profits from licensing its research findings as well as (or instead of) exploiting the research itself, this should increase the incentive to undertake research. Further, the possibility that a firm can obtain a license to use a particular innovation will reduce wasteful R&D that either duplicates existing research effort or is intended merely to invent around an existing patent.

Consider an entrant whose profit (in present value terms) under duopoly is $5 million but who would incur an R&D expenditure of $3 million developing its own product alternative. In the absence of any licensing, the entrant will pursue this investment since it yields a net gain of $2 million. Yet if this is the case, then the monopolist firm will know that whether it licenses or not, it will soon be a duopolist. If the monopolist firm licenses its technology to the entrant for $3 million, the entrant is just as well off and the monopolist now gets the licensing revenue. In addition, society avoids the unnecessary expenditure of $2 million that the entrant would otherwise have made. The moral of this section therefore seems quite clear. Public policy should actively encourage the licensing of innovations as much as possible.

There is, however, need for a cautionary note. Licensing might involve some risks. First, consider the risks associated with licensing based upon an output-related royalty. Imagine as well that the licensing agreement holds for the outstanding duration of the patent that is being licensed since, after that, the information becomes publicly available. If the royalty rate extracts almost all of the additional profits that the licensee might expect to make, there is the risk that the licensee will take the license in order to gain experience with the technology but then actually produce very little during the period of the license agreement, which means, of course, that very little is actually paid for the license. Alternatively, if output is difficult to monitor, the licensee has the incentive to lie about how much is actually being produced. What may be necessary is that the licensor tie the license agreement to some agreed minimum level of output on the part of the licensee but even this is not always easy to negotiate or enforce.

A further risk in licensing is that it can be difficult to write enforceable contracts that limit the ways in which licensees can use the license. Typically, the licensor will want to limit the markets into which the licensee can sell, for example, to avoid direct competition with the licensor or with other licensees. This may be possible within a particular jurisdiction such as the United States, although even here antitrust laws may prevent such market-limiting agreements. But it is almost impossible to write binding contracts that limit the international markets in which licensees can operate. In addition, access to a particular process or product technology may enhance the ability of a licensee to develop related technologies that are not covered by the patent being licensed. Once again, it is almost impossible to write enforceable contracts that protect the licensor from such imitation or at least give the licensor some return from the new technologies that licensees develop.

Licensing raises public policy issues that suggest caution in favoring and promoting every licensing agreement. One danger is that licensing contracts include restrictions on price or geographic territory that create monopolies with exclusive territories—ones that would otherwise be illegal under the antitrust laws. Matters become particularly complicated when, as often happens, one patent leads to another, complementary development. One firm creates, say, a new antibiotic that has some occasional and serious side effects. Then another firm develops a means to undo the side effects of the first firm's drug. The two firms may strike a deal that licenses each to produce the other's product. Yet it is easy to see that this agreement may often include terms that exclude other firms. Such dangers are recognized by U.S. policy, which tends to limit severely the ability of reciprocal licensing agreements to include exclusive provisions. Still, the example serves to make clear that the tension between promoting licensing and realizing its associated benefits, on the one hand, and the potential risk of collusion that licensing may foster, on the other, is real.

Indeed, the increasing complexity of technical advances has resulted in what some might call a "patent thicket." As advance builds on advance, and technical progress increasingly draws from learning in different fields, the technology involved in bringing a new product to market may in fact build on a host of patented techniques each of which is owned by a different entity. The potential licensee then needs the approval of each of these patent holders before proceeding. In turn, this can involve the coordination difficulties of complements that we first described in Chapter 8. Acting individually, each patent-holder may set too high a license fee with the result that all are worse off. Cross-licensing agreements by which firms agree to license their patents to each other and patent pools, by which a group of firms agrees to pool a set of patents and to license them as a package, have become increasingly popular ways to solve the coordination problems inherent in the "patent thicket." They run the risk of permitting cooperation beyond the technological sphere and giving the parties a chance to wield their technological power collectively against potential entrants. However, without such efforts, it may be impossible for any new entrants to cut their way through the thicket and thereby provide any competitive pressure.[11]

23.3

Practice Problem

Two firms compete in a Cournot-type duopoly. The industry demand is given by $P = 100 - 2Q$. Each firm has a constant average and marginal cost of $60.

a. What is the current equilibrium price and quantity in the industry?
b. Suppose that one firm discovers a procedure that lowers its average and marginal cost to $50.
   (i)   If the innovator does not license its product but simply competes as the low-cost firm in a Cournot duopoly, what will be the innovator's profit?
   (ii)   What will be the innovator's profit if it licenses the technology to its competitor at a royalty rate of $10?
   (iii) Suppose instead that the innovator licenses the technology for a fixed fee. What is the highest fee that the non-innovator will be willing to pay. What will the innovator's profits be if it can charge the highest possible such fee?

23.6   RECENT PATENT POLICY DEVELOPMENTS

In the first half of the 1980s a number of events occurred that, together, greatly increased the legal protection of patent rights in the U.S. The first and perhaps most crucial step was a legal reorganization that gave the Court of Appeals for the Federal Circuit (CAFC), in

---

[11]   See Lerner and Tirole (2004).

Washington, D.C., exclusive jurisdiction over patent appeals in an effort to unify the legal treatment of patent rights. This court is widely considered to have a very "pro-patent" view and, until recently, its decisions were left unquestioned by the U.S. Supreme Court. The CAFC emerged as the final and sole arbiter of patent disputes and its pro-patent views became widely reflected in lower court cases. Just how much stronger patent protection was to become became apparent in the 1986 patent infringement suit filed by Polaroid against Kodak regarding Kodak's production and sale of an instant-film and instant-picture camera.

Prior to that decision, losers in a patent infringement case had typically paid small penalties and been permitted to continue to produce so long as they paid appropriate royalties to the winner. However, when Polaroid won the suit Kodak was required to pay very large penalties and, most importantly, forced to stop producing its instant camera. Since shutting down a high-volume production line is very expensive—even if only for a few weeks—the fact that the courts were now willing to impose such an outcome put all firms on notice that patent infringement cases were serious business. Moreover, the Kodak/Polaroid case was quickly followed by very aggressive behavior on the part of one firm, Texas Instruments (TI) in filing infringement suits (mostly against foreign firms) and raising royalty fees that also served to put high technology firms on notice. In the technology sector where reverse engineering has always been important, TI was so aggressive that its royalty fees and court awards began to outstrip its production activities as a source of revenue.

In short, a new legal environment of much stronger protection for patent-holder rights emerged in the U.S. in the 1980s. It may not be surprising then to discover that there was an explosion of patent activity over the next several years. Between 1983 and 2000, the annual number of patent applications doubled while the annual number of patents actually granted rose by an even greater 170 percent.

There has been increasing concern that the strengthened protection of patent rights has become too aggressive. To begin with, recent empirical evidence casts considerable doubt that stronger patent enforcement yields better innovation results. Drawing on a range of sources, Lerner (2000) identified 177 distinct patent policy changes in 60 countries over 150 years such as those that lengthened or broadened patents, those that reduced the patent filing fee, those that required compulsory licensing, and so forth. He then examined the effect of these changes on the rate of patenting. He found that increased patent protection sharply increased patenting by foreign firms but decreased patenting by domestic innovators. The overall effect was positive. However, the inference is that foreign companies used patents to protect themselves against domestic competitors. Hence, while patents may have enhanced international trade, their effect on innovation was negligible.

Moser (2005) constructed internationally comparable data using the catalogues of two nineteenth-century world fairs: the Crystal Palace Exhibition in London, 1851, and the Centennial Exhibition in Philadelphia, 1876. These included innovations that were not patented, as well as those that were, and innovations from countries both with and without patent laws. He found no evidence that patent laws increased levels of innovative activity. Instead, they simply affected the direction of innovation. Relative to countries with strong patent protection, inventors in countries without such protection simply concentrated their efforts in industries where secrecy was easily maintained, leaving the overall rate of innovative efforts unchanged. Similarly, Sakakibara and Branstetter (2001) found no evidence that a strengthening of Japanese patent laws in 1988 led to any increased R&D spending or innovative output.

Fears that patent protection had gone too far reached a dramatic high point in February 2007 when the three million customers of the BlackBerry wireless e-mail service were

Reality Checkpoint

Patent Policy in the Information Age: Getting One (Click) Up On the Competition

The most valuable real estate lots bordering the information superhighway may simply be ideas about how to use this new tool to increase profit. Ideas about how to do business or so-called business methods are different from the technological innovations that we have discussed elsewhere in this chapter. Yet in the information age, they may be just as valuable.

A leading example in this regard is a patent issued to the online store, Amazon.com. Amazon customers shop the site and list the items that they wish to purchase. At the end of their visit, customers simply make one click of their mouse and their order is taken and then shipped. Amazon applied for and received a patent for this 1-Click feature and touts it to all potential customers.

In October, 1999 the traditional "brick and mortar" bookseller, Barnes & Noble, introduced an Express Lane at its recently opened website. The Express Lane checkout also permitted customers to finalize their shopping with one mouse click. Amazon instantly sued, claiming that the Express Lane model was a violation of its 1-Click patent. Amazon won and a federal appeals court subsequently issued an injunction preventing Barnes & Noble from using its Express Lane feature. Ultimately, it dropped the Express Lane and initiated an Express Checkout, which permitted finalizing an order in two clicks.

The 1-Click case is not unique. Business method patents have become common ever since a U.S. Court of Appeals rule in favor of Signature Financial Group's patent for an algorithm to manage mutual fund investments (*State Street Bank and Trust Co., Inc. v. Signature Financial Group*, 149 F.3d 1368, Fed. Cir (1998)). Consider the business method practice called upselling. A customer at Burger King, for instance, might order a Whopper sandwich, an order of french fries, and a small salad for a total of $7.14. When checking out, the cashier might say, "for just 86 cents more, you can also have a soft drink that regularly sells for $1.29." If the customer agrees to this upsale, Burger King obviously receives more revenue. Yet, Burger King will not get to keep all the extra funds. A chunk of it will go to Walker Digital as a licensing fee because Walker (owned by Jay Walker, the founder of Priceline.com), owns a patent on this process and Burger King must pay for it.

Since the *State Street* decision, filings for business method patents have nearly tripled to now reach between 1,000 and 2,000 per year. Such patents raise an interesting qualification to optimal patent policy. Where innovations require lots of development time and expense; where they can be clearly identified; and where they need protection against imitation, a patent award may well be necessary for technical progress to occur. However, when innovations are highly incremental and build on a host of other advances so that it is hard to identify any one actual breakthrough in any one application, a patent system can actually slow down technical progress. Many economists, including Gallini (2002) and Hall (2003), feel business method patents fall in this second category. The irony is that just as the Internet and related developments are making information cheap, the rush to patent business methods and practices may be making the exploitation of that information ever more expensive.

Sources: S. Hansell "Barnes And Noble Injunction Lifted," *New York Times*, February 15, 1991, C1; and J. Angwin "Business Method Patents, Key to Priceline, Draw Growing Protest," *Wall Street Journal*, October 3, 2002, p. B1.

threatened with a shutdown due to a patent dispute. A small Virginia firm, NTP, had developed and patented the technology for a wireless e-mail device in 1990. However, NTP never produced a product nor did it make any effort to license the technology to others. In 1998, the Canadian firm, Research In Motion (RIM), unveiled its first wireless e-mail device. Sales took off sharply. Although RIM claimed that it had developed the technology on its own, NTP filed suit against BlackBerry in 2001. In 2002, a U.S. jury found the Canadian firm guilty of 16 counts of patent infringement. On appeal, seven of these were dismissed in 2004 but that still left 9 outstanding. In 2005, RIM offered $450 million to NTP to settle the case, but that settlement was rejected by the trial judge. In January 2006, the Supreme Court refused to hear any further appeal and a hearing to order a shutdown of the BlackBerry service was scheduled for Friday, February 24, 2006. The hearing did not reach a final decision. However, after further negotiations, RIM and NTP reached a settlement in which RIM made a one-time payment of $615 million to the Virginian firm for unfettered use of the technology. The agreement came even as the U.S. Patent and Trademark Office (USPTO) was conducting a review of the legitimacy of NTP's patents. Many felt that the strong pro-patent laws had effectively allowed NTP to extort the payment from RIM and forced it to rush to a settlement before the USPTO completed its review.

In April 2007, the Supreme Court served notice that it too was concerned about excessive patent protection. (See Reality Checkpoint.) In *KSR International v. Teleflex, Inc* the court ruled that new products that combine elements of pre-existing inventions and that result from nothing more than "ordinary innovation" with no more than predictable results were not entitled to patent protection. The decision was notable for its clear statement that the patent system could be used to undermine innovation and its unanimity. As a result, most experts believe that the decision raised the bar substantially for future patent applications. It also opened the door to a re-examination of existing patents and gave judges much more leeway to dismiss patent infringement suits.

23.7   EMPIRICAL APPLICATION
Patent Law and Practice in the Semiconductor Industry

The semiconductor industry was not immune to the patent fever that spread through America in the last part of the twentieth century. As Hall and Ziedonis (2001) document, patent awards per million dollars of R&D spending in this industry doubled in the ten years following 1982. What makes this increase particularly striking is that semiconductor industry representatives have been surveyed repeatedly and consistently reported that patents are not a very effective way to appropriate the returns on R&D investments. Because the semiconductor industry is one of rapid technological change where product lifecycles are short, semiconductor firms have instead relied on lead time, secrecy, and product design tactics to reap the profits from their innovations. What then is the reason for the increased patent activity by semiconductor firms? How is it related to the changed legal environment?

Hall and Ziedonis (2001) examine the patent explosion in the semiconductor industry using data from 95 industry firms covering the years 1979 to 1995. These firms were awarded over 17,000 patents in this period. Hall and Ziedonis (2001) model these successful patents as the outcome of a patent production process that relates the ith firm's production of patents in year t or p_{it} to a set of variables X_{it} including the firm's R&D spending and its overall size. However, they recognize that p_{it} is what is called a count variable. That is, it counts the number of successes that take place during a time interval of given length. Thus, p_{it} can

Reality Checkpoint

It Was Patently Obvious and Therefore, Not Patent Worthy

On April 30, 2007, the U.S. Supreme Court issued an important ruling that substantially raised the bar for obtaining patents on new products that combine elements of pre-existing inventions. The case involved a patent infringement lawsuit filed by Teleflex, Inc. against KSR International over the development of an adjustable gas pedal for use on cars and trucks equipped with electronic engine controls. The position of the accelerator pedal in many cars is not adjustable. Instead, the driver adjusts the position of the seat until the pedal is a comfortable distance away. However, in the 1970s, a number of inventors began to develop adjustable pedals that could slide forward or backward without changing the effect of depressing the pedal a specific amount. In older cars, that effect is transmitted by means of a cable that typically opens up valves in the fuel injection unit of the engine. In more modern cars, however, the cable has been dispensed with and the mechanical connection has been replaced with a computer sensor that electronically transmits the acceleration or deceleration signal to the engine. KSR is a company with a history of making adjustable mechanical pedals for the major automobile companies. In 1999, it won a contract with General Motors to provide an adjustable pedal with an electronic sensor mounted at the pedal's fixed pivot point to communicate the necessary information. Teleflex, which had a patent for one type of electronic sensor for gasoline pedals, claimed patent infringement and demanded royalties. KSR refused to pay on the ground that Teleflex had combined existing elements including those in other patented sensors in an obvious manner so that its patent was therefore invalid. KSR won in Federal District Court in Detroit, but that decision was overturned in 2005 by the CAFC, the court with exclusive jurisdiction over patent appeals.

For many years, the Supreme Court has let the CAFC judgments stand unreviewed. However, the court now seems to have taken interest in the CAFC decisions. In particular, the court took issue with the way the CAFC employed an approach referred to as the "teaching, suggestion, or motivation" test (TSM test). That approach holds that a patent claim is only proved obvious if "some motivation or suggestion to combine the prior art teachings" can be found in the prior art, the nature of the problem, or the knowledge of a person having ordinary skill in the art. The Supreme Court said that the CAFC was applying the TSM standard too rigidly. In particular, it ruled that when the innovation simply yields predictable results based on existing technology then it is not entitled to patent protection regardless of whether that prediction has actually been tested in practice. The court found that the Teleflex patent on electric sensors was exactly this type of innovation and so, reversed the CAFC judgment and found in favor of KSR.

Because most inventions combine previously known elements, the decision in the *KSR v. Teleflex* case is widely recognized as a signal that two decades of aggressive patent enforcement were coming to an end. Indeed, it was accompanied by a second very similar decision in which the court found for Microsoft against a charge of patent infringement by AT&T. The result of these decisions is almost surely that patents will be harder to obtain and harder to defend.

Sources: *KSR International Co. v. Teleflex Inc.*, 550 U.S. ____(2007); *Microsoft Corporation v. AT&T Corp.* 550 U.S. ____(2007); and L. Greenhouse, "High Court Puts Limits on Patents," *New York Times*, May 1, 2007.

only take discrete integer values and often will be zero. If we consider p_{it} to have a random component, then we need to assume a probability distribution that recognizes these features. The natural choice for this purpose is the Poisson distribution, which gives the probability $f(\lambda, p)$ that there are p occurrences of a random variable in fixed time interval as:

$$f(\lambda, p) = \frac{e^{-\lambda} \lambda^p}{p!} \qquad (23.9)$$

The Poisson distribution has a very nice feature in that it is fully characterized by the parameter λ, which is both its mean and its variance. Thus, Hall and Ziedonis (2001) model patent production as a Poisson process that has a conditional mean λ_{it} that is an exponential function of X_{it} as follows:

$$E(p_{it}|X_{it}) = \lambda_{it} = \exp(X_{it}\beta + \gamma_t) \qquad (23.10)$$

where γ_t is a 1,0 dummy variable for each year reflecting factors in that year that are common to the patenting activity of all semiconductor firms. Of course, we can linearize this relationship by taking logs to yield:

$$\ln \lambda_{it} = X_{it}\beta + \gamma_t \qquad (23.11)$$

Hall and Ziedonis (2001) measure p_{it} as the number of patents per employee. The variables in X_{it} include: (1) the log of firm R&D spending per employee; (2) a 1,0 dummy variable equal to one if the firm reported no R&D spending that year and zero otherwise; (3) the log of firm size measured as the number of employees in thousands; (4) the log of the plant and equipment value per employee as a measure of the capital intensity of the firm's production; (5) a 1,0 dummy variable equal to 1 if the firm entered the market after 1982 and zero otherwise; (6) a 1,0 dummy variable equal to 1 if the firm is a design firm that does no fabrication and zero if it is a manufacturing firm; (7) a 1,0 dummy variable equal to 1 if the firm is Texas Instruments and zero otherwise; and (8) the log of the firm's age.

The first three variables reflect the standard view of patents as the output of a process in which R&D is the input and in which there may be scale economies. The fourth variable allows Hall and Ziedonis (2001) to test the hypothesis that part of the increased patenting following the change in the patent enforcement environment reflects the decision by firms with large sunk costs who cannot afford to get "held up" in a patent dispute, to expand their patent portfolio rapidly to guard against such "hold-ups." The fifth and sixth variables allow them to test a second hypothesis, namely, that another reason for the rise in patent activity was that the new legal environment made it attractive for design firms (who unlike semiconductor manufacturers rely heavily on patents) to enter the market, and thereby changed the mix of firms in the semiconductor industry to one more likely to patent. The seventh variable captures the well-known super-aggressive patenting strategy adopted by TI, while the age variable allows for firm-specific learning.

Hall and Ziedonis (2001) observe the annual number of patents p_{it} by firm i in year t for 95 semiconductor firms from 1979 to 1995, and use these to estimate a Poisson process in which the mean λ is taken to be conditional on a set of firm characteristics X_{it} and time dummies γ_{it}. Because they are estimating a Poisson distribution, the assumptions of Ordinary Least Squares (OLS) do not hold. Instead, Hall and Ziedonis use maximum likelihood estimation

Table 23.3 Parameter estimates for expected patent output by semiconductor firms

Variable	Estimated coefficient	Standard error	Estimated coefficient	Standard error
Log R&D per employee	0.190	(0.084)	0.196	(0.117)
Dummy for no reported R&D	−1.690	(0.830)	−1.690	(0.840)
Log firm size	0.854	(0.032)	0.850	(0.034)
Log firm P&E per employee	0.601	(0.113)	0.603	(0.114)
Dummy for post-1982 entry	0.491	(0.169)	0.491	(0.199)
Dummy for design firm			−0.130	(0.185)
Dummy for Texas Instruments	0.799	(0.111)	0.798	(0.115)
Log of firm age			0.220	(0.146)

(MLE). Because λ is both the mean and the variance of the Poisson distribution, comparing the variance of the data with the mean is a natural test for the appropriateness of the underlying Poisson specification. The results of their two regressions that do best on this test are shown in Table 23.3.

The estimates in both regressions for the first four variables imply roughly constant returns to scale in patent production. As firm size (measured by the number of employees) grows semiconductor firms tend to increase their patent output proportionately. This is similar to the finding of other researchers, e.g., Hall, Griliches, and Hausmann (1986). It is also clear that TI has a markedly higher propensity to patent than do other semiconductor firms consistent with TI's well-known aggressive patenting policy during these years.

Most importantly, both of the key hypotheses are supported by these data. Firms with capital-intensive production as measured by the amount of plant and equipment per employee do significantly more patenting than others do. In addition, it appears that the firms that entered the industry following the 1982 centralization of patent law cases at the CAFC were much more likely to patent than the firms that were already in the industry. The coefficient on the post-1982 entry variable is highly significant in both regressions. While the coefficient on the design firm variable is not significant in the second regression, it is if the post-1982 entry variable is omitted indicating that the entry variable reflects mostly entry by design firms.

In sum, Hall and Ziedonis (2001) interpret their results as indicating two major reasons for the jump in patenting efforts in the semiconductor industry after 1983. One is that the new pro-patent environment and the prospect of having production actually stopped by legal injunction was particularly threatening to capital-intensive firms with heavy sunk costs. The result was that they responded strategically by rapidly accumulating a portfolio of patents to protect their products and processes. The second was that the changed legal environment also induced entry of purely design firms that have an inherently greater propensity to patent their findings in any case.

There is also a third effect revealed by the Hall and Ziedonis (2001) findings. This is that the changed legal framework led all semiconductor firms to patent more. The evidence for this is in the time dummies (not shown). Normalizing so that the effect is zero in 1979, the pattern of these coefficients is seen in Figure 23.3. Here, the dotted line reflects the time dummy coefficients from the first of the two regressions above, while the dashed line reflect the same coefficients in the second regression estimates.

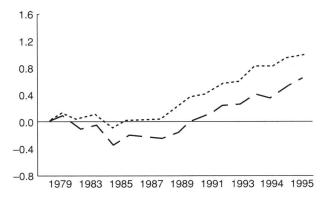

Figure 23.3   Pattern of regression time coefficients in semiconductor patent behavior

What both sets of estimates clearly show is that after 1986, even after controlling for the mix of semiconductor firm characteristics, there was a steady increase in the proclivity to patent with each successive year. The new pro-patent environment is the most obvious explanation for this rise that is common to all semiconductor firms.

Summary

By giving innovators a legally enforceable means of earning a return on their discoveries, patents and copyrights do provide incentives for innovative activity that might otherwise not be undertaken. Yet patents also confer monopoly power on the patent holder, with all the price distortions that such power entails. In addition, patent rules may enhance the ability of existing monopolies to maintain their current dominant position against would-be entrants. One mechanism by which this may occur is through the use of "sleeping patents" designed to buffer the invention against any and all attacks from rival innovations that might permit an entrant to "invent around" the original patent.

Licensing agreements by which firm permit the use of their patented knowledge for a fee can help ameliorate the patent tension. This is because such agreements both permit wider use of the innovation and also allows an innovator to earn a greater return on her R&D investments than she otherwise would receive. However, licensing contracts can be difficult to enforce except by imposing restrictions that can be harmful to competition.

Within the United States, the 1980s marked a sharp increase in the legal protection of patents against infringement. This was followed by an equally sharp increase in both patent applications and patent grants. Empirical evidence from the semiconductor industry suggests that this reflects in part the desire of firms with large sunk investments in products and processes to avoid disruption of their production by accumulating a large patent portfolio and the encouragement of entry by new firms that rely more heavily on patents to appropriate the gains of their innovations. That evidence also confirms that there was a general rise in patent proclivity across all semiconductor firms.

More recently, there has been concern that U.S. patent protection has been overly strong, especially since there is little evidence that it has led to faster innovation. Accordingly, recent court decisions have pared back these protections. Our discussion of licensing and of recent patent legal developments make clear that there is no way to eliminate the tension between allocative efficiency and innovative activity that a patent system raises either in theory or in practice.

Problems

1. Let the inverse demand for a particular product be given by $P = 250 - Q$. The product is offered by two Cournot firms each of which has a current marginal cost of $100. Both firms can invest a sum K to establish a research facility to develop a new process with lower marginal costs. The probability of success is ρ.

   a. Assume that the new process is expected to have marginal costs of $70. Derive a relationship between K and ρ under which
      (i)   neither firm establishes the research facility;
      (ii) only one firm establishes a research facility;
      (iii) both firms establish a research facility.
   b. Can there be "too much" R&D? Illustrate your answers in a diagram with ρ on one axis and K on the other.
   c. Now assume that the marginal costs of the new process are expected to be $40. How does this affect your answers to 1a?

2. In the text of this chapter we considered sleeping patents in the context of a process innovation. The same principles apply in the case of a product innovation. To see why, consider the following example: Assume that there are 100 aspiring Olympic swimmers whose tastes for low-water-resistance colored swimming suits are evenly distributed over the color spectrum from black to yellow. The "length" of this spectrum is normalized to be one unit. Each of these swimmers values the loss of utility from being offered swimming suits in other than their favorite color at $10 per unit of "distance." Each swimmer will buy exactly one swimming suit per period provided that the full price for the suit—the price charged by the firm plus the value of utility loss if there is a color difference between the suits on offer and the swimmer's favorite color—is less than $100 (these are very keen swimmers!). Production of low-water-resistance swimming suits is currently feasible only in black and is controlled by a monopolist who has a patent on the production of the black material. The

marginal cost of making a swimming suit is $25.

   a. What is the current profit-maximizing price per suit and what are the monopolist's per-period profits?

      Now assume that research can be conducted that will allow the swimming suits also to be manufactured in yellow at the same marginal cost of $25.
   b. If the monopolist undertakes the research and introduces the new color what will be the resulting equilibrium prices of black and yellow swimming suits? What is the impact on the monopolist's per-period profit, ignoring research costs?
   c. If a new entrant undertakes the research and introduces the new color, what will be the resulting equilibrium prices of black and yellow swimming suits? What will the entrant's per-period profit be, again ignoring research costs?

3. Return to problem 2, above.
   a. Confirm that the incumbent monopolist will be willing to spend more on researching the new color than the potential entrant.
   b. Assume that the research costs can be split into some amount R, which is pure research cost, and another amount D, which is development cost—the cost of transforming a successful innovation into a viable product. Calculate limits on R and D such that the monopolist will be willing to undertake the research into manufacture of yellow swimming suits and patent it but then leave the patent sleeping.

4. Assume that annual inverse demand for a particular product is $P = 150 - Q$. The product is offered by a pair of Bertrand competitors, each with marginal costs of $75. The discount factor is 0.9. What is the current equilibrium price and total surplus?

5. Return to problem 4. Assume now though that if R&D is conducted at rate x, it incurs one-off costs of $r(x) = 10x^2$ and reduces marginal costs to $(75 - x)$. Suppose that one firm decides to conduct R&D at rate $x = 10$. This research will be protected by a patent of T years.

a. What profit (ignoring the one-off costs of R&D) does the innovating firm make each year during the period of patent protection?
b. What is the new equilibrium price and total surplus once patent protection expires?

6. Use your answers to 5(a) and (b) to write the total net surplus from the innovation as a function of the period of patent protection. Derive (numerically) an approximation to the socially optimal period of patent protection.

7. How are your answers to 5(a) and (b) affected if the innovating firm conducts research at rate $x = 15$?

8. How does the net social surplus change if the innovating firm conducts research at $x = 15$?

9. What research intensity will the firms choose given that the period of patent protection is set optimally?

References

Denicolò, V. 1996. "Patent Races and Optimal Patent Breadth and Length." *Journal of Industrial Economics* 44 (March): 249–65.

Gallini, N. 1992. "Patent Policy and Costly Imitation." *Rand Journal of Economics* 23 (Spring): 52–63.

——. 2002. "The Economics of Patents: Lessons from Recent U.S. Patent Reform." *Journal of Economic Perspectives* 16 (Spring): 131–54.

Gilbert, R. and C. Shapiro. 1990. "Optimal Patent Length and Breadth." *Rand Journal of Economics* 21 (Spring): 106–12.

Giuri, P., Mariani, M., et al. 2005. "Everything You Always Wanted to Know about Inventors (But Never Asked): Evidence From the PatVal-EU Survey." Working Paper 2005/20, Laboratory of Economics and Management, Sant'Anna School of Advanced Studies, Pisa, Italy.

Hall, B. H., Z. Griliches, and J. Hausmann. 1986. "Patents And R and D: Is There A Lag?" *International Economic Review* 27 (June): 265–83.

Hall, B. and R. H. Ziedonis. 2001. "The Patent Paradox Revisited: An Empirical Study of Patenting in the U.S. Semiconductor Industry, 1979–1995." *Rand Journal of Economics* 32 (Spring): 101–28.

Katz, M. and C. Shapiro. 1985. "On the Licensing of Innovation." *Rand Journal of Economics* 16 (Winter): 504–20.

Klemperer, P. 1990. "How Broad Should the Scope of Patent Protection Be?" *Rand Journal of Economics* 21 (Spring): 233–30.

Klette, T., and D. de Meza. 1986. "Is the Market Biased against R&D?" *Rand Journal of Economics* 17 (Spring): 133–9.

Lerner, J. 2000. "150 Years of Patent Protection." Harvard Business School Working Paper 00-039.

Lerner, J. and J. Tirole. 2004. "Efficient Patent Pools." *American Economic Review* 94 (June): 691–711.

Moser, P. 2005. "How Do Patent Laws Influence Innovation? Evidence from Nineteenth-century World Fairs." *American Economic Review* 95 (September): 1214–36.

Nordhaus, W. 1969. *Invention, Growth and Welfare*. Cambridge, MA: MIT Press.

Reinganum, J. 1989. "The Timing of Innovation: Research, Development, and Diffusion." In R. Schmalensee and R. Willig, eds, *The Handbook of Industrial Organization*. Amsterdam: North-Holland, 849–908.

Sakakibara, M. and L. Branstetter. 2001. "Do Stronger Patents Induce More Innovation? Evidence from the 1998 Japanese Patent Law Reforms." *Rand Journal of Economics* 32 (Spring): 77–100.

Scotchmer, S. 2004. *Innovation and Incentives*. Cambridge, MA: MIT Press.

Part VII
Networks and Auctions

In this final part of the text, we explore topics that do not fit easily within our earlier classifications. The first of these is network externalities. For many goods, such as telephones, the value of the product to any one consumer rises as additional consumers buy it. Such network effects greatly alter both the nature of industry competition and the characteristics of the market outcome. Often, network externalities and the complementarities that underlie them give rise to multiple equilibria with no guarantee that the actual equilibrium chosen will be the best of these. Further, because network externalities act much like scale economies except that they work on the demand side, they create strong incentives for firms to operate on a large scale with the result that the market will inevitably be dominated by those few firms that survive. In turn, because not just some profit but a firm's very survival may be at stake, competition in industries with important network effects can be incredibly fierce. We explore these issues in some detail. We also include an empirical study that tries to identify network characteristics in a market for computer software.

In Chapter 25, we switch gears somewhat and turn to the topic of auctions. Auctions have been around for a very long time and, partly because of this historical pedigree, have often been viewed as the paradigm of competitive markets even though few markets might actually be described as auctions. In recent years, however, auctions have re-emerged as a common market arrangement. Financial markets, of course, have long relied on auctions. However, partly because of the privatization movement, governments also have increasingly employed an auction mechanism to sell rail lines, oil facilities and lease tracts, mobile phone licenses, and a host of other assets. Similarly, the rise of e-Bay and other commercial sites offers further evidence of the increased popularity of the auction process.

Our analysis of the auction phenomenon begins with a review of Vickery's (1961) classic piece leading to the Revenue Equivalence Theorem which says that, under certain rather broad conditions, the final auction price is independent of the auction design. We then examine various ways in which this outcome might break down and the auction lead to an inefficient result in which the prize does not go to the buyer who valued it most highly. The interesting feature of such failures is that often they stem from a common source—lack of competition due to either small numbers, or collusive bidding, or both. We then consider how auctions might be alternatively designed to surmount these problems, demonstrating that industrial organization theory has practical insights as well.

24

Network Issues

Microsoft Corporation—perhaps no single firm is more closely associated with the telecommunications revolution that swept through both businesses and households in the last part of the twentieth century than this giant of the software industry. Nor perhaps does any other company better capture the popular view of the opportunities for fame and fortune that the "new economy" presents. Starting out as a simple provider of programming language, Microsoft became the supplier of over 90 percent of the operating systems for personal computers. It holds equally commanding shares in many markets for peripheral programs, such as that for word-processing (*Word*) and electronic spreadsheets (*Excel*). From a small, two-person enterprise with essentially zero net worth in 1975, the firm has grown to a firm of over 30,000 employees with a net worth of over $44 billion in 2007.

Of course, Microsoft is not the only success story of the digital economy age. Among the other Cinderella-firms of recent years is e-Bay, the online auction company. A small startup firm created by Pierre Omidyar in 1995, e-Bay now has over 10 million registered users and conducts over one million person-to-person auctions each day. These transactions initially involved only low-price collectibles, from *Star Wars* action figures to Japanese maple trees. However, the site now brokers trades of many everyday items including toys and games, concert tickets, and even used cars. Prior to the 1990s, direct trade in many items, especially collectibles, had been limited because of the extreme cost of matching a potential buyer with a potential seller. Omidyar was among the first to recognize the enormous potential of the Internet—which makes it easy to disseminate a vast amount of information to a large number of buyers and sellers in a very short time—to solve this problem.

Neither Microsoft nor e-Bay is alone in its respective market. There are other operating system platforms, such as Macintosh or Linux, and other online auction sites. Nevertheless both firms have come to dominate their respective markets. Moreover, each of these markets shares an important feature. One reason that so many people use the *Windows* operating system is that they expect others will use it as well. The more people that use *Windows* the more software that will be written for *Windows* and the more useful therefore *Windows* will be. Similarly, the more buyers that try to buy on e-Bay, the more sellers will want to sell there which in turn attracts more buyers and so on.

When the value of a product to any one consumer increases as the number of other consumers using the product increases, we say that the market for that product exhibits network externalities or demand-side scale economies. When these effects are important, new strategic considerations come into play. In this chapter, we investigate these issues and the type of market outcomes that are likely when important network effects are present.[1]

24.1   MONOPOLY PROVISION OF A NETWORK SERVICE

An early but insightful analysis of network issues is that provided by Rohlfs (1974). Rohlfs approach is quite straightforward and draws attention to the main issues that arise in network settings. It simplifies the supply side by assuming a monopoly so that the analysis can focus on the central demand-side aspects that give rise to network effects. We present a simplified version of Rohlfs model here.

Assume that the monopolist, say a telecommunications firm, charges an access fee but does not impose a per usage charge. That is, the consumer is charged a single price p for "hooking up" to the network but each individual call is free, perhaps because the marginal cost of a call is zero.[2] We will also assume that there is a maximum size of the market, say one million, reflecting the maximum number of consumers who would ever willingly buy the product even if the access fee were zero. By fixing the total amount of potential customers, we can talk interchangeably about the actual number served and the fraction f of the market that is served. That is, if the maximum size of the market is one million, we can characterize a market outcome in which 100,000 purchase the service either in terms of the total output of 100,000 units or the fraction $f = 0.10$ that is served. For our purposes, it is easier to work with f.

Consumers all agree that the service is more valuable the greater the fraction f of the market that signs up for it. However, even if everyone acquires the service ($f = 1$), consumers would still vary in their valuation or willingness to pay for the service. Specifically, we denote the valuation of the ith consumer when $f = 1$, as v_i. These valuations or v_i's are assumed to be uniformly distributed between 0 and \$100. For example, the one percent of consumers who most value the service (roughly about 10,000 individuals in our case) would willingly pay about \$100 for it if all other consumers also acquire it. However, as the fraction of consumers who sign up declines, so does each consumer's willingness to pay. The easiest way to reflect this assumption is that the ith consumer's valuation of the service for any value of f is given by fv_i. The demand by consumer i for a hook up to the communications service is therefore given by

$$q_i^D = \begin{cases} 0 \text{ if } fv_i < p \\ 1 \text{ if } fv_i \geq p \end{cases} \tag{24.1}$$

Again, it is worth pointing out that the influence of network size works here through f. For consumer i, equation (24.1) says that consumer i's willingness to pay for the service fv_i increases with the fraction of potential buyers f that have bought into the service. It is this interdependence between the willingness to pay and the fraction of the market served that leads to network externalities. In addition, each potential user of the network considers only the value to herself of joining the network. What she does not take into account are the

---

[1]   For a formal but very readable introduction to network externalities, see Economides (1996).
[2]   Note that this pricing policy is essentially that of a two-part tariff as described in Chapter 6.

external benefits she creates when she joins the network. By joining she will improve the usefulness of the network to all of the other users since now the network is bigger.

We can use equation (24.1) to calculate the fraction of the market that will sign on to the service at any given price p. As usual, we start by focusing on the marginal consumer denoted by the reservation valuation $\tilde{v}_i$. This is the consumer who is just indifferent between buying into the service network and not buying into it so that $\tilde{v}_i = p/f$. All consumers with a valuation less than $\tilde{v}_i$ will not subscribe to the service. The remainder will subscribe. Since v_i is distributed uniformly between 0 and 100, the fraction of consumers with a valuation below $\tilde{v}_i$ is simply $\tilde{v}_i/100$. Hence, the fraction of consumers f with valuations greater than $\tilde{v}_i$ and who therefore acquire the service is

$$f = 1 - \frac{\tilde{v}_i}{100} = 1 - \frac{p}{100f} \tag{24.2}$$

If we now solve for p we obtain the inverse demand function confronting the monopolist expressed in terms of the fraction f of the maximum potential number of customers who actually buy the service as

$$p = 100f(1 - f) \tag{24.3}$$

This is illustrated in Figure 24.1.

The curve shown in Figure 24.1 is interesting in a number of respects. Note first that for all prices greater than \$25, no equilibrium with a positive value of f exists. If for some reason, the monopolist must charge a price greater than \$25, perhaps to cover fixed costs, then the network will simply fail. This is true even though the network might be socially efficient. For example, when half the market ($f = 0.5$) or 500,000 consumers are served, we know that those who obtain the product are those consumers with v_i values in the range of \$50 to \$100. The average $v_i = \left(\frac{1}{50}\right)\sum_{i=51}^{100} v_i$ value for this group is therefore \$75. With $f = 0.5$, the average actual willingness to pay across these consumers is accordingly $1/2 \times \$75 = \$37.50$. As long

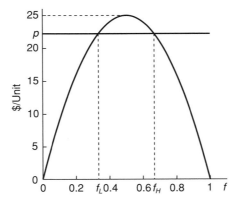

Figure 24.1   Demand to a monopoly provider of a network service
At price p if fewer than f_L consumers subscribe to the network, the equilibrium will fall to $f = 0$. If more than f_L consumers subscribe to the network, the equilibrium will rise to f_H.

as the price is below this amount, consumers as a group gain from having the network service available. Suppose that the monopolist could in fact provide service to 500,000 customers but to do so would require that it sink development costs of $15 million or $30 per customer. The firm would then have to charge a hook-up price of $30 just to break even.

Now $30 is certainly less than $37.50 so such an outcome would be desirable as it would generate net positive consumer gains and no producer losses. Moreover, with an average willingness to pay of $37.50, charging a fee of $30 may also appear to be a price that the market could support. Yet as we have just stated and as Figure 24.1 illustrates, the network will not be viable at this price. Why? Because while the average consumer valuation at $f = 0.5$ is $37.50, there are some current consumers (those for whom $50 \leq v_i < 60) whose willingness to pay is less than $30. As the price rises toward $30, these consumers drop the service. Some (those for whom $50 \leq v_i < 52) drop as soon as the price rises to $26, more drop as it hits $27 and so on. The loss of these consumers, however, reduces the value of the network to those remaining. Those who were previously just willing to pay $30 when the service had 500,000 subscribers, no longer will be willing to do so now that fewer people are signed on. These consumers will also cease to purchase the product reducing still further the network's value to the now even fewer customers left behind. This process will continue until the entire market unravels and the network fails. Here one can see the externality quite explicitly. A consumer does not consider the impact her choice to join or to leave the network has on the value of the network to others.

Next note that for prices less than or equal to $25, there is actually more than one equilibrium value of f. For instance, when $p = 22.22, both $f_L(p) = 1/3$ and $f_H(p) = 2/3$ are possible values for f. Which of these might we expect to occur? Rohlfs points out that the low-fraction equilibrium is actually unstable. Consider, for example, the effect of a small increase in the price or a small loss of customers. Starting from an equilibrium with so few subscribers, this would repeat the outcome described above. As a few consumers leave, the value of being part of the system to those remaining is reduced. Again, the eventual outcome is that all subscribers leave and the network fails. Now consider the impact of a small reduction in the price or the addition of one extra subscriber, again starting from the low-fraction equilibrium. This would increase the value of the service above the reservation price of all consumers in the interval $[0, f_H]$. It would, therefore, lead to the establishment of the high fraction, or $f_H(p)$, equilibrium. These thought experiments suggest that once the fraction $f_L(p)$ of consumers subscribes to the network, it is virtually certain that the high-fraction equilibrium will be attained, since only a trivial price reduction is necessary to do so. For this reason, Rohlfs refer to this lower fraction as a "critical mass" for the network. So long as a fraction of subscribers just a bit greater than this critical mass, $f_L(p)$, can be established, the network will grow to contain the high fraction, $f_H(p)$, of the population.

An important question therefore is whether and how the monopolist can reach the critical mass. For as we have just seen, values of f below the critical mass tend to unravel. That is, an alternative equilibrium that arises at the price of $22.22 is one in which no consumer signs up for the service at all. The reason that this can happen is fairly straightforward. At that price, no individual consumer will wish to sign up for the service unless others do. Accordingly, each consumer holds back from joining until they see some others hooking up. Hence, an outcome in which no one has joined the network can be self-sustaining.

The question as to how to get the network started and grow to a critical mass is an interesting one. One possibility is to provide the service free for a limited period of time. One way to accomplish such selling below cost is to bundle the service free with some other product. Another option is to lease the equipment to potential users with a guarantee that if the service does not achieve critical mass, the lease agreement can be canceled with no penalty. A further possibility, which was employed when fax machines were first being marketed, would be to target groups of large users first. In this regard, national and multinational companies or government agencies are the obvious examples of institutions that might want to operate their own internal networks. The idea is that once the network comes into common use for internal company communications, there will be a demand for it to be extended to those with whom the company does business. Before long, this may grow into a demand by company users of the service for it to be available in their homes.

For the moment, let us assume that the monopolist does achieve the critical mass. What fee will the monopolist charge for its services and how does this compare to the social optimum? In answering this question we will again assume that the monopolist's costs are all fixed and given by F, so that the marginal cost of adding a further subscriber to the network is zero. Let us also assume that the maximum number of individuals who would sign up even at a zero price is N. (In our example above, N = one million.) Then total profit to the monopolist is

$$\pi(f) = pfN - F = 100Nf^2(1 - f) - F \text{ given that } p = 100f(1 - f) \tag{24.4}$$

Maximizing this with respect to f indicates (see the inset) that the monopolist should choose p such that $f^* = 2/3$, implying a profit-maximizing price of $p^* = \$22.22$. As just described, actually getting two-thirds of the market to sign on at a price of $22.22 may be difficult until the critical mass ($f = 1/3$) is reached. Still, it is clear that this should be the monopolist's goal.

How does the combination $p = \$22.22$ and $f = 2/3$ compare with the social optimum? It should not surprise you that the profit-maximizing choice of the monopolist is to serve a smaller market than that which would maximize the total surplus. After all, monopolists achieve their profit by restricting output. The social optimum requires that the market be as large as possible at a price equal to marginal cost. In our case, this means that all N consumers should be served, i.e., $f = 1$.

Derivation Checkpoint

The Profit-Maximizing Network Access Price

Profit is $\pi(f) = pfN = 100Nf^2(1 - f) - F$. Differentiating with respect to f gives the first-order condition:

$$\frac{d\pi(f)}{df} = 100N(2f - 3f^2) = 0$$

This implies that either $f = 0$ or $f = 2/3$. The choice of $f = 0$ generates negative profits so long as $F > 0$. The choice of $f = 2/3$ generates positive operating profits (hopefully, enough to cover fixed costs F). Hence, $f^* = 2/3$ is the optimal choice of market share f. From the inverse demand function,

$$p = 100f(1 - f), \text{ a value of } f = 2/3 \text{ implies a price of } 100 \times \frac{2}{9} = \$22.22.$$

Consider, for example, the numerical example above with N = one million. At the monopolist's profit-maximizing price of \$22.22, two-thirds of the market or 666,666.66 consumers are served. The monopolist therefore earns a profit of \$14.81 million less fixed cost F. Consumer surplus may be calculated as follows. With two-thirds of the market served, all consumers with v_i values in the range \$33.33 $\le v_i \le$ \$100, hook up to the service. Hence, the average value of v_i for this group is \$67.67. Since $f = 2/3$, the average willingness to pay of those consumers served in this equilibrium is $0.67 \times$ \$67.67 $\approx$ \$45. Hence, with p = \$22.22, the average consumer earns a surplus of \$22.78. Multiplying this average surplus by the 666,666.66 consumers yields a total consumer surplus of about \$15,187,000. Accordingly, the monopolist's profit maximizing price and quantity generates a total surplus of \$14.81 million + \$15.19 million = \$30 million *less* the fixed cost F.

Now consider the social optimum in which $f = 1$. With all one million consumers receiving the service, the average value of v_i (and therefore of fv_i) is \$50. Hence, the total value of the service is \$50 million. The total social surplus would then be \$50 million $- F$. Clearly, this exceeds the total surplus under monopoly. Of course, just how the optimal outcome would be achieved in practice is unclear. One way is through subsidization by the government. Alternatively, it could be achieved by creating a legal monopoly and permitting it to price discriminate. A combination of these two strategies is also possible. Indeed, one can think of the postal system as a giant network served by a government monopoly that is both subsidized and that price discriminates (e.g., express versus first class mail).

24.2 NETWORKS, COMPETITION, AND COMPLEMENTARY SERVICES

While the Rohlfs (1974) model focuses on the provision of network services by a monopolist, it makes clear many of the major difficulties that network externalities raise when competition is considered. The market could fail altogether. Alternatively, there could be more than one equilibrium outcome and there is no guarantee that the market will choose the best one. For example, suppose that there are two firms, firm A and firm B, competing for the 1,000,000-customer market above. Suppose further that while fixed costs are zero, each firm now has a positive marginal cost of \$11.11. Consumers buy the service of the network that gives them the biggest net surplus, $f_A v_i - p_A$, and $f_B v_i - p_B$, respectively. In the case of a tie, consumers are split randomly between the two services. One possible equilibrium occurs with each firm setting a price $p_A = p_B$ = marginal cost = \$11.11 and two-thirds of the market being served. The firms offer identical products and, given the tie-breaking assumption, each serves half of the consumers ranging from valuations \$33.33 and up. However, since each firm individually serves only one-third of the market, the valuation of the least valuable consumer in each case is $fv_i = 0.333 \times$ \$33.33 = \$11.11. Neither firm has an incentive to raise its price unilaterally. This would only lose customers and make its network even less valuable to consumers. Nor does either firm have an incentive to lower its price. While this may give it an edge in attracting customers, each one served now involves a loss as the firm would be selling below cost. Hence, $p_A = p_B$ = \$11.11 and two-thirds of market being served is one possible equilibrium.

However, there are two other possible outcomes. They occur when either firm A or firm B has a monopoly with respect to all consumers actually subscribing to a network at the monopoly price while its rival has zero customers at a price equal to or greater than marginal cost. It is easy to show, for example, that with a marginal cost of \$11.11, the monopoly price would be \$23.89 and that at this price, the monopolist would serve about 60.5 percent of the market and earn a profit of \$12.78 on each customer. Suppose that firm A is doing precisely this while firm B is charging a lower price but has zero consumers. Clearly, firm A has no incentive to raise or lower its price since it already has set a price that maximizes its profit. Firm B has no incentive to change its price either. Raising it surely will not help it attract any customers. Yet lowering it won't either because no one will choose a network that has no other customers regardless of the price. Practice Problem 24.1 offers a simple but more complete model of competition with network effects.

24.1

Practice Problem

Two firms are located at opposite ends of a Hotelling line one unit long. Firm A is located at the West end of town ($x = 0$) and firm B is located at the East end of town ($x = 1$). $\bar{N}$ consumers are distributed uniformly along the line. Each buys at most one unit of the good either from firm A or firm B. The net surplus earned by a consumer is: $V + ks_A^e - tx - p_A$ if she buys from firm A, and $V + ks_B^e - t(1 - x) - p_B$, where s_A^e and s_B^e are, respectively, the market shares of consumers that the typical consumer *expects* to purchase good A and good B, respectively. V is large enough that consumers always buy from one of the two firms, i.e., the market is covered. Firms have zero costs and compete in prices, p_A and p_B, respectively. Note that the actual market shares for each good are, respectively: $s^A = x^m$ and $s^B = 1 - x^m$, where x^m is the location of the marginal consumer just indifferent between the two products of the two firms.

a. Assume as a benchmark, no-network-effects case that $k = 0$. Show that prices then are: $p_A = p_B = t$.
b. Now assume that $t > k > 0$.
  (i)   Show that the marginal consumer x^m must satisfy the condition: $2tx^m = t + k(s_A^e - s_B^e) + (p_B - p_A)$.
  (ii) At the time that the marginal consumer confronts a particular set of prices, p_A and p_B, and makes her purchase choice she is aware of her marginal consumer status. She therefore forms the rational expectation that: $s_A^e = x^m$ and $s_B^e = 1 - x^m$. Impose this rational expectation requirement to show that the demand facing firm A, namely $N_A = x^m \bar{N}$ is: $N_A = \left[\dfrac{1}{2} + \dfrac{(p_B - p_A)}{2(t - k)} \right] \bar{N}$
  (iii) Show that profit maximization by firm A implies the best response function: $p_A = \dfrac{t - k}{2} + \dfrac{p_B}{2}$.
  (iv) Use the symmetry condition to show that the equilibrium prices are: $p_A = p_B = t - k$. Compare this result to the no networks effect case of part a.

Competition between two or more firms to establish the network can be particularly fierce if it is possible that only one firm or network survives, i.e., when the market has a "winner take all" feature. The winning network claims the entire (served) population and the loser gets nothing. The market is "tippy" in that once a firm starts to lose customers the value of its product to the remaining customers falls, causing it to lose more customers, its value to fall further, and so on. In such a setting, more than market share is at stake. Survival itself is on the line. Moreover, while this "winner take all" feature would greatly intensify the competition by itself, coupling it with an environment in which pricing below cost may be necessary just to get any network started, makes the competition truly nasty. Some economists have argued that it was precisely this dynamic that was at work in the *Microsoft v. Netscape* case and that what may look like predatory behavior when applied in other markets is really just normal competition when applied in a setting of network goods.[3]

Market problems become particularly difficult when the network is a system comprised of complementary components and when we consider what happens over time. Suppose for instance that the network in question involves the market for digital versatile disc (DVD) movies. The two components to this network are the DVD player and the movie discs themselves. This complementary relationship complicates the network effect. The desired outcome is for sufficiently wide use of DVD players and discs to achieve what appear to be rather sizable scale economies that characterize production, especially disc-making. However, no firm or group of firms will sink the large up-front costs necessary to produce a lot of DVDs unless they are sure that there will be a substantial number of DVD players. Yet consumers may be reluctant to purchase a DVD player until they are sure that there will be a large number of films translated to DVD's for playing. In such a setting one possibility is that the market fails completely because of self-fulfilling expectations. If no consumer expects DVD films to be widely available (or available at a low price), no one will invest in buying a DVD player and, as a result, no firm will produce many DVD films. In turn, this outcome will confirm the initial expectations, justifying the decision not to purchase a DVD player. On the other hand, an alternative outcome is that each consumer expects others to purchase DVD players and therefore anticipates that firms will find it worthwhile to put films on DVDs. In this case, each consumer will purchase a player, inducing firms to produce movie discs, which now confirms this more optimistic expectation. The network externality in this case is reflected in the fact that as I buy a DVD player, I enhance the value of your DVD machine because I increase the likelihood that there will be firms that find it worthwhile to produce DVD films.

The DVD example also highlights another aspect of the multiple equilibria problem, namely, the possibility that the particular equilibrium realized may be one in which the market is "locked" into the wrong or an inferior technology. From a durability and volume of information viewpoint, the DVD technology is undoubtedly superior and less costly way to provide movie rentals than is the VHS technology based on videocassettes and VCRs. However, because the two systems are substitutes and because VHS was the first system to get established, the DVD system has had to attract customers away from VHS in order to gain a footing. It might have been the case that the number of customers so attracted was not sufficiently large in order for the DVD manufacturers to exploit the available scale economies and avoid losses. To reach that volume, each potential DVD consumer needed not only to be convinced of the superiority of the DVD system but also to be sure that others shared that conviction and were willing to act on it. In this case, purely by the historical accident that the videocassette system was developed first, consumers would have been locked into the inferior system.[4]

---

[3]   See Schmalensee (2000) for a clear statement of the view that competition in network or (what he calls) "winner take most" markets is likely to be extremely fierce and easily mistaken for predatory conduct when practiced by a dominant incumbent.

[4]   David (1985) has argued that the standardized QWERTY keyboard used initially by typewriters and now by all PC keyboards, is an example of path dependent lock-in to an inferior technology, with the superior one being the Dvorak keyboard. While Liebowitz and Margolis (1990) cast considerable doubt on this argument, the case nevertheless makes clear that such market failure is a real possibility. See also, Arthur (1989).

To put it somewhat differently, there is "path dependence" so that which system eventually claims the market is the result of an arbitrary process, but one that "locks in" that outcome for a considerable period of time. Instead of the VHS versus DVD example just give, consider a closely related one from the earlier days of home video, namely, the VHS versus Betamax versions of video cassette recorders (VCRs). Imagine that 40 percent of the population has a slight preference for VHS machines *if* the price and market share of these machines are identical to the price and market share of Betamax based products. Similarly, the remaining 60 percent have a slight preference for Betamax. However, these slight preferences can be overcome if one firm has a much larger market share because, again, no one really wants to buy a network product if it does not have a very large network of users. Finally, we assume that all consumers are not initially aware of the general home video market. Instead, they learn of it over time. Each week a few more consumers randomly find out about home videos and decide to buy a VCR of either a VHS or Betamax type.

On average, we would expect each new wave of new consumers to be comprised of 60 percent of Betamax preferring consumers and 40 percent of VHS preferring consumers. However, it is quite possible that, picking randomly, one could get a batch of new consumers who were comprised of say 90 or even 100 percent of those who prefer VHS. Starting from a point in which each system has equal market penetration, such a random draw could easily tip the market heavily in favor of VHS. Once that happens, then even those with a slight preference for Betamax will, in subsequent rounds, choose to buy a VHS machine because that network is so much larger that many more films are going to be printed for it. Hence, the small random draw favoring VHS may tip the entire market in favor of this technology forever even though, at base, Betamax is the superior technology in that most consumers favor it over VHS when all else is equal.

Similarly, Microsoft's dominance may reflect just plain good luck as much as it does superior technology. A key development in this regard came in 1980 when IBM decided to enter the personal computer market in a major way. IBM awarded the contract for its disc operating system to Microsoft and MS-DOS was born. Many analysts think that Microsoft did not have the best product at that time. Yet having the support of IBM was clearly a major advantage in establishing a network of MS-DOS users. Note that the network effect gives Microsoft a strong defense against Linux or Apple or some other product even if it is a better operating system than Windows. Again, the lock in effect raises the possibility that the market may adopt the inferior technology.

24.3 SYSTEMS COMPETITION AND THE BATTLE OVER INDUSTRY STANDARDS

Competition between systems does not always lead to one survivor. There are currently four major suppliers of long distance phone service that dominate the U.S. domestic market. Likewise, there are now three providers of wireless phone serive. When we allow for the coexistence of two or more firms, each operating its own network, a number of additional features enter into the analysis. In such cases, there is the important issue of compatibility. To what extent will the industry adopt a standard product design that enables consumers to "plug in" to any network? If a standard is adopted, what standard will it be? In this section, we address these and related questions using a simple illustrative model described below.

Consider, for example, the question of technology adoption. Assume that two firms have to decide on whether to stick with their individual, existing technology or switch to a new one. To be specific, suppose that the firms estimate the payoffs to their choices to be those shown in Tables 24.1(a) and 24.1(b). The distinction between these two matrices is that in (1) sticking with the old technology is less profitable jointly than incurring the installation costs of switching to the new technology, while in case (2) both firms switching reduces their joint profits.

The payoff received for either firm depends critically on what choice its rival makes. However, there is also a further complication, namely, the issue of compatibility. Suppose that the old technology and the new technology are incompatible in the sense that they cannot be used together. This means that if each firm makes a different choice, they do not derive any network benefits of the type we have introduced previously. By contrast, if they choose the same technologies—whether old or new—then they do enjoy network externalities. Such positive network externalities mean that the payoff to each firm if they choose the same technology is greater than if they choose different technologies. This is illustrated in the payoff matrices by the fact that the payoff to either firm when both firms choose the same technology, no matter which, is greater than the payoff to either firm when they choose different (incompatible) technologies.

Regardless of whether both would do best by switching to the new technology (Table 24.1(a)), or both would do best by avoiding the cost of installing the new equipment and sticking with the existing technology (Table 24.1(b)), it can be seen that there are two Nash equilibria: one in which the two firms stay with the old technology, and the other in which they both switch to the new technology. There is no simple way to pick between these two

Table 24.1 Excess inertia and excess momentum with network externalities (in U.S. dollars, millions)

		Firm 2	
		Old technology	New technology
Firm 1	Old technology	5, 4	3, 2
	New technology	3, 3	6, 7

(a) The new technology is Pareto superior to the old. A Nash equilibrium with both firms staying with the old technology exhibits excess inertia.

		Firm 2	
		Old technology	New technology
Firm 1	Old technology	6, 7	3, 2
	New technology	3, 3	5, 4

(b) The old technology is Pareto superior to the new. A Nash equilibrium with both firms adopting the new technology exhibits excess momentum.

equilibrium outcomes. If the payoffs are as in Table 24.1 (a) and so both switching is efficient, each firm may nevertheless choose not to switch from fear of moving alone into an incompatible technology. Farrell and Saloner (1985) refer to this as a case of excess inertia. Alternatively, with the payoffs of Table 24.1(b), we might find excess momentum with both firms making a costly switch to the new technology out of fear of being stranded alone with the old technology.

There are, of course, ways by which the firms can attempt to avoid either of these unsatisfactory outcomes. For example, the firms might be able to communicate their proposed technology choices—and they have the incentive to do so honestly since lying actually hurts both firms. Coordination may also be more likely if we extend this game over many periods, since then a firm has the potential to correct a "wrong" choice, i.e., one different from that of its rival. Nevertheless, even in these more general settings, Farrell and Saloner show that firms may in particular delay switching technology longer than they should. That is, rather than move promptly to introduce new technology soon, they may wait unduly long until a sufficiently large "bandwagon" has built up. Thus, some theater owners and film producers in the 1920s did not invest in the equipment to show or to make "talking pictures" until they were certain that the new phenomenon would catch on. As a result, the advent of "talkies" may have been suboptimally delayed.

Compatibility is clearly an important factor in technological choice. However, there is a drawback to compatibility. When each firm adopts the same technical standard, their products become very close substitutes and so price competition is likely to be intense. Hence, while product differentiation by means of different technologies incurs the cost of foregoing possible network effects it has the benefit of softening price competition. Firms therefore have to make a judgment in this regard. Choosing the same technology will lead the firms into direct, intratechnology competition of the type discussed throughout the earlier chapters of this book—that is, competition on price, quality, and service. By contrast, the choice of different technologies will lead the firms into intertechnology competition.

Of course, if a firm can establish its technology as the industry standard, the rewards from this kind of competition are likely to be very large indeed. When firms choose to compete in different technologies each is hoping that its technology will someday win the market and become the industry standard. Think of Sony's PlayStation, Nintendo's Wii, and Microsoft's Xbox. These three firms apparently regard the advantages of compatibility to be more than offset by the disadvantages that it would bring in terms of intensified price competition. As a result, the three systems are totally incompatible. Yet each hopes to win the market and to establish its technology as the standard for which all applications, i.e., games are written.

There is no *a priori* means of determining whether rewards will be greater under intratechnology competition "within the market" or intertechnology competition "for the market." There are, however, three main possibilities that we should consider. We illustrate these with three simple games: (1) Tweedledum and Tweedledee; (2) the Battle of the Sexes; and (3) the Pesky Little Brother.[5]

Tweedledum and Tweedledee

Assume that the payoffs for this game of technology choice are given in Table 24.2. There are two Nash equilibria in each of which the firms prefer to adopt incompatible technologies.

---

[5]   This analysis is developed in depth in Besen and Farrell (1994). The language that follows is also borrowed from their discussion.

Table 24.2   Tweedledum and Tweedledee (in U.S. dollars, millions)

		Firm 2	
		Technology A	Technology B
Firm 1	Technology A	3, 2	8, 4
	Technology B	4, 8	2, 3

Two firms prefer to choose incompatible rather than compatible technologies and will become involved in a standards war.

This implies that the firms believe that network externalities are not particularly strong and that any gains from adopting a common technology will be more than offset by the fact that this will lead to particularly fierce intratechnology price competition. They also believe that a battle to establish the industry standard will not significantly delay its adoption by potential consumers and so offers large rewards.

With these payoffs, each firm willingly enters into a battle to have its technology established as the dominant one, i.e., each will push for the Nash equilibrium that favors its own product. In terms of the game matrix, Firm 1 will fight to establish its technology as the "A" technology, thereby defining firm 2's as the lesser "B" technology, and firm 2 will do exactly the same. Besen and Farrell (1994) suggest four forms that this battle can take:

1. *Build on an early lead*: If there are any network externalities at all associated with a particular technology of the type we have discussed, there is considerable benefit to a firm that succeeds in establishing a large installed base of current users. These users will be reluctant to switch to a different technology. At the same time, the existence of such a large installed base makes the technology attractive to new users. (Just think of the choice that a new computer user has to make between buying an IBM compatible running the Windows operating system against a similar machine running Linux or an Apple computer with the Apple operating system.) Under this scenario, there will be intense price competition in the early stages of new technologies as each firm attempts to capture as many customers as possible. Firms will also reveal and perhaps exaggerate their sales figures in order to persuade potential buyers that a large installed base already exists.

2. *Attract suppliers of complements*: As we have pointed out many times, the attractiveness of a product is affected by the number of complementary products that are also available. A computer is of little use except to the most advanced users unless there is a wide range of computer software that will run on it. A Nintendo game machine becomes more attractive as Nintendo or other firms expand the number of games it can play. There is little point in owning a CD player unless recording companies offer a wide range of recordings in CD format.

    Owners of a primary technology such as Dell or Microsoft will likely encourage software developers to produce a wide range of programs that will run on their platform. Indeed, one reason that Apple lost its early lead in personal computers may well have been its reluctance to have its operating system installed in clones. This restriction limited the market penetration of Apple's system and consequently reduced the incentives of software developers to produce Apple-compatible software.

3. *Product preannouncement*: The owner of a particular technology can try to slow the growth of a rival network by regularly "pre-announcing" new products in advance of their actual introduction. The idea is to discourage new buyers from choosing the rival's product with the promise of new "goodies" to come. The long-advertised arrival of Microsoft's Vista program may have been in part an effort to attract new buyers who might otherwise have started out buying an alternative operating system. Such a strategy is not without risk, however. Announcing that a new version of a dominant product is just round the corner may not just cause some new customers to delay their purchase of a rival's product. It may also cause customers already favorable to one's existing product to delay their purchases as well.

4. *Price commitments*: A contractual commitment to achieve and maintain low prices over the long term is a fourth method by which new consumers can be persuaded to adopt a particular technology. This will be especially beneficial if the firm offering the commitment knows that there are significant economies of scale or learning economies in the manufacture of the primary product. In such circumstances, building a large installed base early generates cost reductions that allow the firm to deliver on its low price while maintaining its profitability.

In short, when rival firms compete to establish an industry standard, a variety of strategies and outcomes emerge. Here again we find that such markets are "tippy" with multiple equilibria in which the coexistence of incompatible products may be unstable. The tide of battle can turn rapidly and quite suddenly a dynamic can develop that leads to a single winning standard dominating the market. Moreover, there is no guarantee that the winner will offer the best technology.

The Battle of the Sexes[6]

Rather than fight to have their own technology adopted as the industry standard, firms may agree on the adoption of a common technology. The payoff matrix in this case is as in Tables 24.3(a) and (b). The simplest case is that illustrated in Table 24.3(a). Here, both firms are agreed that they should adopt technology 1. Accordingly, they should be able to establish this technology as a common standard by simple communication between them.

In the case of Table 24.3(b), however, there is no such agreement. The firms would prefer a common standard but they are not agreed on which of the two technologies the standard should be. Firm 1 will fight to establish technology 1 as the standard, and firm 2 will fight to establish technology 2. This is another instance in which commitment plays a crucial role. Firm 1, for example, may be able to persuade firm 2 to accept technology 1 as the standard by irrevocably committing itself to this technology. It could, for example, build an installed base rooted in technology 1. Alternatively, it could invest in production capacity to build more units embodying this technology, or establish a large R&D program devoted to improving this technology. The common intent here is to broadcast the clear message that firm 1 will never give in on its demand that technology 1 be the standard because to do so would cost firm 1 too much to give in.

---

[6]   This title comes from a well-known game in which two individuals, perhaps man and wife, in choosing their entertainment for the night, agree that they would rather be together than apart, but put very different valuations on the entertainment they might share. These could be, for example, going to a ball game or to an opera.

Table 24.3 The Battle of the Sexes (in U.S. dollars, millions)

		Firm 2	
		Technology 1	Technology 2
Firm 1	Technology 1	10, 10	5, 4
	Technology 2	6, 5	8, 8

(a) Agreement on compatible standard and choice of standard.

		Firm 2	
		Technology 1	Technology 2
Firm 1	Technology 1	10, 7	5, 4
	Technology 1	6, 5	8, 12

(b) Agreement to be compatible but disagreement on standard.

Other possible commitments take the form of concessions rather than threats. Thus, firm 1 could offer to license technology 1 to firm 2 for a low fee in return for firm 2 agreeing that technology 1 will be the standard. Alternatively, firm 1 can promise to develop the technology jointly, or it can suggest that the two firms develop a hybrid technology that combines the best features of each.

The Pesky Little Brother

In the Tweedledum and Tweedledee case, the two firms pursue inter-technology competition rather than adopt a common technology and confront each other in the market with technologically undifferentiated products. In the Battle of the Sexes, each firm prefers competition between technically identical products, but the question of which technology is the appropriate standard remains an issue. What these two cases have in common is that there is some degree of consensus, if only on the terms on which competition between the firms will occur. If, however, there are asymmetries between the firms, it may be impossible for them to reach even this limited kind of consensus.

Assume, for example, that firm 1, has established a dominant position with a large installed base and a powerful reputation. It will prefer incompatibility with a small rival in order to hold its customers. The smaller rival, firm 2, will prefer compatibility in order to derive benefits from the network that the larger firm has established. As Besen and Farrell indicate "The firms' problem is like the game between a big brother who wants to be left alone and a pesky little brother who wants to be with his big brother."

The payoff matrix now looks something like Table 24.4. There is no Nash equilibrium (in pure strategies) to this game if the firms make simultaneous choices—the two firms'

Table 24.4 The Pesky Little Brother (in U.S. dollars, millions)

		Firm 2	
		Technology 1	Technology 2
Firm 1	Technology 1	12, 4	16, 2
	Technology 2	15, 2	10, 5

There is no (pure strategy) Nash equilibrium in simultaneous play. Firm 1, the dominant firm (or big brother) prefers that the technologies be incompatible. Firm 2 (the little brother) prefers that they be compatible.

strategic choices are inconsistent.[7] Resolution of the game then comes down again to a question of timing and commitment.

Suppose that the dominant firm must commit to its technology choice first. This is perhaps the most plausible assumption, given that we have motivated the game by describing firm 1 as a pre-existing firm with a large installed base. In this case, the smaller firm 2 may actually enjoy a second-mover advantage. If firm 1 is committed to its existing technology either because it is costly to change or because such change would lose firm 1 the guaranteed patronage it now enjoys from its customers, it may be unable to prevent firm 2 from following. In this case, firm 2's clear choice will be to follow with a compatible system, precisely the outcome firm 1 had hoped to avoid.

Two tactics might be available to firm 1 that would prevent firm 2 from imitating its lead and offer firm 1 relief from its "pesky little brother." These are: (1) aggressive protection of its property rights and (2) changing its technology frequently. The first tactic relates to the use of patents. If the technology the dominant firm has built up is protected by patents, then imitation may be preventable through strict enforcement of the protection such patents give and by building up a stock of sleeping patents that make it difficult for a smaller firm to invent around the current technology.

Alternatively, firm 1 can try to hamper firm 2's imitation efforts by changing its technology frequently. This, of course, can be expensive and runs the risk of alienating users of the existing installed base unless they can be protected by, for example, being given favorable access to the new generation of products. The advantage to this approach is that the target at which the smaller rival is aiming is constantly shifting in ways that are difficult for the small firm to predict. If you really want to avoid your pesky little brother, don't tell him where you are going!

In short, competition over technology has a variety of implications. Often, there may be large social gains from all firms adopting a common technical approach. But the incentive for firms to differentiate their products, as well as the rivalry over which technology should become the industry standard can frequently thwart the realization of such gains. While the gains from price competition are generally clear, the network externality effects make the gains from technology competition more ambiguous.

---

[7] With a game of this type with a finite number of strategies, there is always a Nash equilibrium in mixed strategies in which the firms randomize their choice of technologies, but we shall not consider this equilibrium.

Reality Checkpoint

The Battle for a High (Definition) Standard

In the later 1970s, Sony introduced the BetaMax technology for videocassette recorders (VCR's) and thereby also initiated the war with the Video Home System (VHS), initially engineered by JVC Corporation, over the format standard for VCRs. Of course, Sony eventually lost that war. VHS won out as the standard and a lot of consumers found themselves owning an increasingly obsolete BetaMax machine as more and more films were issued in VHS format. Then DVDs came along. Now, some 30 years later, Sony is involved in another battle over the format for television reproduction technology.

Sony is one of a number of electronics firms pushing the Blu Ray technology for the next generation of DVDs that will support high-density (HD) broadcasts. Its rival, Toshiba, and its allies, however, have opted for a different format known technically as the Advanced Optical Disc (AOD) format. Both technologies use a shorter wavelength blue-violet laser technology, in contrast to the 650nm-wavelength red laser technology used in traditional DVD formats. As a result, the modern technologies use a finer beam and are capable of storing and reading a much greater amount of information than the older DVD technologies.

Each side has a lot at stake and has fought hard to make its technology the industry standard. For its part, Sony has built the Blu Ray technology into its Play Station 3 game console. In addition, it has directed its film studios (including MGM) to issue high-density DVDs only in Blu Ray format, and persuaded both Fox and Disney to do the same with their films. The Toshiba group, which includes Microsoft, has countered by incorporating the AOD format into Microsoft's XBox 360 console and by getting Universal to restrict its high-density DVD film releases to this format, as well. Paramount and Warner are currently issuing HD DVDs in both formats.

All this has been bad news for retailers and consumers. Store owners are not sure which format of film to stock. Customers have been reluctant to buying a high-definition disc player not knowing whether it will become the next BetaMax machine or not. Of course, low sales for HD disc players also means low sales for HD DVDs. The only hope so far has been the emergence of machines that can play both formats. The South Korean firm, LG Electronics has begun to market such a machine and others may soon follow. Unfortunately, the current price for such a machine, just over $1,000, is about the same as one would pay to buy two separate machines, one using Blue Ray technology and one using the AOD format.

At present, Blu Ray seems to have the advantage in terms of support from Hollywood and other film-makers issuing films in its format. Yet the alternative HD machines generally sell for less than a Blu Ray player. So, as of this writing, it remains anyone's guess as to which will format will ultimately win this standards war. Both use a laser that's violet blue but until the battle is over, a lot of people will mostly be seeing red.

Source: N. Wingfield, "Format Face-Off: Bringing the DVD War Home," *Wall Street Journal*, June 20, 2006, p. D1; and W. Mossberg, "Don't Get Caught in a Losing Battle over DVD Technology," *Wall Street Journal*, March 8, 2007, p. B1.

24.4   NETWORK GOODS AND PUBLIC POLICY

Our analysis of network services suggests many ways in which the market mechanism may fail to produce an efficient outcome. In some cases, a socially desirable service may fail to be provided. In other cases, multiple possible outcomes raise the possibility that the market may choose the wrong equilibrium and lock into an inferior technology. Competition may not be a feasible market structure. Moreover, even where feasible, competition may not be a remedy for these failures. To the contrary, competition may intensify the rush to a particular standard or technology, which later is realized to be inferior. Competition may also lead firms to reject compatibility even when it might actually be desirable. When the market will only support one system or network, competition is likely to be very intense and border on predatory conduct. How should public policy deal with these issues?

It is important to understand that in many respects, the problems raised by network effects are not new. The presence of dramatic scale economies and externalities have long been recognized as potential sources of market failure. Large scale economies make marginal cost pricing unlikely because such large scale economies means that marginal cost is below average cost over a wide range of production. Further, even when it is possible to operate at a sufficiently large size that all the scale economies are exploited, doing so will likely imply that there is room for only a few firms. Similarly, externalities always imply a divergence between private and social benefit (or cost) with the result that market outcomes based on the maximizing choices of individuals and firms are not likely to be optimal.

Saying that the problems raised by network effects are not new, however, is not the same thing as saying that they are easy. Three problems are particularly difficult in the case of network goods. The first of these is the problem of detecting or proving anticompetitive behavior. The second is the difficulty of devising an appropriate remedy once anticompetitive actions have been identified. The third is determining the proper role that the government should play in coordinating the technology choices of different firms with a view towards achieving standardization.

Consider the problem of determining anticompetitive tactics. The presence of network externalities requires that the developer of a new product such as a facsimile machine sell to a large number of consumers in order to establish any market at all. In turn, this may well mean pricing below cost, at least initially. This may result in a competitor being driven out of the business. When later, the winning firm raises its price so as to earn a return on its investment, the historical record of selling below cost, eliminating a rival, and then raising price looks a lot like a case of predatory pricing. Indeed, such a record is essentially the evidence called for by Baumol (1979) to determine predation. (See Chapter 13.) Yet such a finding may simply reflect the need to price low so as to penetrate the market and the fact that the market can only support one supplier.

Similarly, the developer of a platform such as Windows or Wii or a DVD player requires that there be a large number of applications (programs, games, or films) available at a low cost in order to gain wide acceptance of the overall system. One way to achieve this aim is to produce and market such complementary goods oneself. Yet to the extent that one can only play Nintendo Wii cartridges on a Nintendo Wii machine the market outcome begins to look like illegal tying or possibly an attempt at foreclosure. To borrow from an example earlier in the text, Microsoft's Windows almost certainly gained from the availability of a compatible, low cost web browser. Yet Microsoft's decision to bundle its Explorer browser with Windows raised substantial concerns of tying with a view to driving Netscape out of the browser business.[8]

---

[8]   This point was made forcibly by Schmalensee (2000). See Fisher (2000) for an opposing point of view. Note that if Schmalensee's argument is that in some industries, e.g., web browsers, only one firm can survive this is really a statement that such a market is a natural monopoly of the type described in Chapter 2. The only difference being that here the scale economy lies on the demand side via the network externality. See also Eisenach and Lenard (1999).

With regard to technology adoption and product improvement, the case of Microsoft is again relevant. Sun Microsystems' Java programming language offered the possibility of greatly enhancing the functionality of Windows. However, this required that Windows be made compatible with Java. Microsoft was generally reluctant to do this at least in part because there was a widespread view that Java could provide the basis for an alternative applications platform if it ever became widely accepted. Making it compatible with Windows would have this effect. So, while providing that compatibility might greatly improve the technology available for PC users, it might also provide an opportunity for entry to a new rival. Does Microsoft's reluctance in this case reflect an illegal effort to deter entry?[9]

As difficult as it is to identify anticompetitive behavior in network or systems markets, devising an appropriate remedy when such actions are discovered is perhaps even more problematic. The just mentioned case of Microsoft and Sun Microsystems is instructive in this connection. Is the appropriate policy to force Microsoft to make Windows compatible with Java? Adoption of such a policy would place the government in the awkward position of pushing a particular technology, and it is far from clear that the government has the skill to do this well. What if *Java* really does not offer any real improvement on the Windows product? Indeed, what if there is an alternative programming language that would offer much greater enhancement? That alternative may never break through if antitrust officials require that Windows work with Java. In other words, antitrust policy may also result in an inferior technology lock-in.

This raises the general question as to the proper role for the government in coordinating the technology choices of different firms with a view towards achieving standardization. Consider the market for mobile telephone service. As a result of legislation by the European Parliament, all mobile phones in Europe adhere to the same technical standard. Consequently, a British resident traveling on the continent can use her mobile phone to make calls in Italy just as easily as she can at home. This was much less feasible for U.S. residents, in part, because there was no centralized authority coordinating the digital standard of American mobile phone companies. Instead, the mobile phone services in the U.S. initially adopted four different standards and inter-service communication was impossible. On the other hand, the presence of these different standards has led to increased competition and technical development. As mobile phone companies in the U.S. have expanded their coverage over wider and wider areas, the regional reach of an American consumer has become comparable to that of a European one with the American consumer enjoying the added benefit of systems competition and technical advance.

24.5   EMPIRICAL APPLICATION
Network Externalities in Computer Software—Spreadsheets

As noted earlier, computer software such as operating systems and web browsers are likely to exhibit important network effects. Users care about being able to run their programs on the computers of their friends or business associates. The more people use a specific software package or the more compatible a software package is with add-on programs, the more valuable it should be. Gandal (1994) offers empirical evidence of this phenomenon from the early days of desktop computing.

---

[9]   Microsoft and Sun eventually did reach an agreement of sorts, but Sun was never happy with it and the agreement was later abandoned.

A spreadsheet was initially a pencil-and-paper operation. Essentially, it was a large sheet of paper with columns and rows organizing all the relevant data about a firm's transactions. Its name comes from the fact that costs or revenues connected to a specific operation were spread or displayed over the sheet in a manner allowing sums over a given row or column. In that way, management is able to focus on a specific factor, say energy costs, in making an informed decision about company operations. The advantage of a spreadsheet format is that if a given cost factor or revenue assumption is changed, decision-makers can trace through the implications of this change rather quickly. However, there is a natural limit to the speed of such adjustments when spreadsheets are "hard copy" and changes must be made by hand.

Beginning about 1980, electronic spreadsheets suitable for use on desktop computers began to make their commercial appearance. The first of these was VisiCalc (Visible Calculator). Computerization greatly enhanced the speed with which managers could assess the impact of cost or revenue changes. It thereby greatly increased the usefulness of spreadsheets in daily operations. Demand for such products grew and so did the supply. Soon, there were a number of spreadsheet programs including SuperCalc, VP Planner, PlanPerfec; Quatro Pro, Multiplan, Excel, and Lotus 1–2–3.

These early products differed both from each other and over time. The earliest versions had very limited, if any, graphing abilities. Some could link entries in one spreadsheet to others in another spreadsheet. Some could not. Only a few were able to link with external data and incorporate that data into the spreadsheet cells directly. The most flexible of all was the Lotus 1–2–3 program. Throughout the late 1980s and into the 1990s, this was the dominant product. Indeed, an important attribute of other spreadsheet programs was whether or not they were Lotus compatible.

Gandal (1994) notes that spreadsheet demand will likely be characterized by important network economies because users like to be able to share their information and the results of their spreadsheet analyses with each other. Gandal then identifies three features of a spreadsheet program that should promote such networking. The first is whether or not the program was compatible with Lotus 1–2–3, the dominant product. This is measured by a variable *LOCOMP* equal to 1 if the program is Lotus compatible and 0 if it is not. The second network attribute is *EXTDAT*. This is a variable that takes on the value 1 if the program can import files from external data sources and 0 if it cannot. The final network feature is another 1,0 variable *LANCOM* that indicates whether or not the program can link independent users through a local area network.

Gandal (1994) hypothesizes that if network externalities are present in the spreadsheet market, then a program's market price will be higher if it has any of the three features just described, i.e., when for that product, any of the variables *LOCOMP*, *EXTDAT*, or *LANCOM* is positive. A function that specifies how product price changes as the product's attributes change is known as an hedonic function. Estimating such functions is usually done by ordinary least squares (OLS) in an hedonic price regression. Gandal (1994) gathered data for 91 computerized spreadsheet products over the six years, 1986 through 1991. His basic regression equation is:

$$\ln p_{it} = \alpha_0 + \alpha_1 TIME87_t + \alpha_2 TIME88_t + \alpha_3 TIME89_t + \alpha_4 TIME90_t + \alpha_5 TIME91_t$$
$$+ \beta_1 LMINRC_{it} + \beta_2 LOTUS_{it} + \beta_3 GRAPHS_{it} + \beta_4 WINDOW_{it}$$
$$+ \gamma_1 LOCOMP_{it} + \gamma_2 EXTDAT_{it} + \gamma_3 LANCOM_{it} + \varepsilon_{it}$$

The dependent variable is the natural log of the price of spreadsheet model *i* in year *t*. Not including the constant, the first five variables are time dummy variables equal to 1 if the year is that indicated by the dummy and zero otherwise. These variables pick up the pure effects of time on spreadsheet program prices while holding the quality attributes fixed. The next four variables are variables that pick up specific features that should add to the value of a spreadsheet program. *LMINRC* is the natural log of the minimum of the maximum number of rows or columns that the spreadsheet can handle. This is meant to capture the sheer computing power of the program. *LOTUS* is a 1,0 dummy variable indicating whether the product is a Lotus spreadsheet. This term captures any brand premium that Lotus enjoyed during these years. GRAPHS is a 1,0 dummy variable indicating whether or not the program can construct pie, bar, and line graphs. *WINDOW* indicates the number of windows a program can handle on a screen simultaneously. Of course, the last three variables are the networking effects described earlier. If there are network externalities, the coefficients on these variables should be significantly positive.

Gandal's (1994) results are presented in the Table 24.5. The first regression shown is the estimated hedonic equation described above. Note that all the attributes hypothesized to raise the value of a spreadsheet program do in fact exert a significantly positive effect on its price. There is a strong brand premium for Lotus. There is an almost as strong premium for programs that have graphing abilities. Most important of all however, the three networking variables are very strongly positive. *LOCOMP*, *EXTDAT*, and *LANCOM* all have a substantial positive effect on a program's price.

Regression 2 shows the effects of allowing the coefficients to change over time. Gandal (1994) splits the sample in half and adds as regressors, values of the independent variables multiplied by 1 if the observation comes in the second half of the sample. Most of these interacted variables are not significant. However, the coefficients on both *MINRC* and *LINKING* do change over time as indicated by the coefficients on *TMINRC* and *TLINKING*. These coefficients are interpreted as the difference between the marginal value of these features in the first half of the sample and that value in the second half of the sample. Note that this

Table 24.5 Hedonic regression results for spreadsheet programs, 1986–91

Variable	Regression 1		Regression 2	
	Coefficient	t-statistic	Coefficient	t-statistic
CONSTANT	3.76	(12.31)	3.12	(9.50)
TIME87	−0.06	(−0.38)	−0.07	(−0.43)
TIME88	−0.44	(−2.67)	−0.45	(−3.03)
TIME89	−0.70	(−4.20)	0.92	(1.71)
TIME90	−0.79	(−4.90)	0.90	(1.67)
TIME91	−0.85	(−5.30)	0.85	(1.59)
LMINRC	0.11	(1.59)	0.26	(3.24)
LOTUS	0.56	(4.36)	0.46	(3.62)
GRAPHS	0.46	(3.51)	0.52	(4.18)
WINDOW	0.17	(2.14)	0.14	(1.92)
LINKING	0.21	(1.91)	0.26	(2.00)
LOCOMP	0.72	(5.28)	0.66	(5.17)
EXTDAT	0.55	(4.05)	0.57	(3.93)
LANCOM	0.21	(1.65)		
TLANCOM			0.61	(3.28)
TLMINRC			−0.34	(−3.07)
TLINKING			−0.31	(−1.49)

Table 24.6   Quality adjusted price indices for spreadsheet programs, 1986–91

	1986	*1987*	*1988*	*1989*	*1990*	*1991*
Price index from regression 1	1.00	0.94	0.64	0.49	0.45	0.42
Price index from regression 2	1.00	0.93	0.64	0.50	0.48	0.46

regression includes *TLANCOM* but not *LANCOM*. This is because connecting to local area networks was generally not possible for any program prior to the second half of the sample.

Gandal (1994) prefers Regression 2 as the better specification of the hedonic price equation. Note again that it implies strong network externalities. The coefficients on *LOCOMP*, *EXTDAT*, and *TLANCOM* are all very significantly positive. Consumers are willing to pay a lot extra for spreadsheets that others can use either because they are Lotus-compatible, can easily import data from external programs, or can exchange information over a local area network. These effects are powerful. Because the dependent variable is the log of the price, the coefficient is easily interpreted as the percentage increase in price a consumer would pay for that feature. Thus, being Lotus-compatible raised the price of a spreadsheet program by 66 percent according to Gandal's (1994) estimates. A program's ability to import data from an external source raised the price by 57 percent.

A frequent use of hedonic price regressions is to construct price indices that trace the movement of a commodity's price over time. This is often difficult to do because we do not have an easy way to adjust for quality. A television set today may cost much more that a television set from 10 years ago. However, it would be wrong to interpret all of that price increase as inflation since today's television set has many more features than that of an earlier set such as high definition, DVD compatibility, and a flat screen, to name just a few. Because the hedonic regression controls explicitly the value of quality features, it permits the easy construction of a quality-corrected price index by focusing on the changes that are due simply to the passage of time, i.e., holding quality constant. In Regression 1, these changes are fully captured by the year specific dummies. Since the dependent variable is ln p_{it}, the predicted price for a spreadsheet of constant quality in any year: $p_{it} = e^{\alpha_t YEAR_t}$ where the $YEAR_t$ variable is the dummy for that observation and α_t is the coefficient estimated for that dummy. If we normalize so that the price index P_t is 1 in the first year of 1986, then equation 1 says that the price index will be $e^{-0.06}$ in 1987; $e^{-0.44}$ in 1988; and so on. For Regression 2, constructing the quality-adjusted price index is slightly more complicated because the value of the some of the attributes also changes over time, but the basic idea is the same. We present Gandal's (1994) estimated spreadsheet price indices for both regressions above (Table 24.6). It indicates that over the six-year period for which Gandal (1994) collected data, the quality-adjusted price of spreadsheet programs—like the price of much software and hardware in this time period, declined substantially. Here, the decline exceeded 50 percent.

Summary

In this chapter, we have investigated the product markets exhibiting important "network externalities." In such markets, the value of the good or service to any one consumer increases as the total number of consumers using the product increases.

Services with important network effects, such as telecommunications and home electronics, play an increasingly large role in modern economies.

Markets with strong network effects present special problems. Competition to establish a network service can be unusually fierce, leading to low prices that can be difficult to distinguish from predation. Often, such competition will result in only one firm surviving so that the market's ultimate structure is one of monopoly. There is also a nontrivial risk that the service will be underdeveloped or not developed at all. Similarly, the course of technical development exhibits a path dependency in which the market may eventually lock into an inferior technology.

There are no easy solutions to the problems raised by network goods. On the one hand, the possibilities for anticompetitive outcomes seem sufficiently clear that such markets necessarily invite examination by the antitrust authorities. Yet it must also be acknowledged that it is not easy either to identify anticompetitive actions clearly or to devise workable remedies to the market failures to which network services are prone. Such tensions have dominated the debate over policies regarding the telecommunications industry and other "new economy" markets in the past. They will no doubt continue to be important in the future.

Problems

1. Two banks compete for the checking and savings deposit business of a small town. Each bank has its own ATM network that works only on its own bankcards, but bank 1 has three times as many ATM machines as bank 2. Depositors value a bank's services as an increasing function of the number of machines on the network. Bank 2 approaches bank 1 and suggests that they merge their ATM networks so that depositors of either bank can use either bank's machines.
    a. Is this merger in the interest of deposit consumers in general?
    b. Do you think that bank 1 will agree with bank 2's proposal?

2. Assume that consumers contemplating buying a network service have reservation prices uniformly distributed on the interval [0, 50] (measured in dollars). Demand by a consumer with reservation price w_i for this service is:

$$q_i^D = \begin{cases} 0 \text{ if } fw_i < p \\ 1 \text{ if } fw_i \geq p \end{cases}.$$

    a. Calculate the demand function for this service.
    b. What is the critical mass if price is set at $5?
    c. What is the profit-maximizing price for the service?

3. Many social customs exhibit network effects. To this end, consider a party given by a group of individuals at a small university. The group is called the Outcasts and has 20 members. It holds a big party on campus each year. These parties are good, but are especially good the more people in attendance. As a result, the number of people who actually come to the Outcasts party depends on how many people are expected to attend. The more people that are expected to attend, the more fun it will be for each attendee and, hence, the more people who actually will come. These effects are captured by the following equation: $A = 20 + 0.95A^e$. Here, A is the number of people actually attending the party. This is equal to the 20 Outcast members plus 0.95 times the number of partygoers A^e that are expected to go.
    a. If potential party attendees are sophisticated and understand the equation describing actual party attendance, how many people are likely to attend the Outcasts party?
    b. Suppose that each party attendee costs the Outcasts $2 in refreshments so that the Outcasts need to charge a fee p for attending the party. Suppose as well that when going to the party requires paying a fee, the equation for attendance is: $A = 20 + 0.95A^e - p$. What value of p should the Outcasts set if they want to maximize their profit from the party? How many people will come to the party at that price?

4. Two firms are competing in their choice of technologies. The payoff matrix for the game between them is given below
    a. Identify constraints on the payoffs a–h that are such that the firms' choices reflect network externalities.

b. Assume that the constraints in (a) are satisfied. Identify further constraints that must be satisfied for the game between the two firms to be of the form

(i)   Tweedledum and Tweedledee,
(ii) the Battle of the Sexes,
(iii) the Pesky Little Brother.

		Firm 2	
		Technology 1	Technology 2
Firm 1	Technology 1	a,b	c,d
	Technology 2	e,f	g,h

References

Arthur, W. Brian. 1989. "Competing Technologies, Increasing Returns, and Lock-in by Historical Events." *Economic Journal* 99 (March): 116–31.

Baumol, W. J. 1979. "Quasi-permanence of Price Reductions: A Policy for Prevention of Predatory Pricing." *Yale Law Journal* 89 (November): 1–26.

Besen, S. M. and J. Farrell. 1994. "Choosing How to Compete: Strategies and Tactics in Standardization." *Journal of Economic Perspectives* 8 (Spring): 117–31.

David, P. A. 1985. "Clio and the Economics of QWERTY." *American Economic Review, Papers and Proceedings* 75 (May): 332–7.

Economides, N. 1996. "The Economics of Networks." *International Journal of Industrial Organization* 14 (October): 673–99.

Eisenach, J. A. and T. M. Lenard. 1999. *Competition, Innovation and the Microsoft Monopoly: Antitrust in the Digital Marketplace*. Amsterdam: Kluwer Academic.

Farrell, J. and G. Saloner. 1985. "Standardization, Compatibility and Innovation." *Rand Journal of Economics* 16 (Spring): 70–83.

Fisher, F. 2000. "The *IBM* and *Microsoft* Cases: What's the Difference?" *American Economic Review* 90 (May): 180–3.

Gandal, N. 1994. "Hedonic Price Indexes for Spreadsheets and A Test for Network Externalities." *Rand Journal of Economics* 25 (Spring): 160–70.

Liebowitz, S. and S. Margolis. 1990. "The Fable of the Keys." *Journal of Law and Economics* 33 (April): 1–25.

Rohlfs, J. 1974. "A Theory of Interdependent Demand for a Communications Service." *Bell Journal of Economics* 5 (Spring): 16–37.

Schmalensee, R. 2000. "Antitrust Issues in Schumpeterian Industries." *American Economic Review, Papers and Proceedings* 90 (May): 192–6.

25

Auctions and Auction Markets

An interesting feature of the telecommunications revolution and the growth of e-commerce over the past 20 years has been the explosion of auction markets. Millions of consumers all over the world now participate daily in auctions. In part, this reflects the fact that auctions are an exciting way to buy and sell. At least as important, however, has been the ability of the Internet to reduce significantly the costs of matching particular buyers and sellers. The leader in this development is, of course, e-Bay which through its operations in the U.S. and elsewhere auctioned over $20 billion worth of goods among over 40 million confirmed users who either bid, bought or sold in 2005.[1]

Auctions, however, started long before the Internet came along. Indeed, they have existed for thousands of years. Herodotus writes of a market for auctioning off wives in Babylonia in 500 BC. In AD 193, the Praetorian Guard auctioned off the rule of the Roman Empire to Marcus Didius Salvius Julianus for a bid of 25,000 sesterces. Today, the two most famous auction houses are probably Sotheby's (U.S.) and Christies (U.K.) each of which dates back to the 1700s. These auction houses specialize in the sale of rare antiques and artwork, goods whose value is difficult to determine because there is a question of taste and opinion and because the value depends on market conditions that are difficult to forecast.

The sale of a good whose value is difficult to assess is exactly the kind of transaction that suits an auction because one needs a sizable number of interested buyers (or sellers) in order to get bids that reflect the spectrum of opinions as to the item's true value. Until recently, it has been much easier to incur the relatively high cost of bringing together such a critical mass of interested buyers for auctions focused on rather specialized markets, such as art, antique furniture, and race horses. Yet as we just noted, recent innovations in information technology and e-commerce have significantly lowered the cost of matching interested buyers and sellers. As a result, auctions are among the most popular sites and the fastest-growing business model on the Internet. Nor is the Internet the only venue for increasing auction use. Many markets that have traditionally been regulated such as electricity and telecommunications now use auctions for trading.

Auctions bring together different people with different values and different information. Whether one considers the potential buyers who go online to e-Bay or those who go to country

---

[1] See Annual Report and the *Silicon Valley Business Journal*, various issues.

auctions, the fact is that the different bidders at any auction will typically have different valuations for the goods being sold at that site. This may simply reflect different preferences. For example, a decorator who prefers a colonial style will value a colonial rocking chair more highly than an Art Deco chair. The reverse is true for the Art Deco decorator. When each participant in an auction has a different or private value for the good being auctioned we say that the auction is a private value auction. Most often individual buyers' private values for the good will be known only to themselves.

Differences in information regarding the value of the good being auctioned, rather than differences in preferences, are another source of variation among auction participants. A common value auction is one in which the good being auctioned has one true value, but this value is not known to potential buyers. Moreover, the information that each potential buyer has for estimating the true value differs across the population of such buyers. A good example of a common value auction is the auction of rights to explore and drill for oil. In this case the bidders are oil companies who have performed tests on the oil tract and have made some estimate of the amount of oil present and then worked out a valuation for the rights to the oil tract. However, because the companies have performed the tests in different places they are likely to have different estimates and different valuations of how much the rights are worth. Yet there is just one true amount of oil present and thus only one true value of the rights to explore and drill for oil on the tract. The weekly bidding on the financial markets for U.S. Treasury securities offers another example of a common value auction.

For the most part in this chapter we will consider single unit auctions or those auctions in which a single unit of some good is to be auctioned. However, in many economic markets, such as in electricity or communications, there are multiple units of the good, which are being auctioned. These auctions are called multi-unit auctions.

25.1 A BRIEF TAXONOMY OF AUCTIONS

Before the advent of the Internet auctions often took place in a crowded room of hushed people. Those who wanted an item being auctioned off would raise their hands in response to the auctioneer's plea "Do I hear $5, do I hear $10 . . . ?" When the auctioneer finally cried "Going, going, gone" the auction ended and the last person to raise their hand won the good at the last price called by the auctioneer. This kind of auction is called an *ascending-bid* or *English* auction. It is probably the arrangement that the word auction first brings to mind for most people. However, the English auction is just one of a number of different auction types and not necessarily the most common. For example, rather than starting low and letting the price of the good rise with each successive bid, the auctioneer could have instead begun the auction with at an extremely high price—one that exceeds anyone's reasonable valuation. The auctioneer could then reduce the price and keep on reducing it until some one in the room raises their hand. This type of auction in which the first one to bid wins the good is called a *descending-bid* auction. It is in fact how flowers have long been sold at auction in Holland and for that reason is often called a *Dutch* auction.

Bidders participating in an ascending bid auction can watch the bidding and have multiple opportunities to place a bid. In a Dutch auction, bidders observe no bids other than the winning one. Once a price is reached at which someone will buy the item, the auction ends. In this respect, the Dutch auction is strategically identical to what is called a *sealed bid* auction. This is an auction in which the seller or auctioneer solicits a single bid in a sealed envelope from each interested buyer. The envelopes are then opened and the highest bidder wins the auction. The similarity with a Dutch auction is that, here again, no bidder can observe any other bids.

Sealed-bid auctions, however, are not all the same. In particular, such auctions are usually divided into one of two types. One of these is referred to as a *first-price* auction while the second is referred to as a *second-price* auction. In a *first-price* auction the highest bidder pays the amount she bid whereas in a *second-price* auction she pays the amount bid by the *next* highest bidder.

25.1

25.1 Show that a dominant bidding strategy in an English auction is to continue bidding as long as the price in the auction is less than your true value of the good.

Practice Problem

25.2   THE REVENUE EQUIVALENCE THEOREM

There is an interesting parallel between the four auction types that was first recognized by Nobel Laureate, William Vickrey in his classic 1961 paper. To see this, let's start by imagining that the chair of the economics department at your university decides to auction off a signed copy of the textbook you are currently reading at an English auction. Let's suppose that you would be willing to pay at most $85.00 to win our book and that, unknown to you, this is the highest valuation of anyone in the class. Suppose further that the class is comprised of 170 students whose individual valuations may be ranked and which run from $0.50 all the way up to your own value of $85, increasing by 50¢ with each student. Bidding starts at $0.50 and you and your classmates raise your hands as the chair bids up the price in 1¢ increments. With this procedure, it is inevitable that the price will eventually rise to the point at which only you and one other bidder remain, namely, at the price of $84.50. At the next round however, when the chair increases the bid to $84.51 your rival will drop out. You will then be the sole student with a hand raised. So you win the auction at a price of $84.51.

Let's now consider what the outcome would have been if instead your chair had auctioned off the textbook using a second-price sealed bid auction. For the moment, let's assume that in this auction all the bidders write their true willingness to pay for the signed text on a piece of paper and put it in a sealed envelope. (We will show below that such a bidding strategy is in fact a dominant strategy in a *second-price* sealed bid auction.) With each student bidding her true reservation price, your bid will be $85 and the next highest bid will be $84.50. You will again be the winner. However, because it is a second-price auction, you will not pay $85, but only $84.50. Note that this is very close to the $84.51 that you paid in the ascending bid auction. In short, if bidding one's true valuation is an optimal strategy, then the English auction and the second price sealed bid auction yield essentially identical outcomes.

Now let's investigate whether bidding based on one's true valuation is indeed optimal. To understand why it is, note that in a *second-price* sealed bid auction, the bid you submit only determines whether or not you win the auction. It does not affect the price that you will actually pay if you do win. That price is determined by the value of the second highest bidder. Therefore, bidding less than your true value of the good will only lower your chance of winning a *second-price* sealed bid auction. It does not change the price that you pay if you do win. There is then no advantage to bidding *less* than your true value. What about bidding more? Increasing your bid above your true willingness to pay will increase the probability that you win only in the case when there is another bidder whose valuation is higher than yours. Otherwise increasing your bid has no effect. Yet if you win in these circumstances you will end up paying the other bidder's valuation—one that is higher than your own. In other words, you will end up paying more for the good than it is worth to you. Therefore, bidding honestly is a dominant strategy in a *second-price* sealed-bid auction. As we have just seen, however, when everyone does this the outcome is equivalent to what occurs in an English auction.

Following Vickrey (1961), we have just established that an English auction and a second-price sealed bid auction yield the same outcome if bidders pursue optimal strategies. This is important. For sellers who want to maximize their revenue from the auction, this fact implies that the choice between these two auction types is irrelevant. The seller will receive the same revenue either way. However, a seller may still wish to consider the two remaining types, the Dutch auction and the first-price sealed bid auction. What will happen in these two cases and how does this compare with the outcome of the English auction process? Here again, Vickrey (1961) provides the key insight.

We have already noted that the Dutch and first price sealed bid auctions are strategically identical. This is because they share two crucial features. One is that is in each case, a bidder has no additional information about the other bidders' valuations before making a bid. Instead, the bidder must simply bid based on her own valuation. The second feature common to these two auction types is that what one bids affects *both* one's chance of winning *and* what one pays. In both the Dutch auction and the first-price sealed-bid auction the winner pays the price that was bid to win the auction. This means that in each setting, bidders need to think strategically about what to bid in these settings.

Consider first a bidder's optimal strategy in a *first-price* sealed bid auction. Suppose that there are N bidders participating in the auction. Each bidder knows, of course, her own private valuation of the good being auctioned. Let us assume as well that each bidder knows the general distribution from which the other bidder's true valuations are draw. With these assumptions, it's easy to see that no bidder has an incentive to submit a bid above her true value. If a bidder did so and won the auction she would end up paying a price greater than her true value, which means she actually loses. We can also see that the bidder who has the highest valuation of the good should, if bidding optimally, win the auction. If the highest valuation bidder did not win because she submitted a bid that lost to say, the second highest bidder then she could always do better by increasing her bid slightly above the value of the bid that won and below her own.

These points suggest a possible winning strategy for any bidder. This is that she bid at least the valuation of the bidder with the next highest valuation. This insures that she will never lose to someone with a lower valuation of the good. The only difficulty is that, by assumption, no bidder knows the next highest valuation. Each only knows her own maximum willingness to pay. So how should a bidder proceed?

Clearly, a bidder needs to make an estimate of the next highest willingness to pay relative to her own. Let's consider how she might do this. Suppose that the bidder knows that all of the N valuations were drawn from a uniform distribution and denote her valuation by v. Because the bidder is particularly interested in the next highest valuation compared with her own she will focus on the distribution of valuations between 0 and v. This means that the bidder acts as though the remaining $N - 1$ bidders have valuations drawn from a uniform distribution over the interval $[0, v]$. The question then becomes what is the best guess of the next highest valuation among these remaining $N - 1$ bids? That is, what is the expected value of the second highest valuation given that hers is the highest of N bids? Let's assume as we did before in the book auction that the values drawn by the other bidders are equally spaced on the interval. This assumption means basically that if we were to draw many, many samples of $N - 1$ values from the uniform distribution over $[0, v]$, then the average value of the highest draw in these samples would be $\dfrac{N-1}{N} v$, while the average value of the second highest would be $\dfrac{N-2}{N} v$, and the average value of the third highest would be $\dfrac{N-3}{N} v$, and so on. The lowest value on average would be $\dfrac{1}{N} v$.

For example, suppose that our bidder's valuation v is equal to \$85 and that there are 170 bidders in total participating in the auction. She can then proceed by assuming that the other bids below hers are equally spaced on the interval $[0, 85]$. The highest valuation in this interval would be $\dfrac{169}{170} \$85 = \$84.50$, the next highest $\dfrac{168}{170} \$85 = \$84$, the next to that $\dfrac{167}{170} \$85 = \$83.50$, and so on. The bidder's optimal strategy in the first price sealed bid auction therefore is to write down a bid of \$84.50. If she writes down more than this, she will pay more on average than is necessary. If she writes down less than this, she will on average lose the auction to someone who values the good less than she does.

The intuition of the foregoing argument is quite general. The bidder's objective is to acquire the auctioned good at the lowest possible price so long as that price does not exceed the bidder's own valuation of the object. For this reason, the bidder should condition her strategy on the assumption that her valuation is the highest because, if it is not, she will not wish to pay the price necessary to win. In turn, acting on the assumption that her valuation is the highest leads the bidder to bid the amount $\dfrac{N-1}{N} v$, which is the expected value of the second highest bidder. Recall however, that the Dutch auction shares all the critical features of a first-price sealed bid auction and so is strategically equivalent to that case. Such strategic equivalence implies that the optimal strategy must be the same in each case. Hence, the optimal strategy in a Dutch auction is for the bidder to raise her hand as soon as the price falls to $\dfrac{N-1}{N} v$. In short, the first-price sealed bid and the Dutch auctions both yield the same outcome. Note also, that this in fact yields the same winning bid as that which results in the English and second-price sealed bid auctions.

25.2

Practice Problem

You are bidding for an original John Lennon hat in a sealed bid first-price auction. You are one of eight bidders in this auction and the most you would be willing to pay for this hat is \$200. Show that your optimal strategy is to submit a bid of \$175.

In short, we have uncovered a very striking result. Regardless of whether the auction is English or Dutch, or first-price or second-price sealed bid, the outcome is the same. The winning bid in all four cases is identical. In our example, it is consistently \$84.50. This remarkable result is quite general and has been codified as auction theory's most well known theorem, the Revenue Equivalence theorem.[2] Informally, the Revenue Equivalence theorem simply states that the expected revenue from an auction is the same regardless of which of the four basic types of auctions are used. A formal statement of Revenue Equivalence is given below.

> *Revenue Equivalence Theorem* (*private values*): Assume that there are N risk-neutral bidders each of which has a privately known valuation v of a good to be sold at auction with v drawn from a continuous distribution $F(v)$ that is strictly increasing over the range $[\underline{v}, \bar{v}]$. Then any auction in which the object always goes to the buyer with the highest value of v, and in which any bidder with a value of $\underline{v}$ enjoys an expected surplus of zero, results in exactly the same expected payment for each bidder v and yields exactly the same revenue to the seller.

The Revenue Equivalence Theorem is a powerful result, in part, because it implies that auction design is not really an issue. There are, however, a number of conditions necessary for Revenue Equivalence to hold. For example, it must be the case that the auctioneer is understood by all bidders to report honestly the true value of the second-highest bid in a second-price sealed bid auction (often called a Vickrey auction in honor of his pioneering work). The problem is that the actual bids tendered are known only to the auctioneer. Consequently, the auctioneer could increase the seller's revenue by pretending that a bid just under the maximum winning bid was received and declaring that this fictitious bid is the second highest price to be paid by the winner. Thus, if six bids of $40, $60, $80, $100, $120, and $140 are submitted, the auctioneer could report that the second-highest bid was actually $139. The bidder offering $140 will still win but pay $19 above what she should have done. If this is a real possibility, then bidders in a Vickrey auction will reduce their bids in order to avoid such "rip-offs."

However, Lucking-Reily (2000) demonstrates that there may be ways to overcome the fear of auctioneer cheating in a Vickrey auction. Proxy bidding, the popular method of bidding on e-Bay, is something of a mix of an English and a Vickrey auction. An online bidder submits a both an initial bid for the object as well as a maximum reservation bid. e-Bay then raises the bid incrementally on behalf of the bidder up to the stated maximum value—a value that is kept secret from other e-Bay users. For example, suppose that you submit an initial bid of $20 for an out-of-print cover from a Grateful Dead album and that you simultaneously disclose to e-Bay that your maximum willingness to pay is $100. If the bidding stops at a price of $57, then that is the price that you will pay for the album cover. Of course, if this happens and if all bidders have, like you, submitted their true maximum willingness to pay then the reason that the bidding stops at $57 is because that is the second highest valuation among all bidders. So, once again, the winning bid will be equal to the second highest valuation.

Of course, it is possible that $57 was not the second highest price and that e-Bay is falsely claiming that value in order to claim a greater payment for itself. However, e-Bay makes considerable effort to persuade buyers that this is not the case. To begin with, e-Bay publishes a list of the losing bidders, their maximum bids and their email addresses after the auction closes. This permits the winning buyer to evaluate e-Bay's claim. In addition, e-Bay charges a relatively low commission from the sale of an object, roughly 5 percent or less.

---

[2] This result was first derived by Vickrey (1961) and then generalized by Myerson (1981) and Riley and Samuelson (1981).

Such a low commission means that e-Bay's primary interest is to encourage trades so as to garner as wide a circle of participants as possible. This too reduces their incentive to cheat. As noted, the great success of e-Bay strongly suggests that these tactics have worked and persuaded bidders to trust e-Bay's auctioneering. Properly designed then, the Vickrey auction should still be revenue equivalent to the others.

25.3   COMMON VALUE AUCTIONS

Suppose your university wants to offer coffee and light meals at the campus center and decides to auction off franchise rights to open a café. The auction type chosen is a first-price sealed bid design. Such an auction is called a common value auction because the café presumably has one true value, common to all participants. However, prior to the actual operation of the café that value is not known. Instead, each firm interested in bidding for the franchise can only estimate that value based on its own market research. Each will try to determine the expected number of students, faculty and staff that will eat there, what they will likely buy and at what price, and how much it will cost to serve them. However, it is crucial to remember that the true value of the café depends on what others are willing to pay for it. That is, although the bidders are different and will submit different bids, they are all trying to guess at the same thing, namely, the true market value of the café. What makes the bidders different here is not their personal valuation of the café but, instead, the fact that each has gathered somewhat different data or acquired different information regarding the café's true value. Presumably, if two bidders had collected exactly the same data they would have submitted identical bids. The usual case though is that each bidder will get a different signal and therefore form his or her own individual idea about the value of the café, even though ultimately that value is common to the entire market.

In general, the Revenue Equivalence Theorem does not hold for common value auctions. This is why our formal statement of the theorem contains the parenthetical phrase (private values). The reason behind this non-equivalence in the case of common values is, however, quite subtle. In what follows, we try to illustrate the argument in an intuitive manner.

25.3.1   The "Winner's Curse"

Consider again our café example. After estimating the expected revenue and cost of operating the café, each firm interested in bidding will have an idea or estimate of what the franchise is worth and can use this estimate in submitting a bid. Of course, no two firms are likely to come up with exactly the same estimate of the café's value. Each firm is likely to survey different students or talk to different suppliers or otherwise base its estimate on information specific to that firm. Indeed, these differences in the information that each firm uses are a major source of the differences in the firms' estimates of the café's value and in the subsequent differences in their submitted bids.

After receiving all the tendered bids, the university will award the franchise to the highest bidder. The winner of the franchise will, of course, be the firm that made the highest bid. Yet in light of how the firms determined the amount of their bids, winning could in fact spell bad news. Because winning means that every other firm bid less for the franchise, it is quite possible that the winner overpaid for the franchise. This downside to winning is a central feature of common value auctions and is called the *winner's curse*. The curse is that the winner of a common value auction often turns out to be the loser because the winner bids too much for the good. The franchise bidders will have collected different information about its true value and the winning bidder is likely the one who has the most optimistic information, and thus made the highest estimate of the value of the franchise. The winner's information is therefore the most likely to be upwardly biased. Consequently, a bid based on that information is likely to be too high.

Bidding in a common value auction therefore requires some sophistication. Let us continue to assume that the auction is a first-price sealed bid type. It should be clear that a bidder should not base his bid solely on the information he collected about the value of the good. He has to think about where this information came from, or alternatively, what kind of information the other bidders were likely to receive. Only by thinking this way can the bidder work out an estimate of the value of the good that will avoid the winner's curse. Suppose, for example, a bidder in our franchise auction knew that there were N bidders including him and that each bidder's estimate came from a uniform distribution, whose minimum is zero and whose maximum is $50,000. The bidder could then work out that the mean value of this distribution is $25,000, and that this value would, in fact, be the best or unbiased guess as to what is the true value of the franchise.

The difficulty is, of course, that a bidder is unlikely to know the upper limit or most optimistic estimate of the franchise's value. The bidder only knows the estimate he received and that the true value is uniformly distributed in the interval $[0, U]$ where U is currently unknown to him. How should he proceed?

Consider a bidder whose research leads to an estimate of $40,000 as the true vale of the café rights. However, he knows that this may well be an overestimate and he wants to avoid the winner's curse. One approach is for our bidder to assume that the estimate his research yielded is, in fact, the highest estimate obtained by any of the bidders. If so, then the bidder can use this information to work out a sensibly lower bid that should avoid the winner's curse.

What the bidder needs to do is to get a measure of the overall distribution of possible estimated values. The mean or average value of that distribution should be a good guess as to the true value of the café rights. He knows that the distribution runs from 0 to U. What he needs now is to get some idea of the value of U. Starting with the assumption that the $40,000 is the highest of all the estimates drawn, let the bidder make our standard assumption that the estimates drawn by the other $N - 1$ bidders are uniformly distributed or equally spaced on the interval $[0, U]$. This assumption means that if we were to draw many, many samples of N values from the uniform distribution then the average value of the *highest* draw in these samples would be $\dfrac{N}{N + 1}U$, where U is the upper limit of the uniform distribution. Since our bidder is assuming that his draw of $40,000 is the highest draw he can work out U from the equation $U = \dfrac{N + 1}{N}\$40,000$. For example, if the number of bidders were 10 in total then $U = \$44,000$.

Why does the bidder assume that his own estimate is the largest? Since U is not known, the bidder recognizes that there is a positive probability that others may have drawn higher estimates. However, in determining his bid what the bidder really cares about is the true value of the café rights *conditional* on his winning. So, the relevance of the higher estimates that others may have drawn is quite limited since if there are such higher estimates he is unlikely to win the café for himself. If our bidder does win the café though, then he can reasonably assume that his estimate was the highest or most optimistic. Since this is the scenario in which the true value of the café is relevant, our bidder will build his bidding strategy around it, i.e., he will work on the assumption that his estimate is the highest and then work out the best bid that minimizes his winner's curse should he actually be the winning bidder.

Once our bidder has assigned some value to the upper limit U of the distribution of estimates, he can work out his best guess regarding the mean value of that distribution. Continuing with our assumption that the distribution of estimates is uniform over the interval $[0, U]$ with $U = \$44,000$, the implied mean would be $22,000. Accordingly this is our bidder's best estimate of the true value of the franchise. Note how much lower this bid is relative to the original value of \$44,000. This reduction in the estimated value of the café rights should therefore be quite effective in eliminating the winner's curse. If all the bidders in the common value auction calculate their bids in this way, each will shade his initial estimate in the same manner. As a result, it will still be the case that the bidder who initially drew the highest estimate will win the auction. However the "curse" of winning will be much reduced.

In short, the prospect of a winner's curse induces buyers in a common value auction to shade their bids below their individual estimate of an item's true value. The worse the winner's curse, the more such shading will occur. This is the intuition as to why, in a formal sense, the Revenue Equivalence Theorem does not generally hold for common value auctions.[3] The reason is that different auction designs have different implications regarding the size of the winner's curse. In an English auction, for example, buyers get more and more information about the possible value as they watch the bid rise with each successive bid. In particular, they get increasing information about the lower bound of estimates for the café's value. In turn, this makes them more confident that the value is indeed high and so reduces the size of the winner's curse. Similarly, a second-price sealed bid auction can also lead to higher offers because the winner only pays the second highest bid. Of course, the weaker is the winner's curse effect the more aggressive will be the bidding and the greater the seller's revenue. The conventional ranking is that revenue is greatest for an English auction, next highest for Vickrey or second-price sealed bid auction and least for a first-price sealed bid auction which is equivalent to the case of a Dutch or descending price auction. However, this convention can break down when one considers slight departures from the standard common value case.[4]

25.3

Practice Problem

Suppose your local town is auctioning off a franchise to sell hot dogs at the July 4 celebration. You and your partner decide to bid for the franchise. Including you there are eight groups bidding in the auction. Your market research on expected attendance, hot dog consumption and costs suggests that the franchise is worth \$2,000. Suppose you believe that your estimate, as well as the other bidders' estimates, are generated independently from a uniform distribution that starts at zero. What is your optimal bid for the franchise assuming that the distribution of values is uniform? If yours is the winning bid are you cursed?

---

[3]   Strictly speaking, it is not so much the common value aspect that generates the break from revenue equivalence as it is the fact that the ascending auction reveals to the ultimate winner information regarding the signals or estimates of those bidders who drop out in a manner which lets him use that information in setting his bids whereas he cannot use that information in a sealed-bid process. Note also that Riley and Li (1997) show that the revenue difference between auction types may in practice be quite small, especially if the seller sets a sensible reserve price below which she will not sell.

[4]   This ranking originates from the famous paper of Milgrom and Weber (1982) on auctions with affiliated bidder values. See also, Milgrom (1989).

25.3.2   Almost Common Value Auctions

In our café example, we assumed that the true value was ultimately the same for everyone. The only difference among the bidders was the initial information that they had regarding precisely what that true value was. However, suppose that one of the bidders is the Starbucks chain and that winning the franchise is more valuable to it. This may be because winning will permit Starbucks to have a monopoly in the area, or because Starbucks can use its experience and buying power to operate the café more efficiently than can the other bidders. Whatever the reason, we will assume that if the café is truly worth v to all the other bidders, then it is worth $v + \$1,000$ to Starbucks. For example, if the true value of the café ultimately turns out to be $25,000 for all the non-Starbucks buyers, it is worth $26,000 to Starbucks. In this case, the café's value is not common to all buyers but the deviation from the common value case is relatively small. For this reason, this setting is often referred to as one of an almost-common value auction.

As it turns out, the small change involved in going from a common value auction to one with an almost common value can have very large consequences, as Klemperer (1998, 2002) in particular has emphasized.. The difference once again has to do with the winner's curse. In our example, all the non-Starbucks bidders face an exaggerated winner's curse. To beat Starbucks in the auction requires an extra large bid, but this just exacerbates the winner's curse. That extra $1,000 that was driving Starbucks' bid will not be there for the non-Starbucks winner who has to outbid Starbucks. Bidders are not stupid, however. The non-Starbucks firms will recognize the exaggerated winner's curse that they face and therefore bid even more conservatively than in our earlier analysis. This permits Starbucks to bid more aggressively because it now faces a reduced winner's curse. Recognizing this makes the others bid less aggressively and so on. The end result is that Starbucks will always win the bidding but that it will do so at a much reduced price relative to that paid in a pure common value auction because of the extra conservative bidding pursued by its rivals. Hence, another reason that Revenue Equivalence may break down is because different auction designs may raise or lower the ability of dominant or advantaged buyers like Starbucks to exploit that uncommon but almost common advantage.[5]

25.4   AUCTION DESIGN: LESSONS FROM INDUSTRIAL ORGANIZATION

Auction markets have become increasingly common. Firms use auctions to purchase supplies, consumers bid for a variety of products through on-line auction sites, and the government auctions off Treasury bonds, mineral rights, and wireless spectrum licenses. In short, auction markets are common. It should come as good news therefore that the tools of industrial organization can yield insight into the operation of such markets. From a public policy perspective, such analysis is likely to be most useful in considering the auctions run by national and local governments. Ideally, such auctions will result in prices that are efficient in that they are close to the true market value of the item in question. In practice, this means that items will be auctioned to those for whom they have the highest (marginal) value. Since this

---

[5]   The "Wallet Game" introduced in Bulow and Klemperer (2002) is a very accessible introduction to the complexities of almost common value auctions

means that the revenue from the auction will be maximized, we can link efficiency to revenue maximization in considering auction design. Therefore, our evaluation of different auction mechanisms will largely be based on which auction design generates the most revenue. For cases in which the government is the seller as in say, the auctioning of airwaves, focusing on revenue maximization is appropriate for another reason as well. This is that the revenue raised can be used to reduce taxes and therefore to alleviate any tax-induced distortions.

Let us start by recognizing that government-run auctions are—except in cases such as auctions of obsolete military weapons—nearly always of the common value or almost common value type. Government bonds, mineral rights, and spectrum licenses are all items whose value to any one buyer depends largely on what other buyers would willingly pay for them. This makes life more difficult because the alternative case of purely private value auctions is certainly much simpler. The Revenue Equivalence Theorem tells us that when bidders all have private values one type of auction is basically as good as another. Moreover, the auction outcome is efficient in that the winner will be the buyer who values the object the most and will pay a price equal to the valuation placed on the object by the buyer with the second-highest valuation, i.e., equal to the item's true opportunity cost as measured by the amount for which the winning bidder could sell it. Common value and almost common value auctions are, on the other hand, different. Here, revenue equivalence does not hold, and so auction design does matter. The source of revenue non-equivalence in this case can often be found in whether the auction design encourages bidders to enter the auction and in whether the design facilitates collusion among the bidders. Entry and collusion are of course issues that lie at the heart of industrial organization.

We begin by observing that our earlier analysis suggests that there is an advantage in an auction design that attracts many bidders. Recall that our optimum bid in the private value case was $\dfrac{N-1}{N} v = v - \dfrac{v}{N}$. Clearly, this bid increases as N grows.

However, it is worth noting that in common value auctions, the winner's curse also intensifies as the number of bidders who enter the auction increases. Recall our earlier café example only now assume that the auction is a Dutch or descending bid type. Suppose as before that you are again thinking of bidding \$22,000. If there are only 4 other bidders and none of them have indicated their willingness to buy as the price nears this point, you might not be too worried. If there are 40 other bidders, however, you might feel a good bit more hesitant. Being the high bidder out of a pool of five does not cause you to question very much your estimate of the café's value. Being the high bidder out of a pool of 41 though is quite different. When there are many bidders, the odds that your high estimate of the café's value is too generous rise considerably because the chances that someone will obtain an estimate far above the café's true value are much greater when there are 41 estimates than when there are five. Thus, the more bidders there are the greater is the potential winner's curse and, therefore, the more each buyer shades her bids. We generally expect an increase in the number of potential buyers to raise the price of a resource whose supply is fixed. Here however, the price-raising effect of more buyers is somewhat offset by the bid-reducing effect that enters into buyers' bidding strategies as they recognize the increasing winner's curse. Revenue maximization requires thinking carefully about which auction design can reduce the winner's curse.

As we noted before, the information revelation that accompanies an ascending auction can help to reduce the winner's curse in a common value auction. However, while an ascending auction reveals information and thus makes bidders more confident about their bid, it has the downside that the winner is unambiguously the one with the most optimistic estimate and this may intensify the winner's curse. Further, while the ascending auction works well in the common value case, it is highly sensitive to the asymmetries that are present in the almost common value auction case. Recall what happened when one of the bidders for our hypothetical café was Starbucks. Because Starbucks valued the café at slightly more than everyone else this intensifies the winner's curse for all other buyers. In turn, this induces all other bidders to shade their bids and thereby reduce the winner's curse that Starbucks faces. Indeed, once other buyers realize Starbucks advantage, they may drop out altogether allowing Starbucks to win the café rights at a very low price. In other words, the information revelation on an ascending auction is almost perfectly designed to reveal Starbucks bidding advantage and thereby result in a low winning bid for Starbucks.

The foregoing point is illustrated by the 1995 ascending auction for mobile phone licenses in the Los Angeles area, a real-world example discussed in Klemperer (2002). Pacific Telephone, the Baby Bell that then supplied fixed line telephone service, was certainly a well-known name in the area, and was widely reported to have made it clear to all potential bidders that it would bid whatever would be necessary to win the California market. While other firms did enter the auction for the Los Angeles license, the number of participants was much less than anticipated and the winning bid (paid by Pacific Telephone) of $26 per head of population was much lower than had been predicted. Indeed, a similar auction in the Chicago area in which consumer demand for mobile phone service was almost certainly *less* than in Los Angeles, resulted in a noticeably higher winning bid of $31 per head of population.

Another drawback to ascending auctions is that they may facilitate collusion. The repeated rounds of bidding do more than just reveal information about other buyers' estimated values. They also permit buyers to communicate and therefore to coordinate their bids. Cramton and Schwartz (1999) demonstrate this point in the context of the 1997 spectrum auctions conducted by the Federal Communications Commission (FCC). These auctions were ascending bid multi-unit auctions. A number of licenses were simultaneously auctioned off in an English auction. Cramton and Schwartz argue that different firms seemed to be signaling in their bids the identity number of the license areas that they were most interested in acquiring by matching the last three digits of their bid with their preferred area code, e.g., bidding $313,378 for license area 378. Such a bid communicates to others that the bidder truly wants this area and will refrain from bidding aggressively for other regions so long as other bidders do not bid aggressively for area 378.

A similar story is told in Klemperer (2002) about a 1999 spectrum auction in Germany. In that case, there were 10 licenses to be auctioned off and bids had to increase by a minimum of 10 percent. One bidder, Mannesman, bid 18.18 million DM per MHz on licenses 1 to 5, and bid 20 million DM per MHz on licenses 6 to 10. Now observe that if you increase 18.18 by 10 percent the result is 20. T-Mobile, the other main bidder for these licenses, later admitted that it made just such a calculation. It concluded that Mannesman's bid represented something of an offer along the following lines: T-Mobile could have licenses 1 to 5 for 20 million DM per Mhz (the minimum amount it would need to beat Mannesman's bid) if it would not make any further bids for licenses 6 to 10. In fact, that is exactly what happened. The auction ended after just two rounds with all 10 licenses going for 20 million DM per Mhz—well below anyone's estimate of the true willingness to pay of either T-Mobil or Mannesman.

Given the uncertain mix of advantages and disadvantages of an ascending auction, many have suggested the use of a first-price sealed bid design. In a sealed bid auction, the bidding process itself cannot be used to coordinate bids or to reveal asymmetries. Indeed, a sealed bid auction tends to encourage less advantaged bidders to participate. To understand why,

Reality Checkpoint
This Wellcome Bid Could Have Been Higher

We have focused on the issues of auctions and auction design from the viewpoint of government auctions of scarce resources such as oil tracts or portions of the radio spectrum. However, the same principles apply for firms at the private level. Here again, the outcome of an auction depends crucially on such features as the number of bidders, the extent of any "winner's curse," and the nature of any asymmetries between bidders, among others.

For example, consider the merger of the two pharmaceutical firms Glaxo and Wellcome in 1995. In that year, Glaxo made an unsolicited bid for Wellcome worth $14 million. At that time, the principal shareholder in Wellcome was the Wellcome Trust, a charity set up by the firm's founder, Sir Henry Wellcome, to finance medical research. Wellcome management was against the deal and sought out alternative buyers including two other drug firms, Zeneca and Roche. In response, Zeneca said it would be willing to bid $15.5 million and Roche suggested it could enter a bid as high as $17 million. However, each noted that it would be very costly to put together a viable bid—including the necessary financing—and so would only submit a bid if they were sure it would win. Glaxo publicly stated though that if another bid did come in, Glaxo would certainly top it. In the end, neither Roche nor Zeneca submitted bids. Without such rival bidders, Wellcome management could not persuade the trust to reject the offer. Glaxo acquired Wellcome for its initial bid of $14 million. Judged by the terms of the drug mergers that quickly followed, e.g., Hoechst and Marion Merrell Dow, this price was about 15 percent below the norm. Glaxo's asymmetric willingness to pay acted to discourage entry by rivals and helped it win Wellcome at a bargain price, saving the firm hundreds of millions, if not over a billion dollars.

Source: R. Stevenson, "Wellcome Fails to Sway Trust on Sale," *New York Times*, January 28, 1995 (p. c1); and "Wellcome Cites Profit Gain in Move Against Glaxo Bid," *New York Times*, February 3, 1995.

consider a simple case with only two bidders. Suppose that both bidders know that each is drawing estimates of the item's worth from a uniform distribution ranging from $0 to $20. Bidder A has drawn a value of $20. Bidder B has drawn a value of $12. Neither of course knows what value the other has drawn. Clearly though, Bidder A will submit a bid fairly well below her value of $20. Bidding $20 means winning with certainty but the net gain is zero. If she submits a bid of $10, however, Bidder A will know that she still has at least a fifty percent chance of winning (if other players do not shade their bids) and enjoying a net of $10. For Bidder B, the temptation to shade her offer is less compelling—especially if she thinks that a rival with a high value is going to underbid a lot. Thus, there is a chance for lower valued bidders to win a first-price sealed bid auction because unlike the ascending auction, the high-valued bidder has no recourse to outbid a rival in a subsequent round. In turn, precisely because a weaker bidder has some chance to win, a sealed bid auction can encourage more entry than an ascending bid auction.

The importance of attracting entry via a sealed bid process was potently illustrated by European mobile telephone auctions in 2000 and 2001. At that time, many governments were using auctions to allocate licenses to provide the so-called third generation (3G) of mobile telephone employing a new transmitting standard (Universal Mobile Telecommunications Service or UMTS). In the Netherlands, there were exactly five incumbent mobile telephone companies and the government chose to auction off exactly five licenses using an ascending bid auction. It is easy to see the asymmetry between the five incumbent firms and any new bidders. The five incumbents clearly valued the new licenses more than an entrant. Thus the five incumbents were advantaged. Without additional entry, the fact that there were exactly five licenses being sold—one for each incumbent—reduced the auction to one that was very much like selling just one license to just one bidder in five separate cases. Yet the use of an ascending auction discouraged such additional participation (and may have permitted coordination between the five incumbents) with the result that only one additional and not very serious bidder emerged. In the end, the auction produced revenues of only 170 euros per capita. This was less than one-fourth the 650 euros per capita earned by a similar auction in the United Kingdom held just a bit earlier and less than one-third the predictions of the Dutch government. In contrast, a year later (after the dot.com and telecommunications booms had ended), the Danish government used a sealed-bid process to allocate four licenses to four incumbents and earned twice as much revenue as expected.

Since both an ascending (second-price sealed bid) and a descending (first-price sealed bid) auction design have potential flaws, many have looked for ways to remedy these shortcomings. One suggestion is for the seller to announce a reserve price below which no bids will be accepted. To return to our earlier example, suppose that our seller knows that Bidder B's values are distributed between $0 and $10 while Bidder A's values are distributed between $10 and $20. If this information is known to the bidders as well, then in a first-priced sealed bid auction, Bidder A will never bid more than $10 and may be tempted to bid a good bit less even when her own value is $20. In an ascending English auction, Bidder A will always win but on average do so while paying only $5. In either case, the seller would do well to introduce a reserve price of $10 as she knows that at least one bidder will always value the item this much. Note how in this case, the reserve price mechanism preserves efficiency and insures that the item goes to the bidder with the highest value. Indeed, if the seller attaches a personal value to the item of above $10, then she should choose that value as her reserve price to maintain an efficient auction outcome.

Another possible design alteration is to conduct a hybrid auction that combines both ascending and sealed-bid features. Klemperer (2002) for example, has suggested an Anglo-Dutch auction comprised of two rounds. The first round is an open ascending auction that ends when just two bidders are left. The second round is then run as a first-price sealed bid auction in which the reserve price is set as the final bid in the first round. The sealed bid procedure guards against collusion in the second round. It also encourages entry in the first round because, again, the sealed bid process permits a lower-valued bidder to win occasionally. At the same time, the first round process helps to establish a meaningful reserve price.

Summary

In this chapter, we have focused on the nature and implication of strategic interaction in the context of auctions. For private value auctions in which each bidder has her own valuation of the auctioned commodity, the four principal auction designs—English, Dutch, first-price sealed bid, and second-price sealed bid—are revenue equivalent. That is, each yields the same winning bid and gives the commodity to the same winning bidder. For common and almost common value auctions, such revenue equivalence does not in general hold. In particular, for these cases, different auction designs can have very different outcomes both in terms of the revenue generated and regarding which bidder wins the auction.

Auctions have been increasingly used by governments to allocate scarce resources and license rights. Contests for ownership of firms and many other private battles can equally be viewed as auction processes. Because these are common or almost common value auctions the link between auction design and auction outcomes is particularly important. In this regard, the key differences between auction designs reflect how each alternative works to modify the "winner's curse," encourage entry, and limit bidder collusion. Typically, an efficient auction will include a

reserve price below which no bids will be accepted. However, setting that price can be difficult. A reserve price that is very low will impose little constraint on bidders' strategies. A price that is too high will deter many bidders. A starting point is for the seller to set a reserve price that is equal to her own valuation of the item.

Problems

1. Consider Practice Problem 25.2 again in which you are bidding for an original John Lennon hat in a sealed bid first-price auction. In this case, however, let there be 20 other bidders in this auction. As before, assume that the most you would be willing to pay for this hat is $200. Show that your optimal strategy is to submit a bid of $190.

2. You are selling your house and want to get the highest price you can for it. What sort of auction would you prefer if:
   a. you expect there to be 25 offers?
   b. you expect the number of offers to be less than four?

3. When more than one buyer submits a bid for the same house, most states have strict laws forbidding real estate brokers to disclose to any one buyer the bid of any other buyer. Based on you're answers to 2a and 2b, what do you think is the justification behind such restrictions?

4. At the time of the 2000 United Kingdom's auction of 3G telecommunication licenses, Britain had four incumbent mobile phone operators. Originally, it also planned to

auction exactly four licenses. (In the end, it sold five.) Had it sold four licenses, the British planned to use a combined Anglo-Dutch approach. Under this design, the auction would proceed as an ascending auction until just five bidders were left. At that point, the auction would switch to a fourth-price sealed bid type in which the four licenses would be allocated to the top four bidders, each paying the price offered by the lowest successful bid. Comment briefly on this model. What economic considerations do you think were behind this auction design?

5. A house painter relates that most of his work is done for established customers for which he has little competition. He says that on these jobs, he submits a cost estimate and usually makes out reasonably well. Occasionally, however, the painter submits bids on jobs for less familiar customers for which business he is usually one of a number of painters the customer is considering. He says that for some reason, these jobs never work out so well and he always tends to lose money on them. Can you explain this result?

References

Bulow, J. and P. Klemperer. 2002. "Prices and the Winner's Curse." *Rand Journal of Economics* 33 (Spring): 1–21.

Cramton, P. and J. A. Schwartz. 2000. "Collusive Bidding: Lessons from FCC Spectrum Auctions." *Journal of Regulatory Economics* 17 (May): 229–52.

Klemperer, P. D. 1998. "Auctions with Almost Common Values: The 'Wallet Game' and its Applications." *European Economic Review* 42 (May): 757–69.

——. 2002. "What Really Matters in Auction Design." *Journal of Economic Perspectives* 16 (Winter): 161–89.

Lucking-Reily, David. 2000. "Vickrey Auctions in Practice: From Nineteenth Century Philately to Twenty-first Century E-Commerce." *Journal of Economic Perspectives* 14 (Summer): 183–92.

Milgrom, P. R. 1989. "Auctions and Bidding: A Primer." *Journal of Economic Perspectives* 3 (Summer): 3–22.

Milgrom, P. R. and R. J. Weber. 1982. "A Theory of Auctions and Competitive Bidding." *Econometrica* 50 (September): 1089–122.

Myerson, R. B. 1981. "Optimal Auction Design." *Mathematics of Operations Research* 6 (February): 58–73.

Riley, J. G. and W. Samuelson. 1981. "Optimal Auctions." *American Economic Review* 71 (June): 381–92.

Riley, J. G. and H. Li. 1997. "Auction Choice." Mimeo. University of California at Los Angeles.

Vickrey, William. 1961. "Counterspeculation, Auctions, and Competitive Sealed Tenders." *Journal of Finance* 16 (March): 8–37.

Answers to Practice Problems

Chapter 2

2.1   a.   Profit maximization implies $MC = 2q + 10 = P$. Hence, $q = (P - 10)/2$.

      b.   With 50 firms, horizontal summation of the individual marginal cost curves yields: $Q^S = 50(P - 10)/2 = 25P - 250$.

      c.   Equilibrium: $P = \$30$ and $Q = 500$.

      d. $q = (P - 10)/2 = 10$. Revenue $= Pq = \$300$. Total cost $= 100 + q^2 + 10q = \$300$. Profit $= 0$.

2.2   a.   Inverse demand curve is: $P = (6,000 - 9Q)/50$. Hence, $MR = 120 - (18Q/50) = 120 - (9Q/25)$.

      b. $MC = 10 + Q/25$. Equate with MR to obtain: $Q = 275$. At this output, $P = \$70.50$.

      c.   Total revenue $= \$19,387.50$. Each plant produces 5.5 units and incurs a total cost of $\$185.25$. Each plant earns a revenue of $\$387.75$. Profit at each plant is $\$202.50$.

2.3   a.   Present value of incremental cash flows from driving out Loew $= -\$100,000 + \dfrac{R}{1 - R}\,\$10,000$

         $= -\$16,629$. Driving out Loew is not a good investment.

      b.   Present value of incremental cash flows from buying Loew $= -\$80,000 + \dfrac{R}{1 - R}\,\$10,000 =$

         $\$3,337$. This is a good investment.

2.4   a.   Consumer surplus is the area of the triangle above the equilibrium price but below the demand curve $= (1/2)(\$120 - \$30)500 = \$22,500$. Producer surplus is the area of the triangle below the equilibrium price but above the supply curve $= (1/2)(\$30 - \$10)500 = \$5,000$. Total surplus $= \$22,500 + \$5,000 = \$27,500$. Note: Surplus is a marginal concept. Producer fixed cost is not considered.

      b.   Total surplus falls by area of deadweight triangle. Height of triangle is given by reduction in output which is $500 - 275 = 225$. Marginal cost at $Q = 275$ is $\$21$. Base of triangle is given by price less marginal $= \$70.50 - \$21 = \$59.50$. So deadweight triangle has area equal to: $= (1/2)(\$49.50)225$ or $\$5,568.75$. The new total surplus is $\$21,931.25$.

2.5   a. $P = MC = \$10$, $Q = 30$.

      b.   Inverse demand is given by: $P = 25 - Q/2$. So, $MR = 25 - Q$. Equating MR and MC ($= \$10$) yields $Q = 15$ and $P = \$17.50$.

      c. $\$56.25$.

Chapter 3

3.1   a. $CR4^A = 70\%$; $CR4^B = 76\%$. $HHI^A = 2,698$; $HHI^B = 1,660$. Industry A has one firm that dominates the industry. Industry B has five firms that control 90 percent of the production. But these five firms may compete fiercely. The Herfindahl–Hirschman Index seems to better capture the greater potential for monopoly power in Industry A.

b. With the merger of the top three firms in Industry A, the new values are: CR4^A = 80%; HHI = 2,892. Both measures rise.

Chapter 4

4.1 In this case, we have discrete and not continuous changes in output. Hence we have to use the average value of marginal cost at output 11. This is calculated as the average of the marginal cost of increasing output from 10 to 11 units ($137) and the marginal cost of increasing output from 11 to 12 units ($165), which is just $151. Average or unit cost at 11 units is equal to $1,407/11 = $127.91. Hence, $S = AC/MC$ = $127.91/151 = 0.847 $\approx$ 0.85.

4.2 a. $AC = TC/q = 50/q + 2 + 0.5q$. $AC(q = 4) = 16.5$; $AC(q = 8) = 12.25$; $AC(q = 10) = 12$; $AC(q = 12) = 12.167$; $AC(q = 15) = 12.833$.

b. $MC = \Delta TC$ per unit change For decreases: $\Delta TC = 50 + 2q + 0.5q^2 - [50 + 2(q - 1) + 0.5(q - 1)^2] = 2 + q - 0.5$. For increases: $\Delta TC = 50 + 2(q + 1) + 0.5(q + 1)^2 - [50 + 2q + 0.5q^2] = 2 + q + 0.5$. The average of these two value is $2 + q$.

c. $S > 1$ for $q < 10$; $S = 1$ for $q = 10$; $S < 1$ for $q > 10$.

Chapter 5

5.1 a. Profit maximizing price for common day/night pricing is P = $7.50. Daytime attendance = 25; Evening attendance = 65. Total daily profit = ($7.50 − $3.00) × 90 = $405.

b. Daytime price = $6.50; daytime attendance = 35. Evening price = $8.50; evening attendance = 55. Total daily attendance is the same. Total daily profit rises to: ($6.50 − $3.00) × 35 + ($8.50 − $3.00) × 55 = $425.

5.2 a. P_B = $5.5, Q_B = 4,500 pints; P_{NY} = $6.00, Q_{NY} = 8,000 pints; P_W = $6.50, Q_W = 5,250 pints.

b. Boston Profit = ($5.50 − $1.00) × 4,500 = $20,250; New York Profit = ($6.00 − $2.00) × 8,000 = $32,000; Washington Profit = ($6.50 − $3.00) × 5,250 = $18,375.

5.3 Without discriminatory pricing, consumer surplus for daytime consumers is: ($10.00 − $7.50) × 25/2 = $31.25. For evening consumers it is: ($14.00 − $7.50) × 65/2 = $211.25. Producer surplus is $405. Total surplus without discriminatory pricing is: $647.50. With discriminatory pricing, consumer surplus for daytime consumers is: ($10.00 − $6.50) × 35/2 = $61.25. For evening consumers it is: (14.00 − $8.50) × 55/2 = $151.25. Producer surplus is $425. Total surplus with discriminatory pricing is: $637.50. Discriminatory pricing has lowered the total surplus by $10.

Chapter 6

6.1 a. If P = $40, then Q = 5. If P = $25, then Q = 10. Hence, slope = $\Delta P/\Delta Q$ = −15/5 = −3. Equation must satisfy: P = Intercept − 3Q and pass through (5, $40). Hence: $P = 55 - 3Q$ is approximation. $MR = 55 - 6Q$, by "twice as steep" rule. Reservation price of consumer with greatest willingness to pay is the price intercept, P = $55.

b. If consumers are now discovered to be willing to buy a second unit at a price $8 below their willingness to pay for a first, then the demand curve for a second unit is just the demand for the first unit shifted down by $8, or $P = 47 - 3Q_2$. Substitution into each demand curve now yields that at P = $33, 7.33 first units and 4.66 second units will be sold, for a total of 12 units.

6.2 a. Price per ride = $k + c$. Admission fee = T = area under demand curve but above $k + c$.

b. Price per ride = 0. Admission fee = entire area under demand curve.

c. The first policy recovers the cost of operating a ride but incurs the cost of charging for tickets. The second policy incurs no ticketing charge but does not recover the cost of each ride.

6.3   a.   Assume high-demand package has 12 units.

	Low-demand customers			High-demand customers		
Number of units in the package	Charge for the package	Profit per package	Consumer surplus from low-demand package	Maximum willingness to pay for 12 units	Charge for package of 12 units	Profit from each package of 12 units
0	0	0	0	$120.00	$120.00	$72.00
1	$11.50	$7.50	$4.00	$120.00	$116.00	$68.00
2	$22.00	$14.00	$8.00	$120.00	$112.00	$64.00
3	$31.50	$19.50	$12.00	$120.00	$108.00	$60.00
4	$40.00	$24.00	$16.00	$120.00	$104.00	$56.00
5	$47.50	$27.50	$20.00	$120.00	$100.00	$52.00
6	$54.00	$30.00	$24.00	$120.00	$96.00	$48.00
7	$59.50	$31.50	$28.00	$120.00	$92.00	$44.00
8	$64.00	$32.00	$32.00	$120.00	$88.00	$40.00
9	$67.50	$31.50	$36.00	$120.00	$84.00	$36.00
10	$70.00	$30.00	$40.00	$120.00	$80.00	$32.00
11	$71.50	$27.50	$44.00	$120.00	$76.00	$28.00
12	$72.00	$24.00	$48.00	$120.00	$72.00	$24.00

b. Four units in low-demand package.
c. Six units in low-demand package.
d. Price of six-unit package = $54; price of 12-unit package = $96.

Chapter 7

7.1   Locate at town center because this permits broadest market access. Optimal price is $P = \$6$. This permits selling to 17 customers: eight to the west; eight to the east; and one also located at the center. Profit = ($6 − $2)17 = $68. Note, demand can be approximated as $P = \$9.75 − Q/4$. Profit maximization then requires $MR = \$9.75 − Q/2 = \$2 \Rightarrow (Q \approx 16$ and $P \approx \$6)$. Let d be the distance from the center (Henry's position) to a customer. With a mobile service, Henry will charge all served customers $10 for smithing. The question is how many to serve. He will earn profit of $8 from consumer at center. He will earn $7.25 from each consumer at #1 East and #1 West, and so on. With the mobile smithy, Henry will serve consumers as long as 0.75 * $d + 2 < 10$, so the maximum distance d that he will travel is $d = 10.67$. This would imply Henry would service 21.33 customers, but since there are only 21 customers, Henry just serves everyone in the town. He earns $10 in revenue from the person at his position, and $10 − 10.5 * \$.75 = 2.125$ from the last person in town in each direction, so his total revenue is the area under the two curves starting at height 10 and declining to height 2.125. Thus total revenue is $2(\frac{1}{2}(7.5 * 10.5) + 2.125 * 10.5) = 123.375$. His total profit is $\Pi = 123.375 − 21 * 2 = \$81.375$. The profit from traveling is clearly greater than the profit from staying in the same place, so Henry should do it.

7.2   a.   The price intercept remains unchanged. The demand curve rotates out along the quantity axis.
b.   If $Z = 1$, $Q = 2$ and $P = \$2$. If $Z = 2$, $Q = 4$ and $P = \$2$. If $Z = 3$, $Q = 6$ and $P = \$2$.
c.   At $Z = 1$, maximum profit is $PQ − Z^2 = \$3$. As $Z = 2$, maximum profit is $PQ − Z^2 = \$4$. At $Z = 3$, maximum profit is $PQ − Z^2 = \$3$. The profit-maximizing choice is $Z = 2$.

7.3 a. Both type 1 and type 2 customers are willing to pay more as quality z increases. The firm should set z as high as possible to 2, so $P_1 = 20(2 - z_1)$ and $P_2 = 10z = 20$.

b. The firm should offer two products only if $20N_1 > 10(N_1 + N_2)$, or $N_1 > N_2$. We know $N_1 = \eta N$ and $N_2 = (1 - \eta)N$. Substituting in, we see that the firm should offer two products only if $\eta > \frac{1}{2}$. If this is the case, the firm should offer a high-quality and a low-quality product. Quality for type 1, $z_1 = 2$, and quality for type 2, $z_2 = 20z_1/(20 - 10) = 2z_1$. $P_1 = 20(2 - z_1)$ and $P_2 = 20 * 10z_1/(20 - 10) = 20z_1$.

c. For $\eta \le 1/2$, profit is increasing in z_2 so the firm will only offer a high quality product of quality $z = 2$. It will therefore set a price of $\theta_2 z = \$10 \times 2 = \$20$ to reach both consumer types and earn a profit of $\$20N$. If $\eta > \theta_2/\theta_1$, and $z_1 = \varepsilon$, the firm will sell its high quality product of quality $z_1 = 2$ at a price of $\$40$ to ηN customers. Because $z_1 = \varepsilon$, the firm's optimal low quality choice is also $20\varepsilon/(20 - 10) = 2\varepsilon$. Hence, it will sell its low quality product at a price of $(20 * 10) * 2\varepsilon/10 = 4\varepsilon$.

Chapter 8

8.1 a. $P_{BASIC} = \$11$; $\pi_{BASIC} = \$24N$; $P_{DISNEY} = \$15$; $\pi_{DISNEY} = \$36N$; where N is the number in each group.

b. $P_{BUNDLE} = \$20$; $P_{BASIC} = \$17$; $P_{DISNEY} = \$17$. Young Adults buy the Disney Channel only. Pensioners buy the Basic Service only. All other groups buy the bundle. Total profit is $4(\$20 - \$6)N + 2(\$17 - \$3)N = \$84N$.

c. New answers to part (a), $P_{BASIC} = \$14$; $P_{DISNEY} = \$15$. New answers to part (b), $P_{BUNDLE} = \$20$; $P_{BASIC} = \$14$; $P_{DISNEY} = \$15$. Pensioners and Hotels buy basic service. Students, Schools, and Young Adults buy Disney. Families may buy the bundle.

8.2 Let Q be measured in thousands. Summing two demand curves yields combined demand of $Q = 28 - 2P$ for $P \le 12$, and $Q = 16 - P$ for $12 < P \le 16$. Assume firm operates where both consumers are served so that $Q = 28 - 2P$ is relevant demand. (This is easy to show.) Profit is $(P - 2)Q + 2S_L$ where S_L is surplus of low demand consumers. In turn, that surplus is given by $(12 - P)^2/2$. So, profit is $(P - 2)(28 - 2P) + (12 - P)^2$. Maximization with respect to P then yields $P = \$4$. If two packages are offered, 8-shot and 14-shot, first note that low demand consumers value eight shots at a total of $(\$8 \times 8)/2 + \$32 = \$64$. So, set $\$64$ as price of the eight-shot camera. High-demand consumers will earn a surplus of $\$32$ on the eight-shot pack. They value a 14-pack camera at $\$126$. So, price of 14-pack camera is $\$126 - \$32 = \$94$. If marginal cost is still $\$2$ per exposure, profit is $(\$64 - \$16) = \$48$ on the 8-shot camera and $(\$94 - \$28) = \$66$ on 14-pack camera. Total profit if there are 1,000 of each, total profit is $\$114,000$.

a. If Rowling sells only the 14-shot package, it can charge $\$126$ to each of the N_h high-demand types and earn $\$94N_h$ in profit. Offering a 10-shot package allows it to earn $\$70 - \$20 = \$50$ from each low demand consumer, but constrains her to lower the price of a 14-shot package to $\$86$ from which it earns $\$86 - \$28 = \$58$ in profit. Total profit from this strategy is therefore $\$50,000 + \$58N_h$. Profit is identical for each strategy when $\$50,000 + \$58N_h = \$94N_h$ or when $N_h = 1,389$. Once there are this many high demand consumers, it is no longer to go after the relatively few low demand ones.

b. From above, offering both types earns a profit of $\$48,000 + \$66N_h$. Otherwise, it earns $\$94N_h$ by offering just the 14-shot camera. This implies that for $N_h \ge 1,714$, only the 14-shot package will be offered.

Chapter 9

9.1 The unique Nash equilibrium is: (Suspense, Suspense). In each of the other three possible outcomes, (Romance, Romance), (Romance, Suspense) and (Suspense, Romance), at least one firm has an incentive to switch its strategy.

9.2   Best response: $q_1 = 22.5 - q_2/2$, and vise-versa for q_2. Hence, $q_1 = q_2 = 15$. $Q = 30$; $P = \$40$; and $\pi_1 = \pi_2 = \$450$.

9.3   Best response function for Untel: $q_U = 2.5 - q_C/2$; best response for Cyrox: $q_C = 2 - q_U/2$. $q_C = 1$; $q_U = 2$; $Q = 3$; $P = \$60$; $\pi_C = \$20$; $\pi_U = \$80$. If $c_C = \$20$, then $q_1 = q_2 = 1.67$; $P = \$53.33$. Hence, $\pi_U = \pi_C = \$55.55$ million.

Chapter 10

10.1   a.   Best response function for q_1 is: $q_1 = 45 - q_2/2$. By symmetry: $q_2 = 45 - q_1/2$. Hence, in equilibrium: $q_1 = q_2 = 30$. Therefore, market price is: $P = \$20 - \$Q/5 = \$8$. $\pi_1 = \pi_2 = \$180$.
         b. $P_1 = P_2 = P = \$2$; and $\pi_1 = \pi_2 = 0$. Market output = 90.

10.2   Market output $Q = q_S + q_R$. At price $P = \$110$, $Q = 2,400$, which is the combined capacity of the two resorts. If Pepall Ridge sets a price $p_{SR} = \$110$, the residual demand curve for Snow Richards is $Q = 8,000 - 60p_{SR}$, or $p_{SR} = 133.33 - Q/60$. The marginal revenue curve is $MR = 133.33 - Q/30$. On the interval $0 \le Q \le 1,400$, marginal revenue is greater than marginal cost, so Snow Richards would increase production to its capacity of 1,400. Conversely, if Snow Richards sets its price $p_{SR} = \$110$, the residual demand curve facing Pepall Ridge is $Q = 7,600 - 60P$, or $P = 126.67 - Q/60$. The marginal revenue curve is $MR = 126.67 - Q/30$. Marginal revenue is greater than marginal cost on the interval $0 \le Q \le 1,000$, so Pepall Ridge will increase production to its capacity of 1,000. Therefore, $p_S = p_R = \$110$ is a Nash equilibrium. $p_{PR} = p_{SR} = \$110$.

10.3   a.   Assume the entire market is served. Best response function for Cheap Cuts: $p_{CC} = \dfrac{p_R + c_{CC} + t}{2}$. Likewise, best response function for the Ritz is: $p_R = \dfrac{p_{CC} + c_R + t}{2}$. For every $1 in one firm's unit cost the rival's optimal price rises by 50 cents.
         b.   Equilibrium prices: $p_{CC} = t + \dfrac{2}{3}c_{CC} + \dfrac{1}{3}c_R = \$18.33$; $p_R = t + \dfrac{1}{3}c_{CC} + \dfrac{2}{3}c_R = \$21.67$. When the two firms had the same unit cost $c = 10$, then $p_{CC} = p_R = \$15$. Prices rise now because c_R has risen and this induces a rise in p_R. In turn, because prices are strategic complements, the rise in p_R permits a similar rise in p_{CC}.

Chapter 11

11.1   a. $q_2 = 70 - q_1/2$.
         b. $q_1 = 70$; $q_2 = 35$; $P = \$95$; profit to firm 1(leader) = \$2,450; profit to firm 2(follower) = \$1,225.
         c. $q_1 = q_2 = 46.67$; $Q = 93.33$; $P = \$106.67$. Profit to firm 1 = profit to firm 2 = \$2,177.77. Firm 1 loses and firm 2 gains as game becomes Cournot rather than Stackelberg. Consumers enjoy more output and lower prices under Stackelberg.

11.2   a.   West End will be on its best response function: $p_{WE} = (p_{EE} + c + t)/2$. Demand for East End is: $p_{EE} = (p_{WE} - p_{EE} + t)N/2t$. Substitution and profit maximization then yields: $p_{EE} = c + 3t/2$ while $p_{WE} = c + 5t/4$, or: $p_{EE} = \$17.50$ and $p_{WE} = \$16.25$. Because of its higher price, East End will serve only 3/8 of the 100 potential customers or 37.5. It earns a profit of $\$7.5 \times 37.5 = \$281.25$. West End serves 62.5 customers and earns a profit of $\$6.25 \times 62.5 = \$390.63$.
         b.   Prices in this sequential price game are higher than they are in the simultaneous game. Prices are strategic complements. With sequential price setting, the firms can exploit this complementarity and coordinate prices to some extent. Note, however, that going first is a disadvantage in this game. While both firms earn more profit than when play is simultaneous, the firm setting its price second earns the most.

11.3 a.

		Player 2	
		Take All	Share
Player 1	Wait	(0, 3)	(1.5, 1.5)
	Grab	(1, 0)	

b.

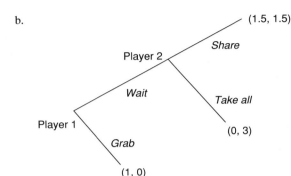

c. Take All is a dominant strategy for Player 2. The promise to play Share is not credible. Anticipating this, Player 1 will Grab the dollar.

Chapter 12

12.1 a. Entrant's residual demand described by: $P = (100 - \bar{Q}) - q$.
b. $q = 30 - \bar{Q}/2$.
c. Entrant profit $= (P - c)q - 100 = [100 - \bar{Q} - q - 40]q - 100$. Substituting in for q, entrant profit $= (30 - \bar{Q}^2/2) = 100 = 0$ if entry is to be deterred. $\bar{Q}_L = 40$, pre-entry price is $P = \$60$. The entrant's best response to $\bar{Q}_L = 40$, is $q = 10$, which would drive the price P to $\$50$ and leave the entrant with zero profit.

12.2 a. Incumbent's marginal cost for output less than $\bar{K}_1$ is 30, hence its best response function for this range of output is: $q_1 = 90/2 - q_2/2 = 45 - q_2/2$. For output greater than or equal to $\bar{K}_1$, Incumbent's marginal cost is 60. Therefore, for this range of output, its best response is $q_1 = 30 - q_2/2$.
b. Entrant's marginal cost is always 60, so its best response function is always $q_2 = 30 - q_1/2$.
c. In this as in most models, the Stackelberg leader always chooses the monopoly output and a rational monopolist. However, a monopoly firm will never keep capacity unused, so it will choose K such that $K_1 = q_1$. Hence, profit $= (90 - q_1)q_I - 30q_I) - 200 = (60 - q_I)q_I - \$200$. Maximization then yields, $60 = 2q_1$ or $q_1 = 30$. Entrant's best response implies that if $q_1 = 30$, $q_2 = 15$. Total output $= 45$. Price $= \$75$. Incumbent profit $= \$(75 - 30)30 - \$30 \times 30 - \$200 = \$250$. Entrant's profit $= 4(75 - 60)15 - \$200 = \$25$.
d. With $K_1 = 40$, it implies that $q_1 = 40$ as well. Entrant's best response then implies that $q_2 = 30 - 40/2 = 10$. Total output is 50, so market price is $\$70$. Entrant's profit is: $\$(70 - 60)q_2 - \$200 = 10 \times \$10 - \$200 = -\$100$. Entrant cannot earn positive profit. So there is no entry incentive.
e. With $K_1 = 32 =$ committed value of q_1, then entrant's best response is $q_2 = 16$. Total output $= 48$ and price is $\$72$. Entrant's profit after entry cost is: $(\$72 - \$60) \times 16 = \$192$. Fixed cost is $\$200$, so net profit is $\$192 - \$200 < 0$. With $K_1 = 32 = q_1$, and no entry, $P = \$88$. Profit $= (\$88 - \$60)32 - \$200 = \$696$.

12.3 a.   The incumbent will fight if $3 > 4 - C$ or if $C > 1$.
      b.   For $C > 1$, the initial expenditure of C implies the incumbent will always fight any entry, so entry does not occur.

           The incumbent therefore earns $\$(8 - C)$ by expending C if $C \geq 3.5 > 1$. If C is not spent, entry will occur and the incumbent earns \$4.50. Expenditure C is only worthwhile if $\$(8 - C) > \$4.50$. If $C > 3.50$, this condition is not satisfied.

Chapter 13

13.1   The bank would have to ask for at least \$137.5 million in a good year. And \$100 million in a bad year. It will then earn \$137.5 with probability 0.4 and \$100 million with probability 0.6 for an average of \$115 million. No, there is no change in the incentive for predation. The bank and Newvel can still expect to make a profit by entering in the second period.

13.2 a. $q_L = 45$, $q_f = 22.5$, $Q = 67.5$, $P = \$32.5$; $\pi_L = \$1,012.5$; $\pi_f = \$506.25$.
      b.   In first period, $q_L = 90$ and $\pi_L = 0$. In second period, $q_L = 45$ and $\pi_L = \$2,025$.
      c.   Offer entrant \$506.25 to stay out in 1st period. Earn $\$2,025 - \$506.25 = \$1,518.75$ in 1st period; \$2,025 in 2nd period.

13.3   Expected predation gain = (prob) $\times$ (\$325 − \$150) million must cover cost = \$30 million. Lowest probability is 17.14 percent.

Chapter 14

14.1   Confess, Confess is the unique Nash equilibrium.

14.2   Third period outcome must be the one-period Nash equilibrium with both producing 40 (thousand) and earning \$1.6 million each. Foreseeing the inevitability of this outcome will thwart any cooperation in periods 1 and 2. The three-period game will simply be played as three one-period games.

14.3 a.   If the firms collude they share the monopoly profit, so if the cartel is sustained we have $\pi^M = \dfrac{(A - c)^2}{8B}$. If the cartel fails, per-period profit is the Cournot–Nash profit $\pi^N = \dfrac{(A - c)^2}{9B}$. Now suppose that one firm sticks by the cartel agreement to produce $(A - c)/4B$ while the other cheats on the agreement. The cheating firm's best response is to produce $3(A - c)/8B$, with profit $\pi^D = \dfrac{9(A - c)^2}{64B}$. Substituting into equation (14.7) and simplifying gives the critical probability-adjusted discount factor $\rho_C^* = \dfrac{9/64 - 1/8}{9/64 - 1/9} = \dfrac{9}{17} = 0.529$.

      b.   If the firms collude they each earn π^M per-period as in part a. If the cartel fails we have $\pi^N = 0$. A firm that cheats on the cartel earns $\pi^D = \dfrac{(A - c)^2}{4B}$. Substituting into equation (14.7) and simplifying gives the critical probability-adjusted discount factor $\rho_B^* = \dfrac{1/4 - 1/8}{1/4 - 0} = \dfrac{1}{2} = 0.5$.

Chapter 15

No Practice Problems in this chapter.

Chapter 16

16.1 a. From equation (16.4) $\pi_i = \$(A - c)^2/B(N + 1)^2$; with $A = \$130$; $c = \$30$; $B = 1$; and $N = 20$
$\Rightarrow \pi_i = \$22.67$.

b. $M = 6$. Hence, by equation (16.7): $\pi_M^C = \pi_{nm}^C = \$100^2/(20 - 6 + 2)^2 = \$39.06 < 6 \times \$22.67$.

c. $M = 17$. $\pi_M^C = \pi_{nm}^C = \$100^2/(20 - 17 + 2)^2 = \$400 > 17 \times \$22.67 = \$385.40$. A merger of 17 firms is barely profitable. Since the profit increases monotonically in M, any merger with fewer firms will be unprofitable.

16.2 a. $q_1 = q_2 = (120 + 30b)/4$; $q_3 = (240 - 90b)/4$; $Q = 120 - 7.5b$, $P = 60.75b$; $\pi_1 = \pi_2 = (120 + 30b)^2/16$; $\pi_3 = (240 - 90b)^2/16$. Hence, b cannot exceed 1.3333.

b. Post-merger market is a symmetric Cournot duopoly with marginal cost $= \$30$ for both firms. Equilibrium has $q_1 = q_2 = 50$. $P = \$80$. Profit to non-merged firm is $\$1,600$. Profit to merged firm is $\$2,500 - \$900a$.

c. Post-merger combined profit $= \$2,500 - \$900a \geq (120 + 30b)^2/16 + (240 - 90b)^2/16 = $ sum of pre-merger separate profits.

16.3 a. $q_i = (A - c)/B(N + 1)$; with $A = \$130$; $c = \$30$; $B = 1$; and $N = 20 \Rightarrow q_i = 4.76$. $Q = 20q_i = 95.24$, $P = \$34.76$.

b. From equation (16.26), $q_L = (A - c)/B(L + 1) = 100/6 = 16.67$. From equation (16.27), $q_f = (A - c)/B(L + 1)(N - L + 1) = 100/6(11) = 1.51$. $Q = 5(16.67) + 10(1.51) = 98.48$.

c. Standard Cournot analysis gives: $q_i = 100/(15 + 1) = 6.25$. $Q = 15q_i = 93.75$.

Chapter 17

17.1 The retailer's marginal revenue curve is $MR = 3,000 - Q$ and the retailer maximizes profit by equating MR and MC, giving $r = 3,000 - Q$, which is also the manufacturer's demand curve. If the retailer has additional marginal costs of c^U then profit maximization gives $3,000 - Q = r + c^U$, which gives $r = (3,000 - c^U) - Q$ as the manufacturer's demand curve.

17.2 a. Profit maximization by WR implies $100 - 2Q = 5 + W_W \Rightarrow W_W = 95 - 2Q = WW$'s demand curve. Profit maximization by WW implies: $95 - 4Q = 5 + W_M \Rightarrow W_M = 90 - 4Q = WM$'s demand curve. Profit maximization by WM implies: $90 - 8Q = 10 \Rightarrow Q = 10$; $W_M = \$50$; $W_W = \$75$; $P = \$90$. $\pi_{WM} = \$400$; $\pi_{WW} = \$200$; $\pi_{WR} = \$100$; total profit = \$700.

b. If WM and WW merge, then the cost of combined operation is \$15. Demand curve facing merged firm is $W_W = 95 - 2Q$. Profit maximization implies: $95 - 4Q = 15 \Rightarrow Q = 20$. Wholesale price to retailer falls to \$55. Price charged to consumers falls to \$80. Profit of the merged firm is $(55 - 15) \times 20 = \$800$. Profit of the retailer is $(80 - 60) \times 20 = \$400$. Total profit has increased, the merged firm has greater profits and the retailer has greater profits. Consumers are offered lower prices. Similarly, if WW and WR the demand to WW remains the same: in direct form $Q_w = (95 - w_w)/2$. Profit to WW is $(w_w - 5 - w_m)Q_w$. Maximizing with respect to w_w gives $w_w = 50 + w_m/2$. So $Q_w = Q_r = Q_m = (90 - w_m)/4$ and the retail price to consumers is $(310 + w_m)/4$. Profit to the merged firm is $(w_m - 5)(90 - w_m)/4 + ((310 + w_w)/4 - 5 - (50 + w_m/2))(90 - w_m)/4$. Maximizing with respect to w_m gives the manufacturing price $w_m = \$36.67$. The wholesale price is \$68.33 and the consumer price is \$86.67. Profit of the merged firm is \$533.33 and of the wholesaler is \$355.38. All firms and consumers benefit as compared to the non-merged case.

c. If all three firms merge, total cost of bringing good to market is \$20. Merged firm faces retail demand of $P = 100 - Q$, hence, $MR = 100 - 2Q = 20$ implies $Q = 40$ and $P = 60$. Merged firm profit is: $\$1,600 > \$1,200$ above.

17.3 a. Suppose that WI sets a wholesale price of w. GI maximizes profit by setting $MC = 0.1 + w = MR = 1 - 2Q_{gb}$ so $Q_{gb} = 0.45 - w/2$. TI maximizes profit by setting $0.1 + w = 0.75 - 0.4Q_{gn}$, so that $Q_{gn} = 1.625 - 2.5w$. This gives aggregate demand for *WI* of $Q = 2.075 - 3w$ or $w = 2.075/3 - Q/3$. Marginal revenue for *WI* is then $MR = 2.075/3 - 2Q/3$ and $MC = 0.1$. This gives profit maximizing total output $Q = 0.8875$. The wholesale price is $w = \$0.396$. Sales in Boston are 0.252 and in New York are 0.635. The price of gizmos in Boston is $0.748 and in New York is $0.623. Profits are: $WI = \$0.263$; $GI = \$0.063$; $TI = \$0.081$.

b. Suppose that *WI* sets a price w_b for widgets in Boston and w_n for widgets in New York. *GI* sets $MR = 1 - 2Q_{gb} = MC = 0.1 + w_b$, giving derived demand to *WI* of $w_b = 0.9 - 2Q_{gb}$. Marginal revenue is $MR = 0.9 - 4Q_{gb}$. Equating with *MC* of 0.1 gives $Q_{gb} = 0.2$. The whole-sale price is $w_b = \$0.5$. The Boston gizmo price is $0.8. Profit of *GI* is $0.04. Profit of *WI* in Boston is $0.08. Similarly, derived demand for *WI* in New York is $w_n = 0.65 - 0.4Q_{gn}$. Equating $MR = 0.65 - 0.8Q_n$ with $MC = 0.1$ gives $Q_n = 0.6875$. Wholesale price is $0.375. The New York gizmo price is $0.6125. Profit of *TI* is $0.095 and of *WI* from sales in New York is $0.189. Profit for *WI* and *TI* increased and for *GI* decreased.

c. Suppose that *WI* merges with *BI* in Boston. Widgets are supplied to *GI* at marginal cost. *GI* equates $MR = 1 - 2Q_{gb} = MC = 0.2$, giving $Q_{gb} = 0.4$. Price of gizmos in Boston = $0.6, profit of the merged firm from Boston is $0.16, aggregate profit is $0.349. Now suppose that *WI* merges with *TI* in New York. Widgets supplied to New York at marginal cost. *GI* sets $MR = 0.75 - 0.4Q_{gn} = MC = 0.2$, giving $Q_{gn} = 1.375$. Price of Gizmos in New York = $0.475. Profit of the merged firm is $0.458. So merger with *TI* is preferred.

d. (i)   Price in Boston rises and in New York falls. Opposite effect on consumer surplus.
    (ii) Price and consumer surplus in Boston is unaffected. Price in New York falls and consumer surplus increases.

17.4 a. Competitive price is equal to marginal cost equals r. Demand facing *WI* is $r = 100 - Q$, so $MR = 100 - 2Q = 10$ for profit maximization, or $Q = 45$ and $r = P = \$55$. *WI* profit is $2,025. Competitive retailers earn zero profit.

b. *WI* is already earning the maximum profit possible in this industry (absent price discrim-ination). Therefore, integration with one or even many downstream retailers cannot raise *WI*'s profits or price P to consumers. Even if *WI* bought all downstream retailers, it would still maximize profits by setting $P = \$55$, selling 45 units and earning $2,025 in profit.

c. Competitive manufacturing price = marginal cost = $10. Competitive retail price = manu-facturing price = $10.

Chapter 18

18.1 a. Wholesale price = $520; Retail price = $760; $Q = 120$.
b. Tiger-el profit = $57,600; Great Toy Store profit = $28,800.
c. $Q = 220$; retail price = $560 (includes $373.33 royalty payment). Tiger-el profit = $82,133.33; Great Toy Store Profit = $32,266.67.

18.2 a. Profit of the retailer is $\pi_r = s(10 - p)(p - 6 - s^2)$. Maximize with respect to p and s to give retail service level, $s = 0.89$; retail price, $p^M = \$8.40$; $Q \approx 143$. Manufacturer's profit $\approx \$143$.
b. Retail service level, $s = 0.775$; retail price, $p^M = \$8.80$; $Q = 93$. Manufacturer's profit = $186. In both (a) and (b), the setting of a wholesale price above cost results in lower retail services, a higher retail price, and less profit to the manufacturer than occurs under integration.

18.3 a. Since cost is zero, revenue and profit maximization are identical. When demand is strong, marginal revenue is $MR^H = 10 - 0.02Q$. Optimal $Q = 500$, implying $P^H = \$5$. When demand is weak, marginal revenue is $MR^L = 10 - Q/15$. Optimal $Q = 150$, implying $P^L = \$5$.
b. Profit maximization requires selling an amount such that $MR = c = 0$. When demand is strong, all 500 units will be sold. When demand is weak, only 150 units will be sold. Expected profit is: $0.5(\$2,500) + 0.5(\$750) = \$1,625$.

    c.   Once bought, the cost of acquiring the stock is sunk. Competitive retailers will sell the entire stock. If demand is strong, the quantity of 500 will sell at the market-clearing price of $5. If demand is weak, the price will fall to $0 and 300 units will be sold.

    d.   Competitive retailers will expect to break even if wholesale price is $2.50. Manufacturer's profit is $1,250.

Chapter 19

19.1   a. $n^* = 2$.

        b. q per division = 15. Π per division = $225. Π per firm = $450 (not including sunk division costs).

        c. $Q = 60$; $P = \$40$.

        d.   Pure monopoly: $P^M = \$62.50$; $Q^M = \$37.50$; $\Pi^M = \$1,406.25$

Chapter 20

20.1   a. $a = 100$ implies $dP/dQ = -0.1$; $a = 1,000$ implies $dP/dQ = -0.0316$.

        b.   (i) $MR = 100 - 0.04Q$.

               (ii) $P = \$80$; $Q = 1,000$.

               (iii)   Price elasticity (absolute value) = 4. Elasticity of sales with respect to advertising = 1/2.

        c.   At $a = 2,500$, $P = \$80$; $Q = 10,000 \Rightarrow$ Advertising/Sales Ratio $= a/PQ = 0.03125$. Dorfman–Steiner condition requires advertising-to-sales ratio = $(1/2)/4 = 1/8$, is not satisfied here. Optimal advertising rate that does satisfy Dorfman–Steiner condition yields: $a = 40,000$; $P = \$80$; $Q = 4,000$.

Chapter 21

21.1   a. $P = c + t = \$5 + \$4 = \$9$.

        b.   Each firm will serve half the market. Each will earn a profit of $\$4N/2 = \$2N = \$2,000$.

        c.   (i)   Original market share = $^1/_2$; new market share = $^1/_2 + 1/2t$. Market share rises by $1/2t$ = 1/8 when $t = 4$.

               (ii)   Original profit = $\$2N$. New profit = $\$3N/2 + \$3N/8 = \$7N/8$. Profit declines by $\$N/8$ or $125 to $1,875.

21.2   a.   As α falls, advertising costs decrease and θ rises. Each firm's message reaches a greater fraction of its potential customers.

        b.   As α falls, more and more customers are fully informed about the availability of sub-stitutes. Resulting price competition leads to a decline in each firm's profit.

21.3   a.   With $\alpha = 100$, the inverse demand curve is: $P = 10 - 10Q$. $MR = 10 - 20Q$. Profit max-imization implies $Q = 0.5$ (one half million) and $P = \$5$. Profit = $\$2.5$ (million) $- \$10,000 \times 100$ advertising expense = $1.5 million.

        b.   With $\alpha = 625$, the inverse demand curve is: $P = 25 - 25Q$. $MR = 25 - 50Q$. Profit max-imization implies $Q = 0.5$ or one half million again. $P = \$12.5$. Profit = $\$6.25$ (million) $- \$5,000 \times 625$ advertising expense = $3,125,000.

Chapter 22

22.1   The monopoly price $= P^M = (A + c)/2B$. With $A = 100$, $B = 1$, and $c = \$28$, $P^M = \$128/2 = \$64$. This exceeds the initial marginal cost of $60, so the innovation does not permit any firm to price as an unconstrained monopolist. To be drastic, an innovation must yield a monopoly price $P^M = (A + c)/2B$ that is less than the marginal cost with the old technology. Since again,

$A = 100$, $B = 2$, and the old technology has a marginal cost of $60, the new marginal cost as a result of the innovation must be no higher than $c = \$20$.

22.2 a. Pre-innovation competitive output is $Q^C = 25$. To be drastic, the innovation must reduce marginal cost below monopoly marginal revenue at $Q = 25$ or below $100 - \$2 * 25 = \$50$.

b. Per-period profit to a monopolist with $c = \$75$ is $156.25. Present value of profit stream is $1,562.50 per-period profit to monopolist with $c = \$60$ is $400. Present value of profit stream is $4,000. Value of innovation to monopolist = $4,000 - \$1,562.50 = \$2,437.50$.

c. $q_1 = q_2 = 8.333$. $Q = 16.67$ and $P = \$83.33$. $\pi_1 = \pi_2 = (\$83.33 - \$75)8.33 = \$69.40$.

d. If firm 1 acquires the innovation: $q_1 = 18.333$; $q_2 = 3.333$. $Q = 21.67$; $P = \$78.33$.

e. Prior to invention, Cournot innovator earns constant per period profit of $\Pi = \$69.40$, or present value of $694. After invention, Cournot innovator earns constant per period profit of $(\$78.33 - \$60)18.333 = \$336$, or present value of $3,360. Net present value of invention to Cournot innovator is: $3,360 - \$694 = \$2,666 > \$2,43.7$ value to monopolist.

Chapter 23

23.1 a. Competition implies $P = MC = \$70$; $Q = 100 - P = 30$.

b. Per period profit to innovator is obtained by selling original 30 units produced at unit cost $\$70 - x$, at price just less than $\$70 = \$30(70 - (70 - x)) = \$30x$. With $R = 0.9091$ and $T = 25$ years, net value to innovator of R&D effort less cost is:
$NV^m(x, T) = \$30x[(1 - 0.9091^{25})/(1 - 0.9091)] - 15x^2$. Maximization implies: $dNV^m/dx = 30[(1 - 0.9091^{25})/(1 - 0.9091)] - 30x = 0$. Hence, $x \approx 10$ and innovator values innovation at: $NV(25) = \$1,500$.

c. If $T = 20$; $x \approx 9.37$ and per period profit $\approx \$281.1$. $NV^m(20) = \$2,633.91 - \$1,316.95 \approx \$1,316.96$.

d. Social welfare gain equals value of innovation to innovator plus increase in consumer surplus. At $P = c = \$70$, consumer surplus is $\$(100 - 70)^2/2 = \$450$. If P falls to $60, consumer surplus is $800. At $P = c = \$60.43$, consumer surplus is $775. Value of consumer surplus gained when $T = 25$ is $\$(800 - 450)\dfrac{0.9091^{25}}{(1 - 0.9091)} \approx \$355.46$. Value of consumer surplus gained when $T = 20$ is $\$(775 - 450)\dfrac{0.9091^{20}}{(1 - 0.9091)} \approx \$531.56$. Reduction in T from 25 to 20 just reduces value of innovation to consumers and producer by $1,855.46 - \$1,848.52$, or about a $7 loss.

23.2 a. $P^M = \$(100 + 50)/2 = \$75$. $Q = (100 - 75)/2 = 12.5$. $\pi^M = \$(75 - 50)12.5 = \$312.50$. Consumer surplus = $\$(100 - 75)^2/4 = \$156.25$.

b. $q_1 = q_2 = (100 - 50)/6 = 8.33$. $Q = 16.67$. $P = 100 - 2Q = \$66.67$. $\pi_1 = \pi_2 = 138.89$. Consumer surplus = $\$(100 - 66.67)^2/4 = \$277.78$.

c. If only one firm does research, the expected profit is $0.8(\$312.50) - K = \$250 - K$. If both do research, the expected profit to each is $0.8(0.2)\$312.50 + 0.8^2(\$138.89) - K = \$138.89 - K$. The payoff matrix is:

		BMI	
		No R&D	R&D
ECN	No R&D	$0, $0	$0, $250 − K
	R&D	$250 − K, $0	$138.89 − K, $138.89 − K

d.   For (no R&D, no R&D) to be a Nash equilibrium, $250 − K < 0$ or $K > \$250$. For (R&D, R&D) to be an equilibrium $138.89 − K > 0$, or $K < \$138.89$.

e.   The expected social surplus with only one lab is $0.8(\$312.50 + \$156.25) − K = \$375 − K$. With two labs it is $2(0.8 \times 0.2[\$312.50 + \$156.25]) + 0.8^2(2 \times \$138.89 + \$277.78) − 2K = \$505.56 − 2K$. Two labs are optimal if $\$505.56 − 2K > \$375 − K$ or $K < \$130.56$.

23.3   a. $P = \$(100 + 120)/3 = \$73.33$. $q_1 = q_2 = 6.67$; $Q = 13.333$. $\pi_1 = \pi_2 = \$88.89$.

   b.   (i)   The innovator's per-period profit is $\pi^I = \$(100 − 100 + 60)^2/18 = \$200$. $q_1 = 10$; $= 5$. Rival earns $50.

   (ii)   This arrangement restores the previous equilibrium. So the innovator earns a per-period profit of $200 plus $10 on each of five units sold or $250 in total. $= \$133.33$. Total profit is $50 greater than without licensing.

   (iii)   If both have marginal cost $= \$50$, Cournot equilibrium is: $q_1 = q_2 = 8.33$. $P = \$66.66$. $\pi_1 = \pi_2 = \$138.89$. Without technology, firm 2 earns profit of $50. Maximum fee it will pay is $138.89 − \$50 = \$88.89$. Without licensing technology firm 1 earns $200. Minimum fee it will accept is $200 − \$138.89 = \$61.11$. Fee must satisfy: $\$61.11 < K < \$88.89$.

Chapter 24

24.1   a.   Best response function for firm A is: $P_A = P_B/2 + t/2$. By symmetry, best response function for firm B is: $P_B = P_A/2 + t/2$. Hence, the Nash equilibrium is: $P_A = P_B = t$.

   b.   (i)   The marginal consumer condition equates: $V + ks_A^e − t_x^m − p_A = V + ks_B^e − t(1 − x^m) − p_B$. Hence, substitution yields $2tx^m = k(s_A^e − s_B^e) + (p_B − p_A) + t$.

   (ii)   Again, substitution of $s_A^e = x^m$ and $s_B^e = (1 − x^m)$ and solving for x^m yields: $x^m =$

$$\frac{1}{2} + \frac{(p_B − p_A)}{2(t − k)}.$$ Total demand for firm A's service then is $x^m N = \left[\dfrac{1}{2} + \dfrac{(p_B − p_A)}{2(t − k)}\right]N.$

   (iii)   Firm A's profit is: $p_A\left[\dfrac{1}{2} + \dfrac{(p_B − p_A)}{2(t − k)}\right]N$. Maximizing this with respect to p_A yields:

$$p_A = \frac{t − k}{2} + \frac{p_B}{2}.$$ An analogous best response function may be similarly derived for firm B.

   (iv)   Imposing symmetry yields $p_A = p_B = t − k$. As k is positive (but presumably less than t), prices are lower than in the no network effects case. Demand is much more sensitive to a price cut now because it attracts more consumers directly and the, by virtue of this, increases the size of the network attracting still more customers.

Chapter 25

25.1   A dominant strategy is one that gives you a payoff greater than any other strategy regardless of what is chosen by other players. The other strategy you could choose is to stop bidding when the price is less than your true valuation.

Suppose that the auction price is p and your true valuation is V. If $p < V$ and you stop bidding your payoff is 0, whereas if you bid $p + \varepsilon < V$ then your payoff is $V − (p + \varepsilon) > 0$. So, for any $p < V$, continuing to bid is a dominant strategy. Of course if $p = V$ then you should stop bidding because to bid $p + \varepsilon > V$ results in a payoff less than zero, which is your payoff from not bidding.

25.2   Your best strategy here is to assume that you are the one with the highest valuation. In other words you assume that the other seven bidders have valuations drawn from a uniform distribution over the interval [0, 200]. If we assume that these bids are evenly spaced out over the interval then the lowest would be 25 (= 1/8 * 200), the next 50 (= 2/8 * 200), the next 75, the next

100, the next 125, the next 150 and finally the highest bid from the other bidders will be 175 (= 7/8 * 200). You should submit a bid of $175 to win the auction.

25.3   You and your partner drew a value of 2,000. Other bidders are drawing other values, and you assume they are drawing from the same uniform distribution on the interval $[0, U]$. You will only win the auction if you have the highest valuation, i.e., if your estimate that the value is 2,000 is the highest estimate. So, you will want to shade your bid. Given that there are 8 groups drawing and you and your partner drew 2,000 you can estimate that the upper value of the distribution, U is that $U = 9/8 * 2,000 = 2,250$. The mean of the distribution is then $1,125. A bid of this amount will greatly reduce your risk of incurring the winner's curse.

Index